# PRENTICE HALL
# LITERATURE

**GRADE 9**

## COMMON CORE EDITION

Upper Saddle River, New Jersey

Boston, Massachusetts

Chandler, Arizona

Glenview, Illinois

**PEARSON**

Acknowledgments appear on page R72, which constitutes an extension of this copyright page.

**PEARSON**

ISBN-13: 978-0-13-319555-2
ISBN-10:  0-13-319555-4

8 9 10 V063 15 14 13 12

# Contributing Authors

*The contributing authors guided the direction and philosophy of* Pearson Prentice Hall Literature. *Working with the development team, they helped to build the pedagogical integrity of the program and to ensure its relevance for today's teachers and students.*

**Grant Wiggins, Ed.D.,** is the President of Authentic Education in Hopewell, New Jersey. He earned his Ed.D. from Harvard University and his B.A. from St. John's College in Annapolis. Grant consults with schools, districts, and state education departments on a variety of reform matters; organizes conferences and workshops; and develops print materials and Web resources on curricular change. He is the coauthor, with Jay McTighe, of Understanding by Design and The Understanding by Design Handbook, the award-winning and highly successful materials on curriculum published by ASCD. His work has been supported by the Pew Charitable Trusts, the Geraldine R. Dodge Foundation, and the National Science Foundation. *The Association for Supervision of Curriculum Development (ASCD), publisher of the "Understanding by Design Handbook" co-authored by Grant Wiggins and registered owner of the trademark "Understanding by Design", has not authorized, approved or sponsored this work and is in no way affiliated with Pearson or its products.*

**Jeff Anderson** has worked with struggling writers and readers for almost 20 years. Anderson's specialty is the integration of grammar and editing instruction into the processes of reading and writing. He has published two books, *Mechanically Inclined: Building Grammar, Usage, and Style into Writer's Workshop* and *Everyday Editing: Inviting Students to Develop Skill and Craft in Writer's Workshop,* as well as a DVD, *The Craft of Grammar.* Anderson's work has appeared in *English Journal.* Anderson won the NCTE Paul and Kate Farmer Award for his *English Journal* article on teaching grammar in context.

**Arnetha F. Ball, Ph.D.,** is a Professor at Stanford University. Her areas of expertise include language and literacy studies of diverse student populations, research on writing instruction, and teacher preparation for working with diverse populations. She is the author of *African American Literacies Unleashed* with Dr. Ted Lardner, and *Multicultural Strategies for Education and Social Change.*

**Sheridan Blau** is Professor of Education and English at the University of California, Santa Barbara, where he directs the South Coast Writing Project and the Literature Institute for Teachers. He has served in senior advisory roles for such groups as the National Board for Professional Teaching Standards, the College Board, and the American Board for Teacher Education. Blau served for twenty years on the National Writing Project Advisory Board and Task Force, and is a former president of NCTE. Blau is the author of *The Literature Workshop: Teaching Texts and Their Readers,* which was named by the Conference on English Education as the 2004 Richard Meade Award winner for outstanding research in English education.

**William G. Brozo, Ph.D.,** is a Professor of Literacy at George Mason University in Fairfax, Virginia. He has taught reading and language arts in junior and senior high school and is the author of numerous texts on literacy development. Dr. Brozo's work focuses on building capacity among teacher leaders, enriching the literate culture of schools, enhancing the literate lives of boys, and making teaching more responsive to the needs of all students. His recent publications include *Bright Beginnings for Boys: Engaging Young Boys in Active Literacy* and the *Adolescent Literacy Inventory.*

**Doug Buehl** is a teacher, author, and national literacy consultant. He is the author of *Classroom Strategies for Interactive Learning* and coauthor of *Reading and the High School Student: Strategies to Enhance Literacy;* and *Strategies to Enhance Literacy and Learning in Middle School Content Area Classrooms.*

**Jim Cummins, Ph.D.,** is a professor in the Modern Language Centre at the University of Toronto. He is the author of numerous publications, including *Negotiating Identities: Education for Empowerment in a Diverse Society.* Cummins coined the acronyms BICS and CAPT to help differentiate the type of language ability students need for success.

**Harvey Daniels, Ph.D.,** has been a classroom teacher, writing project director, author, and university professor. "Smokey" serves as an international consultant to schools, districts, and educational agencies. He is known for his work on student-led book clubs, as recounted in *Literature Circles: Voice and Choice in Book Clubs & Reading Groups* and *Mini Lessons for Literature Circles.* Recent works include *Subjects Matter: Every Teacher's Guide to Content-Area Reading* and *Content Area Writing: Every Teacher's Guide.*

**Jane Feber** taught language arts in  Jacksonville, Florida, for 36 years. Her innovative approach to instruction has earned her several awards, including the NMSA Distinguished Educator Award, the NCTE Edwin A. Hoey Award, the Gladys Prior Award for Teaching Excellence, and the Florida Council of Teachers of English Teacher of the Year Award. She is a National Board Certified Teacher, past president of the Florida Council of Teachers of English and is the author of *Creative Book Reports* and *Active Word Play.*

**Danling Fu, Ph.D.,** is Professor  of Language and Culture in the College of Education at the University of Florida. She researches and provides inservice to public schools nationally, focusing on literacy instruction for new immigrant students. Fu's books include *My Trouble is My English* and *An Island of English* addressing English language learners in the secondary schools. She has authored chapters in the *Handbook of Adolescent Literacy Research* and in *Adolescent Literacy: Turning Promise to Practice.*

**Kelly Gallagher** is a full-time English  teacher at Magnolia High School in Anaheim, California. He is the former co-director of the South Basin Writing Project at California State University, Long Beach. Gallagher wrote *Reading Reasons: Motivational Mini-Lessons for the Middle and High School, Deeper Reading: Comprehending Challenging Texts 4-12,* and *Teaching Adolescent Writers.* Gallagher won the Secondary Award of Classroom Excellence from the California Association of Teachers of English—the state's top English teacher honor.

**Sharroky Hollie, Ph.D.,** is an  assistant professor at California State University, Dominguez Hills, and an urban literacy visiting professor at Webster University, St. Louis. Hollie's work focuses on professional development, African American education, and second language methodology. He is a contributing author in two texts on culturally and linguistically responsive teaching. He is the Executive Director of the Center for Culturally Responsive Teaching and Learning and the co-founding director of the Culture and Language Academy of Success, an independent charter school in Los Angeles.

**Dr. Donald J. Leu, Ph.D.,** teaches  at the University of Connecticut and holds a joint appointment in Curriculum and Instruction and in Educational Psychology. He directs the New Literacies Research Lab and is a member of the Board of Directors of the International Reading Association. Leu studies the skills required to read, write, and learn with Internet technologies. His research has been funded by groups including the U.S. Department of Education, the National Science Foundation, and the Bill & Melinda Gates Foundation.

**Jon Scieszka** founded GUYS READ,  a nonprofit literacy initiative for boys, to call attention to the problem of getting boys connected with reading. In 2008, he was named the first U.S. National Ambassador for Young People's Literature by the Library of Congress. Scieszka taught from first grade to eighth grade for ten years in New York City, drawing inspiration from his students to write *The True Story of the 3 Little Pigs!, The Stinky Cheese Man,* the *Time Warp Trio* series of chapter books, and the *Trucktown* series of books for beginning readers.

**Sharon Vaughn, Ph.D.,** teaches  at the University of Texas at Austin. She is the previous Editor-in-Chief of the *Journal of Learning Disabilities* and the co-editor of *Learning Disabilities Research and Practice.* She is the recipient of the American Education Research Association SIG Award for Outstanding Researcher. Vaughn's work focuses on effective practices for enhancing reading outcomes for students with reading difficulties. She is the author of more than 100 articles and numerous books designed to improve research-based practices in the classroom.

**Karen K. Wixson** is Dean of the  School of Education at the University of North Carolina, Greensboro. She has published widely in the areas of literacy curriculum, instruction, and assessment. Wixson has been an advisor to the National Research Council and helped develop the National Assessment of Educational Progress (NAEP) reading tests. She is a past member of the IRA Board of Directors and co-chair of the IRA Commission on RTI. Recently, Wixson served on the English Language Arts Work Team that was part of the Common Core State Standards Initiative.

*Each unit addresses a BIG Question to enrich exploration of literary concepts and reading strategies.*

## Unit 4: Poetry 602

**How does communication change us?**

**Literary Analysis Workshop**

| | |
|---|---|
| **Literary Skills:** | Figurative and Connotative Language |
| | Tone |
| **Reading Skills:** | Read Fluently |
| | Paraphrase |
| **Writing Workshop:** | Descriptive Essay |
| | Response to Literature |
| **Vocabulary Workshop:** | Connotation and Denotation |
| **Communications Workshop:** | Oral Interpretation of Literature |

## Unit 5: Drama 776

**Do our differences define us?**

**Literary Analysis Workshop**

| | |
|---|---|
| **Literary Skills:** | Dramatic Structure |
| | Character, Plot, and Theme |
| **Reading Skills:** | Summarize |
| | Draw Conclusions |
| **Writing Workshop:** | How-to Essay |
| | Research Report |
| **Vocabulary Workshop:** | Borrowed and Foreign Words |
| **Communications Workshop:** | Multimedia Presentation of a Research Report |

## Unit 6: Themes in Literature: Heroism 1026

**Do heroes have responsibilities?**

**Literary Analysis Workshop**

| | |
|---|---|
| **Literary Skills:** | Theme |
| | Social and Cultural Context |
| **Reading Skills:** | Historical and Cultural Context |
| | Compare and Contrast |
| **Writing Workshop:** | Technical Document |
| | Comparison-and-Contrast Essay |
| **Vocabulary Workshop:** | Idioms, Jargon, and |
| | Technical Terms |
| **Communications Workshop:** | Comparing Media Coverage |

### Resources

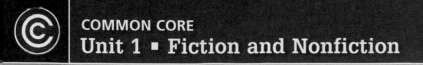

**Can *truth* change?**

★ INFORMATIONAL TEXT HIGHLIGHTED

# Skills at a Glance

This page provides a quick look at the skills you will learn and practice in Unit 1.

## Reading Skills

Make Predictions
 Ask Questions
 Reread or Read Ahead to Verify
  Your Predictions
Author's Purpose
 Preview the Text Before You Read
 Reflect

## Reading for Information

 Read to Perform a Task
 Analyze Structure and Format

## Literary Analysis

Theme
Central Idea
Narrative Essay
Plot
Comparing Points of View
Voice
Character
Comparing Themes
Independent Reading

## Vocabulary

Big Question Vocabulary
Prefixes: *fore-, con-*
Suffixes: *-ate, -tion, -able, -ive*
Roots: *-fin-, -term-*
Using a Dictionary and Thesaurus

## Conventions

Common and Proper Nouns
Abstract and Concrete Nouns
Revising to Correct Use of Possessive Nouns
Personal Pronouns and Reflexive Pronouns
Relative, Interrogative, and Indefinite Pronouns
Revising Pronoun-Antecedent Agreement

## Writing

Writing About the Big Question
Anecdote
Critique
Journal Entry
Character Profile
Timed Writing
Writing Workshop: Narrative Text:
 Autobiographical Narrative
Writing Workshop: Argument:
 Problem-and-Solution Essay

## Speaking and Listening

Interview
Retelling
Giving and Following Oral Instructions

## Research and Technology

Introduction for a Multimedia Presentation
Learning Log

---

### Ⓒ Common Core State Standards Addressed in This Unit

**Reading Literature** RL.9-10.1, RL.9-10.2, RL.9-10.3, RL.9-10.5, RL.9-10.6, RL.9-10.7, RL.9-10.10

**Reading Informational Text** RI.9-10.2, RI.9-10.3, RI.9-10.6, RI.9-10.7, RI.9-10.10

**Writing** W.9-10.1, W.9-10.1.a-1.e, W.9-10.2, W.9-10.2.a, W.9-10.2.b, W.9-10.2.d, W.9-10.2.f, W.9-10.3, W.9-10.3.a–d, W.9-10.4, W.9-10.5, W.9-10.6, W.9-10.9, W.9-10.9.a, W.9-10.9.b, W.9-10.10

**Speaking and Listening** SL.9-10.1, SL.9-10.1.a, SL.9-10.1.c, SL.9-10.1.d, SL.9-10.4, SL.9-10.5

**Language** L.9-10.1, L.9-10.2, L.9-10.2.c, L.9-10.3, L.9-10.4.a–c, L.9-10.5, L.9-10.5.b, L.9-10.6

[For the full wording of the standards, see the standards chart in the front of your textbook.]

## Is conflict *necessary?*

★ INFORMATIONAL TEXT HIGHLIGHTED

**www.PHLitOnline.com**
Interactive resources provide
personalized instruction and
activities online.

# Skills at a Glance

This page provides a quick look at the skills you will learn and practice in Unit 2.

## Reading Skills

Make Inferences
  Use Details as Clues
  Use Your Own Prior Knowledge and Experience
Cause and Effect
  Ask Questions
  Visualize the Action to Analyze Cause and Effect

## Reading for Information

  Critique the Logic of Functional Documents
  Analyze Structure and Format

## Literary Analysis

Character, Plot, and Theme
Text Structure
Plot
Story
Conflict
Irony
Comparing Setting
Characterization
Dialogue and Dialect
Comparing Symbolism and Allegory
Independent Reading

## Vocabulary

Big Question Vocabulary
Prefixes: *de-, inter-*
Suffixes: *-esque, -ant, -ity, -ous*
Roots: *-bene-, -jec(t)-*
Word Origins

## Conventions

The Principal Parts of Regular Verbs
Irregular Verbs
Subjects and Predicates
Active and Passive Voice
Revising Inconsistent Verb Tense
Revising to Correct Faulty Subject-Verb Agreement

## Writing

Writing About the Big Question
Alternative Ending
News Report
Written Presentation
Informal Letter
Timed Writing
Writing Workshop: Narrative Text: Short Story
Writing Workshop: Explanatory Text:
  Cause-and-Effect Essay

## Speaking and Listening

Oral Presentation
Debate
Dialogue
Evaluating a Speech

## Research and Technology

Informative Brochure

---

 **Common Core State Standards Addressed in This Unit**

**Reading Literature** RL.9-10.1, RL.9-10.3, RL.9-10.4, RL.9-10.6, RL.9-10.10

**Reading Informational Text** RI.9-10.3, RI.9-10.10

**Writing** W.9-10.2, W.9-10.2.a–c, W.9-10.2.f, W.9-10.3, W.9-10.3.a–e, W.9-10.4, W.9-10.5, W.9-10.9.a, W.9-10.10

**Speaking and Listening** SL.9-10.1, SL.9-10.1.b, SL.9-10.2, SL.9-10.3, SL.9-10.4

**Language** L.9-10.1, L.9-10.2.c, L.9-10.4, L.9-10.4.b, L.9-10.4.c, L.9-10.6

[For the full wording of the standards, see the standards chart in the front of your textbook.]

**Is *knowledge* the same as *understanding?***

Development of Ideas
Word Choice and Tone
Point of View and
Purpose

Main Idea
Author's Style

Main Idea
Expository Essay

Generate Relevant
Questions

★ INFORMATIONAL TEXT HIGHLIGHTED

**www.PHLitOnline.com**
Interactive resources provide
personalized instruction and
activities online.

# Skills at a Glance

This page provides a quick look at the skills you will learn and practice in Unit 3.

## Reading Skills

Main Idea
  Generate Questions Prior to Reading
  Reread
Evaluate Persuasion
  Reread
  Read Aloud to Hear the Effect

## Reading for Information

  Generate Relevant Questions
  Evaluate Credibility

## Literary Analysis

Development of Ideas
Word Choice and Tone
Point of View and Purpose
Author's Style
Expository Essay
Comparing Biographical Writing
Persuasive Essay
Persuasive Speech
Comparing Humorous Writing
Independent Reading

## Vocabulary

Big Question Vocabulary

Roots: *-viv-, -dur-, -nov-, -temp-,*
  *-potens-, -sum-, -cred-, -duct-*

Words With Multiple
  Meanings

## Conventions

Direct and Indirect Objects
Predicate Nominatives and
  Predicate Adjectives
Revising to Combine Choppy Sentences
Adjectives
Adverbs

Revising to Create Parallelism

## Writing

Writing About the Big Question
Book Jacket Copy
Script
Journal Entries
Abstract
Proposal
Timed Writing
Writing Workshop: Informative Text:
  Business Letter
Writing Workshop: Argument: Editorial

## Speaking and Listening

Panel Discussion
Radio News Report
Delivering a Persuasive Speech

## Research and Technology

Journal Entries
Comparative Chart / Persuasive Speech

---

### Common Core State Standards Addressed in This Unit

**Reading Literature** RL.9-10.6, RL.9-10.10
**Reading Informational Text** RI.9-10.1, RI.9-10.2, RI.9-10.3, RI.9-10.4, RI.9-10.5, RI.9-10.6, RI.9-10.8, RI.9-10.9, RI.9-10.10
**Writing** W.9-10.1, W.9-10.1.a–e, W.9-10.2, W.9-10.2.a, W.9-10.2.d–f, W.9-10.4, W.9-10.5, W.9-10.6, W.9-10.7, W.9-10.8, W.9-10.9, W.9-10.9.b, W.9-10.10
**Speaking and Listening** SL.9-10.1, SL.9-10.3, SL.9-10.4, SL.9-10.5, SL.9-10.6
**Language** L.9-10.1, L.9-10.1.a, L.9-10.3, L.9-10.4, L.9-10.4.a, L.9-10.4.b, L.9-10.4.d, L.9-10.5, L.9-10.5.b, L.9-10.6
[For the full wording of the standards, see the standards chart in the front of your textbook.]

## How does *communication* change us?

# Skills at a Glance

This page provides a quick look at the skills you will learn and practice in Unit 4.

## Reading Skills

Read Fluently

Read in Sentences or Units of Meaning

Read Poems Several Times

Paraphrase

Picture the Action

Break Down Long Sentences

## Reading for Information

Follow Technical Directions

Paraphrase a Text: Main Idea

## Literary Analysis

Poetic Language

Tone

Figurative Language

Sound Devices

Comparing Imagery

Narrative Poetry

Rhyme and Meter

Comparing Lyric Poetry

Independent Reading

## Vocabulary

Big Question Vocabulary

Prefixes: *ana-, mono-, pre-, im-*

Suffixes: *-ment, -ion*

Roots: *-fer-, -vert-*

Connotation and Denotation

## Conventions

Prepositions

Prepositional Phrases

Revising to Vary Sentence Patterns

Appositive Phrase

Infinitives

Using Quotations

## Writing

Writing About the Big Question

Description of a Scene

Editorial

Poem

Timed Writing

Writing Workshop: Informative Text:
  Descriptive Essay

Writing Workshop: Argument:
  Response to Literature

## Speaking and Listening

Impromptu Speech

Illustrated Presentation

Dialogue

Panel Discussion

Oral Interpretation of Literature

---

**Ⓒ Common Core State Standards
Addressed in This Unit**

**Reading Literature** RL.9-10.2, RL.9-10.4, RL.9-10.5, RL.9-10.7, RL.9-10.10

**Reading Informational Text** RI.9-10.2, RI.9-10.4, RI.9-10.5, RI.9-10.10

**Writing** W.9-10.1, W.9-10.2, W.9-10.2.a, W.9-10.2.b, W.9-10.2.d, W.9-10.2.e, W.9-10.3.d, W.9-10.4, W.9-10.5, W.9-10.9.a, W.9-10.10

**Speaking and Listening** SL.9-10.1, SL.9-10.1.a–d, SL.9-10.4, SL.9-10.5, SL.9-10.6

**Language** L.9-10.1, L.9-10.1.b, L.9-10.3, L.9-10.5, L.9-10.6

[For the full wording of the standards, see the standards chart in the front of your textbook.]

**Do our *differences* define us?**

**PHLit Online!**
www.PHLitOnline.com
Interactive resources provide personalized instruction and activities online.

# Skills at a Glance

This page provides a quick look at the skills you will learn and practice in Unit 5.

## Reading Skills

Summarize

Use Text Aids

Read in Sentences

Paraphrase

Break Down Long Sentences

Identify Causes and Effects

Draw Conclusions

Dialogue and Stage Directions

## Reading for Information

Analyze Text Information

Evaluate Sources

## Literary Analysis

Dramatic Structure

Character, Plot, and Theme

Dialogue and Stage Directions

Blank Verse

Dramatic Speeches

Dramatic Irony

Tragedy and Motive

Comparing Archetypal Themes

Comedy

Comparing Satire

Independent Reading

## Vocabulary

Big Question Vocabulary

Prefixes: *trans-, pro-, en-, ambi-*

Roots: *-loque-, -nym-, -nom-*

Borrowed and Foreign Words

## Conventions

Participles and Participial Phrases

Gerunds and Gerund Phrases

Revising to Combine Sentences With Phrases

Main and Subordinate Clauses

Revising to Combine Sentences Using Adverb Clauses

## Writing

Writing About the Big Question

Editorial

Persuasive Letter

Play

Timed Writing

Writing Workshop: Explanatory Text: How-to Essay

Writing Workshop: Informative Text: Research Report

## Speaking and Listening

Staged Performance

Mock Trial

## Research and Technology

Annotated Flowchart

Film Review

Multimedia Presentation

Informational Chart

Multimedia Presentation of a Research Report

---

 **Common Core State Standards Addressed in This Unit**

**Reading Literature** RL.9-10.2, RL.9-10.3, RL.9-10.4, RL.9-10.5, RL.9-10.7, RL.9-10.9, RL.9-10.10

**Reading Informational Text** RI.9-10.3, RI.9-10.10

**Writing** W.9-10.1, W.9-10.1.c, W.9-10.2, W.9-10.2.a, W.9-10.2.b, W.9-10.3, W.9-10.5, W.9-10.7, W.9-10.8, W.9-10.9.a, W.9-10.10

**Speaking and Listening** SL.9-10.1.b, SL.9-10.5

**Language** L.9-10.1, L.9-10.1.b, L.9-10.3, L.9-10.4, L.9-10.4.c, L.9-10.4.d, L.9-10.5.a, L.9-10.6

[For the full wording of the standards, see the standards chart in the front of your textbook.]

THE BIG ?  Do *heroes* have *responsibilities?*

★ INFORMATIONAL TEXT HIGHLIGHTED

**PHLit Online!**
www.PHLitOnline.com
Interactive resources provide personalized instruction and activities online.

# Skills at a Glance

This page provides a quick look at the skills you will learn and practice in Unit 6.

## Reading Skills

Historical and Cultural Context
Use Background and Prior Knowledge
Identify Influences on Your Own Reading and Responses
Comparing and Contrasting Characters
Generate Questions
Use Self-Monitoring Techniques

## Reading for Information

Identify Characteristics of Various Types of Text
Analyze Primary Sources

## Literary Analysis

Theme
Social and Cultural Context
Point of View and Cultural Experience
Epic Hero
Epic Simile
Comparing Contemporary Interpretations
Protagonist and Antagonist
Philosophical Assumptions
Comparing Tall Tale and Myth

## Vocabulary

Big Question Vocabulary
Prefixes: *be-, dis-*
Roots: *-min-, -spect-, -merg-, -fer-*
Idioms, Jargon, and Technical Terms

## Conventions

Simple and Compound Sentences
Complex and Compound-Complex Sentences
Revising to Correct Fragments and Run-ons
Using Commas and Dashes
Colons, Semicolons, and Ellipsis Points
Varying Sentence Structure and Length

## Writing

Writing About the Big Question
Everyday Epic
Biography
Journal Entries
Letter
Timed Writing
Writing Workshop: Explanatory Text: Technical Document
Writing Workshop: Informative Text: Comparison-and-Contrast Essay

## Speaking and Listening

Conversation
Debate
Oral Report
Panel Discussion
Comparing Media Coverage

### Common Core State Standards Addressed in This Unit

**Reading Literature** RL.9-10.2, RL.9-10.3, RL.9-10.4, RL.9-10.6, RL.9-10.7, RL.9-10.10
**Reading Informational Text** RI.9-10.3, RI.9-10.6, RI.9-10.7, RI.9-10.10
**Writing** W.9-10.2, W.9-10.2.a, W.9-10.2.b, W.9-10.3, W.9-10.3.a, W.9-10.3.b, W.9-10.5, W.9-10.9, W.9-10.9.a, W.9-10.10
**Speaking and Listening** SL.9-10.1.a, SL.9-10.1.c, SL.9-10.2
**Language** L.9-10.1, L.9-10.1.b, L.9-10.2, L.9-10.2.a, L.9-10.2.b, L.9-10.4.b, L.9-10.4.c, L.9-10.5, L.9-10.5.a, L.9-10.6
[For the full wording of the standards, see the standards chart in the front of your textbook.]

# Literature

## ▶ Poetry

# Informational Text

## ▶ Functional Text

## ▶ Literature in Context—Reading in Content Areas

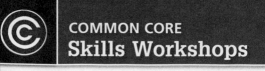

## ▶ Writing Workshops

## ▶ Vocabulary Workshops

## ▶ Communications Workshops

**The Common Core State Standards** will prepare you to succeed in college and your future career. They are separated into four sections—Reading (Literature and Informational Text), Writing, Speaking and Listening, and Language. Beginning each section, the College and Career Readiness Anchor Standards define what you need to achieve by the end of high school. The grade-specific standards that follow define what you need to know by the end of your current grade level.

# ©Common Core Reading Standards

## College and Career Readiness Anchor Standards for Reading

### Key Ideas and Details

1. Read closely to determine what the text says explicitly and to make logical inferences from it; cite specific textual evidence when writing or speaking to support conclusions drawn from the text.

2. Determine central ideas or themes of a text and analyze their development; summarize the key supporting details and ideas.

3. Analyze how and why individuals, events, and ideas develop and interact over the course of a text.

### Craft and Structure

4. Interpret words and phrases as they are used in a text, including determining technical, connotative, and figurative meanings, and analyze how specific word choices shape meaning or tone.

5. Analyze the structure of texts, including how specific sentences, paragraphs, and larger portions of the text (e.g., a section, chapter, scene, or stanza) relate to each other and the whole.

6. Assess how point of view or purpose shapes the content and style of a text.

### Integration of Knowledge and Ideas

7. Integrate and evaluate content presented in diverse formats and media, including visually and quantitatively, as well as in words.

8. Delineate and evaluate the argument and specific claims in a text, including the validity of the reasoning as well as the relevance and sufficiency of the evidence.

9. Analyze how two or more texts address similar themes or topics in order to build knowledge or to compare the approaches the authors take.

### Range of Reading and Level of Text Complexity

10. Read and comprehend complex literary and informational texts independently and proficiently.

## Grade 9 Reading Standards for Literature

### Key Ideas and Details

1. Cite strong and thorough textual evidence to support analysis of what the text says explicitly as well as inferences drawn from the text.

2. Determine a theme or central idea of a text and analyze in detail its development over the course of the text, including how it emerges and is shaped and refined by specific details; provide an objective summary of the text.

3. Analyze how complex characters (e.g., those with multiple or conflicting motivations) develop over the course of a text, interact with other characters, and advance the plot or develop the theme.

### Craft and Structure

4. Determine the meaning of words and phrases as they are used in the text, including figurative and connotative meanings; analyze the cumulative impact of specific word choices on meaning and tone (e.g., how the language evokes a sense of time and place; how it sets a formal or informal tone).

5. Analyze how an author's choices concerning how to structure a text, order events within it (e.g., parallel plots), and manipulate time (e.g., pacing, flashbacks) create such effects as mystery, tension, or surprise.

6. Analyze a particular point of view or cultural experience reflected in a work of literature from outside the United States, drawing on a wide reading of world literature.

### Integration of Knowledge and Ideas

7. Analyze the representation of a subject or a key scene in two different artistic mediums, including what is emphasized or absent in each treatment (e.g., Auden's "Musée des Beaux Arts" and Breughel's *Landscape with the Fall of Icarus*).

8. (Not applicable to literature)

9. Analyze how an author draws on and transforms source material in a specific work (e.g., how Shakespeare treats a theme or topic from Ovid or the Bible or how a later author draws on a play by Shakespeare).

### Range of Reading and Level of Text Complexity

10. By the end of grade 9, read and comprehend literature, including stories, dramas, and poems, in the grades 9–10 text complexity band proficiently, with scaffolding as needed at the high end of the range.

## Grade 9 Reading Standards for Informational Text

### Key Ideas and Details

1. Cite strong and thorough textual evidence to support analysis of what the text says explicitly as well as inferences drawn from the text.

2. Determine a central idea of a text and analyze its development over the course of the text, including how it emerges and is shaped and refined by specific details; provide an objective summary of the text.

3. Analyze how the author unfolds an analysis or series of ideas or events, including the order in which the points are made, how they are introduced and developed, and the connections that are drawn between them.

### Craft and Structure

4. Determine the meaning of words and phrases as they are used in a text, including figurative, connotative, and technical meanings; analyze the cumulative impact of specific word choices on meaning and tone (e.g., how the language of a court opinion differs from that of a newspaper).

5. Analyze in detail how an author's ideas or claims are developed and refined by particular sentences, paragraphs, or larger portions of a text (e.g., a section or chapter).

6. Determine an author's point of view or purpose in a text and analyze how an author uses rhetoric to advance that point of view or purpose.

### Integration of Knowledge and Ideas

7. Analyze various accounts of a subject told in different mediums (e.g., a person's life story in both print and multimedia), determining which details are emphasized in each account.

8. Delineate and evaluate the argument and specific claims in a text, assessing whether the reasoning is valid and the evidence is relevant and sufficient; identify false statements and fallacious reasoning.

9. Analyze seminal U.S. documents of historical and literary significance (e.g., Washington's Farewell Address, the Gettysburg Address, Roosevelt's Four Freedoms speech, King's "Letter from Birmingham Jail"), including how they address related themes and concepts.

### Range of Reading and Level of Text Complexity

10. By the end of grade 9, read and comprehend literary nonfiction in the grades 9–10 text complexity band proficiently, with scaffolding as needed at the high end of the range.

# © Common Core Writing Standards

## College and Career Readiness Anchor Standards for Writing

### Text Types and Purpose

1. Write arguments to support claims in an analysis of substantive topics or texts, using valid reasoning and relevant and sufficient evidence.

2. Write informative/explanatory texts to examine and convey complex ideas and information clearly and accurately through the effective selection, organization, and analysis of content.

3. Write narratives to develop real or imagined experiences or events using effective technique, well-chosen details, and well-structured event sequences.

### Production and Distribution of Writing

4. Produce clear and coherent writing in which the development, organization, and style are appropriate to task, purpose, and audience.

5. Develop and strengthen writing as needed by planning, revising, editing, rewriting, or trying a new approach.

6. Use technology, including the Internet, to produce and publish writing and to interact and collaborate with others.

### Research to Build and Present Knowledge

7. Conduct short as well as more sustained research projects based on focused questions, demonstrating understanding of the subject under investigation.

8. Gather relevant information from multiple print and digital sources, assess the credibility and accuracy of each source, and integrate the information while avoiding plagiarism.

9. Draw evidence from literary or informational texts to support analysis, reflection, and research.

### Range of Writing

10. Write routinely over extended time frames (time for research, reflection, and revision) and shorter time frames (a single sitting or a day or two) for a range of tasks, purposes, and audiences.

## Grade 9 Writing Standards

### Text Types and Purposes

**1.** Write arguments to support claims in an analysis of substantive topics or texts, using valid reasoning and relevant and sufficient evidence.

   a. Introduce precise claim(s), distinguish the claim(s) from alternate or opposing claims, and create an organization that establishes clear relationships among claim(s), counterclaims, reasons, and evidence.

   b. Develop claim(s) and counterclaims fairly, supplying evidence for each while pointing out the strengths and limitations of both in a manner that anticipates the audience's knowledge level and concerns.

   c. Use words, phrases, and clauses to link the major sections of the text, create cohesion, and clarify the relationships between claim(s) and reasons, between reasons and evidence, and between claim(s) and counterclaims.

   d. Establish and maintain a formal style and objective tone while attending to the norms and conventions of the discipline in which they are writing.

   e. Provide a concluding statement or section that follows from and supports the argument presented.

**2.** Write informative/explanatory texts to examine and convey complex ideas, concepts, and information clearly and accurately through the effective selection, organization, and analysis of content.

   a. Introduce a topic; organize complex ideas, concepts, and information to make important connections and distinctions; include formatting (e.g., headings), graphics (e.g., figures, tables), and multimedia when useful to aiding comprehension.

   b. Develop the topic with well-chosen, relevant, and sufficient facts, extended definitions, concrete details, quotations, or other information and examples appropriate to the audience's knowledge of the topic.

   c. Use appropriate and varied transitions to link the major sections of the text, create cohesion, and clarify the relationships among complex ideas and concepts.

   d. Use precise language and domain-specific vocabulary to manage the complexity of the topic.

   e. Establish and maintain a formal style and objective tone while attending to the norms and conventions of the discipline in which they are writing.

   f. Provide a concluding statement or section that follows from and supports the information or explanation presented (e.g., articulating implications or the significance of the topic).

**3.** Write narratives to develop real or imagined experiences or events using effective technique, well-chosen details, and well-structured event sequences.

   a. Engage and orient the reader by setting out a problem, situation, or observation, establishing one or multiple point(s) of view, and introducing a narrator and/or characters; create a smooth progression of experiences or events.

b. Use narrative techniques, such as dialogue, pacing, description, reflection, and multiple plot lines, to develop experiences, events, and/or characters.

c. Use a variety of techniques to sequence events so that they build on one another to create a coherent whole.

d. Use precise words and phrases, telling details, and sensory language to convey a vivid picture of the experiences, events, setting, and/or characters.

e. Provide a conclusion that follows from and reflects on what is experienced, observed, or resolved over the course of the narrative.

## Production and Distribution of Writing

**4.** Produce clear and coherent writing in which the development, organization, and style are appropriate to task, purpose, and audience.

**5.** Develop and strengthen writing as needed by planning, revising, editing, rewriting, or trying a new approach, focusing on addressing what is most significant for a specific purpose and audience.

**6.** Use technology, including the Internet, to produce, publish, and update individual or shared writing products, taking advantage of technology's capacity to link to other information and to display information flexibly and dynamically.

## Research to Build and Present Knowledge

**7.** Conduct short as well as more sustained research projects to answer a question (including a self-generated question) or solve a problem; narrow or broaden the inquiry when appropriate; synthesize multiple sources on the subject, demonstrating understanding of the subject under investigation.

**8.** Gather relevant information from multiple authoritative print and digital sources, using advanced searches effectively; assess the usefulness of each source in answering the research question; integrate information into the text selectively to maintain the flow of ideas, avoiding plagiarism and following a standard format for citation.

**9.** Draw evidence from literary or informational texts to support analysis, reflection, and research.

a. Apply *grades 9–10 Reading standards* to literature (e.g., "Analyze how an author draws on and transforms source material in a specific work [e.g., how Shakespeare treats a theme or topic from Ovid or the Bible or how a later author draws on a play by Shakespeare]").

b. Apply *grades 9–10 Reading standards* to literary nonfiction (e.g., "Delineate and evaluate the argument and specific claims in a text, assessing whether the reasoning is valid and the evidence is relevant and sufficient; identify false statements and fallacious reasoning").

## Range of Writing

**10.** Write routinely over extended time frames (time for research, reflection, and revision) and shorter time frames (a single sitting or a day or two) for a range of tasks, purposes, and audiences.

# © Common Core
## Speaking and Listening Standards

### College and Career Readiness Anchor Standards for Speaking and Listening

#### Comprehension and Collaboration

1. Prepare for and participate effectively in a range of conversations and collaborations with diverse partners, building on others' ideas and expressing their own clearly and persuasively.

2. Integrate and evaluate information presented in diverse media and formats, including visually, quantitatively, and orally.

3. Evaluate a speaker's point of view, reasoning, and use of evidence and rhetoric.

#### Presentation of Knowledge and Ideas

4. Present information, findings, and supporting evidence such that listeners can follow the line of reasoning and the organization, development, and style are appropriate to task, purpose, and audience.

5. Make strategic use of digital media and visual displays of data to express information and enhance understanding of presentations.

6. Adapt speech to a variety of contexts and communicative tasks, demonstrating command of formal English when indicated or appropriate.

## Grade 9 Speaking and Listening Standards

### Comprehension and Collaboration

1. Initiate and participate effectively in a range of collaborative discussions (one-on-one, in groups, and teacher-led) with diverse partners on *grades 9–10 topics, texts, and issues,* building on others' ideas and expressing their own clearly and persuasively.

   a. Come to discussions prepared, having read and researched material under study; explicitly draw on that preparation by referring to evidence from texts and other research on the topic or issue to stimulate a thoughtful, well-reasoned exchange of ideas.

   b. Work with peers to set rules for collegial discussions and decision-making (e.g., informal consensus, taking votes on key issues, presentation of alternate views), clear goals and deadlines, and individual roles as needed.

   c. Propel conversations by posing and responding to questions that relate the current discussion to broader themes or larger ideas; actively incorporate others into the discussion; and clarify, verify, or challenge ideas and conclusions.

   d. Respond thoughtfully to diverse perspectives, summarize points of agreement and disagreement, and, when warranted, qualify or justify their own views and understanding and make new connections in light of the evidence and reasoning presented.

2. Integrate multiple sources of information presented in diverse media or formats (e.g., visually, quantitatively, orally) evaluating the credibility and accuracy of each source.

3. Evaluate a speaker's point of view, reasoning, and use of evidence and rhetoric, identifying any fallacious reasoning or exaggerated or distorted evidence.

### Presentation of Knowledge and Ideas

4. Present information, findings, and supporting evidence clearly, concisely, and logically such that listeners can follow the line of reasoning and the organization, development, substance, and style are appropriate to purpose, audience, and task.

5. Make strategic use of digital media (e.g., textual, graphical, audio, visual, and interactive elements) in presentations to enhance understanding of findings, reasoning, and evidence and to add interest.

6. Adapt speech to a variety of contexts and tasks, demonstrating command of formal English when indicated or appropriate. (See grades 9–10 Language standards 1 and 3 for specific expectations.)

# Ⓒ Common Core Language Standards

## College and Career Readiness Anchor Standards for Language

### Conventions of Standard English

1. Demonstrate command of the conventions of standard English grammar and usage when writing or speaking.

2. Demonstrate command of the conventions of standard English capitalization, punctuation, and spelling when writing.

### Knowledge of Language

3. Apply knowledge of language to understand how language functions in different contexts, to make effective choices for meaning or style, and to comprehend more fully when reading or listening.

### Vocabulary Acquisition and Use

4. Determine or clarify the meaning of unknown and multiple-meaning words and phrases by using context clues, analyzing meaningful word parts, and consulting general and specialized reference materials, as appropriate.

5. Demonstrate understanding of figurative language, word relationships, and nuances in word meanings.

6. Acquire and use accurately a range of general academic and domain-specific words and phrases sufficient for reading, writing, speaking, and listening at the college and career readiness level; demonstrate independence in gathering vocabulary knowledge when considering a word or phrase important to comprehension or expression.

## Grade 9 Language Standards

### Conventions of Standard English

1. Demonstrate command of the conventions of standard English grammar and usage when writing or speaking.
   a. Use parallel structure.
   b. Use various types of phrases (noun, verb, adjectival, adverbial, participial, prepositional, absolute) and clauses (independent, dependent; noun, relative, adverbial) to convey specific meanings and add variety and interest to writing or presentations.

**2.** Demonstrate command of the conventions of standard English capitalization, punctuation, and spelling when writing.

   a. Use a semicolon (and perhaps a conjunctive adverb) to link two or more closely related independent clauses.

   b. Use a colon to introduce a list or quotation.

   c. Spell correctly.

## Knowledge of Language

**3.** Apply knowledge of language to understand how language functions in different contexts, to make effective choices for meaning or style, and to comprehend more fully when reading or listening.

   a. Write and edit work so that it conforms to the guidelines in a style manual (e.g., *MLA Handbook,* Turabian's *Manual for Writers*) appropriate for the discipline and writing type.

## Vocabulary Acquisition and Use

**4.** Determine or clarify the meaning of unknown and multiple-meaning words and phrases based on *grades 9–10 reading and content,* choosing flexibly from a range of strategies.

   a. Use context (e.g., the overall meaning of a sentence, paragraph, or text; a word's position or function in a sentence) as a clue to the meaning of a word or phrase.

   b. Identify and correctly use patterns of word changes that indicate different meanings or parts of speech (e.g., *analyze, analysis, analytical; advocate, advocacy*).

   c. Consult general and specialized reference materials (e.g., dictionaries, glossaries, thesauruses), both print and digital, to find the pronunciation of a word or determine or clarify its precise meaning, its part of speech, or its etymology.

   d. Verify the preliminary determination of the meaning of a word or phrase (e.g., by checking the inferred meaning in context or in a dictionary).

**5.** Demonstrate understanding of figurative language, word relationships, and nuances in word meanings.

   a. Interpret figures of speech (e.g., euphemism, oxymoron) in context and analyze their role in the text.

   b. Analyze nuances in the meaning of words with similar denotations.

**6.** Acquire and use accurately general academic and domain-specific words and phrases, sufficient for reading, writing, speaking, and listening at the college and career readiness level; demonstrate independence in gathering vocabulary knowledge when considering a word or phrase important to comprehension or expression.

# Introductory Unit

# Building Academic Vocabulary

Academic vocabulary is the language you encounter in textbooks and on standardized tests and other assessments. Understanding these words and using them in your classroom discussions and writing will help you communicate your ideas clearly and effectively.

There are two basic types of academic vocabulary: general and domain-specific. **General academic vocabulary** includes words that are not specific to any single course of study. For example, the general academic vocabulary word *analyze* is used in language arts, math, social studies, art, and so on. **Domain-specific academic vocabulary** includes words that are usually encountered in the study of a specific discipline. For example, the words *factor* and *remainder* are most often used in mathematics classrooms and texts.

**Common Core State Standards**

**Language 6.** Acquire and use accurately general academic and domain-specific words and phrases, sufficient for reading, writing, speaking, and listening at the college and career readiness level; demonstrate independence in gathering vocabulary knowledge when considering a word or phrase important to comprehension or expression.

## General Academic Vocabulary

| Word | Definition | Related Words | Word in Context |
|------|-----------|---------------|-----------------|
| ambiguous (am BIHG yoo uhs) *adj* | having more than one meaning; unclear | ambiguity | The story's uncertain ending was ambiguous. |
| appreciate (uh PREE shee ayt) *v.* | be aware of the value of | appreciative appreciating | Once I read Frost's poem, I learned to appreciate his use of symbols. |
| argument (AHR gyuh muhnt) *n.* | persuasive message | argue argumentative | The argument in the essay is well supported. |
| articulate (ahr TIHK yuh layt) *v.* | express an idea clearly | articulating articulated | The writer was able to articulate his ideas clearly. |
| articulate (ahr TIHK yuh liht) *adj.* | able to express clearly | articulating articulated | It is important to be articulate when giving a speech. |
| assumption (uh SUHMP shuhn) *n.* | something taken for granted | assume assuming | My assumption that the character was telling the truth proved wrong. |
| character (KAR ihk tuhr) *n.* | qualities that make a person unique | characteristic characteristically | Jenny's character became clear through her actions and words. |
| circumstance (SUR kuhm stans) *n.* | situation; event | | In that circumstance, I would have done the same thing as that character. |

**Ordinary Language:**
I **like** poems with strong rhymes and rhythms.

**Academic Language:**
I **appreciate** poems with strong rhymes and rhythms.

| Word | Definition | Related Words | Word in Context |
|------|-----------|---------------|-----------------|
| clarify (KLAR uh fy) *v.* | make something more clear or understandable | clarification | More details were needed to clarify the writer's ideas about pollution. |
| compete (kuhm PEET) *v.* | battle against; try to win | competition competitor | The two characters compete in a battle of wits. |
| competition (kom puh TIHSH uhn) *n.* | rivalry; act of competing | compete competitor | There seemed to be a competition between the mother and daughter. |
| comprehend (kom prih HEHND) *v.* | understand | comprehension | It was easy to comprehend the character's motives. |
| comprehension (kom prih HEHN shuhn) *n.* | act of understanding something | comprehend | My comprehension of the poem was hampered by the use of archaic language. |
| concept (KON sehpt) *n.* | idea; notion | conceive conceptualize | The concept of freedom is explored in this essay. |
| context (KON tehkst) *n.* | surrounding text; situation | contextual | In this context, the word *democracy* takes on new meaning. |
| controversy (KON truh vur see) *n.* | discussion of a question in which opposing opinions clash | controversial | The essayist explores the controversy that brewed in the heartland. |
| convince (kuhn VIHNS) *v.* | persuade by argument or evidence | convincing | The writer tries to convince her audience to change their ways. |
| credible (KREHD uh buhl) *adj.* | believable | creed credibility | I found the story's plot to be credible. |
| defend (dih FEHND) *v.* | protect against attack | defense | The writer tries to defend his notions about fairness. |
| determine (dih TUR muhn) *v.* | cause something to happen in a certain way | determination | The character's actions determine his fate. |
| differentiate (dihf uh REHN shee ayt) *v.* | see or express what makes two or more things different from each other | differ different | In this essay, the writer differentiates between students and scholars. |

| Word | Definition | Related Words | Word in Context |
|------|-----------|---------------|-----------------|
| discriminate (dihs KRIHM uh nayt) v. | see the differences between things; act against someone because of prejudice | discrimination | The character was unable to discriminate loyal friends from disloyal ones. |
| discuss (dihs KUHS) v. | talk about; write about | discussion | Discuss your ideas in your response. |
| identify (ahy DEHN tuh fy) v. | say who someone or something is | identification | I will identify three key factors in the story's success. |
| illuminate (ih LOO muh nayt) v. | light up; make something clearer | illumination | Here is my attempt to illuminate my ideas. |
| imitate (IHM uh tayt) v. | copy the actions of another | imitation imitator | The poet uses onomatopoeia to imitate the sounds of a rooster. |
| informed (ihn FAWRMD) v. | gave someone information | inform information | The character informed his teacher that he had finished his test. |
| interpret (ihn TUR priht) v. | understand or explain the meaning of something | interpreter interpretation | How do you interpret the title of this poem? |
| interpretation (ihn tur pruh TAY shuhn) n. | explanation of the meaning of something | interpreter interpret | My interpretation of the theme differs from that of my friend. |
| involvement (ihn VOLV muhnt) n. | state of being included in something | involve | The character's involvement in sports propels the plot. |
| perspective (puhr SPEHK tihv) n. | point of view | | The story is told from the perspective of a three-year-old. |
| speculate (SPEHK yuh layt) v. | think about or make up theories about a subject; guess at | speculative | Speculate about the author's reasons for setting this story in the tundra. |
| standard (STAN duhrd) n. | idea or thing to which other things are compared | standardize | Shakespeare sets the standard by which many playwrights are judged. |
| standard (STAN duhrd) adj. | normal; average | standardize substandard | It is standard practice for stories to center on conflict. |
| unique (yoo NEEK) adj. | one of a kind | uniqueness | The poet has a unique style. |
| verify (VEHR uh fy) v. | make sure something is true; confirm | verification | You should verify the facts before you accept them. |

**Ordinary Language:**
In this essay, I will **talk about** the story's theme.

**Academic Language:**
In this essay, I will **discuss** the story's theme.

# Practice

Examples of various kinds of domain-specific academic vocabulary appear in the charts below. On a separate piece of paper, create your own domain-specific academic vocabulary charts for each domain in which you enter new academic vocabulary words as you learn them.

## Social Studies: Domain-Specific Academic Vocabulary

| Word | Definition | Related Words | Word in Context |
|---|---|---|---|
| entrepreneurship (ahn truh pruh NUR ship) *n.* | willingness to assume the risk and responsibility of starting a business | entrepreneur entrepreneurial | The scholarship rewards entrepreneurship. |
| sovereignty (SOV rin tee) *n.* | independence and self-government | sovereign | The country fought for its sovereignty. |
| capitalism (KAP i tl iz uhm) *n.* | an economic system based on private investment and ownership | capitalist | With capitalism, private individuals or corporations control the wealth. |
| populist (POP yuh list) *adj.* | favoring common people over the wealthy and elite | populism | The politician tried to sway populist groups. |
| impeach (im PEECH) *v.* | accuse a public official of misconduct in office | impeached impeachment | The people will impeach a corrupt official. |

Create a chart for these social studies academic vocabulary words: *enterprise, landmass, ecosystem, market,* and *opportunity.*

## Mathematics: Domain-Specific Academic Vocabulary

| Word | Definition | Related Words | Word in Context |
|---|---|---|---|
| theorem (THEE er uhm) *n.* | an assertion that can be proved true using the rules of logic | theory | The scientist worked hard to prove her theorem. |
| permutation (pur myoo TAY shuhn) *n.* | an ordered arrangement of a set of objects | permuting | The teacher formed a permutation by rearranging the letters. |
| congruent (KONG groo uhnt) *adj.* | exactly equal in size and shape | congruous congruity | The triangles are congruent. |
| logarithm (LAW guh rith uhm) *n.* | the power to which a constant must be raised to equal a specified number | logarithmic | 2 is the logarithm of 100 to the base 10. |
| inverse (in VURS) *adj.* | containing terms of which an increase in one causes a decrease in another | invert | The inverse functions mirrored each other. |

Create a chart for these mathematics academic vocabulary words: *graph, slope, triangle, quadrilateral,* and *diagram.*

## Science: Domain-Specific Academic Vocabulary

| Word | Definition | Related Words | Word in Context |
|------|-----------|---------------|-----------------|
| meiosis (mahy OH sis) *n.* | process of cell division that halves the number of chromosomes | meiotic | The biology video included a section about meiosis. |
| ion (AHY uhn) *n.* | an atom or a group of atoms that has an electric charge | ionic | An ion can carry a positive or negative charge. |
| catalyst (KAT I ist) *n.* | a substance that starts or speeds up a chemical reaction | catalytic | The chemical served as a catalyst in the experiment. |
| power (POU er) *n.* | the rate at which work is done, or energy expended, per unit time | powered powerful | The work done per second is called the power. |
| work (wurk) *n.* | the product of the force applied to a body and the resulting distance the body moves | worked working | How much work needs to be done to pick up the box? |

Create a chart for these science academic vocabulary words: *glacier, tsunami, atomic, tectonic,* and *fracture.*

## Art: Domain-Specific Academic Vocabulary

| Word | Definition | Related Words | Word in Context |
|------|-----------|---------------|-----------------|
| abstract (ab STRAKT) *adj.* | not depicting recognizable scenes or objects | abstraction abstractly | The artist was known for his abstract paintings. |
| tone (tohn) *n.* | a slight modification of a given color | tonal | He chose a tone that matched the color of the leaves. |
| monochrome (MON uh krohm) *adj.* | in the shades of a single color | monochromatic | The red painting was monochromatic. |
| complementary (kom pluh MEN tuh ree) *adj.* | perceived as enhancing each other or another | complement complementariness | The colors in the painting are complementary. |
| proportion (pruh PAWR shuhn) *n.* | relation between parts | proportional proportioned | The figures are drawn in correct proportion. |

Create a chart for these art academic vocabulary words: *outline, still life, sketch, contrast,* and *repetition.*

## Technology: Domain-Specific Academic Vocabulary

| Word | Definition | Related Words | Word in Context |
|------|-----------|---------------|-----------------|
| byte (byt) *n.* | a unit of computer information consisting of eight bits | megabyte gigabyte | The storage device can hold many bytes. |
| processor (PROS es er) *n.* | electronic device that responds to instructions that drive a computer | process processing | The computer processor quickly performs calculations. |
| pixel (PIK suhl) *n.* | any of a number of very small picture elements that make up a picture | pixelated | I could see a single pixel in the magnified picture. |
| application (ap li KAY shuhn) *n.* | software designed to help a user perform specific tasks | apply | The computer application will track the information. |
| streaming (STREE ming) *n.* | technique for transferring data as a continuous stream | stream | The presenter was live streaming a video. |

Create a chart for these technology academic vocabulary words: *graphic, format, copyright, scanner,* and *browser.*

## Increasing Your Word Knowledge

Increase your word knowledge and chances of success by taking an active role in developing your vocabulary. Here are some tips for you.

To own a word, follow these steps:

| Steps to Follow | Model |
|---|---|
| 1. Learn to identify the word and its basic meaning. | The word *examine* means "to look at closely." |
| 2. Take note of the word's spelling. | *Examine* begins and ends with an *e*. |
| 3. Practice pronouncing the word so that you can use it in conversation. | The *e* on the end of the word is silent. Its second syllable gets the most stress. |
| 4. Visualize the word and illustrate its key meaning. | When I think of the word *examine*, I visualize a doctor checking a patient's health. |
| 5. Learn the various forms of the word and its related words. | *Examination* and *exam* are forms of the word *examine*. |
| 6. Compare the word with similar words. | *Examine*, *peruse*, and *study* are synonyms. |
| 7. Contrast the word with similar words. | *Examine* suggests a more detailed study than *read* or *look at*. |
| 8. Use the word in various contexts. | "I'd like to *examine* the footprints more closely." "I will *examine* the use of imagery in this poem." |

## Building Your Speaking Vocabulary

Language gives us the ability to express ourselves. The more words you know, the better able you will be to get your points across. There are two main aspects of language: reading and speaking. Using the steps above will help you to acquire a rich vocabulary. Follow these steps to help you learn to use this rich vocabulary in discussions, speeches, and conversations.

| Steps to Follow | Tip |
|---|---|
| 1. Practice pronouncing the word. | Become familiar with pronunciation guides to allow you to sound out unfamiliar words. Listening to audio books as you read the text will help you learn pronunciations of words. |
| 2. Learn word forms. | Dictionaries often list forms of words following the main word entry. Practice saying word families aloud: "generate," "generated," "generation," "regenerate," "generator." |
| 3. Translate your thoughts. | Restate your own thoughts and ideas in a variety of ways, to inject formality or to change your tone, for example. |
| 4. Hold discussions. | With a classmate, practice using academic vocabulary words in discussions about the text. Choose one term to practice at a time, and see how many statements you can create using that term. |
| 5. Record yourself. | Analyze your word choices by listening to yourself objectively. Note places your word choice could be strengthened or changed. |

# Writing an Objective Summary

The ability to write objective summaries is key to success in college and in many careers. Writing an effective objective summary involves recording the key ideas of a text while demonstrating your understanding.

**Common Core State Standards**

**Literature 2.** Determine a theme or central idea of a text and analyze in detail its development over the course of the text, including how it emerges and is shaped and refined by specific details; provide an objective summary of the text.

## What Is an Objective Summary?

An effective objective summary is a concise, complete, and accurate overview of a text. Following are key elements of an objective summary:

- A good summary focuses on the main theme or central idea of a text and specific, relevant details that support that theme or central idea, while unnecessary supporting details are left out.

- Effective summaries are brief, although the writer must take care not to misrepresent the text by leaving out key elements.

- A summary should accurately capture the essence of the longer text it is describing.

- Finally, the writer must take care to remain objective, or to refrain from inserting his or her own opinions, reactions, or personal connections into the summary.

## What to Avoid in an Objective Summary

- Avoid simply copying a collection of sentences or paragraphs from the original source.

- An objective summary should also not be a long recounting of every event, detail, or point in the original text.

- Finally, a good summary does not include evaluative comments, such as the reader's overall opinion of or reaction to the piece. An objective summary is not the reader's interpretation or critical analysis of the work.

# Model Objective Summary

Note the elements of an effective objective summary, called out in the yellow sidenotes. Then, write an objective summary of a text you have recently read. Review your summary, and delete any unnecessary details, opinions, or evaluations.

### Summary of "Thank You, M'am"

"Thank You, M'am" by Langston Hughes is an ~~amusing~~ story of a young boy who tries to steal a large purse from Mrs. Luella Bates Washington Jones, but he gets more than he expected.

The story begins with a description of a large woman with a heavy purse walking alone at night. A boy tries to snatch her purse, but the weight of the purse causes him to fall on the ground. The woman kicks the boy and then grabs his shirt, picking him up off the ground.

Then, the woman asks the boy if he will run if she lets go. He says yes, so she doesn't let go. The boy tells her he is sorry, and the woman responds by stating that his face is dirty. She begins to drag him down the street, declaring that his face will be washed this evening. ~~The boy looks to be fourteen years old.~~

The boy tells the woman that he just wants to be let go, and the woman responds that he put himself in contact with her, and that contact is going to last awhile. She tells him that he will remember Mrs. Luella Bates Washington Jones.

The boy begins to struggle, but Mrs. Jones pins his arm up and drags him to her room. She asks the boy his name, and he tells her: Roger. She lets go of Roger and commands him to go wash his face. Even though the door is open, he goes to the sink.

Mrs. Jones then asks if Roger tried to steal her purse because he was hungry. He explains that he wanted a pair of blue suede shoes. Mrs. Jones tells him he didn't have to snatch her purse for shoes, but that he could have asked her.

After a long pause, during which Roger once again thinks of running away, Mrs. Jones reveals that she once wanted things she could not get, and she had done things she would not talk about. Mrs. Jones leaves Roger alone with her purse as she goes behind a screen to prepare food. Roger wants her to trust him, so he moves to where she can see him.

After dinner, she gives him ten dollars to buy blue suede shoes and tells him not to steal anymore.

Mrs. Jones then walks him to the door and wishes him good night. Roger is unable to say anything, even "Thank you, M'am" before Mrs. Jones shuts the door. Mrs. Jones was right: the unexpected kindness she showed him means Roger will never forget Mrs. Luella Bates Washington Jones.

A one-sentence synopsis highlighting the theme or central idea of the story can be an effective start to a summary.

The adjective *amusing* marks an opinion and should not be included in an objective summary.

Relating the development of the text in chronological order makes a summary easy to follow.

Unnecessary details should be eliminated.

Not using the woman and the boy's names until this point keeps with the essence of the story.

A key phrase at the end of the story is included in the summary.

The writer's interpretations should not appear in an objective summary.

# Comprehending Complex Texts

 **Common Core
State Standards**

**Literature 10.** By the end of grade 9, read and comprehend literature, including stories, dramas, and poems, in the grades 9–10 text complexity band proficiently, with scaffolding as needed at the high end of the range.

**Informational Text 10.** By the end of grade 9, read and comprehend literary nonfiction in the grades 9–10 text complexity band proficiently, with scaffolding as needed at the high end of the range.

Over the course of your academic years, you will be required to read increasingly complex texts as preparation for college and the workplace. A complex text can be loosely described as a text that contains challenging vocabulary; long, complex sentences; figurative language; multiple levels of meaning; or unfamiliar settings and situations.

The texts in this textbook provide you with a range of readings, from short stories to autobiographies, poetry, drama, myths, and even science and social studies texts. Some of these texts will fall within your comfort zone; others will most likely be more challenging.

## Strategy 1: Multidraft Reading

Good readers develop the habit of revisiting texts in order to comprehend them completely. Just as a musician returns over and over again to a song in order to master it, good readers return to texts to more fully enjoy and comprehend them. To fully understand a text, try this multidraft reading strategy:

### 1st Reading
The first time you read a text, read to gain the basic meaning of the text. If you are reading a narrative text, look for some of the story basics: who did what to whom. If the text is nonfiction, look for the main ideas. If you are reading poetry, read first to get a sense of who the speaker is. Also take note of the setting and situation.

### 2nd Reading
During your second reading of a text, focus on the artistry or effectiveness of the writing. Look for text structures and think about why the author chose those organizational patterns. Then, examine the author's creative uses of language and the effects of that language. For example, has the author used rhyme, figurative language, or words with negative connotations?

### 3rd Reading
After your third reading, compare and contrast the text with others of its kind you have read. For example, if you read a poem in sonnet form, think of other sonnets you have read, and think of ways the poems are alike or different. Evaluate the text's overall effectiveness and its central idea or theme.

# Independent Practice

As you read this poem, practice the multidraft reading strategy by completing a chart like the one below.

## "Memory" by Margaret Walker

I can remember wind-swept streets of cities
on cold and blustery nights, on rainy days;
heads under shabby felts and parasols
and shoulders hunched against a sharp concern;
seeing hurt bewilderment on poor faces,
smelling a deep and sinister unrest
these brooding people cautiously caress;
hearing ghostly marching on pavement stones
and closing fast around their squares of hate.
I can remember seeing them alone,
at work, and in their tenements at home.
I can remember hearing all they said:
their muttering protests their whispered oaths,
and all that spells their living in distress.

## Multidraft Reading Chart

|  | My Understanding |
|---|---|
| **1st Reading**<br>Look for key ideas and details that unlock basic meaning. |  |
| **2nd Reading**<br>Read for deeper meanings. Look for ways in which the author used text structures and language to create effects. |  |
| **3rd Reading**<br>Read to integrate your knowledge and ideas. Connect the text to others of its kind and to your own experience. |  |

# Strategy 2: Close Read the Text

Complex texts require close reading, a careful analysis of the words, phrases, and sentences. When you close read, use the following tips to comprehend the text:

---

### Tips for Close Reading

1. **Break down long sentences** into parts. Look for the subject of the sentence and its verb. Then, identify which parts of the sentence modify, or give more information about, its subject.

2. **Reread passages** to confirm that you understand their meaning.

3. **Look for context clues,** such as

   a. restatement of an idea. For example, in this sentence, "utter defeat" restates the noun *rout*.

      The rugby team celebrated its **rout,** its <u>utter defeat</u>, of its arch rival.

   b. definition of sophisticated words. In this sentence, the underlined information defines the word *fealty*.

      **Fealty** is a <u>pledge of support and allegiance between one person and another</u>.

   c. examples of concepts and topics. In the following passage, the underlined text provides examples of the adjective *serendipitous*.

      <u>Discovering a treasure when cleaning out an attic or bumping into an old friend when taking shelter from a rain storm</u>—these **serendipitous** events never fail to bring a smile to one's face.

   d. contrasts of ideas and topics.

      **Altruism,** <u>unlike selfishness</u>, is a rare quality.

4. **Identify pronoun antecedents.** If long sentences contain pronouns, reread the text to make sure you know to what the pronouns refer.

5. **Look for conjunctions,** such as *and*, *or*, and *yet*, to understand relationships between ideas.

6. **Paraphrase,** or restate in your own words, passages of difficult text in order to check your understanding. Remember that a paraphrase is a restatement of an original text; it is not a summary.

---

# Close-Read Model

As you read this document, take note of the sidenotes that model ways to unlock meaning in the text.

---

### from *The Federalist* No. 2 by John Jay

To the People of the State of New York:

WHEN the people of America reflect that they are now called upon to decide a question, which, in its consequences, must prove one of the most important that ever engaged their attention, the propriety of their taking a very comprehensive, as well as a very serious, view of it, will be evident. Nothing is more certain than the indispensable necessity of government, and it is equally undeniable, that whenever and however it is instituted, the people must cede to it some of their natural rights in order to vest it with requisite powers. It is well worthy of consideration therefore, whether it would conduce more to the interest of the people of America that they should, to all general purposes, be one nation, under one federal government, or that they should divide themselves into separate confederacies, and give to the head of each the same kind of powers which they are advised to place in one national government.

It has until lately been a received and uncontradicted opinion that the prosperity of the people of America depended on their continuing firmly united, and the wishes, prayers, and efforts of our best and wisest citizens have been constantly directed to that object. But politicians now appear, who insist that this opinion is erroneous, and that instead of looking for safety and happiness in union, we ought to seek it in a division of the States into distinct confederacies or sovereignties. However extraordinary this new doctrine may appear, it nevertheless has its advocates; and certain characters who were much opposed to it formerly, are at present of the number. Whatever may be the arguments or inducements which have wrought this change in the sentiments and declarations of these gentlemen, it certainly would not be wise in the people at large to adopt these new political tenets without being fully convinced that they are founded in truth and sound policy.

---

Break down this long sentence into parts. The text highlighted in yellow conveys the basic meaning of the sentence. The text highlighted in blue provides additional information.

Look for antecedents. In this sentence, the noun, *government*, is replaced by the pronoun *it*.

The conjunction *or* indicates that two options are being presented.

Search for context clues. The words in blue are context clues that help you figure out the meaning of the words in yellow.

# Strategy 3: Ask Questions

Be an attentive reader by asking questions as you read. Throughout this textbook, we have provided questions for you following each selection. These questions are sorted into three basic categories that build in sophistication and lead you to a deeper understanding of the texts you read.

Here is an example from this text:

Some questions are about **Key Ideas and Details** in the text. To answer these questions, you will need to locate and cite explicit information in the text or draw inferences from what you have read.

Some questions are about **Craft and Structure** in the text. To answer these questions, you will need to analyze how the author developed and structured the text. You will also look for ways in which the author artfully used language and how those word choices impacted the meaning and tone of the work.

### After You Read — "Before Hip-Hop Was Hip-Hop"

1. **Key Ideas and Details (a)** According to Walker, why did P.S. 141 "crackle" with energy? **(b) Analyze Cause and Effect:** In what ways did hip-hop help Walker and her friends bridge differences?

2. **Key Ideas and Details (a) Draw Conclusions:** Why was it so important for Walker and her friends to define themselves through dress, special language, dance, and music? **(b) Generalize:** What do teenagers use today to express themselves?

3. **Craft and Structure (a)** Is the **tone** of Walker's **essay** personal or impersonal? **(b)** What other adjectives appropriately describe her tone? **(c)** Which details in the first three paragraphs support your answers?

4. **Craft and Structure** What overall **organizational structure** does Walker use to organize her essay?

5. **Craft and Structure (a)** Use a chart like this one to analyze Walker's **style,** noting passages that support your ideas.

| Level of Formality | Word Choice | Sentence Patterns |
|---|---|---|
|  |  |  |

**(b) Collaboration:** In a small group, discuss the examples in your chart and develop a one-sentence description of Walker's writing style.

6. **Integration of Knowledge and Ideas (a) Compare and Contrast:** What differences does Walker find between the music of her youth and today's hip-hop? **(b) Take a Position:** Do you think Walker's judgment is fair or biased? Explain.

7. **Key Ideas and Details** Write an objective summary of "Before Hip-Hop Was Hip-Hop." Remember that an objective summary should not include your personal reaction to the selection, just the most important ideas and details.

Some questions are about the **Integration of Knowledge and Ideas**. These questions ask you to evaluate a text in many different ways, such as comparing texts, analyzing arguments in the text, and using many other methods of thinking critically about a text's ideas.

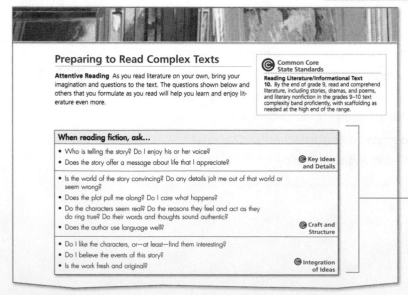

### Preparing to Read Complex Texts

**Attentive Reading** As you read literature on your own, bring your imagination and questions to the text. The questions shown below and others that you formulate as you read will help you learn and enjoy literature even more.

**Common Core State Standards**

**Reading Literature/Informational Text**
**10.** By the end of grade 9, read and comprehend literature, including stories, dramas, and poems, and literary nonfiction in the grades 9–10 text complexity band proficiently, with scaffolding as needed at the high end of the range.

**When reading fiction, ask...**

- Who is telling the story? Do I enjoy his or her voice?
- Does the story offer a message about life that I appreciate?

*Key Ideas and Details*

- Is the world of the story convincing? Do any details jolt me out of that world or seem wrong?
- Does the plot pull me along? Do I care what happens?
- Do the characters seem real? Do the reasons they feel and act as they do ring true? Do their words and thoughts sound authentic?
- Does the author use language well?

*Craft and Structure*

- Do I like the characters, or—at least—find them interesting?
- Do I believe the events of this story?
- Is the work fresh and original?

*Integration of Ideas*

As you read independently, ask similar types of questions to ensure that you fully enjoy and comprehend texts you read for school and for pleasure. We have provided sets of questions for you on the Independent Reading pages at the end of each unit.

INFORMATIONAL TEXT

# Model

Following is an example of a complex text. The sidenotes show sample questions that an attentive reader might ask while reading.

**Sample questions:**

### from "Farewell Address" by General Douglas MacArthur

. . . I have just left your fighting sons in Korea. . . . It was my constant effort to preserve them and end this savage conflict honorably and with the least loss of time and a minimum sacrifice of life. . . . Those gallant men will remain often in my thoughts and in my prayers always.

I am closing my fifty-two years of military service. . . . The world has turned over many times since I took the oath on the plain at West Point . . . but I still remember the refrain of one of the most popular barracks ballads of that day which proclaimed most proudly that old soldiers never die; they just fade away. And like the old soldier of that ballad, I now close my military career and just fade away, an old soldier who tried to do his duty as God gave him the light to see that duty. Good-by.

**Integration of Knowledge and Ideas** What do I know about the Korean War? What can I learn from the General's comments?

**Key Ideas and Details** What ideas are introduced in the first paragraph? How is the second paragraph different in topic? How are the two paragraphs related?

**Craft and Structure** How is the last paragraph a good conclusion? How does the General feel about the Korean War? How does he feel about his career?

INFORMATIONAL TEXT

# Independent Practice

Write three to five questions you might ask yourself as you read this passage from a speech delivered by Andrew Johnson shortly after the death of Abraham Lincoln.

### from "State of the Union Address" by Andrew Johnson

. . . To express gratitude to God in the name of the people for the preservation of the United States is my first duty in addressing you. Our thoughts next revert to the death of the late President by an act of parricidal treason. The grief of the nation is still fresh. It finds some solace in the consideration that he lived to enjoy the highest proof of its confidence by entering on the renewed term of the Chief Magistracy to which he had been elected; that he brought the civil war substantially to a close; that his loss was deplored in all parts of the Union, and that foreign nations have rendered justice to his memory. His removal cast upon me a heavier weight of cares than ever devolved upon any one of his predecessors. To fulfill my trust I need the support and confidence of all who are associated with me in the various departments of Government and the support and confidence of the people.

# Analyzing Arguments

The ability to evaluate an argument, as well as to make one, is an important skill for success in college and in the workplace.

## What Is an Argument?

When you think of the word *argument,* you might think of a disagreement between two people, but an argument is more than that. An argument is a logical way of presenting a belief, conclusion, or stance. A good argument is supported with logical reasoning and relevant evidence.

## Purposes of Argument

There are three main purposes for writing a formal argument:

- to change the reader's mind
- to convince the reader to accept what is written
- to motivate the reader to take action, based on what is written

### Elements of Argument

**Claim** (assertion)—what the writer is trying to prove or the call to action
*Example: Harold would make a good student council president.*

**Grounds** (evidence)—the support used to convince the reader
*Example: He participates in several extracurricular activities, volunteers locally, and earns good grades.*

**Justification**—the link between the grounds and the claim; why the grounds are credible
*Example: School and community involvement suggest he knows his school and town well; good grades indicate intelligence.*

## Addressing the Opposition

While it might be tempting to ignore the opposing side of an issue because you don't agree with it, it is important to present a balanced argument. You can make your argument stronger by refuting the opposition's claim or by demonstrating that you understand it, or perhaps even accept a part or parts of it. When calling someone to action, it is important to address barriers to that action, or to point out ways that the person has already moved in that direction.

 **Common Core State Standards**

**Informational Text 6.** Determine an author's point of view or purpose in a text and analyze how an author uses rhetoric to advance that point of view or purpose.

**Informational Text 8.** Delineate and evaluate the argument and specific claims in a text, assessing whether the reasoning is valid and the evidence is relevant and sufficient; identify false statements and fallacious reasoning.

**Informational Text 9.** Analyze seminal U.S. documents of historical and literary significance (e.g., Washington's Farewell Address, the Gettysburg Address, Roosevelt's Four Freedoms speech, King's "Letter from Birmingham Jail"), including how they address related themes and concepts.

**Language 6.** Acquire and use accurately grade-appropriate general academic and domain-specific words and phrases; gather vocabulary knowledge when considering a word or phrase important to comprehension or expression.

INFORMATIONAL TEXT

# Model Argument

The excerpted speech includes the common elements of arguments.

### from "Remarks on East-West Relations at the Brandenburg Gate in West Berlin," June 12, 1987 by Ronald Reagan

…Behind me stands a wall that encircles the free sectors of this city, part of a vast system of barriers that divides the entire continent of Europe. From the Baltic, south, those barriers cut across Germany in a gash of barbed wire, concrete, dog runs, and guardtowers. Farther south, there may be no visible, no obvious wall. But there remain armed guards and checkpoints all the same—still a restriction on the right to travel, still an instrument to impose upon ordinary men and women the will of a totalitarian state.…

> The first part of the argument describes the setting and context for the call to action.

…Yet I do not come here to lament. For I find in Berlin a message of hope, even in the shadow of this wall, a message of triumph…

…Where four decades ago there was rubble, today in West Berlin there is the greatest industrial output of any city in Germany—busy office blocks, fine homes and apartments, proud avenues, and the spreading lawns of park land. Where a city's culture seemed to have been destroyed, today there are two great universities, orchestras and an opera, countless theaters, and museums. Where there was want, today there's abundance—food, clothing, automobiles …From devastation, from utter ruin, you Berliners have, in freedom, rebuilt a city that once again ranks as one of the greatest on Earth…

> **Grounds:** The free West achieved prosperity, while the Communist East remained in decline.

…In the 1950s, Khrushchev predicted: "We will bury you." But in the West today, we see a free world that has achieved a level of prosperity and well-being unprecedented in all human history. In the Communist world, we see failure, technological backwardness, declining standards of health, even want of the most basic kind-too little food. Even today, the Soviet Union still cannot feed itself. After these four decades, then, there stands before the entire world one great and inescapable conclusion: Freedom leads to prosperity…

> **Justification:** A country achieves prosperity when its people have economic freedom. (The grounds support this idea with the example of the free West vs. the Communist East.)

And now the Soviets themselves may, in a limited way, be coming to understand the importance of freedom. We hear much from Moscow about a new policy of reform and openness. Some political prisoners have been released. Certain foreign news broadcasts are no longer being jammed. Some economic enterprises have been permitted to operate with greater freedom from state control. Are these the beginnings of profound changes in the Soviet state?…

> The opposition's claim is refuted; later, the opposition is acknowledged for the steps they have already taken.

There is one sign the Soviets can make that would be unmistakable, that would advance dramatically the cause of freedom and peace. General Secretary Gorbachev, …if you seek prosperity for the Soviet Union and Eastern Europe… Come here to this gate! Mr. Gorbachev, open this gate! Mr. Gorbachev, tear down this wall!

> **Claim:** The wall dividing West and East Berlin should be torn down.

> The speaker gives a specific call to action.

# The Art of Argument: Rhetorical Devices and Persuasive Techniques

## Rhetorical Devices

Rhetoric is the art of using language in order to make a point or to persuade listeners. Rhetorical devices such as the ones listed below are accepted elements of argument. Their use does not invalidate or weaken an argument. Rather, the use of rhetorical devices is regarded as a key part of an effective argument.

| Rhetorical Devices | Examples |
|---|---|
| **Repetition** The repeated use of certain words, phrases, or sentences | What we long for is freedom. Freedom to work. Freedom to learn. |
| **Parallelism** The repeated use of similar grammatical structures | Good writing entertains; great writing inspires. |
| **Rhetorical Question** Calling attention to an issue by implying an obvious answer | Is there no reasonable solution to this problem? |
| **Sound Devices** The use of alliteration, assonance, rhyme, or rhythm | The path before them was dark, dangerous, and daunting. |
| **Simile and Metaphor** Comparison of two like things or asserting that one thing is another | We are caged birds, unable to fly free. |

## Persuasive Techniques

The persuasive techniques below are often found in advertisements and in other forms of informal persuasion. Although techniques like the ones below are sometimes found in formal arguments, these techniques are usually avoided.

| Persuasive Techniques | Examples |
|---|---|
| **Bandwagon Approach/Anti-Bandwagon Approach** Appeals to a person's desire to belong/Encourages or celebrates individuality | You have to buy one; everyone has one. Be yourself; don't give into peer pressure. |
| **Emotional Appeal** Capitalizes on people's fear, anger, or desire | Without a home security system, your family is in danger. |
| **Endorsement/Testimony** Employs a well-known person to promote a product or idea | I use this product every time before I compete, and it has helped me win. |
| **Loaded Language** Uses words charged with emotion | They live in abject squalor, their hovels not fit for human inhabitation. |
| **"Plain Folks" Appeal** Shows a connection to everyday, ordinary people | I grew up in a hard-working community just like this one. |
| **Hyperbole** Exaggerates to make a point | There are a thousand reasons why I'm right. |

 **EXEMPLAR TEXT**

# Model Speech

The excerpted speech below includes examples of rhetorical devices and persuasive techniques.

---

### from "Remarks to the Senate in Support of a Declaration of Conscience" by Margaret Chase Smith

Mr. President:

I would like to speak briefly and simply about a serious national condition. It is a national feeling of fear and frustration that could result in national suicide and the end of everything that we Americans hold dear...

> This emotional language appeals to national pride.

...The United States Senate has long enjoyed worldwide respect as the greatest deliberative body in the world. But recently that deliberative character has too often been debased to the level of a forum of hate and character assassination sheltered by the shield of congressional immunity....

...I think that it is high time for the United States Senate and its members to do some soul-searching—for us to weigh our consciences—on the manner in which we are performing our duty to the people of America—on the manner in which we are using or abusing our individual powers and privileges. I think that it is high time that we remembered that we have sworn to uphold and defend the Constitution. I think that it is high time that we remembered that the Constitution, as amended, speaks not only of the freedom of speech but also of trial by jury instead of trial by accusation....

> The repetition of the first few words in each sentence gives the speech rhythm.

Whether it be a criminal prosecution in court or a character prosecution in the Senate, there is little practical distinction when the life of a person has been ruined.

Those of us who shout the loudest about Americanism in making character assassinations are all too frequently those who, by our own words and acts, ignore some of the basic principles of Americanism:

The right to criticize;

The right to hold unpopular beliefs;

The right to protest;

The right of independent thought.

The exercise of these rights should not cost one single American citizen his reputation or his right to a livelihood nor should he be in danger of losing his reputation or livelihood merely because he happens to know someone who holds unpopular beliefs. Who of us doesn't? Otherwise none of us could call our souls our own. Otherwise thought control would have set in...

> The rhetorical question assumes that all people listening would answer in the same way.

...The American people are sick and tired of seeing innocent people smeared and guilty people whitewashed...

> The parallelism created by repeated grammatical structures adds to the rhythm of the speech.

---

# Composing an Argument

**Common Core
State Standards**

**Writing 1.a.** Introduce precise, knowledgeable claim(s), distinguish the claim(s) from alternate or opposing claims, and create an organization that establishes clear relationships among claim(s), counterclaims, reasons, and evidence.

**Writing 1.b.** Develop claim(s) and counterclaims fairly, supplying evidence for each while pointing out the strengths and limitations of both in a manner that anticipates the audience's knowledge level and concerns.

**Writing 1.e.** Provide a concluding statement or section that follows from and supports the argument presented.

## Choosing a Topic

You should choose a topic that matters to people—and to you. Brainstorm topics you would like to write about; then, choose the topic that most interests you.

Once you have chosen a topic, you should check to make sure you can make an arguable claim. Ask yourself:

1. What am I trying to prove?
2. Are there people who would disagree with my claim?
3. Do I have evidence to support my claim?

If you are able to put into words what you want to prove and answered "yes" to questions 2 and 3, you have an arguable claim.

## Introducing the Claim and Establishing Its Significance

Before you begin writing, you should consider your audience and how much you think they already know about the topic you have chosen to write about. Then, provide only as much background information as necessary. Remember that you are not writing a summary of the issue—you are crafting an argument.

Once you have provided context for your argument, you should clearly state your claim, or thesis. A written argument's claim often appears in the first paragraph.

## Developing Your Claim with Reasoning and Evidence

Now that you have made your claim, you must support it with evidence, or grounds. A good argument should have at least three solid pieces of evidence to support the claim.

Evidence can range from personal experience to researched data or expert opinion. Knowing your audience's knowledge level, concerns, values, and possible biases can help inform your decision on what kind of evidence will have the strongest impact. Make sure your evidence is up to date and comes from a credible source, and don't forget to credit your sources. *(See page R36 for guidelines on citing sources.)*

You should also address the opposing counterclaim within the body of your argument. Consider points you have made or evidence you have provided that a person might challenge. Decide how best to respond to these counterclaims.

## Writing a Concluding Statement or Section

Restate your claim in the conclusion (not necessarily word for word) and synthesize the evidence you have provided. Make your conclusion compelling enough to be memorable to the reader; leave him or her with something to think about.

# Practice

Complete an outline like the one below to help you plan your own argument.

Brainstorming for Topics:

_____

_____

The Topic That Most Interests Me Is _____ because

_____

Arguable Claim (Thesis): _____

What I Already Know About the Issue: _____

What I Need to Find Out About the Issue:

_____

Who Is My Audience and How Much Does My Audience Know About the Issue?

_____

Possible Sources of Evidence: _____

Grounds to Support My Claim (at least three strong pieces of evidence):

1. _____

2. _____

3. _____

Justifications for My Grounds (why my grounds are allowed to stand as evidence):

1. _____

2. _____

3. _____

Opposing Viewpoints to Consider: _____

# Media Literacy Handbook

**INTRODUCTION:** Today, messages are transmitted across a variety of media modes, such as film, television, radio, and the Internet. As you interact with these messages each day—in images, advertisements, movies, and an array of different contexts—it is important to consider the potential influence of the medium.

- What is the intention of the message?
- How is it communicated?
- How do specific elements of the medium—such as color, image, or font—help convey the message?
- Why might the creator of the message have selected this medium?

These are the key issues of media literacy, the study of messages in the media and their impact.

## Camera Shots and Angles

Filmmakers create camera shots and sequences to help them tell stories. Some shots capture an entire scene; others zoom in on specific characters.

## Special Effects

Filmmakers use special effects to create on-screen illusions that bring the imagination to life.

## Questions About Film Techniques

- What effect is created by the choice of camera angle shown in the image at left? Choose another camera angle and explain how that shot might convey a different message than the one shown here.

- Study the images above. In what way does the use of special effects make the film better for viewers?

## Focus and Framing

A sharp focus captures all details in a photographic image. A softer focus lessens the amount of detail that can be seen. The framing of elements within a photograph directs the eye toward a portion of the image.

## Lighting and Shadow

Lighting techniques are used in photography to enhance mood and direct the viewer's focus.

## Special Techniques

Most images you see today have been manipulated or changed in some way. Even a small change—such as an added graphic element or a difference in shading—can alter the mood of an image.

## Questions About Graphics and Photos

- What would be the effect if the image at left used a different focus?

- In what way does the use of color and light create mood in the photo at left?

- What special techniques were applied to the original photograph shown above? What effect does the use of special techniques create?

**Persuasive Techniques**
Advertisements use carefully selected visual elements to appeal to the viewer's emotions.

## Text and Graphics

Newspaper and magazine layouts are constructed to capture the eye and quickly convey the important ideas of a story. The use of type fonts, images, and page space direct the eye to portions of the printed page.

## Questions About Print Media

- What image or graphic dominates the advertisement at left? How does the image make the advertisement more effective?

- Which of the above grabs your attention: the image or the text on the magazine cover? Explain.

- What do you notice first on the newspaper's front page? What overall effect does the use of type size and fonts create?

# How is this book organized?

- There are six units, each focusing on a specific genre.
- Each unit has a Big Question to get you thinking about important ideas and to guide your reading.
- A Literary Analysis Workshop begins each unit, providing instruction and practice for essential skills.

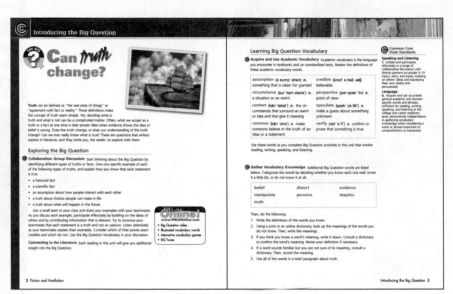

◀ At the beginning of the unit, **Introducing the Big Question** provides a reading focus for the entire unit. Use **academic vocabulary** to think, talk, and write about this question.

A **Literary Analysis Workshop** provides an overview of the unit genre, an in-depth exploration of Common Core State Standards, as well as models and practice opportunities. ▶

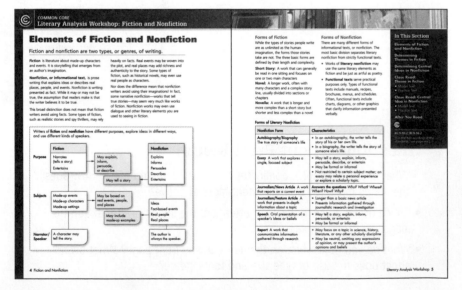

# How are the literary selections organized?

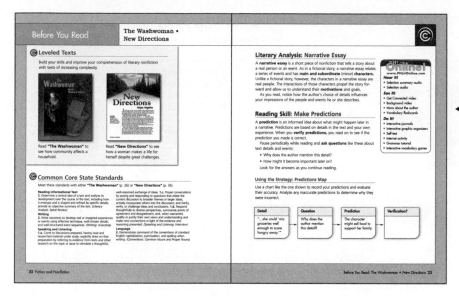

◀ **Before You Read** introduces two selection choices that both teach the same skills. Your teacher will help you choose the selection that is right for you.

**Writing About the Big Question** is a quick-writing activity that helps you connect the Big Question to the selection you are about to read.

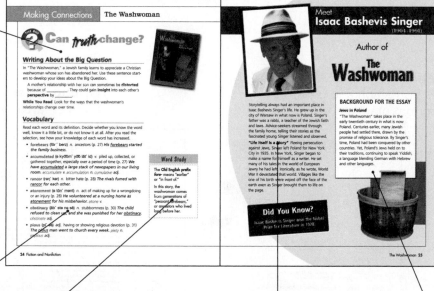

**Vocabulary and Word Study** introduce important selection vocabulary words and teach you about prefixes, suffixes, and roots.

**Meet the Author and Background** teach you about the author's life and provide information that will help you understand the selection.

# How are the literary selections organized? *(continued)*

**After You Read** helps you practice the skills you have learned. ▼

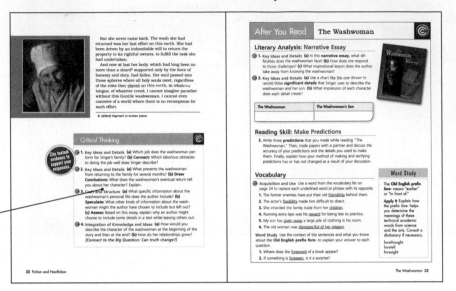

**Critical Thinking** questions help you reflect on what you have read and apply the Big Question to the selection.

**Integrated Language Skills** provides instruction and practice for important grammar skills.

Projects and activities help you deepen your understanding of the selection while strengthening your **writing, listening, speaking, and research skills.**

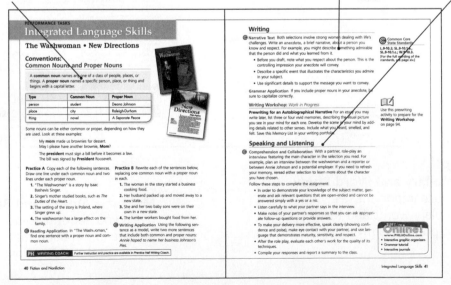

# What special features will I find in this book?

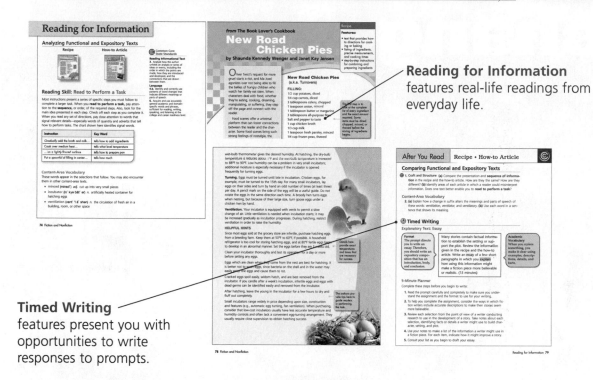

**Reading for Information**
features real-life readings from
everyday life.

**Timed Writing**
features present you with
opportunities to write
responses to prompts.

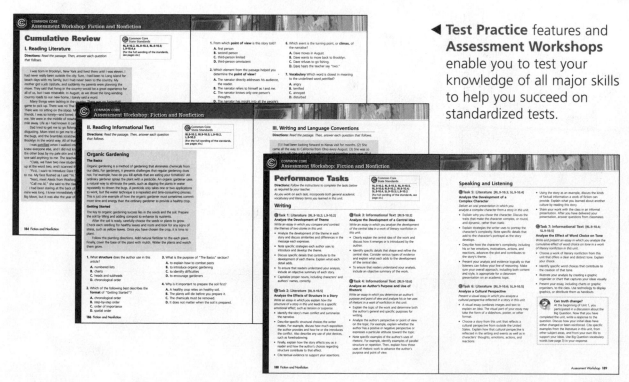

◄ **Test Practice** features and
**Assessment Workshops**
enable you to test your
knowledge of all major skills
to help you succeed on
standardized tests.

# Can *truth* change?

# Fiction and Nonfiction

## PHLit Online!
### www.PHLitOnline.com

*Hear It!*
- Selection summary audio
- Selection audio
- BQ Tunes

*See It!*
- Author videos
- Big Question video
- Get Connected videos
- Background videos
- More about the authors
- Illustrated vocabulary words
- Vocabulary flashcards

*Do It!*
- Interactive journals
- Interactive graphic organizers
- Grammar tutorials
- Interactive vocabulary games
- Test practice

# Can *truth* change?

**Truth** can be defined as "the real state of things" or "agreement with fact or reality." These definitions make the concept of truth seem simple. Yet, deciding what is truth and what is not can be a complicated matter. Often, what we accept as a truth or a fact at one time is later proven false when evidence shows the idea or belief is wrong. Does the truth change, or does our understanding of the truth change? Can we ever really know what is true? These are questions that writers explore in literature, and they invite you, the reader, to explore with them.

## Exploring the Big Question

**Collaboration: Group Discussion** Start thinking about the Big Question by identifying different types of truths or facts. Give one specific example of each of the following types of truths, and explain how you know that each statement is true.

- a historical fact
- a scientific fact
- an assumption about how people interact with each other
- a truth about choices people can make in life
- a truth about what will happen in the future

Join a small team in your class and share your examples with your teammates. As you discuss each example, participate effectively by building on the ideas of others and by contributing information that is relevant. Try to convince your teammates that each statement is a truth and not an opinion. Listen attentively as your teammates explain their examples. Consider which of their points seem credible and which do not. Use the Big Question Vocabulary in your discussion.

**Connecting to the Literature** Each reading in this unit will give you additional insight into the Big Question.

**PHLit**
**Online!**
www.PHLitOnline.com
- Big Question video
- Illustrated vocabulary words
- Interactive vocabulary games
- BQ Tunes

# Learning Big Question Vocabulary

**Common Core State Standards**

**Speaking and Listening**
**1.** Initiate and participate effectively in a range of collaborative discussions with diverse partners on grades 9–10 topics, texts, and issues, building on others' ideas and expressing their own clearly and persuasively.

**Language**
**6.** Acquire and use accurately general academic and domain-specific words and phrases, sufficient for reading, writing, speaking, and listening at the college and career readiness level; demonstrate independence in gathering vocabulary knowledge when considering a word or phrase important to comprehension or expression.

**Acquire and Use Academic Vocabulary** Academic vocabulary is the language you encounter in textbooks and on standardized tests. Review the definitions of these academic vocabulary words.

**assumption** (ə sump´ shən) **n.** something that is taken for granted

**circumstance** (sur´ kəm stans´) **n.** a situation or an event

**context** (kän´ tekst´) **n.** the circumstances that surround an event or idea and that give it meaning

**convince** (kän´ vins´) **v.** make someone believe in the truth of an idea or a statement

**credible** (kred´ ə bəl) **adj.** believable

**perspective** (pər spek´ tiv) **n.** point of view

**speculate** (spek´ yə lāt´) **v.** make a guess about something unknown

**verify** (ver´ ə fī´) **v.** confirm or prove that something is true

Use these words as you complete Big Question activities in this unit that involve reading, writing, speaking, and listening.

**Gather Vocabulary Knowledge** Additional Big Question words are listed below. Categorize the words by deciding whether you know each one well, know it a little bit, or do not know it at all.

| | | |
|---|---|---|
| belief | distort | evidence |
| manipulate | perceive | skeptics |
| truth | | |

Then, do the following:

1. Write the definitions of the words you know.

2. Using a print or an online dictionary, look up the meanings of the words you do not know. Then, write the meanings.

3. If you think you know a word's meaning, write it down. Consult a dictionary to confirm the word's meaning. Revise your definition if necessary.

4. If a word sounds familiar but you are not sure of its meaning, consult a dictionary. Then, record the meaning.

5. Use all of the words in a brief paragraph about truth.

# Elements of Fiction and Nonfiction

## Fiction and nonfiction are two types, or genres, of writing.

**Fiction** is literature about made-up characters and events. It is storytelling that emerges from an author's imagination.

**Nonfiction, or informational text,** is prose writing that explains ideas or describes real places, people, and events. Nonfiction is writing presented as fact. While it may or may not be true, the assumption that readers make is that the writer believes it to be true.

This broad distinction does not mean that fiction writers avoid using facts. Some types of fiction, such as realistic stories and spy thrillers, may rely heavily on facts. Real events may be woven into the plot, and real places may add richness and authenticity to the story. Some types of fiction, such as historical novels, may even use real people as characters.

Nor does the difference mean that nonfiction writers avoid using their imaginations! In fact, some narrative nonfiction—works that tell true stories—may seem very much like works of fiction. Nonfiction works may even use dialogue and other literary elements you are used to seeing in fiction.

Writers of **fiction** and **nonfiction** have different purposes, explore ideas in different ways, and use different kinds of speakers.

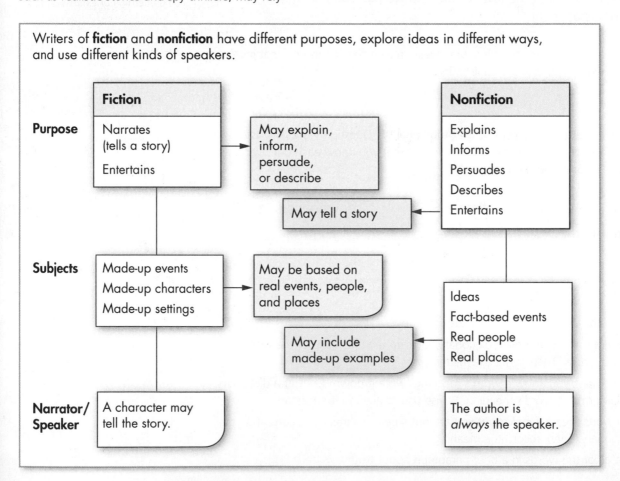

## Forms of Fiction

While the types of stories people write are as unlimited as the human imagination, the forms those stories take are not. The three basic forms are defined by their length and complexity.

**Short Story:** A work that can generally be read in one sitting and focuses on one or two main characters

**Novel:** A longer work, often with many characters and a complex story line, usually divided into sections or chapters

**Novella:** A work that is longer and more complex than a short story but shorter and less complex than a novel

## Forms of Nonfiction

There are many different forms of informational texts, or nonfiction. The most basic division separates literary nonfiction from strictly functional texts.

- Works of **literary nonfiction** may use the same literary elements as fiction and be just as artful as poetry.

- **Functional texts** serve practical purposes only. Types of functional texts include manuals, recipes, brochures, menus, and schedules. Often, functional texts include charts, diagrams, or other graphics that clarify information presented verbally.

 Common Core State Standards

RL.9-10.2; RI.9-10.2
[For the full wording of the standards, see the standards chart in the front of your textbook.]

## Forms of Literary Nonfiction

| Nonfiction Form | Characteristics |
|---|---|
| **Autobiography/Biography** The true story of someone's life | • In an autobiography, the writer tells the story of his or her own life.<br>• In a biography, the writer tells the story of someone else's life. |
| **Essay** A work that explores a single, focused subject | • May tell a story, explain, inform, persuade, describe, or entertain<br>• May be formal or informal<br>• Not restricted to certain subject matter; an essay may relate a personal experience or explore a scholarly topic. |
| **Journalism/News Article** A work that reports on a current event | **Answers the questions** Who? What? Where? When? How? Why? |
| **Journalism/Feature Article** A work that presents in-depth information about a topic | • Longer than a basic news article<br>• Presents information gathered through journalistic research and investigation |
| **Speech** Oral presentation of a speaker's ideas or beliefs | • May tell a story, explain, inform, persuade, or entertain<br>• May be formal or informal |
| **Report** A work that communicates information gathered through research | • May focus on a topic in science, history, literature, or any other scholarly discipline<br>• May be neutral, omitting any expressions of opinion, or may present the author's opinions and beliefs |

# Determining Themes in Fiction

## Works of fiction express themes—messages or insights about life.

**Common Core State Standards**

**Reading Literature**
**2.** Determine a theme or central idea of a text and analyze in detail its development over the course of the text, including how it emerges and is shaped and refined by specific details; provide an objective summary of the text.

A story may take you to whole new worlds, rich with amazing characters, events, and settings. That journey, full of drama, suspense, and intrigue, is a critical element of fiction. However, the true heart of a story is its deeper, underlying meaning—its theme. The theme is not the subject of the story. Rather, it is the insight with which the author explores the subject. This insight can often be expressed as a generalization about people or life.

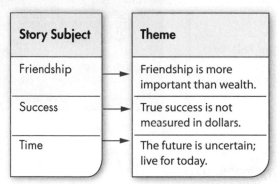

| Story Subject | Theme |
|---|---|
| Friendship | Friendship is more important than wealth. |
| Success | True success is not measured in dollars. |
| Time | The future is uncertain; live for today. |

**Universal Themes** Some themes are timeless, appearing in the literature of nearly all cultures and eras. Such universal themes express fundamental aspects of the human experience, such as the power of love or the danger of greed. Folk tales, fairy tales, epics, and legends often address universal themes, but so do contemporary novels, movies, and even video games.

**Multiple Themes** The length and complexity of some literary works may allow writers to explore more than one unifying thematic insight. Novels, full-length plays, and epic poems may have multiple themes, while short stories usually express a single theme.

**Multiple Interpretations of Theme** Writers use all the details of a story to develop the theme. However, your interpretation of those details and the theme they develop may be very different from someone else's. For example, consider just three of the ways you might interpret the theme of the traditional fairy tale "Beauty and the Beast":

**Example: Beauty and the Beast**
A poor but beautiful young woman falls in love with a rich prince who has been cursed to look like a horrible beast. Her love frees him from the curse, and the two live happily ever after.

**Interpretation of Theme**
1. Real beauty comes from a noble heart.
2. True love sees through outward appearances.
3. True love heals; it frees people from pain.

While all three interpretations center on related ideas—those of beauty, love, and suffering—the particular insight each expresses is slightly different. With more complex texts, such as those that involve multiple characters, locations, and events, interpretations may differ more widely. The best interpretation of a theme will take into account all of a story's critical details. It will show how an author has woven those details together into the unifying pattern of meaning that we call a theme.

# Determining Central Ideas in Nonfiction

## Works of literary nonfiction express central, or main, ideas.

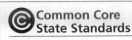 **Common Core State Standards**

**Reading Informational Text**
**2.** Determine a central idea of a text and analyze its development over the course of the text, including how it emerges and is shaped and refined by specific details; provide an objective summary of the text.

**Central, or Main, Ideas** Central ideas are the key arguments, positions, or points writers communicate in works of literary nonfiction. Regardless of the form of the literary work or the subject it addresses, the central idea provides the focus for the writing. All of the other details work to develop and support that idea.

**Author's Purpose and Central Ideas** The author's purpose is his or her main reason for writing. The three main purposes for writing are **to inform or explain, to entertain**, and **to persuade**. Nonfiction writers also have specific purposes for writing. For example, a writer does not merely seek to inform readers in some general way, he or she seeks to inform them about a specific topic. At an even deeper level, the writer seeks to inform readers about a specific idea within the larger topic. That specific idea is the central idea of the text.

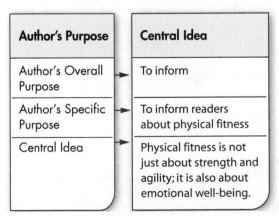

| Author's Purpose | Central Idea |
|---|---|
| Author's Overall Purpose | → To inform |
| Author's Specific Purpose | → To inform readers about physical fitness |
| Central Idea | → Physical fitness is not just about strength and agility; it is also about emotional well-being. |

Central ideas drive all the decisions a writer makes, including how to structure a text to introduce the idea and how to develop, shape, and refine the idea through the use of specific details.

**Central Ideas in Academic Writing** In academic and scholarly writing, such as formal essays and research reports, the writer's overall purpose is usually to inform or to persuade. Often, the writer seeks to do both.

**Example:**
**History Report:** The American Revolution inspired other revolutions throughout the world, including those in France and Haiti.

**Literary Criticism** (essay): The novel's darkest conflict pits two brothers against each other in a battle neither can win.

**Science Report:** Although people have studied nature since antiquity, modern science did not truly begin until 1543, when Copernicus published *On the Revolutions of the Celestial Spheres.*

**Central Ideas in Nonacademic Writing** Magazine articles, memoirs, blogs, and other types of nonfiction may also inform or persuade. Usually, however, at least one purpose is to entertain. The writer's choices of content and structure, including the central ideas and the details that support them, reflect those combined purposes.

**Example:**
**Celebrity Profile:** With dazzling performances in four movies this year alone, she has become the most bankable young actress in Hollywood.

**Memoir:** Raised by a stand-up comedian, I had a childhood that was often exciting but not always funny.

# Close Read: Theme in Fiction

**All the elements of a story, from the title to the characters to individual words, may be clues to the theme.**

Authors of serious fiction almost never state themes directly. Instead, they suggest the theme by weaving meaningful details into the narrative. Reading for theme, then, is like being a detective solving a mystery. You must notice details and analyze how they relate to one another. These relationships may include contrasts, comparisons, repetitions, or other connections.

## Clues to Theme

### Title
The title is the name of a story. Sometimes, the chapters of a novel or sections of a story have their own titles. Titles may give you information about a story's characters, setting, events, and theme. As you read, consider whether the title

- points to a character, an event, an object, or a location in the story;
- suggests emotions or abstract ideas;
- has more than one possible meaning.

### Statements and Observations
A statement or an observation asserts an idea. Characters or the narrator may make statements that suggest or even reveal the theme. As you read, notice

- whether a character or the narrator sums up the story's events;
- whether a character or the narrator makes general observations about characters' emotions.

### Setting
The setting is the time and location of the action in a story. In some stories, the setting is just a backdrop. However, in other stories, the setting can shed light on the theme. As you read, consider

- the importance of the setting to the characters and events;
- whether descriptions of the setting include words with strong emotional associations.

### Characters
Characters are the people who take part in the action of a story. Their motivations, experiences, and reactions almost always relate to the theme. As you read, notice

- what you learn about characters from their statements, thoughts, behavior, and appearance;
- whether characters change and, if so, how they change;
- whether characters learn something and, if so, what they learn.

### Symbols
A symbol is any story element, whether an object, a person, an animal, a place, an action, or an image, that has both a literal and a deeper meaning. Symbols often relate directly to themes. As you read,

- notice story elements that repeat or that have strong emotional content;
- think about the deeper meanings these elements suggest.

### Conflict and Plot
Conflicts are the struggles characters face. Plot is the sequence of events in a story. Conflicts always spark the plot and are key to the theme. As you read, identify

- the problems characters face;
- how or if the conflicts are resolved;
- how characters feel about the resolution.

# Model

**About the Text** This story is set in the United States during the 1950s, when fears of nuclear war ran high. In the story, a mother irons clothes while thinking about her teenage daughter Emily. Earlier in the day, the mother received a visit from a social worker who is concerned about Emily.

---

### from "I Stand Here Ironing" by Tillie Olsen

Ronnie is calling. He is wet and I change him. It is rare there is such a cry now. That time of motherhood is almost behind me when the ear is not one's own but must always be racked and listening for the child cry, the child call. We sit for a while and I hold him, looking out over the city spread in charcoal with its soft aisles of light. *"Shoogily,"* he breathes and curls closer. I carry him back to bed, asleep. *Shoogily*. A funny word, a family word, inherited from Emily, invented by her to say: *comfort.*

In this and other ways she leaves her seal, I say aloud. And startle at my saying it. What do I mean? What did I start to gather together, to try and make coherent? I was at the terrible, growing years. War years. I do not remember them well. I was working, there were four smaller ones now, there was not time for her. She had to help be a mother, and housekeeper, and shopper. She had to set her seal. Mornings of crisis and near hysteria trying to get lunches packed, hair combed, coats and shoes found, everyone to school or Child Care on time, the baby ready for transportation. And always the paper scribbled on by a smaller one, the book looked at by Susan then mislaid, the homework not done. Running out to that huge school where she was one, she was lost, she was a drop; suffering over the unpreparedness, stammering and unsure in her classes.

There was so little time left at night after the kids were bedded down. She would struggle over books, always eating (it was in those years she developed her enormous appetite that is legendary in our family) and I would be ironing, or preparing food for the next day, or writing V-mail to Bill, or tending the baby. Sometimes, to make me laugh, or out of her despair, she would imitate happenings or types at school.

I think I said once: "Why don't you do something like this in the school amateur show?" One morning she phoned me at work, hardly understandable through the weeping: "Mother, I did it. I won, I won; they gave me first prize; they clapped and clapped and wouldn't let me go."

Now suddenly she was Somebody, and as imprisoned in her difference as she had been in anonymity.

---

**Title** The title tells you that ironing is an important activity in this story and key to the theme.

**Statements** The narrator makes numerous statements about Emily's past and future. She often expresses sadness, but also acceptance and a belief that her daughter will survive despite her struggles.

**Setting** The "War years" refers to the World War II era of the 1940s. These details about the ways in which the era affects the narrator and her family are key to the theme.

**Characters** The narrator describes Emily as "stammering and unsure," but then as someone who is in "command." Either way, Emily is "imprisoned." The idea of the circumstances of one's life being akin to a prison is key to the story's theme.

**Model continued**

She began to be asked to perform at other high schools, even colleges, then at city and statewide affairs. The first one we went to, I only recognized her that first moment when thin, shy, she almost drowned herself into the curtains. Then: Was this Emily? The control, the command, the convulsing and deadly clowning, the spell, then the roaring, stamping audience, unwilling to let this rare and precious laughter out of their lives.

Afterwards: You ought to do something about her with a gift like that—but without money or knowing how, what does one do? We have left it all to her, and the gift has as often eddied inside, clogged and clotted, as been used and growing.

She is coming. She runs up the stairs two at a time with her light graceful step, and I know she is happy tonight. Whatever it was that occasioned your call did not happen today.

"Aren't you ever going to finish the ironing, Mother? Whistler painted his mother in a rocker. I'd have to paint mine standing over an ironing board." This is one of her communicative nights and she tells me everything and nothing as she fixes herself a plate of food out of the icebox.

She is so lovely. Why did you want me to come in at all? Why were you concerned? She will find her way.

She starts up the stairs to bed. "Don't get me up with the rest in the morning." "But I thought you were having midterms." "Oh, those," she comes back in, kisses me, and says quite lightly, "in a couple of years when we'll all be atom-dead they won't matter a bit."

She has said it before. She *believes* it. But because I have been dredging the past, and all that compounds a human being is so heavy and meaningful in me, I cannot endure it tonight.

I will never total it all. I will never come in to say: She was a child seldom smiled at. Her father left me before she was a year old. I had to work her first six years when there was work, or I sent her home and to his relatives. There were tears she had care she hated. She was dark and thin and foreign-looking in a world where the prestige went to blondness and curly hair and dimples, she was slow where glibness was prized. She was a child of anxious, not proud, love. We were poor and could not afford for her the soil of easy growth. I was a young mother, I was a distracted mother. There were other children pushing up, demanding. Her younger sister seemed all that she was not. There were years she did not want me to touch her. She kept too much in herself, her life was such she had to keep too much in herself. My wisdom came too late. She has

**Setting** The 1950s setting plays a key role: The daughter believes she has no future. Her certainty pains the mother, who cannot accept such hopelessness.

much to her and probably nothing will come of it. She is a child of her age, of depression, of war, of fear.

Let her be. So all that is in her will not bloom—but in how many does it? There is still enough left to live by. Only help her to know—help make it so there is cause for her to know—that she is more than this dress on the ironing board, helpless before the iron.

**Characters** The daughter's pain is not hers alone. The theme relates both to individual suffering and to that of the entire society.

**Symbols** In this final sentence, we learn that the ironing is symbolic: The narrator does not want her daughter to feel as powerless as a dress "before the iron."

**Determining the Theme** By combining details about the impact of the historical setting on the characters and the hopes that the mother has for her daughter, you might interpret the story's theme in this way: *While historical events and personal circumstances may make life difficult and unfair, people survive.*

# Independent Practice

**About the Selection** This is an excerpt from a novel by Elizabeth McCracken. Set in a small town during the 1950s, the story revolves around James Sweatt, the world's tallest boy. The story is told by Peggy, the town librarian.

## from *The Giant's House* by Elizabeth McCracken

James took out books on astronomy, ornithology:[1] sciences at once about tininess and height. He approached the desk with books he'd liked and asked for more—he knew it was easier to find more books with a good example in hand.

Then one day, in the first months of 1955—I remember looking over his head at some awful persistent Christmas decoration Astoria had stuck to the ceiling— he came to me without books. His height had become unwieldy; he reached out to touch walls as he walked, sometimes leaving marks way above where the other teenage boys smudged their hands. "I want books about people like me," he said.

I thought I knew what he was talking about, but I wanted to be cautious. "What exactly about you?" I asked. I made myself think of all the things he could have meant: Boy Scouts, basketball players. Never jump to conclusions when trying to answer a reference question. Interview the patron.

"Tall people," he said.

"Tall people? Just tall people in general?"

"Very tall people. Like me," he said, clearly exasperated with my playing dumb. "What they do."

"Okay," I told him. "Try the card catalog. Look in the big books on the table— see those books?" I pointed. "Those are books of subject headings for the card catalog. Look under words that you think describe your topic." James was used to me doing this: I gave directions but would not pull the books off the shelf for him. My job was to show people—even people I liked—how to use the library, not to use it for them. "Dig around," I said. "Try height, try stature. Then look in the catalog for books."

He nodded, leaned on the desk, and pushed off.

An hour later he headed out the door.

"Did you find what you needed?" I asked.

"There isn't anything," he said. "There was one book that sort of was about it, but I couldn't find it on the shelf."

**Setting** This section of the story takes place in the library. Identify the types of books James wants to find. What thematic ideas does his search introduce to the story?

**Conflict** Why is the narrator cautious in answering James? How does James's reaction suggest a conflict?

**Character** The narrator says that James "leaned on the desk, and pushed off." What does her observation tell you about the difficulties James faces simply in moving? How does this add to an emerging theme about normality and difference?

---

1. **astronomy, ornithology** Astronomy is the study of the stars and planets. Ornithology is the study of birds.

"There's something," I told him. "Come back. We'll look for it together."

That night after closing, I hunted around myself. The only thing under *stature* was a book about growth and nutrition. I tried our two encyclopedias under height and found passing references. Not much.

In truth, my library was a small-town place, and this was a specialized topic. Still, I was certain I could find more. I got that familiar mania—there is information somewhere here, and I can find it, I have to. A good librarian is not so different from a prospector, her whole brain a divining rod. She walks to books and stands and wonders: here? Is the answer here? The same blind faith in finding, even when hopeless. If someone caught me when I was in the throes of tracking something elusive, I would have told them: but it's out there. I can feel it. God *wants* me to find it.

That night I wandered the reference department, eyed the bindings of the encyclopedias, dictionaries, atlases. James was so big I almost expected to locate him in the gazetteer.[2] I set my hands upon our little card catalog, curled my fingers in the curved handles of the drawers. Then I went to the big volumes of subject headings.

Looking under *height* and *stature* turned up nothing; *anthropometry* was not quite right. Then I realized the word I was looking for: *Giant*.

*Giant* described him. *Giant*, I knew, would lead me to countless things—not just the word, located in indexes and catalogs and encyclopedias, but the idea of Giant, the knowledge that the people that James wanted to read about, people who could be described as like him, were not just tall but giants. I sat in a spindle-backed chair in the reference room, waiting for a minute. Then I checked the volume of the Library of Congress headings. *Giant. See also: dwarfs*.

We did not have a book, but I found several encyclopedia entries. Nowadays I could just photocopy; but that night I wrote down the page and volume numbers, thinking I could not bear to tell him the word to look under. Most of the very tall people mentioned in the encyclopedia had worked in the circus as professional giants, so I went to our books on the circus.

The photographs showed enormous people. Not just tall, though of course they were that, often with an ordinary person posed beside them. The tall people looked twice as big as the ambassador from the normal-sized, as if they were an entirely different race. The books described weak stomachs and legs and bones. Sometimes what made them tall showed in their faces: each feature looked like something disturbed in an avalanche, separate from the others, in danger of slipping off.

**Symbol** What shades of meaning does the word *"Giant"* convey? How might the narrator's discovery of this word point to a theme?

**Conflict** Why is the narrator so worried about telling James to find works under the category "Giant"?

**Statements and Observations** How does the narrator's description of giants help develop a theme? In particular, consider her use of the word *ambassador* to describe the normal-sized people in the photographs.

---

2. **gazetteer** (gaz´ ə tir´) *n.* dictionary or index of geographical names.

Anna Swann, the Nova Scotia Giantess, married Captain Bates, the Kentucky Giant. As a young woman at Barnum's Dime Museum in New York, Miss Swann had been in two fires; in the second she had to be lifted out by a crane. No ordinary over-the-shoulder rescue for a woman better than seven feet tall. She and her husband retired to Ohio, to a specially made house. Their church installed an extra-large pew.

Byrne, the Irish Giant, lived in fear of a certain doctor who lusted after his skeleton; he imagined the doctor's giant kettle ready to boil his bones.

Jack Earle was over seven feet tall, traveled with the circus for years; after his retirement he wrote poetry.

I took comfort in Anna Swann and her husband. They were solid-looking people. Respectable. They'd had two children, though neither survived. The book described them as *in love*, and you could believe that from the pictures: their complementary heights were just a lovely coincidence to their love affair. I found myself that late night a little jealous of Anna Swann and her handsome, bearded captain.

The books said that giants tended to exaggerate their heights for exhibition purposes. I did not know it then, but every person I read about was shorter than James grew to be.

The worst book was called *Medical Curiosities*. I say worst now. That is hindsight. The night I looked, I thought, in fact, that it was the best book—not because it was good or even accurate, but because it had the most pages on the subject I was researching. I found it under the subject heading *Abnormalities, human*. A terrible phrase, and one I knew I could not repeat to James. It was a late-nineteenth-century medical book, described two-headed people and parasitic twins and dwarfs. And giants. Not exactly information, but interesting: giants who had enormous or usual appetites; ones who grew throughout their lives or only after adolescence; professional giants and private citizens.

So I took that book, and the circus books, marked the pertinent places with the old catalog cards I used for scrap, and set them aside. Ready for him, so that he did not have to look in the index, or wander through the pages at all.

"Your tall friend is here," Astoria said to me the next week. I was in my office, reading reviews. "He's looking for you."

James waited for me at the circ desk. "You said we could—"

"I looked," I said. I'd stowed the books beneath the shelf. "Try these out."

He took them to the big table in the front room. Read them. He made the sturdy chair, the same chair I'd sat in the night before, seem tiny.

**Symbols** The narrator finds two different types of books for James. What do these two categories of books suggest about James's situation in life?

Afterward he came up to me.

"How were they?" I asked. "Would you like to take them home?"

He shook his head.

"No," he said. "Thanks."

"Nothing useful here at all?"

"No," he said.

I tried to catch his eye. "Close?"

"Close. I guess." He pointed at *Medical Curiosities*. "I guess that's close."

I picked up the book and opened it to where the marker was, but he'd moved it to another page. A line drawing of a double-bodied baby looked up at me. Horrible. I snapped the book shut.

"I meant medical books," he said. "But new ones. Ones that say what goes wrong. How to cure it."

"Cures," I said. "Oh." Cures for giants? No such thing. No cure for height. Only preventive medicine. I said it as a question. "Cures? For tall people?"

"Yes," he said.

All I wanted was for him to explain it to me. It seemed presumptuous to come to any conclusions myself. I knew what he was talking about. I did. But what he wanted, I couldn't help him with.

Darla, the shelver, came rattling up with her metal cart. "Shelve these?" she said, pointing at the books. The catalog cards I'd used stuck out from the pages; James had lined them up, like a pack of cards he'd shuffled into them. "Hi, Jim," she said.

"Hi." He squinted down at her.

She stared at me; I waited for her to get back to shelving.

"Peggy. Shelve them, or not?"

"Not yet," I said. She sighed and pushed the cart off.

James stood in silence on the other side of the desk. He looked ready to leave.

"You mean how to stop growing," I said.

"Yes." Now he looked at me. "Medicine, or operations, or something."

"I'm not sure we have anything here," I said. That was a lie. I knew we didn't. "A medical library somewhere, perhaps. Or a university library. But really—" I started pulling the bookmarks from the books. I tried to sound gentle. "Really, you should ask your doctor."

"I have," he said. "I've asked a lot of doctors."

**Character** What does James want? What does his desire tell you about the story's theme?

**Theme** How do the characters of the narrator and James help point to a theme about human nature? Explain a possible story theme and cite textual evidence to support your response.

# Close Read: Central Idea in Nonfiction

The central idea is often stated or implied early in a work.
Supporting details develop that idea.

**Central Idea** The central idea is the author's main point in a work of nonfiction. The term also refers to key ideas in individual paragraphs or sections of a work. The main ideas expressed in paragraphs work to develop the central idea of the work as a whole.

**Stated Central Idea** In some nonfiction, the author expresses the central idea in a direct statement. The title of a work may also state the central idea directly.

> **Example:**
> **Here, the author states the central idea in the first sentence:**
> My acting career began early, long before I could actually act. As a baby, I wore elf suits, snowsuits, bunny suits, and my birthday suit to crawl through movie scenes.

**Implied Central Idea** The author may also imply a central idea through a series of related details. You can determine the central idea by identifying how individual details relate to one another. The central idea can then be expressed as a broad statement that accounts for all of the details.

> **Example:**
> Human beings, eagles, owls, hawks, and other predators hunt rabbits for food. Mother rabbits spend only a few minutes in the nest each day, so the babies are often unprotected. Wild rabbits also fall victim to disease and starvation.
>
> **In each sentence, the author discusses a different threat to wild rabbits. The inferred central idea might be stated as follows: Wild rabbits face many dangers.**

## Types of Supporting Details

Writers develop and refine central ideas by using supporting details of many different types. As you read, distinguish between the supporting details and the central concepts they help to shape.

**Facts** are statements that can be proved true.
*Example: Most grocery stores carry a variety of fruits and vegetables.*

**Observations** are eyewitness accounts of experiments or events.
*Example: Adding vinegar to baking soda causes a chemical reaction.*

**Statistics** are numerical data.
*Example: Girls account for 47 percent of all high school soccer players.*

**Personal experience** is the author's own lived experience.
*Example: Riding the rapids was a great adventure.*

**Expert testimony** is information provided by an authoritative person.
*Example: Biologist George Tillman estimates that 50,000 species go extinct every year.*

**Anecdotes** are brief stories that illustrate a point.
*Example: My mother insisted I get out on the ice and skate. "Falling down is part of life," she said.*

**Examples** are specific illustrations of a general concept.
*Example: Hybrid flowers are popular. The "Peace" rose is a favorite among gardeners.*

**Analogies** are comparisons of seemingly unlike situations to show similarities.
*Example: Alice's moods are like a rocket. They go from warm to explosive in seconds.*

# Model

President Franklin Delano Roosevelt delivered this address, known as "The Four Freedoms Speech," at the beginning of his second term in office. Although the United States was not yet involved in World War II, the speech anticipates the ideals for which the nation would fight in that conflict.

## from "State of the Union Address (1941)" by Franklin D. Roosevelt

For there is nothing mysterious about the foundations of a healthy and strong democracy. The basic things expected by our people of their political and economic systems are simple. They are:

Equality of opportunity for youth and for others.

Jobs for those who can work.

Security for those who need it.

The ending of special privilege for the few.

The preservation of civil liberties for all.

The enjoyment of the fruits of scientific progress in a wider and constantly rising standard of living.

These are the simple, basic things that must never be lost sight of in the turmoil and unbelievable complexity of our modern world. The inner and abiding strength of our economic and political systems is dependent upon the degree to which they fulfill these expectations.

Many subjects connected with our social economy call for immediate improvement. As examples:

We should bring more citizens under the coverage of old-age pensions and unemployment insurance.

We should widen the opportunities for adequate medical care.

We should plan a better system by which persons deserving or needing gainful employment may obtain it.

I have called for personal sacrifice. I am assured of the willingness of almost all Americans to respond to that call.

**Observations** Roosevelt begins this section of his address with the observation that the elements of a healthy and strong democracy are those people intuitively understand.

**Examples** Roosevelt cites specific examples of how to improve the social economy.

**Expert Testimony** Roosevelt's expression of confidence in the American people carries all the authority of his office. This statement supports his central idea that the nation can meet the challenges of the day.

# Independent Practice

**About the Selection** Elizabeth McCracken wrote this personal essay in response to a request from her publisher. The title, "Desiderata," means "something wanted, needed, or desired."

**Fact** In her first sentence, McCracken provides a definition, which is a type of fact. Why is this supporting detail important?

**Examples** Which details in the second and third paragraphs support the main idea that McCracken states in the yellow highlighted sentence?

## "Desiderata" by Elizabeth McCracken

Desiderata, I learned in library science school, were the items you needed for an archive to make it useful. Useful, not complete, because there is no such thing as a complete archive. There's always a letter out there you want and need, either in someone else's collection or in an attic or just unfound. You need and want things you don't even know exist. That's how collections work.

I come from a family strong on documents. I have a small archive myself. My grandfather McCracken was a genealogist—I have his history of the McCrackens, a lovely compilation of research on early ancestors and personal remembrances of his own relatives. His wife, my grandmother, wrote stories and poems; I have copies of those, and remember once opening a drawer full of letters she wrote to God, part prayer and part daily correspondence to Someone dear. I have my grandmother Jacobson's collection of family letters; she had 11 brothers and sisters, some who wrote often and some just now and then. I have diplomas of relatives I never met. I have diaries and laundry lists. I love anything written by a relative, any evidence of what they really thought.

And I read these documents fairly regularly. Besides letters from her family, my grandmother also saved letters from Martha, her children's nanny. My mother, who says she had the happiest childhood on record, remembers Martha and her letters as lovely and slightly daffy. Her twin sister, my aunt Carolyn, remembers the letters and the woman as dark and Dickensian,[1] longing for a time that never really existed. I'd always assumed that the truth was somewhere in the middle, but I have the letters and now know that Martha was, at best, weird. She wrote to my travelling grandmother that the twins—The Dollies, she called them—didn't miss her at all. She reported that she took them out to her mother's farm, and couldn't understand why the girls were so upset to be served for dinner the chicken they'd met earlier. She reported on The Dollies' toilet training as if it were grand opera, and the Dollies heroines who wanted only, desperately, to triumph.

I'm glad to know this, I think. Certainly, it's a whole different Martha than the one I knew from my mother's stories. I know Martha now because of all that she reveals of herself, not knowing she was doing it, in her letters.

---

1. **Dickensian** of or relating to English novelist Charles Dickens (1812–1870).

Still, there are many frustrations to family papers. First of all, you may learn things you don't want to know. For instance: some of my grandmother's sisters wanted to sue the widow of one of their brothers. Even in letters from the litigious[2] sisters themselves, this comes across as merely petty and vindictive. There are letters that can break your heart: my Aunt Edna, writing to my grandmother, lamented how poor her health was, how the doctors told her to slow down; I know from the dates that Edna died two weeks later, of a heart attack.

But the major frustration is how incomplete everything is, how incomplete *people* are if you try to meet them this way. The great-aunt who wanted to sue only happened to write it down; maybe she gave up the idea. Maybe she was suffering otherwise—her life was continually tragic in small ways, I know that. Some of the great-aunts I barely know, because they barely wrote. Or rather, I *think* they barely wrote—my grandmother saved every letter some years, and selected letters others. Perhaps those great-aunts simply never made it into the collection.

And then there's my grandmother Jacobson herself. She was a wonderful and complex woman, an attorney and small businessperson who died at home at the age of 90. The pieces of paper I have from her don't conjure her up at all. Her diary (which I don't own but have read) is a very careful record of daily events, nothing more. She doesn't detail worries or doubts, and the fact is she was a worried and somewhat doubtful person. I think she knew that we'd read it, eventually, and didn't want to tell us in her diary anything she hadn't told us already.

One piece of paper I do have: a post-it note from late in her life, which she used to mark a recipe in *The Jewish Cookbook*. It says:

coffee
bananas
bread
milk
wax beans?

and then, in the corner, written diagonally and underlined,

*lottery ticket*.

I know that this dates to a time when she was both worried about money and had become very serious about luck. I don't know how superstitious she'd previously been, but about two years before she died, she began to see luck

**Anecdote** What idea do the anecdotes about the sisters of the narrator's grandmother and the narrator's Aunt Edna help to shape?

**Observations** How does this observation help shape the central idea of McCracken's work? Explain.

**Observation** What idea is developed by McCracken's observations about her grandmother's note?

---

2. **litigious** (li tij´ əs) *adj.* given to carrying out lawsuits; quarrelsome.

**Practice continued**

good and bad, in everything: she read her horoscope, her children's horoscope, the horoscope of everyone who might touch her life that day. She believed in fortune cookies. She told her own fortune playing solitaire. And she bought lottery tickets, not so much because she believed she might win but because not playing meant she did not believe that sudden good things could happen. She was a businessperson, after all: she knew what a bad investment that weekly dollar was.

I love that little green piece of paper. *Desideratum* to me, though less than ephemera[3] to anyone else.

I could tell dozens of other stories from the pages of family papers: my aunt Blanche's pell-mell record of taking care of her favorite sister, Elizabeth, who was dying of Alzheimer's; Blanche has that disease herself now, and you can see the early signs in these notes. My great-uncles' cheery letters from Europe during World War II. A letter my brother wrote to my grandmother when I was four and he was six, thanking her for a gift and then recording that I was resisting writing a thank-you note myself.

Here's a last story. My father's parents were, when I knew them, quiet people. I know now that my version of them is different from anyone else's, but they were my grandparents and I never questioned who I understood them to be. After their deaths, I inherited a cherry chest-of-drawers from their house. I owned this imposing piece of furniture for a few years before I lifted some paper lining from one of the drawers and found a letter. Part of a letter, actually, written by my grandfather to my grandmother before their marriage.

It was one of the most beautiful love letters I've ever read, full of delight for her person and for their love together. It was passionate and thrilled and almost disbelieving of his great fortune, to have found her. I never imagined my grandfather, my quiet careful grandfather, was the sort of man who'd write any kind of love letter, never mind this kind. Wrong again. And my grandmother had saved it for more than fifty years. I wondered whether she took it out and reread it from time to time, or whether she'd forgotten where she'd put it.

My parents were out of town that weekend, and as it happened I'd agreed to pick them up at the airport. I brought the letter to give to my father—if it meant that much to me, I couldn't imagine what it would mean to him. And so, sitting on a bench in Logan,[4] I gave it to him. "Look what I found," I said.

"Oh," he said, perfectly pleased but not surprised. "Another letter. I'll put it with the others."

**Anecdote** What idea does McCracken refine with this anecdote about her grandparents' love letters?

---

3. **ephemera** (e fem′ ər ə) *n.* something, often printed material, meant to last for only a short time.
4. **Logan** Boston's Logan International Airport, named for General Edward Lawrence Logan.

Turns out there were many more—my grandparents had written each other several times a day during their courtship. Which makes it, of course, a happier story.

My question is: was that letter more a *desideratum* for me, or my father? He had the collection, I didn't. Sometimes I regret giving it to him. I've forgotten the exact words my grandfather used, but it doesn't seem right to ask for someone else's love letter back. Someday I'll see it again, I know. Meanwhile, I need it and desire it. I need and desire everything that belongs to my family, and in some ways, I think, that's what I do with my days, writing fiction. I am writing love letters to diaries and post-it notes and telegrams and birthday cards. I am writing love letters to love letters.

**Central Idea** What central idea about desiderata in general and human nature specifically can be supported with the key ideas and details in this work?

---

## After You Read

### *from* The Giant's House • Desiderata

**1. Key Ideas and Details (a)** Write a summary of the excerpt from *The Giant's House.* A summary is a brief version of a text that relates the most important ideas in your own words and in a logical order. Your summary should be understood by someone who has not read the selection. **(b)** Write a summary of "Desiderata."

**2. Key Ideas and Details** What is McCracken's **main purpose** for writing "Desiderata"? Explain.

**3. Key Ideas and Details** Identify one possible **theme** expressed in the excerpt from *The Giant's House.* Note details from the selection that support your answer.

**4. Key Ideas and Details (a)** Identify the key idea in each of the final seven paragraphs of "Desiderata." **(b)** Consider the relationships among the individual key ideas. Then, write a general statement in which you express the central idea of the entire work. Remember that each of the key ideas will support the work's central idea.

**5. Key Ideas and Details (a)** In the excerpt from *The Giant's House,* note two points at which the narrator, Peggy, refers to her training as a librarian. **(b) Analyze:** Do Peggy's efforts for James meet her criteria for being a good librarian? Explain.

**6. Integration of Knowledge and Ideas (a)** In "Desiderata," what frustrations does McCracken experience in "meeting" people through family papers? **(b) Speculate:** Based on this essay, why do you think McCracken became a writer of fiction? Explain.

**7. Integration of Knowledge and Ideas (a)** Complete a chart like the one shown to list sources, including those found on the Internet and in a library, that James could use if he were researching his condition today.

| Research Question | Possible Source |
|---|---|
|  |  |

**(b) Collaboration:** Discuss your chart with a classmate to identify the most valuable resource.

##  Leveled Texts

Build your skills and improve your comprehension of literary nonfiction
with texts of increasing complexity.

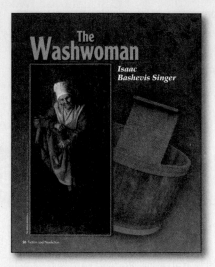

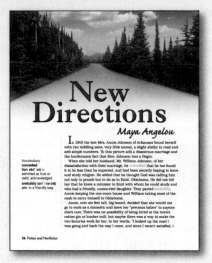

Read **"The Washwoman"** to
see how community affects a
household.

Read **"New Directions"** to see
how a woman makes a life for
herself despite great challenges.

##  Common Core State Standards

Meet these standards with either **"The Washwoman"** (p. 26) or **"New Directions"** (p. 36).

**Reading Informational Text**
**2.** Determine a central idea of a text and analyze its
development over the course of the text, including how
it emerges and is shaped and refined by specific details;
provide an objective summary of the text. *(Literary
Analysis: Spiral Review)*

**Writing**
**3.** Write narratives to develop real or imagined experiences
or events using effective technique, well-chosen details,
and well-structured event sequences. *(Writing: Anecdote)*

**Speaking and Listening**
**1.a.** Come to discussions prepared, having read and
researched material under study; explicitly draw on that
preparation by referring to evidence from texts and other
research on the topic or issue to stimulate a thoughtful,

well-reasoned exchange of ideas. **1.c.** Propel conversations
by posing and responding to questions that relate the
current discussion to broader themes or larger ideas;
actively incorporate others into the discussion; and clarify,
verify, or challenge ideas and conclusions. **1.d.** Respond
thoughtfully to diverse perspectives, summarize points of
agreement and disagreement, and, when warranted,
qualify or justify their own views and understanding and
make new connections in light of the evidence and
reasoning presented. *(Speaking and Listening: Interview)*

**Language**
**2.** Demonstrate command of the conventions of standard
English capitalization, punctuation, and spelling when
writing. *(Conventions: Common Nouns and Proper Nouns)*

# Literary Analysis: Narrative Essay

A **narrative essay** is a short piece of nonfiction that tells a story about a real person or an event. As in a fictional story, a narrative essay relates a series of events and has **main and subordinate** (minor) **characters.** Unlike a fictional story, however, the characters in a narrative essay are real people. The interactions of those characters propel the story forward and allow us to understand their **motivations** and goals.

As you read, notice how the author's choice of details influences your impressions of the people and events he or she describes.

# Reading Skill: Make Predictions

A **prediction** is an informed idea about what might happen later in a narrative. Predictions are based on details in the text and your own experience. When you **verify predictions,** you read on to see if the prediction you made is correct.

Pause periodically while reading and **ask questions** like these about text details and events:

- Why does the author mention this detail?

- How might it become important later on?

Look for the answers as you continue reading.

## Using the Strategy: Predictions Map

Use a chart like the one shown to record your predictions and evaluate their accuracy. Analyze any inaccurate predictions to determine why they were incorrect.

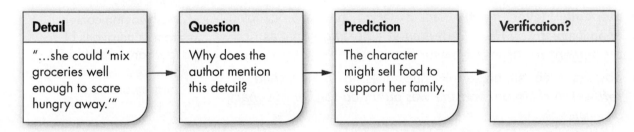

| Detail | Question | Prediction | Verification? |
|--------|----------|------------|---------------|
| "…she could 'mix groceries well enough to scare hungry away.'" | Why does the author mention this detail? | The character might sell food to support her family. | |

**PHLit**
**Online!**
www.PHLitOnline.com

***Hear It!***
- Selection summary audio
- Selection audio

***See It!***
- Get Connected video
- Background video
- More about the author
- Vocabulary flashcards

***Do It!***
- Interactive journals
- Interactive graphic organizers
- Self-test
- Internet activity
- Grammar tutorial
- Interactive vocabulary games

# Can *truth* change?

## Writing About the Big Question

In "The Washwoman," a Jewish family learns to appreciate a Christian washwoman whose son has abandoned her. Use these sentence starters to develop your ideas about the Big Question.

A mother's relationship with her son can sometimes be **distorted** because of _____. They could gain **insight** into each other's **perspective** by _____.

**While You Read** Look for the ways that the washwoman's relationships change over time.

## Vocabulary

Read each word and its definition. Decide whether you know the word well, know it a little bit, or do not know it at all. After you read the selection, see how your knowledge of each word has increased.

- **forebears** (fôr´ berz) *n.* ancestors (p. 27) *His <u>forebears</u> started the family business.*

- **accumulated** (ə kyōōm´ yōō lāt´ id) *v.* piled up, collected, or gathered together, especially over a period of time (p. 27) *We have <u>accumulated</u> a large stack of newspapers in our living room.* accumulate *v.* accumulation *n.* cumulative *adj.*

- **rancor** (raŋ´ kər) *n.* bitter hate (p. 28) *The rivals fumed with <u>rancor</u> for each other.*

- **atonement** (ə tōn´ mənt) *n.* act of making up for a wrongdoing or an injury (p. 28) *He volunteered at a nursing home as <u>atonement</u> for his misbehavior.* atone *v.*

- **obstinacy** (äb´ stə nə sē) *n.* stubbornness (p. 30) *The child refused to clean up, and she was punished for her <u>obstinacy</u>.* obstinate *adj.*

- **pious** (pī´ əs) *adj.* having or showing religious devotion (p. 31) *The <u>pious</u> man went to church every week.* piety *n.* impious *adj.*

### Word Study

The **Old English prefix fore-** means "earlier" or "in front of."

In this story, the washwoman comes from generations of "peasant **forebears**," or ancestors who lived long before her.

## Author of

# The Washwoman

Storytelling always had an important place in Isaac Bashevis Singer's life. He grew up in the city of Warsaw in what now is Poland. Singer's father was a rabbi, a teacher of the Jewish faith and laws. Advice-seekers streamed through the family home, telling their stories as the fascinated young Singer listened and observed.

**"Life Itself Is a Story"** Fleeing persecution against Jews, Singer left Poland for New York City in 1935. In New York, Singer began to make a name for himself as a writer. He set many of his tales in the world of European Jewry he had left. Ironically, as he wrote, World War II devastated that world. Villages like the one of his birth were wiped off the face of the earth even as Singer brought them to life on the page.

## BACKGROUND FOR THE ESSAY

### Jews in Poland

"The Washwoman" takes place in the early twentieth century in what is now Poland. Centuries earlier, many Jewish people had settled there, drawn by the promise of religious tolerance. By Singer's time, Poland had been conquered by other countries. Yet, Poland's Jews held on to their traditions, continuing to speak Yiddish, a language blending German with Hebrew and other languages.

## Did You Know?

Isaac Bashevis Singer won the Nobel Prize for Literature in 1978.

# The Washwoman

## Isaac Bashevis Singer

*The Oldest Inhabitant*, 1876, Julian Alden Weir, Butler Institute of American Art, Youngstown, Ohio

O ur home had little contact with Gentiles.[1] The only Gentile in the building was the janitor. Fridays he would come for a tip, his "Friday money." He remained standing at the door, took off his hat, and my mother gave him six groschen.[2]

Besides the janitor there were also the Gentile washwomen who came to the house to fetch our laundry. My story is about one of these.

She was a small woman, old and wrinkled. When she started washing for us, she was already past seventy. Most Jewish women of her age were sickly, weak, broken in body. All the old women in our street had bent backs and leaned on sticks when they walked. But this washwoman, small and thin as she was, possessed a strength that came from generations of peasant forebears. Mother would count out to her a bundle of laundry that had accumulated over several weeks. She would lift the unwieldy pack, load it on her narrow shoulders, and carry it the long way home. She lived on Krochmalna Street too, but at the other end, near the Wola section. It must have been a walk of an hour and a half.

She would bring the laundry back about two weeks later. My mother had never been so pleased with any washwoman. Every piece of linen sparkled like polished silver. Every piece was neatly ironed. Yet she charged no more than the others. She was a real find. Mother always had her money ready, because it was too far for the old woman to come a second time.

Laundering was not easy in those days. The old woman had no faucet where she lived but had to bring in the water from a pump. For the linens to come out so clean, they had to be scrubbed thoroughly in a washtub, rinsed with washing soda, soaked, boiled in an enormous pot, starched, then ironed. Every piece was handled ten times or more. And the drying! It could not be done outside because thieves would steal the laundry. The wrung-out wash had to be carried up to the attic and hung on clotheslines. In the winter it would become as brittle as glass and almost break when touched. And there was always a to-do with other housewives and washwomen who wanted the attic clothesline for their own use. Only God knows all the old woman had to endure each time she did a wash!

---

1. **Gentiles** (jen´ tīls) *n.* any persons not Jewish; here, specifically Christians.
2. **groschen** (grō´ shən) *n.* Austrian cent or penny.

**Literary Analysis
Narrative Essay**
Which detail in the first paragraph helps you identify this as a narrative essay?

**Vocabulary
forebears** (fôr´ berz´) *n.* ancestors

**accumulated**
(ə kyo͞om´ yo͞o lāt´ id) *v.* piled up, collected, or gathered together, especially over a period of time

▲ **Iron, end of
19th century**

Reading
Check

According to Singer, what is the washwoman's physical appearance?

She could have begged at the church door or entered a home for the penniless and aged. But there was in her a certain pride and love of labor with which many Gentiles have been blessed. The old woman did not want to become a burden, and so she bore her burden. •

My mother spoke a little Polish, and the old woman would talk with her about many things. She was especially fond of me and used to say I looked like Jesus. She repeated this every time she came, and Mother would frown and whisper to herself, her lips barely moving, "May her words be scattered in the wilderness."

The woman had a son who was rich. I no longer remember what sort of business he had. He was ashamed of his mother, the washwoman, and never came to see her. Nor did he ever give her a groschen. The old woman told this without rancor. One day the son was married. It seemed that he had made a good match. The wedding took place in a church. The son had not invited the old mother to his wedding, but she went to the church and waited at the steps to see her son lead the "young lady" to the altar.

The story of the faithless son left a deep impression on my mother. She talked about it for weeks and months. It was an affront not only to the old woman but to the entire institution of motherhood. Mother would argue, "Nu, does it pay to make sacrifices for children? The mother uses up her last strength, and he does not even know the meaning of loyalty."

And she would drop dark hints to the effect that she was not certain of her own children: Who knows what they would do some day? This, however, did not prevent her from dedicating her life to us. If there was any delicacy in the house, she would put it aside for the children and invent all sorts of excuses and reasons why she herself did not want to taste it. She knew charms that went back to ancient times, and she used expressions she had inherited from generations of devoted mothers and grandmothers. If one of the children complained of a pain, she would say, "May I be your ransom and may you outlive my bones!" Or she would say, "May I be the atonement for the least of your fingernails." When we ate she used to say, "Health and marrow in your bones!" The day before the new moon she gave us a kind of candy that was said to prevent parasitic worms. If one of us had something in his eye, Mother would lick the eye clean with her tongue. She also fed us rock candy against coughs, and from time to time she would take us to be blessed against the evil eye. This did not prevent her from studying *The Duties of the Heart*, *The Book of the Covenant*, and other serious philosophic works.

**Vocabulary**
**rancor** (raṅ´ kər)
*n.* bitter hate

Ⓒ
**Spiral Review**
**Central Idea** Compare the washwoman's reaction to her son's faithlessness with the author's description of his mother's reaction to this news. What central idea do these differing reactions suggest the author is developing?

**Vocabulary**
**atonement** (ə tōn´ mənt)
*n.* act of making up for a wrongdoing or an injury

But to return to the washwoman. That winter was a harsh one. The streets were in the grip of a bitter cold. No matter how much we heated our stove, the windows were covered with frostwork and decorated with icicles. The newspapers reported that people were dying of the cold. Coal became dear. The winter had become so severe that parents stopped sending children to cheder,[3] and even the Polish schools were closed.

On one such day the washwoman, now nearly eighty years old, came to our house. A good deal of laundry had accumulated during the past weeks. Mother gave her a pot of tea to warm herself, as well as some bread. The old woman sat on a kitchen chair trembling and shaking, and warmed her hands against the teapot. Her fingers were gnarled from work, and perhaps from arthritis too. Her fingernails were strangely white. These hands spoke of the stubbornness of mankind, of the will to work not only as one's strength permits but beyond the limits of one's power. Mother counted and wrote down the list: men's undershirts, women's vests, long-legged drawers, bloomers, petticoats, shifts, featherbed covers, pillowcases, sheets, and the men's fringed garments. Yes, the Gentile woman washed these holy garments as well.

---

3. **cheder** (khā′ dər) religious school.

▲ **Critical Viewing**
How does this picture of a neighborhood in Poland compare with how you imagine the Singers' neighborhood to look? **[Compare]**

☑ Reading Check
How did the winter weather affect the neighborhood?

The Washwoman **29**

**Literary Analysis**
**Character** What
qualities does the
author describe in the
washwoman that show
she is "a human being,
the crown of creation"?
Explain.

The bundle was big, bigger than usual. When the woman placed it on her shoulders, it covered her completely. At first she swayed, as though she were about to fall under the load. But an inner obstinacy seemed to call out: No, you may not fall. A donkey may permit himself to fall under his burden, but not a human being, the crown of creation.

It was fearful to watch the old woman staggering out with the enormous pack, out into the frost, where the snow was dry as salt and the air was filled with dusty white whirlwinds, like goblins dancing in the cold. Would the old woman ever reach Wola?

She disappeared, and Mother sighed and prayed for her.

Usually the woman brought back the wash after two or, at the most, three weeks. But three weeks passed, then four and five, and nothing was heard of the old woman. We remained without linens. The cold had become even more intense. The telephone wires were now as thick as ropes. The branches of the trees looked like glass. So much snow had fallen that the streets had become uneven, and sleds were able to glide down many streets as on the slopes of a hill.

Kindhearted people lit fires in the streets for vagrants[4] to warm themselves and roast potatoes in, if they had any to roast.

**A**t first she swayed, as though she were about to fall under the load.

For us the washwoman's absence was a catastrophe. We needed the laundry. We did not even know the woman's address. It seemed certain that she had collapsed, died. Mother declared she had had a premonition, as the old woman left our house that last time, that we would never see our things again. She found some old torn shirts and washed and mended them. We mourned, both for the laundry and for the old, toil-worn woman who had grown close to us through the years she had served us so faithfully. •

More than two months passed. The frost had subsided, and then a new frost had come,

---

4. **vagrants** (vā´ grənts) *n.* people who wander from place to place, especially those without regular jobs.

a new wave of cold. One evening, while Mother was sitting near the kerosene lamp mending a shirt, the door opened and a small puff of steam, followed by a gigantic bundle, entered. Under the bundle tottered the old woman, her face as white as a linen sheet. A few wisps of white hair straggled out from beneath her shawl. Mother uttered a half-choked cry. It was as though a corpse had entered the room. I ran toward the old woman and helped her unload her pack. She was even thinner now, more bent. Her face had become more gaunt, and her head shook from side to side as though she were saying no. She could not utter a clear word, but mumbled something with her sunken mouth and pale lips.

After the old woman had recovered somewhat, she told us that she had been ill, very ill. Just what her illness was, I cannot remember. She had been so sick that someone had called a doctor, and the doctor had sent for a priest. Someone had informed the son, and he had contributed money for a coffin and for the funeral. But the Almighty had not yet wanted to take this pain-racked soul to Himself. She began to feel better, she became well, and as soon as she was able to stand on her feet once more, she resumed her washing. Not just ours, but the wash of several other families too.

"I could not rest easy in my bed because of the wash," the old woman explained. "The wash would not let me die."

"With the help of God you will live to be a hundred and twenty," said my mother, as a benediction.

"God forbid! What good would such a long life be? The work becomes harder and harder . . . my strength is leaving me . . . I do not want to be a burden on anyone!" The old woman muttered and crossed herself, and raised her eyes toward heaven.

Fortunately there was some money in the house and Mother counted out what she owed. I had a strange feeling: the coins in the old woman's washed-out hands seemed to become as worn and clean and pious as she herself was. She blew on the coins and tied them in a kerchief. Then she left, promising to return in a few weeks for a new load of wash.

**Reading Skill**
**Make Predictions**
Was your earlier prediction about the old woman accurate? Why or why not?

◄ **Critical Viewing**
What do you think it would be like to wash clothes using a washboard and tub like these? **[Speculate]**

**Vocabulary**
**pious** (pī′ əs) *adj.* having or showing religious devotion

**Reading Check**
Why does the washwoman do other people's laundry?

But she never came back. The wash she had returned was her last effort on this earth. She had been driven by an indomitable will to return the property to its rightful owners, to fulfill the task she had undertaken.

And now at last her body, which had long been no more than a shard[5] supported only by the force of honesty and duty, had fallen. Her soul passed into those spheres where all holy souls meet, regardless of the roles they played on this earth, in whatever tongue, of whatever creed. I cannot imagine paradise without this Gentile washwoman. I cannot even conceive of a world where there is no recompense for such effort.

---

5. (shärd) fragment or broken piece.

## Critical Thinking

Cite textual evidence to support your responses.

1. **Key Ideas and Details (a)** Which job does the washwoman perform for Singer's family? **(b) Connect:** Which laborious obstacles to doing the job well does Singer describe?

2. **Key Ideas and Details (a)** What prevents the washwoman from returning to the family for several months? **(b) Draw Conclusions:** What does the washwoman's eventual return tell you about her character? Explain.

3. **Craft and Structure (a)** What specific information about the washwoman's personal life does the author include? **(b) Speculate:** What other kinds of information about the washwoman might the author have chosen to include but left out? **(c) Assess:** Based on this essay, explain why an author might choose to include some details in a text while leaving others out.

4. **Integration of Knowledge and Ideas (a)** How would you describe the character of the washwoman at the beginning of the story and then at the end? **(b)** How do her relationships grow? *[Connect to the Big Question: Can truth change?]*

## Literary Analysis: Narrative Essay

**1. Key Ideas and Details (a)** In this **narrative essay,** what difficulties does the washwoman face? **(b)** How does she respond to those challenges? **(c)** What inspirational lesson does the author take away from knowing the washwoman?

**2. Key Ideas and Details (a)** Use a chart like the one shown to record three **significant details** that Singer uses to describe the washwoman and her son. **(b)** What impression of each character does each detail create?

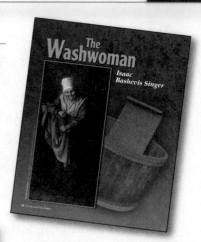

| The Washwoman | The Washwoman's Son |
| --- | --- |
|  |  |

## Reading Skill: Make Predictions

**3.** Write three **predictions** that you made while reading "The Washwoman." Then, trade papers with a partner and discuss the accuracy of your predictions and the details you used to make them. Finally, explain how your method of making and verifying predictions has or has not changed as a result of your discussion.

## Vocabulary

**Acquisition and Use** Use a word from the vocabulary list on page 24 to replace each underlined word or phrase with its opposite.

**1.** The former enemies have put their old <u>friendship</u> behind them.

**2.** The actor's <u>flexibility</u> made him difficult to direct.

**3.** She inherited the family trade from her <u>children</u>.

**4.** Running extra laps was his <u>reward</u> for being late to practice.

**5.** My son has <u>given away</u> a large pile of clothing in his room.

**6.** The old woman was <u>disrespectful of her religion</u>.

**Word Study** Use the context of the sentences and what you know about the **Old English prefix *fore-*** to explain your answer to each question.

**1.** Where does the <u>foreword</u> of a book appear?

**2.** If something is <u>foreseen</u>, is it a surprise?

### Word Study

The **Old English prefix *fore-*** means "earlier" or "in front of."

**Apply It** Explain how the prefix *fore-* helps you determine the meanings of these technical academic words from science and the arts. Consult a dictionary if necessary.

**forethought**
**foretell**
**foresight**

**Can truth change?**

## Writing About the Big Question

In "New Directions," Mrs. Annie Johnson finds herself on her own with two young children. Use these sentence starters to develop your ideas about the Big Question.

The **truth** about a person can change as a result of _____.

We see things differently as **circumstances** change because _____.

**While You Read** Look for the ways Annie Johnson's situation changes over time, and decide whether she really has set off in a new direction.

## Vocabulary

Read each word and its definition. Decide whether you know the word well, know it a little bit, or do not know it at all. After you read, see how your knowledge of each word has increased.

- **conceded** (kən sēd´ əd) *v.* admitted as true or valid; acknowledged (p. 36) *Julie conceded that she had made an awful mistake.* concede *v.* concession *n.*

- **amicably** (am´ i kə blē) *adv.* in a friendly way (p. 36) *Luckily, they settled their disagreements amicably before the problem escalated into something violent.* amicable *adj.*

- **meticulously** (mə tik´ yōō ləs lē) *adv.* very carefully and precisely (p. 37) *She meticulously applied her makeup.* meticulous *adj.*

- **balmy** (bäm´ ē) *adj.* having the qualities of balm; soothing, mild, pleasant (p. 38) *It was a balmy spring day with sunshine and a warm breeze.* balm *n.* balminess *n.*

- **ominous** (äm´ ə nəs) *adj.* threatening (p. 38) *The sound of the thunder seemed ominous.* ominously *adv.* omen *n.*

- **unpalatable** (un pal´ it ə bəl) *adj.* distasteful; unpleasant (p. 38) *She thought changing soiled diapers was her most unpalatable chore.* palate *n.* palatable *adj.*

### Word Study

The **Latin prefix con-** means "with" or "together."

If a person **concedes**, he or she yields to or gives in. In the story, Annie Johnson's husband *concedes* that their marriage is not going to work.

## Author of

# New Directions

Maya Angelou's life is a story of overcoming hardships and succeeding. She was raised in rural, segregated Arkansas. In 1940, she moved to San Francisco, where she worked as a waitress, cook, and dancer. In the 1950s, Angelou went to New York, where she discovered her talents as a writer.

**"I am human, and nothing human can be alien to me."** Angelou wrote these words, and she lives by them. She went on to become a poet, a playwright, an editor, an actress, a director, and a teacher. Her many literary honors include a nomination for a Pulitzer Prize. She also read one of her poems at President Bill Clinton's inauguration in January 1993.

## BACKGROUND FOR THE STORY

### Limited Options

In the early 1900s, job opportunities were limited for many Americans—particularly African Americans like Annie Johnson, the main character in "New Directions." At that time, the most common jobs available for African American women were cleaning, child care, and general household labor. For women who had families, caring for someone else's household was an extra burden.

## DID YOU KNOW?

Angelou's first name is Marguerite. Her brother gave her the nickname Maya when she was a child.

# New Directions

## Maya Angelou

In 1903 the late Mrs. Annie Johnson of Arkansas found herself with two toddling sons, very little money, a slight ability to read and add simple numbers. To this picture add a disastrous marriage and the burdensome fact that Mrs. Johnson was a Negro.

When she told her husband, Mr. William Johnson, of her dissatisfaction with their marriage, he conceded that he too found it to be less than he expected, and had been secretly hoping to leave and study religion. He added that he thought God was calling him not only to preach but to do so in Enid, Oklahoma. He did not tell her that he knew a minister in Enid with whom he could study and who had a friendly, unmarried daughter. They parted amicably, Annie keeping the one-room house and William taking most of the cash to carry himself to Oklahoma.

Annie, over six feet tall, big-boned, decided that she would not go to work as a domestic and leave her "precious babes" to anyone else's care. There was no possibility of being hired at the town's cotton gin or lumber mill, but maybe there was a way to make the two factories work for her. In her words, "I looked up the road I was going and back the way I come, and since I wasn't satisfied, I

**Vocabulary**
**conceded** (kən sēd´ əd)
*v.* admitted as true or valid; acknowledged

**amicably** (am´ i kə blē)
*adv.* in a friendly way

decided to step off the road and cut me a new path." She told herself that she wasn't a fancy cook but that she could "mix groceries well enough to scare hungry away and from starving a man."

She made her plans meticulously and in secret. One early evening to see if she was ready, she placed stones in two five-gallon pails and carried them three miles to the cotton gin. She rested a little, and then, discarding some rocks, she walked in the darkness to the saw mill five miles farther along the dirt road. On her way back to her little house and her babies, she dumped the remaining rocks along the path.

That same night she worked into the early hours boiling chicken and frying ham. She made dough and filled the rolled-out pastry with meat. At last she went to sleep.

The next morning she left her house carrying the meat pies, lard, an iron brazier,[1] and coals for a fire. Just before lunch she appeared in an empty lot behind the cotton gin. As the dinner noon bell rang, she dropped the savors into boiling fat and the aroma rose and floated over to the workers who spilled out of the gin, covered with white lint, looking like specters.

Most workers had brought their lunches of pinto beans and biscuits or crackers, onions and cans of sardines, but they were tempted by the hot meat pies which Annie ladled out of the fat. She wrapped them in newspapers, which soaked up the grease, and offered them for sale at a nickel each. Although business was slow, those first days Annie was determined. She balanced her appearances between the two hours of activity.

---

1. **brazier** (brā′ zhər) *n.* A brazier is a pan or bowl that holds burning coals or charcoal as a heat source for cooking. In some braziers, food is placed on a grill directly over the flames. Johnson uses hers to heat a pot of boiling fat so that she can deep-fry her pies.

**Vocabulary**
**meticulously** (mə tik′ yoo ləs lē) *adv.* very carefully and precisely

**Reading Skill**
**Make Predictions**
What prediction can you make about Annie's plans? Why?

*As the dinner noon bell rang, she dropped the savors into boiling fat and the aroma rose....*

◄ **Critical Viewing**
Judging from this photograph, why do you think Annie Johnson felt that lumber workers would want to buy her pies?
**[Draw Conclusions]**

**Spiral Review**
**Central Idea** In this section, how does the author interweave personal examples with factual information to support the central idea?

So, on Monday if she offered hot fresh pies at the cotton gin and sold the remaining cooled-down pies at the lumber mill for three cents, then on Tuesday she went first to the lumber mill presenting fresh, just-cooked pies as the lumbermen covered in sawdust emerged from the mill.

For the next few years, on balmy spring days, blistering summer noons, and cold, wet, and wintry middays, Annie never disappointed her customers, who could count on seeing the tall, brown-skin woman bent over her brazier, carefully turning the meat pies. When she felt certain that the workers had become dependent on her, she built a stall between the two hives of industry and let the men run to her for their lunchtime provisions.

She had indeed stepped from the road which seemed to have been chosen for her and cut herself a brand-new path. In years that stall became a store where customers could buy cheese, meal, syrup, cookies, candy, writing tablets, pickles, canned goods, fresh fruit, soft drinks, coal, oil, and leather soles for worn-out shoes.

Each of us has the right and the responsibility to assess the roads which lie ahead, and those over which we have traveled, and if the future road looms ominous or unpromising, and the roads back uninviting, then we need to gather our resolve and, carrying only the necessary baggage, step off that road into another direction. If the new choice is also unpalatable, without embarrassment, we must be ready to change that as well.

## Critical Thinking

Cite textual evidence to support your responses.

1. **Key Ideas and Details (a)** Why does Annie Johnson have to find a source of income? **(b)** Why does she decide against a job as a domestic? **(c) Infer:** What does Annie Johnson's decision suggest about the kind of mother she is?

2. **Key Ideas and Details (a)** What does Annie Johnson decide to do to earn a living? **(b) Evaluate:** How would you describe Annie Johnson's abilities as a businessperson? Explain your response.

3. **Craft and Structure (a)** What details in the text show that Annie Johnson's business grows? **(b) Draw Conclusions:** What does her achievement suggest about the human spirit in general?

4. **Integration of Knowledge and Ideas (a)** How does the truth of Annie's life change? **(b)** Do you think that taking a "new direction" in life is worth the risk of failure? Explain. *[Connect to the Big Question: Can truth change?]*

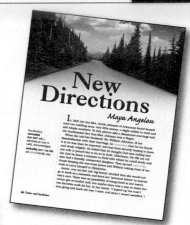

## Literary Analysis: Narrative Essay

**1. Key Ideas and Details (a)** In this **narrative essay,** what problem sets the story in motion? **(b)** How is the problem overcome?

**2. Key Ideas and Details (a)** Use a chart like the one shown to record three **significant details** Angelou uses to describe Annie Johnson and her husband. **(b)** What impression of each character does each of these details create?

| Annie Johnson | Annie Johnson's Husband |
|---|---|
|  |  |

## Reading Skill: Make Predictions

**3.** Write three **predictions** that you made while reading "New Directions." Then, trade papers with a partner and discuss the accuracy of your predictions and the details you used to make them. Finally, explain how your method of making and verifying predictions has or has not changed as a result of your discussion.

## Vocabulary

**Acquisition and Use** Use a word from the vocabulary list on page 34 to replace each underlined word or phrase with its opposite.

**1.** When people act in a friendly manner, they behave <u>viciously</u>.

**2.** Some people think that spinach is <u>delicious</u>.

**3.** The rumble of a volcano is an <u>encouraging</u> sound.

**4.** You can avoid mistakes on tests by checking your work <u>carelessly</u>.

**5.** Ralph finally <u>did not admit</u> his participation in the prank.

**6.** A <u>chilly</u> wind was blowing on that summer day.

**Word Study** Use the context of the sentences and what you know about the **Latin prefix *con-*** to explain your answer to each question.

**1.** What does it mean if something is <u>concentrated</u>?

**2.** How does a person <u>contend</u> with problems?

### Word Study

The **Latin prefix *con-*** means "with" or "together."

**Apply It** Explain how the prefix *con-* helps you determine the meanings of these technical academic words from science and social studies. Consult a dictionary if necessary.

**convex**
**concentric**
**confederate**

# Integrated Language Skills

## The Washwoman • New Directions

### Conventions:
### Common Nouns and Proper Nouns

A **common noun** names any one of a class of people, places, or things. A **proper noun** names a specific person, place, or thing and begins with a capital letter.

| Type | Common Noun | Proper Noun |
| --- | --- | --- |
| person | student | Deana Johnson |
| place | city | Raleigh-Durham |
| thing | novel | *A Separate Peace* |

Some nouns can be either common or proper, depending on how they are used. Look at these examples:

> My **mom** made us brownies for dessert.
> May I please have another brownie, **Mom**?

> The **president** must sign a bill before it becomes a law.
> The bill was signed by **President** Roosevelt.

**Practice A** Copy each of the following sentences. Draw one line under each common noun and two lines under each proper noun.

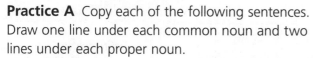

1. "The Washwoman" is a story by Isaac Bashevis Singer.
2. Singer's mother studied books, such as *The Duties of the Heart.*
3. The setting of the story is Poland, where Singer grew up.
4. The washwoman has a large effect on the family.

**Reading Application** In "The Washwoman," find one sentence with a proper noun and common noun.

**Practice B** Rewrite each of the sentences below, replacing one common noun with a proper noun.

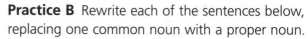

1. The woman in the story started a business cooking food.
2. Her husband packed up and moved away to a new state.
3. She and her two baby sons were on their own in a new state.
4. The lumber workers bought food from her.

**Writing Application** Using the following sentence as a model, write two more sentences that include both common and proper nouns: *Annie hoped to name her business Johnson's Pies.*

**PH WRITING COACH** Further instruction and practice are available in *Prentice Hall Writing Coach.*

# Writing

**Narrative Text** Both selections involve strong women dealing with life's challenges. Write an **anecdote,** a brief narrative, about a person you know and respect. For example, you might describe something admirable that the person did and what you learned from it.

- Before you draft, note what you respect about the person. This is the controlling impression your anecdote will convey.
- Describe a specific event that illustrates the characteristics you admire in your subject.
- Use significant details to support the message you want to convey.

**Grammar Application** If you include proper nouns in your anecdote, be sure to capitalize correctly.

## Writing Workshop: *Work in Progress*

**Prewriting for an Autobiographical Narrative** For an essay you may write later, list three or four vivid memories, describing the visual picture you see in your mind for each one. Develop the scene in your mind by adding details related to other senses. Include what you heard, smelled, and felt. Save this Memory List in your writing portfolio.

# Speaking and Listening

**Comprehension and Collaboration** With a partner, role-play an **interview** featuring the main character in the selection you read. For example, plan an interview between the washwoman and a reporter or between Annie Johnson and a potential employer. If you need to refresh your memory, reread either selection to learn more about the character you have chosen.

Follow these steps to complete the assignment:

- In order to demonstrate your knowledge of the subject matter, generate and ask relevant questions that are open-ended and cannot be answered simply with a yes or a no.
- Listen carefully to what your partner says in the interview.
- Make notes of your partner's responses so that you can ask appropriate follow-up questions or provide answers.
- To make your delivery more effective, speak clearly (showing confidence and poise), make eye contact with your partner, and use language that demonstrates maturity, sensitivity, and respect.
- After the role play, evaluate each other's work for the quality of its techniques.
- Compile your responses and report a summary to the class.

**Common Core State Standards**

L.9-10.2; W.9-10.3; SL.9-10.1.a, SL.9-10.1.c
[For the full wording of the standards, see page 22.]

Use this prewriting activity to prepare for the **Writing Workshop** on page 94.

**PHLit Online!**
www.PHLitOnline.com
- Interactive graphic organizers
- Grammar tutorial
- Interactive journals

## © Leveled Texts

Build your skills and improve your comprehension of fiction with texts of increasing complexity.

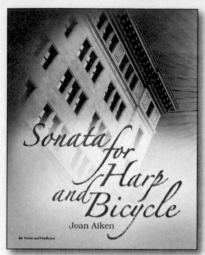

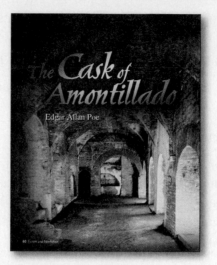

Read **"Sonata for Harp and Bicycle"** to see how a man solves a ghostly problem.

Read **"The Cask of Amontillado"** to see how a man seeks revenge.

##  Common Core State Standards

Meet these standards with either **"Sonata for Harp and Bicycle"** (p. 46) or **"The Cask of Amontillado"** (p. 60).

**Reading Literature**
**5.** Analyze how an author's choices concerning how to structure a text, order events within it, and manipulate time create such effects as mystery, tension, or surprise. *(Literary Analysis: Plot)*

**Spiral Review: RL.9-10.2**

**Writing**
**9.** Draw evidence from literary or informational texts to support analysis, reflection, and research. *(Writing: Critique)*

**Speaking and Listening**
**1.** Initiate and participate effectively in a range of collaborative discussions with diverse partners, building on others' ideas and expressing their own clearly and persuasively. **1.a.** Come to discussions prepared, having read and researched material under study; explicitly draw on that preparation by referring to evidence from texts and other research on the topic or issue to stimulate a thoughtful, well-reasoned exchange of ideas. *(Speaking and Listening: Retell a Story)*

**Language**
**5.** Demonstrate understanding of figurative language, word relationships, and nuances in word meanings. *(Vocabulary: Analogy)*

**6.** Acquire and use accurately general academic and domain-specific words and phrases, sufficient for reading and listening at the college and career readiness level; demonstrate independence in gathering vocabulary knowledge when considering a word or phrase important to comprehension or expression. *(Vocabulary: Word Study)*

# Literary Analysis: Plot

**Plot** is the sequence of events in a narrative. It is structured around a **conflict,** or problem, and it can be divided into the following parts:

- **Exposition:** characters and setting are introduced
- **Rising Action:** central conflict begins
- **Climax:** high point of intensity in the conflict is reached
- **Falling Action:** conflict's intensity lessens
- **Resolution:** conflict concludes and loose ends are tied up

Writers use a variety of techniques, or *stylistic devices*, to keep readers interested in the plot. One of these devices, **foreshadowing,** is the use of clues to hint at events that will happen later in a story. Authors use this technique to create **suspense,** a feeling of tension that keeps readers wondering what will happen next.

# Reading Skill: Make Predictions

A **prediction** is an idea you develop about what will happen later in a narrative. It is based on details in the text combined with your own experience. As you read, notice details that may foreshadow future events. Next, make predictions based on those details, and then **read ahead to verify your predictions.** If a prediction turns out to be wrong, evaluate your reasoning by asking questions like these:

- Did you misread details?
- Did the author purposely create false expectations in order to surprise you later in the story?

**Revise,** or change, your prediction based on your evaluation.

## Using the Strategy: Predictions Map

Use a chart like the one shown to record and evaluate your predictions. Analyze any inaccurate predictions to determine why they were incorrect.

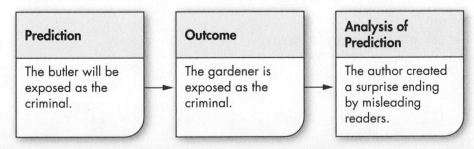

| Prediction | Outcome | Analysis of Prediction |
|---|---|---|
| The butler will be exposed as the criminal. | The gardener is exposed as the criminal. | The author created a surprise ending by misleading readers. |

# Can *truth* change?

## Writing About the Big Question

In "**Sonata for Harp and Bicycle**," miscommunication leads to tragedy and a curse on a building. Use these sentence starters to develop your ideas about the Big Question:

You can change your own fate by _____.

**Evidence** can change our **beliefs** because _____.

**While You Read** Look for the ways the main character takes charge of his life to change the truth of his situation.

## Vocabulary

Read each word and its definition. Decide whether you know the word well, know it a little bit, or do not know it at all. After you have read the selection, see how your knowledge of each word has increased.

- **encroaching** (en krōch´ iŋ) *adj.* intruding (p. 47) *The encroaching weeds are taking over the lawn.* encroach *v.* encroachment *n.*

- **tantalizingly** (tan´ tə līz´ iŋ lē) *adv.* in a teasing way (p. 48) *He held the ball tantalizingly out of reach.* tantalize *v.* tantalizing *adj.*

- **furtive** (fʉr´ tiv) *adj.* sneaky; hidden (p. 50) *With a furtive wink, he let his best friends in on the joke.* furtively *adv.*

- **menacing** (men´ əs iŋ) *adj.* threatening (p. 51) *The menacing cat stalked the little bird.* menace *v.* menace *n.*

- **reciprocate** (ri sip´ rə kāt´) *v.* return (p. 52) *Because Julio invited Mary to the party, she decided to reciprocate the offer by asking him to the game.* reciprocal *adj.*

- **preposterous** (prē päs´ tər əs) *adj.* so contrary to common sense as to be laughable; absurd; ridiculous (p. 53) *The high ticket prices for the show were preposterous.* preposterously *adv.*

### Word Study

The **suffix -*ate*** means "to become or form," and it often indicates the word is a verb.

In this story, the main character **reciprocates** the love of his admirer, forming a reciprocal, or shared, relationship.

# Meet
# Joan Aiken
(1924–2004)

## Author of
## *Sonata for Harp and Bicycle*

The daughter of an American poet, Conrad Aiken, and a Canadian mother, Jessie MacDonald, Joan Aiken was born in England and grew up there. She lived with her family in an eerie old house, an experience that helped foster her fascination with mystery and the unexplained. Her mother's second husband was another writer, Martin Armstrong. Not surprisingly, Aiken knew when she was very young that she would become a writer someday.

**The "Family Trade"** Aiken began writing when she was five and published her first story at sixteen. After spending some time working in London for a magazine, an advertising agency, and the United Nations, she decided to pursue what she called "the family trade." Her many literary works include novels, poems, plays, and stories for both children and adults.

## BACKGROUND FOR THE STORY

### Sonata

A sonata (sə nät´ ə) is a musical composition in several movements, or parts. Sonatas are often written for solo piano or for piano and another instrument. In titling her story "Sonata for Harp and Bicycle," Joan Aiken playfully suggests a musical structure that will, like a sequence of chords, be resolved harmoniously at the end.

### Did You Know?

Aiken did not attend a school until she was twelve. Before then, she was taught at home.

# Sonata for Harp and Bicycle

Joan Aiken

"**N**o one is allowed to remain in the building after five o'clock," Mr. Manaby told his new assistant, showing him into the little room that was like the inside of a parcel.

"Why not?"

"Directorial policy," said Mr. Manaby. But that was not the real reason.

Gaunt and sooty, Grimes Buildings lurched up the side of a hill toward Clerkenwell.[1] Every little office within its dim and crumbling exterior owned one tiny crumb of light—such was the proud boast of the architect—but toward evening the crumbs were collected as by an immense vacuum cleaner, absorbed and demolished, yielding to an uncontrollable mass of dark that came tumbling in through windows and doors to take their place. Darkness infested the building like a flight of bats returning willingly to roost.

"Wash hands, please. Wash hands, please," the intercom began to bawl in the passages at a quarter to five. Without much need of prompting, the staff hustled like lemmings along the corridors to green- and blue-tiled washrooms that mocked with an illusion of cheerfulness the encroaching dusk.

"All papers into cases, please," the voice warned, five minutes later. "Look at your desks, ladies and gentlemen. Any documents left lying about? Kindly put them away. Desks must be left clear and tidy. Drawers must be shut."

A multitudinous shuffling, a rustling as of innumerable bluebottle flies might have been heard by the attentive

---

1. **Clerkenwell** district of London.

**Vocabulary**
**encroaching**
(en krōch´ iŋ) *adj.*
intruding

Reading
Check
What is the new assistant told about being in the building after five o'clock?

ear after this injunction, as the employees of Moreton Wold and Company thrust their papers into cases, hurried letters and invoices into drawers, clipped statistical abstracts together and slammed them into filing cabinets, dropped discarded copy into wastepaper baskets. Two minutes later, and not a desk throughout Grimes Buildings bore more than its customary coating of dust.

"Hats and coats on, please. Hats and coats on, please. Did you bring an umbrella? Have you left any shopping on the floor?" At three minutes to five the homegoing throng was in the lifts[2] and on the stairs; a clattering, staccato-voiced flood darkened momentarily the great double doors of the building, and then as the first faint notes of St. Paul's[3] came echoing faintly on the frosty air, to be picked up near at hand by the louder chimes of St. Biddulph's-on-the-Wall, the entire premises of Moreton Wold stood empty.

"But why is it?" Jason Ashgrove, the new copywriter, asked his secretary one day. "Why are the staff herded out so fast? Not that I'm against it, mind you; I think it's an admirable idea in many ways, but there is the liberty of the individual to be considered, don't you think?"

"Hush!" Miss Golden, the secretary, gazed at him with large and terrified eyes. "You mustn't ask that sort of question. When you are taken onto the Established Staff you'll be told. Not before."

"But I want to know now," Jason said in discontent. "Do you know?"

"Yes, I do," Miss Golden answered tantalizingly. "Come on, or we shan't have finished the Oat Crisp layout by a quarter to." And she stared firmly down at the copy in front of her, lips folded, candyfloss hair falling over her face, lashes hiding eyes like peridots,[4] a girl with a secret.

Jason was annoyed. He rapped out a couple of rude and witty rhymes which Miss Golden let pass in a withering silence.

"What do you want for your birthday, Miss Golden? Sherry? Fudge? Bubble bath?"

"I want to go away with a clear conscience about Oat Crisps," Miss Golden retorted. It was not true; what she chiefly wanted was Mr. Jason Ashgrove, but he had not realized this yet.

"Come on, don't tease! I'm sure you haven't been on the Established Staff all that long," he coaxed her. "What happens when one is taken on, anyway? Does the Managing Director have us up for a confidential chat? Or are we given a little book called *The Awful Secret of Grimes Buildings*?"

---

2. **lifts** *n.* British term for elevators.
3. **St. Paul's** famous church in London.
4. **peridots** (per´ i däts´) *n.* yellowish-green gems.

**Literary Analysis**
**Plot**
What problem is introduced in Jason's conversation with Miss Golden?

**Vocabulary**
**tantalizingly** (tan´ tə līz´ iŋ lē) *adv.* in a teasing way

© **Spiral Review**
**Theme** Which details hint that Jason and Miss Golden are secretly in love? What theme, or insight into people, is suggested by these details?

Miss Golden wasn't telling. She opened her drawer and took out a white towel and a cake of rosy soap.

"Wash hands, please! Wash hands, please!"

Jason was frustrated. "You'll be sorry," he said. "I shall do something desperate."

"Oh no, you mustn't!" Her eyes were large with fright. She ran from the room and was back within a couple of moments, still drying her hands.

"If I took you out for a coffee, couldn't you give me just a tiny hint?"

Side by side Miss Golden and Mr. Ashgrove ran along the green-floored passages, battled down the white marble stairs among the hundred other employees from the tenth floor, the nine hundred from the floors below.

He saw her lips move as she said something, but in the clatter of two thousand feet the words were lost.

"—fire escape," he heard, as they came into the momentary hush of the carpeted entrance hall. And "—it's to do with a bicycle. A bicycle and a harp."

"I don't understand."

Now they were in the street, chilly with the winter dusk smells of celery on carts, of swept-up leaves heaped in faraway parks, and cold layers of dew sinking among the withered evening primroses in the bombed areas. London lay about them wreathed in twilit mystery and fading against the barred and smoky sky. Like a ninth wave the sound of traffic overtook and swallowed them.

"Please tell me!"

But, shaking her head, she stepped onto a scarlet homebound bus and was borne away from him.

Jason stood undecided on the pavement, with the crowds dividing around him as around the pier of a bridge. He scratched his head, looked about him for guidance.

An ambulance clanged, a taxi hooted, a drill stuttered, a siren wailed on the river, a door slammed, a brake squealed, and close beside his ear a bicycle bell tinkled its tiny warning.

A bicycle, she had said. A bicycle and a harp.

Jason turned and stared at Grimes Buildings.

Somewhere, he knew, there was a back way in, a service entrance. He walked slowly past the main doors, with their tubs of

### Reading Skill
### Make Predictions

Which text clue leads you to predict that a romance will develop between Jason and Miss Golden? Explain.

### Reading Check

What question does Jason Ashgrove want Miss Golden to answer?

**Vocabulary**
**furtive** (fur´ tiv) *adj.*
sneaky; hidden

snowy chrysanthemums, and up Glass Street. A tiny furtive wedge of darkness beckoned him, a snicket, a hacket, an alley carved into the thickness of the building. It was so narrow that at any moment, it seemed, the overtopping walls would come together and squeeze it out of existence.

Walking as softly as an Indian, Jason passed through it, slid by a file of dustbins,[5] and found the foot of the fire escape. Iron treads rose into the mist, like an illustration to a Gothic[6] fairy tale.

He began to climb.

When he had mounted to the ninth story he paused for breath. It was a lonely place. The lighting consisted of a dim bulb at the foot of every flight. A well of gloom sank beneath him. The cold fingers of the wind nagged and fluttered at the tails of his jacket, and he pulled the string of the fire door and edged inside.

**Literary Analysis**
**Plot**
How do Jason's actions increase the suspense of the narrative?

Grimes Buildings were triangular, with the street forming the base of the triangle, and the fire escape the point. Jason could see two long passages coming toward him, meeting at an acute angle where he stood. He started down the left-hand one, tiptoeing in the cavelike silence. Nowhere was there any sound, except for the faraway drip of a tap. No night watchman would stay in the building; none was needed. Burglars gave the place a wide berth.

**▼ Critical Viewing**
What advantages would patrolling corridors on a bicycle offer as opposed to patrolling on foot? **[Evaluate]**

Jason opened a door at random; then another. Offices lay everywhere about him, empty and forbidding. Some held lipstick-stained tissues, spilled powder, and orange peels; others were still foggy with cigarette smoke. Here was a Director's suite of rooms—a desk like half an acre of frozen lake, inch-thick carpet, roses, and the smell of cigars. Here was a conference room with scattered squares of doodled blotting paper. All equally empty.

He was not sure when he first began to notice the bell. Telephone, he thought at first, and then he remembered that all the outside lines were disconnected at five. And

---

5. **dustbins** *n.* British term for garbage cans.
6. **Gothic** *adj.* mysterious.

this bell, anyway, had not the regularity of a telephone's double ring: there was a tinkle, and then silence; a long ring, and then silence; a whole volley of rings together, and then silence.

Jason stood listening, and fear knocked against his ribs and shortened his breath. He knew that he must move or be paralyzed by it. He ran up a flight of stairs and found himself with two more endless green corridors beckoning him like a pair of dividers.

Another sound now: a waft of ice-thin notes, riffling up an arpeggio[7] like a flurry of snowflakes. Far away down the passage it echoed. Jason ran in pursuit, but as he ran the music receded. He circled the building, but it always outdistanced him, and when he came back to the stairs he heard it fading away to the story below.

He hesitated, and as he did so heard again the bell; the bicycle bell. It was approaching him fast, bearing down on him, urgent, menacing. He could hear the pedals, almost see the shimmer of an invisible wheel. Absurdly, he was reminded of the insistent clamor of an ice-cream vendor, summoning children on a sultry Sunday afternoon.

There was a little fireman's alcove beside him, with buckets and pumps. He hurled himself into it. The bell stopped beside him, and then there was a moment while his heart tried to shake itself loose in his chest. He was looking into two eyes carved out of expressionless air; he was held by two hands knotted together out of the width of dark.

"Daisy, Daisy?" came the whisper. "Is that you, Daisy? Have you come to give me your answer?"

Jason tried to speak, but no words came.

"It's not Daisy! Who are you?" The sibilants[8] were full of threat. "You can't stay here. This is private property."

He was thrust along the corridor. It was like being pushed by a whirlwind—the fire door opened ahead of him without a touch, and he was on the openwork platform, clutching the slender railing. Still the hands would not let him go.

"How about it?" the whisper mocked him. "How about jumping? It's an easy death compared with some."

Jason looked down into the smoky void. The darkness nodded to him like a familiar.[9]

"You wouldn't be much loss, would you? What have you got to live for?"

**Literary Analysis
Plot**
What earlier details foreshadowed this mysterious ringing?

**Vocabulary
menacing** (men´ əs iŋ) *adj.* threatening

*He hesitated, and as he did so heard again the bell; the bicycle bell.*

Reading Check
What makes the ringing sound that Jason hears inside the Grimes Buildings?

---

7. **arpeggio** (är pej´ ō) *n.* notes of a chord played one after the other instead of together.
8. **sibilants** (sib´ əl əntz) *n.* hissing sounds.
9. **a familiar** *n.* a spirit.

Miss Golden, Jason thought. She would miss me. And the syllables Berenice Golden lingered in the air like a chime. Drawing on some unknown deposit of courage he shook himself loose from the holding hands and ran down the fire escape without looking back.

Next morning when Miss Golden, crisp, fragrant, and punctual, shut the door of Room 492 behind her, she stopped short of the hat-pegs with a horrified gasp.

"Mr. Ashgrove, your hair!"

"It makes me look more distinguished, don't you think?" he said.

It had indeed this effect, for his impeccable dark cut had turned to a stippled silver which might have been envied by many a diplomat.

"How did it happen? You've not—" her voice sank to a whisper—"*you've not been in Grimes Buildings after dark?*"

"Miss Golden—Berenice," he said earnestly. "Who was Daisy? Plainly you know. Tell me the story."

"Did you see him?" she asked faintly.

"Him?"

"William Heron—The Wailing Watchman. Oh," she exclaimed in terror, "I can see you did. Then you are doomed—doomed!"

"If I'm doomed," said Jason, "let's have coffee, and you tell me the story quickly."

"It all happened over fifty years ago," said Berenice, as she spooned out coffee powder with distracted extravagance. "Heron was the night watchman in this building, patrolling the corridors from dusk to dawn every night on his bicycle. He fell in love with a Miss Bell who taught the harp. She rented a room—this room—and gave lessons in it. She began to reciprocate his love, and they used to share a picnic supper every night at eleven, and she'd stay on a while to keep him company. It was an idyll,[10] among the fire buckets and the furnace pipes.

**10. idyll** (ī´ dəl) *n.* romantic scene, usually in the country.

► **Critical Viewing**
The harp is an important part of this mystery. Describe the sound you think this instrument would make.
**[Speculate]**

**Vocabulary**
**reciprocate** (ri sip´ rə kāt´) *v.* return

"On Halloween he had summoned up the courage to propose to her. The day before he had told her he was going to ask her a very important question, and he came to the Buildings with a huge bunch of roses and a bottle of wine. But Miss Bell never turned up.

"The explanation was simple. Miss Bell, of course, had been losing a lot of sleep through her nocturnal romance, and so she used to take a nap in her music room between seven and ten, to save going home. In order to make sure that she would wake up, she persuaded her father, a distant relative of Graham Bell,[11] to attach an alarm-waking fixture to her telephone which called her every night at ten. She was too modest and shy to let Heron know that she spent those hours in the building, and to give him the pleasure of waking her himself.

"Alas! On this important evening the line failed, and she never woke up. The telephone was in its infancy at that time, you must remember.

"Heron waited and waited. At last, mad with grief and jealousy, having called her home and discovered that she was not there, he concluded that she had betrayed him; he ran to the fire escape, and cast himself off it, holding the roses and the bottle of wine.

"Daisy did not long survive him but pined away soon after. Since that day their ghosts have haunted Grimes Buildings, he vainly patrolling the corridors on his bicycle, she playing her harp in the room she rented. But they never meet. And anyone who meets the ghost of William Heron will himself, within five days, leap down from the same fatal fire escape."

She gazed at him with tragic eyes.

"In that case we must lose no time," said Jason, and he enveloped her in an embrace as prompt as it was ardent. Looking down at the gossamer hair sprayed across his pin-stripe, he added, "Just the same it is a preposterous situation. Firstly, I have no intention of jumping off the fire escape—" here, however, he repressed a shudder as he remembered the cold, clutching hands of the evening before— "and secondly, I find it quite nonsensical that those two inefficient ghosts have spent fifty years in this building without coming across each other. We must remedy the matter, Berenice. We must not begrudge our new-found happiness to others."

He gave her another kiss so impassioned that the electric typewriter against which they were leaning began chattering to itself in a frenzy of enthusiasm.

---

11. **Graham Bell** Alexander Graham Bell (1847–1922), the inventor of the telephone.

**Literary Analysis**
**Plot**
How does this new information increase the suspense of the narrative?

**Reading Skill**
**Make Predictions**
What do you think Jason might do to "remedy the matter"?

**Vocabulary**
**preposterous** (prē päs´ tər əs) *adj.* so contrary to common sense as to be laughable; absurd; ridiculous

Reading Check
According to Berenice, what happens to anyone who meets the ghost of William Heron?

"This very evening," he went on, looking at his watch, "we will put matters right for that unhappy couple and then, if I really have only five more days to live, which I don't for one moment believe, we will proceed to spend them together, my bewitching Berenice, in the most advantageous manner possible."

She nodded, spellbound.

"Can you work a switchboard?" he added. She nodded again. "My love, you are perfection itself. Meet me in the switchboard room then, at ten this evening. I would say, have dinner with me, but I shall need to make one or two purchases and see an old R.A.F.[12] friend. You will be safe from Heron's curse in the switchboard room if he always keeps to the corridors."

"I would rather meet him and die with you," she murmured.

"My angel, I hope that won't be necessary. Now," he said, sighing, "I suppose we should get down to our day's work."

Strangely enough the copy they wrote that day, although engendered from such agitated minds, sold more packets of Oat Crisps than any other advertising matter before or since.

That evening when Jason entered Grimes Buildings he was carrying two bottles of wine, two bunches of red roses, and a large canvas-covered bundle. Miss Golden, who had concealed herself in the switchboard room before the offices closed for the night, eyed these things with surprise.

"Now," said Jason, after he had greeted her, "I want you first to ring our own extension."

"No one will reply, surely?"

"I think she will reply."

Sure enough, when Berenice rang Extension 170 a faint, sleepy voice, distant and yet clear, whispered, "Hullo?"

"Is that Miss Bell?"

"Yes."

Berenice went a little pale. Her eyes sought Jason's and, prompted by him, she said formally, "Switchboard here, Miss Bell. Your ten o'clock call."

"Thank you," the faint voice said. There was a click and the line went blank.

"Excellent," Jason remarked. He unfastened his package and slipped its straps over his shoulders. "Now plug into the intercom."

Berenice did so, and then said, loudly and clearly, "Attention. Night watchman on duty, please. Night watchman on duty. You have

**Reading Skill**
**Make Predictions**
What do you predict Jason will do with the two bunches of roses? Why?

12. **R.A.F.** Royal Air Force.

an urgent summons to Room 492. You have an urgent summons to Room 492." The intercom echoed and reverberated through the empty corridors, then coughed itself to silence.

"Now we must run. You take the roses, sweetheart, and I'll carry the bottles."

Together they raced up eight flights of stairs and along the passages to Room 492. As they neared the door a burst of music met them—harp music swelling out, sweet and triumphant. Jason took a bunch of roses from Berenice, opened the door a little way, and gently deposited them, with a bottle, inside the door. As he closed it again Berenice said breathlessly, "Did you see anyone?"

"No," he said. "The room was too full of music." She saw that his eyes were shining.

They stood hand in hand, reluctant to move away, waiting for they hardly knew what. Suddenly the door opened again. Neither Berenice nor Jason, afterward, would speak of what they saw but each was left with a memory, bright as the picture on a Salvador Dali[13] calendar, of a bicycle bearing on its saddle a harp, a bottle of wine, and a bouquet of red roses, sweeping improbably down the corridor and far, far away.

Reading Check

What is Jason carrying as he enters the Grimes Buildings?

---

13. **Salvador Dali** (sal´ və dôr´ dä´ lē) (1904–1989) modern artist famous for his unusual pictures.

"We can go now," Jason said.

He led Berenice to the fire door, tucking the bottle of Médoc in his jacket pocket. A black wind from the north whistled beneath them as they stood on the openwork platform, looking down.

"We don't want our evening to be spoiled by the thought of a curse hanging over us," he said, "so this is the practical thing to do. Hang onto the roses." And holding his love firmly, Jason pulled the rip cord of his R.A.F. friend's parachute and leaped off the fire escape.

A bridal shower of rose petals adorned the descent of Miss Golden, who was possibly the only girl to be kissed in midair in the district of Clerkenwell at ten minutes to midnight on Halloween.

**Reading Skill**
**Make Predictions**
Do the events at the end of the story verify your predictions? Why or why not?

## Critical Thinking

Cite textual evidence to support your responses.

1. **Key Ideas and Details (a)** What three important objects does Miss Golden mention to Jason as they leave the Grimes Buildings at five o'clock? **(b) Connect:** How does he use this information?

2. **Craft and Structure (a)** Who is in love in the main plot of the story? In the ghost-story subplot? **(b) Analyze:** How do these two love plots connect?

3. **Key Ideas and Details** What actions does Jason take to avoid the curse that awaits those who see Heron's ghost?

4. **Integration of Knowledge and Ideas (a)** How does Jason react to the news of the curse? **(b) Analyze Cause and Effect:** How do his actions help change the "truth"? *[Connect to the Big Question: Can truth change?]*

## Literary Analysis: Plot

**© 1. Key Ideas and Details** Using a chart like this one, identify two key events in the **rising action,** one that marks the **climax,** and one in the **falling action.** Discuss your choices with a partner.

**© 2. Craft and Structure (a)** Identify a passage that **foreshadows** Jason's entering the Grimes Buildings after hours.
**(b)** Explain how foreshadowing increases the story's **suspense.**

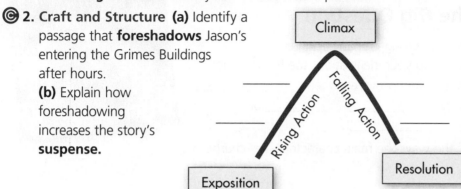

## Reading Skill: Make Predictions

**3.** What **prediction** did you make when Jason entered the Grimes Buildings after closing and heard a bicycle bell? **(b)** What details helped you make your prediction?

**4.** Was your prediction **verified** by later story events? Explain.

## Vocabulary

**© Acquisition and Use** An **analogy** shows the relationship between pairs of words. Use a word from the vocabulary list on page 44 to complete each analogy. For each case, your choice should create a word pair that matches the relationship between the first two words.

**1.** angry : shout :: _____ : whisper

**2.** steal : take :: _____ : give

**3.** hopelessly : far :: _____ : near

**4.** ending : concluding :: _____ : infringing

**5.** criticizing : praising :: _____ : comforting

**6.** funny : serious :: _____ : reasonable

**Word Study** Use the context of the sentences and what you know about the **suffix -ate** to explain your answer to each question.

**1.** What does someone do if they *participate* in an activity?

**2.** If a question is *complicated*, is it easy?

### Word Study

The **suffix -ate** means "to become or form."

**Apply It** Explain how the suffix *-ate* contributes to the meaning of these words. Use a dictionary if necessary.

**depreciate**
**captivate**
**duplicate**

# Can *truth* change?

## Writing About the Big Question

In "The Cask of Amontillado," a wronged man seeks revenge. Use these sentence starters to develop your ideas about the Big Question.

The **truth** about a person can be discovered when _____.

It can either be **verified** by _____ or **distorted** by _____.

**While You Read** Look for the ways the main character takes charge of his life.

## Vocabulary

Read each word and its definition. Decide whether you know the word well, know it a little bit, or do not know it at all. After you have read the selection, see how your knowledge of each word has increased.

- **precluded** (prē klōōd´ id) *v.* prevented (p. 61) *When his injury precluded any chance of victory, the fans lost hope.* preclude *v.* include *v.*

- **retribution** (re´ trə byōō´ shən) *n.* payback; punishment for a misdeed (p. 61) *He wanted retribution for an insult he had received.* tribute *n.*

- **afflicted** (ə flikt´ əd) *v.* suffering or sickened (p. 63) *The old man was afflicted with a rare type of pneumonia.* affliction *n.* afflict *v.*

- **explicit** (eks plis´ it) *adj.* clearly stated (p. 63) *I could not ignore her explicit refusal.* explicate *v.*

- **recoiling** (ri koil´ iŋ) *v.* staggering back (p. 65) *Wendy, recoiling in horror, shrieked at the rattlesnake in her path.* recoil *v.* recoil *n.*

- **subsided** (səb sīd´ əd) *v.* settled down; became less active or intense (p. 67) *As we walked away from the beach, the sound of the waves subsided.* subside *v.* subsidiary *n.*

### Word Study

The **suffix -tion** means "the act of." It usually indicates the word is a noun.

In this story, the ghost seeks **retribution**, or the act of revenge, for his lost life and love.

# Meet
# Edgar Allan Poe
## (1809–1849)

## Author of

# The Cask of Amontillado

One of the first great American storytellers, Edgar Allan Poe made the most of a short, tragic life. Orphaned at the age of three, Poe was raised by foster parents, the Allans, from whom he took his middle name. The Allans were good to Poe and gave him an education, but he had to leave college when his foster father refused to pay Poe's gambling debts. Poe found some happiness when he married Virginia Clemm. However, her early death from tuberculosis in 1847 caused Poe to become increasingly antisocial. In 1849, he was discovered in a delirious condition on a Baltimore street, and three days later he was dead.

**An Inspiration to Later Generations**
Like few others, Poe blazed trails for future writers. His work helped to define the short story, and his dark imagination helped establish the genre of horror literature now popularized by writers like Stephen King.

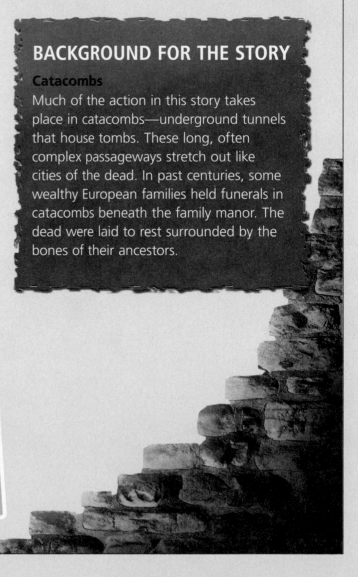

## BACKGROUND FOR THE STORY

**Catacombs**
Much of the action in this story takes place in catacombs—underground tunnels that house tombs. These long, often complex passageways stretch out like cities of the dead. In past centuries, some wealthy European families held funerals in catacombs beneath the family manor. The dead were laid to rest surrounded by the bones of their ancestors.

## Did You Know?
Poe invented the genre of the detective story with his tale "The Murders in the Rue Morgue."

# The Cask of Amontillado [1]

## Edgar Allan Poe

The thousand injuries of Fortunato I had borne as I best could, but when he ventured upon insult I vowed revenge. You, who so well know the nature of my soul, will not suppose, however, that I gave utterance to a threat. At *length* I would be avenged; this was a point definitely settled—but the very definitiveness with which it was resolved precluded the idea of risk. I must not only punish but punish with impunity.[2] A wrong is unredressed when retribution overtakes its redresser. It is equally unredressed when the avenger fails to make himself felt as such to him who has done the wrong.

It must be understood that neither by word nor deed had I given Fortunato cause to doubt my good will. I continued, as was my wont, to smile in his face, and he did not perceive that my smile *now* was at the thought of his immolation.[3]

**Vocabulary**

**precluded** (prē klōōd´ id) *v.* prevented

**retribution** (re´ trə byōō´ shən) *n.* payback; punishment for a misdeed

**Reading Check** ☑

Why does the narrator vow revenge on Fortunato?

---

1. **Amontillado** (ə män´ tə ya´ dō) *n.* a pale, dry sherry.
2. **impunity** (im pyōō´ nə tē´) *n.* freedom from consequences.
3. **immolation** (im´ ə lā´ shən) *n.* destruction.

He had a weak point—this Fortunato—although in other regards he was a man to be respected and even feared. He prided himself on his connoisseurship[4] in wine. Few Italians have the true virtuoso[5] spirit. For the most part their enthusiasm is adopted to suit the time and opportunity, to practice imposture upon the British and Austrian millionaires. In painting and gemmary, Fortunato, like his countrymen, was a quack, but in the matter of old wines he was sincere. In this respect I did not differ from him materially; I was skillful in the Italian vintages myself, and bought largely whenever I could.

It was about dusk, one evening during the supreme madness of the carnival season, that I encountered my friend. He accosted me with excessive warmth, for he had been drinking much. The man wore motley.[6] He had on a tight-fitting parti-striped dress, and his head was surmounted by the conical cap and bells. I was so pleased to see him that I thought I should never have done wringing his hand.

I said to him, "My dear Fortunato, you are luckily met. How remarkably well you are looking today. But I have received a pipe[7] of what passes for Amontillado, and I have my doubts."

"How?" said he. "Amontillado? A pipe? Impossible! And in the middle of the carnival!"

"I have my doubts," I replied: "and I was silly enough to pay the full Amontillado price without consulting you in the matter. You were not to be found, and I was fearful of losing a bargain."

"Amontillado!"

"I have my doubts."

"Amontillado!"

"And I must satisfy them."

"Amontillado!"

"As you are engaged, I am on my way to Luchesi. If any one has a critical turn it is he. He will tell me—"

"Luchesi cannot tell Amontillado from sherry."

"And yet some fools will have it that his taste is a match for your own."

"Come, let us go."

---

4. **connoisseurship** (kän´ ə sʉr´ ship) *n.* expert judgment.
5. **virtuoso** (vʉr´ cho͞o ō´ sō) *adj.* masterly skill in a particular field.
6. **motley** (mät´ lē) *n.* a clown's multicolored costume.
7. **pipe** (pīp) *n.* large barrel, holding approximately 126 gallons.

"Whither?"

"To your vaults."

"My friend, no; I will not impose upon your good nature. I perceive you have an engagement. Luchesi—"

"I have no engagement—come."

"My friend, no. It is not the engagement, but the severe cold with which I perceive you are afflicted. The vaults are insufferably damp. They are encrusted with niter."

"Let us go, nevertheless. The cold is merely nothing. Amontillado! You have been imposed upon. And as for Luchesi, he cannot distinguish sherry from Amontillado."

Thus speaking, Fortunato possessed himself of my arm; and putting on a mask of black silk and drawing a *roquelaure*[8] closely about my person, I suffered him to hurry me to my palazzo.

There were no attendants at home; they had absconded to make merry in honor of the time. I had told them that I should not return until the morning, and had given them explicit orders not to stir from the house. These orders were sufficient, I well knew, to insure their immediate disappearance, one and all, as soon as my back was turned.

I took from their sconces two flambeaux, and giving one to Fortunato, bowed him through several suites of rooms to the archway that led into the vaults. I passed down a long and winding staircase, requesting him to be cautious as he followed. We came at length to the foot of the descent, and stood together upon the damp ground of the catacombs of the Montresors.

The gait of my friend was unsteady, and the bells upon his cap jingled as he strode.

"The pipe," he said.

"It is farther on," said I; "but observe the white webwork which gleams from these cavern walls."

He turned towards me, and looked into my eyes with two filmy orbs that distilled the rheum of intoxication.

"Niter?" he asked, at length.

"Niter," I replied. "How long have you had that cough?"

---

8. *roquelaure* (räk´ ə lôr) *n.* knee-length cloak.

**Vocabulary**

**afflicted** (ə flikt´ əd) *v.* suffering or sickened

**Vocabulary**

**explicit** (eks plis´ it) *adj.* clearly stated

*It was about dusk, one evening during the supreme madness of the carnival season, that I encountered my friend.*

**Reading Check**
What common interest does the narrator share with Fortunato?

"Ugh! ugh! ugh!—ugh! ugh! ugh!—ugh! ugh! ugh!—ugh! ugh! ugh!—ugh! ugh! ugh!"

My poor friend found it impossible to reply for many minutes.

"It is nothing," he said, at last.

"Come," I said, with decision, "we will go back; your health is precious. You are rich, respected, admired, beloved; you are happy, as once I was. You are a man to be missed. For me it is no matter. We will go back; you will be ill, and I cannot be responsible. Besides, there is Luchesi—"

"Enough," he said; "the cough is a mere nothing; it will not kill me. I shall not die of a cough."

"True—true," I replied; "and, indeed, I had no intention of alarming you unnecessarily—but you should use all proper caution. A draft of this Médoc will defend us from the damps."

Here I knocked off the neck of a bottle which I drew from a long row of its fellows that lay upon the mold.

"Drink," I said, presenting him the wine.

He raised it to his lips with a leer. He paused and nodded to me familiarly, while his bells jingled.

"I drink," he said "to the buried that repose around us."

"And I to your long life."

He again took my arm, and we proceeded.

"These vaults," he said, "are extensive."

"The Montresors," I replied, "were a great and numerous family."

"I forget your arms."

"A huge human foot d'or, in a field azure; the foot crushes a serpent rampant whose fangs are imbedded in the heel."

"And the motto?"

"*Nemo me impune lacessit.*"[9]

"Good!" he said.

The wine sparkled in his eyes and the bells jingled. My own fancy grew warm with the Médoc. We had passed through long walls of piled skeletons, with casks and puncheons[10] intermingling, into the inmost recesses of the catacombs. I paused again, and this time I made bold to seize Fortunato by an arm above the elbow.

---

9. *Nemo me impune lacessit* Latin for "No one attacks me with impunity."
10. puncheons (pun´ chənz) *n.* large barrels.

"The niter!" I said; "see, it increases. It hangs like moss upon the vaults. We are below the river's bed. The drops of moisture trickle among the bones. Come, we will go back ere it is too late. Your cough—"

"It is nothing," he said; "let us go on. But first, another draft of the Médoc."

I broke and reached him a flagon of De Grâve. He emptied it at a breath. His eyes flashed with a fierce light. He laughed and threw the bottle upwards with a gesticulation I did not understand.

I looked at him in surprise. He repeated the movement—a grotesque one.

"You do not comprehend?" he said.

"Not I," I replied.

"Then you are not of the brotherhood."

"How?"

"You are not of the masons."[11]

"Yes, yes," I said; "yes, yes."

"You? Impossible! A mason?"

"A mason," I replied.

"A sign," he said, "a sign."

"It is this," I answered, producing from beneath the folds of my *roquelaure* a trowel.

"You jest," he exclaimed, recoiling a few paces. "But let us proceed to the Amontillado."

"Be it so," I said, replacing the tool beneath the cloak and again offering him my arm. He leaned upon it heavily. We continued our route in search of the Amontillado. We passed through a range of low arches, descended, passed on, and descending again, arrived at a deep crypt, in which the foulness of the air caused our flambeaux rather to glow than flame.

At the most remote end of the crypt there appeared another less spacious. Its walls had been lined with human remains,

---

11. **masons** *n.* the Freemasons, an international secret society.

## LITERATURE IN CONTEXT

### Literature Connection

**Poe and the Gothic Tradition**
The literary genre known as gothic fiction emerged in England in the late 1700s in works like *Castle of Otranto* (1765) by Horace Walpole and *The Mysteries of Udolpho* (1794) by Ann Radcliffe. The word *gothic* was originally used to describe a style of building that was common in the late Middle Ages. To writers in the eighteenth century, the cold chambers and secret passages of such buildings suggested mystery and dark tales of vengeance and passion.

Edgar Allan Poe translated the imagery and atmosphere of British gothic fiction to an American landscape, pioneering an American gothic tradition. Contemporary writers like Stephen King and Anne Rice, as well as countless filmmakers, carry on that tradition today.

### Connect to the Literature

What qualities of gothic fiction do you find in "The Cask of Amontillado"? Explain.

**Vocabulary**
**recoiling** (ri koil´ iŋ) *v.* staggering back

**Reading Check**
Where does Montresor bring Fortunato?

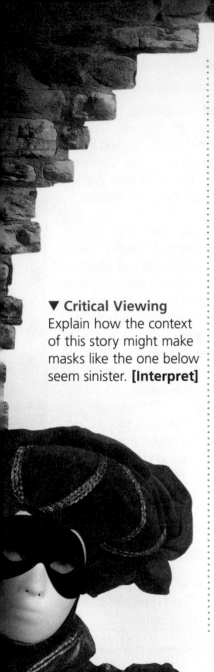

▼ **Critical Viewing**
Explain how the context of this story might make masks like the one below seem sinister. **[Interpret]**

piled to the vault overhead, in the fashion of the great catacombs of Paris. Three sides of this interior crypt were still ornamented in this manner. From the fourth side the bones had been thrown down, and lay promiscuously upon the earth, forming at one point a mound of some size. Within the wall thus exposed by the displacing of the bones, we perceived a still interior crypt or recess, in depth about four feet, in width three, in height six or seven. It seemed to have been constructed for no especial use within itself, but formed merely the *interval* between two of the colossal supports of the roof of the catacombs, and was backed by one of their circumscribing walls of solid granite.

It was in vain that Fortunato, uplifting his dull torch, endeavored to pry into the depth of the recess. Its termination the feeble light did not enable us to see.

"Proceed," I said: "herein is the Amontillado. As for Luchesi—"

"He is an ignoramus," interrupted my friend, as he stepped unsteadily forward, while I followed immediately at his heels. In an instant he had reached the extremity of the niche, and finding his progress arrested by the rock, stood stupidly bewildered. A moment more and I had fettered him to the granite. In its surface were two iron staples, distant from each other about two feet, horizontally. From one of these depended a short chain, from the other a padlock. Throwing the links about his waist, it was but the work of a few seconds to secure it. He was too much astounded to resist. Withdrawing the key I stepped back from the recess.

"Pass your hand," I said, "over the wall; you cannot help feeling the niter. Indeed, it is very damp. Once more let me implore you to return. No? Then I must positively leave you. But I must first render you all the little attentions in my power."

"The Amontillado!" ejaculated my friend, not yet recovered from his astonishment.

"True," I replied; "the Amontillado."

As I said these words I busied myself among the pile of bones of which I have before spoken. Throwing them aside, I soon uncovered a quantity of building stone and mortar. With these materials and with the aid of my trowel, I began vigorously to wall up the entrance of the niche.

I had scarcely laid the first tier of the masonry when I discovered that the intoxication of Fortunato had in a great measure worn off. The earliest indication I had of this was a low moaning cry from the depth of the recess. It was not the cry of a drunken man. There was then a long and obstinate silence. I laid the second tier, and the third, and the fourth; and then I heard the furious vibrations of the chain. The noise lasted for several minutes, during which, that I might hearken to it with the more satisfaction, I ceased my labors and sat down upon the bones. When at last the clanking subsided, I resumed the trowel, and finished without interruption the fifth, the sixth, and the seventh tier. The wall was now nearly upon a level with my breast. I again paused, and holding the flambeaux over the masonwork, threw a few feeble rays upon the figure within.

A succession of loud and shrill screams, bursting suddenly from the throat of the chained form, seemed to thrust me violently back. For a brief moment I hesitated, I trembled. Unsheathing my rapier, I began to grope with it about the recess; but the thought of an instant reassured me. I placed my hand upon the solid fabric of the catacombs, and felt satisfied. I reapproached the wall; I replied to the yells of him who clamored. I reechoed, I aided, I surpassed them in volume and in strength. I did this, and the clamorer grew still.

It was now midnight, and my task was drawing to a close. I had completed the eighth, the ninth, and the tenth tier. I had finished a portion of the last and the eleventh; there remained but a single stone to be fitted and plastered in. I struggled with its weight; I placed it partially in its destined position. But now there came from out the niche a low laugh that erected the hairs upon my head. It was succeeded by a sad voice, which I had difficulty in recognizing as that of the noble Fortunato. The voice said—

"Ha! ha! ha!—he! he! he!—a very good joke, indeed—an excellent jest. We will have many a rich laugh about it at the palazzo—he! he! he!—over our wine—he! he! he!"

"The Amontillado!" I said.

"He! he! he!—he! he! he!—yes, the Amontillado. But is it not getting late? Will not they be awaiting us at the palazzo, the Lady Fortunato and the rest? Let us be gone."

"Yes," I said, "let us be gone."

*"For the love of God, Montresor!"*

**Vocabulary**
**subsided** (səb sīd´ əd) *v.* settled down; became less active or intense

**Reading Skill**
**Make Predictions**
Does this scene in which Montresor imprisons Fortunato verify your earlier predictions? Explain.

**Reading Check**
How does Fortunato become locked in the chains so easily?

*It was now midnight, and my task was drawing to a close.*

"Yes," I said, "for the love of God!"

But to these words I hearkened in vain for a reply. I grew impatient. I called aloud—

"Fortunato!"

No answer. I called again—

"Fortunato!"

No answer still. I thrust a torch through the remaining aperture and let it fall within. There came forth in return only a jingling of the bells. My heart grew sick; it was the dampness of the catacombs that made it so. I hastened to make an end of my labor. I forced the last stone into its position; I plastered it up. Against the new masonry I reerected the old rampart of bones. For the half of a century no mortal has disturbed them. *In pace requiescat!*[12]

12. *In pace requiescat!* Latin for "May he rest in peace!"

**Spiral Review**

**Theme** How many years have passed since Montresor took revenge on Fortunato? What insight into revenge does this detail suggest? Explain.

## Critical Thinking

Cite textual evidence to support your responses.

**1. Key Ideas and Details (a)** How does Montresor describe Fortunato's strengths and weaknesses early in the story? **(b) Analyze:** Which character traits make Fortunato easy prey for Montresor?

**2. Key Ideas and Details (a)** What specific steps does Montresor take to ensure that his plan works? **(b) Interpret:** Why does Montresor keep urging Fortunato to turn back?

**3. Craft and Structure (a) Assess:** Does Montresor express any regret or ever question whether this punishment is fair, just, or rational? **(b) Evaluate:** What does your answer tell you about Montresor's character?

**4. Integration of Knowledge and Ideas** Montresor acts as both victim and judge in this story. Do you think that Montresor sees the truth and acts appropriately? Explain. *[Connect to the Big Question: Can truth change?]*

## Literary Analysis: Plot

© **1. Key Ideas and Details** Using a chart like the one shown, identify two key events in the **rising action,** the event that marks the **climax,** and one event in the **falling action.** Then, discuss your choices with a partner.

© **2. Craft and Structure (a)** Identify a passage that **foreshadows** Fortunato's fate. **(b)** Explain how the foreshadowing adds to the story's **suspense.**

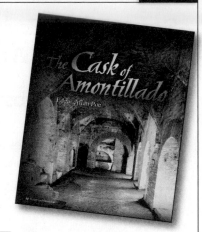

Climax

Rising Action    Falling Action

Exposition    Resolution

## Reading Skill: Make Predictions

**3. (a)** What **prediction** did you make after reading about Montresor's and Fortunato's shared interest in wine?
**(b)** What details helped you make your prediction?

**4.** Was your prediction **verified** by later story events? Explain.

## Vocabulary

© **Acquisition and Use** An **analogy** shows the relationship between pairs of words. Use a word from the vocabulary list on page 58 to complete each analogy. For each case, your choice should create a word pair that matches the relationship between the first two words.

**1.** conversation: dialogue :: _____ : revenge

**2.** harmed : helped :: _____ : allowed

**3.** delicious : food :: _____ : instructions

**4.** graceful : awkward :: _____ : increased

**5.** humor : laughing :: disgust : _____

**6.** enormous : gigantic :: troubled : _____

**Word Study** Use the context of the sentences and what you know about the **suffix -tion** to explain your answer to each question.

**1.** What is audience *participation?*

**2.** If you make a *contribution* to a cause, what have you done?

### Word Study

The **suffix -tion** means "the act of."

**Apply It** The suffix *-tion* often indicates that a word is a noun. Identify another form of each word below by changing the suffix.

**reconciliation**
**compensation**
**induction**

# Integrated Language Skills

## Sonata for Harp and Bicycle • The Cask of Amontillado

### Conventions: Abstract and Concrete Nouns

A **concrete noun** names a person, place, or thing that can be seen or recognized through any of the five senses.

An **abstract noun** names an idea, an action, a condition, or a quality—something that cannot be recognized through the senses.

| Abstract Noun | Concrete Noun |
| --- | --- |
| Fortunato discovered Montresor's *intention*, but it was too late. | William Heron patrolled the halls on a *bicycle*. |

**Practice A** Tell whether the underlined word in each sentence is a concrete noun or an abstract noun. Then, use the word in an original sentence about the story.

1. Mr. Manaby instructed Jason, the new <u>assistant</u>, to leave at five.

2. What went on in the building after five was a <u>mystery</u> to Jason.

3. He did not seem to have <u>fear</u> of the curse.

4. He wanted to know why he could not stay later at <u>work</u>.

5. He found answers by taking a tremendous <u>risk</u>.

© **Reading Application** In "Sonata for Harp and Bicycle," find one sentence with a concrete noun and one with an abstract noun.

**Practice B** Identify an abstract and a concrete noun in each sentence. Then, use one of the words in an original sentence.

1. Montresor held vengeance in his heart.

2. He lured Fortunato to the catacombs with a falsehood.

3. The men were supposedly on the search for a cask of wine.

4. Instead, Fortunato met a horrid fate after reading Montresor's letters.

5. Montresor felt no remorse after carrying out his plan.

© **Writing Application** Using these two sentences as models, write two more sentences that follow the pattern of presenting and describing nouns: *The wine sparkled in his eyes and bells jingled. The joy glowed on his face and his keys jangled.*

**PH WRITING COACH** | Further instruction and practice are available in *Prentice Hall Writing Coach.*

# Writing

**Explanatory Text** Each of these stories presents readers with a compelling plot. Write a **critique** analyzing and evaluating the suspense and the ending of either "Sonata for Harp and Bicycle" or "The Cask of Amontillado."

- Before you draft, list the qualities a suspenseful story should have. Then, list the qualities that make a satisfactory ending for you.
- Use your lists to evaluate the suspense, the ending of the story, and the author's use of devices, such as foreshadowing. Note specific details from the story that demonstrate your ideas.
- As you write your critique, consult your checklists, using them as evidence to support your analysis.

**Grammar Application** As you write, consider your noun choices. Use abstract nouns to describe ideas or qualities and concrete nouns to refer to physical things.

## Writing Workshop: *Work in Progress*

**Prewriting for an Autobiographical Narrative** Review the Memory List in your writing portfolio. Next to each scene description, **describe your reaction** in the situation. Save this Reaction Work in your writing portfolio.

# Speaking and Listening

**Comprehension and Collaboration** With a partner, **retell** one of the stories from another point of view. For example, you might tell "Sonata for Harp or Bicycle" from Miss Golden's point of view or "The Cask of Amontillado" from Fortunato's point of view. Refresh your memory by rereading your chosen selection. Follow these steps to complete the assignment.

- Identify an audience and the type of information they will need.
- Make language choices appropriate for the audience and the story, using words and expressions consistent with the narrator's character.
- As you speak, use facial expressions and body movements effectively to convey the narrator's personality.
- Make eye contact with your audience to engage them in the story.
- Vary your intonation to reflect the emotions of the narrator.
- After you and your partner have presented your work, evaluate each other's presentations in a thoughtful, well-reasoned discussion.

**Common Core State Standards**

L.9-10.3; W.9-10.9; SL.9-10.1, SL.9-10.1.a
[For the full wording of the standards, see page 42.]

Use this prewriting activity to prepare for the **Writing Workshop** on page 94.

**PHLit Online!**
www.PHLitOnline.com
- Interactive graphic organizers
- Grammar tutorial
- Interactive journals

# Test Practice: Reading

## Make Predictions

### Fiction Selection

**Directions:** *Read the selection. Then, answer the questions.*

**The Great Skate**

All Martina ever wanted was to learn how to ride a skateboard. Despite Martina's pleading, any attempt at using her older bother's board would invite a shrieking response. "Don't touch that!" he would shout. Seeing her determination, Martina's mother bought her a skateboard. Practicing secretly every day, Martina built her skills and her confidence. When she finally felt ready to prove her ability, Martina asked one last time to use her brother's board. Surprisingly, he gave in to the request but with little encouragement. "Okay, little girl, give it your best shot," he laughed. Martina smiled as her hands gripped the rough edges of the board. She knew she would skate away his sarcasm.

1. Based on clues in the title and the first sentence, which would be the best prediction?
   A. The story will be about a rivalry between Martina and her brother.
   B. The story will be about the history of skateboarding.
   C. The story will be about Martina learning to ride a skateboard.
   D. The story will be about Martina competing on a skateboard.

2. Which clue from the text supports the prediction that Martina will learn to skateboard well?
   A. Her older brother was so good he competed.
   B. Her mom gave Martina her own board because she was so determined.
   C. One day, she begged her brother to let her try his board.
   D. Martina hated it when her brother called her "little girl."

3. Based on clues in the text, what did you predict Martina's brother would say when she asked one last time to try his board?
   A. "Don't touch that!"
   B. "Sure. No problem."
   C. "What board?"
   D. "You'd better ask Mom."

4. Based on clues in the text, what do you predict will happen once Martina takes her brother's board?
   A. She will ride well and impress him.
   B. She will fall as he expects her to.
   C. She will tell him she has her own board.
   D. She will break his skateboard.

### Writing for Assessment

In a brief paragraph, explain your thinking process in predicting what will happen when Martina takes the board. Which details from the text support your prediction?

## Nonfiction Selection

**Directions:** *Read the selection. Then, answer the questions.*

Skateboarding grew out of surfing. Surfers had to depend on the weather and the perfect conditions to catch a wave. Instead of waiting for the perfect wave, they invented the skateboard and started "surfing" on land. The first skateboards were difficult to steer and ride. The wheels were also very hard, so the ride was bumpy. Over the years, many improvements have been made to skateboards. Even though the popularity of skateboarding declined for a while, it is now very popular again. Skateboarding is even considered to be an extreme sport.

1. Based on the first sentence in the selection, which is the best prediction about its content?
   A. It will be about skateboarding history.
   B. It will be about surfing history.
   C. It will be about a famous skateboarder.
   D. It will give specific instructions on how to skateboard.

2. What information would support a prediction about the safety of the original skateboards?
   A. Skateboarding grew out of surfing.
   B. The first skateboards were difficult to steer and ride.
   C. They invented the skateboard and started "surfing" on land.
   D. Skateboarding is even considered to be an extreme sport.

3. Which information would support a prediction about the decline in popularity of skateboarding?
   A. Skateboards were easier to maneuver.
   B. Skate parks closed because of accidents.
   C. Rollerblades became popular.
   D. People's interest in skateboarding grew.

4. Based on the information in the text, which is the best prediction for the future of skateboarding?
   A. People will lose interest in skateboarding as a sport.
   B. Skateboarding will be eliminated from extreme sports.
   C. Skateboarding will continue to progress in popularity.
   D. Skateboarders will stick with the inventions they now have.

## Writing for Assessment

**Connect Across Texts**
If Martina and her brother had been alive when skateboards were first invented, do you think that would have affected Martina's ability to learn how to skateboard? Write a paragraph, in which you use details from the two passages to support your answer.

**PHLit**
**Online!**
www.PHLitOnline.com
- Online practice
- Instant feedback

# Reading for Information

## Analyzing Functional and Expository Texts

**Recipe**

**How-to Article**

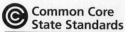

**Common Core
State Standards**

**Reading Informational Text**
**3.** Analyze how the author unfolds an analysis or series of ideas or events, including the order in which the points are made, how they are introduced and developed, and the connections that are drawn between them.

**Language**
**4.b.** Identify and correctly use patterns of word changes that indicate different meanings or parts of speech.
**6.** Acquire and use accurately general academic and domain-specific words and phrases, sufficient for reading, writing, speaking, and listening at the college and career readiness level.

## Reading Skill: Read to Perform a Task

Most instructions present a series of specific steps you must follow to complete a larger task. When you **read to perform a task,** pay attention to the **sequence,** or order, of the required steps. Also, look for the main idea presented in each step. Check off each step as you complete it. When you read any set of directions, pay close attention to words that signal relevant details—especially words of quantity and adverbs that tell how to perform tasks. The chart shown here identifies signal words.

| Instruction | Key Word |
|---|---|
| *Gradually* add the broth and milk… | tells how to add ingredients |
| Cook over *medium* heat… | tells what level temperature |
| …on a *lightly* floured surface | tells how to prepare pan |
| Put a *spoonful* of filling in center… | tells how much |

### Content-Area Vocabulary

These words appear in the selections that follow. You may also encounter them in other content-area texts.

- **minced** (minsd´) *adj.* cut up into very small pieces

- **incubator** (in´ kyə bāt´ ər) *n.* artificially heated container for hatching eggs

- **ventilation** (vent´ 'l ā´ shən) *n.* the circulation of fresh air in a building, room, or other space

*from* **The Book Lover's Cookbook**

# New Road Chicken Pies

## by Shaunda Kennedy Wenger and Janet Kay Jensen

**Recipe**

**Features:**

- text that provides how-to directions for cooking or baking
- listing of ingredients, precise measurements, and cooking times
- step-by-step instructions for combining and preparing ingredients

Oliver Twist's request for more gruel starts a riot, and Ma Joad agonizes over not being able to fill the bellies of hungry children who watch her family eat stew. When characters deal with food, whether they're eating, cooking, dreaming, manipulating, or suffering, they step off the page and connect with the reader.

Food scenes offer a universal platform that can foster connections between the reader and the character. Some food scenes bring such strong feelings of nostalgia, the experience between the fiction of the story, the reality of the present, and the memories of the past blur to the point where we question, Could I have known this author? Could I have known this character?

This recipe links the real-life experience of preparing and eating delicious meat-pies to the characters and events in Maya Angelou's story "New Directions."

> The introduction describes the way in which a recipe can connect readers to literary characters.

## New Road Chicken Pies
(a.k.a. Turnovers)

### FILLING:
1/2 cup potatoes, diced
1/4 cup carrots, diced
3 tablespoons celery, chopped
1 teaspoon onion, **minced**
1 tablespoon butter or margarine
3 tablespoons all-purpose flour
Salt and pepper to taste
1 cup chicken broth
1/3 cup milk
1 teaspoon fresh parsley, minced
1/4 cup frozen peas, thawed
1 1/2 cups chicken, cooked & diced

### PASTRY DOUGH:
2/3 cup shortening or margarine
2 cups all-purpose flour
1/2 teaspoon salt
5 to 7 tablespoons water
1 egg white
1 teaspoon water

> The first step is to look at the complete list of every ingredient and the exact amount required. Some items must be *diced, chopped, minced,* or *thawed* before the mixing of ingredients begins.

# New Road Chicken Pies
*continued*

Boil the potatoes, carrots, celery, and onions until tender, about 6 to 8 minutes. Drain and set aside. In a separate saucepan, melt the butter or margarine over medium heat. Whisk in the flour, salt, and pepper. Gradually add the broth and milk, whisking continually to keep sauce smooth. Cook over medium heat until thickened. Stir in the cooked vegetables, parsley, peas, and chicken and continue cooking until warmed through.

Prepare pastry by mixing the shortening or margarine, sugar, flour, and salt in a bowl with a fork or pastry blender until the mixture is crumbly. Add water 1 tablespoon at a time until dough is pliable. Work dough into a ball with hands after last tablespoon of water is added.

With a rolling pin, roll the pastry dough out to a 1/4-inch thickness on a lightly floured surface. Cut 4-inch or 5-inch-diameter circles from the dough. Put a spoonful of filling in center of each circle. Fold to a half-moon shape. Press edges together to make a seam. Crimp edges with a fork, dipping tines in flour as needed to keep from sticking to dough.

In a small bowl, whisk together egg white and 1 teaspoon water. Brush egg white mixture onto the tops of the turnovers with a pastry brush. Cut a small slit in the top of each turnover. Bake on ungreased cookie sheet at 375° for 15 to 20 minutes or until golden brown.

**MAKES 8 TO 10 TURNOVERS**

> The recipe gives instructions in a specific order. First the vegetables must be cooked, and then they can be added to the sauce.

> The last line provides the number of servings the recipe makes. If you want to make 16–20 turnovers, you would double the quantities of the ingredients.

# Incubating Eggs in Small Quantities

**Ursula K. Abbott, Professor Emerita; Ralph A. Ernst, Extension Poultry Specialist; and Francine A. Bradley, Extension Poultry Specialist**

Department of Animal Science, University of California, Davis

To hatch a small number of eggs, buy or build an **incubator** that provides controlled conditions. You might want a model with transparent sides or top so you can watch the hatching. An alternative that is frequently overlooked is natural incubation under a broody hen. Each hen can cover 12 to 14 chicken eggs, 9 to 11 duck eggs, or 4 to 6 goose eggs. General purpose breeds like New Hampshires and Plymouth Rocks make better setters than Leghorns.

> The authors provide relevant details about a variety of incubators to help readers decide which type would best suit their needs.

## INCUBATION PERIODS

| | |
|---|---|
| Japanese quail | 17-18 days |
| Chicken | 21 days |
| Pheasants, Chukar partridge, Bobwhite and Valley quail | 24 days |
| Turkeys, guinea fowl, peafowl, most ducks | 28 days |
| Most geese | 30 days |
| Muscovy ducks, Canadian and Egyptian geese | 35 days |

> This chart of the various incubation periods tells readers what to expect from each type of egg.

## INCUBATING CONDITIONS

> Read this section carefully to ensure that you understand the details about temperature and humidity.

**Temperature.** Incubators with fans are set at 99 1/2°F to 99 3/4°F; incubators with gravity **ventilation** are set at temperatures of 101°F to 103°F as measured at the top of the egg. Lethal temperatures are 103°F in fan-ventilated incubators, and 107°F in gravity-ventilated incubators. To regulate temperature, humidity, etc., follow the manufacturer's directions if available.

**Humidity.** During incubation, a relative humidity of about 60 percent is satisfactory; at hatching it should be raised to about 70 percent. Trays of water inside the incubator furnish these humidity levels. In fan-ventilated machines, humidity is measured indirectly but quite accurately by a wet-bulb thermometer (a thermometer with its bulb wrapped in a damp cloth). At 99.5°F dry bulb, a reading of 85°F to 86°F on the

wet-bulb thermometer gives the desired humidity. At hatching, the dry-bulb temperature is reduced about 1°F and the wet-bulb temperature is increased to 88°F to 90°F. Low humidity can be a problem in very small incubators; additional moisture is especially necessary if the incubator is opened frequently for turning eggs.

**Turning.** Eggs must be turned until late in incubation. Chicken eggs, for example, must be turned to the 15th day. For many small incubators, lay eggs on their sides and turn by hand an odd number of times (at least three) per day. A pencil mark on the side of the egg will be a useful guide. Do not rotate the eggs in the same direction each time. A broody hen turns eggs when nesting, but because of their large size, turn goose eggs under a chicken hen by hand.

**Ventilation.** Your incubator is equipped with vents to permit a slow change of air. Little ventilation is needed when incubation starts; it may be increased gradually as incubation progresses. During hatching, restrict ventilation in order to raise the humidity.

## HELPFUL HINTS

Since most eggs sold at the grocery store are infertile, purchase hatching eggs from a breeding farm. Keep them at 50°F to 60°F, if possible. A household refrigerator is too cool for storing hatching eggs, and at 80°F fertile eggs begin to develop in an abnormal manner. Set the eggs before they are 2 weeks old.

Clean your incubator thoroughly and test its operation for a day or more before setting any eggs.

Eggs which are clean when they come from the nest are best for hatching. It is better not to wash eggs, since bacteria on the shell and in the water may easily enter the eggs and cause them to rot.

Cracked eggs spoil easily, seldom hatch, and are best removed from the incubator. If you candle after a week's incubation, infertile eggs and eggs with dead germs can be identified easily and removed from the incubator.

After hatching, leave the young in the incubator for a few hours to dry and fluff out completely.

Small incubators range widely in price depending upon size, construction and features (e.g., automatic egg turning, fan ventilation). When purchasing, consider that low-cost incubators usually have less accurate temperature and humidity controls and often lack a convenient egg-turning arrangement. They usually require close supervision to obtain hatching success.

> Details here provide exact temperatures and times that are necessary for success.

> The authors provide tips here to guide readers in performing the task.

## Comparing Functional and Expository Texts

**1. Craft and Structure** **(a)** Compare the presentation and **sequence of information** in the recipe and the how-to article. How are they the same? How are they different? **(b)** Identify areas of each article in which a reader could misinterpret information. Does one text better enable you to **read to perform a task**?

### Content-Area Vocabulary

**2. (a)** For each of the following words, explain how a change in suffix alters the meanings and parts of speech of the base word *ventilate*: *ventilation, ventilator,* and *ventilating*. **(b)** Use each word in a sentence that shows its meaning.

## Timed Writing

### Explanatory Text: Essay

> **Format**
> The prompt directs you to write an essay. Therefore, you should write an expository composition that has an introduction, body, and conclusion.

Many stories contain factual information to establish the setting or support the plot. Review the information given in the recipe and the how-to article. Write an essay of a few short paragraphs in which you explain how using this information might make a fiction piece more believable or realistic. (15 minutes)

> **Academic Vocabulary**
> When you *explain* something, you make it clear using examples, descriptions, details, and facts.

### 5-Minute Planner

Complete these steps before you begin to write:

**1.** Read the prompt carefully and completely to make sure you understand the assignment and the format to use for your writing.

**2.** To help you complete the assignment, consider the ways in which fiction writers include accurate descriptions to make their stories seem more believable.

**3.** Review each selection from the point of view of a writer conducting research to use in the development of a story. Take notes about each selection, identifying facts or details a writer might use to build character, setting, and plot.

**4.** Use your notes to make a list of the information a writer might use in a fiction piece. For each item, indicate how it might improve a story.

**5.** Consult your list as you begin to draft your essay.

# Comparing Literary Works

## Comparing Points of View

**Narrative point of view** is the perspective from which a story is narrated, or told.

- **First-person point of view:** The narrator is a character who participates in the action and uses the first-person pronouns *I* and *me*.

- **Third-person point of view:** The narrator is not a character in the story but a voice outside it. The narrator uses the third-person pronouns *he, she, him, her, they,* and *them* to refer to all characters. There are two kinds of third-person point of view. In the **third-person omniscient point of view,** the narrator knows everything, including the thoughts of all the characters. In the **third-person limited point of view,** the narrator sees and reports things through one character's eyes.

These selections are written using different points of view. As you read, complete a Venn diagram like this one to compare and contrast how the point of view affects the way you understand the characters and the plot of each story.

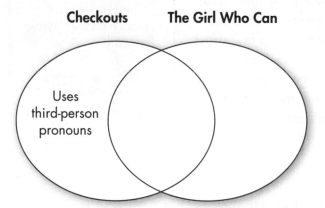

Checkouts     The Girl Who Can

Uses third-person pronouns

### Common Core State Standards

**Reading Literature**
**6.** Analyze a particular point of view or cultural experience reflected in a work of literature from outside the United States, drawing on a wide reading of world literature.

**Writing**
**2.a.** Introduce a topic; organize complex ideas, concepts, and information to make important connections and distinctions; include formatting, graphics, and multimedia when useful to aiding comprehension.

**Cultural perspective** is another, related, element of many literary works. A character's perspective or outlook may also be referred to as point of view. This perspective can be strongly influenced by the customs and beliefs of the place and time in which he or she lives. Notice how the perspective of the girl in each story is affected by her culture's ideas and attitudes about the roles of women.

PHLit Online!
www.PHLitOnline.com

- Vocabulary flashcards
- Interactive journals
- More about the authors
- Selection audio
- Interactive graphic organizers

## Writing About the Big Question

Although the characters in these stories seem sure of certain things, when circumstances change, new possibilities—and new questions—emerge. Use these sentence starters to develop your ideas about the Big Question.

People may have **assumptions** about others or themselves based on _____.

Those **beliefs** can be changed when _____.

# Meet the Authors

## Cynthia Rylant (b. 1954)
### Author of "Checkouts"

Cynthia Rylant spent four years as a child living with her grandparents in a small town in West Virginia. With no public library and little money to buy books, she started reading comic books. Once in college, she discovered great literature, but she did not consider becoming a writer until she took a job as a librarian and began reading children's books.

**Writing About Her Life** In her work, Rylant draws upon her experiences as a young adult. "The best writing," she says, "is that which is most personal, most revealing." She has written many award-winning stories, poems, and novels.

## Ama Ata Aidoo (b. 1942)

### Author of "The Girl Who Can"

Ama Ata Aidoo was born in Ghana, Africa, where her father was a village chief. He wanted his daughter to have a Western education and sent her to a university in Cape Coast, Ghana. Aidoo earned her bachelor's degree in English and later taught at universities in Ghana and the United States.

**Works and Themes** Aidoo has written plays, short stories, poetry, and novels. Her fiction, written in English, often explores the conflicts between Western and African cultures and the roles of women in modern society.

# Checkouts

## Cynthia Rylant

Her parents had moved her to Cincinnati, to a large house with beveled glass[1] windows and several porches and the history her mother liked to emphasize. You'll love the house, they said. You'll be lonely at first, they admitted, but you're so nice you'll make friends fast. And as an impulse tore at her to lie on the floor, to hold to their ankles and tell them she felt she was dying, to offer anything, anything at all, so they might allow her to finish growing up in the town of her childhood, they firmed their mouths and spoke from their chests and they said, It's decided.

They moved her to Cincinnati, where for a month she spent the greater part of every day in a room full of beveled glass windows, sifting through photographs of the life she'd lived and left behind. But it is difficult work, suffering, and in its own way a kind of art, and finally she didn't have the energy for it anymore, so she emerged from the beautiful house and fell in love with a bag boy at the supermarket. Of course, this didn't happen all at once, just like that, but in the sequence of things that's exactly the way it happened.

She liked to grocery shop. She loved it in the way some people love to drive long country roads, because doing it she could think and relax and wander. Her parents wrote up the list and handed it to her and off she went without complaint to perform what they regarded as a great sacrifice of her time and a sign that she was indeed a very nice girl. She had never told them how much she loved grocery shopping, only that she was "willing" to do it. She had an intuition which told her that her parents were not safe for sharing such strong, important facts about herself. Let them think they knew her.

---

**1. beveled** (bev´ əld) **glass** *n.* glass having angled or slanted edges.

Once inside the supermarket, her hands firmly around the handle of the cart, she would lapse into a kind of reverie and wheel toward the produce. Like a Tibetan monk in solitary meditation, she calmed to a point of deep, deep happiness; this feeling came to her, reliably, if strangely, only in the supermarket.

Then one day the bag boy dropped her jar of mayonnaise and that is how she fell in love.

He was nervous—first day on the job—and along had come this fascinating girl, standing in the checkout line with the unfocused stare one often sees in young children, her face turned enough away that he might take several full looks at her as he packed sturdy bags full of food and the goods of modern life. She interested him because her hair was red and thick, and in it she had placed a huge orange bow, nearly the size of a small hat. That was enough to distract him, and when finally it was her groceries he was packing, she looked at him and smiled and he could respond only by busting her jar of mayonnaise on the floor, shards of glass and oozing cream decorating the area around his feet.

She loved him at exactly that moment, and if he'd known this perhaps he wouldn't have fallen into the brown depression he fell into, which lasted the rest of his shift. He believed he must have looked the fool in her eyes, and he envied the sureness of everyone around him: the cocky cashier at the register, the grim and harried store manager, the bland butcher, and the brazen bag boys who smoked in the warehouse on their breaks. He wanted a second chance. Another chance to be confident and say witty things to her as he threw tin cans into her bags, persuading her to allow him to help her to her car so he might learn just a little about her, check out the floor of the

**Then one day the bag boy dropped her jar of mayonnaise and that is how she fell in love.**

**Literary Analysis**
**Point of View**
How does the use of pronouns in this paragraph show that this story is being told from the third-person point of view?

**Vocabulary**
**reverie** (rev´ ə rē) *n.* dreamy thinking and imagining

**Literary Analysis**
**Point of View**
Whose thoughts and feelings are expressed in this paragraph?

**Reading Check**
At first, why does the girl fascinate the boy?

car for signs of hobbies or fetishes and the bumpers for clues as to beliefs and loyalties.

But he busted her jar of mayonnaise and nothing else worked out for the rest of the day.

Strange, how attractive clumsiness can be. She left the supermarket with stars in her eyes, for she had loved the way his long nervous fingers moved from the conveyor belt to the bags, how deftly (until the mayonnaise) they had picked up her items and placed them in her bags. She had loved the way the hair kept falling into his eyes as he leaned over to grab a box or a tin. And the tattered brown shoes he wore with no socks. And the left side of his collar turned in rather than out.

The bag boy seemed a wonderful contrast to the perfectly beautiful house she had been forced to accept as her home, to the history she hated, to the loneliness she had become used to, and she couldn't wait to come back for more of his awkwardness and dishevelment.

Incredibly, it was another four weeks before they saw each other again. As fate would have it, her visits to the supermarket never coincided with his schedule to bag. Each time she went to the store, her eyes scanned the checkouts at once, her heart in her mouth. And each hour he worked, the bag boy kept one eye on the door, watching for the red-haired girl with the big orange bow.

Yet in their disappointment these weeks there was a kind of ecstasy. It is reason enough to be alive, the hope you may see again some face which has meant something to you. The anticipation of meeting the bag boy eased the girl's painful transition into her new and jarring life in Cincinnati. It provided for her an anchor amid all that was impersonal and unfamiliar, and she spent less time on thoughts of what she had left behind as she concentrated on what might lie ahead. And for the boy, the long and often tedious hours at the supermarket which provided no challenge other than that of showing up the following workday . . . these hours became possibilities of mystery and romance for him as he watched the electric doors for the girl in the orange bow.

*Strange, how attractive clumsiness can be.*

And when finally they did meet up again, neither offered a clue to the other that he, or she, had been the object of obsessive thought for weeks. She spotted him as soon as she came into the store, but she kept her eyes strictly in front of her as she pulled out a cart and wheeled it toward the produce. And he, too, knew the instant she came through the door—though the orange bow was gone, replaced by a small but bright yellow flower instead—and he never once turned his head in her direction but watched her from the corner of his vision as he tried to swallow back the fear in his throat.

It is odd how we sometimes deny ourselves the very pleasure we have longed for and which is finally within our reach. For some perverse reason she would not have been able to articulate, the girl did not bring her cart up to the bag boy's checkout when her shopping was done. And the bag boy let her leave the store, pretending no notice of her.

This is often the way of children, when they truly want a thing, to pretend that they don't. And then they grow angry when no one tried harder to give them this thing they so casually rejected, and they soon find themselves in a rage simply because they cannot say yes when they mean yes. Humans are very complicated. (And perhaps cats, who have been known to react in the same way, though the resulting rage can only be guessed at.)

The girl hated herself for not checking out at the boy's line, and the boy hated himself for not catching her eye and saying hello, and they most sincerely hated each other without having ever exchanged even two minutes of conversation.

Eventually—in fact, within the week—a kind and intelligent boy who lived very near her beautiful house asked the girl to a movie and she gave up her fancy for the bag boy at the supermarket. And the bag boy himself grew so bored with his job that he made a desperate search for something better and ended up in a bookstore where scores of fascinating girls lingered like honeybees about a hive. Some months later the bag boy and the girl with the orange bow again crossed paths, standing in line with their dates at a movie theater, and, glancing toward the other, each smiled slightly, then looked away, as strangers on public buses often do, when one is moving off the bus and the other is moving on.

**Vocabulary**
**perverse** (pər vurs´) *adj.*
different from what is considered right or reasonable

**Literary Analysis**
**Point of View**
Which details in this paragraph might be omitted if the story were told from the third-person limited point of view? Explain.

## Critical Thinking

1. **Key Ideas and Details** **(a)** What do the boy and girl think about while they are apart? **(b) Speculate:** How do you think the two characters feel when they see each other at the movie theater?

2. **Key Ideas and Details** **Draw Conclusions:** Does the experience described in the story seem like a missed opportunity or a necessary outcome? Explain.

3. **Key Ideas and Details** **(a) Summarize:** Why do the boy and girl never act on their feelings? **(b) Make a Judgment:** Do you agree that "humans are very complicated"? Explain, using details from the story.

4. **Integration of Knowledge and Ideas** **(a)** Is the situation described in this story a common cultural experience for American teenagers? Explain. **(b) Speculate:** How might the story be different if it were set in a culture that limits the independence of teenage girls? *[Connect to the Big Question: Can truth change?]*

Cite textual evidence to support your responses.

# The Girl Who Can

## Ama Ata Aidoo

They say that I was born in Hasodzi; and it is a very big village in the central region of our country, Ghana. They also say that when all of Africa is not choking under a drought, Hasodzi lies in a very fertile lowland in a district known for its good soil. Maybe that is why any time I don't finish eating my food, Nana says, "You Adjoa, you don't know what life is about . . . you don't know what problems there are in this life . . ."

As far as I could see, there was only one problem. And it had nothing to do with what I knew Nana considered as "problems," or what Maami thinks of as "the problem." Maami is my mother. Nana is my mother's mother. And they say I am seven years old. And my problem is that at this seven years of age, there are things I can think in my head, but which, maybe, I do not have the proper language to speak them out with. And that, I think, is a very serious problem because it is always difficult to decide whether to keep quiet and not say any of the things that come into my head, or say them and get laughed at. Not that it is easy to get any grown-up to listen to you, even when you decide to take the risk and say something serious to them.

Take Nana. First, I have to struggle to catch her attention. Then I tell her something I had taken a long time to figure out. And then you know what always happens? She would at once stop whatever she is doing and, mouth open, stare at me for a very long time. Then, bending and turning her head slightly, so that one ear comes down towards me, she'll say in that voice: "Adjoa, you say what?" After I have repeated whatever I had said, she would either, still in that voice, ask me "never, never, but NEVER to repeat THAT," or she would immediately burst out laughing. She would laugh and laugh and laugh, until tears run down her cheeks and she would stop whatever she is doing and wipe away the tears with the hanging edges of her cloth. And she would continue laughing until she is completely tired. But then, as soon as another person comes by, just to make sure she doesn't forget whatever it was I had said, she would repeat it to her. And then, of course, there would be two old people laughing and screaming with tears running down their faces. Sometimes this show continues until there are three, four or even more of such laughing and screaming tear-faced grownups. And all that performance for whatever I'd said? I find something quite confusing in all this. That is, no one ever explains to me why sometimes I shouldn't repeat some things I say; while at other times, some other things I say would not only be all right, but would be considered so funny they would be repeated so many times for so many people's enjoyment. You see how neither way of hearing me out can encourage me to express my thoughts too often?

◄ **Critical Viewing**
Describe the feelings the girl in the photograph expresses. **[Interpret]**

**Vocabulary**
**fertile** (furt′ 'l) *adj.* rich in nutrients that promote growth

**Literary Analysis**
**Point of View**
Which pronouns in this paragraph show that this story is being told from the first-person point of view?

**Reading Check**
What does the narrator say is her problem?

The Girl Who Can **87**

Like all this business to do with my legs. I have always wanted to tell them not to worry. I mean Nana and my mother. It did not have to be an issue for my two favorite people to fight over. I didn't want to be told not to repeat it or for it to be considered so funny that anyone would laugh at me until they cried. After all, they were my legs . . . When I think back on it now, those two, Nana and my mother must have been discussing my legs from the day I was born. What I am sure of is that when I came out of the land of sweet, soft silence into the world of noise and comprehension, the first topic I met was my legs.

That discussion was repeated very regularly.

Nana: "Ah, ah, you know, Kaya, I thank my God that your very first child is female. But Kaya, I am not sure about her legs. Hm . . . hm . . . hm . . ."

And Nana would shake her head.

Maami: "Mother, why are you always complaining about Adjoa's legs? If you ask me . . ."

Nana: "They are too thin. And I am not asking you!"

Nana has many voices. There is a special one she uses to shut everyone up.

"Some people have no legs at all," my mother would try again with all her small courage.

"But Adjoa has legs," Nana would insist; "except that they are too thin. And also too long for a woman. Kaya, listen. Once in a while, but only once in a very long while, somebody decides — nature, a child's spirit mother, an accident happens, and somebody gets born without arms, or legs, or both sets of limbs. And then let me touch wood; it is a sad business. And you know, such things are not for talking about every day. But if any female child decides to come into this world with legs, then they might as well be legs."

"What kind of legs?" And always at that point, I knew from her voice that my

mother was weeping inside. Nana never heard such inside weeping. Not that it would have stopped Nana even if she had heard it. Which always surprised me. Because, about almost everything else apart from my legs, Nana is such a good grown-up. In any case, what do I know about good grown-ups and bad grown-ups? How could Nana be a good grown-up when she carried on so about my legs? All I want to say is that I really liked Nana except for that.

Nana: "As I keep saying, if any woman decides to come into this world with her two legs, then she should select legs that have meat on them: with good calves. Because you are sure such legs would support solid hips. And a woman must have solid hips to be able to have children."

"Oh, Mother." That's how my mother would answer. Very, very quietly. And the discussion would end or they would move on to something else.

Sometimes, Nana would pull in something about my father:

How, "Looking at such a man, we have to be humble and admit that after all, God's children are many . . ."

How, "After one's only daughter had insisted on marrying a man like that, you still have to thank your God that the biggest problem you got later was having a granddaughter with spindly legs that are too long for a woman, and too thin to be of any use."

The way she always added that bit about my father under her breath, she probably thought I didn't hear it. But I always heard it. Plus, that is what always shut my mother up for good, so that even if I had not actually heard the words, once my mother looked like even her little courage was finished, I could always guess what Nana had added to the argument.

"Legs that have meat on them with good calves to support solid hips . . . to be able to have children."

So I wished that one day I would see, for myself, the legs of any woman who had had children. But in our village, that is not easy. The older women wear long wrap-arounds[1] all the time. Perhaps if they let me go bathe in the river in the evening, I could have checked. But I never had the chance. It took a lot of begging just to get my mother and Nana to let me go splash around in the shallow end of the river with my friends, who were other little girls like me. For proper baths, we used the small bathhouse behind our hut. Therefore, the only naked female legs I have ever really seen are those of other little girls like me, or older girls in the school. And those of my mother and Nana: two pairs of legs which must surely belong to the approved kind; because Nana gave birth to my mother

---

1. **wrap-arounds** (rap´ ə roundz´) *n.* a type of garment that is open down the side and is wrapped around the body.

**Literary Analysis**
**Point of View**
What do we learn about the narrator's inner feelings from the words in this paragraph?

**Vocabulary**
**humble** (hum´ bəl)
*adj.* modest; having humility

When I think back on it now, those two, Nana and my mother must have been discussing my legs from the day I was born.

Reading Check

According to the narrator, which topic makes the mother weep inside?

The Girl Who Can **89**

and my mother gave birth to me. In my eyes, all my friends have got legs that look like legs, but whether the legs have got meat on them to support the kind of hips that . . . that I don't know.

According to the older boys and girls, the distance between our little village and the small town is about five kilometers. I don't know what five kilometers mean. They always complain about how long it is to walk to school and back. But to me, we live in our village, and walking those kilometers didn't matter. School is nice. School is another thing Nana and my mother discussed often and appeared to have different ideas about. Nana thought it would be a waste of time. I never understood what she meant. My mother seemed to know—and disagreed. She kept telling Nana that she—that is, my mother—felt she was locked into some kind of darkness because she didn't go to school. So that if I, her daughter, could learn to write and read my own name and a little besides—perhaps be able to calculate some things on paper—that would be good. I could always marry later and maybe . . .

Nana would just laugh. "Ah, maybe with legs like hers, she might as well go to school."

Running with our classmates on our small sports field and winning first place each time never seemed to me to be anything about which to tell anyone at home. This time it was different. I don't know how the teachers decided to let me run for the junior section of our school in the district games. But they did.

When I went home to tell my mother and Nana, they had not believed it at first. So Nana had taken it upon herself to go and "ask into it properly." She came home to tell my mother that it was really true. I was one of my school's runners.

"Is that so?" exclaimed my mother. I know her. Her mouth moved as though she was going to tell Nana, that, after all, there was a secret about me she couldn't be expected to share with anyone. But then Nana herself looked so pleased, out of surprise, my mother shut her mouth up. In any case, since the first time they heard the news, I have often caught Nana staring at my legs with a strange look on her face, but still pretending like she was not looking. All this week, she has been washing my school uniform herself. That is a big surprise. And she didn't stop at that,

▼ **Critical Viewing**
How does your image of the narrator compare to the girls in this photograph? **[Compare]**

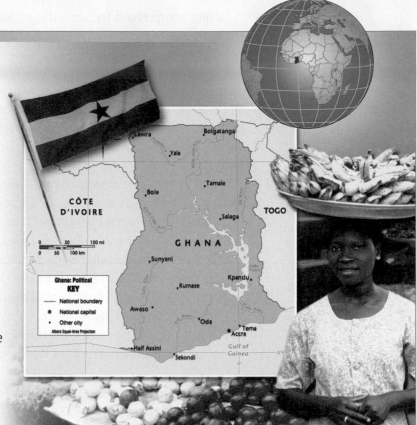

## LITERATURE IN CONTEXT

### Social Studies Connection

**Country Profile: Ghana**

**Location:** southern coast of West Africa bordering the Atlantic Ocean

**Climate:** tropical; wet in the south and dry in the north

**Terrain:** low fertile plains and plateaus

**Population:** 20.2 million

### Connect to the Literature

Adjoa says that she lives in a fertile lowland of central Ghana. What benefits and challenges might this region's climate and terrain present for a runner like Adjoa?

she even went to Mr. Mensah's house and borrowed his charcoal pressing iron. Each time she came back home with it and ironed and ironed and ironed the uniform, until, if I had been the uniform, I would have said aloud that I had had enough.

Wearing my school uniform this week has been very nice. At the parade, on the first afternoon, its sheen caught the rays of the sun and shone brighter than anybody else's uniform. I'm sure Nana saw that too, and must have liked it. Yes, she has been coming into town with us every afternoon of this district sports week. Each afternoon, she has pulled one set of fresh old cloth from the big brass bowl to wear. And those old clothes are always so stiffly starched, you can hear the cloth creak when she passes by. But she walks way behind us schoolchildren. As though she was on her own way to some place else.

Yes, I have won every race I ran for my school, and I have won the cup for the best all-round junior athlete. Yes, Nana said that she didn't care if such things are not done. She would do it. You know what she did? She carried the gleaming cup on her back. Like they do with babies, and other very precious things. And this time, not taking the trouble to walk by herself.

**Spiral Review
Theme** How does Nana's behavior toward Adjoa connect to a possible theme?

Reading Check

After learning about her running talent, what does Nana do with the narrator's uniform?

The Girl Who Can **91**

When we arrived in our village, she entered our compound to show the cup to my mother before going to give it back to the headmaster.

Oh, grown-ups are so strange. Nana is right now carrying me on her knee, and crying softly. Muttering, muttering, muttering that: "saa, thin legs can also be useful . . . thin legs can also be useful . . ." that "even though some legs don't have much meat on them, to carry hips . . . they can run. Thin legs can run . . . then who knows? . . ."

I don't know too much about such things. But that's how I was feeling and thinking all along. That surely, one should be able to do other things with legs as well as have them because they can support hips that make babies. Except that I was afraid of saying that sort of thing aloud. Because someone would have told me never, never, but NEVER to repeat such words. Or else, they would have laughed so much at what I'd said, they would have cried.

It's much better this way. To have acted it out to show them, although I could not have planned it.

As for my mother, she has been speechless as usual.

Oh, grown-ups are so strange.

## Critical Thinking

1. **Key Ideas and Details (a)** Why does Nana criticize the narrator's legs? **(b) Draw Conclusions:** How does this criticism reveal Nana's fears for the narrator's future? Explain.

2. **Integration of Knowledge and Ideas (a)** What are Nana's feelings about the narrator going to school? **(b) Compare and Contrast:** How do the mother's feelings about school differ from Nana's? **(c) Make Generalizations:** Based on these details, what kind of lives do you think many women in Ghana are expected to lead?

3. **Key Ideas and Details (a) Infer:** After Adjoa is chosen for the district games, why does Nana keep staring at her legs? **(b) Draw Conclusions:** Why does Nana iron Adjoa's school uniform so carefully?

4. **Key Ideas and Details (a) Analyze:** At the end of the story, Adjoa says it was much better to "have acted it out to show them." What has she acted out? **(b) Evaluate:** Was it "better," as Adjoa says? Explain.

5. **Integration of Knowledge and Ideas** Do the narrator's legs mean the same thing to her and her family at the end of the selection as they do at the beginning? Use details to support your answer. *[Connect to the Big Question: Can truth change?]*

## Comparing Points of View

© **1. Key Ideas and Details** Use a chart like the one shown to note the actions, thoughts, and feelings of the listed characters in both stories.

| Checkouts | Actions | Thoughts | Feelings |
|---|---|---|---|
| Girl | | | |
| Boy | | | |
| **The Girl Who Can** | **Actions** | **Thoughts** | **Feelings** |
| Nana | | | |
| Adjoa | | | |

© **2. Craft and Structure (a)** Which details from your chart show that the **third-person omniscient point of view** in "Checkouts" gives readers insight into the inner lives of all the characters? Explain. **(b)** Which details show that the **first-person point of view** in "The Girl Who Can" lets the reader understand the narrator best of all? Explain.

## ⏱ Timed Writing

### Explanatory Text: Essay

Compare and contrast the main character in "Checkouts" with the narrator in "The Girl Who Can." In an essay, analyze the way in which the development of each character is shaped by the narrative point of view. Also, consider the cultural perspectives that contribute to the portrayal of each character. **(30 minutes)**

### 5-Minute Planner

1. Read the prompt carefully and completely.

2. Organize your ideas to make important connections by answering these questions:

   • Who are the narrators in the two stories?

   • How do you know what each girl is thinking?

   • Do both narrators seem equally reliable? Why or why not?

   • How does each girl's culture influence her perspective?

3. Reread the prompt, and then draft your essay.

# Writing Workshop

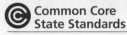 **Common Core State Standards**

**Writing**

**3.** Write narratives to develop real or imagined experiences or events using effective technique, well-chosen details, and well-structured event sequences.

**3.a.** Engage and orient the reader by setting out a problem, situation, or observation, establishing one or multiple point(s) of view, and introducing a narrator and/or characters; create a smooth progression of experiences or events.

**3.c.** Use a variety of techniques to sequence events so that they build on one another to create a coherent whole.

**3.d.** Use precise words and phrases, telling details, and sensory language to convey a vivid picture of the experiences, events, setting, and/or characters.

**5.** Develop and strengthen writing as needed by planning, revising, editing, rewriting, or trying a new approach, focusing on addressing what is most significant for a specific purpose and audience.

## Write a Narrative

### Narration: Autobiographical Narrative

**Defining the Form** An **autobiographical narrative** describes real events in the writer's life and shares the lessons or wisdom the writer gained from the experiences. You might use elements of autobiographical narration in letters, journals, reflective essays, or persuasive essays.

**Assignment** Write an autobiographical narrative about an event that taught you a valuable lesson. Include the following elements:

✓ a *sequence of events* involving you, the writer

✓ a *problem, or conflict,* and a lesson you learned from it

✓ details that locate scenes and incidents in specific places

✓ your thoughts, feelings, or views about the significance of events

✓ error-free grammar, including *correct use of possessive nouns*

To preview the criteria on which your autobiographical narrative may be judged, see the rubric on page 99.

 **Writing Workshop:** *Work in Progress*

Review the work you did on pages 41 and 71.

## Prewriting/Planning Strategy

> **Reading-Writing Connection**
>
> To get a feel for auto-biographical narratives, read "My English" by Julia Alvarez on page 114.

**Structure the sequence.** Create a detailed record of events by making a timeline like the one shown. Write down the first incident related to your subject and record subsequent incidents in the order and place in which they occurred. Note the significance of each event so that you will be able to communicate it to your audience in your essay.

 **Timeline**

**Event 2:** Dad took off training wheels.

**Event 4:** Improved riding. Tried other activities.

**Event 1:** Dreamed of riding bike with no training wheels.

**Event 3:** Rode two-wheeled bike and fell.

SIX TRAITS WRITER'S TOOLBOX SIX TRAITS

**Word Choice** | Ideas | Conventions | Sentence Fluency | Voice | Organization

## Painting a Picture with Words

Word choice is the specific language a writer uses to tell a story. By choosing the right words in your narrative, you can make the people, places, and events you describe as real for your reader as they are for you.

**Choosing Details** Remember that your readers can only see what you show them with words. As you write, do not just list events; use details to show readers what happened and how it felt. Add life to your story with precise descriptions. The chart shown below gives a spectrum of tips that will help you elaborate further on an idea.

| Story Element | Elaboration Tip |
|---|---|
| Experience | Explain its main effect on you. |
| Time and Place | Describe impressions using sensory details. |
| Suspense | Add details that raise the tension and heighten the story's problem. |
| Main Events of Story | Include thoughts or feelings that occurred to you at the time of the events. |
| Story Outcome | Consider other possible outcomes of events. |

**Avoiding Vague Language** A good story not only describes an event; it makes readers feel as if they were there. To be sure that your readers understand what you are trying to communicate, avoid words that are vague. Instead, use language that creates a clear image in readers' minds.

**Vague:** There was a *beautiful* tree in the playground.

**Precise:** In the playground stood an *old oak* tree with *thick branches that stretched at least twenty feet in every direction.*

**Vague:** It was a *hot* day.

**Precise:** It was the kind of day *when the sun is so bright that it hurts your eyes and the sidewalk scorches your feet if you walk barefoot.*

**Evaluating Word Choice** Check your writing to be sure you have used precise words. If you find that a word you are using does not capture the meaning you are trying to communicate, use a *thesaurus* to find a more precise word. Then, check a *dictionary* to be sure that you are using the new word correctly.

# Drafting Strategies

**Identify your main point.** As you draft, think about why this experience matters to you. To convey that importance to readers, clearly state the main problem you faced and what you learned from it. Then, organize your details to highlight the significance of that main point.

**Pace the action.** Details and description add substance to your essay, but too much can slow the pace, or flow, of the story. Be sure that every detail you include has a clear purpose and keeps the reader engaged.

- Emphasize the central conflict that sets the story in motion.

- Create suspense by withholding some details until later in the narrative.

- Conclude by reflecting on the experience and telling what you learned from it.

Use a flow chart like the one shown below to help you decide which details to include in your narrative and the most effective time to reveal them.

**Common Core State Standards**

**Writing**

**3.b.** Use narrative techniques, such as dialogue, pacing, description, reflection, and multiple plot lines, to develop experiences, events, and/or characters.

**3.e.** Provide a conclusion that follows from and reflects on what is experienced, observed, or resolved over the course of the narrative.

| Detail | Purpose | Best Use of Detail |
|---|---|---|
| I put my good-luck penny in my pocket the first time I rode without training wheels, but it fell out while I was riding. | This detail shows that it was courage and hard work, not luck, that helped me ride without training wheels. | Reveal that I put the penny in my pocket early in the narrative. Delay revealing that it fell out until the end, when I explain what I learned. |

# Revising Strategy

**Vary your sentence beginnings.** Even though your narrative is about you, avoid beginning every sentence with *I*. Circle the first word in each sentence in your draft. Then, consider varying sentence beginnings to make your story more interesting.

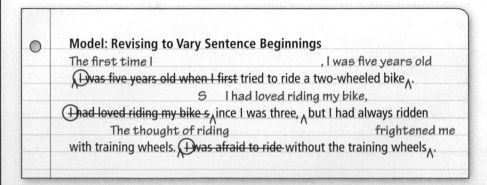

**Model: Revising to Vary Sentence Beginnings**

The first time I                                    , I was five years old
~~I was five years old when I first~~ tried to ride a two-wheeled bike ^.
                            S    I had loved riding my bike,
~~I had loved riding my bike s~~ince I was three, ^ but I had always ridden
            The thought of riding                        frightened me
with training wheels. ~~I was afraid to ride~~ without the training wheels ^.

# Revising to Correct Use of Possessive Nouns

Possessive nouns show to whom places or things belong. A possessive noun is usually formed by adding an apostrophe and an *s* ('s) to a noun.

| Noun | Possessive Noun |
|------|-----------------|
| the homework of the *student* | the *student's* homework |

Because they modify other nouns, possessive nouns function in sentences as adjectives.

**Forming Possessive Nouns Correctly**

**Singular Nouns**

- Add an apostrophe and an *s* to show the possessive case of most singular nouns.

   the radiator of the car ⟶ the car's radiator

- When a singular noun ends in *s,* you may still be able to add an apostrophe and *s.* However, if the apostrophe and *s* make the word difficult to pronounce, the apostrophe may be used alone.

   the sleeve of the dress ⟶ the dress's sleeve
   the poetry of Burns ⟶ Burns' poetry

**Plural Nouns**

- Add an apostrophe to show the possessive case of plural nouns ending in *s* or *es:* the *representatives'* decision.

- Add an apostrophe and *s* to show the possessive case of plural nouns that do not end in *s* or *es:* the *men's* books.

**Compound Nouns**

- Add an apostrophe and *s* to the last word of a compound noun: the *Prime Minister's* visit.

- Add only an apostrophe if the last word of a compound noun ends in *s:* the *House of Representatives'* decision.

**Grammar in Your Writing**

Review the draft of your autobiographical narrative, highlighting all the possessive nouns. Check that you have used singular possessives and plural possessives correctly. Correct any errors you find.

> **PH WRITING COACH**
>
> Further instruction and practice are available in *Prentice Hall Writing Coach*.

## True Friend

Late one Thursday night in July, my sister and I were packing for our upcoming trip to youth camp. This was my first time attending the camp, but it would be my older sister Phoebe's third experience. Everything was running smoothly until my mother called from downstairs, "Don't forget to grab a sleeping bag from my closet!" Our mother never dreamed such a simple statement would start a desperate dash by both of us to seize the most coveted sleeping bag in our household.

The night-sky blue, extra long, brand new, one hundred percent fleece sleeping bag with a built-in pillow was one-of-a-kind. By comparison, the old sleeping bag, with a broken zipper and a small hole forming at the bottom, looked even worse. Phoebe and I reached for the beautiful new bag at the exact same moment. Insulting remarks sailed from our lips as we each grabbed it. Our stomps and yells attracted our parents to the fight scene. I began to argue that I had reached the bag first, when my sister simply let go, returned to her room, and slammed the door. She was so thoroughly angry we did not speak again that night.

As the weekend progressed, our relationship did not improve. Even worse, she had shared the story with her friends. Phoebe's words were so moving, they convinced her friends to embark on a personal voyage to "get me." As a result, I spent the getaway with a target on my back.

As the skinny new kid at the camp, terror struck my heart when I heard a rumor about the plot against me. By Sunday morning, the plan, "Operation Little Brother," was all set. My sister's friends were on a mission.

I was shooting hoops in the gym that morning when my sister's friends appeared. I looked frantically for an escape but was quickly surrounded. The assailants closed to within inches of me when a familiar voice echoed through the emptiness of the open gymnasium. My sister walked calmly between her friends and me and said, "Do not bother him or you will feel the wrath of Phoebe." I was in awe. With this statement, "Operation Little Brother" came to an abrupt end. The sister I was feuding with had just saved me. Her friends never bothered me again.

On the trip home I asked her to explain her unlikely action. She simply replied, "I still don't like you, but I would dislike myself even more if I ever abandoned a friend in trouble." Since then, I have often modeled my actions to emulate my sister's behavior that day. I have learned that even when I am angry, I must stand up for my friends. My sister has taught me many things, but the most important lesson is how to be a true friend.

Jonathan's use of dialogue helps to make this opening scene more real and vivid.

The detailed description of the sleeping bag helps to establish the conflict.

Here, the conflict intensifies.

Jonathan uses specific details to paint a picture of the problem he faces.

The dialogue and description help to convey the drama of the moment and make it seem real.

Jonathan concludes by drawing an important lesson from his experience.

# Editing and Proofreading

Check your draft for errors in grammar, spelling, and punctuation.

**Focus on Dates and Facts.** Review your manuscript to make sure you have provided accurate factual information. Capitalize the proper names of people or places and use correct punctuation when including dates.

# Publishing and Presenting

Consider one of the following ways to share your writing.

**Present an oral narrative.** Mark up a copy of your autobiographical narrative, underlining any thoughts or conversations that you believe your audience would enjoy. As you present to your classmates, emphasize those passages. Be sure to pace the presentation of actions to accommodate changes in time or mood. When you are done, gracefully accept your classmates' applause and praise.

**Post your essay.** With your classmates, create a bulletin board display of the narratives. Have each writer supply a short comment about the event or idea that inspired his or her writing.

# Reflecting on Your Writing

**Writer's Journal** Jot down your answers to this question:
*How did writing about events help you to understand them better?*

# Rubric for Self-Assessment

Find evidence in your writing to address each category. Then, use the rating scale to grade your work.

## Spiral Review

Earlier in the unit, you learned about **common and proper nouns** (p. 40) and **abstract and concrete nouns** (p. 70). Check the capitalization of the common and proper nouns in your narrative. Review your essay to be sure you have used these types of nouns correctly.

| Criteria | Rating Scale | | | | |
|---|---|---|---|---|---|
| | *not very* | | | | *very* |
| **Focus:** How central are you to the action of the story? | 1 | 2 | 3 | 4 | 5 |
| **Organization:** How clearly organized is the sequence of events? | 1 | 2 | 3 | 4 | 5 |
| **Support/Elaboration:** How powerfully are sensory details used to locate scenes in specific places? | 1 | 2 | 3 | 4 | 5 |
| **Style:** How clearly do you convey your insights, thoughts, and feelings? | 1 | 2 | 3 | 4 | 5 |
| **Conventions:** How correct is your grammar—especially your use of possessive nouns? | 1 | 2 | 3 | 4 | 5 |
| **Word Choice:** How precise is the language used to describe the people, places, and events in your narrative? | 1 | 2 | 3 | 4 | 5 |

## Ⓒ Leveled Texts

Build your skills and improve your comprehension of narrative nonfiction with texts of increasing complexity.

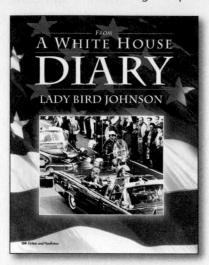

Read from **A White House Diary** to learn first-hand what happened on the day a president was assassinated.

Read **"My English"** to learn how a Spanish-speaking child makes English her language.

## Ⓒ Common Core State Standards

Meet these standards with either the excerpt from **A White House Diary** (p. 104) or **"My English"** (p. 114).

**Reading Informational Text**

**6.** Determine an author's point of view or purpose in a text and analyze how an author uses rhetoric to advance that point of view or purpose. *(Literary Analysis: Voice; Reading Skill: Author's Purpose)*

**7.** Analyze various accounts of a subject told in different mediums, determining which details are emphasized in each account. *(Analyze Media)*

**Spiral Review: RI.9-10.2**

**Writing**

**4.** Produce clear and coherent writing in which the development, organization, and style are appropriate to task, purpose, and audience. *(Writing: Journal Entry)*

**Speaking and Listening**

**5.** Make strategic use of digital media in presentations to enhance understanding of findings, reasoning, and evidence and to add interest. *(Research and Technology: Multimedia Presentation Introduction)*

**Language**

**1.** Demonstrate command of the conventions of standard English grammar and usage when writing or speaking. *(Conventions: Pronouns)*

**6.** Acquire and use accurately grade-appropriate general academic and domain-specific words and phrases; gather vocabulary knowledge when considering a word or phrase important to comprehension or expression. *(Vocabulary: Word Study)*

# Literary Analysis: Voice

**Voice** is the way a writer sounds on the page. It is related to both the author's *point of view*—his or her unique way of seeing a topic—and his or her *style*, or distinct way of using language. For example, a writer's voice may be sophisticated, blunt, or breathless. The following elements contribute to an author's voice:

- *word choice:* the kinds of words the author chooses
- *tone,* or *attitude:* the way the writer feels about the subject
- *sentence structure:* the arrangement of words in sentences

Voice is a key element in all literature. However, it may be particularly evident in **autobiographical writing,** in which the author relates his or her own life story. As you read, notice how details capture the author's voice, or personality, on the page.

# Reading Skill: Author's Purpose

An **author's purpose** is his or her main reason for writing. General purposes for writing are to inform, to persuade, and to narrate. Authors also have specific purposes for writing. For example, an author may write to expose a social problem or to describe an adventure. The author's purpose shapes the decisions he or she makes about every element of the work. To better understand what you read, **preview the text** to identify the author's purpose.

- Notice information or ideas conveyed in the title.
- Look for any organizing features, such as subheads.
- Identify the subject of photos, illustrations, or diagrams.

## Using the Strategy: Author's Purpose Map

As you preview, use an organizer like the one shown to jot down ideas about the author's specific purpose. Later, as you read the full text, confirm whether your ideas are correct.

| Text Feature | Insight About Purpose |
|---|---|
|  |  |
|  |  |
|  |  |

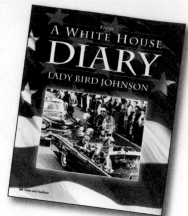

## Can *truth* change?

## Writing About the Big Question

In this passage from *A White House Diary*, Lady Bird Johnson recalls details about the day President John F. Kennedy was assassinated. Use these sentence starters to develop your ideas about the Big Question.

Abrupt changes in **circumstances** can _____.

Accepting the **truth** of these changes can be difficult because _____.

**While You Read** Look for details that show how the author's feelings and attitudes shift as a result of her eyewitness observations during these historic days.

## Vocabulary

Read each word and its definition. Decide whether you know the word well, know it a little bit, or do not know it at all. After you read, see how your knowledge of each word has increased.

- **tumultuous** (tōō mul′ chōō əs) *adj.* greatly disturbed; in an uproar (p. 107) *The year we moved cross-country was a tumultuous one for the whole family.* tumult *n.*

- **implications** (im′ pli kā′ shənz) *n.* indirect results (p. 108) *He did not think about the implications of his decision to change jobs.* implicate *v.* imply *v.*

- **confines** (kän′ fīnz) *n.* boundaries or bounded region; border; limit (p. 109) *Please, stay within the confines of this yard.* confine *v.* confinement *n.* confined *adj.*

- **desolate** (des′ ə lit) *adj.* forlorn; wretched (p. 109) *Living alone on a desolate mountain top would make most people feel lonely.* desolate *v.* desolation *n.*

- **poignant** (pɔin′ yənt) *adj.* emotionally touching (p. 109) *The moment of farewell is often very poignant.* poignancy *n.*

- **immaculate** (i mak′ yə lit) *adj.* perfectly correct; without a flaw, fault, or error (p. 109) *My mother kept an immaculate house, with nothing out of place.* immaculately *adv.*

### Word Study

The **Latin root -fin-** means "end."

In this selection, the author describes the **confines** of a plane, emphasizing the tight, enclosed space on board the aircraft.

# Meet
# Lady Bird Johnson
## (1912–2007)

## Author of
# A WHITE HOUSE
# DIARY

Texas-born Claudia Alta Taylor received her nickname when a nurse said the two-year-old was "as pretty as a lady bird." A graduate of the University of Texas, Lady Bird met and married Lyndon Johnson, then a young congressional aide, in 1934. Even though she was a shy woman, Lady Bird was a valued advisor and effective campaigner for her husband, who said that voters "would happily have elected her over me."

**Living History** When President Kennedy was assassinated, Vice President Lyndon Johnson became president, and Lady Bird became First Lady of the United States. In this role, she made many contributions to her husband's agenda, including the launch of Head Start, a project that makes early childhood education available to all children.

## BACKGROUND FOR THE MEMOIR

### The Assassination of JFK

President John F. Kennedy was a young, vibrant, and popular leader who had been elected in 1960. His assassination on November 22, 1963, was a stunning and unforgettable event. As the news media reported the tragedy, people wept openly in the streets. A mournful nation agreed with Lyndon B. Johnson, JFK's successor, when he said, "We have suffered a loss that cannot be weighed."

## DID YOU KNOW?

In 1982, Lady Bird Johnson founded the National Wildflower Research Center in Austin, Texas.

From

# A WHITE HOUSE
# DIARY

## LADY BIRD JOHNSON

## Dallas, Friday, November 22, 1963

It all began so beautifully. After a drizzle in the morning, the sun came out bright and clear. We were driving into Dallas. In the lead car were President and Mrs. Kennedy, John and Nellie Connally,[1] a Secret Service[2] car full of men, and then our car with Lyndon and me and Senator Ralph Yarborough.

The streets were lined with people—lots and lots of people— the children all smiling, placards, confetti, people waving from windows. One last happy moment I had was looking up and seeing Mary Griffith leaning out of a window waving at me. (Mary for many years had been in charge of altering the clothes which I purchased at Neiman-Marcus.)

Then, almost at the edge of town, on our way to the Trade Mart for the Presidential luncheon, we were rounding a curve, going down a hill, and suddenly there was a sharp, loud report. It sounded like a shot. The sound seemed to me to come from a building on the right above my shoulder. A moment passed, and then two more shots rang out in rapid succession. There had been such a gala air about the day that I thought the noise must come from firecrackers—part of the celebration. Then the Secret Service men were suddenly down in the lead car. Over the car radio system, I heard "Let's get out of here!" and our Secret Service man, Rufus Youngblood, vaulted over the front seat on top of Lyndon, threw him to the floor, and said, "Get down."

---

1. **John and Nellie Connally** John Connally, then governor of Texas, and his wife, Nellie.
2. **Secret Service** division of the U.S. Treasury Department, responsible for protecting the president.

**Reading Skill**
**Author's Purpose**
What does this sub-head tell you about the author's purpose in this part of the diary?

**Literary Analysis**
**Voice**
What do the details about firecrackers tell you about the writer's attitude toward the events she describes?

Reading Check
What was Lady Bird Johnson's last happy moment on this day?

**November 22, 1963**

President John F. Kennedy and his wife, Jackie, arrive in Dallas, Texas.

**November 22, 1963**

The President, First Lady, and Texas Governor Connally ride through Dallas.

**November 22, 1963**

President Kennedy smiles at the crowd in his last moments.

*from* A White House Diary  **105**

**Spiral Review**
**Central Idea** What is the central, or most important, idea conveyed so far?

Senator Yarborough and I ducked our heads. The car accelerated terrifically—faster and faster. Then, suddenly, the brakes were put on so hard that I wondered if we were going to make it as we wheeled left and went around the corner. We pulled up to a building. I looked up and saw a sign, "HOSPITAL." Only then did I believe that this might be what it was. Senator Yarborough kept saying in an excited voice, "Have they shot the President? Have they shot the President?" I said something like, "No, it can't be."

As we ground to a halt—we were still the third car—Secret Service men began to pull, lead, guide, and hustle us out. I cast one last look over my shoulder and saw in the President's car a bundle of pink, just like a drift of blossoms, lying on the back seat. It was Mrs. Kennedy lying over the President's body.

The Secret Service men rushed us to the right, then to the left, and then onward into a quiet room in the hospital—a very small room. It was lined with white sheets, I believe.

People came and went—Kenny O'Donnell, the President's top aide, Congressman Homer Thornberry, Congressman Jack Brooks. Always there was Rufe right there and other Secret Service agents—Emory Roberts, Jerry Kivett, Lem Johns, and Woody Taylor. People spoke of

## LITERATURE IN CONTEXT

### History Connection

**The Legacy of JFK**
At the age of 43, John Fitzgerald Kennedy became the youngest president in American history. He brought to the White House a new energy, optimism, and hope for the future. The initiatives he sought changed America.

◄ Kennedy, shown here with astronaut John Glenn, committed the nation to space exploration.

### Connect to the Literature

How does information about President Kennedy's ideas help explain the intense grief most Americans felt at his death?

◄ Kennedy initiated the Civil Rights Act. Johnson, with Dr. Martin Luther King, Jr., at his side, signed it into law in 1965.

▲ Kennedy established the Peace Corps in 1961. To date, 170,000 volunteers have served in 137 countries.

how widespread this might be. There was talk about where we would go—to the plane, to our house, back to Washington. •

Through it all Lyndon was remarkably calm and quiet. He suggested that the Presidential plane ought to be moved to another part of the field. He spoke of going back out to the plane in unmarked black cars. Every face that came in, you searched for the answer. I think the face I kept seeing the answer on was the face of Kenny O'Donnell, who loved President Kennedy so much.

It was Lyndon who spoke of it first, although I knew I would not leave without doing it. He said, "You had better try to see Jackie and Nellie." We didn't know what had happened to John.

I asked the Secret Service if I could be taken to them. They began to lead me up one corridor and down another. Suddenly I found myself face to face with Jackie in a small hallway. I believe it was right outside the operating room. You always think of someone like her as being insulated, protected. She was quite alone. I don't think I ever saw anyone so much alone in my life. I went up to her, put my arms around her, and said something to her. I'm sure it was something like "God, help us all," because my feelings for her were too tumultuous to put into words.

And then I went to see Nellie. There it was different, because Nellie and I have gone through so many things together since 1938. I hugged her tight and we both cried and I said, "Nellie, John's going to be all right." And Nellie said, "Yes, John's going to be all right." Among her many other fine qualities, she is also strong.

I turned and went back to the small white room where Lyndon was. Mac Kilduff, the President's press man on this trip, and Kenny O'Donnell were coming and going. I think it was from Kenny's face that I first knew the truth and from Kenny's voice that I first heard

▼ **Analyze Media**
Based on the photos shown below and Mrs. Johnson's account, explain how different types of media can emphasize different aspects of an event. **[Analyze]**

**Vocabulary**
**tumultuous**
(tōō mul´ chōō əs) *adj.*
greatly disturbed; in an uproar

**Reading Check**
Where were the Johnsons taken after the shots were fired?

**Dealey Plaza**

This is the site of JFK's assassination.

**November 22, 1963**

Spectators drop to the ground moments after shots are fired at President Kennedy.

**November 22, 1963**

Mourners lay flowers along the street, weeping for their fallen president.

*from* A White House Diary **107**

▼ Analyze Media  The central photo below and the first paragraph on page 109 address the same moment. Do you learn different things about that moment from the two texts? [Analyze]

Vocabulary
**implications**
(im´ pli kā´ shənz) *n.*
indirect results

the words "The President is dead." Mr. Kilduff entered and said to Lyndon, "Mr. President."

It was decided that we would go immediately to the airport. Hurried plans were made about how we should get to the cars and who was to ride in which car. Our departure from the hospital and approach to the cars was one of the swiftest walks I have ever made.

We got in. Lyndon told the agents to stop the sirens. We drove along as fast as we could. I looked up at a building and there, already, was a flag at half-mast. I think that was when the enormity of what had happened first struck me.

When we got to the field, we entered *Air Force One*[3] for the first time. There was a TV set on and the commentator was saying, "Lyndon B. Johnson, now President of the United States." The news commentator was saying the President had been shot with a 30-30 rifle. The police had a suspect. They were not sure he was the assassin.

On the plane, all the shades were lowered. We heard that we were going to wait for Mrs. Kennedy and the coffin. There was a telephone call to Washington—I believe to the Attorney General.[4]

It was decided that Lyndon should be sworn in here as quickly as possible, because of national and world implications, and because we did not know how widespread this was as to intended victims. Judge Sarah Hughes, a Federal Judge in Dallas—and I am glad it was she— was called and asked to come in a hurry to administer the oath.

---

3. *Air Force One*  name of the airplane officially assigned to transport the president of the United States.
4. **Attorney General**  chief law officer of the nation, head of the U.S. Department of Justice; at the time, the position was held by Robert Kennedy, JFK's brother.

November 22, 1963

Vice President Johnson responds to the news of Kennedy's death.

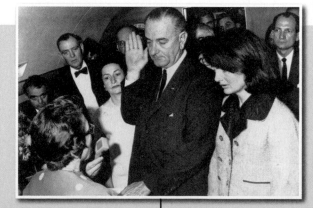

November 22, 1963

Lyndon B. Johnson is sworn in as the thirty-sixth U.S. president.

November 22, 1963

The coffin of John F. Kennedy is removed from Air Force One.

Mrs. Kennedy had arrived by this time, as had the coffin. There, in the very narrow confines of the plane—with Jackie standing by Lyndon, her hair falling in her face but very composed, with me beside him, Judge Hughes in front of him, and a cluster of Secret Service people, staff, and Congressmen we had known for a long time around him—Lyndon took the oath of office.

It's odd the little things that come to your mind at times of utmost stress, the flashes of deep compassion you feel for people who are really not at the center of the tragedy. I heard a Secret Service man say in the most desolate voice—and I hurt for him: "We never lost a President in the Service." Then, Police Chief Curry of Dallas came on the plane and said, "Mrs. Kennedy, believe me, we did everything we possibly could." That must have been an agonizing moment for him.

We all sat around the plane. The casket was in the corridor. I went in the small private room to see Mrs. Kennedy, and though it was a very hard thing to do, she made it as easy as possible. She said things like, "Oh, Lady Bird, we've liked you two so much. . . . Oh, what if I had not been there. I'm so glad I was there."

I looked at her. Mrs. Kennedy's dress was stained with blood. One leg was almost entirely covered with it and her right glove was caked, it was caked with blood—her husband's blood. Somehow that was one of the most poignant sights—that immaculate woman exquisitely dressed, and caked in blood.

I asked her if I couldn't get someone in to help her change and she said, "Oh, no. Perhaps later I'll ask Mary Gallagher but not right now." And then with almost an element of fierceness—if a person

**Reading Skill**
**Author's Purpose**
What is the writer's purpose in including the comments of the Secret Service man?

**Reading Check**
How did Mrs. Johnson first know that the President was dead?

**November 22, 1963**

President Johnson prepares to make his first address to a grieving nation.

**November 25, 1963**

John F. Kennedy, Jr., salutes his father's coffin.

**A Nation Mourns**

The flag on the White House is lowered to half-mast.

*from A White House Diary* **109**

that gentle, that dignified, can be said to have such a quality—she said, "I want them to see what they have done to Jack."

I tried to express how we felt. I said, "Oh, Mrs. Kennedy, you know we never even wanted to be Vice President and now, dear God, it's come to this." I would have done anything to help her, but there was nothing I could do, so rather quickly I left and went back to the main part of the airplane where everyone was seated.

The flight to Washington was silent, each sitting with his own thoughts. One of mine was a recollection of what I had said about Lyndon a long time ago—he's a good man in a tight spot. I remembered one little thing he had said in that hospital room— "Tell the children to get a Secret Service man with them."

Finally we got to Washington, with a cluster of people waiting and many bright lights. The casket went off first, then Mrs. Kennedy, and then we followed. The family had come to join her. Lyndon made a very simple, very brief, and, I think, strong statement to the people there. Only about four sentences. We got in helicopters, dropped him off at the White House, and I came home in a car with Liz Carpenter.[5]

---

5. **Liz Carpenter** Mrs. Johnson's press secretary.

## Critical Thinking

1. **Key Ideas and Details (a)** What does Mrs. Kennedy say when Mrs. Johnson offers to find someone to help her change her clothes? **(b) Interpret:** What does Mrs. Kennedy mean? **(c) Analyze:** Why do you think Mrs. Johnson reports this detail?

2. **Key Ideas and Details (a)** What comment about her husband does Mrs. Johnson recall on the flight back to Washington? **(b) Interpret:** What character traits does this comment suggest President Johnson possesses? Explain. **(c) Support:** Which details from the selection show that Mrs. Johnson possesses similar character traits?

3. **Craft and Structure Evaluate:** Do you think Mrs. Johnson effectively expresses what it felt like to live through this historic incident? Explain.

4. **Integration of Knowledge and Ideas** How do the events of November 22, 1963, change what Lady Bird Johnson thinks of as her everyday reality? *[Connect to the Big Question: Can truth change?]*

Cite textual evidence to support your responses.

---

### Literary Analysis
**Voice**
What does this passage reveal about Mrs. Johnson's attitude toward Mrs. Kennedy?

*The flight to Washington was silent, each sitting with his own thoughts.*

## Literary Analysis: Voice

**ⓒ 1. Craft and Structure (a)** Complete a chart like the one shown to find examples of Johnson's **word choice, attitude,** and **sentence structure.**

| Voice | | |
|---|---|---|
| **Word Choice** | **Attitude** | **Sentence Structure** |
| | | |

**(b)** Using examples from your chart, describe Johnson's **voice.**

**ⓒ 2. Key Ideas and Details (a)** What details about Lyndon Johnson are emphasized in Lady Bird Johnson's **autobiographical writing? (b)** What are two other details that reflect Mrs. Johnson's perspective?

## Reading Skill: Author's Purpose

**3.** Review the notes you made in your **preview** of the excerpt. Which of your ideas about the **author's purpose** were confirmed as you read the selection? Which were not? Explain.

**4. (a)** What general purpose do you think Mrs. Johnson had in writing this portion of *A White House Diary*? Explain. **(b)** What more specific purpose do you think she had? Explain.

## Vocabulary

**ⓒ Acquisition and Use** An **analogy** shows the relationship between pairs of words. To complete each analogy, use a word from the vocabulary list on page 102. Your choice should create a word pair that matches the relationship between the first two words given.

**1.** weak : strong :: calm : _____
**2.** rain : flood :: choice : _____
**3.** laughter : humorous :: sadness : _____
**4.** troubled : carefree :: _____ : delighted
**5.** steep : precipitous :: _____ : perfect
**6.** vital : necessary :: _____ : bounds

**Word Study** Use the context of the sentences and what you know about the **Latin root -fin-** to explain your answer to each question.

**1.** If you have a *definite* opinion, are you uncertain?
**2.** Do you think of the *infinity* of space as limitless?

> ### Word Study
>
> The **Latin root -fin-** means "end."
>
> **Apply It** Explain how the root *-fin-* contributes to the meanings of these words. Consult a dictionary if necessary.
>
> finish
> final
> refine

# Can *truth* change?

## Writing About the Big Question

In "My English," Alvarez describes how her view of her place in the world changes as she learns English. Use these sentence starters to develop your ideas about the Big Question.

Learning a language can affect our **perspective** because_____.

We may make **assumptions** about people from other cultures because _____.

**While You Read** Look for details that show how the author's confidence in herself changes as she learns English.

## Vocabulary

Read each word and its definition. Decide whether you know the word well, know it a little bit, or do not know it at all. After you read, see how your knowledge of each word has increased.

- **bilingual** (bi liŋ´ gwəl) *adj.* using two languages (p. 114) *The bilingual student speaks Spanish and English.* linguistics *n.*

- **countenance** (koun´ tə nəns) *n.* face (p. 116) *The child's overjoyed countenance showed her relief at being home.*

- **ponderously** (pän´ dər əs lē) *adv.* in a labored, boring, and serious way (p. 117) *The telemarketer ponderously explained the rules of the service contract.* ponderous *adj.* ponder *v.*

- **enumerated** (ē nōō´ mər āt id) *v.* named one by one; specified, as in a list (p. 118) *Joel enumerated the names of video games he likes to play.* enumerate *v.* enumerable *adj.* numeral *n.*

- **interminably** (in tʉr´ mi nə blē) *adv.* endlessly (p. 119) *To the tired audience, the speaker seemed to go on interminably.* interminable *adj.* terminal *adj.* terminal *n.* terminate *v.*

- **accentuated** (ak sen´ chōō āt id) *v.* emphasized; heightened the effect of (p. 119) *Her new haircut accentuated her graceful neck.* accentuate *v.* accent *n.*

### Word Study

The **Latin root -term-** means "limit, end, boundary."

The teacher in this essay does not make the class diagram sentences **interminably**, or in a way that has no end.

# Meet
# Julia Alvarez

(b. 1950)

## Author of

# My English

When her family fled the Dominican Republic and returned to New York, Julia Alvarez was ten years old, and Spanish was her primary language. Painfully aware of not fitting in, Julia took refuge in reading and making up stories. She says, "I landed, not in the United States, but in the English language. That became my new home."

**"I write to find out who I am."** Alvarez attended Middlebury College, where she won several poetry awards. She later earned a master's degree in creative writing from Syracuse University. Alvarez says that writing is "a way to understand yourself." Her writing has been praised for its humor, sensitivity, and insight.

### Did You Know?

One of Julia Alvarez's books, *In the Time of the Butterflies*, was made into a film starring Salma Hayek.

## BACKGROUND FOR THE AUTOBIOGRAPHY

**Alvarez's Two Nationalities**

Julia Alvarez, the author of "My English," was born in New York but grew up in the Dominican Republic, a small Caribbean nation. An independent state since 1844, the Dominican Republic has often struggled with foreign conquest, political unrest, and dictatorship. Alvarez's family was forced to return to New York in 1960 because her father had participated in a movement against the brutal Dominican dictator Raphael Trujillo.

# My English

## Julia Alvarez

**M**ami and Papi used to speak it when they had a secret they wanted to keep from us children. We lived then in the Dominican Republic, and the family as a whole spoke only Spanish at home, until my sisters and I started attending the Carol Morgan School, and we became a bilingual family. Spanish had its many tongues as well. There was the castellano[1] of Padre[2] Joaquín from Spain, whose lisp we all loved to imitate. Then the educated español my parents' families spoke, aunts and uncles who were always correcting us children, for we spent most of the day with the maids

---

1. **castellano** (cä´ stä yä´ nō) *Spanish for "Castilian," the most widely spoken dialect of the Spanish language.*
2. **Padre** (pä´ drä) *"Father" (Spanish), a form of address for a Roman Catholic priest.*

and so had picked up their "bad Spanish." Campesinas,[3] they spoke a lilting, animated campuno,[4] ss swallowed, endings chopped off, funny turns of phrases. This campuno was my true mother tongue, not the Spanish of Calderón de la Barca or Cervantes or even Neruda,[5] but of Chucha and Iluminada and Gladys and Ursulina from Juncalito and Licey and Boca de Yuma and San Juan de la Maguana.[6] Those women yakked as they cooked, they storytold, they gossiped, they sang—boleros, merengues, canciones, salves.[7] Theirs were the voices that belonged to the rain and the wind and the teeny, teeny stars even a small child could blot out with her thumb.

Besides all these versions of Spanish, every once in a while another strange tongue emerged from my papi's mouth or my mami's lips. What I first recognized was not a language, but a tone of voice, serious, urgent, something important and top secret being said, some uncle in trouble, someone divorcing, someone dead. *Say it in English so the children won't understand.* I would listen, straining to understand, thinking that this was not a different language but just another and harder version of Spanish. *Say it in English so the children won't understand.* From the beginning, English was the sound of worry and secrets, the sound of being left out.

I could make no sense of this "harder Spanish," and so I tried by other means to find out what was going on. I knew my mother's face by heart. When the little lines on the corners of her eyes crinkled, she was amused. When her nostrils flared and she bit her lips, she was trying hard not to laugh. She held her head down, eyes glancing up, when she thought I was lying. Whenever she spoke that gibberish English, I translated the general content by watching the Spanish expressions on her face.

---

3. **Campesinas** (cäm pä sē′ näs) simple rural women; peasant women (Spanish).
4. **campuno** (cäm pōō′ nō) Spanish dialect spoken in rural areas of the Dominican Republic.
5. **Calderón de la Barca** (cäl de rôn′ dā lä bär′ cä) . . . **Cervantes** (ser vän′ tes) . . . **Neruda** (nā rōō′ dä) important literary figures.
6. **Juncalito** (hōōŋ cä lē′ tō) . . . **Licey** . . . **Boca de Yuma** (bō′ cä dä yōō′ mä) . . . **San Juan de la Maguana** (sän hwän′ dā lä mä gwä′ nä) small rural villages in the Dominican Republic.
7. **boleros** (bō ler′ ōs) . . . **merengues** (mə reŋ′ gäs) . . . **canciones** (cän sē ō′ nes) . . . **salves** (säl′ ves) Spanish and Latin American songs and dances.

**Reading Check**
According to Alvarez, how does English sound?

Soon, I began to learn more English, at the Carol Morgan School. That is, when I had stopped gawking. The teacher and some of the American children had the strangest coloration: light hair, light eyes, light skin, as if Ursulina had soaked them in bleach too long, to' deteñío.[8] I did have some blond cousins, but they had deeply tanned skin, and as they grew older, their hair darkened, so their earlier paleness seemed a phase of their acquiring normal color. Just as strange was the little girl in my reader who had a *cat* and a *dog*, that looked just like un gatito y un perrito. Her mami was *Mother* and her papi *Father*. Why have a whole new language for school and for books with a teacher who could speak it teaching you double the amount of words you really needed?

*Butter, butter, butter, butter.* All day, one English word that had particularly struck me would go round and round in my mouth and weave through all the Spanish in my head until by the end of the day, the word did sound like just another Spanish word. And so I would say, "Mami, please pass la mantequilla." She would scowl and say in English, "I'm sorry, I don't understand. But would you be needing some butter on your bread?" ●

Why my parents didn't first educate us in our native language by enrolling us in a Dominican school, I don't know. Part of it was that Mami's family had a tradition of sending the boys to the States to boarding school and college, and she had been one of the first girls to be allowed to join her brothers. At Abbot Academy,[9] whose school song was our lullaby as babies ("Although Columbus and Cabot[10] never heard of Abbot, it's quite the place for you and me"), she had become quite Americanized. It was very important, she kept saying, that we learn our English. She always used the possessive pronoun: *your* English, an inheritance we had come into and must wisely use. Unfortunately, my English became all mixed up with our Spanish.

Mix-up, or what's now called Spanglish, was the language we spoke for several years. There wasn't a sentence that wasn't colonized by an English word. At school, a Spanish word would suddenly slide into my English like someone butting into line. Teacher, whose face I was learning to read as minutely as my mother's, would scowl but no smile played on her lips. Her pale skin made her strange countenance hard to read, so that I often misjudged how much I could get away with. Whenever I made a

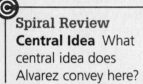

**Literary Analysis**
**Voice**
Which words and phrases here convey the writer's uncertainty about English and her unwillingness to learn it?

**Spiral Review**
**Central Idea** What central idea does Alvarez convey here?

**Vocabulary**
**countenance**
(koun´ tə nəns) *n.* face

---

8. **to' deteñío** (tō dā tān yē´ ō) all washed out; completely colorless (Spanish).
9. **Abbot Academy** boarding school for girls in Andover, Massachusetts; merged in 1973 with the neighboring boys' school, Phillips Academy.
10. **Cabot** (kab´ ət) John Cabot (1450–1499), Italian explorer who sailed in the service of England and was the first European to discover the coast of North America in 1497.

mistake, Teacher would shake her head slowly, "In English, YU-LEE-AH, there's no such word as *columpio.* Do you mean a *swing?*"

I would bow my head, humiliated by the smiles and snickers of the American children around me. I grew insecure about Spanish. My native tongue was not quite as good as English, as if words like *columpio* were illegal immigrants trying to cross a border into another language. But Teacher's discerning grammar-and-vocabulary-patrol ears could tell and send them back.

Soon, I was talking up an English storm. "Did you eat English parrot?" my grandfather asked one Sunday. I had just enlisted yet one more patient servant to listen to my rendition of "Peter Piper picked a peck of pickled peppers" at breakneck pace. "Huh?" I asked impolitely in English, putting him in his place. *Cat got your tongue? No big deal! So there! Take that! Holy Toledo!* (Our teacher's favorite "curse word.") *Go jump in the lake! Really dumb. Golly. Gosh.* Slang, clichés, sayings, hotshot language that our teacher called, ponderously, idiomatic expressions. Riddles, jokes, puns, conundrums. *What is yellow and goes click-click? Why did the chicken cross the road? See you later, alligator.* How wonderful to call someone an alligator and not be scolded for being disrespectful. In fact, they were supposed to say back, *In a while, crocodile.*

There was also a neat little trick I wanted to try on an English-speaking adult at home. I had learned it from Elizabeth, my smart-alecky friend in fourth grade, whom I alternately worshiped and resented. I'd ask her a question that required an explanation, and she'd answer, "Because . . ." "Elizabeth, how come you didn't go to Isabel's birthday party?" "Because . . ." "Why didn't you put your name in your reader?" "Because . . ." I thought that such a cool way to get around having to come up with answers. So, I practiced saying it under my breath, planning for the day I could use it on an unsuspecting English-speaking adult.

One Sunday at our extended family dinner, my grandfather sat down at the children's table to chat with us. He was famous, in fact, for the way he could carry on adult conversations with his grandchildren. He often spoke to us in English so that we could practice speaking it outside the classroom. He was a Cornell[11] man, a United Nations representative from our country. He gave speeches in English. Perfect English, my mother's phrase. That

---

11. **Cornell** Cornell University in Ithaca, New York.

**Literary Analysis**
**Voice**
How would you describe the author's voice, based on her examples of idiomatic expressions?

**Vocabulary**
**ponderously**
(pän´ dər əs lē) *adv.*
in a labored, boring, and serious way

**Reading Check**
Which language did Alvarez learn to speak first—English or Spanish?

Sunday, he asked me a question. I can't even remember what it was because I wasn't really listening but lying in wait for my chance. "Because . . .," I answered him. Papito waited a second for the rest of my sentence and then gave me a thumbnail grammar lesson, "*Because* has to be followed by a clause."

"Why's that?" I asked, nonplussed.[12]

"Because," he winked. "Just because."

A beginning wordsmith, I had so much left to learn; sometimes it was disheartening. Once Tío[13] Gus, the family intellectual, put a speck of salt on my grandparents' big dining table during Sunday dinner. He said, "Imagine this whole table is the human brain. Then this teensy grain is all we ever use of our intelligence!" He enumerated geniuses who had perhaps used two grains, maybe three: Einstein, Michelangelo, da Vinci, Beethoven. We children believed him. It was the kind of impossible fact we thrived on, proving as it did that the world out there was not drastically different from the one we were making up in our heads.

Later, at home, Mami said that you had to take what her younger brother said "with a grain of salt." I thought she was still referring to Tío Gus's demonstration, and I tried to puzzle out what she was saying. Finally, I asked what she meant. "Taking what someone says with a grain of salt is an idiomatic expression in English," she explained. It was pure voodoo is what it was—what later I learned poetry could also do: a grain of salt could symbolize both the human brain and a condiment for human nonsense. And it could be itself, too: a grain of salt to flavor a bland plate of American food.

When we arrived in New York, I was shocked. A country where everyone spoke English! These people must be smarter, I thought. Maids, waiters, taxi drivers, doormen, bums on the street, all spoke this difficult language. It took some time before I understood that Americans were not necessarily a smarter, superior race. It was as natural for them to learn their mother tongue as it was for a little Dominican baby to learn Spanish. It came with "mother's milk," my mother explained, and for a while I thought a mother tongue was a mother tongue because you got it from your mother's milk along with proteins and vitamins.

Soon it wasn't so strange that everyone was speaking in English instead of Spanish. I learned not to hear it as English, but as sense. I no longer strained to understand, I understood. I relaxed in this second language. Only when someone with a heavy southern or

---

**Vocabulary**
**enumerated**
(ē nōō′ mər āt id) *v.*
named one by one;
specified, as in a list

**Reading Skill**
**Author's Purpose**
Why do you think the writer includes these details about Mami's comments?

*"Taking what someone says* **with a grain of salt** *is an idiomatic expression in English," she explained.*

---

12. **nonplussed** (nän plüst′) *v.* confused; baffled.
13. **Tío** (tē′ ō) "Uncle" (Spanish).

British accent spoke in a movie, or at church when the priest droned his sermon—only then did I experience that little catch of anxiety. I worried that I would not be able to understand, that I wouldn't be able to "keep up" with the voice speaking in this acquired language. I would be like those people from the Bible we had studied in religion class, whom I imagined standing at the foot of an enormous tower[14] that looked just like the skyscrapers around me. They had been punished for their pride by being made to speak different languages so that they didn't understand what anyone was saying.

But at the foot of those towering New York skyscrapers, I began to understand more and more—not less and less—English. In sixth grade, I had one of the first in a lucky line of great English teachers who began to nurture in me a love of language, a love that had been there since my childhood of listening closely to words. Sister Maria Generosa did not make our class interminably diagram sentences from a workbook or learn a catechism[15] of grammar rules. Instead, she asked us to write little stories imagining we were snowflakes, birds, pianos, a stone in the pavement, a star in the sky. What would it feel like to be a flower with roots in the ground? If the clouds could talk, what would they say? She had an expressive, dreamy look that was accentuated by the wimple[16] that framed her face.

Supposing, just supposing . . . My mind would take off, soaring into possibilities, a flower with roots, a star in the sky, a cloud full of sad, sad tears, a piano crying out each time its back was tapped, music only to our ears.

---

14. **enormous tower** a reference to the Tower of Babel in Genesis 11:1–9. According to Genesis, early Babylonians tried to build a tower to heaven, but they were thwarted when God caused them to speak many languages rather than one.
15. **catechism** (kat´ ə kiz´ əm) *n.* short book written in question-and-answer format.
16. **wimple** (wim´ pəl) *n.* cloth worn around the head, neck, and chin by some nuns.

▼ **Critical Viewing**
Based on these photographs, why do you think Alvarez might have found New York to be both intimidating and exciting? **[Analyze]**

**Vocabulary**
**interminably**
(in tʉr´ mi nə blē) *adv.* endlessly

**accentuated**
(ak sen´ cho͞o āt id) *v.* emphasized; heightened the effect of

**Reading Check**
To what city does Alvarez's family relocate?

Sister Maria stood at the chalkboard. Her chalk was always snapping in two because she wrote with such energy, her whole habit[17] shaking with the swing of her arm, her hand tap-tap-tapping on the board. "Here's a simple sentence: 'The snow fell.'" Sister pointed with her chalk, her eyebrows lifted, her wimple poked up. Sometimes I could see wisps of gray hair that strayed from under her headdress. "But watch what happens if we put an adverb at the beginning and a prepositional phrase at the end: 'Gently, the snow fell on the bare hills.'"

I thought about the snow. I saw how it might fall on the hills, tapping lightly on the bare branches of trees. Softly, it would fall on the cold, bare fields. On toys children had left out in the yard, and on cars and on little birds and on people out late walking on the streets. Sister Marie filled the chalkboard with snowy print, on and on, handling and shaping and moving the language, scribbling all over the board until English, those verbal gadgets, those tricks and turns of phrases, those little fixed units and counters, became a charged, fluid mass that carried me in its great fluent waves, rolling and moving onward, to deposit me on the shores of my new homeland. I was no longer a foreigner with no ground to stand on. I had landed in the English language.

---

**17. habit** (hab′ it) *n.* robe or dress worn by some nuns.

*I was no longer a foreigner with no ground to stand on. I had landed in the English language.*

Cite textual evidence to support your responses.

## Critical Thinking

1. **Key Ideas and Details (a)** When Julia Alvarez was young, at what times did her parents speak English at home? **(b) Infer:** Why do you think Alvarez says that English was the "sound of being left out"?

2. **Key Ideas and Details (a)** What method does Sister Maria Generosa use to teach Alvarez English? **(b) Compare and Contrast:** How does this method differ from the way she was taught at the Carol Morgan School? **(c) Assess:** Which method does Alvarez prefer? Why?

3. **Craft and Structure Evaluate:** How well do you think Alvarez succeeds in portraying the growth of her relationship with the English language? Use details from the text to support your answer.

4. **Integration of Knowledge and Ideas** How do Alvarez's ideas about English change as she learns the language? *[Connect to the Big Question: Can truth change?]*

## Literary Analysis: Voice

**1. Craft and Structure (a)** Complete a chart like the one shown to find examples of Alvarez's **word choice, attitude,** and **sentence structure. (b)** Using examples from your chart, describe Alvarez's **voice** in this work of nonfiction.

| Voice | | |
|---|---|---|
| **Word Choice** | **Attitude** | **Sentence Structure** |
| | | |

**2. Key Ideas and Details (a)** Which aspects of learning English does the author emphasize in this example of **autobiographical writing? (b)** Note two details that reflect her individual point of view.

## Reading Skill: Author's Purpose

**3.** Review the notes you made in your **preview** of "My English." Which of your ideas about the **author's purpose** were confirmed as you read the selection? Which were not? Explain.

**4. (a)** What general purpose do you think Alvarez had in writing this essay? Explain. **(b)** What more specific purpose or purposes do you think she had for writing? Support your answer.

## Vocabulary

**Acquisition and Use** An **analogy** shows the relationship between pairs of words. To complete each analogy, use a word from the vocabulary list on page 112. For each case, your choice should create a word pair that matches the relationship between the first two words given.

**1.** happily : sadly :: _____ : quickly
**2.** bipartisan : party :: _____ : language
**3.** frame : photograph :: _____ : expression
**4.** counted : tally :: _____ : list
**5.** terrific : great :: _____ : highlighted
**6.** boldly : meekly :: _____ : lightly

**Word Study** Use the context of the sentences and what you know about the **Latin root -term-** to explain your answer to each question.

**1.** If you are *determined*, are you likely to quit?
**2.** If a worker is *terminated*, has he or she been fired?

### Word Study

The **Latin root -term-** means "limit, end, boundary."

**Apply It** Explain how the root contributes to the meanings of these words. Consult a dictionary if necessary.

**terminal**
**exterminate**
**determination**

# Integrated Language Skills

## *from* **A White House Diary • My English**

## Conventions: Pronouns

A **pronoun** is a word that stands for a noun or for a word that takes the place of a noun.

A **personal pronoun** refers to the person speaking (first person), the person spoken to (second person), or the person or thing spoken about (third person).

**Reflexive pronouns** end in *-self* or *-selves* and are used to indicate that someone or something performs an action to, for, or upon himself, herself, or itself.

|  | **First Person** | **Second Person** | **Third Person** |
|---|---|---|---|
| **Personal Pronouns** | **Singular:** I, me, my, mine <br> **Plural:** we, us, our, ours | **Singular:** you, your, yours <br> **Plural:** you, your, yours | **Singular:** he, she, him, her, his, hers, it, its <br> **Plural:** they, them, their, theirs |
| **Reflexive Pronouns** | **Singular:** myself <br> **Plural:** ourselves | **Singular:** yourself <br> **Plural:** yourselves | **Singular:** himself, herself, itself <br> **Plural:** themselves |

**Practice A** Identify the pronouns in each sentence and indicate whether they are personal or reflexive. Look for a word, or antecedent, to which the pronoun refers.

1. At first, Lady Bird Johnson was herself unsure of what had happened.
2. Mrs. Kennedy said, "I want them to see what they have done to Jack."
3. If you were alive in 1963, you would still remember the events of November 22.

© **Reading Application** In *A White House Diary*, find one sentence that uses a personal pronoun and one that uses a reflexive pronoun.

**Practice B** Identify the pronouns in each sentence and indicate whether they are personal or reflexive. Rewrite sentences with reflexive pronouns to eliminate the reflexive pronoun.

1. Her parents were themselves well educated.
2. Alvarez found herself in a class where her writing was encouraged.
3. She enjoyed talking to her grandfather.

© **Writing Application** Using this sentence as a model, write two or more sentences that include both personal and reflexive pronouns: *Julia Alvarez writes about her parents speaking English between themselves.*

**PH** **WRITING COACH** | Further instruction and practice are available in *Prentice Hall Writing Coach*.

# Writing

 **Narrative Text** Both selections deal with the experience of going through a tough time. Write a **journal entry** about an event or subject of importance to you. Model your writing on either *A White House Diary* or "My English." As you prepare to write, consider these questions about your topic:

- Who was affected by the event, and in what way?
- What specific words, images, sights, sounds, or smells does this event call to mind?
- Has this subject always been important to you? Why or why not?
- How does this subject influence your outlook on the world?

**Grammar Application** Use personal, reflexive, and reciprocal pronouns correctly in your writing.

## Writing Workshop: *Work in Progress*

**Prewriting for Problem-Solution Essay** Think of issues that concern people in your school or community. Jot down several problems. As you write, use a narrative format, describing events in the order they occurred. Put these Problem Notes in your writing portfolio for development later.

# Research and Technology

 **Build and Present Knowledge** Each of these selections is based on actual historical events. Using presentation software, prepare an **introduction for a multimedia presentation** about one of these two topics suggested by the reading:

- First ladies in American history and how the role of the first lady has changed over time
- Immigration to the United States since 1800, the reasons people left their home countries, and what they sought in the United States

Follow these steps to complete the assignment:

- Choose your topic and conduct research to learn more.
- Identify the main idea and key points of your presentation.
- Create a strong opening statement that captures your audience's interest and introduces the main idea of your topic.
- Choose appropriate media to present your topic. Use available technologies to achieve your purpose, displaying information on charts, maps, or graphs when appropriate.
- Provide an overview of your presentation so your audience knows what your focus will be.

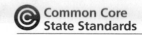 **Common Core State Standards**

L.9-10.1, L.9-10.6; W.9-10.4; SL.9-10.5
[For the full wording of the standards, see page 100.]

Use this prewriting activity to prepare for the **Writing Workshop** on page 172.

**PHLit**
**Online!**
www.PHLitOnline.com
- Interactive graphic organizers
- Grammar tutorial
- Interactive journals

## © Leveled Texts

Build your skills and improve your comprehension of fiction with texts of increasing complexity.

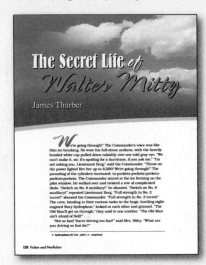

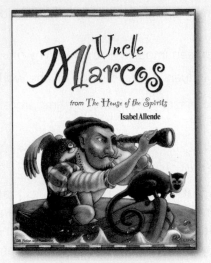

Read **"The Secret Life of Walter Mitty"** to learn how a man lives an imaginary life of adventure in his own mind.

Read **"Uncle Marcos"** to learn about an eccentric uncle's fabulously memorable life.

## © Common Core State Standards

Meet these standards with either **"The Secret Life of Walter Mitty"** (p. 128) or **"Uncle Marcos"** (p. 138).

**Reading Literature**

**3.** Analyze how complex characters develop over the course of a text, interact with other characters, and advance the plot or develop the theme. *(Literary Analysis: Character)*

**Spiral Review: RL.9-10.2**

**Writing**

**4.** Produce clear and coherent writing in which the development, organization, and style are appropriate to task, purpose, and audience. *(Writing: Character Profile)*

**6.** Use technology, including the Internet, to produce, publish, and update individual or shared writing products, taking advantage of technology's capacity to link to other information and to display information flexibly and dynamically. *(Research and Technology: Learning Log)*

**Language**

**1.** Demonstrate command of the conventions of standard English grammar and usage when writing or speaking. *(Conventions: Pronouns)*

**4.a.** Use context as a clue to the meaning of a word or phrase. *(Vocabulary: Word Study)*

**6.** Acquire and use accurately general academic and domain-specific words and phrases, sufficient for reading and listening at the college and career readiness level; demonstrate independence in gathering vocabulary knowledge when considering a word or phrase important to comprehension or expression. *(Vocabulary: Word Study)*

# Literary Analysis: Character

A **character** is a person or an animal who takes part in the action of a literary work. You can learn about a character through the character's words and actions, the author's narration, and what others say about the character.

- A **round character** is complex, showing many different qualities—revealing faults as well as virtues. In contrast, a **flat character** is one-dimensional, showing a single trait.

- A **dynamic character** develops, changes, and learns something during the course of a story—unlike a **static character,** who remains the same.

The main character of a story tends to be a round character and usually is a dynamic one. The main character's development and growth are often central to a story's plot and theme. As you read, consider the traits that make characters seem round or flat, dynamic or static.

# Reading Skill: Author's Purpose

An **author's purpose** is his or her main reason for writing. In fiction, the specific purpose is often expressed in the story's theme, message, or insight. Pause periodically while reading and **reflect** on the story's details and events to determine the author's purpose for relating this particular story. Ask questions such as the following:

- *What significance might this event have?*

- *Why does the author include this detail?*

Based on your reflections, formulate ideas about what the author's purpose might be.

### Using the Strategy: Author's Purpose Map

Use a chart like the one shown to organize your thoughts.

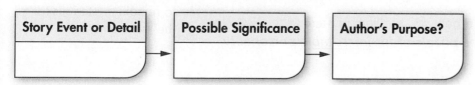

| Story Event or Detail | Possible Significance | Author's Purpose? |
|---|---|---|
| | | |

**www.PHLitOnline.com**

*Hear It!*
- Selection summary audio
- Selection audio

*See It!*
- Get Connected video
- Background video
- More about the author
- Vocabulary flashcards

*Do It!*
- Interactive journals
- Interactive graphic organizers
- Self-test
- Internet activity
- Grammar tutorial
- Interactive vocabulary games

# Can *truth* change?

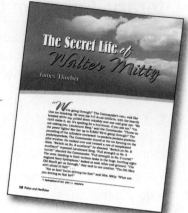

## Writing About the Big Question

In "The Secret Life of Walter Mitty," Mitty lives two lives: the one dominated by his wife and the one of his imagination. Use these sentence starters to develop your ideas about the Big Question.

Compared to our everyday life, the life of our imagination is _____.

**Truth** can change in our imagination because _____.

**While You Read** Look for details in the text that show how important Mitty's imagination is in his daily life.

## Vocabulary

Read each word and its definition. Decide whether you know the word well, know it a little bit, or do not know it at all. After you read, see how your knowledge of each word has increased.

- **distraught** (di strôt´) *adj.* very troubled or confused (p. 130) *She was distraught over losing her wallet.*

- **insolent** (in´ sə lənt) *adj.* boldly disrespectful (p. 130) *Her insolent words offended the guests. insolence n. insolently adv.*

- **insinuatingly** (in sin´ yōō āt´ iŋ lē) *adv.* suggesting indirectly (p. 131) *My friend looked at me insinuatingly, as if she thought I had taken the money from her purse. insinuate v. insinuation n.*

- **pandemonium** (pan´ də mō´ nē əm) *n.* any place or scene of wild disorder, noise, or confusion (p. 132) *When the band left the stage, the crowd erupted into pandemonium.*

- **derisive** (di rī´ siv) *adj.* showing contempt or ridicule (p. 134) *With a derisive laugh, the bully pushed the little boy off the swing. derision n. deride v.*

- **inscrutable** (in skrōōt´ ə bəl) *adj.* baffling; mysterious (p. 134) *No one has ever solved the puzzle of his inscrutable personality.*

### Word Study

The **Latin suffix -able** means "can or will" or "capable of being."

Thurber closes the story by describing Mitty as **inscrutable** to the end. The word choice indicates that Mitty is able to remain mysterious to the last moment.

# Meet
# James Thurber
### (1894–1961)

## Author of
# The Secret Life of Walter Mitty

James Thurber was a rare writer who expressed his comic genius in both words and pictures. He wrote stories, plays, essays, and poems, and he was also a great cartoonist. Born in Ohio, he joined the staff of *The New Yorker* magazine in 1927. "The Secret Life of Walter Mitty" was published in that magazine in 1939, becoming an instant success.

**Humor and Anxiety** Many of Thurber's stories and sketches grew directly out of his own life. As he put it, "Humor is a kind of emotional chaos told about calmly and quietly in retrospect." Thurber's characters try to stand up to the surprises of the modern world. Whether they succeed or fail, they always strike readers as authentic and very funny.

## BACKGROUND FOR THE STORY

**Reality and Imagination**

Psychologists say that a person's thoughts are often a series of seemingly unconnected reflections. An event in the real world can prompt unpredictable mental responses, such as memories, snippets of songs, or daydreams. In Thurber's story, random events cause Walter Mitty's thoughts to jump back and forth between his exciting "secret" life and his humdrum everyday existence.

### *Did You Know?*

Thurber offered a Hollywood producer $10,000 not to make a movie about Walter Mitty. The movie was made anyway in 1947. A new version is in development.

# The Secret Life of *Walter Mitty*

## James Thurber

"*W*e're going through!" The Commander's voice was like thin ice breaking. He wore his full-dress uniform, with the heavily braided white cap pulled down rakishly over one cold gray eye. "We can't make it, sir. It's spoiling for a hurricane, if you ask me." "I'm not asking you, Lieutenant Berg," said the Commander. "Throw on the power lights! Rev her up to 8,500! We're going through!" The pounding of the cylinders increased: ta-pocketa-pocketa-pocketa-*pocketa-pocketa*. The Commander stared at the ice forming on the pilot window. He walked over and twisted a row of complicated dials. "Switch on No. 8 auxiliary!" he shouted. "Switch on No. 8 auxiliary!" repeated Lieutenant Berg. "Full strength in No. 3 turret!" shouted the Commander. "Full strength in No. 3 turret!" The crew, bending to their various tasks in the huge, hurtling eight-engined Navy hydroplane,[1] looked at each other and grinned. "The Old Man'll get us through," they said to one another. "The Old Man ain't afraid of Hell!" . . .

"Not so fast! You're driving too fast!" said Mrs. Mitty. "What are you driving so fast for?"

---

**1. hydroplane** (hī´drō plān´) *n.* seaplane.

"Hmm?" said Walter Mitty. He looked at his wife, in the seat beside him, with shocked astonishment. She seemed grossly unfamiliar, like a strange woman who had yelled at him in a crowd. "You were up to fifty-five," she said. "You know I don't like to go more than forty. You were up to fifty-five." Walter Mitty drove on toward Waterbury in silence, the roaring of the SN202 through the worst storm in twenty years of Navy flying fading in the remote, intimate airways of his mind. "You're tensed up again," said Mrs. Mitty. "It's one of your days. I wish you'd let Dr. Renshaw look you over."

Walter Mitty stopped the car in front of the building where his wife went to have her hair done. "Remember to get those overshoes while I'm having my hair done," she said. "I don't need overshoes," said Mitty. She put her mirror back into her bag. "We've been all through that," she said, getting out of the car. "You're not a young man any longer." He raced the engine a little. "Why don't you wear your gloves? Have you lost your gloves?" Walter Mitty reached in a pocket and brought out the gloves. He put them on, but after she had turned and gone into the building and he had driven on to a red light, he took them off again. "Pick it up, brother!" snapped a cop as the light changed, and Mitty hastily pulled on his gloves and lurched ahead. He drove around the streets aimlessly for a time, and then he drove past the hospital on his way to the parking lot.

**Reading Skill**
**Author's Purpose**
Pause to reflect. What does the phrase "intimate airways of his mind" suggest about the author's purpose in writing this story?

Reading Check
Why is Mrs. Mitty upset?

**Vocabulary**

**distraught** (di strôt´)
*adj.* very troubled
or confused

. . . "It's the millionaire banker, Wellington McMillan," said the pretty nurse. "Yes?" said Walter Mitty, removing his gloves slowly. "Who has the case?" "Dr. Renshaw and Dr. Benbow, but there are two specialists here, Dr. Remington from New York and Mr. Pritchard-Mitford from London. He flew over." A door opened down a long, cool corridor and Dr. Renshaw came out. He looked distraught and haggard. "Hello, Mitty," he said. "We're having the devil's own time with McMillan, the millionaire banker and close personal friend of Roosevelt. Obstreosis of the ductal tract.[2] Tertiary. Wish you'd take a look at him." "Glad to," said Mitty.

In the operating room there were whispered introductions: "Dr. Remington, Dr. Mitty. Mr. Pritchard-Mitford, Dr. Mitty." "I've read your book on streptothricosis," said Pritchard-Mitford, shaking hands. "A brilliant performance, sir." "Thank you," said Walter Mitty. "Didn't know you were in the States, Mitty," grumbled Remington. "Coals to Newcastle,[3] bringing Mitford and me up here for tertiary." "You are very kind," said Mitty. A huge, complicated machine, connected to the operating table, with many tubes and wires, began at this moment to go pocketa-pocketa-pocketa. "The new anesthetizer is giving way!" shouted an intern. "There is no one in the East who knows how to fix it!" "Quiet, man!" said Mitty, in a low, cool voice. He sprang to the machine, which was now going pocketa-pocketa-queep-pocketa-queep. He began fingering delicately a row of glistening dials. "Give me a fountain pen!" he snapped. Someone handed him a fountain pen. He pulled a faulty piston out of the machine and inserted the pen in its place. "That will hold for ten minutes," he said. "Get on with the operation." A nurse hurried over and whispered to Renshaw, and Mitty saw the man turn pale. "Coreopsis has set in," said Renshaw nervously. "If you would take over, Mitty?" Mitty looked at him and at the craven figure of Benbow, who drank, and at the grave, uncertain faces of the two great specialists. "If you wish," he said. They slipped a white gown on him; he adjusted a mask and drew on thin gloves; nurses handed him shining . . .

"Back it up, Mac! Look out for that Buick!" Walter Mitty jammed on the brakes. "Wrong lane, Mac," said the parking-lot attendant, looking at Mitty closely. "Gee. Yeh," muttered Mitty. He began cautiously to back out of the lane marked "Exit Only." "Leave her sit there," said the attendant. "I'll put her away." Mitty got out of the car. "Hey, better leave the key." "Oh," said Mitty, handing the man the ignition key. The attendant vaulted into the car, backed it up with insolent skill, and put it where it belonged.

*Someone handed him a fountain pen.*

**Literary Analysis**
**Character**
How does this shift
in scenes show that
Walter Mitty is a
multidimensional
character?

**Vocabulary**
**insolent** (in´ sə lənt)
*adj.* boldly disrespectful

2. **obstreosis of the ductal tract** Thurber has invented this and other medical terms.
3. **coals to Newcastle** The proverb "bringing coals to Newcastle"
   means bringing things to a place unnecessarily—Newcastle, England,
   was a coal center and so did not need coal brought to it.

They're so cocky, thought Walter Mitty, walking along Main Street; they think they know everything. Once he had tried to take his chains off, outside New Milford, and he had got them wound around the axles. A man had had to come out in a wrecking car and unwind them, a young, grinning garageman. Since then Mrs. Mitty always made him drive to a garage to have the chains taken off. The next time, he thought, I'll wear my right arm in a sling; they won't grin at me then. I'll have my right arm in a sling and they'll see I couldn't possibly take the chains off myself. He kicked at the slush on the sidewalk. "Overshoes," he said to himself, and he began looking for a shoe store.

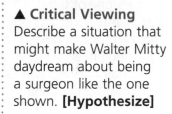

When he came out into the street again, with the overshoes in a box under his arm, Walter Mitty began to wonder what the other thing was his wife had told him to get. She had told him, twice, before they set out from their house for Waterbury. In a way he hated these weekly trips to town—he was always getting something wrong. Kleenex, he thought, Squibb's, razor blades? No. Toothpaste, toothbrush, bicarbonate, carborundum, initiative and referendum?[4] He gave it up. But she would remember it. "Where's the what's-its-name?" she would ask. "Don't tell me you forgot the what's-its-name." A newsboy went by shouting something about the Waterbury trial.

. . . "Perhaps this will refresh your memory." The District Attorney suddenly thrust a heavy automatic at the quiet figure on the witness stand. "Have you ever seen this before?" Walter Mitty took the gun and examined it expertly. "This is my Webley-Vickers 50.80," he said calmly. An excited buzz ran around the courtroom. The Judge rapped for order. "You are a crack shot with any sort of firearms, I believe?" said the District Attorney, insinuatingly. "Objection!" shouted Mitty's attorney. "We have shown that the defendant

---

**4. carborundum** (kär´ bə run´ dəm), **initiative** (i ni´ shē ə tiv) **and referendum** (ref´ ə ren´ dəm) Thurber is purposely making a nonsense list; *carborundum* is a hard substance used for scraping, *initiative* is a process by which citizens may introduce ideas for laws, and *referendum* is a process by which citizens may vote on laws.

▲ **Critical Viewing**
Describe a situation that might make Walter Mitty daydream about being a surgeon like the one shown. **[Hypothesize]**

**Vocabulary**
**insinuatingly**
(in sin´ yōō āt´ iŋ lē)
*adv.* suggesting indirectly

**Reading Check**
Why does Mitty say that next time he will wear his arm in a sling?

## Social Studies Connection

### The Royal Air Force

Although he is American, Mitty fantasizes about being a brave and handsome English officer, a bomber pilot in the Royal Air Force (RAF). The RAF was officially formed in 1918 and distinguished itself in numerous air battles during World War I. RAF pilots would earn even greater distinction in the Battle of Britain during World War II. The reference to "Von Richtman's circus" recalls one of the RAF's finest moments—the shooting down in 1918 of Baron Manfred von Richthofen, also known as "The Red Baron," who was Germany's greatest fighter pilot.

### Connect to the Literature

What elements of life in the RAF would Mitty enjoy?

**Vocabulary**
**pandemonium**
(pan´ də mō´ nē əm)
*n.* any place or scene of wild disorder, noise, or confusion

could not have fired the shot. We have shown that he wore his right arm in a sling on the night of the fourteenth of July." Walter Mitty raised his hand briefly and the bickering attorneys were stilled. "With any known make of gun," he said evenly, "I could have killed Gregory Fitzhurst at three hundred *feet with my left hand*." Pandemonium broke loose in the courtroom. A woman's scream rose above the bedlam and suddenly a lovely, dark-haired girl was in Walter Mitty's arms. The District Attorney struck at her savagely. Without rising from his chair, Mitty let the man have it on the point of the chin. "You miserable cur!" . . .

"Puppy biscuit," said Walter Mitty. He stopped walking and the buildings of Waterbury rose up out of the misty courtroom and surrounded him again. A woman who was passing laughed. "He said 'Puppy biscuit,'" she said to her companion. "That man said 'Puppy biscuit' to himself." Walter Mitty hurried on. He went into an A. & P., not the first one he came to but a smaller one farther up the street. "I want some biscuit for small, young dogs," he said to the clerk. "Any special brand, sir?" The greatest pistol shot in the world thought a moment. "It says 'Puppies Bark for It' on the box," said Walter Mitty.

His wife would be through at the hairdresser's in fifteen minutes, Mitty saw in looking at his watch, unless they had trouble drying it; sometimes they had trouble drying it. She didn't like to get to the hotel first;

she would want him to be there waiting for her as usual. He found a big leather chair in the lobby, facing a window, and he put the overshoes and the puppy biscuit on the floor beside it. He picked up an old copy of *Liberty* and sank down into the chair. "Can Germany Conquer the World Through the Air?" Walter Mitty looked at the pictures of bombing planes and of ruined streets.

. . . "The cannonading has got the wind up in young Raleigh,[5] sir," said the sergeant. Captain Mitty looked up at him through tousled hair. "Get him to bed," he said wearily. "With the others. I'll fly alone." "But you can't, sir," said the sergeant anxiously. "It takes two men to handle that bomber and the Archies[6] are pounding hell out of the air. Von Richtman's circus[7] is between here and Saulier." "Somebody's got to get that ammunition dump," said Mitty. "I'm going over. Spot of brandy?" He poured a drink for the sergeant and one for himself. War thundered and whined around the dugout and battered at the door. There was a rending of wood and splinters flew through the room. "A bit of a near thing," said Captain Mitty carelessly. "The box barrage is closing in," said the sergeant. "We only live once, Sergeant," said Mitty, with his faint, fleeting smile. "Or do we?" He poured another brandy and tossed it off. "I never see a man could hold his brandy like you, sir," said the sergeant. "Begging your pardon, sir." Captain Mitty stood up and strapped on his huge Webley-Vickers automatic. "It's forty kilometers through hell, sir," said the sergeant. Mitty finished one last brandy. "After all," he said softly, "what isn't?" The pounding of the cannon increased; there was the rat-tat-tatting of machine guns, and from somewhere came the menacing pocketa-pocketa-pocketa of the new flame-throwers. Walter Mitty walked to the door of the dugout humming "Auprés de Ma Blonde."[8] He turned and waved to the sergeant. "Cheerio!" he said. . . .

Something struck his shoulder. "I've been looking all over this hotel for you," said Mrs. Mitty. "Why do you have to hide in this old chair? How did you expect me to find you?" "Things close in," said Walter Mitty vaguely. "What?" Mrs. Mitty said. "Did you get the what's-its-name? The puppy biscuit? What's in that box?" "Overshoes," said Mitty. "Couldn't you have put them on in the store?"

---

5. **has got the wind up in young Raleigh** has made young Raleigh nervous.
6. **Archies** slang term for antiaircraft guns.
7. **Von Richtman's circus** a fictional German airplane squadron.
8. **"Auprés de Ma Blonde"** (ō prä´ də mä blôn´ də) "Next to My Blonde," a popular French song.

**Spiral Review**
**Theme** What insight into daily life is suggested by the contrast between Mitty's daydreams and his reality?

*"We only live once, Sergeant,"* said Mitty, with his faint, fleeting smile.

**Reading Check**
What triggers Mitty's daydream about being a military Captain?

**Vocabulary**
**derisive** (di rī′siv) *adj.*
showing contempt
or ridicule


**Literary Analysis**
**Character**
How do Walter Mitty's
responses in this
paragraph indicate
that he is a complex
character?


**Vocabulary**
**inscrutable** (in skrōōt′
ə bəl) *adj.* baffling;
mysterious

"I was thinking," said Walter Mitty. "Does it ever occur to you that I am sometimes thinking?" She looked at him. "I'm going to take your temperature when I get you home," she said.

They went out through the revolving doors that made a faintly derisive whistling sound when you pushed them. It was two blocks to the parking lot. At the drugstore on the corner she said, "Wait here for me. I forgot something. I won't be a minute." She was more than a minute. Walter Mitty lighted a cigarette. It began to rain, rain with sleet in it. He stood up against the wall of the drugstore, smoking. . . . He put his shoulders back and his heels together. "To hell with the handkerchief," said Walter Mitty scornfully. He took one last drag on his cigarette and snapped it away. Then, with that faint, fleeting smile playing about his lips, he faced the firing squad; erect and motionless, proud and disdainful, Walter Mitty the Undefeated, inscrutable to the last.

## Critical Thinking

*Cite textual evidence to support your responses.*

1. **Key Ideas and Details (a)** What distraction jars Mitty out of his first daydream? **(b) Compare and Contrast:** Explain how Mitty's behavior in this daydream differs from his behavior in real life.

2. **Key Ideas and Details (a)** In the "real world," what tasks are Mitty and his wife carrying out? **(b) Infer:** What deeds is Mitty attempting to accomplish in his fantasy life? **(c) Compare and Contrast:** How do the tasks of his daily life compare to those of his fantasy life?

3. **Key Ideas and Details (a) Infer:** Which aspects of Mitty's personality trigger his final daydream? **(b) Draw Conclusions:** In what ways is this daydream a comment on his fate in real life?

4. **Key Ideas and Details (a) Evaluate:** Do Mitty's daydreams help him in any way or do they hurt him? Identify three details from the story that support your evaluation. **(b) Discuss:** Share your responses with a small group and discuss the differences and similarities among them.

5. **Integration of Knowledge and Ideas** Does Walter Mitty rely on daydreams to change the truth of his everyday life? *[Connect to the Big Question: Can truth change?]*

## Literary Analysis: Character

**1. Key Ideas and Details** Mitty wants to be like the heroes in his daydreams. **(a)** Using a chart like the one shown, identify one detail from each of Mitty's daydreams and the quality that each detail reveals.

| Details of Daydreams | | Desired Character Traits |
|---|---|---|
| "The Old Man'll get us through." | → | Leadership |

**(b)** Briefly describe the **character** of the man Mitty wants to be.

**2. Craft and Structure** Review the characters of Walter and Mrs. Mitty. **(a)** Determine whether each character is **round** or **flat.** Explain your responses. **(b)** Determine whether each character is **static** or **dynamic.** Explain.

## Reading Skill: Author's Purpose

**3. (a)** What specific **purpose** might James Thurber have had for creating the character of Walter Mitty? **(b)** Identify three details from the story that support your responses, and explain how **reflecting** on them helped you determine Thurber's purpose.

## Vocabulary

**Acquisition and Use** Review the vocabulary list for "The Secret Life of Walter Mitty" on page 126. Then, decide whether each of the following statements is true or false. Explain your answers.

**1.** Someone who is *distraught* is likely to behave in a calm manner.

**2.** Coaches encourage their players to be *insolent.*

**3.** *Inscrutable* handwriting is difficult to interpret.

**4.** If you speak *insinuatingly*, you say exactly what you mean.

**5.** A *derisive* comment shows great kindness.

**6.** *Pandemonium* might result if you gave unlimited candy to kindergarten students.

**Word Study** Use the context of sentences and what you know about the **Latin suffix -able** to explain your answer to each question.

**1.** Should you give up when facing an *achievable* goal?

**2.** If two bicycles are *comparable*, are they much alike?

### Word Study

The **Latin suffix -able** means "can or will" or "capable of being."

**Apply It** Explain how the suffix contributes to the meanings of these words. Consult a dictionary if necessary.

**unpalatable**
**interminable**
**portable**

# Can *truth* change?

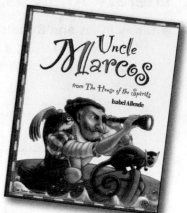

## Writing About the Big Question

In "Uncle Marcos," the narrator describes the fantastic escapades of an uncle who is not satisfied with the ordinary. Use these sentence starters to develop your ideas about the Big Question.

A person who **believes** strongly in impractical and impossible things may _____ .

**Manipulating** the **truth** can be _____ because _____ .

**While You Read** Look for details that show how Uncle Marcos created his own realities.

## Vocabulary

Read each word and its definition. Decide whether you know the word well, know it a little bit, or do not know it at all. After you read, see how your knowledge of each word has increased.

- **pallid** (pal´ id) *adj.* pale (p. 139) *The flu gave him a weak and pallid appearance.* *pallidness n. pallidly adv. pallor n.*

- **impassive** (im pas´ iv) *adj.* showing no emotion (p. 141) *She wanted to cry, but her face remained impassive as she watched her daughter leave for college.* *passive adj.*

- **conspicuous** (kən spik´ yo͞o əs) *adj.* attracting attention by being unexpected, unusual or outstanding (p. 141) *Renee felt conspicuous in her red coat and hat.* *inconspicuous adj.*

- **disconsolately** (dis kän´ sə lit lē) *adv.* very unhappily (p. 144) *He gazed disconsolately as his friends drove to the game without him.* *disconsolate adj. consolation n. console v.*

- **pertinent** (pʉrt´ 'n ənt) *adj.* relevant; to the point (p. 146) *Your outrageous comments are not at all pertinent to our discussion.* *pertinence n. impertinent adj.*

- **unrequited** (un ri kwīt´ id) *adj.* not returned or repaid (p. 146) *Romance novels sometimes describe the sadness of unrequited love.*

### Word Study

The **Latin suffix -ive** means "of, belonging to, or quality of."

In this story, Uncle Marcos cannot believe that any woman could remain **impassive** when listening to a barrel organ. He thinks the organ must surely evoke the quality of passion.

Author of

## Uncle Marcos

The daughter of diplomats, Isabel Allende grew up in the South American country of Chile. Her uncle was the Chilean president Salvador Allende. When his government was overthrown in 1973, Allende fled to Venezuela. She lived there in exile until 1988, when she moved to California.

**Family and Fiction** "Uncle Marcos" is excerpted from Allende's first novel, *The House of the Spirits*, which was inspired by her own remarkable family. Allende's family stories, however, are usually told with large helpings of imagination. She delights in blending the real and the imaginary. Allende once summed up her profession by quoting her granddaughter. Asked what it means to have a great imagination, the child replied, "You can remember what never happened."

### BACKGROUND FOR THE STORY

**Magical Realism**

Imagine a world in which people float in the air and rain falls continuously for years. Such fantastic details fill stories and novels by a group of writers, including Isabel Allende, who are called magical realists. Works of magical realism blend fantastic details with realistic ones to stretch the boundaries of readers' imaginations.

## Did You Know?

Allende's first novel, *The House of the Spirits*, began as a letter to her 100-year-old grandfather.

# Uncle Marcos

## from *The House of the Spirits*

### Isabel Allende

It had been two years since Clara had last seen her Uncle Marcos, but she remembered him very well. His was the only perfectly clear image she retained from her whole childhood, and in order to describe him she did not need to consult the daguerreotype[1] in the drawing room that showed him dressed as an explorer leaning on an old-fashioned double-barreled rifle with his right foot on the neck of a Malaysian tiger, the same triumphant position in which she had seen the Virgin standing between plaster clouds and *pallid* angels at the main altar, one foot on the vanquished devil. All Clara had to do to see her uncle was close her eyes and there he was, weather-beaten and thin, with a pirate's mustache through which his strange, sharklike smile peered out at her. It seemed impossible that he could be inside that long black box that was lying in the middle of the courtyard.

Each time Uncle Marcos had visited his sister Nivea's home, he had stayed for several months, to the immense joy of his nieces and nephews, particularly Clara, causing a storm in which the sharp lines of domestic order blurred. The house became a clutter of trunks, of animals in jars of formaldehyde,[2] of Indian lances and sailor's bundles. In every part of the house people kept tripping over his equipment, and all sorts of unfamiliar animals appeared that had traveled from remote lands only to meet their death beneath Nana's irate broom in the farthest corners of the house. Uncle Marcos's manners were those of a cannibal, as Severo put it. He spent the whole night making incomprehensible movements in the drawing room; later they turned out to be exercises designed to perfect the mind's control over the body and to improve digestion. He performed alchemy[3] experiments in the kitchen, filling the house with fetid smoke and ruining pots and pans with solid substances that stuck to their bottoms and were impossible to remove. While

**Vocabulary**
**pallid** (pal′ id) *adj.* pale

Reading
Check
What happens to the order of the house when Uncle Marcos visits?

---

1. **daguerreotype** (də ger′ ō tīp′) *n.* early type of photograph.
2. **formaldehyde** (for mal′ də hīd′) *n.* solution used as a preservative.
3. **alchemy** (al′ kə mē) *n.* early form of chemistry with philosophic and magical associations.

▲ Barrel organ

the rest of the household tried to sleep, he dragged his suitcases up and down the halls, practiced making strange, high-pitched sounds on savage instruments, and taught Spanish to a parrot whose native language was an Amazonic dialect. During the day, he slept in a hammock that he had strung between two columns in the hall, wearing only a loincloth that put Severo in a terrible mood but that Nivea forgave because Marcos had convinced her that it was the same costume in which Jesus of Nazareth had preached. Clara remembered perfectly, even though she had been only a tiny child, the first time her Uncle Marcos came to the house after one of his voyages. He settled in as if he planned to stay forever. After a short time, bored with having to appear at ladies' gatherings where the mistress of the house played the piano, with playing cards, and with dodging all his relatives' pressures to pull himself together and take a job as a clerk in Severo del Valle's law practice, he bought a barrel organ and took to the streets with the hope of seducing his Cousin Antonieta and entertaining the public in the bargain. The machine was just a rusty box with wheels, but he painted it with seafaring designs and gave it a fake ship's smokestack. It ended up looking like a coal stove. The organ played either a military march or a waltz, and in between turns of the handle the parrot, who had managed to learn Spanish although he had not lost his foreign accent, would draw a crowd with his piercing shrieks. He also plucked slips of paper from a box with his beak, by way of selling fortunes to the curious. The little pink, green, and blue papers were so clever that they always divulged the exact secret wishes of the customers. Besides fortunes there were little balls of sawdust to amuse the children. The idea of the organ was a last desperate attempt to win the hand of Cousin Antonieta after more conventional means of courting her had failed. Marcos thought no

> *The organ played either a military march or a waltz...*

woman in her right mind could remain impassive before a barrel-organ serenade. He stood beneath her window one evening and played his military march and his waltz just as she was taking tea with a group of female friends. Antonieta did not realize the music was meant for her until the parrot called her by her full name, at which point she appeared in the window. Her reaction was not what her suitor had hoped for. Her friends offered to spread the news to every salon[4] in the city, and the next day people thronged the downtown streets hoping to see Severo del Valle's brother-in-law playing the organ and selling little sawdust balls with a motheaten parrot, for the sheer pleasure of proving that even in the best of families there could be good reason for embarrassment. In the face of this stain to the family reputation, Marcos was forced to give up organ grinding and resort to less conspicuous ways of winning over his Cousin Antonieta, but he did not renounce his goal. In any case, he did not succeed, because from one day to the next the young lady married a diplomat who was twenty years her senior; he took her to live in a tropical country whose name no one could recall, except that it suggested negritude,[5] bananas, and palm trees, where she managed to recover from the memory of that suitor who had ruined her seventeenth year with his military march and his waltz. Marcos sank into a deep depression that lasted two or three days, at the end of which he announced that he would never marry and that he was embarking on a trip around the world. He sold his organ to a blind man and left the parrot to Clara, but Nana secretly poisoned it with an overdose of cod-liver oil, because no one could stand its lusty glance, its fleas, and its harsh, tuneless hawking of paper fortunes and sawdust balls. •

That was Marcos's longest trip. He returned with a shipment of enormous boxes that were piled in the far courtyard, between the chicken coop and the woodshed, until the winter was over. At the first signs of spring he had them transferred to the parade grounds, a huge park where people would gather to watch the soldiers file by on Independence Day, with the goosestep they had learned from the Prussians. When the crates were opened, they were found to contain

---

4. **salon** (sə län´) *n.* regular gathering of distinguished guests that meets in a private home.
5. **negritude** (neg´ rə tood´) *n.* blacks and their cultural heritage.

**Vocabulary**
**impassive** (im pas´ iv)
*adj.* showing no emotion

**Literary Analysis**
**Character** In what way does Uncle Marcos's behavior suggest that he is a multidimensional character?

**Vocabulary**
**conspicuous**
(kən spik´ yoo əs) *adj.* attracting attention by being unexpected, unusual or outstanding

☑ Reading Check
What does Uncle Marcos do with the barrel organ?

loose bits of wood, metal, and painted cloth. Marcos spent two weeks assembling the contents according to an instruction manual written in English, which he was able to decipher thanks to his invincible imagination and a small dictionary. When the job was finished, it turned out to be a bird of prehistoric dimensions, with the face of a furious eagle, wings that moved, and a propeller on its back. It caused an uproar. The families of the oligarchy[6] forgot all about the barrel organ, and Marcos became the star attraction of the season. People took Sunday outings to see the bird; souvenir vendors and strolling photographers made a fortune. Nonetheless, the public's interest quickly waned. But then Marcos announced that as soon as the weather cleared he planned to take off in his bird and cross the mountain range. The news spread, making this the most talked-about event of the year. The contraption lay with its stomach on terra firma,[7] heavy and sluggish and looking more like a wounded duck than like one of those newfangled airplanes they were starting to produce in the United States. There was nothing in its appearance to suggest that it could move, much less take flight across the snowy peaks. Journalists and the curious flocked to see it. Marcos smiled his immutable[8] smile before the avalanche of questions and posed for photographers without offering the least technical or scientific explanation of how he hoped to carry out his plan. People came from the provinces to see the sight. Forty years later his great-nephew Nicolás, whom Marcos did not live to see, unearthed the desire to fly that had always existed in the men of his lineage. Nicolás was interested in doing it for commercial reasons, in a gigantic hot-air sausage on which would be printed an advertisement for carbonated drinks. But when Marcos announced his plane trip, no one believed that his contraption could be put to any practical use. The appointed day dawned full of clouds, but so many people had turned out that Marcos did not want to disappoint them. He showed up punctually at the appointed spot and did not once look up at the sky, which was growing darker and darker with thick gray clouds. The astonished crowd filled all the nearby streets, perching on rooftops and the balconies of the nearest houses and squeezing into the park.

**Spiral Review**

**Theme** What insights into human nature are suggested by the various reactions to Uncle Marcos and his giant bird? Explain.

▼ **Critical Viewing**

In this story, a man builds a flying machine. Which character traits might you find in someone who would try to do this? **[Speculate]**

6. **oligarchy** (äl´ i gar´ kē) *n.* government ruled by a few.
7. **terra firma** (ter´ a fʉr´ ma) *n.* Latin term meaning "firm earth; solid ground."
8. **immutable** (im myōōt´ ə bəl) *adj.* never changing.

No political gathering managed to attract so many people until half a century later, when the first Marxist candidate attempted, through strictly democratic channels, to become President. Clara would remember this holiday as long as she lived. People dressed in their spring best, thereby getting a step ahead of the official opening of the season, the men in white linen suits and the ladies in the Italian straw hats that were all the rage that year. Groups of elementary-school children paraded with their teachers, clutching flowers for the hero. Marcos accepted their bouquets and joked that they might as well hold on to them and wait for him to crash, so they could take them directly to his funeral. The bishop himself, accompanied by two incense bearers, appeared to bless the bird without having been asked, and the police band played happy, unpretentious music that pleased everyone. The police, on horseback and carrying lances, had trouble keeping the crowds far enough away from the center of the park, where Marcos waited dressed in mechanic's overalls, with huge racer's goggles and an explorer's helmet. He was also equipped with a compass, a telescope, and several strange maps that he had traced himself based on various theories of Leonardo da Vinci and on the polar knowledge of the Incas.[9] Against all logic, on the second try the bird lifted off without mishap and with a certain elegance, accompanied by the creaking of its skeleton and the roar of its motor. It rose flapping its wings and disappeared into the clouds, to a send-off of applause, whistlings, handkerchiefs, drumrolls, and the sprinkling of holy water. All that remained on earth were the comments of the amazed crowd below and a multitude of experts, who attempted to provide a reasonable explanation of the miracle. Clara continued to stare at the sky long after her uncle had become invisible. She thought she saw him ten minutes later, but it was only a migrating sparrow. After three days the initial euphoria that had accompanied the first airplane flight in the country died down and no one gave the episode another thought, except for Clara, who continued to peer at the horizon.

---

9. **Leonardo da Vinci** (lē′ ə när′ dō də vin′ chē) **. . . Incas** Leonardo da Vinci (1452–1519) was an Italian painter, sculptor, architect, and scientist. The Incas were Native Americans who dominated ancient Peru until the Spanish conquest.

**Reading Skill**
**Author's Purpose**
What does the statement "Clara would remember this holiday as long as she lived" suggest about the author's purpose in this story?

> *A*gainst all logic, on the second try the bird lifted off without mishap...

**Reading Check**
Where does Uncle Marcos plan to fly in his flying machine?

After a week with no word from the flying uncle, people began to speculate that he had gone so high that he had disappeared into outer space, and the ignorant suggested he would reach the moon. With a mixture of sadness and relief, Severo decided that his brother-in-law and his machine must have fallen into some hidden crevice of the cordillera,[10] where they would never be found. Nivea wept disconsolately and lit candles to San Antonio, patron of lost objects. Severo opposed the idea of having masses said, because he did not believe in them as a way of getting into heaven, much less of returning to earth, and he maintained that masses and religious vows, like the selling of indulgences, images, and scapulars,[11] were a dishonest business. Because of his attitude, Nivea and Nana had the children say the rosary,[12] behind their father's back for nine days. Meanwhile, groups of volunteer explorers and mountain climbers tirelessly searched peaks and passes, combing every accessible stretch of land until they finally returned in triumph to hand the family the mortal remains of the deceased in a sealed black coffin. The intrepid traveler was laid to rest in a grandiose funeral. His death made him a hero and his name was on the front page of all the papers for several days. The same multitude that had gathered to see him off the day he flew away in his bird paraded past his coffin. The entire family wept as befit the occasion, except for Clara, who continued to watch the sky with the patience of an astronomer. One week after he had been buried, Uncle Marcos, a bright smile playing behind his pirate's mustache, appeared in person in the doorway of Nivea and Severo del Valle's house. Thanks to the surreptitious[13] prayers of the women and children, as he himself admitted, he was alive and well and in full possession of his faculties, including his sense of humor. Despite the noble lineage of his aerial maps, the flight had been a failure. He had lost his airplane and had to return on foot, but he had not broken any bones and his adventurous spirit was intact. This confirmed the family's eternal devotion to San Antonio, but was not taken as a warning by future generations, who also tried to fly, although by different means. Legally, however, Marcos was a corpse. Severo del Valle was obliged to use all his legal ingenuity to bring his brother-in-law back to life and the full rights of citizenship. When the coffin was pried open in the presence of the appropriate authorities, it was found to contain a bag of sand. This discovery ruined the

**Reading Skill**
**Author's Purpose**
What do the narrator's observations about Marcos suggest about the author's purpose?

**Literary Analysis**
**Character**
Which details in this passage indicate that Marcos has changed since the beginning of the story?

---

10. **cordillera** (kôr´ dil yer´ ə) *n.* system or chain of mountains.
11. **indulgences, images, and scapulars** (skap´ yə lərz) Indulgences are pardons for sins; images are pictures or sculptures of religious figures; scapulars are garments worn by Roman Catholics as tokens of religious devotion.
12. **say the rosary** use a set of beads to say prayers.
13. **surreptitious** (sʉr´ əp tish´ əs) *adj.* secretive.

reputation, up till then untarnished, of the volunteer explorers and mountain climbers, who from that day on were considered little better than a pack of bandits.

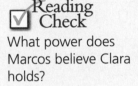

● Marcos's heroic resurrection made everyone forget about his barrel-organ phase. Once again he was a sought-after guest in all the city's salons and, at least for a while, his name was cleared. Marcos stayed in his sister's house for several months. One night he left without saying goodbye, leaving behind his trunks, his books, his weapons, his boots, and all his belongings. Severo, and even Nivea herself, breathed a sigh of relief. His visit had gone on too long. But Clara was so upset that she spent a week walking in her sleep and sucking her thumb. The little girl, who was only seven at the time, had learned to read from her uncle's storybooks and been closer to him than any other member of the family because of her prophesying powers. Marcos maintained that his niece's gift could be a source of income and a good opportunity for him to cultivate his own clairvoyance.[14] He believed that all human beings possessed this ability, particularly his own family, and that if it did not function well it was simply due to a lack of training. He bought a crystal ball in the Persian bazaar, insisting that it had magic powers and was from the East (although it was later found to be part of a buoy from a fishing boat), set it down on a background of black velvet, and announced that he could tell people's fortunes, cure the evil eye, and improve the quality of dreams, all for the modest sum of five centavos.[15] His first customers were the maids from around the neighborhood. One of them had been accused of stealing, because her employer had misplaced a valuable ring. The crystal ball revealed the exact location of the object in question: it had rolled beneath a wardrobe. The next day there was a line outside the front door of the house. There were coachmen, storekeepers, and milkmen; later a few municipal employees and distinguished ladies made a discreet appearance, slinking along the side walls of the house to keep from being recognized. The customers were

> *A*fter a week with no word from the flying uncle, people began to speculate that he had gone so high that he had disappeared into outer space...

**Reading Check**

What power does Marcos believe Clara holds?

---

14. **clairvoyance** (kler voi´ əns) *n.* supposed ability to perceive unseen things.
15. **centavos** (sen tä´ vōs) *n.* coins equal to 1/100 of a *cruzeiro*, the basic monetary unit of Brazil.

received by Nana, who ushered them into the waiting room and collected their fees. This task kept her busy throughout the day and demanded so much of her time that the family began to complain that all there ever was for dinner was old string beans and jellied quince.[16] Marcos decorated the carriage house with some frayed curtains that had once belonged in the drawing room but that neglect and age had turned to dusty rags. There he and Clara received the customers. The two divines wore tunics "color of the men of light," as Marcos called the color yellow. Nana had dyed them with saffron powder, boiling them in pots usually reserved for rice and pasta. In addition to his tunic, Marcos wore a turban around his head and an Egyptian amulet around his neck. He had grown a beard and let his hair grow long and he was thinner than ever before. Marcos and Clara were utterly convincing, especially because the child had no need to look into the crystal ball to guess what her clients wanted to hear. She would whisper in her Uncle Marcos's ear, and he in turn would transmit the message to the client, along with any improvisations of his own that he thought pertinent. Thus their fame spread, because all those who arrived sad and bedraggled at the consulting room left filled with hope.

Unrequited lovers were told how to win over indifferent hearts, and the poor left with foolproof tips on how to place their money at the dog tracks. Business grew so prosperous that the waiting room was always packed with people, and Nana began to suffer dizzy spells from being on her feet so many hours a day. This time Severo had no need to intervene to put a stop to his brother-in-law's venture, for both Marcos and Clara, realizing that their unerring guesses could alter the fate of their clients, who always followed their advice to the letter, became frightened and decided that this was a job for swindlers. They abandoned their carriage-house oracle and split the profits, even though the only one who had cared about the material side of things had been Nana. •

Of all the del Valle children, Clara was the one with the greatest interest in and stamina for her uncle's stories. She could repeat each and every one of them. She knew by heart words from several dialects of the Indians, was acquainted with their customs, and could describe the exact way in which they pierced their lips and earlobes with wooden shafts, their initiation rites, the names of the most poisonous snakes, and the appropriate antidotes for each. Her uncle was so eloquent that the child could feel in her own skin the burning sting of snakebites, see reptiles slide across the carpet between the legs of the jacaranda[17] room divider, and hear the

**Vocabulary**
**pertinent** (pʉrt´ 'n ənt)
*adj.* relevant; to the point
**unrequited** (un ri kwīt´ id) *adj.* not returned or repaid

**Literary Analysis**
**Character**
Which details in this paragraph indicate that Clara, like Marcos, is a complex character?

---

16. **quince** (kwins) hard, gold or greenish-yellow apple-shaped fruit.
17. **jacaranda** (jak´ ə ran´ də) type of tropical American tree.

shrieks of macaws behind the drawing-room drapes. She did not hesitate as she recalled Lope de Aguirre's search for El Dorado,[18] or the unpronounceable names of the flora and fauna her extraordinary uncle had seen; she knew about the lamas who take salt tea with yak lard and she could give detailed descriptions of the opulent women of Tahiti, the rice fields of China, or the white prairies of the North, where the eternal ice kills animals and men who lose their way, turning them to stone in seconds. Marcos had various travel journals in which he recorded his excursions and impressions, as well as a collection of maps and books of stories and fairy tales that he kept in the trunks he stored in the junk room at the far end of the third courtyard. From there they were hauled out to inhabit the dreams of his descendants, until they were mistakenly burned half a century later on an infamous pyre.

Now Marcos had returned from his last journey in a coffin. He had died of a mysterious African plague that had turned him as yellow and wrinkled as a piece of parchment. When he realized he was ill, he set out for home with the hope that his sister's ministrations and Dr. Cuevas's knowledge would restore his health and youth, but he was unable to withstand the sixty days on ship and died at the latitude of Guayaquil,[19] ravaged by fever and hallucinating about musky women and hidden treasure. The captain of the ship, an Englishman by the name of Longfellow, was about to throw him overboard wrapped in a flag, but Marcos, despite his savage appearance and his delirium, had made so many friends on board and seduced so many women that the

---

18. **Lope de Aguirre's** (lō′ pā dā ä gēr′ rās) **. . . El Dorado** Lope de Aguirre was a Spanish adventurer (1518–1561) in colonial South America who searched for a legendary country called El Dorado, which was supposedly rich in gold.
19. **Guayaquil** (gwī′ ä kēl′) seaport in western Ecuador.

## LITERATURE IN CONTEXT

### Humanities Connection

**Magical Realists**

The literary movement known as Magical Realism is most closely associated with the wonder-filled novels and short stories of a group of twentieth-century Latin American authors. Isabel Allende is an important writer in this group. The great Argentinian writer Jorge Luis Borges is another. His style often combines realistic characters and events with details that seem to come out of dreams and myths. Gabriel García Márquez of Colombia is often considered the central figure of the movement. His works chronicle the lives of passionate and sympathetic characters who experience miraculous happenings and strange, unearthly events.

### Connect to the Literature

What elements of "Uncle Marcos" confirm that it belongs to the literary movement known as Magical Realism?

**Reading Check**

Who loves hearing Marcos's stories the most?

passengers prevented him from doing so, and Longfellow was obliged to store the body side by side with the vegetables of the Chinese cook, to preserve it from the heat and mosquitoes of the tropics until the ship's carpenter had time to improvise a coffin. At El Callao[20] they obtained a more appropriate container, and several days later the captain, furious at all the troubles this passenger had caused the shipping company and himself personally, unloaded him without a backward glance, surprised that not a soul was there to receive the body or cover the expenses he had incurred. Later he learned that the post office in these latitudes was not as reliable as that of far-off England, and that all his telegrams had vaporized en route. Fortunately for Longfellow, a customs lawyer who was a friend of the del Valle family appeared and offered to take charge, placing Marcos and all his paraphernalia in a freight car, which he shipped to the capital to the only known address of the deceased: his sister's house. . . .

---

**20. El Callao** (kə yä´ ō) seaport in western Peru.

## Critical Thinking

Cite textual evidence to support your responses.

1. **Key Ideas and Details (a)** What does Uncle Marcos do to try to win the hand of Cousin Antonieta? **(b) Connect:** Is her reaction what Uncle Marcos expects? Use details from the text to explain.

2. **Key Ideas and Details (a)** What does Uncle Marcos make from the materials he brings back in "enormous boxes"?
**(b) Infer:** What do you think motivates Uncle Marcos to undertake this project?

3. **Key Ideas and Details (a) Compare and Contrast:** Compare and contrast Clara's reaction to her uncle's disappearance with those of the others. **(b) Interpret:** What does Clara's reaction show about her personality and relationship to Uncle Marcos? Explain.

4. **Key Ideas and Details (a) Draw Conclusions:** What life lessons can people learn from the character of Uncle Marcos?
**(b) Discuss:** Share your responses with a group and discuss similarities and differences among them. **(c) Reflect:** How has the discussion affected your response?

5. **Integration of Knowledge and Ideas (a)** How is Uncle Marcos's reality different from that of the narrator and other characters?
**(b)** Which reality do you think is truer? Defend your answers.
*[Connect to the Big Question: Can truth change?]*

## Literary Analysis: Character

© **1. Key Ideas and Details (a)** Using a chart like the one shown, list at least three of Uncle Marcos's projects or adventures. Then, identify a quality that each project or adventure reveals.

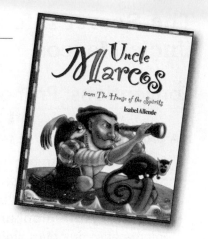

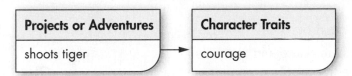

| Projects or Adventures | | Character Traits |
|---|---|---|
| shoots tiger | → | courage |

**(b)** Based on his projects and adventures, summarize the **character** of Uncle Marcos in a few sentences.

© **2. Craft and Structure** Review the characters of Clara and Uncle Marcos. **(a)** Determine whether each character is **round** or **flat.** Explain your responses. **(b)** Explain whether each character is **static** or **dynamic.**

## Reading Skill: Author's Purpose

**3. (a)** What specific **purpose** might Isabel Allende have had for creating the character of Uncle Marcos? **(b)** Identify three details from the story that support your response and explain how **reflecting** on them helped you determine Allende's purpose.

## Vocabulary

© **Acquisition and Use** Review the vocabulary list for "Uncle Marcos" on page 136. Then, decide whether each of the following statements is true or false. Explain your answers.

**1.** Something that looks *pallid* is full of color.

**2.** Sighing *disconsolately* is a good way to express enthusiasm.

**3.** *Unrequited* love is symbolized by a wedding.

**4.** Standing on your head in public would be considered *conspicuous*.

**5.** A *pertinent* detail has absolutely nothing to do with the topic.

**6.** You can easily read the mood of an *impassive* person.

**Word Study** Use the context of the sentences and what you know about the **Latin suffix -ive** to explain your answer to each question.

**1.** Do *permissive* parents allow their children their freedom?

**2.** If people are *cooperative*, will they refuse to work together?

---

### Word Study

The **Latin suffix -ive** means "of, belonging to, or quality of."

**Apply It** Explain how the suffix contributes to the meanings of these words. Consult a dictionary if necessary.

**derisive**
**collective**
**festive**

# Integrated Language Skills

## The Secret Life of Walter Mitty • Uncle Marcos

### Conventions: Pronouns

A **pronoun** is a word that stands for a noun.

- A **relative pronoun** begins a subordinate clause and connects it to another idea in the sentence. The five relative pronouns are *that, which, who, whom,* and *whose.*
- An **interrogative pronoun** is used to begin a question. The five interrogative pronouns are *what, which, who, whom,* and *whose.*
- **Indefinite pronouns** refer to people, places, or things, often without specifying which ones.

| Indefinite Pronouns | | | | | | |
|---|---|---|---|---|---|---|
| **Singular** | | | | **Plural** | **Singular or Plural** | |
| another | either | much | one | both | all | most |
| anybody | everybody | neither | other | few | any | none |
| anyone | everyone | nobody | somebody | many | more | some |
| anything | everything | no one | someone | others | | |
| each | little | nothing | something | several | | |

**Practice A** Identify the pronouns in each sentence, and tell whether each one is relative, interrogative, or indefinite.

1. No one knew about Mitty's daydreams.
2. Who doesn't daydream occasionally?
3. Mitty was a courageous pilot who saved his crew from certain death.
4. Mitty, whose wife was getting her hair done, waited quietly in the hotel.

© **Reading Application** Find an example of sentences using a relative, an interrogative, and an indefinite pronoun in "The Secret Life of Walter Mitty."

**Practice B** Complete each sentence by adding a relative, an interrogative, or an indefinite pronoun that makes sense.

1. Has _____ heard Uncle Marcos's stories?
2. People _____ listen to him find him hard to believe.
3. The adventures _____ Uncle Marcos had sometimes embarrassed his family.
4. _____ of them were surprised by his flying.

© **Writing Application** Use this sentence as a model to write five sentences. Substitute the italicized word or words with the same part speech. *Many of them came from a country that is in Asia.*

**PH WRITING COACH** Further instruction and practice are available in *Prentice Hall Writing Coach.*

# Writing

 **Informational Text** Both of these selections present memorable characters who entertain readers. Using details from the story you read, write a **character profile.** If you read "The Secret Life of Walter Mitty," choose one of the heroic personalities in Mitty's daydreams. If you read "Uncle Marcos," write a profile of Uncle Marcos.

- Begin by jotting down details that capture the character's appearance, personality, and achievements.
- Decide on a single impression to convey about the character.
- Organize and present details to create an impression.
- Maintain a consistent tone and focus throughout the piece.

**Grammar Application** Check your character profile to be sure that you have used relative, interrogative, and indefinite pronouns correctly.

### Writing Workshop: *Work in Progress*

**Prewriting for Problem-Solution Essay** Review the Problem Notes you created in your writing portfolio. To build on this work, provide three specific examples of the problem and three examples of solutions. Put these Problem/Solution Notes in your writing portfolio.

# Research and Technology

 **Build and Present Knowledge** Literature often suggests great topics for further research. Use a variety of sources from both the library and the Internet to research information for a **learning log,** a written record of information you learn about a topic. Use any available reliable sources, including speeches, journals, and news sources. Follow reliable links within sources to locate additional useful information. Analyze the information to compare your findings to details and descriptions in the story you read.

- If you read "The Secret Life of Walter Mitty," research scientific facts and theories about daydreams. Record your research in a learning log. Decide whether Mitty's daydreams reflect the facts you have learned.
- If you read "Uncle Marcos," research the history of human flight. Look for historic details that can be compared to the descriptions of flight given in the story. Record your research in a learning log. Decide if Allende's description of flight is realistic or fantastic.

If possible, incorporate graphics, visuals, or audio files into your log. Then, present the log to a small group, explaining how you researched and created it.

**Common Core State Standards**

L.9-10.1, L.9-10.6; W.9-10.4, W.9-10.6
[For the full wording of the standards, see page 124.]

Use this prewriting activity to prepare for the **Writing Workshop** on page 172.

**PHLit Online!**
www.PHLitOnline.com
- Interactive graphic organizers
- Grammar tutorial
- Interactive journals

# Test Practice: Reading

## Author's Purpose

### Fiction Selection

**Directions:** *Read the selection. Then, answer the questions.*

Juan slowly walked home from school, wondering what he could possibly do for his science fair project. As he ambled down his block, he noticed the gigantic mounds of garbage on the curb waiting to be taken to a landfill. "Something's got to be done about all this garbage!" Juan thought, and the idea for his science project hit him. He decided to pre-pare a presentation on recycling. First, he weighed how much garbage his family threw out in a week. Then, Juan and his family removed the recy-clable glass and plastic from their trash and weighed it again. Finally, they took out the paper they were throwing away and weighed the remaining trash. Juan and his family were shocked by the difference in the weight of their garbage.

1. The author most likely includes the line, "Something's got to be done about this garbage!" to show that Juan is—
   A. genuinely concerned about the garbage.
   B. going to win first prize at the science fair.
   C. wondering what to do for his project.
   D. walking home from school.

2. Why does the author include the description of Juan seeing the mounds of garbage?
   A. It adds realism and interest to the story.
   B. It gives Juan's inspiration for his project.
   C. It provides crucial details about the setting.
   D. It shows that Juan is conscientious.

3. The author says, "the idea for his science fair project hit him" to show that Juan has—
   A. tripped over the mounds of garbage.
   B. created a prize-winning presentation.
   C. decided what to study for the science fair.
   D. given up on his science fair project.

4. For what purpose does the author describe the steps in Juan's project?
   A. to entertain the reader with humor
   B. to make the story longer
   C. to make the story realistic
   D. to show how to recycle

5. What is the author's main purpose in writing this story?
   A. to inspire people to recycle
   B. to call for more garbage collection
   C. to persuade us to complete science projects
   D. to show the importance of science on the environment

### Writing for Assessment

How do you think Juan feels about the environment? Write a brief paragraph and use details from the text to support your response.

## Nonfiction Selection

**Directions:** *Read the selection. Then, answer the questions.*

Recycling saves on the amount of garbage we make and helps us keep our planet healthy. Even if you recycle just a small amount of material, you can have a positive impact on the environment. Some materials can be reused in their present state, such as using a tire for a flower planter. Other materials can be recycled into new products. Plastic, for example, is processed and reused to create new plastic items. Whatever way you choose to recycle, you do the earth a favor. Recycling helps lower greenhouse gases and decreases the space we need for landfills. Overall, recycling is a friend to the environment. You can make a difference. Why not recycle something today?

1. What is the general purpose of this article?
   A. to entertain
   B. to reflect
   C. to describe
   D. to persuade

2. Why do you think the author ends the article with a question?
   A. to call the audience to action
   B. to make the audience look for an answer
   C. to teach the audience about landfills
   D. to eliminate the need for questioning the author

3. For what purpose does the author give examples of how materials can be recycled?
   A. to provide ideas for recycling plastic
   B. to explain how recycling works
   C. to convince the reader to do Earth a favor
   D. to show the advantages of reusing products

4. Which sentence *best* reveals the author's purpose in this selection?
   A. Some materials can be reused in their present state, such as using a tire for a flower planter.
   B. Other materials can be recycled into new products.
   C. Whatever way you choose to recycle, you do the earth a favor.
   D. Recycling is expensive and unnecessary.

5. What would be the *best* title for this article?
   A. The Environment
   B. Recycling Saves Lives
   C. How I Started Recycling
   D. Why Everyone Should Recycle

## Writing for Assessment

**Connecting Across Texts**
In what ways would this article be helpful to Juan as he completes his science fair project? Write a paragraph in which you use specific details from both passages to explain why Juan should read this article as he prepares his presentation on recycling.

www.PHLitOnline.com
• Online practice
• Instant feedback

# Reading for Information

## Analyzing Functional Texts

### Schedule

### Brochure

### Ⓒ Common Core State Standards

**Reading Informational Text**
**3.** Analyze how the author unfolds an analysis or series of ideas or events, including the order in which the points are made, how they are introduced and developed, and the connections that are drawn between them.

**Language**
**4.b.** Identify and correctly use patterns of word changes that indicate different meanings or parts of speech.

## Reading Skill: Analyze Structure and Format

The structure of a text is the way in which it is organized. Format refers to the layout and other features that clarify the structure. When you **analyze structure and format,** you identify organizational elements in a text and consider how they help convey information. In functional texts, such as schedules and brochures, information might be presented in graphic formats, such as tables or charts. Understanding how such features connect with verbal elements can help you locate useful information.

The following chart shows some common structural features and the purposes they achieve.

| Structural Features of Schedules | Structural Features of Brochures |
|---|---|
| • **headings:** show where to find categories of information<br>• **rows and columns:** formatted information allows for easy scanning across and down the page<br>• **graphics:** call attention to important information | • **headings and subheadings:** help readers to locate information on a topic<br>• **lists:** provide a quick way to reference essential information<br>• **photographs and other images:** convey visual information |

## Content-Area Vocabulary

These words appear in the selections that follow. You may also encounter them in other content-area texts.

- **obstructions** (əb struk′shən) *n.* objects that block access; obstacles

- **complement** (kom plə ment′) *n.* object or action that makes something else whole or complete

- **cosmetic** (koz met′ik) *adj.* dealing with physical beauty or outward appearances

# Pascack Valley Line Train Schedule

**Schedule**

**Features:**
- data, such as departure and arrival times
- organization by day of the week, time, and location
- tables and charts
- headings and sub-headings

This feature is specially formatted so that readers can easily see an important fare policy.

AVOID THE $5 SURCHARGE
Buy before you board

The heading shows the train's final destination, as well as the days of the week the trains run.

## To Hoboken Monday – Friday

| | AM | | Off-peak roundtrip fares are not valid to New York, Secaucus or Hoboken | | | | | |
|---|---|---|---|---|---|---|---|---|
| TRAINS<br>Departing from: | 1600 | 1602 | 1604 | 1606 | 1608 | 1610 | 1612 | 1614 |
| METRO-NORTH STATION<br>**PEARL RIVER** | 5 15 | 5 38 | 6 04 | 6 35 | 6 45 | 7 05 | 7 24 | 7 38 |
| **Montvale** | 5 18 | 5 41 | 6 07 | | 6 48 | 7 08 | 7 28 | 7 41 |
| **Park Ridge** | 5 20 | 5 43 | 6 09 | | 6 50 | 7 11 | 7 30 | 7 44 |

| Arriving at: | | | | | | | | |
|---|---|---|---|---|---|---|---|---|
| **HOBOKEN** | 6 14 | 6 37 | 7 07 | 7 18 | 7 49 | 8 07 | 8 19 | 8 41 |
| via PATH | 6 24 | 6 44 | 7 14 | 7 32 | 8 01 | 8 19 | 8 31 | 8 49 |
| arrive World Trade Center | 6 34 | 6 54 | 7 25 | 7 43 | 8 12 | 8 30 | 8 42 | 9 00 |
| via FERRY | 6 30 | 6 50 | 7 16 | 7 32 | 7 56 | 8 20 | 8 28 | 8 52 |
| arrive World Financial Center | 6 40 | 7 00 | 7 26 | 7 42 | 8 06 | 8 30 | 8 38 | 9 02 |

The chart uses different colors to separate information and make it easier to read.

## FARE OPTIONS saving you time and money

**We want to make your travel convenient and economical, so we offer lots of options:**

**Monthly Passes** Unlimited trips within a calendar month; can be purchased beginning the 20th of the month prior and are valid until noon on the first commuting weekday of the following month.

**Weekly Passes** Unlimited trips from 12:01 a.m. Saturday to 6:00 a.m. on the following Saturday.

**10-Trip Tickets** Ten one-way trips.

**One-Way Tickets** One continuous trip.

**Off-Peak Roundtrip Tickets (ORT)** One-way travel in the direction indicated on the ticket. Not valid for AM peak travel to/via, or PM peak travel from/via New York, Secaucus, Newark or Hoboken.

**One-Way Reduced Tickets** One-way travel valid for senior citizens, passengers with disabilities, and children.

**Student Monthly Passes** A good reason to stay in school. Ask a ticket agent for details.

**Group Rates** Travel cheaper together.

The main headings draw the reader's attention to important information.

## KNOW BEFORE YOU GO

**Personal Items** Keep aisle ways clear of **obstructions** at all times. Store larger items in the overhead racks or under the seats.

**Pets** Only service animals accompanying customers with disabilities or their trainers, police dogs and small pets in carry-on travel cages are allowed on-board NJ TRANSIT trains.

**Smoking** Smoking is not allowed on any trains, in any stations, or on any platforms.

**Electronic Devices and Cell Phones** Listen or speak at a volume that does not disturb other passengers.

**Bicycles** You can bring collapsible bicycles on all trains at all times. Standard frame bicycles are permitted in accessible cars only except aboard weekday peak period trains or on major holidays. NJ TRANSIT conductors may use their judgment based on crowding and capacity, to make exceptions. Note that a customer with a disability is given priority over a customer with a bicycle.

## WE'RE ACCESSIBLE AT MANY STATIONS

Stations with this symbol are accessible to customers using mobility assist devices. For assistance on or off the train, please inform the train crew. Customers traveling from Hoboken, please arrive 15 minutes before your scheduled train departure and notify an NJ TRANSIT representative for assistance.

Icons are used along with boldface headings to provide visual information.

### Pascack Valley Line

- SPRING VALLEY ♿
- Nanuet ♿
- Pearl River
- Montvale ♿
- Park Ridge
- Woodcliff Lake
- Hillsdale
- Westwood ♿
- Emerson
- Oradell
- River Edge
- North Hackensack
- Anderson Street
- Essex Street ♿
- Teterboro
- Wood-Ridge
- Secaucus Junction ♿
- HOBOKEN ♿

This part of the schedule shows stops on the train line and stations that are accessible to people using wheelchairs or other mobility devices.

# Georgia's Official Transportation History Museum

## DULUTH, GEORGIA

The Southern Railway Museum occupies a 34-acre site in Duluth, Georgia, in northeast suburban Atlanta. In operation since 1970, SRM features about 90 items of rolling stock including historic Pullman cars and classic steam locomotives. During the spring, summer, and fall, the museum is open Thursday, Friday, and Saturday. During the winter, we're open on Saturdays. For more details, please see our Events Calendar.

Ride in restored cabooses behind steam or diesel locomotives, stand next to the massive driving wheels of the locomotive that once pulled passenger trains to Key West on the "railroad that went to sea," tour the business car that helped bring the Olympics to Atlanta, pose on the platform of the private car once used by President Warren G. Harding, and see just how green Southern Railway green can be as you walk the length of the diesel-electric locomotive that ran the point on the last *Crescent* before AMTRAK assumed control of the famous train.

| LOCOMOTIVE | STATUS AS OF SPRING 2006 |
| --- | --- |

**SOUTHERN #8202  SW-7** Built c. 1950 by EMD for Georgia Southern, & Florida Railroad. Previously numbered 1100 and used for yard switching until 1981.

**OPERATIONAL**

Photographs show the design and purpose of each train.

**SOUTHERN #6901  E8** Built in 1951 by the Electro-Motive Division of General Motors. Routinely powered the Atlanta-Washington D.C. portion of the famous *Crescent* passenger train. Was lead engine when operation of the *Crescent* formally changed from the Southern Railway to Amtrak in 1979. Originally numbered 2924.

**PERMANENT EXHIBIT**

## SOUTHERN FT B-UNIT #960604 STEAM HEAT & TRAINLINE POWER

**EXHIBIT**

Constructed as a **complement** to the full diesel locomotive ("A" unit), these "B" units are essentially locomotives without cabs. Originally containing both diesel engines and steam generators (for passenger car heating), this unit has been modified to hold only steam generation equipment.

The headings allow readers to easily locate information about particular exhibits.

## NEW YORK, ONTARIO, AND WESTERN #104 (FORMERLY HARTWELL #5) GE 44-TON

**OPERATIONAL, NORMAL POWER FOR TRAIN RIDE**

Built 1941 by General Electric for the New York, Ontario & Western Railroad as #104. The museum staff completed a **cosmetic** restoration of the locomotive in 2005.

Here's the engine's previous paint scheme ⟶

## GEORGIA RAILROAD #1026 EMD GP 7

**EXHIBIT**

Acquired by the museum in 2004 from Tennessee Valley Railway Museum, the locomotive was repainted to it's original 1950 paint scheme before being delivered in January 2006.

## Comparing Functional and Expository Texts

**1. Key Ideas and Details** **(a)** Summarize the information you learn from the maps and charts of the train schedule. **(b)** What information is conveyed in the visual elements of the brochure? **(c) Analyze:** What purposes do the graphic elements in each document serve? **(d) Evaluate:** Which graphics do you find more effective in meeting their intended purpose? Explain.

### Content-Area Vocabulary

**2. (a)** For each of the following words, explain how a change in suffix alters the meaning and part of speech of the base word *obstruct*: *obstruction*, *obstructive*, and *obstructed*. **(b)** Use each word in a sentence that reveals its meaning.

## ⏱ Timed Writing

### Explanatory Text: Description

> **Format**
> The prompt directs you to write a description of a scene. Therefore, be sure your response is specific to the situation as it is described in the prompt.

> Write a description of a scene at a train station. Describe what you would see if you were on the station's platform waiting to board a train. Use the information in the train schedule for ideas about what kinds of details to include. (20 minutes)

> **Academic Vocabulary**
> When you *describe* something, you use words and details to create a vivid picture in your readers' minds.

### 5-Minute Planner

Complete these steps before you begin to write:

**1.** Read the prompt to be sure you understand the assignment.

**2.** Review the train schedule to find details that you can include in your description. **TIP** Use structural features such as subheadings and boldface type to quickly locate information in the document.

**3.** Make a list of the details that you want to use in your writing. Then, make a quick sketch of the train station scene as you picture it in your mind, including details from your list.

**4.** Use your sketch and your list of details for your description.

## Comparing Themes

**Theme** is the message or insight about life that is conveyed in a short story, a play, or another literary work. Sometimes it is explicit, or stated directly. More often, it is implicit, or expressed indirectly, through the words and actions of the characters or the events of a story. The way theme is developed depends in part on the **genre**, or form, of the work.

- **Nonfiction:** In nonfiction literature, such as essays or articles, the meaning or insight is usually referred to as the **central idea.** The central idea is generally stated directly. A thesis statement expressing that idea may appear at the beginning of the work. Key ideas and supporting details presented throughout the work develop the central idea in a systematic way.

- **Fiction and poetry:** In fiction and poetry, the theme is often implicit. Readers can figure it out by looking at story events, the words and actions of characters, and patterns of related images and ideas called *motifs.* As readers make connections between various literary elements, the thematic message emerges.

Works of nonfiction and fiction can express similar central ideas and themes. Nonfiction and fiction can address the same concerns and subjects.

The following selections share a similar basic topic: the effects of human behavior on the environment. However, "If I Forget Thee, Oh Earth . . ." is a short story, and *Silent Spring* is nonfiction. Because they represent two different genres, the two works develop meaning in different ways. As you read, complete a Venn diagram like the one shown to analyze how theme and central ideas develop.

**If I Forget Thee, Oh Earth**          **Silent Spring**

Deals with environmental issues.

www.PHLitOnline.com

- Vocabulary flashcards
- Interactive journals
- More about the authors
- Selection audio
- Interactive graphic organizers

# Can *truth* change?

## Writing About the Big Question

Some people feel that the condition of Earth is a constant, unchangeable truth. Use these sentence starters to develop your ideas about the Big Question.

I **speculate** that in 100 years, Earth will be _____.

My **assumptions** are based on _____.

# Meet the Authors

## Arthur C. Clarke (1917–2008)

### Author of "If I Forget Thee, Oh Earth . . ."

Born in England, Arthur C. Clarke was both a writer and a scientist. He wrote his first science-fiction stories during his teens, and he later published more than fifty works of fiction and nonfiction.

**A True Scientist** Although best known for his science fiction, Clarke was a serious scientist as well. In 1945, he published a technical article called "Extra-Terrestrial Relays" in which he established the principles of the satellite communications system we have today.

## Rachel Carson (1907–1964)

### Author of *Silent Spring*

Even as a young girl, Rachel Carson thought of herself as a writer, and she entered college to pursue that goal. Once there, she renewed an interest in nature and switched her major to marine biology. She later earned a master's degree in zoology.

**Environmental Activist** Carson had long been worried about the overuse of pesticides. "Everything which meant most to me as a naturalist was being threatened," she said, and she felt that the most important thing she could do was publicize the facts. *Silent Spring* became one of the most influential environmental books ever written. Carson died of cancer before she witnessed the major impact of her book.

# "If I Forget Thee, Oh Earth..."

## Arthur C. Clarke

**Literary Analysis**
**Theme** What information about Marvin's environment appears in this description of the Farmlands?

**Vocabulary**
**purged** (pʉrjd) *v.*
cleansed

When Marvin was ten years old, his father took him through the long, echoing corridors that led up through Administration and Power, until at last they came to the uppermost levels of all and were among the swiftly growing vegetation of the Farmlands. Marvin liked it here: it was fun watching the great, slender plants creeping with almost visible eagerness toward the sunlight as it filtered down through the plastic domes to meet them. The smell of life was everywhere, awakening inexpressible longings in his heart: no longer was he breathing the dry, cool air of the residential levels, purged of all smells but the faint tang of ozone.[1] He wished he could stay here for a little while, but Father would not let him. They went onward until they had reached the entrance to the Observatory, which he had never visited: but they did not stop, and Marvin knew

---

**1. ozone** (ō′ zōn′) *n.* form of oxygen with a sharp odor.

with a sense of rising excitement that there could be only one goal left. For the first time in his life, he was going Outside.

There were a dozen of the surface vehicles, with their wide balloon tires and pressurized cabins, in the great servicing chamber. His father must have been expected, for they were led at once to the little scout car waiting by the huge circular door of the airlock. Tense with expectancy, Marvin settled himself down in the cramped cabin while his father started the motor and checked the controls. The inner door of the lock slid open and then closed behind them: he heard the roar of the great air pumps fade slowly away as the pressure dropped to zero. Then the "Vacuum" sign flashed on, the outer door parted, and before Marvin lay the land which he had never yet entered.

He had seen it in photographs, of course: he had watched it imaged on television screens a hundred times. But now it was lying all around him, burning beneath the fierce sun that crawled so slowly across the jet-black sky. He stared into the west, away from the blinding splendor of the sun—and there were the stars, as he had been told but had never quite believed. He gazed at them for a long time, marveling that anything could be so bright and yet so tiny. They were intense unscintillating points, and suddenly he remembered a rhyme he had once read in one of his father's books:

**Twinkle, twinkle, little star,**

**How I wonder what you are.**

Well, he knew what the stars were. Whoever asked that question must have been very stupid. And what did they mean by "twinkle"? You could see at a glance that all the stars shone with the same steady, unwavering light. He abandoned the puzzle and turned his attention to the landscape around him.

They were racing across a level plain at almost a hundred miles an hour, the great balloon tires sending up little spurts of dust behind them. There was no sign of the Colony: in the few minutes while he had been gazing at the stars, its domes and radio towers had fallen below the horizon. Yet there were other indications of man's presence, for about a mile ahead Marvin could see the curiously shaped structures clustering round the head of a mine. Now and then a puff of vapor would emerge from a squat smokestack and would instantly disperse.

They were past the mine in a moment: Father was driving with a reckless and exhilarating skill as if—it was a strange thought to come into a child's mind—he were trying to escape from something. In a few minutes they had reached the edge of the plateau on which the Colony had been built. The ground fell sharply away beneath them in a dizzying slope whose lower stretches were lost in shadow.

**Literary Analysis**
**Theme** What do the words "burning beneath the fierce sun" suggest about what Marvin is observing?

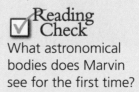

Reading Check
What astronomical bodies does Marvin see for the first time?

### Science Connection

**International Space Station**
In Arthur C. Clarke's story, a space colony is all that remains of the human species. If the idea of a space colony seems implausible, consider the fact that a small colony is being developed directly over your head in the form of an International Space Station. Sixteen nations are contributing scientific and technological resources to build the Station, which has been under construction since 1998. The Space Station will be used for experiments and research, and it will also provide insight into the way humans can learn to live and work in outer space. The first astronaut crew arrived at the Station in November of 2000, and since then, people have lived and worked continuously at the Station, more than 200 miles above Earth.

### Connect to the Literature

How do you think the astronauts' feelings about living in outer space compare to Marvin's feelings?

Ahead, as far as the eye could reach, was a jumbled wasteland of craters, mountain ranges, and ravines. The crests of the mountains, catching the low sun, burned like islands of fire in a sea of darkness: and above them the stars still shone as steadfastly as ever.

There could be no way forward—yet there was. Marvin clenched his fists as the car edged over the slope and started the long descent. Then he saw the barely visible track leading down the mountainside, and relaxed a little. Other men, it seemed, had gone this way before.

Night fell with a shocking abruptness as they crossed the shadow line and the sun dropped below the crest of the plateau. The twin searchlights sprang into life, casting blue-white bands on the rocks ahead, so that there was scarcely need to check their speed. For hours they drove through valleys and past the foot of mountains whose peaks seemed to comb the stars, and sometimes they emerged for a moment into the sunlight as they climbed over higher ground.

And now on the right was a wrinkled, dusty plain, and on the left, its ramparts and terraces rising mile after mile into the sky, was a wall of mountains that marched into the distance until its peaks sank from sight below the rim of the world. There was no sign that men had ever explored this land, but once they passed the skeleton of a crashed rocket, and beside it a stone cairn[2] surmounted by a metal cross.

It seemed to Marvin that the mountains stretched on forever: but at last, many hours later, the range ended in a towering, precipitous headland[3] that rose steeply from a cluster of little hills. They drove down into a shallow valley that curved in a great arc toward the far side of the mountains: and as they did so, Marvin slowly realized that something very strange was happening in the land ahead.

The sun was now low behind the hills on the right: the valley before them should be in total darkness. Yet it was awash with a cold white radiance that came spilling over the crags beneath which they were driving. Then, suddenly, they were out in the open plain, and the source of the light lay before them in all its glory.

---

2. **cairn** (kern) *n.* a cone-shaped pile of stones built as a monument.
3. **precipitous headland** (prē sip´ ə təs hed´ land´) *n.* steep cliff that juts out over water.

It was very quiet in the little cabin now that the motors had stopped. The only sound was the faint whisper of the oxygen feed and an occasional metallic crepitation as the outer walls of the vehicle radiated away their heat. For no warmth at all came from the great silver crescent that floated low above the far horizon and flooded all this land with pearly light. It was so brilliant that minutes passed before Marvin could accept its challenge and look steadfastly into its glare, but at last he could discern the outlines of continents, the hazy border of the atmosphere, and the white islands of cloud. And even at this distance, he could see the glitter of sunlight on the polar ice.

It was beautiful, and it called to his heart across the abyss of space. There in that shining crescent were all the wonders that he had never known—the hues of sunset skies, the moaning of the sea on pebbled shores, the patter of falling rain, the unhurried benison of snow. These and a thousand others should have been his rightful heritage, but he knew them only from the books and ancient records, and the thought filled him with the anguish of exile.

Why could they not return? It seemed so peaceful beneath those lines of marching cloud. Then Marvin, his eyes no longer blinded by the glare, saw that the portion of the disk that should have been in darkness was gleaming faintly with an evil phosphorescence[4] and he remembered. He was looking upon the funeral pyre of a world— upon the radioactive aftermath of Armageddon.[5] Across a quarter of a million miles of space, the glow of dying atoms was still visible, a perennial reminder of the ruinous past. It would be centuries yet before that deadly glow died from the rocks and life could return again to fill that silent, empty world.

And now Father began to speak, telling Marvin the story which until this moment had meant no more to him than the fairy tales he had once been told. There were many things he could not understand: it was impossible for him to picture the glowing, multicolored pattern of life on the planet he had never seen. Nor could he comprehend the forces that had destroyed it in the end, leaving the Colony, preserved by its isolation, as the sole survivor. Yet he could share the agony of those final days, when the Colony had learned at last that never again would the supply ships come flaming down through the stars with gifts from home. One by one the radio stations had ceased to call: on the shadowed globe the lights of the cities had dimmed and died, and they were alone at last, as no men had ever been alone before, carrying in their hands the future of the race.

---

4. **phosphorescence** (fäs´ fə res´ əns) *n.* emission of light resulting from exposure to radiation.
5. **Armageddon** (är´ mə ged´ 'n) *n.* in the Bible, the place where the final battle between good and evil is to be fought.

**Literary Analysis**
**Theme** Which details in these paragraphs provide an insight into what Marvin and others in his colony have lost?

**Vocabulary**
**perennial** (pə ren´ ē əl) *adj.* happening over and over; perpetual

**Reading Check**
What does Marvin notice in a portion of the disk?

Then had followed the years of despair, and the long-drawn battle for survival in their fierce and hostile world. That battle had been won, though barely: this little oasis of life was safe against the worst that Nature could do. But unless there was a goal, a future toward which it could work, the Colony would lose the will to live, and neither machines nor skill nor science could save it then.

So, at last, Marvin understood the purpose of this pilgrimage. He would never walk beside the rivers of that lost and legendary world, or listen to the thunder raging above its softly rounded hills. Yet one day—how far ahead?—his children's children would return to claim their heritage. The winds and the rains would scour the poisons from the burning lands and carry them to the sea, and in the depths of the sea they would waste their venom until they could harm no living things. Then the great ships that were still waiting here on the silent, dusty plains could lift once more into space, along the road that led to home.

That was the dream: and one day, Marvin knew with a sudden flash of insight, he would pass it on to his own son, here at this same spot with the mountains behind him and the silver light from the sky streaming into his face.

He did not look back as they began the homeward journey. He could not bear to see the cold glory of the crescent Earth fade from the rocks around him, as he went to rejoin his people in their long exile.

## Critical Thinking

Cite textual evidence to support your responses.

© **1. Key Ideas and Details (a)** At the end of the story, what does Marvin realize? **(b) Draw Conclusions:** What was the purpose of Marvin's trip with his father?

© **2. Craft and Structure (a) Infer:** What evidence from the text indicates that the story is set on the moon? **(b) Analyze:** How does the choice of setting make the story more realistic?

© **3. Integration of Knowledge and Ideas (a) Infer:** How did Earth come to be destroyed? **(b) Speculate:** What suggestions do you think Clarke might have offered today to prevent a situation like this from occurring?

© **4. Integration of Knowledge and Ideas** How does the truth about the moon and Earth shift for Marvin after his trip with his father? *[Connect to the Big Question: Can truth change?]*

# from Silent Spring

## Rachel Carson

There was once a town in the heart of America where all life seemed to live in harmony with its surroundings. The town lay in the midst of a checkerboard of prosperous farms, with fields of grain and hillsides of orchards where, in spring, white clouds of bloom drifted above the green fields. In autumn, oak and maple and birch set up a blaze of color that flamed and flickered across a backdrop of pines. Then foxes barked in the hills and deer silently crossed the fields, half hidden in the mists of the fall mornings.

Along the roads, laurel, viburnum and alder, great ferns and wildflowers delighted the traveler's eye through much of the year. Even in winter the roadsides were places of beauty, where

**Literary Analysis
Central Idea** Which details in this paragraph paint a picture of the beauty and energy of nature? Explain.

countless birds came to feed on the berries and on the seed heads of the dried weeds rising above the snow. The countryside was, in fact, famous for the abundance and variety of its bird life, and when the flood of migrants was pouring through in spring and fall people traveled from great distances to observe them. Others came to fish the streams, which flowed clear and cold out of the hills and contained shady pools where trout lay. So it had been from the days many years ago when the first settlers raised their houses, sank their wells, and built their barns.

Then a strange blight crept over the area and everything began to change. Some evil spell had settled on the community: mysterious maladies swept the flocks of chickens; the cattle and sheep sickened and died. Everywhere was a shadow of death. The farmers spoke of much illness among their families. In the town the doctors had become more and more puzzled by new kinds of sickness appearing among their patients. There had been several sudden and unexplained deaths, not only among adults but even among children, who would be stricken suddenly while at play and die within a few hours.

There was a strange stillness. The birds, for example— where had they gone? Many people spoke of them, puzzled and disturbed. The feeding stations in the backyards were deserted. The few birds seen anywhere were moribund; they trembled violently and could not fly. It was a spring without voices. On the mornings that had once throbbed with the dawn chorus of robins, catbirds, doves, jays, wrens, and scores of other bird voices there was now no sound; only silence lay over the fields and woods and marsh.

On the farms the hens brooded, but no chicks hatched. The farmers complained that they were unable to raise any pigs—the litters were small and the young survived only a few days. The apple trees were coming into bloom but no bees droned among the blossoms, so there was no pollination and there would be no fruit.

The roadsides, once so attractive, were now lined with browned and withered vegetation as though swept by fire. These, too, were silent, deserted by all living things. Even

▶ **Critical Viewing** What details in this picture indicate that a "strange blight" may have affected this area? **[Connect]**

**Vocabulary**
**blight** (blīt) *n.* something that destroys or prevents growth
**maladies** (mal´ ə dēz) *n.* diseases

**Vocabulary**
**moribund** (môr´ i bund´) *adj.* slowly dying

the streams were now lifeless. Anglers[1] no longer visited them, for all the fish had died.

In the gutters under the eaves and between the shingles of the roofs, a white granular powder still showed a few patches; some weeks before it had fallen like snow upon the roofs and the lawns, the fields and streams.

No witchcraft, no enemy action had silenced the rebirth of new life in this stricken world. The people had done it themselves.

This town does not actually exist, but it might easily have a thousand counterparts in America or elsewhere in the world. I know of no community that has experienced all the misfortunes I describe. Yet every one of these disasters has actually happened somewhere, and many real communities have already suffered a substantial number of them. A grim specter has crept upon us almost unnoticed, and this imagined tragedy may easily become a stark reality we all shall know.

*The people had done it themselves.*

---

**1. anglers** (aŋ′ glərz) *n.* people who fish with a line and hook.

## Critical Thinking

Cite textual evidence to support your responses.

© 1. **Key Ideas and Details (a)** What is the condition of life at the beginning of this excerpt? **(b) Compare and Contrast:** How does the condition of life change as the narrative continues?

© 2. **Key Ideas and Details (a)** What happens to the farm animals and the vegetation? **(b) Infer:** What causes this sudden change?

© 3. **Craft and Structure (a)** What information about the town does Carson reveal at the end of the excerpt? **(b) Speculate:** Do you think the narrative would be more effective if the town was real? Why or why not?

© 4. **Integration of Knowledge and Ideas (a)** According to Carson, who caused the environmental problems? **(b) Speculate:** What suggestions do you think Carson would make to people today?

© 5. **Integration of Knowledge and Ideas** Do you think most Americans' understanding of environmental issues has changed since Carson first wrote *Silent Spring*? Why or why not?
*[Connect to the Big Question: Can truth change?]*

## Comparing Themes

ⓒ **1. Key Ideas and Details** Use a chart like the one shown to analyze the theme expressed in "If I Forget Thee, Oh Earth . . ." and the central idea expressed in the excerpt from *Silent Spring.* First, list important details from each selection and what you think the details mean. Use this information to suggest the theme or central idea of the selection.

| Details from "If I Forget Thee, Oh Earth..." | What They Mean | Theme |
|---|---|---|
|  |  |  |
| Details from *Silent Spring* | What They Mean | Central Idea |
|  |  |  |

ⓒ **2. Craft and Structure (a)** Using details from the chart, explain how the theme and central idea in the two selections are similar. **(b)** How is the meaning or insight expressed differently in each one?

## ⏱ Timed Writing

### Reflective Text: Essay

Write an essay in which you compare your reactions to the way "If I Forget Thee, Oh Earth . . ." and the excerpt from *Silent Spring* explore a theme and a central idea. In your response, consider how the genre of each selection affects your reading experience. **(25 minutes)**

### 5-Minute Planner

**1.** Read the prompt carefully and completely.

**2.** Jot down your answers to these questions to help organize your thoughts:

- Do you feel more affected by the experiences of the character Marvin or by the words of Rachel Carson, the author of *Silent Spring*?
- Which genre do you find more effective in shaping meaning and expressing ideas—fiction or nonfiction? Why?
- Why do you think an author would choose one genre over another when conveying an important insight or idea?

**3.** Decide on a structure for your essay. Plan the points you will cover in each paragraph.

**4.** Reread the prompt and then draft your essay.

# Writing Workshop

## Write Arguments

### Argument: Problem-and-Solution Essay

Some forms of writing engage us in the struggles and resolutions of our daily lives. In a **problem-and-solution essay,** an author identifies a problem and then argues for a possible solution. You might use this type of writing in letters, memos, proposals, or editorials.

**Assignment** Write a problem-and-solution essay about an issue that confronts your school or community. Your essay should feature the following elements:

✓ a statement of the *problem* and a suggested *solution*

✓ *valid reasoning* and *evidence*, such as *facts* and *expert opinions*, that show the problem's scope and support an effective solution

✓ formal and objective *language* appropriate to your audience

✓ logical *organization* and a *concluding statement* or section that supports your argument

✓ *error-free grammar*, including correct use of pronouns

To preview problem-and-solution essay criteria, see page 179.

 **Writing Workshop:** *Work in Progress*

Review the work you did on pages 123 and 151.

**WRITE GUY**
*Jeff Anderson, M.Ed.*

## What Do You Notice?

### Powerful Diction

Read the following sentences from Rachel Carson's *Silent Spring* several times.

*A grim specter has crept upon us almost unnoticed, and this imagined tragedy may easily become a stark reality we all shall know.*

What do you notice about the passage? Discuss your observations with a partner. Then, discuss Carson's diction, or word choice. Consider how you might use vivid word choices in your own writing.

**Writing**

**1.** Write arguments to support claims in an analysis of substantive topics or texts, using valid reasoning and relevant and sufficient evidence.

**1.b.** Develop claim(s) and counterclaims fairly, supplying evidence for each while pointing out the strengths and limitations of both in a manner that anticipates the audience's knowledge level and concerns.

**1.d.** Establish and maintain a formal style and objective tone while attending to the norms and conventions of the discipline in which they are writing.

**Reading-Writing Connection**

To get a feel for the use of problem-and-solution structure in a speech, read "First Inaugural Address" by Franklin Delano Roosevelt on page 552.

# Prewriting/Planning Strategies

**Choose a topic.** To select a topic for your problem-and-solution essay, use one of the following strategies:

- **Media Scan** Review local newspapers and television news programs for items about issues and problems in your community. List problems for which you can imagine practical solutions, and select one as your topic.

- **Sentence Starters** Complete the following sentence starters and jot down any associated ideas that come to mind. Then, choose one of the issues generated by the sentence starters as your topic.

  **One issue that needs to be addressed is _____**
  **The biggest problem people my age face is _____**
  **Life would be better in my community if _____**
  **The world would be a much better place if _____**

www.PHLitOnline.com
- Author video: Writing Process
- Author video: Rewards of Writing

**Create a problem profile.** Once you have chosen a topic, create a profile like the one shown to help you focus your essay on a specific aspect of the problem. Answer the following questions about the problem:

- Who is affected by the problem?
- What causes the problem to occur?
- Is there more than one cause of the problem?
- What are some possible solutions to the problem?

| Problem Profile |
| --- |
| **Problem:** Litter is creating an unsafe and unsightly environment. |
| **Who is affected?** Everyone on Earth |
| **What causes the problem?** <br> Lack of: <br> • responsibility <br> • environmental education <br> • sense of ownership |
| **What are the possible solutions?** Stiffer fines, more policing, more environmental education, volunteer trash pickup |

**Consider your audience.** Once you have clearly defined the problem, collect the details and information you will need to start your draft. Assess all possible solutions and weed out the less practical ones. Then, determine whom you want to reach with your essay and which aspects of the problem affect them most. For example, if you are trying to reach community leaders, you may shape your message differently than if you are trying to reach a peer group. As you narrow your focus, identify the ideas that will have the strongest impact on your target audience.

# Drafting Strategies

**Engage your audience immediately.** To make the problem real to your audience, consider one of these strategies for starting your essay:

- **Personal example:** Provide a detail from your own experience.

- **Anecdote:** Give a factual account of how the problem has already affected others.

- **Scenario:** Present a hypothetical but realistic picture of future consequences if the problem is not addressed.

**Outline the problem clearly.** Use an organizer like the one shown to display aspects of the central problem, their causes, and their direct effects on people's lives. Then, select and develop only those details that will make the problem clear, significant, and urgent to your audience.

**Common Core
State Standards**

**Writing**

**1.a.** Introduce precise claim(s), distinguish the claim(s) from alternate or opposing claims, and create an organization that establishes clear relationships among claim(s), counterclaims, reasons, and evidence.

**1.e.** Provide a concluding statement or section that follows from and supports the argument presented.

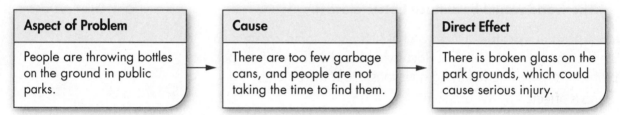

| Aspect of Problem | Cause | Direct Effect |
|---|---|---|
| People are throwing bottles on the ground in public parks. | There are too few garbage cans, and people are not taking the time to find them. | There is broken glass on the park grounds, which could cause serious injury. |

**Select convincing details.** You cannot "prove" your solution in advance, but you can persuade the audience that your proposal is likely to work by using the following types of evidence. Make sure that you research your evidence using reliable sources.

- **Statistics:** Provide relevant numerical data.

- **Expert opinions:** Include the advice of those who have training or experience related to your topic problem. Integrate quotations and citations from experts to support the evidence.

- **Comparable situations:** Describe other real-life difficulties that were resolved by actions similar to the ones you propose.

Use primary and secondary sources that are appropriate to your purpose and audience. To maintain the flow of ideas, explain the value of each quotation you include and make sure that you establish clear connections among the various types of evidence you use.

**Address readers' concerns.** Anticipate arguments that you might get from people with differing opinions. Include one or two skeptical questions to show you know both sides of the issue. Then, provide well-supported answers and a concluding statement that supports your argument.

# Writers on Writing

## Elizabeth McCracken On Word Choice

Elizabeth McCracken is the author of *The Giant's House* (p. 12) and "Desiderata" (p. 18).

One of the best things about writing my novel *Niagara Falls All Over Again,* which tells the story of a comedy team, was that I could watch videotapes of old TV shows and movies, and claim that I was working. My favorite tapes were old episodes of a show that my beloved comic duo Abbott and Costello hosted once a month. This passage is basically just a description of what I saw when I was "working," watching *The Colgate Comedy Hour.*

*"Write about your most beloved obsessions."*
—Elizabeth McCracken

**Professional Model:**

### from *Niagara Falls All Over Again*

We broke into television as the once-a-month hosts of a weekly hour-long live variety show. By 1951, our movie career was mostly over, and we were back where we'd begun, except famous, rich, and middle-aged: a thin man and a fat man on a stage, willing to do anything for a laugh. We were shameless. We insulted the band leader, we knocked down scenery on purpose, we tried to crack each other up. We broke props we'd need later, just so we could improvise first about the breakage, and then about the lack of props. Our old wheezing vaudeville jokes were new again, thanks to the postwar baby boom: the country was full of brand-new people with blissfully unsophisticated senses of humor. You could see Rocky search for the red light that told us which camera was paying attention, doing a slow burn and then saying, "Watch me, camera two," and tipping his hat. . . .

I have a weakness for repetition, both straight repeats (like all the *We*'s) and slight variations, like *break, broke.*

Some writers say, Avoid adverbs. It's true that some people use adverbs to do the work that verbs and adjectives should do, but I use *blissfully* here as a joke—most people wouldn't see a lack of sophistication as *blissful.*

He's wearing a bowler hat. I draw my characters' clothing when I write (though I'm a very poor artist). I know them better if I know what they wear.

# Revising Strategies

**Support your generalizations.** Look at each paragraph in your essay to be certain that the details you have used support or explain the main idea that is expressed in the topic sentence. Use the following strategy to revise your paragraphs:

1. Highlight your topic sentence, the general statement in which you summarize the main idea of the paragraph.

2. Underline the sentences that develop and support this idea.

3. Eliminate any sentences that do not support the main idea or that simply restate it.

> **Model: Revising to Support Generalizations**
> Litter can be dangerous, as well as unsightly. <u>When glass bottles are left on the ground, they eventually break into tiny, sharp pieces. These pieces of glass are hard to see and could easily cut someone walking barefoot or diving for a soccer ball.</u> ~~Also, broken bottles are more difficult to recycle.~~

**Evaluate your vocabulary.** Review your draft as if you were a member of your target audience. Find specialized or technical terms that need to be defined. Look for vocabulary that seems too difficult or easy for your readers. Then, adjust your language so that it is appropriate for your target audience. Be sure to maintain a formal style and objective tone. Use resources and reference materials to select more effective and precise language. Even if you simplify your language to address the needs of your audience, make sure to maintain a formal, academic style and objective tone.

| General Audience | Target Audience of Experts |
|---|---|
| Another way to fight fatigue is to exercise. | Another way to raise low levels of blood sugar is to get more exercise. |

## Peer Review

Exchange drafts with a partner. Review each other's work, circling words that are either too specialized and technical or too simple and basic for your target audiences. Use reference materials such as a dictionary or thesaurus to suggest more effective and precise language. Review your concluding section, and make sure it sums up your argument and supports the evidence you presented. Discuss your decisions with your partner and make the revisions you think will improve your writing.

**Writing**

**1.c.** Use words, phrases, and clauses to link the major sections of the text, create cohesion, and clarify the relationships between claim(s) and reasons, between reasons and evidence, and between claim(s) and counterclaims.

**1.d.** Establish and maintain a formal style and objective tone while attending to the norms and conventions of the discipline in which they are writing.

**1.e.** Provide a concluding statement or section that follows from and supports the argument presented.

**Language**

**6.** Acquire and use accurately general academic and domain-specific words and phrases, sufficient for reading, writing, speaking, and listening at the college and career readiness level; demonstrate independence in gathering vocabulary knowledge when considering a word or phrase important to comprehension or expression.

# Revising Pronoun-Antecedent Agreement

**Pronouns** are words that take the place of nouns. **Antecedents** are the nouns that the pronouns refer to.

**Identifying Errors in Pronoun-Antecedent Agreement.** Pronouns "disagree" with their antecedents when they are mismatched in number, person, or gender. A pronoun should agree with its antecedent in number:

**Incorrect:** *Anne and Natasha* reminded *her* parents.
**Correct:** *Anne and Natasha* reminded *their* parents. (plural)

**Incorrect:** *Neither Carl nor Jeff* remember *their* ID number.
**Correct:** *Neither Carl nor Jeff* remembers *his* ID number. (singular)

A pronoun should agree with its antecedent in person:

**Incorrect:** When a *person* hurries, *you* may fall.
**Correct:** When a *person* hurries, *he or she* may fall. (third-person singular)
**Correct:** When *people* hurry, *they* may fall. (third-person plural)

> **PH WRITING COACH**
> Further instruction and practice are available in *Prentice Hall Writing Coach.*

**Fixing Errors in Pronoun-Antecedent Agreement.** To correct errors, first identify the antecedent of each pronoun. As you work through each paragraph of your draft, consider the following:

| Gender of Third-Person Singular Pronouns | | |
|---|---|---|
| **Masculine** | **Feminine** | **Neuter** |
| he, him, his, himself | she, her, hers, herself | it, its, itself |

1. For compound antecedents joined by *and,* use a plural personal pronoun.

2. For singular antecedents joined by *or* or *nor,* use a singular personal pronoun.

3. Check every occurrence of the pronoun *you* to make sure that you have not made a shift in person.

**Grammar in Your Writing**

Review the first and last paragraphs in your draft. Underline each antecedent and circle each pronoun. Check the marked words for pronoun-antecedent agreement and fix any errors.

# Student Model: Naomi Barrowclough, Maplewood, NJ

**Common Core State Standards**

**Language**
**2.c.** Spell correctly.

## Environmental Un-Consciousness

During a recent Earth Day cleanup, I became disgusted by the amount of trash I picked up within a two-hour period. People had thrown little papers, bits of plastic, and candy wrappers until the mess formed a multicolored carpet over the green grass. Those who litter may not realize that litter creates serious environmental problems.

We've all been told not to litter, but it does not seem to sink in. One person may think his or her contribution is only a microscopic addition when viewed against the whole. But if every person shared this sense of irresponsibility, Earth would soon be overwhelmed by pollution.

Litter is harmful for many reasons. For one, roadside litter eventually washes into waterways and oceans—water we use for drinking and recreation. Also, animals might entangle themselves or mistake trash for food and swallow it. In our public spaces, children spend a great deal of time in areas where they could be physically harmed by the pollution caused by litter.

There is no simple solution to the problem of litter, only an array of possible solutions with one strategy in common: Create a feeling of ownership over public spaces. Some of the most popular sites for litter are beaches and parks because people feel no sense of ownership over these places. These same people would never litter in their own homes.

To create a feeling of ownership, it is necessary to educate children early about the environmental consequences of littering. According to research done by Keep America Beautiful, a non-profit organization, most people do not feel responsible for public spaces. They think "someone else" will clean up. To change this attitude, schools could lead field trips to local beaches or parks where students pick up trash and test water quality. If kids have to fish two shopping carts from the side of a stream, as I did, they might think twice about throwing something else on the ground. If they see that contaminated water is harmful to both humans and wildlife, they might stop someone they see littering.

There is no easy way to stop littering. Fines and policing alone will not do the trick because people will just look before they litter. Until people understand that littering is irresponsible and has devastating environmental consequences, they will continue to litter. The solution lies in education and creating a sense of ownership about our public spaces.

In the opening paragraph, Naomi provides a general statement of the problem.

Here, the author provides greater detail to explain the problem more fully.

Naomi introduces a general solution here.

In this paragraph, specific strategies for achieving the solution are introduced.

In the final paragraph, Naomi addresses a potential concern and then restates her solution.

# Editing and Proofreading

Check your draft for errors in spelling, grammar, and punctuation.

**Focus on spelling.** As you proofread, circle any words that you are not sure how to spell, frequently misspell, or seldom use. Then, use reference resources, such as a dictionary or a thesaurus, to confirm the correct spelling. Follow these steps to find spellings in a dictionary:

- **Check the first letters of a word.** Think of homophones for that sound.
- **Check the other letters.** Once you spell the first sound correctly, try sounding out the rest of the word. Look for likely spellings in the dictionary. If you do not find your word, look for more unusual spellings of the sound.

# Publishing and Presenting

To make the best use of your problem-and-solution essay, share it with people who can help you make a difference.

**Send a letter.** Send your essay to the appropriate government official, agency, or organization. When you receive a response, share it with your classmates in a presentation. Save both the essay and response in your portfolio.

**Make a speech.** Deliver your essay as a speech to a group from your school or a community that shares your concerns about the problem. Then, lead a question-and-answer session. Be sure to restate your answers if the audience seems confused. Report any consequences of your speech to your classmates.

# Reflecting on Your Writing

**Writer's Journal.** Jot down your answers to this question.

*How did writing about the problem help you to better understand it?*

## Rubric for Self-Assessment

Find evidence in your writing to address each category. Then, use the rating scale to grade your work.

| Criteria | Rating Scale |
|---|---|
| | not very        very |
| **Focus:** How adequately do you explore the problem in the essay? | 1  2  3  4  5 |
| **Organization:** How well do you organize the steps of the solution? | 1  2  3  4  5 |
| **Support/Elaboration:** How convincing are your facts, details, and reasons? | 1  2  3  4  5 |
| **Style:** How appropriate is the language for the audience's knowledge level? | 1  2  3  4  5 |
| **Conventions:** How correct is your grammar, especially your use of pronouns? | 1  2  3  4  5 |

**Spiral Review**

Earlier in this unit, you learned about **personal and reflexive pronouns** (p. 122) and **relative, interrogative, and indefinite pronouns** (p. 150). Check your essay to be sure that you have used these pronouns correctly.

**PH | WRITING COACH**

Further instruction and practice are available in *Prentice Hall Writing Coach*.

# Vocabulary Workshop

## Using a Dictionary and Thesaurus

A **dictionary** is a resource that provides different kinds of information to help readers, writers, and speakers use words correctly. Consult a dictionary to find how to pronounce a word, its part of speech, and its history, or etymology. Look at this dictionary entry for the word *poet*.

**Dictionary**

> **poet** (pō´ət) *n.* [ME < OFr. *poete* < L *poeta* < Gr *poietes*, one who makes, poet < *poiein*, to make: see POEM] **1.** a person who writes poems or verses **2.** a person who displays imaginative power and beauty of thought, language, etc.

The pronunciation uses letters, symbols, and accent marks to show how the word is pronounced. A key to these letters and symbols usually appears at the bottom of the dictionary page or in the front of the dictionary. The key includes a common word to show how the symbols are pronounced.

A **thesaurus** is a book of synonyms. Use it to find the exact word to fit your meaning and to vary word selection to avoid repetition. A thesaurus can also help you locate words that share **denotations,** or dictionary definitions, but have different **connotations,** or shades of meaning.

**Thesaurus**

> **teaching** *n.* teaching, education, schooling, instruction, tuition, coaching, tutoring
> *v.* teach, educate, instruct, give information, give lessons in, school, edify

Many types of dictionaries can be found in the reference section of your library. Also look for them online and on CD-ROMs and DVDs.

**Common Core State Standards**

**Language**
**4.c.** Consult general and specialized reference materials, both print and digital, to find the pronunciation of a word or determine or clarify its precise meaning, its part of speech, or its etymology.
**5.b.** Analyze nuances in the meanings of words with similar denotations.

**Practice A** Look up each word in a dictionary. Write the part of speech and the first definition for each word.

**1.** eminent   **2.** misconstrue   **3.** anecdote

**4.** illiterate   **5.** diversion   **6.** perceive

**Practice B** Use a dictionary to answer questions 1 through 8.

**1.** Which syllable receives the heaviest accent in the word *integrity*?

**2.** Can *wane* be properly used as a noun? If so, what does it mean?

**3.** What word can be used to replace *agitate* in this sentence? "Jonathan began to *agitate* the fish tank."

**4.** What is the adverb form of the word *dire*?

**5.** What part of speech is *expire*?

**6.** Does the vowel sound in *fray* sound like the vowel in *at, ate,* or *car*?

**7.** Which syllable of *upheaval* receives the heaviest accent?

**8. (a)** Note two words with similar denotations you might use to replace *melancholy* in this sentence. "At the end of her vacation, Alice felt melancholy." **(b)** For each word, explain how the connotations of the replacement words change the overall meaning of the sentence.

**Activity** Form a small group with classmates. Write a sentence about a story that you know. Then, pass your sentence to another student. That student should change the sentence that he or she receives by replacing one word with a synonym. See how long your group can keep passing the sentence on and coming up with new words while keeping the original sentence's meaning. Group members may use a thesaurus if they need help.

**Comprehension and Collaboration**

How do you pronounce these words: *feint, insignia, valise*? Look up each word in a dictionary, study the pronunciation, and practice saying it. Then, compare your pronunciations of the words with those of three other students. If you disagree, review the pronunciation key and decide who's correct.

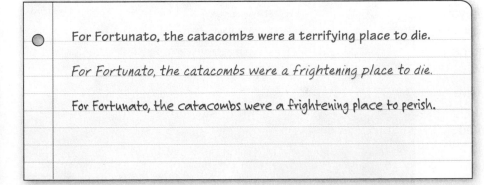

For Fortunato, the catacombs were a terrifying place to die.

For Fortunato, the catacombs were a frightening place to die.

For Fortunato, the catacombs were a frightening place to perish.

# Communications Workshop

## Giving and Following Oral Instructions

**Common Core State Standards**

**Speaking and Listening**
**4.** Present information, findings, and supporting evidence clearly, concisely, and logically such that listeners can follow the line of reasoning and the organization, development, and style are appropriate to task, purpose, and audience.

You can give and follow oral directions to perform specific tasks, answer questions, solve problems, and complete processes.

### Learn the Skills

Use the strategies to complete the activity on page 183.

**Present information.** When you give instructions, explain complex processes in easy-to-follow steps. Ask questions to be sure that your audience understands.

**Listen attentively.** When you follow instructions, listen carefully. Repeat the steps to the instructor to show that you understand. If you are confused, ask the instructor to explain.

**Use instructions for different purposes.** Give and follow complex oral directions for each of the following purposes. Work with a partner to complete these practice exercises.

- **Perform specific tasks.** Draw a design using only straight lines. Do not let your partner see your drawing. Then, give your partner step-by-step instructions for drawing the design. Finally, compare your drawings to see how well the instructions were given and followed.

- **Answer questions.** Ask your partner how to get from school to a place he or she knows well. Follow your partner's instructions by tracing the route on a map.

- **Solve problems.** Name a problem you face, such as staying organized or managing your time. Ask your partner for instructions that will help you solve this problem. Report back to your partner after you have followed the instructions.

- **Complete processes.** Give instructions for completing a process you have learned in school, such as solving an equation.

# Practice the Skills

**© Presentation of Knowledge and Ideas** Use what you've learned in this workshop to perform the following task.

> ## ACTIVITY: Give Complex Oral Instructions
>
> Choose a specific task or process that would help your classmates solve a problem that they face. Give complex oral instructions that tell the class how to perform this task. Answer the following questions in your presentation:
> - What are you teaching your classmates to do?
> - How could your directions help your classmates solve a problem?
> - What materials will your classmates need to follow the directions?
> - How will your classmates know when they have completed the process correctly?
> - What are the steps in the task or process?

As your classmates make their presentations, follow their directions. Use the Presentation Checklist below to analyze their presentations, and let your classmates use the checklist to analyze your presentation.

---

### Presentation Checklist

**Presentation Content**
Does the presentation meet all of the requirements of the activity?
Check all that apply.
❏ It gives listeners instructions to complete a task or process.
❏ It helps listeners solve a problem.
❏ It answers the questions outlined in the activity assignment.

**Presentation Delivery**
Did the speaker give the instructions clearly? Check all that apply.
❏ The speaker gave instructions in logical, easy-to-follow steps.
❏ The speaker asked questions to check that the audience understood the steps.
❏ The speaker gave clear answers to questions asked by the audience.

---

**© Comprehension and Collaboration** After your presentation, ask your classmates to tell you how they rated you on the Presentation Checklist. While your classmates give their presentations, follow their instructions and use the checklist to rate them. As a group, discuss which presentations were the easiest to follow and why.

# Cumulative Review

**Common Core State Standards**

RL.9-10.2, RL.9-10.3, RL.9-10.5; L.9-10.4.a
[For the full wording of the standards, see the standards chart in the front of your textbook.]

## I. Reading Literature

**Directions:** *Read the passage. Then, answer each question that follows.*

I was born in Brooklyn, New York and lived there until I was eleven. I had never really been outside the city. Sure, I had been to Long Island for beach days with my family, but I had never been to the country. My mother got a job Upstate, and suddenly my parents were planning the move. They said that living in the country would be a great experience for all of us, but I was miserable. In August, as we drove the long winding country roads to our new home, I barely said a word.

Many things were lacking in the country. There was no basketball game to pick up. There was no Thai food. There was no skateboarding. There was no sitting on the stoop. Most importantly, there were no old friends. I was so lonely—and bored. It was just my mom, my dad, and me. We were in the middle of nowhere with the closest neighbor over a mile away. Life as I had known it came to an end that August day.

Dad tried to get me to go fishing, but I thought the whole idea was disgusting. Mom tried to get me to walk in the woods, but I didn't like all the bugs, and the brambles scratched my legs. I wanted to go back to Brooklyn in the worst way. All of that would soon change.

I was <u>petrified</u> when I walked into my homeroom. Everyone there knew everyone else, and I did not know anyone. I was set apart from all the other boys by my pale skin and long hair. I sat in the back, and no one said anything to me. The teacher came in and introduced herself.

"Class, we have two new students with us this year." My ears perked up at the word *two,* and I scanned the room for another outsider.

"First, I want to introduce Dave from Brooklyn." The teacher pointed to me. My face flushed as I said "Hi."

"Next, meet Alexis from Washington, D.C."

"Call me Al," she said to the class, looking as lost as I felt.

I had been staring at the back of her head. Her hair was as short as mine was long. I knew immediately that this was not only the year of the Big Move, but it was also the year of the New Best Friend.

1. From which **point of view** is this story told?

   A. first person
   B. second person
   C. third-person limited
   D. third-person omniscient

2. Which element from the passage helped you determine the **point of view**?

   A. The narrator directly addresses his audience, the reader.
   B. The narrator refers to himself as *I* and *me*.
   C. The narrator knows only one person's thoughts.
   D. The narrator has insight into all the people's thoughts.

3. Which word best describes the **author's voice**?

   A. formal
   B. casual
   C. friendly
   D. sarcastic

4. Which of the following sentences is an example of **foreshadowing**?

   A. All of that would soon change.
   B. I had never really been outside of the city.
   C. I wanted to go back to Brooklyn in the worst way.
   D. The teacher pointed to me.

5. Which event occurs during the **rising action** of the narrative?

   A. Dave is born in Brooklyn.
   B. Dave makes a new friend.
   C. Dave's mom gets a job Upstate.
   D. Dave meets Alexis.

6. Which event is the turning point, or **climax,** of the narrative?

   A. Dave moves in August.
   B. Dave wants to move back to Brooklyn.
   C. Dave refuses to go fishing.
   D. Dave hears the teacher say "two."

7. **Vocabulary** Which word is closest in meaning to the underlined word *petrified*?

   A. angry
   B. terrified
   C. annoyed
   D. disturbed

8. How is the conflict in the story resolved?

   A. Dave makes a new friend in the city.
   B. Dave wants to return to Brooklyn.
   C. Dave's mom does not like her job.
   D. Dave goes fishing with his dad.

9. In what way does the choice of narrator affect the description of the country in paragraph 2?

   A. Life in the country seems frightening.
   B. The country appears to offer lots of fun activities.
   C. Moving to the country sounds like a good idea.
   D. The country seems to lack a lot of things that life in the city has to offer.

## ⏱ Timed Writing

10. In a well-developed essay, **identify** the conflict in this story. **Explain** how the author of the text establishes the conflict. Cite evidence from the text to support your analysis. [20 minutes]

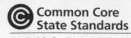
# II. Reading Informational Text

**Directions:** *Read the passage. Then, answer each question that follows.*

> **Common Core State Standards**
>
> **RI.9-10.2, RI.9-10.5; L.9-10.2, L.9-10.3**
> [For the full wording of the standards, see the standards chart in the front of your textbook.]

## Organic Gardening

### The Basics

Organic gardening is a method of gardening that eliminates chemicals from our diets. For gardeners, it presents challenges that regular gardening does not. For example, how do you kill aphids that are eating your tomatoes? An ordinary gardener sprays the plant with a pesticide. An organic gardener uses a natural way to eliminate the pests, such as dipping the plants in water repeatedly to drown the bugs. A pesticide only takes one or two applications to work, but the water technique is a repeated and time-consuming process. This is just one example of how the organic gardener must sometimes commit more time and energy than the ordinary gardener to provide a healthy crop.

### Getting Started

The key to organic gardening success lies in the seeds and the soil. Prepare the soil by tilling and adding compost to enhance its nutrients.

After the soil is ready, carefully choose the seeds or plants to grow. Check each seedling for healthy leaves and roots and look for any signs of stress, such as yellow leaves. Once you have chosen the crop, it is time to plant.

Follow the planting directions. Add natural fertilizer to the each plant. Finally, cover the base of the plant with mulch. Water the plants and watch them grow.

**1.** What **structure** does the author use in this article?

   **A.** numbered lists

   **B.** charts

   **C.** heads and subheads

   **D.** chronological order

**2.** Which of the following *best* describes the **format** of "Getting Started"?

   **A.** chronological order

   **B.** step-by-step order

   **C.** order of importance

   **D.** spatial order

**3.** What is the purpose of "The Basics" section?

   **A.** to explain how to combat pests

   **B.** to introduce organic gardening

   **C.** to identify difficulties

   **D.** to encourage gardeners

**4.** Why is it important to prepare the soil first?

   **A.** A healthy crop relies on healthy soil.

   **B.** The plants will die before you prepare it.

   **C.** The chemicals must be removed.

   **D.** It does not matter when the soil is prepared.

# III. Writing and Language Conventions

**Directions:** *Read the passage. Then, answer each question that follows.*

> (1) I had been looking forward to Nanas visit for months. (2) She came all the way to California from Ohio every August. (3) She was so much fun. (4) She and I did something special together every year. (5) A week before her visit, my cousin invited me to come with his family to Yellowstone National Park. (6) I had never been there before, and I couldn't believe I had the chance to go. (7) Only after the phone call did I realize that the trip was the exact same week Nana was coming. (8) In the end, I weighed the pros and cons and decided to stay for Nana. (9) I only saw her twice a year. (10) Besides, Yellowstone will always be there for me to visit. (11) I had to make a decision.

1. Which revision corrects the illogical **sequence of events**?

   A. Combine sentences 1 and 2.
   B. Eliminate sentence 3.
   C. Break sentence 6 into two sentences.
   D. Move sentence 11 after sentence 7.

2. Which **detail** would most vividly support sentence 4?

   A. She taught me to fish, to cook, and to sew.
   B. She spent a lot of time with Mom.
   C. We didn't do much but talk.
   D. She traveled alone all the way there.

3. Which revision would you make to sentences 2, 3, and 4 to make the writing more interesting?

   A. Change the verb tense.
   B. Vary the sentence beginnings.
   C. Put them in a different order.
   D. Add punctuation.

4. What is the correct way to form the **possessive** in sentence 1?

   A. Nanas
   B. Nana's
   C. Nanas'
   D. Nana

5. Which revision is the most effective way to vary the beginning of sentence 4?

   A. We did something special every year.
   B. Her and I did something special every year.
   C. Every year, we did something special.
   D. Special things were done by us every year.

6. Which is the proper **possessive** form of the **plural** noun *families*?

   A. familys'
   B. familie's
   C. family's
   D. families'

# Performance Tasks

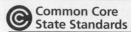

**Common Core State Standards**

RL.9-10.2, RL.9-10.3, RL.9-10.5, RL.9-10.6; RI.9-10.2, RI.9-10.4; SL.9-10.4, SL.9-10.5; L.9-10.2
[For full wording of the standards, see the standards chart in the front of your textbook.]

**Directions:** *Follow the instructions to complete the tasks below as required by your teacher.*

*As you work on each task, incorporate both general academic vocabulary and literary terms you learned in this unit.*

## Writing

### Task 1: Literature [RL.9-10.2; L.9-10.2]
**Analyze the Development of Theme**

*Write an essay in which you compare and contrast the themes of two stories in this unit.*

- Analyze the development of the theme in each story and discuss similarities and differences in the message each expresses.

- Note specific strategies each author uses to introduce and develop the theme.

- Discuss specific details that contribute to the development of each theme. Explain what each detail adds.

- To ensure that readers understand your analysis, include an objective summary of each story.

- Capitalize proper nouns, including characters' and authors' names, correctly.

### Task 2: Literature [RL.9-10.5]
**Analyze the Effects of Structure in a Story**

*Write an essay in which you explain how the structure of a story in this unit leads to a specific emotional effect, such as tension or suspense.*

- Identify the story's main conflict and summarize the narrative.

- Describe specific structural choices the writer makes. For example, discuss how much exposition the author provides and how he or she introduces the conflict. Also describe any use of plot devices, such as foreshadowing.

- Finally, explain how the story affects you as a reader and how the author's choices regarding structure contribute to that effect.

- Cite textual evidence to support your assertions.

### Task 3: Informational Text [RI.9-10.2]
**Analyze the Development of a Central Idea**

*Write an essay in which you analyze the development of the central idea in a work of literary nonfiction in this unit.*

- Clearly explain the central idea of the work and discuss how it emerges or is introduced by the author.

- Identify specific details that shape and refine the central idea. Consider various types of evidence and explain what each adds to the development of the central idea.

- To ensure that readers understand your analysis, include an objective summary of the work.

### Task 4: Informational Text [RI.9-10.6]
**Analyze an Author's Purpose and Use of Rhetoric**

*Write an essay in which you determine an author's purpose and point of view and analyze his or her uses of rhetoric in a work of nonfiction in this unit.*

- Explain the topic of the work and determine both the author's general and specific purposes for writing.

- Analyze the author's perspective or point of view on the topic. For example, explain whether the author has a positive or negative perspective or expresses a particular attitude toward the topic.

- Note specific examples of the author's uses of rhetoric. For example, identify examples of parallel structure or repetition. Then, explain how those uses of rhetoric work to advance the author's purpose and point of view.

# Speaking and Listening

## @ Task 5: Literature [RL.9-10.3; SL.9-10.4]
### Analyze the Development of a Complex Character

*Deliver an oral presentation in which you analyze a complex character from a story in this unit.*

- Explain why you chose the character. Discuss the traits that make the character complex, or round, and dynamic, rather than static.

- Explain strategies the writer uses to portray the character's complexity. Note specific details that add to the character's portrayal as the story develops.

- Describe how the character's complexity, including his or her emotions, motivations, actions, and reactions, advances the plot and contributes to the story's theme.

- Present your analysis and evidence logically so that listeners can follow your line of reasoning. Make sure your overall approach, including both content and style, is appropriate for a classroom presentation on an academic topic.

## @ Task 6: Literature [RL.9-10.6; SL.9-10.5]
### Analyze a Cultural Perspective

*Present a visual essay in which you analyze a cultural perspective reflected in a story in this unit.*

- A visual essay combines images and text to explain an idea. The visual part of your essay may take the form of a slideshow, poster, or other format.

- Choose a story from this unit that reflects a cultural perspective from outside the United States. Explain how that cultural perspective is reflected in the setting and events as well as in characters' thoughts, emotions, actions, and reactions.

- Using the story as an example, discuss the kinds of factual information a work of fiction can provide. Explain what you learned about another culture by reading this story.

- Share your work with the class in an informal presentation. After you have delivered your presentation, answer questions from classmates.

## @ Task 7: Informational Text [RI.9-10.4; SL.9-10.5]
### Analyze the Effect of Word Choice on Tone

*Write and present an essay in which you analyze the cumulative effect of word choice on tone in a work of literary nonfiction in this unit.*

- Choose a work of literary nonfiction from this unit that offers a clear and distinct tone. Explain your choice.

- Identify specific word choices that contribute to the creation of that tone.

- Illustrate your analysis by creating a graphic organizer or chart that captures your ideas visually.

- Present your essay, including charts or graphic organizers, to the class. Use technology to display graphics, or distribute them as handouts.

---

**Can truth change?**
At the beginning of Unit 1, you participated in a discussion about the Big Question. Now that you have completed the unit, write a response to the question. Discuss how your initial ideas have either changed or been reinforced. Cite specific examples from the literature in this unit, from other subject areas, and from your own life to support your ideas. Use Big Question vocabulary words (see page 3) in your response.

# Featured Titles

In this unit, you have read a variety of fiction and literary nonfiction. Continue to read both genres on your own. Select books that you enjoy, but challenge yourself to explore new topics, new authors, and works of increasing depth and complexity. The titles suggested below will help you get started.

## Literature

### The Red Badge of Courage
by Stephen Crane

In this groundbreaking **novel,** Henry Fleming is a soldier who must conquer his terror of battle or live in shame. He discovers the truth about himself in the midst of the Civil War, the bloodiest conflict in American history.

### Journey Home
by Yoshiko Uchida
Aladdin Books, 1978

As World War II rages overseas, prejudice against Japanese Americans runs rampant in the United States. Yuki and her family, just released from an internment camp, must deal with this climate of fear and anger on their journey home, as described in this gripping **historical novel.**

### Fahrenheit 451
by Ray Bradbury                    EXEMPLAR TEXT

In a desolate future, firemen no longer put out fires—they start them, using books as fuel. This **science-fiction novel** critiques thoughtless conformity, the media, and what the author saw as the abuses of technology.

### Six Characters in Search of an Author
by Luigi Pirandello
Signet Classics, 1970

Imagine your family walking into a theater and demanding that the actors portray your relationships on stage. This **play,** a classic of modern theater, explores that idea.

## Complete Stories and Poems of Edgar Allan Poe
EXEMPLAR TEXT

"The Raven," Poe's narrative poem that mixes sorrow with supernatural gloom, is just one of the classic **poems** and **stories** included in this volume.

## Informational Texts

### I Know Why the Caged Bird Sings
by Maya Angelou                    EXEMPLAR TEXT

Maya Angelou's **memoir** of her Arkansas childhood is a classic of twentieth-century literature. This coming-of-age story reveals the author's strength and resilience in the face of racism, trauma, and poverty.

### Up Close: Rachel Carson
by Ellen Levine

With a love of nature and a passion for science, Rachel Carson revolutionized the world's thinking about the environment. This **biography** tells the story of her struggle to protect the beauty of nature for us all.

### Rosa Parks: My Story
by Rosa Parks with Jim Haskins

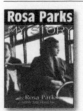

In this **autobiography,** Rosa Parks tells the story of how her refusal to give up a bus seat to a white man in 1955 inspired a year of boycotts, lawsuits, and, ultimately, a new future for civil rights in America.

# Preparing to Read Complex Texts

**Attentive Reading** As you read literature on your own, bring your imagination and questions to the text. The questions shown below and others that you formulate as you read will help you learn and enjoy literature even more.

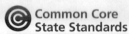 **Common Core State Standards**

**Reading Literature/Informational Text 10.** By the end of grade 9, read and comprehend literature, including stories, dramas, and poems, and literary nonfiction in the grades 9–10 text complexity band proficiently, with scaffolding as needed at the high end of the range.

## When reading fiction, ask yourself...

- Who is telling the story? Do I enjoy his or her voice?
- Does the story offer a message about life that I appreciate?

**Ⓒ Key Ideas and Details**

- Is the world of the story convincing? Do any details jolt me out of that world or seem wrong?
- Does the plot pull me along? Do I care what happens?
- Do the characters seem real? Do the reasons they feel and act as they do ring true? Do their words and thoughts sound authentic?
- Does the author use language well?

**Ⓒ Craft and Structure**

- Do I like the characters, or at least find them interesting?
- Do I believe the events of this story?
- Is the work fresh and original?

**Ⓒ Integration of Ideas**

## When reading nonfiction, ask yourself...

- Who is the author? Why did he or she write the work?
- Does the work meet my expectations?
- Are the ideas exciting? Do they give me a new way of looking at a topic? Do I learn something?
- Has the author made me care about the subject?

**Ⓒ Key Ideas and Details**

- Does the author organize ideas so that I can follow them?
- Does the author use strong, varied, and convincing evidence?
- Does the author use language well?
- Does the work ring true? Is any aspect of the work exaggerated?

**Ⓒ Craft and Structure**

- Do I agree or disagree with the author's ideas?
- Does the author omit viewpoints I think are important?

**Ⓒ Integration of Ideas**

# Is *conflict* necessary?

# Short Stories

## PHLit Online!
www.PHLitOnline.com

### Hear It!
- Selection summary audio
- Selection audio
- BQ Tunes

### See It!
- Author videos
- Big Question video
- Get Connected videos
- Background videos
- More about the authors
- Illustrated vocabulary words
- Vocabulary flashcards

### Do It!
- Interactive journals
- Interactive graphic organizers
- Grammar tutorials
- Interactive vocabulary games
- Test practice

 **Is** *conflict* **necessary?**

A **conflict** is a struggle between opposing forces. A conflict might be as small as an argument between friends or as large as a war between nations. It might also involve just one person who faces a personal challenge or a hard decision. Conflicts occur frequently in literature and in life, but are they necessary? Conflicts can be difficult for the people involved in them, but can a conflict also have a positive outcome?

## Exploring the Big Question

© **Collaboration: Group Discussion** Start thinking about the Big Question by identifying different types of conflicts and what can happen as a result of them. Make a list of some different conflicts you have either read about or experienced. Describe one specific example of each of the following:

- An argument or a disagreement between friends
- A contest or competition between teams
- A struggle to make a decision
- A controversy in the news
- A problem that must be solved

Share your examples with a group. Talk about both the causes and the effects of each conflict. Consider the positive and negative effects that each conflict might have for each person involved.

Before you begin the discussion, establish rules that will allow you to manage conflicts within your own group. For example, agree upon specific goals you want to achieve, how you will handle disagreements, and timeframes for completing your objectives. Write down the rules and refer to them as needed as you conduct your discussion.

**Connecting to the Literature** Each reading in this unit will give you additional insight into the Big Question.

**www.PHLitOnline.com**

- Big Question video
- Illustrated vocabulary words
- Interactive vocabulary games
- BQ Tunes

# Learning Big Question Vocabulary

**Acquire and Use Academic Vocabulary** Academic vocabulary is the language you encounter in textbooks and on standardized tests. Review the definitions of these academic vocabulary words.

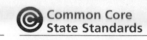

**Common Core**
**State Standards**

**Speaking and Listening**
**1.b.** Work with peers to set rules for collegial discussions and decision-making, clear goals and deadlines, and individual roles as needed.

**Language**
**6.** Acquire and use accurately general academic and domain-specific words and phrases, sufficient for reading, writing, speaking, and listening at the college and career readiness level; demonstrate independence in gathering vocabulary knowledge when considering a word or phrase important to comprehension or expression.

> **appreciate** (ə prē′ shē āt′) **v.** be aware of the value of something
>
> **argument** (är′ gyo͞o mənt) **n.** disagreement; dispute
>
> **articulate** (är tik′yo͞o lāt′) **v.** express clearly
>
> **compete** (kəm pēt′) **v.** try to win
>
> **competition** (käm′ pə tish′ ən) **n.** contest or match
>
> **controversy** (kän′trə vur′ sē) **n.** disagreement, often public

Use these words as you complete Big Question activities that involve reading, writing, speaking, and listening.

**Gather Vocabulary Knowledge** Additional Big Question words are listed below. Categorize the words by deciding whether you know each one well, know it a little bit, or do not know it at all.

| | | |
|---|---|---|
| amicably | equity | mediate |
| antagonize | grievance | survival |
| cooperate | issue | war/battle |
| differences | | |

Then, do the following:

1. Write the definitions of the words you know.
2. Consult a dictionary to confirm the word's meaning. Revise your definition if necessary.
3. Using a print or an online dictionary, look up the meanings of the words you do not know. Then, write the meanings.
4. If a word sounds familiar but you are not sure of its meaning, consult a dictionary. Then, record the meaning.
5. Use all of the words in a brief paragraph about the necessity of conflict. Choose punctuation for effect.

# Elements of a Short Story

In a short story, elements such as characters, setting, plot, and conflict combine to create a unified impression, or main effect.

**Short stories** are brief fictional narratives intended to be read in a single sitting. Because of a short story's length, the narration and character portrayals must be focused and compressed, adding a special energy and depth to the form. As a result, a good short story leaves the reader with a unified, strong impression—its **main effect.** Each element of a story can contribute to this effect.

**Characters** The **characters** are the people or animals who take part in the action of the story. Details in the story help readers understand characters' **traits,** or qualities, and **motives,** or reasons for acting. The main effect of a story often involves a change or revelation experienced by a character.

**Setting** The **setting** of a story is the time and place of its action. Often, a short story takes place in a single, unified setting. The setting often contributes to a story's **mood**—the general feeling the story conveys.

**Plot** The **plot** of a story is the sequence of events it tells. Plot often contributes to the unified effect of a story by building toward a **climax,** or turning point, in which a character reaches an insight or undergoes a change.

**Conflict** A plot is driven by a **conflict,** or struggle between two opposing forces. Short stories usually focus on one central conflict.

- An **internal conflict** takes place in the mind of a character. The character struggles to make a decision or overcome feelings.

- An **external conflict** takes place between a character and an outside force, such as another character or a force of nature.

**Theme and Symbols** As the elements of a story combine to create a unified effect, they also suggest a **theme,** or insight into life. Most often, readers come to understand the theme by making inferences from key elements, including symbols. A **symbol** is an object or a story element that stands for a larger meaning.

**The elements of a short story are interrelated and contribute to a unified effect.**

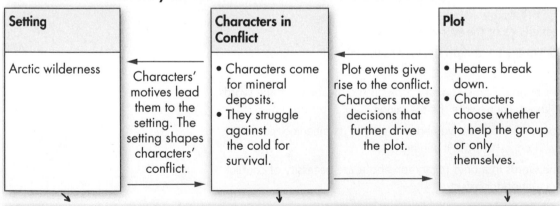

| Setting | | Characters in Conflict | | Plot |
|---|---|---|---|---|
| Arctic wilderness | Characters' motives lead them to the setting. The setting shapes characters' conflict. | • Characters come for mineral deposits.<br>• They struggle against the cold for survival. | Plot events give rise to the conflict. Characters make decisions that further drive the plot. | • Heaters break down.<br>• Characters choose whether to help the group or only themselves. |

**Main Effect:** Characters' fear and greed create a sickening sense of chaos until one character rallies them.

## Plot Structure in a Short Story

No matter what tales short stories tell, many stories share a basic plot structure. Understanding this structure can help you appreciate how a short story builds to a satisfying conclusion.

In the section of the plot called the **exposition,** the author introduces the setting and the characters. This section often includes an **inciting event**—an event that establishes the **conflict,** or struggle between opposing forces, that drives the story. Types of conflicts include

- a struggle between two characters;
- a struggle between a character and an outside force, such as nature;
- a struggle within the mind of a character, such as a struggle with guilt.

The next part of a typical plot is the **rising action,** which includes events and complications that intensify the conflict. The rising action leads to the **climax,** which is the turning point in the story—the moment of highest tension or suspense. The climax is the part of the story that makes readers want to read on to find out what happens next.

The **falling action** sets up the story's ending. The intensity of the conflict lessens and events wind down, leading to the **resolution,** or **denouement,** which shows the outcome of the conflict. In some stories, the conflict is settled, meaning that the central problem is solved; in other stories, the conflict may be left unsettled. In still other stories, the ending may revisit the characters after time has passed to show how the situation changes after the conflict is resolved. Look at the example in the chart below.

### Example: Plot Structure

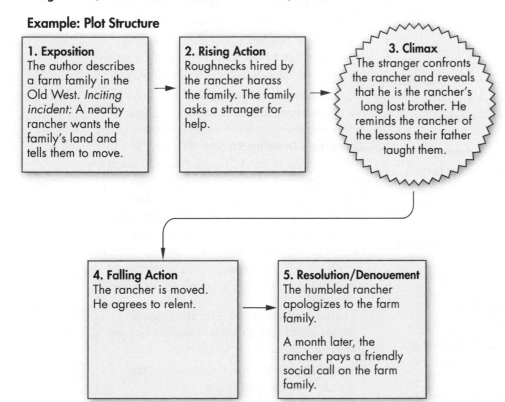

**1. Exposition**
The author describes a farm family in the Old West. *Inciting incident:* A nearby rancher wants the family's land and tells them to move.

**2. Rising Action**
Roughnecks hired by the rancher harass the family. The family asks a stranger for help.

**3. Climax**
The stranger confronts the rancher and reveals that he is the rancher's long lost brother. He reminds the rancher of the lessons their father taught them.

**4. Falling Action**
The rancher is moved. He agrees to relent.

**5. Resolution/Denouement**
The humbled rancher apologizes to the farm family.

A month later, the rancher pays a friendly social call on the farm family.

# Analyzing Character

An author develops **characters** in ways that advance a story's **plot**.

**Common Core
State Standards**

**Reading Literature**

**3.** Analyze how complex characters develop over the course of a text, interact with other characters, and advance the plot or develop the theme.

**5.** Analyze how an author's choices concerning how to structure a text, order events within it, and manipulate time create such effects as mystery, tension, or surprise.

## Developing Complex Characters

In the best short stories, the main characters are interesting and **complex,** or well-rounded. Complex characters share these qualities:

- They show multiple or even contradictory **traits,** or qualities.
- They struggle with conflicting **motivations,** or reasons for acting as they do.
- They may change by the end of the story.

---

**Example: Complex Character**

**Contradictory Traits** Bob's ability to organize ideas leads the debate team to victory—but his room is a mess.

**Conflicting Motives** After high school, Bob wants to stay near his friends; he also wants to go to the best college he can.

**Change** After making a new friend on a trip, Bob decides he will move away for college.

---

**Characterization** To create and **develop** a character, a writer will use techniques of **characterization.**

- In **direct characterization,** the narrator makes direct statements about a character's personality:
  *Afshin focused on just one thing at a time, but the depth of his focus was remarkable. Before a race, his single-minded trance could only be broken by the sound of the starter's whistle.*
- In **indirect characterization,** readers learn what characters are like by analyzing what they say and do as well as how other characters respond to them:
  *Summer or winter, in sun, wind, or rain, Jess rose before dawn and jogged the two-mile loop around the reservoir. After a quick shower and two chocolate donuts, she always felt ready to face the day.*

## How Characters Advance a Story

**Characters Advance the Plot** As characters interact with one another and struggle to overcome problems, their choices move the story along. A character's action—or decision *not* to take action—can lead to new plot developments and may intensify the conflict, heightening tension or suspense in the story.

---

**Example:**

**Conflict** Cindy is friendly with Matilda. Cindy's friends Staci and Ashley do not like Matilda and put pressure on Cindy to shun her.

**Characters' Interactions** Cindy decides that Staci and Ashley are being unfair and makes a point of attending a school game with Matilda.

**Result: Intensified Conflict** Staci and Ashley invite everyone to their party except Cindy.

---

**Characters Develop Theme** As in real life, a character's struggles with a situation can teach a general lesson. In this way, characters help develop a story's **theme**—the central insight that it conveys. As you read a short story, pay close attention to the ways that characters change and to the lessons that they learn. These details will point you toward the story's theme.

---

**Example:**

**Character's Experience** After struggling to please her friends, Cindy realizes that they are shallow and decides to let them go.

**Theme** As people grow, they may outgrow their friendships with others.

---

# Analyzing Structure and Theme

An author **structures** a story in ways that create interest and help develop the **theme**.

**Common Core State Standards**

**Reading Literature**
**5.** Analyze how an author's choices concerning how to structure a text, order events within it, and manipulate time create such effects as mystery, tension, or surprise.

## Structuring a Text for Effect

The way in which an author structures or organizes information in a story can create effects like tension, mystery, and surprise.

**Plot Structure** Authors make decisions about the order in which to present information as well as the pacing of events.

• **Openings** The opening establishes the general feeling of a story.

---

**Examples of Some Story Openings**

**Focus on Setting:** *The hospital waiting room was empty at that hour of the night. It was so quiet I could hear the second hand on the large wall clock toll each passing second.*

**Focus on Character:** *I'll never forget my grandfather. He was the most charming man I ever met.*

**in medias res** (Latin for "in the middle of things"): *"Someone call for help!" shouted a man at the side of the road.*

---

• **Sequence** Narrators tell plot events mainly in **chronological order**—the order in which events occurred. However, they may break from chronological order for effect.
**Flashbacks** are sections of a narrative that describe a time before the present time of the story. A flashback might give insight into a character's motivations. **Foreshadowing** gives readers hints about what will happen later in the story, as when a narrator says, "That would be the last time they spoke." Foreshadowing can create **suspense,** or a reader's feeling of anxious uncertainty about the outcome.

• **Pacing** refers to the "speed" with which a narrator relates events. For example, by describing a scene at length and giving many descriptive details, the narrator "slows down" the pace. This effect can be used to heighten suspense, as in the following example:

---

**Example: Slow Pace**
Beads of sweat stood out on Agent Vole's forehead. As he struggled with the ropes that bound him, he could hear each beat of his heart, rapid but distinct. Ba-dum, ba-dum. With each beat, the second hand on the timing device clicked one notch closer to catastrophe.

---

• A narrative can also create a sensation of "speed" and excitement by moving quickly from one idea to another in a scene that is loaded with tension.

**Point of View** The **point of view,** or narrative perspective, from which a story is told determines the information an author includes. There are three main points of view:

• **Third-person omniscient:** The narrator is outside the events of the story and tells the thoughts and feelings of all characters.
• **Third-person limited:** The narrator is outside the story but tells the thoughts and feelings of only one character.
• **First-person:** The narrator is a character in the story and uses the pronouns *I* and *me*.

Point of view can be used to achieve striking effects. For example, if the first-person narrator is naive, or unsophisticated, the reader may know more about what is going on than the narrator, creating an effect known as **dramatic irony.**

# Close Read: Elements of a Short Story

**Short stories create a main effect and convey a theme by telling how complex characters interact and struggle to resolve a conflict.**

A short story is like a small but powerful machine. Conflict, the motor, drives events of the plot toward a resolution, brought about by the characters' actions. Along the way, characters may grow or change. As you read a short story, use these tips to analyze its elements.

## Tips for Analyzing Elements of Short Stories

### Plot and Conflict
The plot is the sequence of events. Plot events are driven by a conflict, or struggle between opposing forces. As you read, identify

- how the story begins and ends;
- the main conflict and how events intensify it;
- breaks from chronological order, including flashbacks (shifts to the past) or foreshadowing (hints of future events);
- how the conflict is resolved.

### Characters
The characters are the people who take part in the action of the story. As you read, think about

- characters' actions, thoughts, statements, and appearance;
- how complex, or many-sided, they are;
- whether characters learn something and if so, what they learn;
- how their actions drive the plot;
- how their experiences develop the theme.

### Point of View
Point of view is the perspective from which a story is told. As you read, determine

- whether the story is told from third-person omniscient, third-person limited, or first-person point of view;
- how the point of view shapes the story, either by excluding certain information or by making certain information available.

### Setting
The setting is the time and place of the story. It may simply be the backdrop against which actions take place, or it may be a crucial element of the conflict. As you read, consider

- the conflict and where it takes place;
- whether the setting affects what the characters say and do.

### Main Effect
The elements of a well-constructed short story combine to create one main effect. Notice

- the feeling that accompanies the climax— horror, amusement, pity, and so on;
- how the story impacts your understanding or view of a situation or character.

### Theme and Symbols
The theme, or insight, a story conveys may be reinforced by a symbol—an object or story element that stands for a larger idea. Think about

- what the characters learn about themselves or life;
- whether or not characters change;
- whether elements in the story are treated as symbols, and if so, what they stand for.

# Model

**About the Text** Nobel Prize-winning author Ernest Hemingway (1899–1961) pioneered a distinctive narrative style in his fiction. In 1938, Hemingway went to Spain as a reporter to cover events in the Spanish Civil War (1936–1939), a bloody conflict that divided the country and drew the attention of the world. He originally wrote this story as a news dispatch, but later rewrote it as a short story.

## "Old Man at the Bridge" by Ernest Hemingway

An old man with steel rimmed spectacles and very dusty clothes sat by the side of the road. There was a pontoon bridge across the river and carts, trucks, and men, women and children were crossing it. The mule-drawn carts staggered up the steep bank from the bridge with soldiers helping push against the spokes of the wheels. The trucks ground up and away heading out of it all and the peasants plodded along in the ankle deep dust. But the old man sat there without moving. He was too tired to go any farther.

It was my business to cross the bridge, explore the bridgehead beyond and find out to what point the enemy had advanced. I did this and returned over the bridge. There were not so many carts now and very few people on foot, but the old man was still there.

"Where do you come from?" I asked him.

"From San Carlos," he said, and smiled.

That was his native town and so it gave him pleasure to mention it and he smiled.

"I was taking care of animals," he explained.

"Oh," I said, not quite understanding.

"Yes," he said, "I stayed, you see, taking care of animals. I was the last one to leave the town of San Carlos."

He did not look like a shepherd nor a herdsman and I looked at his black dusty clothes and his gray dusty face and his steel rimmed spectacles and said, "What animals were they?"

"Various animals," he said, and shook his head. "I had to leave them."

I was watching the bridge and the African looking country of the Ebro Delta and wondering how long now it would be before we would see the enemy, and listening all the while for the first noises that would signal that ever mysterious event called contact, and the old man still sat there.

"What animals were they?" I asked.

"There were three animals altogether," he explained. "There were two goats and a cat and then there were four pairs of pigeons."

"And you had to leave them?" I asked.

"Yes. Because of the artillery. The captain told me to go because of the artillery."

**Setting** This description of wartime activities establishes the setting.

**Point of View** The story is told by a first-person narrator. While he can share his own thoughts and feelings, he does not know those of the old man, adding to the old man's mystery.

**Characters** The old man's pleasure at naming his hometown conveys his simplicity and innocence.

**Plot and Conflict** The narrator's expectation of the enemy's arrival—and the implication that violence is imminent—contrasts with the old man's passivity. The contrast heightens the conflict.

**Model continued**

**Theme** The old man describes himself as "without politics." His statement develops the theme: War affects even those who do not take sides.

**Plot and Conflict** The repetitive dialogue heightens the conflict between the old man's lack of action and the narrator's concern. It advances the plot by showing that the narrator has done all that he can.

**Main Effect** Through the old man's incomprehension of the danger facing him, Hemingway achieves his main effect: a glimpse of the dull horror of war.

**Theme** This conclusion points to a theme: *War has innocent victims. It displaces, disorients, and may even destroy them.*

"And you have no family?" I asked, watching the far end of the bridge where a few last carts were hurrying down the slope of the bank.

"No," he said, "only the animals I stated. The cat, of course, will be all right. A cat can look out for itself, but I cannot think what will become of the others."

"What politics have you?" I asked.

"I am without politics," he said. "I am seventy-six years old. I have come twelve kilometers now and I think now I can go no further."

"This is not a good place to stop," I said. "If you can make it, there are trucks up the road where it forks for Tortosa."

"I will wait a while," he said, "and then I will go. Where do the trucks go?"

"Towards Barcelona," I told him.

"I know no one in that direction," he said, "but thank you very much. Thank you again very much."

He looked at me very blankly and tiredly, then said, having to share his worry with some one, "The cat will be all right, I am sure. There is no need to be unquiet about the cat. But the others. Now what do you think about the others?"

"Why they'll probably come through it all right."

"You think so?"

"Why not," I said, watching the far bank where now there were no carts.

"But what will they do under the artillery when I was told to leave because of the artillery?"

"Did you leave the dove cage unlocked?" I asked.

"Yes."

"Then they'll fly."

"Yes, certainly they'll fly. But the others. It's better not to think about the others," he said.

"If you are rested I would go," I urged. "Get up and try to walk now."

"Thank you," he said and got to his feet, swayed from side to side and then sat down backwards in the dust.

"I was taking care of animals," he said dully, but no longer to me. "I was only taking care of animals."

There was nothing to do about him. It was Easter Sunday and the Fascists[1] were advancing toward the Ebro. It was a gray overcast day with a low ceiling so their planes were not up. That and the fact that cats know how to look after themselves was all the good luck that old man would ever have.

---

1. **Fascists** Right-wing members of the military and their supporters who, aided by Nazi Germany and Fascist Italy, fought to control Spain during the Spanish Civil War.

# Independent Practice

**About the Text** Wayson Choy (b. 1939) is a contemporary Canadian writer. During World War II, while Choy's immigrant parents worked, he was cared for by Chinatown's village elders in Vancouver, Canada. The vivid myths that they shared during his childhood inspired him to tell his own tales.

## "The Jade Peony"[1] by Wayson Choy

When Grandmama died at 83 our whole household held its breath. She had promised us a sign of her leaving, final proof that her present life had ended well. My parents knew that without any clear sign, our own family fortunes could be altered, threatened. My stepmother looked endlessly into the small cluttered room the ancient lady had occupied. Nothing was touched; nothing changed. My father, thinking that a sign should appear in Grandmama's garden, looked at the frost-killed shoots and cringed: *no, that could not be it.*

My two older teenage brothers and my sister, Liang, age 14, were embarrassed by my parents' behavior. What would all the white people in Vancouver[2] think of us? We were Canadians now, *Chinese-Canadians,* a hyphenated reality that my parents could never accept. So it seemed, for different reasons, we all held our breath waiting for *something.*

I was eight when she died. For days she had resisted going into the hospital . . . *a cold*, *just a cold* . . . and instead gave constant instruction to my stepmother and sister on the boiling of ginseng roots mixed with bitter extract. At night, between wracking coughs and deadly silences, Grandmama had her back and chest rubbed with heated camphor oil and sipped a bluish decoction of an herb called Peacock's Tail. When all these failed to abate her fever, she began to arrange the details of her will. This she did with my father, confessing finally: "I am too stubborn. The only cure for old age is to die."

My father wept to hear this. I stood beside her bed; she turned to me. Her round face looked darker, and the gentleness of her eyes, the thin, arching eyebrows, seemed weary. I brushed the few strands of gray, brittle hair from her face; she managed to smile at me. Being the youngest, I had spent nearly all my time with her and could not imagine that we would ever be parted. Yet when she spoke, and her voice hesitated, cracked, the somber shadows of her room chilled me. Her wrinkled brow grew wet with fever, and her small body seemed even more diminutive.

"I—I am going to the hospital, Grandson." Her hand reached out for mine. "You know, Little Son, whatever happens I will never leave you." Her palm felt plush and warm, the slender, old fingers boney and firm, so magically strong was her grip that I could not imagine how she could ever part from me. Ever.

**Plot and Conflict** What information does the narrator give readers in the opening paragraph?

**Point of View** From what point of view is the story told? How does this point of view determine the information the narrator can share?

**Characters** How does the physical description of Grandmama contribute to your understanding of her character?

---

1. **Jade Peony** (pē′ ə nē) jade is a hard, dense gemstone; a peony is a common garden flower, the Chinese variety of which produces large, single blossoms in early summer.
2. **Vancouver** (van kōō′ vər) large city in the province of British Columbia, Canada.

## Practice continued

**Plot** What important information do you learn in this passage, which flashes back to events before the beginning of the story and then returns to the present?

**Symbols** How do you know the jade peony is an important symbol? What is its connection to the windchimes?

**Setting** How does the setting influence the characters' reactions to Grandmama's quest?

**Conflict** What conflict between Grandmama and other family members is established here?

**Theme and Symbols** What theme concerning tradition and the past does the father's reaction develop? How is it connected to the symbol of the jade peony?

Her hands were magical. My most vivid memories are of her hands: long, elegant fingers, with impeccable nails, a skein of fine, barely-seen veins, and wrinkled skin like light pine. Those hands were quick when she taught me, at six, simple tricks of juggling, learnt when she was a village girl in Southern Canton; a troupe of actors had stayed on her father's farm. One of them, "tall and pale as the whiteness of petals," fell in love with her, promising to return. In her last years his image came back like a third being in our two lives. He had been magician, acrobat, juggler, and some of the things he taught her she had absorbed and passed on to me through her stories and games. But above all, without realizing it then, her hands conveyed to me the quality of their love.

Most marvelous for me was the quick-witted skill her hands revealed in making windchimes for our birthdays: windchimes in the likeness of her lost friend's only present to her, made of bits of string and scraps, in the center of which once hung a precious jade peony. This wondrous gift to her broke apart years ago, in China, but Grandmama kept the jade pendant in a tiny red silk envelope, and kept it always in her pocket, until her death.

These were not ordinary, carelessly made chimes, such as those you now find in our Chinatown stores, whose rattling noises drive you mad. But making her special ones caused dissension in our family, and some shame. Each one that she made was created from a treasure trove of glass fragments and castaway costume jewelry, in the same way that her first windchime had been made. The problem for the rest of the family was in the fact that Grandmama looked for these treasures wandering the back alleys of Keefer and Pender Streets, peering into our neighbors' garbage cans, chasing away hungry, nervous cats and shouting curses at them.

"All our friends are laughing at us!" Older Brother Jung said at last to my father, when Grandmama was away having tea at Mrs. Lim's.

"We are not poor," Oldest Brother Kiam declared, "Yet she and Sek-Lung poke through those awful things as if—" he shoved me in frustration and I stumbled against my sister, "—they were beggars!"

"She will make Little Brother crazy!" Sister Liang said. Without warning, she punched me sharply in the back; I jumped. "You see, look how *nervous* he is!"

I lifted my foot slightly, enough to swing it back and kick Liang in the shin. She yelled and pulled back her fist to punch me again. Jung made a menacing move towards me.

"Stop this, all of you!" My father shook his head in exasperation. How could he dare tell the Grand Old One, his aging mother, that what was somehow appropriate in a poor village in China, was an abomination here. How could he prevent me, his youngest, from accompanying her? If she went walking into those alleyways alone she could well be attacked by hoodlums. "She is not a beggar looking for food. She is searching for—for. . . ."

My stepmother attempted to speak, then fell silent. She, too, seemed perplexed and somewhat ashamed. They all loved Grandmama, but she was *inconvenient*, unsettling.

As for our neighbors, most understood Grandmama to be harmlessly crazy, others that she did indeed make lovely toys but for what purpose? *Why*? they asked, and the stories she told me, of the juggler who smiled at her, flashed in my head.

Finally, by their cutting remarks, the family did exert enough pressure so that Grandmama and I no longer openly announced our expeditions. Instead, she took me with her on "shopping trips," ostensibly for clothes or groceries, while in fact we spent most of our time exploring stranger and more distant neighborhoods, searching for splendid junk: jangling pieces of a vase, cranberry glass fragments embossed with leaves, discarded glass beads from Woolworth[3] necklaces. . . . We would sneak them all home in brown rice sacks, folded into small parcels, and put them under her bed. During the day when the family was away at school or work, we brought them out and washed every item in a large black pot of boiling lye[4] and water, dried them quickly, carefully, and returned them, sparkling, under her bed.

Our greatest excitement occurred when a fire gutted the large Chinese Presbyterian Church, three blocks from our house. Over the still-smoking ruins the next day, Grandmama and I rushed precariously over the blackened beams to pick out the stained glass that glittered in the sunlight. Small figure bent over, wrapped against the autumn cold in a dark blue quilted coat, happily gathering each piece like gold, she became my spiritual playmate: "There's a good one! *There!*"

Hours later, soot-covered and smelling of smoke, we came home with a carton full of delicate fragments, still early enough to steal them all into the house and put the small box under her bed. "These are special pieces," she said, giving the box a last push, "because they come from a sacred place." She slowly got up and I saw, for the first time, her hand begin to shake. But then, in her joy, she embraced me. Both of our hearts were racing, as if we were two dreamers. I buried my face in her blue quilt, and for a moment, the whole world seemed silent.

"My juggler," she said, "he never came back to me from Honan[5]. . . perhaps the famine. . . ." Her voice began to quake. "But I shall have my sacred windchime . . . I shall have it again."

One evening, when the family was gathered in their usual places in the parlor, Grandmama gave me her secret nod: a slight wink of her eye and a flaring of her nostrils. There was *trouble* in the air. Supper had gone badly, school examinations were due, father had failed to meet an editorial deadline at the *Vancouver Chinese Times*. A huge sigh came from Sister Liang.

**Characters** How do other characters' reactions to Grandmama add to your understanding of her personality?

**Characters** How do the interactions of characters advance the plot in this section?

**Point of View** How does the narrator's point of view determine which information is presented and how?

**Plot** In what ways do Grandmama's musings both flash back to earlier events and foreshadow the future?

---

3. **Woolworth** a variety store belonging to the chain founded by Frank Woolworth in 1879.
4. **lye** (lī) *n.* substance derived from wood ashes, commonly used in making soap or for washing.
5. **Honan** (hō´ nän´) province in east central China.

**Practice continued**

"But it is useless this Chinese they teach you!" she lamented, turning to Stepmother for support. Silence. Liang frowned, dejected, and went back to her Chinese book, bending the covers back.

"Father," Oldest Brother Kiam began, waving his bamboo brush in the air, "you must realize that this Mandarin only confuses us. We are Cantonese[6] speakers. . . ."

"And you do not complain about Latin, French or German in your English school?" Father rattled his newspaper, a signal that his patience was ending.

"But, Father, those languages are *scientific*," Kiam jabbed his brush in the air. "We are now in a scientific, logical world."

Father was silent. We could all hear Grandmama's rocker.

"What about Sek-Lung?" Older Brother Jung pointed angrily at me. "He was sick last year, but this year he should have at least started Chinese school, instead of picking over garbage cans!"

**Characters** What do you learn about Older Brother and Father from this dialogue?

"He starts next year," Father said, in a hard tone that immediately warned everyone to be silent. Liang slammed her book.

Grandmama went on rocking quietly in her chair. She complimented my mother on her knitting, made a remark about the "strong beauty" of Kiam's brushstrokes which, in spite of himself, immensely pleased him. All this babbling noise was her family torn and confused in a strange land: everything here was so very foreign and scientific.

**Plot** The narrator goes back in time to explain why he was not yet attending school. Why do you think he gives this information now, rather than at the beginning of the story?

The truth was, I was sorry not to have started school the year before. In my innocence I had imagined going to school meant certain privileges worthy of all my brothers' and sister's complaints. The fact that my lung infection in my fifth and sixth years, mistakenly diagnosed as TB,[7] earned me some reprieve, only made me long for school the more. Each member of the family took turns on Sunday, teaching me or annoying me. But it was the countless hours I spent with Grandmama that were my real education. Tapping me on my head she would say, "Come, Sek-Lung, we have *our* work," and we would walk up the stairs to her small crowded room. There, in the midst of her antique shawls, the old ancestral calligraphy and multi-colored embroidered hangings, beneath the mysterious shelves of sweet herbs and bitter potions, we would continue doing what we had started that morning: the elaborate windchime for her death.

**Setting** How does the description of Grandmama's room reflect her values? How might spending time in this room have influenced Sek-Lung?

"I can't last forever," she declared, when she let me in on the secret of this one. "It will sing and dance and glitter," her long fingers stretched into the air, pantomiming the waving motion of her ghost chimes; "My spirit will hear its sounds and see its light and return to this house and say goodbye to you."

---

6. **Mandarin** (man´ də rin) **. . . Cantonese** (kan´ tə nēz´) Mandarin is the most commonly spoken form of Chinese; Cantonese is a variety of Chinese spoken in some parts of China, including the cities of Canton and Hong Kong, and by most Chinese emigrants.
7. **TB** (tē´ bē´) *n.* abbreviation for tuberculosis, a contagious disease that begins in the lungs.

Deftly she reached into the carton she had placed on the chair beside me. She picked out a fish-shape amber piece, and with a long needle-like tool and a steel ruler, she scored[8] it. Pressing the blade of a cleaver against the line, with the fingers of her other hand, she lifted up the glass until it cleanly *snapped* into the exact shape she required. Her hand began to tremble, the tips of her fingers to shiver, like rippling water.

"You see that, Little One?" She held her hand up. "That is my body fighting with Death. He is in this room now."

My eyes darted in panic, but Grandmama remained calm, undisturbed, and went on with her work. Then I remembered the glue and uncorked the jar for her. Soon the graceful ritual movements of her hand returned to her, and I became lost in the magic of her task: she dabbed a cabalistic[9] mixture of glue on one end and skillfully dropped the braided end of a silk thread into it. This part always amazed me: the braiding would slowly, *very* slowly, *unknot,* fanning out like a prized fishtail. In a few seconds the clear, homemade glue began to harden as I blew lightly over it, welding to itself each separate silk strand.

Each jam-sized pot of glue was precious; each large cork had been wrapped with a fragment of pink silk. I remember this part vividly, because each cork was treated to a special rite. First we went shopping in the best silk stores in Chinatown for the perfect square of silk she required. It had to be a deep pink, a shade of color blushing toward red. And the tone had to match—as closely as possible—her precious jade carving, the small peony of white and light-red jade, her most lucky possession. In the center of this semi-translucent carving, no more than an inch wide, was a pool of pink light, its veins swirling out into the petals of the flower.

"This color is the color of my spirit," she said, holding it up to the window so I could see the delicate pastel against the broad strokes of sunlight. She dropped her voice, and I held my breath at the wonder of the color. "This was given to me by the young actor who taught me how to juggle. He had four of them, and each one had a center of this rare color, the color of Good Fortune." The pendant seemed to pulse as she turned it: "Oh, Sek-Lung! He had white hair and white skin to *his toes!* It's *true,* I saw him bathing." She laughed and blushed, her eyes softened at the memory. The silk had to match the pink heart of her pendant: the color was magical for her, to hold the unraveling strands of her memory. . . .

It was just six months before she died that we really began to work on her last windchime. Three thin bamboo sticks were steamed and bent into circlets; 30 exact lengths of silk thread, the strongest kind, were cut and braided at both ends and glued to stained glass. Her hands worked on their own command, each hand racing with a life of its own: cutting, snapping, braiding, knotting. . . .

**Theme** What possible theme is developed through the contrast between Grandmama's and Sek-Lung's responses to the thought of death?

**Symbols** How does this description connect the jade peony with Grandmama's spirit in youth and old age?

**Plot** How does this discussion bring the story full circle, back to the beginning discussion of "signs"?

8. **scored** (skôrd) *v.* put a notch or groove in.
9. **cabalistic** (kab´ ə lis´ tik) *adj.* relating to a secret or mystical belief or practice.

**Practice continued**

**Plot and Conflict**
What conflict does Grandmama face?

**Main Effect** To what main effect of the story does this passage contribute? Explain.

**Symbols** How do the characters react to the white cat? What do their reactions suggest about the cat's symbolic meaning?

**Plot and Conflict**
How does Grandmama's reaction suggest a resolution to the central conflict she has faced throughout the story?

Sometimes she breathed heavily and her small body, growing thinner, sagged against me. *Death*, I thought, *He is in this room,* and I would work harder alongside her. For months Grandmama and I did this every other evening, a half dozen pieces each time. The shaking in her hand grew worse, but we said nothing. Finally, after discarding hundreds, she told me she had the necessary 30 pieces. But this time, because it was a sacred chime, I would not be permitted to help her tie it up or have the joy of raising it. "Once tied," she said, holding me against my disappointment, "not even I can raise it. Not a sound must it make until I have died."

"What will happen?"

"Your father will then take the center braided strand and raise it. He will hang it against my bedroom window so that my ghost may see it, and hear it, and return. I must say goodbye to this world properly or wander in this foreign land forever."

"You can take the streetcar!" I blurted, suddenly shocked that she actually meant to leave me. I thought I could hear the clear-chromatic chimes, see the shimmering colors on the wall: I fell against her and cried, and there in my crying I knew that she would die. I can still remember the touch of her hand on my head, and the smell of her thick woolen sweater pressed against my face. "I will always be with you, Little Sek-Lung, but in a different way . . . you'll see."

Months went by, and nothing happened. Then one late September evening, when I had just come home from Chinese School, Grandmama was preparing supper when she looked out our kitchen window and saw a cat—a long, lean white cat— jump into our garbage pail and knock it over. She ran out to chase it away, shouting curses at it. She did not have her thick sweater on and when she came back into the house, a chill gripped her. She leaned against the door: "That was not a cat," she said, and the odd tone of her voice caused my father to look with alarm at her. "I can not take back my curses. It is too late." She took hold of my father's arm: "It was all white and had pink eyes like sacred fire."

My father started at this, and they both looked pale. My brothers and sister, clearing the table, froze in their gestures.

"The fog has confused you," Stepmother said. "It was just a cat."

But Grandmama shook her head, for she knew it was a sign. "I will not live forever," she said. "I am prepared."

The next morning she was confined to her bed with a severe cold. Sitting by her, playing with some of my toys, I asked her about the cat: "Why did father jump at the cat with the pink eyes? He didn't see it, you did."

"But he and your mother know what it means."

"What?"

"My friend, the juggler, the magician, was as pale as white jade, and he had pink eyes." I thought she would begin to tell me one of her stories, a tale of enchantment or of a wondrous adventure, but she only paused to swallow; her eyes glittered, lost in memory. She took my hand, gently opening and closing her fingers over it. "Sek-Lung," she sighed, "*he* has come back to me."

Then Grandmama sank back into her pillow and the embroidered flowers lifted to frame her wrinkled face. I saw her hand over my own, and my own began to tremble. I fell fitfully asleep by her side. When I woke up it was dark and her bed was empty. She had been taken to the hospital and I was not permitted to visit.

A few days after that she died of the complications of pneumonia. Immediately after her death my father came home and said nothing to us, but walked up the stairs to her room, pulled aside the drawn lace curtains of her window and lifted the windchimes to the sky.

I began to cry and quickly put my hand in my pocket for a handkerchief. Instead, caught between my fingers, was the small, round firmness of the jade peony. In my mind's eye I saw Grandmama smile and heard, softly, the pink center beat like a beautiful, cramped heart.

**Plot** How does the pacing accelerate at the end of the story? What is the effect of this acceleration?

**Theme and Symbols** What theme is emphasized by the final paragraph of the story? How does the symbol of the jade peony help convey this theme?

# After You Read — The Jade Peony

1. **Key Ideas and Details (a) Explain:** Citing details from the story, explain who gave the grandmother her first windchime. **(b) Infer:** Why do you think the making of windchimes was such a meaningful activity in the grandmother's later years?

2. **Key Ideas and Details (a) Compare and Contrast:** How do Sek-Lung's reactions to his grandmother's activities differ from those of the other family members? **(b) Analyze:** How do you explain these differing attitudes?

3. **Craft and Structure (a) Identify:** Who is the narrator of the story? **(b) Analyze:** How does the narrator's unique perspective on events help develop the character of the grandmother and the characters of other family members? **(c) Analyze:** How does the narrator's perspective help develop the conflict between the grandmother and other family members?

4. **Key Ideas and Details (a) Collaborate:** With a partner, complete a chart like the one shown to examine key details and symbols in the story. List events, actions, or descriptions that seem important.

| What It Says | What It Means | Why It Is Important |
|---|---|---|
|  |  |  |

**(b) Interpret:** Based on your chart, draw a conclusion about the underlying theme, or message, of this story. Support your answer with story details.

5. **Integration of Knowledge and Ideas Evaluate:** Does the theme of the story apply to everyone, or is it limited to people in certain situations? Explain.

## Ⓒ Leveled Texts

Build your skills and improve your comprehension of short stories with texts of increasing complexity.

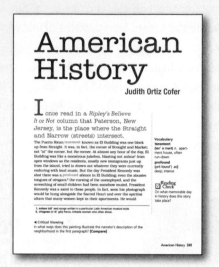

Read **"The Most Dangerous Game"** to find out about a great hunter who meets a challenging opponent.

Read **"American History"** to see how a teenager experiences a national tragedy and a personal crisis.

## Ⓒ Common Core State Standards

Meet these standards with either **"The Most Dangerous Game"** (p. 214) or **"American History"** (p. 240).

**Reading Literature**
**1.** Cite strong and thorough textual evidence to support analysis of what the text says explicitly as well as inferences drawn from the text. *(Reading Skill: Make Inferences)*
**5.** Analyze how an author's choices concerning how to structure a text, order events within it, and manipulate time create such effects as mystery, tension, or surprise. *(Literary Analysis: Spiral Review)*

**Writing**
**3.e.** Provide a conclusion that follows from and reflects on what is experienced, observed, or resolved over the course of the narrative. *(Writing: Alternative Ending)*

**Speaking and Listening**
**4.** Present information, findings, and supporting evidence clearly, concisely, and logically such that listeners can follow

the line of reasoning and the organization, development, substance, and style are appropriate to purpose, audience, and task. *(Speaking and Listening: Oral Presentation)*

**Language**
**1.** Demonstrate command of the conventions of standard English grammar and usage when writing or speaking. *(Conventions: Regular Verbs)*
**6.** Acquire and use accurately grade-appropriate general academic and domain-specific words and phrases; gather vocabulary knowledge when considering a word or phrase important to comprehension or expression. *(Vocabulary: Context Clues)*

# Literary Analysis: Conflict

**Conflict** is a struggle between opposing forces.

- In an **external conflict,** a character clashes with an outside force—for example, another character, society, or nature.

- In an **internal conflict,** a character grapples with his or her own opposing feelings, beliefs, needs, or desires.

Conflict drives the plot of most stories. Its solution usually occurs near the end of the story, in the **resolution.** When a story's conflict is left unresolved, the character may have an **epiphany,** or sudden flash of insight, that changes his or her feelings about the conflict. Some epiphanies can also lead to a plot's resolution, or result from one. As you read, analyze the conflicts that characters face and decide which ones truly are resolved.

# Reading Skill: Make Inferences

**Inferences** are logical assumptions about information or ideas that are not directly stated in a piece of writing.

When you make inferences, you use details as clues to develop ideas about unstated information and concepts in a text. To make inferences as you read a story, for example, ask questions such as these about characters' feelings and behavior:

- What does this detail show about the reasons for a character's actions or words?

- What does this passage say about the character's unstated feelings?

## Using the Strategy: Inferences Chart

Use an **inferences chart** like this one to track your thinking as you read.

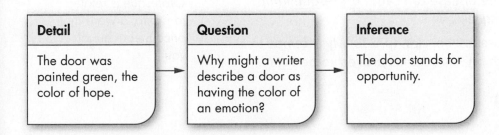

| Detail | Question | Inference |
|---|---|---|
| The door was painted green, the color of hope. | Why might a writer describe a door as having the color of an emotion? | The door stands for opportunity. |

## Is *conflict* necessary?

### Writing About the Big Question

In "The Most Dangerous Game," a hunter faces a life-threatening conflict. Use these sentence starters to develop your ideas about the Big Question.

To succeed in a fight for **survival,** a person needs to _____ because _____.

**Competition** is important for our personal growth because _____.

**While You Read** Consider the conflict at the heart of hunting. Keep track of the ways in which the hunter tries to ensure his survival.

### Vocabulary

Read each word and its definition. Decide whether you know the word well, know it a little bit, or do not know it at all. After you have read the selection, see how your knowledge of each word has increased.

- **palpable** (pal′ pə bəl) *adj.* able to be felt; easily perceived (p. 215) *The tension during the exam was palpable.* *palpate v.*

- **indolently** (in′ də lənt lē) *adv.* lazily; idly (p. 217) *The sleepy cat yawned indolently.* *indolent adj. indolence n.*

- **naive** (nä ēv′) *adj.* unsophisticated (p. 225) *How naive you are to trust everyone you meet!* *naiveté n. naively adv.*

- **scruples** (scrōō′ pəlz) *n.* misgivings about something one feels is wrong (p. 225) *Her scruples prevented her from lying.* *scrupulous adj. unscrupulous adj.*

- **grotesque** (grō tesk′) *adj.* having a strange, bizarre design; shocking or offensive (p. 227) *The disease can cause grotesque lumps under the skin.* *grotesquely adv.*

- **futile** (fyōōt′ 'l) *adj.* useless; hopeless (p. 230) *My attempt to catch the mouse with my bare hands proved to be futile.* *futility n. futilely adv.*

### Word Study

The **Latin suffix -esque,** which forms adjectives, means "in the style or manner of."

In this story, the hunter sees many **grotesque** things—things that remind him of death—on the island he visits. *Grotesque* is related to *grotto,* a word that once meant burial vault.

## Author of
*The Most Dangerous Game*

Richard Connell seemed destined to become a writer: he was a sports reporter at the age of ten! At sixteen, he was editing his father's newspaper, the *Poughkeepsie News-Press,* in upstate New York. Connell attended Harvard University, where he worked on the *Daily Crimson* and the *Lampoon,* an early version of the humor magazine *National Lampoon.* During World War I, Connell edited his army division's newspaper.

**From Page to Screen** In 1924, Connell published "The Most Dangerous Game." In 1936, he settled in Beverly Hills, California, where he started working as a screenwriter. Twice nominated for Academy Awards, he became one of the most successful screenwriters of his day.

## BACKGROUND FOR THE STORY

**Tests of Survival**

As civilizations advance, people no longer need to struggle for their basic survival. Nevertheless, some people still enjoy testing their bravery and physical skills in competitions. Today, computer games sometimes feature death-defying challenges. As this story shows, the sport of big-game hunting once served a similar purpose.

### Did You Know?
When "The Most Dangerous Game" was first published, it won the prestigious O. Henry Memorial Award for short fiction.

# The Most Dangerous Game

## Richard Connell

"**O**ff there to the right—somewhere—is a large island," said Whitney. "It's rather a mystery—"

"What island is it?" Rainsford asked.

"The old charts call it 'Ship-Trap Island,'" Whitney replied. "A suggestive name, isn't it? Sailors have a curious dread of the place. I don't know why. Some superstition—"

"Can't see it," remarked Rainsford, trying to peer through the dank tropical night that was palpable as it pressed its thick warm blackness in upon the yacht.

"You've good eyes," said Whitney, with a laugh, "and I've seen you pick off a moose moving in the brown fall bush at four hundred yards, but even you can't see four miles or so through a moonless Caribbean[1] night."

"Not four yards," admitted Rainsford. "Ugh! It's like moist black velvet."

"It will be light in Rio," promised Whitney. "We should make it in a few days. I hope the jaguar guns have come from Purdey's. We should have some good hunting up the Amazon. Great sport, hunting."

"The best sport in the world," agreed Rainsford.

"For the hunter," amended Whitney. "Not for the jaguar."

"Don't talk rot, Whitney," said Rainsford. "You're a big-game hunter, not a philosopher. Who cares how a jaguar feels?"

---

1. **Caribbean** (kar´ ə bē´ ən) the Caribbean Sea, a part of the Atlantic Ocean, bounded by the north coast of South America, Central America, and the West Indies.

◀ **Critical Viewing**
Based on the details in this image, what do you think this story will be about? **[Speculate]**

**Vocabulary**
**palpable** (pal´ pə bəl) *adj.* able to be felt; easily perceived

**Reading Check**
What do Rainsford and Whitney see from the ship?

"Perhaps the jaguar does," observed Whitney.

"Bah! They've no understanding."

"Even so, I rather think they understand one thing—fear. The fear of pain and the fear of death."

"Nonsense," laughed Rainsford. "This hot weather is making you soft, Whitney. Be a realist. The world is made up of two classes—the hunters and the huntees. Luckily, you and I are the hunters. Do you think we've passed that island yet?"

"I can't tell in the dark. I hope so."

"Why?" asked Rainsford.

"The place has a reputation—a bad one."

"Cannibals?" suggested Rainsford.

"Hardly. Even cannibals wouldn't live in such a God-forsaken place. But it's gotten into sailor lore, somehow. Didn't you notice that the crew's nerves seemed a bit jumpy today?"

"They were a bit strange, now you mention it. Even Captain Nielsen—"

"Yes, even that tough-minded old Swede, who'd go up to the devil himself and ask him for a light. Those fishy blue eyes held a look I never saw there before. All I could get out of him was: 'This place has an evil name among sea-faring men, sir.' Then he said to me, very gravely: 'Don't you feel anything?'—as if the air about us was actually poisonous. Now, you mustn't laugh when I tell you this—I did feel something like a sudden chill.

"There was no breeze. The sea was as flat as a plate-glass window. We were drawing near the island then. What I felt was a—a mental chill; a sort of sudden dread."

"Pure imagination," said Rainsford. "One superstitious sailor can taint the whole ship's company with his fear."

"Maybe. But sometimes I think sailors have an extra sense that tells them when they are in danger. Sometimes I think evil is a tangible thing—with wave lengths, just as sound and light have. An evil place can, so to speak, broadcast vibrations of evil. Anyhow, I'm glad we're getting out of this zone. Well, I think I'll turn in now, Rainsford."

"I'm not sleepy," said Rainsford. "I'm going to smoke another pipe on the afterdeck."

"Good night, then, Rainsford. See you at breakfast."

"Right. Good night, Whitney." •

There was no sound in the night as Rainsford sat there, but the muffled throb of the engine that drove the yacht swiftly through the darkness, and the swish and ripple of the wash of the propeller.

Rainsford, reclining in a steamer chair, indolently puffed on his favorite brier. The sensuous drowsiness of the night was on him. "It's so dark," he thought, "that I could sleep without closing my eyes; the night would be my eyelids—"

An abrupt sound startled him. Off to the right he heard it, and his ears, expert in such matters, could not be mistaken. Again he heard the sound, and again. Somewhere, off in the blackness, someone had fired a gun three times.

Rainsford sprang up and moved quickly to the rail, mystified. He strained his eyes in the direction from which the reports had come, but it was like trying to see through a blanket. He leaped upon the rail and balanced himself there, to get greater elevation; his pipe, striking a rope, was knocked from his mouth. He lunged for it; a short, hoarse cry came from his lips as he realized he had reached too far and had lost his balance. The cry was pinched off short as the blood-warm waters of the Caribbean Sea closed over his head.

**Vocabulary**
**indolently** (in´ də lənt lē)
*adv.* lazily; idly

Reading Check

What "two classes" does Rainsford believe make up the world?

**Literary Analysis**
**Conflict** With what
external conflict is
Rainsford suddenly
confronted?

▶ **Critical Viewing**
What does the wildness
of the island in the
picture tell you about the
island itself? **[Infer]**

He struggled up to the surface and tried to cry out, but the wash from the speeding yacht slapped him in the face and the salt water in his open mouth made him gag and strangle. Desperately he struck out with strong strokes after the receding lights of the yacht, but he stopped before he had swum fifty feet. A certain cool-headedness had come to him; it was not the first time he had been in a tight place. There was a chance that his cries could be heard by someone aboard the yacht, but that chance was slender, and grew more slender as the yacht raced on. He wrestled himself out of his clothes, and shouted with all his power. The lights of the yacht became faint and ever-vanishing fireflies; then they were blotted out entirely by the night.

Rainsford remembered the shots. They had come from the right, and doggedly he swam in that direction, swimming with slow, deliberate strokes, conserving his strength. For a seemingly endless time he fought the sea. He began to count his strokes; he could do possibly a hundred more and then—

Rainsford heard a sound. It came out of the darkness, a high screaming sound, the sound of an animal in an extremity of anguish and terror.

He did not recognize the animal that made the sound; he did not try to; with fresh vitality he swam toward the sound. He heard it again; then it was cut short by another noise, crisp, staccato.

"Pistol shot," muttered Rainsford, swimming on.

Ten minutes of determined effort brought another sound to his ears—the most welcome he had ever heard—the muttering and growling of the sea breaking on a rocky shore. He was almost on the rocks before he saw them; on a night less calm he would have been shattered against them. With his remaining strength he dragged himself from the swirling waters. Jagged crags appeared to jut into the opaqueness, he forced himself upward, hand over hand. Gasping, his hands raw, he reached a flat place at the top. Dense jungle came down to the very edge of the cliffs. What perils that tangle of trees and underbrush might hold for him did not concern Rainsford just then. All he knew was that he was safe from his enemy, the sea, and that utter weariness was on him. He flung himself down at the jungle edge and tumbled headlong into the deepest sleep of his life. ●

When he opened his eyes he knew from the position of the sun that it was late in the afternoon. Sleep had given him new vigor; a sharp hunger was picking at him. He looked about him, almost cheerfully.

"Where there are pistol shots, there are men. Where there are men, there is food," he thought. But what kind of men, he wondered, in so forbidding a place? An unbroken front of snarled and ragged jungle fringed the shore.

He saw no sign of a trail through the closely knit web of weeds and trees; it was easier to go along the shore, and Rainsford floundered along by the water. Not far from where he had landed, he stopped.

Some wounded thing, by the evidence a large animal, had thrashed about in the underbrush; the jungle weeds were crushed down and the moss was lacerated; one patch of weeds was stained crimson. A small, glittering object not far away caught Rainsford's eye and he picked it up. It was an empty cartridge.

"A twenty-two," he remarked. "That's odd. It must have been a fairly large animal too. The hunter had his nerve with him to tackle it with a light gun. It's clear that the brute put up a fight. I suppose the first three shots I heard was when the hunter flushed his quarry and wounded it. The last shot was when he trailed it here and finished it."

**Reading Skill
Make Inferences**
What inferences does Rainsford make based on the evidence of pistol shots?

**Reading Check**
As Rainsford swims for shore, what sounds does he hear coming out of the darkness?

He examined the ground closely and found what he had hoped to find—the print of hunting boots. They pointed along the cliff in the direction he had been going. Eagerly he hurried along, now slipping on a rotten log or a loose stone, but making headway; night was beginning to settle down on the island.

Bleak darkness was blacking out the sea and jungle when Rainsford sighted the lights. He came upon them as he turned a crook in the coast line, and his first thought was that he had come upon a village, for there were many lights. But as he forged along he saw to his great astonishment that all the lights were in one enormous building—a lofty structure with pointed towers plunging upward into the gloom. His eyes made out the shadowy outlines of a palatial château;[2] it was set on a high bluff, and on three sides of it cliffs dived down to where the sea licked greedy lips in the shadows.

"Mirage," thought Rainsford. But it was no mirage, he found, when he opened the tall spiked iron gate. The stone steps were real enough; the massive door with a leering gargoyle[3] for a knocker was real enough; yet about it all hung an air of unreality.

He lifted the knocker, and it creaked up stiffly, as if it had never before been used. He let it fall, and it startled him with its booming loudness. He thought he heard steps within; the door remained closed. Again Rainsford lifted the heavy knocker, and let it fall. The door opened then, opened as suddenly as if it were on a spring, and Rainsford stood blinking in the river of glaring gold light that poured out. The first thing Rainsford's eyes discerned was the largest man Rainsford had ever seen—a gigantic creature, solidly made and black-bearded to the waist. In his hand the man held a long-barreled revolver, and he was pointing it straight at Rainsford's heart.

Out of the snarl of beard two small eyes regarded Rainsford.

"Don't be alarmed," said Rainsford, with a smile which he hoped was disarming. "I'm no robber. I fell off a yacht. My name is Sanger Rainsford of New York City."

The menacing look in the eyes did not change. The revolver pointed as rigidly as if the giant were a statue. He gave no sign that he understood Rainsford's words, or that he had even heard them. He was dressed in uniform, a black uniform trimmed with gray astrakhan.[4]

"I'm Sanger Rainsford of New York," Rainsford began again. "I fell off a yacht. I am hungry."

The man's only answer was to raise with his thumb the hammer of his revolver. Then Rainsford saw the man's free hand go to his forehead in a military salute, and he saw him click his heels together and stand at attention. Another man was coming down

**Reading Skill**
**Make Inferences**
Which details here lead you to infer that the two men Rainsford meets have a shared military past? Explain.

---

2. **palatial** (pə lā´ shəl) *château* (sha tō´) a mansion as luxurious as a palace.
3. **gargoyle** (gär´ goil´) *n.* strange and distorted animal form projecting from a building.
4. **astrakhan** (as´ trə kən) *n.* loosely curled fur made from the skins of very young lambs.

the broad marble steps, an erect, slender man in evening clothes. He advanced to Rainsford and held out his hand.

In a cultivated voice marked by a slight accent that gave it added precision and deliberateness, he said: "It is a very great pleasure and honor to welcome Mr. Sanger Rainsford, the celebrated hunter, to my home."

Automatically Rainsford shook the man's hand.

"I've read your book about hunting snow leopards in Tibet, you see," explained the man. "I am General Zaroff."

Rainsford's first impression was that the man was singularly handsome; his second was that there was an original, almost bizarre quality about the general's face. He was a tall man past middle age, for his hair was a vivid white; but his thick eyebrows and pointed military mustache were as black as the night from which Rainsford had come. His eyes, too, were black and very bright. He had high cheek bones, a sharp-cut nose, a spare, dark face, the face of a man used to giving orders, the face of an aristocrat. Turning to the giant in uniform, the general made a sign. The giant put away his pistol, saluted, withdrew.

"Ivan is an incredibly strong fellow," remarked the general, "but he has the misfortune to be deaf and dumb. A simple fellow, but, I'm afraid, like all his race, a bit of a savage."

"Is he Russian?"

"He is a Cossack," said the general, and his smile showed red lips and pointed teeth. "So am I."

"Come," he said, "we shouldn't be chatting here. We can talk later. Now you want clothes, food, rest. You shall have them. This is a most restful spot."

Ivan had reappeared, and the general spoke to him with lips that moved but gave forth no sound.

"Follow Ivan, if you please, Mr. Rainsford," said the general. "I was about to have my dinner when you came. I'll wait for you. You'll find that my clothes will fit you, I think."

It was to a huge, beam-ceilinged bedroom with a canopied bed big enough for six men that Rainsford followed the silent giant. Ivan laid out an evening suit, and Rainsford, as he put it on, noticed that it came from a London tailor who ordinarily cut and sewed for none below the rank of duke.

The dining room to which Ivan conducted him was in many ways remarkable. There was a medieval magnificence about it; it suggested a baronial hall of feudal times with its oaken panels,

Reading Check

What type of building does Rainsford encounter on the island he reaches?

its high ceiling, its vast refectory table where twoscore men could sit down to eat. About the hall were the mounted heads of many animals—lions, tigers, elephants, moose, bears; larger or more perfect specimens Rainsford had never seen. At the great table the general was sitting, alone.

"You'll have a cocktail, Mr. Rainsford," he suggested. The cocktail was surpassingly good; and, Rainsford noted, the table appointments were of the finest—the linen, the crystal, the silver, the china.

They were eating *borsch*, the rich, red soup with whipped cream so dear to Russian palates. Half apologetically General Zaroff said: "We do our best to preserve the amenities of civilization here. Please forgive any lapses. We are well off the beaten track, you know. Do you think the champagne has suffered from its long ocean trip?"

"Not in the least," declared Rainsford. He was finding the general a most thoughtful and affable host, a true cosmopolite.[5] But there was one small trait of the general's that made Rainsford uncomfortable. Whenever he looked up from his plate he found the general studying him, appraising him narrowly.

"Perhaps," said General Zaroff, "you were surprised that I recognized your name. You see, I read all books on hunting published in English, French, and Russian. I have but one passion in my life, Mr. Rainsford, and it is the hunt."

"You have some wonderful heads here," said Rainsford as he ate a particularly well cooked filet mignon. "That Cape buffalo is the largest I ever saw."

"Oh, that fellow. Yes, he was a monster."

"Did he charge you?"

"Hurled me against a tree," said the general. "Fractured my skull. But I got the brute."

"I've always thought," said Rainsford, "that the Cape buffalo is the most dangerous of all big game."

For a moment the general did not reply; he was smiling his curious red-lipped smile. Then he said slowly: "No. You are wrong, sir. The Cape buffalo is not the most dangerous big game." He sipped his wine. "Here in my preserve on this island," he said in the same slow tone, "I hunt more dangerous game."

Rainsford expressed his surprise. "Is there big game on this island?"

The general nodded. "The biggest."

"Really?"

"Oh, it isn't here naturally, of course. I have to stock the island."

"What have you imported, general?" Rainsford asked. "Tigers?"

The general smiled. "No," he said. "Hunting tigers ceased to

---

**Literary Analysis**
**Conflict** Explain how Rainsford's discomfort in this passage is both an internal and an external conflict.

---

5. **cosmopolite** (käz mäp´ ə lït´) *n.* person at home in all parts of the world.

interest me some years ago. I exhausted their possibilities, you see. No thrill left in tigers, no real danger. I live for danger, Mr. Rainsford."

The general took from his pocket a gold cigarette case and offered his guest a long black cigarette with a silver tip; it was perfumed and gave off a smell like incense.

"We will have some capital hunting, you and I," said the general. "I shall be most glad to have your society."

"But what game—" began Rainsford.

"I'll tell you," said the general. "You will be amused, I know. I think I may say, in all modesty, that I have done a rare thing. I have invented a new sensation. May I pour you another glass of port, Mr. Rainsford?"

"Thank you, general."

The general filled both glasses, and said: "God makes some men poets. Some He makes kings, some beggars. Me He made a hunter. My hand was made for the trigger, my father said. He was a very rich man with a quarter of a million acres in the Crimea,[6] and he was an ardent sportsman. When I was only five years old he gave me a little gun, specially made in Moscow for me, to shoot sparrows with. When I shot some of his prize turkeys with it, he did not punish me; he complimented me on my marksmanship. I killed my first bear in the Caucasus[7] when I was ten. My whole life has been one prolonged hunt. I went into the army—it was expected of noblemen's sons—and for a time commanded a division of Cossack cavalry, but my real interest was always the hunt. I have hunted every kind of game in every land. It would be impossible for me to tell you how many animals I have killed."

The general puffed at his cigarette.

"After the debacle[8] in Russia I left the country, for it was imprudent for an officer of the Czar to stay there. Many noble Russians lost everything. I, luckily, had invested heavily in American securities, so I shall never have to open a tea room in Monte Carlo or drive a taxi in Paris. Naturally, I continued to hunt—grizzlies in your Rockies, crocodiles in the Ganges, rhinoceroses in East Africa. It was in Africa that the Cape buffalo hit me and laid me up for six months. As soon as I recovered I started for the Amazon to hunt jaguars, for I had heard they were unusually cunning. They weren't." The Cossack sighed. "They were no match at all for a hunter with his wits about him, and a high-

"Here in my preserve on this island," he said in the same slow tone, "I hunt more dangerous game."

**Reading Skill**
**Make Inferences**
How do the details about Zaroff's life support the inference that he feels neither guilt nor fear concerning hunting?

Reading
Check
Why does Zaroff recognize Rainsford's name?

---

6. **Crimea** (krī mē´ ə) region in southwestern Ukraine extending into the Black Sea.
7. **Caucasus** (kô´ kə səs) mountain range between the Black and Caspian seas.
8. **debacle** (di bä´ kəl) *n.* bad defeat (Zaroff is referring to the Russian Revolution of 1917, a defeat for upper-class Russians like himself).

powered rifle. I was bitterly disappointed. I was lying in my tent with a splitting headache one night when a terrible thought pushed its way into my mind. Hunting was beginning to bore me! And hunting, remember, had been my life. I have heard that in America business men often go to pieces when they give up the business that has been their life."

"Yes, that's so," said Rainsford.

The general smiled. "I had no wish to go to pieces," he said. "I must do something. Now, mine is an analytical mind, Mr. Rainsford. Doubtless that is why I enjoy the problems of the chase."

"No doubt, General Zaroff."

"So," continued the general, "I asked myself why the hunt no longer fascinated me. You are much younger than I am, Mr. Rainsford, and have not hunted as much, but you perhaps can guess the answer."

"What was it?"

"Simply this: hunting had ceased to be what you call 'a sporting proposition.' It had become too easy. I always got my quarry. Always. There is no greater bore than perfection."

The general lit a fresh cigarette.

"No animal had a chance with me any more. That is no boast; it is a mathematical certainty. The animal had nothing but his legs and his instinct. Instinct is no match for reason. When I thought of this it was a tragic moment for me, I can tell you."

Rainsford leaned across the table, absorbed in what his host was saying.

"It came to me as an inspiration what I must do," the general went on.

"And that was?"

The general smiled the quiet smile of one who has faced an obstacle and surmounted it with success. "I had to invent a new animal to hunt," he said.

"A new animal? You're joking."

"Not at all," said the general. "I never joke about hunting. I needed a new animal. I found one. So I bought this island, built this house, and here I do my hunting. The island is perfect for my purpose—there are jungles with a maze of trails in them, hills, swamps—"

"But the animal, General Zaroff?"

"Oh," said the general, "it supplies me with the most exciting hunting in the world. No other hunting compares with it for an instant. Every day I hunt, and I never grow bored now, for I have a quarry with which I can match my wits."

Rainsford's bewilderment showed in his face.

**Literary Analysis**
**Conflict** How was the "tragic moment" Zaroff refers to the sign of an internal conflict?

"I wanted the ideal animal to hunt," explained the general. "So I said: 'What are the attributes of an ideal quarry?' And the answer was, of course: 'It must have courage, cunning, and, above all, it must be able to reason.'"

"But no animal can reason," objected Rainsford.

"My dear fellow," said the general, "there is one that can."

"But you can't mean—" gasped Rainsford.

"And why not?"

"I can't believe you are serious, General Zaroff. This is a grisly joke."

"Why should I not be serious? I am speaking of hunting."

"Hunting? General Zaroff, what you speak of is murder."

The general laughed with entire good nature. He regarded Rainsford quizzically. "I refuse to believe that so modern and civilized a young man as you seem to be harbors romantic ideas about the value of human life. Surely your experiences in the war—"

"Did not make me condone cold-blooded murder," finished Rainsford stiffly.

Laughter shook the general. "How extraordinarily droll you are!" he said. "One does not expect nowadays to find a young man of the educated class, even in America, with such a naive, and, if I may say so, mid-Victorian point of view.[9] It's like finding a snuff-box in a limousine. Ah, well, doubtless you had Puritan ancestors. So many Americans appear to have had. I'll wager you'll forget your notions when you go hunting with me. You've a genuine new thrill in store for you, Mr. Rainsford."

"Thank you, I'm a hunter, not a murderer."

"Dear me," said the general, quite unruffled, "again that unpleasant word. But I think I can show you that your scruples are quite ill founded."

"Yes?"

"Life is for the strong, to be lived by the strong, and, if need be, taken by the strong. The weak of the world were put here to give the strong pleasure. I am strong. Why should I not use my gift? If I wish to hunt, why should I not? I hunt the scum of the earth—sailors from tramp ships—lascars,[10] blacks, Chinese, whites, mongrels—a thoroughbred horse or hound is worth more than a score of them."

"But they are men," said Rainsford hotly.

"Precisely," said the general. "That is why I use them. It gives me pleasure. They can reason, after a fashion. So they are dangerous."

"But where do you get them?"

The general's left eyelid fluttered down in a wink. "This island is called Ship-Trap," he answered. "Sometimes an angry god of the

---

9. **mid-Victorian point of view** a point of view emphasizing proper behavior and associated with the time of Queen Victoria of England (1819–1901).
10. **lascars** (las´ kərz) *n.* Indian or East Indian sailors, employed on European ships.

high seas sends them to me. Sometimes, when Providence is not so kind, I help Providence a bit. Come to the window with me."

Rainsford went to the window and looked out toward the sea.

"Watch! Out there!" exclaimed the general, pointing into the night. Rainsford's eyes saw only blackness, and then, as the general pressed a button, far out to sea Rainsford saw the flash of lights.

The general chuckled. "They indicate a channel," he said, "where there's none: giant rocks with razor edges crouch like a sea monster with wide-open jaws. They can crush a ship as easily as I crush this nut." He dropped a walnut on the hardwood floor and brought his heel grinding down on it. "Oh, yes," he said, casually, as if in answer to a question, "I have electricity. We try to be civilized here."

**Reading Skill**
**Make Inferences**
Based on this description, what can you infer about the method Zaroff uses to lure his quarry to the island?

"Civilized? And you shoot down men?"

A trace of anger was in the general's black eyes, but it was there for but a second, and he said, in his most pleasant manner: "Dear me, what a righteous young man you are! I assure you I do not do the thing you suggest. That would be barbarous. I treat these visitors with every consideration. They get plenty of good food and exercise. They get into splendid physical condition. You shall see for yourself tomorrow."

"What do you mean?"

"We'll visit my training school," smiled the general. "It's in the cellar. I have about a dozen pupils down there now. They're from the Spanish bark San Lucar that had the bad luck to go on the rocks out there. A very inferior lot, I regret to say. Poor specimens and more accustomed to the deck than to the jungle."

He raised his hand, and Ivan, who served as waiter, brought thick Turkish coffee. Rainsford, with an effort, held his tongue in check.

"It's a game, you see," pursued the general blandly. "I suggest to one of them that we go hunting. I give him a supply of food and an excellent hunting knife. I give him three hours' start. I am to follow, armed only with a pistol of the smallest caliber and range. If my quarry eludes me for three whole days, he wins the game. If I find him"—the general smiled—"he loses."

"Suppose he refuses to be hunted?"

**Literary Analysis**
**Conflict** Is Zaroff's statement that his captives do not have to participate in the hunt true? Explain.

"Oh," said the general, "I give him his option, of course. He need not play the game if he doesn't wish to. If he does not wish to hunt, I turn him over to Ivan. Ivan once had the honor of serving as official knouter[11] to the Great White Czar, and he has his own ideas of sport. Invariably, Mr. Rainsford, invariably they choose the hunt."

"And if they win?"

The smile on the general's face widened. "To date I have not lost," he said.

---

**11. knouter** (nout′ ər) *n.* someone who beats criminals with a leather whip, or knout.

Then he added, hastily: "I don't wish you to think me a braggart, Mr. Rainsford. Many of them afford only the most elementary sort of problem. Occasionally I strike a tartar.[12] One almost did win. I eventually had to use the dogs."

"The dogs?"

"This way, please. I'll show you."

The general steered Rainsford to a window. The lights from the windows sent a flickering illumination that made grotesque patterns on the courtyard below, and Rainsford could see moving about there a dozen or so huge black shapes; as they turned toward him, their eyes glittered greenly.

"A rather good lot, I think," observed the general. "They are let out at seven every night. If anyone should try to get into my house—or out of it—something extremely regrettable would occur to him." He hummed a snatch of song from the Folies Bergère.[13]

"And now," said the general, "I want to show you my new collection of heads. Will you come with me to the library?"

"I hope," said Rainsford, "that you will excuse me tonight, General Zaroff. I'm really not feeling at all well."

"Ah, indeed?" the general inquired solicitously. "Well, I suppose that's only natural, after your long swim. You need a good, restful night's sleep. Tomorrow you'll feel like a new man, I'll wager. Then we'll hunt, eh? I've one rather promising prospect—"

Rainsford was hurrying from the room.

"Sorry you can't go with me tonight," called the general. "I expect rather fair sport—a big, strong black. He looks resourceful—Well good night, Mr. Rainsford; I hope you have a good night's rest."

The bed was good, and the pajamas of the softest silk, and he was tired in every fiber of his being, but nevertheless Rainsford could not quiet his brain with the opiate of sleep. He lay, eyes wide open. Once he thought he heard stealthy steps in the corridor outside his room. He sought to throw open the door; it would not

---

**12. tartar** (tärt´ ər) *n.* stubborn, violent person.
**13. Folies** (fô´ lē) **Bergère** (ber zher') musical theater in Paris.

▲ **Critical Viewing**
Why might Zaroff have used dogs like these on his hunts? **[Connect]**

**Vocabulary**
**grotesque** (grō tesk´) *adj.* having a strange, bizarre design; shocking or offensive

**Reading Skill**
**Make Inferences**
What kind of heads do you think Zaroff wants to show Rainsford? Explain.

Reading Check
Who are the "pupils" in Zaroff's cellar?

open. He went to the window and looked out. His room was high up in one of the towers. The lights of the château were out now, and it was dark and silent, but there was a fragment of sallow moon, and by its wan light he could see, dimly, the courtyard; there, weaving in and out in the pattern of shadow, were black, noiseless forms; the hounds heard him at the window and looked up, expectantly, with their green eyes. Rainsford went back to the bed and lay down. By many methods he tried to put himself to sleep. He had achieved a doze when, just as morning began to come, he heard, far off in the jungle, the faint report of a pistol. ●

General Zaroff did not appear until luncheon. He was dressed faultlessly in the tweeds of a country squire. He was solicitous about the state of Rainsford's health.

"As for me," sighed the general, "I do not feel so well. I am worried, Mr. Rainsford. Last night I detected traces of my old complaint."

To Rainsford's questioning glance the general said: "Ennui. Boredom."

Then, taking a second helping of crêpes suzette, the general explained: "The hunting was not good last night. The fellow lost his head. He made a straight trail that offered no problems at all. That's the trouble with these sailors; they have dull brains to begin with, and they do not know how to get about in the woods. They do excessively stupid and obvious things. It's most annoying. Will you have another glass of Chablis, Mr. Rainsford?"

"General," said Rainsford firmly, "I wish to leave this island at once."

The general raised his thickets of eyebrows; he seemed hurt. "But, my dear fellow," the general protested, "you've only just come. You've had no hunting—"

"I wish to go today," said Rainsford. He saw the dead black eyes of the general on him, studying him. General Zaroff's face suddenly brightened.

He filled Rainsford's glass with venerable Chablis from a dusty bottle.

"Tonight," said the general, "we will hunt—you and I."

Rainsford shook his head. "No, general," he said. "I will not hunt."

The general shrugged his shoulders and delicately ate a hothouse grape. "As you wish, my friend," he said. "The choice rests entirely with you. But may I not venture to suggest that you will find my idea of sport more diverting than Ivan's?"

He nodded toward the corner to where the giant stood, scowling, his thick arms crossed on his hogshead of chest.

"You don't mean—" cried Rainsford.

**Literary Analysis**
**Conflict** How does Rainsford's statement about wishing to leave make his internal conflict an external one?

**Reading Skill**
**Make Inferences**
What inference can you make about the hunting trip Zaroff is suggesting?

"My dear fellow," said the general, "have I not told you I always mean what I say about hunting? This is really an inspiration. I drink to a foeman worthy of my steel—at last."

The general raised his glass, but Rainsford sat staring at him.

"You'll find this game worth playing," the general said enthusiastically. "Your brain against mine. Your woodcraft against mine. Your strength and stamina against mine. Outdoor chess! And the stake is not without value, eh?"

"And if I win—" began Rainsford huskily.

"I'll cheerfully acknowledge myself defeated if I do not find you by midnight of the third day," said General Zaroff. "My sloop will place you on the mainland near a town."

The general read what Rainsford was thinking.

"Oh, you can trust me," said the Cossack. "I will give you my word as a gentleman and a sportsman. Of course you, in turn, must agree to say nothing of your visit here."

"I'll agree to nothing of the kind," said Rainsford.

"Oh," said the general, "in that case— But why discuss that now? Three days hence we can discuss it over a bottle of Veuve Cliquot, unless—"

The general sipped his wine.

Then a businesslike air animated him. "Ivan," he said to Rainsford, "will supply you with hunting clothes, food, a knife. I suggest you wear moccasins; they leave a poorer trail. I suggest too that you avoid the big swamp in the southeast corner of the island. We call it Death Swamp. There's quicksand there. One foolish fellow tried it. The deplorable part of it was that Lazarus followed him. You can imagine my feelings, Mr. Rainsford. I loved Lazarus; he was the finest hound in my pack. Well, I must beg you to excuse me now. I always take a siesta after lunch. You'll hardly have time for a nap, I fear. You'll want to start, no doubt. I shall not follow till dusk. Hunting at night is so much more exciting than by day, don't you think? Au revoir,[14] Mr. Rainsford, au revoir."

General Zaroff, with a deep, courtly bow, strolled from the room.

From another door came Ivan. Under one arm he carried khaki hunting clothes, a haversack of food, a leather sheath containing a long-bladed hunting knife; his right hand rested on a cocked revolver thrust in the crimson sash about his waist. . . .

Rainsford had fought his way through the bush for two hours. "I must keep my nerve. I must keep my nerve," he said through tight teeth.

---

14. **Au** (ō´) **revoir** (rə vwär´) French for "until we meet again."

"My dear fellow," said the general, "have I not told you I always mean what I say about hunting?"

Reading Check

What two suggestions does Zaroff give Rainsford before they begin the hunt?

**Vocabulary**
**futile** (fyo͞ot´ 'l) *adj.*
useless; hopeless

▼ **Critical Viewing**
How does this picture
support Rainsford's
thought that straight
flight through the jungle
is futile? **[Support]**

He had not been entirely clear-headed when the château gates
snapped shut behind him.

His whole idea at first was to put distance between himself and
General Zaroff, and, to this end, he had plunged along, spurred on
by the sharp rowels of something very like panic. Now he had got a
grip on himself, had stopped, and was taking stock of himself and
the situation.

He saw that straight flight was futile; inevitably it would bring him
face to face with the sea. He was in a picture with a frame of water,
and his operations, clearly, must take place within that frame.

"I'll give him a trail to follow," muttered Rainsford, and he struck
off from the rude paths he had been following into the trackless
wilderness. He executed a series of intricate loops; he doubled on
his trail again and again, recalling all the lore of the fox hunt, and
all the dodges of the fox. Night found him leg-weary, with his hands

and face lashed by the branches, on a thickly wooded ridge. He knew it would be insane to blunder on through the dark, even if he had the strength. His need for rest was imperative and he thought: "I have played the fox, now I must play the cat of the fable." A big tree with a thick trunk and outspread branches was nearby, and, taking care to leave not the slightest mark, he climbed up into the crotch, and stretching out on one of the broad limbs, after a fashion, rested. Rest brought him new confidence and almost a feeling of security. Even so zealous a hunter as General Zaroff could not trace him there, he told himself; only the devil himself could follow that complicated trail through the jungle after dark. But, perhaps, the general was a devil—

An apprehensive night crawled slowly by like a wounded snake, and sleep did not visit Rainsford, although the silence of a dead world was on the jungle. Toward morning when a dingy gray was varnishing the sky, the cry of some startled bird focused Rainsford's attention in that direction. Something was coming through the bush, coming slowly, carefully, coming by the same winding way Rainsford had come. He flattened himself down on the limb, and through a screen of leaves almost as thick as tapestry, he watched. The thing that was approaching was a man.

It was General Zaroff. He made his way along with his eyes fixed in utmost concentration on the ground before him. He paused, almost beneath the tree, dropped to his knees and studied the ground. Rainsford's impulse was to hurl himself down like a panther, but he saw the general's right hand held something metallic—a small automatic pistol.

The hunter shook his head several times, as if he were puzzled. Then he straightened up and took from his case one of his black cigarettes; its pungent incense-like smoke floated up to Rainsford's nostrils.

Rainsford held his breath. The general's eyes had left the ground and were traveling inch by inch up the tree. Rainsford froze there, every muscle tensed for a spring. But the sharp eyes of the hunter stopped before they reached the limb where Rainsford lay; a smile spread over his brown face. Very deliberately he blew a smoke ring into the air; then he turned his back on the tree and walked carelessly away, back along the trail he had come. The swish of the underbrush against his hunting boots grew fainter and fainter.

The pent-up air burst hotly from Rainsford's lungs. His first thought made him feel sick and numb. The general could follow a trail through the woods at night; he could follow an extremely difficult trail; he must have uncanny powers; only by the merest chance had the Cossack failed to see his quarry.

**Spiral Review**
**Pacing** The author shows Rainsford resting and waiting. How does the slower pace of this scene help to create tension in the story?

**Reading Skill**
**Make Inferences**
Which details in the description of Zaroff's searching the tree suggest that he knows Rainsford is there?

Reading
Check
On the first night of the hunt, where does Rainsford attempt to hide from Zaroff?

Rainsford's second thought was even more terrible. It sent a shudder of cold horror through his whole being. Why had the general smiled? Why had he turned back?

Rainsford did not want to believe what his reason told him was true, but the truth was as evident as the sun that had by now pushed through the morning mists. The general was playing with him! The general was saving him for another day's sport! The Cossack was the cat; he was the mouse. Then it was that Rainsford knew the full meaning of terror.

"I will not lose my nerve. I will not."

He slid down from the tree, and struck off again into the woods. His face was set and he forced the machinery of his mind to function. Three hundred yards from his hiding place he stopped where a huge dead tree leaned precariously on a smaller, living one. Throwing off his sack of food, Rainsford took his knife from its sheath and began to work with all his energy.

The job was finished at last, and he threw himself down behind a fallen log a hundred feet away. He did not have to wait long. The cat was coming again to play with the mouse. •

Following the trail with the sureness of a bloodhound, came General Zaroff. Nothing escaped those searching black eyes, no crushed blade of grass, no bent twig, no mark, no matter how faint, in the moss. So intent was the Cossack on his stalking that he was upon the thing Rainsford had made before he saw it. His foot touched the protruding bough that was the trigger. Even as he touched it, the general sensed his danger and leaped back with the agility of an ape. But he was not quite quick enough; the dead tree, delicately adjusted to rest on the cut living one, crashed down and struck the general a glancing blow on the shoulder as it fell; but for his alertness, he must have been smashed beneath it. He staggered, but he did not fall; nor did he drop his revolver. He stood there, rubbing his injured shoulder, and Rainsford, with fear again gripping his heart, heard the general's mocking laugh ring through the jungle.

"Rainsford," called the general, "if you are within the sound of my voice, as I suppose you are, let me congratulate you. Not many men know how to make a Malay mancatcher. Luckily, for me, I too have hunted in Malacca. You are proving interesting, Mr. Rainsford. I am going now to have my wound dressed; it's only a slight one. But I shall be back. I shall be back."

When the general, nursing his bruised shoulder, had gone, Rainsford took up his flight again. It was flight now, a desperate, hopeless flight, that carried him on for some hours. Dusk came, then darkness, and still he pressed on. The ground grew softer

**Literary Analysis**
**Conflict** Who seems to be winning the conflict at this point in the story? Explain.

## History Connection

### World War I Trenches

When Rainsford digs himself in, he is drawing on his experiences as a soldier. During World War I (1914–1918), European armies on both sides dug hundreds of miles of deep, narrow ditches. The soldiers lived in these trenches, from where they would charge the enemy's trenches.

◀ Soldiers' equipment included masks to protect them from mustard gas and other chemical weapons.

### LIFE IN THE TRENCHES

- Throughout the war, approximately seven thousand British soldiers were killed, wounded, or disabled every day while serving in the trenches.

- Soldiers living in trenches were plagued by lice, rats, beetles, and frogs.

- The trenches smelled terrible due to dead bodies, overflowing latrines, and unwashed men.

A single pair of trench rats could produce as many as 880 offspring in one year.
▼

### Connect to the Literature

Rainsford says his time in the trenches was "placid" compared to his experience on the island. How does this information about trenches clarify his fear?

under his moccasins; the vegetation grew ranker, denser; insects bit him savagely. Then, as he stepped forward, his foot sank into the ooze. He tried to wrench it back, but the muck sucked viciously at his foot as if it were a giant leech. With a violent effort, he tore his foot loose. He knew where he was now. Death Swamp and its quicksand.

His hands were tight closed as if his nerve were something tangible that someone in the darkness was trying to tear from his grip. The softness of the earth had given him an idea. He stepped back from the quicksand a dozen feet or so, and, like some huge prehistoric beaver, he began to dig.

Rainsford had dug himself in in France when a second's delay meant death. That had been a placid pastime compared to his digging now. The pit grew deeper; when it was above his shoulders, he climbed out and from some hard saplings cut stakes and

**Reading Check**
What toll does Rainsford's trap take on Zaroff?

sharpened them to a fine point. These stakes he planted in the bottom of the pit with the points sticking up. With flying fingers he wove a rough carpet of weeds and branches and with it he covered the mouth of the pit. Then, wet with sweat and aching with tiredness, he crouched behind the stump of a lightning-charred tree.

He knew his pursuer was coming; he heard the padding sound of feet on the soft earth, and the night breeze brought him the perfume of the general's cigarette. It seemed to Rainsford that the general was coming with unusual swiftness; he was not feeling his way along, foot by foot. Rainsford, crouching there, could not see the general, nor could he see the pit. He lived a year in a minute. Then he felt an impulse to cry aloud with joy, for he heard the sharp crackle of the breaking branches as the cover of the pit gave way; he heard the sharp scream of pain as the pointed stakes found their mark. He leaped up from his place of concealment. Then he cowered back. Three feet from the pit a man was standing, with an electric torch in his hand.

"You've done well, Rainsford," the voice of the general called. "Your Burmese tiger pit has claimed one of my best dogs. Again you score. I think, Mr. Rainsford, I'll see what you can do against my whole pack. I'm going home for a rest now. Thank you for a most amusing evening."

At daybreak Rainsford, lying near the swamp, was awakened by a sound that made him know that he had new things to learn about fear. It was a distant sound, faint and wavering, but he knew it. It was the baying of a pack of hounds.

Rainsford knew he could do one of two things. He could stay where he was and wait. That was suicide. He could flee. That was postponing the inevitable. For a moment he stood there, thinking. An idea that held a wild chance came to him, and, tightening his belt, he headed away from the swamp.

The baying of the hounds drew nearer, then still nearer, nearer, ever nearer. On a ridge Rainsford climbed a tree. Down a watercourse, not a quarter of a mile away, he could see the bush moving. Straining his eyes, he saw the lean figure of General Zaroff; just ahead of him Rainsford made out another figure whose wide shoulders surged through the tall jungle weeds; it was the giant Ivan, and he seemed pulled forward by some unseen force; Rainsford knew that Ivan must be holding the pack in leash.

They would be on him any minute now. His mind worked frantically. He thought of a native trick he had learned in Uganda. He slid down the tree. He caught hold of a springy young sapling and to it he fastened his hunting knife, with the blade pointing down the trail; with a bit of wild grapevine he tied back the sapling. Then he ran for his life. The hounds raised their voices as they hit the fresh scent. Rainsford knew now how an animal at bay feels.

He had to stop to get his breath. The baying of the hounds stopped abruptly, and Rainsford's heart stopped too. They must have reached the knife.

He shinnied excitedly up a tree and looked back. His pursuers had stopped. But the hope that was in Rainsford's brain when he climbed died, for he saw in the shallow valley that General Zaroff was still on his feet. But Ivan was not. The knife, driven by the recoil of the springing tree, had not wholly failed.

"Nerve, nerve, nerve!" he panted, as he dashed along. A blue gap showed between the trees dead ahead. Ever nearer drew the hounds. Rainsford forced himself on toward that gap. He reached it. It was the shore of the sea. Across a cove he could see the gloomy gray stone of the château. Twenty feet below him the sea rumbled and hissed. Rainsford hesitated. He heard the hounds. Then he leaped far out into the sea. . . .

When the general and his pack reached the place by the sea, the Cossack stopped. For some minutes he stood regarding the blue-green expanse of water. He shrugged his shoulders. Then he sat down, took a drink of brandy from a silver flask, lit a perfumed cigarette, and hummed a bit from *Madame Butterfly*.[15]

General Zaroff had an exceedingly good dinner in his great paneled dining hall that evening. With it he had a bottle of Pol Roger and half a bottle of Chambertin. Two slight annoyances kept him from perfect enjoyment. One was the thought that it would be difficult to replace Ivan; the other was that his quarry had escaped him; of course the American hadn't played the game—so thought the general as he tasted his after-dinner liqueur. In his library he

---

15. *Madame Butterfly* an opera by Giacomo Puccini.

**Literary Analysis**
**Conflict** What new internal conflict does the sound of the baying dogs create for Rainsford?

Reading Check
What does Rainsford do when he reaches the edge of the cliff?

read, to soothe himself, from the works of Marcus Aurelius.[16] At ten he went up to his bedroom. He was deliciously tired, he said to himself, as he locked himself in. There was a little moonlight, so, before turning on his light, he went to the window and looked down at the courtyard. He could see the great hounds, and he called: "Better luck another time," to them. Then he switched on the light.

A man, who had been hiding in the curtain of the bed, was standing there.

"Rainsford!" screamed the general. "How in God's name did you get here?"

"Swam," said Rainsford. "I found it quicker than walking through the jungle."

The general sucked in his breath and smiled. "I congratulate you," he said. "You have won the game."

Rainsford did not smile. "I am still a beast at bay," he said, in a low, hoarse voice. "Get ready, General Zaroff."

The general made one of his deepest bows. "I see," he said. "Splendid! One of us is to furnish a repast for the hounds. The other will sleep in this very excellent bed. On guard, Rainsford. . . ."

He had never slept in a better bed, Rainsford decided.

---

**16. Marcus Aurelius** (ô rē´ lē əs) Roman emperor and philosopher (A.D. 121–180).

## Critical Thinking

Cite textual evidence to support your responses.

ⓒ **1. Key Ideas and Details (a)** According to Zaroff, what is the most dangerous game? **(b) Make a Judgment:** Based on this attitude, would you call Zaroff "civilized"? Why or why not?

ⓒ **2. Key Ideas and Details (a)** Near the end, with what words does Zaroff congratulate Rainsford? **(b) Infer:** What action does Rainsford then take?

ⓒ **3. Integration of Knowledge and Ideas Speculate:** How might Rainsford's experience on the island change him? Use evidence from the text to support your answer.

ⓒ **4. Integration of Knowledge and Ideas (a)** In what sense is conflict a "necessary" part of the hunting experience? **(b)** Why does Zaroff consider it necessary to increase the conflict in his hunts? *[Connect to the Big Question: Is conflict necessary?]*

## Literary Analysis: Conflict

**1. Key Ideas and Details (a)** What is the main **conflict** in this story? Explain. **(b)** Is the main conflict primarily **internal** or **external**? Explain.

**2. Key Ideas and Details** Use a chart like the one shown to provide specific details that reveal conflicts other than the main conflict.

| Rainsford vs. Nature | Rainsford vs. Himself |
|---|---|
|  |  |

**3. Integration of Knowledge and Ideas** Is there a **resolution** in this story or does Rainsford experience an **epiphany** with no real end to the conflict? Support your answer.

## Reading Skill: Make Inferences

**4. (a)** Identify three **inferences** you made while reading this story and the details you used to make them. **(b)** Did making inferences improve your understanding of the story? Explain your response.

**5. (a)** Write two **inferences** you made about Whitney. Compare the inferences you made with a partner's inferences. **(b)** Based on your ideas, discuss how the story would be different if it had been Whitney on the island with Zaroff.

## Vocabulary

**Acquisition and Use** Use a word from the vocabulary list on page 212 to fill in the blank in each sentence. Then, explain the **context clues,** or key words and phrases, in each sentence that helped you.

**1.** His cheating at the game demonstrated a lack of _____.

**2.** At the wedding, the joy in the air seemed _____.

**3.** She tried to climb, but her high heels made her efforts _____.

**4.** The lazy sloth hung _____ from the tree branch.

**5.** Only a very _____ person would believe in the Tooth Fairy.

**6.** The _____ necklace was made of beads that looked like skulls.

**Word Study** Use the context of the sentences and what you know about the **Latin suffix -esque** to explain your answer to each question.

**1.** Why do people like to visit *picturesque* places?

**2.** If a film is called *Disneyesque,* whose movies does it resemble?

### Word Study

The **Latin suffix -esque** means "in the style or manner of."

**Apply It** Explain how the suffix *-esque* contributes to the meanings of these words. Consult a dictionary if necessary.

statuesque
Lincolnesque
tabloidesque

# Is *conflict* necessary?

## Writing About the Big Question

In "American History," a teenage girl wrestles with personal feelings while the adults around her try to grasp a tragic historic event. Use these sentence starters to develop your ideas about the Big Question.

For both individuals and countries, historic events often involve conflict because _____.

Fighting the same **battle** allows people to overlook the **differences** among them because _____.

**While You Read** Think about how Elena prioritizes the thoughts that compete for her attention.

## Vocabulary

Read each word and its definition. Decide whether you know the word well, know it a little bit, or do not know it at all. After you read, see how your knowledge of each word has increased.

- **tenement** (ten´ ə mənt) *n.* apartment house, often run-down (p. 241) *Many families lived in the large tenement.*

- **profound** (prō found´) *adj.* deep; intense (p. 241) *Mia felt profound sorrow when her dog died.* profoundly *adv.*

- **discreet** (di skrēt´) *adj.* careful about one's actions; prudent; keeping silent or preserving confidences (p. 244) *Please, be discreet when you talk to the press about our agreement.* discreetly *adv.* discretion *n.* indiscreet *adj.* indiscretion *n.*

- **vigilant** (vij´ ə lənt) *adj.* watchful (p. 245) *The bodyguard kept a vigilant eye on the candidate.* vigil *n.* vigilance *n.*

- **elation** (ē lā´ shən) *n.* exultant joy or pride; high spirits (p. 249) *She danced with elation when she saw the new puppy.* elate *v.* elated *adj.*

- **dilapidated** (də lap´ ə dāt´ ed) *adj.* broken down (p. 250) *The old furniture was dilapidated and worn.*

### Word Study

The **Latin suffix -ant** is often used to form adjectives. It usually means "performing an action."

In this story, a mother is **vigilant** about her daughter. She watches closely—keeps vigil—to make sure her daughter focuses on the right things.

# Meet
# Judith Ortiz Cofer
(b. 1952)

## Author of
# American History

Judith Ortiz Cofer spent her childhood in two different cultures. Born in Puerto Rico, she moved with her parents to Paterson, New Jersey, when she was four years old. She grew up mostly in Paterson, but she also spent time in Puerto Rico with her *abuela* (grandmother).

**The Art of Storytelling** It was from her grandmother that Ortiz Cofer learned the art of storytelling. "When my *abuela* sat us down to tell a story," she says, "we learned something from it, even though we always laughed. That was her way of teaching." In her own work, Ortiz Cofer teaches readers about the richness and difficulty of coming of age in two cultures at once.

## BACKGROUND FOR THE STORY

**The Kennedy Assassination**

On November 22, 1963, President John F. Kennedy was shot and killed in Dallas, Texas, and the United States was plunged into mourning. Most people who lived through that time can still remember where they were when they heard the news. Kennedy's assassination and the nation's grief defined a generation. Key events in "American History" take place on that fateful day.

## Did You Know?

Ortiz Cofer teaches for Operation Homecoming, a writing program for U.S. military personnel.

*Sunday Afternoon - Stickball Game,* 1953, Ralph Fasanella. Courtesy A.C.A. Galleries, N.Y.

# American History

## Judith Ortiz Cofer

I once read in a *Ripley's Believe It or Not* column that Paterson, New Jersey, is the place where the Straight and Narrow (streets) intersect.

The Puerto Rican tenement known as El Building was one block up from Straight. It was, in fact, the corner of Straight and Market; not "at" the corner, but *the* corner. At almost any hour of the day, El Building was like a monstrous jukebox, blasting out *salsas*[1] from open windows as the residents, mostly new immigrants just up from the island, tried to drown out whatever they were currently enduring with loud music. But the day President Kennedy was shot there was a profound silence in El Building; even the abusive tongues of *viragoes*,[2] the cursing of the unemployed, and the screeching of small children had been somehow muted. President Kennedy was a saint to these people. In fact, soon his photograph would be hung alongside the Sacred Heart and over the spiritist altars that many women kept in their apartments. He would

---

**1.** *salsas* (säl´ səs) songs written in a particular Latin American musical style.
**2.** *viragoes* (vi rä´ gōz) fierce, irritable women who often shout.

**Vocabulary**
**tenement**
(ten´ ə mənt) *n.* apartment house, often run-down

**profound**
(prō found´) *adj.* deep; intense

**Reading Check**
On what memorable day in history does this story take place?

◄ **Critical Viewing**
In what ways does this painting illustrate the narrator's description of the neighborhood in the first paragraph? **[Compare]**

become part of the hierarchy of martyrs they prayed to for favors that only one who had died for a cause would understand.  •

On the day that President Kennedy was shot, my ninth grade class had been out in the fenced playground of Public School Number 13. We had been given "free" exercise time and had been ordered by our P.E. teacher, Mr. DePalma, to "keep moving." That meant that the girls should jump rope and the boys toss basketballs through a hoop at the far end of the yard. He in the meantime would "keep an eye" on us from just inside the building.

It was a cold gray day in Paterson. The kind that warns of early snow. I was miserable, since I had forgotten my gloves, and my knuckles were turning red and raw from the jump rope. I was also taking a lot of abuse from the black girls for not turning the rope hard and fast enough for them.

▶ **Critical Viewing**
In what ways is this school scene similar to your school? In what ways is it different? **[Compare and Contrast]**

"Hey, Skinny Bones, pump it, girl. Ain't you got no energy today?" Gail, the biggest of the black girls who had the other end of the rope, yelled, "Didn't you eat your rice and beans and pork chops for breakfast today?"

The other girls picked up the "pork chops" and made it into a refrain: "pork chop, pork chop, did you eat your pork chop?" They entered the double ropes in pairs and exited without tripping or missing a beat. I felt a burning on my cheeks and then my glasses fogged up so that I could not manage to coordinate the jump rope with Gail. The chill was doing to me what it always did, entering my bones, making me cry, humiliating me. I hated the city, especially in winter. I hated Public School Number 13. I hated my skinny flat-chested body, and I envied the black girls who could jump rope so fast that their legs became a blur. They always seemed to be warm while I froze.

**Reading Skill**
**Make Inferences**
Which details in this passage lead you to infer that the narrator is fond of Eugene?

There was only one source of beauty and light for me that school year. The only thing I had anticipated at the start of the semester. That was seeing Eugene. In August, Eugene and his family had moved into the only house on the block that had a yard and trees. I could see his place from my window in El Building. In fact, if I sat on the fire escape I was literally suspended above Eugene's backyard. It was my favorite spot to read my library books in the summer. Until that August the house had been occupied by an old Jewish couple. Over the years I had become part of their family, without their knowing it, of course. I had a view of their kitchen and their backyard, and though I could not hear what they said, I knew when they were arguing, when one of them was sick, and many other things. I knew all this by watching them at mealtimes. I could see their kitchen table, the sink, and the stove. During good times, he sat at the table and read his newspapers while she fixed the meals. If they argued, he would leave and the old woman would sit and stare at nothing for a long time. When one of them was sick, the other would come and get things from the kitchen and carry them out on a tray. The old man had died in June. The last week of school I had not seen him at the table at all. Then one day I saw that there was a crowd in the kitchen. The old woman had finally emerged from the house on the arm of a stocky, middle-aged woman, whom I had seen there a few times before, maybe her daughter. Then a man had carried out suitcases. The house had stood empty for weeks. I had had to resist the temptation to climb down into the yard and water the flowers the old lady had taken such good care of.

By the time Eugene's family moved in, the yard was a tangled mass of weeds. The father had spent several days mowing, and

## Reading Check

Who is Eugene, and how does the narrator become aware of him?

There was only one source of beauty and light for me that school year.

▲ **Critical Viewing**
Which description from
the selection does
this painting suggest?
**[Connect]**

**Vocabulary**
**discreet** (di skrēt´)
*adj.* careful about
one's actions; prudent;
keeping silent or
preserving confidences

when he finished, from where I sat, I didn't see the red, yellow, and purple clusters that meant flowers to me. I didn't see this family sit down at the kitchen table together. It was just the mother, a red-headed tall woman who wore a white uniform—a nurse's, I guessed it was; the father was gone before I got up in the morning and was never there at dinner time. I only saw him on weekends when they sometimes sat on lawn chairs under the oak tree, each hidden behind a section of the newspaper; and there was Eugene. He was tall and blond, and he wore glasses. I liked him right away because he sat at the kitchen table and read books for hours. That summer, before we had even spoken one word to each other, I kept him company on my fire escape.

Once school started I looked for him in all my classes, but P.S. 13 was a huge, overpopulated place and it took me days and many discreet questions to discover that Eugene was in honors classes for all his subjects; classes that were not open to me because English was not my first language, though I was a straight A student. After much maneuvering, I managed "to run into him" in the hallway where his locker was—on the other side of the building from mine—and in study hall at the library, where he first seemed to notice me but did not speak; and finally, on the way home after school one day when I decided to approach him directly, though my stomach was doing somersaults.

I was ready for rejection, snobbery, the worst. But when I came up to him, practically panting in my nervousness, and blurted out: "You're Eugene. Right?" he smiled, pushed his glasses up on his nose, and nodded. I saw then that he was blushing deeply. Eugene liked me, but he was shy. I did most of the talking that day. He nodded and smiled a lot. In the weeks that followed, we walked home together. He would linger at the corner of El Building for a few minutes then walk down to his two-story house. It was not until Eugene moved into that house that I noticed that El Building blocked most of the sun, and that the only spot that got a little sunlight during the day was the tiny square of earth the old woman had planted with flowers.

I did not tell Eugene that I could see inside his kitchen from my bedroom. I felt dishonest, but I liked my secret sharing of his evenings, especially now that I knew what he was reading since we chose our books together at the school library.

One day my mother came into my room as I was sitting on the windowsill staring out. In her abrupt way she said: "Elena, you are acting 'moony.' " *Enamorada* [3] was what she really said, that is—like a girl stupidly infatuated. Since I had turned fourteen . . . my mother had been more vigilant than ever. She acted as if I was going to go crazy or explode or something if she didn't watch me and nag me all the time about being a *señorita* [4] now. She kept talking about virtue, morality, and other subjects that did not interest me in the least. My mother was unhappy in Paterson, but my father had a good job at the blue jeans factory in Passaic and soon, he kept assuring us, we would be moving to our own house there. Every Sunday we drove out to the suburbs of Paterson, Clifton, and Passaic, out to where people mowed grass on Sundays in the summer, and where children made snowmen in the winter from pure white snow, not like the gray slush of Paterson which seemed to fall from the sky in that hue. I had learned to listen to my parents' dreams, which were spoken in Spanish, as fairy tales, like the stories about life in the island paradise of Puerto Rico before I was born. I had been to the island once as a little girl, to grandmother's funeral, and all I remembered was wailing women in black, my mother becoming hysterical and being given a pill that

**Literary Analysis**
**Conflict** What internal conflict does the narrator experience as she prepares to approach Eugene?

**Vocabulary**
**vigilant** (vij´ ə lənt)
*adj.* watchful

**Reading Check**
According to her mother, how does Elena seem to feel about Eugene?

**Spiral Review**
**Plot Devices** This story can be seen as having a parallel plot structure. What are the two story lines that the author develops?

**Literary Analysis**
**Conflict** What external conflict does Eugene experience at school?

made her sleep two days, and me feeling lost in a crowd of strangers all claiming to be my aunts, uncles, and cousins. I had actually been glad to return to the city. We had not been back there since then, though my parents talked constantly about buying a house on the beach someday, retiring on the island—that was a common topic among the residents of El Building. As for me, I was going to go to college and become a teacher.

But after meeting Eugene I began to think of the present more than of the future. What I wanted now was to enter that house I had watched for so many years. I wanted to see the other rooms where the old people had lived, and where the boy spent his time. Most of all, I wanted to sit at the kitchen table with Eugene like two adults, like the old man and his wife had done, maybe drink some coffee and talk about books. I had started reading *Gone with the Wind.* I was enthralled by it, with the daring and the passion of the beautiful girl living in a mansion, and with her devoted parents and the slaves who did everything for them. I didn't believe such a world had ever really existed, and I wanted to ask Eugene some questions since he and his parents, he had told me, had come up from Georgia, the same place where the novel was set. His father worked for a company that had transferred him to Paterson. His mother was very unhappy, Eugene said, in his beautiful voice that rose and fell over words in a strange, lilting way. The kids at school called him "the hick" and made fun of the way he talked. I knew I was his only friend so far, and I liked that, though I felt sad for him sometimes. "Skinny Bones" and the "Hick" was what they called us at school when we were seen together.  •

The day Mr. DePalma came out into the cold and asked us to line up in front of him was the day that President Kennedy was shot. Mr. DePalma, a short, muscular man with slicked-down black hair, was the science teacher, P.E. coach, and disciplinarian at P.S. 13. He was the teacher to whose homeroom you got assigned if you were a troublemaker, and the man called out to break up playground fights, and to escort violently angry teenagers to the office. And Mr. DePalma was the man who called your parents in for "a conference."

That day, he stood in front of two rows of mostly black and Puerto Rican kids, brittle from their efforts to "keep moving" on a November day that was turning bitter cold. Mr. DePalma, to our complete shock, was crying. Not just silent adult tears, but really sobbing. There were a few titters from the back of the line where I stood shivering.

"Listen," Mr. DePalma raised his arms over his head as if he were about to conduct an orchestra. His voice broke, and he covered his face with his hands. His barrel chest was heaving. Someone giggled behind me.

"Listen," he repeated, "something awful has happened." A strange gurgling came from his throat, and he turned around and spat on the cement behind him.

"Gross," someone said, and there was a lot of laughter.

"The president is dead, you idiots. I should have known that wouldn't mean anything to a bunch of losers like you kids. Go home." He was shrieking now. No one moved for a minute or two, but then a big girl let out a "Yeah!" and ran to get her books piled up with the others against the brick wall of the school building. The others followed in a mad scramble to get to their things before somebody caught on. It was still an hour to the dismissal bell.

A little scared, I headed for El Building. There was an eerie feeling on the streets. I looked into Mario's drugstore, a favorite hangout for the high school crowd, but there were only a couple of old Jewish men at the soda bar talking with the short order cook in tones that sounded almost angry, but they were keeping their voices low. Even the traffic on one of the busiest intersections in Paterson—Straight Street and Park Avenue—seemed to be moving slower. There were no horns blasting that day. At El Building, the usual little group of unemployed men were not hanging out on the front stoop making it difficult for women to enter the front door. No music spilled out from open doors in the hallway. When I walked into our apartment, I found my mother sitting in front of the grainy picture of the television set.

She looked up at me with a tear-streaked face and just said: "*Dios mío*,"[5] turning back to the set as if it were pulling at her eyes. I went into my room.

Though I wanted to feel the right thing about President Kennedy's death, I could not fight the

---

5. *Dios mío* (dē′ ōs mē′ ō) Spanish for "My God!"

**Reading Skill**
**Make Inferences**
Which details in Elena's description of her walk home let you infer the anguish people feel over the assassination of the president?

◀ **Critical Viewing**
What lines in the story help you to understand this image? **[Connect]**

Reading Check

How does Mr. DePalma's reaction to the news of Kennedy's assassination differ from the students' reaction?

feeling of elation that stirred in my chest. Today was the day I was to visit Eugene in his house. He had asked me to come over after school to study for an American history test with him. We had also planned to walk to the public library together. I looked down into his yard. The oak tree was bare of leaves and the ground looked gray with ice. The light through the large kitchen window of his house told me that El Building blocked the sun to such an extent that they had to turn lights on in the middle of the day. I felt ashamed about it. But the white kitchen table with the lamp hanging just above it looked cozy and inviting. I would soon sit there, across from Eugene, and I would tell him about my perch just above his house. Maybe I should.

In the next thirty minutes I changed clothes, put on a little pink lipstick, and got my books together. Then I went in to tell my mother that I was going to a friend's house to study. I did not expect her reaction.

"You are going out *today?*" The way she said "today" sounded as if a storm warning had been issued. It was said in utter disbelief. Before I could answer, she came toward me and held my elbows as I clutched my books.

"*Hija,*[6] the president has been killed. We must show respect. He was a great man. Come to church with me tonight."

She tried to embrace me, but my books were in the way. My first impulse was to comfort her, she seemed so distraught, but I had to meet Eugene in fifteen minutes.

"I have a test to study for, Mama. I will be home by eight."

"You are forgetting who you are, *Niña.*[7] I have seen you staring down at that boy's house. You are heading for humiliation and

---

6. *Hija* (ē´ hä) Spanish for "daughter."
7. *Niña* (nē´ nyä) Spanish for "child."

**Vocabulary**
**elation** (ē lā´ shən)
*adj.* exultant joy or pride; high spirits

**Literary Analysis**
**Conflict** On the evening of the assassination, how do Elena's plans conflict with her mother's?

**Reading Check**
How does Elena feel about studying with Eugene?

"*Hija,* the president has been killed. We must show respect. He was a great man."

▲ **Critical Viewing**
What is striking about this image? **[Respond]**

**Vocabulary**
**dilapidated** (də lap´ə dāt´ əd) *adj.* broken down

**Reading Skill**
**Make Inferences**
Based on the description of the woman's face, what do you think she was doing before Elena arrived?

pain." My mother said this in Spanish and in a resigned tone that surprised me, as if she had no intention of stopping me from "heading for humiliation and pain." I started for the door. She sat in front of the TV holding a white handkerchief to her face. •

I walked out to the street and around the chain-link fence that separated El Building from Eugene's house. The yard was neatly edged around the little walk that led to the door. It always amazed me how Paterson, the inner core of the city, had no apparent logic to its architecture. Small, neat, single residences like this one could be found right next to huge, dilapidated apartment buildings like El Building. My guess was that the little houses had been there first, then the immigrants had come in droves, and the monstrosities had been raised for them—the Italians, the Irish, the Jews, and now us, the Puerto Ricans and the blacks. The door was painted a deep green: *verde,* the color of hope, I had heard my mother say it: *Verde-Esperanza.*[8]

I knocked softly. A few suspenseful moments later the door opened just a crack. The red, swollen face of a woman appeared. She had a halo of red hair floating over a delicate ivory face—the face of a doll—with freckles on the nose. Her smudged eye make-up made her look unreal to me, like a mannequin seen through a warped store window.

"What do you want?" Her voice was tiny and sweet-sounding, like a little girl's, but her tone was not friendly.

"I'm Eugene's friend. He asked me over. To study." I thrust out my books, a silly gesture that embarrassed me almost immediately.

---

**8. Verde-Esperanza** (ver´ dā es pā rän´ zä) Spanish for "green-hope."

"You live there?" She pointed up to El Building, which looked particularly ugly, like a gray prison with its many dirty windows and rusty fire escapes. The woman had stepped halfway out and I could see that she wore a white nurse's uniform with "St. Joseph's Hospital" on the name tag.

"Yes. I do."

She looked intently at me for a couple of heartbeats, then said as if to herself, "I don't know how you people do it." Then directly to me: "Listen. Honey. Eugene doesn't want to study with you. He is a smart boy. Doesn't need help. You understand me. I am truly sorry if he told you you could come over. He cannot study with you. It's nothing personal. You understand? We won't be in this place much longer, no need for him to get close to people—it'll just make it harder for him later. Run back home now."

I couldn't move. I just stood there in shock at hearing these things said to me in such a honey-drenched voice. I had never heard an accent like hers, except for Eugene's softer version. It was as if she were singing me a little song.

"What's wrong? Didn't you hear what I said?" She seemed very angry, and I finally snapped out of my trance. I turned away from the green door, and heard her close it gently.

Our apartment was empty when I got home. My mother was in someone else's kitchen, seeking the solace she needed. Father would come in from his late shift at midnight. I would hear them talking softly in the kitchen for hours that night. They would not discuss their dreams for the future, or life in Puerto Rico, as they often did; that night they would talk sadly about the young widow and her two children, as if they were family. For the next few days, we would observe *luto*[9] in our apartment; that is, we would practice restraint and silence—no loud music or laughter. Some of the women of El Building would wear black for weeks.

That night, I lay in my bed trying to feel the right thing for our dead president. But the tears that came up from a deep source inside me were strictly for me. When my mother came to the door, I pretended to be sleeping. Sometime during the night, I saw from my bed the streetlight come on. It had a pink halo around it. I went to my window and pressed my face to the cool glass. Looking up

---

9. *luto* (lo͞o′ tō) Spanish for "mourning."

**Literary Analysis**
**Conflict** How do Eugene's mother's comments change the story's conflict?

The door was painted a deep green: verde, the color of hope, I had heard my mother say it: *Verde-Esperanza.*

**Reading Check**
How does Eugene's mother react to Elena's visit to their house?

**Literary Analysis**

**Conflict** How does the contrast between the white snow falling and the gray snow touching the ground reflect Elena's feelings for Eugene?

at the light I could see the white snow falling like a lace veil over its face. I did not look down to see it turning gray as it touched the ground below.

## Critical Thinking

1. **Key Ideas and Details (a)** In the first paragraph, what words does Elena use to describe her building? **(b)** How does she describe Eugene's house from her fire escape? **(c) Compare and Contrast:** Based on these descriptions, explain the contrast in Elena's feelings toward her own home and toward Eugene's house.

2. **Key Ideas and Details (a)** What subject is Elena going to study with Eugene? **(b) Interpret:** What other reasons might Ortiz Cofer have for calling this story "American History"?

3. **Key Ideas and Details (a) Analyze:** Where is Elena's mother and what is she doing when Elena returns from Eugene's house? **(b) Analyze:** In the last scene of the story, why does Elena say that her tears are just for herself?

4. **Integration of Knowledge and Ideas (a)** For Elena, which problem in the story—the national one or the personal one—is more important? **(b)** Are these conflicts necessary for Elena's personal growth and understanding of the world? Explain your response. *[Connect to the Big Question: Is conflict necessary?]*

## Literary Analysis: Conflict

**1. Key Ideas and Details (a)** What is the main **conflict** in this story? Explain. **(b)** Is the main conflict primarily **internal** or **external**? Explain your response.

**2. Key Ideas and Details** Use a chart like the one shown to provide specific details that reveal conflicts other than the main conflict.

| Elena vs. Another Person | Elena vs. Herself |
|---|---|
|  |  |

**3. Key Ideas and Details (a)** What realization about life's disappointments does Elena come to at the end of the story? **(b)** Does this **epiphany** lead to a clear **resolution?** Support your answer with details from the story.

## Reading Skill: Make Inferences

**4. (a)** Identify three **inferences** you made while reading this story. **(b)** Identify the details you used in order to make those inferences.

**5.** Explain how making inferences improved your understanding of the story.

## Vocabulary

**Acquisition and Use** Use a word from the "American History" vocabulary list on page 238 to fill in each blank. Then, explain the **context clues,** or key words and phrases, in each sentence that helped you.

**1.** During the blackout, the guard was more _____ than usual.

**2.** The _____ car had no wheels and was covered in rust.

**3.** She felt a _____ sense of pride as she graduated with honors.

**4.** The serene garden contrasted with the bustling _____.

**5.** We shouted with _____ when our team won the game.

**6.** I remained _____, even though I was desperate to tell the secret.

**Word Study** Use the context of the sentences and what you know about the **Latin suffix -ant** to explain your answer to each question.

**1.** Would it be easy to get along with a *compliant* person?

**2.** Why is a baby *reliant* upon her parents?

### Word Study

The **Latin suffix -ant** often means "performing an action."

**Apply It** Explain how the suffix -*ant* contributes to the meanings of these words. Consult a dictionary if necessary.

**defiant**
**repentant**
**errant**

# Integrated Language Skills

## The Most Dangerous Game • American History

### Conventions: Regular Verbs

The **principal parts** of a verb are the present, the present participle, the past, and the past participle.

Most verbs in the English language are **regular verbs** that use predictable patterns. By using various **principal parts,** you can show how actions take place in time and add variety and interest to sentences.

The **present** tense describes action happening now or in the future. The **present participle** is formed by adding *-ing* to the present form. The **future** tense is achieved by adding *will* to the present form as a helping verb. The **past** tense describes events that happened already. To form the past and **past participle,** add *-ed* to the present form (the participle uses *have, has*, or *had* as a helping verb). If the present form ends in -e, that -e is usually dropped when adding an ending. Finally, the **present progressive** shows continuing action and uses a form of *be* as a helping verb.

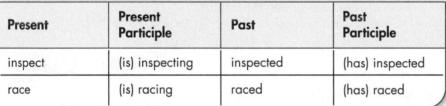

| Present | Present Participle | Past | Past Participle |
|---------|--------------------|------|-----------------|
| inspect | (is) inspecting | inspected | (has) inspected |
| race | (is) racing | raced | (has) raced |

**Practice A** Identify the principal part of each underlined verb.

1. Rainsford <u>discovered</u> a mysterious island.
2. The gunshots had <u>awakened</u> the night.
3. Now he is <u>running</u> toward a cliff.
4. Soon, he will <u>confront</u> the foe in his fight.

**© Reading Application** Find four sentences in "The Most Dangerous Game" that use regular verbs. Change each sentence by using a different principal part.

**Practice B** Complete each sentence with a regular verb, using the form in parentheses.

1. Kennedy's death (past) Elena's mother.
2. Elena is (present participle) about Eugene.
3. Eugene's family has (past participle) next door.
4. Elena will (future) with him after school.

**© Writing Application** Look back to the image on page 250 in "American History." Write four sentences about it using a different principal part for each.

**PH WRITING COACH** Further instruction and practice are available in *Prentice Hall Writing Coach.*

# Writing

 **Narrative Text** Each of these stories may leave readers with more questions than answers. Write an **alternative ending** to "American History" or "The Most Dangerous Game."

- Create an ending that flows logically from earlier events.
- Focus on presenting a satisfactory resolution to the conflict.
- Make your ending consistent with your understanding of the characters.
- Include dialogue and details to show how the characters feel and think.

**Grammar Application** As you write, use the principal parts of verbs correctly to show actions as they occur in time.

**Writing Workshop:** *Work in Progress*

**Prewriting for Narration: Short Story** To prepare for writing a short story, create a Character Profile. Name a character and develop information about his or her gender, age, appearance, background, interests, and longings. Save the profile in your portfolio.

# Speaking and Listening

 **Presentation of Ideas** In a group, prepare an **oral presentation** using print and nonprint media.

- If you read "American History," discuss the effect of President Kennedy's assassination upon the American public.
- If you read "The Most Dangerous Game," discuss two or three big-game species mentioned in the story. Include key facts about each one, including any threats that the species faces today.

Follow these steps to write a speech on the topic:

- Choose questions that the speech should answer. Then, gather information from primary and secondary sources.
- Organize the information that you wish to share. You may need to do additional research to supplement what you already have.
- Write an introduction and conclusion for the speech. The introduction should grab the audience's attention and the conclusion should summarize key points in a memorable way.
- Use vivid language to make the speech interesting.
- Gather images, either print or nonprint, that illustrate the speech and decide how you want to display them.

Practice your presentation. Rehearse to make sure that you can operate multimedia equipment. If necessary, revise your presentation so that points will be clearer or more interesting.

 **Common Core State Standards**

L.9-10.1, L.9-10.6;
W.9-10.3.e; SL.9-10.4
[For the full wording of the standards, see page 210.]

Use this prewriting activity to prepare for the **Writing Workshop** on page 306.

**PHLit Online!**
www.PHLitOnline.com
- Interactive graphic organizers
- Grammar tutorial
- Interactive journals

## ⓒ Leveled Texts

Build your skills and improve your comprehension of short stories with texts of increasing complexity.

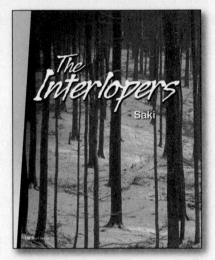

Read **"The Gift of the Magi"** to learn about a husband and wife who seek the perfect present for each other.

Read **"The Interlopers"** to see how enemies become each other's only hope for survival.

## ⓒ Common Core State Standards

Meet these standards with either **"The Gift of the Magi"** (p. 260) or **"The Interlopers"** (p. 270).

**Reading Literature**

**1.** Cite strong and thorough textual evidence to support analysis of what the text says explicitly as well as inferences drawn from the text. *(Reading Skill: Make Inferences)*

**Writing**

**3.** Write narratives to develop real or imagined experiences or events using effective technique, well-chosen details, and well-structured event sequences. *(Writing: News Report)*

**3.c.** Use a variety of techniques to sequence events so that they build on one another to create a coherent whole.

**Speaking and Listening**

**4.** Present information, findings, and supporting evidence clearly, concisely, and logically such that listeners can follow the line of reasoning and the organization, development, substance, and style are appropriate to purpose, audience, and task. *(Speaking and Listening: Debate)*

**Language**

**1.** Demonstrate command of the conventions of standard English grammar and usage when writing or speaking. *(Conventions: Irregular Verbs)*

# Literary Analysis: Irony

**Irony** is a *contradiction* between appearance and reality—it is the difference between what is expected and what actually happens.

In **situational irony,** something happens in the story that contradicts the expectations of a character or the reader. For example, a runner who trains hard would be expected to do well in a race. It would be ironic if she trained so hard that she overslept and missed the race.

A **surprise ending** often presents a situational irony. The turn of events may be startling, but writers using irony usually build clues into the story that make the ending logical, just the same.

Ironies and surprise endings usually help convey the story's *theme*, or message. As you read, watch for surprises and think about what each one may mean.

# Reading Skill: Make Inferences

An **inference** is a logical assumption that you make based on details in a text. The author may state some information directly, but most of the ideas in a story are suggested through details. When reading short stories, **use your own prior knowledge and experience** to make inferences. As you learn, watch movies and plays, and observe the world every day, you gather knowledge and experiences.

- When you read something new, look for ways in which the characters and situations resemble ones you have seen before.

- Then, apply that knowledge and experience to make inferences.

## Using the Strategy: Inferences Chart

Use a **flowchart** like this one to make inferences as you read.

| Detail | My Experience | Inference |
|---|---|---|
| The king yawns when he is told that his people are starving. | The best leaders are those who show concern for their people. | The author wants me to believe that the king is a bad leader. |

# Is *conflict* necessary?

## Writing About the Big Question

In "The Gift of the Magi," Jim and Della want to exchange Christmas presents, but money is an issue. Use these sentence starters to develop your ideas about the Big Question.

When money is tight, it may be hard to show you **appreciate** others because _____. To resolve this problem, you might _____ or _____.

**While You Read** Think about the similarities in the ways that Della and Jim try to overcome their Christmastime conflict.

## Vocabulary

Read each word and its definition. Decide whether you know the word well, know it a little bit, or do not know it at all. After you read, see how your knowledge of each word has increased.

- **instigates** (in´ stə gāts´) *v.* urges on; stirs up (p. 261) *When he is not watched carefully, he instigates trouble.* instigation n.

- **depreciate** (dē prē´ shē āt´) *v.* reduce in value (p. 262) *Items that do not depreciate are good investments.* depreciation n.

- **cascade** (kas kād´) *n.* a small steep waterfall; anything suggesting such a waterfall (p. 262) *Her hair flowed down her back like a cascade.* cascade v. cascading v.

- **faltered** (fôl´ tərd) *v.* acted hesitantly; showed uncertainty (p. 262) *The manager faltered in her decision to hire the inexperienced worker.* falter v.

- **prudence** (prōō´ dəns) *n.* a sensible and careful attitude that makes you avoid some risks (p. 263) *Her prudence resulted in a substantial amount of savings.* prudent adj. imprudence n.

- **discreet** (di skrēt´) *adj.* careful about what one says or does (p. 265) *Being discreet is a good way to avoid hurting other people's feelings.* discretion n. indiscreet adj. indiscretion adj.

### Word Study

The **Latin prefix de-** has various meanings, including "down."

In this story, Della's hair is said to **depreciate** a queen's treasures. Her hair is so lovely that, by comparison, it brings down the price and value of jewels.

# Meet
# O. Henry
## (1862–1910)

## Author of
# The Gift of the Magi

William Sydney Porter, better known as O. Henry, dropped out of school at sixteen to work in his uncle's drugstore. In 1882, he left his home in North Carolina to seek his fortune in Texas. He worked on a ranch, then at a bank, and eventually started writing sketches. He became a reporter, columnist, and cartoonist for the *Houston Post*.

**Writing Stories in Prison** In 1896, Porter was jailed for his involvement in a bank scandal. While in prison, he began writing stories. When he was released, Porter changed his name to O. Henry, moved to New York City, and developed into one of America's most celebrated writers of short fiction.

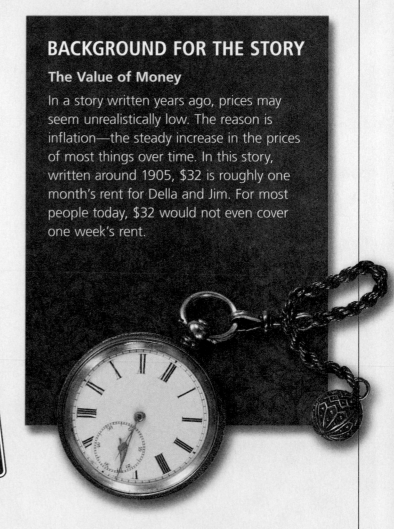

## BACKGROUND FOR THE STORY

### The Value of Money

In a story written years ago, prices may seem unrealistically low. The reason is inflation—the steady increase in the prices of most things over time. In this story, written around 1905, $32 is roughly one month's rent for Della and Jim. For most people today, $32 would not even cover one week's rent.

## Did You Know?

Since 1919, the O. Henry Awards for short fiction have been given to the best short stories written each year.

# The Gift of the Magi

### ❧ O. HENRY ❧

One dollar and eighty-seven cents. That was all. And sixty cents of it was in pennies. Pennies saved one and two at a time by bulldozing the grocer and the vegetable man and the butcher until one's cheeks burned with the silent imputation of parsimony[1] that such close dealing implied. Three times Della counted it. One dollar and eighty-seven cents. And the next day would be Christmas.

There was clearly nothing to do but flop down on the shabby little couch and howl. So Della did it. Which instigates the moral reflection that life is made up of sobs, sniffles, and smiles, with sniffles predominating.

While the mistress of the home is gradually subsiding from the first stage to the second, take a look at the home. A furnished flat at $8 per week. It did not exactly beggar description,[2] but it certainly had that word on the lookout for the mendicancy squad.[3]

In the vestibule below was a letter-box into which no letter would go, and an electric button from which no mortal finger could coax a ring. Also appertaining thereunto was a card bearing the name "Mr. James Dillingham Young."

The "Dillingham" had been flung to the breeze during a former period of prosperity when its possessor was being paid $30 per week. Now, when the income was shrunk to $20, the letters of "Dillingham" looked blurred, as though they were thinking seriously of contracting to a modest and unassuming D. But whenever Mr. James Dillingham Young came home and reached his flat above he was called "Jim" and greatly hugged by Mrs. James Dillingham Young, already introduced to you as Della. Which is all very good.

Della finished her cry and attended to her cheeks with the powder rag. She stood by the window and looked out dully at a gray cat walking a gray fence in a gray backyard. Tomorrow would be Christmas Day, and she had only $1.87 with which to buy

**Vocabulary**
**instigates** (in´ stə gāts´) *v.* urges on; stirs up

**Reading Skill**
**Make Inferences** Based on this paragraph, what can you infer about Jim and the kind of person he would like to be?

Reading
Check

How much money does Della have to buy a present for Jim?

---

1. **imputation** (im´ pyo͞o tā´ shən) **of parsimony** (pär´ sə mō´ nē) accusation of stinginess.
2. **beggar description** make description seem inadequate or useless.
3. **it certainly . . . mendicancy** (men´ di kən sē) **squad** it would have been noticed by the police who arrest beggars.

▲ **Critical Viewing**
How do you think Della felt in a street like this one as she approached Madame Sofronie's shop? **[Analyze]**

**Vocabulary**
**depreciate** (dē prē´ shē āt´) *v.* reduce in value

**cascade** (kas kād´) *n.* a small steep water-fall; anything suggesting such a waterfall

**faltered** (fôl´ tərd) *v.* acted hesitantly; showed uncertainty

Jim a present. She had been saving every penny she could for months, with this result. Twenty dollars a week doesn't go far. Expenses had been greater than she had calculated. They always are. Only $1.87 to buy a present for Jim. Her Jim. Many a happy hour she had spent planning for something nice for him. Something fine and rare and sterling—something just a little bit near to being worthy of the honor of being owned by Jim.

There was a pier glass between the windows of the room. Perhaps you have seen a pier glass in an $8 flat. A very thin and very agile person may, by observing his reflection in a rapid sequence of longitudinal strips, obtain a fairly accurate conception of his looks. Della, being slender, had mastered the art.

Suddenly she whirled from the window and stood before the glass. Her eyes were shining brilliantly, but her face had lost its color within twenty seconds. Rapidly she pulled down her hair and let it fall to its full length.

Now, there were two possessions of the James Dillingham Youngs in which they both took a mighty pride. One was Jim's gold watch that had been his father's and his grandfather's. The other was Della's hair. Had the Queen of Sheba lived in the flat across the airshaft, Della would have let her hair hang out the window some day to dry just to depreciate Her Majesty's jewels and gifts. Had King Solomon been the janitor, with all his treasures piled up in the basement, Jim would have pulled out his watch every time he passed, just to see him pluck at his beard from envy.

So now Della's beautiful hair fell about her rippling and shining like a cascade of brown waters. It reached below her knee and made itself almost a garment for her. And then she did it up again nervously and quickly. Once she faltered for a minute and stood still while a tear or two splashed on the worn red carpet.

On went her old brown jacket; on went her old brown hat. With a whirl of skirts and with the brilliant sparkle still in her eyes, she fluttered out the door and down the stairs to the street.

Where she stopped the sign read: "Mme. Sofronie. Hair Goods of All Kinds." One flight up Della ran, and collected herself, panting. Madame, large, too white, chilly, hardly looked the "Sofronie."

"Will you buy my hair?" asked Della.

"I buy hair," said Madame. "Take yer hat off and let's have a sight at the looks of it."

Down rippled the brown cascade.

"Twenty dollars," said Madame, lifting the mass with a practiced hand.

"Give it to me quick," said Della.

Oh, and the next two hours tripped by on rosy wings. Forget the hashed metaphor. She was ransacking the stores for Jim's present.

She found it at last. It surely had been made for Jim and no one else. There was no other like it in any of the stores, and she had turned all of them inside out. It was a platinum fob chain simple and chaste in design, properly proclaiming its value by substance alone and not by meretricious ornamentation—as all good things should do. It was even worthy of The Watch. As soon as she saw it she knew that it must be Jim's. It was like him. Quietness and value—the description applied to both. Twenty-one dollars they took from her for it, and she hurried home with the 87 cents. With that chain on his watch Jim might be properly anxious about the time in any company. Grand as the watch was he sometimes looked at it on the sly on account of the old leather strap that he used in place of a chain. •

When Della reached home her intoxication gave way a little to prudence and reason. She got out her curling irons and lighted the gas and went to work repairing the ravages made by generosity added to love. Which is always a tremendous task, dear friends—a mammoth task.

Within forty minutes her head was covered with tiny, close-lying curls that made her look wonderfully like a truant schoolboy. She looked at her reflection in the mirror long, carefully, and critically.

**Vocabulary**
**prudence** (proo´ dəns)
*n.* a sensible and careful attitude that makes you avoid some risks

Reading
Check

What does Della sell for twenty dollars?

"If Jim doesn't kill me," she said to herself, "before he takes a second look at me, he'll say I look like a Coney Island[4] chorus girl. But what could I do—oh! what could I do with a dollar and eighty-seven cents?"

At 7 o'clock the coffee was made and the frying-pan was on the back of the stove hot and ready to cook the chops.

Jim was never late. Della doubled the fob chain in her hand and sat on the corner of the table near the door that he always entered. Then she heard his step on the stair away down on the first flight, and she turned white for just a moment. She had a habit of saying little silent prayers about the simplest everyday things, and now she whispered: "Please God, make him think I am still pretty."

The door opened and Jim stepped in and closed it. He looked thin and very serious. Poor fellow, he was only twenty-two—and to be burdened with a family! He needed a new overcoat and he was without gloves.

Jim stopped inside the door, as immovable as a setter at the scent of quail. His eyes were fixed upon Della, and there was an expression in them that she could not read, and it terrified her. It was not anger, nor surprise, nor disapproval, nor horror, nor any of the sentiments that she had been prepared for. He simply stared at her fixedly with that peculiar expression on his face.

Della wriggled off the table and went for him.

"Jim, darling," she cried, "don't look at me that way. I had my hair cut off and sold it because I couldn't have lived through Christmas without giving you a present. It'll grow out again—you won't mind, will you? I just had to do it. My hair grows awfully fast. Say 'Merry Christmas!' Jim, and let's be happy. You don't know what a nice—what a beautiful, nice gift I've got for you."

"You've cut off your hair?" asked Jim, laboriously, as if he had not arrived at that patent fact yet even after the hardest mental labor.

"Cut it off and sold it," said Della. "Don't you like me just as well, anyhow? I'm me without my hair, ain't I?"

Jim looked about the room curiously.

"You say your hair is gone?" he said, with an air almost of idiocy.

> "...I couldn't have lived through Christmas without giving you a present."

---

4. **Coney** (kō´ nē) **Island** beach and amusement park in Brooklyn, New York.

"You needn't look for it," said Della. "It's sold, I tell you—sold and gone, too. It's Christmas Eve, boy. Be good to me, for it went for you. Maybe the hairs of my head were numbered," she went on with a sudden serious sweetness, "but nobody could ever count my love for you. Shall I put the chops on, Jim?"

Out of his trance Jim seemed quickly to wake. He enfolded his Della. For ten seconds let us regard with discreet scrutiny some inconsequential object in the other direction. Eight dollars a week or a million a year—what is the difference? A mathematician or a wit would give you the wrong answer. The Magi brought valuable gifts, but that was not among them. This dark assertion will be illuminated later on.

Jim drew a package from his overcoat pocket and threw it upon the table.

"Don't make any mistake, Dell," he said, "about me. I don't think there's anything in the way of a haircut or a shave or a shampoo that could make me like my girl any less. But if you'll unwrap that package you may see why you had me going a while at first."

White fingers and nimble tore at the string and paper. And then an ecstatic scream of joy; and then, alas! a quick feminine change to hysterical tears and wails, necessitating the immediate employment of all the comforting powers of the lord of the flat.

For there lay The Combs—the set of combs, side and back, that Della had worshipped for long in a Broadway window. Beautiful combs, pure tortoise shell, with jeweled rims—just the shade to wear in the beautiful vanished hair. They were expensive combs, she knew, and her heart had simply craved and yearned over them without the least hope of possession. And now, they were hers, but the tresses that should have adorned the coveted adornments were gone.

But she hugged them to her bosom, and at length she was able to look up with dim eyes and a smile and say: "My hair grows so fast, Jim!"

And then Della leaped up like a little singed cat and cried, "Oh, oh!"

Jim had not yet seen his beautiful present. She held it out to him eagerly upon her open palm. The dull precious metal seemed to flash with a reflection of her bright and ardent spirit.

Vocabulary
**discreet** (di skrēt´) *adj.* careful about what one says or does

**Literary Analysis**
**Irony** In what way does Jim's gift to Della create an ironic situation?

Reading Check

How does Jim react to Della's newly cut hair?

The Gift of the Magi **265**

"Isn't it a dandy, Jim? I hunted all over town to find it. You'll have to look at the time a hundred times a day now. Give me your watch. I want to see how it looks on it."

Instead of obeying, Jim tumbled down on the couch and put his hands under the back of his head and smiled.

"Dell," said he, "let's put our Christmas presents away and keep 'em a while. They're too nice to use just at present. I sold the watch to get the money to buy your combs. And now suppose you put the chops on."

The Magi, as you know, were wise men—wonderfully wise men— who brought gifts to the Babe in the manger. They invented the art of giving Christmas presents. Being wise, their gifts were no doubt wise ones, possibly bearing the privilege of exchange in case of duplication. And here I have lamely related to you the uneventful chronicle of two foolish children in a flat who most unwisely sacrificed for each other the greatest treasures of their house. But in a last word to the wise of these days let it be said that of all who give gifts these two were the wisest. Of all who give and receive gifts, such as they are wisest. Everywhere they are wisest. They are the magi.

## Critical Thinking

1. **Key Ideas and Details (a)** What does Della do to get money for Jim's present? **(b) Infer:** What does her action suggest about her character?

2. **Key Ideas and Details (a)** How does Jim react when he first sees that Della has cut her hair? **(b) Analyze:** Why does Della misunderstand Jim's reaction?

3. **Integration of Knowledge and Ideas Draw Conclusions:** O. Henry says that these "two foolish children" were "the wisest." How do you think he would define wisdom? Explain your response.

4. **Integration of Knowledge and Ideas (a)** What internal conflict occurs for both Jim and Della? **(b)** Do you think that this is a necessary conflict? Explain. *[Connect to the Big Question: Is conflict necessary?]*

## Literary Analysis: Irony

© **1. Key Ideas and Details (a)** Identify **irony** in the story by using a chart like the one shown. In the first box, note the outcome that Jim and Della expect when they present their gifts to each other. In the second box, describe what actually happens.

| What Characters Expect | → | What Actually Happens |
| --- | --- | --- |
|  |  |  |

**(b)** What message about life does this situational irony convey?

© **2. Craft and Structure (a)** Which details in the story make its **surprise ending** seem like a logical outcome of events? **(b)** Why do you think surprise endings are such a popular device in literature and movies?

## Reading Skill: Make Inferences

**3. (a)** What **inferences** do you think O. Henry intended readers to make about the characters of Jim and Della? **(b)** Which details in the text support your inferences?

**4.** In what ways do your prior knowledge and experience of characters like Jim and Della help you make inferences about them? Use details from the text to explain your response.

## Vocabulary

© **Acquisition and Use** Explain why each statement below is true or false.

**1.** One who *instigates* conflict might be called a "problem solver."

**2.** After six years of hard use, a car will *depreciate* in value.

**3.** Only a *discreet* person should be trusted with a secret.

**4.** It is a sign of *prudence* to drive a car before you have your license.

**5.** In a fireworks display, a shell might create a sparkling *cascade*.

**6.** The horse *faltered* in the home stretch and won as a result.

**Word Study** Use the context of the sentences and what you know about the **Latin prefix de-** to explain your answer to each question.

**1.** If you were to *depress* a friend, would he feel better?

**2.** What happens to food when people *devour* it?

### Word Study

The **Latin prefix de-** has various meanings, including "down."

**Apply It** Explain how the prefix de- contributes to the meanings of these words. Consult a dictionary if necessary.

**descend**
**decline**
**depose**

**Is** *conflict* **necessary?**

## Writing About the Big Question

In "The Interlopers," men from feuding families face a situation that makes them rethink their hatred for each other. Use these sentence starters to develop your ideas about the Big Question.

In a longtime feud, the people involved may struggle to resolve their **issues amicably** because _____.

Those in **competition** often **antagonize** each other because _____.

**While You Read** Consider the men's reasons for continuing the feud and their reasons for ending it.

## Vocabulary

Read each word and its definition. Decide whether you know the word well, know it a little bit, or do not know it at all. After you read, see how your knowledge of each word has increased.

- **precipitous** (prē sip′ ə təs) *adj.* steep; sheer (p. 272) *At the edge of the cliff, you will face a* <u>precipitous</u> *drop.* precipice *n.*

- **acquiesced** (ak′ wē est′) *v.* agreed quietly without protest or enthusiasm (p. 272) *The boy sullenly* <u>acquiesced</u> *to the demand that he take out the garbage.* acquiescence *n.*

- **feud** (fyo͞od) *n.* a long and violent quarrel, especially between clans or families, often characterized by killing (p. 272) *The* <u>feud</u> *between the Hatfields and the McCoys lasted for almost 30 years.* feud *v.*

- **disputed** (di spyo͞ot′ id) *adj.* contested; argued about (p. 272) *The* <u>disputed</u> *border between the yards had been a source of conflict for many years.* dispute *n.* dispute *v.*

- **condolences** (kən dō′ lən səz) *n.* expressions of sympathy with another in grief (p. 274) *The mourners shared their* <u>condolences</u>.

- **interlopers** (in′ tər lō′ pərz) *n.* people who intrude or meddle in other peoples' business or lives (p. 275) *Even though we had been invited to the party, we felt like unwelcome* <u>interlopers</u>.

### Word Study

The **Latin prefix** *inter-* means "between."

This is the story of **interlopers,** describing those who leap or intrude into each other's affairs and find themselves unwelcome.

Author of

# The Interlopers

Saki is the pen name of the British writer H. H. Munro. Munro was born in Burma and sent at age two to live in England. As a young adult, he returned to Burma to serve in the police force. However, poor health forced him to return to England, where he began work as a journalist.

**Talent and Tragedy** In 1904, Munro published a collection of short stories entitled *Reginald*. He went on to write several more collections of stories and two novels. The abrupt ending of Saki's own life was as shocking as one of his plot twists: When World War I broke out, he enlisted in the British army and was killed fighting in France.

## BACKGROUND FOR THE STORY

### Family Feuds

A feud is a bitter, prolonged fight, typically between families or clans, that may continue for years or even generations. The brutality of a feud can make for gripping drama, as it does in "The Interlopers."

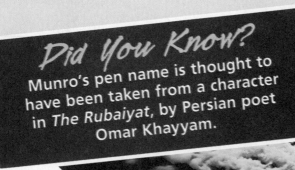

## Did You Know?

Munro's pen name is thought to have been taken from a character in *The Rubaiyat*, by Persian poet Omar Khayyam.

# The Interlopers

## Saki

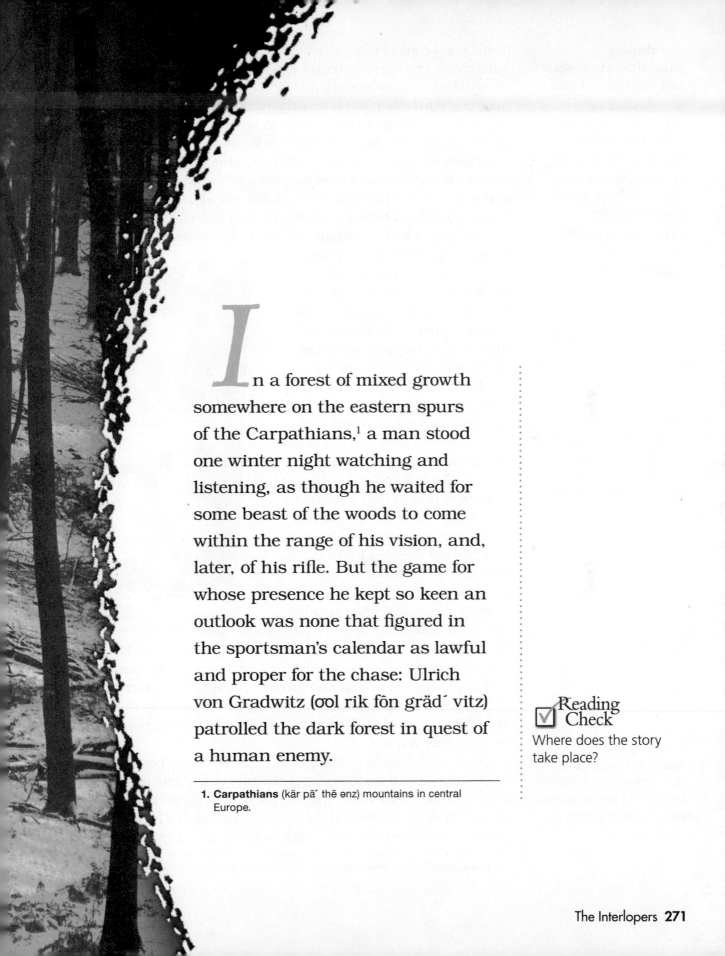

*I*n a forest of mixed growth somewhere on the eastern spurs of the Carpathians,[1] a man stood one winter night watching and listening, as though he waited for some beast of the woods to come within the range of his vision, and, later, of his rifle. But the game for whose presence he kept so keen an outlook was none that figured in the sportsman's calendar as lawful and proper for the chase: Ulrich von Gradwitz (ool rik fôn gräd´ vitz) patrolled the dark forest in quest of a human enemy.

---

1. **Carpathians** (kär pā´ thē ənz) mountains in central Europe.

## Reading Check

Where does the story take place?

**Vocabulary**

**precipitous** (prē´ sip ə təs) *adj.* steep; sheer

**acquiesced** (ak´ wē est´) *v.* agreed quietly without protest or enthusiasm

**feud** (fyōod) *n.* a long and violent quarrel, especially between clans or families

**disputed** (di spyōot´ əd) *adj.* contested; argued about

**Reading Skill**
**Make Inferences** What can you infer about the characters from their unwillingness to compromise?

**Reading Skill**
**Make Inferences** How does your knowledge of feuds help you infer the reason Ulrich hopes to meet Znaeym?

The forest lands of Gradwitz were of wide extent and well stocked with game; the narrow strip of precipitous woodland that lay on its outskirt was not remarkable for the game it harbored or the shooting it afforded, but it was the most jealously guarded of all its owner's territorial possessions. A famous lawsuit, in the days of his grandfather, had wrested it from the illegal possession of a neighboring family of petty landowners; the dispossessed party had never acquiesced in the judgment of the Courts, and a long series of poaching affrays[2] and similar scandals had embittered the relationships between the families for three generations. The neighbor feud had grown into a personal one since Ulrich had come to be head of his family; if there was a man in the world whom he detested and wished ill to it was Georg Znaeym (gà´ ôrg znä´ im), the inheritor of the quarrel and the tireless game-snatcher and raider of the disputed border-forest. The feud might, perhaps, have died down or been compromised if the personal ill will of the two men had not stood in the way; as boys they had thirsted for one another's blood, as men each prayed that misfortune might fall on the other, and this wind-scourged winter night Ulrich had banded together his foresters to watch the dark forest, not in quest of four-footed quarry, but to keep a lookout for the prowling

thieves whom he suspected of being afoot from across the land boundary. The roebuck which usually kept in the sheltered hollows during a storm wind, were running like driven things tonight, and there was movement and unrest among the creatures that were wont to sleep through the dark hours. Assuredly there was a disturbing element in the forest, and Ulrich could guess the quarter from whence it came.  ●

He strayed away by himself from the watchers whom he had placed in ambush on the crest of the hill, and wandered far down the steep slopes amid the wild tangle of undergrowth, peering through the tree trunks and listening through the whistling and skirling of the wind and the restless beating of the branches for

---

**2. poaching** (pōch´ iŋ) **affrays** (ə frà´z´) disputes about hunting on someone else's property.

sight or sound of the marauders. If only on this wild night, in this dark, lone spot, he might come across Georg Znaeym, man to man, with none to witness—that was the wish that was uppermost in his thoughts. And as he stepped round the trunk of a huge beech he came face to face with the man he sought.

The two enemies stood glaring at one another for a long silent moment. Each had a rifle in his hand, each had hate in his heart and murder uppermost in his mind. The chance had come to give full play to the passions of a lifetime. But a man who has been brought up under the code of a restraining civilization cannot easily nerve himself to shoot down his neighbor in cold blood and without word spoken, except for an offense against his hearth and honor. And before the moment of hesitation had given way to action a deed of Nature's own violence overwhelmed them both. A fierce shriek of the storm had been answered by a splitting crash over their heads, and ere they could leap aside a mass of falling beech tree had thundered down on them. Ulrich von Gradwitz found himself stretched on the ground, one arm numb beneath him and the other held almost as helplessly in a tight tangle of forked branches, while both legs were pinned beneath the fallen mass.

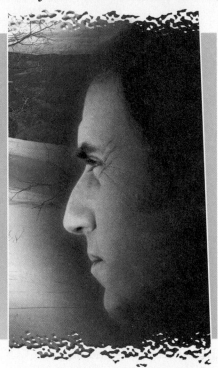

His heavy shooting-boots had saved his feet from being crushed to pieces, but if his fractures were not as serious as they might have been, at least it was evident that he could not move from his present position till someone came to release him. The descending twigs had slashed the skin of his face, and he had to wink away some drops of blood from his eyelashes before he could take in a general view of the disaster. At his side, so near that under ordinary circumstances he could almost have touched him, lay Georg Znaeym, alive and struggling, but obviously as helplessly pinioned down as himself. All round them lay a thick-strewn wreckage of splintered branches and broken twigs.

Relief at being alive and exasperation at his captive plight brought a strange medley of pious thank-offerings and sharp

*The two enemies stood glaring at one another for a long silent moment.*

**Literary Analysis**
**Irony** Each character wishes harm to the other. What is the irony in how the wish is fulfilled?

**Reading Check**
What happens to the two men when the tree falls?

curses to Ulrich's lips. Georg, who was nearly blinded with the blood which trickled across his eyes, stopped his struggling for a moment to listen, and then gave a short, snarling laugh.

**Literary Analysis**
**Irony** What is ironic about Georg's joy over catching Ulrich?

"So you're not killed, as you ought to be, but you're caught, anyway," he cried; "caught fast. Ho, what a jest, Ulrich von Gradwitz snared in his stolen forest. There's real justice for you!"

And he laughed again, mockingly and savagely.

"I'm caught in my own forest land," retorted Ulrich. "When my men come to release us you will wish, perhaps, that you were in a better plight than caught poaching on a neighbor's land, shame on you."

Georg was silent for a moment; then he answered quietly:

"Are you sure that your men will find much to release? I have men, too, in the forest tonight, close behind me, and *they* will be here first and do the releasing. When they drag me out from under these branches it won't need much clumsiness on their part to roll this mass of trunk right over on the top of you. Your men will find you dead under a fallen beech tree. For form's sake I shall send my condolences to your family."

**Vocabulary**
**condolences** (kən dō´ lən səz) *n.* expressions of sympathy with another in grief

"It is a useful hint," said Ulrich fiercely. "My men had orders to follow in ten minutes' time, seven of which must have gone by already, and when they get me out—I will remember the hint. Only as you will have met your death poaching on my lands I don't think I can decently send any message of condolence to your family."

"Good," snarled Georg, "good. We fight this quarrel out to the

death, you and I and our foresters, with no cursed interlopers to come between us. Death and damnation to you, Ulrich von Gradwitz."

"The same to you, Georg Znaeym, forest-thief, game-snatcher."

Both men spoke with the bitterness of possible defeat before them, for each knew that it might be long before his men would seek him out or find him; it was a bare matter of chance which party would arrive first on the scene.

Both had now given up the useless struggle to free themselves from the mass of wood that held them down; Ulrich limited his endeavors to an effort to bring his one partially free arm near enough to his outer coat pocket to draw out his wine flask. Even when he had accomplished that operation it was long before he could manage the unscrewing of the stopper or get any of the liquid down his throat. But what a heaven-sent draft it seemed! It was an open winter, and little snow had fallen as yet, hence the captives suffered less from the cold than might have been the case at that season of the year; nevertheless, the wine was warming and reviving to the wounded man, and he looked across with something like a throb of pity to where his enemy lay, just keeping the groans of pain and weariness from crossing his lips.

"Could you reach this flask if I threw it over to you?" asked Ulrich suddenly; "there is good wine in it, and one may as well be as comfortable as one can. Let us drink, even if tonight one of us dies."

▲ **Critical Viewing**
What are some dangers the characters might face in a setting like this one? **[Analyze]**

**Vocabulary**
**interlopers** (in´ tər lō´ pərz) *n.* people who intrude or meddle in other peoples' business or lives

**Reading Check**
What is each man's hope for rescue?

The Interlopers **275**

"No, I can scarcely see anything; there is so much blood caked round my eyes," said Georg, "and in any case I don't drink wine with an enemy."

Ulrich was silent for a few minutes, and lay listening to the weary screeching of the wind. An idea was slowly forming and growing in his brain, an idea that gained strength every time that he looked across at the man who was fighting so grimly against pain and exhaustion. In the pain and languor that Ulrich himself was feeling the old fierce hatred seemed to be dying down.

"Neighbor," he said presently, "do as you please if your men come first. It was a fair compact. But as for me, I've changed my mind. If my men are the first to come you shall be the first to be helped, as though you were my guest. We have quarreled like devils all our lives over this stupid strip of forest, where the trees can't even stand upright in a breath of wind. Lying here tonight, thinking, I've come to think we've been rather fools; there are better things in life than getting the better of a boundary dispute. Neighbor, if you will help me to bury the old quarrel I—I will ask you to be my friend."

Georg Znaeym was silent for so long that Ulrich thought, perhaps, he had fainted with the pain of his injuries. Then he spoke slowly and in jerks.

"How the whole region would stare and gabble if we rode into the market square together. No one living can remember seeing a Znaeym and a von Gradwitz talking to one another in friendship. And what peace there would be among the forester folk if we ended our feud tonight. And if we choose to make peace among our people there is none other to interfere, no interlopers from outside . . . You would come and keep the Sylvester night beneath my roof, and I would come and feast on some high day at your castle . . . I would never fire a shot on your land, save when you invited me as a guest; and you should come and shoot

**Reading Skill**
**Make Inferences** What can you infer that Georg is considering during this long silence?

**Literary Analysis**
**Irony** What is surprising about this new meaning of interlopers?

with me down in the marshes where the wildfowl are. In all the countryside there are none that could hinder if we willed to make peace. I never thought to have wanted to do other than hate you all my life, but I think I have changed my mind about things too, this last half-hour. And you offered me your wine flask . . . Ulrich von Gradwitz, I will be your friend."

For a space both men were silent, turning over in their minds the wonderful changes that this dramatic reconciliation would bring about. In the cold, gloomy forest, with the wind tearing in fitful gusts through the naked branches and whistling round the tree trunks, they lay and waited for the help that would now bring release and succor to both parties. And each prayed a private prayer that his men might be the first to arrive, so that he might be the first to show honorable attention to the enemy that had become a friend. ●

Presently, as the wind dropped for a moment, Ulrich broke silence.

"Let's shout for help," he said; "in this lull our voices may carry a little way."

"They won't carry far through the trees and undergrowth," said Georg, "but we can try. Together, then."

The two raised their voices in a prolonged hunting call.

"Together again," said Ulrich a few minutes later, after listening in vain for an answering halloo.

"I heard something that time, I think," said Ulrich.

"I heard nothing but the pestilential wind," said Georg hoarsely.

There was silence again for some minutes, and then Ulrich gave a joyful cry.

"I can see figures coming through the wood. They are following in the way I came down the hillside."

Both men raised their voices in as loud a shout as they could muster.

"They hear us! They've stopped. Now they see us. They're running down the hill toward us," cried Ulrich.

"How many of them are there?" asked Georg.

"I can't see distinctly," said Ulrich; "nine or ten."

"Then they are yours," said Georg; "I had only seven out with me."

**Spiral Review**
**Conflict** What contrast in this paragraph hints that the men's friendship may be short lived?

**Literary Analysis**
**Irony** In what way is the two men's cooperation an ironic situation?

> *In the cold, gloomy forest, with the wind tearing in fitful gusts through the naked branches and whistling round the tree trunks...*

**Reading Check**
What do the men agree to do?

**Literary Analysis**

**Irony** In what way does the story's surprise ending make the title ironic?

"They are making all the speed they can, brave lads," said Ulrich gladly.

"Are they your men?" asked Georg. "Are they your men?" he repeated impatiently as Ulrich did not answer.

"No," said Ulrich with a laugh, the idiotic chattering laugh of a man unstrung with hideous fear.

"Who are they?" asked Georg quickly, straining his eyes to see what the other would gladly not have seen.

"*Wolves.*"

## Critical Thinking

Cite textual evidence to support your responses.

1. **Key Ideas and Details (a)** Whose family won possession of the disputed land in the lawsuit? **(b) Interpret:** Why does Georg not consider himself a poacher?

2. **Key Ideas and Details (a)** In what condition does the fallen tree leave each man? **(b) Draw Conclusions:** Why do the men decide finally to end their feud?

3. **Integration of Knowledge and Ideas (a) Evaluate:** Considering the cause of their predicament, do you think the two men deserved their fate? Why or why not? **(b) Discuss:** Share your ideas with a partner and then explain how your answer has grown or changed.

4. **Integration of Knowledge and Ideas (a)** How long has the controversy between Ulrich and Georg been going on? **(b)** Why does it take special courage for Ulrich and Georg to consider the conflict no longer "necessary"? *[Connect to the Big Question: Is conflict necessary?]*

## Literary Analysis: Irony

**©** **1. Key Ideas and Details (a)** Identify **irony** in the story by using a chart like the one shown. In the first box, note the outcome that Ulrich and Georg expect when they first confront each other in the forest. In the second box, describe what actually happens.

| What Characters Expect | → | What Actually Happens |
|---|---|---|
|  |  |  |

    **(b)** What message about life does this **situational irony** convey?

**©** **2. Craft and Structure (a)** Which **nuances,** or subtle details, in "The Interlopers" make its **surprise ending** seem like a logical outcome of events? **(b)** Is the ending certain, or is it ambiguous—open to many interpretations? Explain your response.

## Reading Skill: Make Inferences

**3. (a)** What **inferences** do you think Saki intended readers to make about the characters of Ulrich and Georg? **(b)** Which details in the text support your inferences?

**4.** In what ways do your prior knowledge and experience of characters help you to make inferences about Ulrich and Georg?

## Vocabulary

**©** **Acquisition and Use** Explain why each statement is true or false.

**1.** A beach generally has a *precipitous* slope down to the water.

**2.** It is proper to express *condolences* to one who has suffered a loss.

**3.** *Interlopers* are people who are always welcome.

**4.** A *feud* between powerful families could endanger a community.

**5.** People involved in a *disputed* matter enjoy each other's company.

**6.** If protesters did not obey a curfew, they would have *acquiesced*.

**Word Study** Use the context of the sentences and what you know about the **Latin prefix *inter-*** to explain your answer to each question.

**1.** Does an *international* crisis affect more than one country?

**2.** Where is an *intertidal* zone located?

### Word Study

The **Latin prefix *inter-*** means "between."

**Apply It** Explain how the prefix *inter-* contributes to the meanings of these words. Consult a dictionary if necessary.

**intercept**
**intermission**
**interstate**

# Integrated Language Skills

## The Gift of the Magi • The Interlopers

## Conventions: Irregular Verbs

**Irregular verbs** form their principal parts in a variety of ways.

**Regular verbs** form the present participle by adding *-ing* to the present form. They form the past and past participle by adding *-ed* to the present form. **Irregular verbs** also form the present participle by adding *-ing* to the present form. However, they form the past and past participle in a variety of ways. Here are a few of the most common examples:

| Present | Past | Past Participle |
| --- | --- | --- |
| be (am, is, are) | was, were | (has) been |
| buy | bought | (has) bought |
| choose | chose | (has) chosen |
| come | came | (has) come |
| give | gave | (has) given |
| go | went | (has) gone |
| have | had | (has) had |
| see | saw | (has) seen |
| sell | sold | (has) sold |
| speak | spoke | (has) spoken |
| take | took | (has) taken |
| write | wrote | (has) written |

**Practice A** Use the correct form of each verb in parentheses.

1. O. Henry has (write) a great story.
2. Della (sell) her hair to (buy) Jim a watch fob.
3. Jim (choose) a set of combs for Della.
4. By the end, the husband and wife have (speak) of their love and have (see) its power.

© **Reading Application** Find five irregular verbs that appear in "The Gift of the Magi." Write the principal parts of each.

**Practice B** Revise each sentence by correcting the mistakes in the principal parts of verbs.

1. In the forest, Ulrich speaked to himself.
2. Georg has chose to trespass on my land.
3. Suddenly, Ulrich seen Georg, rifle in hand.
4. What cause for hatred have these men gave?

© **Writing Application** Rewrite the following sentence, replacing the underlined words with these phrases: take cover, be afraid, speak quietly, write wills. *While they waited for the wolves, they _became_ _friends_.*

**PH WRITING COACH**  Further instruction and practice are available in *Prentice Hall Writing Coach*.

# Writing

**Narrative Text** These selections present conflicts that end in irony. Write a **news report** about the experiences characters face in either story.

- First, gather facts by asking the questions *Who? What? Where? When? Why?* and *How?* Write an opening paragraph or lead that summarizes events and grabs the reader's interest.
- Include quotations to show characters' reactions. Choose logical points where quotations will integrate smoothly into the narrative.
- Read your lead paragraph to a classmate. Revise unclear parts.
- Add several more paragraphs, providing details that tell the rest of the story.

**Grammar Application** Make sure to form the principal parts of irregular verbs correctly.

**Writing Workshop:** *Work in Progress*

**Prewriting for Narration: Short Story** Using the Character Profile from your portfolio, write a letter from your character to a best friend, telling about an important event. Describe the event in detail and show why it is important. Save this letter in your portfolio.

# Speaking and Listening

**Presentation of Ideas** With a group of classmates, use your persuasive skills to present a **debate.**

- If you read "The Gift of the Magi," debate whether sacrifice is the best expression of love.
- If you read "The Interlopers," debate which character is entitled to the disputed land.

Follow these steps to complete the assignment:

- Prepare an argument that expresses your opinion.
- Choose supporting evidence. Look for specific ways in which the story supports your claim. Find events, quotations from dialogue, comments from the narrator, and so on. If necessary, do additional research to find outside evidence, such as statistics or quotations from experts to back up your ideas.
- Anticipate opposing arguments. Consider what the other side may say. Be ready with a response and evidence to support it.
- After the teams have debated, ask the audience to evaluate the presentation and decide which team was more persuasive.

**Common Core State Standards**

**L.9-10.1; W.9-10.3, W.9-10.3.c.; SL.9-10.4**
[For the full wording of the standards, see page 256.]

Use this prewriting activity to prepare for the **Writing Workshop** on page 306.

**PHLit Online!**
www.PHLitOnline.com
- Interactive graphic organizers
- Grammar tutorial
- Interactive journals

# Test Practice: Reading

## Make Inferences

### Fiction Selection

**Directions:** *Read the selection. Then, answer the questions.*

Carmen stared at the Departures board and swallowed hard. In about an hour, she would be taking her first airplane flight. "Everything will be fine, *querida*," Mama whispered. "Your *abuelo* will be waiting for you in Phoenix—ready with a joke, I'm sure." Mama smiled the way she only did when she spoke of her father. "You need to go through security on your own now and wait at gate 23. Please call me on your cell phone if you have any problems. Have fun in Phoenix!" Mama kissed Carmen on the cheek and then stepped back. Carmen turned. Feeling more alone than she ever had felt before, Carmen put her bag on the conveyer belt and stepped through the metal detector.

**1.** It would be reasonable to infer that events in this passage take place
   **A.** in Phoenix, Arizona.
   **B.** in Carmen's home.
   **C.** at an airport.
   **D.** on an airplane.

**2.** Based on details in the passage, how do you think Carmen feels about making this trip?
   **A.** apologetic
   **B.** nervous
   **C.** proud
   **D.** disillusioned

**3.** Which detail is most helpful in making an inference about the meaning of *abuelo*?
   **A.** Mama smiles the way she only does when she is speaking of her father.
   **B.** In a little while, *abuelo* will see Carmen in Phoenix.
   **C.** Carmen feels very alone as she steps through the metal detector.
   **D.** *Abuelo* will probably tell Carmen a joke when she arrives in Phoenix.

**4.** From the tone of Mama's words, which of the following would be a reasonable inference?
   **A.** Mama does not want Carmen to go to Phoenix.
   **B.** Mama wants to help Carmen feel more comfortable flying alone.
   **C.** Mama thinks that making jokes is a waste of time.
   **D.** Mama wishes that she was going to Phoenix to see *abuelo*.

### Writing for Assessment

What might readers **infer** about Carmen's thoughts as her plane departs for Phoenix? Write a one paragraph journal entry from Carmen's point of view describing what she is thinking and feeling at the beginning of the flight. Use details from the passage to develop your ideas.

# Nonfiction Selection

**Directions:** *Read the selection. Then, answer the questions.*

The career of Bessie Coleman, the first African American pilot, began with a joke. When her brother John came home after World War I, he laughed about French women who were pilots. Inspired, Coleman went to France in 1920 and finished the ten-month training course in seven months. Coleman soon was performing in air shows in the United States, attracting crowds with her stunts. She also started plans for a flight school for African Americans. A test plane's malfunction ended her life in 1926, but Coleman's dream of a flight school was fulfilled by others.

**1.** Which of the following details helps readers infer that there were few women pilots in the 1920s?
- **A.** Bessie Coleman became the first African American pilot.
- **B.** Bessie Coleman performed in air shows.
- **C.** World War I, in Europe, had just ended.
- **D.** John Coleman treated the idea of women pilots as a joke.

**2.** Details about Coleman's training help readers infer that Coleman—
- **A.** wanted to become a pilot as quickly as possible.
- **B.** hoped to become a commercial pilot, not a stunt pilot.
- **C.** was the only woman in her class to earn a pilot's license.
- **D.** often was made fun of by her classmates.

**3.** Which of the following would *not* be a reasonable inference, based on the passage?
- **A.** Coleman wanted to help other people fulfill their dreams.
- **B.** Since Coleman's time, other African Americans have become pilots.
- **C.** After World War I, the only jobs for pilots were in air shows.
- **D.** It takes several months of training for a person to become a pilot.

**4.** Which word *best* describes Bessie Coleman, based on details in the passage?
- **A.** impractical
- **B.** creative
- **C.** determined
- **D.** thoughtless

## Writing for Assessment

**Connecting Across Texts**
Suppose that Bessie Coleman and Carmen had a conversation about flying. What might they say to each other? Write a **dialogue** of at least ten lines between Bessie and Carmen. Incorporate details from the two passages.

**PHLit Online!**
www.PHLitOnline.com
- Online practice
- Instant feedback

# Reading for Information

## Analyzing Functional and Expository Texts

**Signs and Instructions**

**Technical Instructions**

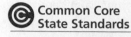 **Common Core State Standards**

**Reading Informational Text**
**3.** Analyze how the author unfolds an analysis or series of ideas or events, including the order in which the points are made, how they are introduced and developed, and the connections that are drawn between them.

**Writing**
**1.** Write arguments to support claims in an analysis of substantive topics or texts, using valid reasoning and relevant and sufficient evidence.

**Language**
**4.b.** Identify and correctly use patterns of word changes that indicate different meanings or parts of speech.

## Reading Skill: Critique the Logic of Functional Documents

Because instructions give important information or help people perform a task, they should be clear and logical. To **critique the logic** of functional documents, look at how the writer identifies the steps in a process and the order in which each one should be completed. Consider whether the organization suits the information. Also, notice how the writer uses text features, such as the ones listed in the chart, to clarify ideas.

| Text Features | Description |
|---|---|
| Subheads | Boldfaced words that identify the main idea of each section |
| Highlighted text | Boldfaced, italicized, uppercase words that emphasize important information |
| Charts, graphs, maps | Graphic organizers that order information in a clear, easy-to-understand form |
| Illustrations and diagrams | Graphic organizers that show ideas described in the text |
| Captions | Brief information that describes an illustration, diagram, or other graphic organizer |

### Content-Area Vocabulary

These words appear in the selections that follow. You may also encounter them in other content-area texts.

- **generated** (jen´ ə rāt´ d) *v.* caused to be; brought into being; produced
- **carabiners** (ker ə 'bē nərz) *n.* hooks used for climbing
- **substantial** (səb stan´ shəl) *adj.* large; important; ample

# BEACH SAFETY GUIDE
## HIGH SURF SIGN

It is logical that *warning* is the boldest word on the sign. The background for the word is orange—a color often used on warning signs and safety devices.

A simple picture illustrates the danger.

**WARNING LEVEL:** *DANGEROUS*…a potential for loss of *life* or *limb* exists.

**CONDITION:** Large powerful waves are **generated** by winds and storms at sea, sometimes thousands of miles from the Hawaiian Islands. Seasonal high surf occurs on all shores of Oahu. Typically, shorelines facing North, East and West receive high surf during winter months. Shores facing Southeast and Southwest receive high surf during summer months. Surf on the North shore may reach heights of twenty-five feet plus—on the West shore, *fifteen* feet plus!

**INSTRUCTIONS:** If you're uncertain of your abilities, don't go into the ocean during high surf; heed all posted high surf warnings!

The uppercase red letters in each heading let readers know that they are reading important information.

# BEACH SAFETY GUIDE
## STRONG CURRENT SIGN

**WARNING**

**STRONG CURRENT**

YOU COULD BE SWEPT AWAY FROM SHORE AND COULD DROWN

IF IN DOUBT, DON'T GO OUT

> A specific warning message is stated briefly and clearly. The most important words are printed in the largest letters.

**WARNING LEVEL:** *DANGEROUS…a potential for loss of life or limb exists.*

**CONDITION:** These are swift moving channels of water against which it is difficult to swim. Strong currents frequently accompany high surf and rapid tide changes and can be recognized as a turbulent channel of water between areas where waves are breaking.

> The information in the instructions is logically and simply stated.

**INSTRUCTIONS:** When caught in a strong current —Try to keep a level head. Don't panic! Wave one or both hands in the air, and scream or call for help. Swim diagonally to the current, not against it.

## OCEAN SAFETY TIPS:

> The tips reinforce warnings and instructions and clear up any misunderstandings readers might have.

- Swim in Lifeguarded Areas.
- Never Swim Alone.
- Don't Dive Into Unknown Water or Into Shallow Breaking Waves.
- Ask a Lifeguard About <u>Beach and Surf Conditions</u> Before Swimming.
- If You Are Unable to Swim Out of a Strong Current, Signal for Help.
- Rely on Your Swimming Ability Rather Than a Flotation Device.
- Look For, Read and Obey All <u>Beach Safety Signs and Symbols</u>.
- If In Doubt, Just Stay Out!

# ROCK CLIMBING EQUIPMENT AND TECHNIQUES

THE FOLLOWING DESCRIBES one way of using ropes and equipment to climb safely. It also describes how to descend after climbing.

## Top-Roping and Belaying

In top-roping, a rope from the top of the climb always holds the climber, making most slips off the climb harmless. As shown above, the climber is attached to one end of the rope, the middle is passed through an anchor at the top of the climb, and the other end is held by the belayer.

The anchor at the top of the climb is assembled from loops of webbing connected to **carabiners** attached securely to the rock. The rope is passed through some of the carabiners, and the others are attached to either pieces of protection, wedged into a convenient crack, or bolts, which other climbers have drilled into the rock.

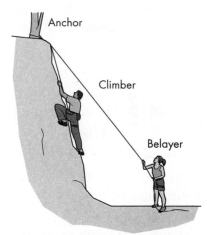

Anchor

Climber

Belayer

The anchor's carabiners with the rope passing through are suspended below the top of the climb to prevent the rope from rubbing. When bolts or protection are far from the top of the climb, **substantial** lengths of webbing are needed to place the carabiners correctly.

Not all climbs can be top-roped because of two requirements:

1. There must be a safe way to the top to set the anchor before the climber starts. Most popular top-roped climbs have an easy way to hike to the top.

2. The climb may be no longer than half the length of the rope; when the climber starts, the rope must cross the full length of the climb twice.

The belayer stops the rope with a belay device attached to his harness if the climber slips. The belay device makes it easy to apply enough friction to stop a falling climber. If there is some danger of the belayer being lifted into the air, he can be anchored down.

The belayer must keep the slack in the rope to a minimum since when a climber slips, any slack must be taken up before the rope can stop the fall. To take up this slack, the belayer pulls the rope downward as the climber climbs. While doing this, the belayer must never release the rope fully to ensure the climber could never fall far.

## Rappeling

Rappeling is a scheme for lowering yourself with the rope. As shown above, the center of the rope is passed through an anchor at the top of the climb. The person descending wears a harness and attaches himself to the rope with a belay device, which he uses to control his descent.

Unlike climbing, it is best to be nearly horizontal while rappeling. In this position, the body is pointing more directly at the rock, giving the feet better friction and leading to more control.

Starting a rappel is the most difficult part. It is very disconcerting to switch from standing to being supported completely by the rope. Moreover, it is necessary to get below the anchor before

the rope can help. If the anchor is below the top of the climb, climbing down is necessary.

Once everybody has descended, the rope is recovered by pulling it through the anchor. The anchor cannot be recovered, but this is not usually a problem. In many cases, other climbers have placed a permanent anchor at the top, often a pair of bolts drilled into the rock connected to a ring with some chains. Another possibility is to use the base of a tree as an anchor. Since the rope is under little tension when it is pulled through the anchor, this abrades the rope and tree only slightly, and can be done occasionally.

A single rope can only be used to descend half a rope-length, but two ropes can be tied together to rappel a full rope-length. This is useful, for example, when descending a multi-pitch lead climb via the same route used for the ascent. The belay stations, usually spaced a full rope-length, can be used as rappel anchors. Three or more ropes cannot be used to rappel in this manner, since doing so would require rappeling past a knot and pulling a knot through the anchor, which are generally impossible.

Anchor

Diagrams illustrate the descriptions in the text, making it easy for readers to understand the technique. Labels identify important parts of the equipment.

Instructions outline the sequence of steps necessary to complete the task safely.

## Comparing Functional and Expository Texts

 **1. Craft and Structure (a)** How is the organization of the information used in the signs and instructions document different from the organization used in the technical instructions? **(b) Critique the logic** of the organization of each document by explaining how it does or does not suit the information.

**2. Craft and Structure** For each document, identify specific text features that clarify the order of ideas or help draw connections among them.

### Content-Area Vocabulary

**3. (a)** Explain how a change in prefix or suffix alters the meanings and parts of speech of the base word *generate*: *generation, generative,* and *regenerate.* **(b)** Use each word in a sentence that shows its meaning.

## Timed Writing

### Argumentative Text: Speech

**Format and Audience**
The prompt directs you to write a brief speech for your community, so your remarks should be three to five paragraphs long and should address the concerns of your audience.

People are often injured when they take unintentional risks. Write a brief speech for your community, urging people to observe safety signs and to follow equipment instructions exactly. Use the information in the signs and technical instructions to support your ideas. (25 minutes)

**Academic Vocabulary**
When you *support* your ideas, you use details and examples to show that your ideas are reasonable and correct.

### 5-Minute Planner

Complete these steps before you begin to write:

**1.** Read the prompt carefully. Look for key words and instructions that tell what you should include in your speech.

**2.** Review the signs and technical instructions. Consider the importance of the details presented, including the sequence of the information.

**3.** Jot down the main ideas you will cover in outline form.

**4.** Use your outline to organize your ideas as you write. **TIP:** Check your outline and make sure you have put new ideas in the best place.

## Comparing Setting

The **setting** of a story is the time and place in which it occurs. The time may include not only the *historical period* but also a year or an hour. "Place" may mean the social, economic, or *cultural environment*, not just the location. Cultural aspects of setting may be present in a variety of ways:

- the values and beliefs the characters hold
- the details of daily life, such as characters' work, food, or clothing
- the types of language, such as non-English words or slang, that characters use. To build setting, a writer may include *idioms*, or phrases whose meanings differ from those of the individual words.
- the themes and issues of the historical period

The importance of setting varies from story to story. Sometimes, the setting is only a backdrop for the action. In such a story, the setting could change, but events would remain the same. However, in some stories, the setting shapes the characters and plot. For example, cultural expectations may cause characters to take specific actions. Vivid descriptive details that focus on setting often create a story's mood, or emotional atmosphere, and even hint at what may happen to characters as the plot unfolds.

These two stories are set in very different places. However, culture and belief systems play a role in both. Use a chart like this to identify details suggesting the place, time, issues, and culture of each story.

|  | Place: | Time: | Culture: |
|---|---|---|---|
| **The Man to Send Rain Clouds** |  |  |  |
| **Old Man of the Temple** |  |  |  |

**Cultural Perspectives** An author may express a distinct point of view, or attitude, toward the cultural setting of a story. That perspective may be positive, negative, mixed, or neutral. For example, an author may show that certain cultural values limit or complicate characters' lives. As you read, consider whether the author expresses a particular point of view toward the culture reflected in each story.

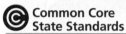

**Common Core State Standards**

**Reading Literature**

**4.** Determine the meaning of words and phrases as they are used in the text, including figurative and connotative meanings; analyze the cumulative impact of specific word choices on meaning and tone.

**6.** Analyze a particular point of view or cultural experience reflected in a work of literature from outside the United States, drawing on a wide reading of world literature.

**Writing**

**2.** Write informative/explanatory texts to examine and convey complex ideas, concepts, and information clearly and accurately through the effective selection, organization, and analysis of content.

www.PHLitOnline.com

- Vocabulary flashcards
- Interactive journals
- More about the authors
- Selection audio
- Interactive graphic organizers

# Is *conflict* necessary?

## Writing About the Big Question

In both of these stories, the authors show the modern world in conflict with traditional ways. Use these sentence starters to develop your ideas:

The modern world sometimes **competes** with traditional ways because _____.

When these **differences** can be resolved, _____.

# Meet the Authors

## Leslie Marmon Silko (b. 1948)

### Author of "The Man to Send Rain Clouds"

Storytelling has always been an important part of Leslie Marmon Silko's life. Raised on the Laguna Pueblo reservation in New Mexico, she grew up listening to tribal stories told by her great-grandmother and great aunts. She has said that the oral tradition is "a collective memory and depends upon the whole community."

**The Old and the New** In her stories, novels, and poems, Silko explores what life is like for Native Americans in today's world. Many of her works capture the contrast between traditional values and beliefs and elements of modern life.

## R. K. Narayan (1906–2001)

### Author of "Old Man of the Temple"

R. K. Narayan was born in the city of Madras in southern India. He was one of nine children in a middle-class family. After briefly working as a teacher, he became a writer. In 1960, his novel *The Guide* won India's highest literary honor.

**Combining Themes** Within a career that spanned nearly seventy years, Narayan wrote more than fifteen novels—as well as collections of short stories and essays. His works skillfully combine Western plots and themes with Indian subject matter.

# The Man
# to Send Rain
# Clouds

## Leslie Marmon Silko

**T**hey found him under a big cottonwood tree. His Levi jacket and pants were faded light blue so that he had been easy to find. The big cottonwood tree stood apart from a small grove of winterbare cottonwoods which grew in the wide, sandy arroyo.[1] He had been dead for a day or more, and the sheep had wandered and scattered up and down the arroyo. Leon and his brother-in-law, Ken, gathered the sheep and left them in the pen at the sheep camp before they returned to the cottonwood tree. Leon waited under the tree while Ken drove the truck through the deep sand to the edge of the arroyo. He squinted up at the sun and unzipped his jacket—it sure was hot for this time of year. But high and northwest the blue mountains were still in snow. Ken came sliding down the low, crumbling bank about fifty yards down, and he was bringing the red blanket.

Before they wrapped the old man, Leon took a piece of string out of his pocket and tied a small gray feather in the old man's long white hair. Ken gave him the paint. Across the brown wrinkled forehead he drew a streak of white and along the high cheekbones he drew a strip of blue paint. He paused and watched Ken throw pinches of corn meal and pollen into the wind that fluttered the small gray feather. Then Leon painted with yellow under the old man's broad nose, and finally, when he had painted green across the chin, he smiled.

"Send us rain clouds, Grandfather." They laid the bundle in the back of the pickup and covered it with a heavy tarp before they started back to the pueblo.

They turned off the highway onto the sandy pueblo road. Not long after they passed the store and post office they saw Father Paul's car coming toward them. When he recognized their faces he slowed his car and waved for them to stop. The young priest rolled down the car window.

"Did you find old Teofilo?" he asked loudly.

Leon stopped the truck. "Good morning, Father. We were just out to the sheep camp. Everything is O.K. now."

"Thank God for that. Teofilo is a very old man. You really shouldn't allow him to stay at the sheep camp alone."

"No, he won't do that any more now."

"Well, I'm glad you understand. I hope I'll be seeing you at Mass[2] this week—we missed you last Sunday. See if you can get old Teofilo to come with you." The priest smiled and waved at them as they drove away.

---

1. **arroyo** (ə rȯiˊ ō) *n.* a dry gully or hollow in the earth's surface.
2. **Mass** (mas) *n.* church service celebrated by Roman Catholics.

Reading Check

How do Leon and Ken prepare the old man's body before they move it?

Louise and Teresa were waiting. The table was set for lunch, and the coffee was boiling on the black iron stove. Leon looked at Louise and then at Teresa.

"We found him under a cottonwood tree in the big arroyo near sheep camp. I guess he sat down to rest in the shade and never got up again." Leon walked toward the old man's bed. The red plaid shawl had been shaken and spread carefully over the bed, and a new brown flannel shirt and pair of stiff new Levi's were arranged neatly beside the pillow. Louise held the screen door open while Leon and Ken carried in the red blanket. He looked small and shriveled, and after they dressed him in the new shirt and pants he seemed more shrunken.

It was noontime now because the church bells rang the Angelus.[3] They ate the beans with hot bread, and nobody said anything until after Teresa poured the coffee.

Ken stood up and put on his jacket. "I'll see about the gravediggers. Only the top layer of soil is frozen. I think it can be ready before dark."

Leon nodded his head and finished his coffee. After Ken had been gone for a while, the neighbors and clanspeople came quietly to embrace Teofilo's family and to leave food on the table because the gravediggers would come to eat when they were finished.

The sky in the west was full of pale yellow light. Louise stood outside with her hands in the pockets of Leon's green army jacket that was too big for her. The funeral was over, and the old men had taken their candles and medicine bags[4] and were gone. She waited until the body was laid into the pickup before she said anything to Leon. She touched his arm, and he noticed that her hands were still dusty from the corn meal that she had sprinkled around the old man. When she spoke, Leon could not hear her.

"What did you say? I didn't hear you."

"I said that I had been thinking about something."

"About what?"

"About the priest sprinkling holy water for Grandpa. So he won't be thirsty."

Leon stared at the new moccasins that Teofilo had made for the ceremonial dances in the summer. They were nearly hidden by the red blanket. It was getting colder, and the wind pushed gray dust down the narrow pueblo road. The sun was approaching the long mesa where it disappeared during the winter. Louise stood there shivering and watching his face. Then he zipped up his jacket and opened the truck door. "I'll see if he's there."

3. **Angelus** (an´ jə ləs) *n.* bell rung at morning, noon, and evening to announce a prayer.
4. **medicine bags** bags containing objects that were thought to have special powers.

Ken stopped the pickup at the church, and Leon got out: and then Ken drove down the hill to the graveyard where people were waiting. Leon knocked at the old carved door with its symbols of the Lamb.[5] While he waited he looked up at the twin bells from the king of Spain with the last sunlight pouring around them in their tower.

The priest opened the door and smiled when he saw who it was. "Come in! What brings you here this evening?"

The priest walked toward the kitchen, and Leon stood with his cap in his hand, playing with the earflaps and examining the living room—the brown sofa, the green armchair, and the brass lamp that hung down from the ceiling by links of chain. The priest dragged a chair out of the kitchen and offered it to Leon.

"No thank you, Father. I only came to ask you if you would bring your holy water to the graveyard."

The priest turned away from Leon and looked out the window at the patio full of shadows and the dining-room windows of the nuns' cloister[6] across the patio. The curtains were heavy, and the light

▲ **Critical Viewing**
How does the scene depicted in this painting compare to the images described in the story?
**[Compare and Contrast]**

What do the old men take with them when the funeral is over?

---

5. **the Lamb** Jesus Christ, as the sacrificial Lamb of God.
6. **cloister** (klȯis´ tər) *n.* place devoted to religious seclusion.

**Vocabulary**
**penetrated** (pen′ i trāt′
əd) *v.* broke through

from within faintly penetrated; it was impossible to see the nuns inside eating supper. "Why didn't you tell me he was dead? I could have brought the Last Rites[7] anyway."

Leon smiled. "It wasn't necessary, Father."

The priest stared down at his scuffed brown loafers and the worn hem of his cassock. "For a Christian burial it was necessary."

His voice was distant, and Leon thought that his blue eyes looked tired.

"It's O.K. Father, we just want him to have plenty of water."

The priest sank down into the green chair and picked up a glossy missionary magazine. He turned the colored pages full of lepers and pagans[8] without looking at them.

**Literary Analysis**
**Setting** What details
of Leon's request to the
priest combine Christian
and Pueblo beliefs?

"You know I can't do that, Leon. There should have been the Last Rites and a funeral Mass at the very least."

Leon put on his green cap and pulled the flaps down over his ears. "It's getting late, Father. I've got to go."

When Leon opened the door Father Paul stood up and said, "Wait." He left the room and came back wearing a long brown overcoat. He followed Leon out the door and across the dim churchyard to the adobe steps in front of the church. They both stooped to fit through the low adobe entrance. And when they started down the hill to the graveyard only half of the sun was visible above the mesa.

The priest approached the grave slowly, wondering how they had managed to dig into the frozen ground; and then he remembered that this was New Mexico, and saw the pile of cold loose sand beside the hole. The people stood close to each other with little clouds of steam puffing from their faces. The priest looked at them and saw a pile of jackets, gloves, and scarves in the yellow, dry tumbleweeds that grew in the graveyard. He looked at the red blanket, not sure that Teofilo was so small, wondering if it wasn't some perverse Indian trick—something they did in March to ensure a good harvest—wondering if maybe old Teofilo was actually at sheep camp corraling the sheep for the night. But there he was, facing into a cold dry wind and squinting at the last sunlight, ready to bury a red wool blanket while the faces of his parishioners were in shadow with the last warmth of the sun on their backs.

**Vocabulary**
**perverse** (pər vʉrs′) *adj.*
deviating from what is
considered right

His fingers were stiff, and it took him a long time to twist the lid off the holy water. Drops of water fell on the red blanket and soaked into dark icy spots. He sprinkled the grave and the water disappeared almost before it touched the dim, cold sand; it reminded him of something—he tried to remember what it was,

---

**7. Last Rites** religious ceremony for a dying person or for someone who has just died.
**8. pagans** (pā′ gənz) *n.* people who are not Christians, Muslims, or Jews.

because he thought if he could remember he might understand this. He sprinkled more water; he shook the container until it was empty, and the water fell through the light from sundown like August rain that fell while the sun was still shining, almost evaporating before it touched the wilted squash flowers.

# HE SPRINKLED THE GRAVE AND THE WATER DISAPPEARED ALMOST BEFORE IT TOUCHED THE DIM, COLD SAND...

The wind pulled at the priest's brown Franciscan robe[9] and swirled away the corn meal and pollen that had been sprinkled on the blanket. They lowered the bundle into the ground, and they didn't bother to untie the stiff pieces of new rope that were tied around the ends of the blanket. The sun was gone, and over on the highway the eastbound lane was full of headlights. The priest walked away slowly. Leon watched him climb the hill, and when he had disappeared within the tall, thick walls, Leon turned to look up at the high blue mountains in the deep snow that reflected a faint red light from the west. He felt good because it was finished, and he was happy about the sprinkling of the holy water; now the old man could send them big thunderclouds for sure.

9. **Franciscan** (fran sis´ kən) **robe** robe worn by a member of the Franciscan religious order, founded in 1209 by Saint Francis of Assisi.

**Literary Analysis**
**Setting** Which details in the last paragraph reflect Native American practices and beliefs? Explain.

## Critical Thinking

Cite textual evidence to support your responses.

1. **Key Ideas and Details (a)** What do Leon and Ken find at the beginning of the story? **(b) Infer:** Why does Leon avoid telling Father Paul about Teofilo?

2. **Key Ideas and Details Infer:** What insight into the Pueblo people does Father Paul gain during the ceremony?

3. **Integration of Knowledge and Ideas (a) Draw Conclusions:** What do Leon's thoughts after Teofilo's burial reveal about his views of death? **(b) Compare and Contrast:** What does the ending reveal about the contrasts between Pueblo and Christian beliefs?

4. **Integration of Knowledge and Ideas** Why does Father Paul decide that the conflict over modern and traditional death rituals is not "necessary"? *[Connect to the Big Question: Is conflict necessary?]*

# Old Man of the Temple

## R. K. NARAYAN

# The Talkative Man said:

It was some years ago that this happened. I don't know if you can make anything of it. If you do, I shall be glad to hear what you have to say; but personally I don't understand it at all. It has always mystified me. Perhaps the driver was drunk; perhaps he wasn't.

I had engaged a taxi for going to Kumbum, which, as you may already know, is fifty miles from Malgudi.[1] I went there one morning and it was past nine in the evening when I finished my business and started back for the town. Doss [däs], the driver, was a young fellow of about twenty-five. He had often brought his car for me and I liked him. He was a well-behaved, obedient fellow, with a capacity to sit and wait at the wheel, which is really a rare quality in a taxi driver. He drove the car smoothly, seldom swore at passers-by, and exhibited perfect judgment, good sense, and sobriety; and so I preferred him to any other driver whenever I had to go out on business.

---

1. **Malgudi** (mäl gōō' dē) fictional town about which Narayan often writes.

**Critical Viewing**
What mysterious events might occur in a temple like this?
**[Speculate]**

**Literary Analysis**
**Setting** Which details in this paragraph describe the place and the time in which the story occurs?

**Spiral Review**
**Character** Which details suggest that the narrator is a round, or complex, character rather than a flat character?

It was about eleven when we passed the village Koopal [kōō päl′], which is on the way down. It was the dark half of the month and the surrounding country was swallowed up in the night. The village street was deserted. Everyone had gone to sleep; hardly any light was to be seen. The stars overhead sparkled brightly. Sitting in the back seat and listening to the continuous noise of the running wheels, I was half lulled into a drowse.

All of a sudden Doss swerved the car and shouted: "You old fool! Do you want to kill yourself?"

I was shaken out of my drowse and asked: "What is the matter?"

Doss stopped the car and said, "You see that old fellow, sir. He is trying to kill himself. I can't understand what he is up to."

I looked in the direction he pointed and asked, "Which old man?"

"There, there. He is coming towards us again. As soon as I saw him open that temple door and come out I had a feeling, somehow, that I must keep an eye on him."

I took out my torch, got down, and walked about, but could see no one. There was an old temple on the roadside. It was utterly in ruins; most portions of it were mere mounds of old brick; the walls were awry; the doors were shut to the main doorway, and brambles and thickets grew over and covered them. It was difficult to guess with the aid of the torch alone what temple it was and to what period it belonged.

"The doors are shut and sealed and don't look as if they had been opened for centuries now," I cried.

"No, sir," Doss said coming nearer. "I saw the old man open the doors and come out. He is standing there; shall we ask him to open them again if you want to go in and see?"

I said to Doss, "Let us be going. We are wasting our time here."

We went back to the car. Doss sat in his seat, pressed the self-starter, and asked without turning his head, "Are you permitting this fellow to come with us, sir? He says he will get down at the next milestone."

"Which fellow?" I asked.

Doss indicated the space next to him.

"What is the matter with you, Doss? Have you had a drop of drink or something?"

"I have never tasted any drink in my life, sir," he said, and added, "Get down, old boy. Master says he can't take you."

"Are you talking to yourself?"

"After all, I think we needn't care for these unknown fellows on the road," he said.

"Doss," I pleaded. "Do you feel confident you can drive? If you feel dizzy don't drive."

"Thank you, sir," said Doss. "I would rather not start the car now. I am feeling a little out of sorts." I looked at him anxiously. He closed his eyes, his breathing became heavy and noisy, and gradually his head sank.

"Doss, Doss," I cried desperately. I got down, walked to the front seat, opened the door, and shook him vigorously. He opened his eyes, assumed a hunched-up position, and rubbed his eyes with his hands, which trembled like an old man's.

"Do you feel better?" I asked.

"Better! Better! Hi! Hi!" he said in a thin, piping voice.

"What has happened to your voice? You sound like someone else," I said.

"Nothing. My voice is as good as it was. When a man is eighty he is bound to feel a few changes coming on."

"You aren't eighty, surely," I said.

"Not a day less," he said. "Is nobody going to move this vehicle? If not, there is no sense in sitting here all day. I will get down and go back to my temple."

"I don't know how to drive," I said. "And unless you do it, I don't see how it can move."

"Me!" exclaimed Doss. "These new chariots! God knows what they are drawn by, I never understand, though I could handle a pair of bullocks² in my time. May I ask a question?"

"Go on," I said.

"Where is everybody?"

"Who?"

"Lots of people I knew are not to be seen at all. All sorts of new fellows everywhere, and nobody seems to care. Not a soul comes near the temple. All sorts of people go about but not one who cares to stop and talk. Why doesn't the king ever come this way? He used to go this way at least once a year before."

"Which king?" I asked.

"Let me go, you idiot," said Doss, edging towards the door on which I was leaning. "You don't seem to know anything." He pushed me aside, and got down from the car. He stooped as if he had a big hump on his back, and hobbled along towards the temple. I followed

---

2. **bullocks** (bŏŏl´ əks) *young bulls.*

▲ **Critical Viewing**
How does the man in this picture compare to your vision of the old man in the story? **[Compare and Contrast]**

 Reading Check

How old does Doss say he is when he wakes up?

### Culture Connection

**Hinduism**
Hinduism is the religion of the majority of people in India, the setting for "Old Man of the Temple." Drawing from a set of beliefs that are thousands of years old, Hinduism teaches that death is a temporary stage in an endless cycle of reincarnation, or rebirths. The actions that someone performs in one life, good and bad, will determine the conditions of future rebirths.

### Connect to the Literature

Which aspects of Hinduism does Narayan include in this story?

him, hardly knowing what to do. He turned and snarled at me: "Go away, leave me alone. I have had enough of you."

"What has come over you, Doss?" I asked.

"Who is Doss, anyway? Doss, Doss, Doss. What an absurd name! Call me by my name or leave me alone. Don't follow me calling 'Doss, Doss.'"

"What is your name?" I asked.

"Krishna Battar [krish´ nə bə tar´], and if you mention my name people will know for a hundred miles around. I built a temple where there was only a cactus field before. I dug the earth, burnt every brick, and put them one upon another, all single-handed. And on the day the temple held up its tower over the surrounding country, what a crowd gathered! The king sent his chief minister . . ."

"Who was the king?"

"Where do you come from?" he asked.

"I belong to these parts certainly, but as far as I know there has been only a collector at the head of the district. I have never heard of any king."

"Hi! Hi! Hi!" he cackled, and his voice rang through the gloomy silent village. "Fancy never knowing the king! He will behead you if he hears it."

"What is his name?" I asked.

This tickled him so much that he sat down on the ground, literally unable to stand the joke any more. He laughed and coughed uncontrollably.

"I am sorry to admit," I said, "that my parents have brought me up in such utter ignorance of worldly affairs that I don't know even my king. But won't you enlighten me? What is his name?"

"Vishnu Varma [vish´ n⁻oo vär´ mə], the emperor of emperors . . ."

I cast my mind up and down the range of my historical knowledge but there was no one by that name. Perhaps a local chief of pre-British days, I thought.

"What a king! He often visited my temple or sent his minister for the Annual Festival of the temple. But now nobody cares."

"People are becoming less godly nowadays," I said. There was silence for a moment. An idea occurred to me, I can't say why. "Listen to me," I said. "You ought not to be here any more."

"What do you mean?" he asked, drawing himself up, proudly.

"Don't feel hurt; I say you shouldn't be here any more because you are dead."

"Dead! Dead!" he said. "Don't talk nonsense. How can I be dead when you see me before you now? If I am dead how can I be saying this and that?"

"I don't know all that," I said. I argued and pointed out that according to his own story he was more than five hundred years old, and didn't he know that man's longevity was only a hundred? He constantly interrupted me, but considered deeply what I said.

He said: "It is like this . . . I was coming through the jungle one night after visiting my sister in the next village. I had on me some money and gold ornaments. A gang of robbers set upon me. I gave them as good a fight as any man could, but they were too many for me. They beat me down and knifed me; they took away all that I had on me and left thinking they had killed me. But soon I got up and tried to follow them. They were gone. And I returned to the temple and have been here since . . ."

I told him, "Krishna Battar, you are dead, absolutely dead. You must try and go away from here."

"What is to happen to the temple?" he asked.

"Others will look after it."

"Where am I to go? Where am I to go?"

"Have you no one who cares for you?" I asked.

"None except my wife. I loved her very much."

"You can go to her."

"Oh, no. She died four years ago . . ."

Four years! It was very puzzling. "Do you say four years back from now?" I asked.

"Yes, four years ago from now." He was clearly without any sense of time.

So I asked, "Was she alive when you were attacked by thieves?"

"Certainly not. If she had been alive she would never have allowed me to go through the jungle after nightfall. She took very good care of me."

"See here," I said. "It is imperative you should go away from here. If she comes and calls you, will you go?"

"How can she when I tell you that she is dead?"

I thought for a moment. Presently I found myself saying, "Think of her, and only of her, for a while and see what happens. What was her name?"

"Seetha [sē´ thə], a wonderful girl . . ."

"Come on, think of her." He remained in deep thought for a while. He suddenly screamed, "Seetha is coming! Am I dreaming or what? I will go with her . . ." He stood up, very erect; he appeared to have

**Literary Analysis**

**Setting** What details of setting are revealed through the old man's story of the robbery?

> "Don't feel hurt; I say you shouldn't be here any more because you are dead."

Reading Check

Based on the old man's story, how old does the narrator think the old man is?

lost all the humps and twists he had on his body. He drew himself up, made a dash forward, and fell down in a heap.

Doss lay on the rough ground. The only sign of life in him was his faint breathing. I shook him and called him. He would not open his eyes. I walked across and knocked on the door of the first cottage. I banged on the door violently.

Someone moaned inside, "Ah, it is come!"

Someone else whispered, "You just cover your ears and sleep. It will knock for a while and go away." I banged on the door and shouted who I was and where I came from.

I walked back to the car and sounded the horn. Then the door opened, and a whole family crowded out with lamps. "We thought it was the usual knocking and we wouldn't have opened if you hadn't spoken."

"When was this knocking first heard?" I asked.

"We can't say," said one. "The first time I heard it was when my grandfather was living; he used to say he had even seen it once or twice. It doesn't harm anyone, as far as I know. The only thing it does is bother the bullock carts passing the temple and knock on the doors at night . . ."

I said as a venture, "It is unlikely you will be troubled any more."

It proved correct. When I passed that way again months later I was told that the bullocks passing the temple after dusk never shied now and no knocking on the doors was heard at nights. So I felt that the old fellow had really gone away with his good wife.

## Critical Thinking

**1. Key Ideas and Details (a)** Early in the story, what does Doss say he sees when the car swerves? **(b) Analyze:** Why doesn't the narrator believe Doss?

**2. Key Ideas and Details (a) Summarize:** Describe Doss's transformation. Use details. **(b) Analyze:** How does the narrator react to these changes?

**3. Key Ideas and Details (a) Summarize:** How does the narrator finally get the ghost to leave?

**4. Integration of Knowledge and Ideas Evaluate:** How would you respond to the narrator's invitation to "hear what you have to say" about his story?

**5. Integration of Knowledge and Ideas** Use details from the story to explain what this story teaches about conflicts between the past and the present. *[Connect to the Big Question: Is conflict necessary?]*

## Comparing Setting

**1. Key Ideas and Details (a)** Describe the place, time, and culture of each story. **(b)** For each story, note at least two details that describe specific aspects of the setting—the geographical location, the time, and the cultural environment. As you reread, use a chart like the one shown to record specific details. Pay particular attention to the cultural experiences reflected in each work.

|  | Place: | Time: | Culture: |
|---|---|---|---|
| **The Man to Send Rain Clouds** |  |  |  |
| **Old Man of the Temple** |  |  |  |

**2. Key Ideas and Details** If the setting were changed, could either story take place without being totally different? Explain.

## ⏱ Timed Writing

### Explanatory Text: Essay

In an essay, compare and contrast the way the setting in each story, including the values and attitudes held by people in that time and place, influences the characters and story events. Support your analysis with the details about the setting you gathered while reading. **(40 minutes)**

### 5-Minute Planner

**1.** Read the prompt carefully and completely.

**2.** Gather your ideas. Consider these questions before you write.

- How do the characters in each story live?
- What cultural values, themes, and issues are present in each story?
- Does the setting itself affect the events in each story?
- Do any characters in either story change their thinking or behavior because of the setting? Explain.

**3.** Use the details from your chart to consider the similarities and differences.

**4.** Reread the prompt, and then draft your essay.

# Writing Workshop

 **Common Core
State Standards**

**Writing**

**3.** Write narratives to develop real
or imagined experiences or events
using effective technique, well-
chosen details, and well-
structured event sequences.

**3.a.** Engage and orient the
reader by setting out a problem,
situation, or observation,
establishing one or multiple
point(s) of view, and introducing a
narrator and/or characters; create
a smooth progression of
experiences or events.

**3.e.** Provide a conclusion that
follows from and reflects on what
is experienced, observed, or
resolved over the course of the
narrative.

## Write a Narrative

### Narration: Short Story

**Defining the Form** Stories are one of the oldest and most familiar forms
of literature. A traditional **short story** is a brief fictional narrative composed of plot, setting, and characters. You might use elements of this type
of writing in science fiction, mysteries, and autobiographies.

**Assignment** Write a short story that presents characters in a specific setting
and engaged in a specific conflict that is resolved. Include these elements:

  ✓ a *main character* who takes part in the action

  ✓ details that establish a particular *time, place,* and *mood*

  ✓ a *conflict,* or problem, that is introduced, developed, and resolved,
    including a smooth progression of experiences or events

  ✓ a central *theme,* or message about life

  ✓ *dialogue* between characters

  ✓ a narrator's *point of view*

  ✓ error-free grammar, including *correct use of verbs*

To preview story criteria, see the rubric on page 311.

 **Writing Workshop:** *Work in Progress*

Review the work you did on pages 255 and 281.

## Prewriting/Planning Strategy

**Develop characters.** Use a chart like the one shown to help you think
about each character and the conflict he or she might face. Match a character with a conflict to begin generating ideas for a story. Then, consider
how you would have the conflict play out in the character's life.

| Potential Characters | Potential Conflicts |
|---|---|
| A business man | loses family heirloom |
| An elderly woman | wins lottery |
| A teenage girl | cheats on exam |
| A mechanic | loses job |
| A sports player | moves to a new town |

# Developing the Plot

The **organization** of a story includes several elements, which are often presented in a particular order. The major building blocks of a story's plot include the following:

**Exposition:** introduction of the characters, setting, and basic situation

**Inciting Incident:** introduction of a central conflict

**Rising Action:** development of the conflict

**Climax:** the high point of interest or suspense

**Falling Action:** winding down of the conflict

**Resolution:** general insight about or change in the main character

**Decide who and what your story is about.** Think about the characters, the setting, and the basic situation. Then, introduce these elements in the exposition of your story.

**Identify the conflict, or problem.** Consider your main character and his or her feelings about the basic situation of the story. Ask yourself these questions to develop the conflict:

• How does he or she react to the conflict?

• How does his or her reaction lead to the development of the conflict?

• What external circumstances add to the character's reactions and actions?

Use your answers to plan the inciting incident and rising action.

**Decide how the conflict will play out.** After the development of the inciting incident and rising action, think about the most interesting and effective way for the conflict to be developed and resolved. Consider what will be the high point of anxiety or the possible turning point in the conflict. Use these considerations to construct the climax of your story.

**Decide what will happen in the end.** Everything that happens after the climax is a simple wrapping up of the loose ends. This part of the story is also a place where you can express the moral or lesson of the story. You might present this insight both indirectly through the events and directly through narration. Think about what your character learned through the conflict and use that knowledge to express the insight he or she gained.

# Drafting Strategies

**Develop the narrator's point of view.** Decide how your story will be told. The narrator may be a character within the story or someone who simply reports on the action. Your narrator may be biased toward one character or outcome. Think about all of these options as you begin crafting your story. It is important to give your narrator a consistent voice to relate the story's events and to express his or her observations.

**Create realistic dialogue between characters.** Effective dialogue does not sound stiff and unnatural. It should sound like real people speaking to one another. Try writing a dialogue between characters. Then, read the dialogue aloud with a friend or by yourself. As you listen, decide whether your dialogue sounds natural.

**Show, don't tell.** Use descriptions, dialogue, movements, gestures, and *characters' interior monologues* to make events and characterization vivid for your readers. For example, do not simply report that a street was noisy—provide details that help readers hear the commotion. You might write that the character thought, "How can I possibly think with all these blaring horns?" Additionally, you can add *sensory details*—words that appeal to the senses of sight, smell, taste, touch, and hearing. Appeal to as many senses as possible to bring the scene to life for readers.

**Common Core State Standards**

**Writing**

**3.a.** Engage and orient the reader by setting out a problem, situation, or observation, establishing one or multiple point(s) of view, and introducing a narrator and/or characters; create a smooth progression of experiences or events.

**3.b.** Use narrative techniques, such as dialogue, pacing, description, reflection, and multiple plot lines, to develop experiences, events, and/or characters.

**3.c.** Use a variety of techniques to sequence events so that they build on one another to create a coherent whole.

**3.d.** Use precise words and phrases, telling details, and sensory language to convey a vivid picture of the experiences, events, setting, and/or characters.

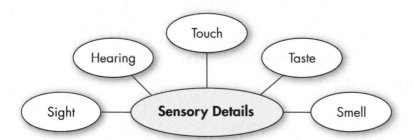

# Revising Strategies

**Maintain an effective sequence of events.** Every detail in your story should deepen your portrayal of the characters or increase the tension of the conflict. Review your draft, noting any interruptions to the momentum of your plot. Consider modifying or deleting such interruptions.

**Use active language.** To create dynamic sentences, choose the active voice instead of the passive voice. Make sure that the subjects in your sentences perform the actions.

- **Passive Voice:** The problem was solved by Curtis.

- **Active Voice:** Curtis solved the problem.

# Revising Inconsistent Verb Tenses

A **tense** is a form of a verb that expresses the time of an action. The six verb tenses are present, present perfect, past, past perfect, future, and future perfect. Inconsistent use of verb tenses causes confusion in a story.

| Uses of Past and Future Perfect Tense | |
|---|---|
| Past action of condition completed before another | I had been to the museum before it was remodeled. |
| Future action of condition completed before another | I will have seen that movie before it will be on television. |
| Continuing past action interrupted by another | I had been on the telephone when you rang the doorbell. |
| Continuing future action interrupted by another | By the time I will graduate, I will have been in school for thirteen years. |

**Identifying Inconsistent Verb Tenses** Inconsistent verb tense occurs when a sentence begins in one tense and incorrectly switches to another. Shifts in tense should always reflect a logical sequence.

**Incorrect:** I *will be* on time today, and I *was* on time tomorrow.
**Correct:** I *was* on time today, and I *will be* on time tomorrow.
Perfect tenses can clarify a sequence of actions.

**Unclear:** By the time she *will arrive*, we *will start* the meeting.
**Clear:** By the time she *will arrive*, we *will have started* the meeting.

**Fixing Errors** Scan your draft for shifts in tense.

1. **Identify the reason for each shift.** Correct unnecessary shifts.

2. **Determine which actions happened first.** When two actions occur at different times in the past, use the past perfect tense for the earlier action. When two actions will occur at different times in the future, use the future perfect tense for the earlier action.

**Grammar in Your Writing**

Review a passage of your draft that includes both narrative and dialogue. Underline any shifts in tense that you find. Be sure that the shift represents a clear and logical time order. Fix any inconsistent tenses.

**PH** **WRITING COACH**

Further instruction and practice are available in *Prentice Hall Writing Coach*.

**Common Core
State Standards**

**Language**
**2.c.** Spell correctly.

## The Oil Slick

The Oil Slick is a place where I play baseball with a bunch of friends. We call the field the "Oil Slick" because a boat carrying gallons of oil once sailed by. The boat sprang a leak, polluting the water around it. The Oil Slick also has a big hole in the outfield. . . .

My nickname is Giant. It suits me because I am the tallest player on the team. . . . I only know the nicknames of the others on my team. They're called Ant, Dash, Rip, X-Ray, Target, Eye, Animal, Uno, and Cover. . . .

This morning, I headed out to the Oil Slick, ready to play. However, before we started, Uno held a meeting. "As you know," he said, "there is a hole in the outfield."

"Who can tell me why the hole is there?" There was silence until Uno spoke again. "That's what I thought," he said. "Some people say there's treasure buried on this field. Somebody probably tried to dig for it, and they left that hole behind. I thought maybe we should dig, too, but then I figured that'd be stupid. It's probably just a rumor. We wouldn't find anything, diggin' holes."

Silence again until someone shouted. "Let's play already!" Everyone went to their positions and the game started. . . .

Rip hit the ball and it flew past the right-fielder, Eye. Concentrating on the ball, Eye ran toward the hole. He didn't know when to stop and he fell. . . .

We all ran and looked down the hole. Nobody had ever bothered to really look before, and it was deep—much deeper than we thought. Hoping to find Eye, we jumped in. . . .

When we saw what the hole truly was, we forgot about Eye. We had expected dirt, rocks—the usual stuff you'd find in a hole. Instead, we saw smooth walls, stretching into the distance. All this time, without ever suspecting it, we had been playing above a maze of tunnels. . . .

We headed down the tunnel to our right. . . .These weren't ordinary tunnels. They had the names of famous baseball players carved right into the walls. Then, we noticed something strange. There were other, different words painted on the wall, and what they said scared us all: "Your friend is here. Don't try to find him. Or else."

We continued through the tunnels until we emerged in a room which . . . had a sign that said, "You Found Him." Sure enough, there was Eye, leaning against a wall. He saw us and shouted, "Go! Now!"

But it was too late. A door slammed shut and we were trapped. Then, we heard a familiar voice. "You saw the warnings, but you didn't stop. Now you are trapped and the treasure is mine!". . .

Randy starts the story with a detailed description of an interesting setting.

The characters' quirky nicknames help the writer create a sense of what each one is like.

Randy uses dialogue to introduce the mystery of the hole in the field—the source of the story's conflict. Notice the correct use of punctuation to show Uno's direct words.

The conflict intensifies here.

# Editing and Proofreading

Check your draft for errors in spelling, punctuation, and grammar.

**Focus on spelling.** Often, the addition of a suffix does not require a spelling change to the base word. Sometimes, though, spelling changes are required. For example, you may need to drop final *e*'s or change final *y*'s to *i*. The final consonant in a word or its internal spelling may also need to change, as in *suspend-suspension* and *maintain-maintenance*. Consult a dictionary to double-check your spelling.

**Use punctuation for effect.** Use a style guide to be sure you have correctly punctuated dialogue in your story. In addition, occasionally use punctuation to emphasize characters' emotions. For example, exclamation points suggest excitement while ellipses (a series of three periods) suggest hesitation or wandering thoughts.

**Spiral Review**

Earlier in the unit, you learned about **regular verbs** (p. 254) and **irregular verbs** (p. 280). Check the use of all verbs in your narrative to be sure you have used them consistently and correctly.

## Publishing and Presenting

Consider one of the following ways to share your writing:

**Deliver an oral presentation.** Read your story aloud to your classmates. Get feedback from your classmates and make necessary revisions.

**Create an anthology.** Work with your class to illustrate and collect your stories in a single binder. Contribute the anthology to the school library.

## Reflecting on Your Writing

**Writer's Journal** Jot down your answer to this question:

*How might your experience writing a story help with other writing you do?*

## Rubric for Self-Assessment

Find evidence in your writing to address each category. Then, use the rating scale to grade your work.

| Criteria | Rating Scale |
| --- | --- |
| | not very                very |
| **Focus:** How clear is the story's theme or message? | 1   2   3   4   5 |
| **Organization:** How clearly do you introduce, develop, and resolve the conflict? | 1   2   3   4   5 |
| **Support/Elaboration:** How well do you use details to establish time, place, and mood? | 1   2   3   4   5 |
| **Style:** How well do you describe the characters and setting? | 1   2   3   4   5 |
| **Conventions:** How correct is your grammar, especially your use of verb tenses? | 1   2   3   4   5 |

## Leveled Texts

Build your skills and improve your comprehension of short stories with texts of increasing complexity.

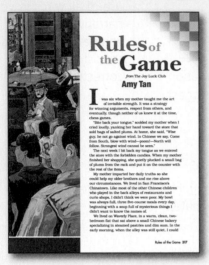

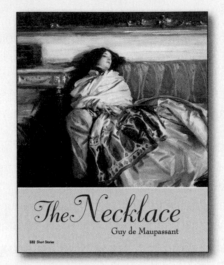

Read **"Rules of the Game"** to learn how a daughter's success leads to a new set of problems.

Read **"The Necklace"** to see the disastrous effects of a woman's wish for social acceptance.

## Common Core State Standards

Meet these standards with either **"Rules of the Game"** from *The Joy Luck Club* (p. 316) or **"The Necklace"** (p. 332).

**Reading Literature**
**3.** Analyze how complex characters develop over the course of a text, interact with other characters, and advance the plot or develop the theme. *(Literary Analysis: Characterization)*

**Writing**
**4.** Produce clear and coherent writing in which the development, organization, and style are appropriate to task, purpose, and audience. *(Writing: Written Presentation)*

**Speaking and Listening**
**2.** Integrate multiple sources of information presented in diverse media or formats evaluating the credibility and accuracy of each source. *(Research and Technology: Informative Brochure)*

**Language**
**6.** Acquire and use accurately grade-appropriate general academic and domain-specific words and phrases; gather vocabulary knowledge when considering a word or phrase important to comprehension or expression. *(Vocabulary: Latin Roots)*

# Literary Analysis: Characterization

A **character** is a person, an animal, or even an object that participates in the action and experiences the events of a literary work. Writers communicate a character's traits and personality through these **characterization** techniques:

- **Direct characterization:** The writer (speaking through a narrator) simply tells readers about a character.
- **Indirect characterization:** The writer gives clues to a character by presenting the character's actions, words, and thoughts and by showing how others react to the character.

## Using the Strategy: Characterization Chart

Use a **characterization chart** like this one to explore characters as they are developed over the course of the story.

| Story Details | What They Show About the Character |
|---|---|
| Narrator's comments | |
| Character's thoughts and words | |
| Character's actions | |
| Character's appearance | |
| What others say or think about character | |

# Reading Skill: Cause and Effect

A **cause** is an event, action, or feeling that produces a result. An **effect** is the result produced. A single cause may produce several effects. For example, a poor student starts to do well in school. Her success results in greater self-esteem. Effects, in turn, may become causes. For example, that same student's new confidence leads her to audition for a play.

As you read, ask questions like these to analyze cause and effect:

- What happened?
- Why did it happen?
- What happens as a result?
- Does that result cause something else to happen?

# Is *conflict* necessary?

## Writing About the Big Question

In "Rules of the Game," a girl learns some important life lessons while working to master chess. Use these sentence starters to develop your ideas about the Big Question:

**Competition** can cause internal conflicts because _____.

Overcoming conflict while playing a game can help us **battle** through other real-life struggles because _____.

**While You Read** Look for ways in which Waverly starts treating her mother like a chess opponent.

## Vocabulary

Read each word and its definition. Decide whether you know the word well, know it a little bit, or do not know it at all. After you read, see how your knowledge of each word has increased.

- **pungent** (pun´ jənt) *adj.* producing a sharp smell (p. 318) *We could smell the <u>pungent</u> Indian spices as we walked into the apartment.* pungency *n.* pungently *adv.*

- **benevolently** (bə nev´ ə lənt lē) *adv.* in a well-meaning way (p. 322) *The helpful officer smiled <u>benevolently</u> at the children.* benevolent *adj.* benevolence *n.*

- **retort** (ri tôrt´) *n.* sharp or clever reply (p. 322) *Her quick <u>retort</u> silenced her critic.* retort *v.*

- **prodigy** (präd´ ə jē) *n.* person who is amazingly talented or intelligent, especially a child of unusual genius (p. 324) *The six-year-old concert pianist was a <u>prodigy</u>.*

- **malodorous** (mal ō´ dər əs) *adj.* having a bad smell (p. 325) *The bag was filled with <u>malodorous</u> garbage.* malodorously *adv.* malodorousness *n.* odor *n.*

- **concessions** (kən sesh´ ənz) *n.* things given or granted as privileges (p. 326) *I had to make a lot of <u>concessions</u> to get my brother to give me his game tickets.* concede *v.* concessionary *adj.*

### Word Study

The **Latin root -*bene*-** means "well."

In this story, an elderly man who is playing chess in the park smiles **benevolently** at Waverly. His smile shows that he wishes her well.

## Meet
# Amy Tan
### (b. 1952)

## Author of
# Rules of the Game

As a child, Amy Tan did not imagine that she would become a successful novelist. Her parents, who had emigrated from China to the San Francisco Bay area, wanted her to become a doctor. Doubting her abilities in science, Tan instead majored in English in college. She went on to become a successful business writer.
**Finding Herself in Fiction** When she reached her mid-thirties, Tan began writing stories. While she was surprised by the pleasure writing fiction gave her, she was even more surprised by the content of her work. Tan had tried to play down her ethnicity, but in her fiction, she found herself exploring the experiences of Chinese American women. In 1985, Tan wrote "Rules of the Game," which she later included in her best-selling first novel, *The Joy Luck Club*.

### Did You Know?

When she was eight years old, Tan's essay "What the Library Means to Me" won first prize in a local contest.

**316** Short Stories

# Rules of the Game

*from* The Joy Luck Club

## Amy Tan

I was six when my mother taught me the art of invisible strength. It was a strategy for winning arguments, respect from others, and eventually, though neither of us knew it at the time, chess games.

"Bite back your tongue," scolded my mother when I cried loudly, yanking her hand toward the store that sold bags of salted plums. At home, she said, "Wise guy, he not go against wind. In Chinese we say, Come from South, blow with wind—poom!—North will follow. Strongest wind cannot be seen."

The next week I bit back my tongue as we entered the store with the forbidden candies. When my mother finished her shopping, she quietly plucked a small bag of plums from the rack and put it on the counter with the rest of the items.

My mother imparted her daily truths so she could help my older brothers and me rise above our circumstances. We lived in San Francisco's Chinatown. Like most of the other Chinese children who played in the back alleys of restaurants and curio shops, I didn't think we were poor. My bowl was always full, three five-course meals every day, beginning with a soup full of mysterious things I didn't want to know the names of.

We lived on Waverly Place, in a warm, clean, two-bedroom flat that sat above a small Chinese bakery specializing in steamed pastries and dim sum. In the early morning, when the alley was still quiet, I could smell fragrant red beans as they were cooked down to a pasty sweetness. By daybreak, our flat was heavy with the odor of fried sesame balls and sweet curried chicken crescents. From my bed, I would listen as my father got ready for work, then locked the door behind him, one-two-three clicks.

At the end of our two-block alley was a small sandlot playground with swings and slides well-shined down the middle with use. The play area was bordered by wood-slat benches where old-country people sat cracking roasted watermelon seeds with their golden teeth and scattering the husks to an impatient gathering of gurgling pigeons. The best playground, however, was the dark alley itself. It was crammed with daily mysteries and adventures. My brothers and I would peer into the medicinal herb shop, watching old Li dole out onto a stiff sheet of white paper the right amount of insect shells, saffron-colored seeds and pungent leaves for his ailing customers. It was said that he once cured a woman dying of an ancestral curse that had eluded the best of American doctors. Next to the pharmacy was a printer who specialized in gold-embossed wedding invitations and festive red banners.

Farther down the street was Ping Yuen Fish Market. The front window displayed a tank crowded with doomed fish and turtles struggling to gain footing on the slimy green-tiled sides. A hand-written sign informed tourists, "Within this store, is all for food, not for pet." Inside, the butchers with their bloodstained white smocks deftly gutted the fish while customers cried out their orders and shouted, "Give me your freshest," to which the butchers always protested, "All are freshest." On less crowded market days, we would inspect the crates of live frogs and crabs which we were warned not to poke, boxes of dried cuttlefish, and row upon row of iced prawns, squid, and slippery fish. The sanddabs made me shiver each time; their eyes lay on one flattened side and reminded me of my mother's story of a careless girl who ran into a crowded street and was crushed by a cab. "Was smash flat," reported my mother.

At the corner of the alley was Hong Sing's, a four-table cafe with a recessed stairwell in front that led to a door marked "Tradesmen." My brothers and I believed the bad people emerged from this door at night. Tourists never went to Hong Sing's,

**Vocabulary**
**pungent** (pun´ jənt) *adj.* producing a sharp smell

**Spiral Review**
**Setting** What do details tell you about the cultural environment in which the narrator grew up?

**Literary Analysis**
**Characterization**
What does this quotation reveal about the narrator's mother?

since the menu was printed only in Chinese. A Caucasian man with a big camera once posed me and my playmates in front of the restaurant. He had us move to the side of the picture window so the photo would capture the roasted duck with its head dangling from a juice-covered rope. After he took the picture, I told him he should go into Hong Sing's and eat dinner. When he smiled and asked me what they served, I shouted, "Guts and duck's feet and octopus gizzards!" Then I ran off with my friends, shrieking with laughter as we scampered across the alley and hid in the entryway grotto of the China Gem Company, my heart pounding with hope that he would chase us.

My mother named me after the street that we lived on: Waverly Place Jong, my official name for important American documents. But my family called me Meimei [mā′ mā′], "Little Sister," I was the youngest, the only daughter. Each morning before school, my mother would twist and yank on my thick black hair until she had formed two tightly wound pigtails. One day, as she struggled to weave a hard-toothed comb through my disobedient hair, I had a sly thought.

I asked her, "Ma, what is Chinese torture?" My mother shook her head. A bobby pin was wedged between her lips. She wetted her palm and smoothed the hair above my ear, then pushed the pin in so that it nicked sharply against my scalp.

"Who say this word?" she asked without a trace of knowing how wicked I was being. I shrugged my shoulders and said, "Some boy in my class said Chinese people do Chinese torture."

"Chinese people do many things," she said simply. "Chinese people do business, do medicine, do painting. Not lazy like American people. We do torture. Best torture." •

My older brother Vincent was the one who actually got the chess set. We had gone to the annual Christmas party held at the First Chinese Baptist Church at the end of the alley. The missionary ladies had put together a Santa bag of gifts donated by members of another church. None of the gifts had names on them. There were separate sacks for boys and girls of different ages.

One of the Chinese parishioners had donned a Santa Claus costume and a stiff paper beard with cotton balls glued to it. I think the only children who thought he was the real thing were too young to know that Santa Claus was not Chinese. When my turn came up, the Santa man asked me how old I was. I thought it was a trick question; I was seven according to the American formula and eight by the Chinese calendar. I said I was born on March 17, 1951. That seemed to satisfy him. He then solemnly asked if I had been a very,

**Literary Analysis**
**Characterization**
What does Mrs. Jong's response to the accusation that Chinese people do torture reveal about her personality?

Reading Check
What gift does Vincent receive at the Christmas party?

very good girl this year and did I believe in Jesus Christ and obey my parents. I knew the only answer to that. I nodded back with equal solemnity.

Having watched the other children opening their gifts, I already knew that the big gifts were not necessarily the nicest ones. One girl my age got a large coloring book of biblical characters, while a less greedy girl who selected a small box received a glass vial of lavender toilet water. The sound of the box was also important. A ten-year-old boy had chosen a box that jangled when he shook it. It was a tin globe of the world with a slit for inserting money. He must have thought it was full of dimes and nickels, because when he saw that it had just ten pennies, his face fell with such undisguised disappointment that his mother slapped the side of his head and led him out of the church hall, apologizing to the crowd for her son who had such bad manners he couldn't appreciate such a fine gift.

As I peered into the sack, I quickly fingered the remaining presents, testing their weight, imagining what they contained. I chose a heavy, compact one that was wrapped in shiny silver foil and a red satin ribbon. It was a twelve-pack of Life Savers and I spent the rest of the party arranging and rearranging the candy tubes in the order of my favorites. My brother Winston chose wisely as well. His present turned out to be a box of intricate plastic parts; the instructions on the box proclaimed that when they were properly assembled he would have an authentic miniature replica of a World War II submarine.

Vincent got the chess set, which would have been a very decent present to get at a church Christmas party except it was obviously used and, as we discovered later, it was missing a black pawn and a white knight. My mother graciously thanked the unknown benefactor, saying, "Too good. Cost too much." At which point, an old lady with fine white, wispy hair nodded toward our family and said with a whistling whisper, "Merry, merry Christmas."

When we got home, my mother told Vincent to throw the chess set away. "She not want it. We not want it," she said, tossing her head stiffly to the side with a tight, proud smile. My brothers had deaf ears. They were already lining up the chess pieces and reading from the dog-eared instruction book. •

I watched Vincent and Winston play during Christmas week. The chess board seemed to hold elaborate secrets waiting to be untangled. The chessmen were more powerful than Old Li's magic herbs that cured ancestral curses. And my brothers wore such serious faces that I was sure something was at stake that was greater than avoiding the tradesmen's door to Hong Sing's.

"Let me! Let me!" I begged between games when one brother or the other would sit back with a deep sigh of relief and victory, the other annoyed, unable to let go of the outcome. Vincent at first refused to let me play, but when I offered my Life Savers as replacements for the buttons that filled in for the missing pieces, he relented. He chose the flavors: wild cherry for the black pawn and peppermint for the white knight. Winner could eat both. As our mother sprinkled flour and rolled out small doughy circles for the steamed dumplings that would be our dinner that night, Vincent explained the rules, pointing to each piece. "You have sixteen pieces and so do I. One king and queen, two bishops, two knights, two castles, and eight pawns. The pawns can only move forward one step, except on the first move. Then they can move two. But they can only take men by moving crossways like this, except in the beginning, when you can move ahead and take another pawn."

"Why?" I asked as I moved my pawn. "Why can't they move more steps?"

"Because they're pawns," he said.

"But why do they go crossways to take other men? Why aren't there any women and children?"

"Why is the sky blue? Why must you always ask stupid questions?" asked Vincent. "This is a game. These are the rules. I didn't make them up. See. Here. In the book." He jabbed a page with a pawn in his hand. "Pawn. P-A-W-N. Pawn. Read it yourself."

My mother patted the flour off her hands. "Let me see book," she said quietly. She scanned the pages quickly, not reading the foreign English symbols, seeming to search deliberately for nothing in particular.

"This American rules," she concluded at last. "Every time people come out from foreign country, must know rules. You not know, judge say, Too bad, go back. They not telling you why so you can use their way go forward. They say, Don't know why, you find out yourself. But they knowing all the time. Better you take it, find out why yourself." She tossed her head back with a satisfied smile.

I found out about all the whys later. I read the rules and looked up all the big words in a dictionary. I borrowed books from the Chinatown library. I studied each chess piece, trying to absorb the power each contained.

**Literary Analysis**
**Characterization**
What do you learn about Vincent based on this conversation?

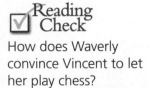

Reading Check

How does Waverly convince Vincent to let her play chess?

**Endgame**
Endgame describes a tense period in a chess game when the end seems close at hand. With fewer pieces left, lines of attack and defense become clearer to both players. Mistakes are magnified in an endgame, when victory and defeat can be determined by a single ill-considered move. In this story, Waverly develops a keen aware- ness of the strategies needed to secure a victory in the endgame.

### Connect to the Literature

Why might it be difficult for a young beginning chess player like Waverly to master the endgame?

**Vocabulary**
**benevolently** (bə nev´ ə lənt lē) *adv.* in a well-meaning way

**retort** (ri tôrt´) *n.* sharp or clever reply

I learned about opening moves and why it's important to control the center early on; the shortest distance between two points is straight down the middle. I learned about the middle game and why tactics between two adversaries are like clashing ideas; the one who plays better has the clearest plans for both attacking and getting out of traps. I learned why it is essential in the endgame to have foresight, a mathematical understanding of all possible moves, and patience; all weaknesses and advantages become evident to a strong adversary and are obscured to a tiring opponent. I discovered that for the whole game one must gather invisible strengths and see the endgame before the game begins.

I also found out why I should never reveal "why" to others. A little knowledge withheld is a great advantage one should store for future use. That is the power of chess. It is a game of secrets in which one must show and never tell.

I loved the secrets I found within the sixty-four black and white squares. I carefully drew a handmade chessboard and pinned it to the wall next to my bed, where at night I would stare for hours at imaginary battles. Soon I no longer lost any games or Life Savers, but I lost my adversaries. Winston and Vincent decided they were more interested in roaming the streets after school in their Hopalong Cassidy cowboy hats. ●

On a cold spring afternoon, while walking home from school, I detoured through the playground at the end of our alley. I saw a group of old men, two seated across a folding table playing a game of chess, others smoking pipes, eating peanuts, and watching. I ran home and grabbed Vincent's chess set, which was bound in a cardboard box with rubber bands. I also carefully selected two prized rolls of Life Savers. I came back to the park and approached a man who was observing the game.

"Want to play?" I asked him. His face widened with surprise and he grinned as he looked at the box under my arm.

"Little sister, been a long time since I play with dolls," he said, smiling benevolently. I quickly put the box down next to him on the bench and displayed my retort.

Lau Po, as he allowed me to call him, turned out to be a much better player than my brothers. I lost many games and many Life

Savers. But over the weeks, with each diminishing roll of candies, I added new secrets. Lau Po gave me the names. The Double Attack from the East and West Shores. Throwing Stones on the Drowning Man. The Sudden Meeting of the Clan. The Surprise from the Sleeping Guard. The Humble Servant Who Kills the King. Sand in the Eyes of Advancing Forces. A Double Killing Without Blood.

There were also the fine points of chess etiquette. Keep captured men in neat rows, as well-tended prisoners. Never announce "Check" with vanity, lest someone with an unseen sword slit your throat. Never hurl pieces into the sandbox after you have lost a game, because then you must find them again, by yourself, after apologizing to all around you. By the end of the summer, Lau Po had taught me all he knew, and I had become a better chess player.

A small weekend crowd of Chinese people and tourists would gather as I played and defeated my opponents one by one. My mother would join the crowds during these outdoor exhibition games. She sat proudly on the bench, telling my admirers with proper Chinese humility, "Is luck."

A man who watched me play in the park suggested that my mother allow me to play in local chess tournaments. My mother smiled graciously, an answer that meant nothing. I desperately wanted to go, but I bit back my tongue. I knew she would not let me play among strangers. So as we walked home I said in a small voice that I didn't want to play in the local tournament. They would have American rules. If I lost, I would bring shame on my family.

"Is shame you fall down nobody push you," said my mother.

During my first tournament, my mother sat with me in the front row as I waited for my turn. I frequently bounced my legs to unstick them from the cold metal seat of the folding chair. When my name was called, I leapt up. My mother unwrapped something in her lap. It was her chang, a small tablet of red jade which held the sun's fire. "Is luck," she whispered, and tucked it into my dress pocket. I turned to my opponent, a fifteen-year-old boy from Oakland. He looked at me, wrinkling his nose.

*By the end of summer, Lau Po had taught me all he knew . . .*

**Reading Skill
Cause and Effect**
What does Waverly anticipate would be the effect of her expressing her desire to play in local chess tournaments?

**Reading
Check**
How does Waverly's mother respond to Waverly's admirers in the park?

**Reading Skill**
**Cause and Effect**
How does Waverly's mindset affect the outcome of the match?

As I began to play, the boy disappeared, the color ran out of the room, and I saw only my white pieces and his black ones waiting on the other side. A light wind began blowing past my ears. It whispered secrets only I could hear.

"Blow from the South," it murmured. "The wind leaves no trail." I saw a clear path, the traps to avoid. The crowd rustled. "Shhh! Shhh!" said the corners of the room. The wind blew stronger. "Throw sand from the East to distract him." The knight came forward ready for the sacrifice. The wind hissed, louder and louder. "Blow, blow, blow. He cannot see. He is blind now. Make him lean away from the wind so he is easier to knock down."

"Check," I said, as the wind roared with laughter. The wind died down to little puffs, my own breath. ●

My mother placed my first trophy next to a new plastic chess set that the neighborhood Tao society had given to me. As she wiped each piece with a soft cloth, she said, "Next time win more, lose less."

"Ma, it's not how many pieces you lose," I said. "Sometimes you need to lose pieces to get ahead."

"Better to lose less, see if you really need."

At the next tournament, I won again, but it was my mother who wore the triumphant grin.

**Literary Analysis**
**Characterization**
What do Waverly's mother's comments here reveal indirectly about her ambitions for Waverly?

"Lost eight piece this time. Last time was eleven. What I tell you? Better off lose less!" I was annoyed, but I couldn't say anything.

I attended more tournaments, each one farther away from home. I won all games, in all divisions. The Chinese bakery downstairs from our flat displayed my growing collection of trophies in its window, amidst the dust-covered cakes that were never picked up. The day after I won an important regional tournament, the window encased a fresh sheet cake with whipped-cream frosting and red script saying, "Congratulations, Waverly Jong, Chinatown Chess Champion." Soon after that, a flower shop, headstone engraver, and funeral parlor offered to sponsor me in national tournaments. That's when my mother decided I no longer had to do the dishes. Winston and Vincent had to do my chores.

"Why does she get to play and we do all the work," complained Vincent.

**Vocabulary**
**prodigy** (präd´ ə jē) *n.* person who is amazingly talented or intelligent, especially a child of unusual genius

"Is new American rules," said my mother. "Meimei play, squeeze all her brains out for win chess. You play, worth squeeze towel."

By my ninth birthday, I was a national chess champion. I was still some 429 points away from grand-master status, but I was touted as the Great American Hope, a child prodigy and a girl to boot. They ran a photo of me in *Life* magazine next to a quote in which Bobby Fischer[1] said, "There will never be a woman grand master." "Your move, Bobby," said the caption.

The day they took the magazine picture I wore neatly plaited braids clipped with plastic barrettes trimmed with rhinestones. I was playing in a large high school auditorium that echoed with phlegmy coughs and the squeaky rubber knobs of chair legs sliding across freshly waxed wooden floors. Seated across from me was an American man, about the same age as Lau Po, maybe fifty. I remember that his sweaty brow seemed to weep at my every move. He wore a dark, malodorous suit. One of his pockets was stuffed with a great white kerchief on which he wiped his palm before sweeping his hand over the chosen chess piece with great flourish.

In my crisp pink-and-white dress with scratchy lace at the neck, one of two my mother had sewn for these special occasions, I would clasp my hands under my chin, the delicate points of my elbows poised lightly on the table in the manner my mother had shown me for posing for the press. I would swing my patent leather shoes back and forth like an impatient child riding on a school bus. Then I would pause, suck in my lips, twirl my chosen piece in midair as if undecided, and then firmly plant it in its new threatening place, with a triumphant smile thrown back at my opponent for good measure.

---

1. **Bobby Fischer** (1943–2008), this American chess prodigy attained the top rank of grandmaster in 1958.

**Vocabulary**
**malodorous**
(mal ō´ dər əs) *adj.*
having a bad smell

Reading
Check
Why does Waverly no longer have to do her chores?

I no longer played in the alley of Waverly Place. I never visited the playground where the pigeons and old men gathered. I went to school, then directly home to learn new chess secrets, cleverly concealed advantages, more escape routes.

But I found it difficult to concentrate at home. My mother had a habit of standing over me while I plotted out my games. I think she thought of herself as my protective ally. Her lips would be sealed tight, and after each move I made, a soft "Hmmmmph" would escape from her nose.

"Ma, I can't practice when you stand there like that," I said one day. She retreated to the kitchen and made loud noises with the pots and pans. When the crashing stopped, I could see out of the corner of my eye that she was standing in the doorway. "Hmmmmph!" Only this one came out of her tight throat.

**Vocabulary**
**concessions** (kən sesh′ ənz) *n.* things given or granted as privileges

My parents made many concessions to allow me to practice. One time I complained that the bedroom I shared was so noisy that I couldn't think. Thereafter, my brothers slept in a bed in the living room facing the street. I said I couldn't finish my rice; my head didn't work right when my stomach was too full. I left the table with half-finished bowls and nobody complained. But there was one duty I couldn't avoid. I had to accompany my mother on Saturday market days when I had no tournament to play. My mother would proudly walk with me, visiting many shops, buying very little. "This my daughter Wave-ly Jong," she said to whoever looked her way.

One day, after we left a shop I said under my breath, "I wish you wouldn't do that, telling everybody I'm your daughter." My mother stopped walking. Crowds of people with heavy bags pushed past us on the sidewalk, bumping into first one shoulder, then another.

**Reading Skill**
**Cause and Effect**
In what ways does Waverly's success at chess affect her family life? Explain.

"Aiii-ya. So shame be with mother?" She grasped my hand even tighter as she glared at me.

I looked down. "It's not that, it's just so obvious. It's just so embarrassing."

"Embarrass you be my daughter?" Her voice was cracking with anger.

"That's not what I meant. That's not what I said."

"What you say?"

I knew it was a mistake to say anything more, but I heard my voice speaking. "Why do you have to use me to show off? If you want to show off, then why don't you learn to play chess?" My mother's eyes turned into dangerous black slits. She had no words for me, just sharp silence.

I felt the wind rushing around my hot ears. I jerked my hand out of my mother's tight grasp and spun around, knocking into an old woman. Her bag of groceries spilled to the ground.

"Aii-ya! Stupid girl!" my mother and the woman cried. Oranges and tin cans careened down the sidewalk. As my mother stooped to help the old woman pick up the escaping food, I took off.

I raced down the street, dashing between people, not looking back as my mother screamed shrilly, "Meimei! Meimei!" I fled down an alley, past dark curtained shops and merchants washing the grime off their windows. I sped into the sunlight, into a large street crowded with tourists examining trinkets and souvenirs. I ducked into another dark alley, down another street, up another alley. I ran until it hurt and I realized I had nowhere to go, that I was not running from anything. The alleys contained no escape routes.

My breath came out like angry smoke. It was cold. I sat down on an upturned plastic pail next to a stack of empty boxes, cupping my chin with my hands, thinking hard. I imagined my mother, first walking briskly down one street or another looking for me, then giving up and returning home to await my arrival. After two hours, I stood up on creaking legs and slowly walked home.

The alley was quiet and I could see the yellow lights shining from our flat like two tiger's eyes in the night. I climbed the sixteen steps to the door, advancing quietly up each so as not to make any warning sounds. I turned the knob; the door was locked. I heard a chair moving, quick steps, the locks turning—click! click! click!—and then the door opened.

"About time you got home," said Vincent. "Boy, are you in trouble."

He slid back to the dinner table. On a platter were the remains of a large fish, its fleshy head still connected to bones swimming upstream in vain escape. Standing there waiting for my punishment, I heard my mother speak in a dry voice.

"We not concerning this girl. This girl not have concerning for us."

Nobody looked at me. Bone chopsticks clinked against the insides of bowls being emptied into hungry mouths.

I walked into my room, closed the door, and lay down on my bed. The room was dark, the ceiling filled with shadows from the dinnertime lights of neighboring flats.

*My mother had a habit of standing over me while I plotted out my games.*

**Reading Check**
What do Waverly and her mother argue about at the market?

**Reading Skill
Cause and Effect**
Why do you think Waverly and her mother stop speaking to each other?

*"Strongest wind cannot be seen."*

In my head, I saw a chessboard with sixty-four black and white squares. Opposite me was my opponent, two angry black slits. She wore a triumphant smile. "Strongest wind cannot be seen," she said.

Her black men advanced across the plane, slowly marching to each successive level as a single unit. My white pieces screamed as they scurried and fell off the board one by one. As her men drew closer to my edge, I felt myself growing light. I rose up into the air and flew out the window. Higher and higher, above the alley, over the tops of tiled roofs, where I was gathered up by the wind and pushed up toward the night sky until everything below me disappeared and I was alone.

I closed my eyes and pondered my next move.

## Critical Thinking

Cite textual evidence to support your responses.

© **1. Key Ideas and Details (a)** Early in the story, what happens when Waverly asks for a bag of salted plums? **(b) Connect:** What happens when she stops asking? **(c) Apply:** How does Waverly later apply that strategy to her desire to play chess competitively?

© **2. Key Ideas and Details (a)** How does Mrs. Jong teach Waverly rules of behavior? **(b) Connect:** How does Waverly translate these rules into strategies for winning at chess? **(c) Extend:** How does she use these rules against her mother?

© **3. Integration of Knowledge and Ideas Speculate:** Who do you think will "win" the game between Waverly and her mother? Use details from the text to explain.

© **4. Integration of Knowledge and Ideas (a)** Is it necessary for Waverly to oppose her mother at the market? **(b)** How do their personal and cultural differences make it "necessary" for Waverly to see her mother on the other side of the chess board? *[Connect to the Big Question: Is conflict necessary?]*

## Literary Analysis: Characterization

ⓒ **1. Key Ideas and Details** Describe the **character** of Waverly. Support your response with examples of her actions, behavior, words, and thoughts, along with details about the effect she has on other people.

ⓒ **2. Craft and Structure (a)** Is the conversation in which Waverly and Mrs. Jong discuss Chinese torture an example of **direct** or **indirect characterization?** Explain your response. **(b)** What do you learn about Mrs. Jong's character from this exchange?

## Reading Skill: Cause and Effect

**3.** Use a chart like the one shown to **analyze cause and effect** in this story. **(a)** Note two causes for Waverly's success with chess. **(b)** List three effects of her success.

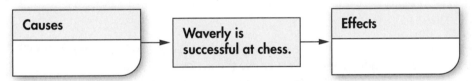

| Causes | | Waverly is successful at chess. | | Effects |
|---|---|---|---|---|

**4. (a)** Why does Mrs. Jong give Waverly special privileges? **(b)** How do these privileges affect Waverly and her relationship with her mother? Use details from the text to explain your response.

## Vocabulary

ⓒ **Acquisition and Use** Tell whether each sentence below makes sense. Use the meaning of the italicized vocabulary word to explain your answer.

**1.** The *pungent* scent of the baking pie drew the hungry crowd.

**2.** The girl was wary when the lady *benevolently* distributed cookies.

**3.** The audience was bored by the comedian's brilliant *retort*.

**4.** He gave his wife a bottle of expensive, *malodorous* perfume.

**5.** During play rehearsals, Mom made some *concessions* regarding my homework.

**6.** With his average talent, the violin *prodigy* amazed no one.

**Word Study** Use the context of the sentences and what you know about the **Latin root -bene-** to explain your answer to each question.

**1.** Would you appreciate what a *benefactor* would do for you?

**2.** What are some of the *benefits* of exercise?

### Word Study

The **Latin root -bene-** means "well."

**Apply It** Explain how the root -bene- contributes to the meanings of these words. Consult a dictionary if necessary.

**beneficial**
**benediction**
**beneficiary**

**Is** *conflict* **necessary?**

## Writing About the Big Question

In "The Necklace," a woman is jealous of people with greater wealth and social standing. Use these sentence starters to develop your ideas about the Big Question.

Jealousy can lead to many conflicts because_____.

Learning to **appreciate** who we are and what we have can help us avoid conflict because _____.

**While You Read** Consider how a jealous attitude creates both internal and external conflict.

## Vocabulary

Read each word and its definition. Decide whether you know the word well, know it a little bit, or do not know it at all. After you read, see how your knowledge of each word has increased.

- **rueful** (rōō′ fəl) *adj.* feeling sorrow or regret (p. 333) *With a rueful sigh, she picked up the pieces of the broken dish.* rue *v.*

- **resplendent** (ri splen′ dənt) *adj.* shining brightly (p. 336) *The winner's face was resplendent as he accepted the prize.* splendor *n.* splendid *adj.*

- **dejection** (dē jek′ shən) *n.* lowness of spirits; depression (p. 339) *I suffered dejection when I lost the spelling bee.* deject *v.* dejected *adj.*

- **fortitude** (fôrt′ ə tōōd′) *n.* the strength to bear misfortune and pain (p. 340) *Lucy met each problem with fortitude and a sense of humor.* forte *n.*

- **disheveled** (di shev′ əld) *adj.* untidy (p. 341) *Val's disheveled hair showed that it was very windy outside.* dishevel *v.*

- **profoundly** (prō found′ lē) *adv.* deeply (p. 342) *We were all profoundly moved by the long-lost brothers' reunion.* profound *adj.*

### Word Study

The **Latin root** *-jec(t)-* means "to throw."

In this story, the Loisels feel **dejection.** A problem has made them feel gloomy; literally, it has thrown them down emotionally.

## Author of

# The Necklace

Perhaps the best-known short-story writer in the world, Guy de Maupassant (gē´ də mō pä sän´) wrote tales that are realistic and pessimistic, and often offer surprise endings.

**Friendship with Writers** Following his army service, Maupassant settled in Paris, where he began to develop his skills as a writer, guided by the famous French author Gustave Flaubert. Maupassant also joined a circle of writers led by French novelist Emile Zola. With Zola's encouragement, Maupassant published his first short story, "Ball of Fat," in 1880. The story earned him immediate fame and freed him to write full time. "The Necklace" is perhaps his most widely read story.

## BACKGROUND FOR THE STORY

### European Society

During the nineteenth century, the old social order in Europe changed. Previously, society had been divided into two main classes: nobles, who owned land, and peasants, who farmed it. However, as industry spread, a new middle class emerged and people could rise—or sink— in social position. Some sought to own material goods as a mark of higher social standing.

### Did You Know?

Maupassant wrote more than 300 short stories, six novels, and other books.

# The Necklace

Guy de Maupassant

$S$he was one of those pretty, charming young women who are born, as if by an error of Fate, into a petty official's family.

She had no dowry,[1] no hopes, not the slightest chance of being appreciated, understood, loved, and married by a rich and distinguished man; so she slipped into marriage with a minor civil servant at the Ministry of Education.

Unable to afford jewelry, she dressed simply: but she was as wretched as a déclassée, for women have neither caste nor breeding—in them beauty, grace, and charm replace pride of birth. Innate refinement, instinctive elegance, and suppleness of wit give them their place on the only scale that counts, and these qualities make humble girls the peers of the grandest ladies.

She suffered constantly, feeling that all the attributes of a gracious life, every luxury, should rightly have been hers. The poverty of her rooms—the shabby walls, the worn furniture, the ugly upholstery—caused her pain. All these things that another woman of her class would not even have noticed, tormented her and made her angry. The very sight of the little Breton girl who cleaned for her awoke rueful thoughts and the wildest dreams in her mind. She dreamt of thick-carpeted reception rooms with Oriental hangings, lighted by tall,

---

1. **dowry** (dou´ rē) n. property that a woman brought to her husband at marriage.

**Literary Analysis**
**Characterization**
What does the author tell you directly about the young woman in the first two paragraphs?

**Vocabulary**
**rueful** (rōō´ fəl) adj. feeling sorrow or regret

Reading Check
Why does the woman suffer constantly?

bronze torches, and with two huge footmen in knee breeches, made drowsy by the heat from the stove, asleep in the wide armchairs. She dreamt of great drawing rooms upholstered in old silks, with fragile little tables holding priceless knick-knacks, and of enchanting little sitting rooms redolent of perfume, designed for tea-time chats with intimate friends—famous, sought-after men whose attentions all women longed for.

When she sat down to dinner at her round table with its three-day-old cloth, and watched her husband opposite her lift the lid of the soup tureen and exclaim, delighted: "Ah, a good homemade beef stew! There's nothing better . . ." she would visualize elegant dinners with gleaming silver amid tapestried walls peopled by knights and ladies and exotic birds in a fairy forest; she would think of exquisite dishes served on gorgeous china, and of gallantries whispered and received with sphinx-like smiles while eating the pink flesh of trout or wings of grouse.

She had no proper wardrobe, no jewels, nothing. And those were the only things that she loved—she felt she was made for them. She would have so loved to charm, to be envied, to be admired and sought after.

She had a rich friend, a schoolmate from the convent she had attended, but she didn't like to visit her because it always made her so miserable when she got home again. She would weep for whole days at a time from sorrow, regret, despair, and distress.

Then one evening her husband arrived home looking triumphant and waving a large envelope.

"There," he said, "there's something for you."

She tore it open eagerly and took out a printed card which said:

"The Minister of Education and Madame Georges Ramponneau [ma dam′ zhôrzh ram pə nō′] request the pleasure of the company of M. and Mme. Loisel [lwa zel′] at an evening reception at the Ministry on Monday, January 18th."

Instead of being delighted, as her husband had hoped, she tossed the invitation on the table and muttered, annoyed:

"What do you expect me to do with that?"

"Why, I thought you'd be pleased, dear. You never go out and this would be an occasion for you, a great one! I had a lot of trouble getting it. Everyone wants an invitation; they're in great demand and there are only a few reserved for the employees. All the officials will be there."

She looked at him, irritated, and said impatiently:

"I haven't a thing to wear. How could I go?"

**Literary Analysis**
**Characterization**
What does the husband's comment in this paragraph reveal indirectly about his character?

**Reading Skill**
**Cause and Effect**
Why do visits to her rich friend always fill the young woman with despair?

It had never even occurred to him. He stammered:

"But what about the dress you wear to the theater? I think it's lovely. . . ."

He fell silent, amazed and bewildered to see that his wife was crying. Two big tears escaped from the corners of her eyes and rolled slowly toward the corners of her mouth. He mumbled:

"What is it? What is it?"

But, with great effort, she had overcome her misery; and now she answered him calmly, wiping her tear-damp cheeks:

"It's nothing. It's just that I have no evening dress and so I can't go to the party. Give the invitation to one of your colleagues whose wife will be better dressed than I would be."

He was overcome. He said:

"Listen, Mathilde [ma tēld´], how much would an evening dress cost—a suitable one that you could wear again on other occasions, something very simple?"

She thought for several seconds, making her calculations and at the same time estimating how much she could ask for without eliciting an immediate refusal and an exclamation of horror from this economical government clerk.

At last, not too sure of herself, she said:

"It's hard to say exactly but I think I could manage with four hundred francs."

He went a little pale, for that was exactly the amount he had put aside to buy a rifle so that he could go hunting the following summer near Nanterre, with a few friends who went shooting larks around there on Sundays.

However, he said:

"Well, all right, then. I'll give you four hundred francs. But try to get something really nice." ●

As the day of the ball drew closer, Madame Loisel seemed depressed, disturbed, worried—despite the fact that her dress was ready. One evening her husband said:

"What's the matter? You've really been very strange these last few days."

And she answered:

"I hate not having a single jewel, not one stone, to wear. I shall look so dowdy.[2] I'd almost rather not go to the party."

---

2. **dowdy** (dou´dē) *adj.* shabby.

**Reading Skill
Cause and Effect**
Why is the husband surprised by his wife's reaction to the party invitation?

> *S*he had no proper wardrobe, no jewels, nothing. And those were the only things that she loved—she felt she was made for them.

Reading Check
What does Monsieur Loisel give up to make his wife happy?

He suggested:

"You can wear some fresh flowers. It's considered very chic[3] at this time of year. For ten francs you can get two or three beautiful roses."

That didn't satisfy her at all.

"No . . . there's nothing more humiliating than to look poverty-stricken among a lot of rich women."

Then her husband exclaimed:

"Wait—you silly thing! Why don't you go and see Madame Forestier [fôr əs tyā′] and ask her to lend you some jewelry. You certainly know her well enough for that, don't you think?"

She let out a joyful cry.

"You're right. It never occurred to me."

The next day she went to see her friend and related her tale of woe.

Madame Forestier went to her mirrored wardrobe, took out a big jewel case, brought it to Madame Loisel, opened it, and said:

"Take your pick, my dear."

Her eyes wandered from some bracelets to a pearl necklace, then to a gold Venetian cross set with stones, of very fine workmanship. She tried on the jewelry before the mirror, hesitating, unable to bring herself to take them off, to give them back. And she kept asking:

"Do you have anything else, by chance?"

"Why yes. Here, look for yourself. I don't know which ones you'll like."

All at once, in a box lined with black satin, she came upon a superb diamond necklace, and her heart started beating with overwhelming desire. Her hands trembled as she picked it up. She fastened it around her neck over her high-necked dress and stood there gazing at herself ecstatically.

Hesitantly, filled with terrible anguish, she asked:

"Could you lend me this one—just this and nothing else?"

"Yes, of course."

She threw her arms around her friend's neck, kissed her ardently, and fled with her treasure.

The day of the party arrived. Madame Loisel was a great success. She was the prettiest woman there—resplendent, graceful, beaming, and deliriously happy. All the men looked at her, asked who she was, tried to get themselves introduced to her. All the minister's aides wanted to waltz with her. The minister himself noticed her.

---

3. **chic** (shēk) *adj.* fashionable.

**Vocabulary**
**resplendent** (ri splen′ dənt) *adj.* shining brightly

▲ **Critical Viewing**
What key part of the story could this image illustrate? **[Connect]**

She danced enraptured—carried away, intoxicated with pleasure, forgetting everything in this triumph of her beauty and the glory of her success, floating in a cloud of happiness formed by all this homage, all this admiration, all the desires she had stirred up—by this victory so complete and so sweet to the heart of a woman. •

When she left the party, it was almost four in the morning. Her husband had been sleeping since midnight in a small, deserted

Reading
Check

How does Madame Loisel feel at the ball?

▲ Critical Viewing
What details in this
painting suggest the
setting of the story?
[Connect]

sitting room, with three other gentlemen whose wives were having a
wonderful time.

He brought her wraps so that they could leave and put them
around her shoulders—the plain wraps from her everyday life
whose shabbiness jarred with the elegance of her evening dress.
She felt this and wanted to escape quickly so that the other women,
who were enveloping themselves in their rich furs, wouldn't see her.

Loisel held her back.

"Wait a minute. You'll catch cold out there. I'm going to call a
cab."

But she wouldn't listen to him and went hastily downstairs.
Outside in the street, there was no cab to be found; they set out to
look for one, calling to the drivers they saw passing in the distance.

They walked toward the Seine,[4] shivering and miserable. Finally,
on the embankment, they found one of those ancient nocturnal
broughams[5] which are only to be seen in Paris at night, as if they
were ashamed to show their shabbiness in daylight.

---

4. **Seine** (sān) river flowing through Paris.
5. **broughams** (brōōmz) *n.* horse-drawn carriages.

It took them to their door in the Rue des Martyrs, and they went sadly upstairs to their apartment. For her, it was all over. And he was thinking that he had to be at the Ministry by ten.

She took off her wraps before the mirror so that she could see herself in all her glory once more. Then she cried out. The necklace was gone; there was nothing around her neck.

Her husband, already half undressed, asked:

"What's the matter?"

She turned toward him in a frenzy:

"The . . . the . . . necklace—it's gone."

He got up, thunderstruck.

"What did you say? . . . What! . . . Impossible!"

And they searched the folds of her dress, the folds of her wrap, the pockets, everywhere. They didn't find it.

He asked:

"Are you sure you still had it when we left the ball?"

"Yes. I remember touching it in the hallway of the Ministry."

"But if you had lost it in the street, we would have heard it fall. It must be in the cab."

"Yes, most likely. Do you remember the number?"

"No. What about you—did you notice it?"

"No."

They looked at each other in utter dejection. Finally Loisel got dressed again.

"I'm going to retrace the whole distance we covered on foot," he said, "and see if I can't find it."

And he left the house. She remained in her evening dress, too weak to go to bed, sitting crushed on a chair, lifeless and blank.

Her husband returned at about seven o'clock. He had found nothing.

He went to the police station, to the newspapers to offer a reward, to the offices of the cab companies—in a word, wherever there seemed to be the slightest hope of tracing it.

She spent the whole day waiting, in a state of utter hopelessness before such an appalling catastrophe.

Loisel returned in the evening, his face lined and pale; he had learned nothing.

"You must write to your friend," he said, "and tell her that you've broken the clasp of the necklace and that you're getting it mended. That'll give us time to decide what to do."

*He brought her wraps so that they could leave and put them around her shoulders—the plain wraps from her everyday life...*

**Vocabulary**
**dejection** (di jek´ shən) *n.* lowness of spirits; depression

**Literary Analysis**
**Characterization**
What do the Loisels' actions after the necklace is lost reveal about their individual characters?

Reading Check
When does Madame Loisel discover the necklace is missing?

**Reading Skill**
**Cause and Effect**
What fear prevents
the Loisels from telling
Madame Forestier the
necklace was lost?

She wrote the letter at his dictation.

By the end of the week, they had lost all hope.

Loisel, who had aged five years, declared:

"We'll have to replace the necklace."

The next day they took the case in which it had been kept and went to the jeweler whose name appeared inside it. He looked through his ledgers:

"I didn't sell this necklace, madame. I only supplied the case."

Then they went from one jeweler to the next, trying to find a necklace like the other, racking their memories, both of them sick with worry and distress.

In a fashionable shop near the Palais Royal, they found a diamond necklace which they decided was exactly like the other. It was worth 40,000 francs. They could have it for 36,000 francs.

They asked the jeweler to hold it for them for three days, and they stipulated that he should take it back for 34,000 francs if the other necklace was found before the end of February.

Loisel possessed 18,000 francs left him by his father. He would borrow the rest.

He borrowed, asking a thousand francs from one man, five hundred from another, a hundred here, fifty there. He signed promissory notes,[6] borrowed at exorbitant rates, dealt with usurers and the entire race of moneylenders. He compromised his whole career, gave his signature even when he wasn't sure he would be able to honor it, and horrified by the anxieties with which his future would be filled, by the black misery about to descend upon him, by the prospect of physical privation and moral suffering, went to get the new necklace, placing on the jeweler's counter 36,000 francs.

When Madame Loisel went to return the necklace, Madame Forestier said in a faintly waspish tone:

"You could have brought it back a little sooner! I might have needed it."

She didn't open the case as her friend had feared she might. If she had noticed the substitution, what would she have thought? What would she have said? Mightn't she have taken Madame Loisel for a thief? •

Madame Loisel came to know the awful life of the poverty-stricken. However, she resigned herself to it with unexpected fortitude. The crushing debt had to be paid. She would pay it. They dismissed the maid; they moved into an attic under the roof.

She came to know all the heavy household chores, the loathsome work of the kitchen. She washed the dishes, wearing

**Vocabulary**
**fortitude**
(fôrt´ ə to͞od´) *n.* the
strength to bear mis-
fortune and pain

---

6. **promissory** (präm´ i sôr´ ē) **notes** written promises to pay back borrowed money.

down her pink nails on greasy casseroles and the bottoms of saucepans. She did the laundry, washing shirts and dishcloths which she hung on a line to dry; she took the garbage down to the street every morning, and carried water upstairs, stopping at every floor to get her breath. Dressed like a working-class woman, she went to the fruit store, the grocer, and the butcher with her basket on her arm, bargaining, outraged, contesting each sou[7] of her pitiful funds.

Every month some notes had to be honored and more time requested on others.

Her husband worked in the evenings, putting a shopkeeper's ledgers in order, and often at night as well, doing copying at twenty-five centimes a page.

And it went on like that for ten years.

After ten years, they had made good on everything, including the usurious rates and the compound interest.

Madame Loisel looked old now. She had become the sort of strong woman, hard and coarse, that one finds in poor families. Disheveled, her skirts askew, with reddened hands, she spoke in a loud voice, slopping water over the floors as she washed them. But sometimes, when her husband was at the office, she would sit down by the window and muse over that party long ago when she had been so beautiful, the belle of the ball.

How would things have turned out if she hadn't lost that necklace? Who could tell? How strange and fickle life is! How little it takes to make or break you!

Then one Sunday when she was strolling along the Champs Elysées[8] to forget the week's chores for a while, she suddenly caught sight of a woman taking a child for a walk. It was Madame Forestier, still young, still beautiful, still charming.

Madame Loisel started to tremble. Should she speak to her? Yes, certainly she should. And now that she had paid everything back, why shouldn't she tell her the whole story?

She went up to her.

"Hello, Jeanne."

The other didn't recognize her and was surprised that this plainly dressed woman should speak to her so familiarly. She murmured:

"But . . . madame! . . . I'm sure . . . You must be mistaken."

"No, I'm not. I am Mathilde Loisel."

---

7. **sou** (sōō) *n.* former French coin, worth very little; the centime (sän» tèm«), mentioned later, was also of little value.
8. **Champs Elysées** (shän zā lē zā') fashionable street in Paris.

**Spiral Review**
**Setting** How does the class-based nature of the Loisels' society influence their behavior?

**Vocabulary**
**disheveled**
(di shev′ əld) *adj.* untidy

**Reading Skill**
**Cause and Effect**
What causes Madame Loisel to tremble at the sight of Madame Forestier?

**Reading Check**
How has Madame Loisel's appearance changed?

> *S*he had become the sort of strong woman, hard and coarse, that one finds in poor families.

Her friend gave a little cry.

"Oh! Oh, my poor Mathilde, how you've changed!"

"Yes, I've been through some pretty hard times since I last saw you and I've had plenty of trouble—and all because of you!"

"Because of me? What do you mean?"

"You remember the diamond necklace you lent me to wear to the party at the Ministry?"

"Yes. What about it?"

"Well, I lost it."

"What are you talking about? You returned it to me."

"What I gave back to you was another one just like it. And it took us ten years to pay for it. You can imagine it wasn't easy for us, since we were quite poor. . . . Anyway, I'm glad it's over and done with."

Madame Forestier stopped short.

"You say you bought a diamond necklace to replace that other one?"

"Yes. You didn't even notice then? They really were exactly alike."

And she smiled, full of a proud, simple joy.

Madame Forestier, profoundly moved, took Mathilde's hands in her own.

"Oh, my poor, poor Mathilde! Mine was false. It was worth five hundred francs at the most!"

**Vocabulary**
**profoundly** (prō found′ lē) *adv.* deeply

## Critical Thinking

**Cite textual evidence to support your responses.**

1. **Key Ideas and Details (a)** As the story begins, why is Madame Loisel unhappy with her life? **(b) Infer:** Do you think the author wants readers to sympathize with her unhappiness? Explain your response.

2. **Key Ideas and Details (a)** How does Monsieur Loisel respond to Madame Loisel's disappointment? **(b) Compare and Contrast:** How is Monsieur Loisel different from his wife? Use details from the text to explain.

3. **Integration of Knowledge and Ideas (a) Interpret:** How does the change in Madame Loisel's appearance illustrate the internal and external conflicts of the story? **(b) Draw Conclusions:** What is the effect of this change?

4. **Integration of Knowledge and Ideas (a)** What external conflict is proven unnecessary by the end of the story? **(b)** Could a change in Madame Loisel's attitude have prevented her internal conflict? *[Connect to the Big Question: Is conflict necessary?]*

## Literary Analysis: Characterization

© 1. **Key Ideas and Details** Describe Madame Loisel's **character.** Support your answer with at least one example of each of the following methods of **indirect characterization** in the story: **(a)** Madame Loisel's actions, **(b)** her words and thoughts, and **(c)** her effect on other people.

© 2. **Craft and Structure (a)** Is the conversation on the day of the ball in which the Loisels discuss Madame's attire an example of indirect characterization or **direct characterization**? Explain your response. **(b)** What do you learn about both Monsieur and Madame Loisel's characters from this exchange?

## Reading Skill: Cause and Effect

3. Use a chart like the one shown to **analyze cause and effect** in this story. Note two causes and two effects for Madame Loisel's decision to borrow the necklace from Madame Forestier.

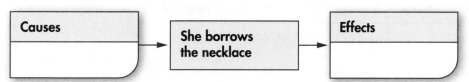

4. Does Madame Loisel cause her own suffering? Explain.

## Vocabulary

© **Acquisition and Use** Tell whether each sentence below makes sense. Use the meaning of the italicized vocabulary word to explain your answer.

1. With a *rueful* smile, she described the fun she had had at the fair.
2. The tired campers were *resplendent* as they hiked in the rain.
3. Alan went to the interview *disheveled* and wearing a new suit.
4. The class was *profoundly* moved by the story of the heroic dog.
5. One of my grandfather's greatest qualities is his *fortitude.*
6. With great *dejection,* the family celebrated the engagement.

**Word Study** Use the context of the sentences and what you know about the **Latin root -*jec(t)*-** to explain your answer to each question.

1. Why might a player be *ejected* from a basketball game?
2. Could you challenge an idea by raising an *objection* to it?

### Word Study

The **Latin root -*jec(t)*-** means "to throw."

**Apply It** Explain how the root -*jec(t)*- contributes to the meanings of these words. Consult a dictionary if necessary.
**project** *v.*
**reject** *v.*
**trajectory**

# Integrated Language Skills

## Rules of the Game • The Necklace

### Conventions: Subjects and Predicates

The **subject** is the word or group of words that tells whom or what a sentence is about.

The **predicate** is the verb or verb phrase that tells what the subject of a sentence does or is.

A complete sentence needs both a subject and a predicate. The underlined words in these examples are the simple subject and simple predicate, or the noun and verb that make a sentence complete.

| Subject | Predicate |
|---|---|
| <u>Conflict</u> between family members | <u>is</u> not unusual. |
| Madame Loisel's <u>desire</u> for status | <u>has created</u> a conflict with her husband. |
| <u>Waverly</u> | <u>argues</u> dramatically with her mother in the market. |

**Practice A** Add a subject or predicate to complete each sentence. Identify the subject and predicate in the completed sentence.

1. _____ watched Vincent and Winston's chess games.
2. The book of rules _____.
3. Her interest in the game _____.
4. _____ soon made Waverly a skillful player.

**Ⓒ Writing Application** Create four new sentences by changing the subject and the predicate in the example sentence. *Chess has been my favorite game since I was ten.*

**Practice B** Identify the subject and predicate in each sentence.

1. Madame Loisel felt great dissatisfaction.
2. Her dreams of wealth and recognition caused trouble.
3. The necklace from Madame Forestier disappeared after a party.
4. Its replacement cost Madame Loisel and her husband ten years of hardship.

**Ⓒ Reading Application** Choose two sentences in "The Necklace." Identify the subject and predicate in each sentence.

**PH WRITING COACH** Further instruction and practice are available in *Prentice Hall Writing Coach*.

# Writing

**Common Core State Standards**

L.9-10.6; W.9-10.4; SL.9-10.2
[For the full wording of the standards, see page 312.]

**Informative Text** Each of these stories deals with people learning lessons. Think about a lesson that you could teach the main characters in "The Necklace" or "Rules of the Game." Create a **written presentation** that details your ideas.

- Make notes about an issue that the characters face. Consider what you might teach them and how best to convey your ideas.

- Based on your audience, purpose, and point of view as an outsider, choose an appropriate genre and text structure. For example, you might write an essay, or you might tell a story with a moral.

- As you revise, check that your presentation is organized logically. Add transitions where needed and vary your sentences for meaning, interest, and style.

**Grammar Application** As you write, check that subjects and predicates agree in number and tense.

**Writing Workshop:** *Work in Progress*

**Prewriting for Exposition: Cause-and-Effect Essay** It often is easier to see effects than to understand causes. For a cause-and-effect essay you may write, list ten effects for which you do not know the cause. Put this "What's the Cause?" list into your writing portfolio.

Use this prewriting activity to prepare for the **Writing Workshop** on page 402.

# Research and Technology

**Build and Present Knowledge** The characters in these stories need facts in order to succeed. With a few classmates, make an **informative brochure.**

- If you read "The Necklace," make a brochure about the qualities and uses of diamonds.

- If you read "Rules of the Game," make a brochure about the history, rules, and strategies of chess. Follow these steps.

- **Gather information** on the topic, evaluating sources as you take notes on library and authoritative Internet sources. Develop clear questions to help you gather details from a variety of sources.

- **Organize your coverage.** Plan the sections for the brochure. Decide whether illustrations should convey some of the information (for example, diagrams of chess moves).

- **Design and present your brochure.** Add visual elements but avoid a "cluttered" look. Use diverse media or formats to present your brochure to the class.

www.PHLitOnline.com
- Interactive graphic organizers
- Grammar tutorial
- Interactive journals

## ⓒ Leveled Texts

Build your skills and improve your comprehension of short stories
with texts of increasing complexity.

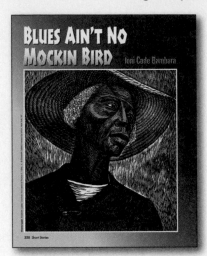

Read **"Blues Ain't No Mockin Bird"** to find out what happens when two photographers clash with a strong-willed woman.

Read **"The Invalid's Story"** to see how a master humorist takes a somber train ride and makes it comical.

## ⓒ Common Core State Standards

Meet these standards with either **"Blues Ain't No Mockin Bird"** (p. 350) or **"The Invalid's Story"** (p. 362).

**Reading Literature**
**4.** Determine the meaning of words and phrases as they are used in the text, including figurative and connotative meanings; analyze the cumulative impact of specific word choices on meaning and tone. (*Literary Analysis: Dialogue and Dialect*)

**Spiral Review: RL.9-10.3**

**Writing**
**3.a.** Engage and orient the reader by setting out a problem, situation, or observation, establishing one or multiple point(s) of view, and introducing a narrator and/or characters; create a smooth progression of experiences or events. (*Writing: Informal Letter*)

**Speaking and Listening**
**4.** Present information, findings, and supporting evidence clearly, concisely, and logically such that listeners can follow the line of reasoning and the organization, development, substance, and style are appropriate to purpose, audience, and task. (*Speaking and Listening: Dialogue*)

**Language**
**1.** Demonstrate command of the conventions of standard English grammar and usage when writing or speaking. (*Conventions: Active and Passive Voice*)

**6.** Acquire and use accurately grade-appropriate general academic and domain-specific words and phrases; gather vocabulary knowledge when considering a word or phrase important to comprehension or expression. (*Vocabulary: Analogies*)

# Literary Analysis: Dialogue and Dialect

**Dialogue** is a conversation between or among characters in a literary work. In prose, dialogue is usually set off by quotation marks, and a new paragraph indicates a change in speaker. Writers use dialogue for these purposes:

- to reveal character traits and relationships
- to advance the action of the plot and develop the conflict
- to add variety, color, and realism to narratives
- to develop the **tone** of the work—the writer's attitude toward his or her subject and audience

To make characters and settings vivid, authors may write dialogue reflecting characters' **dialect.** Dialect is a way of speaking that is common to people of a region or group. The words, pronunciations, and grammar of a dialect differ from those of the standard form of a language.

As you read, notice passages of dialogue and dialect, and determine what they show about the characters and the setting. In addition, consider how they affect the tone of the story.

# Reading Skill: Cause and Effect

A **cause** is an event, an action, or a feeling that produces a result. An **effect** is the result produced. When reading a story, **visualize the action to analyze cause and effect.**

- Use text details to picture the setting, characters, and action.
- Use the details of your mental picture to help you identify the relationships between actions and events.

## Using the Strategy: Cause-and-Effect Chart

Use a **flow chart** like this one to follow cause-and-effect relationships as you read.

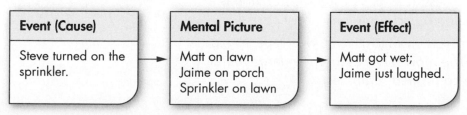

| Event (Cause) | Mental Picture | Event (Effect) |
|---|---|---|
| Steve turned on the sprinkler. | Matt on lawn<br>Jaime on porch<br>Sprinkler on lawn | Matt got wet;<br>Jaime just laughed. |

## Is *conflict* necessary?

### Writing About the Big Question

In "Blues Ain't No Mockin Bird," an elderly woman finds it necessary to fight with people who threaten something important to her. Use these sentence starters to develop your ideas about the Big Question.

People will **battle** to protect _____ because _____.

Personal feelings and **issues** spark conflicts between people because _____.

**While You Read** Compare the responses of the various characters to the situation that antagonizes Granny, and look for the successful resolution of the conflict.

### Vocabulary

Read each word and its definition. Decide whether you know the word well, know it a little bit, or do not know it at all. After you read, see how your knowledge of each word has increased.

- **ladle** (lād′ 'l) *n.* a long-handled, cuplike spoon for dipping out liquids (p. 351) *The waiter used a <u>ladle</u> to put soup into my bowl.* *ladle v.*

- **raggedy** (rag′ i dē) *adj.* torn and in bad condition (p. 354) *I always wear <u>raggedy</u> old clothes to work in the garden.* *ragged adj.*

- **stalks** (stôks) *v.* walks in a stiff, haughty, or grim manner (p. 355) *An angry man <u>stalks</u> out of the room in a huff.* *stalk n. stalker n.*

- **formality** (fôr mal′ ə tē) *n.* attention to established rules or customs (p. 356) *His <u>formality</u> conveyed respect for his guests.* *formal adj. formalize v. informal adj.*

- **reckless** (rek′ lis) *adj.* careless; rash (p. 356) *<u>Reckless</u> driving is a serious offense.* *recklessly adv. recklessness n.*

- **reels** (rēlz) *n.* frames or spools on which thread, wire, tape, film, or a net is wound (p. 357) *The movies were stored on large metal <u>reels</u> in a temperature-controlled room.* *reel v.*

### Word Study

The **Latin suffix -*ity*** forms nouns from adjectives. It means "the quality of showing a certain characteristic."

This story describes someone who dislikes the **formality** of the title *Miss*. She thinks it has a "too formal" quality.

## Author of
# BLUES AIN'T NO MOCKIN BIRD

Toni Cade Bambara was a social activist and a writer of short stories, a novel, plays, television scripts, and documentaries. She started writing when she was in kindergarten and had her first story published when she was a senior in college.

**"I write because I must,"** Bambara said. "If there were no more presses, no more publishing houses, I'd still be writing." She was equally devoted to social change and worked to improve the condition of African Americans. Her writing echoes that concern. Her stories are often praised for their vivid portrayals of the daily lives of African Americans in the twentieth century.

### BACKGROUND FOR THE STORY

**Hawks**

Hawks are large, predatory birds. They are fiercely territorial, and they often keep the same mate for life. Usually, hawks hunt rabbits, squirrels, and other birds. However, in rural areas they may kill and eat chickens. For a poor rural family like the one in this story, defending the family's flock of chickens from hawks is a matter of survival. Sometimes, when a farmer kills a hawk that has attacked his chickens, he displays it to frighten off other hawks.

### DID YOU KNOW?

Bambara was born Miltona Cade but added *Bambara* after discovering it on her great-grandmother's sketchbook. *Bambara* is also the name of an African tribe known for its textiles.

# Blues Ain't No Mockin Bird

## Toni Cade Bambara

*Sharecropper,* Elizabeth Catlett, Courtesy The Estate of Thurlow E. Tibbs, Jr., © Elizabeth Catlett/Licensed by VAGA, New York, NY

**T**he puddle had frozen over, and me and Cathy went stompin in it. The twins from next door, Tyrone and Terry, were swingin so high out of sight we forgot we were waitin our turn on the tire. Cathy jumped up and came down hard on her heels and started tap-dancin. And the frozen patch splinterin every which way underneath kinda spooky. "Looks like a plastic spider web," she said. "A sort of weird spider, I guess, with many mental problems." But really it looked like the crystal paperweight Granny kept in the parlor. She was on the back porch, Granny was, making the cakes drunk. The old ladle dripping rum into the Christmas tins, like it used to drip maple syrup into the pails when we lived in the Judson's woods, like it poured cider into the vats when we were on the Cooper place, like it used to scoop buttermilk and soft cheese when we lived at the dairy.

"Go tell that man we ain't a bunch of trees."

"Ma'am?"

"I said to tell that man to get away from here with that camera." Me and Cathy look over toward the meadow where the men with the station wagon'd been roamin around all mornin. The tall man with a huge camera lassoed to his shoulder was buzzin our way.

"They're makin movie pictures," yelled Tyrone, stiffenin his legs and twistin so the tire'd come down slow so they could see.

"They're makin movie pictures," sang out Terry.

"That boy don't never have anything original to say," say Cathy grown-up.

By the time the man with the camera had cut across our neighbor's yard, the twins were out of the trees swingin low and Granny was onto the steps, the screen door bammin soft and scratchy against her palms. "We thought we'd get a shot or two of the house and everything and then—"

"Good mornin," Granny cut him off. And smiled that smile.

"Good mornin," he said, head all down the way Bingo does when you yell at him about the bones on the kitchen floor. "Nice place you got here, aunty. We thought we'd take a—"

"Did you?" said Granny with her eyebrows. Cathy pulled up her socks and giggled.

**Literary Analysis**
**Dialogue and Dialect**
Which features of the title and opening paragraph show that this story is written in dialect?

**Vocabulary**
**ladle** (lād´ 'l) *n.* a long-handled, cuplike spoon for dipping out liquids

◄ **Critical Viewing**
As you read, compare Granny with the woman in the illustration.
**[Compare and Contrast]**

**Reading Skill**
**Cause and Effect**
Which details in the text help you to visualize the effect that the camera crew has on Granny?

Reading Check

What are the men doing on Granny's property?

"Nice things here," said the man, buzzin his camera over the yard. The pecan barrels, the sled, me and Cathy, the flowers, the printed stones along the driveway, the trees, the twins, the toolshed.

"I don't know about the thing, the it, and the stuff," said Granny, still talkin with her eyebrows. "Just people here is what I tend to consider."

Camera man stopped buzzin. Cathy giggled into her collar.

"Mornin, ladies," a new man said. He had come up behind us when we weren't lookin. "And gents," discoverin the twins givin him a nasty look. "We're filmin for the county," he said with a smile. "Mind if we shoot a bit around here?"

"I do indeed," said Granny with no smile. Smilin man was smiling up a storm. So was Cathy. But he didn't seem to have another word to say, so he and the camera man backed on out the yard, but you could hear the camera buzzin still. "Suppose you just shut that machine off," said Granny real low through her teeth, and took a step down off the porch and then another.

"Now, aunty," Camera said, pointin the thing straight at her.

"Your mama and I are not related."

Smilin man got his notebook out and a chewed-up pencil. "Listen," he said movin back into our yard, "we'd like to have a statement from you . . . for the film. We're filmin for the county, see. Part of the food stamp campaign. You know about the food stamps?"

Granny said nuthin.

"Maybe there's somethin you want to say for the film. I see you grow your own vegetables," he smiled real nice. "If more folks did that, see, there'd be no need—"

Granny wasn't sayin nuthin. So they backed on out, buzzin at our clothesline and the twins' bicycles, then back on down to the meadow. The twins were danglin in the tire, lookin at Granny. Me and Cathy were waitin, too, cause Granny always got somethin to say. She teaches steady with no let-up. "I was on this bridge one time," she started off. "Was a crowd cause this man was goin to jump, you understand. And a minister was there and the police and some other folks. His woman was there, too."

"What was they doin?" asked Tyrone.

"Tryin to talk him out of it was what they was doin. The minister talkin about how it was a mortal sin, suicide. His woman takin bites out of her own hand and not even knowin it, so nervous and cryin and talkin fast."

"So what happened?" asked Tyrone.

"So here comes . . . this person . . . with a camera, takin pictures of the man and the minister and the woman. Takin pictures of the man in his misery about to jump, cause life so bad and people been messin with him so bad. This person takin up the whole roll of film practically. But savin a few, of course."

"Of course," said Cathy, hatin the person. Me standin there wonderin how Cathy knew it was "of course" when I didn't and it was *my* grandmother.

After a while Tyrone say, "Did he jump?"

"Yeh, did he jump?" say Terry all eager. And Granny just stared at the twins till their faces swallow up the eager and they don't even care any more about the man jumpin. Then she goes back onto the porch and lets the screen door go for itself. I'm lookin to Cathy to finish the story cause she knows Granny's whole story before me even. Like she knew how come we move so much and Cathy ain't but a third cousin we picked up on the way last Thanksgivin visitin. But she knew it was on account of people drivin Granny crazy till she'd get up in the night and start packin. Mumblin and

**Reading Check**

How does Granny respond when "Smilin" asks her to make a statement?

**Vocabulary**
**raggedy** (rag´ i dē)
*adj.* torn and in
bad condition

packin and wakin everybody up sayin, "Let's get on away from here before I kill me somebody." Like people wouldn't pay her for things like they said they would. Or Mr. Judson bringin us boxes of old clothes and raggedy magazines. Or Mrs. Cooper comin in our kitchen and touchin everything and sayin how clean it all was. Granny goin crazy, and Granddaddy Cain pullin her off the people, sayin, "Now, now, Cora." But next day loadin up the truck, with rocks all in his jaw, madder than Granny in the first place.

"I read a story once," said Cathy soundin like Granny teacher. "About this lady Goldilocks who barged into a house that wasn't even hers. And not invited, you understand. Messed over the

## LITERATURE IN CONTEXT

### Science Connection

**Hawks: Tales and Truths**
A variety of hawk species, including the Northern Goshawk and the Coopers hawk, are sometimes called chickenhawks, although no such species exists. This name comes from the belief that hawks prey on chickens. While hawks do sometimes eat chickens, in reality, raccoons pose greater threats to small barnyard animals.

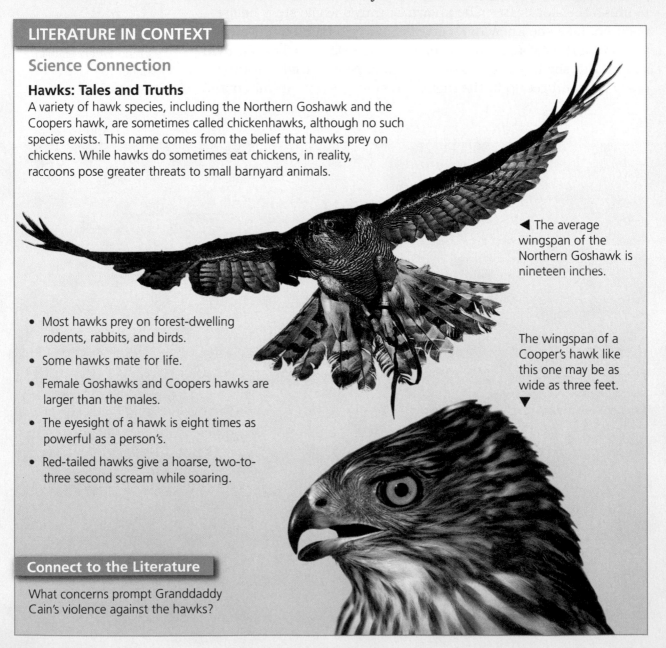

◀ The average wingspan of the Northern Goshawk is nineteen inches.

- Most hawks prey on forest-dwelling rodents, rabbits, and birds.

- Some hawks mate for life.

- Female Goshawks and Coopers hawks are larger than the males.

- The eyesight of a hawk is eight times as powerful as a person's.

- Red-tailed hawks give a hoarse, two-to-three second scream while soaring.

The wingspan of a Cooper's hawk like this one may be as wide as three feet.
▼

### Connect to the Literature

What concerns prompt Granddaddy Cain's violence against the hawks?

people's groceries and broke up the people's furniture. Had the nerve to sleep in the folks' bed."

"Then what happened?" asked Tyrone. "What they do, the folks, when they come in to all this mess?"

"Did they make her pay for it?" asked Terry, makin a fist. "I'd've made her pay me."

I didn't even ask. I could see Cathy actress was very likely to just walk away and leave us in mystery about this story which I heard was about some bears.

"Did they throw her out?" asked Tyrone, like his father sounds when he's bein extra nasty-plus to the washin-machine man.

"Woulda," said Terry. "I woulda gone upside her head with my fist and—"

"You woulda done whatcha always do—go cry to Mama, you big baby," said Tyrone. So naturally Terry starts hittin on Tyrone, and next thing you know they tumblin out the tire and rollin on the ground. But Granny didn't say a thing or send the twins home or step out on the steps to tell us about how we can't afford to be fightin amongst ourselves. She didn't say nuthin. So I get into the tire to take my turn. And I could see her leanin up against the pantry table, staring at the cakes she was puttin up for the Christmas sale, mumblin real low and grumpy and holdin her forehead like it wanted to fall off and mess up the rum cakes.

Behind me I hear before I can see Granddaddy Cain comin through the woods in his field boots. Then I twist around to see the shiny black oilskin cuttin through what little left there was of yellows, reds, and oranges. His great white head not quite round cause of this bloody thing high on his shoulder, like he was wearin a cap on sideways. He takes the shortcut through the pecan grove, and the sound of twigs snapping overhead and underfoot travels clear and cold all the way up to us. And here comes Smilin and Camera up behind him like they was goin to do somethin. Folks like to go for him sometimes. Cathy say it's because he's so tall and quiet and like a king. And people just can't stand it. But Smilin and Camera don't hit him in the head or nuthin. They just buzz on him as he **stalks** by with the chicken hawk slung over his shoulder, squawkin, drippin red down the back of the oilskin. He passes the porch and stops a second for Granny to see he's caught the hawk at last, but she's just starin and mumblin, and not at the hawk. So he nails the bird to the toolshed door, the hammerin crackin through the eardrums. And the bird flappin himself to death and droolin down the door to paint the gravel in the driveway red, then brown, then black. And the two men movin up on tiptoe like they was invisible or we were blind, one.

**Literary Analysis**
**Dialogue and Dialect**
What does the idiom "gone upside her head" probably mean?

**Vocabulary**
**stalks** (stôks) *v.* walks in a stiff, haughty, or grim manner

Reading Check
What does Granddaddy do with the hawk?

**Vocabulary**
**formality** (fôr mal´ ə tē)
*n.* attention to estab-
lished rules or customs
**reckless** (rek´ lis) *adj.*
careless; rash

**Reading Skill**
**Cause and Effect**
How does the arrival
of the screaming hawk
affect the film crew?
How does it affect
Granddaddy Cain?

"Get them persons out of my flower bed, Mister Cain," say Granny moanin real low like at a funeral.

"How come your grandmother calls her husband 'Mister Cain' all the time?" Tyrone whispers all loud and noisy and from the city and don't know no better. Like his mama, Miss Myrtle, tell us never mind the formality as if we had no better breeding than to call her Myrtle, plain. And then this awful thing—a giant hawk—come wailin up over the meadow, flyin low and tilted and screamin, zigzaggin through the pecan grove, breakin branches and hollerin, snappin past the clothesline, flyin every which way, flyin into things reckless with crazy.

"He's come to claim his mate," say Cathy fast, and ducks down. We all fall quick and flat into the gravel driveway, stones scrapin my face. I squinch my eyes open again at the hawk on the door, tryin to fly up out of her death like it was just a sack flown into by mistake. Her body holdin her there on that nail, though. The mate beatin the air overhead and clutchin for hair, for heads, for landin space.

The camera man duckin and bendin and runnin and fallin, jigglin the camera and scared. And Smilin jumpin up and down swipin at the huge bird, tryin to bring the hawk down with just his raggedy ole cap. Granddaddy Cain straight up and silent, watchin the circles of the hawk, then aimin the hammer off his wrist. The giant bird fallin, silent and slow. Then here comes Camera and Smilin all big and bad now that the awful screechin thing is on its back and broken, here they come. And Granddaddy Cain looks up at them like it was the first time noticin, but not payin them too much mind cause he's listenin, we all listenin, to that low groanin music comin from the porch. And we figure any minute, somethin in my back tells me any minute now, Granny gonna bust through that screen with somethin in her hand and murder on her mind. So Granddaddy say above the buzzin, but quiet, "Good day, gentlemen." Just like that. Like he'd invited them in to play cards and they'd stayed too long and all the sandwiches were gone and Reverend Webb was droppin by and it was time to go.

They didn't know what to do. But like Cathy say, folks can't stand Granddaddy tall and silent and like a king. They can't neither. The smile the men smilin is pullin the mouth back and showin the teeth. Lookin like the wolf man, both of them. Then Granddaddy holds his hand out—this huge hand I used to sit in when I was a baby and he'd carry me through the house to my mother like I was a gift on a tray. Like he used to on the trains. They called the other men just waiters. But they spoke of Granddaddy separate and said, The Waiter. And said he had engines in his feet and motors in his hands and couldn't no train throw him off and couldn't nobody turn him round. They were big enough for motors, his hands were. He held that one hand out all still and it gettin to be not at all a hand but a person in itself.

"He wants you to hand him the camera," Smilin whispers to Camera, tiltin his head to talk secret like they was in the jungle or somethin and come upon a native that don't speak the language. The men start untyin the straps, and they put the camera into that great hand speckled with the hawk's blood all black and crackly now. And the hand don't even drop with the weight, just the fingers move, curl up around the machine. But Granddaddy lookin straight at the men. They lookin at each other and everywhere but at Granddaddy's face.

"We filmin for the county, see," say Smilin. "We puttin together a movie for the food stamp program . . . filmin all around these parts. Uhh, filmin for the county."

"Can I have my camera back?" say the tall man with no machine on his shoulder, but still keepin it high like the camera was still there or needed to be. "Please, sir."

Then Granddaddy's other hand flies up like a sudden and gentle bird, slaps down fast on top of the camera and lifts off half like it was a calabash[1] cut for sharing.

"Hey," Camera jumps forward. He gathers up the parts into his chest and everything unrollin and fallin all over. "Whatcha tryin to do? You'll ruin the film." He looks down into his chest of metal **reels** and things like he's protectin a kitten from the cold.

"You standin in the misses' flower bed," say Granddaddy. "This is our own place."

The two men look at him, then at each other, then back at the mess in the camera man's chest, and they just back off. One sayin over and over all the way down to the meadow, "Watch it, Bruno. Keep ya fingers off the film." Then Granddaddy picks up the hammer and jams it into the oilskin pocket, scrapes his boots, and goes into the house. And you can hear the squish of his boots

1. **calabash** (kal´ ə bash´) *n.* large gourd-like fruit.

**Vocabulary**
**reels** (rēlz) *n.* frames or spools on which thread, wire, tape, film, or a net is wound

Reading Check

How does Granddaddy Cain react to the camera men's visit?

**Reading Skill**
**Cause and Effect**
In what way does visualizing this scene help you understand the effects of Granddaddy's action?

headin through the house. And you can see the funny shadow he throws from the parlor window onto the ground by the string-bean patch. The hammer draggin the pocket of the oilskin out so Granddaddy looked even wider. Granny was hummin now—high not low and grumbly. And she was doin the cakes again, you could smell the molasses from the rum.

"There's this story I'm goin to write one day," say Cathy dreamer. "About the proper use of the hammer."

"Can I be in it?" Tyrone say with his hand up like it was a matter of first come, first served.

"Perhaps," say Cathy, climbin onto the tire to pump us up. "If you there and ready."

## Critical Thinking

**Cite textual evidence to support your responses.**

1. **Key Ideas and Details (a)** Why are the photographers filming in the area? **(b) Infer:** What message does Granny give the men through her speech and actions?

2. **Key Ideas and Details** Make a chart like the one shown below. **(a) Compare:** In the first column, write the ways that Camera and Smilin are like the hawks. **(b) Connect:** In the second column, write the ways that Granddaddy's actions are like the actions of the male hawk.

3. **Integration of Knowledge and Ideas Discuss:** Share your chart with a partner, and discuss your responses. Then, in the third column, explain whether you think the hawks represent Granddaddy and Granny, Smilin and Camera, or both pairs.

| Hawks and Camera and Smilin | Hawks and Granddaddy | What the Hawks Represent |
|---|---|---|
|  |  |  |

4. **Integration of Knowledge and Ideas (a)** Why does Granddaddy become involved in the story's conflict? **(b)** Why is his way of handling the conflict successful, when Granny's is not? *[Connect to the Big Question: Is conflict necessary?]*

## Literary Analysis: Dialogue and Dialect

© **1. Key Ideas and Details** Identify one example of **dialogue** that indicates the tension is increasing between Granny and the filmmakers.

© **2. Key Ideas and Details** Identify one example of dialogue that shows Granny is tough.

© **3. Craft and Structure (a)** Explain how the spelling and grammar used in the following passage indicate that it is an example of **dialect.** "Granny always got somethin to say. She teaches steady with no let-up." **(b)** Rewrite the passage in Standard English. **(c)** Explain how the use of dialect makes the characters and setting more vivid.

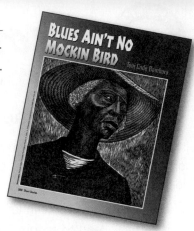

## Reading Skill: Cause and Effect

**4. (a)** What is the **cause** of Granddaddy's decision to disassemble the men's camera? **(b)** What is the **effect** of Granddaddy's action on the cameramen? **(c)** What is the effect on Granny?

**5.** Which visual details in the story help you explain the causes and effects of Granddaddy's decision to ruin the film?

## Vocabulary

© **Acquisition and Use** In vocabulary study, **analogies** show the relationships between pairs of words. Use a word from the "Blues Ain't No Mockin Bird" vocabulary list on page 348 to complete each analogy. In each, your choice should create a word pair that matches the relationship between the first two words given. Explain the relationship that the pairs in each set share.

**1.** solution : intelligent :: accident : _____

**2.** sportsmanship : game :: _____ : ceremony

**3.** fork : meat :: _____ : soup

**4.** frowns : scowls :: walks : _____

**5.** powerful : weak :: unworn : _____

**6.** carton : eggs :: _____ : film

**Word Study** Use the context of the sentences and what you know about the **Latin suffix -ity** to explain your answer to each question.

**1.** If a plan is referred to as a *possibility,* might it be used?

**2.** When people take a *sensitivity* training class, what do they learn?

# Is *conflict* necessary?

## Writing About the Big Question

In "The Invalid's Story," the two main characters try to resolve a problem but do not have all the facts. Use these sentence starters to develop your ideas about the Big Question.

Lack of information can lead to a humorous conflict because _____.

It can also lead to serious **issues** and sometimes **controversy** because _____.

**While You Read** Look for ways in which the lack of information makes the problem more intense—and funnier—as time passes.

## Vocabulary

Read each word and its definition. Decide whether you know the word well, know it a little bit, or do not know it at all. After you read, see how your knowledge of each word has increased.

- **prodigious** (prō dij´ əs) *adj.* enormous (p. 364) *The Grand Canyon is a <u>prodigious</u> natural wonder.* *prodigiously adv. prodigiousness n.*

- **deleterious** (del´ ə tir´ ē əs) *adj.* harmful to health or well-being (p. 365) *Too much sun can be <u>deleterious</u> to one's skin.* *deleteriously adv. deleteriousness n.*

- **ominous** (äm´ ə nəs) *adj.* threatening (p. 365) *The black storm clouds coming from the West were <u>ominous</u>.* *ominously adv. ominousness n. omen n.*

- **judicious** (jōō dish´ əs) *adj.* showing good judgment (p. 366) *Her decision to stay indoors during the storm was <u>judicious</u>.* *judiciously adv. judiciousness n. judge n. judge v.*

- **placidly** (plas´ id lē) *adv.* calmly; quietly (p. 366) *He smiled <u>placidly</u>, content with his own thoughts.* *placid adj. placidity n.*

- **desultory** (des´ əl tôr´ ē) *adj.* random (p. 367) *They wandered through the park in a <u>desultory</u> way, with no clear destination.* *desultorily adv.*

### Word Study

The **Latin suffix -ous** (or **-ious** or **-uous**) forms adjectives. It means "like" or "pertaining to."

In this story, the narrator talks about "an **ominous** stillness." The stillness feels like an omen, something that foretells a future danger.

# Meet
# Mark Twain
### (1835–1910)

## Author of
# The Invalid's Story

Born Samuel Clemens, Mark Twain grew up in the Mississippi River town of Hannibal, Missouri. He worked as a riverboat pilot, printer, prospector, reporter, and at many other jobs. Primarily, however, Clemens was a writer of comic stories, sketches, and novels. The most famous humorist of his day, he traveled the world entertaining people with his witty lectures.

**"By the mark—twain"** was a cry heard on the riverboats of Clemens's youth. It meant that the water was two fathoms deep—deep enough for a riverboat to pass unharmed. Harkening back to his youth working on those boats, Clemens took the name Mark Twain at age twenty-seven. Under that name, he wrote some of the most beloved fiction in American literature.

## BACKGROUND FOR THE STORY
### Nineteenth-Century Train Travel

In the late nineteenth century, when this story takes place, trains were the fastest way to travel and transport cargo. Nonetheless, train cars in which people with cargo had to travel were uncomfortable. The cars were poorly ventilated boxes on wheels, and had only small windows.

## Did You Know?
Mark Twain was the first writer to turn himself into a business. He even trademarked his name!

# The Invalid's Story

## Mark Twain

I seem sixty and married, but these effects are due to my condition and sufferings, for I am a bachelor, and only forty-one. It will be hard for you to believe that I, who am now but a shadow, was a hale, hearty man two short years ago—a man of iron, a very athlete!—yet such is the simple truth. But stranger still than this fact is the way in which I lost my health. I lost it through helping to take care of a box of guns on a two-hundred-mile railway journey one winter's night. It is the actual truth, and I will tell you about it.

I belong in Cleveland, Ohio. One winter's night, two years ago, I reached home just after dark, in a driving snowstorm, and the first thing I heard when I entered the house was that my dearest boyhood friend and schoolmate, John B. Hackett, had died the day before, and that his last utterance had been a desire that I would take his remains home to his poor old father and mother in Wisconsin. I was greatly shocked and grieved, but there was no time to waste in emotions; I must start at once. I took the card, marked "Deacon Levi Hackett, Bethlehem, Wisconsin," and hurried off through the whistling storm to the railway station. Arrived there I found the long white-pine box which had been described to me; I fastened the card to it with some tacks, saw it put safely aboard the express car, and then ran into the eating room to provide myself with a sandwich and some cigars. When I returned, presently, there was my coffin-box back again, apparently, and a young fellow examining around it, with a card in his hands, and some tacks and

**Reading Check**

What was John B. Hackett's dying wish?

**Vocabulary**
**prodigious** (prō dij´
əs) *adj.* enormous

a hammer! I was astonished and puzzled. He began to nail on his card, and I rushed out to the express car, in a good deal of a state of mind, to ask for an explanation. But no—there was my box, all right, in the express car; it hadn't been disturbed. [The fact is that without my suspecting it a prodigious mistake had been made. I was carrying off a box of guns which that young fellow had come to the station to ship to a rifle company in Peoria, Illinois, and he had got my corpse.] Just then the conductor sang out "All aboard," and I jumped into the express car and got a comfortable seat on a bale of buckets. The expressman was there, hard at work—a plain man of fifty, with a simple, honest, good-natured face, and a breezy, practical heartiness in his general style. As the train moved off a stranger skipped into the car and set a package of peculiarly mature and capable Limburger cheese[1] on one end of my coffin-box—I mean my box of guns. That is to say, I know now that it was Limburger cheese, but at that time I never had heard of the article in my life, and of course was wholly ignorant of its character. Well, we sped through the wild night, the bitter storm raged on, a cheerless misery stole over me, my heart went down, down, down! The old expressman made a brisk remark or two about the tempest and the arctic weather, slammed his sliding doors to, and bolted them, closed his window down tight, and then went bustling around, here and there and yonder, setting things to rights, and all the time contentedly humming "Sweet By and By" in a low tone, and flatting a good deal. Presently I began to detect a most evil and searching odor stealing about on the frozen air. This depressed my spirits still more, because of course I attributed it to my poor departed friend. There was something infinitely saddening about his calling himself to my remembrance in this dumb, pathetic way, so it was hard to

▶ **Critical Viewing**
This potbellied stove would have been found in a train car in the late 1800s. What challenges did train travel pose at that time in history?
**[Analyze]**

---

1. **Limburger cheese** cheese with a strong odor.

keep the tears back. Moreover, it distressed me on account of the old expressman, who, I was afraid, might notice it. However, he went humming tranquilly on, and gave no sign; and for this I was grateful. Grateful, yes, but still uneasy; and soon I began to feel more and more uneasy every minute, for every minute that went by that odor thickened up the more, and got to be more and more gamy and hard to stand. Presently, having got things arranged to his satisfaction, the expressman got some wood and made up a tremendous fire in his stove. This distressed me more than I can tell, for I could not but feel that it was a mistake. I was sure that the effect would be deleterious upon my poor departed friend. Thompson—the expressman's name was Thompson, as I found out in the course of the night—now went poking around his car, stopping up whatever stray cracks he could find, remarking that it didn't make any difference what kind of a night it was outside, he calculated to make us comfortable, anyway. I said nothing, but I believed he was not choosing the right way. Meantime he was humming to himself just as before; and meantime, too, the stove was getting hotter and hotter, and the place closer and closer. I felt myself growing pale and qualmish,[2] but grieved in silence and said nothing. Soon I noticed that the "Sweet By and By" was gradually fading out; next it ceased altogether, and there was an ominous stillness. After a few moments Thompson said—

"Pfew! I reckon it ain't no cinnamon't I've loaded up thish-year stove with!"

He gasped once or twice, then moved toward the cof—gun-box, stood over that Limburger cheese part of a moment, then came back and sat down near me, looking a good deal impressed. After a contemplative pause, he said, indicating the box with a gesture—

"Friend of yourn?"

"Yes," I said with a sigh.

"He's pretty ripe, ain't he!"

> ## "Pfew! I reckon it ain't no cinnamon't I've loaded up thish-year stove with!"

Nothing further was said for perhaps a couple of minutes, each being busy with his own thoughts; then Thompson said, in a low awed voice—

"Sometimes it's uncertain whether they're really gone or not— seem gone, you know—body warm, joints limber—and so, although you think they're gone, you don't really

---

2. **qualmish** (kwäm´ ish) *adj.* suddenly sick.

**Vocabulary**
**deleterious** (del´ ə tir´ ē əs) *adj.* harmful to health or well-being

**Vocabulary**
**ominous** (äm´ ə nəs) *adj.* threatening

**Reading Skill**
**Cause and Effect**
When you picture this scene, what details explain the cause of Thompson's gasp?

Reading Check
What does the narrator say depressed his spirits?

know. I've had cases in my car. It's perfectly awful, becuz you don't know what minute they'll rise up and look at you!" Then, after a pause, and slightly lifting his elbow toward the box,—"But he ain't in no trance! No, sir, I go bail for him!"

We sat some time, in meditative silence, listening to the wind and the roar of the train; then Thompson said, with a good deal of feeling:

"Well-a-well, we've all got to go, they ain't no getting around it. Man that is born of woman is of few days and far between, as Scriptur'[3] says. Yes, you look at it any way you want to, it's awful solemn and cur'us: they ain't nobody can get around it; all's got to go—just everybody, as you may say. One day you're hearty and strong"—here he scrambled to his feet and broke a pane and stretched his nose out at it a moment or two, then sat down again while I struggled up and thrust my nose out at the same place, and this we kept on doing every now and then—"and next day he's cut down like the grass, and the places which knowed him then knows him no more forever, as Scriptur' says. Yes'ndeedy, it's awful solemn and cur'us; but we've all got to go, one time or another; they ain't no getting around it."

There was another long pause; then—

"What did he die of?"

I said I didn't know.

"How long has he ben dead?"

It seemed judicious to enlarge the facts to fit the probabilities; so I said:

"Two or three days."

But it did no good: for Thompson received it with an injured look which plainly said, "Two or three years, you mean." Then he went right along, placidly ignoring my statement, and gave his views at considerable length upon the unwisdom of putting off burials too long. Then he lounged off toward the box, stood a moment, then came back on a sharp trot and visited the broken pane, observing:

"'Twould 'a' ben a durn sight better, all around, if they'd started him along last summer."

Thompson sat down and buried his face in his red silk handkerchief, and began to slowly sway and rock his body like one who is doing his best to endure the almost unendurable. By this

**Spiral Review**
**Character** What do you learn about Thompson's view of life, based on his comments to the narrator?

**Vocabulary**
**judicious** (jo͞o dish´ əs) *adj.* showing good judgment

**placidly** (plas´ id lē) *adv.* calmly; quietly

...he scrambled to his feet and broke a pane and stretched his nose out at it a moment or two...

3. **Scriptur'** scripture; the Bible.

time the fragrance—if you may call it fragrance—was just about suffocating, as near as you can come at it. Thompson's face was turning gray: I knew mine hadn't any color left in it. By and by Thompson rested his forehead in his left hand, with his elbow on his knee, and sort of waved his red handkerchief toward the box with his other hand, and said:

"I've carried a many a one of 'em—some of 'em considerable overdue, too—but, lordy, he just lays over 'em all!—and does it easy. Cap, they was heliotrope[4] to him!"

This recognition of my poor friend gratified me, in spite of the sad circumstances, because it had so much the sound of a compliment.

Pretty soon it was plain that something had got to be done. I suggested cigars. Thompson thought it was a good idea. He said:

"Likely it'll modify him some."

We puffed gingerly along for a while, and tried hard to imagine that things were improved. But it wasn't any use. Before very long, and without any consultation, both cigars were quietly dropped from our nerveless fingers at the same moment. Thompson said, with a sigh:

"No, Cap, it don't modify him worth a cent. Fact is, it makes him worse, becuz it appears to stir up his ambition. What do you reckon we better do, now?"

I was not able to suggest anything: indeed, I had to be swallowing and swallowing all the time, and did not like to trust myself to speak. Thompson fell to maundering, in a desultory and low-spirited way, about the miserable experiences of this night: and he got to referring to my poor friend by various titles—sometimes military ones, sometimes civil ones; and I noticed that as fast as my poor friend's effectiveness grew, Thompson promoted him accordingly—gave him a bigger title. Finally he said:

"I've got an idea. Suppos'n' we buckle down to it and give the Colonel a bit of a shove toward t'other end of the car?—about ten foot, say. He wouldn't have so much influence, then, don't you reckon?"

I said it was a good scheme. So we took in a good fresh breath at the broken pane, calculating to hold it till we got through: then we went there and bent over that deadly cheese and took a grip on the box. Thompson nodded "All ready," and then we threw ourselves forward with all our might: but Thompson slipped, and slumped down with his nose on the cheese, and his breath got loose. He gagged and gasped, and floundered up and made a break for the door, pawing the air and saying hoarsely, "Don't hender me!—

---

4. **heliotrope** (hē´ lē ə trōp´) *n.* a sweet-smelling plant.

**Literary Analysis**
**Dialogue and Dialect** Which features of Thompson's speech in this passage reflect a particular dialect?

**Vocabulary**
**desultory**
(des´ əl tôr´ ē)
*adj.* random

Reading Check
How do the men use the window to lessen the effect of the odor?

### Cultural Connection

**Limburger Cheese**
The foul stench that torments the narrator and Thompson comes from a package of Limburger cheese. This cheese was first made in Belgium and is now made in Germany and in the United States. It is notorious for its strong odor. The cheese is made from cow's milk and is "ripened" for about three months under specially controlled conditions. This ripening process gives Limburger cheese its distinctive smell and flavor. The cheese continues to ripen during shipping and its odor can become extremely intense.

### Connect to the Literature

Why do you think the narrator and Thompson are so confused about the source of the smell in the train car?

gimme the road! I'm a-dying; gimme the road!" Out on the cold platform I sat down and held his head awhile, and he revived. Presently he said:

"Do you reckon we started the Gen'rul any?"

I said no: we hadn't budged him.

"Well, then, that idea's up the flume. We got to think up something else. He's suited wher' he is, I reckon; and if that's the way he feels about it, and has made up his mind that he don't wish to be disturbed, you bet he's a-going to have his own way in the business. Yes, better leave him right wher' he is, long as he wants it so; becuz he holds all the trumps, don't you know, and so it stands to reason that the man that lays out to alter his plans for him is going to get left."

But we couldn't stay out there in that mad storm; we should have frozen to death. So we went in again and shut the door, and began to suffer once more and take turns at the break in the window. By and by, as we were starting away from a station where we had stopped a moment Thompson pranced in cheerily, and exclaimed:

"We're all right, now! I reckon we've got the Commodore this time. I judge I've got the stuff here that'll take the tuck out of him."

It was carbolic acid. He had a carboy of it. He sprinkled it all around everywhere; in fact he drenched everything with it, rifle-box, cheese and all. Then we sat down, feeling pretty hopeful. But it wasn't for long. You see the two perfumes began to mix, and then—well, pretty soon we made a break for the door; and out there Thompson swabbed his face with his bandanna and said in a kind of disheartened way:

"It ain't no use. We can't buck agin him. He just utilizes everything we put up to modify him with, and gives it his own flavor and plays it back on us. Why, Cap, don't you know, it's as much as a hundred times worse in there now than it was when he first got a-going. I never did see one of 'em warm up to his work so, and take such a dumnation interest in it. No, sir, I never did, as long as I've ben on the road: and I've carried a many a one of 'em, as I was telling you."

We went in again after we were frozen pretty stiff; but my, we couldn't stay in, now. So we just waltzed back and forth, freezing, and thawing, and stifling, by turns. In about an hour we stopped at another station; and as we left it Thompson came in with a bag, and said—

"Cap, I'm a-going to chance him once more—just this once; and if we don't fetch him this time, the thing for us to do, is to just throw up the sponge and withdraw from the canvass. That's the way I put it up." •

He had brought a lot of chicken feathers, and dried apples, and leaf tobacco, and rags, and old shoes, and sulphur, and asafetida, and one thing or another: and he piled them on a breadth of sheet iron in the middle of the floor, and set fire to them.

When they got well started, I couldn't see, myself, how even the corpse could stand it. All that went before was just simply poetry to that smell—but mind you, the original smell stood up out of it just as sublime as ever—fact is, these other smells just seemed to give it a better hold: and my, how rich it was! I didn't make these reflections there—there wasn't time—made them on the platform. And breaking for the platform, Thompson got suffocated and

**Reading Skill**
**Cause and Effect**
What is the result of Thompson's final attempt to deal with the odor?

But we couldn't stay out there in that mad storm; we should have frozen to death.

fell: and before I got him dragged out, which I did by the collar, I was mighty near gone myself. When we revived, Thompson said dejectedly:

"We got to stay out here, Cap. We got to do it. They ain't no other way. The Governor wants to travel alone, and he's fixed so he can outvote us."

And presently he added:

"And don't you know, we're pisoned. It's our last trip, you can make up your mind to it. Typhoid fever is what's going to come of this. I feel it a-coming right now. Yes, sir, we're elected, just as sure as you're born."

We were taken from the platform an hour later, frozen and insensible, at the next station, and I went straight off into a virulent fever, and never knew anything again for three weeks. I found out, then, that I had spent that awful night with a harmless box of rifles and a lot of innocent cheese; but the news was too late to save me; imagination had done its work, and my health was permanently shattered; neither Bermuda nor any other land can ever bring it back to me. This is my last trip; I am on my way home to die.

**Reading Skill**
**Cause and Effect**
What effect does the experience on the train have on the narrator's health?

## Critical Thinking

1. **Key Ideas and Details (a)** What do the men believe is creating the awful smell? **(b) Connect:** What is actually creating the smell?

2. **Key Ideas and Details Compare and Contrast:** In what ways does the contrast between what the men think is true and what is really true contribute to the humor?

3. **Key Ideas and Details** Make a chart with three columns. **(a) Compare:** In the first column, write a list of sad details in the story. **(b) Connect:** In the second column, write the details that add humor to the story. **(c) Discuss and Evaluate:** Share your chart with a partner and discuss your responses. Then, in the third column, explain whether you think the story is sad, funny, or both.

4. **Integration of Knowledge and Ideas (a)** For the story to be funny, why is it critical that the narrator doesn't have all the information? **(b)** If this conflict were avoided, what would be the effect on the story? *[Connect to the Big Question: Is conflict necessary?]*

Cite textual evidence to support your responses.

| **The Invalid's Story**

## Literary Analysis: Dialogue and Dialect

© **1. Key Ideas and Details** Identify one example of **dialogue** in the story that indicates the smell is increasing. Explain your choice.

© **2. Key Ideas and Details** Identify an example of dialogue that shows that Thompson and the narrator do not know each other well. Explain your choice.

© **3. Craft and Structure (a)** In what way do the spelling, grammar, and words used in this passage indicate it is an example of **dialect?**

"No, Cap, it don't modify him worth a cent. Fact is, it makes him worse, becuz it appears to stir up his ambition. What do you reckon we better do, now?"

**(b)** Rewrite the passage in Standard English. **(c)** Explain how the use of dialect makes the characters and setting more vivid.

## Reading Skill: Cause and Effect

**4. (a)** What is the **cause** of the smell in the express car? **(b)** What **effect** does the smell have on Thompson and the narrator?

**5.** Which visual details in the story help you to explain why the characters are mistaken about the true cause of the smell?

## Vocabulary

© **Acquisition and Use** In vocabulary study, **analogies** show the relationships between pairs of words. Use a word from the vocabulary list on page 360 to complete each analogy so that the relationship in the second pair of words matches that in the first pair. Explain the relationships.

**1.** comedy : humorous :: measles : _____

**2.** graceful : clumsy :: _____ : foolish

**3.** tiny : small :: _____ : large

**4.** systematic : reliable :: _____ : unpredictable

**5.** violently : angry :: _____ : content

**6.** praise : joyful :: warning : _____

**Word Study** Use the context of the sentences and what you know about the **Latin suffix -ous** (or **-ious** or **-uous**) to explain your answers.

**1.** If a sport is *hazardous,* could you be seriously hurt playing it?

**2.** How do most people react to *ridiculous* events?

### Word Study

The **Latin suffix -ous** (or **-ious** or **-uous**) means "like" or "pertaining to."

**Apply It** Explain how the suffix **-ous** contributes to the meanings of these words. You may consult a dictionary if necessary.

**glorious**
**mysterious**
**tumultuous**

# Integrated Language Skills

## Blues Ain't No Mockin Bird • The Invalid's Story

### Conventions: Active and Passive Voice

A verb in the **active voice** expresses an action done **by** its subject.

A verb in the **passive voice** expresses an action done **to** its subject.

The "voice" of a verb tells whether the subject *performs* an action (active voice) or *receives* an action (passive voice).

| Active Voice | Passive Voice |
|---|---|
| Bambara and Twain have written stories about memorable conflicts. (The subjects, *Bambara* and *Twain*, perform the action of the verb, *have written*.) | Stories about memorable conflicts have been written by Bambara and Twain. (The subject, *stories*, receives the action of the verb, *have been written*.) |

Use the active voice for lively, direct writing. Use the passive voice to de-emphasize the performer of the action or when the performer is unknown.

**Practice A** Identify the verb or verb phrase in each sentence. Tell whether the writer has used the active voice or the passive voice.

1. Granny is bothered by the unwelcome visitors.

2. She watches them in angry silence.

3. Granddaddy Cain greets Camera and Smilin.

4. They are frightened by his size and power.

**Ⓒ Writing Application** Rewrite the sentences in Practice A. If the verb is in the active voice, use the passive voice. If the verb is in the passive voice, use the active voice. Explain the effect of each change.

**Practice B** Rewrite the following sentences using the active voice. You may need to add words to indicate who performed the action.

1. The cheese had been placed on the box.

2. "The Invalid's Story" was written by Mark Twain.

3. The coffin was sent to Wisconsin by train.

4. A foul odor was detected by the narrator.

**Ⓒ Speaking Application** Look at the image on page 369 of "The Invalid's Story." Write four sentences based on this image, using the active voice twice and the passive voice twice. With a partner, discuss which sentences are more effective and why.

**PH WRITING COACH**  Further instruction and practice are available in *Prentice Hall Writing Coach*.

# Writing

**Common Core State Standards**

L.9-10.1, L.9-10.6; W.9-10.3.a.; SL.9-10.4
[For the full wording of the standards, see page 346.]

**Narrative Text** Write an **informal letter** from the point of view of a character in "Blues Ain't No Mockin Bird" or "The Invalid's Story." Choose a character who is not the narrator.

- Before writing, list the personality traits of your character.

- Write to a friend or relative, describing the story events and their significance from your character's point of view.

- Refer to your list as you write. Make sure that your details and language are consistent with the traits that you listed.

**Grammar Application** Check your letter to be sure that you have used active voice whenever possible.

## Writing Workshop: *Work in Progress*

**Prewriting for Exposition: Cause-and-Effect Essay** Review the "What's the Cause?" list in your writing portfolio. Highlight the effect that interests you the most. Then, list several questions to help you define the cause for this effect. Save this Highlighted Cause List.

Use this prewriting activity to prepare for the **Writing Workshop** on page 402.

# Speaking and Listening

**Presentation of Ideas** In both of these stories, dialogue and dialect are important elements. With a partner, prepare and deliver a **dialogue.**

- If you read "Blues Ain't No Mockin Bird," have Camera and Smilin discuss their experience with Granny and Granddaddy.

- If you read "The Invalid's Story," have the narrator discuss his "shattered" health with a doctor.

Follow these steps to complete the assignment:

- Decide what the dialogue will reveal about the story events and the personalities of the speakers.

- Outline a "plot." Decide how the dialogue should begin and end. Choose at least one event for the middle of the dialogue (for example, having a character re-enact an important moment from the story). Build the dialogue around that "plot."

- Use language that is appropriate to the characters' situations and personalities, but be polite.

- After you have presented your dialogue, invite questions from the audience. If you wish, answer in character.

**PHLit Online!**
www.PHLitOnline.com
- Interactive graphic organizers
- Grammar tutorial
- Interactive journals

# Test Practice: Reading

## Cause and Effect

### Fiction Selection

**Directions:** *Read the selection. Then, answer the questions.*

Just before the bell, Jeff stumbled into math class. Maya watched with concern as he plopped into his seat and wearily rubbed his face. Throughout the class, Jeff kept pinching himself to stay awake. Afterward, Maya confronted him, wanting to know what was wrong. Jeff sighed. "I wouldn't admit this to just anyone, Maya, but since you're my best friend . . . It's this science project. My partner isn't doing his share of the work, and I can't let his laziness hurt my grade. To make things worse, the topic we picked is a lot harder than we'd planned. I've had only three hours of sleep each night this week, and I'm feeling pretty sick."

**1.** Jeff pinches himself during math class in order to—

    **A.** attract Maya's attention.
    **B.** keep himself from falling asleep.
    **C.** prevent himself from getting sick.
    **D.** receive a warning from the teacher.

**2.** Which of the following statements is *not* a cause of Jeff's poor condition?

    **A.** He has failed to get approval for an easier science project.
    **B.** His science partner is not doing an equal share of work.
    **C.** He has experienced a lack of sleep for several nights in a row.
    **D.** He is worried about getting a good grade in science.

**3.** Jeff decides to explain his dilemma to Maya because he—

    **A.** wants her help with the science project.
    **B.** wants to ask her on a date.
    **C.** needs her to take him to the school nurse.
    **D.** trusts her as his closest friend.

**4.** Jeff believes that not spending extra time on his science project will result in which of the following effects?

    **A.** His science partner will get all the credit for the work.
    **B.** He will look foolish to his classmates.
    **C.** His teacher will not give him a good grade.
    **D.** He will have to repeat the class in summer school.

### Writing for Assessment

In a paragraph, explain why Jeff is upset and having trouble sleeping. Use details from the passage to support your answer.

# Nonfiction Selection

**Directions:** *Read the selection. Then, answer the questions.*

If you have trouble sleeping, you are in good company: About 50 million American adults suffer from sleep deprivation. Some causes, such as drinking caffeine in the evening, are avoidable. Certain medical conditions, such as asthma and depression, can interfere with sleep—and so can some medications. Sleep deprivation is something you should take seriously. It can leave you without the energy or physical strength to meet the day's demands. You may find it harder to think clearly, to solve problems, or to remember things, too. Irritability, moodiness, and anxiety often can be traced to a lack of sleep.

**1.** Based on the passage, what is *not* usually a cause of sleep deprivation?

   **A.** depression

   **B.** consuming caffeinated products

   **C.** consuming dairy products

   **D.** some medications

**2.** According to the passage, which cause-and-effect relationship is correct?

   **A.** Irritability causes sleep problems.

   **B.** Too much sleep may cause memory problems.

   **C.** Asthma may interfere with sleep.

   **D.** Sleeping less can give you more energy.

**3.** The passage explains that sleep deprivation may result in—

   **A.** moodiness and an inability to solve problems.

   **B.** asthma and emotional irritability.

   **C.** weight loss and anxiety.

   **D.** anxiety and an increased need for medication.

**4.** Which of the following statements *best* describes one way to avoid sleep deprivation?

   **A.** Discontinue all prescription medications.

   **B.** Take sleeping pills and high-potency vitamins.

   **C.** Stop drinking caffeinated soda in the evening.

   **D.** Spend time exercising just before bedtime.

## Writing for Assessment

**Connecting Across Texts**

In the first passage, Jeff experiences sleep deprivation. Think about the causes and effects of sleep deprivation. In a short paragraph, give Jeff advice about what he might do. Use details from both passages to support your response.

www.PHLitOnline.com
- Online practice
- Instant feedback

# Reading for Information

## Analyzing Functional Texts

**User Guide**

**Application**

**Common Core State Standards**

**Language**

**4.c.** Consult general and specialized reference materials, both print and digital, to find the pronunciation of a word or determine or clarify its precise meaning, its part of speech, or its etymology.

**6.** Acquire and use accurately grade-appropriate general academic and domain-specific words and phrases; demonstrate independence in gathering vocabulary knowledge when considering a word or phrase important to comprehension or expression.

## Reading Skills: Analyze Structure and Format

Dictionaries, applications, and other **functional** texts often use headings, labels, graphics, and other features to set off specific types of information. These documents are functional because they provide information to help people perform tasks. When working with such documents, **analyze structure and format** by identifying their text features and considering how they clarify information. The questions in this chart can help you locate and understand text features in functional documents. Think about how these features help the author convey information clearly.

| Questions to Ask About Structure and Format |
| --- |
| Are there special instructions or information? |
| What are the main headings on the page? |
| How is certain information labeled or highlighted? |
| What features have been pointed out? Why? |

### Content-Area Vocabulary

These words appear in the selections that follow. You may also encounter them in other content-area texts.

- **homographs** (hom´ ə grafs) *n.* words that are spelled the same way but have different meanings

- **idiomatic** (id´ ē ə mat´ ik) *adj.* typical of the natural way in which people using their own language speak or write

- **certifications** (sér´ tə fə kā´ shənz) *n.* official documents that state that people are qualified and allowed to do certain jobs

# Spanish-English Dictionary User Guide

User Guide

**Features:**

- explanations of word meanings
- a pronunciation key
- labeled features of entries
- explanations of abbreviations

In these bilingual dictionary entries, Spanish words are formatted in bold type to make them easy to find.

**Gender**

**American use**

**Keyword**

**apartamento,** *n.m.* flat, (*Am.*) apartment.

**casar** (1), *v.t.* to marry, mate, couple, unite in marriage, join in wedlock; (*fig.*) to join, unite; to suit, match (*things* or *colours*); (*paint.*) to blend; (*typ.*) to impose; *casar una cosa con otra,* to match one thing with another. — **casar(se),** *v.i.* (*v.r.*) to marry, get married, wed; *casarse por poderes,* to marry by proxy; *antes que te cases, mira lo que haces,* look before you leap; *casarse en segundas nupcias,* to remarry.

**casar** (2), *v.t.* (*law*) to annul, abrogate, repeal.

**casar** (3), *n.m.* hamlet, small village.

**Homographs**

**Feminine forms**

**hito, -ta,** *a.* adjoining (*house* or *street*); firm, fixed; black (*horse*); — *n.m.* boundary mark; landmark; milestone; hob and quoits; (*artill.*) target; *a hito,* fixedly, firmly; *dar en el hito,* to hit the nail on the head; *mirar de hito en hito,* to look up and down. — *n.f.* headless nail, brad.

**Translation**

**horma,** *n.f.* form, mould; boot-tree, shoe-tree, shoemaker's last; block, hatter's block; (*mas.*) dry wall; (*Cub.*, *Per.*) sugar-loaf mould; (*coll.*) *hallar la horma de su zapato,* to meet one's match or Waterloo.

**medir** [8], *v.t.*, *v.i.* to measure; to scan. — **medirse,** *v.r.* to act with moderation.

**Figurative expressions**

**Examples of use**

**Specialized vocabulary**

**Appropriate context**

**Stylistic level**

**Parts of speech**

**Idiomatic usage**

**Different meanings**

**Cross-reference to verb tables**

**Mode of verb**

This guide includes several entries from the dictionary. The labels point out specific features that are part of most entries.

The structure of labels that the user guide includes explain abbreviations used in the entries.

C
DE
D
FH
E
IL
EF
MO
GH
PR
IJ
KO
S
PR
TU
SZ
VZ

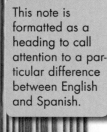

This guide explains how letters are pronounced in Spanish. It is structured in categories to help readers find information.

# Key to Spanish Pronunciation

## Vowels

| | |
|---|---|
| i | seen |
| e | late |
| a | past (Northern English) |
| o | soldier |
| u | boot |

## Diphthongs

| | |
|---|---|
| ie | *Yale* |
| ei | *paying* |
| eu | pear, *July*; *e-u* run together |
| ai, ay | sky |
| au | cow |
| oi, oy | boy |
| ue | way |

## Consonants

| | |
|---|---|
| b, v (*initial*) | best |
| b, v (*intervocalic*) | like *b* without lips touching |
| c (*before a, o, u or consonant*), k, qu | kind |
| c (*before e or i*), z | think |
| ch | choose |
| d (*initial*) | dear |
| d (*intervocalic*) | there |
| f | find |
| g (*before a, o, u or consonant*) | gain |

| | |
|---|---|
| g (*before e or i*), j | loch (Scots) |
| h | honour |
| l | long |
| ll | million |
| m | mice |
| n | banner |
| ñ | onion |
| p | copper |
| r | large (Scots) |
| rr | round (Scots) |
| s | goose |
| t | tank |
| w | like Spanish b, v |
| x (*intervocalic*) | axe or pigskin or eggs |
| x (*before consonant*) | extreme or paste |
| y | yellow |

## American Spanish

The following are the main features which distinguish the pronunciation of American from that of Castilian Spanish; they also occur in Southern Spain

| | |
|---|---|
| c (*before e or i*), z | goose |
| ll (*in many regions of Spain and of Spanish America*) | yellow |
| ll (*Argentina, Uruguay*) | pleasure |
| s (*at end of word or before a consonant; in parts of Southern Spain and America*) | hail |

The pronunciation of Spanish spoken in Spain differs from the Spanish spoken in Latin America. These notes point out key distinctions.

This note is formatted as a heading to call attention to a particular difference between English and Spanish.

# Note on Spanish Gender

As a general rule, nouns ending in *-a*, *-ción*, *-gión*, *-sión*, *-tión*, *-xión*, *-dad*, *-tad*, *-tud*, *-ez* and *-umbre* are feminine; all other nouns are masculine. In the body of the text genders are given only where this rule does not apply or in order to clarify its application.

# State of Georgia Job Application

**Features:**
- spaces for providing requested information
- a line for the applicant's signature
- text written for a specific audience

### STATE OF GEORGIA
### APPLICATION FOR EMPLOYMENT
*An Equal Opportunity Employer*

**Daytime Telephone Number**

☐☐☐ — ☐☐☐ — ☐☐☐☐

**E-mail Address**

| Last Name | First Name | Middle Initials |
| --- | --- | --- |
| Street or Mailing Address | | Apartment No. |

| City | State | Zip Code | County |
| --- | --- | --- | --- |

This part of the application captures contact information. Headings indicate where the applicant should fill in information.

**EMPLOYMENT ELIGIBILITY:** To be employed by the State of Georgia, you must meet certain State and Federal employment eligibility requirements. These include (but are not limited to) United States citizenship or authorization to work in this country, positive rehire status if previously employed by the State, and no felony convictions (for some jobs). Please answer the following questions.

| 1. Are you a United States citizen? | 2. Are you an alien authorized to work in the Utited States? | 3. Have you ever been dismissed from any State of Georgia government position? | 4. Have you ever been convicted of a felony? |
| --- | --- | --- | --- |
| ☐YES ☐NO | ☐YES ☐NO ☐N/A | ☐ YES ☐ NO **If YES, attach an explanation.** | ☐ YES ☐ NO **If YES, attach an explanation.** |

**TYPE OF WORK:** JOB TITLE AND JOB CODE REQUIRED. If you do not know the correct job titles, information is available at the various State of Georgia agency personnel offices, the Georgia Merit System Office in Atlanta, or the Georgia Department of Labor Career Centers.

Bold and upper-case letters give the applicant important information for completing the application.

| Specific Job Title Sought | Job Code | Specific Job Title Sought | Job Code |
| --- | --- | --- | --- |
| 1. | | 2. | |

**EDUCATION:**

| High School Graduate or Equivalent (GED)? ☐Yes ☐No | Vocational/Business School: | No. of Months: | Field of Study: | Completed: Yes☐ No☐ Date: (Mo/Yr) |
| --- | --- | --- | --- | --- |

| **PLEASE LIST EXACT COLLEGE HOURS:** | | CREDIT RECEIVED | | FIELD/AREA OF CONCENTRATION | | | | TYPE OF DEGREE | DATE DEGREE COMPLETED |
| --- | --- | --- | --- | --- | --- | --- | --- | --- | --- |
| COLLEGES/UNIVERSITIES | CITY and STATE | Qtr Hrs | Sem Hrs | Major | Hrs | Minor | Hrs | (BA/BS/ MA/PhD) | (Mo./Yr.) |
| | | | | | | | | | |
| | | | | | | | | | |

This section is structured as rows and columns, so that applicants can provide information in an organized way.

**LANGUAGE SKILLS:** ☐ **Multilingual (Specify languages)**_____ ☐ **Sign Language**

**GEORGIA LICENSES AND** CERTIFICATIONS:

| Type of License/Certificate | License/Certificate Number | Expiration (Mo./Yr.) | Specialization/ Endorsements |
| --- | --- | --- | --- |
| Current Valid Driver's License ☐Yes ☐No | | | |
| Current Valid Commercial Driver's License (CDL): ☐A ☐B ☐C | | | |
| Teacher Certified in Georgia: Type of Certificate Held: | | | |
| Georgia Peace Officer Standards and Training Certificate (POST) | | | |
| Other Professional License/Certificate: _____ | | | |

**WORK HISTORY:** Describe your work history below beginning with your current or most recent job. Include military and volunteer experience. If you worked for the same employer but held different jobs describe each separately. Describe in detail the specific duties beginning with your primary duties. If you need more space, print out the supplemental work history page and attach to the application. Failure to give complete and detailed information regarding each job held may result in your disqualification from employment consideration. You may submit a resume to document your work background. However, if the resume does not contain all information requested in the Work History section, please fill in that information on the application. Include additional documents as requested.

| Current or Last Employer: | | | Your Job Title: | | |
|---|---|---|---|---|---|
| Address | | | From (mo/yr) | To (mo/yr) | Hours per Week: |
| City | State | Zip Code | Check all that apply:<br>☐ Volunteer ☐ Intern ☐ Paid | | Annual Salary |
| Your Supervisor's Name and Title | | | May We Contact Employer?<br>☐ YES ☐ NO | Your Supervisor's Phone Number<br>(    ) | |
| Reason for Leaving | | | # and types of employees you supervised: | | |

Describe in detail your job duties.

Related Computer Skills:

| Current or Last Employer: | | | Your Job Title: | | |
|---|---|---|---|---|---|
| Address | | | From (mo/yr) | To (mo/yr) | Hours per Week: |
| City | State | Zip Code | Check all that apply:<br>☐ Volunteer ☐ Intern ☐ Paid | | Annual Salary |
| Your Supervisor's Name and Title | | | May We Contact Employer?<br>☐ YES ☐ NO | Your Supervisor's Phone Number<br>(    ) | |
| Reason for Leaving | | | # and types of employees you supervised: | | |

Describe in detail your job duties.

Related Computer Skills:

**CERTIFICATION: Read carefully before signing and dating. Unsigned applications will not be processed.** I certify that all information on this application is correct. I authorize any agent or employee of the State to verify this information and to release it to anyone who may consider me for appointment. I understand that intentionally providing false information on this form or attachments is a violation of state law. **I also understand that applications submitted electronically, via e-mail or similar media, are not valid unless I enter my name in the signature field below and such action shall constitute an electronic signature.**

**Signature:**                                          **Date:**

Each section asks for special information needed to complete the application. It is formatted with lines running across the page. Lines are also used to separate different parts of the application.

The structure of the application includes a place for applicants to sign to show that they have been truthful in filling out the required information.

## Comparing Functional Texts

**1. Craft and Structure (a)** Compare the **structures and formats** of the user guide and the job application. What elements do the texts have in common? **(b)** How do the graphics and headings help the user perform tasks efficiently?

**2. Craft and Structure (a)** Using the guide on pages 377 and 378, supply the precise meaning of the Spanish word *casar* and explain how it is pronounced. **(b)** Identify the text features that helped you locate this information.

### Content-Area Vocabulary

**3. (a)** Identify two sets of *homographs* in English and list their meanings. **(b)** The Greek root *-phon-* means "sound." What kind of words are homophones? **(c)** Explain why *fly off the handle* is an *idiomatic,* not a literal, expression.

## Timed Writing

### Explanatory Text: Report

**Format and Audience**
The prompt directs you to write a brief report for job applicants. Include information from your source and formal language appropriate to your audience and purpose.

Write a brief report that summarizes the Georgia job application for prospective applicants. Include an explanation of how knowing this information before filling out the application might be helpful to job applicants. (20 minutes)

**Academic Vocabulary**
When you *summarize,* you prepare a brief statement of the most important information and details of a text.

### 5-Minute Planner

Complete these steps before you begin to write:

**1.** Review the application and take notes about its most important elements. Use the application's structure and format to guide you.
**TIP** Consider questions prospective job applicants might have, and note details that address those points.

**2.** Consider your notes and what might be most helpful to an applicant.

**3.** Think about how best to structure your report, and make a quick outline. Refer to your outline and notes as you write.

## Comparing Symbolism and Allegory

Works of literature can have two levels of meaning. The first level is literal—the text means exactly what it says. In some works, however, the text suggests a second, more abstract meaning. This second, deeper layer of meaning is often symbolic or allegorical.

- A **symbol** is a person or thing that represents both itself and a larger idea. For example, a dove can be a symbol of peace, and a voyage can represent the journey of life. **Symbolism** is the use of symbols to convey ideas. Writers may use traditional, or conventional, symbols that readers recognize easily, such as a rose signifying love. Writers may also create their own personal symbols within literary works. As you read, consider whether characters, objects, details, or even the setting of a story may suggest another level of meaning.

- An **allegory** is a story or poem in which every element has parallel literal and symbolic meanings. For example, in an allegory about a sailor crossing the ocean, the sailor could represent all people; storms at sea could represent life's troubles; and sails could represent the help of friends. To appreciate an allegory, consider both levels of meaning. To interpret an allegory, ask yourself what each particular element in a story might stand for. A true allegory will have a one-to-one correspondence of literal meaning to symbolic meaning throughout the narrative.

Only one of the following stories is an allegory, but both use symbols. As you read, fill out a chart like the one shown. Afterward, determine which story uses symbols to enhance the meaning and which is a true allegory.

### Common Core State Standards

**Reading Literature**

**4.** Determine the meaning of words and phrases as they are used in the text, including figurative and connotative meanings; analyze the cumulative impact of specific word choices on meaning.

**Writing**

**2.** Write informative/explanatory texts to examine and convey complex ideas, concepts, and information clearly and accurately through the effective selection, organization, and analysis of content.

|  | The Scarlet Ibis | The Golden Kite, the Silver Wind |
|---|---|---|
| **Symbol** | rotting brown petals | city wall shaped like a club |
| **Meaning** | the end of summer | a community's desire to protect itself |

**www.PHLitOnline.com**

- Vocabulary flashcards
- Interactive journals
- More about the authors
- Selection audio
- Interactive graphic organizers

## Writing About the Big Question

In both of these stories, **competitiveness** leads to conflict. Complete these sentences to develop your ideas about the Big Question:

Some people like to **compete** because _____.

To prevent a **competition** from turning into a conflict, you might _____.

# Meet the Authors

## James Hurst (b. 1922)

### Author of "The Scarlet Ibis"

James Hurst grew up along the coast of North Carolina, a place of quiet landscapes and violent storms. After studying chemical engineering and opera and serving in the army during World War II, Hurst took a job at a New York bank. For thirty-four years, he worked as a banker and spent his evenings writing stories.

**Creating Symbolism** "The Scarlet Ibis," published in 1960, is Hurst's best-known story. Hurst has said that he "wanted [the ibis] to represent [the character of Doodle]—not Doodle's physical self, but his spirit."

## Ray Bradbury (b. 1920)

### Author of "The Golden Kite, the Silver Wind"

Born in Waukegan, Illinois, Ray Bradbury grew up in Arizona and California. He has been writing for more than sixty years and has published more than 500 stories. His work has earned him many honors, including the World Fantasy Award for lifetime achievement and the Grand Master Award from the Science Fiction Writers of America.

**Writing to Entertain** Bradbury is best known for his works of fantasy and science fiction. "I write for fun," Bradbury has said. "I don't see myself as a philosopher. That's awfully boring. . . . My goal is to entertain myself and others."

# The Scarlet Ibis

## James Hurst

▶ **Critical Viewing**
What could you infer about the childhood of someone living in the location pictured? **[Interpret]**

**Literary Analysis**
**Symbolism and Allegory** What details about the flowers, weeds, and the oriole nest in the opening paragraph symbolize death?

It was in the clove of seasons, summer was dead but autumn had not yet been born, that the ibis lit in the bleeding tree. The flower garden was stained with rotting brown magnolia petals and ironweeds grew rank amid the purple phlox. The five o'clocks by the chimney still marked time, but the oriole nest in the elm was untenanted and rocked back and forth like an empty cradle. The last graveyard flowers were blooming, and their smell drifted across the cotton field and through every room of our house, speaking softly the names of our dead.

It's strange that all this is still so clear to me, now that the summer has long since fled and time has had its way. A grindstone stands where the bleeding tree stood, just outside the kitchen door, and now if an oriole sings in the elm, its song seems to die up in the leaves, a silvery dust. The flower garden is prim, the house a gleaming white, and the pale fence across the yard stands straight and spruce. But sometimes (like right now), as I sit in the cool, green-draped parlor, the grindstone begins to turn, and time with all its changes is ground away—and I remember Doodle.

Doodle was just about the craziest brother a boy ever had. Of course, he wasn't a crazy crazy like old Miss Leedie, who was in love with President Wilson and wrote him a letter every day, but was a nice crazy, like someone you meet in your dreams. He was born when I was six and was, from the outset, a disappointment. He seemed all head, with a tiny body which was red and shriveled like an old man's. Everybody thought he was going to die—everybody

except Aunt Nicey, who had delivered him. She said he would live because he was born in a caul[1] and cauls were made from Jesus' nightgown. Daddy had Mr. Heath, the carpenter, build a little mahogany coffin for him. But he didn't die, and when he was three months old Mama and Daddy decided they might as well name him. They named him William Armstrong, which was like tying a big tail on a small kite. Such a name sounds good only on a tombstone.

I thought myself pretty smart at many things, like holding my breath, running, jumping, or climbing the vines in Old Woman Swamp, and I wanted more than anything else someone to race to Horsehead Landing, someone to box with, and someone to perch with in the top fork of the great pine behind the barn, where across the fields and swamps you could see the sea. I wanted a brother. But Mama, crying, told me that even if William Armstrong lived, he would never do these things with me. He might not, she sobbed, even be "all there." He might, as long as he lived, lie on the rubber sheet in the center of the bed in the front bedroom where the white marquisette curtains billowed out in the afternoon sea breeze, rustling like palmetto fronds.[2]

It was bad enough having an invalid brother, but having one who possibly was not all there was unbearable, so I began to make plans to kill him by smothering him with a pillow. However, one afternoon as I watched him, my head poked between the iron posts of the foot of the bed, he looked straight at me and grinned. I skipped through the rooms, down the echoing halls, shouting, "Mama, he smiled. He's all there! He's all there!" and he was.

---

1. **caul** (kôl) *n.* membrane enclosing a baby at birth.
2. **palmetto** (pal met´ ō) **fronds** (frändz) *n.* palm leaves.

**Literary Analysis**
**Symbolism and Allegory** In what ways does the caul symbolize life and hope?

*It's strange that all this is still so clear to me, now that the summer has long since fled and time has had its way.*

**Reading Check**
Who is Doodle?

## LITERATURE IN CONTEXT

### Science Connection

**Scarlet Ibis**
Found mostly in the South American tropics, the strikingly beautiful scarlet ibis is a wading bird with long legs, a long, slender neck, black-tipped wings, and a wingspan of more than three feet. It seldom appears in the United States north of Florida.

### Connect to the Literature

Why would the discovery of a scarlet ibis in coastal North Carolina, the setting of this story, be unexpected and dramatic?

When he was two, if you laid him on his stomach, he began to try to move himself, straining terribly. The doctor said that with his weak heart this strain would probably kill him, but it didn't. Trembling, he'd push himself up, turning first red, then a soft purple, and finally collapse back onto the bed like an old worn-out doll. I can still see Mama watching him, her hand pressed tight across her mouth, her eyes wide and unblinking. But he learned to crawl (it was his third winter), and we brought him out of the front bedroom, putting him on the rug before the fireplace. For the first time he became one of us.

As long as he lay all the time in bed, we called him William Armstrong, even though it was formal and sounded as if we were referring to one of our ancestors, but with his creeping around on the deerskin rug and beginning to talk, something had to be done about his name. It was I who renamed him. When he crawled, he crawled backwards, as if he were in reverse and couldn't change gears. If you called him, he'd turn around as if he were going in the other direction, then he'd back right up to you to be picked up. Crawling backward made him look like a doodle-bug, so I began to call him Doodle, and in time even Mama and Daddy thought it was a better name than William Armstrong. Only Aunt Nicey disagreed. She said caul babies should be treated with special respect since they might turn out to be saints. Renaming my brother was perhaps the kindest thing I ever did for him, because nobody expects much from someone called Doodle.

Although Doodle learned to crawl, he showed no signs of walking, but he wasn't idle. He talked so much that we all quit listening to what he said. It was about this time that Daddy built him a go-cart and I had to pull him around. At first I just paraded him up and down the piazza, but then he started crying to be taken out into the yard and it ended up by my having to lug him wherever I went. If I so much as picked up my cap, he'd start crying to go with me and Mama would call from wherever she was, "Take Doodle with you."

He was a burden in many ways. The doctor had said that he mustn't get too excited, too hot, too cold, or too tired and that he must always be treated gently. A long list of don'ts went with him, all of which I ignored once we got out of the house. To discourage his coming with me, I'd run with him across the ends of the cotton rows and careen him around corners on two wheels. Sometimes I accidentally turned him over, but he never told Mama. His skin was very sensitive, and he had to wear a big straw hat whenever he went out. When the going got rough and he had to cling to the sides of the go-cart, the hat slipped all the way down over his ears. He was a sight. Finally, I could see I was licked. Doodle was my brother and he was going to cling to me forever, no matter what I did, so I dragged him across the burning cotton field to share with him the only beauty I knew, Old Woman Swamp. I pulled the go-cart through the saw-tooth fern, down into the green dimness where the palmetto fronds whispered by the stream. I lifted him out and set him down in the soft rubber grass beside a tall pine. His eyes were round with wonder as he gazed about him, and his little hands began to stroke the rubber grass. Then he began to cry.

"For heaven's sake, what's the matter?" I asked, annoyed.

"It's so pretty," he said. "So pretty, pretty, pretty."

After that day Doodle and I often went down into Old Woman Swamp. I would gather wildflowers, wild violets, honeysuckle, yellow jasmine, snakeflowers, and water lilies, and with wire grass we'd weave them into necklaces and crowns. We'd bedeck ourselves with our handiwork and loll about thus beautified, beyond the touch of the everyday world. Then when the slanted rays of the sun burned orange in the tops of the pines, we'd drop our jewels into the stream and watch them float away toward the sea.

There is within me (and with sadness I have watched it in others) a knot of cruelty borne by the stream of love, much as our blood sometimes bears the seed of our destruction, and at times I was mean to Doodle. One day I took him up to the barn loft and showed him his casket, telling him how we all had believed he would die. It was covered with a film of Paris green[3] sprinkled to kill the rats, and screech owls had built a nest inside it.

Doodle studied the mahogany box for a long time, then said, "It's not mine."

"It is," I said. "And before I'll help you down from the loft, you're going to have to touch it."

"I won't touch it," he said sullenly.

"Then I'll leave you here by yourself," I threatened, and made as if I were going down.

Doodle was frightened of being left. "Don't go leave me, Brother," he cried, and he leaned toward the coffin. His hand, trembling, reached out, and when he touched the casket he screamed. A screech owl flapped out of the box into our faces, scaring us and covering us with Paris green. Doodle was paralyzed, so I put him on my shoulder and carried him down the ladder, and even when we were outside in the bright sunshine, he clung to me, crying, "Don't leave me. Don't leave me."

---

3. **Paris green** poisonous green powder used chiefly as an insecticide.

Literary Analysis
**Symbolism and Allegory** Which details in this paragraph symbolize life and beauty?

Reading Check

What does the narrator force Doodle to touch?

The Scarlet Ibis **387**

When Doodle was five years old, I was embarrassed at having a brother of that age who couldn't walk, so I set out to teach him. We were down in Old Woman Swamp and it was spring and the sick-sweet smell of bay flowers hung everywhere like a mournful song. "I'm going to teach you to walk, Doodle," I said.

He was sitting comfortably on the soft grass, leaning back against the pine. "Why?" he asked.

I hadn't expected such an answer. "So I won't have to haul you around all the time."

"I can't walk, Brother," he said.

"Who says so?" I demanded.

"Mama, the doctor—everybody."

"Oh, you can walk," I said, and I took him by the arms and stood him up. He collapsed onto the grass like a half-empty flour sack. It was as if he had no bones in his little legs.

"Don't hurt me, Brother," he warned.

"Shut up. I'm not going to hurt you. I'm going to teach you to walk." I heaved him up again, and again he collapsed.

This time he did not lift his face up out of the rubber grass. "I just can't do it. Let's make honeysuckle wreaths."

"Oh yes you can, Doodle," I said. "All you got to do is try. Now come on," and I hauled him up once more.

It seemed so hopeless from the beginning that it's a miracle I didn't give up. But all of us must have something or someone to be proud of, and Doodle had become mine. I did not know then that pride is a wonderful, terrible thing, a seed that bears two vines, life and death. Every day that summer we went to the pine beside the stream of Old Woman Swamp, and I put him on his feet at least a hundred times each afternoon. Occasionally I too became discouraged because it didn't seem as if he was trying, and I would say, "Doodle, don't you want to learn to walk?"

He'd nod his head, and I'd say, "Well, if you don't keep trying, you'll never learn." Then I'd paint for him a picture of us as old men, white-haired, him with a long white beard and me still pulling him around in the go-cart. This never failed to make him try again.

Finally one day, after many weeks of practicing, he stood alone for a few seconds. When he fell, I grabbed him in my arms and hugged him, our laughter pealing through the swamp like a ringing bell. Now we knew it could be done. Hope no longer hid in the dark palmetto thicket but perched like a cardinal in the lacy toothbrush tree, brilliantly visible. "Yes, yes," I cried, and he cried it too, and the grass beneath us was soft and the smell of the swamp was sweet.

With success so imminent, we decided not to tell anyone until he could actually walk. Each day, barring rain, we sneaked into Old

**Literary Analysis**
**Symbolism and Allegory** How is pride like "a seed that bears two vines"?

**Vocabulary**
**imminent** (im´ ə nənt) *adj.* likely to happen soon

*Two Boys in a Punt,* 1915–Cover Illustration, *Popular Magazine,* N.C. Wyeth (1882–1945), Private Collection, Photography courtesy of Brandywine River Museum.

Woman Swamp, and by cotton-picking time Doodle was ready to show what he could do. He still wasn't able to walk far, but we could wait no longer. Keeping a nice secret is very hard to do, like holding your breath. We chose to reveal all on October eighth, Doodle's sixth birthday, and for weeks ahead we mooned around the house, promising everybody a most spectacular surprise. Aunt Nicey said that, after so much talk, if we produced anything less tremendous than the Resurrection,[4] she was going to be disappointed.

At breakfast on our chosen day, when Mama, Daddy, and Aunt Nicey were in the dining room, I brought Doodle to the door in the go-cart just as usual and had them turn their backs, making them cross their hearts and hope to die if they peeked. I helped Doodle up, and when he was standing alone I let them look. There wasn't a sound as Doodle walked slowly across the room and sat down at his place at the table. Then Mama began to cry and ran over to him, hugging him and kissing him. Daddy hugged him too, so I went to Aunt Nicey, who was thanks praying in the doorway, and began to waltz her around. We danced together quite well until she came down on my big toe with her brogans, hurting me so badly I thought I was crippled for life.

Doodle told them it was I who had taught him to walk, so everyone wanted to hug me, and I began to cry.

"What are you crying for?" asked Daddy, but I couldn't answer. They did not know that I did it for myself; that pride, whose slave I was, spoke to me louder than all their voices, and that Doodle walked only because I was ashamed of having a crippled brother.

---

4. **the Resurrection** (rez´ ə rek´ shən) the rising of Jesus Christ from the dead after his death and burial.

◀ **Critical Viewing**
What can you tell about the brothers' relationship from the illustration and the details in the story? **[Interpret]**

*"I'm going to teach you to walk, Doodle," I said.*

☑ **Reading Check**
What surprise do the boys present?

**Literary Analysis**
**Symbolism and Allegory** How might the peacock and the boy symbolize death?

Within a few months Doodle had learned to walk well and his go-cart was put up in the barn loft (it's still there) beside his little mahogany coffin. Now, when we roamed off together, resting often, we never turned back until our destination had been reached, and to help pass the time, we took up lying. From the beginning Doodle was a terrible liar and he got me in the habit. Had anyone stopped to listen to us, we would have been sent off to Dix Hill.

My lies were scary, involved, and usually pointless, but Doodle's were twice as crazy. People in his stories all had wings and flew wherever they wanted to go. His favorite lie was about a boy named Peter who had a pet peacock with a ten-foot tail. Peter wore a golden robe that glittered so brightly that when he walked through the sunflowers they turned away from the sun to face him. When Peter was ready to go to sleep, the peacock spread his magnificent tail, enfolding the boy gently like a closing go-to-sleep flower, burying him in the gloriously iridescent, rustling vortex.[5] Yes, I must admit it. Doodle could beat me lying.

Doodle and I spent lots of time thinking about our future. We decided that when we were grown we'd live in Old Woman Swamp and pick dog-tongue for a living. Beside the stream, he planned, we'd build us a house of whispering leaves and the swamp birds would be our chickens. All day long (when we weren't gathering dog-tongue) we'd swing through the cypresses on the rope vines, and if it rained we'd huddle beneath an umbrella tree and play stickfrog. Mama and Daddy could come and live with us if they wanted to. He even came up with the idea that he could marry Mama and I could marry Daddy. Of course, I was old enough to know this wouldn't work out, but the picture he painted was so beautiful and serene that all I could do was whisper Yes, yes.

**Vocabulary**
**infallibility** (in fal´ ə bil´ ə tē) *n.* condition of not being likely to fail

Once I had succeeded in teaching Doodle to walk, I began to believe in my own infallibility and I prepared a terrific development program for him, unknown to Mama and Daddy, of course. I would teach him to run, to swim, to climb trees, and to fight. He, too, now believed in my infallibility, so we set the deadline for these accomplishments less than a year away, when, it had been decided, Doodle could start to school.

That winter we didn't make much progress, for I was in school and Doodle suffered from one bad cold after another. But when spring came, rich and warm, we raised our sights again. Success lay at the end of summer like a pot of gold, and our campaign got off to a good start. On hot days, Doodle and I went down to Horsehead Landing and I gave him swimming lessons or showed him how to row a boat. Sometimes we descended into the cool

---

**5. vortex** (vôr´ teks´) *n.* rushing whirl, drawing in all that surrounds it.

greenness of Old Woman Swamp and climbed the rope vines or boxed scientifically beneath the pine where he had learned to walk. Promise hung about us like the leaves, and wherever we looked, ferns unfurled and birds broke into song.

That summer, the summer of 1918, was blighted. In May and June there was no rain and the crops withered, curled up, then died under the thirsty sun. One morning in July a hurricane came out of the east, tipping over the oaks in the yard and splitting the limbs of the elm trees. That afternoon it roared back out of the west, blew the fallen oaks around, snapping their roots and tearing them out of the earth like a hawk at the entrails of a chicken. Cotton bolls were wrenched from the stalks and lay like green walnuts in the valleys between the rows, while the cornfield leaned over uniformly so that the tassels touched the ground. Doodle and I followed Daddy out into the cotton field, where he stood, shoulders sagging, surveying the ruin. When his chin sank down onto his chest, we were frightened, and Doodle slipped his hand into mine. Suddenly Daddy straightened his shoulders, raised a giant knuckly fist, and with a voice that seemed to rumble out of the earth itself began cursing heaven, hell, the weather, and the Republican Party. Doodle and I, prodding each other and giggling, went back to the house, knowing that everything would be all right.

**Literary Analysis**
**Symbolism and Allegory** What might the "blighted" summer symbolize?

And during that summer, strange names were heard through the house: Chateau-Thierry, Amiens, Soissons, and in her blessing at the supper table, Mama once said, "And bless the Pearsons, whose boy Joe was lost at Belleau Wood."[6]

So we came to that clove of seasons. School was only a few weeks away, and Doodle was far behind schedule. He could barely clear the ground when climbing up the rope vines and his swimming was certainly not passable. We decided to double our efforts, to make that last drive and reach our pot of gold. I made him swim until he turned blue and row until he couldn't lift an oar. Wherever we went, I purposely walked fast, and although he kept up, his face turned red and his eyes became glazed. Once, he could go no further, so he collapsed on the ground and began to cry.

*Success lay at the end of summer like a pot of gold...*

"Aw, come on, Doodle," I urged. "You can do it. Do you want to be different from everybody else when you start school?"

"Does it make any difference?"

"It certainly does," I said. "Now, come on," and I helped him up.

As we slipped through dog days, Doodle began to look feverish, and Mama felt his forehead, asking him if he felt ill. At night he didn't sleep well, and sometimes he had nightmares, crying out until I touched him and said, "Wake up, Doodle. Wake up."

**Reading Check**
What plan does the narrator make for Doodle's future?

---

6. **Chateau-Thierry** (sha′ tō′ tē er′ ē), **Amiens** (á myan′), **Soissons** (swä sôn′), . . . **Belleau** (be lò′) **Wood** places in France where battles were fought during World War I.

▼ **Critical Viewing**
How would you react
if this exotic bird—an
ibis—showed up in your
backyard? **[Relate]**

**Vocabulary**
**precariously** (pri ker´ ē
əs lē) *adv.* insecurely

It was Saturday noon, just a few days before school was to start. I should have already admitted defeat, but my pride wouldn't let me. The excitement of our program had now been gone for weeks, but still we kept on with a tired doggedness. It was too late to turn back, for we had both wandered too far into a net of expectations and had left no crumbs behind.

Daddy, Mama, Doodle, and I were seated at the dining-room table having lunch. It was a hot day, with all the windows and doors open in case a breeze should come. In the kitchen Aunt Nicey was humming softly. After a long silence, Daddy spoke. "It's so calm, I wouldn't be surprised if we had a storm this afternoon."

"I haven't heard a rain frog," said Mama, who believed in signs, as she served the bread around the table.

"I did," declared Doodle. "Down in the swamp."

"He didn't," I said contrarily.

"You did, eh?" said Daddy, ignoring my denial.

"I certainly did," Doodle reiterated, scowling at me over the top of his iced-tea glass, and we were quiet again.

Suddenly, from out in the yard, came a strange croaking noise. Doodle stopped eating, with a piece of bread poised ready for his mouth, his eyes popped round like two blue buttons. "What's that?" he whispered.

I jumped up, knocking over my chair, and had reached the door when Mama called, "Pick up the chair, sit down again, and say excuse me."

By the time I had done this, Doodle had excused himself and had slipped out into the yard. He was looking up into the bleeding tree. "It's a great big red bird!" he called.

The bird croaked loudly again, and Mama and Daddy came out into the yard. We shaded our eyes with our hands against the hazy glare of the sun and peered up through the still leaves. On the topmost branch a bird the size of a chicken, with scarlet feathers and long legs, was perched precariously. Its wings hung down loosely, and as we watched, a feather dropped away and floated slowly down through the green leaves.

"It's not even frightened of us," Mama said.

"It looks tired," Daddy added. "Or maybe sick."

Doodle's hands were clasped at his throat, and I had never seen him stand still so long. "What is it?" he asked.

Daddy shook his head. "I don't know, maybe it's—"

At that moment the bird began to flutter, but the wings were uncoordinated, and amid much flapping and a spray of flying feathers, it tumbled down, bumping through the limbs of the bleeding tree and landing at our feet with a thud. Its long, graceful neck jerked twice into an S, then straightened out, and the bird was still. A white veil came over the eyes and the long white beak unhinged. Its legs were crossed and its clawlike feet were delicately curved at rest. Even death did not mar its grace, for it lay on the earth like a broken vase of red flowers, and we stood around it, awed by its exotic beauty.

"It's dead," Mama said.

"What is it?" Doodle repeated.

"Go bring me the bird book," said Daddy.

I ran into the house and brought back the bird book. As we watched, Daddy thumbed through its pages. "It's a scarlet ibis," he said, pointing to a picture. "It lives in the tropics— South America to Florida. A storm must have brought it here."

Sadly, we all looked back at the bird. A scarlet ibis! How many miles it had traveled to die like this, in our yard, beneath the bleeding tree.

"Let's finish lunch," Mama said, nudging us back toward the dining room.

"I'm not hungry," said Doodle, and he knelt down beside the ibis.

"We've got peach cobbler for dessert," Mama tempted from the doorway.

Doodle remained kneeling. "I'm going to bury him."

"Don't you dare touch him," Mama warned. "There's no telling what disease he might have had."

"All right," said Doodle. "I won't."

Daddy, Mama, and I went back to the dining-room table, but we watched Doodle through the open door. He took out a piece of string from his pocket and, without touching the ibis, looped one end around its neck. Slowly, while singing softly "Shall We Gather at the River," he carried the bird around to the front yard and dug a hole in the flower garden, next to the petunia bed. Now we were watching him through the front window, but he didn't know it. His awkwardness at digging the hole with a shovel whose handle was twice as long as he was made us laugh, and we covered our mouths with our hands so he wouldn't hear.

When Doodle came into the dining room, he found us seriously eating our cobbler. He was pale and lingered just inside the screen door. "Did you get the scarlet ibis buried?" asked Daddy.

Doodle didn't speak but nodded his head.

"Go wash your hands, and then you can have some peach cobbler," said Mama.

"I'm not hungry," he said.

**Literary Analysis**
**Symbolism and Allegory** In what ways are the bird's uncoordinated movements similar to Doodle's? Explain.

*On the topmost branch a bird the size of a chicken, with scarlet feathers and long legs, was perched precariously.*

Reading Check
What does Doodle find in the bleeding tree?

**Spiral Review**
**Plot Devices** What future event might the strange episode of the scarlet ibis foreshadow?

**Literary Analysis**
**Symbolism and Allegory** What might "black clouds" symbolize? Explain.

"Dead birds is bad luck," said Aunt Nicey, poking her head from the kitchen door. "Specially red dead birds!"

As soon as I had finished eating, Doodle and I hurried off to Horsehead Landing. Time was short, and Doodle still had a long way to go if he was going to keep up with the other boys when he started school. The sun, gilded with the yellow cast of autumn, still burned fiercely, but the dark green woods through which we passed were shady and cool. When we reached the landing, Doodle said he was too tired to swim, so we got into a skiff and floated down the creek with the tide. Far off in the marsh a rail was scolding, and over on the beach locusts were singing in the myrtle trees. Doodle did not speak and kept his head turned away, letting one hand trail limply in the water.

After we had drifted a long way, I put the oars in place and made Doodle row back against the tide. Black clouds began to gather in the southwest, and he kept watching them, trying to pull the oars a little faster. When we reached Horsehead Landing, lightning was playing across half the sky and thunder roared out, hiding even the sound of the sea. The sun disappeared and darkness descended, almost like night. Flocks of marsh crows flew by, heading inland to their roosting trees, and two egrets, squawking, arose from the oyster-rock shallows and careened away.

Doodle was both tired and frightened, and when he stepped from the skiff he collapsed onto the mud, sending an armada of fiddler crabs rustling off into the marsh grass. I helped him up, and as he wiped the mud off his trousers, he smiled at me ashamedly. He had failed and we both knew it, so we started back home, racing the storm. We never spoke (What are the words that can solder cracked pride?), but I knew he was watching me, watching for a sign of mercy. The lightning was near now, and from fear he walked so close behind me he kept stepping on my heels. The faster I walked, the faster he walked, so I began to run. The rain was coming, roaring through the pines, and then, like a bursting Roman candle, a gum tree ahead of us was shattered by a bolt of lightning. When the deafening peal of thunder had died, and in the moment before the rain arrived, I heard Doodle, who had fallen behind, cry out, "Brother, Brother, don't leave me! Don't leave me!"

The knowledge that Doodle's and my plans had come to naught was bitter, and that streak of cruelty within me awakened. I ran as fast as I could, leaving him far behind with a wall of rain dividing us. The drops stung my face like nettles, and the wind flared the wet glistening leaves of the bordering trees. Soon I could hear his voice no more.

I hadn't run too far before I became tired, and the flood of childish spite evanesced as well. I stopped and waited for Doodle. The sound of rain was everywhere, but the wind had died and it fell straight down in parallel paths like ropes hanging from the sky. As I waited, I peered through the downpour, but no one came. Finally I went back and found him huddled beneath a red nightshade bush beside the road. He was sitting on the ground, his face buried in his arms, which were resting on his drawn-up knees. "Let's go, Doodle," I said.

He didn't answer, so I placed my hand on his forehead and lifted his head. Limply, he fell backwards onto the earth. He had been bleeding from the mouth, and his neck and the front of his shirt were stained a brilliant red.

"Doodle! Doodle!" I cried, shaking him, but there was no answer but the ropy rain. He lay very awkwardly, with his head thrown far back, making his vermilion neck appear unusually long and slim. His little legs, bent sharply at the knees, had never before seemed so fragile, so thin.

I began to weep, and the tear-blurred vision in red before me looked very familiar. "Doodle!" I screamed above the pounding storm and threw my body to the earth above his. For a long long time, it seemed forever, I lay there crying, sheltering my fallen scarlet ibis from the heresy[7] of rain.

---

7. **heresy** (her′ ə sē) *n.* idea opposed to the beliefs of a religion or philosophy.

**Literary Analysis**
**Symbolism and Allegory** How are the details about the blood as well as Doodle's position beneath the bush similar to what happened to the scarlet ibis?

## Critical Thinking

Cite textual evidence to support your responses.

@ 1. **Key Ideas and Details  Analyze:** Why does the narrator cry when everyone congratulates him for teaching Doodle to walk?

@ 2. **Key Ideas and Details  Analyze:** What do the narrator's tears reveal about his conflicted, or mixed, feelings?

@ 3. **Key Ideas and Details  (a)** What does Doodle do with the dead ibis? **(b) Compare and Contrast:** How does Doodle's reaction to the dead bird compare to those of his family members? Support your answer with details from the text. **(c) Infer:** What do you think motivates Doodle to treat the ibis as he does?

@ 4. **Integration of Knowledge and Ideas** As a child, the narrator sets demanding competitive goals for Doodle. **(a)** Why do you think Doodle strives for these goals even though he does not have a competitive nature? **(b)** In what way do those goals reflect the conflict that the narrator feels about Doodle? *[Connect to the Big Question: Is conflict necessary?]*

# The Golden Kite, the Silver Wind

## Ray Bradbury

▼ **Critical Viewing**
How are the leader in this painting and the Mandarin in the story both similar and different? **[Compare and Contrast]**

*Background* "The Golden Kite, the Silver Wind" was written during the Cold War, a period of intense rivalry between the United States and the former Soviet Union that shaped world politics in the second half of the twentieth century. During this time, each action by one country—the creation of a weapon, the launching of a satellite—was countered by a reaction from the other country. As you read, think about the parallels between the story events and the conflicts of the Cold War.

"In the shape of a pig?" cried the Mandarin.[1]

"In the shape of a pig," said the messenger, and departed.

"Oh, what an evil day in an evil year," cried the Mandarin. "The town of Kwan-Si, beyond the hill, was very small in my childhood. Now it has grown so large that at last they are building a wall."

"But why should a wall two miles away make my good father sad and angry all within the hour?" asked his daughter quietly.

"They build their wall," said the Mandarin, "in the shape of a pig! Do you see? Our own city wall is built in the shape of an orange. That pig will devour us, greedily!"

"Ah."

They both sat thinking.

Life was full of symbols and omens. Demons lurked everywhere, Death swam in the wetness of an eye, the turn of a gull's wing meant rain, a fan held so, the tilt of a roof, and, yes, even a city wall was of immense importance. Travelers and tourists, caravans, musicians, artists, coming upon these two towns, equally judging the portents,[2] would say, "The city

---

1. **Mandarin** (man´ də rin) *n.* a high official of China; here, the ruling leader.
2. **portents** (pôr´ tents´) *n.* things that are thought to be signs of events to come; omens.

shaped like an orange? No! I will enter the city shaped like a pig and prosper, eating all, growing fat with good luck and prosperity!"

The Mandarin wept. "All is lost! These symbols and signs terrify. Our city will come on evil days."

"Then," said the daughter, "call in your stonemasons and temple builders. I will whisper from behind the silken screen and you will know the words."

The old man clapped his hands despairingly. "Ho, stonemasons!

"Ho, builders of towns and palaces!"

The men who knew marble and granite and onyx and quartz came quickly. The Mandarin faced them most uneasily, himself waiting for a whisper from the silken screen behind his throne. At last the whisper came.

"I have called you here," said the whisper.

"I have called you here," said the Mandarin aloud, "because our city is shaped like an orange, and the vile city of Kwan-Si has this day shaped theirs like a ravenous pig—"

Here the stonemasons groaned and wept. Death rattled his cane in the outer courtyard. Poverty made a sound like a wet cough in the shadows of the room.

"And so," said the whisper, said the Mandarin, "you raisers of walls must go bearing trowels and rocks and change the shape of our city!"

The architects and masons gasped. The Mandarin himself gasped at what he had said. The whisper whispered. The Mandarin went on: "And you will change our walls into a club which may beat the pig and drive it off!"

The stonemasons rose up, shouting. Even the Mandarin, delighted at the words from his mouth, applauded, stood down from his throne. "Quick!" he cried. "To work!"

When his men had gone, smiling and bustling, the Mandarin turned with great love to the silken screen. "Daughter," he whispered, "I will embrace you." There was no reply. He stepped around the screen, and she was gone.

Such modesty, he thought. She has slipped away and left me with a triumph, as if it were mine.

The news spread through the city; the Mandarin was acclaimed. Everyone carried stone to the walls. Fireworks were set off and the demons of death and poverty did not linger, as all worked together. At the end of the month the wall had been changed. It was now a mighty bludgeon with which to drive pigs, boars, even lions, far away. The Mandarin slept like a happy fox every night.

"I would like to see the Mandarin of Kwan-Si when the news is

**Literary Analysis**
**Symbolism and Allegory** What qualities do the people believe the image of a pig symbolizes?

**Vocabulary**
**ravenous** (rav´ ə nəs) *adj.* wildly hungry

*Life was full of symbols and omens.*

Reading Check

Who whispers to the king from behind a silken screen?

himself from a mountain! A little more of that wine, oh Daughter-
who-thinks-like-a-son."

But the pleasure was like a winter flower; it died swiftly. That
very afternoon the messenger rushed into the courtroom. "Oh,
Mandarin, disease, early sorrow, avalanches, grasshopper plagues,
and poisoned well water!"

The Mandarin trembled.

"The town of Kwan-Si," said the messenger, "which was built like
a pig and which animal we drove away by changing our walls to a
mighty stick, has now turned triumph to winter ashes. They have
built their city's walls like a great bonfire to burn our stick!"

The Mandarin's heart sickened within him, like an autumn
fruit upon an ancient tree. "Oh, gods! Travelers will spurn us.
Tradesmen, reading the symbols, will turn from the stick, so easily
destroyed, to the fire, which conquers all!"

"No," said a whisper like a snowflake from behind the silken
screen.

"No," said the startled Mandarin.

"Tell my stonemasons," said the whisper that was a falling drop
of rain, "to build our walls in the shape of a shining lake."

The Mandarin said this aloud, his heart warmed.

"And with this lake of water," said the whisper and the old man,
"we will quench the fire and put it out forever!"

The city turned out in joy to learn that once again they had been
saved by the magnificent Emperor of ideas. They ran to the walls
and built them nearer to this new vision, singing, not as loudly as
before, of course, for they were tired, and not as quickly, for since it
had taken a month to rebuild the wall the first time, they had had
to neglect business and crops and therefore were somewhat weaker
and poorer.

There then followed a succession of horrible and wonderful days,
one in another like a nest of frightened boxes.

"Oh, Emperor," cried the messenger, "Kwan-Si has rebuilt their
walls to resemble a mouth with which to drink all our lake!"

"Then," said the Emperor, standing very close to his silken screen,
"build our walls like a needle to sew up that mouth!"

"Emperor!" screamed the messenger. "They make
their walls like a sword to break your needle!"

The Emperor held, trembling, to the silken screen.
"Then shift the stones to form a scabbard to sheathe that
sword!"[3]

---

3. **scabbard** (skab´ ərd) **to sheathe** (shēth) **that sword!** case to hold the blade of
the sword.

**Literary Analysis**
**Symbolism and
Allegory** In what ways
does the "winter flower"
describe the fleeting
pleasure the Mandarin
feels?

**Vocabulary**
**spurn** (spʉrn) *v.* reject
with contempt or disdain

"Mercy," wept the messenger the following morn, "they have worked all night and shaped their walls like lightning which will explode and destroy that sheath!"

Sickness spread in the city like a pack of evil dogs. Shops closed. The population, working now steadily for endless months upon the changing of the walls, resembled Death himself, clattering his white bones like musical instruments in the wind. Funerals began to appear in the streets, though it was the middle of summer, a time when all should be tending and harvesting. The Mandarin fell so ill that he had his bed drawn up by the silken screen and there he lay, miserably giving his architectural orders. The voice behind the screen was weak now, too, and faint, like the wind in the eaves.

"Kwan-Si is an eagle. Then our walls must be a net for that eagle. They are a sun to burn our net. Then we build a moon to eclipse their sun!"

Like a rusted machine, the city ground to a halt.

At last the whisper behind the screen cried out:

"In the name of the gods, send for Kwan-Si!"

Upon the last day of summer the Mandarin Kwan-Si, very ill and withered away, was carried into our Mandarin's courtroom by four starving footmen. The two mandarins were propped up, facing each other. Their breaths fluttered like winter winds in their mouths. A voice said:

"Let us put an end to this."

The old men nodded.

"This cannot go on," said the faint voice. "Our people do nothing but rebuild our cities to a different shape every day, every hour. They have no time to hunt, to fish, to love, to be good to their ancestors and their ancestors' children."

"This I admit," said the mandarins of the towns of the Cage, the Moon, the Spear, the Fire, the Sword and this, that, and other things.

"Carry us into the sunlight," said the voice.

The old men were borne out under the sun and up a little hill. In the late summer breeze a few very thin children were flying dragon kites in all the colors of the sun, and frogs and grass, the color of the sea and the color of coins and wheat.

The first Mandarin's daughter stood by his bed.

"See," she said.

"Those are nothing but kites," said the two old men.

"But what is a kite on the ground?" she said. "It is nothing. What does it need to sustain it and make it beautiful and truly spiritual?"

"The wind, of course!" said the others.

"And what do the sky and the wind need to make them beautiful?"

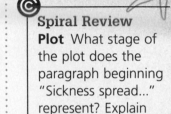

**Spiral Review**
**Plot** What stage of the plot does the paragraph beginning "Sickness spread..." represent? Explain your answer.

*L*ike a rusted machine, the city ground to a halt.

Reading Check

What kind of wall does the daughter suggest should be built to defeat Kwan-Si's sun?

**Literary Analysis**
**Symbolism and Allegory** What kind of relationship do the kite and the wind symbolize?

"A kite, of course—many kites, to break the monotony, the sameness of the sky. Colored kites, flying!"

"So," said the Mandarin's daughter. "You, Kwan-Si, will make a last rebuilding of your town to resemble nothing more nor less than the wind. And we shall build like a golden kite. The wind will beautify the kite and carry it to wondrous heights. And the kite will break the sameness of the wind's existence and give it purpose and meaning. One without the other is nothing. Together, all will be beauty and cooperation and a long and enduring life."

Whereupon the two mandarins were so overjoyed that they took their first nourishment in days, momentarily were given strength, embraced, and lavished praise upon each other, called the Mandarin's daughter a boy, a man, a stone pillar, a warrior, and a true and unforgettable son. Almost immediately they parted and hurried to their towns, calling out and singing, weakly but happily.

And so, in time, the towns became the Town of Golden Kite and the Town of the Silver Wind. And harvestings were harvested and business tended again, and the flesh returned, and disease ran off like a frightened jackal. And on every night of the year the inhabitants in the Town of the Kite could hear the good clear wind sustaining them. And those in the Town of the Wind could hear the kite singing, whispering, rising, and beautifying them.

"So be it," said the Mandarin in front of his silken screen.

## Critical Thinking

1. **Key Ideas and Details (a) Interpret:** How do the townspeople react to the repeated directions to rebuild? **(b) Analyze Cause and Effect:** How does the competition between the towns affect the people's health and well-being? Explain.

2. **Integration of Knowledge and Ideas (a) Evaluate:** Should the people have continued to follow the Mandarin as a leader?

3. **Integration of Knowledge and Ideas (a) Evaluate:** Why are walls built as a kite and the wind more effective for a peaceful and harmonious relationship between the two towns? **(b) Draw Conclusions:** What lesson does this story teach for today's world?

4. **Integration of Knowledge and Ideas (a)** Why do the two Mandarins feel that their cities must compete in wall-building? **(b)** To end their conflict, what must the Mandarins realize is more important than this competition? Explain your answer.
*[Connect to the Big Question: Is conflict necessary?]*

Cite textual evidence to support your responses.

## Comparing Symbolism and Allegory

**1. Key Ideas and Details** Use a chart like the one shown to analyze how the characters, events, and setting in "The Golden Kite, the Silver Wind" could be **symbols** for Cold War leaders and events.

| Symbol | Qualities | Meaning |
|---|---|---|
| Mandarin | Leader of his town; worried about losing business and reputation | Leader of a nation who wants to stay on top |
| Mandarin's daughter | | |
| Walls | | |

**2. Key Ideas and Details (a)** In "The Scarlet Ibis," what does the ibis symbolize? **(b)** Which details support your conclusion? Explain.

**3. Craft and Structure** Based on your analysis of the **symbolism** in the stories, which of these selections is an **allegory?** Explain.

**4. Craft and Structure** Based on these stories, why do you think writers might use symbolism in their work?

## ⏱ Timed Writing

### Explanatory Text: Essay

Write an essay in which you compare the use of symbolism in "The Scarlet Ibis" and "The Golden Kite, the Silver Wind." Use details from the texts to support your responses. **(30 minutes)**

### 5-Minute Planner

1. Read the prompt carefully and completely.
2. Gather your ideas. Consider these questions before you write.
   - What message or lesson does the author of each story express?
   - How do both authors use symbols to develop a message?
3. Decide on an organizational strategy.
   - Block: Discuss one story, and then another.
   - Point by Point: Discuss one aspect of each story's symbolism at a time.
4. Reread the prompt, and then draft your essay.

# Writing Workshop

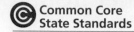 **Common Core State Standards**

**Writing**

**2.** Write informative/explanatory texts to examine and convey complex ideas, concepts, and information clearly and accurately through the effective selection, organization, and analysis of content.

**2.a.** Introduce a topic; organize complex ideas, concepts, and information to make important connections and distinctions; include formatting, graphics, and multimedia when useful to aiding comprehension.

**2.b.** Develop the topic with well-chosen, relevant, and sufficient facts, extended definitions, concrete details, quotations, or other information and examples appropriate to the audience's knowledge of the topic.

**5.** Develop and strengthen writing as needed by planning, revising, editing, rewriting, or trying a new approach, focusing on addressing what is most significant for a specific purpose and audience.

## Write Explanatory Text

### Exposition: Cause-and-Effect Essay

**Defining the Form** Whether the subject is human nature, historical trends, or weather patterns, cause-and-effect reasoning explains why things happen. A **cause-and-effect essay** examines the relationship between or among two or more events, explaining how one causes another. You may use elements of this type of writing in science reports, history papers, and health articles, for example.

**Assignment** Write a cause-and-effect essay to explain an event or a condition in a subject area that interests you, such as business, the arts, technology, history, sports, or music. Include these elements:

✓ a clear *identification of a cause-and-effect relationship*

✓ an *analysis of specific aspects of the cause* or causes that produce the effects

✓ *facts, details, examples, and reasons that support your assertions* and *anticipate readers' questions*

✓ a *logical organization* clarified by smooth transitions

✓ error-free grammar, including correct *subject-verb agreement*

To preview the criteria on which your cause-and-effect essay may be judged, see the rubric on page 409.

 **Writing Workshop:** *Work in Progress*

Review the work you did on pages 345 and 373.

## WRITE GUY
*Jeff Anderson, M.Ed.*

### What Do You Notice?

**Sentence Structure**

Read and reread this passage from Elizabeth McCracken's "Desiderata."

*I could tell dozens of other stories from the pages of family papers: my aunt Blanche's pell-mell record of taking care of her favorite sister, Elizabeth, who was dying of Alzheimer's; Blanche has that disease herself now, and you can see the early signs in these notes. My great-uncles' cheery letters from Europe during World War II.*

Jot down what you notice about the passage. Then, consider how you might use examples to affect the audience of your own essay.

**Reading-Writing Connection**

To get a feel for cause-and-effect essays, read the excerpt from *Silent Spring* by Rachel Carson on page 167.

# Prewriting/Planning Strategies

**Examine current events.** Scan newspapers or magazines for headlines that interest you. Use a three-column chart to speculate about possible causes and effects: In the middle column, write the event; in the left column, write the possible causes; in the right column, note possible effects. Notice how the event listed in the chart below—team wins championship—is an effect of the causes listed in the left column— practice, focus, and individual performance—as well as a cause of the effects listed in the right column—increased fan interest, harder to buy tickets, and revenue for city.

**PHLit**
**Online!**
www.PHLitOnline.com
• Author video: Writing Process
• Author video: Rewards of Writing

| Causes | Event | Effects |
|--------|-------|---------|
| • practice, focus<br>• individual performance | Team wins championship. | • increased fan interest<br>• harder to buy tickets<br>• revenue for city |

**List and freewrite.** Jot down any interesting events that come to mind from the worlds of business, science, technology, the arts, nature, politics, and sports. Then, circle the item that most intrigues you. Freewrite for three minutes about that topic. As you write, note any causes and effects that come to mind. You can develop your topic from ideas you uncover in your freewriting.

**Categorize to narrow your topic.** You may find that your topic is too broad to manage in the scope of a single essay. Break your subject into smaller categories. For example, if your topic is about a record-breaking sports event, you might create categories such as "key player," "great coach," and "new equipment." Choose a more focused topic that interests you from your list of categories.

**Chart causes and effects.** Using an index card or a self-sticking note, write the central event or circumstance that is your subject. Explore the causes that produced the event and the effects the event produced. Write those factors on separate cards or notes. Write key details related to each cause and effect on the cards or notes. Then, arrange the cards or notes in a logical sequence.

# Drafting Strategies

 **Common Core State Standards**

**Writing**

**2.a.** Introduce a topic; organize complex ideas, concepts, and information to make important connections and distinctions; include formatting, graphics, and multimedia when useful to aiding comprehension.

**2.b.** Develop the topic with well-chosen, relevant, and sufficient facts, extended definitions, concrete details, quotations, or other information and examples appropriate to the audience's knowledge of the topic.

**2.e.** Establish and maintain a formal style and objective tone while attending to the norms and conventions of the discipline in which they are writing.

**Choose a structure.** In your opening paragraph, introduce your topic and show why it is important. Here are two possibilities for organizing the body paragraphs of your essay:

- **Chronological order** is particularly valuable when describing a sequence of causes and effects. You can start with the cause and then continue by describing its effects. You can also start with the effect and then list its causes one at a time. Keep in mind, however, that a time-order relationship is not in itself proof of cause and effect.

- **Order of importance** organization can be structured in two ways. You can begin with your most important point and follow it with less important points—this approach grabs a reader's attention. Alternatively, you can begin with your least important point and build toward your most important point, which creates drama.

**Use logical evidence and an objective tone.** As you build support for your ideas, avoid opinions and trivial details. Rely instead on facts, statistics, and persuasive examples. Strengthen your ideas even more by using a formal writing style and an objective, serious tone.

- **Unsupported assertion:** Members of the royal family probably liked the color purple more than any other color.

- **Convincing support:** According to a primary-source historical document, members of the royal family believed the color purple symbolized power and prosperity.

**Use the TRI method to develop paragraphs.** Follow these steps:

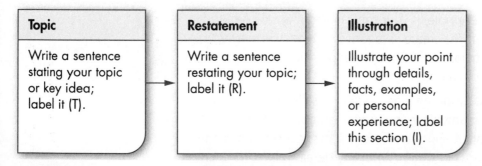

| Topic | Restatement | Illustration |
|---|---|---|
| Write a sentence stating your topic or key idea; label it (T). | Write a sentence restating your topic; label it (R). | Illustrate your point through details, facts, examples, or personal experience; label this section (I). |

You can use the TRI pattern to shift the sequence to suit the information you present and add variety to your writing.

**Example:** Originally, the color purple was associated with royalty. **(T)** Only kings, queens, and members of the nobility wore purple-colored clothing. **(R)** In England, Queen Elizabeth I actually made a law prohibiting anyone except herself and her relatives from wearing purple. **(I)**

## Writers on Writing

# Wayson Choy On Showing Cause and Effect

Wayson Choy is the author of "The Jade Peony" (p. 203).

An origami butterfly sits on my computer to remind me that just as a butterfly must first go through various stages, my first draft will be "re-created" many times before it can take flight. During that process, I keep in mind that a sense of cause and effect is as important in fiction as in nonfiction. So, I hone the action and dialogue "to show, not tell about" the causes and effects in my characters' lives. The following draft from my novel *All That Matters* demonstrates how I do that.

*I aim for "showing, not telling."*
—Wayson Choy

### Professional Model:

### from *All That Matters*

   I had given up a late afternoon soccer practice to do some serious studying for Mr. Eades's first English test. There were plenty of others like us, books opened, eyes focused. Jenny pointed to the library seat across from hers, and her eyes said, *No fooling around!* ~~Truth was, she took her English studies more seriously than she took me. It was frustrating. I just wanted to be with her. She was always in charge.~~

   As she pushed my books across the table, I thought that she and I should have, two months ago, declared ourselves an official couple, especially after our fifth double date together. But Jenny didn't want that.

   "Too showy," she had told me. "Maybe after we graduate. Next year."

   She folded both our school sweaters together and neatly draped them over one of the empty chairs.

I needed to expand this account with more details to show causes and effects in the relationship between the narrator and his girlfriend, Jenny.

These two sentences tell that Jenny is an in-control girl who takes charge of the narrator. But I wanted to show it through dialogue and actions.

The act of folding the sweaters symbolizes Jenny's shaping of the relationship.

# Revising Strategies

**Clarify cause-and-effect relationships.** Review your entire draft, focusing on the causes and effects you have presented. With two highlighters, use one color to mark phrases that show causes and the other to mark effects. Add details to strengthen connections, insert transitional words to make links clear, and eliminate causes or effects that do not support your main point. Provide a clear concluding statement that follows logically from the information that preceded it and that supports your main idea.

### Model: Revising to Clarify Cause and Effect

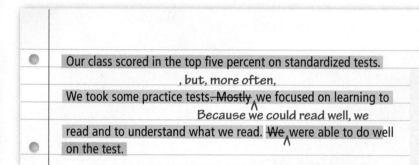

Our class scored in the top five percent on standardized tests.

~~, but, more often,~~

We took some practice tests. ~~Mostly~~ we focused on learning to

*Because we could read well, we*

read and to understand what we read. ~~We~~ were able to do well on the test.

> This writer adds transitional words and phrases to clarify the cause-and-effect relationships.

**Combine short sentences.** If you find too many short sentences, look for places to combine them using the following strategies:

- Combine two sentences using subordinating clauses that start with conjunctions such as *after, although, despite, if,* and *whenever.* Use subordinating conjunctions to show a relationship between ideas.

- Use coordinating conjunctions such as *and, but, or, nor, for, so,* and *yet* to combine ideas of equal importance.

**Example:   Short Sentences:**
The team members lost hope. They found an unlikely inspiration to continue.

**Combined:**
The team members lost hope, but they found an unlikely inspiration to continue.

## Peer Review

Ask a partner to read your draft, and then have a discussion about your work. Your reader should discuss the clarity of the cause-and-effect relationships presented throughout your essay. Consider modifying sentences, omitting or adding transitions, or reordering paragraphs to improve the logical flow of your ideas as needed.

# Revising to Correct Faulty Subject-Verb Agreement

For a subject and verb to agree, they must agree in number.

**Identifying Errors in Subject-Verb Agreement** Agreement errors may occur with compound subjects, subjects joined by *or* or *nor*, and indefinite pronouns as subjects. Below, subjects are underlined and verbs italicized.

**Compound Subject:**
The coach and the captain *is going* *are going* to attend.

**Subject Joined by *Or* or *Nor*:**
Either Jason or his brother *are bringing* *is bringing* the snacks.

**Indefinite Pronoun as Subject:**
Everybody who supports our ideas *are helping* *is helping*.

If a plural subject is joined to a singular subject by *or* or *nor*, the verb should agree with the subject that is closer to it.

**Correct:** Either the coach or the co-captains *are going* to speak.
**Correct:** Either the co-captains or the coach *is going* to speak.

**Fixing Errors** To correct subject and verb agreement, follow these steps:

1. **Identify whether the subject in a sentence is singular or plural.**

2. **Select the matching form of the verb:**
   - For compound subjects joined by *and*, use plural verb forms.
   - For singular subjects joined by *or* or *nor*, use singular verb forms.
   - When the subject is an indefinite pronoun, use the appropriate verb form. Use this chart for guidance.

> **PH** **WRITING COACH**
>
> Further instruction and practice are available in *Prentice Hall Writing Coach*.

| Indefinite Pronouns | |
|---|---|
| **Always Singular** | anybody, anyone, anything, each, either, every, everybody, everyone, everything, neither, nobody, no one, nothing, somebody, someone, something |
| **Always Plural** | both, few, many, others, several |
| **Singular or Plural** | all, any, more, most, none, some |

**Grammar in Your Writing**

Scan several paragraphs in your draft and underline all compound subjects and indefinite pronouns. In each case, make sure that the verb form you have used agrees with the subject.

# Student Model: Glen Milner, Charlotte, NC

**Common Core State Standards**

Language
**2.c.** Spell correctly.

## Climate Effects of the North Atlantic Current

The oceans have been around since the beginning of time, yet we know relatively little about them. They are constantly moving and changing, turning up water that has been down in the depths for hundreds of years. One of these currents is the North Atlantic, also known as the Great Ocean Conveyor Belt.

The level of impact the current has on climate and the causes that change it are widely debated. The presumption held by most scientists is that we are currently experiencing global warming. Other theories state that global warming may influence the North Atlantic Current. This, consequently, may cause the exact opposite of warming— an ice age.

Models have shown that any change in speed or location of the current may well cause a rapid climate shift of great magnitude (Burroughs 17). This shift would be caused by two key changes: a decrease in salinity and an increase in the temperature of water in the North Atlantic Current. These factors would, in turn, cause the current to slow down or shut down, sending the Northern Hemisphere into an ice age.

The North Atlantic Current is a complicated system that runs for thousands of miles and combines water from all oceans. It moves heat from the tropics to the northern Atlantic. Robert Kunzig, the author of *The Restless Sea: Exploring the World Beneath the Waves* . . ., said that oceanographers call this the "global journey" of the Thermohaline Circulation, which is run by heat and salt (268). It is called a conveyor belt because warm water moves north on surface currents and then back south in deep cold-water currents, folding over itself like a conveyor belt. The heat has a drastic effect on the climate for the Northern Hemisphere. Without it, the average temperature would be much lower.

The mechanisms by which the current works are very simple. As the water moves north, it cools down. In addition, its salinity rises because winds that blow east to west across the equator transport moisture from the Atlantic to the Pacific, leaving the Atlantic more saline. The water that feeds the Atlantic from the Mediterranean is also salty because it is nearly landlocked and moisture evaporates from the Mediterranean, leaving it saltier (Mayewski 105). As the temperature decreases and salinity increases, the water becomes denser, causing it to sink. As it sinks, it spreads out deep in the ocean basin where it is pulled back toward the equator, thus creating the conveyor-like characteristics. . . .

Direct statements of fact form the basis of the essay.

Glen builds interest by acknowledging that there are differing opinions on the topic.

The coordinating conjunction *consequently* is particularly useful in a cause-and-effect essay.

The writer takes the knowledge level of his audience into account and provides explanations of scientific concepts. He supports his ideas with research.

Glen uses chronological order to explain the way the ocean currents work.

# Editing and Proofreading

Check your draft for errors in spelling, grammar, and punctuation.

**Focus on spelling.** Double-check your spelling of words like *unnecessary* and *dissatisfied* in which a prefix is added to a base word that begins with a consonant. In most cases, the spelling of the base word does not change.

**Focus on sentence clarity.** Ensure that your sentences are clear by checking that the subjects agree with the verbs. In addition, read each sentence to be sure that each one expresses a complete thought.

# Publishing and Presenting

Consider one of the following ways to share your work with others:

**Present your essay.** Use photographs, charts, and diagrams to help you explain the topic of your article. Include definitions of any challenging or specialized vocabulary your listeners will need to know in order to understand the information. Ask friends in the audience to provide feedback notes on your presentation.

**Submit your essay for publication.** If your essay focuses on a matter of local interest, send it to your school or community newspaper.

# Reflecting on Your Writing

**Writer's Journal** Jot down your answer to this question:
*How did writing about the topic help you understand it?*

# Rubric for Self-Assessment

Find evidence in your writing to address each category. Then, use the rating scale to grade your work.

**Spiral Review**
Earlier in this unit, you learned about **subjects and predicates** (p. 344) and **active and passive voice** (p. 372). Check your essay for correct subject-predicate agreement and for appropriate and effective use of active and passive voice.

| Criteria | Rating Scale |
|---|---|
| | not very       very |
| **Focus:** How clearly do you identify and explore the cause-and-effect relationship? | 1   2   3   4   5 |
| **Organization:** How logical is your organization? | 1   2   3   4   5 |
| **Support/Elaboration:** How effective are your facts, details, and reasons? | 1   2   3   4   5 |
| **Style:** How well do you use transitional words and phrases? | 1   2   3   4   5 |
| **Conventions:** How correct is your grammar, especially your use of subject-verb agreement? | 1   2   3   4   5 |

# Vocabulary Workshop

## Etymology: Words from Mythology

**Common Core
State Standards**

**Language**

**4.** Determine or clarify the meaning of unknown and multiple-meaning words and phrases based on grades 9–10 reading and content, choosing flexibly from a range of strategies.

**4.c.** Consult general and specialized reference materials, both print and digital, to find the pronunciation of a word or determine or clarify its precise meaning, its part of speech, or its etymology.

The words that make up the English language come from a variety of sources. A word's **origin,** or source, is shown in its etymology. A word's **etymology** identifies the language in which the word first appeared and tells how its spelling and meaning have changed over time. The following excerpt from a dictionary entry shows the etymology of the word *make*.

### Sample Dictionary Entry

Middle English (Dictionaries usually list abbreviations at the front or back of the book.)

The Middle English source word

**make** (māk) *vt.* [ME *maken* < OE *macian*, akin to Ger *machen* < IE base *\*mag-*, to knead, press, stretch > MASON, Gr *magis*, kneaded mass, paste, dough, *mageus*, kneader]

This symbol means "derived from."

Many English words are derived from Greek, Roman, and Norse mythology. Having some knowledge of myths from these cultures can help you to understand the origins and meaning of new words. This chart shows some examples.

| Word | Definition | Origin |
|------|-----------|--------|
| narcissistic | showing excessive self-love | reference to Narcissus, a young man in Greek mythology who falls in love with his own reflection |
| mercurial | lively and quick-witted | reference to Mercury, a god in Roman mythology who is swift and clever |
| Wednesday | the fourth day of the week | Old Norse word *Othinsdagr,* which means "Odin's day," a reference to the chief god in Norse mythology |

**Practice A** Look up each word in a print, digital, or online dictionary. Identify the original Greek, Latin, or Old Norse source word and its meaning.

1. skill
2. salute
3. antique

4. crisis
5. ship
6. north

**Practice B** Find each underlined word in a print, digital, or online dictionary that provides word etymologies. Write the word's definition, and then use its etymology to explain how the original source word relates to the word's use in the sentence.

1. When the ambulance sounded its <u>siren</u>, cars moved out of its way.

2. She seemed to be in a <u>hypnotic</u> state.

3. A <u>witness</u> came forward and told what she saw.

4. When the mouse saw the cat, he made a quick <u>escape</u>.

5. The club's <u>slogan</u> is "Do your best!"

6. We had to <u>pay</u> a fee before entering the park.

7. I <u>regret</u> that I will be unable to attend the event.

8. The Sampsons have a <u>robot</u> that cleans the bottom of their pool.

9. He apologized for <u>spilling</u> the milk.

**Activity** Prepare a note card like the one shown for each of these words: *derive, choice, tantalize, window,* and *curfew.* Look up each word in a dictionary and record some details about the word's origin, including notes about how older words from other languages influenced its meaning. Then, write the word's modern meaning. Finally, write a sentence using the word.

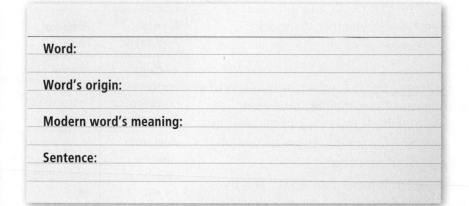

| Word: |
|---|
| Word's origin: |
| Modern word's meaning: |
| Sentence: |

**Comprehension and Collaboration**

Work with three classmates to research the following characters from Greek and Roman mythology. Then, use a dictionary to find an English word that is based on the character's name. Finally, write a few sentences that explain how the word's meaning relates to the character.

**Mars**
**Vulcan**
**Jove**

# Communications Workshop

## Evaluating a Speech

**Common Core State Standards**

**Speaking and Listening**

**3.** Evaluate a speaker's point of view, reasoning, and use of evidence and rhetoric, identifying any fallacious reasoning or exaggerated or distorted evidence.

When you hear a formal speech or an informal talk, strive to be an active listener. Assess the credibility of the message and the effectiveness of the speaker's techniques. Learning how to evaluate a speech will make you a critical listener, allow you to judge the value of what you hear, and give you a solid basis for improving your own oral presentations.

### Learn the Skills

**Create a context.** When listening to a speech or an informal talk, consider the following questions:

- What is the speaker's purpose?
- What knowledge of the subject does the speaker have?
- What traditional, cultural, or historical influences shape the message?
- As a listener, what prior knowledge do you bring to the topic?

**Evaluate the development of arguments.** A good speaker presents arguments that are clearly and logically stated and fully supported with evidence in the form of facts, statistics, anecdotes, and expert opinions. As you listen, ask yourself whether the speaker's information is accurate, complete, and relevant. Is important information deliberately or unintentionally excluded? Does the speaker have a point of view—the perspective from which he or she speaks—that might lead to bias, or a focus on only one side of an argument? Assess whether the speaker's use of facts is fair or biased. Try to anticipate weaknesses in certain types of arguments.

**Note the speaker's choice of language.** Listen for the speaker's use of words and phrases with positive or negative connotations, or associations. Note repetition of key words or stress given to certain phrases. Be alert to the fact that some speakers, as a substitute for good evidence or logical argument, may rely on emotionally "loaded" language.

**Note the speaker's technique.** A speech is more than words. Use the following questions to analyze nonverbal elements:

- Is the speaker's tone of voice, word choice, and rate of speaking appropriate for the audience, subject, and occasion?
- What is the effect of the speaker's nonverbal signals, such as eye contact, facial expressions, and gestures?
- When and why does the speaker pause, speak more loudly or softly, or speak more rapidly or slowly?

| Type of Argument | Potential Flaw |
|---|---|
| **Analogy:** compares one situation to another | Are the two situations really alike? |
| **Authority:** cites the opinion of an expert | Is the expert knowledgeable and unbiased? |
| **Emotion:** appeals to the audience's feelings | Is the full argument balanced between logic and emotion? |
| **Causation:** shows a cause-and-effect relationship | Does the speaker oversimplify his or her arguments? |

# Practice the Skills

**Ⓒ Presentation of Knowledge and Ideas** Use what you've learned in this workshop to perform the following task.

> ## ACTIVITY: Evaluate a Speech
>
> As a class, view a political speech or a televised editorial. Then, use the evaluation tools from this workshop and the following questions to write a two-paragraph evaluation of the speech or editorial. In your evaluation, assess the content (including point of view, use of supporting details, and word choice) and technique (including tone, stresses, pauses, and non-verbal gestures).
>
> - What is the speaker's point of view?
> - Does the speaker use logical reasoning? How can you tell?
> - Are the speaker's points supported with facts, details, and opinions from experts?
> - Was the information presented unbiased?
> - Did the speaker exclude any important information?
> - How do you think the speech or editorial could be improved?

**Ⓒ Comprehension and Collaboration** After you have listened to the speech or editorial and have drafted your evaluation, form groups and discuss your findings, noting what you thought were the strongest and weakest parts of the speech. As you listen to classmates, jot down notes on your classmates' views. Then, as a group, review and fill in the following Evaluation Checklist. When you have finished, share your results with the rest of the class and discuss your reasoning.

> ## Evaluation Checklist
>
> ### Speech Content
> Rate the speaker's content on a scale of 1 (very poor) to 5 (excellent) for each of these items. Explain your ratings.
>
> - met the needs of the audience     Rating: ___
> - achieved its purpose     Rating: ___
> - was appropriate to the occasion     Rating: ___
> - used effective main and supporting ideas     Rating: ___
> - included convincing facts and expert opinions     Rating: ___
>
> ### Speech Delivery
> Rate the speaker's delivery on a scale of 1 (very poor) to 5 (excellentl) for each of these items. Explain your ratings.
>
> - formal language     Rating: ___
> - eye contact     Rating: ___
> - effective speaking rate     Rating: ___
> - pauses for effect     Rating: ___
> - appropriate volume     Rating: ___
> - enunciation     Rating: ___
> - appropriate gestures     Rating: ___
> - conventions of language     Rating: ___

# Cumulative Review

 Common Core
State Standards

RL.9-10.1, RL.9-10.3, RL.9-10.4,
RL.9-10.5; W.9-10.10
[For the full wording of the standards,
see the standards chart in the front of
your textbook.]

## I. Reading Literature

**Directions:** *Read the passage. Then, answer each question that follows.*

It was Nicole's first year of high school. She was so nervous that her mom desperately wanted to help. To ease Nicole's transition, her mom decided that Nicole should try out for the marching band flag corps. Nicole's mom had been in the flag corps when she was young, and she had met some of her best friends there.

"I'm a total <u>klutz</u>," Nicole said. "I don't think I can do it." Nicole neglected to mention that she had no desire to join the flag corps. Practicing every night after school in the blazing heat did not appeal to her. Spending every weekend at football games and competitions sounded incredibly boring. Because Nicole's mom was so excited, though, Nicole couldn't bear to disappoint her.

"You'll absolutely love it," Nicole's mom said. "It is so much fun. You'll meet a whole new group of friends. It was the best thing I ever did!"

"Okay," Nicole agreed reluctantly. "I'll try it." Nicole did not have a lot of confidence about making the flag corps. She had never been coordinated—she was more of a bookworm than an athlete. Night after night, though, Nicole diligently practiced with her mom. After weeks of practice, she wasn't *so* bad.

Finally, the day of tryouts arrived. Nicole's mom was far more nervous than Nicole. Nicole, however, was apprehensive for another reason. She didn't want to join the flag corps, yet she didn't want to disappoint her mother. She felt totally and completely stuck. After weighing her options, she finally knew what she had to do.

A month later, on a Saturday afternoon, Nicole could hear her mother cheering boisterously from the audience. Nicole had just scored the winning point for the quiz bowl team. It turns out that Nicole had not tried out for the flag corps after all. She knew that finding an activity was a good idea, but the flag corps was not the one for her. Quiz bowl, though, was perfect. She made many new friends who shared her interests. Instead of being upset, Nicole's mom was happy her daughter had found a way to meet new people and do something that she enjoyed.

1. What **internal conflict** does Nicole face?

    **A.** She wants to join the flag corps but doesn't want to disappoint her mother.
    **B.** She doesn't want to be in the flag corps or disappoint her mother.
    **C.** She joins the flag corps but she is clumsy.
    **D.** She doesn't know what she wants to do her first year of high school.

2. What **external conflict** does Nicole face?

    **A.** her own clumsiness
    **B.** her mother
    **C.** students at high school
    **D.** blazing heat

3. Which of the following is *not* part of this story's **setting?**

    **A.** a quiz bowl
    **B.** Nicole's home
    **C.** a football game
    **D.** the beginning of the school year

4. Which of the following is an example of **direct characterization?**

    **A.** It was Nicole's first year of high school.
    **B.** "You'll absolutely love it," Nicole's mom said.
    **C.** She was more of a bookworm than an athlete.
    **D.** Nicole had just scored the winning point for the quiz bowl team.

5. Which of the following is an example of **indirect characterization?**

    **A.** Nicole practiced diligently with her mom.
    **B.** But Nicole's mom was so excited, Nicole couldn't bear to disappoint her.
    **C.** She knew she had to find something that she was interested in.
    **D.** It was Nicole's first year of high school.

6. What does the **dialogue** reveal about Nicole's feelings?

    **A.** She is hesitant about joining the flag corps.
    **B.** She wants to argue with her mother.
    **C.** She cannot express herself clearly.
    **D.** She is angry at her mother for making her try out.

7. **Vocabulary** Which is the best definition of the underlined word *klutz?*

    **A.** a boring person
    **B.** a foolish person
    **C.** a clumsy person
    **D.** a confused person

8. How is the **conflict** in the story resolved?

    **A.** Nicole does what her mother wants.
    **B.** Nicole joins the quiz bowl instead of the flag corps.
    **C.** Nicole's mother is disappointed with her.
    **D.** Nicole doesn't make the team in tryouts.

9. Which of the following expectations creates a **surprise ending?**

    **A.** The reader expects Nicole to join the flag corps.
    **B.** The reader expects Nicole to fail the tryouts.
    **C.** The reader expects Nicole to join the quiz team.
    **D.** The reader expects Nicole's mom to be disappointed.

### ◈ Timed Writing

10. Write an informative essay in which you identify and explain the **situational irony** in this story. In your essay, be sure to describe the clues that led you to expect a different story outcome.

**GO ON**

## II. Reading Informational Text

**Directions:** *Read the passage. Then, answer each question that follows.*

**Common Core State Standards**

**RI.9-10.4, RI.9-10.5; L.9-10.1, L.9-10.2**
[For the full wording of the standards, see the standards chart in the front of your textbook.]

# History of the Bicycle

The early history of the bicycle is sparsely recorded, leading to many debates. One thing that is known for sure is that the late nineteenth century gave rise to the bicycle's popularity.

### The Nineteenth Century

Bicycles were originally powered by riders who pushed against the ground with their feet to get moving. In the 1860s, inventors added pedals to bicycles. At that time, France was the home of the bicycle. The word *bicycle* comes from the French word *bicyclette*. In models at that time, the front wheel was a bit larger than the back. The iron frame and iron wheels made for an uncomfortable ride. This version of the bicycle was appropriately nicknamed the "boneshaker."

In the 1870s, interest moved to Britain and development continued there. The British introduced the "ordinary," a bicycle with solid rubber tires, a large front wheel, and a small back wheel. The ordinary proved to be hazardous. By 1885, the "safety" was invented, in which the front wheel size was reduced and the rear wheel enlarged.

In the 1890s, bicycling around the world boomed. Bicycles provided a means of transportation for men, women, and children.

### The Twentieth Century

In the early 1900s, the automobile was introduced and mass transit improved, giving the bicycle a second-class status. However, a <u>resurgence</u> of popularity came in the 1950s and 1960s with huge sales of the banana seat bicycles. The 1970s saw the invention of the 10-speed and a huge growth in the bicycle industry. In the 1980s and 1990s, the popularity of the mountain bike grew.

### Bicycling Today

Today, bicyclers can choose from a variety of bicycles. Some of the most predominant styles are the mountain bike, the racing bike, and the hybrid (a cross between the two). Bicycling has reached a new level of popularity.

---

**1. Vocabulary** What is the *best* definition for the underlined word *resurgence*?

   **A.** decline

   **B.** revival

   **C.** surprise

   **D.** group

**2.** What **text feature** does the author use in this article?

   **A.** bulleted lists

   **B.** time lines

   **C.** heads and subheads

   **D.** outlines

# III. Writing and Language Conventions

**Directions:** *Read the passage. Then, answer each question that follows.*

(1) Jeff's face felt hot as the redness crawled up her cheeks. (2) Every time she introduced herself, she heard, "Isn't Jeff a boy's name?" (3) It was worse when she was little. (4) Everyone thought she is a boy. (5) Now it was just embarrassing. (6) She wanted to introduce herself to him. (7) As she struggled through the crowd in the cafeteria, she noticed that Joe, the attractive boy from her English class, was there. (8) Then, his friend had to ask that question. (9) His friends chuckled, but Joe smiled kindly. (10) When lunch was over, Jeff walk away brokenhearted. (11) She knew she would never talk to Joe again. (12) Suddenly, a tap was felt on her shoulder. (13) "Jeff is a great name. It makes you special," said Joe. (14) A smile spread across Jeff's face. (15) Maybe she needed to be proud of being different.

**1.** Which of the following revisions *best* corrects the inconsistent **verb tense** in sentence 4?

  **A.** Change *is* to *were*.
  **B.** Change *is* to *was*.
  **C.** Change *is* to *will be*.
  **D.** Leave as is.

**2.** Which revision to sentence 9 helps to highlight Jeff's **internal conflict?**

  **A.** His friends chuckled as Jeff knew they would, but Joe smiled kindly.
  **B.** Joe smiled kindly even though his friends chuckled.
  **C.** His friends chuckled, but Joe smiled kindly.
  **D.** His friends chuckled and Jeff felt herself tingle with embarrassment, but Joe smiled kindly.

**3.** Which revision shows the *best* way to correct the use of **passive voice** in sentence 12?

  **A.** Suddenly, she tapped on her shoulder.
  **B.** Suddenly, on her shoulder a tap was felt by Jeff.
  **C.** Suddenly, a tap is felt by Jeff on her shoulder.
  **D.** Suddenly, she felt a tap on her shoulder.

**4.** Which revision to sentence 8 would help clarify the event being described?

  **A.** Then his friend had to ask that question: What's your name?
  **B.** Then his friend had to ask that same old question.
  **C.** The question Jeff dreaded was asked by his friend.
  **D.** Then his friend, whom Jeff didn't know, had to ask that question.

**5.** Which of the following revisions is the *best* way to correct the **verb tense** shift in sentence 10?

  **A.** Change *was* to *is*.
  **B.** Change *walk* to *walks*.
  **C.** Change *walk* to *walked*.
  **D.** Change *walk* to *will walk*.

**6.** Which revision would *best* clarify the **sequence of events** in this passage?

  **A.** Switch sentence 12 and sentence 13.
  **B.** Switch sentence 5 and sentence 6.
  **C.** Switch sentence 7 and sentence 8.
  **D.** Switch sentence 6 and sentence 7.

# Performance Tasks

**Common Core
State Standards**

RL.9-10.1, RL.9-10.3, RL.9-10.4,
RL.9-10.5; W.9-10.9.a; SL.9-10.1,
SL.9-10.4; L.9-10.6
[For the full wording of the standards,
see the standards chart in the front of
your textbook.]

**Directions:** *Follow the instructions to complete the tasks below
as required by your teacher.*

*As you work on each task, incorporate both general academic
vocabulary and literary terms you learned in this unit.*

## Writing

### Task 1: Literature [RL.9-10.3; W.9-10.9.a]
**Analyze a Complex Character**

*Write an essay in which you analyze the development
of a complex character from a story in this unit.*

- State which story and character you chose and
  why. Explain what qualities make the character
  complex. Provide a brief summary of the story's
  plot and your character's role in it.

- Explain how the author uses characterization—
  direct, indirect, or both—to develop the character.
  Cite details, including dialogue and descriptions of
  interactions between characters.

- Explain how your character changes and develops
  over the course of the story. Discuss how these
  changes help to advance the plot or develop the
  story's theme.

- Use proper language conventions, including
  correct subject and predicate agreement.

### Task 2: Literature [RL.9-10.5; W.9-10.9.a]
**Analyze Situational Irony in a Short Story**

*Analyze how an author's use of situational irony in a
story from this unit creates surprise.*

- State which story you chose and briefly summarize
  the plot.

- Explain what is ironic in the plot and show what
  happens that contradicts the expectations of
  characters or the reader.

- Explain how the story's surprise ending still makes
  sense and fits with details or ideas from earlier in
  the work.

- Provide specific examples from the text to support
  your analysis.

- Use active rather than passive voice whenever
  possible.

### Task 3: Literature [RL.9-10.1; W.9-10.9.a]
**Make and Support Inferences About a Main
Character**

*Write an essay in which you explain how making
inferences about a main character affected your
understanding of a story from this unit.*

- Introduce the story's characters, setting, and plot,
  and explain the main character's role in the story.

- Identify three inferences you made about the
  main character while reading this story. Cite
  specific details you used to make them.

- Show how making inferences led you to an
  understanding of the main character. For
  example, you might show how specific details
  suggest a character's personality traits, such as
  kindness, or help you predict the character's
  actions.

### Task 4: Literature [RL.9-10.5; W.9-10.9.a]
**Analyze Plot Structure**

*Write an essay in which you analyze how events in a
story from this unit are ordered by cause-and-effect
relationships.*

- Identify a story from this unit in which cause-and-
  effect relationships play a key role. Briefly
  summarize the plot.

- Describe how the story's plot follows a series of
  causes and effects. Explain how these causes and
  effects are introduced and developed in the
  different stages of the plot—the exposition, rising
  action, climax, and resolution.

- Cite examples from the story that clearly show
  how one event causes or influences another.
  Explain how events lead to the story's resolution
  or to a character's epiphany.

# Speaking and Listening

## Task 5: Literature [RL.9-10.4; SL.9-10.4]
### Analyze How Language Evokes a Sense of Time and Place

*Deliver an oral presentation in which you analyze how the language in a story from this unit creates a vivid picture of the setting (time and place).*

- Identify the story you chose and explain the setting—where and when it takes place.

- Provide examples of words the author chose to evoke this time and place. Identify descriptive language, as well as language specific to a certain region or era. Explain how these word choices help to paint a picture of the physical setting while also building a specific mood in the story.

- Clarify the meanings of any words that might be unfamiliar to your listeners.

- Include a visual image that captures an aspect of the story's setting. It might illustrate the location or simply suggest a similar mood. Explain why you chose this image.

- Present your findings and supporting evidence clearly so your audience can follow your reasoning.

## Task 6: Literature [RL.9-10.3; SL.9-10.4]
### Analyze Character and Theme

*Deliver an oral presentation in which you analyze how a complex character contributes to the expression of the theme in a story from this unit.*

- Deliver your presentation as the character you chose. Tell the story from your point of view, describing why you, as the character, think, feel, and behave as you do.

- As the character, explain your understanding of other characters. Consider how other characters react similarly or differently to events.

- As the character, explain the insight about life or human nature your story expresses.

- Use language similar to that used by the character in the story.

- Present information clearly, concisely, and logically so that listeners can follow your reasoning.

## Task 7: Literature [RL.9-10.5; SL.9-10.1; L.9-10.6]
### Analyze Conflict

*Deliver an oral presentation in which you analyze the conflict in a short story from this unit.*

- Identify a short story from this unit that you feel has a rich and interesting conflict.

- Outline the plot points of the story and explain whether the main conflict is external, internal, or both.

- Use specific evidence from the story to show how the conflict unfolds. Explain how characters, dialogue, and setting contribute to the conflict and to its resolution.

- Use visual aids to help present your analysis to the class. For example, you might create a plot diagram on poster board to help your listeners follow your ideas.

- After your speech, invite questions from the audience. Answer questions thoughtfully, using correct academic language and literary terms.

**Is conflict necessary?**
At the beginning of Unit 2, you participated in a discussion of the Big Question. Now that you have completed the unit, write a response to the question. Discuss how your initial ideas have changed or been reinforced. Support your response with at least one example from literature and one example from an additional subject area or your own life. Use Big Question vocabulary words (see p. 195) in your response.

# Featured Titles

In this unit, you have read a variety of short stories. Continue to read on your own. Select works that you enjoy, but challenge yourself to explore new authors and works of increasing depth and complexity. The titles suggested below will help you get started.

## Literature

### The Tragedy of Macbeth
by William Shakespeare           EXEMPLAR TEXT

This spine-tingling **drama** is one of William Shakespeare's most popular plays. *The Tragedy of Macbeth* explores the dangers of unrestrained ambition as Macbeth and his scheming wife Lady Macbeth murder his competitors in a plot to seize the throne of Scotland.

### Diary of a Madman and Other Stories
by Nikolai Gogol
Signet Classic, 2005           EXEMPLAR TEXT

Written in diary form, this **novel** tells the story of a government clerk who loses his mind. At the beginning of the story, the narrator writes rationally. As the story progresses, however, the narrator descends deeper into madness. The volume also includes the author's classic story, "The Nose."

### Stories by O. Henry
by O. Henry           EXEMPLAR TEXT

O. Henry is considered one of America's greatest short story writers, famous for his colorful characters and surprise endings. This collection of **short stories** includes "The Gift of the Magi" and other famous tales.

### The Sea-Wolf and Selected Stories
by Jack London
Signet Classic, 2005

Captain Wolf Larsen believes the weak do not deserve to live; his crewman, Humphrey van Weyden, strongly disagrees. This tale of bitter conflict and other **short stories** in this collection whisk readers into a world of peril and adventure.

### The Left Hand of Darkness
by Ursula K. Le Guin
Ace Books, 1969

In this innovative **science-fiction novel,** Genly Ai is a government representative sent to the isolated planet of Gethen to mend relationships among an evolving galactic civilization. To do so, he must overcome his own prejudices as well as those of the people he encounters.

### The Joy Luck Club
by Amy Tan           EXEMPLAR TEXT

Amy Tan's best-selling **novel** explores the lives of Chinese American families who meet to play games and share meals. Told from the perspective of several female family members, the novel explores parent-child relationships and the dynamics of immigrant families.

## Informational Texts

### Literature of the Expanding Frontier

As pioneers spread across the Western frontier, they brought with them their passion for life and their hope for the future. This collection of **stories, poems, songs,** and **personal accounts** captures the spirits of everyone from Chinese immigrants building the nation's railroads to Native Americans dealing with the influx of new people as they all face the challenges of living together in the wilderness.

# Preparing to Read Complex Texts

**Attentive Reading** As you read literature on your own, bring your imagination and questions to the text. The questions shown below and others that you ask as you read will help you learn and enjoy literature even more.

 **Common Core State Standards**

**Reading Literature/Informational Text**
**10.** By the end of grade 9, read and comprehend literature, including stories, dramas, poems, and literary nonfiction in the grades 9–10 text complexity band proficiently, with scaffolding as needed at the high end of the range.

## When reading short stories, ask yourself...

- Who is narrating the story? Is this voice part of the story or an outside observer?
- Do I find the narrator's voice interesting and engaging? Why or why not?
- Who is the story's main character? Is he or she interesting to me? Why or why not?
- Which characters do I like or admire? Which do I dislike? How do my reactions to the characters make me feel about the story as a whole?
- Is the setting of the story—the place, time, and society—believable and interesting? Why or why not?
- What does the story mean to me? Does it convey a theme or insight that I find important and true? Why or why not?

**Ⓒ Key Ideas and Details**

- What aspects of the story grab my attention right away? Which fail to grab my attention?
- Do I find anything about the story confusing? Do my questions get answered? Why or why not?
- Is there anything different or unusual in the way the story is structured? Do I find that structure interesting or distracting?
- Are there any passages or details that I find especially strong or beautiful?
- Do I understand why characters act and feel as they do? Do their thoughts and actions seem real? Why or why not?
- What questions do I have about the characters and events?

**Ⓒ Craft and Structure**

- Does the story remind me of others I have read? If so, how?
- Have I gained new knowledge from reading this story? If so, what have I learned?
- Would I recommend this story to others? If so, to whom?
- Would I like to read other stories by this author? Why or why not?

**Ⓒ Integration of Ideas**

# Is *knowledge* the same as *understanding?*

# Types of Nonfiction

## PHLit Online!
www.PHLitOnline.com

### Hear It!
- Selection summary audio
- Selection audio
- BQ Tunes

### See It!
- Author videos
- Big Question video
- Get Connected videos
- Background videos
- More about the authors
- Illustrated vocabulary words
- Vocabulary flashcards

### Do It!
- Interactive journals
- Interactive graphic organizers
- Grammar tutorials
- Interactive vocabulary games
- Test practice

## Is *knowledge the same as understanding?*

We are constantly working to learn more about the world. We find information in a variety of sources, and we struggle to comprehend the facts. We may study books, interpret charts, and conduct further research. We may talk to others to gain insight. We may have gained knowledge, but when do we know that we truly understand? For example, does practicing soccer prepare us to play soccer? Does reading about relationships help us get along, or do we have to experience a friendship to truly understand?

## Exploring the Big Question

**Collaboration: Group Discussion** Begin thinking about the Big Question by analyzing what you know and how you know it. List topics that you have knowledge about and also understand. Describe an example from each of these categories.

- A grandparent or older adult you know well
- A concept you have learned in school
- A speech you have read over and over
- An argument you have had that still bothers you
- Something you have read about but also experienced
- The memory of an important event in your life

Share your list in a group. Talk about any differences you discover between your knowledge and your understanding of these topics.

Before you begin the discussion, set rules that will lead to a cooperative exchange. For example, consider any specific goals you want to achieve, whether to assign a mediator, and how you will handle disagreements. Capture the rules in a format everyone can use as the discussion takes place.

**Connecting to the Literature** Each reading in this unit will give you additional insight into the Big Question.

**PHLit**
**Online!**
www.PHLitOnline.com
- Big Question video
- Illustrated vocabulary words
- Interactive vocabulary games
- BQ Tunes

# Learn Big Question Vocabulary

**Acquire and Use Academic Vocabulary** Academic vocabulary is the language you encounter in textbooks and on standardized tests. Review the definitions of these academic vocabulary words.

> **ambiguous** (am big′ yōō əs) *adj.* having more than one meaning; able to be interpreted in different ways
>
> **clarify** (klar′ ə fī) *v.* make something more clear or understandable
>
> **comprehend** (käm′ prē hend′) *v.* understand
>
> **concept** (kän′ sept′) *n.* idea; notion
>
> **interpret** (in tʉr′ prət) *v.* understand or explain the meaning of a concept or idea

Use these words as you complete Big Question activities that involve reading, writing, speaking, and listening.

**Gather Vocabulary Knowledge** Additional Big Question words are listed below. Categorize the words by deciding whether you know each one well, know it a little bit, or do not know it at all.

| | | |
|---|---|---|
| **connection** | **insight** | **senses/sensory** |
| **fact** | **instinct** | **sources** |
| **feeling** | **research** | **statistics** |
| **information** | | |

Then, do the following:

1. Write the definitions of the words you know.
2. Consult a dictionary to confirm each word's meaning. Revise your definitions if necessary.
3. Using a print or an online dictionary, look up the meanings of the words you do not know. Then, write the meanings.
4. If a word sounds familiar but you are not sure of its meaning, consult a dictionary. Then, record the meaning.
5. Use all of the words in a brief paragraph about knowledge and understanding. Choose words and phrases that convey your ideas precisely.

**Common Core State Standards**

**Speaking and Listening**
**1.b.** Work with peers to set rules for collegial discussions and decision-making, clear goals and deadlines, and individual roles as needed.

**Language**
**6.** Acquire and use accurately grade-appropriate general academic and domain-specific words and phrases, sufficient for reading, writing, speaking, and listening at the college and career readiness level; demonstrate independence in gathering vocabulary knowledge when considering a word or phrase important to comprehension or expression.

# Elements of Essays, Articles, and Speeches

Essays, articles, and speeches organize factual information to present a picture of a topic—often from a particular point of view.

An essay can make you laugh. An article can make you cry. A speech can change your mind. Like all **nonfiction,** these forms of writing present facts or discuss real life.

- In an **essay,** an author supports a **thesis**—a central idea about a topic. In doing so, the author conveys his or her **point of view,** or perspective, on the topic.

- An **article** provides information about a topic. Articles are often divided into sections introduced by subheads. Each subhead names the central idea of the section it introduces. Many articles are written from an objective point of view—they give just the facts.

- A **speech** is a nonfiction text that a speaker delivers, or says, to an audience. Like the author of an essay, a speaker usually presents a thesis and expresses his or her point of view.

An author's approach to a topic depends on his or her **purpose,** or reason for writing. An author's purpose is related to the effect he or she wishes to have on readers. There are three main purposes for writing.

- **To inform,** or provide facts and explain how they relate to one another

- **To persuade,** or try to influence an audience's attitudes or actions

- **To entertain,** or engage and move the emotions of an audience

To achieve his or her purpose, a writer uses techniques such as these:

- **organizing information** in ways that make it clear (as when writing to inform) or dramatic (as when writing to persuade or to entertain)

- **choosing language** that makes ideas clear (as when writing to inform) or that creates **tone,** or conveys the writer's attitude (as when writing to persuade)

When you read nonfiction, analyze each element in the chart below.

## Key Elements of Nonfiction

| Element | Definition |
|---|---|
| Thesis or Central Idea | the main idea the author wants the audience to understand and remember |
| Purpose | the reason the author is writing about the topic |
| Organizational Structure | the order in which information and ideas are presented and the connections that are drawn between and among them |
| Tone | the author's attitude toward the topic and audience as conveyed in his or her word choices |
| Word Choice | the author's use of language devices, such as **figurative language,** or language that is not meant to be taken literally, and **rhetoric,** or the patterning of words |

## Types of Essays and Articles

The chart below explains five major types of essays.

> **Types of Essays**
> - **Narrative essays** tell the story of actual experiences or events.
> - **Expository essays** inform readers about a topic and explain the ideas it involves.
> - **Persuasive,** or **argumentative, essays** are written to convince audiences to accept an author's **claim,** or position on an issue, or to motivate audiences to take a particular course of action.
> - **Descriptive essays** give vivid details about a person, place, or thing to help readers picture it.
> - **Reflective essays** explore the meaning of an experience or offer the author's thoughts or feelings.

Authors may combine elements of different types of essays. For instance, in an argumentative essay persuading readers to adopt dogs from shelters, an author might include vivid descriptions of homeless dogs.

There are many types of articles. Two main types are news articles and feature articles.

> **Two Types of Articles**
> - **News articles** provide facts about current events. These articles usually answer the questions *Who? What? Where? When? Why?* and *How?* and are written from an objective, or neutral, point of view.
> - **Feature articles** provide facts about topics of current interest such as fashion trends or developments in science. These articles are often written in a friendly, conversational style.

## Types of Speeches

What a writer says in a speech is shaped by its **occasion,** or the event at which the speech will be delivered, as well as by its **audience,** or the people to whom the speech will be addressed. The following chart gives examples of several common types of speeches, along with a possible occasion and audience for each.

> **Speech of Public Advocacy:** a formal, prepared speech intended to persuade an audience to take action
>
> *Example:* an argumentative speech that describes a community problem and proposes a possible solution
>
> *Delivered by:* a citizen
>
> *Occasion:* a city council meeting
>
> *Audience:* the city council; fellow citizens
>
> **Talk:** an informal speech presented in a conversational style
>
> *Example:* a report on a science fair
>
> *Delivered by:* a student
>
> *Occasion:* a science club meeting
>
> *Audience:* student members of the club
>
> **Impromptu Speech:** a speech presented with little or no preparation, often in a conversational style
>
> *Example:* a speech of celebration
>
> *Delivered by:* the subject's friend
>
> *Occasion:* a birthday party
>
> *Audience:* the person whose birthday is being celebrated, along with the guests

 Common Core State Standards

RI.9-10.3, RI.9-10.4, RI.9-10.5, RI.9-10.6
[For the full wording of the standards, see the standards chart in the front of your textbook.]

# Analyzing the Development and Organization of Ideas

An author uses different methods to **introduce** and **develop** ideas, presenting supporting details in logical order to achieve a purpose.

**Common Core State Standards**

**Reading Informational Text**
**3.** Analyze how the author unfolds an analysis or series of ideas or events, including the order in which the points are made, how they are introduced and developed, and the connections that are drawn between them.
**5.** Analyze in detail how an author's ideas or claims are developed and refined by particular sentences, paragraphs, or larger portions of a text.

**Introducing and Developing Ideas** In a nonfiction work, the author will present ideas in a particular order and style. First, the author introduces the topic and key ideas. If these ideas are likely to be unfamiliar to readers, the author may introduce them with a familiar example or a simple comparison, as in this example:

> **Example: Sun Static**
> Although the sun is about 93 million miles away, solar activity can affect communications here on Earth. To understand why, picture water boiling in a pot. Bubbles on the surface burst and release steam. Similarly, solar flares on the surface of the sun can release particles that travel to the Earth.

Then, the author **develops,** or elaborates on, ideas, explaining them and showing the connections from one idea to the next. Details that illustrate, expand on, or prove the author's ideas are called **supporting details.** Here are some types of supporting details:

- **Statements of fact,** or statements that can be proved true
- **Statistics,** or numbers used to compare members of a group of people or things
- **Examples,** or specific cases
- **Descriptions,** or details that tell what something looks like, tastes like, and so on
- **Reasons,** or claims that justify a belief
- **Expert opinions,** or the judgments of people with special knowledge of a subject

**Overall Organizational Structures** To develop ideas and show the connections among them, an author needs to present information in a clear order. An author's purpose for writing will help her or him choose an overall **structure,** or pattern of organization, as in these examples:

- A news report about a space shuttle launch written to inform might present events in **chronological order,** or the order in which they happened. This order will aid readers in following the series of events.

- A feature article comparing the space shuttle program with older programs might use **comparison-and-contrast organization,** grouping details according to their similarities and differences.

- An editorial about the space shuttle program written to persuade readers to support the program might have a **cause-and-effect organization.** By clearly showing how the program leads to important medical discoveries, for example, this organization could help convince readers.

Each part of a work plays its role in the development of ideas. For example, the author may organize the work into **sections,** or parts. In this case, each **paragraph** in a section would elaborate on the main idea of the section. In turn, each **sentence** within a paragraph would help develop the main idea of that paragraph. In this way, the various parts of a text work together to support the author's main idea, or thesis.

# Analyzing Word Choice and Rhetoric

To achieve their purpose and to convey a point of view, authors use tools such as **word choice** and **rhetoric.**

 **Common Core State Standards**

**Reading Informational Text**
**4.** Determine the meaning of words and phrases as they are used in a text, including figurative, connotative, and technical meanings; analyze the cumulative impact of specific word choices on meaning and tone.
**6.** Determine an author's point of view or purpose in a text and analyze how an author uses rhetoric to advance that point of view or purpose.

Whether an author's **purpose** is to inform, to persuade, or to entertain readers, the author will use words in ways designed to achieve his or her goal.

**Diction** An author's choice of words is called diction. By using simple diction—choosing familiar words—an author can make ideas clear. By using **technical language,** or language specific to a discipline, an author can be precise. By choosing words with strong **connotations,** or associations, an author can shape readers' views. For example, calling a situation *disastrous* creates one picture; calling it *challenging* creates another.

**Tone** Word choice creates tone, or conveys an attitude toward the topic and audience. An author's tone may be formal or informal, solemn or playful, joyous or annoyed, and so on. For example, this sentence has a tone of outrage: *That scoundrel will disgrace our city!*

**Figurative Language** Authors also convey point of view using figurative language, or language not meant to be taken literally. Here are three common figures of speech:

- A **simile** is an indirect comparison that contains the word *like* or *as: It was as tricky as skateboarding during an earthquake.*

- A **metaphor** describes one thing as if it were another, without using the words *like* or *as: Friendship is a warm place on a cold day.*

- **Personification** gives human traits to a nonhuman subject: *The winter wind slapped my face with its icy hands.*

**Rhetorical Devices and Purpose** Rhetorical devices are patterns of words and ideas used to emphasize points and to make them more memorable. If an author's purpose is to inform, he or she may use rhetorical devices to help readers remember key points. If an author's purpose is to persuade, he or she may use rhetorical devices that appeal to readers' emotions. Rhetorical devices include the following:

> **Rhetorical Devices**
>
> **Repetition** is the reuse of a key word, phrase, or idea:
> *He plays with skill. He plays with passion. He plays in a style all his own.*
>
> **Parallel structure** is the use of similar grammatical structures to express related ideas:
> *The eagle soared above the treetops, into the heavens, and beyond reach.*
>
> **Restatement** is the expression of the same idea in different words to strengthen a point:
> *Aspire to greatness.* (Restatement 1:) *Aim high,* (Restatement 2:) *and dream big.*
>
> **Rhetorical questions** are inquiries that have obvious answers and that are asked for effect:
> *Is it really so much trouble to recycle? Isn't saving our planet worth your time?*

# Close Read: Development of Ideas

## To understand literary nonfiction, determine the author's purpose and point of view and analyze ways in which the author develops ideas.

To paint a clear picture or to make a strong argument, authors of literary nonfiction select, organize, and make connections between details—they develop ideas. Starting from a central idea or thesis, an author provides readers with supporting information that helps them understand and accept that idea or thesis. To ensure effective development, an author uses a variety of tools, from organizational structure to tone. These tools help an author fulfill his or her purpose and convey a point of view. To guide you in analyzing an author's development of ideas, follow the tips in this chart.

### Tips for Analyzing Literary Nonfiction

**Purpose and Point of View**
- Determine whether the author includes only details meant to inform or whether some details are meant to persuade or to entertain.
- To determine the author's point of view, look for a direct statement of opinion, such as "We need year-round schools."
- If there is no direct statement of opinion, infer point of view from word choices such as *good* or *unfair*.

**Rhetorical Devices**
- Look for instances of repetition, parallel structure, restatement, and rhetorical questions.
- Consider in each case how the device expresses the author's point of view and helps fulfill his or her purpose.

**Central Idea and Support**
- Identify the author's central idea or thesis—the main point the work makes.
- If the author does not directly state this point, infer it based on the details he or she includes.
- For each new idea or detail the author presents, ask yourself, In what way does this point relate to the main idea?

**Figurative Language**
- Look for similes, metaphors, and personification.
- Determine in each case what the figure of speech shows about the author's point of view and purpose.

**Organizational Structures**
Identify the overall structure of the work—chronological order, for example, or cause-and-effect. Take note of the transition words that the author uses between paragraphs, such as *First, Most important,* and *Due to,* as clues to its organization.

**Tone and Word Choice**
- Notice whether the words the author chooses are formal or informal, technical or everyday, emotionally charged or objective.
- Determine the reasons for the author's word choice, including the tone these choices create—what attitude toward the subject or audience they convey.

# Model 1

**About the Text** Learned Hand (1872–1961) was a U.S. federal judge for more than half a century. On May 21, 1944, he delivered the following address in New York City's Central Park to a crowd of over one million people. His audience had gathered to attend a patriotic event called "I Am an American Day."

The annual event drew an extraordinary number of people that year because it came at a critical time in U.S. history. As World War II raged on, many Americans wanted to show support for their country. Among the Americans who attended the event that day were 150,000 newly naturalized citizens, who had come to pledge their allegiance to the United States. Hand delivered his inspirational address just before that ceremony.

## "I Am an American Day" Address by Learned Hand

We have gathered here to affirm a faith, a faith in a common purpose, a common conviction, a common devotion. Some of us have chosen America as the land of our adoption; the rest have come from those who did the same. For this reason we have some right to consider ourselves a picked group, a group of those who had the courage to break from the past and brave the dangers and the loneliness of a strange land. What was the object that nerved us, or those who went before us, to this choice? We sought liberty; freedom from oppression, freedom from want, freedom to be ourselves. This we then sought; this we now believe that we are by way of winning. What do we mean when we say that first of all we seek liberty? I often wonder whether we do not rest our hopes too much upon constitutions, upon laws and upon courts. These are false hopes; believe me, these are false hopes. Liberty lies in the hearts of men and women; when it dies there, no constitution, no law, no court can save it; no constitution, no law, no court can even do much to help it. While it lies there it needs no constitution, no law, no court to save it. And what is this liberty which must lie in the hearts of men and women? It is not the ruthless, the unbridled will; it is not freedom to do as one likes. That is the denial of liberty, and leads straight to its overthrow. A society in which men recognize no check upon their freedom soon becomes a society where freedom is the possession of only a savage few; as we have learned to our sorrow.

What then is the spirit of liberty? I cannot define it; I can only tell you my own faith. The spirit of liberty is the spirit which is not too sure that it is right; the spirit of liberty is the spirit which seeks to understand the minds of other men and women; the spirit of liberty is the spirit which weighs their interests alongside its own without bias; the spirit of liberty remembers that not even a

---

**Point of View** Hand defines the occasion for the address and identifies his common bond with the audience. In doing so, he begins to reveal his beliefs about what it means to be an American.

**Rhetorical Devices** Notice Hand's use of questions followed by answers stated in parallel form. With each question, Hand introduces a different aspect of his topic: liberty. With each answer, he refines his explanation of liberty, using parallelism to state the explanation in a moving, memorable way. Repeating this pattern creates clear connections between ideas.

**Central Idea and Support** Here Hand states a central idea— liberty depends on the people, not on laws.

© EXEMPLAR TEXT

## Model 1 continued

**Tone and Word Choice** Hand adopts the tone of a preacher, using language that refers to the Bible as he claims a divine right to liberty and freedom. Figurative language adds a poetic quality.

sparrow falls to earth unheeded; the spirit of liberty is the spirit of Him who, near two thousand years ago, taught mankind that lesson it has never learned, but has never quite forgotten; that there may be a kingdom where the least shall be heard and considered side by side with the greatest. And now in that spirit, that spirit of an America which has never been, and which may never be; nay, which never will be except as the conscience and courage of Americans create it; yet in the spirit of that America which lies hidden in some form in the aspirations of us all; in the spirit of that America for which our young men are at this moment fighting and dying; in that spirit of liberty and of America I ask you to rise and with me pledge our faith in the glorious destiny of our beloved country.

# Model 2

**About the Text** In this famous speech, Patrick Henry (1736–1799) denounces the British king and urges the colonists to fight for independence. Addressing the Virginia Provincial Convention on the eve of the American Revolution, in 1775, Henry gives a fiery defense of liberty. While many of the speakers at the convention argued for a peaceful compromise with Britain, Henry called for armed resistance. His speech fanned the flames of revolution, and in 1776, the colonies declared their independence.

### "Speech to the Virginia Convention" by Patrick Henry

Mr. President: No man thinks more highly than I do of the patriotism, as well as abilities, of the very worthy gentlemen who have just addressed the house. But different men often see the same subject in different lights; and, therefore, I hope it will not be thought disrespectful to those gentlemen, if, entertaining, as I do, opinions of a character very opposite to theirs, I shall speak forth my sentiments freely and without reserve. This is no time for ceremony. The question before the house is one of awful moment[1] to this country. For my own part, I consider it as nothing less than a question of freedom or slavery. And in proportion to the magnitude of the subject ought to be the freedom of the debate. It is only in this way that we can hope to arrive at truth, and fulfill the great responsibility which we hold to God and our country. Should I keep back my opinions at such a time, through fear of giving offense, I should consider myself as guilty of treason toward my country, and of an act of disloyalty toward the Majesty of Heaven, which I revere above all earthly kings.

Mr. President, it is natural to man to indulge in the illusions of hope. We are apt to shut our eyes against a painful truth, and listen to the song of that siren till

**Point of View** In his opening, Henry begins to lay out his point of view: British rule is depriving colonists of their liberty.

---

1. **moment** *n.* importance.

she transforms us into beasts.[2] Is this the part of wise men, engaged in a great and arduous struggle for liberty? Are we disposed to be of the number of those who having eyes see not, and having ears hear not, the things which so nearly concern their temporal salvation? For my part, whatever anguish of spirit it may cost, I am willing to know the whole truth; to know the worst and to provide for it.

I have but one lamp by which my feet are guided, and that is the lamp of experience. I know of no way of judging of the future but by the past. And judging by the past, I wish to know what there has been in the conduct of the British ministry for the last ten years to justify those hopes with which gentlemen have been pleased to solace[3] themselves and the house? Is it that insidious smile with which our petition has been lately received? Trust it not, sir; it will prove a snare to your feet. Suffer not yourselves to be betrayed with a kiss.[4] Ask yourselves how this gracious reception of our petition comports with those warlike preparations which cover our waters and darken our land. Are fleets and armies necessary to a work of love and reconciliation? Have we shown ourselves so unwilling to be reconciled that force must be called in to win back our love? Let us not deceive ourselves, sir. These are the implements of war and subjugation—the last arguments to which kings resort.

I ask gentlemen, sir, what means this martial array, if its purpose be not to force us to submission? Can gentlemen assign any other possible motive for it? Has Great Britain any enemy in this quarter of the world, to call for all this accumulation of navies and armies? No, sir, she has none. They are meant for us: they can be meant for no other. They are sent over to bind and rivet upon us those chains which the British ministry have been so long forging.

And what have we to oppose to them? Shall we try argument? Sir, we have been trying that for the last ten years. Have we anything new to offer upon the subject? Nothing. We have held the subject up in every light of which it is capable; but it has been all in vain. Shall we resort to entreaty and humble supplication?[5] What terms shall we find which have not been already exhausted? Let us not, I beseech you, sir, deceive ourselves longer. Sir, we have done everything that could be done to avert the storm which is now coming on. We have petitioned; we have remonstrated; we have supplicated; we have prostrated ourselves before the throne, and have implored its interposition[6] to

**Rhetorical Devices**
Henry makes his point of view clear using rhetorical questions and charged language. His listeners will want to be counted as "wise men," not as "those who . . . see not."

**Word Choice** Henry uses the connotations, or emotional associations, of *insidious*—meaning "evil" or "treacherous"— to create a memorable image of British power.

---

2. **listen . . . beasts** In Homer's epic poem the *Odyssey*, the enchantress Circe transforms men into beasts after charming them with her singing.
3. **solace** (sä´ lis) *v.* comfort.
4. **betrayed with a kiss** In the Bible, in Luke 22:47–48, Judas kisses Jesus to identify Jesus to the officials who have come to arrest him.
5. **supplication** (sup´ lə kā´ shən) *n.* a plea; a humble request.
6. **interposition** (in´ tər pə zish´ ən) *n.* intervention.

© EXEMPLAR TEXT

**Model 2 continued**

**Organizational Structures** Henry carefully builds his argument. First, he explains why he needs to speak freely and urges others not to deceive themselves. Next, he explains the motives of the British and then shows the ineffectiveness of the colonists' response. Only after carefully preparing listeners does he now speak directly of armed rebellion.

**Figurative Language** At the climax of his speech, Henry repeats a vivid metaphor—the British are putting the Americans in chains—to drive home his point and accomplish his purpose: persuading the colonists to revolt.

arrest the tyrannical hands of the ministry and Parliament. Our petitions have been slighted; our remonstrances have produced additional violence and insult; our supplications have been disregarded; and we have been spurned with contempt from the foot of the throne! In vain, after these things, may we indulge the fond[7] hope of peace and reconciliation. There is no longer any room for hope. If we wish to be free, if we mean to preserve inviolate those inestimable privileges for which we have been so long contending, if we mean not basely to abandon the noble struggle in which we have been so long engaged, and which we have pledged ourselves never to abandon until the glorious object of our contest shall be obtained—we must fight! I repeat it, sir, we must fight! An appeal to arms and to the God of Hosts is all that is left us!

They tell us, sir, that we are weak—unable to cope with so formidable an adversary. But when shall we be stronger? Will it be the next week, or the next year? Will it be when we are totally disarmed, and when a British guard shall be stationed in every house? Shall we gather strength by irresolution and inaction? Shall we acquire the means of effectual resistance by lying supinely on our backs and hugging the delusive phantom of hope until our enemies shall have bound us hand and foot? Sir, we are not weak, if we make a proper use of those means which the God of nature hath placed in our power. Three millions of people, armed in the holy cause of liberty, and in such a country as that which we possess, are invincible by any force which our enemy can send against us. Besides, sir, we shall not fight our battles alone. There is a just God who presides over the destinies of nations and who will raise up friends to fight our battles for us. The battle, sir, is not to the strong alone; it is to the vigilant, the active, the brave. Besides, sir, we have no election;[8] if we were base enough to desire it, it is now too late to retire from the contest. There is no retreat but in submission and slavery! Our chains are forged! Their clanging may be heard on the plains of Boston! The war is inevitable—and let it come! I repeat it, sir, let it come!

It is in vain, sir, to extenuate[9] the matter. Gentlemen may cry, "Peace, peace"—but there is no peace. The war is actually begun! The next gale that sweeps from the north[10] will bring to our ears the clash of resounding arms! Our brethren are already in the field! Why stand we here idle? What is it that gentlemen wish? What would they have? Is life so dear, or peace so sweet, as to be purchased at the price of chains and slavery? Forbid it, Almighty God! I know not what course others may take; but as for me, give me liberty or give me death!

---

7. **fond** *adj.* foolish.
8. **election** *n.* choice.
9. **extenuate** (ek sten′ yo͞o āt′) *v.* treat as less serious.
10. **The next gale . . . north** In Massachusetts, north of Virginia, some colonists had already shown open resistance to the British.

# Independent Practice

**About the Text** Rebecca Walker's lively interest in youth culture is evident in this essay. She is a writer of magazine articles, books, and essays. At the age of twenty-five, she was named by *Time* magazine as one of fifty influential American leaders under the age of forty.

## "Before Hip-Hop Was Hip-Hop" by Rebecca Walker

If you ask most kids today about hip-hop, they'll spit out the names of recording artists they see on TV: Eminem, P. Diddy, J. Lo, Beyonce. They'll tell you about the songs they like and the clothes they want to buy. They'll tell you about the indisputable zones of hip-hop like "EO" (East Orange, New Jersey), the "ATL" (Atlanta, Georgia), and the "West Side" (Los Angeles, California), neighborhoods they feel they know because they've seen them in all the glossiest, "flossiest" music videos. Hip-hop is natural to these kids, like air or water, just there, a part of the digital landscape that streams through their lives.

I watch this cultural sea change with fascination. It astounds me that hip-hop has grown into a global industry, a force that dominates youth culture from Paris to Prague, Tokyo to Timbuktu. I can't believe that in small, all-white towns like Lincoln, Nebraska, high school boys wear their clothes in the latest "steelo": pants sagging off their waists, sports jerseys hanging to their knees, baseball hats cocked to one side. Even in the pueblos of Mexico, where mariachi bands and old school crooners still rule, it is hip-hop that sells cars, sodas, and children's toys on TV.

The vast empire of hip-hop amazes me because I knew hip-hop before it was hip-hop. I was there when it all began.

Way back then, in what today's ninth graders might call the ancient eighties, there was no MTV or VH-1. We found out about music by listening to the radio, flipping through the stacks at the record store, or buying "mix tapes" from local deejays at two dollars apiece. Back then, we carried combs in our back pockets and clipped long strands of feathers to the belt loops of our designer jeans. We wore our names in cursive gold letters around our necks or in big brass letters on our belt buckles. We picked up words and inverted them, calling something that we thought was really cool, "hot," and something that had a whole lot of life, "def."

We didn't know a whole new language was rolling off our tongues as we flipped English upside down and pulled some Spanish and even a few words from Africa into our parlance. We didn't know that young people for years to come would recycle our fashions and sample the bass lines from our favorite tracks. We thought we were just being kids and expressing ourselves, showing the grown-ups we were different from them in a way that was safe and fun. In fact we were at the epicenter[1] of one of America's most significant cultural revolutions, making it happen. Who knew?

Not me.

---

**Tone and Word Choice** Does Walker's choice of words create a formal tone or an informal tone? Explain.

**Purpose** What specific purpose does this statement suggest?

**Central Idea and Support** How do these examples help elaborate on Walker's central idea?

**Rhetorical Devices** Why does the author ask this question and then answer it?

---

1. **epicenter** (ep´ i sent´ ər) *n.* focal or central point.

## Practice continued

**Organizational Structures** What organizational structure does this statement suggest?

**Rhetorical Devices** What effect does Walker create by using repetition and parallel phrasing to list examples?

**Central Idea and Support** What central idea in the paragraph do these examples support?

When I moved from Washington, D.C., to the Bronx the summer before seventh grade, I had one box of records, mostly albums I had ordered from the Columbia Record Club. In 1982, if you promised to buy a record a month for one whole year, the Club sent you eight records for a penny. I had Bruce Springsteen's "The River," REO Speedwagon's "The Letter," "Belladonna" by Stevie Nicks. I had "Stairway to Heaven," by Led Zeppelin and the soundtrack from the movie *Saturday Night Fever,* which I played so many times I thought my mother would go crazy from listening to me belt out the lyrics with those lanky, swanky Bee Gees.

Along with my albums I had loads of 45s, what today we would call singles, little records with just two songs on them, that I bought at the record store near my school for just a dollar a piece. I had Chaka Khan's "I'm Every Woman," and Luther Vandross' "Never Too Much," and Chuck Brown and Soul Searcher's big hit, "Bustin' Loose." I had Michael Jackson's "Rock with You" and even Aretha Franklin's cover of "You Make Me Feel Like a Natural Woman," which I sang along to in the mornings as I styled my hair.

If you had asked me then about rap music I would have shrugged my shoulders and looked at you like you were crazy. Rap music? What's that?

But then I started seventh grade and my whole world turned upside down. At Public School 141, I went to classes with kids from all over the Bronx. There were kids whose families came from Puerto Rico and the Dominican Republic, and kids whose families came from Russia and China. There were kids who were African-American and kids who were Irish-American, kids who were Italian-American and kids who were Greek-American. There were kids whose families were poor, kids whose families were well off, and kids whose families were somewhere in between. Some were Jewish, and others devout Catholics. Some were Muslim. Some of the Asian kids were even Buddhist.

The charge created by so many different elements coming together was palpable.[2] The school crackled with energy, and as you can imagine, things weren't always smooth. There were some pretty entrenched[3] cliques, and a few vicious fights in the schoolyard. But there was also so much "flavor." You could hear Spanish spoken with a thick "Nuyorican" accent to a kid wearing a "yamulke." A seemingly reserved Asian-American girl would get out of her parents' car, wait for them to drive off, and then unzip her coat to reveal a fire engine red Adidas sweatsuit. A guy in a preppy, button-down shirt would "sport" gold chains with pendants of every denomination: the Jewish Star of David, the Arabic lettering for Allah, and a shiny gold cross. He was everything, that was his "steelo," and everyone gave him "props" for it.

---

2. **palpable** (pal′ pə bəl) *adj.* able to be touched, felt, or handled; tangible.
3. **entrenched** (en trencht′) *adj.* securely established; unmovable.

When I got to 141, I felt like a blank canvas. Nothing had prepared me for the dynamism, the screaming self-expression of the place and its students. For the first few weeks I secretly studied the habits of the seventh, eighth and ninth graders with whom I walked the halls and shared the cafeteria. I was transfixed by the way they infused their words with attitude and drama, moving their hands and heads as they spoke. I was captivated by the way many of them walked and ran and joked with each other with confidence and bravado.[4] I noted what they wore and how they wore it: the razor sharp creases of their Jordache jeans, the spotless sneakers with the laces left loose and untied.

Slowly, I began to add some of what I saw into my "look." I convinced my grandmother to buy me a name chain to wear around my neck, and my stepmother to buy me dark dyed designer jeans. I bought my first pair of Nike sneakers, red, white and blue Air Cortez's, with money I saved from my allowance.

One by one, I started to make friends—Diane, Loida, James, Jesus, Maya. When James and Jesus weren't making fun of me for being so "square," they took me to parties on the Grand Concourse, the big boulevard lined with old apartment buildings and department stores that ran through the Bronx. The parties were incredible, filled with young people who didn't drink, smoke or fight, but who just wanted to dance and laugh and ooh and ahhh over the "scratching" sounds and funky beats the DJ's coaxed out of their turntables.

A lot of the kids at the parties were "breakers" or "poppers and lockers," which meant they could breakdance, a style of movement that blends the Brazilian martial art of Capoeira with a dance called the Robot, and incorporates classical dance moves as well. The "breakers" moved in "crews" that competed against each other.

Standing in a circle we watched as members of the different groups "moonwalked" into the center, and then hurled themselves to the floor, spinning on their heads, kicking their legs into the air, and making elaborate hand gestures, each more intricate and acrobatic than the last. Everyone at the party who wasn't "breaking" was a judge by default, and we registered our scores by clapping and yelling.

When Loida and Diane weren't "capping on" or making fun of my clothes, they were "hipping" me to Kiss 98.7 and WBLS, the radio stations that had started to slip some of the songs we liked into their rotation. Songs like "Planet Rock" by Soul Sonic Force and "Take Me Home" by Lisa Lisa and the Cult Jam. After school and on the weekends, they took me to the street vendors that sold the accessories we all coveted: the big knockoff Porsche sunglasses everybody wanted but not everybody could afford, and the heavy gold chains people collected around their necks like so many pieces of string. Loida and Diane also

**Figurative Language** In what ways was Walker like a "blank canvas"?

**Point of View** What is Walker's perspective on the young people she met at the parties?

**Word Choice** Why does Walker define these technical, dance-related terms?

**Central Idea and Support** How do these examples help support Walker's central idea?

---

**4. bravado** (brə vä´ dō) *n.* pretended courage or defiant confidence.

## Practice continued

took me around the city on the bus, familiarizing me with the routes of the M1 and M3 and M7, showing me all the different neighborhoods like Little Italy and Chinatown, Bed-Stuy and Harlem.

I remember looking out the big sliding glass windows of the bus at the lines drawn in concrete and glass and thinking that while the world outside seemed so divided, inside, in my circle, among my friends, those lines didn't seem to exist. Loida was Dominican and Diane was Puerto Rican. Our friend Mary was Irish-American, and Lisa was Italian-American. Maya's family was from Haiti. Julius was Russian-American. We were different ages, with different likes and dislikes, but we were united in our love of hip-hop. We loved the "dope"[5] beats, the ever changing and ever expanding lexicon[6], the outrageous dance moves, the cocky swagger, the feeling that we were part of something dynamic and "fresh"[7] that was bigger than any one of us. That world, that other realm that we created on the streets and in our minds, that streamed from the radio in the privacy of our bedrooms and coursed between us as we talked on the phone, that was where we lived.

That was where we felt free.

Looking back on it now, I can see that hip-hop was born of the diversity I found at 141. Unlike the hip-hop of today, it didn't come pre-packaged from a marketing department with millions of dollars to spend. Our hip-hop was the product of a bunch of kids from a bunch of different places trying to talk to each other, trying to create a common language that could cut through the many languages people spoke at home. Intuitively, kids were making a community where there was none; we were affirming our sameness in a world that seemed to only emphasize our difference. That desire to come together irrespective of superficial differences and sometimes in celebration of them, was what gave hip-hop authenticity, that was what kept it honest and as crucial to our well being as food. It's what kept it real.

I can't say much about hip-hop today, but I can say that old hip-hop, original hip-hop, changed my life forever. I only lived in the "Boogie Down Bronx" for a year, but those twelve months gave me so much. I learned that art could bring people together and make them forget their differences. I learned how good it could feel to move with a "posse," a group of friends who had my back no matter what. I learned that I could express myself and communicate with others through what I wore and how I walked and what music I liked. I learned that it doesn't take money or a special degree to transform the grit and drive and hardness of the city into something beautiful.

---

**Central Idea and Support** Which details support the central idea highlighted in blue?

**Rhetorical Devices** Analyze the effect Walker creates through the use of repetition and parallelism. Does she emphasize key ideas? Stir emotions? Something else? Explain.

**Purpose** How do these statements help fulfill Walker's specific purpose for writing?

**Point of View** What is Walker's point of view on the twelve months she spent in the Bronx?

---

5. **dope** (dōp) *adj.* slang term meaning "great; irresistible."
6. **lexicon** (lek´ si kän´) *n.* the special vocabulary of a particular subject.
7. **fresh** (fresh) *adj.* slang term meaning "new."

Loyalty. Community. Self-confidence. Creativity. Hip-hop taught me more about real life than anything I learned that year in class.

I hope when kids today look at shiny videos by their favorite hip-hop artists, they will see through the expensive cars and exotic locations, the women in skimpy outfits and the men trying to approximate a "gangsta" lean. I hope they will remember that hip-hop was born without a formula and without a lot of expensive props or violent undertones. I hope they will marvel at the fact that in the early days of hip-hop, young people were making it up as they went along, following their hearts, following what felt good. I hope they will think about what it takes to create culture that is unique and transcendent and honest, and I hope they begin to dream about creating a new world for themselves.

I hope hip-hop inspires them to make their own revolution.

**Rhetorical Devices**
How does Walker's use of repetition and parallelism help create clear connections between ideas?

## After You Read — "Before Hip-Hop Was Hip-Hop"

**©️ 1. Key Ideas and Details (a)** According to Walker, why did P.S. 141 "crackle" with energy? **(b) Analyze Cause and Effect:** In what ways did hip-hop help Walker and her friends bridge differences?

**©️ 2. Key Ideas and Details (a) Draw Conclusions:** Why was it so important for Walker and her friends to define themselves through dress, special language, dance, and music? **(b) Generalize:** What do teenagers use today to express themselves?

**©️ 3. Craft and Structure (a)** Is the **tone** of Walker's **essay** personal or impersonal? **(b)** What other adjectives appropriately describe her tone? **(c)** Which details in the first three paragraphs support your answers?

**©️ 4. Craft and Structure** What overall **organizational structure** does Walker use to organize her essay?

**©️ 5. Craft and Structure (a)** Use a chart like this one to analyze Walker's **style,** noting passages that support your ideas.

| Level of Formality | Word Choice | Sentence Patterns |
|---|---|---|
|  |  |  |

**(b) Collaborate:** In a small group, discuss the examples in your chart and develop a one-sentence description of Walker's writing style.

**©️ 6. Integration of Knowledge and Ideas (a) Compare and Contrast:** What differences does Walker find between the music of her youth and today's hip-hop? **(b) Take a Position:** Do you think Walker's judgment is fair or biased? Explain.

**©️ 7. Key Ideas and Details** Write an objective summary of "Before Hip-Hop Was Hip-Hop." Do not include your personal reaction to the essay.

## Ⓒ Leveled Texts

Build your skills and improve your comprehension of literary nonfiction with texts of increasing complexity.

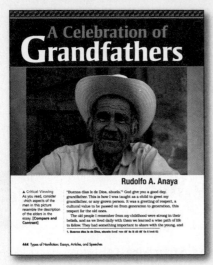

Read **"A Celebration of Grandfathers"** to know the strength and wisdom of older people.

Read **"On Summer"** to glimpse life when it is lived to the fullest.

## Ⓒ Common Core State Standards

Meet these standards with either **"A Celebration of Grandfathers"** (p. 444) or **"On Summer"** (p. 456).

### Reading Informational Text

**1.** Cite strong and thorough textual evidence to support analysis of what the text says explicitly as well as inferences drawn from the text. *(Reading Skill: Main Idea)*

**2.** Determine a central idea of a text and analyze in detail its development, including how it is shaped and refined by specific details. *(Reading Skill: Main Idea)*

**Spiral Review: RI.9-10.6**

### Writing

**2.** Write informative/explanatory texts to examine and convey complex ideas, concepts, and information clearly and accurately through the effective selection, organization, and analysis of content. *(Writing: Book Jacket Copy)*

### Speaking and Listening

**1.** Initiate and participate effectively in a range of collaborative discussions with diverse partners. *(Speaking and Listening: Panel Discussion)*

### Language

**1.** Demonstrate command of the conventions of standard English grammar and usage when writing or speaking. *(Conventions: Direct and Indirect Objects)*

**6.** Acquire and use accurately grade-appropriate general academic and domain-specific words and phrases; gather vocabulary knowledge when considering a word or phrase important to comprehension or expression. *(Vocabulary: Word Study)*

# Literary Analysis: Author's Style

An **author's style** is his or her unique way of using language. Elements that contribute to an author's style include the following:

- **Diction:** the words the author uses
- **Syntax:** the arrangement of words in sentences
- **Tone:** the author's attitude toward the audience or subject

A writer's diction and syntax might be described as *formal* or *informal*, *technical* or *ordinary*, or *sophisticated* or *down-to-earth*. His or her tone might be described as *serious, playful,* or *harsh.* An author's style affects the writer's ability to communicate ideas to readers.

# Reading Skill: Main Idea

The **main, or central, idea** is the key message, insight, or opinion in a work of nonfiction. In some works, the author states his or her central idea directly. In other works the author suggests the central idea but does not state it explicitly. **Supporting details** give further information about the main idea. These details can include facts, statistics, quotations, or anecdotes. To **identify the main idea and supporting details** in a work, **generate questions prior to reading.** Before you read, ask yourself questions such as these:

- Does the author state the central idea or merely suggest it through details?
- Does the title shed light on the central idea?
- How might events in the author's life influence his or her attitude?
- What does the author want me to know?

As you read, look for details that answer these questions and point to the main idea.

## Using the Strategy: Main Idea Chart

Record questions, details, and main ideas on a chart like this one.

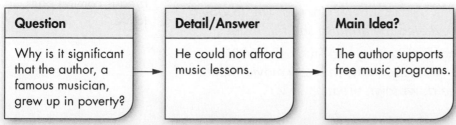

| Question | Detail/Answer | Main Idea? |
|---|---|---|
| Why is it significant that the author, a famous musician, grew up in poverty? | He could not afford music lessons. | The author supports free music programs. |

**PHLit Online!**
**www.PHLitOnline.com**

*Hear It!*
- Selection summary audio
- Selection audio

*See It!*
- Get Connected video
- Background video
- More about the author
- Vocabulary flashcards

*Do It!*
- Interactive journals
- Interactive graphic organizers
- Self-test
- Internet activity
- Grammar tutorial
- Interactive vocabulary games

A Celebration of **Grandfathers**

Rudolfo A. Anaya

444 Types of Nonfiction: Essays, Articles, and Speeches

## Writing About the Big Question

"A Celebration of Grandfathers" explains how the author's grandfather and people of his generation lived and what they valued. Use these sentence starters to develop your ideas about the Big Question.

Knowing what people do and how they live can give **insight** into who they are because _____.

People of different ages often **interpret** ideas and events differently because _____.

**While You Read** Look for details that help you understand the author's grandfather.

## Vocabulary

Read each word and its definition. Decide whether you know the word well, know it a little bit, or do not know it at all. After you read, see how your knowledge of each word has increased.

- **nurturing** (nʉr´ chər iŋ) *n.* the raising or promoting the development of (p. 445) *Nurturing their children is the most important job of parents.* nurture *n.* nurture *v.*

- **perplexes** (pər pleks´ əz) *v.* confuses or puzzles (p. 445) *His odd behavior perplexes them.* perplex *v.* perplexing *adj.* perplexity *n.*

- **absurdity** (ab sʉr´ də tē) *n.* something ridiculous or nonsensical (p. 445) *To our surprise, our reasonable request was treated as an absurdity.* absurd *adj.* absurdly *adv.*

- **permeate** (pʉr´ mē āt´) *v.* spread or flow throughout (p. 446) *It didn't take long for the odor to permeate the entire apartment.* permeation *n.* permeable *adj.* permeating *v.*

- **anguish** (aŋ´ gwish) *n.* great pain or suffering (p. 450) *The troubled expression on her face revealed the anguish she felt inside.*

- **revival** (ri vī´ vəl) *n.* a bringing or coming back into use, attention, or being after a decline (p. 451) *Hopefully, the new movie theater will spark a revival of the downtown area.* revive *v.*

### Word Study

The **Latin root -viv-** means "to live."

In this selection, the author describes the **revival** of the valley where the author's grandfather lived. The word suggests that the area is coming back to life.

Author of

# A Celebration of Grandfathers

Born in New Mexico, Rudolfo A. Anaya is considered the founder of modern Chicano literature. His first novel, *Bless Me, Ultima*, was praised for its depiction of the culture and history of New Mexico. Today, it is widely accepted as a classic of American literature.

**A Storytelling Tradition** "I am an oral storyteller," Anaya explains, "but now I do it on the printed page." Anaya's storytelling reflects his interest in the folk tales of his native Hispanic culture, which combines Spanish, Mexican, and Central American influences. Anaya has won a number of awards, including a PEN Center West Award for his 1992 novel *Albuquerque*. He is currently a professor of English at the University of New Mexico.

## BACKGROUND FOR THE ESSAY

**New Mexican Culture**

Native Americans occupied present-day New Mexico thousands of years before the Spanish arrived in the late 1500s. The area remained under Spanish and then Mexican rule until 1848, when the United States gained control of it. Since then, people from all over the world have settled in New Mexico. As a result, the region has become a kind of cultural crossroads.

## Did You Know?

As a teenager, Anaya was paralyzed after he dove into an irrigation ditch and fractured two vertebrae in his neck. He recovered, but the ordeal forever changed his outlook on life.

# A Celebration of Grandfathers

## Rudolfo A. Anaya

**▲ Critical Viewing**
As you read, consider
which aspects of the
man in this picture
resemble the description
of the elders in the
essay. **[Compare and
Contrast]**

"Buenos días le de Dios, abuelo."[1] God give you a good day,
grandfather. This is how I was taught as a child to greet my
grandfather, or any grown person. It was a greeting of respect, a
cultural value to be passed on from generation to generation, this
respect for the old ones.

The old people I remember from my childhood were strong in their
beliefs, and as we lived daily with them we learned a wise path of life
to follow. They had something important to share with the young, and

---

1. **Buenos días le de Dios, abuelo** (bwā´ nəs dē´ äs lā dä dē´ ōs ä bwä lō)

when they spoke the young listened. These old abuelos and abuelitas[2] had worked the earth all their lives, and so they knew the value of nurturing, they knew the sensitivity of the earth. The daily struggle called for cooperation, and so every person contributed to the social fabric, and each person was respected for his contribution.

The old ones had looked deep into the web that connects all animate and inanimate forms of life, and they recognized the great design of the creation.

These *ancianos*[3] from the cultures of the Río Grande, living side by side, sharing, growing together, they knew the rhythms and cycles of time, from the preparation of the earth in the spring to the digging of the acequias[4] that brought the water to the dance of harvest in the fall. They shared good times and hard times. They helped each other through the epidemics and the personal tragedies, and they shared what little they had when the hot winds burned the land and no rain came. They learned that to survive one had to share in the process of life.

Hard workers all, they tilled the earth and farmed, ran the herds and spun wool, and carved their saints and their kachinas[5] from cottonwood late in the winter nights. All worked with a deep faith which perplexes the modern mind.

Their faith shone in their eyes; it was in the strength of their grip, in the creases time wove into their faces. When they spoke, they spoke plainly and with few words, and they meant what they said. When they prayed, they went straight to the source of life. When there were good times, they knew how to dance in celebration and how to prepare the foods of the fiestas.[6] All this they passed on to the young, so that a new generation would know what they had known, so the string of life would not be broken. •

Today we would say that the old abuelitos lived authentic lives.

Newcomers to New Mexico often say that time seems to move slowly here. I think they mean they have come in contact with the inner strength of the people, a strength so solid it causes time itself to pause. Think of it. Think of the high, northern New Mexico villages, or the lonely ranches on the open llano.[7] Think of the Indian pueblo[8] which lies as solid as rock in the face of time. Remember the old people whose eyes seem like windows that peer into a distant past that makes absurdity of our contemporary

---

2. **abuelitas** (ä bwä lē´ täs) *n.* Spanish for *grandmothers.*
3. *ancianos* (än cē ä´ nōs) n. Spanish for *old people; ancestors.*
4. **acequias** (ä sä kē´ əs) *n.* Spanish for *irrigation ditches.*
5. **kachinas** (kə chē´ nez) *n.* Spanish for *small wooden dolls, representing the spirit of an ancestor or a god.*
6. **fiestas** (fē es´ tez) *n.* Spanish for *celebrations; feasts.*
7. **llano** (yä´ nō) *n.* Spanish for *plain.*
8. **pueblo** (pweb´ lō) *n.* Spanish for *village or town.*

**Literary Analysis**
**Style and Tone**
What is the author's tone as he discusses the *ancianos?*

**Vocabulary**
**nurturing** (nur´ chər in) *n.* the raising or promoting the development of
**perplexes** (pər pleks´ əz) *v.* confuses or puzzles
**absurdity** (ab sur´ də tē) *n.* something ridiculous or nonsensical

Reading Check
What work did the *ancianos* do?

world. That is what one feels when one encounters the old ones and their land, a pausing of time.

We have all felt time stand still. We have all been in the presence of power, the knowledge of the old ones, the majestic peace of a mountain stream or an aspen grove or red buttes rising into blue sky. We have all felt the light of dusk permeate the earth and cause time to pause in its flow.

I felt this when first touched by the spirit of Ultima, the old *curandera*[9] who appears in my first novel, *Bless Me, Ultima*. This is how the young Antonio describes what he feels:

> When she came the beauty of the llano unfolded before my eyes, and the gurgling waters of the river sang to the hum of the turning earth. The magical time of childhood stood still, and the pulse of the living earth pressed its mystery into my living blood. She took my hand, and the silent, magic powers she possessed made beauty from the raw, sun-baked llano, the green river valley, and the blue bowl which was the white sun's home. My bare feet felt the throbbing earth, and my body trembled with excitement. Time stood still . . .

At other times, in other places, when I have been privileged to be with the old ones, to learn, I have felt this inner reserve of strength upon which they draw. I have been held motionless and speechless by the power of curanderas. I have felt the same power when I hunted with Cruz, high on the Taos [tä´ ōs] mountain, where it was more than the incredible beauty of the mountain bathed in morning light, more than the shining of the quivering aspen, but a connection with life, as if a shining strand of light connected the particular and the cosmic. That feeling is an epiphany of time, a standing still of time.

But not all of our old ones are curanderos or hunters on the mountain. My grandfather was a plain man, a farmer from Puerto de Luna[10] on the Pecos River. He was probably a descendent of those people who spilled over the mountain from Taos, following the Pecos River in search of farmland. There in that river valley he settled and raised a large family.

Bearded and walrus-mustached, he stood five feet tall, but to me as a child he was a giant. I remember him most for his silence. In the summers my parents sent me to live with him on his farm, for I was to learn the ways of a farmer. My uncles also lived in that valley, the valley called Puerto de Luna, there where only the flow of

---

**9. curandera** (kōō rän dä´ rä) *n.* Spanish for *medicine woman.*
**10. Puerto de Luna** (pwer´ tō dä lōō´ ne) *n.* Port of the Moon, the name of a town.

---

**Vocabulary**
**permeate** (pʉr´ mē āt´)
*v.* spread or flow throughout

**Literary Analysis**
**Style** How does Anaya's use of Spanish words add to his message of being connected to his culture?

**Spiral Review**
**Author's Point of View** In what way does the author's sense of awe about his subject relate to his purpose for writing?

the river and the whispering of the wind marked time. For me it was a magical place.

I remember once, while out hoeing the fields, I came upon an anthill, and before I knew it I was badly bitten. After he had covered my welts with the cool mud from the irrigation ditch, my grandfather calmly said: "Know where you stand." That is the way he spoke, in short phrases, to the point. ●

One very dry summer, the river dried to a trickle, there was no water for the fields. The young plants withered and died. In my sadness and with the impulses of youth I said, "I wish it would rain!" My grandfather touched me, looked up into the sky and whispered, "Pray for rain." In his language there was a difference. He felt connected to the cycles that brought the rain or kept it from us. His prayer was a meaningful action, because he was a participant with the forces that filled our world, he was not a bystander.

A young man died at the village one summer. A very tragic death. He was dragged by his horse. When he was found I cried, for the boy was my friend. I did not understand why death had come to one so young. My grandfather took me aside and said: "Think of the death of the trees and the fields in the fall. The leaves fall, and everything rests, as if dead. But they bloom again in the spring. Death is only this small transformation in life."

These are the things I remember, these fleeting images, few words.

I remember him driving his horse-drawn wagon into Santa Rosa in the fall when he brought his harvest produce to sell in the town. What a tower of strength seemed to come in that small man huddled on the seat of the giant wagon. One click of his tongue and the horses obeyed, stopped or turned as he wished. He never raised his whip. How unlike today when so much teaching is done with loud words and threatening hands.

*Woodcutter and Burro* ("El Lenador"), 1934, Tom Lea, on long-term loan to the New Mexico Museum of Art from the U.S. General Services Administration, Works Project Administration. Photograph by Blair Clark.

▲ **Critical Viewing**
How does the farmer in this painting compare with your image of the author's grandfather? **[Compare and Contrast]**

Reading Check

Why did Anaya's parents send him to stay with his grandfather in the summer?

A Celebration of Grandfathers  **447**

**Reading Skill**
**Main Idea** What main idea about the loss of values does Anaya state here?

▼ **Critical Viewing**
Why do you think a writer like Anaya might find this New Mexican landscape inspiring?
**[Speculate]**

I would run to greet the wagon, and the wagon would stop. "Buenos días le de Dios, abuelo," I would say. This was the prescribed greeting of esteem and respect. Only after the greeting was given could we approach these venerable old people. "Buenos días te de Dios, mi hijo,"[11] he would answer and smile, and then I could jump up on the wagon and sit at his side. Then I, too, became a king as I rode next to the old man who smelled of earth and sweat and the other deep aromas from the orchards and fields of Puerto de Luna.

We were all sons and daughters to him. But today the sons and daughters are breaking with the past, putting aside los abuelitos. The old values are threatened, and threatened most where it comes to these relationships with the old people. If we don't take the time to watch and feel the years of their final transformation, a part of our humanity will be lessened.

I grew up speaking Spanish, and oh! how difficult it was to learn English. Sometimes I would give up and cry out that I couldn't learn. Then he would say, "Ten paciencia."[12] Have patience.

---

**11. mi hijo** (mē ē′ hō) *n.* Spanish for *my son.*
**12. Ten paciencia** (ten pä sē en′ sē ä) *n.* Spanish for *Have patience.*

*Paciencia*, a word with the strength of centuries, a word that said that someday we would overcome. *Paciencia*, how soothing a word coming from this old man who could still sling hundred-pound bags over his shoulder, chop wood for hours on end, and hitch up his own horses and ride to town and back in one day.

"You have to learn the language of the Americanos,"[13] he said. "Me, I will live my last days in my valley. You will live in a new time, the time of the gringos."[14]

A new time did come, a new time is here. How will we form it so it is fruitful? We need to know where we stand. We need to speak softly and respect others, and to share what we have. We need to pray not for material gain, but for rain for the fields, for the sun to nurture growth, for nights in which we can sleep in peace, and for a harvest in which everyone can share. Simple lessons from a simple man. These lessons he learned from his past which was as deep and strong as the currents of the river of life, a life which could be stronger than death. ●

---

13. **Americanos** (ä mer´ ē kä´ nōs) *n.* Spanish for *Americans.*
14. **gringos** (grin´ gōs) *n.* Spanish for *foreigners; North Americans.*

**Literary Analysis**
**Style** How does the author's repetition of the phrase "We need" add urgency to his message?

Reading
Check
Why does Anaya's grandfather tell him that he must learn English?

*Three Reds,* Courtesy of Patrick Coffaro, Photography courtesy of Joan Cawley Licensing, Ltd.

## Cultural Connection

**Anaya's Best-Known Work**
In this essay, Anaya quotes from his novel *Bless Me, Ultima*. First published in 1972, the novel tells the story of a young boy, Antonio, who lives with his family in Guadalupe, New Mexico. Ultima, who is respected for her healing powers and her knowledge of the uses of plants, comes to live with Antonio's family. Ultima takes the boy under her wing and teaches him about the plants and trees of the area. She also teaches him some important lessons about life.

### Connect to the Literature

Based on what you know about Anaya's writing, how would you expect him to describe the bond between people and the land? Explain your answer.

**Vocabulary**
**anguish** (aŋ´ gwish) *n.*
great pain or suffering

He was a man; he died. Not in his valley, but nevertheless cared for by his sons and daughters and flocks of grandchildren. At the end, I would enter his room which carried the smell of medications and Vicks, the faint pungent odor of urine, and cigarette smoke. Gone were the aroma of the fields, the strength of his young manhood. Gone also was his patience in the face of crippling old age. Small things bothered him; he shouted or turned sour when his expectations were not met. It was because he could not care for himself, because he was returning to that state of childhood, and all those wishes and desires were now wrapped in a crumbling old body.

"Ten paciencia," I once said to him, and he smiled. "I didn't know I would grow this old," he said. "Now, I can't even roll my own cigarettes." I rolled a cigarette for him, placed it in his mouth and lit it. I asked him why he smoked, the doctor had said it was bad for him. "I like to see the smoke rise," he said. He would smoke and doze, and his quilt was spotted with little burns where the cigarettes dropped. One of us had to sit and watch to make sure a fire didn't start.

I would sit and look at him and remember what was said of him when he was a young man. He could mount a wild horse and break it, and he could ride as far as any man. He could dance all night at a dance, then work the acequia the following day. He helped neighbors, they helped him. He married, raised children. Small legends, the kind that make up everyman's life.

He was 94 when he died. Family, neighbors, and friends gathered; they all agreed he had led a rich life. I remembered the last years, the years he spent in bed. And as I remember now, I am reminded that it is too easy to romanticize old age. Sometimes we forget the pain of the transformation into old age, we forget the natural breaking down of the body. Not all go gentle into the last years, some go crying and cursing, forgetting the names of those they loved the most, withdrawing into an internal anguish few of us can know. May we be granted the patience and care to deal with our ancianos.

For some time we haven't looked at these changes and needs of the old ones. The American image created by the mass media is an image of youth, not of old age. It is the beautiful and the young who are praised in this society. If analyzed carefully, we see that same damaging thought has crept into the way society views the old. In response to the old, the mass media have just created old people who act like the young. It is only the healthy, pink-cheeked, outgoing, older persons we are shown in the media. And they are always selling something, as if an entire generation of old people were salesmen in their lives. Commercials show very lively old men, who must always be in excellent health according to the new myth, selling insurance policies or real estate as they are out golfing; older women selling coffee or toilet paper to those just married. That image does not illustrate the real life of the old ones.

Real life takes into account the natural cycle of growth and change. My grandfather pointed to the leaves falling from the tree. So time brings with its transformation the often painful, wearing-down process. Vision blurs, health wanes; even the act of walking carries with it the painful reminder of the autumn of life. But this process is something to be faced, not something to be hidden away by false images. Yes, the old can be young at heart, but in their own way, with their own dignity. They do not have to copy the always-young image of the Hollywood star.

> Real life takes into account the natural cycle of growth and change.

My grandfather wanted to return to his valley to die. But by then the families of the valley had left in search of a better future. It is only now that there seems to be a return to the valley, a revival. The new generation seeks its roots, that value of love for the land moves us to return to the place where our ancianos formed the culture.

I returned to Puerto de Luna last summer, to join the community in a celebration of the founding of the church. I drove by my grandfather's home, my uncles' ranches, the neglected adobe[15] washing down into the earth from whence it came. And I wondered, how might the values of my grandfather's generation live in our own? What can we retain to see us through these hard times? I

---

15. **adobe** (ə dō´ bē) *n.* sun-dried clay brick.

**Vocabulary**
**revival** (ri vī´ vəl) *n.* a bringing or coming back into use, attention, or being after a decline

**Reading Check**
What happens to Anaya's grandfather?

was to become a farmer, and I became a writer. As I plow and plant my words, do I nurture as my grandfather did in his fields and orchards? The answers are not simple.

>
>
> **H**ow strong these people were to leave such a lasting impression.

"They don't make men like that anymore," is a phrase we hear when one does honor to a man. I am glad I knew my grandfather. I am glad there are still times when I can see him in my dreams, hear him in my reverie. Sometimes I think I catch a whiff of that earthy aroma that was his smell, just as in lonely times sometimes I catch the fragrance of Ultima's herbs. Then I smile. How strong these people were to leave such a lasting impression.

So, as I would greet my abuelo long ago, it would help us all to greet the old ones we know with this kind and respectful greeting: "Buenos días le de Dios."

## Critical Thinking

**Cite textual evidence to support your responses.**

Ⓒ **1. Key Ideas and Details (a)** What qualities of old people does Anaya remember from his childhood? **(b) Distinguish:** How are these qualities different from the images that Anaya says have been created by American mass media?

Ⓒ **2. Integration of Knowledge and Ideas** What does the author imply about the "new time" in which his people will live?

Ⓒ **3. Key Ideas and Details (a) Draw Conclusions:** What opinion does Anaya offer on the way people should be treated as they grow old? **(b) Take a Position:** Do you agree with him? Explain. **(c) Discuss:** Share your answers with a partner. Then, explain how your answer has grown or changed as a result of the discussion.

Ⓒ **4. Integration of Knowledge and Ideas (a)** What insights do the quotations from Anaya's grandfather give you? **(b)** How do these insights strengthen your understanding? *[Connect to the Big Question: Is knowledge the same as understanding?]*

## Literary Analysis: Author's Style

© **1. Craft and Structure** At several points in his essay, Anaya strings together sentences that have parallel structure, as in this example: "When they spoke, they spoke plainly and with few words, and they meant what they said. When they prayed, they went straight to the source of life. When there were good times, they knew how to dance in celebration. . . ." What effect does this aspect of the author's **syntax** create? Explain your response.

© **2. Craft and Structure** Use a chart like the one shown to record examples of the **diction** and **tone** Anaya uses. Then, based on his diction and tone, write three adjectives in the center of the chart that describe his **style.**

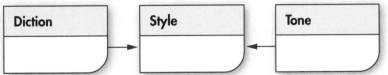

## Reading Skill: Main Idea

**3.** State the **central idea** of Anaya's essay in your own words.

**4. (a)** List three **supporting details** that serve as evidence for the main point that Anaya makes in his essay. **(b)** Does the author adequately support his main idea with details? Why or why not?

## Vocabulary

© **Acquisition and Use** Determine whether each sentence below is true or false. Use the meaning of the italicized word to explain your reasoning.

**1.** A poor instruction manual is one that *perplexes* its readers.

**2.** It is a compliment to have a business idea labeled "an *absurdity*."

**3.** To prevent a stain, allow ink to *permeate* the fabric.

**4.** Comforting someone in *anguish* is a kind action.

**5.** *Nurturing* a plant involves watering and feeding it.

**6.** The closing performance of a play would be a *revival*.

**Word Study** Use the context of the sentences and what you know about the **Latin root -viv-** to explain your answer to each question.

**1.** Do most people *survive* an embarrassing moment?

**2.** Is a *vivid* experience one you're likely to soon forget?

### Word Study

The **Latin root -viv-** means "to live."

**Apply It** Explain how the root -viv- contributes to the meanings of these words. You may consult a dictionary if necessary.

convivial

vivacious

revive

## Writing About the Big Question

**Is *knowledge* the same as *understanding*?**

In "On Summer," Lorraine Hansberry's growing understanding of life has changed her feelings about summer. Use these sentence starters to develop your ideas about the Big Question.

Learning the **facts** of people's lives may change how we **comprehend** them because _____.

When we make a **connection** with something, our **feelings** toward it may change because _____.

**While You Read** Look for details that tell about Hansberry's feelings toward summer.

## Vocabulary

Read each word and its definition. Decide whether you know the word well, know it a little bit, or do not know it at all. After you read, see how your knowledge of each word has increased.

- **aloofness** (ə loof´ nəs) *n.* emotional distance (p. 456) *His aloofness made him appear unfriendly. aloof adj. aloofly adv.*

- **melancholy** (mel´ ən käl´ ē) *adj.* sad; gloomy (p. 456) *The rain set a melancholy mood. melancholy n. melancholic adj.*

- **bias** (bī´ əs) *n.* mental leaning or inclination; partiality (p. 457) *For years, John has had a bias toward Italian restaurants. bias v. biased adj.*

- **duration** (doo rā´ shən) *n.* the time that a thing continues or lasts (p. 457) *To sleep better at night, decrease the duration of your afternoon nap. durable adj. durability n. endure v.*

- **pretentious** (prē ten´ shəs) *adj.* grand in a showy way (p. 460) *His pretentious manner only impressed those who had just met him. pretentiousness n.*

- **apex** (ā´ peks´) *n.* highest point; peak (p. 460) *Playing in the World Series was the apex of his baseball career.*

### Word Study

The **Latin root -dur-** means "to harden," "to hold out," or "to last."

In this story, the narrator describes the long **duration** of a summer day. She means that it seems to last for a very long time.

Author of

## On Summer

Lorraine Hansberry grew up on the South Side of Chicago, where her father prospered as a real-estate broker. At the time, many white people closed their neighborhoods, refusing to sell or rent property to African Americans. Hansberry's father fought this practice, taking his case all the way to the Supreme Court, where he won.

**A Pioneering Playwright** As her father fought to integrate Chicago's neighborhoods, Hansberry laid claim to territories of the imagination. With the 1959 production of her play *A Raisin in the Sun*, she became the first African American woman to have a drama produced on Broadway.

## BACKGROUND FOR THE ESSAY

**The Great Migration**

Beginning in the early 1900s, hundreds of thousands of African Americans left the rural South for northern cities. They fled discrimination and the floods and pests that threatened their livelihood as farmers. Many left relatives behind and, like Hansberry's Chicago family, journeyed south in summertime to visit.

### Did You Know?

A Broadway revival of the play *A Raisin in the Sun* won Tony awards for Phylicia Rashad and Audra McDonald in 2004.

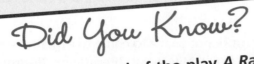

# On Summer

## Lorraine Hansberry

**Vocabulary**
**aloofness** (ə lo͞of′ nəs)
*n.* emotional distance

**melancholy**
(mel′ ən käl′ ē) *adj.*
sad; gloomy

It has taken me a good number of years to come to any measure of respect for summer. I was, being May-born, literally an "infant of the spring" and, during the later childhood years, tended, for some reason or other, to rather worship the cold aloofness of winter. The adolescence, admittedly lingering still, brought the traditional passionate commitment to melancholy autumn—and all that. For the longest kind of time I simply thought that *summer* was a mistake.

In fact, my earliest memory of anything at all is of waking up in a darkened room where I had been put to bed for a nap on a summer's afternoon, and feeling very, very hot. I acutely disliked the feeling then and retained the bias for years. It had originally been a matter of the heat but, over the years, I came actively to associate displeasure with most of the usually celebrated natural features and social by-products of the season: the too-grainy texture of sand; the too-cold coldness of the various waters we constantly try to escape into, and the icky-perspiry feeling of bathing caps.

It also seemed to me, esthetically[1] speaking, that nature had got inexcusably carried away on the summer question and let the whole thing get to be rather much. By duration alone, for instance, a summer's day seemed maddeningly excessive; an utter overstatement. Except for those few hours at either end of it, objects always appeared in too sharp a relief against backgrounds; shadows too pronounced and light too blinding. It always gave me the feeling of walking around in a motion picture which had been too artsily-craftsily exposed. Sound also had a way of coming to the ear without that muting influence, marvelously common to winter, across patios or beaches or through the woods. I suppose I found it too stark and yet too intimate a season.

My childhood Southside summers were the ordinary city kind, full of the street games which other rememberers have turned into fine ballets these days and rhymes that anticipated what some people insist on calling modern poetry:

> Oh, Mary Mack, Mack, Mack
> All dressed in black, black, black
> With the silver buttons, buttons, buttons
> All down her back, back, back
> She asked her mother, mother, mother
> For fifteen cents, cents, cents
> To see the elephant, elephant, elephant
> Jump the fence, fence, fence
> Well, he jumped so high, high, high
> 'Til he touched the sky, sky, sky
> And he didn't come back, back, back
> 'Til the Fourth of Ju-ly, ly, ly!

Evenings were spent mainly on the back porches where screen doors slammed in the darkness with those really very special summertime sounds. And, sometimes, when Chicago nights got too steamy, the whole family got into the car and went to the park and slept out in the

---

1. **esthetically** (es thet´ ik lē) *adv.* artistically.

**Literary Analysis**
**Style** How would you describe Hansberry's tone as she explains her childhood feelings about summer?

**Vocabulary**
**bias** (bī´ əs) *n.* mental leaning or inclination; partiality
**duration** (doo rā´ shən) *n.* the time that a thing continues or lasts

**Literary Analysis**
**Style** What effect does the use of the made-up word "artsily-craftsily" create?

Reading Check
Identify one thing the author dislikes about summer.

**Literary Analysis**
**Style** How does
Hansberry's repeated use
of the word *and* to begin
sentences emphasize the
flow and abundance of
her memories?

Ⓒ

**Spiral Review**
**Author's Point of**
**View** Why do you
think the author chose
to relate this episode
through her childhood
perspective?

open on blankets. Those were, of course, the best times of all because the grownups were invariably reminded of having been children in rural parts of the country and told the best stories then. And it was also cool and sweet to be on the grass and there was usually the scent of freshly cut lemons or melons in the air. And Daddy would lie on his back, as fathers must, and explain about how men thought the stars above us came to be and how far away they were. I never did learn to believe that anything could be as far away as *that.* Especially the stars.

My mother first took us south to visit her Tennessee birthplace one summer when I was seven or eight, I think. I woke up on the back seat of the car while we were still driving through some place called Kentucky and my mother was pointing out to the beautiful hills on both sides of the highway and telling my brothers and my sister about how her father had run away and hidden from his master in those very hills when he was a little boy. She said that his mother had wandered among the wooded slopes in the moonlight and left food for him in secret places. They were very beautiful hills and I looked out at them for miles and miles after that wondering who and what a *master* might be.

I remember being startled when I first saw my grandmother rocking away on her porch. All my life I had heard that she was a great beauty and no one had ever remarked that they meant a half century before. The woman that I met was as wrinkled as a prune and could hardly hear and barely see and always seemed to be thinking of other times. But she could still rock and talk and even make wonderful cupcakes which were like cornbread, only sweet. She was captivated by automobiles and, even though it was well into the Thirties,[2] I don't think she had ever been in one before we came down and took her driving. She was a little afraid of them and could not seem to negotiate the windows, but she loved driving. She died the next summer and that is all that I remember about her, except that she was born in slavery and had memories of it and they didn't sound anything like *Gone With the Wind.*[3]

**Reading Skill**
**Main Idea** What
do these anecdotes
about her trips to
Tennessee add to your
understanding of the
author's childhood
summers?

Like everyone else, I have spent whole or bits of summers in many different kinds of places since then: camps and resorts in the Middle West and New York State; on an island; in a tiny Mexican village; Cape Cod, perched atop the Truro bluffs at Longnook Beach that Millay wrote about; or simply strolling the streets of Provincetown[4] before the hours when the parties begin.

And, lastly, I do not think that I will forget days spent, a few summers ago, at a beautiful lodge built right into the rocky cliffs

---

2. **Thirties** the 1930s.
3. **Gone With the Wind** novel set in the South during the Civil War period.
4. **Provincetown** resort town at the northern tip of Cape Cod, Massachusetts.

of a bay on the Maine coast. We met a woman there who had lived a purposeful and courageous life and who was then dying of cancer. She had, characteristically, just written a book and taken up painting. She had also been of radical viewpoint all her life; one of those people who energetically believe that the world *can* be changed for the better and spend their lives trying to do just that. And that was the way she thought of cancer; she absolutely refused to award it the stature of tragedy, a devastating instance of the brooding doom and inexplicability[5] of the absurdity of human destiny, etc., etc. The kind of characterization given, lately, as we all know, to far less formidable foes in life than cancer.

But for this remarkable woman it was a matter of nature in imperfection, implying, as always, work for man to do. It was an *enemy,* but a palpable one with shape and effect and source; and if it existed, it could be destroyed. She saluted it accordingly, without despondency, but with a lively, beautiful and delightfully ribald anger. There was one thing, she felt, which would prove equal to its relentless ravages and that was the genius of man. Not his mysticism, but man with tubes and slides and the stubborn human notion that the stars are very much within our reach.

---

5. **inexplicability** (in eks′ pli kə bil′ ə tē) *n.* condition of being unexplainable.

▼ **Critical Viewing**
How does this illustration of the Maine coast add to the description in the essay? **[Connect]**

**Reading Check**
Whom does Hansberry visit in Tennessee?

**Literary Analysis**
**Style** What words has Hansberry used to convey her feelings about the woman in Maine?

**Vocabulary**
**pretentious** (prē ten´ shəs) *adj.* grand in a showy way

**apex** (ā´ peks´) *n.* highest point; peak

The last time I saw her she was sitting surrounded by her paintings with her manuscript laid out for me to read, because, she said, she wanted to know what a *young person* would think of her thinking; one must always keep up with what *young people* thought about things because, after all, they were *change.*

Every now and then her jaw set in anger as we spoke of things people should be angry about. And then, for relief, she would look out at the lovely bay at a mellow sunset settling on the water. Her face softened with love of all that beauty and, watching her, I wished with all my power what I knew that she was wishing: that she might live to see at least one more *summer.* Through her eyes I finally gained the sense of what it might mean; more than the coming autumn with its pretentious melancholy; more than an austere and silent winter which must shut dying people in for precious months; more even than the frivolous spring, too full of too many false promises, would be the gift of another summer with its stark and intimate assertion of neither birth nor death but life at the apex; with the gentlest nights and, above all, the longest days.

I heard later that she did live to see another summer. And I have retained my respect for the noblest of the seasons.

## Critical Thinking

*Cite textual evidence to support your responses.*

1. **Key Ideas and Details (a)** When does Hansberry first visit her grandmother? **(b) Infer:** Why do you think she includes the section about her grandmother in her essay? Which details led you to this idea?

2. **Integration of Knowledge and Ideas (a)** When does Hansberry's attitude toward summer begin to change? **(b) Interpret:** At the essay's end, Hansberry calls summer "the noblest of seasons." What do you think she means by this phrase?

3. **Craft and Structure Evaluate:** How clearly do you think Hansberry explains the way her feelings about summer have changed? Explain.

4. **Integration of Knowledge and Ideas (a)** In what way has Hansberry's knowledge of summer stayed the same? **(b)** How has her understanding of summer changed? Use details from the text to explain your response. *[Connect to the Big Question: Is knowledge the same as understanding?]*

## Literary Analysis: Author's Style

© 1. **Craft and Structure** What one word might you use to describe the overall **tone** of "On Summer"? Explain your answer.

© 2. **Craft and Structure** Review the last two paragraphs of "On Summer." Use a chart like the one shown to record examples of the **diction** and **tone** Hansberry uses in describing her associations with summer. Then, based on her diction and tone in these paragraphs, write three adjectives in the center of the chart to describe Hansberry's **style.**

| Diction | | Style | | Tone |
|---------|--|-------|--|------|

## Reading Skill: Main Idea

3. State the **main idea** of "On Summer" in your own words.

4. **(a)** List three **supporting details** that serve as evidence for the main point that Hansberry makes in the essay. **(b)** Does the author adequately support her main idea with details? Explain.

## Vocabulary

© **Acquisition and Use** Determine whether each sentence below is true or false. Use the meaning of the italicized word to explain your reasoning.

1. Greeting a close friend with *aloofness* shows respect.

2. Cheerful songs might change someone's *melancholy* mood.

3. A *pretentious* politician is likely to be unpopular with many voters.

4. One must climb a mountain to reach its *apex*.

5. If a man has a *bias* toward cats, he feels neutral about them.

6. If we stay for the *duration* of the game, we will leave at halftime.

**Word Study** Use the context of sentences and what you know about the **Latin root -dur-** to explain your answer to each question.

1. If a manufacturer claims an item is *durable*, would you expect it to wear out quickly?

2. When a thief is caught *during* a robbery, has he or she been caught in the act?

### Word Study

The **Latin root -dur-** means "to harden," "to hold out," or "to last."

**Apply It** Explain how the root -dur- contributes to the meanings of these words. You may consult a dictionary if necessary.

**obdurate**
**endure**
**duress**

# Integrated Language Skills

## A Celebration of Grandfathers • On Summer

### Conventions: Direct and Indirect Objects

A **direct object** is a noun or pronoun that *receives* the action of an action verb. An **indirect object** appears with a direct object and names the person or thing that something is *given to* or *done for.*

You can determine whether a word is a direct object by asking *Whom?* or *What?* after an action verb. You can tell whether a word is an indirect object by asking *To or for whom?* or *To or for what?* An indirect object can only appear between a subject and a direct object.

| Example | Explanation |
|---|---|
| The family bought **an old house.** | *House* is a direct object—answers the question *Bought what?* |
| The rain pelted **the campers.** | *Campers* is a direct object—answers the question *Pelted whom?* |
| I wrote my **brother letters.** | *Brother* is an indirect object—answers the question *Wrote to whom?* *Letters* is a direct object—answers the question *Wrote what?* |

**Practice A** Identify the direct and indirect objects in each sentence.

1. The author greeted his grandfather.
2. His grandfather usually gave him very good advice.
3. Rudolfo Anaya always showed his grandfather respect.
4. Grandfather drove the huge wagon to market with the produce.

**Practice B** For each item, write an original sentence using the word or phrase as directed in the information in parentheses.

1. winter (as a direct object)
2. Maine coast (as a direct object in a question)
3. author (as an indirect object), manuscript (as a direct object)
4. grandmother (as an indirect object), gift (as a direct object)

© **Reading Application** In the first paragraph of "A Celebration of Grandfathers," find a sentence that uses both a direct and an indirect object.

© **Writing Application** Use this sentence starter to write three sentences about summer that each contain an indirect object (IO) and a direct object (DO): *I gave <u>(IO)/(DO).</u>*

**PH WRITING COACH** | Further instruction and practice are available in *Prentice Hall Writing Coach.*

# Writing

**Informative Text** Both of these selections describe the admiration the main characters have for someone older than they are. Think of an older person whom you admire. Write a few paragraphs of **book jacket copy** for a biography of that person.

- Include some important highlights of the person's life.
- Choose specific details that will make the reader want to know more.

**Grammar Application** Review your draft to identify the direct and indirect objects you have used.

## Writing Workshop: *Work in Progress*

**Prewriting for Business Letters** For a business letter you may write, list consumer items that have not lived up to your expectations. Note what has been disappointing. Then, choose one item and consider information a company representative would need to know. Jot down three questions to be answered. Save this Questions List.

# Speaking and Listening

**Presentation of Ideas** In a small group, hold a **panel discussion** on one of these topics.

- If you read "A Celebration of Grandfathers," discuss Anaya's claim that "the American image created by the mass media is an image of youth, not old age." To get started, think about the age of most people in television and films. Decide what images are conveyed by these actors.

- If you read "On Summer," discuss the pros and cons of each season of the year. To prepare, consider what you like about your favorite season, as well as what others might dislike about that season.

Follow these steps to complete the assignment:

- Prepare notes to use during the discussion. These will help keep you on track and remind you about what you have planned to say.

- During the discussion, clarify and defend your position. Help elaborate on the ideas of other panel members by adding useful supporting details.

- Use precise and relevant evidence such as facts, opinions, quotations, and reasoning to support your points.

- Use props, visual aids, graphs, and electronic media to make your discussion more appealing and persuasive.

**Common Core State Standards**

**L.9-10.1; W.9-10.2; SL.9-10.1**
[For the full wording of the standards, see page 440.]

Use this prewriting activity to prepare for the **Writing Workshop** on page 512.

## Leveled Texts

Build your skills and improve your comprehension of types of nonfiction with texts of increasing complexity.

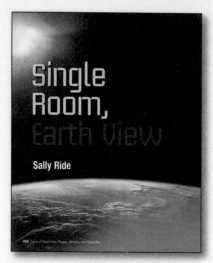

Read **"Single Room, Earth View"** to get an understanding of traveling in space.

Read **"The News"** to learn about and analyze the unique qualities of TV news.

## Common Core State Standards

Meet these standards with either **"Single Room, Earth View"** (p. 468) or **"The News"** (p. 478).

**Reading Informational Text**

**2.** Determine a central idea of a text and analyze its development over the course of the text, including how it emerges and is shaped and refined by specific details; provide an objective summary of the text. *(Literary Analysis: Main Idea)*

**3.** Analyze how the author unfolds an analysis or series of ideas or events, including the order in which the points are made, how they are introduced and developed, and the connections that are drawn between them. *(Literary Analysis: Main Idea)*

**Spiral Review: RI.9-10.4**

**Writing**

**2.** Write informative/explanatory texts to examine and convey complex ideas, concepts, and information clearly and accurately through the effective selection, organization, and analysis of content. *(Writing: Public Service Announcement)*

**7.** Conduct short as well as more sustained research projects to answer a question or solve a problem; narrow or broaden the inquiry when appropriate; synthesize multiple sources on the subject, demonstrating understanding of the subject under investigation. *(Research and Technology: Journal Entries)*

**8.** Gather relevant information from multiple authoritative print and digital sources, using advanced searches effectively; assess the usefulness of each source in answering the research question; integrate information into the text selectively to maintain the flow of ideas. *(Research and Technology: Journal Entries)*

**Speaking and Listening**

**4.** Present information, findings, and supporting evidence clearly, concisely, and logically such that listeners can follow the line of reasoning and the organization, development, substance, and style are appropriate to purpose, audience, and task. *(Writing: Public Service Announcement)*

# Literary Analysis: Expository Essay

An **expository essay** is a short piece of nonfiction that presents information, discusses ideas, or explains a process. An essay writer may use a variety of techniques to introduce and develop ideas and to draw connections between those ideas.

- **Description:** including imagery—language that appeals to the senses—and figurative language, such as simile and metaphor
- **Comparison and contrast:** showing similarities and differences between two or more ideas, people, events, or things
- **Cause and effect:** explaining the relationship between events, actions, or situations by showing how one can result from another

# Reading Skill: Main Idea

The **main, or central, idea** is the key message, insight, or opinion in a work of nonfiction. The author may state the central idea explicitly, or merely suggest it. The **supporting details** are the pieces of evidence a writer uses to prove his or her point. **Reread** to help you **identify the main idea and supporting details** in a work. As you read, follow these steps:

- Note whether the author states the central idea directly. If not, note key details to decide what the main idea might be.
- If a detail does not seem to support that main idea, reread the passage to be sure that you have not misinterpreted it.
- If necessary, revise your assumptions about the main idea.

## Using the Strategy: Cluster Diagram

Record details and main ideas on a cluster diagram like this one.

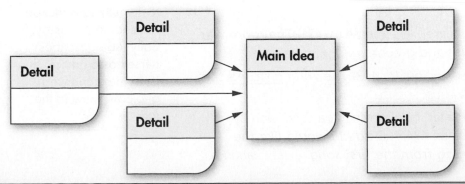

**PHLit Online!**
www.PHLitOnline.com

*Hear It!*
- Selection summary audio
- Selection audio

*See It!*
- Get Connected video
- Background video
- More about the author
- Vocabulary flashcards

*Do It!*
- Interactive journals
- Interactive graphic organizers
- Self-test
- Internet activity
- Grammar tutorial
- Interactive vocabulary games

**Is *knowledge* the same as *understanding*?**

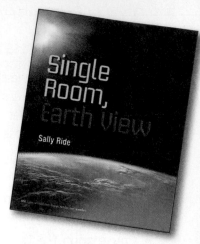

## Writing About the Big Question

In "Single Room, Earth View," astronaut Sally Ride explains what it is like to see Earth from the space shuttle. Use these sentence starters to develop your ideas about the Big Question.

Looking at Earth from space may change how we **comprehend** the world because _____.

Analyzing familiar **concepts** from a different perspective can help us understand them better because _____.

**While You Read** Look for a way in which the writer's knowledge grows into understanding while traveling in space for the first time.

## Vocabulary

Read each word and its definition. Decide whether you know the word well, know it a little bit, or do not know it at all. After you read, see how your knowledge of each word has increased.

- **articulate** (är tik´ yo͞o lit) *adj.* able to express oneself clearly and easily (p. 469) *The candidate is an <u>articulate</u> public speaker.* *articulate v. articulately adv. articulation n.*

- **surreal** (sər rē´ əl) *adj.* strange, like something from a dream (p. 470) *The party was a <u>surreal</u> mixture of men in business suits and punk rockers.* *surrealism n.*

- **novice** (näv´ is) *adj.* new to an activity; inexperienced (p. 470) *For a <u>novice</u> chess player, she shows great patience and maturity.* *nova n. novitiate n.*

- **muted** (myo͞ot´ əd) *adj.* weaker; less intense (p. 471) *The room was furnished in <u>muted</u> blues and greens.* *mute v. mute n.*

- **diffused** (di fyo͞ozd´) *v.* spread out (p. 473) *The wind <u>diffused</u> the confetti over the field.* *diffuse v. diffusion n.*

- **extrapolating** (ek strap´ ə lāt´ iŋ) *v.* arriving at a conclusion by inferring from known facts (p. 474) *I decided I would like the whole CD by <u>extrapolating</u> from the first song.* *extrapolation n.*

### Word Study

The **Latin root -nov-** means "new" or "recent."

Someone who is new to something is inexperienced. In this essay, Sally Ride describes herself as a **novice**. She is an inexperienced geologist, new to the job.

# Meet
# Sally Ride
(b. 1957)

# Author of
# Single Room, Earth View

Although best known as an astronaut, Sally Ride was also a talented athlete in her youth. She was a ranked player on the junior tennis circuit and considered turning professional before deciding to go to college instead.

**The Right Stuff** In 1978, Ride read a newspaper advertisement about NASA's search for astronauts. After extensive testing to be sure she had "the right stuff," NASA chose her as one of six women and twenty-five men accepted from among 8,000 applicants. Five years later, in 1983, she took her historic flight. Ride retired from NASA in 1987 and currently teaches physics at the University of California.

## BACKGROUND FOR THE ESSAY

**First American Woman in Space**

On June 18, 1983, when she worked as a flight engineer and mission specialist aboard the shuttle *Challenger*, Sally Ride became the first American woman in space. Her historic mission allowed her to experience what she recounts in "Single Room, Earth View."

## Did You Know?
Sally Ride holds four degrees from Stanford University, including a Master's and a Doctorate.

# Single Room, Earth View

## Sally Ride

Everyone I've met has a glittering, if vague, mental image of space travel. And naturally enough, people want to hear about it from an astronaut: "How did it feel . . . ?" "What did it look like . . . ?" "Were you scared?" Sometimes, the questions come from reporters, their pens poised and their tape recorders silently reeling in the words; sometimes, it's wide-eyed, ten-year-old girls who want answers. I find a way to answer all of them, but it's not easy.

Imagine trying to describe an airplane ride to someone who has never flown. An articulate traveler could describe the sights but would find it much harder to explain the difference in perspective provided by the new view from a greater distance, along with the feelings, impressions, and insights that go with that new perspective. And the difference is enormous: Spaceflight moves the traveler another giant step farther away. Eight and one-half thunderous minutes after launch, an astronaut is orbiting high above the Earth, suddenly able to watch typhoons form, volcanoes smolder, and meteors streak through the atmosphere below.

◄ **Critical Viewing** Based on this photograph, how might travel in the space shuttle defy description? **[Connect]**

**Vocabulary**
**articulate** (är tik´ yo͞o lit) *adj.* able to express oneself clearly and easily

While flying over the Hawaiian Islands, several astronauts have marveled that the islands look just like they do on a map. When people first hear that, they wonder what should be so surprising about Hawaii looking the way it does in the atlas. Yet, to the astronauts it is an absolutely startling sensation: The islands really *do* look as if that part of the world has been carpeted with a big page torn out of Rand-McNally, and all we can do is try to convey the surreal quality of that scene.●

In orbit, racing along at five miles per second, the space shuttle circles the Earth once every 90 minutes. I found that at this speed, unless I kept my nose pressed to the window, it was almost impossible to keep track of where we were at any given moment—the world below simply changes too fast. If I turned my concentration away for too long, even just to change film in a camera, I could miss an entire land mass. It's embarrassing to float up to a window, glance outside, and then have to ask a crewmate, "What continent is this?"

We could see smoke rising from fires that dotted the entire east coast of Africa, and in the same orbit only moments later, ice floes jostling for position in the Antarctic. We could see the Ganges River dumping its murky, sediment-laden water into the Indian Ocean and watch ominous hurricane clouds expanding and rising like biscuits in the oven of the Caribbean.

Mountain ranges, volcanoes, and river deltas appeared in salt-and-flour relief, all leading me to assume the role of a novice geologist. In such moments, it was easy to imagine the dynamic upheavals that created jutting mountain ranges and the internal wrenchings that created rifts and seas. I also became an instant believer in plate tectonics; India really *is* crashing into Asia, and Saudi Arabia and Egypt really *are* pulling apart, making the Red Sea wider. Even though their respective motion is really no more than mere inches a year, the view from overhead makes theory come alive. Spectacular as the view is from 200 miles up, the Earth is not the awe-inspiring "blue marble" made famous by the photos from the moon. From space shuttle height, we can't see the entire globe at a glance, but we can look down the entire boot of Italy, or up the East Coast of the United

States from Cape Hatteras to Cape Cod. The panoramic view inspires an appreciation for the scale of some of nature's phenomena. One day, as I scanned the sandy expanse of Northern Africa, I couldn't find any of the familiar landmarks—colorful outcroppings of rock in Chad, irrigated patches of the Sahara. Then I realized they were obscured by a huge dust storm, a cloud of sand that enveloped the continent from Morocco to the Sudan.

Since the space shuttle flies fairly low (at least by orbital standards; it's more than 22,000 miles lower than a typical TV satellite), we can make out both natural and manmade features in surprising detail. Familiar geographical features like San Francisco Bay, Long Island, and Lake Michigan are easy to recognize, as are many cities, bridges, and airports. The Great Wall of China is not the only man-made object visible from space.

The signatures of civilization are usually seen in straight lines (bridges or runways) or sharp delineations (abrupt transitions from desert to irrigated land, as in California's Imperial Valley). A modern city like New York doesn't leap from the canvas of its surroundings, but its straight piers and concrete runways catch the eye—and around them, the city materializes. I found Salina, Kansas (and pleased my in-laws, who live there) by spotting its long runway amid the wheat fields near the city. Over Florida, I could see the launch pad where we had begun our trip, and the landing strip, where we would eventually land.

Some of civilization's more unfortunate effects on the environment are also evident from orbit. Oil slicks glisten on the surface of the Persian Gulf, patches of pollution-damaged trees dot the forests of central Europe. Some cities look out of focus, and their colors muted, when viewed through a pollutant haze. Not surprisingly, the effects are more noticeable now than they were a decade ago. An astronaut who has flown in both Skylab and the space shuttle reported that the horizon didn't seem quite as sharp, or the colors quite as bright, in 1983 as they had in 1973.

Of course, informal observations by individual astronauts are one thing, but more precise measurements are continually being made from space: The space shuttle has carried infrared film to document damage to citrus trees in Florida and in rain forests along the Amazon. It has carried even more sophisticated sensors in the payload bay. Here is one example: sensors used to measure atmospheric carbon monoxide levels, allowing scientists to study the environmental effects of city emissions and land-clearing fires.

Most of the Earth's surface is covered with water, and at first glance it all looks the same: blue. But with the right lighting conditions and a couple of orbits of practice, it's possible to make

Ⓒ
**Spiral Review**
**Word Choice and Tone** Do words and phrases such as *sharp delineations, irrigated land,* and *materializes* give this paragraph a formal or informal tone? Explain.

**Literary Analysis Expository Essay** What point about environmental change does Ride support with her descriptions in this paragraph?

**Vocabulary**
**muted** (myo͞ot´ əd) *adj.* weaker; less intense

**Reading Check**
What kinds of structures reveal the "signatures of civilization" from space?

out the intricate patterns in the oceans—eddies and spirals become visible because of the subtle differences in water color or reflectivity.

Observations and photographs by astronauts have contributed significantly to the understanding of ocean dynamics, and some of the more intriguing discoveries prompted the National Aeronautics and Space Administration to fly an oceanographic observer for the express purpose of studying the ocean from orbit. Scientists' understanding of the energy balance in the oceans has increased significantly as a result of the discoveries of circular and spiral eddies tens of kilometers in diameter, of standing waves hundreds of kilometers long, and of spiral eddies that sometimes trail into one another for thousands of kilometers. If a scientist wants to study features on this scale, it's much easier from an orbiting vehicle than from the vantage point of a boat.

Believe it or not, an astronaut can also see the wakes of large ships and the contrails of airplanes. The sun angle has to be just right, but when the lighting conditions are perfect, you can follow otherwise invisible oil tankers on the Persian Gulf and trace major shipping lanes through the Mediterranean Sea. Similarly, when atmospheric conditions allow contrail formation, the thousand-mile-long condensation trails let astronauts trace the major air routes across the northern Pacific Ocean.●

**Literary Analysis**
**Expository Essay**
What relationship between space travel and ocean study does Ride discuss in this passage?

## LITERATURE IN CONTEXT

### Science Connection

#### The Changing Planet: Continental Drift

**350 million years ago**
The continents were once part of a massive land mass.

**54.8 to 33.7 million years ago**
This land mass, named Pangea, started drifting apart 300 hundred million years ago.

**38 to 1.6 million years ago**
The continents are still moving a few inches farther apart each year.

▼ The southern hemisphere "drifting" through time

*Africa* *India* *Australia* *South America* *Antarctica*

**The Evidence:**
Plants and animals in North America and Europe are very similar. Fossils from southern continents show that dinosaurs once roamed the entire area. In Africa and South America, 200 million-year-old matching lava has been found.

#### Connect to the Literature

The theories of plate tectonics and continental drift state that the Earth's crust is made of shifting "plates." What evidence for these theories might an astronaut see from space?

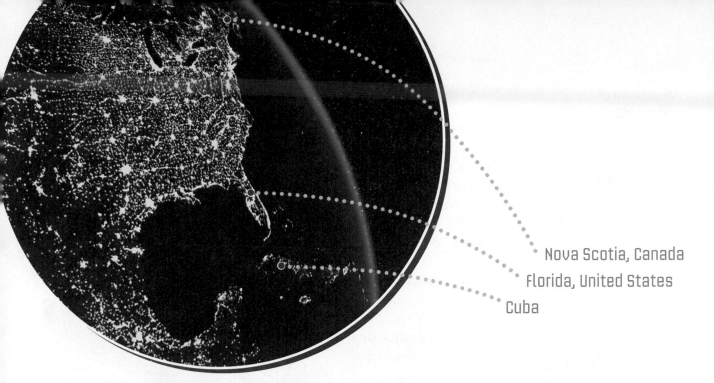

Nova Scotia, Canada
Florida, United States
Cuba

Part of every orbit takes us to the dark side of the planet. In space, night is very, very black—but that doesn't mean there's nothing to look at. The lights of cities sparkle; on nights when there was no moon, it was difficult for me to tell the Earth from the sky—the twinkling lights could be stars or they could be small cities. On one nighttime pass from Cuba to Nova Scotia, the entire East Coast of the United States appeared in twinkling outline.

When the moon is full, it casts an eerie light on the Earth. In its light, we see ghostly clouds and bright reflections on the water. One night, the Mississippi River flashed into view, and because of our viewing angle and orbital path, the reflected moonlight seemed to flow downstream—as if Huck Finn had tied a candle to his raft.

Of all the sights from orbit, the most spectacular may be the magnificent displays of lightning that ignite the clouds at night. On Earth, we see lightning from below the clouds; in orbit, we see it from above. Bolts of lightning are diffused by the clouds into bursting balls of light. Sometimes, when a storm extends hundreds of miles, it looks like a transcontinental brigade is tossing fireworks from cloud to cloud.

As the shuttle races the sun around the Earth, we pass from day to night and back again during a single orbit—hurtling into darkness, then bursting into daylight. The sun's appearance unleashes spectacular blue and orange bands along the horizon, a clockwork miracle that astronauts witness every 90 minutes. But I really can't describe a sunrise in orbit. The drama set against the black backdrop of space and the magic of the materializing colors

**On one nighttime pass from Cuba to Nova Scotia, the entire East Coast of the United States appeared in twinkling outline.**

**Vocabulary**
**diffused** (di fyo͞ozd´)
*v.* spread out

Reading Check
What can astronauts see from space when the light is right?

Part of the
fascination with
space travel is
the element of
the unknown...

can't be captured in an astronomer's equations or an astronaut's photographs.

I once heard someone (not an astronaut) suggest that it's possible to imagine what spaceflight is like by simply extrapolating from the sensations you experience on an airplane. All you have to do, he said, is mentally raise the airplane 200 miles, mentally eliminate the air noise and the turbulence, and you get an accurate mental picture of a trip in the space shuttle.

Not true. And while it's natural to try to liken spaceflight to familiar experiences, it can't be brought "down to Earth"— not in the final sense. The environment is different, the perspective is different. Part of the fascination with space travel is the element of the unknown— the conviction that it's different from earthbound experiences. And it is.

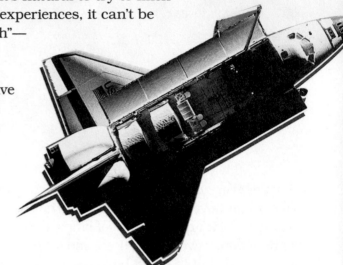

## Critical Thinking

Cite textual
evidence to
support your
responses.

1. **Key Ideas and Details (a)** Which geological features did Ride observe from the shuttle in orbit? **(b) Interpret:** Why do you think Ride found it easier to imagine the workings of geological forces when she saw Earth from space?

2. **Key Ideas and Details (a)** What "unfortunate effects" does Ride say she could see as she orbited Earth? **(b) Analyze:** Why would these effects make colors seen in 1983 seem not as bright as those seen ten years earlier?

3. **Craft and Structure  Assess:** Have Ride's descriptions of Earth changed the way you think about our planet? Explain your answer.

4. **Integration of Knowledge and Ideas** Does Ride's understanding of Earth change as a result of her experience on the space shuttle? Explain. *[Connect to the Big Question: Is knowledge the same as understanding?]*

## Literary Analysis: Narrative Essay

**© 1. Key Ideas and Details** What is the topic of Sally Ride's **expository essay?**

**© 2. Key Ideas and Details (a)** What scientific data does Ride use to make her ideas clear to readers? **(b)** Does this essay persuade you to have a certain opinion? Explain your response. **(c)** How might you extend or elaborate on Ride's ideas and share them with others?

**© 3. Craft and Structure (a)** Using a chart like the one shown, identify passages in which Ride uses **description, comparison and contrast,** or **cause and effect.** Find one example of each technique. **(b)** Explain how each example adds depth and context to the information Ride presents in that passage.

|  | Example | Effect |
|---|---|---|
| **Description** |  |  |
| **Comparison/Contrast** |  |  |
| **Cause and Effect** |  |  |

## Reading Skill: Main Idea

**4.** Summarize the **central idea** of the essay "Single Room, Earth View" in your own words.

**5. (a)** List three **supporting details** that serve as evidence for the points that Sally Ride makes. **(b)** Do you think the author adequately supports her main idea with details? Why or why not?

## Vocabulary

**© Acquisition and Use** Review the vocabulary list on page 466. Then, identify the word in each group that does not belong and explain your response.

**1.** articulate, eloquent, unclear

**2.** novice, expert, veteran

**3.** diffused, scattered, withheld

**4.** extrapolating, concluding, donating

**5.** surreal, odd, normal

**6.** muted, intense, vibrant

**Word Study** Use the context of the sentences and what you know about the **Latin root -nov-** to explain your answer to each question.

**1.** Is a *novel* idea common or unusual?

**2.** Why might a star that suddenly becomes much brighter be called a *nova*?

**Is *knowledge* the same as *understanding*?**

## Writing About the Big Question

In "The News," the author describes the pros and cons of television news. Use these sentence starters to develop your ideas about the Big Question.

We react in different ways to the presentation of news **information** on television and to the presentation in other media because _____.

Television news appeals to the viewers' **senses** by _____ and _____ .

**While You Read** Consider the writer's ideas about television news as a source of information. Then, determine whether he believes watching television news can lead to understanding.

## Vocabulary

Read each word and its definition. Decide whether you know the word well, know it a little bit, or do not know it at all. After you read, see how your knowledge of each word has increased.

- **compensation** (käm´ pən sā´ shən) *n.* anything that makes up for a loss, damage, or debt (p. 478) *They ran out of prizes, so they gave free tickets as <u>compensation</u>. compensate v. compensatory adj.*

- **temporal** (tem´ pə rəl) *adj.* having to do with time (p. 478) *His persistent lateness suggests that he has no <u>temporal</u> sense. tempo n.*

- **medium** (mē´ dē əm) *n.* a particular way of communicating information and news to people, such as a newspaper or a television broadcast (p. 480) *Politicians prefer to use the <u>medium</u> of television. media n. pl.*

- **imposition** (im´ pə zish´ ən) *n.* the introduction of something such as a rule, tax, or punishment (p. 482) *The <u>imposition</u> of the tax on tea caused many colonists to rebel. imposing adj. impose v.*

- **revered** (ri vird´) *adj.* regarded with great respect and awe (p. 483) *Many students came to the retirement party for the <u>revered</u> teacher. revere v. reverence n.*

- **daunting** (dônt´ iŋ) *adj.* intimidating (p. 484) *Climbing Mount Everest is a <u>daunting</u> task. daunt v. dauntless adj.*

### Word Study

The **Latin root -temp-** means "time."

In this selection, the author comments that film alone cannot accurately show the **temporal,** or time, aspects of events.

# Meet
# Neil Postman
## (1931–2003)

## Author of
# The News

Neil Postman was a media critic and a revered professor of communications at New York University, where he taught for more than forty years. He called his field "media ecology," and his great concern was the effect of television on Americans.

**Teachings on Television** Born in New York, Postman received a doctorate in education from Columbia University. He also wrote twenty books and hundreds of articles. One of his most intense arguments is set forth in *The Disappearance of Childhood* (1982), in which he asserts that television exposes children to adult concerns far too early in their lives.

## BACKGROUND FOR THE ESSAY

### Television News

In 1948, only 400,000 American homes had a television. By 1960, more than 46 million American homes had a television, and TV began to take over as the news medium of choice. Today, television news is one of the most influential institutions in American culture.

## Did You Know?

Postman once said, "You have to understand, what Americans do is watch television. I am not saying that's who they are. But that is what they do. Americans . . . watch . . . television."

# The News

## Neil Postman

The whole problem with news on television comes down to this: all the words uttered in an hour of news coverage could be printed on one page of a newspaper. And the world cannot be understood in one page. Of course, there is a compensation: television offers pictures, and the pictures move. It is often said that moving pictures are a kind of language in themselves, and there is a good deal of truth in this. But the language of pictures differs radically from oral and written language, and the differences are crucial for understanding television news.

To begin with, the grammar of pictures is weak in communicating past-ness and present-ness. When terrorists want to prove to the world that their kidnap victims are still alive, they photograph them holding a copy of a recent newspaper. The dateline on the newspaper provides the proof that the photograph was taken on or after that date. Without the help of the written word, film and videotape cannot portray temporal dimensions with any precision. Consider a film clip showing an aircraft carrier at sea. One might be able to identify the ship as Soviet[1] or American, but there would be no way of telling where in the world the carrier was, where it was headed, or when the pictures were taken. It is only through language—words spoken over the pictures or reproduced in them—that the image of the aircraft carrier takes on meaning as a portrayal of a specific event.

---

**1. Soviet** (sō´ vē et´) adj. belonging to the Soviet Union, the formerly socialist nation the main part of which was Russia.

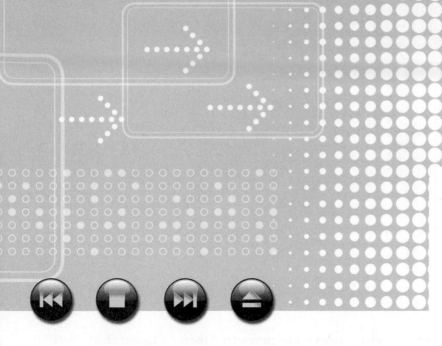

But the language of pictures differs radically from oral and written language, and the differences are crucial for understanding television news.

Still, it is possible to enjoy the image of the carrier for its own sake. One might find the hugeness of the vessel interesting; it signifies military power on the move. There is a certain drama in watching the planes come in at high speeds and skid to a stop on the deck. Suppose the ship were burning: that would be even more interesting. This leads to a second point about the language of pictures. The grammar of moving pictures favors images that change. That is why violence and destruction find their way onto television so often. When something is destroyed violently its constitution is altered in a highly visible way: hence the entrancing power of fire. Fire gives visual form to the ideas of consumption, disappearance, death—the thing which is burned is actually taken away by fire. It is at this very basic level that fires make a good subject for television news. Something was here, now it's gone, and the change is recorded on film.

Earthquakes and typhoons have the same power: before the viewer's eyes the world is taken apart. If a television viewer has relatives in Mexico City and an earthquake occurs there, then she may take an interest in the images of destruction as a report from a specific place and time. That is, she may look to television news for information about an important event. But film of an earthquake can still be interesting if the viewer cares nothing about the event itself. Which is only to say that there is another way of participating in the news—as a spectator who desires to be entertained. Actually to see buildings topple is exciting, no matter where the buildings are. The world turns to dust before our eyes.

**Literary Analysis**
**Expository Essay**
How do details about airplanes and fire support Postman's point that television favors change?

 **Reading Check**
What does Postman mean by the "grammar" of pictures?

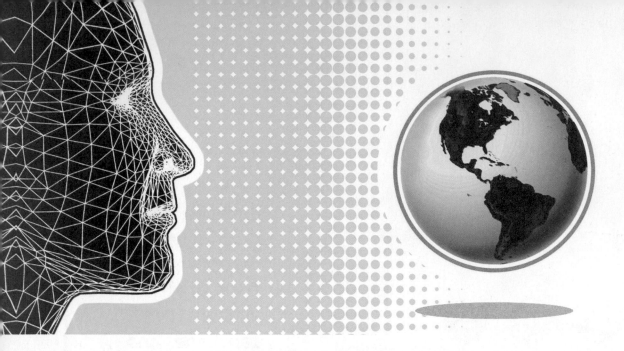

**Vocabulary**
**medium** (mē′ dē əm)
*n.* a particular way
of communicating
information and news
to people, such as
a newspaper or a
television broadcast

Those who produce television news in America know that their
medium favors images that move. That is why they despise "talking
heads," people who simply appear in front of a camera and speak.
When talking heads appear on television, there is nothing to record
or document, no change in process. In the cinema the situation is
somewhat different. On a movie screen, close-ups of a good actor
speaking dramatically can sometimes be interesting to watch.
When Clint Eastwood narrows his eyes and challenges his rival
to shoot first, the spectator sees the cool rage of the Eastwood
character take visual form, and the narrowing of the eyes is
dramatic. But much of the effect of this small movement depends
on the size of the movie screen and the darkness of the theater,
which make Eastwood and his every action "larger than life."

The television screen is smaller than life. It occupies about 15
percent of the viewer's visual field (compared to about 70 percent
for the movie screen). It is not set in a darkened theater closed off
from the world but in the viewer's ordinary living space. This means
that visual changes must be more extreme and more dramatic to be
interesting on television. A narrowing of the eyes will not do. A car
crash, an earthquake, a burning factory are much better.

With these principles in mind, let us examine more closely the
structure of a typical newscast. In America, almost all news shows
begin with music, the tone of which suggests important events
about to unfold. (Beethoven's Fifth Symphony would be entirely
appropriate.) The music is very important, for it equates the news
with various forms of drama and ritual—the opera, for example,
or a wedding procession—in which musical themes underscore the
meaning of the event. Music takes us immediately into the realm

**Literary Analysis**
**Expository Essay**
What topic will Postman
analyze more closely in
this essay?

of the symbolic, a world that is not to be taken literally. After all, when events unfold in the real world, they do so without musical accompaniment. More symbolism follows. The sound of teletype machines can be heard in the studio, not because it is impossible to screen this noise out, but because the sound is a kind of music in itself. It tells us that data are pouring in from all corners of the globe, a sensation reinforced by the world map in the background (or clocks noting the time on different continents).

Already, then, before a single news item is introduced, a great deal has been communicated. We know that we are in the presence of a symbolic event, a form of theater in which the day's events are to be dramatized. This theater takes the entire globe as its subject, although it may look at the world from the perspective of a single nation. A certain tension is present, like the atmosphere in a theater just before the curtain goes up. The tension is represented by the music, the staccato beat of the teletype machines, and the sight of newsworkers scurrying around typing reports and answering phones. As a technical matter, it would be no problem to build a set in which the newsroom staff remained off camera, invisible to the viewer, but an important theatrical effect would be lost. By being busy on camera, the workers help communicate urgency about the events at hand, which it is suggested are changing so rapidly that constant revision of the news is necessary.

The staff in the background also helps signal the importance of the person in the center, the anchorman (or -woman) "in command" of both the staff and the news. The anchorman plays the role of host. He welcomes us to the newscast and welcomes us back from the different locations we visit during filmed reports. His voice, appearance, and manner establish the mood of the broadcast. It would be unthinkable for the anchor to be ugly, or a nervous sort who could not complete a sentence. Viewers must be able to believe in the anchor as a person of authority and skill, a person who would not panic in a crisis—someone to trust.

This belief is based not on knowledge of the anchorman's character or achievements as a journalist, but on his presentation of self while on the air. Does he look the part of a trusted man? Does he speak firmly and clearly? Does he have a warm smile? Does he project confidence without seeming arrogant? The value the anchor must communicate above all else is control. He must be in control of himself, his voice, his emotions. He must know what is coming next in the broadcast, and he must move smoothly and

**Reading Skill**
**Main Idea** How do these descriptive details support Postman's idea that a newscast is a form of theater?

> This theater takes the entire globe as its subject, although it may look at the world from the perspective of a single nation.

Reading Check
What are "talking heads" and why do television producers despise them?

▲ **Critical Viewing**
How does this image relate to the idea of people connecting to their world through the news? **[Interpret]**

**Vocabulary**
**imposition** (im′ pə zish′ ən) *n.* the introduction of something such as a rule, tax, or punishment

confidently from segment to segment. Again, it would be unthinkable for the anchor to break down and weep over a story, or laugh uncontrollably on camera, no matter how "human" these responses may be.

Many other features of the newscast help the anchor to establish the impression of control. These are usually equated with professionalism in broadcasting. They include such things as graphics that tell the viewer what is being shown, or maps and charts that suddenly appear on the screen and disappear on cue, or the orderly progression from story to story, starting with the most important events first. They also include the absence of gaps or "deadtime" during the broadcast, even the simple fact that the news starts and ends at a certain hour. These common features are thought of as purely technical matters, which a professional crew handles as a matter of course. But they are also symbols of a dominant theme of television news: the imposition of an orderly world—called "the news"—upon the disorderly flow of events.

While the form of a news broadcast emphasizes tidiness and control, its content can best be described as chaotic. Because time is so precious on television, because the nature of the medium favors dynamic visual images, and because the pressures of a commercial structure require the news to hold its audience above all else, there is rarely any attempt to explain issues in depth or place events in their proper context. The news moves nervously from a warehouse fire to a court decision, from a guerrilla war to a World Cup match, the quality of the film often determining the length of the story. Certain stories show up only because they offer dramatic pictures. Bleachers collapse in South America: hundreds of people are crushed—a perfect television news story, for the cameras can record the face of disaster in all its anguish. Back in Washington, a new budget is approved by Congress. Here there is nothing to photograph because a budget is not a physical event; it is a document full of language and numbers. So the producers of the news will show a photo of the document itself, focusing on the cover where it says: "Budget of the United States of America." Or sometimes they will send a camera crew to the government printing plant where copies of the budget are produced. That evening, while the contents of the budget are summarized by a voice-over, the viewer sees stacks of documents being loaded into boxes at the government printing plant. Then a few of the budget's more important provisions will be flashed on the screen in written form, but this is such a time-consuming process—using television as a printed page—that the producers keep it to a minimum. In short, the budget is not televisable, and for that reason its time on the news must be brief. The bleacher collapse will get more minutes that evening.

With priorities of this sort, it is almost impossible for the news to offer an adequate account of important events. Indeed, it is the trivial event that is often best suited for television coverage. This is such a commonplace that no one even bothers to challenge it. Walter Cronkite, a revered figure in television and anchorman of the CBS Evening News for many years, has acknowledged several times that television cannot be relied on to inform the citizens of a democratic nation. Unless they also read newspapers and magazines, television viewers are helpless to understand their world, Cronkite has said. No one at CBS has ever disagreed with his conclusion, other than to say, "We do the best we can." •

Of course, it is a tendency of journalism in general to concentrate on the surface of events rather than underlying conditions; this is as true for the newspaper as it is for the newscast. But several features of television undermine whatever efforts journalists may make to give sense to the world. One is that a television broadcast is a series of events that occur in sequence, and the sequence is the same for all viewers. This is not true for a newspaper page, which displays many items simultaneously, allowing readers to choose the order in which they read them. If a newspaper reader wants only a summary of the latest tax bill, he can read the headline and the first paragraph of an article, and if he wants more, he can keep reading. In a sense, then, everyone reads a different newspaper, for no two readers will read (or ignore) the same items.

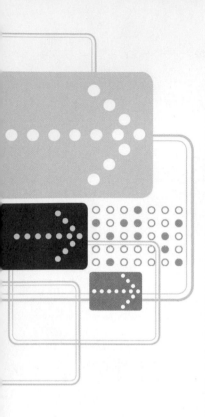

But all television viewers see the same broadcast. They have no choices. A report is either in the broadcast or out, which means that anything which is of narrow interest is unlikely to be included. As NBC News executive Reuven Frank once explained:

> A newspaper, for example, can easily afford to print an item of conceivable interest to only a fraction of its readers. A television news program must be put together with the assumption that each item will be of some interest to everyone that watches. Every time a newspaper includes a feature which will attract a specialized group it can assume it is adding at least a little bit to its circulation. To the degree a television news program includes an item of this sort . . . it must assume that its audience will diminish.

The need to "include everyone," an identifying feature of commercial television in all its forms, prevents journalists from offering lengthy or complex explanations, or from tracing the sequence of events leading up to today's headlines. One of the ironies of political life in modern democracies is that many problems which concern the "general welfare" are of interest only to specialized groups. Arms control, for example, is an issue that literally concerns everyone in the world, and yet the language of arms control and the complexity of the subject are so daunting that only a minority of people can actually follow the issue from week to week and month to month. If it wants to act responsibly, a newspaper can at least make available more information about arms control than most people want. But commercial television cannot afford to do so.

This illustrates an important point in the psychology of television's appeal. Many of the items in newspapers and magazines are not, in a strict sense, demanded by a majority of readers. They are there because some readers might be interested or because the editors think their readers should be interested. On commercial television, "might" and "should" are not the relevant words. The producers attempt to make sure that "each item will be of some interest to everyone that watches," as Reuven Frank put it. What this means is that a newspaper or magazine can challenge its audience in a way that television cannot. Print media have the luxury of suggesting or inviting interest, whereas television must always concern itself with conforming to existing interests. In a way, television is more strictly responsive to the demands of its huge audience. But there is one demand it cannot meet: the desire to be challenged, to be told "this is worth attending to," to be surprised by what one thought would not be of interest.

**Vocabulary**
**daunting** (dônt´ iŋ)
*adj.* intimidating

Another severe limitation on television is time. There is simply not enough of it. The evening news programs at CBS, NBC, and ABC all run for thirty minutes, eight of which are taken up by commercials. No one believes that twenty-two minutes for the day's news is adequate. For years news executives at ABC, NBC, and CBS have suggested that the news be expanded to one hour. But by tradition the half-hour after the national evening news is given over to the hundreds of local affiliate stations around the country to use as they see fit. They have found it a very profitable time to broadcast game shows or half-hour situation comedies, and they are reluctant to give up the income they derive from these programs.

The evening news produced by the three networks is profitable for both the networks and the local stations. The local stations are paid a fee by the network to broadcast the network news, and they profit from this fee since the news—produced by the network—costs them nothing. It is likely that they would also make money from a one-hour newscast, but not as much, they judge, as they do from the game shows and comedies they now schedule.

> The result is that the evening news must try to do what cannot reasonably be done: give a decent account of the day's events in twenty-two minutes.

The result is that the evening news must try to do what cannot reasonably be done: give a decent account of the day's events in twenty-two minutes. What the viewer gets instead is a series of impressions, many of them purely visual, most of them unconnected to each other or to any sense of a history unfolding. Taken together, they suggest a world that is fundamentally ungovernable, where events do not arise out of historical conditions but rather explode from the heavens in a series of disasters that suggest a permanent state of crisis. It is this crisis—highly visual, ahistorical, and unsolvable—which the evening news presents as theater every evening.

The audience for this theater is offered a contradictory pair of responses. On the one hand, it is reassured by the smooth presentation of the news itself, especially the firm voice and steady gaze of the trusty anchorman. Newscasts frequently end with a "human-interest story," often with a sentimental or comic touch.

**Spiral Review**
**Word Choice and Tone** Does the use of words and phrases such as *severe limitation, by tradition, affiliates,* and *situation comedies* contribute to an appropriate tone for the author's message? Explain.

**Literary Analysis**
**Expository Essay**
What sense of the world does television news cause?

**Reading Check**
According to Postman, why are television news broadcasts so short?

Example: a little girl in Chicago writes Gorbachev a letter, and he answers her, saying that he and President Reagan are trying to work out their differences. This item reassures viewers that all is well, leaders are in command, we can still communicate with each other, and so on. But—and now we come to the other hand—the rest of the broadcast has told a different story. It has shown the audience a world that is out of control and incomprehensible, full of violence, disaster, and suffering. Whatever authority the anchorman may project through his steady manner is undermined by the terror inspired by the news itself.

This is where television news is at its most radical—not in giving publicity to radical causes, but in producing the impression of an ungovernable world. And it produces this impression not because the people who work in television are leftists or anarchists.[2] The anarchy in television news is a direct result of the commercial structure of broadcasting, which introduces into news judgments a single-mindedness more powerful than any ideology: the overwhelming need to keep people watching.

---

2. **leftists . . . anarchists** (an´ ər kists´) leftists desire to change the existing political order in the name of greater freedom for all; anarchists oppose any political authority.

## Critical Thinking

*Cite textual evidence to support your responses.*

**1. Key Ideas and Details (a)** According to Postman, what elements make a news broadcast like a form of theater? **(b) Interpret:** What problem does Postman see in the similarity between television news and theater?

**2. Craft and Structure** How does the cause-and-effect text structure in the essay help you connect important ideas? Explain.

**3. Key Ideas and Details (a)** What type of role is an anchorperson supposed to play while presenting the news? **(b) Connect:** How does the impression created by the anchor relate to the "radical" nature of television?

**4. Key Ideas and Details (a)** How long do people in the news business feel the evening news broadcast should have to present the news? **(b) Cause and Effect:** What effects do time limits have on television news?

**5. Integration of Knowledge and Ideas (a)** How does our knowledge of the news affect our understanding of the world? **(b)** How does the changing nature of the news affect this understanding? *[Connect to the Big Question: Is knowledge the same as understanding?]*

## Literary Analysis: Expository Essay

© **1. Key Ideas and Details** What is the purpose of Neil Postman's **expository essay?**

© **2. Key Ideas and Details (a)** What quotations does Postman use to make his ideas clear to readers? **(b)** Does this essay persuade you to have a certain opinion? Explain your response. **(c)** How might you extend or elaborate on Postman's ideas and share them with others?

© **3. Craft and Structure (a)** Using a chart like the one shown, identify passages in which Postman uses **description, comparison and contrast,** or **cause and effect.** Find one example of each technique. **(b)** Explain how each example adds depth and context to the information Postman presents in that passage.

|  | Example | Effect |
|---|---|---|
| **Description** |  |  |
| **Comparison/Contrast** |  |  |
| **Cause and Effect** |  |  |

## Reading Skill: Main Idea

**4.** Summarize the **central idea** of "The News" in your own words.

**5. (a)** List three **supporting details** that serve as evidence for the points that Neil Postman makes. **(b)** Do you think the author adequately supports his main idea with details? Why or why not?

## Vocabulary

© **Acquisition and Use** Review the vocabulary list on page 476. Then, identify the word in each group that does not belong and explain your response.

**1.** compensation, repayment, donation

**2.** temporal, timed, severe

**3.** revered, scorned, ridiculed

**4.** daunting, challenging, tempting

**5.** medium, magazine, memory

**6.** law, imposition, stamp

**Word Study** Use the context of the sentences and what you know about the **Latin root -temp-** to explain your answer to each question.

**1.** Why is it essential for a musician to keep a *tempo*?

**2.** For how long might a *temporary* job last?

### Word Study

The **Latin root -temp-** means "time."

**Apply It** Explain how the root *-temp-* contributes to the meanings of these words. Consult a dictionary if necessary.

**temporize**
**extemporaneous**
**contemporary**

# Integrated Language Skills

## Single Room, Earth View • The News

### Conventions: Predicate Nominatives and Predicate Adjectives

A **predicate nominative** renames the subject of the sentence.

The predicate nominative comes after a linking verb and *renames, identifies, or explains* the subject of the sentence. In a sentence with a predicate nominative, the linking verb acts as an equals sign between the subject and the predicate nominative.

A **predicate adjective** is an adjective that appears with a linking verb and *describes* the subject of the sentence.

|  | Example | Explanation |
|---|---|---|
| **Predicate Nominative** | The winner of the tournament is our *team*. | *Team* renames *winner*. |
|  | That player was the *star*. | *Star* renames *player*. |
| **Predicate Adjective** | The swimmer was *fast*. | *Fast* describes *swimmer*. |
|  | Josh is very *clever*. | *Clever* describes *Josh*. |

**Practice A** Identify the predicate nominatives and predicate adjectives in the following sentences.

1. Sally Ride was the first woman astronaut to join the NASA program.
2. The space shuttle is a plane capable of flying into space.
3. Earth is a beautiful, blue planet.
4. Space is a vast new frontier.
5. When viewed from space, the Earth appears small.

@ **Reading Application** In "Single Room, Earth View," find one sentence with a predicate nominative and one with a predicate adjective.

**Practice B** Add a predicate nominative or a predicate adjective as indicated to complete the sentence.

1. The news anchor is _____. (predicate nominative)
2. News events can be _____. (predicate adjective)
3. That film was _____. (predicate adjective)
4. Media, such as television, tend to be _____. (predicate adjective)

@ **Writing Application** Replace the underlined predicate adjective in the model sentence. Write two sentences with predicate nominatives and two with predicate adjectives. *Typical images in a TV newscast are <u>interesting</u>.*

| PH | WRITING COACH | Further instruction and practice are available in *Prentice Hall Writing Coach*. |

# Writing

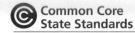

**Common Core State Standards**

W.9-10.2, W.9-10.7, W.9-10.8; SL.9-10.4
[For the full wording of the standards, see page 464.]

**Argument** Write and present to the class a **script for a public service announcement** in which you highlight the rewards of entering a specific profession. If you read "Single Room, Earth View," write a script that NASA might use to attract candidates for astronaut training. If you read "The News," write a script that encourages people to pursue careers in journalism.

As you prepare your script for an oral presentation to the class,

- select details that will persuade people that the job is exciting.
- include visual elements that make the job seem appealing.
- structure your ideas and arguments logically.

**Grammar Application** Make sure to use predicate nominatives and predicate adjectives correctly as you draft your script.

## Writing Workshop: *Work in Progress*

**Prewriting for Business Letters** From your writing portfolio, review the Questions List you generated. Answer each question using specific evidence and crafting each answer to be clear and precise. Then, save your Answers List in your writing portfolio.

Use this prewriting activity to prepare for the **Writing Workshop** on page 512.

# Research and Technology

**Build and Present Knowledge** Using library and Internet resources, conduct research based on the following assignment choices and write two **journal entries.**

- If you read "Single Room, Earth View," research the training that astronauts undergo. Based on this information, write two journal entries that an astronaut might write while in training.
- If you read "The News," research the work television journalists do to prepare a news story. Then, write two journal entries a reporter might write while working on a story.

Follow these steps:

- Prepare clear research questions to guide your research.
- Use libraries, the Internet, personal interviews, and other suitable research methods to gather information.
- Use both primary and secondary sources in your research.
- Analyze and evaluate your sources to determine the usefulness, validity, and reliability of the information.
- Organize information to use in your journal entries.

Share your completed entries with the class.

**www.PHLitOnline.com**
- Interactive graphic organizers
- Grammar tutorial
- Interactive journals

# Test Practice: Reading

## Main Idea

### Fiction Selection

**Directions:** *Read the selection. Then, answer the questions.*

As the storm approached, Emily's mother urged her to bring her car into the garage. "OK, Mom," Emily replied, "as soon as I finish my history homework." She was still reading, however, when the lights went out and the first thunderclap shook the house. Then came a shower of *click* sounds, which immediately turned into *whack* sounds and then into *bam* sounds. It was hail—big hail! "My car!" cried Emily. She ran to the door, but her mother refused to let her go out into the storm. It passed as quickly as it came, leaving a broken windshield and dents in the car's roof. "How could a two-minute storm do so much damage?" Emily wailed.

1. Which detail does *not* support the idea that the thunderstorm was severe?
   A. The storm was accompanied by hail.
   B. A thunderclap shook the house.
   C. The storm passed quickly.
   D. The storm knocked out the lights.

2. What is the *best* statement of the main idea of this passage?
   A. A brief hailstorm damaged Emily's unprotected car.
   B. Hail makes a variety of very noisy sounds.
   C. Emily will need a job to pay for car repairs.
   D. Young people should always listen to their parents.

3. Which detail supports the main idea?
   A. "…the first thunderclap shook the house."
   B. "…her mother refused to let her go out into the storm."
   C. "…a broken windshield and dents in the car's roof."
   D. "Then came a shower of *click* sounds…"

4. Which detail supports the idea that the hailstorm quickly increased in strength?
   A. The storm arrived while Emily was finishing her homework.
   B. The first sign of the storm's arrival was a thunderclap and a power outage.
   C. Emily's mother urged Emily to put the car into the garage.
   D. The sound of the hail went from mild to very loud almost immediately.

## Writing for Assessment

Suppose that Emily had moved the car into the garage before the storm. How would the rest of the passage change? In a detailed paragraph, state a new main idea for the passage. Then, explain how you would change or add details to support the new main idea.

# Nonfiction Selection

**Directions:** *Read the selection. Then, answer the questions.*

A hailstone usually begins in a storm cloud when a droplet of supercooled water freezes onto a snowflake or a dust particle. As the tiny hailstone falls through the cloud, more droplets freeze onto it. Still, the hailstone stays rather small—unless the winds in the storm take control. A strong updraft can carry a hailstone high into the cloud again. When the hailstone falls a second time, it collects another layer of ice. This fall-rise-fall cycle repeats until the hailstone grows too heavy for the updraft to support it; then it falls to the ground. By the time hailstones fall, they can be quite large. The largest hailstone ever recovered in the United States had a circumference of almost 19 inches.

1. Which of the following is the main idea of this passage?
   A. Storm clouds might contain strong updrafts.
   B. Storm winds directly affect the size of hailstones.
   C. Hailstones develop from tiny particles into chunks of ice during the fall-repeat-fall cycle.
   D. The biggest hailstone found in the United States had a circumference of about 19 inches, but hailstones can also be tiny.

2. Which detail gives the most effective support to the main idea?
   A. "a strong updraft can carry a hailstone high into the cloud again"
   B. "then it falls to the ground"
   C. "they can be quite large"
   D. "circumference of almost 19 inches"

3. Which of the following phrases *best* describes the author's purpose in writing about hailstones?
   A. to entertain
   B. to inform
   C. to persuade
   D. to amuse

4. Based on the main idea of this passage, which question would be the *best* guide to further reading?
   A. How do meteorologists predict storms?
   B. Which months of the year have strong storms?
   C. What damage can storm winds cause?
   D. Which types of storms produce hailstones?

## Writing for Assessment

**Connecting Across Texts**
Emily wonders, "How could a two-minute storm do so much damage?" Write a response to her question. Make sure that your response has a main idea. Use details from the two passages to support your answer.

**PHLit**
**Online!**
www.PHLitOnline.com
- Online practice
- Instant feedback

# Reading for Information

## Analyzing Expository Texts

**Technical Document**

**Web Article**

**Common Core State Standards**

**Reading Informational Text**
**5.** Analyze in detail how an author's ideas or claims are developed and refined by particular sentences, paragraphs, or larger portions of a text.

**Language**
**6.** Acquire and use accurately grade-appropriate general academic and domain-specific words and phrases; demonstrate independence in gathering vocabulary knowledge when considering a word or phrase important to comprehension or expression.

## Reading Skill: Generate Relevant Questions

When you read technical documents and articles, you may come across unfamiliar terms and concepts. To gain a full understanding of the text, **generate relevant questions** as you read. Use the following guidelines to help you:

- Preview how the text is structured—that is, how information is organized with headings, lists, introductory sentences, and so on. Previewing sections of text helps you predict what information each section will relate.
- Use your background knowledge of the subject to generate questions that you think each section of text can answer.
- Read each section, looking for answers to your questions. If your questions remain unanswered, generate additional questions for research.

As you read, use a chart like this one to record your prior knowledge, what you learn, and what questions to research.

| What I Know | What I Learned | Relevant Questions |
|---|---|---|
| Part of the shuttle is destroyed when it enters Earth's atmosphere. | The external fuel tank is the part that burns up when the shuttle enters the atmosphere. | What causes the external fuel tank to burn? |

### Content-Area Vocabulary

These words appear in the selections that follow. You may also encounter them in other content-area texts.

- **orbit** (ôr´ bit) *n.* path used by a spacecraft around a planet or star
- **payloads** (pā´ lōdz´) *n.* things that are carried in an aircraft

# NATIONAL AERONAUTICS AND SPACE ADMINISTRATION

## Features:

- technical language
- numeric data or specifications
- diagrams or other graphics
- specific audience

# Space Shuttle Basics

## Shuttle Statistics

### Length

Space Shuttle:
56.14 meters (184.2 feet)
Orbiter:
37.23 meters (122.17 feet)

### Height

Orbiter on runway:
17.27 meters (56.67 feet)

### Wingspan

23.79 meters (78.06 feet)

### Weight*

At liftoff: 2,041,166 kilograms
(4.5 million pounds)

End of mission: 104,326 kilograms
(230,000 pounds)

### Maximum cargo to orbit

28,803 kilograms (63,500 pounds)

### SRB Separation

Two minutes after launch

### External Tank Separation

8.5 minutes after launch

Altitude: 109.26 kilometers  (59 nautical miles)

Velocity: 28,067 kph (17,440 mph)

### Orbit

185 to 643 kilometers  (115 to 400 statute miles)

Velocity: 27,875 kph (17,321 mph)

*weight will vary depending on **payloads** and onboard consumables.

The space shuttle is the world's first reusable spacecraft, and the first spacecraft in history that can carry large satellites both to and from orbit. The shuttle launches like a rocket, maneuvers in Earth orbit like a spacecraft and lands like an airplane. Each of the three space shuttle orbiters now in operation— *Discovery, Atlantis* and *Endeavour*— is designed to fly at least 100 missions. So far, altogether they have flown a combined total of less than one-fourth of that.

*Columbia* was the first space shuttle orbiter to be delivered to NASA's Kennedy Space Center, Fla., in March 1979. *Columbia* and the STS-107 crew were lost Feb. 1, 2003, during re-entry. The orbiter *Challenger* was delivered to KSC in July 1982 and was destroyed in an explosion during ascent in January 1986. *Discovery* was delivered in November 1983. *Atlantis* was delivered in April 1985. *Endeavour* was built as a replacement following the *Challenger* accident and was delivered to Florida in May 1991. An early space shuttle orbiter, the *Enterprise*, never flew in space but was used for approach and landing tests at the Dryden Flight Research Center and several launch pad studies in the late 1970s.

The space shuttle consists of three major components: the orbiter, which houses the crew; a large external fuel tank that holds fuel for the main engines; and two solid rocket boosters, which provide most of the shuttle's lift during the first two minutes of flight. All of the components are reused except for the external fuel tank, which burns up in the atmosphere after each launch.

You can use these diagrams to generate questions about aspects of the shuttle's design.

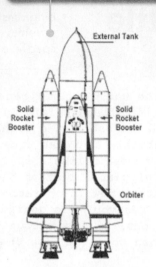

External Tank

Solid Rocket Booster

Solid Rocket Booster

Orbiter

**Space Shuttle**
(launch configuration)

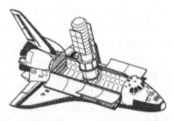

**orbiter flight configuration**
(w/satellite in payload bay)

These lines state one of NASA's objectives. You can use this information to generate questions about the shuttle's future.

The longest the shuttle has stayed in orbit on any single mission is 17.5 days on mission STS-80 in November 1996. Normally, missions may be planned for anywhere from five to 16 days in duration. The smallest crew ever to fly on the shuttle numbered two people on the first few missions. The largest crew numbered eight people. Normally, crews may range in size from five to seven people. The shuttle is designed to reach orbits ranging from about 185 kilometers to 643 kilometers (115 statute miles to 400 statute miles) high.

The shuttle has the most reliable launch record of any rocket now in operation. Since 1981, it has boosted more than 1.36 million kilograms (3 million pounds) of cargo into orbit. More than 600 crew members have flown on its missions. Although it has been in operation for almost 20 years, the shuttle has continually evolved and is significantly different today than when it first was launched. NASA has made literally thousands of major and minor modifications to the original design that have made it safer, more reliable and more capable today than ever before.

Since 1992 alone, NASA has made engine and system improvements that are estimated to have tripled the safety of flying the space shuttle, and the number of problems experienced while a space shuttle is in flight has decreased by 70 percent. During the same period, the cost of operating the shuttle has decreased by one and a quarter billion dollars annually—a reduction of more than 40 percent. At the same time, because of weight reductions and other improvements, the cargo the shuttle can carry has increased by 7.3 metric tons (8 tons).

NASA is prepared to continue flying the shuttle for at least the next decade and plans to continue to improve the shuttle during the next five years, with goals of increasing its safety by improving the highest-risk components. NASA will also be working with the Columbia Accident Investigation Board to correct any problems the board may find as it works to determine the cause of the *Columbia* accident.

In managing and operating the space shuttle, NASA holds the safety of the crew as its highest priority.

Web Article

**Features:**
- content accessed through the Internet
- photos or illustrations
- text that is available to the general public but may be written for a specific audience

# NASA National Aeronautics and Space Administration

## Launch Schedule 101

NASA launches involve many elements: the payloads that give missions their names, the rockets that will carry them into space, launch dates and times, and where the launch will take place. Launch Schedule 101 answers common questions about the NASA launch schedule.

### ▶ How do I read the NASA launch schedule?

The date and time of the most recent update is provided in bold, red text at the top of the page. The schedule is arranged by launch date. The name of the mission is where you'll find an in-depth look at the mission. Next, the launch vehicle for each mission is listed. Look to the last line to find the launch site. ●

A question-and-answer format anticipates what readers want to know about NASA launches.

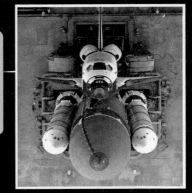

### ▶ What is a launch vehicle?

Simply put, the launch vehicle is the rocket or space shuttle itself, which carries the payload into space. For example, when space shuttle *Discovery* carried the U.S. laboratory Destiny to the International Space Station, the shuttle was the launch vehicle and the lab module was the payload.

### ▶ What is a launch site, and why does NASA use more than one? ●

The launch site is the physical location from which the space shuttle or a rocket takes off. Space shuttles always launch from Kennedy Space Center in Central Florida. Primary rocket launch sites are Cape Canaveral Air Force Station (CCAFS) near Kennedy Space Center and Vandenberg Air Force Base (VAFB) in California. Missions requiring equatorial orbits are typically launched from Cape Canaveral, while those requiring polar orbits are usually launched from Vandenberg. NASA also has secondary launch sites at Kodiak Island, Alaska, and the Kwajalein Atoll in the Republic of the Marshall Islands.

This paragraph mentions locations and technical terms that you can research further.

# NASA | National Aeronautics and Space Administration

## Launch Schedule
### NASA's Shuttle and Rocket Missions

The NASA schedule is easy to decipher by checking out our Launch Schedule 101 that explains how it all works!

Updated: July 11, 2007 - 1 p.m.

**Legend: +Targeted For / *No Earlier Than**

This photograph can help you generate questions about the launch process.

---

**Date:** 2007 Aug. 7+
**Mission:** STS-118
   STS-118 will deliver the S5 Truss and will be the twenty-second mission to the International Space Station.
**Vehicle:** Space Shuttle
**Launch Site:** Kennedy Space Center or Cape Canaveral Air Force Station
**Launch Time:** 7:02 EDT

---

**Date:** 2007 Sept.
**Mission:** Dawn
   The Dawn Mission will be the first time a spacecraft will orbit two planetary bodies on a single voyage as it studies Ceres and Vesta.
**Vehicle:** Delta II
**Launch Site:** Kennedy Space Center or Cape Canaveral Air Force Station

---

**Date:** 2007 Nov. 8*
**Mission:** Missile Defense Agency Block 2010 Spacecraft Risk Reduction
   To be launched by NASA for the Missile Defense Agency (MDA), STSS Block 2010 Spacecraft Risk Reduction serves as a pathfinder for future launch and mission technology for MDA.
**Vehicle:** Delta II
**Launch Site:** Vandenberg Air Force Base

---

**Date:** 2008 March 15+
**Mission:** TacSat-3
   NASA will support the Air Force launch of the TacSat-3 Satellite, managed by the Air Force Research Laboratory's Space Vehicles Directorate. TacSat-3 will demonstrate the capability of furnish real-time data.
**Vehicle:** Minotaur
**Launch Site:** Wallops Flight Facility/Goddard Space Flight Center

## Comparing Expository Texts

**1. Key Ideas and Details (a)** What are two **relevant questions** for research that you can **generate** based on your reading of the technical document and the Web article? **(b)** Does either text answer any of your questions about the other text? Explain your response.

### Content-Area Vocabulary

**2. (a)** Add the suffix -*al* to the base word *orbit*. Using a print or an online dictionary, explain how the suffix alters the meaning of the base word. **(b)** Do the same with the suffix -*er*. **(c)** Use each word in a sentence that shows its meaning.

## Timed Writing

### Informational Text: Explanation

Use information from "Space Shuttle Basics" to explain how the shuttle's solid rocket boosters and external fuel tank function during launches. Be sure to describe the tank and boosters themselves, as well as discuss the purposes they serve. Your explanation should be one paragraph long. (20 minutes)

**Format**
The prompt gives specific directions regarding the length of the assignment.

**Academic Vocabulary**
When you *describe* something, you give details that enhance your reader's understanding of the subject.

### 5-Minute Planner

Complete these steps before you begin to write:

1. Read the prompt carefully and completely.

2. Review the technical document, focusing on passages that discuss the shuttle's solid rocket boosters (SRBs) and external fuel tank. Make notes about their key features.

3. Decide how you will structure your explanation. For example, you might begin by describing the function of the solid rocket boosters and then describe the fuel tank's function. **TIP** Think of questions that a reader might have about the boosters and fuel tank, and then choose the clearest way to answer those questions.

4. Arrange your notes in the form of a list, based on the structure you have chosen. Refer to your list as you write your explanation.

# Comparing Literary Works

## Comparing Biographical Writing

**Biographical writing** is a form of nonfiction in which a writer tells the life story of another person. Important elements of biographical writing include the following:

- **Subject:** The subject of a biography is an important, inspiring, or fascinating figure. The subject may or may not be famous. The more important element is that the biographer presents the subject's life as compelling and worth studying.
- **Writer-Subject Connection:** The biographer usually has an intense interest in and a strong appreciation for his or her subject.
- **Research:** A biographer uses primary-source documents, other works on the subject, and, when possible, interviews with the subject or people connected to him or her.
- **Interpretation:** Biographical writing does not simply involve the telling of a subject's life story or the presentation of facts. Instead, a biographer analyzes and interprets the facts of a subject's life in order to present them in a meaningful way. The order of ideas, the details that support them, and the ways in which the writer connects different aspects of a subject's achievements or personality all contribute to this interpretation.

A biographer may openly state his or her attitude toward the subject. However, he or she may merely suggest that attitude, or **tone,** through word choice and details. As you read the biographies that follow, use an organizer like the one shown below to note details that describe specific aspects of each subject's life. Then, consider the order in which the writer presents these details, the ways in which he or she connects them, and how they support the writer's interpretation of the subject's life.

|  | Lincoln | Ashe |
|---|---|---|
| **Personality** |  |  |
| **Upbringing** |  |  |
| **Relationships** |  |  |
| **Life events** |  |  |
| **Role in major events** |  |  |
| **Influence on others** |  |  |

**Common Core
State Standards**

**Reading Informational Text**

**3.** Analyze how the author unfolds an analysis or series of ideas or events, including the order in which the points are made, how they are introduced and developed, and the connections that are drawn between them.

**Writing**

**2.** Write informative/explanatory texts to examine and convey complex ideas, concepts, and information clearly and accurately through the effective selection, organization, and analysis of content.

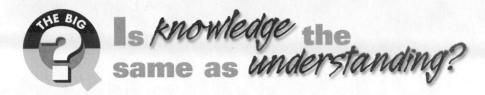

**Is** *knowledge* **the same as** *understanding?*

## Writing About the Big Question

Each of these biographers provides factual details to help readers understand the essence of his subject. Use this sentence starter to develop your ideas about the Big Question.

When I read to learn about someone, I expect to find out _____, _____, and _____.

# Meet the Authors

## Carl Sandburg (1878–1967)
### Author of *A Lincoln Preface*

Between the ages of thirteen and twenty, Carl Sandburg worked as a porter, scene changer, truck handler, dishwasher, and farm worker. Sandburg served briefly in Puerto Rico during the Spanish-American War, which brought on the strong antiwar feelings he would hold throughout his life.

**Childhood Favorite** Even as a child, Sandburg was fascinated by Abraham Lincoln. For thirty years, he collected material about Lincoln, and his single-mindedness paid off. Sandburg's six-volume work about Lincoln is considered the definitive biography.

## John McPhee

© Thomas Victor

### Author of "Arthur Ashe Remembered"

John McPhee's big break as a writer came in 1965, when *The New Yorker* magazine published his profile of Princeton basketball star Bill Bradley. That profile, which became the basis for McPhee's first book, combined two of the author's great loves: sports and his hometown of Princeton, New Jersey, where he still lives today.

**Broader Interests** McPhee continues to write about sports, but he has broadened his subject matter to include the natural world, with books on Alaska, whales, and North American geology. McPhee's extraordinary prose has won many important honors, including a Pulitzer Prize.

# from
# A Lincoln Preface
## Carl Sandburg

Courtesy of The Lincoln Museum, Fort Wayne, Indiana, (#983) – *Lincoln Proclaiming Thanksgiving*, Dean Cornwell

**Background** Ever since the birth of the United States in 1776, the issue of slavery had troubled the nation. Each time a new state entered the Union, Congress debated fiercely over whether it would be a slaveholding or free state. In 1860, when Abraham Lincoln was elected president, he refused to support any congressional proposal that would allow for new slave states. The southern slaveholding states resolved to fight to keep new states open to slavery. This conflict led to the outbreak of the Civil War in April 1861.

In the time of the April lilacs in the year 1865, a man in the City of Washington, D.C., trusted a guard to watch at a door, and the guard was careless, left the door, and the man was shot, lingered a night, passed away, was laid in a box, and carried north and west a thousand miles; bells sobbed; cities wore crepe;[1] people stood with hats off as the railroad burial car came past at midnight, dawn or noon.

During the four years of time before he gave up the ghost, this man was clothed with despotic power, commanding the most powerful armies till then assembled in modern warfare, enforcing drafts of soldiers, abolishing the right of habeas corpus,[2] directing politically and spiritually the wild, massive forces loosed in civil war.

Four billion dollars' worth of property was taken from those who had been legal owners of it, confiscated, wiped out as by fire, at his instigation and executive direction; a class of

**Vocabulary**
**despotic** (des pät´ ik)
*adj.* like an absolute ruler or tyrant

**Reading Check**

What violent event happened in April 1865?

---

1. **crepe** (krāp) *n.* thin, black cloth worn to show mourning.
2. **habeas corpus** (hā´ bē əs kôr´ pəs) *n.* right of an imprisoned person to have a court hearing.

◀ **Critical Viewing** Does this painting portray Lincoln as a man of great power? Explain. **[Make a Judgment]**

▲ **Critical Viewing**
What impression of Lincoln does this painting convey? **[Describe]**

chattel[3] property recognized as lawful for two hundred years went to the scrap pile.

When the woman who wrote *Uncle Tom's Cabin*[4] came to see him in the White House, he greeted her, "So you're the little woman who wrote the book that made this great war," and as they seated themselves at a fireplace, "I do love an open fire: I always had one at home." As they were finishing their talk of the days of blood, he said, "I shan't last long after it's over."

An Illinois Congressman looked in on him as he had his face lathered for a shave in the White House and remarked, "If anybody had told me that in a great crisis like this the people were going out to a little one-horse town and pick out a one-horse lawyer for president, I wouldn't have believed it." The answer was, "Neither would I. But it was a time when a man with a policy would have been fatal to the country. I never had a policy. I have simply tried to do what seemed best each day, as each day came."

"I don't intend precisely to throw the Constitution overboard, but I will stick it in a hole if I can," he told a Cabinet officer. The enemy was violating the Constitution to destroy the Union, he argued, and therefore, "I will violate the Constitution, if necessary, to save the Union." He instructed a messenger to the Secretary of the Treasury, "Tell him not to bother himself about the Constitution. Say that I have that sacred instrument here at the White House, and I am guarding it with great care."

When he was renominated, it was by the device of seating delegates from Tennessee, which gave enough added votes to seat favorable delegates from Kentucky, Missouri, Louisiana, Arkansas, and from one county in Florida. Until late in that campaign of 1864, he expected to lose the November election; military victories brought the tide his way; the vote was 2,200,000 for him and 1,800,000 against him. Among those who bitterly fought him politically, and

---

3. **chattel** (chat´'l) *n.* a movable item of personal property.
4. **woman . . . Cabin** Harriet Beecher Stowe (1811–1896), whose novel stirred up opinion against slavery.

accused him of blunders or crimes, were Franklin Pierce, a former president of the United States; Horatio Seymour, the Governor of New York; Samuel F. B. Morse, inventor of the telegraph; Cyrus H. McCormick, inventor of the farm reaper; General George B. McClellan, a Democrat who had commanded the Army of the Potomac; and the *Chicago Times*, a daily newspaper. In all its essential propositions the Southern Confederacy had the moral support of powerful, respectable elements throughout the North, probably more than a million votes believing in the justice of the cause of the South as compared with the North.

While propagandas raged, and the war winds howled, he sat in the White House, the Stubborn Man of History, writing that the Mississippi was one river and could not belong to two countries, that the plans for railroad connection from coast to coast must be pushed through and the Union Pacific[5] realized.

His life, mind and heart ran in contrasts. When his white kid gloves broke into tatters while shaking hands at a White House reception, he remarked, "This looks like a general bustification." When he talked with an Ohio friend one day during the 1864 campaign, he mentioned one public man, and murmured, "He's a thistle! I don't see why God lets him live." Of a devious Senator, he said, "He's too crooked to lie still!" And of a New York editor, "In early life in the West, we used to make our shoes last a great while with much mending, and sometimes, when far gone, we found the leather so rotten the stitches would not hold. Greeley is so rotten that nothing can be done with him. He is not truthful; the stitches all tear out." As he sat in the telegraph office of the War Department, reading cipher dispatches, and came to the words, Hosanna and Husband, he would chuckle, "Jeffy D.,"[6] and at the words, Hunter and Happy, "Bobby Lee."[7]

While the luck of war wavered and broke and came again, as generals failed and campaigns were lost, he held enough forces of the Union together to raise new armies and supply them, until generals were found who made war as victorious war has always been made, with terror, frightfulness, destruction, and valor and sacrifice past words of man to tell.

A slouching, gray-headed poet,[8] haunting the hospitals at Washington, characterized him as "the grandest figure on the crowded canvas of the drama of the nineteenth century—a Hoosier Michael Angelo."[9]

5. **Union Pacific** railroad chartered by Congress in 1862 to form part of a transcontinental system.
6. **"Jeffy D."** Jefferson Davis (1808–1889), president of the Confederacy.
7. **"Bobby Lee"** Robert E. Lee (1807–1870), commander in chief of the Confederate army.
8. **slouching . . . poet** Walt Whitman (1819–1892).
9. **Michael Angelo** Michelangelo (mī´ kəl an´ jə lō´) (1475–1564), famous Italian artist.

**Literary Analysis
Biographical Writing**
Which details here present Lincoln's strength in the face of opposition? Explain.

His life, mind and heart ran in contrasts.

Reading Check
Under what circumstances was Lincoln willing to violate the Constitution?

His own speeches, letters, telegrams and official messages during that war form the most significant and enduring document from any one man on why the war began, why it went on, and the dangers beyond its end. He mentioned "the politicians," over and again "the politicians," with scorn and blame. As the platoons filed before him at a review of an army corps, he asked, "What is to become of these boys when the war is over?"

He was a chosen spokesman: yet there were times he was silent; nothing but silence could at those times have fitted a chosen spokesman; in the mixed shame and blame of the immense wrongs of two crashing civilizations, with nothing to say, he said nothing, slept not at all, and wept at those times in a way that made weeping appropriate, decent, majestic.

**Literary Analysis**
**Biographical Writing**
What is the writer's tone as he describes Lincoln's emotional state?

His hat was shot off as he rode alone one night in Washington; a son he loved died as he watched at the bed; his wife was accused of betraying information to the enemy, until denials from him were necessary; his best companion was a fine-hearted and brilliant son with a deformed palate and an impediment of speech; when a Pennsylvania Congressman told him the enemy had declared they would break into the city and hang him to a lamp-post, he said he had considered "the violent preliminaries" to such a scene; on his left thumb was a scar where an ax had nearly chopped the thumb off when he was a boy; over one eye was a scar where he had been hit with a club in the hands of a man trying to steal the cargo off a Mississippi River flatboat; he threw a cashiered[10] officer out of his room in the White House, crying, "I can bear censure, but not insult. I never wish to see your face again."

**Vocabulary**
**censure** (sen′ shər) *n.* strong disapproval

**Spiral Review**
**Organization and Structure** How does the author develop the reader's impression of Lincoln in this paragraph and in surrounding paragraphs?

As he shook hands with the correspondent of the London *Times,* he drawled, "Well, I guess the London *Times* is about the greatest power on earth—unless perhaps it is the Mississippi River." He rebuked with anger a woman who got on her knees to thank him for a pardon that saved her son from being shot at sunrise; and when an Iowa woman said she had journeyed out of her way to Washington just for a look at him, he grinned, "Well, in the matter of looking at one another, I have altogether the advantage."

He asked his Cabinet to vote on the high military command, and after the vote, told them the appointment had already been made; one Cabinet officer, who had been governor of Ohio, came away personally baffled and frustrated from an interview, to exclaim, to a private secretary, "That man is the most cunning person I ever saw in my life"; an Illinois lawyer who had been sent on errands carrying his political secrets, said, "He is a trimmer[11] and such a trimmer as the world has never seen."

---

**10. cashiered** (ka shird′) *adj.* dishonorably discharged.
**11. trimmer** (trim′ ər) *n.* person who changes his or her opinion to suit the circumstances.

He manipulated the admission of Nevada as a state in the Union, when her votes were needed for the Emancipation Proclamation, saying, "It is easier to admit Nevada than to raise another million of soldiers." At the same time he went to the office of a former New York editor, who had become Assistant Secretary of War, and said the votes of three congressmen were wanted for the required three-quarters of votes in the House of Representatives, advising, "There are three that you can deal with better than anybody else. . . . Whatever promise you make to those men, I will perform it." And in the same week, he said to a Massachusetts politician that two votes were lacking, and, "Those two votes must be procured. I leave it to you to determine how it shall be done; but remember that I am President of the United States and clothed with immense power, and I expect you to procure those votes." And while he was thus employing every last resource and device of practical politics to constitutionally abolish slavery, the abolitionist[12] Henry Ward Beecher attacked him with javelins of scorn and detestation in a series of editorials that brought from him the single comment, "Is thy servant a dog?"

When the King of Siam sent him a costly sword of exquisite embellishment, and two elephant tusks, along with letters and a photograph of the King, he acknowledged the gifts in a manner as lavish as the Orientals. Addressing the King of Siam as "Great and Good Friend," he wrote thanks for each of the gifts, including "also two elephant's tusks of length and magnitude, such as indicate they could have belonged only to an animal which was a native of Siam." After further thanks for the tokens received, he closed the letter to the King of Siam with strange grace and humor, saying, "I appreciate most highly your Majesty's tender of good offices in forwarding to this Government a stock from which a supply of elephants might be raised on our soil. . . our political jurisdiction, however, does not reach a latitude so low as to favor the multiplication of the elephant, and steam on land as well as water has been our best agent of transportation . . . . Meantime, wishing for your Majesty a long and happy life, and, for

12. **abolitionist** (ab´ ə lish´ ən ist) *n.* person in favor of doing away with slavery in the United States.

## LITERATURE IN CONTEXT

### History Connection

**The Emancipation Proclamation**
On January 1, 1863, Lincoln signed the Emancipation Proclamation, freeing the slaves in all Confederate states. The proclamation was largely a symbolic document because the federal government had no means to enforce it. Nevertheless, it gave Southern blacks cause to hope. Eventually, as Union armies advanced, freeing thousands of slaves, the promise of the proclamation became a reality.

### Connect to the Literature

How were Lincoln's efforts to admit Nevada into the Union related to the passage of the Emancipation Proclamation?

**Reading Check**
Who was Lincoln's best companion?

▲ Abraham Lincoln
in 1863

**Literary Analysis**
**Biographical Writing**
What do you learn
about Lincoln from the
statement overheard by
an Indiana man?

**Vocabulary**
**droll** (drōl) *adj.* funny in
an odd way

the generous and emulous people of Siam, the highest
possible prosperity, I commend both to the blessing of
Almighty God."

He sent hundreds of telegrams, "Suspend death
sentence" or "Suspend execution" of So-and-So, who
was to be shot at sunrise. The telegrams varied oddly
at times, as in one, "If Thomas Samplogh, of the First
Delaware Regiment, has been sentenced to death, and
is not yet executed, suspend and report the case to me."
And another, "Is it Lieut. Samuel B. Davis whose death
sentence is commuted? If not done, let it be done."

While the war drums beat, he liked best of all the
stories told of him, one of two Quakeresses[13] heard
talking in a railway car. "I think that Jefferson will
succeed." "Why does thee think so?" "Because Jefferson
is a praying man." "And so is Abraham a praying man."
"Yes, but the Lord will think Abraham is joking."

An Indiana man at the White House heard him say,
"Voorhees, don't it seem strange to you that I, who could never
so much as cut off the head of a chicken, should be elected, or
selected, into the midst of all this blood?"

A party of American citizens, standing in the ruins of the Forum
in Rome, Italy, heard there the news of the first assassination of the
first American dictator, and took it as a sign of the growing up and
the aging of the civilization on the North American continent. Far
out in Coles County, Illinois, a beautiful, gaunt old woman in a log
cabin said, "I knowed he'd never come back."

Of men taking too fat profits out of the war, he said, "Where the
carcass is there will the eagles be gathered together."

An enemy general, Longstreet, after the war, declared him to have
been "the one matchless man in forty millions of people," while one
of his private secretaries, Hay, declared his life to have been the most
perfect in its relationships and adjustments since that of Christ.

Between the days in which he crawled as a baby on the dirt floor
of a Kentucky cabin, and the time when he gave his final breath
in Washington, he packed a rich life with work, thought, laughter,
tears, hate, love.

With vast reservoirs of the comic and the droll, and
notwithstanding a mastery of mirth and nonsense, he delivered
a volume of addresses and letters of terrible and serious appeal,
with import beyond his own day, shot through here and there with

---

**13. Quakeresses** (kwā′ kər es əz) *n.* female members of the religious group known as the
Society of Friends, or Quakers.

far, thin ironics, with paragraphs having railery[14] of the quality of the Book of Job,[15] and echoes as subtle as the whispers of wind in prairie grass.

Perhaps no human clay pot has held more laughter and tears.

The facts and myths of his life are to be an American possession, shared widely over the world, for thousands of years, as the tradition of Knute or Alfred, Lao-tse or Diogenes, Pericles or Caesar,[16] are kept. This because he was not only a genius in the science of neighborly human relationships and an artist in the personal handling of life from day to day, but a strange friend and a friendly stranger to all forms of life that he met.

He lived fifty-six years of which fifty-two were lived in the West—the prairie years.

---

14. **railery** (rā´ lər ē) *n.* good-natured teasing.
15. **Book of Job** (jōb) *n.* book of the Old Testament in which Job is tested by God.
16. **Knute** (knōōt) **or Alfred, Lao-tse** (lou´ dzu´) **or Diogenes** (dī äj´ ə nēz´) **Pericles** (per´ ə klēz´) **or Caesar** (sē´ zər) well-known thinkers and leaders from different eras and places.

**Literary Analysis**
**Biographical Writing**
According to Sandburg, what personal qualities make Lincoln a great historical figure?

P erhaps no human clay pot has held more laughter and tears.

## Critical Thinking

**1. Key Ideas and Details (a)** To whom did Lincoln refer as "the little woman who wrote the book that made this great war"? **(b) Infer:** Why do you think Lincoln wanted to meet this woman? **(c) Draw Conclusions:** What does Lincoln's interest in meeting this woman say about his character?

*Cite textual evidence to support your responses.*

**2. Key Ideas and Details (a)** How did Lincoln justify admitting Nevada to the Union? **(b) Connect:** What other examples of Lincoln's "practical" politics does the author note? **(c) Make a Judgment:** Does Sandburg seem to admire this aspect of Lincoln's character? Explain.

**3. Key Ideas and Details (a)** According to Sandburg, what aspects of Lincoln's life will be "an American possession, shared widely over the world"? **(b) Interpret:** What does Sandburg mean by this comment?

**4. Integration of Knowledge and Ideas** Sandburg says that Lincoln "packed a rich life with work, thought, laughter, tears, hate, love." Do you believe this better demonstrates Sandburg's knowledge about Lincoln or his understanding of him? Explain. *[Connect to the Big Question: Is knowledge the same as understanding?]*

# Arthur Ashe
## Remembered

### John McPhee

**Background** Arthur Ashe was the first African American man to achieve fame in tennis. When he was six years old, his mother died of heart disease. Ashe's father worked as a caretaker in a neighborhood park, where Ashe spent hours playing on the tennis courts. Ashe went on to win numerous honors in tennis, including the 1968 U.S. Open and the 1975 Wimbledon singles championship. Throughout his life, Ashe devoted himself to issues of human rights, education, and public health. After struggling with heart problems, he contracted AIDS from a transfusion during by-pass surgery. He founded the Arthur Ashe Foundation for the Defeat of AIDS before his death in 1993.

He once described his life as "a succession of fortunate circumstances." He was in his twenties then. More than half of his life was behind him. His memory of his mother was confined to a single image: in a blue corduroy bathrobe she stood in a doorway looking out on the courts and playing fields surrounding their house, which stood in the center of a Richmond playground. Weakened by illness, she was taken to a hospital that day, and died at the age of twenty-seven. He was six.

It was to be his tragedy, as the world knows, that he would leave his own child when she was six, that his life would be trapped in a medical irony as a result of early heart disease, and death would come to him prematurely, as it had to his mother.

His mother was tall, with long soft hair and a face that was gentle and thin. She read a lot. She read a lot to him. His father said of her, "She was just like Arthur Junior. She never argued. She was quiet, easygoing, kindhearted."

If by legacy her son never argued, he was also schooled, instructed, coached not to argue, and as he moved alone into alien country he fashioned not-arguing into an enigma and turned the enigma into a weapon. When things got tough (as I noted in these pages twenty-four years ago[1]), he had control. Even in very tight moments, other players thought he was toying with them. They rarely knew what he was thinking. They could not tell if he was angry. It was maddening, sometimes, to play against him. Never less than candid, he said that what he liked best about himself on a tennis court was his demeanor: "What it is is controlled cool, in a way. Always have the situation under control, even if losing. Never betray an inward sense of defeat."

---

1. **twenty-four years ago** McPhee refers to an article published in 1969.

◀ **Critical Viewing** Based on this photograph, what emotions did Ashe express when he won the Wimbledon Championship in 1975? **[Assess]**

**Vocabulary**
**legacy** (leg´ ə sē) *n.* something handed down from an ancestor
**enigma** (i nig´ mə) *n.* mystery

☑ **Reading Check**
What personality trait did Ashe share with his mother?

**Vocabulary**
**lithe** (līth) *adj.* flexible

And of course he never did—not in the height of his athletic power, not in the statesmanship of the years that followed, and not in the endgame of his existence. If you wished to choose a single image, you would see him standing there in his twenties, his lithe body a braid of cables, his energy without apparent limit, in a court situation indescribably bad, and all he does is put his index finger on the bridge of his glasses and push them back up the bridge of his nose. In the shadow of disaster, he hits out. Faced with a choice between a conservative, percentage return or a one-in-ten flat-out blast, he chooses the blast. In a signature manner, he extends his left arm to point upward at lobs as they fall toward him. His overheads, in fire bursts, put them away. His backhand is, if anything, stronger than his forehand, and his shots from either side for the most part are explosions. In motions graceful and decisive, though, and with reactions as fast as the imagination, he is a master of drop shots, of cat-and-mouse, of miscellaneous dinks and chips and (riskiest of all) the crosscourt half-volley. Other tennis players might be wondering who in his right mind would attempt something like that, but that is how Ashe plays the game: at the tensest moment, he goes for the all but impossible. He is predictably unpredictable. He is unreadable. His ballistic serves move in odd patterns and come off the court in unexpected ways. Behind his impassive face—behind the enigmatic glasses, the lifted chin, the first-mate-on-the-bridge look—there seems to be, even from this distance, a smile.

**Literary Analysis**
**Biographical Writing**
What does this description of Ashe's tennis game reveal about his character?

## Critical Thinking

Cite textual evidence to support your responses.

1. **Key Ideas and Details (a)** According to his father, how was Ashe like his mother? **(b) Summarize:** What does Ashe say he likes best about himself on the court? **(c) Draw Conclusions:** Based on this article, how would you describe Ashe's character?

2. **Key Ideas and Details (a)** How did Ashe once describe his life? **(b) Make a Judgment:** Does this description seem accurate based on the information in this biography?

3. **Key Ideas and Details (a) Summarize:** Summarize Ashe's approach to tennis. **(b) Apply:** In what ways might Ashe's approach to tennis be seen as an approach to life?

4. **Integration of Knowledge and Ideas** Which details in the article helped you understand Ashe better than if you had read only statistics related to his tennis career? Discuss your response with a partner. *[Connect to the Big Question: Is knowledge the same as understanding?]*

## Comparing Points of View

**1. Key Ideas and Details** Identify at least three facts that each author includes about his subject. Then, explain what each fact shows about the subject.

**2. Key Ideas and Details (a)** For each biography, note two statements the biographer makes that are interpretations of information about the subject. **(b)** What does each statement show about the biographer's attitude toward his subject? Explain.

## Timed Writing

### Explanatory Text: Essay

Write an essay in which you compare your reaction to the excerpt from *A Lincoln Preface* to your reaction to "Arthur Ashe Remembered." In your response, explain how the writer's tone affected your reaction. **(25 minutes)**

### 5-Minute Planner

**1.** Read the prompt carefully and completely.

**2.** Gather your ideas. Consider these questions before you write:

- Does each writer clearly convey why his subject is important?

- Did you respond more to the description of Abraham Lincoln or the description of Arthur Ashe? Why?

- What main impression do you think each writer wants to convey?

- Using a chart like the one shown, record your main impression of each author's work, as well as details that support your responses. Use these notes to build your essay.

| Author | Main Impression | Details |
|--------|-----------------|---------|
| Sandburg | | |
| McPhee | | |

**3.** Make a quick outline of your essay, deciding which points you will cover in each section. **TIP** Consider how you will move from one point to the next. As you develop your draft, include transitions that help convey your exact meaning.

**4.** Reread the prompt, and then draft your essay.

# Writing Workshop

## Write Explanatory Text

### Workplace Writing: Business Letter

**Defining the Form** A **business letter** is a piece of correspondence that you write when conducting business or professional matters. Effective business letters are clear, direct, courteous, and well formatted. You might use elements of this type of writing in requests for information, appointments, or interviews; formal complaints or commendations; or proposals.

**Assignment** Write a business letter to a company in which you ask for information about a product or service you are interested in using. Include these elements:

✓ a *heading*, *inside address*, *greeting*, *body*, *closing*, and *signature*

✓ *formal*, *polite language*, a clear *purpose*, and relevant background information

✓ standard *formatting* with consistent spacing and indentation

✓ error-free grammar, including *correct use of compound subjects, objects, and complements*

To preview the criteria on which your business letter may be judged, see the rubric on page 517.

 **Writing Workshop:** *Work in Progress*

Review the work you did on pages 463 and 489.

## Prewriting/Planning Strategy

**Brainstorm and itemize.** Jot down a list of products or services that interest you. Itemize each by noting what you want to learn about this product or service. Search the Internet or phone book to locate each company's address. Then, decide which details of performance, features, price, or reliability matter most to you. Choose a topic from your list.

| Products and Services | Company | Interest |
|---|---|---|
| Bicycle | A Bicycle Shop | What kind of bike is best for me? Which has the most options for the lowest price? |
| Cell Phone | Air Time Cell Phones | Which phone is the cheapest and best? How reliable is the service? |
| Homework Help | A+ Tutors | How often is it provided? What is the improvement rate? What does it cost? |

**Common Core State Standards**

**Writing**

**2.** Write informative/explanatory texts to examine and convey complex ideas, concepts, and information clearly and accurately through the effective selection, organization, and analysis of content.

**2.a.** Introduce a topic; organize complex ideas, concepts, and information to make important connections and distinctions; include formatting when useful to aiding comprehension.

**2.e.** Establish and maintain a formal style and objective tone while attending to the norms and conventions of the discipline in which they are writing.

**4.** Produce clear and coherent writing in which the development, organization, and style are appropriate to task, purpose, and audience.

## Setting Your Tone

The **voice** of a business letter sets the stage for the response you will receive. Busy professionals respond well to concise letters that include only essential information presented in an appropriate, formal style. The voice is created by the use of formal vocabulary and tone. The **tone** is the attitude you take toward the subject of your letter.

**Identifying Audience** If you were writing an e-mail to a close friend, you would likely use slang, abbreviations, and a loose format, if you used a format at all. Your friend would pick up on the casual tone and likely respond in a similar manner. However, when you are writing a business letter, your tone needs to be businesslike. You are not simply chatting with a friend. You want information. You should express yourself clearly and professionally to receive the assistance you need. You might even need to do some research on your topic before you begin to write. Doing so will enable you to ask relevant questions.

**Maintaining Consistency** Use these steps to maintain a formal tone:

- Avoid slang and contractions.

- Replace casual language with formal expressions.

- Include only essential information the person needs to answer your questions.

- Follow formatting conventions.

These two letters request the same information, but they are quite different in tone.

| Casual Letter | Formal Letter |
| --- | --- |
| I love riding bicycles. I have outgrown mine and want a new one really badly. Which is the best kind for me? How much does it cost? | I am planning on purchasing a new bicycle. I like riding on the street, but I mostly ride the bike trails with my parents. Would a mountain bike be best for me? Or would a hybrid better serve my needs? What is the price range for recreational bicycles like these? |

# Drafting Strategies

**Select a format.** Choose a standard business letter format, using a consistent font and spacing. This will contribute to the readability and impact of your letter. You may use block format, in which each part of the letter begins at the left margin. Alternatively, you may use modified block format, in which the heading, closing, and signature are indented to the center of the page. (For a sample business letter, see page R34.) Use the checklist shown here to verify that your draft includes all six elements of a business letter.

**Business Letter Elements**

- ❑ **Heading**—the writer's address and organization (if any) and the date
- ❑ **Inside Address**—where the letter will be sent
- ❑ **Greeting**—a salutation, always punctuated by a colon
- ❑ **Body**—a presentation of the writer's purpose
- ❑ **Closing**—an appropriate farewell
- ❑ **Signature**—a hand-signed name

**Write a memo—Spread the news.** If your purpose is to give information to a number of people, you might choose to send a memo instead of the more formal letter format. A memo has all the information at the top—who wrote it, whom it is to, the date, and the subject. The body of the memo contains the pertinent information. Memos do not have addresses, greetings, or closings.

**E-mail—Take it to the Internet.** E-mail is an efficient way to request or present information. It is less formal than a business letter, but it can be speedier and provide direct access to the source of information. When you write an e-mail, be clear in your subject line. The subject line of an e-mail is much like one in a memo. It should be short and to the point. Include a greeting, a body, a closing, and an electronic signature in your e-mail.

# Revising Strategy

**Highlight the active voice.** A verb in the active voice expresses an action done by its subject. A verb in the passive voice expresses an action done to its subject.

**Passive Voice:** The vacuum cleaner *was broken* by the salesman.

**Active Voice:** The salesman *broke* the vacuum cleaner.

The active voice is preferable because it produces a more direct and forceful sentence than the passive voice. Review your draft, highlighting verbs written in the passive voice; then, rewrite the sentences in the active voice when you can.

**Common Core
State Standards**

**Writing**

**2.a.** Introduce a topic; organize complex ideas, concepts, and information to make important connections and distinctions; include formatting when useful to aiding comprehension.

**2.d.** Use precise language and domain-specific vocabulary to manage the complexity of the topic.

**2.f.** Provide a concluding statement or section that follows from and supports the information or explanation presented.

**6.** Use technology, including the Internet, to produce, publish, and update individual or shared writing products, taking advantage of technology's capacity to link other information and to display information flexibly and dynamically.

# Revising to Combine Choppy Sentences

**Revising to Combine Choppy Sentences** Avoid choppy, disconnected sentences by combining two or more related ideas into a single sentence.

**Methods of Sentence Combining** **Compound verbs**—more than one verb linked to a single subject—can be used to combine two short sentences:

**Choppy:** I *disconnected* my phone. I *brought* it in for service.

**Compound Verb:** I *disconnected* my phone and *brought* it in for service.

**Compound objects**—more than one object linked to a single verb—can help combine sentences.

**Choppy:** I purchased *a scanner.* I purchased *a fax machine.*

**Compound Object:** I purchased *a scanner and a fax machine.*

A third option is the use of **compound predicate nominatives** or **predicate adjectives.**

**Choppy:** My newest device *is a printer.* It is also *a scanner.* It is also *a fax machine.*

**Compound Predicative Nominative:** My newest device *is a printer, scanner, and fax machine.*

**Choppy:** The fax is *automated.* It is *fast.*

**Compound Predicative Adjective:** The fax is *automated and fast.*

**Fixing Choppy Sentences** Scan your draft for sentence variety.

1. **Read your draft aloud.** Listen for overuse of short sentences.

2. **Identify sentences that can be combined.** Look for sentences that share a common subject or a common predicate element.

3. **Use a variety of sentence combining techniques.** Use compound verbs, compound direct objects, or compound predicate nominatives or predicate adjectives to create a wider variety of flowing sentences.

> **PH WRITING COACH**
>
> Further instruction and practice are available in *Prentice Hall Writing Coach.*

### Grammar in Your Writing

Review the body paragraphs in your letter, highlighting central ideas or images. Use various types of phrases and clauses to convey specific meanings and to add interest. Be sure to use punctuation to separate items in a series.

# Student Model: Robin Weber, St. Petersburg, FL

Intelligent Productions
220 Any Street, Suite 112
Any Town, NY 10000
December 13, 2006

Robin uses modified block format.

G-2000 Computers
310 Infinite Loop
Any City, CA 94000

Dear Sir or Madam:

My business is currently in the market for several high-end, reliable server computers. I would like to obtain more information about your line of server products.

Robin's purpose is stated clearly and concisely.

The computers we use are operating twenty-four hours a day, seven days a week, as servers hosting a high-traffic Internet Web site. Therefore, it would be unacceptable for my company to purchase computers that require periods of inactivity in order to remain in working condition. We are also concerned about technical support issues and costs.

In this paragraph, Robin provides important background information.

I would appreciate if you could send me the exact specifications on catalog items number 1444 and 2314. In addition, there is no information on warranties in your product descriptions. Any information you can provide in this regard would be very helpful in making my purchasing decision. Also, would it be possible to obtain a high-volume discount? How would such an order affect delivery time?

The letter includes specific questions that Robin would like answered.

Please send me any information you have on these matters. I look foward to hearing from you.

Sincerely,

*Robin Weber*

Robin Weber

In his conclusion, Robin summarizes the request using polite language.

# Editing and Proofreading

Check your draft for errors in format, grammar, and punctuation.

**Focus on accuracy.** Make certain that the names of individuals and companies are spelled correctly and that the address is complete. Check the capitalizations and abbreviations to ensure they are correct.

# Publishing and Presenting

Consider one of the following ways to share your writing:

**Send your letter.** If your letter is written to an existing business, mail it. When you get a response, share it with classmates.

**Conduct a discussion.** Use your letter to begin a class discussion about the role of communication skills in everyday life. To improve the productivity of the discussion, be open to the variety of ideas your classmates suggest. Make notes on their comments, and add your letter and notes to your writing portfolio.

# Reflecting on Your Writing

**Writer's Journal** Jot down your answer to this question:

*How is business writing different than other types of writing?*

# Rubric for Self-Assessment

Find evidence in your writing to address each category. Then, use the rating scale to grade your work.

**Spiral Review**

Earlier in the unit, you learned about **direct and indirect objects** (p. 462) and **predicate nominatives and predicate adjectives** (p. 488). Before you send your letter, check to be sure you have used these grammatical forms correctly.

| Criteria | Rating Scale | | | | |
|---|---|---|---|---|---|
| | not very | | | | very |
| **Voice:** How well have you maintained a consistently formal tone? | 1 | 2 | 3 | 4 | 5 |
| **Focus:** How clearly have you stated your purpose? | 1 | 2 | 3 | 4 | 5 |
| **Organization:** How thoroughly have you incorporated all the elements of a business letter? | 1 | 2 | 3 | 4 | 5 |
| **Support/Elaboration:** How comprehensive is the background information you provided? | 1 | 2 | 3 | 4 | 5 |
| **Style:** How formal and polite is your use of language? | 1 | 2 | 3 | 4 | 5 |
| **Conventions:** How correct is your grammar, especially your use of compound subjects, objects, and complements? | 1 | 2 | 3 | 4 | 5 |

## ⓒ Leveled Texts

Build your skills and improve your comprehension of types of nonfiction with texts of increasing complexity.

Read **"Carry Your Own Skis"** to discover the real benefits of taking care of yourself.

Read **"Libraries Face Sad Chapter"** to learn why libraries should be treasured and maintained.

## ⓒ Common Core State Standards

Meet these standards with either **"Carry Your Own Skis"** (p. 522) or **"Libraries Face Sad Chapter"** (p. 530).

### Reading Informational Text
**6.** Determine an author's point of view or purpose in a text and analyze how an author uses rhetoric to advance that point of view or purpose. *(Literary Analysis: Spiral Review)*

**8.** Delineate and evaluate the argument and specific claims in a text, assessing whether the reasoning is valid and the evidence is relevant and sufficient; identify false statements and fallacious reasoning. *(Reading Skill: Evaluate Persuasion)*

### Writing
**4.** Produce clear and coherent writing in which the development, organization, and style are appropriate to task, purpose, and audience. *(Writing: Abstract)*

### Speaking and Listening
**4.** Present information, findings, and supporting evidence clearly, concisely, and logically such that listeners can follow the line of reasoning and the organization, development, substance, and style are appropriate to purpose, audience, and task. *(Research and Technology: Persuasive Speech)*

### Language
**1.** Demonstrate command of the conventions of standard English grammar and usage when writing and speaking. *(Conventions: Adjectives)*

**5.** Demonstrate understanding of figurative language, word relationships, and nuances in word meanings. *(Vocabulary: Analogies)*

# Literary Analysis: Persuasive Essay

A **persuasive essay** is a short nonfiction work in which the author's purpose is to convince a reader to think or act in a particular way. Persuasive essays usually include the following persuasive appeals:

- **Appeals to reason:** logical arguments based on verifiable evidence, such as facts, statistics, or expert testimony.
- **Appeals to emotion:** statements intended to affect listeners' feelings about a subject. These statements often include charged language—words with strong positive or negative associations.

As you read persuasive writing, try to identify the **author's motive,** or intent. Ask "Why does the writer include this information?"

# Reading Skill: Evaluate Persuasion

A persuasive argument is composed of a series of **claims.** To **analyze and evaluate an author's argument,** identify passages in which the author makes a claim in support of his or her position. Then, **reread** those passages to test the author's logic and reasoning. Ask yourself the following questions:

- Is the author's argument **credible**—supported by valid and relevant evidence—or is it based on faulty reasoning?
- Is the evidence provided **comprehensive,** or complete?
- Are the writer's **generalizations,** or broad statements, supported by evidence?

## Using the Strategy: Persuasion Analysis Diagram

Use a chart like the one shown to record your analysis of the author's claims. Review your analysis to decide how effectively the author has presented his or her argument.

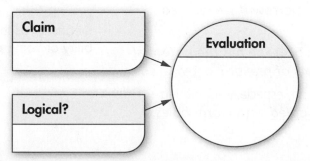

**PHLit**
**Online!**

www.PHLitOnline.com

**Hear It!**
- Selection summary audio
- Selection audio

**See It!**
- Get Connected video
- Background video
- More about the author
- Vocabulary flashcards

**Do It!**
- Interactive journals
- Interactive graphic organizers
- Self-test
- Internet activity
- Grammar tutorial
- Interactive vocabulary games

Is *knowledge* the same as *understanding?*

## Writing About the Big Question

In "Carry Your Own Skis," the author draws an analogy between carrying your own skis and taking responsibility for yourself. Use this sentence starter to develop your ideas about the Big Question.

Personal responsibility is a **concept** that many people do not truly understand because _____ .

**While You Read** Look for details that illustrate the benefits of taking personal responsibility.

## Vocabulary

Read each word and its definition. Decide whether you know the word well, know it a little bit, or do not know it at all. After you read, see how your knowledge of each word has increased.

- **entailed** (en tāld´) *v.* caused or required as a necessary consequence; involved; necessitated (p. 523) *The plan to repaint the house entailed a lot of work.* entail *v.* entailment *n.*

- **inevitability** (in ev´ i tə bil´ ə tē) *n.* quality of being certain to happen; certainty (p. 523) *The inevitability of losing did not keep the team from playing hard.* inevitable *adj.* inevitably *adv.*

- **collective** (kə lek´ tiv) *adj.* put together as a group; gathered into a whole (p. 523) *With our collective friends, we had enough people to get the group rate.* collect *v.* collection *n.* collectively *adv.*

- **forgo** (fôr gō´) *v.* do without; abstain from; give up (p. 523) *The coach said we could forgo practice tomorrow if we worked hard today.* forgone *v.*

- **potential** (pō ten´ shəl) *n.* possibility (p. 524) *She has the potential to be a good player, but she needs lots of practice.* potential *adj.*

- **riddled** (rid´ ´ld) *adj.* very full of something, especially something unpleasant (p. 525) *The old tree was riddled with worm holes.* riddle *v.*

### Word Study

The **Latin root -potens-** means "able" or "having the essence of." The root relates to power and possibility.

When Dolan describes skiing as having the **potential** for fun, she means it has the possibility of being exciting.

Author of
# Carry Your Own Skis

Lian Dolan is one of the "Satellite Sisters," a group of five sisters who host a radio show. Before helping launch the show, Dolan tried everything from working as a waitress to producing films. She also writes the column "The Chaos Chronicles" for *Working Mother* magazine.

**"The Sassiest"** Lian is known as the sassiest of the sisters, and she is not afraid to express her opinions on any topic. Even though Lian is the youngest of the five sisters, she directs all of their writing projects. She enjoys being the "Head Sister," giving orders to her older siblings.

## BACKGROUND FOR THE ESSAY

### Cold-Weather Clothing

Before the development of synthetic, lightweight, waterproof fabrics that "breathe" and keep the wearer dry, keeping warm on the ski slopes meant wearing heavy wool and cotton clothing. Garments made from these fabrics would become wet and cold in the snow, and they would stay wet and cold until removed.

## Did You Know?

The Satellite Sisters live in four different cities on two continents. They link via satellite for their popular radio show.

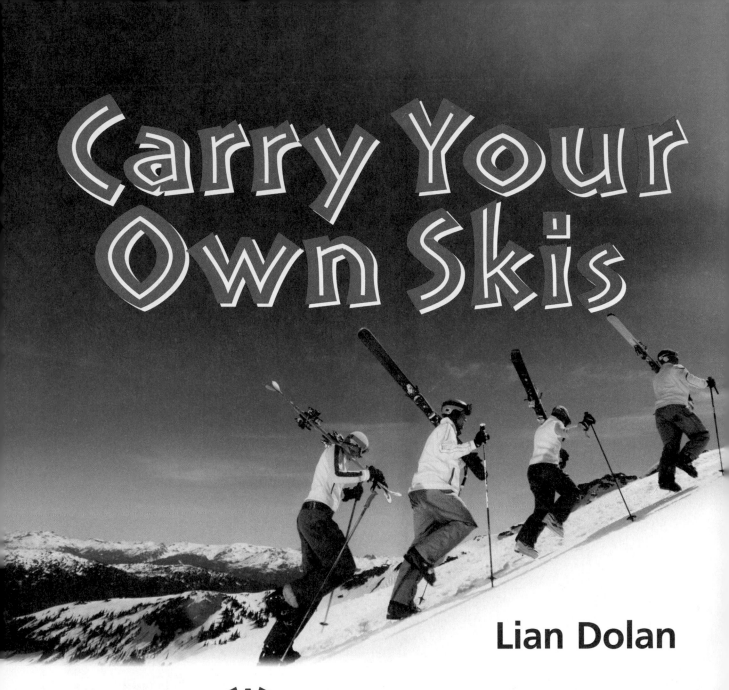

# Carry Your Own Skis

## Lian Dolan

**▲ Critical Viewing**
Based on this photo-
graph, does skiing look
like work or recreation?
Explain. **[Analyze]**

**W**hen my mother was forty, she took up skiing. Or, more
correctly, she and her twin sister took up skiing. They got on a bus,
went to ski camp for a week, and learned to ski. After that, they'd
get in the car and head up to Ladies Day at Powder Hill as often as
they could to practice their stem christies.[1] Don't let the name fool
you, Powder Hill (which later became the more Everest-like "Powder
Ridge") was no pushover bunny slope.[2]

---

1. **stem christies** turns made by angling one ski and then bringing the other into alignment.
2. **bunny slope** gently sloping hill used for practice by beginning skiers.

This was in the mid-sixties, when skiing was work—decades before valet parking, fondue lunches, and gear that actually keeps you dry, warm, and safe. My mother and my aunt took up the kind of skiing that entailed wooden skis, tie boots, and rope tows[3] that could jerk your arm out of its socket. This was the kind of skiing where skiers, not the Sno-Cats, groomed the hill[4] in the morning. Ticket buyers were expected to sidestep up and down slopes and herringbone the lift lines.[5] The typical A-frame lodge had a big fireplace, a couple of bathrooms, rows of picnic tables, and maybe some hot chocolate for sale. At the end of the day, there were no hot toddies by a roaring fire in furry boots or drinks in the hot tub of a slopeside condo. Instead, my mother and her sister faced the inevitability of a station wagon with a dead battery and the long, dark drive back home in wet clothes.

Why did they learn to ski? It wasn't to spend some quality time outdoors together away from their responsibilities at home. They learned to ski so that they could take their collective children skiing, all seventeen of us. My mother's eight children and my aunt's nine. And learn to ski we did, eagerly. There was, however, one rule my mother had about skiing: Carry your own skis.

My mother didn't teach us to ski until we could carry our own skis from the car to the lodge in the morning and—this is key—from the lodge back to the car at the end of the day. Even cold, wet, and tired, we had to get our skis, poles, and boots back to that station wagon on our own. No falling behind. No dragging. And no whining. My mother had the responsibility for her gear, the giant lunch, the car, and the occasional trip to the ER for broken legs. We were in charge of our own gear and meeting at the end of the day. These were the conditions to be allowed to accompany siblings and cousins to the slopes. Carry your own skis or sit in the lodge all day.

No one wanted to get left in the lodge. A cold, wet day on the ice-blue slopes of New England, freezing in leather boots and the generation of ski clothes before microfibers was far preferable to being left out of all that fun. Miss the lunches of soggy tuna fish sandwiches and mini chocolate bars? No way! Sit in the lodge instead of side-slipping your way down a sheet of ice disguised as a trail or tramping through three feet of snow to get the pole you dropped under the chair lift? Not me! Forgo that last run of the day in near darkness, cold and alone and crying because your siblings have skied on ahead without you? Who'd want to miss all that fun? Sitting in the

---

3. **rope tows** moving ropes that skiers hold to be pulled to the top of the hill.
4. **groomed the hill** packed and smoothed the snow.
5. **herringbone the lift lines** walk uphill to chair lift by stepping with skis pointed outward to avoid sliding back down the hill. The skis leave a "herringbone" pattern—a line of connected v-shapes—on the snow.

**Vocabulary**

**entailed** (en tāld´) *v.* caused or required as a necessary consequence; involved; necessitated

**inevitability** (in ev´ i tə bil´ ə tē) *n.* quality of being certain to happen; certainty

**collective** (kə lek´ tiv) *adj.* put together as a group; gathered into a whole

**forgo** (fôr gō´) *v.* do without; abstain from; give up

**Literary Analysis**
**Persuasive Essay**
Which details in this paragraph appeal to the emotions? Explain.

**Reading Check**
Why did Dolan's mother and aunt learn to ski?

lodge all day just wasn't an option once we reached ski age. We were expected to participate. We learned to carry our own skis.

The lesson was simple, really. Be responsible for yourself and your stuff or you miss out. No one wanted to miss out. Getting across the icy parking lot and back seemed a small price to pay for the potential of great fun. And even if you dropped your poles or the bindings cut into your hands or you fell on your rear end, that was part of the experience. The "carry your own skis" mentality filtered into almost every area of our life as we were growing up. Doing homework, getting to practice, applying to college—be responsible for yourself and your stuff or you miss out. •

I began to notice the people who hadn't learned to carry their own skis when I was as young as eleven. I didn't have a name for this concept yet, but I had the notion that maybe other kids operated by a different set of rules. They thought that somewhere, somebody was going to take care of things for them. I remember the girls at summer

◄ **Critical Viewing**
How do you think the girl in this photograph feels about skiing?
**[Speculate]**

camp who never signed up to pack out or pack in for a camping trip, expecting that someone else would provide food or do all the cleanup for them. But me? I would sign up to make the PB&Js and to clean up the mess. I'd load the canoes onto the truck and take 'em off again. And the tent? I'd put it up and I'd take it down. I didn't know any different. As a result, I was invited to go on a lot of camping trips. The lodge and back, baby—that was my attitude.

In high school, the kids who didn't carry their own skis called their parents to bring in assignments they'd forgotten or to ask for a ride home instead of walking or taking the late bus. In college, the no-ski carriers all had pink T-shirts—a sure sign that they had never done laundry before—and they complained about how much work they had. Isn't that what college was about—doing your own laundry and finishing your work? Then you could get to the fun stuff.

The real world is riddled with people who have never learned to carry their own skis—the blame-shifters, the no-RSVPers, the coworkers who never participate in those painful group birthdays except if it's their own. I admit it: I don't really get these people.

I like the folks who clear the dishes, even when they're the guests. Or the committee members who show up on time, assignment completed and ready to pitch in on the next event. Or the neighbor who drives the carpool even though her kids are sick. I get these people. These people have learned to carry their own skis.

In early adulthood, carrying my own skis meant getting a job, paying off my student loans, and working hard for the company that was providing my paycheck. If I did those things, then I could enjoy the other areas of my life. Dull, yes, but freeing, too. When I wasn't responsible for myself or my stuff, I felt lousy. Sometimes I could get to the lodge, but I just couldn't get back to the station wagon at the end of the day. It was an unfamiliar feeling to let someone down by missing a deadline at work or not showing up for an early-morning run. . . . On days like that, the parking lot seemed bigger and icier than I had anticipated.

Now I have a life that includes a husband, two children, a dog, a house, friends, schools, and a radio show that involves lots of other people, including four sisters. The "stuff" of my life may seem much heavier than two skis, two boots, and two poles, but it isn't really—just a little bit trickier to carry. I have to do more balancing and let go of the commitments that I'd probably drop anyway. If I commit to more than I can handle, I miss out. That's when I think of Powder Hill.

**Reading Skill**
**Persuasive Appeals**
How does the author support her claim that being responsible for yourself can be rewarding?

**Vocabulary**
**riddled** (rid´ 'ld) adj. very full of something, especially something unpleasant

**Literary Analysis**
**Persuasive Essay**
What does the paragraph beginning "I like the folks who. . . " suggest the author's motive for writing might be?

# Be responsible for yourself and your stuff or you miss out.

Reading Check
How did Dolan adapt the "carry your own skis" idea to other areas of her life?

The funny thing is, some of the worst moments of my childhood were spent on skis or in pursuit of skiing. The truth is, I didn't really like skiing as a kid. And I wasn't a very good skier. Most days, skiing for me was about freezing rain and constantly trying to catch up to my older, faster, more talented siblings. The hard falls on the hard ice. I can still feel the damp long underwear and the wet wool during the endless ride home. But whether I liked to ski or not didn't really matter. I was expected to learn to ski, and I did. And I also learned that in life you need to be responsible for yourself and your stuff or you miss out. The lodge and back, baby.

## Critical Thinking

**Cite textual evidence to support your responses.**

1. **Key Ideas and Details** **(a)** What is the one rule that Dolan's mother had about skiing? **(b) Make a Judgment:** Do you think Dolan's mother's expectations of her children were reasonable? Why or why not?

2. **Key Ideas and Details** **(a)** What lesson does Dolan say she learned from carrying her own skis? **(b) Connect:** In what other aspects of life does the author say this lesson has guided her behavior?

3. **Integration of Knowledge and Ideas** **(a) Take a Position:** Do you agree or disagree with Dolan's claim that people who do not take responsibility miss out on things? Explain. **(b) Discuss:** Share your response with a partner, and then explain how the discussion has or has not changed your response to the question.

4. **Integration of Knowledge and Ideas** How do the author's family skiing experiences lead to a better understanding of her personal responsibility? *[Connect to the Big Question: Is knowledge the same as understanding?]*

## Literary Analysis: Persuasive Essay

1. **Key Ideas and Details (a)** In this essay, what is the author trying to persuade readers to do? **(b)** What evidence does she use to support her position?

2. **Craft and Structure (a)** Using a chart like the one shown, identify three passages in which Dolan argues for "the 'carry your own skis' mentality." In the right-hand column, indicate whether each passage is an appeal to reason or to emotion, and explain your ideas. **(b)** Which kind of appeals does the author seem to favor—**appeals to reason** or **appeals to emotion**? Explain.

Lian Dolan

| Passage | Reason or Emotion |
|---------|-------------------|
|         |                   |
|         |                   |

3. **Integration of Knowledge and Ideas** What do you think is the **author's motive** for trying to persuade readers to agree with her?

## Reading Skill: Evaluate Persuasion

4. Are the **claims** in this essay well-reasoned and logical? Explain.

5. Which passages are especially convincing? Explain your response.

## Vocabulary

**Acquisition and Use** In vocabulary study, **analogies** show the relationships between pairs of words. Use a word from the vocabulary list on page 520 to complete each analogy. In each, your choice should create a word pair that matches the relationship between the first two words given.

1. conflict : agreement :: uncertainty : _____

2. idea : reality :: _____ : actual

3. soaked : water :: _____ : dents

4. hidden : revealed :: individual : _____

5. accept : attend :: _____ : decline

6. began : started :: caused : _____

**Word Study** Use the context of the sentences and what you know about the **Latin root -potens-** to explain your answers to each question.

1. Is a *potent* smell difficult to notice?

2. Is a *potentate* likely to be a weak person?

### Word Study

The **Latin root -potens-** means "able" or "having the essence of." The root relates to power and possibility.

**Apply It** Explain how the root -potens- contributes to the meanings of these words. Consult a dictionary if necessary.

potency
potentially

# Is *knowledge* the same as *understanding?*

Libraries Face Sad Chapter

Pete Hamill

## Writing About the Big Question

In "Libraries Face Sad Chapter," the author urges readers to contribute to a fund to support public libraries, a source of knowledge. Use these sentence starters to develop your ideas about the Big Question.

Libraries, as a **source** of **information** and a place for **research,** are still important because _____. They can help us **clarify** information we find on the Internet because _____.

**While You Read** Look for facts that support the author's opinion that libraries must be saved. Then, consider whether he has helped you understand the situation he describes.

## Vocabulary

Read each word and its definition. Decide whether you know the word well, know it a little bit, or do not know it at all. After you read, see how your knowledge of each word has increased.

- **volumes** (väl′ yŏŏmz) *n.* books that are either part of a set or combined into one. (p. 531) *My grandfather had random <u>volumes</u> of an old set of encyclopedias stored in the basement.*

- **presumed** (prē zŏŏmd′) *adj.* accepted as true; supposed (p. 531) *Someone who has been arrested is <u>presumed</u> to be innocent until proven guilty. presume v. presumption n. presumptuous adj.*

- **curtailed** (kər tāld′) *v.* cut short; reduced (p. 532) *The game was <u>curtailed</u> by darkness. curtailing v.*

- **medium** (mē′ dē əm) *n.* means of communication (p. 532) *Television may be today's most popular <u>medium</u>. media n. pl.*

- **duration** (dŏŏ rā′ shən) *n.* length of time something lasts (p. 533) *The graduating class remained standing for the <u>duration</u> of the ceremony. durable adj. endure v.*

- **emulate** (em′ yŏŏ lāt) *v.* imitate (a person or thing admired) (p. 534) *Josh tries to <u>emulate</u> his favorite rock star by dying his hair different colors. emulation n.*

### Word Study

The **Latin root -*sum*-** means "to take."

Pete Hamill describes a shelf in the library that was **presumed** to be safe from children. The librarians took for granted that children would not get to the books placed there.

# Meet
# Pete Hamill
## (b. 1935)

## Author of
# Libraries Face Sad Chapter

Pete Hamill has had two novels on *The New York Times* Bestseller List, but he is first and foremost a journalist. After quitting school at sixteen to work in the Brooklyn Navy Yard, Hamill joined the U.S. Navy. He completed his high school education while in the navy. **"The work was everything."** In 1960, Hamill went to work as a reporter for the *New York Post* newspaper. Although he would write for several other newspapers in his career, Hamill loved his job at the *Post*. He wrote, "Nothing before (or since) could compare with walking into the *New York Post* at midnight, being sent into the dark scary city on assignment and coming back to write a story."

## BACKGROUND FOR THE ESSAY

### Public Libraries

Although the first American library was established in 1638, it was not until the 1800s that public libraries became common in the United States. Since then, Americans have come to rely on public libraries as a free source of education, entertainment, and community.

## Did You Know?

During Hamill's long career as a reporter, he covered wars in a number of countries including Vietnam, Nicaragua, Lebanon, and Northern Ireland.

# Libraries Face Sad Chapter

## Pete Hamill

The library was four blocks from where we lived, on the corner of Ninth St. and Sixth Ave., and it was one of the treasure houses of our Brooklyn lives.

This was in the years before television, when we saw movies once a week at the Minerva or the Avon or the RKO Prospect, and fed our imaginations through radio and books. That is, it was in a time when *The Count of Monte Cristo* was as vivid in our minds, and talk, and dreams, as Jack Roosevelt Robinson. Dumas told the story of the count as vividly as Red Barber[1] recited the unfolding tale of No. 42.

We passed into that library between two mock-Corinthian columns that gave the building a majestic aura. For me, every visit was an astonishment. There was a children's room, first seen when I was 8, where I first read the wonderful Babar books, and then moved on to Howard Pyle's *Book of Pirates,* and all of Robert Louis Stevenson, with those rich, golden, mysterious illustrations by N.C. Wyeth.

There were bound volumes of a children's magazine called *St. Nicholas,* full of spidery drawings of animals that talked, and villains who didn't. There were picture books bursting with images of lost cities or the solar system. In that room, I learned that the world was larger than our neighborhood.

And then, at 10 or 11, I found my way into the adult stacks, to borrow books about the daily life of the Romans, the flight of Richard Hannay across Scotland, the conquests of Mexico and Peru, the cases of Sherlock Holmes. On a high shelf, presumed to be safe from the curious eyes of children, was a lavish (in memory) edition of *The Thousand and One Nights.*[2]

No teacher sent us to those leathery cliffs of books. Reading wasn't an assignment; it was a pleasure. We read for the combined thrills of villainy and heroism, along with knowledge of the vast world beyond the parish. Living in those other worlds, we could become other people: Jim Hawkins, or Edmund Dantes, or (most thrillingly) d'Artagnan, with his three musketeers.

We could live in the South Seas, or Paris, or the Rome of Caligula. It never occurred to us that we were inheriting our little share of civilization. But that's what was happening.

---

1. *The Count of Monte Cristo . . .* **Red Barber** *The Count of Monte Cristo* is a nineteenth-century novel by Alexandre Dumas. Jackie Robinson was the first African American major league baseball player. He joined the Brooklyn Dodgers in 1947 and wore number 42. Dodgers games were broadcast on the radio, and the action was described by announcer Red Barber.
2. *The Thousand and One Nights* collection of ancient tales also known as the Arabian Nights. Although many of the tales, including "Aladdin," are now retold as children's stories, the original tellings are full of violence, bloodshed, poisonings, and betrayals.

# Built by Carnegie

The library of my childhood is still there, since 1975 known as the Park Slope Branch of the Brooklyn Public Library. It was built with grant money from my favorite capitalist, Andrew Carnegie, in 1906. But once again, as happened in 1992, the teeming imaginative life of libraries is in danger of being curtailed. Services might be cut. Hours trimmed. Staff reduced. The reason is the same: money, or the lack of it.

Such reductions are absolutely understandable. As we all know, Mayor Bloomberg has more than a $4 billion shortfall[3] that must be made up. Unlike the spend-more tax-less leaders of the federal government, the government of New York City can't print money to keep things going. In this season of post-September 11 austerities,[4] something must give. I hope it isn't the libraries.

The reason is simple: In hard times, libraries are more important than ever. Human beings need what books give them better than any other medium. Since those ancient nights around prehistoric campfires, we have needed myth. And heroes. And moral tales. And information about the world beyond the nearest mountains or oceans.

**Vocabulary**
**curtailed** (kər tāld´) *v.*
cut short; reduced

**Vocabulary**
**medium** (mē´ dē əm) *n.*
means of communication

---

3. **shortfall** (shôrt´ fôl´) *n.* the difference between the amount you have and the amount you need or expect.
4. **austerities** (ô ster´ ə tēz) *n.* acts of self-discipline and self-denial.

▼ **Critical Viewing**
How does this photograph support Hamill's idea that a library is a "treasure house of the imagination"? **[Connect]**

In hard times, libraries are more important than ever.

Today, with books and movies more expensive than ever, and television entertainment in free fall to the lowest levels of stupidity, freely circulating books are an absolute necessity. They are quite simply another kind of food. We imagine, and then we live.

Hard times are also an opportunity. Parents and teachers all moan about the refusal of the young to read. Here is the chance to revive the power of the printed page. The Harry Potter books show that the audience for young readers is potentially immense. A child who starts with Harry Potter can find his or her way to Dumas and Arthur Conan Doyle, to Mark Twain and Walt Whitman, and, yes, to Tolstoy and Joyce and Proust. ●

# Immigrants' Appreciation

For those without money, the road to that treasure house of the imagination begins at the public library. When I was a boy, the rooms were crowded with immigrants and their children. That is, with people who came from places where there were no libraries for the poor. With their children, they built the New York in which we now live.

Today, the libraries of this city are still doing that work. The libraries of Brooklyn and Queens are jammed with the new immigrants and their astonishing children, the people who will build the New York of tomorrow. The older people want information about this new world, and how to get better jobs and green cards and citizenship. Their American children want to vanish into books their parents cannot afford, thus filling themselves with the endless possibilities of the future.

They are no different from the Irish, the Jews and the Italians of my childhood. My father only went to the eighth grade in Belfast. I remember my mother drilling him at our kitchen table for his citizenship test, and I know that he first read the Constitution in a book borrowed from the Prospect Branch of the Brooklyn Public Library. Lying in a darkened bed off that kitchen, I first heard the language of the Bill of Rights.

That process must go on in all the places where the poor now live. If it's impossible for the city to do it, then we must do it ourselves. Bloomberg can give us the hard numbers, explain the shortfall in the library budget and explain how much we need. Then we should try to make it up with the establishment of a private fund to maintain the libraries at full strength for the duration of the crisis.

## LITERATURE IN CONTEXT

### History Connection

Andrew Carnegie (1835–1919) was a Scottish immigrant who became enormously wealthy in the steel business. In 1889, Carnegie published an essay entitled "The Gospel of Wealth." In it, he argued that the rich should use their money for the public good. Under his plan, "the surplus wealth of the few will become, in the best sense, the property of the many." Unlike many other wealthy men of his time, Carnegie acted on his belief. His many charitable acts included the building of more than 2800 public libraries throughout the English-speaking world.

### Connect to the Literature

How do you think Andrew Carnegie would react to the idea of cuts in library funding? Explain.

**Vocabulary**
**duration** (dʊ rā′ shən) *n.* length of time something lasts

**Vocabulary**
**emulate** (em´ yōō lāt)
*v.* imitate (a person
or thing admired)

**Spiral Review**
**Author's Purpose**
What is the author's
purpose for suggesting
a voluntary library tax?

All of us whose lives
have been affected by the
treasures of public libraries
could contribute. The rich
could emulate Carnegie, who
used his wealth to create more
than 1,600 public libraries,
including 65 in New York. But
the middle class could also send in
small amounts from $10 to $50.

This would be a kind of voluntary
tax. On one level, it would be a powerful
pledge to maintain the life of the mind
among all classes in this city. That is
obviously in our own interest. But above
all, it would be a means of honoring the labor of those men and
women who got us here, and who paid taxes to buy books for all
New Yorkers, and first took us by the hand and walked us into the
treasure houses. We who dreamed of Ebbets Field and the Chateau
d'If on the same American nights owe debts to New York that we
can never pay. This is one that must be honored.

## Critical Thinking

**Cite textual evidence to support your responses.**

1. **Key Ideas and Details (a)** What books and magazines does
   Hamill remember from early visits to the library? **(b) Infer:** What
   do these memories suggest about how Hamill felt about the
   library as a child?

2. **Key Ideas and Details (a) Interpret:** What does Hamill mean by
   calling books "another kind of food"? **(b) Draw Conclusions:**
   What does this comparison suggest about the value he places on
   books?

3. **Integration of Knowledge and Ideas (a) Take a Position:** Do
   you agree with Hamill's claims about the importance of free public
   libraries? Explain. **(b) Discuss:** Share your response with a partner,
   and then explain how the discussion has or has not changed your
   response to the question.

4. **Integration of Knowledge and Ideas (a)** What does Hamill
   want you to know about the need for public libraries? **(b)** Do the
   facts he presents make you understand enough to want to act?
   Explain. *[Connect to the Big Question: Is knowledge the same
   as understanding?]*

## Literary Analysis: Persuasive Essay

1. **Key Ideas and Details** **(a)** In this essay, what is the author trying to persuade readers to do? **(b)** What evidence does he use to support his position?

2. **Craft and Structure** **(a)** Using a chart like the one shown, identify three passages in which Hamill asserts his position on public libraries. In the right-hand column, indicate whether each passage is an appeal to reason or to emotion and explain your ideas. **(b)** Which kind of appeals does the author seem to favor—appeals to reason or appeals to emotion? Explain.

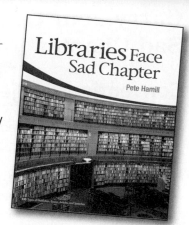

| Passage | Reason or Emotion |
|---|---|
|  |  |
|  |  |

3. **Integration of Knowledge and Ideas** What do you think is the **author's motive** for trying to persuade readers to agree with him?

## Reading Skill: Evaluate Persuasion

4. Are the **claims** in this essay well-reasoned and logical? Explain.

5. Which passages are especially convincing? Explain.

## Vocabulary

**Acquisition and Use** In vocabulary study, **analogies** show the relationships between pairs of words. Use a word from the vocabulary list on page 528 to complete each analogy. In each, your choice should create a word pair that matches the relationship between the first two words.

1. sugar : sweetness :: time : _____

2. bucket : water :: _____ : information

3. arrived : departed :: continued : _____

4. people : groups :: pages : _____

5. knew : guessed :: proved : _____

6. persuade: convince :: mimic : _____

**Word Study** Use the context of the sentences and what you know about the **Latin root -sum-** to explain your answer to each question.

1. If you *resume* an activity, do you stop doing it?

2. Is it wise to make a *presumption* about someone else's wishes?

### Word Study

The **Latin root -sum-** means "to take."

**Apply It** Explain how the root *-sum-* contributes to the meanings of these words. Consult a dictionary if necessary.

**assume**

**sumptuous**

**consume**

# Integrated Language Skills

## Carry Your Own Skis • Libraries Face Sad Chapter

## Conventions: Adjectives

An **adjective** is a word used to give a noun or pronoun a more specific meaning.

Adjectives modify, or change, nouns and pronouns by telling *what kind, which one, how many,* or *how much.*

| Noun/Pronoun | Question | Adjective and Noun/Pronoun |
|---|---|---|
| school | What kind? | martial arts school |
| student | Which one? | involved student |
| cars | How many?/How much? | three cars |

Usually an adjective comes before the noun it modifies. Sometimes, however, the adjective may follow the noun by coming after a linking verb.

**Before**  The *large, yellow* dog is next door.

**After**  The dog next door is *large and yellow.*

**Practice A**  Identify the adjectives in the following sentences. Then, write a new sentence for each, replacing each adjective with a different adjective.

1. The little child carried the heavy skis.

2. The wet, brown sweater was uncomfortable.

3. Her soggy tuna fish sandwich was tasteless.

4. She smiled as she thought about her wonderful day.

5. The ski slope is long and icy.

**Practice B**  Modify each noun in these sentences with one or more adjectives.

1. Most libraries contain books.

2. Children often make animal drawings.

3. The librarian is a lady.

4. Libraries use technology.

5. Libraries need money.

Ⓒ **Reading Application**  Find two sentences in "Carry Your Own Skis" in which an adjective comes before the noun it modifies. Find two sentences in which the adjective follows its noun.

Ⓒ **Writing Application**  Look at the image on page 532. Write four sentences describing what might be going on in this picture. Use at least two adjectives in each sentence and position them both before *and* after the noun.

**PH** **WRITING COACH**  Further instruction and practice are available in *Prentice Hall Writing Coach.*

# Writing

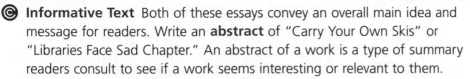 **Informative Text** Both of these essays convey an overall main idea and message for readers. Write an **abstract** of "Carry Your Own Skis" or "Libraries Face Sad Chapter." An abstract of a work is a type of summary readers consult to see if a work seems interesting or relevant to them.

- Clearly state the main point of the **essay.**

- Briefly convey important supporting details.

- Be sure your abstract will help those who have not read the essay.

**Grammar Application** Make sure all adjectives in your abstract are properly placed.

## Writing Workshop: *Work in Progress*

**Prewriting for Editorial** For an editorial you may write, identify and list at least three specific elements of music, fashion, books, or movies that influence you. Put this Cultural Influences List in your writing portfolio.

 **Common Core State Standards**

**L.9-10.1; W.9-10.4; SL.9-10.4**
[For the full wording of the standards, see page 518.]

Use this prewriting activity to prepare for the **Writing Workshop** on page 582.

# Research and Technology

**Build and Present Knowledge** Do research and create a **comparative chart.** Use the chart in preparing and giving a **persuasive speech.**

- If you read "Carry Your Own Skis," research today's popular winter sports. Create a chart that shows which sports have the most participants and largest audience. In your speech, persuade your audience to support one of the less popular sports, making it more visible.

- If you read "Libraries Face Sad Chapter," research the services offered by libraries today. Create a chart that shows the variety of services and the average numbers of people using them. In your speech, persuade your audience to use the library more.

Follow these steps to complete the assignment:

- Follow appropriate conventions for documentation of your source material. Consult page R36 for more information.

- Organize your presentation logically and include an introduction, body, and conclusion.

- Prepare your presentation with your audience in mind, using effective verbal and nonverbal gestures in order to be persuasive.

- Include relevant media to make your chart and oral presentation effective.

**PHLit Online!**
www.PHLitOnline.com
- Interactive graphic organizers
- Grammar tutorial
- Interactive journals

## ⓒ Leveled Texts

Build your skills and improve your comprehension of types of nonfiction with texts of increasing complexity.

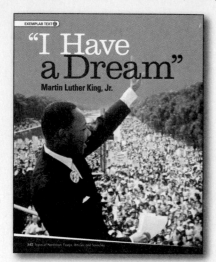

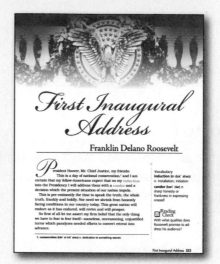

Read **"I Have a Dream"** to discover the power of an idea and a speech.

Read **"First Inaugural Address"** to learn how a president inspired hope during a challenging time.

## ⓒ Common Core State Standards

Meet these standards with either **"I Have a Dream"** (p. 542) or **"First Inaugural Address"** (p. 552).

### Reading Informational Text

**6.** Determine an author's point of view or purpose in a text and analyze how an author uses rhetoric to advance that point of view or purpose. *(Reading Skill: Evaluate Persuasion)*

**8.** Delineate and evaluate the argument and specific claims in a text, assessing whether the reasoning is valid and the evidence is relevant and sufficient; identify false statements and fallacious reasoning. *(Reading Skill: Evaluate Persuasion)*

**9.** Analyze seminal U.S. documents of historical and literary significance, including how they address related themes and concepts. *(Literary Analysis: Persuasive Speech)*

### Writing

**1.** Write arguments to support claims in an analysis of substantive topics or texts, using valid reasoning and relevant and sufficient evidence. *(Writing: Proposal)*

### Speaking and Listening

**3.** Evaluate a speaker's point of view, reasoning, and use of evidence and rhetoric, identifying any fallacious reasoning or exaggerated or distorted evidence. *(Speaking and Listening: Radio News Report)*

### Language

**3.** Apply knowledge of language to understand how language functions in different contexts, to make effective choices for meaning or style, and to comprehend more fully when reading or listening. *(Conventions: Adverbs)*

**6.** Acquire and use accurately grade-appropriate general academic and domain-specific words and phrases; gather vocabulary knowledge when considering a word or phrase important to comprehension or expression. *(Vocabulary: Latin Roots)*

# Literary Analysis: Persuasive Speech

In a **persuasive speech,** a speaker tries to convince listeners to think or act in a certain way. Good persuasive speeches present information and supporting evidence clearly, concisely, and logically so listeners can follow the reasoning. Persuasive speakers often use **rhetorical devices,** patterns of words and ideas that create emphasis and stir emotion. Common rhetorical devices include the following:

- **Parallelism:** repeating a grammatical structure or an arrangement of words to create rhythm and momentum
- **Restatement:** expressing the same idea in different words to clarify and stress key points
- **Repetition:** using the same words frequently to reinforce concepts and unify the speech
- **Analogy:** drawing a comparison that shows a similarity between two unlike things

# Reading Skill: Evaluate Persuasion

**Persuasive techniques** are devices used to influence the audience in favor of the author's argument. In addition to presenting evidence in a persuasive speech, a speaker may also use *emotionally charged language* and rhetorical devices such as those described above.

To analyze and evaluate persuasive techniques, **read aloud to hear the effect.** Notice the emotional impact of certain words and of the rhythm and momentum created by specific word patterns.

As you read, consider the purpose and effect of these techniques and then decide whether the speaker has supported his ideas with valid evidence.

## Using the Strategy: Techniques Chart

Use a chart like this one to analyze the effect of persuasive techniques.

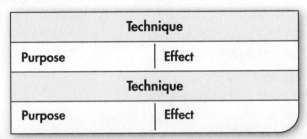

| Technique | |
|---|---|
| **Purpose** | **Effect** |
| Technique | |
| **Purpose** | **Effect** |

**Is** *knowledge* **the same as** *understanding?*

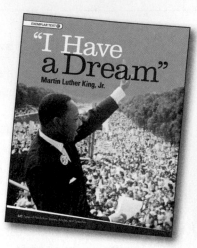

### Writing About the Big Question

In "I Have a Dream," Martin Luther King, Jr., makes a logical and emotional speech to help listeners understand his dream of freedom and equality. Use these sentence starters to develop your ideas about the Big Question.

The **concept** of equality might be **ambiguous** to some people because _____.

To ensure equality exists in our country, we must make **connections** with each other because _____.

**While You Read** Look for the arguments and evidence King uses to help his listeners understand his experience.

### Vocabulary

Read each word and its definition. Decide whether you know the word well, know it a little bit, or do not know it at all. After you read, see how your knowledge of each word has increased.

- **momentous** (mō men´ təs) *adj.* very important (p. 543) *The opening of the new library was a momentous occasion in our town.* *moment n. momentum n.*

- **defaulted** (dē fôlt´ əd) *v.* failed to do something or be somewhere when required or expected; failed to make payment when due (p. 543) *The homeowners defaulted on their loan and lost their house.* *default n. default v.*

- **hallowed** (hal´ ōd) *adj.* sacred (p. 544) *The old battlefield is considered by many to be hallowed ground.* *hallow v.*

- **degenerate** (dē jen´ ər āt´) *v.* grow worse (p. 545) *Don't let this discussion degenerate into a shouting match.* *generate v.*

- **creed** (krēd) *n.* statement of belief (p. 546) *The creed of compassion is preached by many who do not practice it.* *credence n.*

- **oppression** (ə presh´ ən) *n.* keeping others down by the unjust use of power (p. 546) *The oppression of the poor by the rich is the theme of many novels and plays.* *oppress v. oppressive adj.*

**Word Study**

The **Latin root -cred-** means "to trust; to believe."

In this speech, King refers to America's **creed,** or statement of belief, that all people are created equal.

Author of

# "I Have a Dream"

Born in Atlanta, Georgia, Dr. Martin Luther King, Jr., was one of the most charismatic leaders of the civil rights movement. During the 1950s and 1960s, King organized nonviolent protests to bring about equal rights for all Americans.

**A Voice for the Oppressed** King first came to national attention in 1956 in Montgomery, Alabama, when he organized a 382-day boycott by African Americans of the city's segregated buses. He went on to lead other protests and to speak out eloquently against poverty and social injustice. He was assassinated on April 4, 1968. His birthday, January 15, has since become a national holiday.

## BACKGROUND FOR THE SPEECH

### The Civil Rights Movement

The U.S. Constitution guarantees certain rights to all Americans. The struggle of African Americans to have their rights recognized is known as the civil rights movement. Marked by demonstrations and legal challenges, this movement began in the 1950s and was led by figures like Martin Luther King, Jr.

## Did You Know?

At thirty-five, King became the youngest man and only the third black man to be awarded a Nobel Peace Prize.

# "I Have a Dream"

## Martin Luther King, Jr.

Five score years ago, a great American, in whose symbolic shadow we stand today, signed the Emancipation Proclamation. This momentous decree came as a great beacon light of hope to millions of Negro slaves who had been seared in the flames of withering injustice. It came as a joyous daybreak to end the long night of their captivity.

But one hundred years later, the Negro still is not free. One hundred years later, the life of the Negro is still sadly crippled by the manacles of segregation and the chains of discrimination. One hundred years later, the Negro lives on a lonely island of poverty in the midst of a vast ocean of material prosperity. One hundred years later, the Negro is still languished in the corners of American society and finds himself an exile in his own land. So we've come here today to dramatize a shameful condition. •

In a sense we've come to our nation's Capital to cash a check. When the architects of our republic wrote the magnificent words of the Constitution and the Declaration of Independence, they were signing a promissory note[1] to which every American was to fall heir. This note was a promise that all men, yes, black men as well as white men, would be guaranteed the unalienable rights of life, liberty, and the pursuit of happiness.

It is obvious today that America has defaulted on this promissory note insofar as her citizens of color are concerned. Instead of honoring this sacred obligation, America has given the Negro people a bad check; a check which has come back marked "insufficient funds." But we refuse to believe that the bank of justice is bankrupt. We refuse to believe that there are insufficient funds in the great vaults of opportunity of this nation. And so we've come to cash this check—a check that will give us upon demand the riches of freedom and the security of justice. We have also come to

---

1. **promissory** (präm´ i sôr´ ē) **note** written promise to pay a specific amount.

◀ **Critical Viewing** Which details in this photograph demonstrate the importance of the event at which King gave his speech? **[Analyze]**

**Vocabulary**
**momentous**
(mō men´ təs) *adj.*
very important

**defaulted** (dē fôlt´ əd)
*v.* failed to do something or be somewhere when required or expected; failed to make payment when due

**Spiral Review**
**Word Choice** What ideas and images do King's words evoke in the paragraph beginning, "But one hundred years later..."?

**Literary Analysis**
**Persuasive Speech**
Explain King's analogy between a financial transaction and the idea of justice.

**Reading Check**
What injustices are King and his listeners protesting?

"I Have a Dream" **543**

**Vocabulary**
**hallowed** (hal′ ōd)
*adj.* sacred

**Literary Analysis**
**Persuasive Speech**
What idea does King's
repetition of the
word "Now" help to
emphasize?

this hallowed spot to remind America of the fierce urgency of *now*. This is no time to engage in the luxury of cooling off or to take the tranquilizing drug of gradualism.

*Now* is the time to make real the promises of Democracy.

*Now* is the time to rise from the dark and desolate valley of segregation to the sunlit path of racial justice.

*Now* is the time to lift our nation from the quicksands of racial injustice to the solid rock of brotherhood.

*Now* is the time to make justice a reality for all of God's children.

It would be fatal for the nation to overlook the urgency of the moment. This sweltering summer of the Negro's legitimate discontent will not pass until there is an invigorating autumn of freedom and equality. Nineteen sixty-three is not an end, but a beginning. Those who hope that the Negro needed to blow off steam and will now be content will have a rude awakening if the nation returns to business as usual. There will be neither rest nor tranquillity in America until the Negro is granted his citizenship rights. The whirlwinds of revolt will continue to shake the foundations of our nation until the bright day of justice emerges.

But there is something that I must say to my people who stand on the warm threshold which leads into the palace of justice. In the process of gaining our rightful place we must not be guilty of wrongful deeds. Let us not seek to satisfy our thirst for freedom

▼ **Critical Viewing**
Describe King's
expression as he delivers
his speech. **[Analyze]**

by drinking from the cup of bitterness and hatred. We must forever conduct our struggle on the high plane of dignity and discipline. We must not allow our creative protest to degenerate into physical violence. Again and again we must rise to the majestic heights of meeting physical force with soul force. The marvelous new militancy which has engulfed the Negro community must not lead us to a distrust of all white people, for many of our white brothers, as evidenced by their presence here today, have come to realize that their destiny is tied up with our destiny. And they have come to realize that their freedom is inextricably bound to our freedom. We cannot walk alone. ⦁

And as we walk, we must make the pledge that we shall always march ahead. We cannot turn back. There are those who are asking the devotees of civil rights, "When will you be satisfied?" We can never be satisfied as long as the Negro is the victim of the unspeakable horrors of police brutality. We can never be satisfied as long as our bodies, heavy with the fatigue of travel, cannot gain lodging in the motels of the highways and the hotels of the cities. We cannot be satisfied as long as the Negro's basic mobility is from a smaller ghetto to a larger one. We cannot be satisfied as long as a Negro in Mississippi cannot vote and a Negro in New York believes he has nothing for which to vote. No, no, we are not satisfied, and we will not be satisfied until justice rolls down like waters and righteousness like a mighty stream.

I am not unmindful that some of you have come here out of great trials and tribulations. Some of you have come fresh from narrow jail cells. Some of you have come from areas where your quest for freedom left you battered by the storms of persecution and staggered by the winds of police brutality. You have been the veterans of creative suffering. Continue to work with the faith that unearned suffering is redemptive.

Go back to Mississippi, go back to Alabama, go back to South Carolina, go back to Georgia, go back to Louisiana, go back to the slums and ghettos of our northern cities, knowing that somehow this situation can and will be changed. Let us not wallow in the valley of despair.

I say to you today, my friends, so even though we face the difficulties of today and tomorrow, I still have a dream. It is a dream deeply rooted in the American dream.

**Vocabulary**
**degenerate** (dē jen´ ər āt´) v. grow worse

**Literary Analysis**
**Persuasive Speech**
What idea does King restate when he says, "We cannot walk alone"?

Reading Check
According to King, how should his people react to physical force?

**Vocabulary**
**creed** (krēd) *n.*
statement of belief

**oppression**
(ə presh´ ən) *n.* keeping
others down by the
unjust use of power

I have a dream that one day this nation will rise up and live out the true meaning of its creed: "We hold these truths to be self-evident; that all men are created equal."

I have a dream that one day on the red hills of Georgia the sons of former slaves and the sons of former slaveowners will be able to sit down together at the table of brotherhood.

I have a dream that one day even the state of Mississippi, a state sweltering with the heat of injustice, sweltering with the heat of oppression, will be transformed into an oasis of freedom and justice.

I have a dream that my four little children will one day live in a nation where they will not be judged by the color of their skin but by the content of their character.

I have a dream today.

I have a dream that one day down in Alabama, with its vicious racists, with its governor still having his lips dripping with the words of interposition and nullification,[2] one day right down in Alabama little black boys and black girls will be able to join hands with little white boys and white girls as sisters and brothers.

I have a dream today.

I have a dream that one day every valley shall be exalted, every hill and mountain shall be made low, the rough places will be made plains, and the crooked places will be made straight, and the glory of the Lord shall be revealed, and all flesh shall see it together.[3]

This is our hope. This is the faith that I go back to the South with. With this faith we will be able to hew out of the mountain of despair a stone of hope. With this faith we will be able to transform the jangling discords of our nation into a beautiful symphony of brotherhood. With this faith we will be able to work together, to pray together, to struggle together, to go to jail together, to stand up for freedom together, knowing that we will be free one day.

This will be the day when all of God's children will be able to sing with new meaning

My country, 'tis of thee,
Sweet land of liberty,
    Of thee I sing:
Land where my fathers died,
Land of the pilgrims' pride,
From every mountainside
    Let freedom ring.

**Literary Analysis**
**Persuasive Speech**
Identify the parallel clauses in this passage and explain how they emphasize King's ideas.

**Reading Skill**
**Persuasive Techniques**
What idea does King reinforce using the rhythm of repetition?

▶ **Critical Viewing**
Based on this image, in what ways does King use body language to make his speech more effective? **[Interpret]**

---

2. **interposition** (in´ tər pə zish´ ən) **and nullification** (nul´ ə fi kā´ shən) disputed doctrine that a state can reject federal laws considered to be violations of its rights. Governor George C. Wallace used this doctrine to reject federal civil rights legislation.
3. **every valley . . . all flesh shall see it together** reference to a biblical passage (Isaiah 40:4–5). King is likening the struggle of African Americans to the struggle of the Israelites.

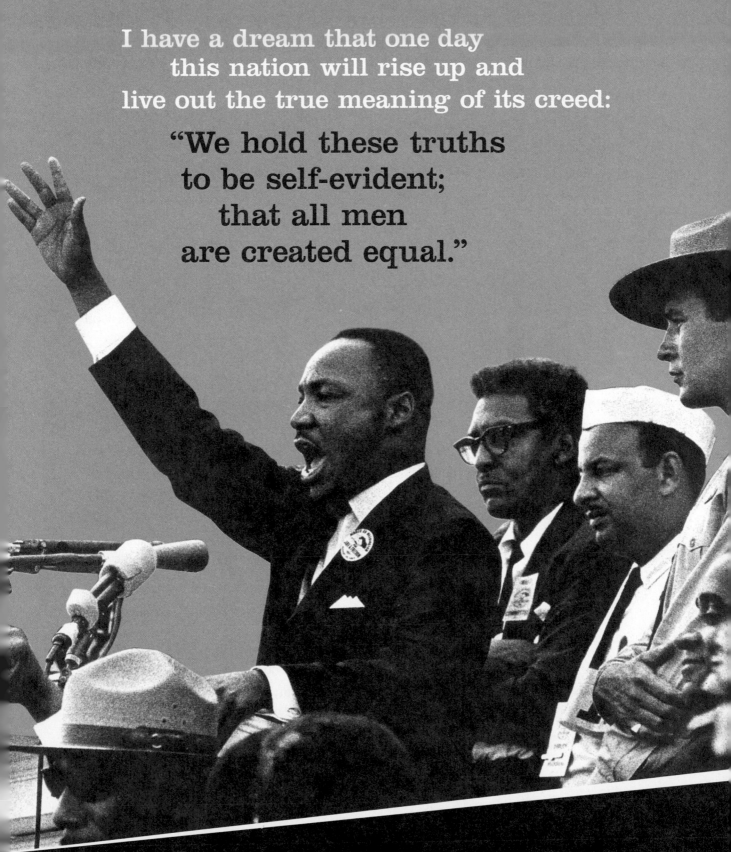

I have a dream that one day
this nation will rise up and
live out the true meaning of its creed:

"We hold these truths
to be self-evident;
that all men
are created equal."

## From every mountainside, let freedom ring.

And if America is to be a great nation this must become true. So let freedom ring from the prodigious hilltops of New Hampshire. Let freedom ring from the mighty mountains of New York. Let freedom ring from the heightening Alleghenies of Pennsylvania!

Let freedom ring from the snowcapped Rockies of Colorado!

Let freedom ring from the curvacious slopes of California!

But not only that; let freedom ring from Stone Mountain of Georgia!

Let freedom ring from Lookout Mountain of Tennessee!

Let freedom ring from every hill and molehill of Mississippi. From every mountainside, let freedom ring.

And when this happens, when we allow freedom to ring, when we let it ring from every village and every hamlet, from every state and every city, we will be able to speed up that day when all of God's children, black men and white men, Jews and Gentiles, Protestants and Catholics, will be able to join hands and sing in the words of the old Negro spiritual, "Free at last! free at last! thank God almighty, we are free at last!"

## Critical Thinking

Cite textual evidence to support your responses.

© **1. Craft and Structure (a)** Which words does King quote from "My Country 'Tis of Thee"? **(b) Interpret:** What impact are these words intended to have on the audience? What message is conveyed? What tone?

© **2. Key Ideas and Details (a)** Which different parts of the United States does King mention in his speech? **(b) Connect:** How does the mention of all of these places help to convey King's central idea and his purpose in the speech?

© **3. Integration of Knowledge and Ideas (a) Hypothesize:** Why do you think "I Have a Dream" has lived on as one of the best-known speeches in modern history? **(b) Make a Judgment:** Do you think it deserves this standing? Explain your response.

© **4. Integration of Knowledge and Ideas (a)** What facts and information does King give to increase your knowledge of equality in America in the 1960s? **(b)** Do the experiences he shares help you understand the importance of his dream? Explain. *[Connect to the Big Question: Is knowledge the same as understanding?]*

## Literary Analysis: Persuasive Speech

**1. Key Ideas and Details** In this **persuasive speech,** what is Martin Luther King, Jr.'s, purpose? Explain.

**2. Craft and Structure** What examples of figurative or connotative words appeal to the audience's emotions? To their reason? Explain.

**3. Craft and Structure** In a chart like this, list examples of **rhetorical devices** in King's speech. Then, describe the effect of each one.

| | Example | Effect |
|---|---|---|
| Restatement | | |
| Repetition | | |
| Parallelism | | |
| Analogy | | |

**4. Key Ideas and Details (a)** What evidence does King use to support his position? **(b)** What details are most valid to his argument? Why?

## Reading Skill: Evaluate Persuasion

**5. (a)** Identify a passage in which King uses emotionally charged language as a **persuasive technique. (b)** What specific purpose do you think King had in using such language? Explain.

**6.** Does King use rhetorical devices effectively? Explain.

## Vocabulary

**Acquisition and Use  Analogies** show the relationships between words. Use a word from page 540 to complete each analogy.

**1.** stumble : rise :: _____ : improve

**2.** oath : office :: _____ : religion

**3.** barren : desert :: _____ : church

**4.** dull : interesting :: trivial : _____

**5.** supportive : harmful :: assistance : _____

**6.** broken : promise :: _____ : agreement

**Word Study** Use the context of the sentences and what you know about the **Latin root -cred-** to explain your answer to each question.

**1.** Should a judge in a criminal trial have *credibility*?

**2.** How would you feel if someone tried to *discredit* you?

### Word Study

The **Latin root -cred-** means "to trust; to believe."

**Apply It** Explain how the root *-cred-* contributes to the meanings of these words. Consult a dictionary if necessary.

credit
credential
incredible

**Is *knowledge* the same as *understanding?***

## Writing About the Big Question

In "First Inaugural Address," President Roosevelt acknowledges the hard realities of the Great Depression and he promises to do whatever is necessary to help the nation recover. Use this sentence starter to develop your ideas about the Big Question.

For leaders to inspire confidence, they must **comprehend** _____ because _____.

**While You Read** Look for evidence that the President understands why people are suffering and also why they should have hope.

## Vocabulary

Read each word and its definition. Decide whether you know the word well, know it a little bit, or do not know it at all. After you read, see how your knowledge of each word has increased.

- **induction** (in duk´ shən) *n.* installation; initiation (p.553) *At his official* <u>induction</u> *into the school's honor society, Pedro gave a speech.* induct *v.* inductee *n.*

- **candor** (kan´ dər) *n.* sharp honesty or frankness in expressing oneself (p. 553) *Joanna spoke with great* <u>candor</u> *about her feelings for her mother.* candid *adj.*

- **abdicated** (ab´ di kāt´ əd) *v.* gave up formally (p. 555) *The king* <u>abdicated</u> *his throne and left the country.* abdicator *n.*

- **discipline** (dis´ ə plin´) *n.* training that develops self-control, character, or efficiency (p. 557) *Working from home requires a great deal of* <u>discipline</u>. discipline *v.* disciplinary *adj.*

- **feasible** (fē´ zə bəl) *adj.* capable of being done or carried out; practicable; possible (p. 559) *Solar heating is both technically and economically* <u>feasible</u>. feasibility *n.*

- **arduous** (är´ jo͞o əs) *adj.* difficult; laborious (p. 559) *Rebuilding the house by ourselves was an* <u>arduous</u> *task.*

### Word Study

The **Latin root -*duct*-** or -*duc*- means "to lead" or "to bring."

Roosevelt speaks during his **induction**—the ceremony that brought him into his role as president of the United States.

Author of

## *First Inaugural Address*

Franklin Delano Roosevelt had a relatively easy life until he was stricken with polio at age 39. Ironically, Roosevelt realized his potential as a leader only after falling victim to this illness. He was twice elected governor of New York; then, in 1932, he defeated President Herbert Hoover to become the nation's thirty-second president. Roosevelt won an unprecedented four terms as president.

**A Leader in Dark Times** Franklin Roosevelt led the nation through two great challenges: the Great Depression and World War II. The war was almost over when the president died of a cerebral hemorrhage in 1945.

## BACKGROUND FOR THE SPEECH

**The Great Depression**

On March 4, 1933, newly elected President Franklin Delano Roosevelt delivered his inaugural address to a nation close to despair. The Great Depression had weighed down American life for more than three years. Americans sat by their radios to hear the new president's address, a speech he had written himself. In this speech, Roosevelt gave Americans hope.

## Did You Know?

Roosevelt's wife, Eleanor, became one of the most active and widely admired first ladies in American history.

# First Inaugural Address

## Franklin Delano Roosevelt

President Hoover, Mr. Chief Justice, my friends:

This is a day of national consecration,[1] and I am certain that my fellow-Americans expect that on my induction into the Presidency I will address them with a candor and a decision which the present situation of our nation impels.

This is pre-eminently the time to speak the truth, the whole truth, frankly and boldly. Nor need we shrink from honestly facing conditions in our country today. This great nation will endure as it has endured, will revive and will prosper.

So first of all let me assert my firm belief that the only thing we have to fear is fear itself—nameless, unreasoning, unjustified terror which paralyzes needed efforts to convert retreat into advance.

---

1. **consecration** (kän′ si krā′ shən) n. dedication to something sacred.

**Vocabulary**

**induction** (in duk′ shən) n. installation; initiation

**candor** (kan′ dər) n. sharp honesty or frankness in expressing oneself

Reading
Check

With what qualities does Roosevelt promise to address his audience?

**Reading Skill**
**Persuasive Techniques**
How do you think
Roosevelt wanted
listeners to respond to
the emotionally charged
language here?

▼ **Critical Viewing**
This is a photograph of
a bread line during the
Great Depression. Why
do you think conditions
like this might have
made Americans fearful?
**[Infer]**

In every dark hour of our national life a leadership of frankness and vigor has met with that understanding and support of the people themselves which is essential to victory. I am convinced that you will again give that support to leadership in these critical days.

In such a spirit on my part and on yours we face our common difficulties. They concern, thank God, only material things. Values have shrunken to fantastic levels; taxes have risen; our ability to pay has fallen, government of all kinds is faced by serious curtailment of income; the means of exchange are frozen in the currents of trade; the withered leaves of industrial enterprise lie on every side; farmers find no markets for their produce; the savings of many years in thousands of families are gone.

More important, a host of unemployed citizens face the grim problem of existence, and an equally great number toil with little return. Only a foolish optimist can deny the dark realities of the moment.

Yet our distress comes from no failure of substance. We are stricken by no plague of locusts.[2] Compared with the perils which our forefathers conquered because they believed and were not afraid, we have still much to be thankful for. Nature still offers

---

2. **plague of locusts** According to Exodus 10:3–20, the plague of locusts was one of ten plagues inflicted by God on the Egyptians as punishment for enslaving the Israelites.

Only a foolish optimist can deny the dark realities of the moment.

her bounty and human efforts have multiplied it. Plenty is at our doorstep, but a generous use of it languishes in the very sight of the supply.

Primarily, this is because the rulers of the exchange of mankind's goods have failed through their own stubbornness and their own incompetence, have admitted that failure and abdicated. Practices of the unscrupulous money changers stand indicted in the court of public opinion, rejected by the hearts and minds of men.

True, they have tried, but their efforts have been cast in the pattern of an outworn tradition. Faced by failure of credit, they have proposed only the lending of more money.

Stripped of the lure of profit by which to induce our people to follow their false leadership, they have resorted to exhortations, pleading tearfully for restored confidence. They know only the rules of a generation of self-seekers.

They have no vision, and when there is no vision the people perish.

The money changers have fled from their high seats in the temple[3] of our civilization. We may now restore that temple to the ancient truths. ●

---

3. **money changers . . . temple** allusion to Matthew 21:12–13, in which Jesus overturns the money changers' tables at the temple in Jerusalem. FDR is comparing those ancient money changers to modern bankers who took great risks with depositors' money and who charged excessive interest rates for loans.

**Literary Analysis**
**Persuasive Speech**
How might this description of national problems have changed people's minds about their troubles?

**Vocabulary**
**abdicated** (ab´ di kāt´ əd) *v.* gave up formally

Reading Check
On whom does Roosevelt place the largest blame for the Great Depression?

The measure of the restoration lies in the extent to which we apply social values more noble than mere monetary profit.

Happiness lies not in the mere possession of money; it lies in the joy of achievement, in the thrill of creative effort.

The joy and moral stimulation of work no longer must be forgotten in the mad chase of evanescent profits. These dark days will be worth all they cost us if they teach us that our true destiny is not to be ministered unto but to minister to ourselves and to our fellow-men.

Recognition of the falsity of material wealth as the standard of success goes hand in hand with the abandonment of the false belief that public office and high political position are to be valued only by the standards of pride of place and personal profit; and there must be an end to a conduct in banking and in business which too often has given to a sacred trust the likeness of callous and selfish wrongdoing.

Small wonder that confidence languishes, for it thrives only on honesty, on honor, on the sacredness of obligations, on faithful protection, on unselfish performance. Without them it cannot live.

Restoration calls, however, not for changes in ethics alone. This nation asks for action, and action now.

Our greatest primary task is to put people to work. This is no unsolvable problem if we face it wisely and courageously. . . .

I favor as a practical policy the putting of first things first. I shall spare no effort to restore world trade by international economic readjustment, but the emergency at home cannot wait on that accomplishment.

The basic thought that guides these specific means of national recovery is not narrowly nationalistic.

It is the insistence, as a first consideration, upon the interdependence of the various elements in, and parts of, the United States—a recognition of the old and permanently important manifestation of the American spirit of the pioneer.

It is the way to recovery. It is the immediate way. It is the strongest assurance that the recovery will endure.

In the field of world policy I would dedicate this nation to the policy of the good neighbor—the neighbor who resolutely respects himself and, because he does so, respects the rights of others—the

**Spiral Review**
**Word Choice** How do Roosevelt's words about the moral stimulation of work create a meaning and tone suitable for the occasion?

> Happiness lies not in the mere possession of money; it lies in the joy of achievement, in the thrill of creative effort.

**Literary Analysis**
**Persuasive Speech**
Identify the parallelism in the paragraph beginning "It is the way . . ." and explain what idea it emphasizes.

neighbor who respects his obligations and respects the sanctity of his agreements in and with a world of neighbors.

If I read the temper of our people correctly, we now realize as we have never before, our interdependence on each other; that we cannot merely take, but we must give as well; that if we are to go forward we must move as a trained and loyal army willing to sacrifice for the good of a common discipline, because, without such discipline, no progress is made, no leadership becomes effective.

We are, I know, ready and willing to submit our lives and property to such discipline because it makes possible a leadership which aims at a larger good. •

### ✓ Reading Check

What does Roosevelt say is the "greatest primary task" facing the nation?

## LITERATURE IN CONTEXT

### Social Studies Connection

**Getting Back to Work: FDR and the WPA**
In 1935, President Roosevelt established the Works Progress Administration (WPA) to aid struggling Americans. At the height of its activity, the WPA provided jobs to one third of the unemployed, ranging from artists to construction workers.

▲ This mural painted by WPA artist William Gropper shows the building of a WPA project dam.

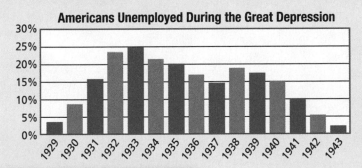

**Americans Unemployed During the Great Depression**

| Year | Percent |
| --- | --- |
| 1929 | 4% |
| 1930 | 9% |
| 1931 | 16% |
| 1932 | 23% |
| 1933 | 25% |
| 1934 | 22% |
| 1935 | 20% |
| 1936 | 17% |
| 1937 | 15% |
| 1938 | 19% |
| 1939 | 17% |
| 1940 | 15% |
| 1941 | 10% |
| 1942 | 5% |
| 1943 | 3% |

**The WPA Projects**

| | | |
| --- | --- | --- |
| WPA workers produced: | 650,000 | miles of roads |
| | 125,000 | public buildings |
| | 75,000 | bridges |
| | 8,000 | parks |
| | 800 | airports |
| WPA artists created: | 2,566 | murals |
| | 100,000 | paintings |
| | 17,700 | sculptures |
| | 300,000 | fine prints |

### Connect to the Literature

President Roosevelt gave his First Inaugural Address in March of 1933. Basing your answer on the chart of unemployment, explain why this was a particularly hard time in American life.

First Inaugural Address **557**

This I propose to offer, pledging that the larger purposes will bind upon us all as a sacred obligation with a unity of duty hitherto evoked only in time of armed strife.

With this pledge taken, I assume unhesitatingly the leadership of this great army of our people, dedicated to a disciplined attack upon our common problems.

Action in this image and to this end is feasible under the forms of government which we have inherited from our ancestors.

Our Constitution is so simple and practical that it is possible always to meet extraordinary needs by changes in emphasis and arrangement without loss of essential form.

That is why our constitutional system has proved itself the most superbly enduring political mechanism the modern world has produced. It has met every stress of vast expansion of territory, of foreign wars, of bitter internal strife, of world relations. . . .

I am prepared under my constitutional duty to recommend the measures that a stricken nation in the midst of a stricken world may require.

These measures, or such other measures as the Congress may build out of its experience and wisdom, I shall seek, within my constitutional authority, to bring to speedy adoption.

But in the event that the Congress shall fail to take one of these two courses, and in the event that the national emergency is still critical, I shall not evade the clear course of duty that will then confront me.

I shall ask the Congress for the one remaining instrument to meet the crisis—broad executive power to wage a war against the emergency as great as the power that would be given me if we were in fact invaded by a foreign foe. •

For the trust reposed in me I will return the courage and the devotion that befit the time. I can do no less.

We face the arduous days that lie before us in the warm courage of national unity; with the clear consciousness of seeking

> Our Constitution is so simple and practical that it is possible always to meet extraordinary needs by changes . . .

**Vocabulary**
**feasible** (fē´ zə bəl)
*adj.* capable of being done or carried out; practicable; possible

**Literary Analysis**
**Persuasive Speech**
What call to action does Roosevelt issue to Congress in this passage?

**Vocabulary**
**arduous** (är´ jo͞o əs)
*adj.* difficult; laborious

◀ **Critical Viewing**
This photograph of President Roosevelt in the Oval Office was taken on the day of his first inauguration. Do you think he projects an image of confidence? Explain. **[Analyze]**

old and precious moral values; with the clean satisfaction that comes from the stern performance of duty by old and young alike.

We aim at the assurance of a rounded and permanent national life.

We do not distrust the future of essential democracy. The people of the United States have not failed. In their need they have registered a mandate that they want direct, vigorous action.

They have asked for discipline and direction under leadership. They have made me the present instrument of their wishes. In the spirit of the gift I take it.

In this dedication of a nation we humbly ask the blessing of God. May He protect each and every one of us. May He guide me in the days to come.

## Critical Thinking

Cite textual evidence to support your responses.

© **1. Craft and Structure (a)** What words does Roosevelt use to describe the leaders who caused the country's financial problems? **(b) Interpret:** What impact are these words intended have on the audience? What message is conveyed? What tone?

© **2. Key Ideas and Details (a)** What does Roosevelt say about Americans from earlier periods in history? **(b) Speculate:** How do you think his listeners felt on hearing about earlier Americans?

© **3. Craft and Structure Make a Judgment:** Roosevelt's speech was made more than seventy years ago to a country in economic ruin. Which parts of the speech do you think would be most appealing to Americans today? Which parts might be less appealing? Explain.

© **4. Integration of Knowledge and Ideas (a)** What information in this speech lets you know that Roosevelt understands the country he is about to lead? **(b)** What is the main thing he wants his listeners to understand? *[Connect to the Big Question: Is knowledge the same as understanding?]*

## Literary Analysis: Persuasive Essay

Ⓒ **1. Key Ideas and Details** In this **persuasive speech,** what is President Roosevelt's purpose? Explain.

Ⓒ **2. Craft and Structure** What examples of figurative or connotative words appeal to the audience's emotions? To their reason? Explain.

Ⓒ **3. Craft and Structure** In a chart like this, list examples in Roosevelt's speech of **rhetorical devices,** and describe the effect of each one.

| | Example | Effect |
|---|---|---|
| Restatement | | |
| Repetition | | |
| Parallelism | | |
| Analogy | | |

Ⓒ **4. Key Ideas and Details (a)** What evidence does Roosevelt use to support his position? **(b)** What details are most valid? Why?

## Reading Skill: Persuasive Techniques

**5. (a)** Identify a passage in which Roosevelt uses emotionally charged language as a **persuasive technique. (b)** What purpose do you think he had in using such language in the passage? Explain.

**6.** Does Roosevelt use rhetorical devices effectively? Explain.

## Vocabulary

Ⓒ **Acquisition and Use Analogies** show relationships between pairs of words. Use a word from page 550 to complete each analogy.

**1.** coach : resigned :: ruler : _____

**2.** vacation : relaxing :: labor : _____

**3.** insecurity : confidence :: deception : _____

**4.** vague : definite :: impossible : _____

**5.** initiation : fraternity :: _____ : military

**6.** left : right :: laxness : _____

**Word Study** Use the context of sentences and what you know about the **Latin root -duct-** or **-duc-** to explain your answer to each question.

**1.** If you *introduce* someone, do you help her meet other people?

**2.** Is a *conductor* someone who watches an orchestra?

### Word Study

The **Latin root -duct-** or **-duc-** means "to lead" or "to bring."

**Apply It** Explain how the root -duct- or -duc- contributes to the meanings of these words. Consult a dictionary if necessary.

**conducive**
**deductible**
**conductivity**

# Integrated Language Skills

## "I Have a Dream" • First Inaugural Address

### Conventions: Adverbs

**Adverbs** are words that modify verbs, adjectives, and other adverbs. They answer the questions *Where? When? In what way?* and *To what extent?* about the words they modify.

An adverb modifying a verb can answer any of the above questions. An adverb modifying an adjective or another adverb will answer only the question *To what extent?*

**Modifying a verb:**
Dave drove the car <u>smoothly.</u> (The adverb *smoothly* modifies the verb *drove*.)

**Modifying an adjective:**
He drove an <u>extremely</u> large car. (The adverb *extremely* modifies the adjective *large*.)

**Modifying another adverb:**
He drove the car <u>very</u> smoothly. (The adverb *very* modifies the adverb *smoothly*.)

**Practice A** Identify the adverbs in the following sentences. Then, tell what question each adverb answers.

1. King stood there waiting to speak.
2. King spoke clearly and passionately before the large audience.
3. The audience was especially attentive to King's words.
4. King spoke more forcefully than people remembered.

**Reading Application** Find three sentences in "I Have a Dream" that include an adverb. Identify the word modified as a verb, an adjective, or another adverb.

**Practice B** In each sentence, identify each adverb and the word it modifies. Then, write a related sentence using a different adverb.

1. Roosevelt spoke compassionately to his audience.
2. Roosevelt often spoke to the nation.
3. Roosevelt very clearly understood the needs of his listeners.
4. Roosevelt was calmly resolute.

**Writing Application** Choose one photo from "First Inaugural Address." Write three sentences to describe the photograph. Use adverbs to modify verbs, adjectives, and adverbs.

**PH WRITING COACH**  Further instruction and practice are available in *Prentice Hall Writing Coach*.

# Writing

**Argument** Both of these speeches use persuasive techniques that inspire listeners. Write a **proposal** to persuade school leaders to invite a great speaker like Dr. King or President Roosevelt to address a school assembly.

- List some issues that concern students at your school, and list details that describe and explain the problem.
- List possible speakers and the issues that each could discuss.
- Choose one speaker, and write a proposal supporting your choice.
- Defend your idea with precise and relevant evidence and logical reasoning, including facts about the speaker and your school. Use logical reasoning to make your case.
- End with an appeal to your principal to act on the proposal.

**Grammar Application** Make sure to use adverbs correctly in your essay.

**Writing Workshop:** *Work in Progress*

**Prewriting for Editorial** Review your Cultural Influences List. Identify one cultural factor that you feel has the greatest effect on you. In a two-column chart, jot down three positive and three negative aspects of this influence. Save this Positive/Negative Chart in your writing portfolio.

Use this prewriting activity to prepare for the **Writing Workshop** on page 582.

# Speaking and Listening

**Presentation of Ideas** Compose a **radio news report** that provides on-the-spot coverage of the speaker whose speech you just read. Include excerpts from the speech, a description of the crowd's reaction and appropriate background information.

- If you read "I Have a Dream," include information about the civil rights movement.
- If you read "First Inaugural Address," include information about the Great Depression.

Follow these steps to complete the assignment:

- Analyze the rhetorical devices and features that made the historical speech you read memorable.
- Consider how the language in the speech and the speaker's delivery would affect the mood and tone of the speech, and imagine how the audience would respond. Choose examples from the speech to quote.
- Add information to provide necessary background for an audience who may not be familiar with the audience or purpose of the speech.
- Broadcast your report to the class, and record it for later evaluation.

## Common Core State Standards

**L.9-10.3; W.9-10.1; SL.9-10.3**
[For the full wording of the standards, see page 538.]

# Test Practice: Reading

## Evaluate Persuasion

### Fiction Selection

**Directions:** *Read the selection. Then, answer the questions.*

David stepped to the front of the class and began his speech: "Scientists say that we need to protect the rain forest, and I agree. Do we want to lose the natural beauty of these areas? Do we want to be denied the medicinal plants that live there? Do we want to see the animals of the rain forest become homeless—or die?" David glanced up and saw his listeners' looks of boredom. He continued, more loudly: "I say no! It's not fair to those parts of the earth, and it's not fair to us!" David waved a sheet of paper over his head as he concluded, "So, if you agree with me, put your name on this petition. Let's get the government to care about this problem!"

**1.** Which type of appeal does David use to open his speech?
   **A.** appeal to evidence
   **B.** appeal to authority
   **C.** appeal to emotion
   **D.** appeal to statistics

**2.** What is David trying to get his listeners to do?
   **A.** join a march protesting the destruction of the rain forest
   **B.** adopt animals made homeless by rain forest destruction
   **C.** sign a petition urging greater protection of the rain forest
   **D.** buy medicines made from plants that grow in the rain forest

**3.** Which of the following strategies is *not* used in David's speech?
   **A.** acknowledgement of opposing viewpoints
   **B.** parallel structure
   **C.** expert opinions
   **D.** clear thesis statement

**4.** The questions beginning with "Do we want . . . " convey a tone of—
   **A.** wishfulness.
   **B.** outrage.
   **C.** determination.
   **D.** wonder.

### Writing for Assessment

Is David's argument well reasoned and logical? Does it convince you to take the action he suggests? Write a paragraph evaluating David's speech. Use details from the passage to support your response.

## Nonfiction Selection

**Directions:** *Read the selection. Then, answer the questions.*

Perhaps the greatest environmental tragedy of our time is the destruction of the Amazon rain forest. The rain forest is home to the most diverse life on Earth. More than 2,000 of the species of rain forest plants are known to have value as medicines, but only about 10 percent of these have been studied. <u>They may disappear before scientists can study and evaluate them</u>. Some organizations, therefore, recommend that nations buy and preserve rain forest land and educate local people about living in the rain forest without destroying it. These are small first steps in saving the rain forest, but they deserve our support.

**1.** Which of the following is an emotionally charged phrase?
- **A.** "only about ten percent of these have been studied"
- **B.** "home to the most diverse life on earth"
- **C.** "Some organizations, therefore, recommend"
- **D.** "greatest environmental tragedy of our time"

**2.** What is the effect of the underlined sentence?
- **A.** It surprises listeners with an unusual analogy.
- **B.** It reminds listeners that the issue is of immediate concern.
- **C.** It comforts listeners with words about hope for the future.
- **D.** It makes listeners feel ashamed of themselves.

**3.** Which of the following details supports the idea that the destruction of the rain forest would be tragic for humanity?
- **A.** Some organizations recommend that nations preserve rain forest land.
- **B.** Many rain forest plants may have undiscovered medicinal value.
- **C.** Life in the rain forest is extremely diverse.
- **D.** Local people can live in harmony with the rain forest.

**4.** The final sentence of the passage—
- **A.** restates the author's main idea.
- **B.** includes a transition to the next idea.
- **C.** provides a call to action.
- **D.** summarizes the author's point of view.

## Writing for Assessment

**Connecting Across Texts**

Write a comparison of the persuasive appeals in these two passages. For each passage, consider the author's motive, the use of rhetorical devices, the inclusion of evidence, and the type of appeal (emotional or logical). Use details from both passages to support your response.

**PHLit**
**Online!**
www.PHLitOnline.com
- Online practice
- Instant feedback

# Reading for Information

## Analyzing Arguments

### Historical Research Study

### Speech

**Common Core State Standards**

**Reading Informational Text**
**6.** Determine an author's point of view or purpose in a text and analyze how an author uses rhetoric to advance that point of view or purpose.
**8.** Delineate and evaluate the argument and specific claims in a text, assessing whether the reasoning is valid and the evidence is relevant and sufficient; identify false statements and fallacious reasoning.
**9.** Analyze seminal U.S. documents of historical and literary significance, including how they address related themes and concepts.

**Language**
**4.b.** Identify and correctly use patterns of word changes that indicate different meanings or parts of speech.

## Reading Skill: Evaluate Credibility

When an author makes an argument, his or her purpose is to convince the audience to adopt a certain position. As a reader or listener, you must **evaluate the credibility** of the argument to determine whether it is valid. Critique the argument to see if generalizations are supported by evidence, and consider the strength of that evidence.

Also note how the structure and tone of the text relate to the author's intent, or purpose. Look for words, phrases, and sentence structures that are repeated, and think about the effect that the author's use of language creates. Ask yourself whether the author is appealing to logic or to emotions. Arguments that appeal only to emotions are not credible.

Use this checklist to help you evaluate an argument's credibility.

---

**Checklist for Evaluating an Author's Argument**

- Does the author present a clear argument?
- Is the argument well-developed and supported by evidence?
- How comprehensive is the evidence?
- Is the argument structured in a logical way?
- Does the author use sound reasoning, or only emotional appeals?

---

## Content-Area Vocabulary

These words appear in the selections that follow. You may also encounter them in other content-area texts.

- **inaugural** (in ô´ gyər əl) *adj.* marking the beginning of an activity or period in office

- **commodities** (kə mod´ ə tēz) *n.* things that are bought and sold

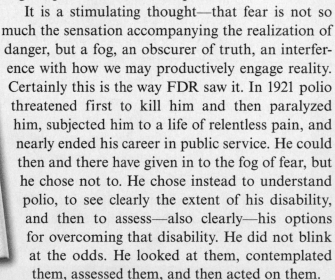

**Features:**
- summary or excerpt of a historical document
- facts and opinions about the document
- explanations and interpretations
- text written for a specific audience

# from **Nothing to Fear:**
## **Lessons in Leadership from FDR**
### *by Alan Axelrod*

*"This great nation will endure as it has endured, will revive and will prosper. So, first of all, let me assert my firm belief that the only thing we have to fear is fear itself—nameless, unreasoning, unjustified terror which paralyzes needed efforts to convert retreat into advance."*

—First **inaugural** address, March 4, 1933

> The study begins with a quotation from a speech by Franklin Delano Roosevelt. It focuses the argument on the famous line, "The only thing we have to fear is fear itself."

In *Defending Your Life*, a charmingly provocative 1991 movie written and directed by its star, Albert Brooks, we discover that the only truly unforgivable sin in life is fear. Killed in a head-on crash with a bus, yuppie Brooks finds himself transported to Judgment City, where he must "defend his life" before a pair of judges who will decide whether he is to be returned to Earth for another crack at life or be permitted to progress to the next plane of existence. His attorney (for the benevolent managers of the universe provide defense assistance) explains to him the nature of fear, which is, he says, a "fog" that obscures everything and that makes intelligent, productive action impossible.

Franklin D. Roosevelt with a local child, 1941.

It is a stimulating thought—that fear is not so much the sensation accompanying the realization of danger, but a fog, an obscurer of truth, an interference with how we may productively engage reality. Certainly this is the way FDR saw it. In 1921 polio threatened first to kill him and then paralyzed him, subjected him to a life of relentless pain, and nearly ended his career in public service. He could then and there have given in to the fog of fear, but he chose not to. He chose instead to understand polio, to see clearly the extent of his disability, and then to assess—also clearly—his options for overcoming that disability. He did not blink at the odds. He looked at them, contemplated them, assessed them, and then acted on them.

Now, more than a decade later, assuming the office of president of the United States, he began by asking the American people to sweep aside the fog of fear, "nameless, unreasoning, unjustified terror which paralyzes needed efforts to convert retreat into advance." He didn't ask them to stop being afraid, but to stop letting fear obscure their vision of reality. He asked the people to confront what they feared, so that they could see clearly what needed to be done and thereby overcome (and the word is significant) the terror that paralyzes.

In the second paragraph of his inaugural speech, FDR lifted the fog of fear. What did he reveal to his audience, the American people?

> Values have shrunken to fantastic levels; taxes have risen; our ability to pay has fallen; government of all kinds is faced by serious curtailment of income; the means of exchange are frozen in the currents of trade; the withered leaves of industrial enterprise lie on every side; farmers find no markets for their produce; the savings of many years in thousands of families are gone.

There is no sugarcoating of reality here! The fog has lifted, the scene is sharply etched and downright frightening: "a host of unemployed citizens face the grim problem of existence, and an equally great number toil with little return. Only a foolish optimist can deny the dark realities of the moment."

FDR did not blink at reality and he did not allow his audience to do so either. He embarked on this catalog of economic disasters by defining them as "our common difficulties," which "concern, thank God, only material things."

The fog was lifted and the president's listeners could see the reality they already knew, a reality of poverty and despair, to be sure; yet with the fog of fear lifted, they could see it in a new light: Our common difficulties "concern, thank God, only material things."

Not one to blink at disaster, FDR also saw a way out of it:

> Yet our distress comes from no failure of substance. We are stricken by no plague of locusts. Compared with the perils which our forefathers conquered because they believed and were not afraid, we have still much to be thankful for. Nature still offers her bounty and human efforts have multiplied it. Plenty is at our doorstep. . .

Lift the fog of fear and you could see that the Great Depression was not of natural, supernatural, or inevitable origin. It was not a plague of biblical proportion. Our kind has conquered worse in the past.

**Axelrod refers back to the "fog" described in the introduction. In later paragraphs, he continues to refer to the "fog of fear." This repetition gives structure to the text.**

**In this paragraph, the author makes a generalization about the speech, then supports the generalization with a direct quotation.**

from
# Radio Address on Drought Conditions

by Franklin Delano Roosevelt
September 6, 1936

I have been on a journey of husbandry. I went primarily to see at first hand conditions in the drought states; to see how effectively Federal and local authorities are taking care of pressing problems of relief and also how they are to work together to defend the people of this country against the effects of future droughts.

I saw drought devastation in nine states.

Roosevelt repeats the word *I* to emphasize his personal experience.

I talked with families who had lost their wheat crop, lost their corn crop, lost their livestock, lost the water in their well, lost their garden and come through to the end of the summer without one dollar of cash resources, facing a winter without feed or food—facing a planting season without seed to put in the ground.

That was the extreme case, but there are thousands and thousands of families on western farms who share the same difficulties.

I saw cattlemen who because of lack of grass or lack of winter feed have been compelled to sell all but their breeding stock and will need help to carry even these through the coming winter. I saw livestock kept alive only because water had been brought to them long distances in tank cars. I saw other farm families who have not lost everything but who, because they have made only partial crops, must have some form of help if they are to continue farming next spring.

Roosevelt gives examples of the hardships he saw to support the argument he is about to make.

I shall never forget the fields of wheat so blasted by heat that they cannot be harvested. I shall never forget field after field of corn stunted, earless and stripped of leaves, for what the sun left the grasshoppers took. I saw brown pastures which would not keep a cow on fifty acres.

Yet I would not have you think for a single minute that there is permanent disaster in these drought regions, or that the picture I saw meant depopulating these areas. No cracked earth, no blistering sun, no burning wind, no grasshoppers, are a permanent match for the indomitable American farmers and stockmen and their wives and children who have carried on through desperate days, and inspire us with their self-reliance, their tenacity and their courage. It was their fathers' task to make homes; it is their task to keep those homes; it is our task to help them with their fight.

First let me talk for a minute about this autumn and the coming winter. We have the option, in the case of families who need actual subsistence, of putting them on the dole or putting them to work. They do not want to go on the dole and they are one thousand percent right. We agree, therefore, that we must put them to work for a decent wage, and when we reach that decision we kill two birds with one stone, because these families will earn enough by working, not only to subsist themselves, but to buy food for their stock, and seed for next year's planting. Into this scheme of things there fit of course the government lending agencies which next year, as in the past, will help with production loans.

Every Governor with whom I have talked is in full accord with this program of doing work for these farm families, just as every Governor agrees that the individual states will take care of their unemployables but that the cost of employing those who are entirely able and willing to work must be borne by the Federal Government. . . .

Spending like this is not waste. It would spell future waste if we did not spend for such things now. These emergency work projects provide money to buy food and clothing for the winter; they keep the livestock on the farm; they provide seed for a new crop, and, best of all, they will conserve soil and water in the future in those areas most frequently hit by drought.

If, for example, in some local area the water table continues to drop and the topsoil to blow away, the land values will disappear with the water and the soil. People on the farms will drift into the nearby cities; the cities will have no farm trade and the workers in the city factories and stores will have no jobs. Property values in the cities will decline. If, on the other hand, the farms within that area remain as farms with better water supply and no erosion, the farm population will stay on the land and prosper and the nearby cities will prosper too. Property values will increase instead of disappearing. That is why it is worth our while as a nation to spend money in order to save money.

. . . The very existence of the men and women working in the clothing factories of New York, making clothes worn by farmers and their families; of the workers in the steel mills in Pittsburgh, in the automobile factories of Detroit, and in the harvester factories of Illinois, depend upon the farmers' ability to purchase the **commodities** they produce. In the same way it is the purchasing power of the workers in these factories in the cities that enables them and their wives and children to eat more beef, more pork, more wheat, more corn, more fruit and more dairy products, and to buy more clothing made from cotton, wool and leather. In a physical and a property sense, as well as in a spiritual sense, we are members one of another.

. . . We are going to have a farm policy that will serve the national welfare. That is our hope for the future.

> The words *spiritual, hope,* and *future* appeal to the audience's emotions.

## Comparing Arguments

 **1. Key Ideas and Details (a)** In what ways are the intent, or purpose, of the historical research study and speech both similar and different? **(b)** When you evaluate the credibility of the arguments made in the two texts, do you find one more credible than the other? Explain your response.

### Content-Area Vocabulary

**2. (a)** For each of the following words, explain how a change in suffix alters the meaning and part of speech of the base word *inaugural: inaugurate, inauguration.* **(b)** Use each word in a sentence that shows its meaning.

##  Timed Writing

### Argument: Essay

**Format**
The prompt directs you to write a brief essay. Therefore, you will need to express your ideas in three to five paragraphs.

> Write a brief essay in which you critique Alan Axelrod's interpretation of Roosevelt's first inaugural address. Analyze the historical research study and decide whether you think Axelrod's points are valid. Support your opinion with examples from the text. (25 minutes)

**Academic Vocabulary**
When you *analyze* a text, you closely examine its information and details.

### 5-Minute Planner

Complete these steps before you begin to write:

1. Read the prompt carefully and completely. Look for key words, like the ones highlighted, that help you understand the assignment.

2. Review the historical research study. Begin by rereading the quotations from Roosevelt's speech. Note your own responses to these passages before rereading Axelrod's comments about them.

3. Make notes about Axelrod's arguments and the evidence he uses to support his points. Be sure to distinguish facts from the author's opinions. Note any generalizations that are not supported by facts.

4. Based on your notes, evaluate the overall strengths and weaknesses of Axelrod's arguments. Write a sentence to sum up your evaluation.

5. Use your notes to prepare a quick outline to organize your critique.

## Comparing Humorous Writing

Humorous writing is intended to make the reader laugh. It can be fiction or nonfiction. One kind of nonfiction is the **humorous essay,** which seeks to entertain but may have a serious message as well.

A **folk tale** is a story passed down from generation to generation that expresses the beliefs and values of its culture. Folk tales typically present simple characters and far-fetched situations. A **humorous folk tale** is meant to entertain and instruct. In humorous writing, authors often include these figures of speech:

- **Hyperbole:** intentional, sometimes outrageous, exaggeration—for example, describing a small patch of ice as a "vast, frozen wasteland"

- **Understatement:** the presentation of an idea, a person, or an event to make it seem less than it is—for example, describing a huge loss as a "minor setback"

Besides these techniques, the writer's **comic diction,** or word choice, may include informal, colloquial language, slang, or other verbal humor.

Use a graphic organizer like the one shown to identify the serious ideas in "The Talk" and "Talk." Then, think about why the authors might have chosen to use humor to explore these issues.

| Funny Detail | Serious Issue |
|---|---|
| "My gangly arms nearly touched my kneecaps." | He was young, and his body was growing in spurts. |

**Cultural context**—the historical and social background of a literary work—can be an important element in humorous writing. This is especially true in folk tales, traditional stories that contain many cultural details. However, every story has a culture behind it. The culture of "Talk" is that of ancient Africa; the culture of "The Talk" is that of mid-century suburban America. The more readers know about the culture in which a story is set, the more they can recognize and understand humorous references. Knowledge of cultural context can also help readers appreciate serious messages contained in amusing works.

 **Common Core State Standards**

**Reading Literature**

**6.** Analyze a particular point of view or cultural experience reflected in a work of literature from outside the United States, drawing on a wide reading of world literature.

**Reading Informational Text**

**4.** Determine the meaning of words and phrases as they are used in the text, including figurative, connotative, and technical meanings; analyze the cumulative impact of specific word choices on meaning and tone.

**Writing**

**2.** Write informative/explanatory texts to examine and convey complex ideas, concepts, and information clearly and accurately through the effective selection, organization, and analysis of content.

**www.PHLitOnline.com**

- Vocabulary flashcards
- Interactive journals
- More about the authors
- Selection audio
- Interactive graphic organizers

# Is *knowledge* the same as *understanding?*

## Writing About the Big Question

In both of these selections, the writers describe serious ideas or **insights** in a humorous way. Use this sentence starter to develop your ideas about the Big Question.

Humor can help **clarify** ideas and build understanding by _____.

# Meet the Authors

## Gary Soto (b. 1952)
### Author of "The Talk"

Gary Soto grew up in a Mexican American section of Fresno, California. As a child, he wanted to be either a priest or a scientist. Then, in high school, he discovered great writers, including John Steinbeck and Robert Frost. In college, Soto started writing poetry.

**Living Through Books** Soto's favorite pastime is reading. He has said, "It appears these days I don't have much of a life because my nose is often stuck in a book. But I discovered that reading builds a life inside the mind."

## Harold Courlander (1908–1996) and George Herzog (1901–1983)
### Retellers of "Talk"

"Talk" is an Ashanti folk tale. The Ashanti live in what is now the West African country of Ghana. They have a history that dates back centuries. "Talk" is retold by Harold Courlander and George Herzog.

**A Distinguished Career** Courlander studied the history and folklore of African and other world cultures. He wrote more than thirty-five fiction and nonfiction books inspired by these studies.

**Music and Culture** Born in Budapest, Hungary, Herzog pioneered the study of the cultural aspects of music. He also taught linguistics and anthropology and published books on folk music.

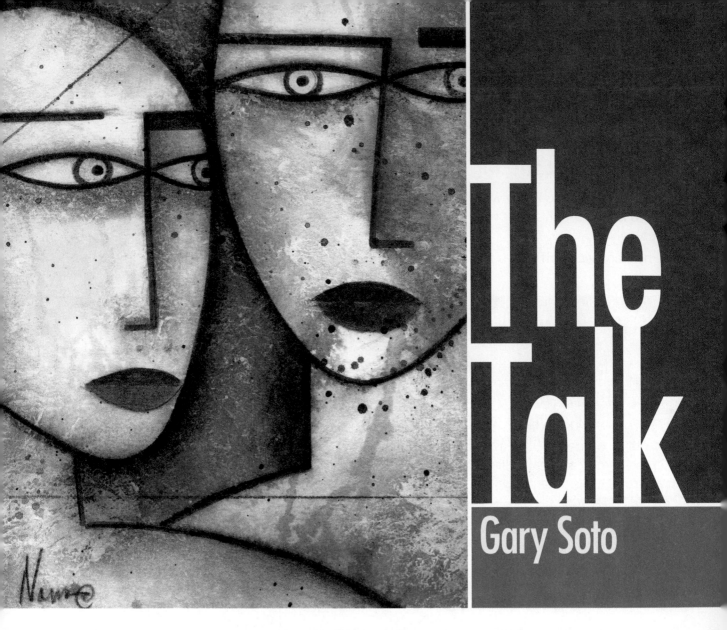

The Talk

Gary Soto

▲ **Critical Viewing**
Based on this image and title, what topics do you think the author of this essay might discuss? Explain. **[Predict]**

My best friend and I knew that we were going to grow up to be ugly. On a backyard lawn—the summer light failing west of the mulberry tree where the house of the most beautiful girl on the street stood—we talked about what we could do: shake the second-base dirt from our hair, wash our hands of frog smells and canal water, and learn to smile without showing our crooked teeth. We had to stop spitting when girls were looking and learn not to pile food onto a fork and into a fat cheek already churning hot grub.

We were twelve, with lean bodies that were beginning to grow in weird ways. First, our heads got large, but our necks wavered, frail as crisp tulips. The eyes stayed small as well, receding into pencil dots on each side of an unshapely nose that cast remarkable shadows when we turned sideways. It seemed that Scott's legs sprouted muscle and renegade veins, but his arms, blue with ink markings, stayed short and hung just below his waist. My gangly arms nearly touched my kneecaps. In this way, I was built for picking up grounders and doing cartwheels, my arms swaying just inches from the summery grass.

We sat on the lawn, with the porch light off, waiting for the beautiful girl to turn on her bedroom light and read on her stomach with one leg stirring the air. This stirred us, and our dream was a clean dream of holding hands and airing out our loneliness by walking up and down the block.

When Scott asked whom I was going to marry, I said a brown girl from the valley. He said that he was going to marry a strawberry blonde who would enjoy Millerton Lake, dirty as it was. I said mine would like cats and the sea and would think nothing of getting up at night from a warm, restless bed and sitting in the yard under the icy stars. Scott said his wife would work for the first year or so, because he would go to trade school[1] in refrigeration. Since our town was made with what was left over after God made hell, there was money in air conditioning, he reasoned.

I said that while my wife would clean the house and stir pots of nice grub, I would drive a truck to my job as a carpenter, which would allow me to use my long arms. I would need only a stepladder to hand a fellow worker on the roof a pinch of nails. I could hammer, saw, lift beams into place, and see the work I got done at the end of the day. Of course, she might like to work, and that would be okay, because then we could buy two cars and wave at each other if we should see the other drive by. In the evenings, we would drink Kool-Aid and throw a slipper at our feisty dog at least a hundred times before we went inside for a Pop-Tart and hot chocolate.

Scott said he would work hard too, but now and then he would find money on the street and the two of them could buy extra things like a second TV for the bedroom and a Doughboy swimming pool for his three kids. He planned on having three kids and a ranch house on the river, where he could dip a hand in the water, drink, and say, "Ahh, tastes good."

But that would be years later. Now we had to do something about our looks. We plucked at the grass and flung it into each other's faces.

"Rotten luck," Scott said. "My arms are too short. Look at 'em."

"Maybe we can lift weights. This would make up for our looks," I said.

"I don't think so," Scott said, depressed. "People like people with nice faces."

---

1. **trade school** school that specializes in teaching the skills needed to work in a particular job.

**Vocabulary**
**renegade** (ren´ ə gād´) *adj.* disloyal; traitorous

**Spiral Review**
**Organization and Structure** As the boys sit in the dark, what does the sense that this is a recurring activity add to your understanding of the story?

**Literary Analysis**
**Humorous Writing** Which details of the boys' youthful dreams might seem funny later in life?

**Vocabulary**
**feisty** (fīs´ tē) *adj.* full of spirit; energetic

**Reading Check**
What are the boys worried they will be like when they grow up?

> "I can't stand it anymore. We have to talk about this."

He was probably right. I turned onto my stomach, a stalk of grass in my mouth. "Even if I'm ugly, my wife's going to be good-looking," I said. "She'll have a lot of dresses and I'll have more shirts than I have now. Do you know how much carpenters make?"

Then I saw the bedroom light come on and the beautiful girl walk into the room drying her hair with a towel. I nudged Scott's short arm and he saw what I saw. We flicked the stalks of grass, stood up, and walked over to the fence to look at her scrub her hair dry. She plopped onto the bed and began to comb it, slowly at first because it was tangled. With a rubber band, she tied it back, and picked up a book that was thick as a good-sized sandwich.

Scott and I watched her read a book, now both legs in the air and twined together, her painted toenails like red petals. She turned the pages slowly, very carefully, and now and then lowered her face into the pillow. She looked sad but beautiful, and we didn't know what to do except nudge each other in the heart and creep away to the front yard.

"I can't stand it anymore. We have to talk about this," Scott said.

"If I try, I think I can make myself better looking," I said. "I read an article about a girl whitening her teeth with water and flour."

So we walked up the street, depressed. For every step I took, Scott took two, his short arms pumping to keep up. For every time Scott said, "I think we're ugly," I said two times, "Yeah, yeah, we're in big trouble."

## Critical Thinking

**Cite textual evidence to support your responses.**

1. **Key Ideas and Details (a)** What jobs do the boys hope to have when they get older? **(b) Infer:** What do the boys' choices of future jobs suggest about their characters? Explain.

2. **Integration of Knowledge and Ideas (a) Infer:** Do you think this is the first time the boys have watched the beautiful girl? Why or why not? **(b) Draw Conclusions:** What do you think the girl in the window represents for the two boys?

3. **Integration of Knowledge and Ideas Speculate:** What advice do you think an adult might give the two boys to help them feel better about themselves?

4. **Integration of Knowledge and Ideas** Soto presents the boys' expectations of the future in a humorous way. What impact does the use of humor have on your understanding of the characters and their plight? *[Connect to the Big Question: Is knowledge the same as understanding?]*

# Talk

**retold by Harold Courlander and George Herzog**

ONCE, not far from the city of Accra on the Gulf of
Guinea, a country man went out to his garden to dig up
some yams to take to market. While he was digging, one of
the yams said to him:

"Well, at last you're here. You never weeded me, but now
you come around with your digging stick. Go away and
leave me alone!"

The farmer turned around and looked at his cow in amazement. The cow was chewing her cud and looking at him.

"Did you say something?" he asked.

The cow kept on chewing and said nothing, but the man's dog spoke up.

"It wasn't the cow who spoke to you," the dog said. "It was the yam. The yam says leave him alone."

The man became angry, because his dog had never talked before, and he didn't like his tone besides. So he took his knife and cut a branch from a palm tree to whip his dog. Just then the palm tree said:

"Put that branch down!"

The man was getting very upset about the way things were going, and he started to throw the palm branch away, but the palm branch said:

"Man, put me down softly!"

He put the branch down gently on a stone, and the stone said:

"Hey, take that thing off me!"

This was enough, and the frightened farmer started to run for his village. On the way he met a fisherman going the other way with a fish trap on his head.

"What's the hurry?" the fisherman asked.

"My yam said, 'Leave me alone!' Then the dog said, 'Listen to what the yam says!' When I went to whip the dog with a palm branch the tree said, 'Put that branch down!' Then the palm branch said, 'Do it softly!' Then the stone said, 'Take that thing off me!'"

"Is that all?" the man with the fish trap asked. "Is that so frightening?"

"Well," the man's fish trap said, "did he take it off the stone?"

"Wah!" the fisherman shouted. He threw the fish trap on the ground and began to run with the farmer, and on the trail they met a weaver with a bundle of cloth on his head.

"Where are you going in such a rush?" he asked them.

"My yam said, 'Leave me alone!'" the farmer said. "The dog said, 'Listen to what the yam says!' The tree said, 'Put that branch down!' The branch said, 'Do it softly!' And the stone said, 'Take that thing off me!'"

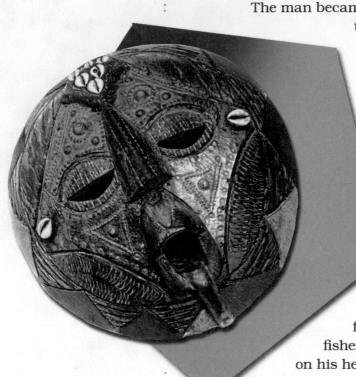

**Literary Analysis**
**Humorous Writing**
How does the fisherman's response, an example of understatement, add humor to this passage?

"And then," the fisherman continued, "the fish trap said, 'Did he take it off?'"

"That's nothing to get excited about," the weaver said, "no reason at all."

"Oh yes it is," his bundle of cloth said. "If it happened to you you'd run too!"

"Wah!" the weaver shouted. He threw his bundle on the trail and started running with the other men.

They came panting to the ford in the river and found a man bathing.

"Are you chasing a gazelle?" he asked them.

The first man said breathlessly:

"My yam talked at me, and it said, 'Leave me alone!' And my dog said, 'Listen to your yam!' And when I cut myself a branch the tree said, 'Put that branch down!' And the branch said, 'Do it softly!' And the stone said, 'Take that thing off me!'"

The fisherman panted:

"And my trap said, 'Did he?'"

The weaver wheezed:

"And my bundle of cloth said, 'You'd run too!'"

"Is that why you're running?" the man in the river asked.

"Well, wouldn't you run if you were in their position?" the river said.

The man jumped out of the water and began to run with the others. They ran down the main street of the village to the house of the chief. The chief's servants brought his stool out, and he came and sat on it to listen to their complaints. The men began to recite their troubles.

"I went out to my garden to dig yams," the farmer said, waving his arms. "Then everything began to talk! My yam said, 'Leave me alone!' My dog said, 'Pay attention to your yam!' The tree said, 'Put that branch down!' The branch said, 'Do it softly!' And the stone said, 'Take it off me!'"

"Wah!" the weaver shouted. He threw his bundle on the trail and started running with the other men.

**Vocabulary**
**wheezed** (wēzd') *v.*
breathed hard with a breathy sound

**Spiral Review**
**Organization and Structure** By this point in the story, what pattern have you noticed in the story's structure?

**Reading Check**
What prompts the man in the river to start to run with the others?

**Vocabulary**
**bulging** (bulj iŋ) *adj.*
swelling

**refrain** (ri frān´) *v.* hold
back

**Literary Analysis**
**Humorous Writing**
How would this folk tale
be different if it ended
with the line "Nonsense
like that upsets the
community"?

"And my fish trap said, 'Well, did he
take it off?'" the fisherman said.

"And my cloth said, 'You'd run
too!'" the weaver said.

"And the river said the same,"
the bather said hoarsely, his
eyes bulging.

The chief listened to them
patiently, but he couldn't
refrain from scowling.

"Now this is really a wild
story," he said at last. "You'd
better all go back to your
work before I punish you for
disturbing the peace."

So the men went away, and
the chief shook his head and
mumbled to himself, "Nonsense
like that upsets the community."

"Fantastic, isn't it?" his stool
said. "Imagine, a talking yam!"

## Critical Thinking

Cite textual
evidence to
support your
responses.

© **1. Key Ideas and Details (a)** Why does the man cut a branch from
the palm tree? **(b) Interpret:** Why does the man want to whip his
dog?

© **2. Key Ideas and Details (a)** What is the fisherman's first response
when he hears the farmer's story? **(b) Interpret:** Why doesn't the
fisherman become frightened when he hears the farmer's story?
**(c) Draw Conclusions:** Why does the fisherman become
frightened only after his fish trap talks to him?

© **3. Key Ideas and Details (a)** How does the chief react when the
men tell him what happened to them? **(b) Speculate:** How do
you think the chief reacted when he heard the stool talk?

© **4. Integration of Knowledge and Ideas (a)** What serious message
can you infer from the understated humor in this folktale? Explain.
**(b)** What might the cultural experience reflected in this tale teach
readers? *[Connect to the Big Question: Is knowledge the
same as understanding?]*

## Comparing Humorous Writing

© **1. Craft and Structure (a)** Use a chart like the one shown to identify at
least one example of hyperbole, one example of understatement, and
one example of comic diction in each piece of humorous writing.
**(b)** Explain how each example adds to the humor of the writing.

| Type | The Talk | Talk |
|------|----------|------|
| Hyperbole | | |
| Understatement | | |
| Comic Diction | | |

© **2. Craft and Structure (a)** Compare the use of informal, colloquial
language in the two stories. **(b)** How does this diction add to the
humor?

© **3. Integration of Knowledge and Ideas** Would you describe the
humor of these selections as harsh or gentle? Explain your answer
using details from the texts.

 **Timed Writing**

### Explanatory Text: Essay

In an essay, discuss and compare the serious ideas expressed in each of
these selections. Consider why the authors chose to present these issues
through humor. Provide evidence from the text to support your response.
**(25 minutes)**

### 5-Minute Planner

**1.** Read the prompt carefully and completely.
**2.** Gather your ideas by jotting down answers to these questions:

- What challenges do the characters in each selection face?

- What specific circumstances or cultural influences do you think might
  have added to those challenges? Note specific supporting details
  from each selection.

- How are humor and seriousness featured alongside one another to
  convey the author's message?

- How does the use of humor help suggest that these challenges can
  be overcome?

**3.** Reread the prompt, and then draft your essay.

# Writing Workshop

## Write an Argument

## Exposition: Editorial

**Defining the Form** One way to take a stand is to write an **editorial.** An editorial is a brief persuasive essay that presents and defends an opinion. Examples include letters to the editor, position papers, and speeches.

**Assignment** Write an editorial about an issue that confronts your school or community. Include these elements:

✓ a clear *thesis statement*—a statement of your position on an issue that offers your *perspective* on the subject

✓ *evidence* that supports your position or *claim* and distinguishes it from an alternate or opposing claim

✓ *organization* of text that makes relationships of ideas clear and links sections through effective word choice

✓ *persuasive techniques* that appeal specifically to your audience

✓ a formal style and objective tone and error-free grammar, including *correct use of parallel structures*

To preview the criteria on which your editorial may be judged, see the rubric on page 589.

 **Writing Workshop:** *Work in Progress*

Review the work you did on pages 537 and 563.

## WRITE GUY
### *Jeff Anderson, M.Ed.*

### What Do You Notice?

**Supporting Evidence**

Read the following sentences from Pete Hamill's "Libraries Face Sad Chapter" several times.

*For those without money, the road to that treasure house of the imagination begins at the public library. When I was a boy, the rooms were crowded with . . . people who came from places where there were no libraries for the poor. With their children, they built the New York in which we now live.*

Discuss your ideas about the passage with a partner. Then, consider how you can use evidence to support the opinions in your editorial.

**Writing**

**1.** Write arguments to support claims in an analysis of substantive topics or texts, using valid reasoning and relevant and sufficient evidence.

**1.a.** Introduce precise claim(s), distinguish the claim(s) from alternate or opposing claims, and create an organization that establishes clear relationships among claim(s), counterclaims, reasons, and evidence.

**7.** Conduct short as well as more sustained research projects to answer a question or solve a problem; narrow or broaden the inquiry when appropriate.

**8.** Gather relevant information from multiple authoritative print and digital sources, using advanced searches effectively.

**Language**

**5.b.** Analyze nuances in the meaning of words with similar denotations.

**Reading-Writing Connection**

To get a feel for an editorial, read "Libraries Face Sad Chapter" by Pete Hamill on page 530.

# Prewriting/Planning Strategies

**Scan newspapers.** Look for relevant information from print and digital sources. Notice articles that describe situations that strike you as unfair, foolish, or harmful. Use one of these news stories as a topic for your editorial.

**Work with a partner.** Pair up with a classmate, and brainstorm for topics that are important to each of you. Select an issue that has compelling arguments. Then, choose a position to support.

**Write a thesis statement.** After reviewing the information you have in hand, decide which part of the issue to address. Write your opinion about the topic in one sentence. That sentence is your thesis statement, an expression of your position that you must now prepare to defend.

**Consider all sides of an issue.** Gather evidence from a wide variety of sources. Use advanced Internet searches to narrow or broaden your topic if needed. In a chart like the one shown, record evidence on both sides of an issue. Anticipate and address readers' potential expectations, biases, and misunderstandings. Do not ignore information that contradicts or opposes your position. Plan to include summaries of opposing positions in order to refute them.

| Support for School Uniforms | Opposition to School Uniforms |
| --- | --- |
| Reduce violence and discrimination | Take choice away from students |
| Create positive school image | Cause resentment among students |

**Appeal to logic and emotion.** Effective persuasion appeals to both logic and emotion—your audience's thoughts and feelings.

- **Logic:** Make a list of ideas, facts, and details that will make people think, analyze, and reason rather than feel.

- **Emotion:** Brainstorm for relevant anecdotes, or brief stories, descriptions, case studies, analogies, and personal examples that will affect readers' emotions. Quickly jot these down. As you work, experiment with language that carries strong emotional connotations:

  - **Neutral connotation:** Megan continues to work.

  - **Strong connotation:** Megan soldiers on.

# Drafting Strategies

**Create a structure for your draft.** Plan a strategy for presenting your ideas. Be sure to structure arguments and ideas in a sustained and logical fashion.

- **Evaluate your arguments.** Review all the points that support your thesis, and consider their impact on your intended audience. Then, rank them according to their persuasiveness.

- **Use an outline.** Use your ranking to write an outline showing order-of-importance organization. Start with your least important point and build toward your most persuasive point. In addition, be sure to indicate where you will address counterarguments. The chart shown demonstrates order-of-importance organization for an editorial.

**Distinguish between fact and opinion.** Your thesis and arguments are statements of opinion that must be validated or supported with evidence. Facts—information that can be proved true—are the strongest evidence. Weak arguments pile opinions on top of opinions; strong arguments back opinions with relevant facts. As you draft, weave together your facts along with details that support them.

**Provide evidence.** For each point you make, produce convincing support. Types of effective evidence include the following:

- **Statistics:** numbers that show the impact of an issue or a proposal
  *If we adopt this plan, we can save $100 every week, or $5,200 a year.*

- **Expert opinions:** the viewpoints or advice of those who have relevant training and experience
  *Dr. Samuel Rothman has published a checklist for those who want to start saving money—and his suggestions are easy to follow.*

- **Personal observations:** your own experiences with the topic
  *It happens every month—I get the paycheck from my job and the money is gone before I know it!*

- **Testimonials:** statements from observers that reinforce an argument
  *Dean Smolens says, "I have been tracking my spending for two weeks, and I have noticed several ways to cut back without making drastic changes."*

**Provide a concluding statement.** Write a strong conclusion that will help readers remember your argument. For example, include a final thought or quotation that summarizes your thesis.

The use of valid and relevant quotations, as well as expressions of accepted beliefs and logical reasoning, may also help clarify your arguments. As you draft, be sure to maintain a formal style and objective tone.

## Common Core State Standards

**Writing**

**1.a.** Introduce precise claim(s), distinguish the claim(s) from alternate or opposing claims, and create an organization that establishes clear relationships among claim(s), counterclaims, reasons, and evidence.

**1.b.** Develop claim(s) and counterclaims fairly, supplying evidence for each while pointing out the strengths and limitations of both in a manner that anticipates the audience's knowledge and concerns.

**1.d.** Establish and maintain a formal style and objective tone while attending to the norms and conventions of the discipline in which they are writing.

**1.e.** Provide a concluding statement or section that follows from and supports the argument presented.

---

**Organizing Your Arguments**

↓

Present thesis statement.

↓

Present arguments to support thesis.

↓

Address counterarguments.

↓

Provide strongest argument in support of thesis.

↓

Provide a logical concluding statement, summarizing argument and supporting thesis.

# Writers on Writing

## Rebecca Walker On Choosing the Right Details

Rebecca Walker is the author of "Before Hip-Hop was Hip-Hop" (p. 435).

This excerpt is from the introductory essay to a book I edited about new perspectives on masculinity. I think about what I am going to write for a long time, maybe months, before committing my thoughts to the page. Long before I sat down to write, I knew I would prompt readers to think about masculinity in new ways by using this personal exchange between my son and me. What I didn't know was how I would finish the piece.

*"Taking one's initial impulse to completion, that's the challenge . . ."*
—Rebecca Walker

---

**Professional Model:**

### from *What Makes a Man*

After a big bowl of his favorite pasta, he sat on a sofa in my study and read his science textbook as I wrote at my desk. . . . As we worked under the soft glow of paper lanterns, . . . I could feel a shift as he began to remember, deep in his body, that he was home, that he was safe, that he didn't have to brace to protect himself from the expectations of the outside world.

An hour or so passed like this before he announced that he had a question. . . . "I've been thinking that maybe I should play sports at school."

. . . I cocked my head to one side. "What brought this on?"

"I don't know," he said. "Maybe girls will like me if I play sports."

*Excuse me?*

My boy is intuitive, smart, and creative . . . At the time he loved animals, Japanese anime, . . . and everything having to do with snowboarding. He liked to help both of his grandmothers in the garden. He read science fiction. . . . and was beginning what I thought would be a lifelong love affair with chess.

*Maybe girls would like him if he played sports?*

I wanted to convey a sense of peace and relaxation, so I added this detail to draw the reader into the tranquility of the "scene."

I used italics here to suggest my surprise and outrage, and to reinforce a direct and intimate connection with the reader.

I included actual things my son enjoyed to add authenticity and texture, and to provide a strong counterpoint to sports.

# Revising Strategies

**Revise to address readers' concerns.** Not all of your readers will agree with your perspective. Show them that you are aware of their potential questions, opposing positions, and counterclaims and that you understand their concerns, biases, and expectations.

- Review your draft and highlight controversial claims that a critic of your position would oppose.

- To make sure you understand each opposing argument, write a summary that captures its main idea and line of reasoning.

- For each claim, develop strong counterarguments that you can support with explanations and evidence.

- Find a point in your editorial where you can include this information smoothly.

**Choose powerful words.** To be persuasive, your essay should include precise words that link major sections together, create a unified whole, and clarify relationships between ideas as they convey meaning and tone.

**Neutral:** Some adults *dislike* today's students' fashions.
**Powerful:** Some adults *deplore* today's students' fashions.

**Neutral:** Joanna *did not want* to wear a uniform.
**Powerful:** Joanna *refused* to wear a uniform.

Check a thesaurus for powerful words like the ones in this chart.

| Ordinary | Powerful |
|---|---|
| Walk | Pace, trudge, scramble, shuffle |
| Like | Be fond of, enjoy, appreciate, adore |
| Nice | Pleasant, kind, gentle, thoughtful |
| Boring | Uninteresting, tedious, dreary, dull, mind-numbing |

## Peer Review

Exchange drafts with a partner. Review each other's work, highlighting weak words that could be replaced by stronger ones. Then, revise your draft, replacing neutral language with words that will encourage your readers to feel and think. After you have made your revisions, exchange drafts with your partner again. Discuss whether the new word choices are more effective.

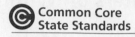
**Common Core State Standards**

**Writing**
**1.c.** Use words, phrases, and clauses to link the major sections of the text, create cohesion, and clarify the relationships between claim(s) and reasons, between reasons and evidence, and between claim(s) and counterclaims.
**5.** Develop and strengthen writing as needed by planning, revising, editing, rewriting, or trying a new approach, focusing on addressing what is most significant for a specific purpose and audience.

**Language**
**1.a.** Use parallel structure.

# Revising to Create Parallelism

**Parallelism** is the use of similar grammatical forms or patterns to express similar ideas. Effective use of parallelism adds rhythm and balance to your writing and strengthens connections among your ideas.

**Identifying Nonparallel Constructions** Parallel constructions place equal ideas in words, phrases, or clauses of similar types. Nonparallel constructions present equal ideas in an unnecessary mix of grammatical forms, producing awkward, distracting shifts for readers.

> **Nonparallel:** Dress codes are <u>less restrictive,</u> <u>less costly,</u> and <u>are not a controversial system.</u>

> **Parallel:** Dress codes are <u>less restrictive,</u> <u>less costly,</u> and <u>less controversial.</u>

**Fixing Nonparallel Constructions** Follow these steps:

1. Identify similar or equal ideas within a sentence.

2. Determine whether the ideas are expressed in the same form—for example, all nouns or all prepositional phrases.

3. Rewrite the sentence so that all the elements match the stronger pattern. Choose forms that produce the smoothest rhythm or require the fewest words.

| Sample Parallel Forms | |
|---|---|
| Nouns | sharp eyes, strong hands, deft fingers |
| Verbs | to ask, to learn, to share |
| Phrases | under a gray sky, near an icy river |
| Adverb clauses | when I am happy, when I am peaceful |
| Adjective clauses | those who read with care, those who act with concern |

## Grammar in Your Writing

Review several paragraphs in your editorial, highlighting any sentences in which you present a series of ideas. Be sure your sentences contain parallel constructions as well as correct subject-verb agreement. Revise your sentences as needed.

# Student Model: Braden Danbury, Cumming, GA

 Common Core State Standards

**Language**
**2.c.** Spell correctly.

## Dress Codes May Succeed Where School Uniforms Have Failed

School uniforms are becoming increasingly popular as a way to combat school violence and discrimination. Uniforms, while they may help somewhat, cause problems of their own. Students argue that it is their right to wear what they choose and uniforms violate that right. A less strict code is the answer to both of these problems, keeping appropriate attire in the school while allowing individuals to choose what they wear.

Uniforms require students to wear specific shirts and pants or skirts, thus eliminating the element of choice. School uniforms may cause friction between students and school officials, which can have negative consequences. Dress codes, on the other hand, are less restrictive than school uniforms and cause less resentment among students. Students enjoy choosing what to wear to school each day, coordinating what they wear with how they feel.

While students' safety is often cited as a leading justification for requiring uniforms, safety hits the bottom of the list in a press release from the National Association of Elementary School Principals. In fact, safety ranks below such trivial things as school image. This calls into question why uniforms are touted as the answer to school safety issues.

Dress codes make the difference where it counts. They keep students safe while forcing them to do nothing other than make sure their clothes meet acceptable standards. An added benefit of dress codes is that schools with uniform policies pay much more than schools with dress codes. Schools with uniforms have to design, order, sell, and distribute the uniforms they wish to have for their school. In addition, school officials spend time and resources making sure they receive payment for uniforms. These expenses may be hidden, but they are real. Dress codes are much less expensive to implement and follow.

With the rise in school violence, students and their dress often come under suspicion and scrutiny. In addition, the wide variety of clothing in our high schools may lead students to make prejudicial judgments about each other. Dress codes address the problems of violence without causing resentment among students. They are less strict, giving the students more freedom in how they dress, while allowing school officials to set general guidelines. The amount of money it would take to implement a dress code is a fraction of the cost of school uniforms. Dress codes are not the only answer, but they are a step toward combating violence and discrimination in the schools.

---

Braden offers a clear thesis statement in the form of a proposal that addresses a key problem.

Braden finds a way to deal with counterarguments based on safety concerns.

Braden offers evidence that supports his position.

Braden restates his thesis and summarizes his evidence. He also offers an additional insight.

# Editing and Proofreading

Review your draft to correct errors in grammar, spelling, and punctuation.

**Focus on spelling.** An editorial that includes spelling errors loses its authority to convince. Check the spelling of each word. Look for words that you frequently misspell, and make sure they are correct. **Content-area words** come from science, history, literature, or other subject areas. While content-area words are not necessarily difficult, they may be unfamiliar to you. These words may have letters that are silent or other challenging letter patterns. Focus on the words you may spell wrong and learn their correct spellings.

**Spiral Review**

Earlier in this unit, you learned about **adjectives** (p. 536) and **adverbs** (p. 562). Check your essay to be sure you have used these grammatical forms correctly.

# Publishing and Presenting

Consider one of the following ways to share your writing:

**Deliver an oral presentation.** Using technology to produce dynamic visuals, present your editorial to the class. As you speak, be sensitive to your audience. If they seem confused or doubtful, modify your word choice to clarify your ideas. After you finish, take a poll to determine whether or not you convinced your audience of your position.

**Submit your editorial to a newspaper.** Send your work to the school or community newspaper, condense it into a letter to the editor, or post it online.

# Reflecting on Your Writing

**Writer's Journal** Jot down your answers to this question:
*How did writing about your topic help you understand it?*

# Rubric for Self-Assessment

Find evidence in your writing to address each category. Then, use the rating scale to grade your work.

| Criteria | Rating Scale |
|---|---|
| | not very         very |
| **Focus:** How clearly does your thesis statement express an opinion? | 1   2   3   4   5 |
| **Organization:** How effectively do you organize your arguments? | 1   2   3   4   5 |
| **Support/Elaboration:** How well do you use evidence to support your position? | 1   2   3   4   5 |
| **Style:** How powerful is your use of persuasive language? | 1   2   3   4   5 |
| **Conventions:** How correct is your grammar, especially your use of parallel structures? | 1   2   3   4   5 |

# Vocabulary Workshop

## Words With Multiple Meanings

Many words in English have **multiple meanings,** or definitions that vary greatly. Look at these sentences. An identification of the word *mine* follows each sentence.

- This book is *mine,* but you are welcome to borrow it. (possessive pronoun)
- The coal *mine* has been in operation for many years. (noun describing a place where coal is dug)
- You can *mine* that report for many good ideas. (verb meaning "take from")

When it is not clear what a word means in a sentence, look for **context clues.** Context clues are in the information surrounding a word and can be used to help you determine the word's meaning. Then, refer to a dictionary and find the definition that fits the context. Notice the context clues in this sentence:

**The three people made a compact to meet again in a year's time.**

- "Three people" suggests that they worked together and "made" the compact.
- The people planned to do something: "meet again."

By checking a dictionary, you will find that *compact* can mean "an agreement between two or more individuals."

**Practice A** Write the meaning of each italicized word in the sentences below. If necessary, consult a dictionary.

1. **(a)** Spinach is a good source of *iron.*
   **(b)** When using an *iron,* make sure that it is not too hot for the fabric.

2. **(a)** The truck moved slowly up the steep *grade.*
   **(b)** My teacher had to stay up most of the night to *grade* the essays.

3. **(a)** The hikers were able to find a *pass* through the mountain.
   **(b)** Were you able to *pass* the entrance exam for the university?

4. **(a)** Cook the sauce over *medium* heat until it begins to boil.
   **(b)** The artist's favorite *medium* is pastels.

**Common Core State Standards**

**Language**

**4.** Determine or clarify the meaning of unknown and multiple-meaning words or phrases based on grades 9–10 reading and content, choosing flexibly from a range of strategies.
**4.a.** Use context as a clue to the meaning of a word or phrase.
**4.d.** Verify the preliminary determination of the meaning of a word or phrase.

**Practice B** Using context clues, write a definition in your own words for the underlined word in each sentence. With a partner, discuss which context clues helped you to determine the meaning of the word. Then, look up the word in a dictionary and confirm or correct your definition.

**www.PHLitOnline.com**
- Illustrated vocabulary words
- Interactive vocabulary games
- Vocabulary flashcards

1. A deeply rounded back gave the violin a <u>rich</u> tone.

2. The <u>stern</u> of the boat swung around, and we floated backward down the stream.

3. George was uncomfortable about taking the money, so he <u>skirted</u> the issue.

4. The kids came <u>thundering</u> down the stairs when they were called for dinner.

5. Which <u>branch</u> of the bank is located nearest to your house?

6. My sister got a ticket for <u>peddling</u> cosmetics door to door without a license.

7. It is important for cooks to keep their cupboards full of the <u>staples</u> they use every day.

8. I wouldn't hire Sue because she has <u>base</u> motives for wanting this job.

9. The child scrambled up the <u>bluff</u> through thorn bushes in pursuit of his runaway cat.

10. The movie does not <u>warrant</u> all the rave reviews it has been getting.

**Activity** Choose five of the underlined words in Practice B. Look in a dictionary to find the multiple meanings of these words. Write each word on a separate note card like the one shown. Fill in the left column of the note card according to one of the word's meanings. Fill in the right-hand column according to another of the word's meanings. Then, trade note cards with a partner, and discuss the different meanings and uses of the words that each of you found.

**Comprehension and Collaboration**

Working with a partner, look up each of these words in a dictionary and talk about their multiple meanings: *scale, review, charge.* Then, write sentences using context clues that clearly show three distinct meanings for each word.

| Word | First Meaning | Second Meaning | |
|------|---------------|----------------|---|
|  |  |  |  |
|  |  |  |  |
|  |  |  |  |
|  |  |  |  |
|  |  |  |  |
|  |  |  |  |
|  |  |  |  |
|  |  |  |  |

# Delivering a Persuasive Speech

The ability to speak persuasively is a valuable life skill that enables you to successfully present ideas and proposals. These speaking strategies can help you refine your persuasive speaking skills.

## Learn the Skills

Use these strategies to complete the activity on page 593.

**Organize your evidence.** Once you have determined your position on an issue or idea, gather and arrange your evidence into an introduction, body, and conclusion. Decide which method of organization will lend power to your speech. For example, you may want to use an order-of-importance organization, beginning with less-important points and leading up to your strongest argument.

**Know your audience.** Understanding your audience will help you present your speech effectively.

- Adjust **word choice, evidence,** and **rhetoric** to the interests, cultural perspectives, and knowledge levels of your listeners.
- **Anticipate questions** and **counterarguments.** Identify fallacious reasoning in counterarguments. You can often disarm skeptical listeners by discussing and refuting their ideas.
- **Respond to the interests of your listeners** by showing how they are affected by the issue and could benefit from your proposals.

**Use rhetorical devices.** Strengthen your appeals to logic and emotion by using rhetorical devices.

- **Parallel structures**—the deliberate repetition of words, sentences, and phrases—help to make your ideas clear and memorable.
- **Rhetorical questions**—questions with obvious answers that support your points—capture the attention of your audience.

**Use your voice and gestures effectively.** Demonstrate confidence in your ideas through your posture, bearing, and facial expression.

- Make eye contact with all your listeners, not just one or two people.
- Vary the volume, tone, and pacing of your voice to emphasize key points and to keep your audience engaged.
- Use hand gestures to support what you are saying.

**Use digital media.** Consider enhancing your presentation by using digital media. Visuals, such as computer-generated charts or graphs, or audio and video clips can emphasize your points and add interest to your speech.

**Common Core State Standards**

**Speaking and Listening**

**3.** Evaluate a speaker's point of view, reasoning, and use of evidence and rhetoric, identifying any fallacious reasoning or exaggerated or distorted evidence.

**4.** Present information, findings, and supporting evidence clearly, concisely, and logically such that listeners can follow the line of reasoning and the organization, development, substance, and style are appropriate to purpose, audience, and task.

**5.** Make strategic use of digital media in presentations to enhance understanding of findings, reasoning, and evidence and to add interest.

**6.** Adapt speech to a variety of contexts and tasks, demonstrating command of formal English when indicated or appropriate.

# Practice the Skills

**Presentation of Knowledge and Ideas** Use what you've learned in this workshop to complete the following activity.

---

### ACTIVITY: Deliver a Persuasive Speech

Develop a persuasive speech in which you take a stand on a current issue. Persuade your audience to agree with your views. Then, poll your classmates to see if your speech has altered their perspectives. Consider these questions as you prepare your speech.

- Which organization of ideas best serves my topic and argument?
- What facts and expert opinions support my claim?
- What counterarguments and questions should I anticipate and address?
- What is the knowledge level and cultural perspective of my audience?
- What rhetorical devices will strengthen my appeal to logic and emotion?

---

Use the Presentation Checklist to help you evaluate your classmates' presentations.

---

### Presentation Checklist

**Persuasive Speech Content**

Rate the speaker's content on a scale of 1(very poor) to 5 (very good) for each of these items. Explain your ratings.

- presented ideas clearly and in a logical order     Rating: ___
- included well-chosen facts and expert opinions     Rating: ___
- anticipated and addressed counterarguments and claims     Rating: ___
- met the knowledge level and perspective of the audience    Rating: ___
- used rhetorical devices effectively     Rating: ___

**Persuasive Speech Delivery**

Rate the speaker's delivery on a scale of 1 (very poor) to 5 (very good) for each of these items. Explain your ratings.

- formal language     Rating: ___     • eye contact     Rating: ___
- effective speaking rate     Rating: ___     • appropriate volume     Rating: ___
- enunciation     Rating: ___     • appropriate gestures     Rating: ___
- conventions of language     Rating: ___

---

**Comprehension and Collaboration** With your classmates, discuss how you evaluated each speaker. As a group, discuss what makes a persuasive speech effective and why.

# Cumulative Review

**Common Core
State Standards**

RI.9-10.1, RI.9-10.2, RI.9-10.4,
RI.9-10.5, RI.9-10.6, RI.9-10.8; L.4.a
[For the full wording of the standards,
see the standards chart in the front of
your textbook.]

## I. Reading Literature

**Directions:** *Read the passage. Then, answer each question that follows.*

The statistics are in on teen smoking, and they are not good. According to the Institute of Medicine of the National Academy of Sciences, it is a fact that teens who watch movies that have characters who smoke are more likely to start the habit. Watching smoking in movies is responsible for 52 percent of young smokers. Smoking in movies is even more effective than cigarette advertising. The best way to slow the pace of teens starting is to limit their access to movies that feature characters who smoke. One way to do that is to require an R rating for movies that contain smoking. Then, teens under 17 will have to be accompanied by a parent to view the movie.

Won't there be a shortage of movies for teens? The idea behind rating smoking movies R is to encourage moviemakers to exclude smoking from PG-13 movies. It is not aimed at limiting the movie market for this audience but at convincing the movie industry to help effect positive change in the lives of young people.

Doesn't requiring an R rating restrict creativity and force censorship? The simple answer is *No.* Moviemakers who want to include smoking can opt for an R rating instead of a PG-13. They have the opportunity to exercise their creativity with few limits under the R rating. In addition, the movie industry is responsible for the rating system, not the government. Therefore, it is not censorship. However, requiring an R rating does provide <u>incentive</u> for moviemakers to omit the smoking scenes because PG-13 movies bring in significantly more money than R movies.

Given the outstanding statistics that prove smoking in movies contributes to teen smoking, one would think the movie industry would be eager to help. However, moviemakers and actors alike have received massive amounts of money for placing brands of cigarettes in their movies. As it stands, the movie industry makes millions from the audience and the tobacco companies, while the tobacco companies make millions from teen smokers. Teens who start smoking at a young age spend their lives addicted to a deadly substance. To give teens a better chance of avoiding the dangerous smoking trap, R ratings should be applied to any movie that includes smoking.

1. Which word best describes the **tone** of this essay?

   A. lighthearted
   B. serious
   C. informal
   D. uncertain

2. What sentence best summarizes the **central idea** of this passage?

   A. Teens should be warned that smoking is unhealthy and dangerous.
   B. Smoking in movies is even more effective than cigarette advertising.
   C. Teens who watch movies with smoking often begin to smoke, so movies with smoking should be rated R to cut teen viewership.
   D. Movies have too great an influence on what teenagers do, and their parents should take a greater interest in what they are watching.

3. What makes the author's statement, that teens who watch movies with smoking will start the habit, more credible and valid?

   A. The author's source is the National Academy of Sciences, a respectable organization.
   B. The author included this information in the first paragraph, so it must be true.
   C. This is a logical conclusion.
   D. Movies that include smoking should be required to have an R rating.

4. Which **supporting detail** serves as evidence for the argument that an R rating would not be too restrictive?

   A. Doesn't requiring an R rating restrict creativity and force censorship?
   B. The simple answer is *No*.
   C. Moviemakers who want to include smoking can opt for an R rating instead of a PG-13.
   D. Therefore, it is not censorship.

5. The opening sentences of paragraph 2 and 3 contain which **rhetorical device?**

   A. parallelism
   B. restatement
   C. rhetorical question
   D. analogy

6. To what does this statement appeal? *Given the outstanding statistics that prove smoking in movies contributes to teen smoking . . .*

   A. reason
   B. sense of humor
   C. emotion
   D. curiosity

7. **Vocabulary** Which word is closest in meaning to the underlined word *incentive*?

   A. motivation
   B. regulation
   C. laws
   D. hope

8. What do you think is the **author's purpose?**

   A. to save people money
   B. to expose the movie industry
   C. to decrease teen cigarette use
   D. to anger the tobacco industry

9. This text is an example of what type of essay?

   A. an expository essay
   B. an informational essay
   C. a narrative essay
   D. a persuasive essay

 Timed Writing

10. In a multi-paragraph essay, **identify** the appeals to reason and emotion in this piece of writing. **Explain** how diction, syntax, and rhetorical devices advance the author's purpose.

 GO ON

## II. Reading Informational Text

**Directions:** *Read the passage. Then, answer each question that follows.*

**Common Core State Standards**

RI.9-10.4, RI.9-10.6; L.3, L.4.a
[For the full wording of the standards, see the standards chart in the front of your textbook.]

## Dog Training: Out With the Old, In With the New

### Alpha Enforcement

Much of dog behavioral training is based on the Alpha dog mentality. This method is based on outdated information. Studies conducted in the 1940s on wolf packs led to training of housedogs in the same way we interpreted wolf behavior—training through physical force.

Alpha enforcement requires the person to handle the dog physically, rolling him or her over to force submission. Little reward is given for fear of upsetting the balance of the hierarchy. This training often results in a submissive dog, but not necessarily a well-adjusted dog. With a few changes, the Alpha dog mentality can work for both pet and human.

### Alpha Mentality

Establishing one's self as the Alpha is not a matter of physical dominance. Doing so is about *mentality*—controlling the dog's access to things he needs. For example, if a dog wants to go outside, have him sit first. If a dog wants food, have him sit again. Wait until the dog performs the desired behavior, and only then reward him. He will quickly learn that to have access to things he wants, he will have to perform a specific task. No fear or aggression is involved between human and dog. Patience, however, is key.

As a dog trainer of ten years, I began my career as an Alpha enforcer and have evolved into true Alpha mentality. Thus, my human and canine clients live happy lives without the presence of fear or physical <u>dominance</u>.

---

1. **Vocabulary** What is the best definition for the underlined word *dominance*?

   **A.** restriction          **C.** skill
   **B.** authority            **D.** decline

2. What is the author's **purpose?**

   **A.** to gain business
   **B.** to share a personal anecdote
   **C.** to present research
   **D.** to explain dog training techniques

3. Which word best describes the author's **tone?**

   **A.** playful          **C.** bitter
   **B.** ironic           **D.** instructive

4. Which of the following questions would a new dog owner be most likely to research after reading this article?

   **A.** Is owning a dog a lot of work?
   **B.** Is "Alpha mentality" training effective?
   **C.** Why do scientists study wolf behavior?
   **D.** Are wolves and dogs very similar?

# III. Writing and Language Conventions

**Directions:** *Read the passage. Then, answer each question that follows.*

(1) 57 Spruce Avenue
Brooklyn, NY 11201

(2) Call Anytime Cell Service
1000 Cellular Circle
Brooklyn, NY 11201

(3) Hello Sir or Madam:
    (4) I am writing to request a termination of my one-year cellular phone contract. (5) I signed the contract three months ago. (6) The service has been sporadic. (7) I am unable to send or receive calls from my home or neighborhood. (8) In addition, when I make calls outside this area the likelihood of the call being dropped is very high.
    (9) I realize that there is normally a termination fee; however, I was assured when the contract was signed by me that I would have no service problems in my area. (10) As a result of my difficulty, I would like the termination fee waived and want to receive a partial refund on the bills I have paid. (11) I need that cash! (12) Please notify me of your plan.
    (13) Sincerely,
    (14) *Katrina Vasquez*
    (15) Katrina Vasquez

**1.** What should be added to the letter's **heading?**

  **A.** the writer's name
  **B.** the date
  **C.** the signature
  **D.** nothing

**2.** What would be the best **salutation** for this letter?

  **A.** Dearest Friend:
  **B.** To You:
  **C.** Dear Sir or Madam:
  **D.** Hello Sir or Madam:

**3.** Which sentences should be combined?

  **A.** sentences 4 and 5
  **B.** sentences 5 and 6
  **C.** sentences 8 and 9
  **D.** sentences 11 and 12

**4.** Which sentence should be removed so that the letter has formal, polite language throughout?

  **A.** sentence 4
  **B.** sentence 6
  **C.** sentence 11
  **D.** sentence 12

**5.** Which phrase in sentence 9 is a use of **passive voice** that should be revised?

  **A.** *was assured*
  **B.** *would have no service*
  **C.** *have no service problems*
  **D.** *was signed by me*

# Performance Tasks

**Directions:** *Follow the instructions to complete the tasks below as required by your teacher.*

*As you work on each task, incorporate both general academic vocabulary and literary terms you learned in this unit.*

Ⓒ **Common Core State Standards**

RI.9-10.3, RI.9-10.4, RI.9-10.5, RI.9-10.6; W.9-10.1, W.9-10.2; SL.9-10.1, SL.9-10.1.a, SL.9-10.1.c, SL.9-10.1.d, SL.9-10.3, SL.9-10.4; L.9-10.1, L.9-10.1.a, L.9-10.3, L.9-10.5

[For the full wording of the standards, see the standards chart in the front of your textbook.]

## Writing

### Ⓒ Task 1: Informational Text [RI.9-10.6]
**Determine an Author's Point of View**

*Write an essay in which you identify the author's purpose and point of view in a work from this unit.*

- Identify the selection you will use as the focus for your essay. State the work's topic and explain the author's general and specific purposes for writing about this topic.

- Describe the author's point of view on the topic. Explain how that perspective influences his or her choice of supporting information and details.

- Evaluate how well the author uses rhetorical devices, such as parallel construction, repetition, and figurative language, to advance his or her point of view. Include examples from the text to support your evaluation.

- Edit your essay to ensure that you have used words that precisely convey your meaning.

### Ⓒ Task 2: Informational Text [RI.9-10.3]
**Analyze the Development of Ideas or Events**

*Write an essay in which you analyze how an author unfolds a series of ideas or events in a work of literary nonfiction in this unit.*

- State which work you chose, and restate its central idea in your own words. Identify key supporting details.

- Describe how the author introduces each idea or event, and note the order in which these points are presented. Explain how this particular sequence is effective in advancing the author's ideas.

- Note any connections that are drawn between ideas or events in the work. Explain how the author makes the connections clear to the reader.

- Use parallel sentence construction as you draw connections or highlight important ideas.

### Ⓒ Task 3: Informational Text [RI.9-10.4]
**Analyze Word Choice**

*Write an essay in which you analyze the way the author's word choice affects the meaning and tone of a nonfiction work from this unit.*

- Identify the work you will discuss and briefly summarize its main idea.

- Describe the author's tone and determine the words and phrases that help convey that tone.

- Describe the effect of unusual words, figures of speech, or technical language on the tone.

- Analyze the cumulative impact of the author's word choice on the overall meaning of the work.

### Ⓒ Task 4: Informational Text [RL.9-10.5]
**Analyze Text Structure**

*Write an essay in which you analyze in detail how the structure of a work in this unit helps develop and refine the author's ideas.*

- State the main ideas or claims presented in the work you have chosen.

- Identify the work's organizational structure—for example, chronological order, comparison-and-contrast, or cause-and-effect.

- Analyze in detail how the text structure helps to develop and refine the author's ideas within paragraphs or sections.

- Conclude by evaluating how well the text's overall structure helps the author achieve his or her purpose.

# Speaking and Listening

## Task 5: Informational Text [RI.9-10.2; SL.9-10.4]
### Determine the Central Idea

*Write and deliver an oral report in which you determine the central idea in a nonfiction work from this unit.*

- Identify the work you will discuss, explain who wrote it, and briefly summarize it.

- State your interpretation of the work's central idea.

- Show how you arrived at your interpretation by explaining how the author introduces and develops the key idea. Cite specific details from the work that support your interpretation.

- Present your information clearly, logically, and concisely. Aid your listeners' understanding by giving them an annotated copy of the work, a list of key supporting details you will discuss, or other helpful information.

- Use the conventions of standard English when presenting your report.

## Task 6: Informational Text [RI.9-10.6; W.9-10.1; SL.9-10.3]
### Evaluate a Speaker's Views

*Deliver an oral presentation in which you evaluate the views expressed by an author of one of the speeches in this unit.*

- Choose a speech from this unit. Then, plan an oral presentation in which you evaluate the writer's point of view, reasoning, supporting evidence, and use of rhetorical devices.

- Analyze the views expressed in the speech. Then, identify examples of strong or weak reasoning and evidence that the writer uses to support his or her argument.

- Evaluate the author's use of rhetorical devices, such as parallel structure, repetition, figures of speech, and other types of forceful language.

- End by expressing your overall evaluation of the speech's validity and effectiveness.

## Task 7: Informational Text [RI.9-10.4; SL.9-10.4]
### Analyze Word Choice, Meaning, and Tone

*Write and deliver a visual presentation in which you analyze the impact of word choice on the meaning and tone of a nonfiction work from this unit.*

- Choose a work that exhibits interesting word choices. Identify at least two key words and phrases from that text.

- For each word or phrase you chose, write a paragraph in which you analyze its figurative, connotative, or technical meanings. Explain how those meanings affect the meaning and tone of the work as a whole.

- Find or create visuals, such as photographs, drawings, charts, or graphs, that illustrate the ideas you expressed in words.

- Organize your written materials and visuals into a presentation that sets out a clear line of reasoning.

- Share your presentation with the class, transitioning logically between reading from your text and showing the visuals.

### Is knowledge the same as understanding?

At the beginning of Unit 3, you participated in a discussion of the Big Question. Now that you have completed the unit, write a response to the question. Have you changed your mind about the relationship between knowledge and understanding after thinking about the selections in this unit? Do you still feel the same way? Support your response with at least one example from the selections you read and one from a different subject area or your own experiences. Use Big Question vocabulary words (see p. 425) in your response.

# Featured Titles

In this unit, you have read a variety of informational texts, including literary nonfiction. Continue to read on your own. Select works that you enjoy, but challenge yourself to explore new topics, new authors, and works of increasing depth and complexity. The titles suggested below will help you get started.

## Informational Texts

### Narrative of Sojourner Truth

Born a slave in New York State, Sojourner Truth became a symbol of freedom and justice for both African Americans and women. Her **autobiographical narrative,** dictated by Truth to a neighbor, reveals the transformation of an illiterate slave into a provocative, passionate speaker who paved the way for African American civil rights and feminism.

### Life by the Numbers
by Keith Devlin
John Wiley & Sons, 1998                    **EXEMPLAR TEXT**

This **nonfiction book** shows readers how math applies to everything: the shape of flowers, the realization of virtual reality, and the physics of sports. The author also provides interesting information about some careers in the field of mathematics.

## Biography and Autobiography

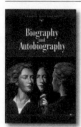

From Doris Kearns Goodwin's recollections of how television revolutionized her neighborhood to Stephen Hawking's story of how he overcame physical limitations, these **biographical** and **autobiographical narratives** give readers fresh perspectives on famous lives.

### Cod: A Biography of the Fish That Changed the World
by Mark Kurlansky                          **EXEMPLAR TEXT**

This **nonfiction book** shows how the cod, a simple fish, fed whole villages, caused several wars, and spurred European transatlantic exploration. On a darker note, Kurlansky describes the dramatic decline of this important species as a result of overfishing.

### Why We Can't Wait
by Martin Luther King, Jr.
Signet, 2000                               **EXEMPLAR TEXT**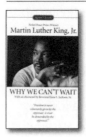

In the 1950s and 60s, Dr. King captured the minds and consciences of a country with his principled stands for justice. This **nonfiction book** is both a description of the Civil Rights movement and a poetic testament to the wisdom and courage of the man who wrote it.

### Abraham Lincoln—DK Biography
by Tanya Lee Stone
Dorling Kindersley Publishing, 2005

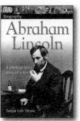

During the perilous days of the Civil War, Abraham Lincoln found himself at the center of events that would transform America as a nation. This **biography** traces Lincoln's life from his boyhood in rural Illinois to the stormy days of his presidency.

## Literature

### The Killer Angels
by Michael Shaara
Ballantine Books, 1974                     **EXEMPLAR TEXT**

This Pulitzer Prize–winning **novel** tells the story of the Battle of Gettysburg, three of the most crucial days of the Civil War. Several points of view are used to draw a complete picture of the moments before and during the battle.

### Words Under the Words: Selected Poems
by Naomi Shihab Nye
Far Corner, 1995

This rich collection of **poetry** reveals how short poems can make big statements about life. Nye explores everything from her Palestinian heritage to the mysterious donor of a music box in poems that burst with imagery and questions and insights about life.

# Preparing to Read Complex Texts

**Attentive Reading** As you read literature on your own, bring your imagination and questions to the text. The questions shown below and others that you ask as you read will help you learn and enjoy literature even more.

 **Common Core State Standards**

**Reading Literature/Informational Text**

**10.** By the end of grade 9, read and comprehend literature, including stories, dramas, poems, and literary nonfiction in the grades 9–10 text complexity band proficiently, with scaffolding as needed at the high end of the range.

## When reading literary nonfiction, ask yourself...

- Who is the author? Why did he or she write the work?
- Are the ideas the author conveys important? Do they merit my attention? If not, why?
- When did the author live and write? Do the attitudes of a particular time and place affect the ideas the author expresses? If so, how?
- Does any one idea strike me as being the most important? Why?
- How might the author's background and life experiences affect his or her views on the topic?
- How might the author's background and life experiences affect his or her use of language?
- How do my life experiences affect what I understand about this work?
- How do my life experiences affect what I feel about the work?
- What can I learn from this text?

**© Key Ideas and Details**

- Does the author order ideas so that I can follow them? If not, what is wrong with the way the text is ordered?
- Does the author capture my interest right from the beginning, or do I have to work to get into the text? Why do I think that is?
- Does the author give me a new way of looking at a topic? If so, how? If not, why?
- Is the author an expert on the topic? How do I know?
- Has the author made me care about the subject? If so, how? If not, why?
- Does the author use strong evidence? Do I find any of the evidence unconvincing? If so, why?

**© Craft and Structure**

- Does the work seem authentic and true? Does any aspect of the work seem exaggerated, false, or unsupported?
- Do I agree or disagree with the author's basic premise? Why?
- Have I read other works about this or a related topic? What does this work add to my knowledge of the topic?
- How would I write about a similar topic? Would I follow a similar approach as the author's, or would I handle the topic differently?

**© Integration of Ideas**

# THE BIG ? How does *communication* change us?

www.PHLitOnline.com

### Hear It!
- Selection summary audio
- Selection audio
- BQ Tunes

### See It!
- Author videos
- Big Question video
- Get Connected videos
- Background videos
- More about the authors
- Illustrated vocabulary words
- Vocabulary flashcards

### Do It!
- Interactive journals
- Interactive graphic organizers
- Grammar tutorials
- Interactive vocabulary games
- Test practice

# How does *communication* change us?

**Communication** involves talking to other people and also listening to them and learning from them. It takes place when you discuss an issue with a friend or react to a piece of writing. Communication is the understanding you get when you read a poem. It is the empathy you feel for others after listening to a news interview with victims of a natural disaster. All of this communication may change us, but how? Does it make us smarter, wiser, kinder, angrier? Does it make us better people, or just more experienced?

## Exploring the Big Question

**Collaboration: Group Discussion** Begin thinking about the Big Question by listing examples of the many ways in which you communicate. Describe an example from each of these categories.

- A discussion with a friend or parent

- A movie that moved you emotionally

- An argument you have had that still bothers you

- A speech or dramatic presentation you gave or heard

- A poem or story you will always remember

- An important conversation you have had

- A commercial or news story that moved you to take action

- A photograph, painting, or song that touched you deeply

  Share your list with a small group. Talk about how these significant communications led to change.

**Connecting to the Literature** Each reading in this unit will give you additional insight into the Big Question.

**PHLit Online!**
www.PHLitOnline.com
- Big Question video
- Illustrated vocabulary words
- Interactive vocabulary games
- BQ Tunes

# Learning Big Question Vocabulary

**Acquire and Use Academic Vocabulary** Academic vocabulary is the language you encounter in textbooks and on standardized tests. Review the definitions of these academic vocabulary words.

> **comprehension** (käm′ prē hen′ shən) *n.* the ability to understand something
>
> **discuss** (di skus′) *v.* talk about with others
>
> **illuminate** (i loo′ mən āt) *v.* light up; make something clear
>
> **informed** (in fôrmd′) *v.* gave someone information; *adj.* having knowledge or information
>
> **interpretation** (in tʉr′ prə tā′ shən) *n.* a way of understanding the meaning of something

Use these words as you complete Big Question activities that involve reading, writing, speaking, and listening.

**Gather Vocabulary Knowledge** Additional Big Question words are listed below. Categorize the words by deciding whether you know each one well, know it a little bit, or do not know it at all.

| | | |
|---|---|---|
| aware | meaning | resolution |
| communication | react | respond |
| empathy | relationship | understanding |
| exchange | | |

Then, do the following:

1. Write the definitions of the words you know.

2. Consult a dictionary to confirm the word's meaning. Revise your definition if necessary.

3. Use all of the words in a brief paragraph about how communication changes us. Write in complete sentences. Avoid fragments or run-on sentences.

**Common Core State Standards**

**Speaking and Listening**
**1.** Initiate and participate effectively in a range of collaborative discussions with diverse partners, building on others' ideas, and expressing their own clearly and persuasively.

**Language**
**6.** Acquire and use accurately grade-appropriate general academic and domain-specific words and phrases, sufficient for reading, writing, speaking, and listening at the college and career readiness level; demonstrate independence in gathering vocabulary knowledge when considering a word or phrase important to comprehension or expression.

# Elements of Poetry

Poetry is imaginative literature that uses precise, musical, and emotionally charged language.

**Poetry** is a literary form that combines the precise meanings of words with their emotional associations and musical qualities, such as rhythm and sounds. There are three main types of poetry:

- **Lyric:** a short poem that expresses the thoughts and feelings of a single speaker
- **Narrative:** a poem that tells a story
- **Dramatic:** a poem that presents the speech of one or more speakers in a dramatic situation

Poems of all types are made up of certain elements. When you read poetry, consider the poem's "voice," structure, and sound.

**Speaker** The speaker in a poem serves the same function as the narrator in a story: to "tell" the poem. In some poems, the speaker is an imagined character. For example, in the poem "Jabberwocky" (page 663), the speaker is not Lewis Carroll, the poet, but the Jabberwock, an imaginary character. Even in personal poems that are based on the poet's life, the speaker is not the poet. Instead, the speaker is a constructed, imagined voice.

**Lines and Stanzas** Most poetry is arranged in lines and **stanzas,** or groupings of lines. Stanzas are named after the number of lines they contain. For example, a couplet consists of two lines, a tercet consists of three lines, and a quatrain consists of four lines.

---

**Example: Quatrain**
Sweetest love, I do not go,
    For weariness of thee,
Nor in hope the world can show
    A fitter love for me
*(from "Song" by John Donne)*

---

In the quatrain, notice that each line *breaks,* or ends, before a complete thought is expressed.

**Rhythm and Meter** Language has its own natural rhythms, created by the stressed and unstressed syllables of words. Poets make use of this innate property of language to create **meter,** or rhythmic patterns built on the arrangement of stressed and unstressed syllables.

Readers identify the kind of meter used in a poem by counting the number and types of stresses in each line. Stressed syllables are marked with an accent symbol (´), and unstressed syllables are marked with a horseshoe symbol (˘). The stressed and unstressed syllables are then divided into units called **feet.** In the following stanza from "The Eagle" (page 647), the vertical lines (|) divide each line into four feet.

---

**Example: Meter**
Thĕ wrín | klĕd seá | bĕneáth | hĭm cráwls,
Hĕ wátch | ĕs fróm | hĭs moúnt | aĭn wálls,
Ănd liké | ă thún | dĕrbólt | hĕ fálls.

---

Each foot is made up of one unstressed syllable and one stressed syllable. This type of foot, called an **iamb,** mimics the rise and fall of the "wrinkled sea" described in the poem. Other types of metrical feet are as follows:

- **Trochee:** a stressed syllable followed by an unstressed syllable, as in the word *twinkle.*
- **Spondee:** two stressed syllables in a row, as in the word *schoolyard*
- **Dactyl:** a stressed syllable followed by two unstressed syllables, as in the word *beautiful*
- **Anapest:** two unstressed syllables followed by a stressed syllable, as in the word *comprehend*

**Rhyme** In addition to meter, poets use other **sound devices,** or techniques that create musical effects. Rhyme is a sound device commonly associated with poetry, although many poems do not rhyme. Types of rhyme include the following:

- **Exact, or true, rhyme:** words that end in both the same vowel and the same consonant sounds
  *Example: sun* and *run*

- **Slant rhyme:** words that end in similar but not exact sounds
  *Example: prove* and *love*

- **End rhyme:** rhyming words that fall at the ends of two or more lines
  *Example: crawls, walls,* and *falls* in the passage from "The Eagle"

- **Internal rhyme:** rhyming words placed within a line
  *Example: The mouse in the house* woke the cat.

**Rhyme Scheme** A set pattern of rhyme is called a **rhyme scheme.** The rhyme scheme of a poem is identified by assigning a different letter of the alphabet to each rhyme. Notice the rhyme scheme of the following stanza from "I Wandered Lonely as a Cloud" (page 627), in which a speaker recalls a field of flowers.

---

**Example: Rhyme Scheme**

| | |
|---|---|
| For oft, when on my couch I lie | **a** |
| In vacant or in pensive mood, | **b** |
| They flash upon that inward eye | **a** |
| Which is the bliss of solitude; | **b** |
| And then my heart with pleasure fills, | **c** |
| And dances with the daffodils. | **c** |

---

Rhyme scheme helps shape the structure of a stanza and clarifies the relationships among the lines. In the example, the *abab* pattern creates a close connection among the first four lines, which describe the speaker's habit of daydreaming about the daffodils. The *cc* rhyme creates a close connection between the last two lines, which sum up the speaker's feelings as he daydreams.

**Other Sound Devices** A poet may use a variety of other sound devices to create musical effects. The chart below explains sound devices that are often used in poetry.

---

**Repetition** is the use of any language element more than once.
**Example:** *Above the town, above the lake, and high above the trees.*

**Alliteration** is the repetition of consonant sounds at the beginning of words.
**Example:** *The snake sneaked past the snail.*

**Assonance** is the repetition of vowel sounds followed by different consonants in two or more stressed syllables.
**Example:** *The green leaves fluttered in the breeze.*

**Consonance** is the repetition of final consonant sounds in stressed syllables with different vowel sounds.
**Example:** *The king sang a song.*

**Onomatopoeia** is the use of words to imitate sounds.
**Example:** *The bees buzzed, and the brook gurgled.*

---

**In This Section**

**Elements of Poetry**

**Analyzing Poetic Language**

**Close Read: Poetic Language and Meaning**

- Model Texts
- Practice Texts

**After You Read**

 Common Core State Standards

**RL.9-10.4**
[For the full wording of the standards, see the standards chart in the front of your textbook.]

# Analyzing Poetic Language

Poets use the **connotations** of words and **figurative language** to express ideas precisely and imaginatively.

**Common Core State Standards**

**Reading Literature 4.** Determine the meaning of words and phrases as they are used in the text, including figurative and connotative meanings; analyze the cumulative impact of specific word choices on meaning and tone.

Poetry relies not only on the sounds and rhythms of language but also on the precise meanings of words. Poets choose each word carefully, considering both its **denotation,** or literal definition, and its **connotation,** or emotional associations.

**Denotative and Connotative Meanings**

Consider the words *thrifty* and *penny-pinching.* Though both words literally mean "careful in the spending of money," their connotative meanings are quite different. *Thrifty* is associated with admirable qualities, such as economy, and therefore conveys a positive attitude. *Penny-pinching* is associated with undesirable qualities, such as stinginess, and therefore conveys a negative attitude. These types of nuances help poets express precise meaning, emotion, and attitudes.

**Meaning and Tone** The connotative meanings of words are especially instrumental in conveying a poem's **tone**—the poet's emotional attitude toward his or her subject. The tone of a poem can be formal, informal, lighthearted, solemn, or anything in between.

As you read the following lines from "I Hear America Singing" (page 750), try to identify the tone that the words create.

**Example:**
I hear America singing, the varied
    carols I hear, . . .
at night the party of young fellows,
    robust, friendly,
Singing with open mouths their strong
    melodious songs.

The positive connotations of the words *singing, carols, robust, friendly, strong,* and *melodious* create a tone that might be described as joyous or cheerful.

**Imagery** Poetic language is also often rich with imagery, or descriptive language that creates word pictures. Through the use of details that appeal to the senses of sight, touch, sound, taste, and smell, poets re-create sensory experiences and emotions in words.

Notice the imagery in the following poem, and analyze the overall impression it creates.

**Example:**
On that long summer day,
    each breath was a labor.
The air was wet wool,
    Heavy and warm.

A thick, yellow haze
    hung over the city,
blocking out buildings,
    blinding the sun.

Not a sound could be heard.
    All was sullen and silent,
save for the whir of
    electric fans.

In the first stanza, the description of the heavy, warm air appeals to the sense of touch. In the second stanza, the description of the yellow haze appeals to the sense of sight. In the third stanza, the onomatopoeic word *whir* appeals to the sense of sound. The overall impression is one of exhaustion and heat.

**Figurative Language** Poetry also often features figurative language, or language that is not meant to be interpreted literally. Most figurative language points out a striking and significant similarity between dissimilar things. Through unexpected comparisons, poets help readers see feelings, experiences, and familiar, everyday objects in a fresh new light.

> **Types of Figurative Language**
>
> A **simile** compares two things using the word *like* or *as: Her visit was as unexpected and welcome as a flower in winter.*
>
> A **metaphor** compares two things by stating one thing in terms of something else: *Her visit was a flower in winter.*
>
> **Personification** gives human qualities or abilities to nonhuman things: *The alarm clock nagged me to get out of bed.*

As you read the following poem, look for examples of each type of figurative language described above.

> **Example:**
> Tall, strong, and silent,
>    the stalks of corn
>     guarded the garden
>     like sentries.
> All ears, they listened
>    for the caws of the crows.
> The birds approached,
>    a hungry, invading force.

In the simile "guarded the garden / like sentries," the cornstalks are compared to watchful soldiers. In a playful example of personification, the ears on the stalks of corn listen for crows. In the metaphor "The birds approached, / a hungry invading force," the crows flying to the garden are compared to an enemy force.

**Free and Formal Verse** The example poem on this page is **free verse**—a type of poetry that exhibits poetic language but does not follow fixed patterns. Free verse may use rhyme, sound devices, varied types of stanzas, and meter but will not do so in a set structure.

By contrast, **formal verse** follows fixed, established patterns. A pattern may require a specific rhyme scheme, meter, line structure, stanza structure, or other element. Throughout history, poets have invented lyric forms. Eventually, some of these forms, including those defined in the chart below, became part of literary tradition.

| Types of Formal Poetry | |
|---|---|
| **Ballad** | a songlike narrative poem, usually written in rhymed stanzas of four to six lines that feature repetition and strong meter |
| **Haiku** | an unrhymed three-line lyric poem, usually focused on images from nature, in which lines 1 and 3 have five syllables and line 2 has seven syllables |
| **English Sonnet** | a fourteen-line lyric poem consisting of three quatrains and a couplet, usually rhymed *abab cdcd efef gg* |
| **Ode** | a lyric poem on a serious subject, usually written in a precise structure |
| **Concrete Poem** | a poem with a shape that suggests its subject; the poet arranges letters, words, punctuation, and lines to create a picture |

The process of formal invention in poetry is ongoing. Today, some poets experiment with forms based on mathematical equations, while others write hypertext poetry—poems that use electronic links online and are different for every reader.

# Close Read: Poetic Language and Meaning

## The elements of poetry combine to build meaning and tone.

Great poems synthesize the poetic elements of language, including sound, rhythms, imagery, and connotations, into works that are wonderful to read and offer profound meanings. To analyze poetry, consider all those elements and identify how they work together to build sound and sense.

**Read aloud.** To begin your analysis, read the poem aloud so that you can hear the language. Make note of sound devices. Consider the voice and character of the speaker. Remember that lines may break before the end of a complete thought, so let the punctuation of the poem guide your reading.

**Read for imagery, figurative language, and structure.** Reread the poem to identify examples of imagery and figurative language, and determine their effects and meanings. Consider any formal elements in the poem and analyze their impact on meaning and tone.

**Read for connotation and tone.** Read the poem again to identify words that suggest a specific tone, paying special attention to the words' connotative meanings.

To guide your analysis of poetry, refer to the chart below, which offers reminders of poetic elements and the ways in which they interact to build meaning and emotional impact in a poem.

## Poetic Elements

**Word Choice and Connotation**
Connotative meanings that carry negative or positive associations provide clues about the ideas and emotions the poem expresses.

**Rhyme**
The repetition of sounds at the ends of words creates musical effects and makes ideas memorable. A regular pattern of rhyme, or rhyme scheme, helps shape stanzas and build relationships among ideas.

**Sensory Language and Imagery**
Word pictures that appeal to the senses express thoughts and feelings. Look for repeated or related images, as these may be clues to a poem's deeper meaning.

**Other Sound Devices**
Repetition, alliteration, assonance, consonance, and onomatopoeia create musical effects and help develop meaning and tone.

**Figurative Language**
Imaginative comparisons, such as similes, metaphors, and personification, make connections among ideas and express shades of meaning.

**Form**
The form of a poem gives structure to the experiences or events it describes. Notice how formal elements in a poem emphasize certain ideas or create a specific emotional quality.

# Model

**About the Text** Sara Teasdale (1884–1933) was born and raised in St. Louis, Missouri. The poem "Barter" is from her collection *Love Songs,* which won the first Pulitzer Prize for poetry, in 1918. A *barter* is a trade or an exchange of items.

## "Barter"
## by Sara Teasdale

Life has loveliness to sell,
    All beautiful and splendid things,
Blue waves whitened on a cliff,
    Soaring fire that sways and sings,
5  And children's faces looking up
Holding wonder like a cup.

Life has loveliness to sell,
    Music like a curve of gold,
Scent of pine trees in the rain,
10     Eyes that love you, arms that hold,
And for your spirit's still delight,
Holy thoughts that star the night.

Spend all you have for loveliness,
    Buy it and never count the cost;
15  For one white singing hour of peace
    Count many a year of strife well lost,
And for a breath of ecstasy
Give all you have been, or could be.

**Rhyme** End rhymes add a musical dimension to the poem and help shape each stanza.

**Figurative Language** The use of personification turns the fire into a living—and joyous—being.

**Figurative Language** The simile allows the reader to "see" music as something tangible and as part of life's "loveliness."

**Other Sound Devices** The alliteration in the repeated "l" and "c" sounds adds to the poem's music.

**Word Choice and Connotation** These words connote powerfully positive emotions and convey a joyful tone.

© **EXEMPLAR TEXT**

# Model

**About the Text** The American poet Emily Dickinson (1830–1886) wrote more than 1,700 brief poems that sparkle with wit and intelligence. She is known for a stylistic use of punctuation, especially exclamation points and dashes, and she often capitalized words within sentences to give them added emphasis.

**Word Choice and Connotation**
Dickinson creates a contrast between darkness, which is associated with fear and death, and light, which is associated with seeing, or understanding.

**Figurative Language**
Dickinson uses metaphors to speak of figurative darknesses. These metaphors suggest periods of great sadness.

**Rhyme** The rhyming words help shape the structure of the stanzas. They support the idea that this experience is a regular occurrence.

**Figurative Language**
The metaphor continues. The "Bravest" people struggle through sadness and sometimes get hurt, but adjust and come to grips with their experiences.

## "We grow accustomed to the Dark—"
### by Emily Dickinson

We grow accustomed to the Dark—
When Light is put away—
As when the Neighbor holds the Lamp
To witness her Goodbye—

5  A Moment—We uncertain step
For newness of the night—
Then—fit our Vision to the Dark—
And meet the Road—erect—

And so of larger—Darknesses—
10  Those Evenings of the Brain—
When not a Moon disclose a sign—
Or Star—come out—within—

The Bravest—grope a little—
And sometimes hit a Tree
15  Directly in the Forehead—
But as they learn to see—

Either the Darkness alters—
Or something in the sight
Adjusts itself to Midnight—
20  And Life steps almost straight.

# Independent Practice

**About the Text** Pat Mora (b. 1942), a bilingual and bicultural Mexican American, often includes Spanish words and phrases in her poems. Her poetry is rich in imagery and feeling, and she often urges her readers to write poems and to "enjoy the word-play." This poem presents a vivid picture of a tornado.

## "Uncoiling" by Pat Mora

With thorns, she scratches
　　on my window, tosses her hair dark with rain,
　　　snares lightning, cholla,[1] hawks, butterfly
　　　　swarms in the tangles.

5　She sighs clouds,
　　　head thrown back, eyes closed, roars
　　　　　　　　　　and rivers leap,
boulders retreat like crabs
into themselves.

10　She spews gusts and thunder,
　　　spooks pale women who scurry to
　　　　lock doors, windows
　　　　　when her tumbleweed skirt starts its spin.

They sing lace lullabies
15　so their children won't hear
　　　her uncoiling
　　　　　through her lips, howling
　　　　　　leaves off trees, flesh
　　　　　　　off bones, until she becomes

20　sound, spins herself
　　　to sleep, sand stinging her ankles,
　　　　whirring into her raw skin like stars.

**Figurative Language** What type of figurative language is introduced in the first stanza? What is the effect?

**Imagery** What emotions do the images in these lines convey?

**Figurative Language** What does this figurative language describe?

**Sound Devices** What sound device is used in these lines? How do the sounds emphasize the action these lines describe?

---

**1. cholla** (cho' yä) *n.* spiny cactus found in the southwestern United States and Mexico.

# Independent Practice

**About the Text** In this poem, the speaker describes her mother who, as a high school student, participated in a speech contest.

**Figurative Language** What type of figurative language is used here? What does it describe?

**Word Choice and Connotation** What does this description of the father suggest about him?

**Sound Devices** What sound devices do you notice in these lines? How do the sounds contribute to the emotion of the poem?

**Figurative Language** What kinds of figurative language appear here? What does this figurative language describe, and what does it suggest?

## "A Voice" by Pat Mora

Even the lights on the stage unrelenting
as the desert sun couldn't hide the other
students, their eyes also unrelenting,
students who spoke English every night

5  as they ate their meat, potatoes, gravy.
Not you. In your house that smelled like
rose powder, you spoke Spanish formal
as your father, the judge without a courtroom

in the country he floated to in the dark
10  on a flatbed truck. He walked slow
as a hot river down the narrow hall
of your house. You never dared to race past him

to say, "Please move," in the language
you learned effortlessly, as you learned to run,
15  the language forbidden at home, though your mother
said you learned it to fight with the neighbors.

You like winning with words. You liked
writing speeches about patriotism and democracy.
You liked all the faces looking at you, all those eyes.
20  "How did I do it?" you ask me now. "How did I do it

when my parents didn't understand?"
The family story says your voice is the voice
of an aunt in Mexico, spunky[1] as a peacock.
Family stories sing of what lives in the blood.

25  You told me only once about the time you went
to the state capitol, your family proud as if
you'd been named governor. But when you looked
around, the only Mexican in the auditorium,

you wanted to hide from those strange faces.
30  Their eyes were pinpricks, and you faked
hoarseness. You, who are never at a loss
for words, felt your breath stick in your throat

---

**1. spunky** (spuŋ′ kē) *adj.* courageous; spirited

like an ice cube. "I can't," you whispered.
"I can't." Yet you did. Not that day but years later.
35    You taught the four of us to speak up.
This is America, Mom. The undoable is done

in the next generation. Your breath moves
through the family like the wind
moves through the trees.

**Form** What type of stanza does the poet use throughout the poem? Why do you think she changes the form at the end?

## After You Read    Uncoiling • A Voice

**1. Key Ideas and Details (a) Infer:** In "Uncoiling," what kind of storm does the speaker describe? **(b) Interpret:** Identify three actions that the storm takes. **(c) Analyze:** How do these actions show the storm's violence?

**2. Craft and Structure (a) Analyze:** In "Uncoiling," what type of figurative language does Mora use to describe the storm? **(b)** What is the effect of this choice?

**3. Key Ideas and Details (a) Interpret:** In "A Voice," which of her mother's childhood accomplishments does the poet celebrate? **(b) Summarize:** What happens to her mother at the state capitol? **(c) Analyze:** According to the speaker, how does the mother turn the pain of that experience into triumph later in life?

**4. Craft and Structure (a)** Note one simile and one metaphor in "A Voice." **(b) Interpret:** Explain the action each example describes.

**5. Craft and Structure (a) Determine:** In "A Voice," the speaker states that family lore describes the mother's voice as being "spunky as a peacock." What type of figurative language is this? **(b) Analyze:** What meaning does this comparison suggest?

**6. Craft and Structure Compare and Contrast:** Compare and contrast the image of the wind in the last stanza of "A Voice" with the image of the wind in "Uncoiling." Explain differences in both tone and meaning.

**7. Integration of Knowledge and Ideas (a)** In the first column of a chart like the one shown, list images of breathing or speaking from the poems. In the second column, note the literal meaning of each image. In the third column, describe each image's effect—the word picture it conveys or the feeling it expresses.

| What It Says | What It Means | Effect |
|---|---|---|
|  |  |  |

**(b) Collaborate:** In a small group, discuss your findings.

## ⓒ Leveled Texts

Build your skills and improve your comprehension of poetry with texts of increasing complexity.

**Poetry Collection 1** includes poems about dreams, the natural world, and love.

**Poetry Collection 2** connects physical and emotional worlds.

## ⓒ Common Core State Standards

Meet these standards with either **Poetry Collection 1** (p. 618) or **Poetry Collection 2** (p. 630).

**Reading Literature**
**4.** Determine the meaning of words and phrases as they are used in a text, including figurative and connotative meanings; analyze the cumulative impact of specific word choices on meaning and tone. *(Literary Analysis: Figurative Language; Literary Analysis: Spiral Review)*

**Writing**
**3.d.** Use precise words and phrases, telling details, and sensory language to convey a vivid picture of the experiences, events, setting, and/or characters. *(Writing: Description of a Scene)*

**Speaking and Listening**
**4.** Present information, findings, and supporting evidence clearly, concisely, and logically such that listeners can

follow the line of reasoning and the organization, development, substance, and style are appropriate to purpose, audience, and task. *(Speaking and Listening: Impromptu Speech)*

**Language**
**1.** Demonstrate command of the conventions of standard English grammar and usage when writing or speaking. *(Conventions: Prepositions)*

**5.** Demonstrate understanding of figurative language, word relationships, and nuances in meanings. *(Vocabulary: Analogies)*

# Literary Analysis: Figurative Language

**Figurative language** is language that is used imaginatively rather than literally. An author's use of figurative language can significantly influence the tone, mood, and theme of a poem. Figurative language includes figures of speech, which are literary devices that make unexpected comparisons or change the usual meanings of words. The following are specific types of figures of speech:

- **Simile:** a comparison of two apparently unlike things using *like, as, than,* or *resembles:* "The morning sun is <u>like</u> a red rubber ball."

- **Metaphor:** a description of one thing as if it were another: "The morning sun is a red rubber ball."

- **Personification:** assignment of human characteristics to a non-human subject: "The <u>sea</u> was <u>angry</u> that day, my friends."

- **Paradox:** a statement, an idea, or a situation that seems contradictory but actually expresses a truth: "The more things change, the more they stay the same."

## Using the Strategy: Figurative Language Chart

Use a **figurative language chart** like the one shown to determine the meaning of each type of figurative language you find as you read the poems that follow.

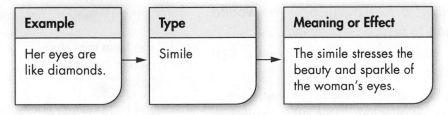

| Example | Type | Meaning or Effect |
|---------|------|-------------------|
| Her eyes are like diamonds. | Simile | The simile stresses the beauty and sparkle of the woman's eyes. |

# Reading Skill: Read Fluently

**Reading fluently** is reading continuously while also comprehending the text and appreciating the writer's artistry. Paying attention to punctuation can help you read poetry fluently. When reading poetry, **read in sentences or units of meaning.** Use punctuation rather than the ends of lines to determine where to pause or stop reading.

# How does communication change us?

## Writing About the Big Question

The poets in this collection communicate ideas that help us think about the world in new ways. Use this sentence starter to develop your ideas about the Big Question.

> When the speaker of a poem asks the audience to **respond** to a question, the reader is pushed to _____ and _____.

**While You Read** Think about what idea or ideas the speaker of each poem is sharing with us. Then, decide how you would respond to any questions the poetry raises.

## Vocabulary

Read each word and its definition. Decide whether you know the word well, know it a little bit, or do not know it at all. After you read, see how your knowledge of each word has increased.

- **deferred** (dē furd´) *adj.* put off until a future time (p. 620) *Jackie* <u>*deferred*</u> *her trip to Italy until she had more money.* defer *v.* deferring *v.* deferral *n.* deference *n.*

- **fester** (fes´ tər) *v.* become infected; form pus (p. 620) *The wound became infected and began to* <u>*fester*</u>. festering *adj.*

- **barren** (bar´ ən) *adj.* empty; having little or no vegetation ( p. 621) *The hillside was* <u>*barren*</u> *after the fire.* barrenness *n.*

- **paradoxical** (par´ ə däk´ si kəl) *adj.* seemingly full of contradictions (p. 623) *I think it is* <u>*paradoxical*</u> *that people in cities could be lonely.* paradox *n.*

- **pensive** (pen´ siv) *adj.* deeply or seriously thoughtful (p. 628) *Everyone remembered the professor as a quiet and* <u>*pensive*</u> *man.* pensively *adv.* pensiveness *n.*

- **solitude** (säl´ ə to͞od´) *n.* the state of being solitary, or alone; seclusion, isolation, or remoteness (p. 628) *I enjoy a quiet moment of* <u>*solitude*</u> *before the guests arrive.* solitary *adj.* sole *adj.*

### Word Study

The **Latin root -fer-** means "bring" or "carry."

The first poem in Poetry Collection 1 is about a dream that has been **deferred**—the dream may have been carried away, or put off until a future time.

# Langston Hughes

**(1902–1967)**

**Author of "Dream Deferred" • "Dreams"** (pp. 620, 621)

Born in Joplin, Missouri, Langston Hughes was the first African American to earn a living by writing literary works. As a young man, he held a variety of jobs—teacher, ranch hand, and farmer, among others. He drew on all of these experiences, but primarily on his perspective as an African American, to create his great body of work.

# Jean de Sponde

**(1557–1595)**

**Author of "Sonnet on Love XIII"** (p. 622)

The French poet Jean de Sponde was a true Renaissance man who served in the court of King Henry IV, dabbled in chemistry, and published scholarly editions of ancient Greek texts. "Sonnet on Love XIII" is part of his finest work, *Sonnets of Love and Death.*

# Gabriela Mistral

**(1889–1957)**

**Author of "Meciendo/Rocking"** (p. 624)

Born in Chile as Lucila Godoy y Alcayaga, this writer formed her pen name from the names of her two favorite poets, the Italian Gabriele D'Annunzio and the French Frederic Mistral. Gabriela Mistral wrote many moving poems about children and motherhood. She was awarded the Nobel Prize in Literature in 1945.

# William Wordsworth

**(1770–1850)**

**Author of "I Wandered Lonely as a Cloud"** (p. 626)

William Wordsworth was born in England's rural Lake District. In 1798, he and fellow poet Samuel Taylor Coleridge published *Lyrical Ballads*—poems that use simple language to exalt everyday life. Emphasizing nature and the imagination, Wordsworth ushered in the age of Romanticism.

*Street Shadows,* 1959, Jacob Lawrence, © ARS, NY/ Photo courtesy of: The Jacob and Gwendolyn Lawrence Foundation / Art Resource, NY

# Dream *Deferred*

## Langston Hughes

▲ **Critical Viewing**
Does the context of this poem make the image above seem hopeless or hopeful? Explain. **[Interpret]**

**Vocabulary**
**deferred** (dē fʉrd´)
*adj.* put off until
a future time

**fester** (fes´ tər) *v.*
become infected;
form pus

*Harlem*

What happens to a dream deferred?

Does it dry up
like a raisin in the sun?
5  Or fester like a sore—
And then run?
Does it stink like rotten meat?
Or crust and sugar over—
like a syrupy sweet?

10  Maybe it just sags
like a heavy load.

*Or does it explode?*

# Dreams
## Langston Hughes

Hold fast to dreams
For if dreams die
Life is a broken-winged bird
That cannot fly.

5  Hold fast to dreams
For when dreams go
Life is a barren field
Frozen with snow.

# Sonnet on Love XIII

## Jean de Sponde

*translated by* David R. Slavitt

**Background** Archimedes (är´ kə mē´ dēz´) (287?–212 B.C.) has been called the founder of theoretical mechanics. He was a brilliant Greek mathematician and inventor who once boasted that, given a place to stand in space and a long enough lever, he could move the Earth itself. Legend has it that when he made a great discovery, he jumped up and shouted "Eureka!" ("I have found it!").

"Give me a place to stand," Archimedes said,
"and I can move the world." Paradoxical, clever,
his remark which first explained the use of the lever
was an academic joke. But if that dead

5  sage could return to life, he would find a clear
demonstration of his idea, which is not
pure theory after all. That putative[1] spot
exists in the love I feel for you, my dear.

What could be more immovable or stronger?
10  What becomes more and more secure, the longer
it is battered by inconstancy and the stress

we find in our lives? Here is that fine fixed point
from which to move a world that is out of joint,
as he could have done, had he known a love like this.

**Vocabulary**
**paradoxical** (par´ ə däk´ si kəl) *adj.* seemingly full of contradictions

**Reading Skill**
**Read Fluently**
Where does the sentence that starts in line 10 end?

---

1. **putative** (py̅o̅o̅t´ ə tiv) *adj.* supposed; known by reputation.

◄ **Critical Viewing** Based on this depiction of Archimedes, how do you think he would have responded to de Sponde's poem? **[Speculate]**

# Meciendo

## Gabriela Mistral

▲ **Critical Viewing**
How well does this photograph illustrate the "loving sea" described in the poem? Explain. **[Evaluate]**

El mar sus millares de olas
mece, divino.
Oyendo a los mares amantes,
mezo a mi niño.

5  El viento errabundo en la noche
mece a los trigos.
Oyendo a los vientos amantes,
mezo a mi niño.

Diós Padre sus miles de mundos
10  mece sin ruido.
Sintiendo su mano en la sombra,
mezo a mi niño.

# Rocking (Meciendo)

## Gabriela Mistral

### translated by Doris Dana

The sea rocks her thousands of waves.
The sea is divine.
Hearing the loving sea,
I rock my son.

5 The wind wandering by night
rocks the wheat.
Hearing the loving wind,
I rock my son.

God, the Father, soundlessly rocks
10 His thousands of worlds.
Feeling His hand in the shadow,
I rock my son.

**Literary Analysis**
**Figurative Language**
What human traits does the wind show in the second stanza?

# I Wandered Lonely as a Cloud

## William Wordsworth

I wandered lonely as a cloud
That floats on high o'er vales[1] and hills,
When all at once I saw a crowd,
A host, of golden daffodils;
5   Beside the lake, beneath the trees,
Fluttering and dancing in the breeze.

Continuous as the stars that shine
And twinkle on the milky way,
They stretched in never-ending line
10  Along the margin of a bay:
Ten thousand saw I at a glance,
Tossing their heads in sprightly dance.
The waves beside them danced; but they
Outdid the sparkling waves in glee;
15  A poet could not but be gay,
In such a jocund[2] company;

---

**1. o'er vales** over valleys.
**2. jocund** (jak´ ənd) *adj.* cheerful.

**Spiral Review**
**Tone** Compare the tone of line 1 to the tone of line 6. In what way has the tone shifted?

**Literary Analysis**
**Figurative Language**
To what does the speaker compare the daffodils in the simile in lines 7–8?

**Vocabulary**

**pensive** (pen´ siv)
*adj.* deeply or seri-
ously thoughtful

**solitude** (säl´ ə tōōd´) *n.*
the state of being soli-
tary, or alone; seclusion,
isolation, or remoteness

I gazed—and gazed—but little thought
What wealth the show to me had brought:

For oft, when on my couch I lie
20 In vacant or in pensive mood,
They flash upon that inward eye
Which is the bliss of solitude;
And then my heart with pleasure fills,
And dances with the daffodils.

## Critical Thinking

**Cite textual evidence to support your responses.**

1. **Key Ideas and Details (a)** To what two things does the speaker in "Dreams" compare life? **(b) Interpret:** Restate in your own words the advice that "Dreams" offers.

2. **Key Ideas and Details (a)** How many questions does "Dream Deferred" ask? Explain. **(b) Contrast:** In what way is the last question different from the others? Explain your response.

3. **Key Ideas and Details (a)** In "I Wandered Lonely as a Cloud," what natural sight does the speaker describe? **(b)** In "Meciendo/ Rocking," what natural sights and sounds does the speaker describe? **(c) Compare and Contrast:** How do the natural sights and sounds affect each of the speakers? Explain how each poem reveals this.

4. **Key Ideas and Details (a) Interpret:** In "Sonnet on Love XIII," to what does the speaker compare his love? **(b) Draw Conclusions:** What does this comparison suggest about the speaker's feelings? Explain your response.

5. **Integration of Knowledge and Ideas (a)** How would you answer the main question posed by the speaker in "Dream Deferred"? Why? **(b)** How does your response to that question grow or change when you read "Dreams"? Explain. *[Connect to the Big Question: How does communication change us?]*

## Literary Analysis: Figurative Language

**1. Craft and Structure (a)** Identify one **simile** in "Dream Deferred" and one **metaphor** in "Dreams." **(b)** Explain what each **figure of speech** contributes to the overall meaning of the poem in which it appears.

**2. Craft and Structure (a)** Identify an example of **personification** in Poetry Collection 1. **(b)** Explain how this use of **figurative language** contributes to the overall effect of the poem in which it appears.

**3. Craft and Structure** Identify and explain the **paradox** in "Sonnet on Love XIII."

## Reading Skill: Read Fluently

**4. (a)** Using a graphic organizer like the one shown, rewrite one stanza in Poetry Collection 1 as a prose paragraph.

| Stanza | Paragraph |
|---|---|
| God, the Father, soundlessly rocks His thousands of worlds. Feeling His hand in the shadow, I rock my son. | God, the Father, soundlessly rocks His thousands of worlds. Feeling His hand in the shadow, I rock my son. |

**(b)** Read the stanza and the paragraph aloud. How does following the punctuation help you **read fluently?**

## Vocabulary

**Acquisition and Use** Vocabulary **analogies** show the relationships between pairs of words. Use a word from the vocabulary list on page 618 to make a word pair that matches the relationship between the first two given words.

**1.** active : exercise :: _____ : ponder

**2.** rainy : weather :: _____ : statement

**3.** empty : full :: _____ : fruitful

**4.** rushed : hurried :: _____ : delayed

**5.** multitude : many :: _____ : one

**6.** burn : blaze :: _____ : rot

**Word Study** Use the context of the sentences and what you know about the **Latin root -fer-** to explain your answer to each question.

**1.** If you *transfer* something, do you keep it in one place?

**2.** Does a *conference* bring people together?

### Word Study

The **Latin root -fer-** means "bring" or "carry."

**Apply It** Explain how the root *-fer-* contributes to the meanings of these words. Consult a dictionary if necessary.

infer
referral
fertile

## Making Connections
**Poetry Collection 2**

All Watched Over... •
"Hope" is the thing... •
Much Madness is divinest... •
The War Against the Trees

# How does *communication* change us?

## Writing About the Big Question

The poets in this collection share thoughts about how technology, war, and even ideas can change both us and the way we regard the world. Use this sentence starter to develop your ideas about the Big Question:

As a result of advances in computer technology, **relationships** between people have become _____ because _____.

**While You Read** Consider what each poem has to say about how people relate to each other and to the world around them.

## Vocabulary

Read each word and its definition. Decide whether you know the word well, know it a little bit, or do not know it at all. After you read, see how your knowledge of each word has increased.

- **abash** (ə bash´) *v.* embarrass (p. 634) *The bully would continuously* <u>abash</u> *his peers to make himself feel more confident.* abashed *adj.* abashedly *adv.* bashful *adj.*

- **discerning** (di sʉrn´ iŋ) *adj.* having good judgment or understanding (p. 635) *The* <u>discerning</u> *viewer will realize what a bad movie this is.* discern *v.* discernment *n.*

- **prevail** (prē vāl´) *v.* gain the advantage or mastery; be victorious; triumph (p. 635) *Good* <u>prevails</u> *over evil in this holiday movie.* prevailing *adj.*

- **preliminaries** (prē lim´ ə ner´ ēz) *n.* steps or events before the main one (p. 637) *The* <u>preliminaries</u>, *especially the national anthem, were more exciting than the game.* preliminary *adj.*

- **subverting** (səb vʉrt´ iŋ) *v.* overthrowing or destroying something established (p. 637) *By* <u>subverting</u> *the monarchy, the revolutionaries hoped to bring freedom.* subvert *v.* subversive *adj.* subversion *n.*

- **seizure** (sē´ zhər) *n.* a sudden and brief loss of consciousness and body control. (p. 637) *One of the customers in the store suffered a* <u>seizure</u> *and fell to the floor.* seize *v.*

### Word Study

The **Latin root -vert-** means "turn."

In the poem "The War Against the Trees," the speaker describes the **subverting** of trees. Bulldozers dig into the roots of the trees and *turn* the trees over from underneath.

# Richard Brautigan

**(1935–1984)**

**Author of "All Watched Over by Machines of Loving Grace"** (p. 632)

With his 1967 novel *Trout Fishing in America*, Richard Brautigan became a spokesperson for the hippie generation. Ironically, he was at least fifteen years older than the hippies and a product of the Beat generation that preceded them. Nevertheless, his writing demonstrates his free spirit. His books present sketches of a counterculture that resists dependence on machines, industry, and business.

# Emily Dickinson

**(1830–1886)**

**Author of "'Hope' is the thing with feathers—"** • **"Much Madness is divinest Sense—"** (pp. 634, 635)

Despite her quiet, outward behavior, Emily Dickinson's inner life overflowed with energy. She produced at least 1,775 poems. Dickinson looked deeply into simple subjects—a fly buzzing, a bird on a walk, the changing seasons. She also made profound explorations of love, death, and the relationship between the human and the divine. She remains unquestionably one of America's finest poets.

# Stanley Kunitz

**(1905–2006)**

**Author of "The War Against the Trees"** (p. 636)

Stanley Kunitz was born in Worcester, Massachusetts, and published his first book of poems in 1930. Kunitz worked as an editor on many small magazines and taught countless young poets. He was named the United States Poet Laureate in 2000.

# All Watched Over by Machines of Loving Grace

## Richard Brautigan

I like to think (and
the sooner the better!)
of a cybernetic meadow
where mammals and computers
5   live together in mutually
programming harmony
like pure water
touching clear sky.

I like to think
   (right now, please!)
10  of a cybernetic forest
filled with pines and electronics
where deer stroll peacefully
past computers
as if they were flowers
15  with spinning blossoms.

I like to think
   (it has to be!)
of a cybernetic ecology
where we are free of our labors
and joined back to nature,
20  returned to our mammal
brothers and sisters,
and all watched over
by machines of loving grace.

**Literary Analysis**
**Figurative Language**
What simile does the speaker use in lines 3–8 to describe the cybernetic meadow?

©

**Spiral Review**
**Tone** What tone is conveyed by the parenthetical expressions in the poem?

# "Hope" is the thing with feathers—
## EMILY DICKINSON

**Reading Skill**
**Read Fluently**
Where in the second stanza could you replace a dash with a period to signify the end of a sentence?

**Vocabulary**
**abash** (ə bash´)
*v.* embarrass

"Hope" is the thing with feathers—
That perches in the soul—
And sings the tune without the words—
And never stops—at all—

5　And sweetest—in the Gale[1]—is heard—
And sore must be the storm—
That could abash the little Bird
That kept so many warm—

I've heard it in the chillest land—
10　And on the strangest Sea—
Yet, never, in Extremity,
It asked a crumb—of Me.

---

**1. Gale** (gāl) *n.* strong wind.

▶ **Critical Viewing**
Why might someone associate birds with hope? **[Speculate]**

# Much Madness is divinest Sense—

## EMILY DICKINSON

Much Madness is divinest Sense—
To a discerning Eye—
Much Sense—the starkest Madness—
'Tis the Majority
5   In this, as All, prevail—
Assent[1]—and you are sane—
Demur[2]—you're straightway dangerous—
And handled with a Chain—

**Vocabulary**
**discerning** (di sʉrn´ iŋ)
*adj.* having good judgment or understanding
**prevail** (prē vāl´) *v.* gain the advantage or mastery; be victorious; triumph

---

1. **assent** (ə sent´) *v.* agree.
2. **demur** (dē mʉr´) *v.* hesitate because of doubts or objections.

# THE WAR AGAINST THE TREES

## STANLEY KUNITZ

The man who sold his lawn to standard oil
Joked with his neighbors come to watch the show
While the bulldozers, drunk with gasoline,
Tested the virtue of the soil
5   Under the branchy sky
By overthrowing first the privet-row.

Forsythia-forays and hydrangea-raids
Were but preliminaries to a war
Against the great-grandfathers of the town,
10   So freshly lopped and maimed.
They struck and struck again,
And with each elm a century went down.

All day the hireling engines charged the trees,
Subverting them by hacking underground
15   In grub-dominions, where dark summer's mole
Rampages through his halls,
Till a northern seizure shook
Those crowns, forcing the giants to their knees.

**Vocabulary**
**preliminaries** (prē lim´ ə ner´ ēz) *n.* steps or events before the main one

**subverting** (səb vʉrt´ iŋ) *v.* overthrowing or destroying something established

**seizure** (sē´ zhər) *n.* a sudden and brief loss of consciousness and body control

**Literary Analysis**
**Figurative Language**
What are the "giants" that are personified in line 18?

◄ **Critical Viewing** What does a tree like the one shown represent to the speaker of the poem? **[Connect]**

I saw the ghosts of children at their games
20 Racing beyond their childhood in the shade,
And while the green world turned its death-foxed page
And a red wagon wheeled,
I watched them disappear
Into the suburbs of their grievous age.

25 Ripped from the craters much too big for hearts
The club-roots bared their amputated coils,
Raw gorgons matted blind, whose pocks and scars
Cried Moon! on a corner lot
One witness-moment, caught
30 In the rear-view mirrors of the passing cars.

## Critical Thinking

Cite textual evidence to support your responses.

@ 1. **Key Ideas and Details (a)** To what does the speaker compare computers in the imaginary world of "All Watched Over by Machines of Loving Grace"? **(b) Interpret:** What does this comparison suggest about the speaker's feelings about computers in the real world?

@ 2. **Key Ideas and Details (a)** In "'Hope' is the thing with feathers—," when does hope sing the sweetest? **(b) Interpret:** Why does hope sing so well at these times? Explain your response.

@ 3. **Key Ideas and Details (a) Interpret:** In "The War Against the Trees," who or what is at war with the trees? **(b) Draw Conclusions:** What does the image of war suggest about the speaker's feelings toward the trees and what is happening to them? Explain how the poem reveals this.

@ 4. **Integration of Knowledge and Ideas (a) Interpret:** In "Much Madness is divinest Sense—," what kind of behavior is considered insane? **(b) Evaluate:** Do you agree with the speaker's ideas? Explain your answer.

@ 5. **Integration of Knowledge and Ideas (a)** Describe the relationship that the speaker of "All Watched Over by Machines of Loving Grace" envisions between people and computers. **(b)** How might people change as a result of this new kind of relationship with computers? Explain. *[Connect to the Big Question: How does communication change us?]*

## Literary Analysis: Figurative Language

1. **Craft and Structure** **(a)** Identify a **simile** and a **metaphor** in Poetry Collection 2. **(b)** Explain what each **figure of speech** contributes to the overall meaning or effect of the poem in which it appears.

2. **Craft and Structure** **(a)** Identify one example of **personification** in Collection 2. **(b)** Explain how this use of **figurative language** contributes to the overall meaning or effect of the poem in which it appears.

3. **Craft and Structure** **(a)** Identify the **paradox** in "Much Madness is divinest Sense—." **(b)** Explain why it is a paradox.

## Reading Skill: Read Fluently

4. **(a)** Using a graphic organizer like the one shown, rewrite one stanza in Poetry Collection 2 as a prose paragraph.

| Stanza | Paragraph |
|---|---|
| I've heard it in the chillest land— And on the strangest Sea— Yet, never, in Extremity, It asked a crumb—of Me. | I've heard it in the chillest land and on the strangest Sea, yet never, in Extremity, it asked a crumb of me. |

**(b)** Read the stanza and the paragraph aloud. How does following punctuation help you **read fluently?**

## Vocabulary

**Acquisition and Use** Vocabulary **analogies** show the relationships between pairs of words. Use a word from the Poetry Collection 2 list on page 630 that creates a word pair matching the relationship between the first two given words.

1. destroying : creating :: _____ : supporting
2. forgiving : fan :: _____ : expert
3. rehearsal : performance :: _____ : championship
4. lose : defeat :: _____ : victory
5. praise : confidence :: _____ : shame
6. house : home :: _____ : attack

**Word Study** Use the context of the sentences and what you know about the **Latin root -vert-** to explain your answer to each question.

1. Is someone who is *introverted* outgoing or shy?
2. What happens to your attention when it gets *diverted*?

### Word Study

The **Latin root -vert-** means "turn."

**Apply It** Explain how the root -vert- contributes to the meanings of these words. Consult a dictionary if necessary.

inversion
revert
vertical

# Integrated Language Skills

## Poetry Collections 1 and 2

### Conventions: Prepositions

**Poetry Collection 1**

A **preposition** is a word that relates a noun or pronoun to another word in the sentence.

The **object of the preposition** is the noun or pronoun at the end of a **prepositional phrase.**

Although most prepositions, such as *at* and *with,* are single words, some prepositions are made up of two or three words. These prepositions are called **compound prepositions.** Some compound prepositions are spelled as a single word, such as *into* and *throughout.* Others, such as *because of* and *in addition to,* are spelled as separate words.

**Poetry Collection 2**

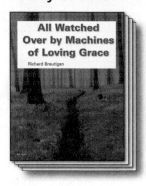

**Common Prepositions:** about, above, across, below, beyond, by, down, except, for, from, in, of, on, over, past, through, to, under, until, up, with

**Prepositional Phrase:** Mr. Johnson ate at a good <u>restaurant</u>. (*restaurant* is the *object of the preposition <u>at</u>*)

**Common Compound Prepositions:** without, underneath, outside, according to, along with, in front of, instead of, next to

**Practice A** Identify the preposition and object of the preposition in each sentence.

1. Hold fast to dreams.
2. I wandered lonely as a cloud.
3. Feeling His hand in the shadow, I rock my son.
4. According to legend, Archimedes shouted "Eureka!" when he made a discovery.

**Ⓒ Reading Application** Find three sentences in "Dream Deferred" that contain a preposition. Identify both the preposition and the object of the preposition in each sentence.

**Practice B** Identify the preposition and object of the preposition in each sentence. Then, rewrite each sentence using a different prepositional phrase.

1. Deer stroll peacefully past computers.
2. I've heard it in the chillest land.
3. The bulldozers rolled across the yard.
4. People stood across the street and watched the bulldozers.

**Ⓒ Writing Application** Write three sentences about the image on page 636, using a compound preposition in each one.

**PH WRITING COACH** Further instruction and practice are available in *Prentice Hall Writing Coach.*

# Writing

**Informative Text** Using one of the scenes described in either Poetry Collection 1 or Poetry Collection 2 as a model, write a **description of a scene** in nature. Using the figurative and connotative language techniques of the author you are emulating, develop your own descriptive word picture in a few paragraphs or a poem.

- Choose a scene that you know firsthand or from photographs.
- List details in the scene that appeal to one or more of the senses.
- Refer to your list of details as you draft your description, and work to establish a controlling impression.

**Grammar Application** Make sure you use prepositions and prepositional phrases correctly in your writing.

**Writing Workshop:** *Work in Progress*

**Prewriting for Descriptive Essay** To prepare for a descriptive essay you may write, make a Sight List of three places. For each place, write ten words that describe how the place looks. Then, choose one place and add a Sensory Word List that describes other characteristics of the place, such as smells or sounds. Save both your Sight List and your Sensory Word List.

# Speaking and Listening

**Comprehension and Collaboration** Use one of the poems in Poetry Collection 1 or Poetry Collection 2 as the basis for an **impromptu speech** about dreams, nature, or love.

- Instead of writing a script or outline, jot down the central point you want to convey. Create concise notes to refer to during your delivery.
- Engage your audience by choosing interesting details that are appropriate to the purpose of your speech.
- As you speak, use a variety of sentence structures. Using a mix of long and short sentences as well as simple and complex sentences will help listeners follow your ideas.
- Make your ideas memorable by using figurative language.
- Use body language and eye contact to convey sincerity.
- Create a rubric so that classmates can assess your speech, and invite them to give you feedback about your performance.

Present your speech before an audience of peers. Evaluate the feedback and make notes about how you can apply it to future speeches.

**Common Core State Standards**

L.9-10.1, L.9-10.5; W.9-10.3.d; SL.9-10.4
[For the full wording of the standards, see page 616.]

Use this prewriting activity to prepare for the **Writing Workshop** on page 686.

www.PHLitOnline.com

- Interactive graphic organizers
- Grammar tutorial
- Interactive journals

## © Leveled Texts

Build your skills and improve your comprehension of poetry with texts of increasing complexity.

The poems in **Poetry Collection 3** use powerful language to make ordinary events extraordinary.

The poems in **Poetry Collection 4** use sounds to add layers of meaning.

## © Common Core State Standards

Meet these standards with either **Poetry Collection 3** (p. 646) or **Poetry Collection 4** (p. 654).

**Reading Literature**
**4.** Determine the meaning of words and phrases as they are used in the text, including figurative and connotative meanings; analyze the cumulative impact of specific word choices on meaning and tone. *(Literary Analysis: Spiral Review)*

**Writing**
**1.** Write arguments to support claims in an analysis of substantive topics or texts, using valid reasoning and relevant and sufficient evidence. *(Writing: Editorial)*

**Speaking and Listening**
**1.** Initiate and participate effectively in a range of collaborative discussions with diverse partners on *grades*

*9–10 topics, texts, and issues,* building on others' ideas and expressing their own clearly and persuasively.

**5.** Make strategic use of digital media in presentations to enhance understanding of findings, reasoning, and evidence and to add interest. *(Speaking and Listening: Illustrated Presentation)*

**Language**
**1.** Demonstrate command of the conventions of standard English grammar and usage when writing or speaking. *(Conventions: Prepositional Phrases)*

**5.** Demonstrate understanding of figurative language, word relationships, and nuances in word meanings. *(Vocabulary: Greek Prefixes)*

# Literary Analysis: Sound Devices

Poets use **sound devices** to emphasize the sound relationships among words. Sound devices, such as those on the following list, also impact the meaning and tone in a poem and help bring it to life for readers.

- **Alliteration:** the repetition of initial consonant sounds in stressed syllables: *"The fair breeze blew, the white foam flew . . ."*
- **Consonance:** the repetition of final consonant sounds in stressed syllables with different vowel sounds, as in *sit* and *cat*
- **Assonance:** the repetition of similar vowel sounds in stressed syllables that end with different consonants, as in *seal* and *meet*
- **Onomatopoeia:** the use of a word whose sound imitates its meaning, such as *pop* or *hiss*

All of these sound devices work to engage the reader's senses and create musical and emotional effects.

# Reading Skill: Read Fluently

**Reading fluently** is reading smoothly and continuously while also comprehending the text. Because poetry is a condensed form of language that employs figurative language, read poems several times to unlock layers of meaning.

## Using the Strategy: Multiple Reading Chart

Use a multiple reading chart such as the one shown to record your understanding of the poems.

|  | My Understanding |
|---|---|
| **1st Reading**<br>• Read for basic meaning. |  |
| **2nd Reading**<br>• Read to unlock deeper meanings. |  |
| **3rd Reading**<br>• Read to recognize and appreciate poet's craft. |  |

## How does *communication* change us?

### Writing About the Big Question

In "Analysis of Baseball," the speaker shares her impressions of "America's pastime." Use these sentence starters to develop your ideas about the Big Question.

Reading someone's **interpretation** of a common experience can **illuminate** one's **understanding** of that experience because

_____.

When people **exchange** stories about the past, they become more **aware** of the present because _____.

**While You Read** Notice when the speaker of a poem describes an experience with which you are familiar, and compare the speaker's response to your own.

### Vocabulary

Read each word and its definition. Decide whether you know the word well, know it a little bit, or do not know it at all. After you read, see how your knowledge of each word has increased.

- **clasps** (klasps) *v.* grips (p. 647) *My mother clasps the steering wheel tightly whenever she approaches a sharp turn in the road.* clasp *n.*

- **azure** (azh´ ər) *adj.* sky blue (p. 647) *She painted the ceiling in her bedroom azure so that it would look like the sky.*

- **analysis** (ə nal´ ə sis) *n.* careful examination by studying something's elements or parts (p. 649) *After a careful analysis of the food sample, the pathologist determined that it had been poisoned.* analyze *v.* analytical *adj.*

- **disgrace** (dis grās´) *n.* loss of respect, honor, or esteem; shame (p. 649) *After scoring on themselves and losing to their rivals as a result, the team left the field in disgrace.* disgraceful *adj.* disgraced *v.*

### Word Study

The **Greek prefix** *ana-* means "up," "back," or "against."

Translated directly from its Greek word parts, the word **analysis** means "a loosening up." In the poem "Analysis of Baseball," the speaker "loosens up" the subject of baseball by describing its most basic parts.

# Walter Dean Myers

**(b. 1937)**

**Author of "Summer"** (p. 646)

Growing up poor in West Virginia and New York City, Walter Dean Myers never imagined himself becoming a writer. Although he was writing poems and stories by his early teens, he believed that his dream of a literary career would never be realized. Myers's dream was fulfilled, however, when he won a writing contest sponsored by the Council on Interracial Books for Children with his book *Where Does a Day Go?*

# Alfred, Lord Tennyson

**(1809–1892)**

**Author of "The Eagle"** (p. 647)

The most popular British poet during his lifetime, Alfred, Lord Tennyson rose from humble beginnings to the position of poet laureate of England. Although he was enthralled by the technological advances of the Victorian Era, Tennyson remained a poet of nature, bringing both imagination and feeling to descriptions of the landscape and its inhabitants.

# May Swenson

**(1919–1989)**

**Author of "Analysis of Baseball"** (p. 648)

May Swenson has been called "one of the surest poets, clear-eyed and absolute." She was born in Logan, Utah, and attended Utah State University. After working for a while as a newspaper reporter, she moved to New York City, where she worked as an editor and as a college lecturer. Her poems were published in such magazines as *The New Yorker, Harper's,* and *The Nation.* Swenson also served as a Chancellor of The Academy of American Poets from 1980 to 1989.

# SUMMER

## Walter Dean Myers

I like hot days, hot days
Sweat is what you got days
Bugs buzzin from cousin to cousin
Juices dripping
5   Running and ripping
Catch the one you love days

Birds peeping
Old men sleeping
Lazy days, daisies lay
10   Beaming and dreaming
Of hot days, hot days,
Sweat is what you got days

▼ **Critical Viewing**
How well does this photograph illustrate the speaker's feelings about summer? Explain. **[Evaluate]**

# The Eagle

## Alfred, Lord Tennyson

He clasps the crag¹ with crooked hands;
Close to the sun in lonely lands,
Ring'd with the azure world, he stands.

The wrinkled sea beneath him crawls;
5    He watches from his mountain walls,
And like a thunderbolt he falls.

---

**1. crag** (krag) *n.* steep, rugged rock that rises above others or projects from a rock mass.

**Vocabulary**
**clasps** (klasps) *v.* grips
**azure** (azh´ ər) *adj.*
sky blue

# Analysis of Baseball

## May Swenson

It's about
the ball,
the bat,
and the mitt.
5   Ball hits
bat, or it
hits mitt.
Bat doesn't
hit ball, bat
10  meets it.
Ball bounces
off bat, flies
air, or thuds
ground (dud)
15  or it
fits mitt.

Bat waits
for ball
to mate.
20  Ball hates
to take bat's
bait. Ball
flirts, bat's
late, don't
25  keep the date.
Ball goes in
(thwack) to mitt,
and goes out
(thwack) back
30  to mitt.

Ball fits
mitt, but
not all
the time.
35  Sometimes
ball gets hit
(pow) when bat
meets it,
and sails
40  to a place
where mitt
has to quit
in disgrace.

**Literary Analysis
Sound Devices** What
final consonant sound is
repeated frequently in
the first ten lines?

**Reading Skill
Read Fluently** After
the first reading, what
would you say is the
basic meaning of the first
stanza?

**Spiral Review
Figurative Language**
What examples of
personification can
you find in the stanza
that runs from lines
17 to 30?

**Vocabulary
analysis** (ə nal′ ə sis)
*n.* careful examination
by studying something's
elements or parts

**disgrace** (dis grās′) *n.*
loss of respect, honor,
or esteem; shame

That's about
45 the bases
loaded,
about 40,000
fans exploded.

It's about
50 the ball,
the bat,
the mitt,
the bases
and the fans.
55 It's done
on a diamond,
and for fun.
It's about
home, and it's
60 about run.

▲ **Critical Viewing**
Which words in the poem might describe the action in this image? **[Connect]**

Cite textual evidence to support your responses.

## Critical Thinking

**1. Key Ideas and Details (a)** In lines 1–2 of "Summer," how does the speaker describe summer? **(b) Interpret:** What kind of juices might be dripping in line 4? **(c) Connect:** In what way is the image in line 4 a continuation of the one in line 2? Explain your response.

**2. Key Ideas and Details (a) Infer:** What is the eagle watching for in line 5 of "The Eagle"? **(b) Interpret:** What is the eagle doing when he "falls" in line 6?

**3. Integration of Knowledge and Ideas Make a Judgment:** Do you think the poem "Analysis of Baseball" can be appreciated by someone who is unfamiliar with the rules of baseball? Why or why not?

**4. Integration of Knowledge and Ideas (a)** How does "Analysis of Baseball" compare with your experience of the sport of baseball? **(b)** Does the poem change how you think about baseball? Why or why not? *[Connect to the Big Question: How does communication change us?]*

## Literary Analysis: Sound Devices

**1. Craft and Structure (a)** For each poem in Poetry Collection 3, use a chart like the one shown to list one example of each **sound device** listed. **(b)** How does each example add to the musical feeling of each poem?

|  | Example | Effect |
|---|---|---|
| Alliteration |  |  |
| Consonance |  |  |
| Assonance |  |  |

**2. Craft and Structure (a)** Identify an example of **onomatopoeia** in "Analysis of Baseball." **(b)** What sound does the word imitate? **(c)** How well does the word imitate the sound? Explain your answer.

**3. Craft and Structure (a)** Which of these poems do you think makes the most effective use of sound devices? **(b)** Discuss your choice with a small group and decide on a single response.

## Reading Skill: Read Fluently

**4.** How did your understanding of the poems deepen with each reading? Give examples.

**5. (a)** How does **reading fluently** help you appreciate a poem's sound devices? **(b)** Which senses, other than your sense of hearing, were most engaged by each poem? Explain.

## Vocabulary

**Acquisition and Use** Identify the word in each group that does not belong with the others. Explain your response.

**1.** clasps, hands, blanket

**2.** azure, bread, green

**3.** analysis, study, recording

**4.** disgrace, pride, approval

**Word Study** Use the context of the sentences and what you know about the **Greek prefix ana-** to explain your answer to each question.

**1.** If something is an *anachronism,* is it in the correct time period?

**2.** Why is a study of *anatomy* important for doctors?

### Word Study

The **Greek prefix ana-** means "up," "back," or "against."

**Apply It** Explain how the prefix *ana-* contributes to the meanings of these words. Consult a dictionary if necessary.

**anagram**

**analogy**

# How does *communication* change us?

## Writing About the Big Question

The speaker in "The Bells" describes a range of ideas associated with the sounds of different bells. Use this sentence starter to develop your ideas about the Big Question.

> By reading about the **meaning** that someone finds in certain sounds, a reader can learn to _____.

**While You Read** Notice when the speaker of a poem mentions a specific sound. Compare the speaker's response to that sound with your own reactions. Notice whether the speaker's response changes how you think about that sound.

## Vocabulary

Read each word and its definition. Decide whether you know the word well, know it a little bit, or do not know it at all. After you have read the selection, see how your knowledge of each word has increased.

- **voluminously** (və loo´ mə nəs lē) *adv.* fully; in great volume (p. 656) *Her coach praised her <u>voluminously</u> at the awards banquet.* *volume n.*

- **endeavor** (en dev´ ər) *n.* an earnest attempt or effort (p. 656) *My <u>endeavor</u> to stay up all night failed when I fell asleep at midnight.* *endeavor v.*

- **palpitating** (pal´ pə tāt´ iŋ) *adj.* beating rapidly; throbbing (p. 656) *The <u>palpitating</u> drums of the pep band excited the fans.*

- **monotone** (män´ ə tōn´) *n.* uninterrupted repetition of the same tone; utterance of successive syllables or words without change of pitch or key (p. 659) *The actor spoke in a <u>monotone</u>, which did nothing to keep me awake during the play.* *monotonous adj. monotony n.*

- **metaphysical** (met´ ə fiz´ i kəl) *adj.* spiritual; beyond the physical (p. 661) *She says that songwriting is <u>metaphysical</u>—the songs come to her in dreams.*

- **jibed** (jībd) *v.* changed direction (p. 661) *As the wind shifted, the crew <u>jibed</u> to keep the sails full.*

### Word Study

The **Greek prefix** **mono-** means "one."

In "The Bells," the speaker describes the "muffled **monotone**" of certain bells. He refers to a kind of ringing that has only one tone, or pitch, that repeats without changing.

# Edgar Allan Poe

**(1809–1849)**

**Author of "The Bells"** (p. 654)

As poems like "The Bells" illustrate, Edgar Allan Poe was a master at using rhythm and sound devices to powerful effect. Many scholars believe that the idea for "The Bells" was suggested to Poe by Marie Louise Shew, a woman with medical training who treated Poe when his health began to fail.

# Yusef Komunyakaa

**(b. 1947)**

**Author of "Slam, Dunk, & Hook"** (p. 660)

Yusef Komunyakaa grew up in Bogalusa, Louisiana. During the mid-1960s, he served in Vietnam as a reporter and an editor for the military newspaper *The Southern Cross*. Komunyakaa later turned his attention to poetry, winning a Pulitzer Prize for his book *Neon Vernacular: New and Selected Poems* (1993). Komunyakaa has said that he likes "connecting the abstract to the concrete."

# Lewis Carroll

**(1832–1898)**

**Author of "Jabberwocky"** (p. 662)

Charles Lutwidge Dodgson was a professor of mathematics and a talented early photographer. Today, he is best remembered for two children's books he wrote under the pen name Lewis Carroll: *Alice's Adventures in Wonderland* (1865) and its sequel, *Through the Looking Glass* (1871). Huge bestsellers almost from the moment they appeared, the Alice books have been the basis of numerous stage plays and films.

# The Bells

## Edgar Allan Poe

### I

Hear the sledges[1] with the bells—
Silver bells!
What a world of merriment their melody foretells!
How they tinkle, tinkle, tinkle,
5      In the icy air of night!
While the stars, that oversprinkle
All the heavens, seem to twinkle
With a crystalline delight;
Keeping time, time, time,
10      In a sort of Runic[2] rhyme,
To the tintinnabulation[3] that so musically wells
From the bells, bells, bells, bells,
Bells, bells, bells—
From the jingling and the tinkling of the bells.


### II

15      Hear the mellow wedding bells,
Golden bells!
What a world of happiness their harmony foretells!
Through the balmy air of night
How they ring out their delight!
20      From the molten golden-notes,

---

**1. sledges** (slej´ ez) *n.* sleighs.
**2. Runic** (rōō´ nik) *adj.* songlike; poetical.
**3. tintinnabulation** (tin´ ti na´ byōo la´ shən) *n.* ringing sound of bells.

**Spiral Review**
**Figurative Language**
How does the author give the stars in lines 6–8 human qualities? What type of figurative language is this an example of?

**Reading Check**
What type of bells does section one describe?

And all in tune,
What a liquid ditty[4] floats
To the turtle-dove[5] that listens, while she gloats
On the moon!
25    Oh, from out the sounding cells,
What a gush of euphony[6] voluminously wells!
How it swells!
How it dwells
On the future! how it tells
30    Of the rapture that impels
To the swinging and the ringing
Of the bells, bells, bells,
Of the bells, bells, bells, bells
Bells, bells, bells—
35    To the rhyming and the chiming of the bells!

### III

Hear the loud alarum[7] bells!
Brazen[8] bells!
What a tale of terror now their turbulency tells!
In the startled ear of night
40    How they scream out their affright!
Too much horrified to speak,
They can only shriek, shriek,
Out of tune,
In a clamorous appealing to the mercy of the fire,
45    In a mad expostulation[9] with the deaf and frantic fire
Leaping higher, higher, higher,
With a desperate desire,
And a resolute endeavor
Now—now to sit or never,
50    By the side of the pale-faced moon.
Oh, the bells, bells, bells!
What a tale their terror tells
Of Despair!
How they clang, and clash, and roar!
55    What a horror they outpour
On the bosom of the palpitating air!

---

**4. ditty** (dit´ ē) *n.* short, simple song.
**5. turtle-dove** (turt´´l duv´) The turtle dove is traditionally associated with love.
**6. euphony** (yo͞o´ fə nē) *n.* pleasing sound.
**7. alarum** (ə ler´ əm) *adj.* sudden call to arms; alarm.
**8. brazen** (brā´ zən) *adj.* made of brass; having the ringing sound of brass.
**9. expostulation** (ek späs´ chə lā´ shən) *n.* objection; complaint.

Yet the ear it fully knows,
By the twanging
And the clanging,
60  How the danger ebbs and flows;
Yet the ear distinctly tells,
In the jangling,
And the wrangling,
How the danger sinks and swells,
65  By the sinking or the swelling in the anger of the bells—
Of the bells—
Of the bells, bells, bells, bells,
Bells, bells, bells—
In the clamor and the clangor of the bells!

**IV**

70  Hear the tolling of the bells—
Iron bells!
What a world of solemn thought their monody[10] compels!

---

**10. monody** (mä´ nə dē) *n.* poem of mourning; a steady sound; music in which one instrument or voice is dominant.

**Literary Analysis
Sound Devices** What is the effect of the repetition in lines 67–68?

**Reading Check**
What kind of story do the alarm bells tell?

In the silence of the night,
How we shiver with affright
75 At the melancholy menace of their tone!
For every sound that floats
From the rust within their throats
Is a groan.
And the people—ah, the people—
80 They that dwell up in the steeple,
All alone,
And who tolling, tolling, tolling,
In that muffled monotone,
Feel a glory in so rolling
85 On the human heart a stone—
They are neither man nor woman—
They are neither brute nor human—
They are Ghouls:[11]
And their king it is who tolls;
90 And he rolls, rolls, rolls,
Rolls
A pæan from the bells!
And his merry bosom swells
With the pæan of the bells!
95 And he dances and he yells;
Keeping time, time, time,
In a sort of Runic rhyme,
To the pæan of the bells—
Of the bells:
100 Keeping time, time, time,
In a sort of Runic rhyme,
To the throbbing of the bells—
Of the bells, bells, bells—
To the sobbing of the bells;
105 Keeping time, time, time,
As he knells, knells, knells,
In a happy Runic rhyme,
To the rolling of the bells—
Of the bells, bells, bells—
110 To the tolling of the bells,
Of the bells, bells, bells, bells,
Bells, bells, bells—
To the moaning and the groaning of the bells.

**Literary Analysis**
**Sound Devices** What alliteration appears in lines 83–85?

**Vocabulary**
**monotone** (män´ ə tōn´) *n.* uninterrupted repetition of the same tone; utterance of successive syllables or words without change of pitch or key

**Reading Skill**
**Read Fluently**
Which repeated words in this stanza might sound like the repetitive tolling of bells?

◄ **Critical Viewing**
Which kind of bells do you think this painting best illustrates? Why? **[Assess]**

---

**11. Ghouls** (go͞olz) *n.* evil spirits that rob graves.

# Slam, Dunk, & Hook

**Yusef Komunyakaa**

Fast breaks. Lay ups. With Mercury's[1]
Insignia[2] on our sneakers,
We outmaneuvered the footwork
Of bad angels. Nothing but a hot
5  Swish of strings like silk
Ten feet out. In the roundhouse[3]
Labyrinth[4] our bodies
Created, we could almost
Last forever, poised in midair
10 Like storybook sea monsters.
A high note hung there
A long second. Off
The rim. We'd corkscrew
Up & dunk balls that exploded
15 The skullcap of hope & good
Intention. Bug-eyed, lanky,
All hands & feet . . . sprung rhythm.
We were metaphysical when girls
Cheered on the sidelines.
20 Tangled up in a falling,
Muscles were a bright motor
Double-flashing to the metal hoop
Nailed to our oak.
When Sonny Boy's mama died
25 He played nonstop all day, so hard
Our backboard splintered.
Glistening with sweat, we jibed
& rolled the ball off our
Fingertips. Trouble
30 Was there slapping a blackjack
Against an open palm.
Dribble, drive to the inside, feint,
& glide like a sparrow hawk.
Lay ups. Fast breaks.
35 We had moves we didn't know
We had. Our bodies spun
On swivels of bone & faith,
Through a lyric slipknot
Of joy, & we knew we were
40 Beautiful & dangerous.

---

1. **Mercury's** Mercury was the Roman god of travel, usually depicted with wings on his feet.
2. **insignia** (in sig´ nē ə) *n.* emblems or badges; logos.
3. **roundhouse** (round´ hous´) *n.* area on the court beneath the basket.
4. **labyrinth** (lab´ ə rin*th*´) *n.* maze.

◄ **Critical Viewing**
Which details in this painting relate to lines in "Slam, Dunk, & Hook"? **[Connect]**

**Vocabulary**
**metaphysical** (met´ ə fiz´ i kəl) *adj.* spiritual; beyond the physical

**jibed** (jībd) *v.* changed direction

**Literary Analysis**
**Sound Devices** What sound does the poet emphasize with the use of assonance in lines 30 and 31?

# Jabberwocky

## Lewis Carroll

'Twas brillig, and the slithy toves
    Did gyre and gimble in the wabe;
All mimsy were the borogoves,
    And the mome raths outgrabe.

5  "Beware the Jabberwock, my son!
    The jaws that bite, the claws that catch!
Beware the Jubjub bird, and shun
    The frumious Bandersnatch!"

He took his vorpal sword in hand:
10     Long time the manxome foe he sought—
So rested he by the Tumtum tree,
    And stood awhile in thought.

And as in uffish thought he stood,
    The Jabberwock, with eyes of flame,
15  Came whiffling through the tulgey wood,
    And burbled as it came!

◄▼ **Critical Viewing**
Which aspects of these illustrations convey the fantastical quality of "Jabberwocky"? **[Analyze]**

**Literary Analysis Sound Devices** What sound or noise does the onomatopoeia *burbled* reflect?

## LITERATURE IN CONTEXT

### Language Connection

**Carroll's Invented Language** In the first chapter of *Through the Looking-Glass,* Alice encounters a creature called a Jabberwock. She cannot understand it, so Humpty Dumpty explains some of the words it uses, including these:

**brillig:** four o'clock in the afternoon, the time when you begin broiling things for dinner

**toves:** creatures that are something like badgers, something like lizards, and something like corkscrews

**gyre:** go round and round like a gyroscope

**gimble:** make holes like a gimlet (a hand tool that bores holes)

**wabe:** grass plot around a sundial

**mome:** having lost the way home

**raths:** something like green pigs

### Connect to the Literature

What challenges do you think Carroll faced in writing a poem with invented language?

One, two! One, two! And through and through
    The vorpal blade went snicker-snack!
He left it dead, and with its head
20    He went galumphing back.

"And hast thou slain the Jabberwock?
    Come to my arms, my beamish boy!
O frabjous day! Callooh! Callay!"
    He chortled in his joy.

25  'Twas brillig, and the slithy toves
    Did gyre and gimble in the wabe;
All mimsy were the borogoves,
    And the mome raths outgrabe.

## Critical Thinking

**Cite textual evidence to support your responses.**

1. **Craft and Structure (a)** In lines 4–5 of "Slam, Dunk, & Hook," what sound does the speaker describe? **(b) Infer:** What action causes this sound?

2. **Key Ideas and Details (a)** In "Jabberwocky," what does the hero do after being warned about the Jabberwock? **(b) Evaluate:** Do you think the poem pokes fun at heroism? Explain your response.

3. **Integration of Knowledge and Ideas Take a Position:** The poet T. S. Eliot once said that poetry can be enjoyed before it is understood. Could "The Bells" be used as evidence to support this idea? Explain your answer.

4. **Integration of Knowledge and Ideas** Do any of the poems in this collection make you think differently about sounds you hear every day? Explain. *[Connect to the Big Question: How does communication change us?]*

## Literary Analysis: Sound Devices

**1. Craft and Structure** **(a)** For each poem in Poetry Collection 4, use a chart like the one shown to give one example of each **sound device** listed. **(b)** How does each example add to the musical feeling of each poem?

|  | Example | Effect |
|---|---|---|
| **Alliteration** |  |  |
| **Consonance** |  |  |
| **Assonance** |  |  |

**2. Craft and Structure** **(a)** Identify an example of **onomatopoeia** in "The Bells." **(b)** What sound does the word imitate? **(c)** How well does the word imitate the sound? Explain your answer.

**3. Craft and Structure** **(a)** Which of these poems do you think makes the most effective use of sound devices? **(b)** Discuss your idea with a small group and decide on a single response.

## Reading Skill: Read Fluently

**4.** How did your understanding of the poems deepen with each reading? Give examples.

**5. (a)** How does **reading fluently** help you appreciate a poem's sound devices? **(b)** Which senses, other than your sense of hearing, were most engaged by each poem? Explain.

## Vocabulary

**Acquisition and Use** Identify the word in each group that does not belong with the others. Explain your response.

**1.** metaphysical, concrete, bodily

**2.** jibed, turn, straight

**3.** voluminously, tiny, huge

**4.** palpitating, pulse, hum

**5.** endeavor, avoid, attempt

**6.** monotone, voice, flower

**Word Study** Use the context of the sentences and what you know about the **Greek prefix mono-** to explain your answer to each question.

**1.** If a painting is *monochromatic,* does it have one color or many?

**2.** If Joe is *monolingual,* how many languages does he speak?

### Word Study

The **Greek prefix mono-** means "one."

**Apply It** Explain how the prefix *mono-* contributes to the meanings of these words. Consult a dictionary if necessary.

**monologue**
**monarch**
**monopoly**

# Integrated Language Skills

## Poetry Collections 3 and 4

### Conventions: Prepositional Phrases

A **prepositional phrase** is a group of words beginning with a prep-osition and ending with a noun or pronoun, called the *object* of the preposition.

A prepositional phrase may function as either an adjective or an adverb, depending on the word it modifies. An adjective phrase modifies a noun or a pronoun by telling *what kind* or *which one.* An adverb phrase modi-fies a verb, an adjective, or an adverb by pointing out *where, when, in what way,* or *to what extent.*

**Adjective phrase:** The players <u>on their team</u> are more experienced. (modifies the noun *players*)

**Adjective phrase:** The flowers <u>with yellow petals</u> are my favorites. (modifies the noun *flowers*)

**Adverb phrase:** They played <u>with more skill</u>. (modifies the verb *played*)

**Adverb phrase:** My parents walked <u>through the door</u> <u>at that moment.</u> (both phrases modify the verb *walked*)

**Practice A** Identify the prepositional phrase in each sentence, and tell whether it functions as an adjective or an adverb.

1. Myers's poem describes the hot days of summer.

2. He clasps the crag with crooked hands.

3. He watches from his mountain walls.

4. Baseball is played on a diamond.

5. Tennyson's poem about the eagle is very descriptive.

© **Reading Application** In "The Eagle," find one prepositional phrase that functions as an adjec-tive and one that functions as an adverb.

**Practice B** Following the instructions in paren-theses, use each prepositional phrase in a sentence of your own.

1. of joyful singing (adjective phrase)

2. in the woods (adverb phrase)

3. under the bridge (adjective phrase)

4. through the hoop (adverb phrase)

© **Writing Application** Following these models, write four sentences. Identify which phrases are used as adjectives and which are used as adverbs.
*Running with a knife is not safe.*
*The child's book was illustrated with animals of many kinds.*

**PH WRITING COACH** Further instruction and practice are available in *Prentice Hall Writing Coach.*

# Writing

© **Argument** Write an **editorial**—a piece of writing that presents one side of an issue—related to one of the poems you read. For example, if you read Tennyson's "The Eagle," you could use it as inspiration to write an editorial about the need to preserve the North American bald eagle. If you read "Slam, Dunk, & Hook," you might use that poem as inspiration to write about the need for more funding for neighborhood sports.

- State the issue clearly and provide support for your opinion.
- Anticipate questions from those who might disagree with you.

Ask several people to respond to your editorial, including someone who disagrees with you, and refute opposing arguments.

**Grammar Application** Make sure to use prepositional phrases correctly in your editorial.

## Writing Workshop: *Work in Progress*

**Prewriting for a Descriptive Essay** Using your Sight List and your Sensory Words List, list three emotions that you associate with the place you chose. Briefly, jot down clue words about the reasons for those emotions. For example, you might list some words related to meaningful events that happened there. Save this Reasons List in your writing portfolio.

# Speaking and Listening

© **Presentation of Ideas** In a group, create an **illustrated presentation** of one of the poems you read. Find photographs or original artwork and, with the group, debate the merits of each choice. Negotiate to reach an agreement about which images best capture the mood of the poem. Then, choose one member of the group to present a dramatic reading of the poem. Have the speaker rehearse in front of the group, and have the group use these questions to assess the speaker's performance:

- Does the speaker maintain eye contact with the audience?
- Does the speaker use a voice register, body movements, and gestures that are appropriate for the occasion and the interests of the audience?
- Does the speaker's delivery convey the mood and tone of the poem in a way that engages the audience? Does the speaker's delivery convey the mood depicted in the images you selected?

Once you have organized your images and rehearsed your dramatic reading, present the images and the reading together to your class. Use other visual aids or electronic media to enhance your presentation.

**Common Core State Standards**

W.9-10.1; SL.9-10.1, SL.9-10.5; L.9-10.1, L.9-10.5
[For the full wording of the standards, see page 642.]

Use this prewriting activity to prepare for the **Writing Workshop** on page 686.

**PHLit Online!**
**www.PHLitOnline.com**
- Interactive graphic organizers
- Grammar tutorial
- Interactive journals

# Test Practice: Reading

## Read Fluently

### Poetry Selection

**Directions:** *Read the selection. Then, answer the questions.*

**The Sky Is Low, the Clouds Are Mean,** *by Emily Dickinson*
The sky is low, the clouds are mean,
A travelling flake of snow
Across a barn or through a rut
Debates if it will go.

5  A narrow wind complains all day
How some one treated him;
Nature, like us, is sometimes caught
Without her diadem.[1]

---

1. **diadem** (dī ə dem') *n.* crown.

**1.** How many sentences are in this poem?
   A. one
   B. two
   C. three
   D. four

**2.** At what points should a reader pause or stop in the first stanza?
   A. after "mean" and after "snow"
   B. at the end of each line
   C. after "mean" and after "go"
   D. only at the end of the stanza

**3.** Which sentence *best* describes the basic meaning of the first stanza?
   A. The gloomy weather outside seems to indicate snow is coming.
   B. Without bad weather, people would not learn to appreciate good weather.
   C. Winter storms are often destructive forces in people's lives.
   D. Nature is beautiful in any season.

**4.** Which lines most clearly point readers to one deeper meaning of this poem?
   A. lines 1 and 2
   B. lines 3 and 4
   C. lines 5 and 6
   D. lines 7 and 8

## Writing for Assessment

Into how many units of meaning would you divide this poem? Write a paragraph in which you explain where you would make these divisions and why.

## Nonfiction Selection

**Directions:** *Read the selection. Then, answer the questions.*

(1) In 1993, a relentless rain fell on the Midwest all spring and almost all summer. (2) There was no place for the water to go except into the rivers, which could not contain the water. (3) The Mississippi, Missouri, and 150 other rivers tore loose from their banks and washed over everything in their paths. (4) Thousands of people evacuated their homes. (5) The rivers destroyed 10,000 homes and put 75 towns under water. (6) Railroads shut down. (7) Airports and Interstate highways closed. (8) In some places, the flood lasted six months. (9) The cleanup, rebuilding, and pervasive moldy odor lasted even longer. (10) It was the worst flood in U.S. history up to that time.

**1.** To read both poetry and prose fluently, readers might do all of the following *except*—
**A.** group words to enhance understanding.
**B.** use punctuation to determine where to stop or pause.
**C.** reread to appreciate the writer's craft.
**D.** stop at the end of each line.

**2.** The reader should expect to read this passage—
**A.** slower than directions for reprogramming a computer.
**B.** at the same rate as a magazine article.
**C.** faster than a grocery list.
**D.** at the same rate as a medical textook.

**3.** At which points should a reader pause or stop in sentence 9?
**A.** Pause after "cleanup" and "rebuilding" and stop after "longer."
**B.** Stop only after "longer."
**C.** Pause after "cleanup," "rebuilding," and "pervasive moldy odor."
**D.** Stop after "rebuilding" and "longer."

**4.** Which sentence best describes the basic meaning of this passage?
**A.** People were probably frightened as they evacuated from their homes.
**B.** Tragedies often either tear people apart or bring them closer together.
**C.** Many highways closed when over 150 rivers flooding in 1993.
**D.** Terrible flooding caused significant damage in the Midwest in 1993.

## Writing for Assessment

**Connecting Across Texts**
Write a two-paragraph "How-to" article for middle school students explaining how to read poetry and prose fluently. Use examples from both of these pieces to illustrate your points.

**www.PHLitOnline.com**
• Online practice
• Instant feedback

# Reading for Information

## Analyzing Functional and Expository Texts

**Technical Directions**

**News Article**

**Common Core State Standards**

**Reading Informational Text**
**4.** Determine the meaning of words and phrases as they are used in text, including figurative, connotative, and technical meanings.
**5.** Analyze in detail how an author's ideas or claims are developed and refined by particular sentences, paragraphs, or larger portions of a text.

**Writing**
**2.** Write informative/explanatory texts to examine and convey complex ideas, concepts, and information clearly and accurately through the effective selection, organization, and analysis of content.

**Language**
**3.** Apply knowledge of language to understand how language functions in different contexts, to make effective choices for meaning or style, and to comprehend more fully when reading or listening.
**6.** Acquire and use accurately grade-appropriate general academic and domain-specific words and phrases, sufficient for reading, writing, speaking, and listening at the college and career readiness level.

## Reading Skill: Follow Technical Directions

In order to properly use a mechanical or digital device, you must understand and **follow technical directions.** Technical directions provide step-by-step instructions on how to use a device correctly. To understand the directions, **analyze the structure, format,** and features of the text. Elements such as bold font, subheadings, and numbered lists can indicate important information and highlight specific sections. Use this checklist to be sure you follow technical directions correctly.

### Checklist for Following Technical Directions

- Analyze the text for clues such as bold or italicized font, numbered lists, headings, and subheadings that highlight specific sections or important information.

- Read all directions carefully and completely, reviewing any sections that are complicated or unclear.

- Follow each step in the exact order given.

- Do not skip any steps.

## Content-Area Vocabulary

These words appear in the selections that follow. You may also encounter them in other content-area texts.

- **blogging** (bläg´ iŋ) *n.* publishing entries on a Web site that consists of an online journal with thoughts, opinions, and links to other sites

- **download** (doun´ lōd´) *v.* transfer data from one computer system to another computer or device

- **democratizing** (di mäk´ rə tīz´ iŋ) *v.* changing a market or governing structure so that power is distributed among larger numbers of people

# How Podcasting Works

### by Stephanie Watson

> This heading clearly states that this section will provide an introduction to the subject of podcasting.

## Introduction to How Podcasting Works

Have you ever dreamed of having your own radio show? Are you a recording artist hoping to have your songs heard by the masses? Decades ago, you would have had to have a lot of connections—or a fortune—to get heard.

> This guide gives background information about podcasting and its purposes.

But now, thanks to the Internet and its instantaneous connection to millions of people, your dreams can become reality. Just as **blogging** has enabled almost anyone with a computer to become a bona fide reporter, a new technology called podcasting is allowing virtually anyone with a computer to become a radio disc jockey, talk show host or recording artist.

If you post it, they will come. Although podcasting is still primarily used by the techie set, it's beginning to catch on with the general public. Log onto one of several podcast sites on the Web, and you can **download** content ranging from music to philosophy. . . . Podcasting combines the freedom of blogging with the technology of MP3 to create an almost endless supply of content. Some say this new technology is **democratizing** the once corporate-run world of radio.

In this article, you'll learn how podcasting works, find out what tools you need to record and receive podcasts and hear what industry analysts have to say about the future of this burgeoning technology.

Podcasting is a free service that allows Internet users to pull audio files (typically MP3s) from a podcasting Web site to listen to on their computer or personal digital audio player. The name comes from a combination of the words **iPod** and **broadcasting**. Even though the name is derived from the iPod, you don't need an iPod to listen to a podcast. You can use virtually any MP3 player or your computer.

> Boldface text highlights key technical words.

Unlike with Internet radio, users don't have to "tune in" to a particular broadcast; instead, they **subscribe** to a podcast, and the audio files are automatically downloaded to their computer via **RSS feed** as often as they request. The technology is similar to that used by TiVo, a personal video recorder that lets users set which programs they'd like to record and then automatically records those programs for later viewing.

## Podcasting History

Podcasting was developed in 2004 by former MTV video jockey Adam Curry and software developer Dave Winer. Curry wrote a program, called iPodder, that enabled him to automatically download Internet radio broadcasts to his iPod. Several developers improved upon his idea, and podcasting was officially born. . . .

Right now, podcasting is free from government regulation. Podcasters don't need to buy a license to broadcast their programming, as radio stations do, and they don't need to conform to the the Federal Communication Commission's (FCC) broadcast decency regulations. . . .

Although several corporations and big broadcast companies have ventured into the medium, many podcasters are amateurs broadcasting from home studios. Because podcasters don't rely on ratings as radio broadcasters do, the subject matter of podcasts can range from the refined to the silly to the excruciatingly mundane. . . .

Several companies are trying to turn podcasting into a profitable business. Podcasting aggregators. . . are including advertising on their sites. The Podcast Network, based in Australia, runs commercials and sponsorships during its audio broadcasts. Television networks have gotten into the action. National Public Radio, the Canadian Broadcasting Corporation and the BBC have begun podcasting some of their shows. Corporations. . . have created their own podcasts to attract consumers.

Some experts say podcasting still has a long way to go before it catches on with the masses. But others believe it will eventually become as popular as text blogging, which grew from a few thousand blogs in the late '90s to more than 7 million today. Some podcasts are already providing thousands of downloads a day.

## Creating and Listening to Podcasts

Virtually anyone with a computer and recording capabilities can create his or her own podcast. Podcasts may include music, comedy, sports, philosophy—even people's rants and raves. Here's how the process works.

**To record a podcast:**

> These sub-headings indicate what type of directions will follow.

1. Plug a USB headset with a microphone into your computer.

2. Install an MP3 recorder for Windows, Mac or Linux.

3. Create an audio file by making a recording (you can talk, sing or record music) and saving it as an MP3 file.

4. Finally, upload the MP3 audio file to one of the podcasting sites.

**To listen to a podcast:**

> Numbered lists provide step-by-step instructions.

1. Go to a podcasting site and download the free software.

2. Click on the hyperlink for each podcast you want. You can listen right away on your computer (both Windows and Mac support podcasting) or download the podcast to your MP3 player.

3. You can also subscribe to one or more RSS feeds. Your podcasting software will check the RSS feeds regularly and automatically pull content that matches your playlist. When you dock your MP3 player to your computer, it automatically updates with the latest content.

News Article

**Features:**

- current or breaking news
- quotations from experts and other qualified sources
- text written for a general audience

# Georgia School Displays iPod Ingenuity

This title explains the topic of the article—that podcasts are being used as sophisticated learning tools.

From eSchool News staff and wire service reports
March 27, 2006

Thanks in part to an enterprising group of faculty who call themselves the iDreamers, Georgia College & State University (GSCU) is quickly becoming a leader in using Apple Computer's near-ubiquitous iPod to enhance education—and school officials say their efforts are helping to retain more students.

More than a third of the rural Georgia school's 300 staff members reportedly use the digital music and video players as

The article is structured by order of importance. The broad topic is stated in the first paragraphs and is followed by details and support.

an education or research tool. Rather than simply making class lectures available for downloading to iPods—a practice now routine at many colleges and even a few high schools—the school's educators are pushing to find more strategic uses of the device.

History professor Deborah Vess asks students to download 39 films to their devices so she doesn't have to spend class time screening the movies. Psychology professor Noland White has found a new-age answer to office hours: a podcast of the week's most frequently-asked questions.

And the campus has organized a group of innovative staff and faculty to conjure up other uses for the technology. Called the iDreamers, the team bats around ideas that could turn the devices into portable yearbooks and replace campus brochures with podcasts.

"The more you free up your classroom for discussion, the more efficient you are," said Dorothy Leland, the school's president.

After Leland and Jim Wolfgang, the school's chief information officer, began seeing iPods around campus in 2002, they decided to explore educational applications for the devices. They started by farming out 50 donated iPods to faculty who offered the best proposals.

Soon Wolfgang's office was flooded with applications from educators suggesting new uses. Now, some 400 college-owned iPods are floating around campus—some loaned to students in certain classes, others available for checkout at libraries.

Hank Edmondson, a government professor known around campus as "The Podfather," was among the first to use iPods to supplement his course lectures. Edmondson makes lectures, language study programs, indigenous music, and thumbnail art sketches available for download to the iPods of students in a three-week, study-abroad program he leads.

During a recent visit to the Prado in Madrid, he recorded a 20-minute lecture on the museum's artwork. Downloading that in advance will let students spend their visit to the museum exploring, not listening to Edmondson talk.

"You want to pack everything in, but you've got a lot of travel time," he said.

Vess said having her history students screen films on their iPods allows her to dedicate class time to discussion and analysis; likewise for the weekly graduate course she teaches on historical methods.

"Now I can devote my whole three hours to Socratic dialogue," she said with a grin.

Although iPods can be useful tools for reviewing coursework, some critics argue donning a pair of earphones is not the same as actively engaging with material in a classroom setting.

Here, an objection to using iPods in an educational environment is followed by details and support that address that objection.

"Learning is through interaction, discussion, critical questioning, and challenging of assumptions," said Donna Qualters, director of the Center for Effective Teaching at Northeastern University in Boston. "Those cannot be duplicated on an iPod—you have to be there to experience that learning."

GCSU officials say the school makes sure its iPod lessons supplement classroom work—not replace it.

"We don't have any project that repeats what's going on in the classroom," Wolfgang said. "All this is value-added."

✳ ✳ ✳

## Comparing Functional and Expository Texts

© **1. Craft and Structure** **(a)** Compare and contrast the **structures and formats** of the **technical directions** and the news article. **(b)** Which text uses structure and format more effectively to help aid reader understanding? Explain your answer.

### Content-Area Vocabulary

**(a)** Explain how *download* can function as either a verb or a noun, depending on the context. **(b)** What suffix could you add to change *download* into an adjective? **(c)** Use all three vocabulary words from page 670 in a paragraph that describes how blogging and podcasting can be viewed as democratizing technologies.

## 🧭 Timed Writing

### Explanatory Text: Letter

> **Format and Audience**
> The prompt directs you to write a letter to fellow students. Therefore, be sure you properly format your response and use formal language that is appropriate for your audience.

> You have just begun posting podcasts that give additional information about a topic discussed in class. Write a letter to fellow students introducing your podcast. Describe your content and explain how to download and listen to the material. Use details and information from both texts to compose your letter. (25 minutes)

> **Academic Vocabulary**
> When you *explain* something, you make it clear by providing details, examples, illustrations, and additional information.

### 5-Minute Planner

Complete these steps before you begin to write:

**1.** Read the prompt carefully and completely. Look for key words that will help you understand the assignment.

**2.** Choose a class subject to serve as the topic of your podcast. Make notes about what topic ideas to include in your podcast.

**3.** Review the technical directions and news article. Scan the texts to locate information that would be helpful in composing your letter. Make notes about details you find that should be included.

**4.** Consider the steps that students will need to take to access your podcast. Determine the clearest way to present the information so that students will be able to follow the technical directions you are providing. Then, create an outline of the body for your letter.

**5.** Refer to your outline and notes as you draft your letter.

## Comparing Imagery

**Imagery** is language that appeals to one or more of the senses—sight, hearing, touch, taste, and smell. The use of imagery allows writers to express their ideas with vividness and immediacy. Images create mental pictures for readers and help them connect their own experiences to the worlds the writers describe. The emotional responses writers evoke through the use of vivid imagery allow a poem or other work to come to life in readers' minds. Interpretations of imagery may differ as readers view a work through the lens of their own life experiences.

Comparing imagery is important in analyzing the aesthetic qualities of a variety of selections. These are the stylistic qualities that make a poem's language beautiful. Writers, for example, often include patterns of images. By recognizing these image patterns, or motifs, you can better appreciate differences and similarities among selections.

As you read, use a chart like this one to compare images and the senses they address.

**Poem: "There Is No Word for Goodbye"**

| Sensory Language | Imagery | Effect |
|---|---|---|
| "wind–tanned skin" | brownish, weathered skin | The reader can see and feel Sokoya's skin. |
|  |  |  |
|  |  |  |
|  |  |  |
|  |  |  |
|  |  |  |

**Common Core State Standards**

**Reading Literature**

**4.** Determine the meaning of words and phrases as they are used in a text, including figurative and connotative meanings; analyze the cumulative impact of specific word choices on meaning and tone.

**Writing**

**2.** Write informative/explanatory texts to examine and convey complex ideas, concepts, and information clearly and accurately through the effective selection, organization, and analysis of content.

**PHLit Online!**
www.PHLitOnline.com

- Vocabulary flashcards
- Interactive journals
- More about the authors
- Selection audio
- Interactive graphic organizers

# How does *communication* change us?

## Writing About the Big Question

In these selections, the writers want you to see an experience as clearly as they do. Use this sentence starter to develop your ideas.

Seeing the world through someone else's eyes may help a person become **aware** of _____.

# Meet the Authors

## Mary Tall Mountain (1918–1991)

### Author of "There Is No Word for Goodbye" (p. 678)

An Athabaskan Indian, Mary Tall Mountain was born in Alaska. When Tall Mountain was six, her mother died, and she was adopted by a family who removed her from her culture. In "There Is No Word For Goodbye," Tall Mountain reconnects with her Native American roots

## Naomi Shihab Nye (b. 1952)

### Author of "Daily" (p. 679)

Naomi Shihab Nye, a successful poet, was born to a Palestinian father and an American mother. Of poems, she has said, "I liked the space around them, and the way they took you to a deeper, quieter place, almost immediately."

## David T. Hilbun (b. 1992)

### Author of "Hope" (p. 680)

David T. Hilbun has been publishing his work since he was in the first grade. He wrote "Hope" after Hurricane Katrina for his eighth grade English class. "I'm not sure yet what I plan to do in the future," Hilbun says, "but I do want to continue writing in some fashion."

## Tyroneca "Ty" Booker (b. 1987)

### Author of "The Day of the Storm" (p. 682)

Tyroneca Booker resides in Louisiana. Booker's piece, "The Day of the Storm," was written in an English course when she was asked to reflect on Hurricane Katrina. She says, "I wrote from my heart, a very true account of what life was like during and after these powerful storms."

# THERE IS NO WORD FOR GOODBYE

## Mary Tall Mountain

Literary Analysis
**Imagery** Which words suggest that Sokoya is an elder?

Sokoya, I said, looking through
    the net of wrinkles into
    wise black pools
    of her eyes.

5    What do you say in Athabaskan
    when you leave each other?
    What is the word
    for goodbye?

Literary Analysis
**Imagery** Which details in lines 9–12 appeal to the sense of touch?

A shade of feeling rippled
10    the wind-tanned skin.
    Ah, nothing, she said,
    watching the river flash.

She looked at me close.
    We just say, Tlaa. That means,
15    See you.
    We never leave each other.
    When does your mouth
    say goodbye to your heart?

She touched me light
20    as a bluebell.
    You forget when you leave us,
    You're so small then.
    We don't use that word.

We always think you're coming back,
25    but if you don't,
    we'll see you some place else.
    You understand.
    There is no word for goodbye.

*Sokoya:* Aunt (mother's sister)

# DAILY

## Naomi Shihab Nye

These shriveled seeds we plant,
corn kernel, dried bean,
poke into loosened soil,
cover over with measured fingertips

5      These T-shirts we fold into
perfect white squares

These tortillas we slice and fry to crisp strips
This rich egg scrambled in a gray clay bowl

This bed whose covers I straighten
10     smoothing edges till blue quilt fits brown blanket
and nothing hangs out

This envelope I address
so the name balances like a cloud
in the center of the sky

15     This page I type and retype
This table I dust till the scarred wood shines
This bundle of clothes I wash and hang and wash again
like flags we share, a country so close
no one needs to name it

20     The days are nouns; touch them
The hands are churches that worship the world

**Vocabulary**
**shriveled** (shriv´ əld) *adj.*
shrunken and wrinkled

**Literary Analysis**
**Imagery** To which
senses does the imagery
of the bed covers
appeal?

**Vocabulary**
**scarred** (skärd) *adj.*
marked or dented

## Critical Thinking

1. **Key Ideas and Details Infer:** In "There Is No Word for Goodbye," why might the speaker want to know the word for goodbye? Support your answer.

2. **Key Ideas and Details (a)** Identify five tasks described in "Daily." **(b) Infer:** Does the speaker seem to take pleasure in doing these tasks? Explain.

3. **Integration of Knowledge and Ideas (a)** What are these writers' messages about life? **(b)** How might readers benefit from understanding these views? *[Connect to the Big Question: How does communication change us?]*

# Hope

## David T. Hilbun
8th Grade, Paul Breaux Middle School, Lafayette, Louisiana

**Literary Analysis**
**Imagery** To which senses does the imagery in the first paragraph appeal?

"Adam, get behind me!" his dad called over the roaring winds and splashing waves. Adam's reply was cut off by the crash of a huge oak tree being ripped out of the dirt and slamming into the ground a few meters away with the force of a stick of dynamite. "Quick, into the storm cellar!" The storm cellar had been designed by Adam's dad years ago. It was made of 6-inch solid steel and had enough MRE's[1] to feed 12 hungry people for a week.

They made it to the door and were able to get inside. Fretful, cold, and frightened, they got out of the storm. In their "secret place," as Adam called it when he was littler, they felt strangely peaceful. Maybe it was the knowledge that they both were safe, maybe it was the comfort of the cellar, they didn't know, but at least they had each other.

Over time, the noise outside got worse and worse. At one point, it was so loud that it felt as if a huge gong were crashing inside their heads. Suddenly, the noise stopped.

---

**1. MRE's:** prepared foods; acronym for Meals Ready to Eat.

"What's going on, Dad?" Adam asked.

"I think the eyewall passed over us," he said. "We can probably go outside for a little while."

Outside was a scene of total destruction. Their house was gone, a few planks in its place.

The school was wrecked, the remains of an airliner strewn all over the football field. But worst, they saw a huge fallen tree. Sticking out from under it was a human arm.

Feeling sick, Adam turned to go underground when the eyewall passed over. Hundred-mile-an-hour winds lifted Adam into the air. Screaming, flipping over and over, he bid a mental farewell to his father and a mental hello to his mother. Crying, thinking all hope was lost, he was miraculously caught by his dad. Inch by inch, they made their way back to the cellar, where they waited out the storm.

Finally, it was over. They looked around at the scene surrounding them in awestruck silence. Luckily, there were no bodies this time.

Too shocked to cry, too scared to do anything but stand there, Adam and his dad looked at each other.

After a time, the shock wore off. They walked around. Adam motioned his dad over.

"Look," he said simply, smiling.

And there, amid all the destruction, was a single green plant.

**Vocabulary**
**miraculously** (mi rak´ yoo ləs le) *adv.* in an amazing way; as though by a miracle
**awestruck** (ô´ struk) *adj.* filled with wonder
**amid** (ə mid´) *prep.* among; in the middle of

## Critical Thinking

1. **Key Ideas and Details (a)** Where do Adam and his father go when the storm hits? **(b) Infer:** Why do you think Adam's father had built the storm shelter?

2. **Key Ideas and Details (a)** What do Adam and his father find when they leave the shelter the first time? **(b) Infer:** What makes Adam feel sick?

3. **Key Ideas and Details (a)** What do Adam and his father find when they emerge from the shelter the last time? **(b) Interpret:** Why is the plant so meaningful to Adam?

4. **Integration of Knowledge and Ideas (a)** Why might readers who have experienced a tragic storm be interested in Hilbun's narrative? **(b)** Does this story change the way you regard storms? Why or why not? *[Connect to the Big Question: How does communication change us?]*

Cite textual evidence to support your responses.

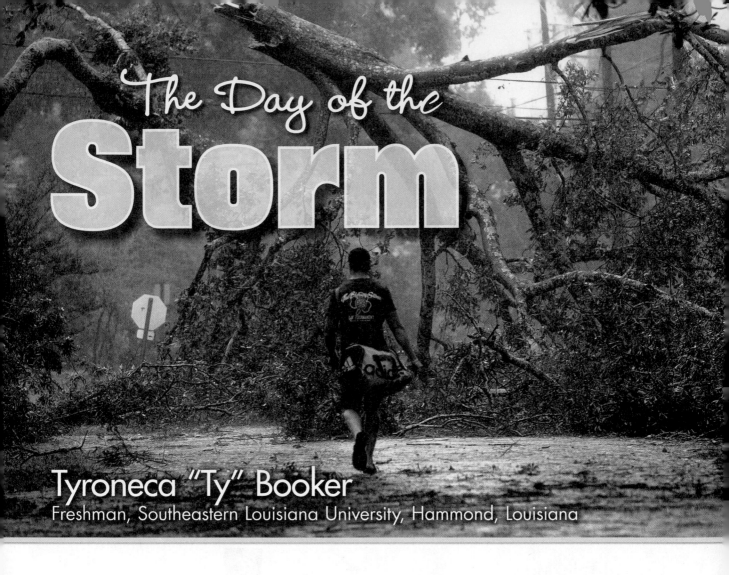

# The Day of the Storm

## Tyroneca "Ty" Booker
Freshman, Southeastern Louisiana University, Hammond, Louisiana

**Vocabulary**
**emitting** (e mit´ inj) *v.*
sending out

I don't watch much T.V., so to hear a hurricane was heading for Louisiana was a scare. Earlier in the week, I was talking to my sister and she had informed me a storm was brewing in the Gulf. I paid little to no attention because every storm since Andrew in '98 was supposedly due to hit Louisiana directly and didn't. As a matter of fact, Andrew is the only "big" storm I can remember. Vivid images come to mind—pine trees, emitting their signature smells from the freshly cracked wood, lie in the street like barricades. For about a week my family survived on Cheerios and Spam; it was all we had. Since then, a hurricane only meant a day or two off from school, and Louisiana dodging the bullet one more time. Friday, August 26th, my cousin and I drove to New Orleans to pick up another relative. We took for granted the scenery and simple pleasures of the city. We never realized what lay ahead.

I have always been a hard-headed person, so this particular weekend I'd decided to stay on campus. My cousin traveled back to Baton Rouge alone to go to work, while I stayed in Hammond, ignorant of the events ahead. On Saturday, the calls flooded my cell phone. Everyone called to tell me about Katrina. I finally, after 20 phone calls, decided to turn on the T.V. There she was: coming straight for New Orleans. I was only a city or two away. Every channel and every news bulletin carried the same, yet simple message: Get out while you can! As I watched her turn like a propeller, it all became grim reality—we were going to be hit and hit hard. I had nowhere to go. Here I was on the fourth floor of Livingston Hall in my room with a category five hurricane headed for a city only 52 miles away.

I knew I needed to stock up on food if I was going to be here to endure the storm. Cayman's was closed, and the Lion's Den wasn't an option. The only thing I had was my SLU ID, so I decided to make a "vending-machine run." After three trips to the electric snack havens, I'd figured that I had enough. The last time I walked across the barren, deserted parking lot, a man in Army fatigues caught my eye. Curiosity took over, and I went to inquire as to why he was on campus.

He proceeded to explain that the Kinesiology and Health Studies building was being used as shelter for ill people. As he continued to ramble on, my thoughts began to come into focus—this was serious. I pretended to listen, but only a few words stuck out in my mind: dorms closed. University Center, shelter. I thanked him, walked away, and those words formed themselves into two ton bricks, each falling upon me like rain: each one came faster than the one before. I realized he had just told me we had to evacuate the dorms, and take shelter in the University Center. I panicked, packed up my belongings as if it were check-out time, and waited for the all-call.[1] At about 5:15 p.m., the clouds couldn't take the pressure as they succumbed to the rain, surrendering themselves peacefully without a fight. The wind picked up, and here I was running to the University Center on North Campus with the few belongings that I could grab. The wind began to howl like a werewolf in the night— this was the one! Katrina was here, and she was as strong as two oxen.

I made it into the University Center, soaked but safe. I looked around, found a spot and made myself at home. I drifted off into a deep sleep, the last peaceful night of rest I would get for a while. When I did awake, I heard the University President, Randy Moffett, on the loudspeaker telling us that Katrina was in fact here, and she

---

1. **all-call** phone system used to contact students at Southeastern Louisiana University.

**Literary Analysis**
**Imagery** To which sense does the image "turn like a propeller" appeal?

**Vocabulary**
**succumbed** (sə kumd) v. gave way; yielded

**Reading Check**
What did Ty learn from the man in army fatigues?

**Literary Analysis**
**Imagery** How does the writer's use of imagery in this paragraph help you understand her experience?

**Vocabulary**
**submerged** (səb murjd′) *adj.* covered with water or the like

was marking her territory all around us as he spoke. He told us we were in the worst two or three hours of the storm, and we had no water or lights, until the generators could be powered up. I went to the window looking out on University Avenue, and surveyed old oak trees thrown around as if they were small branches. As I took all this in, I couldn't help but think—this isn't the worst, this is only the beginning.

When we were let out of the University Center on Tuesday, August 30th, the water was on, but cold, and there was still no electricity. I came back to a dank, dark dorm room, but I was thankful to have survived and to have a place to call home to come to. Later in the day, my cousin came back to pick me up; I was relieved, and cried tears of joy. I was grateful to be back in Baton Rouge with my family, and out of harm's way. However, once I arrived, I realized the devastation Katrina's wrath caused along the Gulf Coast. When I turned on the T.V. I thought it was something unreal. I couldn't even have imagined what I saw—houses submerged to their roof, a whole city flooded. It was then that I thanked the heavens above allowing me to be fortunate, and it was then that I vowed never to take life's simple gifts for granted.

## Critical Thinking

Cite textual evidence to support your responses.

1. **Key Ideas and Details (a)** How does the writer prepare for evacuating the dorm? **(b) Deduce:** Why does she take so few belongings with her to the University Center?

2. **Key Ideas and Details (a)** What does the university president tell those gathered in the University Center during the height of the storm? **(b) Infer:** What does the writer think about the president's announcement? **(c) Make a Judgment:** Was she correct about the president's prediction? Explain.

**Integration of Knowledge and Ideas (a) Interpret:** In the final paragraph, what does the writer mean when she says she "realized the devastation of Katrina's wrath"? **(b) Draw Conclusions:** What do you think the writer learned from her experiences? Share your response with a partner.

3. **Integration of Knowledge and Ideas (a)** How does the news coverage of Katrina affect the writer's thoughts and actions before, during, and after the storm? **(b)** How does reading this account change your own understanding of hurricanes? *[Connect to the Big Question: How does communication change us?]*

## Comparing Imagery

© **1. Craft and Structure** For each selection, find examples of imagery that appeal to as many senses as you can. Create a chart like the one below to identify and describe examples in each selection. Make a chart for each sense.

| Selection | Image Appealing to Touch |
|---|---|
| "There Is No Word For Goodbye" | |
| "Daily" | |
| "Hope" | |
| "The Day of the Storm" | |

© **2. Craft and Structure (a)** Do any of the selections include imagery that appeals to the sense of taste? **(b)** Do any of the selections include imagery that appeals to the sense of smell? Give examples.

## ⏱ Timed Writing

### Explanatory Text: Essay

In an essay, compare and contrast the effects of the writers' use of imagery in each selection. Provide evidence from the texts to support your response. **(35 minutes)**

### 5-Minute Planner

1. Read the prompt carefully and completely.

2. Consider these questions and jot down your responses.

   • In "There Is No Word For Goodbye," how do the images of Sokoya help you understand the speaker's feelings for her aunt?

   • In "Daily," how does the imagery help you understand the speaker's affection for ordinary things?

   • In "Hope," how does the sound image help convey fear?

   • In "Day of the Storm," how does the writer use images to help convey a picture of the deserted campus?

   • What effect does the imagery in these works have on the reader?

3. Reread the prompt, then reference your notes as you draft your essay.

# Writing Workshop

 **Common Core State Standards**

**Writing**

**2.** Write informative/explanatory texts to examine and convey complex ideas, concepts, and information clearly and accurately through the effective selection, organization, and analysis of content.

**2.a.** Introduce a topic; organize complex ideas, concepts, and information to make important connections and distinctions.

**2.d.** Use precise language and domain-specific vocabulary to manage the complexity of the topic.

**4.** Produce clear and coherent writing in which the development, organization, and style are appropriate to task, purpose, and audience.

**Language**

**5.** Demonstrate understanding of figurative language, word relationships, and nuances in word meanings.

## Write an Informative Text

### Description: Descriptive Essay

**Defining the Form** Descriptive writing begins not in your imagination, but in your senses—in your ability to notice physical details. While valuable on its own, description also helps you share an experience, portray a person, and convey meaning and tone. Use descriptive elements in autobiographical writing, travel reports, and character sketches.

**Assignment** Write a description of a place that you enjoy or that is meaningful to you. Include these elements:

✓ *sensory details* that recreate sights, sounds, smells, tastes, and textures

✓ precise *word choice* that brings the subject into focus

✓ *figurative language*, such as metaphor, simile, and personification

✓ logical and consistent *organization*

✓ error-free grammar, especially your use of *prepositional phrases*

To preview the criteria on which your descriptive essay may be judged, see the rubric on page 691.

 **Writing Workshop:** *Work in Progress*

Review the work you did on pages 641 and 667.

## Prewriting/Planning Strategies

**Keep a walking journal.** Be alert to the sights, sounds, smells, tastes, and textures you encounter in your daily routine. Jot down ideas about the places you visit. Choose for your topic the location that presents the most possibilities for description.

**Use trigger words.** A single word or object can trigger a flood of ideas. For example, words like *friendship* or *fire* may remind you of people or places or evoke an emotion in you. Objects like a leaf or a blue ribbon may be equally suggestive. Working with a group, take turns calling out trigger words. As each person takes a turn, jot down whatever comes to mind. When the activity is finished, review your notes and choose a topic.

## Perfecting Your Description

**Word choice** is the specific language a writer selects in order to create a strong impression. It has been said that you can travel the globe between the covers of a book. This is made possible by quality descriptions. Vivid detail has the ability to transport the reader to different places and times. You can affect your audience in the same way by following these tips.

**Bringing the Scene to Life** Descriptive writers attempt to bring a scene or subject to life by including details that appeal to as many senses as possible. Not only do the details need to be sensory, they also need to be specific. Precise and vivid description will allow you to achieve your purpose: helping your audience to imagine and experience what you are describing.

**Choosing Vivid Words** As you draft, you might use generic words to simply get your ideas down. However, you should review your essay, circling vague or dull word choices. Consider replacements that paint a clear and colorful picture of your subject. Also, consider adding descriptors to enhance your scene. You can use a thesaurus to help you.

**PH WRITING COACH**

Further instruction and practice are available in *Prentice Hall Writing Coach*.

| Dull | Vivid |
| --- | --- |
| The air was *really* cold. | The air was *piercingly* cold. |
| The snow was *bright* white. | The snow was *blinding*. |
| The sun *came* out from behind a cloud. | The sun *peeked* out from behind a cloud. |

**Using Figurative Language** Use similes and metaphors in your descriptions to capture your readers' interest.

A **simile** is a comparison of two unlike things using *like* or *as*.

During the storm, the wind tore through the tree branches like a power saw.

A **metaphor** compares two unlike things without using *like* or *as*.

Tree trunks were matchsticks as they snapped in the winds.

**Being Precise** Remember that providing a good description does not mean using a lot of words to describe one thing. Rather, it means choosing the exact words that express your perception of the subject.

# Drafting Strategies

**Choose an effective organization.** The following are two structures that work well with descriptive essays:

- **Spatial organization:** Describe your subject systematically from left to right, front to back, or top to bottom. Like a photographer, pan your "camera" over your subject, using transitional words and phrases like *above, below,* or *in the distance* that show spatial relationships.

- **Time-order organization:** Describe your subject as you first approach it and then as you move through or around it. In addition to words expressing spatial relationships, use words showing time-order relationships, such as *initially, meanwhile,* or *finally.*

**Think about your audience.** Consider your readers' knowledge of the place you are describing. If the place is unfamiliar, include more clarifying details that set context. If the place is familiar, draw your readers in by acknowledging shared experience.

# Revising Strategies

**Strengthen your main impression.** A memorable, descriptive essay conveys a single, strong impression of its subject. Review your work, adding details that support the main impression. Eliminate details that are irrelevant or distracting.

### First Draft

The air was piercingly cold. The snow was blinding. The sun peeked out from behind a cloud. I sat perfectly still. I kept thinking about how hungry I was. Finally a deer walked by. It was just what I had been waiting for!

### Revision

The air was piercingly cold. The snow was blinding. Then, the sun peeked out from behind a cloud. I sat perfectly still, waiting for signs of wildlife. Just then a magnificent buck meandered by in the distance. I was astounded by his strength and beauty.

**Choose vivid words.** Review your essay, circling vague or dull word choices. Consider replacements that paint a clear and colorful picture of your subject.

**Dull:** The air was *really* cold.
**Vivid:** The air was *shockingly* cold.

 **Common Core State Standards**

**Writing**

**2.a.** Introduce a topic; organize complex ideas, concepts, and information to make important connections and distinctions.

**2.d.** Use precise language and domain-specific vocabulary to manage the complexity of the topic.

**4.** Produce clear and coherent writing in which the development, organization, and style are appropriate to task, purpose, and audience.

**Language**

**1.b.** Use various types of phrases and clauses to convey special meanings and add variety and interest to writing or presentations.

# Revising to Vary Sentence Patterns

Overuse of the basic subject-verb pattern can make your writing stiff. To add interest, begin some sentences with prepositional phrases.

**Identifying Prepositional Phrases** A preposition is a word that relates a noun or pronoun to another word in the sentence. The combination of preposition and accompanying noun or pronoun—the object of the preposition—is called a prepositional phrase.

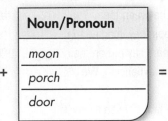

| Preposition | | Noun/Pronoun | | Prepositional Phrase |
|---|---|---|---|---|
| over | | moon | | over the moon |
| under | + | porch | = | under the porch |
| behind | | door | | behind the red door |

Many prepositions express spatial relationships. Appropriate use of such prepositions to begin sentences can clarify descriptive writing.

**Varying Sentences** In the following example, subjects are italicized, verbs are underlined, and prepositional phrases appear in parentheses.

> **Overuse of subject-verb pattern:** The *cave* <u>was</u> <u>hidden</u> (behind the trees). The *ground* <u>was</u> smooth (in front of it). *I* <u>pulled</u> away dead branches. *I* <u>saw</u> large paw prints (on the cave's dirt floor).
>
> **Revision:** The cave was hidden behind the trees. In front of it, the ground was smooth. I pulled away dead branches. On the cave's dirt floor, I saw large paw prints.

Follow these steps to vary your sentences in your writing.

1. Read your draft aloud, listening for places where you overuse the subject-verb sentence pattern.

2. Rewrite some sentences to begin with a prepositional phrase.

3. If an introductory prepositional phrase contains four or more words, set it off with a comma.

**PH WRITING COACH**
Further instruction and practice are available in *Prentice Hall Writing Coach.*

**Grammar in Your Writing**
Review the first and last paragraphs of your descriptive essay, looking for opportunities to vary a monotonous subject-verb sequence of sentences. Rewrite some sentences by beginning them with prepositional phrases.

# Student Model: Zachary DeBoer, Raleigh, NC

 **Common Core State Standards**

**Language**
**2.c.** Spell correctly.

## Ziggy's Coffeehouse

As I enter the gates of the fenced-in courtyard of the humble coffeehouse, smooth stones crunch beneath my shoes and strings of Christmas lights twinkle like the stars overhead. A stranger takes my five-dollar bill and makes a mark on my hand. The freezing winter air is perfectly still while I walk up the ramp and step into the mildly dilapidated structure. Inside I am met by a sound check of guitars vibrating through speakers. I am surrounded by wood; wood floors, wood ceiling, wood walls; acoustic trampolines that make the music bounce around like mad. The guys and girls in the band tonight are good friends of mine. As they run through their set list, there is a strong sense of camaraderie between them. They dream of record deals and radio play and 25-city tours. Perhaps they imagine that their venue is not a small café, but a mammoth, sold-out arena. They put on their best performance, playing just for us and singing: "We should be dancing. We need be dancing."

The place smells like aged wood and fresh coffee, but my lack of even a few dollar bills means I'll be drinking water tonight. There are three platforms in the cafe; the lowest has a set of double doors on the stage right side that have been swung open. The heat lamps radiate warmth as the frigid air rushes in from the doors, like a cold front passing through on a hot September day. On the second tier, those who prefer to act like adults sip their skinny decaf lattes. They seem mildly interested in the music, but most are there for the lack of something better to do. Are they swaying because of the music or because they have put a bit too much sugar in their coffees? Outside in the parking lot, kids talk cars and sports and who knows what else? I'm so captivated by the band that my ears can't tell. They laugh intermittently, oblivious to the music playing inside.

On the lowest level, immediately in front of the stage, the real fans are found. We push the tables back and dance around like no one is watching us and we sing along with the songs we know at the top of our lungs. This is where we artists are, the free spirits, the *real* cool kids. I don't know most of them but I feel a connection with all of them. We are friends now, brothers and sisters, united by the music. We jump up and down, careful not to bump into each other or the tables; we are captivated by the music but respectful of those around us. We have been liberated from the bonds of everyday life. We are transported to a state of bliss. We are not escaping reality; instead, we are experiencing true reality. As the soft lights from the stage shine onto the mellow brown of the all-wood venue, I realize: On this night, at this moment, there is nowhere else I'd rather be than this place.

Zachary uses sensory details to make this introduction vivid and interesting.

Zachary does not limit himself to describing the setting; he imagines the thoughts and feelings of the people, as well.

Zachary uses details related to all the senses, including smell and taste.

Zachary pays attention to all elements of the scene.

Zachary uses description to make a meaningful point.

# Editing and Proofreading

Check your draft for errors in spelling, grammar, and punctuation.

**Focus on transitions.** Make sure that you use transition words accurately and punctuate them correctly. If you begin a sentence with a transitional word or phrase, set it off with a comma.

**Focus on spelling.** When adding suffixes to words ending in silent *e*, drop the *e* when the suffix begins with a vowel, as in *amaze/amazing*. Keep the *e* when the suffix begins with a consonant, as in *amaze/amazement*.

# Publishing and Presenting

Consider one of the following ways to share your writing.

**Prepare an oral presentation.** Present your descriptive essay, making sure to establish your point of view on the subject matter as well as your relationship to the topic. Include effective and factual descriptions of appearance, concrete images, shifting perspectives, and sensory details.

**Create a visitor's guide.** With classmates, assemble several essays that describe places of interest in your community and create a guidebook. If possible, provide copies of the guidebook to your local library, town hall, or chamber of commerce for distribution to the public.

# Reflecting on Your Writing

**Writer's Journal** Jot down your answer to this question:

*How did describing your subject help you to understand it?*

# Rubric for Self-Assessment

Find evidence in your writing to address each category. Then, use the rating scale to grade your work.

| Criteria | Rating Scale<br>not very 1 2 3 4 very 5 |
|---|---|
| **Focus:** How clearly do you describe your subject? | 1  2  3  4  5 |
| **Organization:** How logical and consistent is your organization? | 1  2  3  4  5 |
| **Support/Elaboration:** How well do you use a variety of sensory details? | 1  2  3  4  5 |
| **Style:** How effective is your use of figurative language? | 1  2  3  4  5 |
| **Conventions:** How correct is your grammar, especially your use of prepositional phrases? | 1  2  3  4  5 |
| **Word Choice:** How precise is your word choice? | 1  2  3  4  5 |

**Spiral Review**

**Prepositional Phrases** Earlier in this unit you learned about **prepositions** (p. 640) and **prepositional phrases** (p. 666). Review your essay to be sure you have used prepositions and prepositional phrases correctly and effectively.

**Leveled Texts**

Build your skills and improve your comprehension of poetry with texts of increasing complexity.

**Poetry Collection 5** includes poems with a unique mood or feeling.

**Poetry Collection 6** includes poems with a thought-provoking setting.

 **Common Core State Standards**

Meet these standards with either **Poetry Collection 5** (p. 696) or **Poetry Collection 6** (p. 706).

**Reading Literature**

**4.** Determine the meaning of words and phrases as they are used in the text, including figurative and connotative meanings; analyze the cumulative impact of specific word choices on meaning and tone. *(Literary Analysis: Spiral Review)*

**5.** Analyze how an author's choices concerning how to structure a text, order events within it, and manipulate time create such effects as mystery, tension, or surprise. *(Literary Analysis: Narrative Poetry)*

**Writing**

**4.** Produce clear and coherent writing in which the development, organization, and style are appropriate to task, purpose, and audience. *(Writing: Description of a Scene)*

**Speaking and Listening**

**1.a.** Come to discussions prepared, having read and researched material under study; explicitly draw on

that preparation to stimulate a thoughtful, well-reasoned exchange of ideas. **1.b.** Work with peers to set rules for collegial discussions and decision-making, clear goals and deadlines, and individual roles as needed. **1.c.** Propel conversations by posing and responding to questions that relate the current discussion to broader themes or larger ideas; actively incorporate others into the discussion; and clarify, verify, or challenge ideas and conclusions. *(Speaking and Listening: Role-Play a Dialogue)*

**Language**

**1.b.** Use various types of phrases and clauses to convey specific meanings and add variety and interest to writing or presentations. *(Conventions: Appositive Phrases)*

# Literary Analysis: Narrative Poetry

**Narrative poetry** tells a story and includes the same literary elements as narrative prose: a plot, or sequence of events; specific settings; and people or characters who participate in the action.

Like short stories, narrative poems convey a **mood,** or **atmosphere**—an overall feeling created by the setting, plot, specific word choices, and images. For example, a fast-paced plot may create an exciting mood. A mysterious, recurring image may create a suspenseful mood.

The choice of a speaker, or narrator, affects the meaning, tone, and mood of the poem. The speaker's point of view and personality affects how the reader responds to the poem.

# Reading Skill: Paraphrase

**Paraphrasing** is restating in your own words what someone else has written or said. A paraphrase retains the meaning but is simpler. Paraphrasing is especially useful in comprehending poems that contain **figurative language**—words that are used imaginatively rather than literally. To paraphrase a narrative poem, picture the action.

- Based on details in the poem, form a mental image of the setting, the characters, and the characters' actions.

- To be sure that your mental picture is accurate, continue to pay attention to the poet's description of the scene.

- Then, describe your mental image of the scene.

## Using the Strategy: Paraphrase Chart

Use a **paraphrase chart** like the one shown to record your paraphrases.

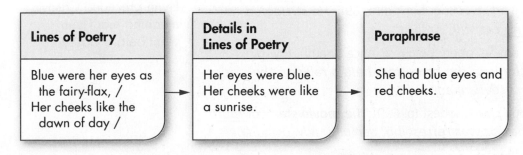

| Lines of Poetry | Details in Lines of Poetry | Paraphrase |
|---|---|---|
| Blue were her eyes as the fairy-flax, / Her cheeks like the dawn of day / | Her eyes were blue. Her cheeks were like a sunrise. | She had blue eyes and red cheeks. |

How does *communication* change us?

### Writing About the Big Question

In "Casey at the Bat," the fans of a baseball team voice their enthusiastic support for their star player. Use this sentence starter to develop your ideas about the Big Question.

> When a crowd communicates its support or disapproval, an athlete might **react** by _____.

**While You Read** Think about what effect the crowd's cheering has on Casey and his performance in "Casey at the Bat."

### Vocabulary

Read each word and its definition. Decide whether you know the word well, know it a little bit, or do not know it at all. After you read, see how your knowledge of each word has increased.

- **pallor** (pal´ ər) *n.* unnatural paleness (p. 697) *His pallor made us realize just how ill he was.* pale *adj.* pallid *adj.*

- **preceded** (prē cēd´ əd) *v.* came before in time, place, order, rank, or importance (p. 697) *The police car preceded the floats in the annual parade.* precede *v.* preceding *adj.* precedence *n.*

- **multitude** (mul´ tə tōōd) *n.* a large number of persons or things, especially when gathered together or considered as a unit (p. 697) *I like to read books that have a multitude of characters.* multitudinous *adj.*

- **writhing** (rīth´ iŋ) *adj.* twisting; turning (p. 698) *He struggled to hold the writhing cat still.* writhe *v.*

- **defiance** (dē fī´ əns) *n.* open, bold resistance to authority (p. 698) *In defiance of the law, the protestors held a rally on the steps of city hall.* defy *v.* defiant *adj.*

- **demure** (di myŏŏr´) *adj.* modest (p. 699) *The movie star's demure and proper behavior was refreshing.* demurely *adv.* demureness *n.*

### Word Study

The **Latin prefix** *pre-* means "before."

In "Casey at the Bat," the speaker says that Flynn **preceded** Casey, meaning that Flynn went before Casey.

# Meet the Authors

## Ernest Lawrence Thayer

**(1863–1940)**

**Author of "Casey at the Bat"** (p. 696)

It is not surprising that "Casey at the Bat" reads like a sports story in verse. The poet, Ernest Lawrence Thayer, worked for many years as a sports reporter on the staff of newspapers in New York and California. "Casey at the Bat" first appeared in the *San Francisco Examiner* in 1888. It became so popular that in 1953 it inspired an operetta called *The Mighty Casey*.

## William Stafford

**(1914–1993)**

**Author of "Fifteen"** (p. 699)

William Stafford was raised in Kansas. He did not publish his first book, *West of Your City,* until he was 46. However, he made up for lost time after that, publishing many collections, including *Traveling Through the Dark.* Fellow poet Robert Bly has said that Stafford's poems are "spoken like a friend over coffee."

## Sandra Cisneros

**(b. 1954)**

**Author of "Twister Hits Houston"** (p. 700)

Sandra Cisneros was born in Chicago, but her family moved frequently between Chicago and Mexico City. She began her first novel, *The House on Mango Street,* while she was still a college student. Cisneros has worked with high-school students, serving as poet-in-residence in several schools. She has received many awards for her writing.

▲ **Critical Viewing** Compare and contrast the stance and attitude of the batter in this painting with Casey's stance and attitude in the poem. **[Compare and Contrast]**

# CASEY AT THE BAT

## ERNEST LAWRENCE THAYER

It looked extremely rocky for the Mudville nine that day;
The score stood two to four, with but an inning left to play.
So, when Cooney died at second, and Burrows did the same,
A pallor wreathed the features of the patrons of the game.

5  A straggling few got up to go, leaving there the rest,
With that hope which springs eternal within the human breast.
For they thought: "If only Casey would get a whack at that,"
They'd put even money now, with Casey at the bat.

But Flynn preceded Casey, and likewise so did Blake,
10  And the former was a pudd'n, and the latter was a fake.
So on that stricken multitude a deathlike silence sat;
For there seemed but little chance of Casey's getting to the bat.

But Flynn let drive a "single," to the wonderment of all.
And the much-despised Blakey "tore the cover off the ball."
15  And when the dust had lifted, and they saw what had occurred,
There was Blakey safe at second, and Flynn a-huggin' third.

Then from the gladdened multitude went up a joyous yell—
It rumbled in the mountaintops, it rattled in the dell;
It struck upon the hillside and rebounded on the flat;
20  For Casey, mighty Casey, was advancing to the bat.

There was ease in Casey's manner as he stepped into his place,
There was pride in Casey's bearing and a smile on Casey's face;
And when responding to the cheers he lightly doffed his hat,
No stranger in the crowd could doubt 'twas Casey at the bat.

**Vocabulary**
**writhing** (rīth´ in) *v.*
twisting; turning

**defiance** (dē fī´ əns)
*n.* open, bold resis-
tance to authority

25 Ten thousand eyes were on him as he rubbed his hands with
dirt,
Five thousand tongues applauded when he wiped them on his
shirt;
Then when the writhing pitcher ground the ball into his hip,
Defiance glanced in Casey's eye, a sneer curled Casey's lip.

And now the leather-covered sphere came hurtling through the
air,
30 And Casey stood a-watching it in haughty grandeur there.
Close by the sturdy batsman the ball unheeded sped;
"That ain't my style," said Casey. "Strike one," the umpire said.

**Spiral Review**
**Diction and**
**Syntax** How does
word choice and word
arrangement in this
stanza help convey the
feelings of the crowd?

From the benches, black with people, there went up a muffled
roar,
Like the beating of the storm waves on the stern and distant
shore.
35 "Kill him! kill the umpire!" shouted someone on the stand;
And it's likely they'd have killed him had not Casey raised his
hand.

With a smile of Christian charity great Casey's visage shone;
He stilled the rising tumult, he made the game go on;
He signaled to the pitcher, and once more the spheroid flew;
40 But Casey still ignored it, and the umpire said, "Strike two."

"Fraud!" cried the maddened thousands, and the echo
answered "Fraud!"
But one scornful look from Casey and the audience was awed;
They saw his face grow stern and cold, they saw his muscles
strain,
And they knew that Casey wouldn't let the ball go by again.

**Literary Analysis**
**Narrative Poetry** In
what way does the
poem's mood change in
this stanza?

45 The sneer is gone from Casey's lips, his teeth are clenched in
hate.
He pounds with cruel vengeance his bat upon the plate:
And now the pitcher holds the ball, and now he lets it go,
And now the air is shattered by the force of Casey's blow.

Oh, somewhere in this favored land the sun is shining bright,
50 The band is playing somewhere, and somewhere hearts are
light:
And somewhere men are laughing, and somewhere children
shout,
But there is no joy in Mudville: Mighty Casey has struck out.

# Fifteen

## William Stafford

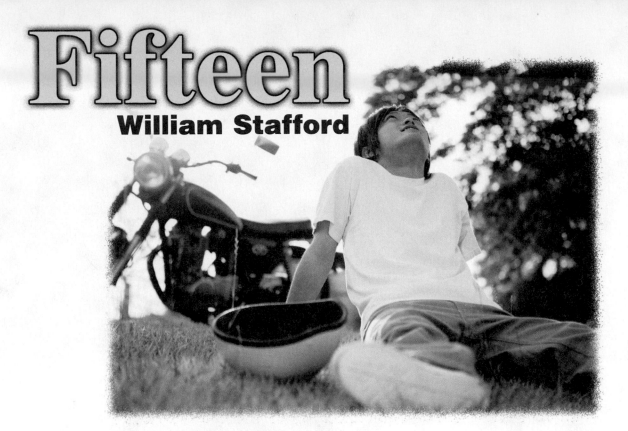

South of the bridge on Seventeenth
I found back of the willows one summer
day a motorcycle with engine running
as it lay on its side, ticking over
5  slowly in the high grass. I was fifteen.

I admired all that pulsing gleam, the
shiny flanks, the demure headlights
fringed where it lay; I led it gently
to the road and stood with that
10  companion, ready and friendly. I was fifteen.

We could find the end of a road, meet
the sky on out Seventeenth. I thought about
hills, and patting the handle got back a
confident opinion. On the bridge we indulged
15  a forward feeling, a tremble. I was fifteen.

Thinking, back farther in the grass I found
the owner, just coming to, where he had flipped
over the rail. He had blood on his hand, was pale—
I helped him walk to his machine. He ran his hand
20  over it, called me a good man, roared away.

I stood there, fifteen.

**Vocabulary**
**demure** (di myoor´)
*adj.* modest

**Reading Skill**
**Paraphrase** Picture the
action in lines 11 and
12, and then restate the
phrase "meet the sky" in
your own words.

# TWISTER *HITS* HOUSTON

## Sandra Cisneros

Papa was on the front porch.
Mama was in the kitchen.
Mama was trying
to screw a lightbulb into a fixture.
5  Papa was watching the rain.
Mama, it's a cyclone for sure,
he shouted to his wife in the kitchen.
Papa who was sitting on his front porch
when the storm hit
10  said the twister ripped
the big black oak to splinter,

◀ **Critical Viewing**
How does the power
of the tornado in this
photograph add to
your understanding of
the poem? **[Connect]**

**Reading Skill**
**Paraphrase** Restate the description in line 14 of the twister banging the back door.

tossed a green sedan into his garden,
and banged the back door
like a mad cat wanting in.
15 Mama who was in the kitchen
said Papa saw everything,
the big oak ripped to kindling,[1]
the green sedan land out back,
the back door slam and slam.
20 I missed it.
Mama was in the kitchen Papa explained.
Papa was sitting on the front porch.
The light bulb is still sitting
where I left it. Don't matter now.
25 Got no electricity anyway.

---

1. **kindling** (kind′ liŋ) *n.* bits of dry wood used for starting fires.

## Critical Thinking

Cite textual evidence to support your responses.

1. **Key Ideas and Details (a)** In "Casey at the Bat," what details does the speaker use to describe Casey? **(b) Infer:** What does the description suggest about Casey's personality? **(c) Draw Conclusions:** How might his personality have affected the game's outcome?

2. **Key Ideas and Details (a)** In the third stanza of "Fifteen," what does the speaker imagine doing with the motorcycle? **(b) Interpret:** What does the motorcycle represent to him? Explain your response.

3. **Key Ideas and Details (a)** What does the speaker's father do throughout the storm in "Twister Hits Houston"? **(b) Make a Judgment:** Is his behavior appropriate for the situation? Explain your answer.

4. **Integration of Knowledge and Ideas** What role, if any, do you think the crowd played in Casey's performance in "Casey at the Bat"? Explain. *[Connect to the Big Question: How does communication change us?]*

## Literary Analysis: Narrative Poetry

**© 1. Craft and Structure (a)** Using a chart like the one shown, identify and describe the story elements in each **narrative poem. (b)** Explain why you think each writer chose poetry to bring these elements to life.

|  | Setting | Characters | Plot |
|---|---|---|---|
| "Casey at the Bat" |  |  |  |
| "Fifteen" |  |  |  |
| "Twister Hits Houston" |  |  |  |

**© 2. Craft and Structure (a)** In "Fifteen," how would you describe the speaker's personality? **(b)** Identify three phrases in "Fifteen" that contribute to the poem's **mood,** or **atmosphere,** of longing. Explain each choice.

**© 3. Integration of Knowledge and Ideas (a)** Do you think a poem is an effective way to tell a story? Why or why not? **(b)** Share your response with a partner, and then explain whether his or her response changed your own.

## Reading Skill: Paraphrase

**4. (a) Paraphrase** lines 29 through 32 of "Casey at the Bat."
**(b)** Explain how picturing the action helped you restate the lines.

## Vocabulary

**© Acquisition and Use** In vocabulary study, **analogies** show the relationships between pairs of words. Use a word from the list on page 694 to make a word pair that matches the relationship between the first two given words.

**1.** flapping : bird :: _____ : snake
**2.** blush : red :: _____ : white
**3.** boastful : proud :: _____ : humble
**4.** approval : happy :: _____ : angry
**5.** club : member :: _____ : individual
**6.** early : late :: _____ : followed

**Word Study** Use the context of the sentences and what you know about the **Latin prefix pre-** to explain your answer to each question.

**1.** If you want to *prevent* a fire, when should you take action against it?

**2.** Are there any records of *prehistoric* events?

### Word Study

The **Latin prefix *pre-*** means "before."

**Apply It** Explain how the prefix *pre-* contributes to the meanings of these words. Consult a dictionary if necessary.

predict
preview
preface

# How does *communication* change us?

## Writing About the Big Question

In "The Writer," a father is moved by the sound of his daughter typing a story. Use this sentence starter to develop your ideas about the Big Question.

Having **empathy** for someone who is in a difficult situation might make a person realize that _____.

**While You Read** Consider how the speaker in "The Writer" is affected by his young daughter's attempt to write a story.

## Vocabulary

Read each word and its definition. Decide whether you know the word well, know it a little bit, or do not know it at all. After you read, see how your knowledge of each word has increased.

- **impenetrable** (im pen´ i trə bəl) *adj.* that cannot be passed through; that cannot be solved or understood (p. 706) *I could not see my hand in front of my face in the impenetrable darkness of the cave.* impenetrability *n.* penetrate *v.*

- **archaic** (är kā´ ik) *adj.* from an earlier time; ancient (p. 707) *Some people say the old song is timeless; others say it is archaic.*

- **iridescent** (ir´ i des´ ənt) *adj.* showing colors that seem to change in different lights (p. 709) *The silvery scales of the fish were iridescent in the sunlight.* iridescence *n.*

- **pondered** (pän´ dərd) *v.* thought deeply about (p. 711) *After hearing the inspirational speaker, Ralph pondered the meaning of life.* ponder *v.* ponderous *adj.*

- **beguiling** (bē gīl´ iŋ) *v.* tricking; charming (p. 712) *The children's innocence was beguiling their parents.* guile *n.*

- **respite** (res´ pit) *n.* rest; relief (p. 713) *The rain provided a respite from the long dry spell.*

## Word Study

The **Latin prefix im-** means "not."

In "The Horses," the speaker refers to an "**im**penetrable sorrow." If something is impenetrable, it cannot be penetrated, or pierced. An impenetrable sorrow is a deep sadness that cannot be relieved.

## Edwin Muir

**(1887–1959)**

**Author of "The Horses"** (p. 706)

An author of numerous books of poetry as well as several novels, Edwin Muir had visions of the future that were rooted in his past. He spent his early years on a farm in the Orkney Islands, north of Scotland. Much of the imagery in his poetry comes from these islands.

## Richard Wilbur

**(b. 1921)**

**Author of "The Writer"** (p. 708)

As a young man, Richard Wilbur planned to be a cartoonist. Instead, he became an award-winning poet. By the time he was thirty, Wilbur had published two collections of poetry and established himself as an important young writer. In 1987, Wilbur was appointed Poet Laureate of the United States.

## Edgar Allan Poe

**(1809–1849)**

**Author of "The Raven"** (p. 710)

One of the first great American storytellers, Edgar Allan Poe often explored dark and bizarre events in his stories and poems. His inspiration may have come from his own life, which was often filled with sadness. He found some happiness in his marriage to Virginia Clemm, but after her death, Poe became depressed and antisocial. Many of his poems and stories focus on an ideal love that is lost.

# THE HORSES

## EDWIN MUIR

Barely a twelvemonth after
The seven days war that put the world to sleep,
Late in the evening the strange horses came.
By then we had made our covenant with silence,
5   But in the first few days it was so still
We listened to our breathing and were afraid.
On the second day
The radios failed; we turned the knobs; no answer.
On the third day a warship passed us, heading north,
10  Dead bodies piled on the deck. On the sixth day
A plane plunged over us into the sea. Thereafter
Nothing. The radios dumb;
And still they stand in corners of our kitchens,
And stand, perhaps, turned on, in a million rooms
15  All over the world. But now if they should speak,
If on a sudden they should speak again,
If on the stroke of noon a voice should speak,
We would not listen, we would not let it bring
That old bad world that swallowed its children quick
20  At one great gulp. We would not have it again.
Sometimes we think of the nations lying asleep,
Curled blindly in impenetrable sorrow,
And then the thought confounds us with its strangeness.

The tractors lie about our fields; at evening
25  They look like dank sea-monsters couched and waiting.
We leave them where they are and let them rust:

▶ **Critical Viewing** Do these horses appear "stubborn and shy" like the ones described in the poem? Explain. **[Compare and Contrast]**

'They'll moulder away and be like other loam'.[1]
We make our oxen drag our rusty ploughs,
Long laid aside. We have gone back
30  Far past our fathers' land.
                    And then, that evening
Late in the summer the strange horses came.
We heard a distant tapping on the road,
A deepening drumming; it stopped, went on again
35  And at the corner changed to hollow thunder.
We saw the heads
Like a wild wave charging and were afraid.
We had sold our horses in our fathers' time
To buy new tractors. Now they were strange to us
40  As fabulous steeds set on an ancient shield
Or illustrations in a book of knights.
We did not dare go near them. Yet they waited,
Stubborn and shy, as if they had been sent
By an old command to find our whereabouts
45  And that long-lost archaic companionship.
In the first moment we had never a thought
That they were creatures to be owned and used.
Among them were some half-a-dozen colts
Dropped in some wilderness of the broken world,
50  Yet new as if they had come from their own Eden.[2]
Since then they have pulled our ploughs and borne our loads,
But that free servitude still can pierce our hearts.
Our life is changed; their coming our beginning.

**Reading Skill
Paraphrase** Picture the
scene here and para-
phrase lines 31–35.

**Vocabulary
archaic** (är kā´ ik)
*adj.* from an ear-
lier time; ancient

---

**1. loam** (lōm) *n.* dark, rich soil.
**2. Eden** in the Bible, the garden where life began with Adam and Eve; paradise.

# The Writer

## RICHARD WILBUR

**Literary Analysis**
**Narrative Poetry** What details about the characters and setting are introduced in the first stanza?

In her room at the prow[1] of the house
Where light breaks, and the windows are tossed with linden,[2]
My daughter is writing a story.

I pause in the stairwell, hearing
5   From her shut door a commotion of typewriter-keys
Like a chain hauled over a gunwale.[3]

Young as she is, the stuff
Of her life is a great cargo, and some of it heavy:
I wish her a lucky passage.

10   But now it is she who pauses,
As if to reject my thought and its easy figure.
A stillness greatens, in which

The whole house seems to be thinking,
And then she is at it again with a bunched clamor
15   Of strokes, and again is silent.

---

**1. prow** (prou) *n.* front part of a ship or boat.
**2. linden** (lin´ dən) *n.* type of tree.
**3. gunwale** (gun´ əl) *n.* upper edge of the side of a ship or boat.

I remember the dazed starling [4]
Which was trapped in that very room, two years ago;
How we stole in, lifted a sash

And retreated, not to affright it;
20  And how for a helpless hour, through the crack of the door,
We watched the sleek, wild, dark

And iridescent creature
Batter against the brilliance, drop like a glove
To the hard floor, or the desk-top,

25  And wait then, humped and bloody,
For the wits to try it again; and how our spirits
Rose when, suddenly sure,

It lifted off from a chair-back,
Beating a smooth course for the right window
30  And clearing the sill of the world.

It is always a matter, my darling,
Of life or death, as I had forgotten. I wish
What I wished you before, but harder.

---

4. **starling** (stär´ liŋ) *n.* bird with black feathers that shine in a greenish or purplish way.

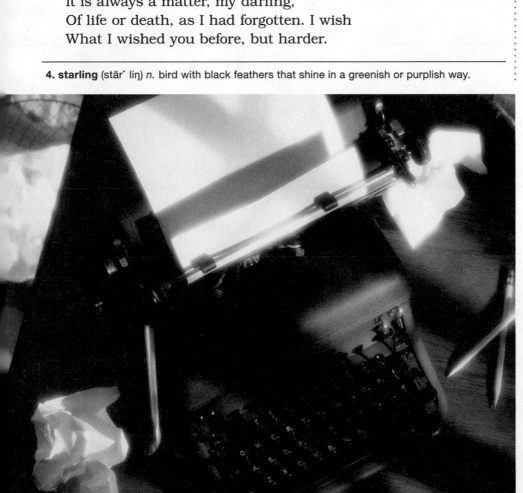

# The Raven

## Edgar Allan Poe

Once upon a midnight dreary, while I pondered, weak and weary,
    Over many a quaint and curious volume of forgotten lore,
    While I nodded, nearly napping, suddenly there came a tapping,
    As of someone gently rapping, rapping at my chamber door.
5    "'Tis some visitor," I muttered, "tapping at my chamber door—
        Only this, and nothing more."

Ah, distinctly I remember it was in the bleak December,
    And each separate dying ember wrought its ghost upon the floor.
    Eagerly I wished the morrow—vainly I had tried to borrow
10    From my books surcease[1] of sorrow—sorrow for the lost Lenore—
    For the rare and radiant maiden whom the angels name Lenore—
        Nameless here for evermore.

And the silken, sad, uncertain rustling of each purple curtain
    Thrilled me—filled me with fantastic terrors never felt before;
15    So that now, to still the beating of my heart, I stood repeating
    "'Tis some visitor entreating entrance at my chamber door—
    Some late visitor entreating entrance at my chamber door—
        This it is and nothing more."

Presently my soul grew stronger; hesitating then no longer,
20    "Sir," said I, "or Madam, truly your forgiveness I implore;
    But the fact is I was napping, and so gently you came rapping,
    And so faintly you came tapping, tapping at my chamber door,
    That I scarce was sure I heard you"—here I opened wide the door—
        Darkness there, and nothing more.

25    Deep into that darkness peering, long I stood there wondering, fearing,
    Doubting, dreaming dreams no mortal ever dared to dream before;
    But the silence was unbroken, and the darkness gave no token,
    And the only word there spoken was the whispered word, "Lenore!"
    This I whispered, and an echo murmured back the word, "Lenore!"
30        Merely this, and nothing more.

Then into the chamber turning, all my soul within me burning,
    Soon I heard again a tapping somewhat louder than before.
    "Surely," said I, "surely that is something at my window lattice;
    Let me see, then, what thereat[2] is, and this mystery explore—

---

1. **surcease** (sʉr sēs´) n. end.
2. **thereat** (ther at´) adv. there.

**Vocabulary**
**pondered** (pän´ dərd) v. thought deeply about

**Literary Analysis**
**Narrative Poetry**
Which details provide information about the setting and the speaker?

**Reading Skill**
**Paraphrase** Picture the action the speaker describes, and paraphrase this stanza.

**Literary Analysis**
**Narrative Poetry** How has the speaker's emotional state changed since the first stanza?

Reading Check
What sorrow is the speaker hoping to ease by reading?

**Reading Skill**
**Paraphrase** In your own words, describe how the raven behaved as it entered the chamber.

**Vocabulary**
**beguiling** (bē gīl´ iŋ) *v.* tricking; charming

**Spiral Review**
**Diction and Syntax** Which words in lines 43–48 help create a dark and gloomy tone?

35    Let my heart be still a moment and this mystery explore—
        'Tis the wind, and nothing more!"
    Open here I flung the shutter, when, with many a flirt[3] and flutter,
    In there stepped a stately raven of the saintly days of yore;
    Not the least obeisance[4] made he; not an instant stopped or stayed he;
40    But, with mien[5] of lord or lady, perched above my chamber door—
    Perched upon a bust of Pallas just above my chamber door—
        Perched, and sat, and nothing more.

    Then this ebony bird beguiling my sad fancy[6] into smiling,
    By the grave and stern decorum of the countenance[7] it wore,
45    "Though thy crest be shorn and shaven, thou," I said, "art sure no craven,[8]
    Ghastly grim and ancient raven wandering from the Nightly shore—
    Tell me what thy lordly name is on the Night's Plutonian[9] shore!"
        Quoth[10] the raven, "Nevermore."

    Much I marveled this ungainly fowl to hear discourse so plainly,
50    Though its answer little meaning—little relevancy bore;
    For we cannot help agreeing that no sublunary[11] being
    Ever yet was blessed with seeing bird above his chamber door—
    Bird or beast upon the sculptured bust above his chamber door,
        With such name as "Nevermore."

55    But the raven, sitting lonely on the placid bust, spoke only
    That one word, as if his soul in that one word he did outpour.
    Nothing farther then he uttered—not a feather then he fluttered—
    Till I scarcely more than muttered, "Other friends have flown before—
    On the morrow *he* will leave me, as my hopes have flown before."
60        Quoth the raven, "Nevermore."

    Wondering at the stillness broken by reply so aptly spoken,
    "Doubtless," said I, "what it utters is its only stock and store,

---

  **3. flirt** (flʉrt) *n.* quick, uneven movement.
  **4. obeisance** (ō bā´ səns) *n.* bow or another sign of respect.
  **5. mien** (mēn) *n.* manner.
  **6. fancy** (fan´ sē) *n.* imagination.
  **7. countenance** (kount´'n əns) *n.* facial appearance.
  **8. craven** (krā´ vən) *n.* coward (usually an adjective).
  **9. Plutonian** (plo͞o tō´ nē ən) *adj.* like the underworld, ruled by the ancient Roman god Pluto.
**10. quoth** (kwōth) *v.* said.
**11. sublunary** (sub lo͞on´ ər ē) *adj.* earthly.

Caught from some unhappy master whom unmerciful Disaster
Followed fast and followed faster—so, when Hope he would
    adjure,[12]
65    Stern Despair returned, instead of the sweet Hope he dared
    adjure—
        That sad answer, 'Nevermore.'"

But the raven still beguiling all my sad soul into smiling,
Straight I wheeled a cushioned seat in front of bird, and
    bust, and door;
Then upon the velvet sinking, I betook myself to linking
70    Fancy unto fancy, thinking what this ominous bird of yore—
What this grim, ungainly, ghastly, gaunt, and ominous bird
    of yore
        Meant in croaking "Nevermore."

This I sat engaged in guessing, but no syllable expressing
To the fowl whose fiery eyes now burned into my bosom's core;
75    This and more I sat divining,[13] with my head at ease reclining
On the cushion's velvet lining that the lamplight gloated o'er,
But whose velvet violet lining with the lamplight gloating o'er,
        *She* shall press, ah, nevermore!

Then, methought, the air grew denser, perfumed from
    an unseen censer[14]
80    Swung by angels whose faint footfalls tinkled on the tufted floor.
"Wretch," I cried, "thy God hath lent thee—by these angels
    he hath sent thee
Respite—respite and Nepenthe[15] from thy memories of Lenore!
Let me quaff this kind Nepenthe and forget this lost Lenore!"
        Quoth the raven, "Nevermore."

85    "Prophet!" said I, "thing of evil!—prophet still, if bird or devil!—
Whether Tempter sent, or whether tempest tossed thee here
    ashore,
Desolate, yet all undaunted, on this desert land enchanted—
On this home by Horror haunted—tell me truly, I
    implore—
Is there—is there balm in Gilead?[16]—tell me—tell me, I
    implore!"
90        Quoth the raven, "Nevermore."

---

**12. adjure** (ə jŏŏr´) *v.* appeal to; ask earnestly.
**13. divining** (də vīn´ iŋ) *v.* guessing.
**14. censer** (sen´ sər) *n.* container for burning incense.
**15. Nepenthe** (nē pen´ *th*ē) *n.* drug believed by the ancient Greeks to cause
    forgetfulness of sorrow.
**16. balm** (bäm) **in Gilead** (gil´ ē əd) cure for suffering; the Bible refers to a
    medicinal ointment, or balm, made in a region called Gilead.

**Literary Analysis**
**Narrative Poetry** What
two conflicts or problems
does the speaker face in
this stanza?

**Vocabulary**
**respite** (res´ pit)
*n.* rest; relief

Reading
Check
What one word does the
raven repeat?

"Prophet!" said I, "thing of evil!—prophet still, if bird or devil!
By that Heaven that bends above us—by that God we both
    adore—
Tell this soul with sorrow laden if, within the distant Aidenn,[17]
It shall clasp a sainted maiden whom the angels name Lenore—
95   Clasp a rare and radiant maiden whom the angels name Lenore."
        Quoth the raven, "Nevermore."

"Be that word our sign of parting, bird or fiend!" I shrieked,
    upstarting—
"Get thee back into the tempest and the Night's Plutonian shore!
Leave no black plume as a token of that lie thy soul hath spoken!
100  Leave my loneliness unbroken!—quit the bust above my door!
Take thy beak from out my heart, and take thy form from
    off my door!"
        Quoth the raven, "Nevermore."

And the raven, never flitting, still is sitting, still is sitting
On the pallid bust of Pallas just above my chamber door;
105  And his eyes have all the seeming of a demon that is dreaming,
And the lamplight o'er him streaming throws his shadow on
    the floor;
And my soul from out that shadow that lies floating on the floor
        Shall be lifted—nevermore!

**17. Aidenn** name meant to suggest Eden, or paradise.

**Literary Analysis**
**Narrative Poetry** How does the mood here compare with the mood at the beginning of the poem? Explain.

## Critical Thinking

**Cite textual evidence to support your responses.**

@ **1. Key Ideas and Details (a)** What happens to the tractors in "The Horses"? **(b) Interpret:** Why does the poet place the tractors and the horses side by side?

@ **2. Key Ideas and Details Analyze:** Why does the speaker of "The Writer" recall the incident of the trapped starling? Explain your answer.

@ **3. Key Ideas and Details (a)** In the first line of "The Raven," which two adjectives does the speaker use to describe his state of mind? **(b) Draw Conclusions:** How would you describe the speaker's state of mind at the end of the poem? **(c) Analyze Cause and Effect:** What has caused the speaker to change?

@ **4. Integration of Knowledge and Ideas** How is the speaker in "The Writer" affected by his daughter's struggle to write her story? *[Connect to the Big Question: How does communication change us?]*

## Literary Analysis: Narrative Poetry

ⓒ **1. Craft and Structure (a)** Using a chart like the one shown, identify and describe the story elements in each **narrative poem. (b)** Explain why you think each writer chose poetry to bring these elements to life.

|  | Setting | Characters | Plot |
|---|---|---|---|
| "The Horses" |  |  |  |
| "The Writer" |  |  |  |
| "The Raven" |  |  |  |

ⓒ **2. Craft and Structure (a)** In "The Raven," how would you describe the speaker's personality? **(b)** Identify three lines or phrases in "The Raven" that contribute to the poem's mysterious and frantic **mood,** or **atmosphere.** Explain your choices.

ⓒ **3. Integration of Knowledge and Ideas (a)** Do you think a poem is an effective way to tell a story? Why or why not? **(b)** Share your response with a partner, and then explain if his or her response changed your own.

## Reading Skill: Paraphrase

**4. (a) Paraphrase** lines 37 through 39 of "The Raven." **(b)** Explain how picturing the action helped you restate the lines.

## Vocabulary

ⓒ **Acquisition and Use** In vocabulary study, **analogies** show the relationships between pairs of words. Use a word from the list on page 704 to make a word pair that matches the relationship between the first two given words.

**1.** stale : fresh :: _____ : modern

**2.** exercise : tiredness :: _____ : rest

**3.** teaching : professor :: _____ : trickster

**4.** clear : glass :: _____ : steel

**5.** kicked : foot :: _____ : mind

**6.** spicy : bland :: _____ : dull

**Word Study** Use the context of the sentences and what you know about the **Latin prefix im-** to explain your answer to each question.

**1.** Is it possible to move an *immovable* object?

**2.** How likely is it that an *improbable* event will occur?

### Word Study

The **Latin prefix im-** means "not."

**Apply It** Explain how the prefix *im-* contributes to the meanings of these words. Consult a dictionary if necessary.

impassive
impersonal
impartial

# Integrated Language Skills

## Poetry Collections 5 and 6

**Poetry Collection 5**

### Conventions: Appositive Phrases

An **appositive phrase** is a noun or pronoun with modifiers that add information to the noun or pronoun it follows.

An appositive phrase is set off with commas and functions as a unit that identifies, renames, or explains the word that comes before it. Notice that appositive phrases do not contain any verbs.

Using appositives is a good way to make your writing more concise. Notice how combining sentences using an appositive phrase (underlined) makes the revised version more concise than the original.

**Poetry Collection 6**

| Less Concise | Revision With Appositive |
|---|---|
| "The Raven" is a poem by Edgar Allan Poe. Edgar Allan Poe was one of the first great American writers. | "The Raven" is a poem by Edgar Allan Poe, <u>one of the first great American writers</u>. |

**Practice A** Identify the appositive phrase in each sentence.

1. "Casey at the Bat" takes place in Mudville, a fictional town.

2. The crowd cheered for Casey, the best player on the team.

3. In "Fifteen," a poem by William Stafford, the speaker finds a motorcycle by the side of a road.

4. Houston, the largest city in Texas, is the setting for Cisneros's poem.

**Practice B** For each item, combine the two sentences using an appositive phrase.

1. The raven perches on a bust of Pallas. Pallas was an ancient Greek goddess.

2. Muir grew up in Orkney. Orkney is a group of islands north of Scotland.

3. "The Writer" is one of Richard Wilbur's most famous poems. "The Writer" was published in 1969.

4. The speaker and his daughter watched as the bird tried to fly through the window. The bird was a starling.

© **Writing Application** Rewrite lines 9 and 10 of "Casey at the Bat" as two sentences. Use an appositive phrase in each one.

© **Writing Application** Write two sentences about the opening image of "The Raven" on page 710. Use an appositive phrase in each one.

**PH** **WRITING COACH** Further instruction and practice are available in *Prentice Hall Writing Coach*.

# Writing

**Informative Text** Imagine you have been hired by a movie studio to make a short film based on one of the poems you read. Write a **description of the scene** that could be used to develop a script.

- Jot down details about the characters, setting, and action.

- Explain the mood you want to set and note how details about characters, setting, and action can evoke this mood.

- Consider the technology you might use to produce the scene. Suggest camerawork, lighting, and other elements, such as sights, sounds, movements, and gestures that should appear in the scene.

Share the poem and your proposed scene with the class, describing the technology you would use in the scene. Ask for feedback from your classmates to determine if your scene conveys the mood of the poem.

**Grammar Application** Make sure you correctly use appositive phrases to add variety and interest to your writing.

**Writing Workshop:** *Work in Progress*

**Prewriting for a Response to Literature** To prepare for a response to literature you may write, review these poems or review "Uncoiling" and "A Voice" at the beginning of Unit 4. Identify the character in each poem that makes the strongest impression on you. Jot down details that help give you that impression. Put your Character Descriptions in your writing portfolio.

# Speaking and Listening

**Presentation of Ideas** With a partner, role-play a **dialogue** between either the speaker and the motorcyclist in "Fifteen" or the father and the daughter in "The Writer."

- Negotiate as partners to determine who will play each character.

- Before writing, review the poem to find relevant details.

- Analyze the situation in the poem to determine each character's concerns or interests.

- Use conventional styles, including humor, expressions, slang, or more formal words, suitable for each character.

- Decide on a voice, body movements, and language choices that are appropriate for each character.

- Use appropriate eye contact while both speaking and listening.

As you role-play your dialogue, listen carefully to what the other character says, interpreting and evaluating his or her intent.

**Common Core State Standards**

L.9-10.1.b; W.9-10.4; SL.9-10.1.a, SL.9-10.1.b, SL.9-10.1.c
[For the full wording of the standards, see page 692.]

Use this prewriting activity to prepare for the **Writing Workshop** on page 756.

www.PHLitOnline.com
- Interactive graphic organizers
- Grammar tutorial
- Interactive journals

## ⓒ Leveled Texts

Build your skills and improve your comprehension of poetry with texts of increasing complexity.

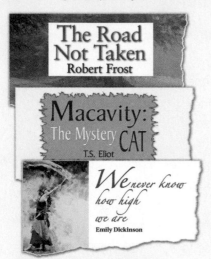

**Poetry Collection 7** explores the nature of heroism and making crucial decisions.

**Poetry Collection 8** explores the emotions and roles people take on in life.

## ⓒ Common Core State Standards

Meet these standards with either **Poetry Collection 7** (p. 724) or **Poetry Collection 8** (p. 732).

**Reading Literature**

**2.** Determine a theme or central idea of a text. *(Reading Skill: Paraphrasing)*

**4.** Determine the meaning of words and phrases as they are used in the text, including figurative and connotative meanings; analyze the cumulative impact of specific word choices on meaning and tone. *(Literary Analysis: Spiral Review)*

**7.** Analyze the representation of a subject or a key scene in two different artistic mediums. *(Analyze Representations)*

**Writing**

**4.** Produce clear and coherent writing in which the development, organization, and style are appropriate to task, purpose, and audience. *(Writing: Poem)*

**Speaking and Listening**

**1.a.** Come to discussions prepared, having read and researched material under study; explicitly draw on that preparation to stimulate a thoughtful, well-reasoned exchange of ideas. **1.c.** Propel conversations by posing and responding to questions that relate the current discussion to broader themes or larger ideas; actively incorporate others into the discussion; and clarify, verify, or challenge ideas and conclusions. **1.d.** Respond thoughtfully to diverse perspectives, summarize points of agreement and disagreement, and, when warranted, qualify or justify their own views and understanding, and make new connections in light of the evidence and reasoning presented. *(Speaking and Listening: Panel Discussion)*

**Language**

**1.b.** Use various types of phrases and clauses to convey specific meanings and add variety and interest to writing or presentations. *(Conventions: Infinitive Phrases)*

# Literary Analysis: Rhyme and Meter

Rhyme and meter are two literary devices often used in poetry. **Rhyme** is the repetition of sounds at the ends of words. There are several types of rhyme:

- **Exact rhyme:** the repetition of words that end with the same vowel and consonant sounds, as in *love* and *dove*

- **Slant rhyme:** the repetition of words that end with similar sounds but do not rhyme perfectly, as in *prove* and *glove*

- **End rhyme:** the rhyming of words at the ends of lines

- **Internal rhyme:** the rhyming of words within a line

A **rhyme scheme** is a regular pattern of end rhymes in a poem or stanza, in which a letter is assigned to each set of rhyming sounds. For example, in "Ring Out, Wild Bells," Alfred, Lord Tennyson uses the rhyme scheme *abba*:

| | |
|---|---|
| Ring out, wild bells, to the wild sky, | a |
| The flying cloud, the frosty light: | b |
| The year is dying in the night; | b |
| Ring out, wild bells, and let him die. | a |

Lewis Carroll opens "Jabberwocky" with the rhyme scheme *abab*:

| | |
|---|---|
| 'Twas brillig, and the slithy toves | a |
| Did gyre and gimble in the wabe; | b |
| All mimsy were the borogroves, | a |
| And the mome raths outgrabe. | b |

**Meter** is the rhythmical pattern in a line of poetry that results from the arrangement of stressed (ˊ) and unstressed (˘) syllables. The stress goes on the syllable that is accented in natural speech. Reading the line aloud reveals the steady rhythmic pulse of the stressed syllables:

The flyĭng clóud, thĕ fróstў líght

Hálf ă leăgue, hálf ă leăgue, / Hálf ă leăgue ońwărd

Each meter is named based on its length and rhythmical pattern. A common pattern uses *iambs*, beats in which the stress is on the second syllable, such as hĕlló or ălóud. In *iambic pentameter,* each line contains five iambs.

Shăll Í / cŏmpáre / thĕe tó / ă súm / mĕr's dáy?

Thŏu árt / mŏre lóve / Ĭy ánd / mŏre témp / ĕr áte.

## Literary Analysis: Rhyme and Meter (continued)

An *iambic dimeter* would consist of two iambs, a *trimeter* would consist of three iambs, a *tetrameter* would consist of four iambs, and so on. See the chart below for examples of these metric groupings.

| Iambic Meter | Example |
|---|---|
| Dimeter (2 beats per line) | And for / redress<br>Of all / my pain, |
| Trimeter (3 beats per line) | We romped / until / the pans<br>Slid from / the kitch / en shelf; |
| Tetrameter (4 beats per line) | I think / that I / shall ne / ver see<br>a po / em love / ly as / a tree. |

Not all poems include rhyme, a rhyme scheme, or a regular meter. Nonmetrical poetry, or poems that do not contain a regular pattern of meter, are known as **free verse.**

"Uncoiling" by Pat Mora is written as free verse:

With thorns she scratches
    on my window, tosses her hair dark with rain,
        snares lightning, cholla, hawks, butterfly
          swarms in the tangles.

Poems that do not rhyme but consist of iambic pentameter are known as **blank verse.** William Shakespeare wrote many of his plays in blank verse as in this line from *Romeo and Juliet*:

But soft! / What light / through yon / der win / dow breaks?
It is / the east, / and Ju / liet is / the sun!

Poets often use one or more rhyming techniques to create musical effects and achieve a sense of unity in their poems.

As you read the poetry in this collection, notice their specific rhyme and meter and the effect of these poetic elements.

- Look for examples of different types of rhyme.
- Determine if the lines follow a rhyme scheme.
- Notice whether or not the lines follow a regular meter.

# Reading Skill: Paraphrase

**Paraphrasing** is restating in your own words what someone else has written or said. A paraphrase should retain the essential meaning and central ideas of the original but should be simpler to read and to understand. One way to simplify the text that you are paraphrasing is to **break down long sentences.** Follow these steps:

- Divide long sentences into parts and paraphrase those parts.
- If a sentence contains multiple subjects or verbs, see if it can be separated into smaller sentences that each contain one subject and one verb.
- If a sentence contains colons, semicolons, or dashes, create separate sentences by treating those punctuation marks as periods.
- If a sentence contains long phrases or long passages in parentheses, turn each phrase or parenthetical passage into a separate sentence.

Poets often write sentences that span several lines to give their poems fluidity. By breaking down long sentences and paraphrasing them, you can better understand how the poet gradually develops his or her central idea.

Paraphrasing can particularly help you synthesize content that comes from several works by the same author addressing a single issue. It can give you a more comprehensive picture of the author.

## Using the Strategy: Paraphrase Chart

As you read poetry and break down long sentences, use a **paraphrase chart** like the one shown to record your work.

| Original Lines | Lines in Smaller Sentences | Paraphrase |
|---|---|---|
| I celebrate myself and sing myself, / And what I assume you shall assume, / For every atom belonging to me as good belongs to you.<br>—Walt Whitman | I celebrate myself. I sing myself. What I assume you shall assume. Every atom belonging to me as good belongs to you. | I celebrate myself and share my joy with you. What is mine is also yours. |

# How does *communication* change us?

## Writing About the Big Question

In the last poem in Collection 7, the speaker claims that "We never know how high we are / Till we are asked to rise." Use this sentence starter to develop your ideas about the Big Question.

> A person can make someone else **aware** of his or her potential by _____.

**While You Read** Consider whether it is true that people achieve more when more is asked of them.

## Vocabulary

Read each word and its definition. Decide whether you know the word well, know it a little bit, or do not know it at all. After you read, see how your knowledge of each word has increased.

- **diverged** (dī vʉrjd´) *v.* branched out in different directions (p. 725) *When the highway <u>diverged</u>, we were not sure which way to go.* diverge *v.* divergence *n.* diverging *adj.* diversity *n.*

- **bafflement** (baf´ əl mənt) *n.* puzzlement; bewilderment (p. 726) *To the <u>bafflement</u> of many, the jet pilot was afraid of heights.* baffle *v.* baffling *adj.*

- **depravity** (dē prav´ ə tē) *n.* crookedness; corruption (p. 727) *The criminal's <u>depravity</u> was well-known, and his arrest was cheered.* depraved *adj.* deprave *v.*

- **rifled** (rī´ fəld) *v.* ransacked and robbed; searched quickly through a cupboard or drawer (p. 727) *My little sister <u>rifled</u> through my drawer and took my favorite sweater.* rifle *v.*

- **disclosed** (dis klōzd´) *v.* revealed; made known (p. 727) *John <u>disclosed</u> the location of his hidden treasure.* disclose *v.* disclosure *n.*

- **warp** (wôrp) *v.* twist; distort (p. 728) *Skilled artists can <u>warp</u> wood into different shapes.* warped *adj.*

### Word Study

The **Latin suffix *-ment*** means "act" or "resulting state of."

In "Macavity: The Mystery Cat," the speaker refers to Macavity as "the **bafflement** of Scotland Yard." Bafflement is the resulting state of being baffled, or puzzled, the speaker means that Macavity is the reason Scotland Yard is puzzled.

# Robert Frost

**(1874–1963)**

**"The Road Not Taken"** (p. 724)

In January 1961, when John F. Kennedy became president of the United States, he called on fellow New Englander Robert Frost to recite two poems at the inauguration. At the time, Frost was America's most famous living poet. He became famous when *A Boy's Will* (1913) and *North of Boston* (1914) won wide praise in both the United Kingdom and the United States.

# T. S. Eliot

**(1888–1965)**

**"Macavity: The Mystery Cat"** (p. 726)

A whimsical poem like "Macavity: The Mystery Cat" was a rarity in the writing of Thomas Stearns Eliot. He was better known for serious, philosophical poems. Born in the United States, Eliot settled in the United Kingdom. He became a highly influential poet and won the Nobel Prize in 1948.

# Emily Dickinson

**(1830–1886)**

**"We never know how high we are"** (p. 728)

Emily Dickinson's life in Amherst, Massachusetts, seemed to be quiet and uneventful. Yet, the emotional power of her poems shows the wide range of her energy and imagination. She found profound meanings in simple subjects, and her poems still delight readers.

# The Road Not Taken

## Robert Frost

Two roads diverged in a yellow wood,
And sorry I could not travel both
And be one traveler, long I stood
And looked down one as far as I could
5   To where it bent in the undergrowth;

Then took the other, as just as fair,
And having perhaps the better claim,
Because it was grassy and wanted wear;
Though as for that, the passing there
10  Had worn them really about the same,

And both that morning equally lay
In leaves no step had trodden black.
Oh, I kept the first for another day!
Yet knowing how way leads on to way,
15  I doubted if I should ever come back.

I shall be telling this with a sigh
Somewhere ages and ages hence:
Two roads diverged in a wood, and I—
I took the one less traveled by,
20  And that has made all the difference.

**Vocabulary**
**diverged** (dī vʉrjd´) v.
branched out in different directions

**Reading Skill**
**Paraphrase** In your own words, restate the decision the speaker makes in lines 6–8.

**Literary Analysis**
**Rhyme and Meter**
What is the rhyme scheme of stanza four?

◄ **Analyze Representations** How is the speaker's description of the woods similar to or different from the photograph? **[Compare and Contrast]**

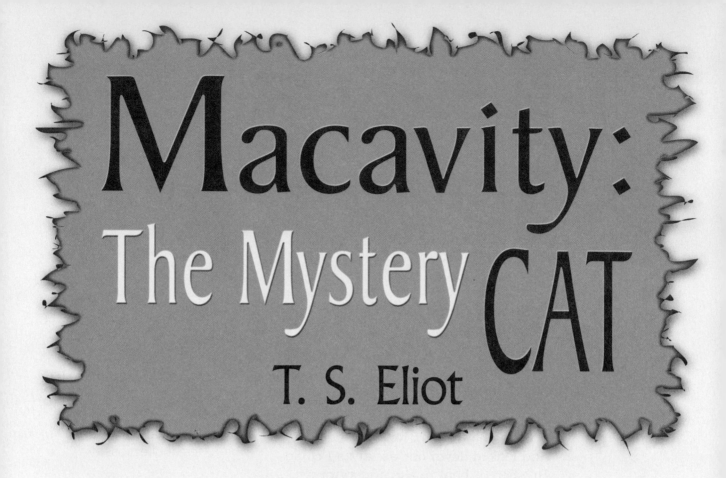

# Macavity: The Mystery CAT

## T. S. Eliot

**Vocabulary**
**bafflement** (baf´ əl mənt) *n.* puzzle- ment; bewilderment

Macavity's a Mystery Cat: he's called the Hidden Paw—
For he's the master criminal who can defy the Law.
He's the bafflement of Scotland Yard,[1] the Flying Squad's[2]
     despair:
5 For when they reach the scene of crime—*Macavity's not*
     *there!*

**Literary Analysis**
**Rhyme and Meter**
What type of rhyme does this stanza contain?

Macavity, Macavity, there's no one like Macavity,
He's broken every human law, he breaks the law of gravity.
His powers of levitation would make a fakir[3] stare,
10 And when you reach the scene of crime—*Macavity's not there!*
You may seek him in the basement, you may look up in the
     air—
But I tell you once and once again, *Macavity's not there!*

Macavity's a ginger cat, he's very tall and thin;
15 You would know him if you saw him, for his eyes are sunken in.

---

1. **Scotland Yard** London police.
2. **Flying Squad** criminal-investigation department.
3. **fakir** (fə kir´) *n.* Muslim or Hindu beggar who claims to perform miracles.

His brow is deeply lined with thought, his head is highly
      domed;
His coat is dusty from neglect, his whiskers are uncombed.
He sways his head from side to side, with movements like a
20       snake;
And when you think he's half asleep, he's always wide awake.

Macavity, Macavity, there's no one like Macavity,
For he's a fiend in feline shape, a monster of depravity.
You may meet him in a by-street, you may see him in the
25       square—
But when a crime's discovered, then *Macavity's not there!*

He's outwardly respectable. (They say he cheats at cards.)
And his footprints are not found in any file of Scotland Yard's.
And when the larder's looted, or the jewel-case is rifled,
30 Or when the milk is missing, or another Peke's[4] been stifled,
Or the greenhouse glass is broken, and the trellis past repair—
Ay, there's the wonder of the thing! *Macavity's not there!*

And when the Foreign Office find a Treaty's gone astray,
Or the Admiralty lose some plans and drawings by the way,
35 There may be a scrap of paper in the hall or on the stair—
But it's useless to investigate—*Macavity's not there!*
And when the loss has been disclosed, the Secret Service say:
'It *must* have been Macavity!'—but he's a mile away.
You'll be sure to find him resting, or a-licking of his thumbs,
40 Or engaged in doing complicated long division sums.

Macavity, Macavity, there's no one like Macavity,
There never was a Cat of such deceitfulness and suavity.
He always has an alibi, and one or two to spare:
At whatever time the deed took place—MACAVITY WASN'T
45       THERE!
And they say that all the Cats whose wicked deeds are widely
      known
(I might mention Mungojerrie, I might mention Griddlebone)
Are nothing more than agents for the Cat who all the time
50 Just controls their operations: the Napoleon of Crime![5]

**Vocabulary**
**depravity** (dē prav´
ə tē) *n.* crooked-
ness; corruption

**rifled** (rī´ fəld) *v.* ransacked and robbed;
searched quickly through
a cupboard or drawer

**Vocabulary**
**disclosed** (dis klōzd´) *v.*
revealed; made known

**Reading Skill**
**Paraphrase** Break down
the sentence in lines
43–45 into three smaller
sentences. Restate each
sentence in your own
words.

---

**4. Peke** short for Pekingese, a small dog with long, silky hair and a pug nose.
**5. the Napoleon of Crime** criminal mastermind; emperor of crime—just as Napoleon
Bonaparte (1769–1821) was a masterful military strategist who had himself crowned
emperor.

*Bubbles,* Watercolor, 39" x 29", by Scott Burdick, Courtesy of the artist

**Vocabulary**
**warp** (wôrp) *v.*
twist; distort

# *We never know how high we are*

## Emily Dickinson

We never know how high we are
Till we are asked to rise
And then if we are true to plan
Our statures touch the skies—
The Heroism we recite
Would be a normal thing
Did not ourselves the Cubits[1] warp
For fear to be a King—

---

**1. Cubits** (kyoo′ bitz) *n.* ancient measure using the length of the arm from the end of the middle finger to the elbow (about 18–22 inches).

## Critical Thinking

Cite textual evidence to support your responses.

**©1. Key Ideas and Details (a)** In "The Road Not Taken," what does the traveler do when faced with a divide in the road?
**(b) Interpret:** What details tell you he is happy with his decision?

**©2. Key Ideas and Details Speculate:** Which qualities of cats might have caused T. S. Eliot to associate them with criminal activities in "Macavity: The Mystery Cat"? Explain.

**©3. Craft and Structure Interpret:** How does figurative language affect the tone in "Macavity: The Mystery Cat"? Explain.

**©4. Integration of Knowledge and Ideas (a)** According to "We never know how high we are," what happens when people are asked to rise to an occasion? **(b)** Do you agree with that claim? Why or why not? *[Connect to the Big Question: How does communication change us?]*

## Literary Analysis: Rhyme and Meter

© **1. Craft and Structure** Identify two lines in "The Road Not Taken" that illustrate both **exact rhyme** and **end rhyme.** Explain your choices.

© **2. Craft and Structure** Which two words in line 31 of "Macavity: The Mystery Cat" illustrate both **slant rhyme** and **internal rhyme?**

© **3. Craft and Structure (a)** Use letters to identify the **rhyme scheme** in "We never know how high we are." **(b)** In what way does the shift in rhyme scheme midway through the poem help to signal a turning point in the poem's message?

© **4. Craft and Structure (a)** Which poem has lines with a more regular **meter:** "The Road Not Taken" or "We never know how high we are"? Explain. **(b)** Which do you find more enjoyable to read—lines with a regular meter or lines with an irregular meter? Explain.

## Reading Skill: Paraphrase

**5. (a) Paraphrase** the first stanza of "The Road Not Taken" by re-writing it as a series of sentences. **(b)** In what way does **breaking down long sentences** make this poem's meaning clearer?

## Vocabulary

© **Acquisition and Use** Decide if each statement is true or false. Then, explain your answer.

**1.** Reporters are taught to *warp* the facts of events they cover.

**2.** Two people whose opinions *diverged* would be in disagreement.

**3.** *Bafflement* is a likely reaction to a bizarre event.

**4.** Laws are written to encourage *depravity* in society.

**5.** A closet is tidier after it has been *rifled.*

**6.** Information that has been *disclosed* is no longer secret.

**Word Study** Use the context of the sentences and what you know about the **Latin suffix -*ment*** to explain your answer to each question.

**1.** Would an *amusement* park entertain you?

**2.** When you make an *improvement,* do you make something better or worse?

### Word Study

The **Latin suffix -*ment*** means "act or resulting state of."

**Apply It** Explain how the suffix -*ment* contributes to the meanings of these words. Consult a dictionary if necessary.

**contentment**
**excitement**
**abasement**

# How does *communication* change us?

## Writing About the Big Question

The speaker of "The Seven Ages of Man" compares the people of the world to actors in a play. Use this sentence starter to develop your ideas about the Big Question.

**Communication** between two people can seem like action in a play when _____.

**While You Read** Look for ways in which people's lives and interactions can resemble actors playing roles. Then, consider how this knowledge might offer a useful way to look at life.

## Vocabulary

Read each word and its definition. Decide whether you know the word well, know it a little bit, or do not know it at all. After you have read the selection, see how your knowledge of each word has increased.

- **stranded** (strand´ əd) *adj.* in a place or situation which one needs help to leave (p. 732) *The stranded airline passengers had to spend the night in the terminal.* strand *v.*

- **languid** (laŋ´ gwid) *adj.* drooping; weak (p. 732) *The heat of the summer afternoon made us all feel languid.* languish *v.*

- **woeful** (wō´ fəl) *adj.* full of sorrow (p. 735) *His woeful story brought us to tears.* woe *n.* woefully *adv.*

- **treble** (treb´ əl) *n.* high-pitched voice or sound (p. 735) *The harsh treble of her alarm clock woke everyone in the house.*

- **oblivion** (ə bliv´ ē ən) *n.* forgetfulness; the state of being unconscious or unaware (p. 735) *While sleeping, most people are in a state of total oblivion.* oblivious *adj.*

- **suffice** (sə fīs´) *v.* be enough (p. 736) *Five tables will suffice for a party of this size.* sufficient *adj.*

### Word Study

The **Latin suffix -ion** means "act or condition of." It usually indicates a noun.

Someone who is oblivious is unaware. In "The Seven Ages of Man," the speaker refers to a man's final stage as "mere **oblivion**," a condition of complete unawareness.

# E. E. Cummings

**(1894–1962)**

**"maggie and milly and molly and may"** (p. 732)

Born in Cambridge, Massachusetts, Edward Estlin Cummings graduated from Harvard University. Both as poet and playwright, Cummings became notorious for his unconventional style, which reflects his individualistic outlook. Much of his work is playful and lyrical, and he often disregarded rules of grammar, spelling, and punctuation.

# William Shakespeare

**(1564–1616)**

**"The Seven Ages of Man"** (p. 734)

William Shakespeare forged a perfect blend of high drama and exalted language. He wrote more than three dozen plays, and because of the timelessness of his themes and the beauty of his language, lines from his plays are quoted more often than those of any other writer. "The Seven Ages of Man" from the play *As You Like It,* is considered one of his best monologues. (For more on William Shakespeare, see p. 802.)

# Robert Frost

**(1874–1963)**

**"Fire and Ice"** (p. 736)

Like the title of his poem "Fire and Ice," Robert Frost seemed warm to some people, cold to other people. All agreed, however, that poetry came first in his life. Frost produced a large body of work and became the most popular American poet of his time, winning four Pulitzer Prizes.

# maggie and milly and molly and may

## E. E. Cummings

maggie and milly and molly and may
went down to the beach (to play one day)

and maggie discovered a shell that sang
so sweetly she couldn't remember her troubles, and

5   milly befriended a stranded star
whose rays five languid fingers were;

and molly was chased by a horrible thing
which raced sideways while blowing bubbles: and

may came home with a smooth round stone
10  as small as a world and as large as alone.

For whatever we lose (like a you or a me)
it's always ourselves we find in the sea

**Vocabulary**
**stranded** (strand´ əd) *adj.* in a place or situation which one needs help to leave
**languid** (laŋ´ gwid) *adj.* drooping; weak

**Literary Analysis**
**Rhyme and Meter**
What type of rhyme does Cummings use in the first and last stanzas?

▶ **Critical Viewing** How well does this photograph illustrate the "stranded star" in the poem? **[Evaluate]**

*The Seven Ages of Man*, Folger Shakespeare Library, Washington, D.C.

# The Seven Ages of Man

## William Shakespeare

All the world's a stage,
And all the men and women merely players:[1]
They have their exits and their entrances;
And one man in his time plays many parts,
His acts being seven ages. At first the infant,
Mewling[2] and puking in the nurse's arms.
And then the whining schoolboy, with his satchel,
And shining morning face, creeping like snail
Unwillingly to school. And then the lover,
Sighing like furnace, with a woeful ballad
Made to his mistress' eyebrow. Then a soldier,
Full of strange oaths, and bearded like the pard,[3]
Jealous in honor,[4] sudden and quick in quarrel,
Seeking the bubble reputation
Even in the cannon's mouth. And then the justice,[5]
In fair round belly with good capon[6] lined,
With eyes severe and beard of formal cut,
Full of wise saws and modern instances;[7]
And so he plays his part. The sixth age shifts
Into the lean and slippered pantaloon,[8]
With spectacles on nose and pouch on side,
His youthful hose[9] well saved, a world too wide
For his shrunk shank;[10] and his big manly voice,
Turning again toward childish treble, pipes
And whistles in his sound. Last scene of all,
That ends this strange eventful history,
Is second childishness, and mere oblivion,
Sans[11] teeth, sans eyes, sans taste, sans everything.

5 (line marker)
10 (line marker)
15 (line marker)
20 (line marker)
25 (line marker)

---

1. **players** actors.
2. **Mewling** (myōōl´ iŋ) v. whimpering; crying weakly.
3. **pard** (pärd) n. leopard or panther.
4. **Jealous in honor** very concerned about his honor.
5. **justice** judge.
6. **capon** (kā´ pän´) n. roasted chicken.
7. **wise saws and modern instances** sayings, and examples that show the truth of the sayings.
8. **pantaloon** (pan´ tə lōōn´) n. thin, foolish old man who is a character in old comedies.
9. **hose** (hōz) n. stockings.
10. **shank** (shaŋk) n. leg.
11. **sans** (sanz) prep. without; lacking.

**Literary Analysis**
**Rhyme and Meter**
What is the pattern of stressed and unstressed syllables in lines 2–4?

**Vocabulary**
**woeful** (wō´ fəl) adj. full of sorrow

**Spiral Review**
**Figurative Language**
Why might a person's reputation be like a bubble?

**Vocabulary**
**treble** (treb´ əl) n. high-pitched voice or sound
**oblivion** (ə bliv´ ē ən) n. forgetfulness; the state of being unconscious or unaware

◄ **Analyze Representations**
How do the images in this stained-glass window add to your understanding of the poem? **[Relate]**

# FIRE AND ICE
## Robert Frost

**Vocabulary**
**suffice** (sə fīs´)
*v.* be enough

Some say the world will end in fire,
Some say in ice.
From what I've tasted of desire
I hold with those who favor fire.
5   But if it had to perish twice,
I think I know enough of hate
To say that for destruction ice
Is also great
And would suffice.

## Critical Thinking

*Cite textual evidence to support your responses.*

1. **Key Ideas and Details  (a)** In "maggie and milly and molly and may," what experience does each character have? **(b) Connect:** How does each character's experience support the conclusion in the poem's final line?

2. **Key Ideas and Details  (a)** In "Fire and Ice," which emotions does the speaker associate with fire and ice? **(b) Interpret:** Why are fire and ice fitting metaphors for these emotions? **(c) Discuss:** Share your answers with a partner or group, and explain how the poem's message applies to teenagers.

3. **Integration of Knowledge and Ideas** Does "The Seven Ages of Man" in any way change your perspective on the stages of life and the "roles" people play? Explain your response. *[Connect to the Big Question: How does communication change us?]*

## Literary Analysis: Rhyme and Meter

**1. Craft and Structure** Identify two lines in "maggie and milly and molly and may" that illustrate both **exact rhyme** and **end rhyme**. Explain your choices.

**2. Craft and Structure** Which two words in line 17 of "The Seven Ages of Man" illustrate both **slant rhyme** and **internal rhyme?**

**3. Craft and Structure (a)** Use letters to identify the **rhyme scheme** in "Fire and Ice." **(b)** In what way does the shift in rhyme scheme midway through the poem help signal a turning point in the poem's message?

**4. Craft and Structure (a)** Which poem has lines with a more regular **meter:** "Fire and Ice" or "The Seven Ages of Man"? Explain. **(b)** Which do you find more enjoyable to read—lines with a regular meter or lines with an irregular meter? Explain.

## Reading Skill: Paraphrase

**5. (a) Paraphrase** the first ten lines of "maggie and milly and molly and may" by rewriting them as a series of sentences. **(b)** In what way does **breaking down long sentences** make this poem's meaning more clear?

## Vocabulary

**Acquisition and Use** Decide if each statement is true or false. Then, explain your answer.

**1.** If something will *suffice,* it will be satisfactory.

**2.** A captain should avoid letting his ship become *stranded.*

**3.** Coaches hope their players will be *languid* during a game.

**4.** A *woeful* sight is likely to inspire pity.

**5.** A *treble* is a deep sound like a foghorn.

**6.** Sleep is a kind of *oblivion.*

**Word Study** Use the context of the sentences and what you know about the **Latin suffix -ion** to explain your answer to each question.

**1.** Could complicated directions lead to *confusion*?

**2.** Is *precision* a good quality for a surgeon to possess?

### Word Study

The **Latin suffix -ion** means "act or condition of." It usually indicates a noun.

**Apply It** Explain how the suffix -ion contributes to the meanings of these words. Consult a dictionary if necessary.

derision
opinion
illusion

# Integrated Language Skills

## Poetry Collections 7 and 8

### Conventions: Infinitives

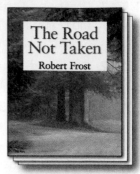

An **infinitive** is a verb form that generally appears with the word *to* and acts as a noun, adjective, or adverb.

An **infinitive phrase** is an infinitive with modifiers, complements, or a subject. Like infinitives, infinitive phrases can function as nouns, adjectives, or adverbs.

| Infinitive | Infinitive Phrase |
|---|---|
| **Used as a Noun**<br>*To write* requires dedication. | **Used as a Noun**<br>*To win a Pulitzer Prize* is an honor. |
| **Used as an Adjective**<br>E. E. Cummings is a good poet *to study.* | **Used as an Adjective**<br>Cummings had a desire *to write unconventional poetry.* |
| **Used as an Adverb**<br>When Shakespeare sat down *to work,* he used a quill dipped in ink. | **Used as an Adverb**<br>Shakespeare wrote his plays *to be performed on a stage.* |

Infinitives include *to* and a verb, as in *to hear*; prepositional phrases include *to* and a noun or pronoun, as in *to the house.*

**Practice A** Identify the infinitive or infinitive phrase and its function in each sentence.

1. It is important to learn about these poets.
2. One needs confidence to be a king.
3. The speaker of "The Road Not Taken" chose to take the more difficult path.
4. The police have failed to catch Macavity.

**Practice B** Identify the infinitive or infinitive phrase in each sentence. Then, rewrite the sentence using a different infinitive or infinitive phrase.

1. Maggie went down to the beach to play.
2. Frost uses ice to represent hate.
3. To pass through seven ages is man's destiny.
4. "The Seven Ages of Man" is not the only speech to be quoted by other writers.

Ⓒ **Reading Application** Find two infinitives or infinitive phrases in "Macavity: The Mystery Cat" and identify each one's function.

Ⓒ **Writing Application** Write two sentences about the beach image on page 733. Use an infinitive or an infinitive phrase in each one.

| PH WRITING COACH | Further instruction and practice are available in *Prentice Hall Writing Coach.* |

# Writing

**Poetry** Each poem in both collections has a specific rhyme scheme. Write a **poem** using the same rhyme scheme and format as a poem in Collection 7 or Collection 8.

- Choose a poem and identify its rhyme scheme.
- Decide on a topic, an event, an experience, or an emotion to use as the subject of your poem.
- Brainstorm for a list of images, precise details, phrases, or vivid words.
- Draft your lines, making them rhyme only after you have expressed your ideas and feelings.

Share your poem with a classmate. Ask him or her to identify the poem's rhyme scheme and discuss the way the rhythm and word choice affect the mood of the poem.

**Grammar Application** Make sure you correctly use infinitives and infinitive phrases in your writing.

### Writing Workshop: *Work in Progress*

**Prewriting for a Response to Literature** Review your Character Descriptions, and write a one-sentence conclusion about each character. Save this Draft Thesis in your writing portfolio.

# Speaking and Listening

**Presentation of Ideas** With classmates, hold a **panel discussion** about possible interpretations of a poem by Robert Frost.

Conduct research about the poet's extensive works. Assemble an electronic database of texts by and about Robert Frost. Identify primary and secondary sources about Frost's poetry. Consider these questions:

- What topics and themes does Frost's work often address?
- What style does he most frequently use?
- What have others said about his works?

Write concise notes for use during the discussion. Be sure to convey your sources' information accurately and coherently.

When you are ready to hold your discussion, follow these steps:

- Begin by stating the purpose of the discussion.
- Use listening strategies to interpret and summarize others' comments.
- Then, look for connections between the ideas expressed by other panel members. Use these connections to develop a position statement that is acceptable to most panelists.

**Common Core State Standards**

L.9-10.1.b; W.9-10.4; SL.9-10.1.a, SL.9-10.1.c, SL.9-10.1.d
[For the full wording of the standards, see page 718.]

Use this prewriting activity to prepare for the **Writing Workshop** on page 756.

# Test Practice: Reading

## Paraphrase

### Fiction Selection

**Directions:** *Read the selection. Then, answer the questions.*

(1) Tom stared in disbelief at the bottle. (2) He remembered the day six months ago. (3) It was his birthday, and the last day before his grandfather moved to Florida. (4) It had been his grandfather's idea. (5) They had written a note and sealed it in the bottle, and Tom had thrown it into the surf. (6) "The world is small," his grandfather had said with a wink, "your bottle will be back." (7) Tom had wanted to hear from someone far away, but as weeks passed he gave up hope. (7) Like his grandfather, the bottle seemed to be gone forever. (8) Tom was wrong. (9) Today's mail had brought a package, and inside was the bottle. (10) It had been found by strangers an ocean away. (11) Tom grinned as he noticed a second piece of mail—a postcard from his grandfather.

**1.** Which of the following is the *best* paraphrase of sentence 1?
   A. Tom was surprised to see the bottle.
   B. Tom didn't believe it was a bottle.
   C. Tom was dreaming about a bottle.
   D. Tom was thinking of something else.

**2.** Which of the following is the *best* paraphrase of sentence 5?
   A. Tom's grandfather had the brilliant idea to throw a bottle into the ocean on Tom's birthday.
   B. Tom and his grandfather did many enjoyable activities together.
   C. Tom and his grandfather put a bottle with a message inside into the ocean.
   D. Tom's grandfather wrote a detailed note including an address, and then Tom and his grandfather sent the bottle into the ocean to see what would happen.

**3.** In sentence 4, Tom's grandfather had an idea to—
   A. celebrate Tom's birthday with a trip to the beach.
   B. put a note in a bottle and throw it in the sea.
   C. send the bottle back to the sender.
   D. mail the bottle to Tom as a souvenir.

**4.** If you were paraphrasing this passage, you might do all of the following *except*—
   A. picture the action.
   B. break down long sentences.
   C. make sure your paraphrase has the same essential meaning.
   D. replace simple words with more difficult words.

### Writing for Assessment

Use details from this passage to write a one-sentence paraphrase describing what Tom received in the mail and why it was significant.

## Nonfiction Selection

**Directions:** *Read the selection. Then, answer the questions.*

(1) In 1977, the National Aeronautics and Space Administration (NASA) launched two spacecraft, *Voyagers 1* and *2*. (2) Their mission was to analyze Jupiter and Saturn, but scientists knew they could go beyond and enter deep space, where they might be found by extraterrestrials. (3) Therefore, NASA packed a record with images, natural sounds, greetings from Earth, and other data and sealed it inside the *Voyagers*. (4) It was like putting a message in a bottle and casting it into the sea of space. (5) In 2007, *Voyagers 1* and *2* were still traveling. (6) *Voyager 1* was 9.5 billion miles from Earth. (7) Will they be found? (8) Will our message ever be read?

1. Which sentence best states the main idea of the passage?
   A. NASA sent *Voyagers 1* and *2* to collect data and to send a "message in a bottle" to space.
   B. The primary mission of *Voyagers 1* and *2* was to study Jupiter and Saturn.
   C. NASA is an organization that focuses on space exploration.
   D. *Voyagers 1* and *2* have traveled billions of miles into deep space, where they might be found by extraterrestrials.

2. The pronoun *they* in sentence 7 refers to—
   A. scientists.
   B. NASA.
   C. aliens.
   D. *Voyagers 1* and *2*.

3. Which of the following is the *best* paraphrase of sentence 2?
   A. NASA built the spacecraft to study Jupiter and Saturn but scientists hoped the spacecraft would be found by aliens.
   B. The spacecraft could go into deep space and be found by aliens.
   C. NASA scientists knew the spacecraft could enter deep space.
   D. The mission was to find life on other planets.

4. For a paraphrase of sentence 3 which word is the best replacement for *data?*
   A. material
   B. sounds
   C. information
   D. messages

## Writing for Assessment

**Connecting Across Texts**

Write a brief essay in which you describe how the *Voyager* spacecraft and Tom's bottle are alike. Use details from both passages, restated in your own words, to support your response.

**www.PHLitOnline.com**
- Online practice
- Instant feedback

# Reading for Information

## Analyzing Expository Texts

**Case Study**

**News Article**

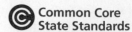 **Common Core State Standards**

**Reading Informational Text**
**2.** Determine a central idea of a text and analyze its development over the course of the text, including how it emerges and is shaped and refined by specific details; provide an objective summary of the text.

**Language**
**6.** Acquire and use accurately general academic and domain-specific words and phrases, sufficient for reading, writing, speaking, and listening at the college and career readiness level; demonstrate independence in gathering vocabulary knowledge when considering a word or phrase important to comprehension or expression.

## Reading Skill: Paraphrase a Text: Main Idea

**Paraphrasing a text**—putting the ideas into your own words—helps you determine the **central idea.** Clearly stating information allows you to judge the significance of ideas in order to decide which are most important. Paraphrasing ideas will also enable you to more easily **find connections** between those ideas and ideas in other sources that deal with related topics. Use this checklist to find connections.

---

**To Paraphrase and Connect Ideas:**

- Paraphrase the ideas in the first source.
- Use your paraphrase to determine the central ideas.
- Find similar or related ideas in the second source.
- Connect ideas from the two sources by drawing conclusions based on your paraphrases of the central ideas.

---

## Content-Area Vocabulary

These words appear in the selections that follow. You may also encounter them in other content-area texts.

- **artificial intelligence** (ärt´ ə fish´ əl in tel´ ə jəns) *n.* the ability of a computer to complete tasks that require intelligence when done by humans

- **robotics** (rō bät´ iks) *n.* the study, design, manufacture, and use of robots

- **stimuli** (stim´ yə lī´) *n.* things that provoke responses

Case Study

**Features:**

- explanation of what is being studied and why
- facts, examples, and quotations
- text written for a specific audience

# Careers in Robotics: A Case Study

*Think you'll never use high school math? Think again . . .*

Gil Jones and Matt Zucker may seem like regular guys just out of college—but they have one of the coolest jobs around! They are both software engineers for a company that makes underwater robots, otherwise known as autonomous underwater vehicles (AUVs). AUVs are small, unmanned submarines that use on-board **artificial intelligence** to complete survey tasks with little or no human supervision.

Although Matt and Gil do the same job now, the difference in how they got there shows there really is no single path to **robotics**.

> Paraphrasing these first two paragraphs will help you determine the main idea of the case study.

## Getting There

"I was a classic underachiever in high school," says Matt. "I got into college by the skin of my teeth. Once I got into college, though, I realized I wanted to focus on my interests. Studying something I liked really made it all worthwhile." In college at Vassar, Matt took his interests in biology and computers even further. He took classes in psychology, philosophy, anthropology, human brain and behavior, and artificial intelligence to work his way to a degree in cognitive science. His main interest? Helping robots and computers learn complex behaviors.

Gil, on the other hand, was a good student in high school, but didn't start out in robotics either—he was more interested in political science. At Swarthmore College, he was inspired by computer science. "I wanted to focus on artificial intelligence. I took an artificial intelligence class where we started playing with toy robots, using Handyboards and sensors." Gil really got interested in robotics through AAAI robotics competitions (imagine creating a robot that can serve hors d'oeuvres!), and when he graduated with a degree in computer science, a lot of his experience was with robots.

> Paraphrasing the three paragraphs in this section will clarify how the subjects of the case study, Matt and Gil, got their starts in robotics.

The bottom line, both Gil and Matt agree, is that you don't have to go to an engineering school. Liberal arts universities and colleges will also give you the skills you need to do robotics. If you're interested in a lot of things—physics, math, science, engineering, communications, and others—you'll do well.

## Landing the Job

Both Gil and Matt did summer internships during college that provided them with work experience and an idea of how to get a job in robotics. During one summer, Gil worked for the Naval Research Laboratory doing software artificial intelligence research and then, after graduating, spent the summer preparing for another AAAI competition. When one of his friends got a job at a robotics company, Gil learned about the company and then applied to be a software engineer. Matt got an internship at the same company during the summer between his junior and senior years and was then offered a job following graduation. What's their best advice for getting internships and jobs? Perseverance! "Just find someone who works in robotics and ask them for advice," says Matt. Gil adds, "Sometimes it's difficult to get in, but keep trying. Think about doing an internship for free. Often internships are the first step through the door."

## Research, Programming, and . . . Cruising(?)

One of the great things about this job is the variety. Sometimes they spend all day reading up on robotics research, sometimes they spend all day in front of a computer . . . and sometimes they spend all day hanging out on a boat testing the robot in the ocean! "You're making something that has a purpose, something that's part of a bigger project," says Gil. "You get to see if what you did worked. Of course, that means you're entirely responsible." Another perk, according to Matt, is that "you usually get to learn something big and new every few weeks." One warning: Pay attention in high school math classes. "You'll use trigonometry like crazy!"

## Next Steps

The final paragraph of the text often contains key details. Paraphrasing will ensure you understand these points.

Both Matt and Gil plan on going back to school sometime to do graduate work. Matt wants to study computer science, focusing on computer graphics and computer-human interfaces. Eventually, he wants to be a professor. Gil plans to go back to school specifically in robotics. He finds underwater robotics exciting because it requires autonomy, but there are a lot of other cool areas of robotics he'd like to explore. The draw for both of them is that robotics is a quickly changing and very open field. As they point out, "You can do new stuff in any of the related areas and that's exciting!"

# TEAM BUILDS 'SOCIABLE' ROBOT

**Elizabeth A. Thompson, News Office**

**Features:**

- information on current events
- descriptions, examples, and quotations
- text written for a general or specific audience

**February 14, 2001**

"Hello, Kismet," said Cynthia Breazeal in a singsong voice. Leaning closer to the object of her attention, she asked, "Are you going to talk to me?"

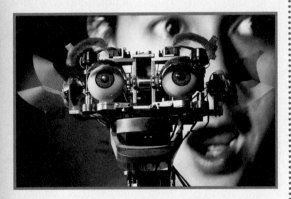

The exchange could be familiar to any parent, but Kismet is not a child. It's a robotic head that can interact with humans in a human-like way via myriad facial expressions, head positions, and tones of voice. "The goal is to build a socially intelligent machine that learns things as we learn them, through social interactions," said Dr. Breazeal, a postdoctoral associate at MIT's Artificial Intelligence Laboratory and leader of the Kismet team.

> Paraphrase the doctor's quote to be sure you understand it fully.

Building a sociable machine, she believes, is also key to building a smarter machine. Most current robots are programmed to be very good at a specific task—say, navigating a room—but they can't do much more. "Can we build a much more open-ended learning system?" asks Dr. Breazeal.

"I'm building a robot that can leverage off the social structure that people already use to help each other learn. If we can build a robot that can tap into that system, then we might not have to program in every piece of its behavior."

## INSPIRED BY KIDS

The work, which began in 1997, is heavily inspired by child developmental psychology. "The robot starts off in a rather helpless and primitive condition, and requires the help of a sophisticated and benevolent caretaker to learn and develop," Dr. Breazeal said. Even Kismet's physical features—which include big blue eyes, lips, ears and eyebrows—are patterned after features known to elicit a caregiving response from human adults.

> Paraphrase complex sentences and ideas like the ones in this paragraph to clarify the information.

The eyes, in particular, are actually sensors that allow the robot to glean information from its environment, such as whether something is being jiggled next to its face. Kismet can then respond to such **stimuli**—by moving its head back if an object gets too close, for example—and communicate a number of emotion-like processes (such as happiness, fear and disgust).

A human wears a microphone to talk to the robot, which also has microphones in its ears. The latter will eventually be used for sound localization.

The robot's features, behavior and "emotions" work together so it can "interact with humans in an intuitive, natural way,"

Dr. Breazeal said. For example, if an object is too close for the robot's cameras to see well, Kismet backs away. "This behavior, by itself, aids the cameras somewhat by increasing the distance between Kismet and the human," Dr. Breazeal said. "But the behavior can have a secondary and greater effect through social amplification. A withdrawal response is a strong social cue for the human to back away."

Kismet, she noted, is the exact opposite of HAL, the menacing robot in the movie *2001: A Space Odyssey*. "HAL is simply a glowing red light with no feedback as to what the machine is thinking. That's why it's so eerie. Kismet, on the other hand, both gives and takes feedback to communicate."

"I think people are often afraid that technology is making us less human. Kismet is a counterpoint to that; it really celebrates our humanity. This is a robot that thrives on social interactions."

## MAKING IT LIFELIKE

To make Kismet as lifelike as possible, Dr. Breazeal and colleagues have not only incorporated findings from developmental psychology, but have also invited the comments of cartoon animators. "How do you make something that's not alive appear lifelike? That's what animators do so well," Dr. Breazeal explained.

> The first paragraph under a subheading often contains the main ideas of that paragraph. Paraphrasing will make these ideas clear.

The proverbial wizard behind the curtain (or in this case, wall) is a bank of some 15 computers. These process software programs that allow the robot to perceive its environment, analyze what it finds and react.

In experiments over the last year or so, the researchers have been exploring how the

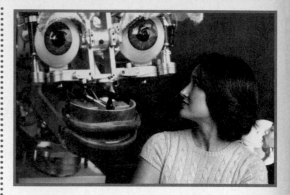

robot interacts with people who aren't familiar with it. Are Kismet's actions and emotions understandable? Do people use those actions as feedback to adjust their own responses? Conversely, is the robot correctly "reading" its visitors?

Results to date are encouraging. For example, many of the people who've met Kismet have told Dr. Breazeal that the robot has a real presence. "It seems to really impact them on an emotional level, to the point where they tell me that when I turn Kismet off, it's really jarring. That's powerful. It means that I've really captured something in this robot that's special. That kind of reaction is also critical to the robot's design and purpose."

Once Kismet's social skills are optimized, "we can move on to other forms of learning," Dr. Breazeal said. In early work to that end, the researchers are teaching Kismet how to use its voice to negotiate the social world. "We want it to be able to get people to do things for it, much like a very young child."

The algorithms that are crucial to this will allow the robot to "learn" by trial and error. When it first attempts a task, it won't be very good. The robot will "remember" its mistakes, however, and make incremental improvements as it goes along. It can then apply what it's learned to completing the same task under different conditions.

## Comparing Expository Texts

© **1. Key Ideas and Details (a) Paraphrase** the second paragraphs of the case study and the news article. **(b)** Determine the **central idea** in each paraphrase. **(c)** Connect the texts by comparing and contrasting the central ideas.

## Content-Area Vocabulary

**2. (a)** Remove the *s* from the word *robotics*. Using a print or an online dictionary, explain how removing the letter *s* reveals a different word with a different part of speech.
**(b)** Then, use the words *robotics* and *robotic* in sentences that show their meaning.

## Timed Writing

### Argument: Persuasive Essay

> **Format**
> The prompt directs you to write a persuasive essay. Therefore, be sure your response includes an introduction, body paragraphs with strong supporting details, and a conclusion.

Robert Collier said, "Success is the sum of small efforts, repeated day in and day out." Write a persuasive essay in response to this quote. Support or refute it using details from both texts. (30 minutes)

> **Academic Vocabulary**
> When you *support* a quote, you show that it is true. When you *refute* a quote, you show that it is not true.

### 5-Minute Planner

Complete these steps before you begin to write:

**1.** Read the prompt carefully and completely. Look at the highlighted words to help you understand the assignment.

**2.** Determine whether you agree or disagree with the quote.

**3.** Review the case study and the news article to find support for your opinion. Identify and make notes about connections between the ideas in the texts to build a strong, convincing argument.
**TIP** Paraphrasing short sections of texts can help you connect ideas.

**4.** Decide in what order you will present your supporting details. Then, create a brief outline for your essay.

**5.** Refer to your notes and outline as you draft your persuasive essay.

# Comparing Literary Works

## Comparing Forms of Lyric Poetry

**Lyric poetry** has a musical quality that expresses the thoughts and feelings of a speaker. It does not tell a complete story, but it does describe an emotion or a mood, often by using vivid imagery. A lyric poem is relatively short and produces a single effect. Poets can use a variety of **lyric forms** or structures to explore topics and themes, and create different effects.

- A **sonnet** is a fourteen-line poem that is usually written in iambic pentameter and often rhymes. Two common sonnet types are the Italian, or Petrarchan, and the English, or Shakespearean, sonnet.

- A **haiku** is a classical Japanese form of poetry. Haiku is an unrhymed verse form arranged into three lines of five, seven, and five syllables. The author of a haiku often uses a striking image from nature to convey a strong emotion.

- A **free verse** poem does not follow a regular pattern of rhythm or rhyme. The poet may use sound and rhythmic devices and even rhyme—but not in a regular pattern.

Each of the following poems depicts one speaker's thoughts. As you read, consider how the poet's choice of a particular lyric form adds to the poem's meaning. Use this chart and the other information on this page to help you understand how each poem's structure enhances its message.

### Common Core State Standards

**Reading Literature**
**5.** Analyze how an author's choices concerning how to structure a text, order events within it, and manipulate time create such effects as mystery, tension, or surprise.

**Writing**
**2.a.** Introduce a topic; organize complex ideas, concepts, and information to make important connections and distinctions; include formatting, graphics, and multimedia when useful to aiding comprehension.

| Shakespearean Sonnet | |
|---|---|
| **Formatting:** usually presented with no spaces between the stanzas, which are unified by their distinct ideas and rhyme schemes | **Three quatrains (four-line stanzas):** each explores a different aspect of the poem's theme |
| **Final couplet:** the two lines at the end of a sonnet, which present a concluding comment | **Rhyme scheme:** the lines in each quatrain follow a regular pattern of *abab cdcd efef gg* |

www.PHLitOnline.com

- Vocabulary flashcards
- Interactive journals
- More about the authors

- Selection audio
- Interactive graphic organizers

## Writing About the Big Question

In few words, the speakers in these poems communicate intense thoughts and feelings. Use this sentence starter to develop your ideas.

A powerful piece of writing can make readers **aware** of _____.

# Meet the Authors

## Walt Whitman (1819–1892)

### Author of "I Hear America Singing" (p. 750)

American poet Walt Whitman celebrated individual freedom. He published his first book of poetry, *Leaves of Grass*, at his own expense. Now, *Leaves of Grass* is known as a very influential volume in American literature.

## Bashō and Chiyojo
### (1644–1694)     (1703–1775)

### Authors of "Three Haiku" (p. 751)

One of the greatest Japanese poets, Bashō raised the haiku from a comic form to a high art. In his youth, he lived in luxury, but he later devoted himself to haiku. Chiyojo was the wife of a samurai's servant. After her husband died, she became a nun and studied poetry.

◄ Bashō

## Alice Walker (b. 1944)

### Author of "Women" (p. 752)

From the age of eight, Alice Walker kept a journal and wrote poems. Today, Walker is an acclaimed novelist, essayist, and poet. Her works include the novel *The Color Purple*, which was made into a movie and a Broadway show.

## William Shakespeare (1564–1616)

### Author of "Sonnet 30" (p. 754)

English poet and playwright William Shakespeare is one of the most beloved writers of all time. Experts believe Shakespeare possessed the largest vocabulary of any writer in history. His many plays, including *Romeo and Juliet*, are still performed around the world.

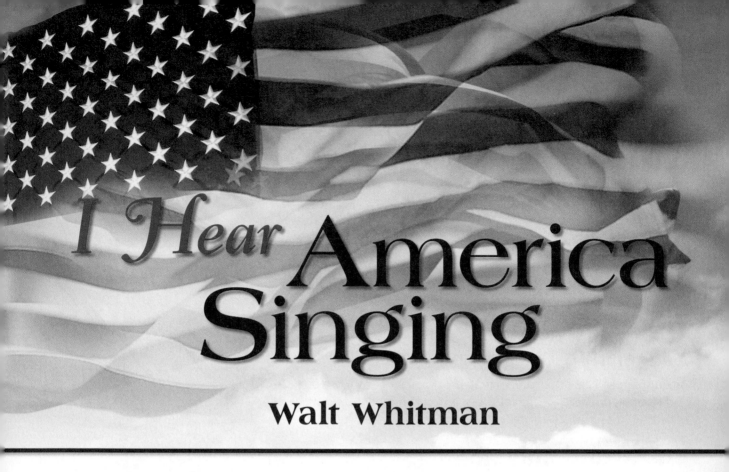

# I Hear America Singing

## Walt Whitman

**Literary Analysis**
**Lyric Poetry** Which word in the opening line helps identify this as a lyric poem?

I hear America singing, the varied carols I hear,
Those of mechanics, each one singing his as it should be blithe and strong,
The carpenter singing his as he measures his plank or beam,
The mason singing his as he makes ready for work, or leaves off work,
5　The boatman singing what belongs to him in his boat, the deckhand singing on the steamboat deck,
The shoemaker singing as he sits on his bench, the hatter singing as he stands,
The wood-cutter's song, the ploughboy's on his way in the morning, or at noon intermission or at sundown,
The delicious singing of the mother, or of the young wife at work, or of the girl sewing or washing,
Each singing what belongs to him or her and to none else,
10　The day what belongs to the day—at night the party of young fellows, robust, friendly,
Singing with open mouths their strong melodious songs.

**Vocabulary**
**intermission** (in´ tər mish´ ən) *n.* any kind of break; more specifically, a break during a performance

# Three Haiku

## translated by Daniel C. Buchanan

Temple bells die out.
The fragrant blossoms remain.
A perfect evening!

     —Bashō

Dragonfly catcher,
How far have you gone today
In your wandering?

     —Chiyojo

Bearing no flowers,
I am free to toss madly
Like the willow tree.

     —Chiyojo

**Literary Analysis**
**Lyric Poetry** What impression does the speaker convey by comparing herself to a willow tree?

## Critical Thinking

Cite textual evidence to support your responses.

1. **Key Ideas and Details (a)** Identify three singers Whitman names. **(b) Interpret:** What does Whitman mean when he says he hears their songs?

2. **Integration of Knowledge and Ideas Generalize:** How does the language of haiku, works from a non–English-speaking literary tradition, differ from the language in poems you have read from English-speaking literary traditions?

3. **Key Ideas and Details (a)** In Bashō's haiku, what dies out and what remains? **(b) Interpret:** To which senses does Bashō's haiku appeal? **(c) Analyze:** Why are these senses most appropriate in a poem about evening?

4. **Craft and Structure Assess:** Would the first haiku by Chiyojo be as effective if it had been written as a statement rather than as a question? Explain.

5. **Integration of Knowledge and Ideas** Which of these poems causes you to see something from a different or more intense point of view? Use details from the poem you select to explain your response. *[Connect to the Big Question: How does communication change us?]*

The Quiltmakers 22 11/16" x 24", Paul Goodnight, Color Circle Art Publishing Inc.

# Women ALICE WALKER

**Background** In "Women," the speaker praises African American women who fought for public school desegregation in the American South. Until the 1950s, African American and white students attended different schools in the South. In 1954, the U.S. Supreme Court ruled that segregated public schooling was unconstitutional.

They were women then
My mama's generation
Husky of voice—Stout of
Step
5   With fists as well as
Hands
How they battered down
Doors
And ironed
10   Starched white
Shirts
How they led
Armies
Headragged Generals
15   Across mined
Fields
Booby-trapped
Kitchens
To discover books
20   Desks
A place for us
How they knew what we
Must know
Without knowing a page
25   Of it
Themselves.

Vocabulary
stout (stout) adj. sturdy

**Literary Analysis**
**Lyric Poetry** What emotion or feeling does the phrase "Headragged Generals" evoke?

◀ **Critical Viewing**
Is the artist's attitude toward these women similar to the one expressed by the poet? **[Compare]**

## Critical Thinking

1. **Craft and Structure** **(a)** List three images in the poem that convey the women's determination to help their children. **(b) Assess:** Which image did you find the most powerful? Why?

2. **Key Ideas and Details** **(a)** What do the women want to "discover" and for whom? **(b) Interpret:** In lines 22–26, why is the women's knowledge so remarkable?

3. **Integration of Knowledge and Ideas** **(a)** What message about education do the women communicate with their actions? Use details to support your answer. **(b)** What impact do you think this message had on their children? Explain your answer. *[Connect to the Big Question: How does communication change us?]*

Cite textual evidence to support your responses.

# SONNET 30

## WILLIAM SHAKESPEARE

**Vocabulary**
**woes** (wōz) *n.* great sorrows

**wail** (wāl)) *n.* lament; cry of deep sorrow

When to the sessions of sweet silent thought
I summon up remembrance of things past,
I sigh the lack of many a thing I sought,
And with old woes new wail my dear times waste:[1]
5  Then can I drown an eye, unused to flow,
For precious friends hid in death's dateless[2] night,
And weep afresh love's long since cancelled woe,
And moan the expense[3] of many a vanished sight:
Then can I grieve at grievances foregone,[4]
10  And heavily from woe to woe tell o'er[5]
The sad account of fore-bemoanèd moan,[6]
Which I new pay as if not paid before.
But if the while I think on thee, dear friend,
All losses are restored and sorrows end.

---

1. **And . . . waste** and by grieving anew for past sorrows, ruin the precious present.
2. **dateless** endless.
3. **expense** loss.
4. **foregone** past and done with.
5. **tell o'er** count up.
6. **fore-bemoanèd moan** sorrows suffered in the past.

## Critical Thinking

Cite textual evidence to support your responses.

1. **Key Ideas and Details (a) Infer:** In line 5, what does "drown an eye" mean? **(b) Analyze Cause and Effect:** What causes the speaker to "drown an eye"? Why?

2. **Key Ideas and Details (a) Clarify:** What is the speaker describing in lines 10–12? **(b) Relate:** Why might someone spend time doing this?

3. **Integration of Knowledge and Ideas** In what ways could the speaker's words change a person's response to a disappointment or personal loss? *[Connect to the Big Question: How does communication change us?]*

## Comparing Forms of Lyric Poetry

© **1. Craft and Structure** Both "I Hear America Singing" and "Women" are **free verse,** with a form imposed by the poet. **(a)** Compare the emotions conveyed in these poems. **(b)** Which poem follows more of a pattern? Explain.

© **2. Craft and Structure** Compare and contrast the subjects and structure of the three **haiku** to the three poems from English-speaking traditions.

© **3. Craft and Structure** In his **sonnet,** Shakespeare presents an idea or a question in the first quatrain (four lines), explores the idea in the next two quatrains, and reaches a conclusion in the final couplet. Use a chart like the one shown to analyze the content of "Sonnet 30."

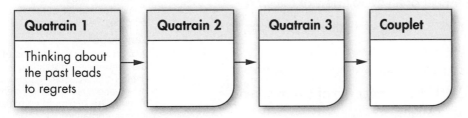

| Quatrain 1 | → | Quatrain 2 | → | Quatrain 3 | → | Couplet |
|---|---|---|---|---|---|---|
| Thinking about the past leads to regrets | | | | | | |

## 🕐 Timed Writing

### Explanatory Text: Essay

In an essay, compare the ways the structure of the different lyric forms affect the meanings of these poems. Choose two poems and structures to discuss. Cite textual evidence to support your response. **(30 minutes)**

### 5-Minute Planner

**1.** Read the prompt carefully and completely.

**2.** Gather your ideas by jotting down answers to these questions:

- How does the free verse structure of Whitman's and Walker's poems help the strength of each poem's message?

- How does the strict form of the haiku help to capture the feeling of a brief moment in time?

- How would the meaning of "Sonnet 30" be different without the final two lines?

**3.** Reread the prompt. Then, refer to your notes as you draft your essay.

# Writing Workshop

 **Common Core State Standards**

**Writing**
**2.** Write informative/explanatory texts to examine and convey complex ideas, concepts, and information clearly and accurately through the effective selection, organization, and analysis of content.
**4.** Produce clear and coherent writing in which the development, organization, and style are appropriate to task, purpose, and audience.
**9.a.** Draw evidence from literary or informational texts to support analysis, reflection and research. Apply grades 9-10 reading standards to literature.
**10.** Write routinely over extended time frames and shorter time frames for a range of tasks, purposes, and audiences.

**Language**
**2.b.** Demonstrate command of the conventions of standard English capitalization, punctuation, and spelling when writing. Use a colon to introduce a list or quotation.

## Write Explanatory Texts

### Exposition: Response to Literature

**Defining the Form** A formal **response to literature** gives you an opportunity to analyze and reflect on a specific work. You might use elements of this type of writing in journals, critical reviews, literary analyses, and annotated bibliographies.

**Assignment** Write a response to a work of literature that engages you as a reader. Include these elements:

- ✓ an *analysis* of the work's content, its related ideas, and its effect on you
- ✓ a *thesis statement* that characterizes your response
- ✓ a *focus* on a single aspect or an overall view of the work
- ✓ *evidence from the text,* including embedded quotations, to support your opinions
- ✓ a *tone* that suits your purpose for writing and audience
- ✓ error-free grammar, including correct use of colons when introducing lists or quotations

To preview the criteria on which your response to literature may be judged, see the rubric on page 763.

 **Writing Workshop:** *Work in Progress*

If you have completed the Work-in-Progress assignments on pages 717 and 739, use these ideas as you complete the Writing Workshop.

### WRITE GUY
*Jeff Anderson, M.Ed.*

## What Do You Notice?

### Direct Quotations

The following excerpt is from *Nothing to Fear: Lessons in Leadership from FDR* by Alan Axelrod. Read the excerpt several times.

*There is no sugarcoating of reality here! The fog has lifted, the scene is sharply etched and downright frightening: "a host of unemployed citizens face the grim problem of existence, and an equally great number toil with little return."*

Jot down what you find effective about the use of a quotation in this excerpt. As you work on your response to literature, think of ways you can best use direct quotations to support your ideas.

**Reading-Writing Connection**

To get a feel for responses to literature, read the excerpt from *Nothing to Fear: Lessons in Leadership from FDR* by Alan Axelrod on page 567.

# Prewriting/Planning Strategies

**Make a top-ten list.** Think of stories, poems, or other works of litera-ture that you found memorable. Create a top-ten list of these titles and authors. Next to each entry, briefly note your initial reactions to the work and any ideas you might want to share about it. Review your list and choose one work as your topic.

**Clarify your purpose.** Determine the specific purpose, or goal, of your essay. For example, you may want to share your enthusiasm for a new writer, find fresh insights into a well-known poem, or analyze the mean-ing of a short story. Write a statement of purpose for your essay. Use both the title and the author's name in your statement:

- **Example of statement of purpose:** *In this essay, I will analyze the character of General Zaroff in Richard Connell's short story "The Most Dangerous Game."*

**Identify types of details you will need.** The purpose or goal of your essay determines the kinds of details you need to include. Consider these tips:

- **To praise,** include concrete details about what you liked.

- **To analyze,** support your ideas with evidence from the selection as well as other outside resources.

- **To explain a personal response,** show how the work connects to your own experiences and ideas.

**Find supporting evidence.** Return to the work of literature you have selected to find examples, excerpts, and direct quotations that relate to your topic. Consider how well your research supports your own responses. Prepare a series of index cards, with one card for every idea you want to prove. Write your main point or idea across the top of the card. Underneath, write your notes on the details you gath-ered from the text to support that point or idea.

By breaking down the details and referring them back to your purpose, you will be able to present complex ideas in a sustained and compelling manner.

---

**Identifying Supporting Evidence**

**Thesis: What I want to prove:**
General Zaroff's civilized exterior conceals a ruthless, heartless murderer.

**How I can prove it:**
His elegant castle is also a prison.

**Explain in detail:**
Zaroff makes Rainsford comfortable in the castle in order to make him healthy and, therefore, the hunt more intriguing.

---

# Drafting Strategies

 **Common Core State Standards**

**Writing**

**2.b.** Develop the topic with well-chosen, relevant, and sufficient facts, extended definitions, concrete details, quotations, or other information and examples appropriate to the audience's knowledge of the topic.

**5.** Develop and strengthen writing as needed by planning, revising, editing, rewriting, or trying a new approach, focusing on addressing what is most significant for a specific purpose and audience.

**Identify your thesis.** Your draft should have a clear thesis statement that you will develop and support throughout your essay. Review your notes to draft a single sentence that combines the statement of purpose you wrote earlier with the ideas and evidence you have accumulated. Use the following thesis statement to direct the writing of your essay.

> **Example of thesis statement:** *In Richard Connell's short story "The Most Dangerous Game," the character of General Zaroff reveals the murderous mind lurking behind an illusion of refinement.*

**Organize your ideas.** Create an organizational chart like the one shown to present your ideas in a logical way. Your introduction should include your thesis, and every body paragraph should provide its support.

**Organize Your Ideas**

**Introduction**
- Grab attention
- Identify author and title
- Offer brief summary
- State thesis

**Body**
- Present supporting ideas
- Introduce each new idea in a new paragraph
- Use details to support each idea

**Conclusion**
- Restate thesis
- Make a final point or present a final question or insight

**Consider your audience.** The nature of your audience—who they are and what they know—influences the amount and kind of information you include in your response to literature. For example, if your audience already knows the work, limit the background information and proceed to your core ideas. If your audience is unfamiliar with the work, give more context and explanation.

**Provide supporting details.** Include evidence from the literary work for every claim you make in your essay. Consider these suggestions:

- **Quotations** can illustrate a character's attitude, a writer's word choice, or an essayist's opinion. Be sure that quotations are exact and enclosed in quotation marks.

- **Examples** of a character's actions or of a specific literary element can enhance your analysis.

- **Paraphrases,** or restatements in your own words, can help you explain a writer's theme, discuss the conflict, analyze a character, or clarify key ideas. Paraphrases must accurately reflect the original text.

Avoid padding your draft with irrelevant passages or unnecessary summaries of the plot. Focus on conveying the point of your essay.

# Writers on Writing

## Pat Mora On Responding to Literature

Pat Mora is the author of "Uncoiling" (p. 613) and
"A Voice" (p. 614).

Many of my best teachers are authors I will never meet. In the essay "Unseen Teachers," I explore how authors help me experience the world more intensely. Literature and all forms of art can make us more human.

This passage from the essay was inspired by a quotation from Southwest artist Georgia O'Keeffe saying that she was trying to prompt the viewer to notice. As I tried to show, writers who see their work as part of a group's struggle for justice do the same

*"I love
words
and their
interweavings."*
—Pat Mora

### Professional Model:

### from "Unseen Teachers," from *Nepantla*

I still smile at her [Georgia O'Keeffe's] laughing confession that by painting huge flowers, she forced us to notice. . . .

We too seek to force a society to notice the bitter and the sweet. Often we both participate in our communities and are solitary writers, a tension. The mere cover of Denise Levertov's *The Poet in the World* reminds me of her firm conviction: "Both life and poetry fade, wilt, shrink when they are divorced." Lorna Dee Cervantes, Sandra Cisneros, Alice Walker, Lucille Clifton, Amy Tan, Joy Harjo, and Linda Hogan are thick in the struggle of their people, and their writing is part of that struggle. Though the daily realities—high dropout rates, low per capita income, high unemployment—continue, these women teach me that the arrangement and rearrangement of work on the page is neither elitist nor irrelevant. It is the appropriate task of the person who weaves words for people's use.

I love art and often get ideas in museums. Many readers know O'Keeffe's paintings of flowers. Here, they make my thesis colorful and concrete.

I debated what names to include and what realities to list. These authors support the diversity that's a theme for the book.

Braids or weaves, I wondered? Both, like writing, are hand activities. I chose weaves because weavers create both basic items of clothing and beautiful art pieces.

# Revising Strategies

**Revise to eliminate unnecessary information.** Use words and phrases to convey ideas precisely by reviewing your draft to eliminate extra details. Identify instances in which the information you provide may not support your main idea, but may actually distract from it. Follow these steps:

- Underline your thesis and the main ideas of each paragraph.

- Highlight sentences that do not support your thesis.

- Consider revising details to make a tighter connection to your main idea.

- Eliminate any paragraphs or details that do not clearly contribute to your analysis.

**Check words of praise or criticism.** Review your response to literature, making sure your word choices are precise and that they accurately reflect your purpose, your audience, and your attitude toward the literary work.

**Vague:**    This *factual* account of the author's life is *interesting.*

**Precise:**    This *honest* account of the author's life *captures* the reader's attention.

In addition, pay close attention to the degree, or form, of the adjectives you use, especially when making comparisons. Use the degree that accurately reflects your meaning. The **comparative** degree, which is usually formed by adding *-er* to the adjective or by using the word *more,* is used to compare two items. The **superlative** degree, which is usually formed by adding *-est* to the adjective or by using the word *most,* is used to compare more than two items.

**Comparative degree:**    Zaroff is a *more disagreeable* character than Rainsford. (*Compares two items*)

**Superlative degree:**    Zaroff is the *most disagreeable* character in the story. (*Compares more than two items*)

## Peer Review

Exchange drafts with a partner. Review each other's work, circling words that convey approval or criticism. Underline words that express degrees of comparison. Determine whether you have used these words correctly and whether they are precise or vague. Then, revise your draft, replacing vague, dull, or incorrect language with choices that pinpoint your meaning. As you revise, be sure to maintain a consistency in style and tone throughout your work.

**Common Core State Standards**

**Writing**
**2.d.** Use precise language and domain-specific vocabulary to manage the complexity of the topic.
**5.** Develop and strengthen writing as needed by planning, revising, editing, rewriting, or trying a new approach, focusing on addressing what is most significant for a specific purpose and audience.

**Language**
**2.b.** Use a colon to introduce a list or quotation.

# Using Quotations

Direct quotations are passages from a work of literature taken word for word. Indirect quotations are paraphrases of the words from literature.

**Punctuating Direct Quotations** All direct quotations in the running text must be enclosed in quotation marks. A direct quotation is usually preceded by a comma and sometimes by a colon. It is followed by its corresponding page number enclosed in parentheses. The period or comma from the quotation follows the page number. See the example below.

**Example of direct quotations in running text:**

*Rainsford is horrified when he realizes the truth of his situation: "The Cossack was the cat; he was the mouse" (232).*

When you quote a passage from the text that runs more than four lines, set it off from the text by indenting it ten spaces. In this case, do not use quotation marks. This type of quotation is often preceded by a colon. Also, the end punctuation comes before the page number citation.

**Example of block indented quotations:**

*As Rainsford awaits Zaroff's discovery of him, he breathes a sigh of relief when Zaroff leaves. Then the horror of the situation hits him:*

> *Rainsford did not want to believe what his reason told him was true, but the truth was as evident as the sun that had by now pushed through the morning mists. The general was playing with him! The general was saving him for another day's sport! (231)*

*Zaroff's true character becomes apparent to Rainsford in this moment.*

**Punctuating Indirect Quotations** Because indirect quotations are paraphrases of the text, you do not need to put them in quotation marks.

**Example of indirect quotation in running text:**

*When Rainsford realizes that Zaroff is playing a game of cat and mouse, he is horrified.*

**Grammar in Your Writing**

Scan your essay to identify any direct quotations. Make sure they have quotation marks at the beginning and end of the quotation. Check whether your end punctuation is inside or outside of the quotation marks. Most periods and commas should be inside. Revise punctuation that is incorrect.

---

**PH WRITING COACH**

Further instruction and practice are available in *Prentice Hall Writing Coach*.

## Characterization of General Zaroff

What lies at the heart of a refined man? In Richard Connell's short story "The Most Dangerous Game," the deranged, yet cunning and elegant General Zaroff shares his taste for hunting with an unsuspecting visitor. Although he is civilized in his dress and habits, Zaroff's beliefs reveal a murderous mind behind the illusion of a charming, charismatic man.

When we first encounter General Zaroff, our initial reaction is one of delight and admiration for his wealth and charm. Zaroff lives in a massive castle, feasts on the finest delicacies, and wears expensive clothes. His luxurious surroundings and lifestyle reflect a highly civilized, eloquent, and proper gentleman. As readers soon learn, however, there is more to Zaroff than food and elegance.

Beneath Zaroff's fine qualities lies an overwhelming attitude of arrogance. This attitude comes from his firm belief that his way of thinking is superior to that of the average person. Zaroff also fancies himself a phenomenal hunter: "My hand was made for the trigger," he claims. It is this deadly mixture of arrogance, superior hunting skills, and belief that it is natural for the strong to prevail over the weak that makes him disregard the value of human life.

Zaroff's extreme beliefs lead him to conclude that only the intelligent mind of a human being can provide him with the dangerous game he desires. Rationalizing that "the weak were created to please the strong," he chooses to hunt humans instead of animals. Unfortunately, Rainsford steps into this situation. The major conflicts in "The Most Dangerous Game" demonstrate what happens during such an inhumane hunt.

However, the general's arrogance and disregard for human life blind him to the fear and desperation of his prey. His attitude leads to his own demise at the hands of Rainsford, his prey. The characterization of Zaroff as a murderer hiding behind a mask of civility shows that beneath even the most beautiful rose can lie a sharp and deadly thorn.

The title indicates that the essay will focus on a single character.

Jeff uses vivid language to state his thesis clearly.

Direct quotations provide evidence for this understanding of Zaroff.

Jeff concludes his response with an illuminating analogy that neatly summarizes his analysis.

# Editing and Proofreading

Review your draft to correct errors in spelling, grammar, and punctuation.

**Correcting Common Usage Problems** *Among* and *between* are not interchangeable. *Among* always implies three or more elements, whereas *between* is generally used with only two elements. *Like, as, as if,* and *as though* are not interchangeable. *Like* is a preposition meaning "similar to" or "such as." It should not be used in place of *as, as if,* or *as though,* which are conjunctions that introduce clauses.

# Publishing and Presenting

Consider one of the following ways to share your writing:

**Deliver an oral presentation.** Read your response to literature aloud. Have a copy of the literary work on hand in the event that your class-mates wish to read or review it.

**Publish a collection of responses to literature.** Gather the essays of several of your classmates. Organize them in a binder and make the collection available in the school library.

# Reflecting on Your Writing

**Writer's Journal** Jot down your answer to this question: *How did writing about the work help you to understand it?*

# Rubric for Self-Assessment

Find evidence in your writing to address each category. Then, use the rating scale to grade your work.

**Spiral Review**
Earlier in this unit, you learned about **appositive phrases** (p. 716) and **infinitives and infinitive phrases** (p. 738). Check your response to literature to be sure you have used these correctly.

| Criteria | Rating Scale | | | | |
| --- | --- | --- | --- | --- | --- |
| | not very | | | | very |
| **Focus:** How clearly have you stated your purpose? | 1 | 2 | 3 | 4 | 5 |
| **Organization:** How well have you crafted a thesis statement and a clear analysis of the literary work? | 1 | 2 | 3 | 4 | 5 |
| **Support/Elaboration:** How comprehensive is the background information you provided? | 1 | 2 | 3 | 4 | 5 |
| **Style:** How formal is your use of language? | 1 | 2 | 3 | 4 | 5 |
| **Conventions:** Have you accurately quoted from the literary work and correctly punctuated your quotations? | 1 | 2 | 3 | 4 | 5 |

# Vocabulary Workshop

## Connotation and Denotation

**Common Core
State Standards**

**Language**
**3.** Apply knowledge of language to understand how language functions in different contexts, to make effective choices for meaning and style, and to comprehend more fully when reading or listening.
**5.b.** Analyze nuances in the meaning of words with similar denotations.

The **denotation** of a word is its direct, dictionary meaning. Its **connotations** include the ideas, images, and feelings that are associated with the word. Consider the words *fragrance, smell,* and *stench.* These words are synonyms, which means they share a similar denotation—having a scent or odor. However, their connotations are very different.

The connotation of *smell* is about the same as its denotation. It has a neutral connotation and can be defined as "the quality that you recognize by using your nose." The connotation of *fragrance* is positive, suggesting a pleasant, sweet smell or scent. *Stench* has negative connotations, suggesting a foul, unpleasant odor. The following graphic shows the positive, neutral, and negative connotations of some synonyms.

| Positive → | Neutral → | Negative |
|---|---|---|
| fragrance | smell | stench |
| modest | shy | mousy |
| inquisitive | curious | nosy |
| home | house | shack |

**Practice A** Choose the word that has the more neutral connotation.

1. On Friday, the Bridgeport Wolves (defeated, crushed) the North Point Beacons.

2. Helen was embarrassed by her (sloppy, untidy) appearance.

3. Julian remained (silent, sullen) as I told him the news.

4. Because of the weekend-long festival, the street was (filthy, dirty).

5. The (tyrant, leader) signed the new legislation into law.

6. She seemed (surprised, staggered) by the question.

**Practice B** Rewrite each sentence, replacing the italicized word with a word that has a more positive connotation. Use a dictionary or thesaurus if necessary.

1. Adrian is too *cheap* to spend money on a ticket to the play.
2. I've been around Elena long enough to appreciate her *cunning*.
3. Jevon's *arrogance* makes him a natural leader.
4. When I told him the joke, Marcus *cackled* uncontrollably.
5. Michelle was *lazy* and spent the day reading.
6. The boy and his *cronies* are playing ball.
7. I would never forgive him for his *treachery*.
8. Ana was *stubborn* and kept practicing to make the team.
9. Janine was *disgusted* when her friend moved out of town.
10. The *old* man walked slowly across the street.

**Activity** Prepare four note cards with the headings as shown below. Then, write a sentence for each of these words: *argue, fashionable, rumpled, chuckle.* Using a dictionary and thesaurus, write four synonyms for each word. Then, circle the synonym whose connotation best matches the meaning of the word used in your sentence. Compare cards with a partner. See if you chose the same synonyms. Talk about the differences in connotations of the words.

**Comprehension and Collaboration**

Write sentences to show how the connotations of the words in each pair differ: *visionary, dreamer; investigate, snoop; clumsy, awkward.* Use a dictionary and thesaurus if you need to. Meet with a group and compare your sentences and talk about the connotations of the words.

| Word: |
| --- |
| Sentence: |
| Synonyms: |

# Communications Workshop

## Oral Interpretation of Literature

**Common Core State Standards**

**Speaking and Listening**
**6.** Adapt speech to a variety of contexts and tasks, demonstrating command of formal English when indicated or appropriate.

An oral interpretation of literature can be fun: sharing stories, poems, or plays aloud is an activity that is enjoyable for people of all ages. An oral interpretation of literature is also challenging: in order to present one well, you must have a strong comprehension of the work and its meaning. As you prepare your interpretation and engage with the work in a detailed, specific way, you will increase your understanding of the literary work. In presenting the interpretation, you will share your appreciation with others. The following strategies can help you prepare and deliver your oral interpretation.

## Learn the Skills

**Understand the literature.** Your interpretation should demonstrate an accurate understanding of the literary work's content and meaning. Make sure you are thoroughly familiar with your selection.

**Rehearse the interpretation.** Make a copy of the literary work to mark performance notes as you practice. Plan and practice appropriate gestures, facial expressions, intonations, and timing until they feel natural. If certain words or phrases become stumbling points, memorize them to assure confidence and poise. Always practice aloud. Use the checklist shown here to help you prepare.

**Consider your audience.** Provide context to help your audience better understand the literary work you are presenting. Write an introduction to help your readers visualize the situation and characters. You may also include information about the author, including his or her style and the circumstances in which he or she wrote the selection.

Your familiarity with the selection should give you the freedom to maintain eye contact with your audience as you read.

**Practice reading poetry.** Use the poem's punctuation, not the ends of lines, as cues to pause when reading. Avoid lapsing into sing-song rhythms; instead, maintain a flow that sounds like natural speech. Vary your volume and pace to create emphasis.

**Practice reading stories and plays.** When expressing a character's quoted words, use a change in intonation to distinguish speech from narration. Modulate your vocal inflections, facial expressions, and posture to indicate whether a speaker is male or female, adult or child.

---

**Oral Interpretation Tips**

- Read the text multiple times.
- Mark performance notes and cues on your reading copy.
- Choose appropriate gestures, costumes, and props to suggest characters or situations.
- Vary your pace and tone of voice to create emphasis.

# Practice the Skills

**Presentation of Knowledge and Ideas** Use what you've learned in this workshop to complete the following activity.

---

**ACTIVITY: Prepare and Deliver an Oral Presentation**

Choose a favorite poem, story, or dramatic speech and prepare an oral interpretation using the strategies outlined in this workshop. Remember that your interpretation should enhance the literature's meaning for your audience. Consider these questions as you prepare and rehearse your presentation:

• What is the knowledge level and cultural perspective of my audience? What context best sets up my presentation?
• How will I organize and present ideas in my introduction?
• What props or costume will best enhance my presentation?
• What gestures are most appropriate for this work of literature?
• What pace and tone of voice best enhance this particular piece?

---

Use the Presentation Checklist below to analyze your classmates' presentations.

---

**Presentation Checklist**

**Presentation Content**
Determine whether or not the speaker provided support for the audience's understanding.
❑ considered audience and provided context
❑ provided organized and informative introduction
❑ included props and costumes effectively

**Presentation Delivery**
Determine whether or not the speaker engaged with the audience.
❑ appropriate eye contact
❑ effective speaking rate and volume
❑ effective tone of voice
❑ appropriate gestures
Comments on most effective elements of presentation: _____

---

**Comprehension and Collaboration** With your classmates, discuss how you evaluated each presenter. As a group, discuss what makes an oral presentation effective and why.

# Cumulative Review

Common Core
State Standards

RL.9-10.4; L.9-10.5, L.9-10.6
[For the full wording of the standards, see the standards chart in the front of your textbook.]

## I. Reading Literature

**Directions:** *Read the passage. Then, answer each question that follows.*

Early in the morning, Samantha and her father drove to the trailhead. She and her father had been planning this trip for two years, and they could not wait. They began the hike soon after dawn.

The uphill climb was a challenge as Samantha walked with pounds of gear on her back. She was barely aware of it by the time they reached the top of the hill because of the beauty of the surrounding woods. She saw a flock of turkeys to start. "Gobble, gobble," the jakes called to the hens. The birds had their own special language. They chatted like old married couples.

As Samantha and her father continued, her father motioned for her to stop as he pointed to the right. Just within sight, Samantha could see a black bear with two cubs. She knew she had to be very quiet. She heard the pounding of the drum of her heart in her ears. The cubs rolled around and <u>frolicked</u> happily as they followed their mother into the distance. Samantha could hardly believe her luck to see a bear on the first day.

The wind whipped through the trees, their new leaves singing a beautiful song to Samantha. The branches and dead leaves crackled under her feet. She imagined being an explorer in the 1600s, before there were trails and markers to guide the way. At lunch she returned from her daydream and was thankful to have the convenience and comforts of the twenty-first century. She loved her energy bars.

They climbed higher and hiked farther. The woods became denser and darker. The sun was setting in the west when Samantha's father suggested they set up camp for the night. They gathered firewood and stones to make a circle for the fire. After starting the fire, they set up their tents and prepared their provisions for dinner. The tight blanket of night covered the surrounding forest. All Samantha could see was a small circle of light cast by the campfire. She didn't want to admit it, but she was a little scared. She and her father had been planning this trip for two years. Now they were resting for the night after hiking for eight hours. Her legs felt like rubber because she was so exhausted, but she was so pleased to be on the hike.

Samantha was satisfied with a fine day of adventure. Though she was nervous to sleep deep in the woods, she was excited to see what the next day held in store for her and her father. Maybe she would see a coyote, she thought, as she heard distant howls echo through the forest.

1. The author of this story most likely uses **figurative language** in order to—

   A. explain a complicated concept.
   B. add suspense to the plot of the story.
   C. characterize Samantha and her father.
   D. describe the hike in an original way.

2. Which is an example of a **simile?**

   A. They began the hike soon after dawn.
   B. The birds had their own special language.
   C. Now they were resting for the night after hiking for eight hours.
   D. Her legs felt like rubber because she was so exhausted.

3. Which **sound device** is used in the phrase *barely aware?*

   A. alliteration
   B. assonance
   C. rhyme
   D. onomatopoeia

4. Which sentence contains an example of a **metaphor?**

   A. Just within sight, Samantha could see a black bear with her two cubs.
   B. She knew she had to be very quiet.
   C. She could hear the pounding of the drum of her heart in her ears.
   D. Samantha was satisfied with a fine day of adventure.

5. Which sentence contains an example of **onomatopoeia?**

   A. She saw a flock of turkeys to start.
   B. "Gobble, gobble," the jakes called to the hens.
   C. She and her father stopped and stared at the big birds' stepping and strutting.
   D. They chatted like old married couples.

6. Which sentence contains an example of **personification?**

   A. The wind whipped through the trees, their new leaves singing a beautiful song to Samantha.
   B. The branches and dead leaves crackled under her feet.
   C. She imagined being an explorer in the 1600s, before there were trails and markers to guide the way.
   D. Samantha could hardly believe her luck to see a bear on the first day.

7. **Vocabulary** Which word is closest in meaning to the underlined word *frolicked?*

   A. cried        C. played
   B. hunted       D. studied

8. Which phrase is an example of **alliteration?**

   A. climbed higher
   B. denser and darker
   C. setting in the west
   D. circle for the fire

9. Which phrase is an example of **consonance?**

   A. gathered firewood
   B. tight blanket of night
   C. held in store
   D. distant howls

 Timed Writing

10. **Identify** three examples of figurative language in this passage. In a paragraph, **explain** how the use of figurative language impacts meaning and tone.

 GO ON

# II. Reading Informational Text

**Directions:** *Read the passages. Then, answer each question that follows.*

 **Common Core
State Standards**

RI.9-10.2; L.9-10.3, L.9-10.4.a, L.9-10.5
[For the full wording of the standards, see the standards chart in the front of your textbook.]

### MP3 Mania!

The new wave in technology is the MP3 format for music files. Long gone are the days of vinyl records, cassettes, and even CDs. What was once considered new technology is now overshadowed by MP3 files. Who needs to carry around bulky CDs when your whole music collection can be stored on a palm-sized MP3 player? With this <u>revolutionary</u>, new technology, you can not only carry around your entire CD collection but you can also purchase files on the Internet, totally bypassing the need for storage space outside of the computer and player. MP3s provide hours of entertainment without the hassles of bulky players and the need for excess storage.

### Simple Instructions for MP3 Players

MP3 files have brought music into the computer age. With this technology, you can carry your entire music library in a tiny player. All you need is a computer, an MP3 player, and a USB cord. Follow these directions to start rocking.

**Step 1.** Download the music from your CDs onto your computer. Your computer should come equipped with a program to store and access music. Insert the CD, choose Download, and let the computer do the work.

**Step 2.** Connect your MP3 player to your computer with the USB cord. Your computer will update your MP3 player, loading all your music onto it.

**Step 3.** Allow the battery of your MP3 player to charge as it is connected to the computer. Your player will alert you when the battery is charged.

**Step 4.** Disconnect your player and follow the manual to play your music.

1. **Vocabulary** What is the *best* definition for the underlined word *revolutionary?*

   **A.** causing a change
   **B.** more affordable
   **C.** upsetting
   **D.** without consequences

2. What **central idea** do these texts share?

   **A.** MP3s are better than old music formats.
   **B.** MP3s are simple to use and easy to find.
   **C.** MP3s are overrated and difficult.
   **D.** MP3s are fun to share with friends.

3. To convert to MP3 format, you must first—

   **A.** allow your MP3 player battery to charge.
   **B.** download your CDs onto your computer.
   **C.** use the USB cord to connect your player.
   **D.** disconnect your player from the computer.

4. According to these texts, why is the MP3 format so good?

   **A.** It is inexpensive.
   **B.** It is convenient.
   **C.** It is complex.
   **D.** It involves computers.

# III. Writing and Language Conventions

**Directions:** *Read the passage. Then, answer each question that follows.*

(1) The smell of turkey filled my room, and before my eyes even opened, my mouth widened to a smile. (2) This was Thanksgiving, my favorite holiday, and all the members of my huge family had already arrived. (3) I heard the soft murmur of voices bubbling up from the kitchen. (4) I ran downstairs to greet my aunts, uncles, and cousins. (5) Later, dinner was ready. (6) I loved the steaming turkey. (7) I loved the seasoned stuffing, too. (8) I loved the conversation, my favorite part of Thanksgiving. (9) My cousin Ana talked about her surfing lessons in Florida. (10) My uncle Charlie told a funny story about his New Orleans jazz band. (11) When my family described their lives all over the country, I felt like I got to visit each place without leaving my home. (12) My grandpa Joe explained how he dug himself out of his house when three feet of snow fell on his home in Buffalo.

**1.** Which choppy sentences should be combined?

  **A.** Sentences 1 and 2

  **B.** Sentences 2 and 3

  **C.** Sentences 3 and 4

  **D.** Sentences 4 and 5

**2.** In what way should sentences 6, 7, and 8 be combined to vary the **sentence patterns?**

  **A.** I loved the steaming turkey and seasoned stuffing, but my favorite part of Thanksgiving was the conversation.

  **B.** I loved the steaming turkey, seasoned stuffing, and the conversation.

  **C.** I loved the steaming turkey, and I loved the seasoned stuffing, but also the conversation.

  **D.** Although I loved the Thanksgiving conversation, I loved the turkey and stuffing as well.

**3.** How could you improve the organization?

  **A.** Combine sentence 10 with sentence 11.

  **B.** Delete sentence 5.

  **C.** Switch sentence 1 with sentence 2.

  **D.** Move sentence 12 before sentence 11.

**4.** To incorporate **figurative language** into sentence 1, add—

  **A.** "as wide as the sea" after "smile."

  **B.** "delicious" before "smell."

  **C.** "bed" before "room,"

  **D.** "that morning" after "opened."

**5.** Which sentence contains an example of **sensory language?**

  **A.** Sentence 2

  **B.** Sentence 3

  **C.** Sentence 5

  **D.** Sentence 10

**6.** Which transition word or phrase should replace "Later" in sentence 5 to be more precise?

  **A.** Sometime on Thanksgiving,

  **B.** That day,

  **C.** Now,

  **D.** Within three hours,

# Performance Tasks

**Directions:** *Follow the instructions to complete the tasks below as required by your teacher.*

*As you work on each task, incorporate both general academic vocabulary and literary terms you learned in this unit.*

**Common Core State Standards**

RL.9-10.4, RL.9-10.5; RI.9-10.3; W.9-10.2.b, W.9-10.2.e, W.9-10.2.f, W.9-10.7, W.9-10.9.a; SL.9-10.2, SL.9-10.4

[For the full wording of the standards, see the standards chart in the front of your textbook.]

## Writing

### Task 1: Literature [RL.9-10.4; W.9-10.9.a]
**Analyze Figurative Language in a Poem**

*Write an essay in which you analyze the figurative language in a poem from this unit.*

- State which poem you chose, and explain why you chose it.
- Identify a key metaphor, simile, or other example of figurative language in the poem. Explain why this figurative language is important to the poem's meaning.
- Analyze the meaning of the figurative language. Explain your analysis clearly.
- Explain how the figurative language contributes to the tone of the poem. For example, explain how the poet's word choices build or maintain a sense of formality or informality. Cite details to support your ideas.
- Edit your essay for correct punctuation and spelling.

### Task 2: Literature [RL.9-10.5; W.9-10.9.a]
**Analyze the Structure in a Narrative Poem**

*Analyze how a poet uses structure to present events in a narrative poem from this unit. Consider how the order of events creates an effect such as mystery or suspense.*

- Give a brief summary of the plot.
- Describe how the poem is structured, or arranged in lines and stanzas.
- Explain how the poet uses the structure to organize information and tell the story. For example, consider how the poet uses the structure

to introduce characters, describe the setting, or show action.
- Explain how other structural elements, such as rhyme scheme, add to the poem.
- Consider whether the poet uses any devices to manipulate time. For example, explain whether the poet uses a flashback or alters the pacing. Explain the effects of these choices.
- Cite specific details from the poem to support your analysis.

### Task 3: Literature [RL.9-10.5; W.9-10.2.b]
**Compare Forms of Lyric Poetry**

*Compare two different forms of lyric poetry from this unit, and show how the form of each helps to express the speaker's thoughts and feelings.*

- Review the different forms of lyric poetry from this unit—sonnet, haiku, and free verse. Choose two poems, each with a different structure, as the basis for your comparison.
- Analyze each poem, explaining its structure and form.
- Show how each poem's structure aids the speaker in conveying important thoughts and feelings. Provide specific examples from each poem.
- Compare and contrast the structures of the two poems, explaining how the patterns of rhythm or rhyme affect the overall mood and feeling each expresses.
- Finally, evaluate the two poems, explaining which poem, in your opinion, better uses its structure to convey the speaker's ideas. Use text evidence to support your judgments.

# Speaking and Listening

## @Task 4: Literature [RL.9-10.4; SL.9-10.4]
### Analyze How Word Choice Affects the Tone of a Poem

*Write and deliver an oral presentation in which you analyze how the poet's word choice in a poem affects its tone.*

- Introduce the poem and briefly summarize it. If the poem is short, read it aloud.

- Describe the tone of the poem. Cite specific words that help to develop this tone. Be sure to explain how a variety of different words combine to create an overall effect.

- Provide a concluding statement that follows from and supports the information you presented earlier.

- Organize your findings and supporting evidence logically so your audience can follow your reasoning.

- As you speak, maintain consistency in your style and tone.

## @Task 5: Informational Text [RI.9-10.3; SL.9-10.4]
### Deliver a Speech Analyzing a Central Idea

*Deliver a speech in which you analyze the central idea expressed in a nonfiction work from this unit.*

- State which work you will discuss and provide an objective summary of the piece. Then, explain the central idea and analyze how the details in the text develop and support the central idea. Include details from the beginning, middle, and end of the work.

- Cite strong and thorough textual evidence to support your analysis.

- Use appropriate and varied transitions to link the major ideas in your speech.

- Present information clearly, concisely, and logically so that listeners can follow your reasoning.

- Conclude with a statement that supports the information you have presented.

## @Task 6: Literature [RL.9-10.2; W.9-10.7; SL.9-10.2]
### Deliver a Multimedia Presentation on Your Research of a Poet

*Deliver a multimedia presentation in which you explain how the theme expressed in a poem from this unit reflects the poet's life experiences.*

- To gather materials for your presentation, conduct research on the poet's life and literary influences. Find texts, images, and, if possible, audio or video clips that you can use in your presentation.

- Identify the poet and poem you will discuss. State the poem's theme and cite details that support your interpretation.

- Explain how the theme expressed in this poem relates to aspects of the poet's life or work. Use evidence from your research and from the poem to support your ideas.

- If possible, use digital media such as digital images, audio, or even video to provide evidence and to add interest to your presentation.

- End with a conclusion that supports the information you presented.

**How does communication change us?**
At the beginning of Unit 4, you participated in a discussion about the Big Question. Now that you have completed the unit, write a response to the question. Discuss how your initial ideas have either changed or been reinforced. Cite specific examples from the literature in this unit, from other subject areas, and from your own life to support your ideas. Use Big Question vocabulary words (see p. 605) in your response.

# Featured Titles

In this unit, you have read a wide variety of poems by many different poets. Continue to read on your own. Select works that you enjoy, but challenge yourself to explore new poets and works of increasing depth and complexity. The titles suggested below will help you get started.

## Literature

### The Sonnets
by William Shakespeare
Signet Classic, 1999     **EXEMPLAR TEXT**

 Shakespeare wrote and published about 150 sonnets, which became some of the most well-known verse in literature. In these **poems,** he offers his observations about love, time, and beauty. Included in this volume is "Sonnet 73."

### The Collected Poetry of W. H. Auden
    **EXEMPLAR TEXT**

 Often referred to as one of the twentieth century's most influential poets, Auden is renowned for his range and depth. He wrote **poems** that describe countless aspects of life, from the ordinary to the profound.

### The Collected Poems of Emily Dickinson
    **EXEMPLAR TEXT**

 In contrast to her current reputation as an important poet, Emily Dickinson was little known during her lifetime. Shy, Dickinson spent most of her time at home, reading and writing. In one of the best-known **poems** in this collection, the now-famous recluse wrote: "I'm nobody! Who are you?"

### Reflections on a Gift of Watermelon Pickle

 Voices from a variety of backgrounds and cultures blend in the second edition of this collection of modern **poems.** Skilled poets such as Sandra Cisneros and Li-Young Lee capture the world around us in their verses.

## Trouble the Water: 250 Years of African-American Poetry
Edited by Jerry W. Ward, Jr.     **EXEMPLAR TEXT**

 African American heritage comes alive in this collection of **poems** covering 300 years. From the spirituals sung in the days of slavery to vibrant poems from the 1990s, this volume spans many aspects of the African American experience. This collection contains poems by Countee Cullen and Alice Walker.

### The Book Thief
by Markus Zusak     **EXEMPLAR TEXT**

Death is the narrator of this **novel** about a nine-year-old girl who goes to live in a tough German neighborhood in the late 1930s. The fast-paced action of this book complements the poetic language.

## Informational Texts

### House of Houses
by Pat Mora
Beacon Press, 1997

 In this **memoir,** five generations of Pat Mora's Mexican American family come alive to retell their stories and weave in and out of each others' lives. In the retelling, history is shared and their understanding of one another is changed.

### The Hot Zone: A Terrifying True Story
by Richard Preston     **EXEMPLAR TEXT**

 This **nonfiction thriller** dramatizes a real-life outbreak of the Ebola virus in an animal laboratory located in a Washington, D.C., suburb. Known for its chilling suspense, this "bio-thriller" was a best-seller when it first appeared and has fascinated readers ever since.

# Preparing to Read Complex Texts

**Attentive Reading** As you read literature on your own, bring your imagination and questions to the text. The questions shown below and others that you ask as you read will help you learn and enjoy literature even more.

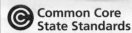

**Common Core State Standards**

**Reading Literature/Informational Text**

**10.** By the end of grade 9, read and comprehend literature, including stories, dramas, poems, and literary nonfiction in the grades 9–10 text complexity band proficiently, with scaffolding as needed at the high end of the range.

---

## When reading poetry, ask yourself...

- What, if anything, do I understand about the poem from its title?
- Who is the speaker of the poem? What is the speaker telling me?
- What subject matter does the poem address?
- Is the poem telling a story? If so, who are the characters, and what are they doing?
- What theme, meaning, or insight does the poem express? Are there any lines or sections that simply state that theme? If so, which ones? If not, which details help me understand the poem's deeper meaning?

**Key Ideas and Details**

- How does the poem look on the page? How does the poem's appearance affect the way I read it?
- Is the poem an example of a particular form, such as sonnet, ballad, or haiku? If so, what do I expect from the poem based on its form?
- Is the poem an example of free verse? If so, does it have any formal elements?
- How does the form affect what I understand and feel about the poem?
- What do I notice about the stanzas? Are they always a set number of lines, or do they vary in length? What new idea or piece of information does each stanza give me?
- What do I notice about the way the poem sounds? Does the poet use repetition? Does the poet use rhyme, and, if so, what kind? Does the poet use other sound devices?
- How do sound devices affect my enjoyment of the poem? How do they emphasize the meaning?
- What do I notice about any symbols or images? Does any one symbol or image repeat? What connections do I see between the symbol or image and the poem's deeper meaning?

**Craft and Structure**

- Even if I do not understand every word, do I like this poem? Why or why not?
- Has the poem helped me understand something in a new way? If so, how?
- In what ways is this poem similar to others I have read? In what ways is it different from others I have read?
- What insights have I gained from reading this poem?
- Would I like to read more poems by this poet? Why or why not?
- Could this poem serve as an inspiration to other writers, artists, or musicians? Why or why not?

**Integration of Ideas**

THE BIG
**Q?**

# Do our *differences* define us?

## PHLit Online!
www.PHLitOnline.com

### Hear It!
- Selection summary audio
- Selection audio
- BQ Tunes

### See It!
- Author videos
- Big Question video
- Get Connected videos
- Background videos
- More about the authors
- Illustrated vocabulary words
- Vocabulary flashcards

### Do It!
- Interactive journals
- Interactive graphic organizers
- Grammar tutorials
- Interactive vocabulary games
- Test practice

# Do our *differences* define us?

The **differences** among human beings can certainly be obvious, like hair color, height, or the accents that mark our speech. Other, more subtle differences may be noticed only when we get to know each other. These differences might show up in our values and in the mannerisms and traditions that are rooted in our individual culture. While differences make us unique, they may also put us at odds with each other. Do our differences define who we are?

## Exploring the Big Question

**Collaboration: One-on-One Discussion** Start thinking about the Big Question by listing examples of ways in which people may differ. List differences that you have observed or read about among people. Describe one specific example of each of these differences.

- physical appearance
- culture or family traditions
- personal style, such as the way people dress and talk
- values
- personal opinions
- personality traits
- interests, sports, or hobbies

Share your list with a partner. Talk about whether these differences help to define the people around us or whether people are more than just the sum of their individual attributes and interests. Use the Big Question Vocabulary in your discussion.

**Connecting to the Literature** Each reading in this unit will give you additional insight into the Big Question.

**PHLit.**
**Online!**
**www.PHLitOnline.com**
- Big Question video
- Illustrated vocabulary words
- Interactive vocabulary games
- BQ Tunes

# Learning Big Question Vocabulary

**Acquire and Use Academic Vocabulary** Academic vocabulary is the language you encounter in textbooks and on standardized tests. Review the definitions of these academic vocabulary words.

---

**defend** (dē fend´) *v.* protect against attack

**determine** (dē tūr´ mən) *v.* cause something to happen in a certain way

**differentiate** (dif´ ər en´ shē āt´) *v.* distinguish between items or ideas

**discriminate** (di skrim´i nāt´) *v.* recognize differences; act because of prejudice

**unique** (yoo nēk´) *adj.* one of a kind

---

Use these words as you complete Big Question activities in this unit that involve reading, writing, speaking, and listening.

**Gather Vocabulary Knowledge** Additional Big Question words are listed below. Categorize the words by deciding whether you know each one well, know it a little bit, or do not know it at all.

---

| | | |
|---|---|---|
| accept | assimilated | background |
| conformity | culture | differences |
| individuality | similarity | understanding |
| values | | |

---

Then, do the following:

1. Write the definitions of the words you know.

2. Consult a dictionary to confirm the meanings of the words whose definitions you wrote down. Revise your definitions if necessary.

3. Using a print or an online dictionary, look up the meanings of the words you are unsure of or do not know. Then, write definitions for those words.

4. Use all of the words in a brief paragraph about how strongly our differences define us.

**Common Core State Standards**

**Speaking and Listening**

**1.** Initiate and participate effectively in a range of collaborative discussions (one-on-one, in groups, and teacher-led) with diverse partners, building on others' ideas and expressing their own clearly and persuasively.

**Language**

**6.** Acquire and use accurately grade-appropriate general academic and domain-specific words and phrases, sufficient for reading, writing, speaking, and listening at the college and career readiness level; demonstrate independence in gathering vocabulary knowledge when considering a word or phrase important to comprehension or expression.

# Elements of Drama

## Drama is narrative, or storytelling, written for performance.

A **drama** is a play, a story written to be performed by actors on a stage or in a film. Sometimes, people use the word *drama* to refer to a work about a serious subject. However, the broad genre of drama includes every type of performed narrative work, whether lighthearted or serious.

Like other works of narrative literature, dramatic works feature **characters,** or personalities who take part in the action of the story. The main characters face a **conflict,** a struggle or problem that propels the sequence of events called the **plot.** The highest point of interest in the plot, the **climax,** occurs during the point of greatest tension between characters. As the story winds down, the **resolution** of the conflict leads to the conclusion of the play.

**Acts** are the basic units of organization in a drama. Acts are often further divided into **scenes.** A scene may move the action to a new setting or time of day, it may introduce new characters, or it may shift a play's mood. For example, an evening scene may follow a daytime scene, or a comic scene may lighten the mood of a serious play.

The author of a play, called a **playwright** or **dramatist,** writes the **script,** or text of the story. The script contains **dialogue,** or the characters' spoken words. It also contains **stage directions,** which are instructions about how the play should be performed. In some plays, the playwright gives detailed stage directions, while in others he or she provides few or none at all.

All the elements of drama combine in performance to produce an illusion of reality known as **dramatic effect.** Dramatic effect allows viewers to believe in the events of the story, even though they know the play is artificial. Through this effect, the dramatist explores a **theme**—a deeper meaning or insight about life.

| The Elements of Drama | |
|---|---|
| **Acts and Scenes** | Acts and scenes are the basic sections of drama. A drama may consist of one or more acts, each of which may contain any number of scenes. |
| **Stage Directions** | Stage directions are the playwright's instructions about how a play should be performed. They are usually set in italics and/or set off by brackets. They may include the following information:<br>• Background about the setting or characters<br>• Abbreviations for where actors should move or say their lines—for example, *D.S.* means downstage, or closer to the audience, while *U.S.* means upstage, or farther from the audience<br>• Details about physical elements of the performance, such as sets, lighting, and costumes |
| **Sets** | Sets are constructions that define the area in which the play's action occurs. Sets may be realistic and look like actual places. They may also be abstract or minimalist and merely suggest real places. |
| **Props** | Props are movable objects, like swords or pens, that actors use on stage. |

## Forms of Drama

The ancient Greeks, who developed drama as an organized literary form, created two basic types of plays. We still use these two categories to define dramatic forms.

- A **tragedy** traces the downfall of the main character, often called the **tragic hero.** In classical drama, the tragic hero is always an important person, such as a general or a king. The hero is admirable but is defeated by a **tragic flaw**—a mistake or a character defect.

- A **comedy** has a happy ending. Comedies usually feature a series of events in which the order or balance of the world is disrupted. A comic ending restores order and harmony.

Comedies are often funny, but humor is not their defining trait. The main distinction between tragedy and comedy is how the story ends: tragedies end in death, defeat, or exile, while comedies end in weddings, births, reunions, or other positive, joyful events.

**Dramatic Structures** Classical dramas, such as most works written by the ancient Greeks and by Shakespeare, take place in five acts and are called **five-act plays.** The acts follow the structure of most narrative works: **Act 1** = introduction/exposition; **Act 2** = rising action; **Act 3** = climax; **Act 4** = falling action; **Act 5** = resolution.

In some dramatic works, the five segments of plot are compressed into fewer acts. For example, many **screenplays,** or scripts written for films, occur in three acts. Act 1 introduces the main characters and the basic situation. Act 2 sets up a problem. Act 3 provides the resolution.

**One-act plays** are dramatic works that are organized in a single act. The one act may still contain multiple scenes.

## Types of Dramatic Speeches

In most dramatic works, dialogue is the playwright's main tool for developing characters and furthering the plot. Ancient Greek playwrights also used the convention of the **chorus,** a group of observers who were part of the play but not part of the story. The chorus provided background information and reacted to the events that unfolded on stage.

In some modern dramas, a **narrator** replaces the chorus. The narrator is a personality or voice that comments on but does not participate in the story. In some films, for example, an unseen narrator may introduce the story as a whole, set up a scene, or tell viewers about a character.

Playwrights use other types of dramatic speeches to supplement dialogue and reveal the thoughts, feelings, and motivations of the characters. The main types of dramatic speeches are explained in the chart below.

**In This Section**

**Elements of Drama**

**Analyzing Character Development**

**Close Read: Character, Plot, and Theme**
- Model Text
- Practice Text

**After You Read**

 Common Core State Standards

RL.9-10.3
[For the full wording of the standards, see the standards chart in the front of your textbook.]

## Types of Dramatic Speeches

| Type of Speech | Definition | Examples from *The Tragedy of Romeo and Juliet* |
| --- | --- | --- |
| Monologue | A long, uninterrupted speech delivered by a character to other characters on stage | Romeo speaks about love to Benvolio. *(p. 813, line 171)* |
| Soliloquy | A speech in which a character, alone on stage, reveals private thoughts that the audience is allowed to overhear | Juliet reveals her private thoughts. *(p. 871, line 17)* |
| Aside | A brief remark a character makes to the audience rather than to other characters | Juliet tells the audience that Romeo is no villain. *(p. 885, line 83)* |

# Analyzing Character Development

Characters' reactions to conflict propel the plot and point to thematic meanings.

**Common Core State Standards**

**Reading Literature**
**3.** Analyze how complex characters develop over the course of a text, interact with other characters, and advance the plot or develop the theme.

## Characters and Conflict

In both tragedies and comedies, characters face **conflicts,** or struggles between opposing forces. There are two main types of conflict: external and internal.

- **External Conflict:** a struggle against an outside force, such as an enemy, nature, or the pressures of society

> **Example:**
> Romeo and Juliet struggle against pressures from their feuding families.

- **Internal Conflict:** a struggle posed by a character's own beliefs, thoughts, or feelings

> **Example:**
> As she enacts the plan that will allow her to join Romeo, Juliet struggles with her fears.

The most interesting dramatic works feature important conflicts that engage the audience. For tragic characters, the conflict is often literally life threatening. For comic characters, the conflict is often symbolically life threatening. For example, the hero in a romantic comedy may not win the woman of his dreams. The quality of his life, if not its substance, is at risk.

**Protagonist and Antagonist** Most plays focus on a single main character—the protagonist. The character who opposes the main character and either creates or adds to the conflict is called the antagonist.

**Complex Characters** Great dramas present interesting characters, both protagonists and antagonists, whose stories are compelling to audiences. Such characters are complex, which means they have strengths and weaknesses and experience mixed emotions. Complex characters have multiple motivations, or a variety of reasons for feeling and behaving as they do. In literary terms, complex characters are round, rather than flat, and dynamic, rather than static.

### Character Types

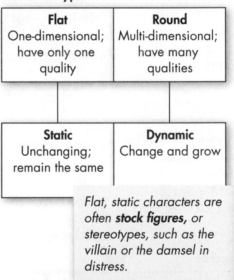

A play is, in part, an exploration of a round, dynamic character's journey from one state of being to another. By dramatizing that journey, a playwright also explores insights into the human condition, or thematic meaning.

## Character Development

In any work of literature, a writer uses the tools of character development, or **characterization,** to show what characters are like. There are two general approaches available to a writer: direct and indirect characterization.

In **direct characterization,** a writer simply tells the audience about a character. In dramatic works, direct characterization may appear in stage directions. Alternatively, the chorus, a narrator, or another character might tell the audience what a character is like. For example, in Shakespeare's *The Tragedy of Julius Caesar,* Caesar describes the suspicious character of Cassius:

*He is a great observer, and he looks*
*Quite through the deeds of men.*

In **indirect characterization,** the writer shows the audience what a character is like in any of the following ways:

- Descriptions of a character's physical appearance

- The character's own words

- The character's actions and behavior

- Other characters' reactions to the character

An actor brings a character to life on the stage or in a movie by using his or her voice, facial expressions, gestures, and body language, as well as the pitch and phrasing of his or her speech. Costumes and sets then help to emphasize elements of a character's personality. However, when you read a drama, you must use textual clues to understand characters' motivations, feelings, actions, and thoughts.

**Clues to Characterization When Reading Drama** Playwrights help readers understand complex characters by using dialogue, stage directions, punctuation, and word choice to show emotions, relationships, and differences in characters' status, education, and environment. As you read drama, look for these clues to complex characters.

---

**Examples: Characterization in Drama**

**Punctuation Showing Emotion:** That's unbelievable! You mean—the bank will give us the loan?

**Stage Directions Showing Attitude:** *[Stanley runs to Anna, arms outstretched.]*

**Dialogue Suggesting Social Class:** Really, Madam. I don't see why we can't just enjoy our tea!

**Word Choice Showing Relationships:** You're fantastic, sweet pea! You rustled up my favorite meal!

---

**Dramatic Speeches** The different types of dramatic speeches, described on page 781, also provide critical clues to characters' motivations and actions. For example, in a monologue or soliloquy, a character can explain what he or she thinks and feels. The audience learns about the character's conflicts and even his or her secrets. Such speeches help propel the plot because they explain why characters do what they do. Often, these types of speeches also express ideas that are key to the play's theme.

**Characters and Theme** There are many ways in which characters provide clues to a play's theme. To determine and analyze the theme of a drama, pay attention to characters' words, motivations, actions, and reactions. Ask yourself questions such as the following:

- How do the characters respond to conflicts?

- What are their reasons for responding as they do?

- What change or growth do characters undergo as a result of their experiences?

- What central ideas are emphasized throughout the drama through the words and actions of the characters?

- What insights about life or the human condition do these ideas convey?

# Close Read: Character, Plot, and Theme

Complex characters advance the plot and develop the theme in drama.

Audiences have been entertained by dramatic works for thousands of years. However, powerful dramas offer more than just entertainment; they provide thematic insights into life and human nature. When you read or watch drama, look for relationships among the characters and events to arrive at your interpretation of a play's deeper meaning. The questions shown below can help you find thematic connections among the characters and events of a play.

## Clues to Analyzing Character, Plot, and Theme in Drama

### Characters
- Who is the protagonist? What qualities make this character special or important?
- Who is the antagonist? How is he or she similar to or different from the protagonist?
- What do characters want? What do they do to achieve their goals?
- Are all characters round and dynamic, or are some characters flat or static?

### Characterization
- Do you find any examples of direct characterization? If so, what do they tell you about characters?
- Do you notice examples of indirect characterization, such as descriptions of characters' appearance; characters' actions; characters' statements; other characters' words and reactions?
- What do details of indirect characterization tell you about characters' feelings, thoughts, motivations, behaviors, and actions?

### Actions and Events
- What do characters do?
- How do characters' actions cause other events?
- How do characters react to events or others' actions?

### Stage Directions
- Does the playwright offer direct statements about the setting, characters, or conflicts?
- Does the playwright include explanatory details about how characters speak, move, or feel?
- Do stage directions suggest characters' emotions through specific word choices or punctuation?

### Conflicts
- What is the main conflict?
- Are there any other conflicts?
- Are the conflicts primarily external or internal?
- How do different characters react to the conflicts?
- What bigger ideas do these conflicts suggest?

### Dialogue and Dramatic Speeches
- What do the characters say to each other? What do they hide from each other?
- What do characters' word choices tell you about them?
- Do characters share information with the audience but not with one another? If so, what do you learn about them?

# Model

**About the Text** *The Glass Menagerie* helped open the door to fame and fortune for its playwright, Tennessee Williams. The drama, which was first produced in Chicago in 1944, tells the story of the struggling Wingfield family. Years earlier, the family was abandoned by the father. The mother, Amanda, is now a desperate, fading Southern belle. Her son, Tom, wants to be a poet instead of an ambitious businessman who could support the family. Amanda's daughter, Laura, is so painfully shy she can barely leave the house and spends her time arranging her collection of glass animals.

In the following scene, Tom and Amanda discuss the friend from work whom Tom has invited for dinner.

---

### from *The Glass Menagerie* by Tennessee Williams

**Tom:** What are you doing?

**Amanda:** I'm brushing that cowlick down! *[She attacks his hair with the brush.]* What is this young man's position at the warehouse?

**Tom:** *[submitting grimly to the brush and the interrogation]:* This young man's position is that of a shipping clerk, Mother.

**Amanda:** Sounds to me like a fairly responsible job, the sort of a job *you* would be in if you just had more *get-up.* What is his salary? Have you any idea?

**Tom:** I would judge it to be approximately eighty-five dollars a month.

**Amanda:** Well—not princely, but—

**Tom:** Twenty more than I make.

**Amanda:** Yes, how well I know! But for a family man, eighty-five dollars a month is not much more than you can just get by on. . . .

**Tom:** Yes, but Mr. O'Connor is not a family man.

**Amanda:** He might be mightn't he? Some time in the future?

**Tom:** I see. Plans and provisions.

---

**Stage Directions** The word *attack* provides a clue to Amanda's feelings of anger toward Tom. The word *grimly* suggests Tom's response to his mother.

**Dialogue** Amanda reveals the source of her irritation—she believes her son lacks ambition. The quick pace of the dialogue suggests that Amanda and Tom have discussed this topic many times before.

© **EXEMPLAR TEXT**

## Model continued

**Conflict** Amanda fears for her family. Tom longs to pursue his own life. The conflict between Amanda and Tom drives both this scene and the events of the play as a whole.

**Characterization** Amanda's memories of her girlhood are romantic and idealized. Tom's understanding of her "tragic mistake" shows his sense of painful truths she chooses to ignore.

**AMANDA:** You are the only young man that I know of who ignores the fact that the future becomes the present, the present the past, and the past turns into everlasting regret if you don't plan for it!

**TOM:** I will think that over and see what I can make of it.

**AMANDA:** Don't be supercilious with your mother! Tell me some more about this—what do you call him?

**TOM:** James D. O'Connor. The D. is for Delaney.

**AMANDA:** Irish on *both* sides! *Gracious!* And doesn't drink?

**TOM:** Shall I call him up and ask him right this minute?

**AMANDA:** The only way to find out about those things is to make discreet inquiries at the proper moment. When I was a girl in Blue Mountain and it was suspected that a young man drank, the girl whose attentions he had been receiving, if any girl *was,* would sometimes speak to the minister of his church, or rather her father would if her father was living, and sort of feel him out on the young man's character. That is the way such things are discreetly handled to keep a young woman from making a tragic mistake!

**TOM:** Then how did you happen to make a tragic mistake?

**AMANDA:** That innocent look of your father's had everyone fooled! He *smiled*— the world was *enchanted!* No girl can do worse than put herself at the mercy of a handsome appearance! I hope that Mr. O'Connor is not too good-looking.

# Independent Practice

**About the Text** Gary Blackwood's novel *The Shakespeare Stealer,* which he adapted into this play, is set in England in 1601, during the period when playwright William Shakespeare was writing his most famous works. In this opening scene from the play, Widge, an orphan who knows a method for writing quickly, is given a task that will lead him into Shakespeare's world.

---

## from *The Shakespeare Stealer* by Gary Blackwood

### Prologue

**SANDER.** I bid you welcome. For an hour or so

I ask you to imagine, if you will,
That this poor stage is not a stage at all
But England, some four hundred years ago.
That the actors who—I hope—will soon appear
Are something more than they appear to be,
That they are not mere shadows on a stage
But men and women of another age.

### Act I

*At the rear of the playing area is a shallow, two-story set with a narrow flight of steps leading to the upper story. In the center of the upper story is a single wide doorway draped with a curtain. The lower story has two smaller openings, one at Left and one at Right, also covered by curtains. At various times, this set will represent DR. TIMOTHY BRIGHT's apothecary, with WIDGE's living quarters upstairs; SIMON BASS's house; and the backstage area at the Globe Theatre. At Lights Up, it is Dr. BRIGHT's apothecary in Berwick-in-Elmet, Yorkshire, c. 1601. A table at Center contains glass and earthenware jars and beakers. One of the containers bubbles over a pot filled with burning pitch. WIDGE sits on a stool at the table, copying something from a small bound notebook onto loose sheets of paper, using a plumbago pencil—a stick of graphite wrapped in paper, similar to a grease pencil or charcoal pencil. WIDGE is a slight boy of fourteen with a "pudding basin," or bowl, haircut. He wears a working-class tunic. All is quiet and peaceful for a long moment. Then the audience is startled by the entrance of DR. TIMOTHY BRIGHT, a florid, overweight man in his forties or fifties, who is slightly deaf. He strides on brandishing a walking stick, and roaring—but he is nearly as comical as he is menacing.*

---

**Dramatic Speeches**
How does Sander's speech emphasize the artificiality of a play? What deeper meanings might this suggest?

**Stage Directions**
What do you learn about Widge in these stage directions?

**Characterization**
In what ways is the description of Bright's entrance an example of both direct and indirect characterization?

## Practice continued

**Dialogue** What do Bright's word choices and actions tell you about him?

**Actions and Events** What has Widge been accused of doing? Why do you think this information is included in the first scene of the play?

**BRIGHT.** You! . . . clod-pated drivel! *(WIDGE reacts, knocking a beaker to the floor, where it shatters, enraging BRIGHT even more)* You . . . halfwitted hoddypeak! Do you know what you've done?!

**WIDGE.** *(Puts the table between himself and BRIGHT)* I—I didn't mean to! I'll clean it up at once!

**BRIGHT.** Not *that,* you simpleton! This! *(He waves a paper about)* It's from the bishop's secretary. I've been accused of stealing sermons from my fellow rectors! How in heaven's name did the bishop get wind of this? Have you let a hint drop to anyone of what you were up to? Anyone at all?

**WIDGE.** Nay, I never! So help me God and halidom!

**BRIGHT.** Has anyone shown any signs of suspecting you?

**WIDGE.** Nay, no one.

**BRIGHT.** You're lying. No, don't bother to deny it. I've the proof here. The rector at Leeds caught you red-handed. Isn't that so? Isn't that so?

**WIDGE.** *(murmurs)* Aye.

**BRIGHT.** What's that? Speak up, boy!

**WIDGE.** Aye! It was a fortnight ago. 'A spotted me scribbling away, and afore I could make me escape, 'a collared me and snatched away me table-book!

**BRIGHT.** Why did you not tell me this sooner?

**WIDGE.** I was afeared. I kenned you'd be angry.

**BRIGHT.** You were right. But . . . if he took away your transcription of his sermon, then . . . then whose sermon was it that I . . . *(he doesn't want to say "stole")* . . . used as my model last Sunday?

**WIDGE.** Well . . . I—I wrote it all out as best I could remember . . .

**BRIGHT.** *You?* I delivered a sermon composed by my idle-headed apprentice? You deceitful little whelp! When will you learn not to lie to me? Well, by St. Pintle, I'll teach you right from wrong! Come here! *(WIDGE dodges the man's grasp, circling the table, but then he slips on the contents of the broken beaker,*

*and is caught. BRIGHT raises the stick as if to strike; WIDGE cowers and flinches. But then BRIGHT tosses him aside and, puffing with the exertion, plops down on the stool)* Ahh, what's the use of it? If I haven't beaten some sense into you by now, I never will. *(shakes his head)* When I think of all I've done for you, all the years I've invested in you. When I took you in five years ago—

**WIDGE:** Seven.

**BRIGHT.** Eh? What's that?

**WIDGE.** It's been seven years, sir.

**BRIGHT.** That's beside the point. When I took you in, you were a feckless illiterate orphan with no prospects whatever in the world. I taught you to read and cipher, taught you about medicine, even taught you my system of swift writing, and this is what I get in return? *(waves the paper)* If someone were to offer it, I'd sell your services for a farthing; it's far more than you're worth. Yes, and I expect you'd jump at the chance to change masters, wouldn't you? Eh? *(The way WIDGE hangs his head makes it clear that he would)* Well, all I can say is, be careful what you wish for, boy. There are far worse places than this, believe me, and far worse masters than me.

**WIDGE.** *(aside)* Aye, the Devil, for one.

**BRIGHT.** What's that?

**WIDGE.** Nothing. *(He sets about cleaning up the broken beaker, while BRIGHT checks his boiling potion. The silence is broken by the sound of an iron door knocker pounding O.S. Right)*

**BRIGHT.** Yes, yes, coming. Bloody patients. Why can't they be sick in the daytime? *(He crosses to Left, reaches O.S. to open a door, then backs up as FALCONER enters, a tall figure in a hooded cloak, looking as grim as Death. Beneath the cloak he carries a rapier. We seldom see his face, but when he does reveal a glimpse of it, we see that he has a bushy, dark beard and a hooked nose. A nasty scar disfigures one side of his face)* G-good evening, sir. How may I serve you?

**FALCONER.** *(seems to reach for his rapier, but instead takes a leatherbound book from beneath his cloak. In a deep, almost spectral voice)* This is yours, is it not?

---

**Conflict** What do these stage directions and dialogue add to your understanding of Dr. Bright and Widge? How does this interaction reveal at least one of the play's conflicts?

**Dramatic Speeches** Why does Widge speak this line in confidence to the audience?

**Characterization** How is this passage about Falconer an example of indirect characterization? What does it tell you about Falconer's character?

**Practice continued**

**BRIGHT.** *(moves hesitantly closer to the man)* Why, yes. Yes, it is. It's a copy of my book on charactery.

**FALCONER.** Does it work?

**BRIGHT.** I beg your pardon?

**FALCONER.** Your system of charactery. Does it work?

**BRIGHT.** Of course it works. Using my system of swift writing, one may without effort transcribe the written or the spoken word—

**FALCONER.** How long does it take?

**BRIGHT.** As I was about to say, one may set down speech as rapidly as it is spoken—

**FALCONER.** *(impatient)* Yes, yes, but how long to learn it?

**BRIGHT.** Well, that depends upon the aptitude of the—

**FALCONER.** How *long*?

**BRIGHT.** *(nervously, stretching the truth)* Oh, two months, perhaps three. Well, let's say four. Five, at the outside.

**FALCONER.** *(tosses the book rather contemptuously onto the table)* To how many have you taught this system of yours?

**BRIGHT.** Let me see . . . There's my apprentice, here, and then . . .

**FALCONER.** How many?

**BRIGHT.** Well . . . one, actually.

**FALCONER.** And how proficient is he?

**BRIGHT.** Oh, quite proficient. Extremely. *(WIDGE is surprised to hear this)*

**FALCONER.** Show me.

**BRIGHT.** *(to WIDGE)* Are you deaf, boy? The gentleman wishes a demonstration of your skill.

**WIDGE.** *(picks up notebook and pencil)* What must I write?

**FALCONER.** Write this: "I hereby convey to the bearer of this paper the services of my former apprentice—"

**Dialogue** Why is Widge surprised at Bright's words? What does his reaction tell you about his relationship with Bright?

**WIDGE.** Go on. I've kept up wi' you.

**FALCONER.** Your name.

**WIDGE.** Pardon?

**FALCONER.** What is your *name*?

**BRIGHT.** Widge. It's Widge. *(laughs as if to show that he realizes how odd it sounds)*

**FALCONER.** "—my former apprentice, Widge, in consideration of which I have accepted the amount of ten pounds sterling."

**BRIGHT.** *(staggered)* Ten p—?!

**WIDGE.** Is that all, then?

**FALCONER.** Let me see it. *(WIDGE hands him the notebook. Skeptical)* You've copied down every word?

**WIDGE.** Aye.

**FALCONER.** Read it back.

**WIDGE.** *(takes notebook)* "I hereby convey to the bearer of this paper the services of my former apprentice, Widge, in consideration—" *(the meaning of the words finally sinks in)* Do you—does this mean—?

**FALCONER.** Copy it out, now, in a normal hand.

**BRIGHT.** *(when WIDGE hesitates)* Go on. Do as he says! *(While WIDGE copies it out, FALCONER takes out a purse and counts out ten sovereigns onto the table, with BRIGHT watching greedily)*

**FALCONER.** If there's anything you want to take along, you'd best fetch it now, boy. I'll be outside. *(to BRIGHT)* Where can I water my horse?

**BRIGHT.** On the north side of the house, there's a trough. *(to WIDGE)* Go on, lad. *(through the following WIDGE goes upstairs, collects his meager belongings, including a leather wallet on a strap. To FALCONER)* I hope you'll keep a close eye on the boy. *(The concern this implies is belied by BRIGHT's next line)* He can be sluggish if you don't stir him from time to time with a stick. *(FALCONER exits)* Move your bones, boy, before he changes his mind. *(WIDGE descends the stairs reluctantly)*

**Dialogue** What does Widge's noticeably different way of speaking tell you about his character? How does his speech distinguish him from Bright and Falconer?

**Actions and Events** How does this demonstration of Widge's writing advance the plot? What is the importance of his writing ability?

**Characterization**
Why does Widge ask this question? What does the request reveal about his character?

**Stage Directions**
What do the stage directions suggest about Falconer's and Widge's journey up to this point? What do they suggest about their current situation?

**Conflict** How does Falconer react to the thief's challenge? What does his reaction show about his character?

**WIDGE.** Must I go with him, then?

**BRIGHT.** *(busy fondling the sovereigns)* Eh? Of course you must. He's paid for you, and far more handsomely than I would have dreamed.

**WIDGE.** Will you not bid me farewell, at least, sir?

**BRIGHT.** *(perfunctorily)* Of course, of course. Fair 'chieve you, boy, fair 'chieve you.

**Transition**

*(FALCONER enters at Down Right, looking about warily, trailed by WIDGE, who is rubbing his backside)*

**WIDGE.** Gog's blood, I'm glad to be off that horse.

**FALCONER.** It won't be for long. Here. *(Hands WIDGE a journey cake, nibbles at one himself, still looking about alertly. They pass a flask of something back and forth)*

**WIDGE.** When will we be at our destination?

**FALCONER.** When we get there.

**WIDGE.** These woods are much more . . . wild than around Berwick, and more dense. It feels almost as though they're closing in on us. *(shivers)*

**FALCONER.** Stop your wagging tongue. You'll have every cutpurse within a league down upon us.

**WIDGE.** Cutpurse? *(looks about even more fearfully)* You mean . . . there are thieves in these woods? *(realizes he's still talking)* Sorry.

*(Horse whinnies O.S. Right. FALCONER reacts, abruptly puts away the flask and loosens his rapier in its sheath, looking about and listening intently. THREE THIEVES enter at Left, one armed with a pistol, two with swords)*

**THIEF #1.** Don't move, if you value your life.

**FALCONER.** *(unexpectedly amiable)* God rest you, gentlemen.

**THIEF #1.** God, is it? Don't tell me you're a parson.

**FALCONER.** No, no. Far from it.

**THIEF #1.** Good. I don't like doing business with parsons. They're too parsimonious. *(Laughs)* All right, let's have it, then.

**FALCONER.** Have what?

**THIEF #1.** *(Laughs again)* Have what, 'a says! Have what? Why, have a pot of ale wi' us, of course. *(More soberly)* Come now, enough pleasantries. Let's have your purse, man.

**FALCONER.** *(Pulls out his hefty purse. Still amiable)* Ah. Forgive me for not taking your meaning.

**THIEF #1.** Oh, aye, an you forgive *me* for taking your purse.

*(FALCONER steps to the man, who holds out a hand for the purse. Instead of handing it over, FALCONER swings it swiftly upward, catching THIEF #1 alongside the head. The man cries out, crumples to the ground; his pistol goes off wildly. The other thieves spring forward. FALCONER draws his rapier, parries an ineffectual blow, kicks the man in the groin. WIDGE picks up a rock, but has no chance to use it. FALCONER grasps the third man's blade in his cloak-wrapped hand, yanks it away, and slices the man's ribs with his own sword. With the thieves lying about groaning, FALCONER lifts his purse with the point of his sword, flips it in the air, catches it, then shakes a single coin from it and throws it at the men's feet)*

**FALCONER.** If this is a toll road, you might simply have tolled me.

**THIEF #1.** *(laughs, then groans in pain)* Would that you had been a parson after all.

**FALCONER.** *(to WIDGE)* Come. *(starts Off Right)*

**WIDGE.** What you did back there—I've never seen the like of it.

**FALCONER.** Yes, well, you haven't seen much, have you?

## Transition

*(A bed has been brought on upstairs, and a writing desk and two chairs downstairs. FALCONER and WIDGE enter at Right. WIDGE is walking stiffly, wincing)*

**WIDGE.** Are we in London, then?

**FALCONER.** *(scoffing)* Hardly. This is Leicester.

*(LIBBY, a sympathetic, plain woman in a maid's garb, emerges from one of the downstairs doorways)*

**LIBBY.** Welcome back, sir.

---

**Actions and Events**
What does the action described here show about Falconer? How does this action affect Widge?

**Character** What new character is introduced in this scene? Why might it be important that she is described as "sympathetic"?

**Practice continued**

**FALCONER.** The boy will be staying the night. Show him to the garret. *(Exits upstage)*

**LIBBY.** Yes, sir. *(looking WIDGE over)* Where you from, then?

**WIDGE.** Berwick-in-Elmet.

**LIBBY.** Where's *that*?

**WIDGE.** Up Yorkshire way. Near Leeds.

**LIBBY.** I see. Well, come. We'd best get you to your room. *(Leads him up the steps)* I'll bring you some food up in a bit. Here you are. It's not much.

**WIDGE.** More than I'm used to. Mind you, it could be a pit of snakes for all I care, I'm that exhausted. *(sinks down on the bed)* You didn't seem surprised at all, that 'a came back wi' me in tow.

**LIBBY.** Nothing the master does surprises me. Have a good rest.

### Transition

*(WIDGE wakes up, rubs eyes, looks around at the unfamiliar surroundings then hobbles downstairs. LIBBY is at the bottom of the steps)*

**LIBBY.** I was just coming to wake you. The master said to bring you to him as soon as you were up. I don't think he expected you to sleep so late. *(They cross to where SIMON BASS sits at the writing desk. He is played by the same actor who plays FALCONER, minus the hooded cloak, the curly black wig, the hooked nose, the swarthy skin, the beard, the scar, and the high boots that make him several inches taller. BASS is much more approachable and genial, but a prickliness lurks beneath the surface)*

**WIDGE.** Will 'a be cross wi' me, do you wis?

**LIBBY.** I can't say. He's a queer one, the master is. *(sotto voce)* Not to tell him I said so, now. *(Leaning into desk area)* I've brought the boy, sir.

**BASS.** *(without turning; we still assume it's FALCONER sitting there)* Come in, Widge. *(WIDGE enters the "room," clearly awed by the furnishings)* Sit down.

**WIDGE.** Eh? Oh. *(sits)* Sorry. It's just that I've never seen such a grand room, with so many books, not even at Squire Cheyney's.

**BASS.** Wait until you see the houses in London. *(He turns, rises. We and WIDGE get our first good look at him. WIDGE is obviously bewildered)*

**Dialogue** What does Libby's line reveal about Falconer? What does it show about her relationship with him?

**Stage Directions** What critical information about Bass and Falconer do you learn from these stage directions?

**Characterization** How does Widge's reaction to the setting show his inexperience and reveal important information about Bass?

**WIDGE.** Who—who are you?

**BASS.** My name is Simon Bass. I'm your new master.

**WIDGE.** But—but I thought—

**BASS.** You thought the one who brought you here was to be your master.

**WIDGE.** Aye.

**BASS.** *(shrugs)* Falconer is not the most communicative of men, I warrant, nor the most genial. But he is reliable and effective. I could not go to Yorkshire myself . . . for various reasons. He got you here safe and sound, it appears.

**WIDGE.** *(squirming on his sore rear end)* Well, *safe,* at any rate.

**BASS.** Let's get down to business. You'll want to know what's expected of you.

**WIDGE.** Aye.

**BASS.** Very well. The first thing I expect is for you to say "yes," rather than "*aye.*" I'd just as soon you did not sound like a complete rustic. Understood?

**WIDGE.** Aye—I mean, yes.

**BASS.** Excellent. Now, when you go to London—

**WIDGE.** London?

**BASS.** Yes. It's a large city to the south.

**WIDGE.** I ken that, but—

**BASS.** Let me finish, then ask questions. You will be attending a play called *The Tragedy of Hamlet, Prince of Denmark.* You will copy down the play, every word of it, in Dr. Bright's charactery, and then you will deliver it to me. *(WIDGE looks uncomfortable)* Do you have some objection to that?

**WIDGE.** Nay, not especially. It's only words, after all. It's just that— Well, when a wight back home caught me copying his sermons, 'a got very upset wi' me.

**BASS.** Then you'll have to make certain you don't get caught, won't you? You will use a small tablebook, easily concealed . . . *(rummages through his desk)* You see how easily it's concealed? Even I can't find it. Ah, here it is. *(hands it to WIDGE)* Keep it in your wallet. You have a plumbago pencil?

**Dialogue** What do Bass's words indicate about his attitude toward Widge? What might this attitude mean for their relationship?

**Practice continued**

**Character** Is Bass a round, or complex, character? Is WIdge a round character? Explain your answers.

WIDGE. Ay—Yes. An I might ask—for what purpose am I to do this?

BASS. Does it matter?

WIDGE. Nay; I was only curious. The only plays I've ever seen are the ones the church does at Easter and Yuletide, and those certainly didn't seem worth stealing.

BASS. *(being prickly now)* I would prefer it if you did not use that term. I am not a thief. I am a man of business, and one of my more profitable ventures is a company of players. They are not so successful as the Lord Chamberlain's Men or the Admiral's Men, of course, but they draw a sizable audience here in the Midlands. If we could stage a current work, by a well-known poet, we could double our profits. Now, sooner or later someone will pry this *Tragedy of Hamlet* from the grasp of its author, Mr. Shakespeare, just as they have his earlier plays. I would like that someone to be me. If I wait for others to do it, they will do a botched job, cobbled together from various sources, none of them very reliable. Mr. Shakespeare deserves better. He is a poet of quality, perhaps of genius, and if his work is to be borrowed, it should be done properly. That is your mission. If you fulfill it satisfactorily, the reward will be considerable.

WIDGE. And . . . what an I do not?

BASS. Falconer will make certain that you do.

WIDGE. Oh. I didn't ken that 'a would go wi' me.

BASS. Did you suppose I would send you off to London on your own? I might as well send you to Guiana. Go and rest now, or soak your haunches, or whatever you will. You'll be leaving for London early in the morning. *(He exits. WIDGE shuffles downstage as LIBBY enters at Left)*

**Conflict** What is Widge's new conflict?

**Theme** Considering Widge's inexperience and his treatment thus far by his masters, what might be one theme of this play?

1. **Key Ideas and Details (a)** Which details in the stage directions show that the play is set in Shakespearean England? **(b) Identify:** Which lines of dialogue establish the play's setting?

2. **Key Ideas and Details (a)** What does the opening scene tell you about Widge, Dr. Bright, and their relationship? **(b) Infer:** Which details indicate that Widge is a complex character?

3. **Craft and Structure  Generalize:** Based on this excerpt, how do you think this play differs from Blackwood's novel?

4. **Craft and Structure (a)** What is the climax of this excerpt? **(b) Analyze:** How do plot events and character development lead up to this climax?

5. **Integration of Knowledge and Ideas (a) Speculate:** The excerpt ends with uncertainty about whether Widge will comply with Falconer's request. What do you think Widge will do? **(b) Infer:** What theme is suggested by Widge's conflict? Use details from the text to support your answer.

6. **Integration of Knowledge and Ideas Compare and Contrast:** Do you see any similarities between Bass's plan and modern-day practices involving music or movies? Explain.

7. **Integration of Knowledge and Ideas (a)** Use a chart like the one shown to explore how characters use props to reveal their personalities. **(b)** In the first column, list props that are used by Dr. Bright, Widge, and Falconer. In the second column, record how the characters use each prop. In the third column, describe what their actions show about their personalities.

| Prop | How It Is Used | What It Shows |
|---|---|---|
|  |  |  |

**(c) Collaborate:** Compare charts with a partner. How do the other students' details add to your understanding of the characters?

# Preparing to Read
# *The Tragedy of Romeo and Juliet*

*The works of William Shakespeare are among the greatest achievements of the Renaissance.*

## Historical Background: Elizabethan England

**The Rebirth of Learning** Sometime around the year 1350, at the end of the Middle Ages, Italian city-states, such as Venice and Genoa, began to trade extensively with the East. With trade came more knowledge and growing curiosity about the world. Soon, Italy was leading the way in a flowering of European learning known as the Renaissance (**ren´ ə sans´**). Commerce, science, and the arts blossomed as people shifted their focus to the interests and pursuits of human life here on earth. The astronomers Copernicus and Galileo questioned long-held beliefs to prove that the world was round and that it circled the sun, not vice versa. Navigators, including Christopher Columbus and Ferdinand Magellan, braved the seas in tiny boats to explore new lands and seek new trade routes. Religious thinkers, such as Martin Luther and John Calvin, challenged the authority of the Roman Catholic Church and spurred the Protestant Reformation. Artists, including Michelangelo and Leonardo da Vinci, painted and sculpted lifelike human beings. Writers, such as Miguel de Cervantes and William Shakespeare, wrote insightfully about complex human personalities in fiction and drama.

**The Renaissance in England** The Renaissance was slow to come to England. The delay was caused mainly by civil war between two great families, or houses, claiming the English throne—the House of York and the House of Lancaster. The conflict ended in 1485 when Henry Tudor of the House of Lancaster took the throne as King Henry VII. After a successful rule in which English commerce expanded, he was succeeded by his son Henry VIII, whose reign was filled with turmoil. Henry sought a divorce from the Spanish princess Catherine of Aragon so that he could remarry and possibly have a son. He was convinced that only a male would be strong enough to hold the throne. When the Pope refused to grant the divorce, Henry renounced the Roman Catholic Church and made England a Protestant nation. Ironically, his remarriage, to a woman named Anne Boleyn, produced not a son but a daughter, Elizabeth. Even more ironically, when Elizabeth took the throne, she proved to be one of the strongest monarchs that England has ever known.

▲ Elizabeth ruled from 1558 to 1603, but her reign was so successful that the entire Renaissance in England is often called the Elizabethan Age.

The symbol of the House of York was a white rose, while the symbol of the House of Lancaster was a red rose. For that reason, the civil wars fought between the two houses were called the Wars of the Roses. Shakespeare wrote several plays about English monarchs involved in these conflicts.

**The Elizabethan World** The reign of Elizabeth I is often seen as a golden age in English history. Treading a moderate and frugal path, Elizabeth brought economic and political stability to the nation, thus allowing commerce and culture to thrive. Advances in mapmaking helped English explorers sail the Old World and claim lands in the New. Practical inventions improved transportation at home. Craft workers created lovely wares for the homes of the wealthy. Musicians composed fine works for the royal court, and literature thrived, peaking with the plays of William Shakespeare.

London became a bustling capital on the busy River Thames (**temz**), where ships from all over the world sailed into port. The city attracted newcomers from the countryside and immigrants from foreign lands. Streets were narrow, dirty, and crowded, but they were also lined with shops where vendors sold merchandise from near and far. English women enjoyed more freedoms than did women elsewhere in Europe, and the class system was more fluid as well. To be sure, those of different ranks led very different lives. Yet even the lowborn were able to attend one of the city's most popular new amusements: the theater.

▼ In 1796, more than 200 years after the defeat of the Spanish Armada, English artist Philippe-Jacques de Loutherbourg painted this image of those dramatic events.

### Elizabeth I and the Spanish Armada

In 1588, King Phillip of Spain sent an armada, or fleet of military ships, to invade England. At the time, Spain was the most powerful nation on earth. Nevertheless, the English soundly defeated the invading forces. The victory cemented Elizabeth's popularity with her people. Prior to the battle, the Queen visited her troops to inspire them to fight. Here is a portion of the speech she delivered:

> . . . And therefore I am come amongst you at this time, not as for my recreation or sport, but being resolved, in the midst and heat of the battle, to live or die amongst you all; to lay down, for my God, and for my kingdom, and for my people, my honor and my blood, even the dust. I know I have but the body of a weak and feeble woman; but I have the heart of a king, and of a king of England too. . . .

# Theater in Elizabethan England

*Elizabethan audiences included all levels of society, from the "groundlings," who paid a penny entrance fee, to the nobility.*

During the Middle Ages, simple religious plays were performed at inns, in castle halls, and on large wagons at pageants. In early Elizabethan times, acting companies still traveled the countryside to perform their plays. However, the best companies acquired noble patrons, or sponsors, who then invited the troupes to perform in their homes. At the same time, Elizabethan dramatists began to use the tragedies and comedies of ancient Greece and Rome as models for their plays. By the end of the sixteenth century, many talented playwrights had emerged, including Christopher Marlowe, Ben Jonson, and, of course, William Shakespeare.

**England's First Theater** England's first successful public theater opened in 1576. Known simply as the Theatre, it was built by an actor named James Burbage. Since officials had banned the performance of plays in London, Burbage built his theater in an area called Shoreditch, just outside the London city walls. Some of Shakespeare's earliest plays were first performed here, including *The Tragedy of Romeo and Juliet*, which probably starred James Burbage's son, Richard, as Romeo.

When the lease on the Theatre expired, Richard Burbage, in charge of the company after his father died, decided to move the company to Southwark (suth´ərk), just across the River Thames from London proper. The Shoreditch landlord had been causing problems, and Southwark was emerging as a popular theater district. Using timbers from the old theater building, Burbage had a new theater built, bigger and better than the one before. It opened in 1599 and was called the Globe. Under that name it would become the most famous theater in the history of the English stage, for many more of Shakespeare's plays were first performed there.

> Audience members ate and drank while they watched the plays and apparently made a lot of noise. In 1990, archaeologists found the remains of the foundation of the original Globe Theatre. They also found the discarded shells of the many hazelnuts audiences munched on while watching performances.

> During Shakespeare's day, acting companies were entirely male. Women did not perform because it was considered improper. The roles of women were usually played by boys of about eleven or twelve—that is, before their voices changed.

◄ This photograph of the reconstructed Globe Theatre was made with a special lens. It shows the pit, where the groundlings stood to watch the show, as well as the sheltered galleries.

**Theater Layout** No floor plans of the Theatre or the Globe survive, but people's descriptions and sketches of similar buildings suggest what they were like. They were either round or octagonal, with a central stage open to the sky. This stage stretched out into an area called the pit, where theatergoers called groundlings paid just a penny to stand and watch the play. The enclosure surrounding this open area consisted of two or three galleries, or tiers. The galleries accommodated audience members who paid more to watch the play while under shelter from the elements, and with some distance from the groundlings. The galleries probably also included a few elegant box seats where members of the nobility could both watch the play and be seen by the masses.

**Staging the Play** The enclosure directly behind the stage was used not for seating but for staging the play. Actors entered and left the stage from doors at stage level. The stage also had a trap door through which mysterious characters, such as ghosts or witches, could disappear suddenly. Some space above the backstage area was used for storage or dressing rooms. The first gallery, however, was visible to the audience and used as a second stage. It would have been on a second stage like this that the famous balcony scene in *Romeo and Juliet* was performed.

These open-air theaters did not use artificial light. Instead, performances took place in the afternoon, when it was still light outside. There was also no scenery in the theaters of Shakespeare's day. Instead, the setting for each scene was communicated through dialogue. With no need for set changes, scenes could follow one another in rapid succession. Special effects were simple—smoke might billow at the disappearance of a ghost, for example. By contrast, costumes were often elaborate. The result was a fast-paced, colorful production that lasted about two hours.

**The Blackfriars** In 1609, Shakespeare's acting company began staging plays in the Blackfriars Theatre as well as the Globe. Located in London proper, the Blackfriars was different from the earlier theaters in which Shakespeare's plays were performed. It was an indoor space with no open area for groundlings. Instead, it relied entirely on a wealthier clientele. It was also one of the first English theaters to use artificial lighting, an innovation that allowed for nighttime performances.

## The Globe Theatre

The three-story structure, open to the air, could house as many as 3,000 people in the pit and surrounding galleries.

**KEY**

1. The hut, housing machinery used to lower characters and props to the stage
2. The stage trap, often used for the entrances and exits of special characters, such as ghosts or witches
3. The stage
4. The pit, where groundlings stood to watch the show
5. The galleries

# Before You Read | The Tragedy of Romeo and Juliet, Act I

## © Drama

Build your skills and improve your comprehension of drama with this selection.

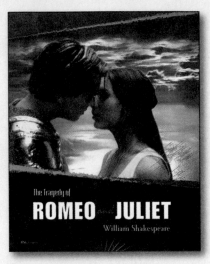

The Tragedy of
**ROMEO** and **JULIET**
William Shakespeare

Read **Romeo and Juliet** to learn about the tragedy of a passionate love torn apart by conflict.

##  Common Core State Standards

Meet these standards with **The Tragedy of Romeo and Juliet,** Act I (p. 806).

**Reading Literature**

**2.** Provide an objective summary of the text. *(Reading: Summarize)*

**3.** Analyze how complex characters develop over the course of a text. *(Literary Analysis: Spiral Review)*

**5.** Analyze how an author's choices concerning how to structure a text, order events within it, and manipulate time create such effects as mystery, tension, or surprise. *(Literary Analysis: Dialogue and Stage Directions)*

**Writing**

**1.** Write arguments to support claims in an analysis of substantive topics or texts, using valid reasoning and relevant and sufficient evidence. *(Writing: Persuasive Letter)*

**4.** Produce clear and coherent writing in which the development, organization, and style are appropriate to task, purpose, and audience. *(Writing: Editorial)*

**7.** Conduct short as well as more sustained research projects to answer a question or solve a problem. *(Research and Technology: Annotated Flowchart; Multimedia Presentation)*

**Speaking and Listening**

**1.** Initiate and participate effectively in a range of collaborative discussions.

**4.** Present information, findings, and supporting evidence clearly, concisely, and logically such that listeners can follow the line of reasoning. *(Research and Technology: Annotated Flowchart; Multimedia Presentation)*

**Language**

**1.** Demonstrate command of the conventions of standard English grammar and usage when writing or speaking. *(Conventions: Participles and Participial Phrases, Gerunds and Gerund Phrases)*

# Literary Analysis: Dialogue and Stage Directions

**Dialogue** is conversation between characters. In prose, dialogue is usually set off with quotation marks. In drama, it generally follows the name of the speaker, as in this example:

> **BENVOLIO.** My noble uncle, do you know the cause?
> **MONTAGUE.** I neither know it nor can learn of him.

Dialogue reveals the personalities and relationships of the characters and advances the action of the play. Dialogue captures the language of the time in which a play is set. As you read, note the words characters use to express themselves.

**Stage directions** are notes in a play that describe how the work should be performed, or staged. They describe scenes, lighting, sound effects, and character actions. They are usually set in italics and are sometimes set off in brackets or parentheses, as in this example:

> *Scene iii.* FRIAR LAWRENCE's cell.
> [*Enter* FRIAR LAWRENCE *alone, with a basket.*]

As you read, notice how the dialogue and stage directions work together to help you "see" and "hear" the play in your mind.

# Reading Skill: Summarize

**Summarizing** is briefly stating the main ideas in a piece of writing. Pausing to summarize as you read helps you check your comprehension before you read further. To be sure that you understand Shakespeare's language before you summarize, **use text aids**—the numbered explanations that appear with the text.

- If you are confused by a passage, check to see if there is a footnote or side note and read the corresponding explanation.

- **Reread** the passage, using the information from the note to be sure you grasp the meaning of the passage.

## Using the Strategy: Summarizing Chart

As you read, use a chart like this one to summarize each scene.

| Act I | |
|---|---|
| **Scene** | **Summary of Action** |
| | |
| | |
| | |

# William Shakespeare (1564–1616)

## SHAKESPEARE'S PLAYS AND POETRY ARE REGARDED AS THE FINEST WORKS EVER WRITTEN IN ENGLISH.

*William Shakespeare is revered as England's greatest writer. Four centuries after his death, his plays are still read and performed every single day. Who was this remarkable author of so many masterpieces? In actual fact, we know very little about him.*

**From Stratford to London** Shakespeare grew up in Stratford-upon-Avon, a busy market town on the Avon River about seventy-five miles northwest of London. Church and town records indicate that his mother, Mary Arden, was the daughter of a wealthy farmer who owned the land on which Shakespeare's grandfather lived. Shakespeare's father, John, was a prosperous merchant who also served for a time as Stratford's mayor. Shakespeare most likely went to the local grammar school, where he would have studied Latin and Greek as well as English and world history. He would eventually put all those lessons to use in plays about historical figures, such as Julius Caesar and King Henry IV.

In 1582, when he was eighteen, Shakespeare married a woman named Anne Hathaway and with her had three children, including a set of twins. The next decade of his life is shrouded in mystery, but by 1592 he had moved to London, where he gravitated to the theater. Starting off as an actor, he soon began writing plays as well. By 1594 he had become the principal playwright of the Lord Chamberlain's Men, the Burbages' acting company. Some of the early plays Shakespeare wrote at this time include the romantic comedy *The Taming of the Shrew* and the romantic tragedy *The Tragedy of Romeo and Juliet*.

Shakespeare was not just a performer and a playwright, however; he was also part owner of the theater company. This meant that he earned money in three ways—from fees for his plays, from his acting salary, and from his share of the company's profits. Those profits rose substantially after the Lord Chamberlain's Men moved to the Globe Theatre, where as many as 3,000 people might attend a single performance. It was at the Globe that many of Shakespeare's later masterpieces premiered, probably beginning with *The Tragedy of Julius Caesar* in 1599.

**The King's Players** In 1603 Queen Elizabeth I died, and her Scottish cousin took the throne as James I. Partial to the theater, James was particularly supportive of the Lord Chamberlain's Men, which had emerged as one of the two best acting companies in the land. Not only did it have a brilliant playwright in William Shakespeare, but it also had a fine actor in Richard Burbage, who starred in most of Shakespeare's plays. In 1606, flattered by the king's patronage, the company changed its name to the King's Men. It is believed that Shakespeare wrote his great Scottish play, *The Tragedy of Macbeth*, to appeal particularly to James I.

Three years later, the King's Men began performing at the Blackfriars Theatre, using the Globe only in summer months. By utilizing this indoor theater in winter, the King's Men further increased profits. The company did so well that Shakespeare was soon able to retire. In 1610, he moved back to Stratford-upon-Avon, buying one of the finest homes in town. He died of unknown causes in 1616.

# Shakespeare Says . . .

Shakespeare's impact on the English language has been enormous. Not only did he coin new words and new meanings for old words, but he also used many expressions that have become part of our everyday speech. Here are just a few examples:

| Expression and Source | Meaning |
|---|---|
| Eat out of house and home *(Henry VI, Part II)* | Eat so much that it makes the provider poor |
| For ever and a day *(The Taming of the Shrew)* | Indefinitely; with no end in sight |
| Give the devil his due *(Henry IV, Part I)* | Recognize an opponent's achievement |
| Greek to me *(Julius Caesar)* | Completely unintelligible to me |
| Green-eyed monster *(Othello)* | Jealousy |
| In a pickle *(The Tempest)* | In trouble |
| In stitches *(Twelfth Night)* | Laughing so hard it hurts |
| Lay it on with a trowel *(As You Like It)* | Flatter excessively |
| Makes your hair stand on end *(Hamlet)* | Really frightens you |
| The milk of human kindness *(Macbeth)* | Compassion |
| A plague on both your houses *(Romeo and Juliet)* | I'm fed up with both sides (in an argument) |
| Salad days *(Anthony and Cleopatra)* | Green, or naïve, youth |
| Star-crossed lovers *(Romeo and Juliet)* | Ill-fated lovers |
| Wear your heart upon your sleeve *(Othello)* | Show your love to all |
| Won't budge an inch *(The Taming of the Shrew)* | Will not give in; stands firm |

# The Tragedy of Romeo and Juliet, Act 1

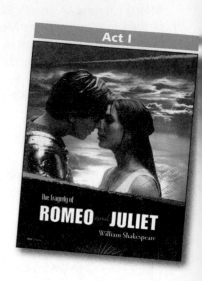

Act I

## Do our *differences* define us?

## Writing About the Big Question

In *The Tragedy of Romeo and Juliet,* two young people from families locked in a deadly feud fall in love. That difference defines their relationship and forces the plot toward tragic consequences. Use this sentence starter to develop your ideas about the Big Question.

When family **differences** stand between two people, it can be destructive because _____.

**While You Read** Look for ways in which family background influences the love between Romeo and Juliet.

## Vocabulary

Read each word and its definition. Decide whether you know the word well, know it a little bit, or do not know it at all. After you read, see how your knowledge of each word has increased.

- **pernicious** (pər nish´ əs) *adj.* causing great injury or ruin (p. 811) *The spy's activities had a* <u>pernicious</u> *effect on the top-secret project.* perniciously *adv.*

- **adversary** (ad´ vər ser´ ē) *n.* a person who opposes or fights against another (p. 811) *Standing tall and trying to look brave, Pam faced her* <u>adversary</u> *in fencing.* adverse *adj.* adversarial *adj.*

- **augmenting** (ôg ment´ iŋ) *v.* increasing; enlarging (p. 812) *With small deposits each week, our family is* <u>augmenting</u> *its savings.* augmentable *adj.* augmentation *n.*

- **grievance** (grēv´ əns) *n.* injustice; complaint (p. 813) *The board investigated the worker's* <u>grievance</u> *against his supervisor.*

- **oppression** (ə presh´ ən) *n.* feeling of being weighed down with worries or problems (p. 813) *He could not pay all of his bills, and this caused a feeling of* <u>oppression.</u> oppress *v.* oppressive *adj.*

- **transgression** (trans gresh´ ən) *n.* wrong-doing; sin (p. 813) *Stealing from the poor is a* <u>transgression</u> *against humanity.* transgress *v.* transgressor *n.*

### Word Study

The **Latin prefix** *trans-* means "across," "over," or "through."

In the play, Romeo describes his friend's sympathy for him as love's **transgression.** The word suggests that love has crossed a boundary and unfairly involved his friend.

## Background for the Play

# Star-Crossed Lovers

Written in 1594 or 1595, when Shakespeare was still a fairly young man, *The Tragedy of Romeo and Juliet* is a play about young love. The basic plot is simple: Two teenagers from feuding families fall in love and marry against their families' wishes, with tragic results. The story is set in Verona, Italy, and is based on an Italian legend that was fairly well known in England at the time.

**Shakespeare's Sources** Elizabethan writers deeply respected Italy as the birthplace of the Renaissance and often drew on Italian sources for inspiration. In 1562, an English poet named Arthur Brooke wrote *The Tragicall History of Romeus and Juliet*, a long narrative poem based on the Romeo and Juliet legend. Three years later, a prose version of the legend also appeared in England. Scholars believe, however, that Brooke's poem was Shakespeare's chief source.

That poem contains a great deal of moralizing, stressing the disobedience of the young lovers, along with fate, as the cause of their doom. Shakespeare's portrayal of the young lovers is more sympathetic, but he does stress the strong role that fate plays in their tragedy. In fact, at the very start of the play, the Chorus describes Romeo and Juliet as "star-crossed lovers," indicating that their tragic ending is written in the stars, or fated by forces beyond their control.

**The Play Through the Centuries** Of all the love stories ever written, *The Tragedy of Romeo and Juliet* may well be the most famous. Acting celebrities down through the centuries have played the leading roles—Edwin Booth and Ellen Terry in the nineteenth century, for example, and John Gielgud and Judi Dench in the twentieth. There have been dozens of film versions of the play, numerous works of art depicting its scenes, over twenty operatic versions, a famous ballet version by Prokofiev, and an equally famous musical overture by Tchaikovsky. The play is often adapted to reflect the concerns of different eras: *West Side Story*, for example, adapts the story as a musical set amid the ethnic rivalries of 1950s New York City; *Romanoff and Juliet* is a comedy of the Cold War set during the 1960s. One of the most recent popular adaptations was the 1996 film *Romeo + Juliet* starring Leonardo di Caprio and Claire Danes, which sets the play in Verona Beach, California.

### Elizabethan Language

English has changed a great deal since Shakespeare's time. Some of the words he uses are now archaic, or outdated. For instance, Shakespeare uses *anon* for "soon" and *haply* for "perhaps." He also uses outdated grammatical forms, such as the pronouns *thou, thee, thy,* and *thine* instead of *you, your,* and *yours*. In addition, Shakespeare's verbs often have archaic endings: *cometh* for "come," for example, and *dost* for "do." Word order, too, is sometimes different from modern English, especially in questions. For instance, instead of "What do you say?" Shakespeare writes, "What say you?" The numbered marginal notes that accompany the text of the play will help you with the unfamiliar language.

# The Tragedy of

# ROMEO *and* JULIET

## William Shakespeare

# Characters

**CHORUS**

**ESCALUS,** Prince of Verona

**PARIS,** a young count, kinsman to the Prince

**MONTAGUE**

**CAPULET**

**AN OLD MAN,** of the Capulet family

**ROMEO,** son to Montague

**MERCUTIO,** kinsman to the Prince and
   friend to Romeo

**BENVOLIO,** nephew to Montague and
   friend to Romeo

**TYBALT,** nephew to Lady Capulet

**FRIAR LAWRENCE,** Franciscan

**FRIAR JOHN,** Franciscan

**BALTHASAR,** servant to Romeo

**SAMPSON,** servant to Capulet

**GREGORY,** servant to Capulet

**PETER,** servant to Juliet's nurse

**ABRAM,** servant to Montague

**AN APOTHECARY**

**THREE MUSICIANS**

**AN OFFICER**

**LADY MONTAGUE,** wife to Montague

**LADY CAPULET,** wife to Capulet

**JULIET,** daughter to Capulet

**NURSE TO JULIET**

**CITIZENS OF VERONA,** Gentlemen
   and Gentlewomen of both houses,
   Maskers, Torchbearers, Pages, Guards,
   Watchmen, Servants, and Attendants

# Prologue

*Scene: Verona; Mantua*

*[Enter* CHORUS.*]*

    **CHORUS.** Two households, both alike in dignity.[1]
      In fair Verona, where we lay our scene,
    From ancient grudge break to new mutiny,[2]
      Where civil blood makes civil hands unclean.[3]
5  From forth the fatal loins of these two foes
      A pair of star-crossed[4] lovers take their life;
    Whose misadventured piteous overthrows[5]
      Doth with their death bury their parents' strife.
    The fearful passage of their death-marked love,
10     And the continuance of their parents' rage,
    Which, but[6] their children's end, naught could remove,
      Is now the two hours' traffic[7] of our stage;
    The which if you with patient ears attend,
    What here shall miss, our toil shall strive to mend.[8] *[Exit.]*

1. **dignity** high social rank.
2. **mutiny** violence.
3. **Where . . . unclean** in which the blood of citizens stains citizens' hands.
4. **star-crossed** ill-fated by the unfavorable positions of the stars.
5. **Whose . . . overthrows** whose unfortunate, sorrowful destruction.
6. **but** except.
7. **two hours' traffic** two hours' business.
8. **What . . . mend** What is not clear in this prologue we actors shall try to clarify in the course of the play.

# ACT I

**Scene i. Verona. A public place.**

*[Enter* SAMPSON *and* GREGORY, *with swords and bucklers,[1] of the house of Capulet.]*

**SAMPSON.** Gregory, on my word, we'll not carry coals.[2]

**GREGORY.** No, for then we should be colliers.[3]

**SAMPSON.** I mean, an we be in choler, we'll draw.[4]

**GREGORY.** Ay, while you live, draw your neck out of collar.[5]

5   **SAMPSON.** I strike quickly, being moved.

**GREGORY.** But thou art not quickly moved to strike.

**SAMPSON.** A dog of the house of Montague moves me.

**GREGORY.** To move is to stir, and to be valiant is to stand. Therefore, if thou art moved, thou run'st away.

10   **SAMPSON.** A dog of that house shall move me to stand. I will take the wall[6] of any man or maid of Montague's.

**GREGORY.** That shows thee a weak slave; for the weakest goes to the wall.

**SAMPSON.** 'Tis true; and therefore women, being the weaker
15   vessels, are ever thrust to the wall. Therefore I will push Montague's men from the wall and thrust his maids to the wall.

**GREGORY.** The quarrel is between our masters and us their men.

20   **SAMPSON.** Tis all one. I will show myself a tyrant. When I have fought with the men, I will be civil with the maids—I will cut off their heads.

**GREGORY.** The heads of the maids?

**SAMPSON.** Ay, the heads of the maids or their maidenheads.
25   Take it in what sense thou wilt.

**GREGORY.** They must take it in sense that feel it.

---

**Side notes:**

1. **bucklers** small shields.
2. **carry coals** endure insults.
3. **colliers** sellers of coal.
4. **an . . . draw** If we are angered, we'll draw our swords.
5. **collar** hangman's noose.

6. **take the wall** assert superiority by walking nearer the houses and therefore farther from the gutter.

**Literary Analysis
Dialogue and Stage
Directions** What does this conversation among servants reveal about the Montagues?

**SAMPSON.** Me they shall feel while I am able to stand; and 'tis known I am a pretty piece of flesh.

**GREGORY.** 'Tis well thou art not fish; if thou hadst, thou hadst
30   been Poor John. Draw thy tool![7] Here comes two of the house of Montagues.

[*Enter two other Servingmen,* ABRAM *and* BALTHASAR.]

**SAMPSON.** My naked weapon is out. Quarrel! I will back thee.

**GREGORY.** How? Turn thy back and run?

**SAMPSON.** Fear me not.

35   **GREGORY.** No, marry. I fear thee!

**SAMPSON.** Let us take the law of our sides;[8] let them begin.

**GREGORY.** I will frown as I pass by, and let them take it as they list.[9]

**SAMPSON.** Nay, as they dare. I will bite my thumb[10] at them,
40   which is disgrace to them if they bear it.

**ABRAM.** Do you bite your thumb at us, sir?

**SAMPSON.** I do bite my thumb, sir.

**ABRAM.** Do you bite your thumb at us, sir?

**SAMPSON.** [*Aside to* GREGORY] Is the law of our side if I say ay?

45   **GREGORY.** [*Aside to* SAMPSON] No.

**SAMPSON.** No, sir, I do not bite my thumb at you, sir; but I bite my thumb, sir.

**GREGORY.** Do you quarrel, sir?

**ABRAM.** Quarrel, sir? No, sir.

50   **SAMPSON.** But if you do, sir, I am for you. I serve as good a man as you.

**ABRAM.** No better.

**SAMPSON.** Well, sir.

[*Enter* BENVOLIO.]

55   **GREGORY.** [*Aside to* SAMPSON.] Say "better." Here comes one of my master's kinsmen.

**SAMPSON.** Yes, better, sir.

**ABRAM.** You lie.

---

7. **tool** weapon.

**Reading Skill**
**Summarize** How does footnote 8 help you understand Sampson's logic in line 36?

8. **take . . . sides** make sure the law is on our side.
9. **list** please.
10. **bite . . . thumb** make an insulting gesture.

**Literary Analysis**
**Dialogue and Stage Directions** Which words in the stage directions in line 44 clarify that Sampson is not speaking to Abram?

Reading Check
With which family are the quarreling servants affiliated?

11. **swashing** hard downward swordstroke.

12. **heartless hinds** cowardly servants. *Hind* also means "a female deer."

**SAMPSON.** Draw, if you be men. Gregory, remember thy swashing[11] blow. *[They fight.]*

60 **BENVOLIO.** Part, fools!
Put up your swords. You know not what you do.

*[Enter* TYBALT.*]*

**TYBALT.** What art thou drawn among these heartless hinds?[12]
Turn thee, Benvolio; look upon thy death.

**BENVOLIO.** I do but keep the peace. Put up thy sword,
65    Or manage it to part these men with me.

**TYBALT.** What, drawn, and talk of peace? I hate the word
As I hate hell, all Montagues, and thee.
Have at thee, coward! *[They fight.]*

*[Enter an* OFFICER, *and three or four* CITIZENS *with clubs or partisans.*[13]*]*

13. **partisans** spearlike weapons with broad blades.

14. **bills** weapons consisting of hook-shaped blades with long handles.

**OFFICER.** Clubs, bills,[14] and partisans! Strike! Beat them down!
70    Down with the Capulets! Down with the Montagues!

*[Enter old* CAPULET *in his gown, and his* WIFE.*]*

**CAPULET.** What noise is this? Give me my long sword, ho!

**LADY CAPULET.** A crutch, a crutch! Why call you for a sword?

**CAPULET.** My sword, I say! Old Montague is come
And flourishes his blade in spite[15] of me.

15. **spite** defiance.

*[Enter old* MONTAGUE *and his* WIFE.*]*

---

## LITERATURE IN CONTEXT

### History Connection

**Prince of Verona**
When Prince Escalus intervenes in the fight between the Capulets and the Montagues, he does so under his authority as the podesta, or "chief magistrate," of Verona. The powers and duties of the podesta combined those of a modern mayor, chief of police, and head of the local militia. Scholars believe that Shakespeare based the character of Prince Escalus on Bartolomeo della Scala, who ruled the northern Italian city of Verona during the early fourteenth century.

### Connect to the Literature

Which part of his authority is Prince Escalus exercising in this scene—mayor, police chief, or head of the army? Explain.

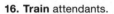

75 **MONTAGUE.** Thou villain Capulet!—Hold me not; let me go.

**LADY MONTAGUE.** Thou shalt not stir one foot to seek a foe.

[*Enter* PRINCE ESCALUS, *with his Train.*[16]]

    **PRINCE.** Rebellious subjects, enemies to peace,
        Profaners[17] of this neighbor-stainèd steel—
        Will they not hear? What, ho! You men, you beasts,
80    That quench the fire of your pernicious rage
        With purple fountains issuing from your veins!
        On pain of torture, from those bloody hands
        Throw your mistempered[18] weapons to the ground
        And hear the sentence of your moved prince.
85    Three civil brawls, bred of an airy word
        By thee, old Capulet, and Montague,
        Have thrice disturbed the quiet of our streets
        And made Verona's ancient citizens
        Cast by their grave beseeming ornaments[19]
90    To wield old partisans, in hands as old,
        Cank'red with peace, to part your cank'red hate.[20]
        If ever you disturb our streets again,
        Your lives shall pay the forfeit of the peace.
        For this time all the rest depart away.
95    You, Capulet, shall go along with me;
        And, Montague, come you this afternoon,
        To know our farther pleasure in this case,
        To old Freetown, our common judgment place.
        Once more, on pain of death, all men depart.

[*Exit all but* MONTAGUE, *his* WIFE, *and* BENVOLIO.]

100 **MONTAGUE.** Who set this ancient quarrel new abroach?[21]
        Speak, nephew, were you by when it began?

    **BENVOLIO.** Here were the servants of your adversary
        And yours, close fighting ere I did approach.
        I drew to part them. In the instant came
105    The fiery Tybalt, with his sword prepared;
        Which, as he breathed defiance to my ears,
        He swung about his head and cut the winds,
        Who, nothing hurt withal, hissed him in scorn.
        While we were interchanging thrusts and blows,
110    Came more and more, and fought on part and part,[22]
        Till the Prince came, who parted either part.

    **LADY MONTAGUE.** O, where is Romeo? Saw you him today?
        Right glad I am he was not at this fray.

---

**16. Train** attendants.
**17. Profaners** those who show disrespect or contempt.

**Vocabulary**
**pernicious** (pər nish′ əs)
*adj.* causing great injury or ruin

**18. mistempered** hardened for a wrong purpose; bad-tempered.

**19. Cast . . . ornaments** put aside their dignified and appropriate clothing.
**20. Cank'red . . . hate** rusted from lack of use, to put an end to your malignant feuding.

**Reading Skill**
**Summarize** Summarize the warning that the Prince issues to the Montagues and Capulets in this speech.

**21. Who . . . abroach?** Who reopened this old fight?

**Vocabulary**
**adversary** (ad′ vər ser′ ē)
*n.* a person who opposes or fights against another

**22. on . . . part** on one side and the other.

**Reading Check**
Who stops the brawl between the Montagues and the Capulets?

**BENVOLIO.** Madam, an hour before the worshiped sun
115     Peered forth the golden window of the East,
        A troubled mind drave me to walk abroad:
        Where, underneath the grove of sycamore
        That westward rooteth from this city side,
        So early walking did I see your son.
120     Towards him I made, but he was ware[23] of me
        And stole into the covert[24] of the wood.
        I, measuring his affections[25] by my own,
        Which then most sought where most might not be found,[26]
        Being one too many by my weary self,
125     Pursued my humor not pursuing his,[27]
        And gladly shunned who gladly fled from me.

**MONTAGUE.** Many a morning hath he there been seen,
        With tears augmenting the fresh morning's dew,
        Adding to clouds more clouds with his deep sighs;
130     But all so soon as the all-cheering sun
        Should in the farthest East begin to draw
        The shady curtains from Aurora's bed,
        Away from light steals home my heavy[28] son
        And private in his chamber pens himself,
135     Shuts up his windows, locks fair daylight out,
        And makes himself an artificial night.
        Black and portentous[29] must this humor prove
        Unless good counsel may the cause remove.

**BENVOLIO.** My noble uncle, do you know the cause?

140 **MONTAGUE.** I neither know it nor can learn of him.

**BENVOLIO.** Have you importuned[30] him by any means?

**MONTAGUE.** Both by myself and many other friends;
        But he, his own affections' counselor,
        Is to himself—I will not say how true—
145     But to himself so secret and so close,
        So far from sounding[31] and discovery,
        As is the bud bit with an envious worm
        Ere he can spread his sweet leaves to the air
        Or dedicate his beauty to the sun.
150     Could we but learn from whence his sorrows grow,
        We would as willingly give cure as know.

[*Enter* ROMEO.]

---

**23. ware** aware; wary.
**24. covert** hidden place.
**25. measuring . . . affections** judging his feelings.
**26. Which . . . found** which wanted to be where there was no one else.
**27. Pursued . . . his** followed my own mind by not following after Romeo.

**Vocabulary**
**augmenting** (ôg ment´ iŋ) *v.* increasing; enlarging

**28. heavy** sad; moody.

**29. portentous** promising bad fortune.

**30. importuned** questioned deeply.

**31. sounding** understanding.

**BENVOLIO.** See, where he comes. So please you step aside;
I'll know his grievance, or be much denied.

**MONTAGUE.** I would thou wert so happy by thy stay
155　To hear true shrift.³² Come, madam, let's away.

[*Exit* MONTAGUE *and* WIFE.]

**BENVOLIO.** Good morrow, cousin.

**ROMEO.**　　　　　　　　　　Is the day so young?

**BENVOLIO.** But new struck nine.

**ROMEO.**　　　　　　　　　Ay me! Sad hours seem long.
Was that my father that went hence so fast?

**BENVOLIO.** It was. What sadness lengthens Romeo's hours?

160　**ROMEO.** Not having that which having makes them short.

**BENVOLIO.** In love?

**ROMEO.** Out—

**BENVOLIO.** Of love?

**ROMEO.** Out of her favor where I am in love.

165　**BENVOLIO.** Alas that love, so gentle in his view,³³
Should be so tyrannous and rough in proof!³⁴

**ROMEO.** Alas that love, whose view is muffled still,³⁵
Should without eyes see pathways to his will!
Where shall we dine? O me! What fray was here?
170　Yet tell me not, for I have heard it all.
Here's much to do with hate, but more with love.³⁶
Why then, O brawling love, O loving hate,
O anything, of nothing first created!
O heavy lightness, serious vanity,
175　Misshapen chaos of well-seeming forms,
Feather of lead, bright smoke, cold fire, sick health,
Still-waking sleep, that is not what it is!
This love feel I, that feel no love in this.
Dost thou not laugh?

**BENVOLIO.**　　　　　　　No, coz,³⁷ I rather weep.

**ROMEO.** Good heart, at what?

180　**BENVOLIO.**　　　　　　　At thy good heart's oppression.

**ROMEO.** Why, such is love's transgression.
Griefs of mine own lie heavy in my breast,

Which thou wilt propagate, to have it prest
With more of thine.³⁸ This love that thou hast shown
185  Doth add more grief to too much of mine own.
Love is a smoke made with the fume of sighs;
Being purged, a fire sparkling in lovers' eyes;
Being vexed, a sea nourished with loving tears.
What is it else? A madness most discreet,³⁹
190  A choking gall,⁴⁰ and a preserving sweet.
Farewell, my coz.

**BENVOLIO.**                    Soft!⁴¹ I will go along.
And if you leave me so, you do me wrong.

**ROMEO.** Tut! I have lost myself; I am not here;
This is not Romeo, he's some other where.

195  **BENVOLIO.** Tell me in sadness,⁴² who is that you love?

**ROMEO.** What, shall I groan and tell thee?

**BENVOLIO.**                              Groan? Why, no;
But sadly tell me who.

**ROMEO.** Bid a sick man in sadness make his will.
Ah, word ill urged to one that is so ill!
200  In sadness, cousin, I do love a woman.

**BENVOLIO.** I aimed so near when I supposed you loved.

**ROMEO.** A right good markman. And she's fair I love.

**BENVOLIO.** A right fair mark, fair coz, is soonest hit.

**ROMEO.** Well, in that hit you miss. She'll not be hit
205  With Cupid's arrow. She hath Dian's wit,⁴³
And, in strong proof⁴⁴ of chastity well armed,
From Love's weak childish bow she lives uncharmed.
She will not stay⁴⁵ the siege of loving terms,
Nor bide th' encounter of assailing eyes,
210  Nor ope her lap to saint-seducing gold.
O, she is rich in beauty; only poor
That, when she dies, with beauty dies her store.⁴⁶

**BENVOLIO.** Then she hath sworn that she will still live chaste?

**ROMEO.** She hath, and in that sparing make huge waste;
215  For beauty, starved with her severity,

◀ **Critical Viewing** What does this photograph reveal about Romeo's feelings? **[Analyze]**

Cuts beauty off from all posterity.[47]
She is too fair, too wise, wisely too fair
To merit bliss by making me despair.[48]
She hath forsworn to[49] love, and in that vow
220  Do I live dead that live to tell it now.

**BENVOLIO.** Be ruled by me; forget to think of her.

**ROMEO.** O, teach me how I should forget to think!

**BENVOLIO.** By giving liberty unto thine eyes.
Examine other beauties.

**ROMEO.**                                   'Tis the way
225  To call hers, exquisite, in question more.[50]
These happy masks that kiss fair ladies' brows,
Being black puts us in mind they hide the fair.
He that is strucken blind cannot forget
The precious treasure of his eyesight lost.
230  Show me a mistress that is passing fair:
What doth her beauty serve but as a note
Where I may read who passed that passing fair?[51]
Farewell. Thou canst not teach me to forget.

**BENVOLIO.** I'll pay that doctrine, or else die in debt.[52]          [*Exit all.*]

### Scene ii. A street.

[*Enter* CAPULET, COUNTY PARIS, *and the* CLOWN, *his servant.*]

**CAPULET.** But Montague is bound as well as I,
In penalty alike; and 'tis not hard, I think,
For men so old as we to keep the peace.

**PARIS.** Of honorable reckoning[1] are you both,
5      And pity 'tis you lived at odds so long.
But now, my lord, what say you to my suit?

**CAPULET.** But saying o'er what I have said before:
My child is yet a stranger in the world,
She hath not seen the change of fourteen years;
10     Let two more summers wither in their pride
Ere we may think her ripe to be a bride.

**PARIS.** Younger than she are happy mothers made.

**CAPULET.** And too soon marred are those so early made.
Earth hath swallowed all my hopes[2] but she;
15     She is the hopeful lady of my earth.[3]
But woo her, gentle Paris, get her heart;
My will to her consent is but a part.

47. **in . . . posterity** By denying herself love and marriage, she wastes her beauty, which will not live on in future generations.
48. **She . . . despair** She is being too good—she will earn happiness in heaven by dooming me to live without her love.
49. **forsworn to** sworn not to.

50. **'Tis . . . more** That way will only make her beauty more strongly present in my mind.

51. **who . . . fair** who surpassed in beauty that very beautiful woman.
52. **I'll . . . debt** I will teach you to forget, or else die trying.

1. **reckoning** reputation.

2. **hopes** children.

3. **She . . . earth** My hopes for the future rest in her; she will inherit all that is mine.

Reading Check

What advice does Benvolio give to Romeo about the woman he loves?

An she agree, within her scope of choice
Lies my consent and fair according voice,[4]
20   This night I hold an old accustomed feast,
Whereto I have invited many a guest,
Such as I love; and you among the store,
One more, most welcome, makes my number more.
At my poor house look to behold this night
25   Earth-treading stars[5] that make dark heaven light.
Such comfort as do lusty young men feel
When well-appareled April on the heel
Of limping Winter treads, even such delight
Among fresh fennel buds shall you this night
30   Inherit at my house. Hear all, all see,
And like her most whose merit most shall be;
Which, on more view of many, mine, being one,
May stand in number, though in reck'ning none.[6]
Come, go with me. [*To* SERVANT, *giving him a paper*]
    Go, sirrah, trudge about
35   Through fair Verona; find those persons out
Whose names are written there, and to them say
My house and welcome on their pleasure stay.[7]

[*Exit with* PARIS.]

**SERVANT.** Find them out whose names are written here? It is
written that the shoemaker should meddle with his yard and
40   the tailor with his last, the fisher with his pencil and the
painter with his nets;[8] but I am sent to find those persons
whose names are here writ, and can never find what names
the writing person hath here writ. I must to the learned.
In good time![9]

[*Enter* BENVOLIO *and* ROMEO.]

45   **BENVOLIO.** Tut, man, one fire burns out another's burning;
One pain is less'ned by another's anguish;
Turn giddy, and be holp by backward turning;[10]
One desperate grief cures with another's languish.
Take thou some new infection to thy eye,
50   And the rank poison of the old will die.

**ROMEO.** Your plantain leaf[11] is excellent for that.

**BENVOLIO.** For what, I pray thee?

**ROMEO.**                       For your broken shin.

**BENVOLIO.** Why, Romeo, art thou mad?

---

**4. an . . . voice** If she agrees, I will consent to and agree with her choice.

**5. Earth-treading stars** young ladies.

**6. Which . . . none** If you look at all the young girls, you may see her as merely one among many, and not worth special admiration.

**7. stay** await.

**Reading Skill**
**Summarize** Use footnote 8 to help you summarize the servant's remarks here.

**8. shoemaker . . . nets** The servant is confusing workers and their tools. He intends to say that people should stick with what they know.

**9. In good time!** Just in time! The servant has seen Benvolio and Romeo, who can read.

**10. Turn . . . turning** If you are dizzy from turning one way, turn the other way.

**11. plantain leaf** leaf used to stop bleeding.

**ROMEO.** Not mad, but bound more than a madman is;
     Shut up in prison, kept without my food,
     Whipped and tormented and—God-den,[12] good fellow.

**SERVANT.** God gi' go-den. I pray, sir, can you read?

**ROMEO.** Ay, mine own fortune in my misery.

**SERVANT.** Perhaps you have learned it without book.
     But, I pray, can you read anything you see?

**ROMEO.** Ay, if I know the letters and the language.

**SERVANT.** Ye say honestly. Rest you merry.[13]

**ROMEO.** Stay, fellow; I can read. [*He reads the letter.*]
     "Signior Martino and his wife and daughters;
     County Anselm and his beauteous sisters;
     The lady widow of Vitruvio;
     Signior Placentio and his lovely nieces;
     Mercutio and his brother Valentine;
     Mine uncle Capulet, his wife and daughters;
     My fair niece Rosaline; Livia;
     Signior Valentio and his cousin Tybalt;
     Lucio and the lively Helena."
     A fair assembly. Whither should they come?

**SERVANT.** Up.

**ROMEO.** Whither? To supper?

**SERVANT.** To our house.

**ROMEO.** Whose house?

**SERVANT.** My master's.

**ROMEO.** Indeed I should have asked you that before.

**SERVANT.** Now I'll tell you without asking. My master is the
     great rich Capulet; and if you be not of the house of
     Montagues, I pray come and crush a cup of wine. Rest you
     merry.                                  [*Exit.*]

**BENVOLIO.** At this same ancient[14] feast of Capulet's
     Sups the fair Rosaline whom thou so loves;
     With all the admirèd beauties of Verona.
     Go thither, and with unattainted[15] eye
     Compare her face with some that I shall show,
     And I will make thee think thy swan a crow.

**ROMEO.** When the devout religion of mine eye
     Maintains such falsehood, then turn tears to fires:

Line numbers: 55, 60, 65, 70, 75, 80, 85, 90

12. **God-den** good afternoon; good evening.

13. **Rest you merry** May God keep you happy—a way of saying farewell.

**Literary Analysis**
**Dialogue and Stage Directions** What important information in the stage directions clarifies Romeo's speech here?

14. **ancient** long-established; traditional.
15. **unattainted** unprejudiced.

**Reading Check**
Why does Capulet's servant talk to Romeo and Benvolio?

And these, who, often drowned, could never die,
Transparent heretics, be burnt for liars![16]
One fairer than my love? The all-seeing sun
95  Ne'er saw her match since first the world begun.

**BENVOLIO.** Tut! you saw her fair, none else being by,
Herself poised with herself in either eye;[17]
But in that crystal scales[18] let there be weighed
Your lady's love against some other maid
100  That I will show you shining at this feast,
And she shall scant show well that now seems best.

**ROMEO.** I'll go along, no such sight to be shown,
But to rejoice in splendor of mine own.[19]                    [*Exit all.*]

**Scene iii. *A room in Capulet's house.***

[*Enter* CAPULET's WIFE, *and* NURSE.]

**LADY CAPULET.** Nurse, where's my daughter? Call her forth to
me.

**NURSE.** Now, by my maidenhead at twelve year old,
I bade her come. What, lamb! What, ladybird!
God forbid, where's this girl? What, Juliet!

[*Enter* JULIET.]

5  **JULIET.** How now? Who calls?

**NURSE.**                                        Your mother.

**JULIET.**                                                Madam, I am here.
What is your will?

**LADY CAPULET.** This is the matter—Nurse, give leave[1] awhile;
We must talk in secret. Nurse, come back again.
I have rememb'red me; thou's hear our counsel.[2]
10  Thou knowest my daughter's of a pretty age.

**NURSE.** Faith, I can tell her age unto an hour.

**LADY CAPULET.** She's not fourteen.

**NURSE.**                                        I'll lay fourteen of my teeth—
And yet, to my teen[3] be it spoken, I have but four—
She's not fourteen. How long is it now
To Lammastide?[4]

15  **LADY CAPULET.**        A fortnight and odd days.[5]

**NURSE.** Even or odd, of all days in the year,
Come Lammas Eve at night shall she be fourteen.

---

**16. When . . . liars!** When I see Rosaline as just a plain-looking girl, may my tears turn to fire and burn my eyes out!

**17. Herself . . . eye** Rosaline compared with no one else.

**18. crystal scales** your eyes.

**19. mine own** my own love, Rosaline.

**1. give leave** Leave us alone.
**2. thou's . . . counsel** You shall hear our conference.

**3. teen** sorrow.
**4. Lammastide** August 1, a holiday celebrating the summer harvest.

**5. A fortnight and odd days** two weeks plus a few days.

Susan and she (God rest all Christian souls!)
Were of an age.[6] Well, Susan is with God;

20  She was too good for me. But, as I said,
On Lammas Eve at night shall she be fourteen;
That shall she, marry; I remember it well.
'Tis since the earthquake now eleven years.
And she was weaned (I never shall forget it),

25  Of all the days of the year, upon that day;
For I had then laid wormwood to my dug,
Sitting in the sun under the dovehouse wall.
My lord and you were then at Mantua.
Nay, I do bear a brain. But, as I said,

30  When it did taste the wormwood on the nipple
Of my dug and felt it bitter, pretty fool,
To see it tetchy and fall out with the dug!
Shake, quoth the dovehouse! 'Twas no need, I trow,
To bid me trudge.

35  And since that time it is eleven years,
For then she could stand high-lone; nay, by th' rood,
She could have run and waddled all about;
For even the day before, she broke her brow;
And then my husband (God be with his soul!

40  'A was a merry man) took up the child.
"Yea," quoth he, "dost thou fall upon thy face?
Thou wilt fall backward when thou hast more wit;
Wilt thou not, Jule?" and, by my holidam,
The pretty wretch left crying and said, "Ay."

45  To see now how a jest shall come about!
I warrant, and I should live a thousand years,
I never should forget it. "Wilt thou not, Jule?" quoth he,
And, pretty fool, it stinted and said, "Ay."

**LADY CAPULET.** Enough of this. I pray thee hold thy peace.

50  **NURSE.** Yes, madam. Yet I cannot choose but laugh
To think it should leave crying and say, "Ay."
And yet, I warrant, it had upon it brow
A bump as big as a young cock'rel's stone;
A perilous knock; and it cried bitterly.

55  "Yea," quoth my husband, "fall'st upon thy face?
Thou wilt fall backward when thou comest to age,
Wilt thou not, Jule?" It stinted and said, "Ay."

**JULIET.** And stint thou too, I pray thee, nurse, say I.

**NURSE.** Peace, I have done. God mark thee to His grace!

6. **Susan . . . age** Susan, the Nurse's child, and Juliet were the same age.

**Literary Analysis**
**Dialogue and Stage Directions** What do the Nurse's words here reveal about her devotion to Juliet?

**Literary Analysis**
**Dialogue and Stage Directions** What does this conversation reveal about the Nurse's personality?

Reading Check

How old is Juliet?

60   Thou wast the prettiest babe that e'er I nursed.
     And I might live to see thee married once,
     I have my wish.

     **LADY CAPULET.** Marry, that "marry" is the very theme
        I came to talk of. Tell me, daughter Juliet,
65      How stands your dispositions to be married?

     **JULIET.** It is an honor that I dream not of.

     **NURSE.** An honor? Were not I thine only nurse,
        I would say thou hadst sucked wisdom from thy teat.

     **LADY CAPULET.** Well, think of marriage now. Younger than you,
70      Here in Verona, ladies of esteem,
        Are made already mothers. By my count,
        I was your mother much upon these years
        That you are now a maid.[7] Thus then in brief;
        The valiant Paris seeks you for his love.

75   **NURSE.** A man, young lady! Lady, such a man
        As all the world—Why, he's a man of wax.[8]

     **LADY CAPULET.** Verona's summer hath not such a flower.

     **NURSE.** Nay, he's a flower, in faith—a very flower.

     **LADY CAPULET.** What say you? Can you love the gentleman?
80      This night you shall behold him at our feast.
        Read o'er the volume of young Paris' face,
        And find delight writ there with beauty's pen;
        Examine every married lineament,
        And see how one another lends content;[9]
85      And what obscured in this fair volume lies
        Find written in the margent[10] of his eyes.
        This precious book of love, this unbound lover,
        To beautify him only lacks a cover.[11]
        The fish lives in the sea, and 'tis much pride
90      For fair without the fair within to hide.
        That book in many's eyes doth share the glory,
        That in gold clasps locks in the golden story;
        So shall you share all that he doth possess,
        By having him making yourself no less.

95   **NURSE.** No less? Nay, bigger! Women grow by men.

     **LADY CAPULET.** Speak briefly, can you like of Paris' love?

     **JULIET.** I'll look to like, if looking liking move;[12]
        But no more deep will I endart mine eye

**Reading Skill**

**Summarize** Use the information in footnote 8 and the dialogue to help you summarize the Nurse's opinion of Paris.

Than your consent gives strength to make it fly.[13]

[*Enter* SERVINGMAN.]

100 **SERVINGMAN.** Madam, the guests are come, supper served up,
    you called, my young lady asked for, the nurse cursed in the
    pantry, and everything in extremity. I must hence to wait. I
    beseech you follow straight.                                    [*Exit.*]

    **LADY CAPULET.** We follow thee. Juliet, the County stays.[14]

105 **NURSE.** Go, girl, seek happy nights to happy days.    [*Exit all.*]


*Scene iv. A street.*

[*Enter* ROMEO, MERCUTIO, BENVOLIO, *with five or six other* MASKERS;
TORCHBEARERS.]

    **ROMEO.** What, shall this speech[1] be spoke for our excuse?
        Or shall we on without apology?

    **BENVOLIO.** The date is out of such prolixity.[2]
        We'll have no Cupid hoodwinked with a scarf,
5       Bearing a Tartar's painted bow of lath,
        Scaring the ladies like a crowkeeper,
        Nor no without-book prologue, faintly spoke
        After the prompter, for our entrance;
        But, let them measure us by what they will,
10      We'll measure them a measure and be gone.

    **ROMEO.** Give me a torch. I am not for this ambling.
        Being but heavy,[3] I will bear the light.

    **MERCUTIO.** Nay, gentle Romeo, we must have you dance.

    **ROMEO.** Not I, believe me. You have dancing shoes
15      With nimble soles; I have a soul of lead
        So stakes me to the ground I cannot move.

    **MERCUTIO.** You are a lover. Borrow Cupid's wings
        And soar with them above a common bound.

    **ROMEO.** I am too sore enpiercèd with his shaft
20      To soar with his light feathers; and so bound
        I cannot bound a pitch above dull woe.
        Under love's heavy burden do I sink.

    **MERCUTIO.** And, to sink in it, should you burden love—
        Too great oppression for a tender thing.

**Literary Analysis
Dialogue and Stage
Directions** What does
the dialogue reveal about
Juliet's attitude toward
marriage and Paris?

13. **But . . . fly** But I will not
    look harder than you want
    me to.
14. **the County stays** The
    Count, Paris, is waiting.

1. **this speech** Romeo
   asks whether he and
   his companions, being
   uninvited guests,
   should follow custom by
   announcing their arrival in
   a speech.
2. **The . . . prolixity** Such
   wordiness is outdated.
   In the following lines,
   Benvolio says, in sum,
   "Let us forget about
   announcing our entrance
   with a show. The other
   guests can look over as
   they see fit. We will dance
   a while, then leave."
3. **heavy** weighed down with
   sadness.

Reading
Check

Why has Lady Capulet
come to talk to Juliet?

**Literary Analysis**
**Dialogue and Stage Directions** What contrast between Mercutio and Romeo does the dialogue reveal?

13. **Take . . . wits** Understand my intended meaning. That shows more intelligence than merely following what your senses perceive.

14. **Queen Mab** the queen of fairyland.
15. **atomies** creatures.

25 **ROMEO.** Is love a tender thing? It is too rough,
Too rude, too boist'rous, and it pricks like thorn.

**MERCUTIO.** If love be rough with you, be rough with love.
Prick love for pricking, and you beat love down.
Give me a case to put my visage[4] in.
30 A visor for a visor![5] What care I
What curious eye doth quote deformities?[6]
Here are the beetle brows shall blush for me.

**BENVOLIO.** Come, knock and enter; and no sooner in
But every man betake him to his legs.[7]

35 **ROMEO.** A torch for me! Let wantons light of heart
Tickle the senseless rushes[8] with their heels;
For I am proverbed with a grandsire phrase,[9]
I'll be a candleholder and look on;
The game was ne'er so fair, and I am done.[10]

40 **MERCUTIO.** Tut! Dun's the mouse, the constable's own word![11]
If thou art Dun,[12] we'll draw thee from the mire
Of this sir-reverence love, wherein thou stickest
Up to the ears. Come, we burn daylight, ho!

**ROMEO.** Nay, that's not so.

**MERCUTIO.**                    I mean, sir, in delay
45 We waste our lights in vain, like lights by day.
Take our good meaning, for our judgment sits
Five times in that ere once in our five wits.[13]

**ROMEO.** And we mean well in going to this masque,
But 'tis no wit to go.

**MERCUTIO.**                Why, may one ask?

**ROMEO.** I dreamt a dream tonight.

50 **MERCUTIO.**                          And so did I.

**ROMEO.** Well, what was yours?

**MERCUTIO.**                          That dreamers often lie.

**ROMEO.** In bed asleep, while they do dream things true.

**MERCUTIO.** O, then I see Queen Mab[14] hath been with you.
She is the fairies' midwife, and she comes
55 In shape no bigger than an agate stone
On the forefinger of an alderman,
Drawn with a team of little atomies[15]
Over men's noses as they lie asleep;

Her wagon spokes made of long spinners'[16] legs,
60   The cover, of the wings of grasshoppers;
Her traces, of the smallest spider web;
Her collars, of the moonshine's wat'ry beams;
Her whip, of cricket's bone; the lash, of film;[17]
Her wagoner, a small gray-coated gnat,
65   Not half so big as a round little worm
Pricked from the lazy finger of a maid;
Her chariot is an empty hazelnut,
Made by the joiner squirrel or old grub,[18]
Time out o' mind the fairies' coachmakers.
70   And in this state she gallops night by night
Through lovers' brains, and then they dream of love;
On courtiers' knees, that dream on curtsies straight;
O'er lawyers' fingers, who straight dream on fees;
O'er ladies' lips, who straight on kisses dream,
75   Which oft the angry Mab with blisters plagues,
Because their breath with sweetmeats[19] tainted are.
Sometimes she gallops o'er a courtier's nose,
And then dreams he of smelling out a suit;[20]
And sometime comes she with a tithe pig's[21] tail
80   Tickling a parson's nose as 'a lies asleep,
Then he dreams of another benefice.[22]
Sometime she driveth o'er a soldier's neck,
And then dream he of cutting foreign throats,
Of breaches, ambuscadoes,[23] Spanish blades,
85   Of healths[24] five fathom deep; and then anon

16. **spinners** spiders.
17. **film** spider's thread.

18. **old grub** insect that bores holes in nuts.
19. **sweetmeats** candy.

20. **smelling . . . suit** finding someone who has a petition (suit) for the king and who will pay the courtier to gain the king's favor for the petition.
21. **tithe pig** pig donated to a parson.
22. **benefice** church appointment that included a guaranteed income.
23. **ambuscadoes** ambushes.
24. **healths** toasts ("To your health!").

Reading Check

How does Romeo feel about going to the Capulets' feast?

25. **plats** tangles.
26. **elflocks** tangled hair.

27. **carriage** posture.

**Reading Skill**
**Summarize** Review
Mercutio's speech and
summarize his ideas
about Queen Mab.

**Literary Analysis**
**Dialogue and Stage**
**Directions** What do
Mercutio's comments
about dreams reveal
about his character?

**Reading Skill**
**Summarize** Use
footnote 28 to help you
summarize Romeo's
response to Benvolio.

28. **my mind . . . death** My
mind is fearful that some
future event, fated by the
stars, shall start to run its
course tonight and cut my
life short.

1. **trencher** wooden platter.

Drums in his ear, at which he starts and wakes,
And being thus frighted, swears a prayer or two
And sleeps again. This is that very Mab
That plats[25] the manes of horses in the night
90  And bakes the elflocks[26] in foul sluttish hairs,
Which once untangled much misfortune bodes.
This is the hag, when maids lie on their backs,
That presses them and learns them first to bear,
Making them women of good carriage.[27]
This is she—

95  **ROMEO.**      Peace, peace, Mercutio, peace!
Thou talk'st of nothing.

**MERCUTIO.**               True, I talk of dreams;
Which are the children of an idle brain,
Begot of nothing but vain fantasy;
Which is as thin of substance as the air,
100  And more inconstant than the wind, who woos
Even now the frozen bosom of the North
And, being angered, puffs away from thence,
Turning his side to the dew-dropping South.

**BENVOLIO.** This wind you talk of blows us from ourselves.
105  Supper is done, and we shall come too late.

**ROMEO.** I fear, too early; for my mind misgives
Some consequence yet hanging in the stars
Shall bitterly begin his fearful date
With this night's revels and expire the term
110  Of a despisèd life, closed in my breast,
By some vile forfeit of untimely death.[28]
But he that hath the steerage of my course
Direct my sail! On, lusty gentlemen!

**BENVOLIO.** Strike, drum.

[*They march about the stage, and retire to one side.*]

**Scene v. A hall in Capulet's house.**

[SERVINGMEN *come forth with napkins.*]

**FIRST SERVINGMAN.** Where's Potpan, that he helps not to
take away? He shift a trencher![1] He scrape a trencher!

**SECOND SERVINGMAN.** When good manners shall lie all in one
or two men's hands, and they unwashed too, 'tis a foul thing.

**FIRST SERVINGMAN.** Away with the joint-stools, remove the
    court cupboard, look to the plate. Good thou, save me a
    piece of marchpane,[2] and, as thou loves me, let the porter
    let in Susan Grindstone and Nell. Anthony and Potpan!

**SECOND SERVINGMAN.** Ay, boy, ready.

10 **FIRST SERVINGMAN.** You are looked for and called for,
    asked for and sought for, in the great chamber.

**THIRD SERVINGMAN.** We cannot be here and there too.
    Cheerly, boys! Be brisk awhile, and the longest liver
    take all.                                      [*Exit.*]

[*Enter* CAPULET, *his* WIFE, JULIET, TYBALT, NURSE, *and all the* GUESTS
*and* GENTLEWOMEN *to the* MASKERS.]

15 **CAPULET.** Welcome, gentlemen! Ladies that have their toes
    Unplagued with corns will walk a bout[3] with you.
    Ah, my mistresses, which of you all
    Will now deny to dance? She that makes dainty,[4]
    She I'll swear hath corns. Am I come near ye now?
20     Welcome, gentlemen! I have seen the day
    That I have worn a visor and could tell
    A whispering tale in a fair lady's ear,
    Such as would please. 'Tis gone, 'tis gone, 'tis gone.
    You are welcome, gentlemen! Come, musicians,
        play.
                               [*Music plays, and they dance.*]
25     A hall,[5] a hall! Give room! And foot it, girls.
    More light, you knaves, and turn the tables up,
    And quench the fire; the room is grown too hot.
    Ah, sirrah, this unlooked-for sport comes well.
    Nay, sit; nay, sit, good cousin Capulet;
30     For you and I are past our dancing days.
    How long is't now since last yourself and I
    Were in a mask?

**SECOND CAPULET.** By'r Lady, thirty years.

**CAPULET.** What, man? 'Tis not so much, 'tis not so
      much;
    'Tis since the nuptial of Lucentio,
35     Come Pentecost as quickly as it will,
    Some five-and-twenty years, and then we masked.

**SECOND CAPULET.** 'Tis more, 'tis more. His son is elder, sir;
    His son is thirty.

2. **marchpane** marzipan, a
confection made of sugar
and almonds.

3. **walk a bout** dance a turn.
4. **makes dainty** hesitates;
acts shy.

5. **A hall** clear the floor, make
room for dancing.

**Spiral Review**
**Character** What do
lines 15 through 32
reveal about Capulet?

Reading
Check

What does Romeo fear
might happen in the near
future?

▲ ▶ **Critical Viewing**
What can you tell about Romeo and Juliet's feelings for each other at this point from these images? **[Draw Conclusions]**

**Literary Analysis**
**Dialogue and Stage Directions** What do the stage direction in line 40 and the dialogue that follows reveal about Romeo?

6. **ward** minor.
7. **Forswear** deny.
8. **antic face** strange, fantastic mask.
9. **fleer** mock.

**CAPULET.**          Will you tell me that?
His son was but a ward[6] two years ago.

40  **ROMEO.** [*To a* SERVINGMAN] What lady's that which doth
        enrich the hand
     Of yonder knight?

**SERVINGMAN.** I know not, sir.

**ROMEO.** O, she doth teach the torches to burn bright!
     It seems she hangs upon the cheek of night
45   As a rich jewel in an Ethiop's ear—
     Beauty too rich for use, for earth too dear!
     So shows a snowy dove trooping with crows
     As yonder lady o'er her fellows shows.
     The measure done, I'll watch her place of stand
50   And, touching hers, make blessèd my rude hand.
     Did my heart love till now? Forswear[7] it, sight!
     For I ne'er saw true beauty till this night.

**TYBALT.** This, by his voice, should be a Montague.
     Fetch me my rapier, boy. What! Dares the slave
55   Come hither, covered with an antic face,[8]
     To fleer[9] and scorn at our solemnity?
     Now, by the stock and honor of my kin,
     To strike him dead I hold it not a sin.

**CAPULET.** Why, how now, kinsman? Wherefore storm you so?

6C  **TYBALT.** Uncle, this is a Montague, our foe,
     A villain, that is hither come in spite

To scorn at our solemnity this night.

**CAPULET.** Young Romeo is it?

**TYBALT.**                     'Tis he, that villain Romeo.

**CAPULET.** Content thee, gentle coz,[10] let him alone.
65     'A bears him like a portly gentleman,[11]
    And, to say truth, Verona brags of him
    To be a virtuous and well-governed youth.
    I would not for the wealth of all this town
    Here in my house do him disparagement.[12]
70     Therefore be patient; take no note of him.
    It is my will, the which if thou respect,
    Show a fair presence and put off these frowns,
    An ill-beseeming semblance[13] for a feast.

**TYBALT.** It fits when such a villain is a guest.
    I'll not endure him.

75 **CAPULET.**            He shall be endured.
    What, goodman[14] boy! I say he shall. Go to![15]
    Am I the master here, or you? Go to!
    You'll not endure him, God shall mend my soul![16]
    You'll make a mutiny among my guests!
80     You will set cock-a-hoop.[17] You'll be the man!

**TYBALT.** Why, uncle, 'tis a shame.

**CAPULET.**                Go to, go to!
    You are a saucy boy. Is't so, indeed?
    This trick may chance to scathe you.[18] I know what.
    You must contrary me! Marry, 'tis time—
85     Well said, my hearts!—You are a princox[19]—go!
    Be quiet, or—more light, more light!—For shame!
    I'll make you quiet. What!—Cheerly, my hearts!

10. **coz** Here, "coz" is used as a term of address for a relative.
11. **'A . . . gentleman** He behaves like a dignified gentleman.
12. **disparagement** insult.
13. **ill-beseeming semblance** inappropriate appearance.
14. **goodman** term of address for someone below the rank of gentleman.
15. **Go to!** expression of angry impatience.
16. **God . . . soul!** expression of impatience, equivalent to "God save me!"
17. **You will set cock-a-hoop** You want to swagger like a barnyard rooster.

**Literary Analysis**
**Dialogue** What does the dialogue between Capulet and Tybalt show about their relationship?

18. **This . . . you** This trait of yours may turn out to hurt you.
19. **princox** rude youngster; wise guy.

**Reading Check**

How does Capulet respond when Tybalt says he will not tolerate Romeo's presence at the party?

20. **Patience . . . meeting**
enforced self-control
mixing with strong anger.

**TYBALT.** Patience perforce with willful choler meeting[20]
　　Makes my flesh tremble in their different greeting.
90　I will withdraw; but this intrusion shall,
　　Now seeming sweet, convert to bitt'rest gall.　　[*Exit.*]

**ROMEO.** If I profane with my unworthiest hand
　　This holy shrine,[21] the gentle sin is this:
　　My lips, two blushing pilgrims, ready stand
95　　To smooth that rough touch with a tender kiss.

21. **shrine** Juliet's hand.

**JULIET.** Good pilgrim, you do wrong your hand too much,
　　Which mannerly devotion shows in this;
　　For saints have hands that pilgrims' hands do touch
　　And palm to palm is holy palmers'[22] kiss.

22. **palmers** pilgrims who
at one time carried palm
branches from the Holy
Land.
23. **move** initiate involvement
in earthly affairs.

100　**ROMEO.** Have not saints lips, and holy palmers too?

**JULIET.** Ay, pilgrim, lips that they must use in prayer.

**ROMEO.** O, then, dear saint, let lips do what hands do!
　　They pray; grant thou, lest faith turn to despair.

**JULIET.** Saints do not move,[23] though grant for prayers' sake.

105　**ROMEO.** Then move not while my prayer's effect I take.
　　Thus from my lips, by thine my sin is purged.　　[*Kisses her.*]

**JULIET.** Then have my lips the sin that they have took.

**ROMEO.** Sin from my lips? O trespass sweetly urged![24]
　　Give me my sin again.　　　　　　　　[*Kisses her.*]

**JULIET.**　　　　　　　　You kiss by th' book.[25]

**Literary Analysis**
**Dialogue and Stage**
**Directions** What do
the dialogue and stage
directions in this passage
reveal about Romeo's
and Juliet's feelings?

110　**NURSE.** Madam, your mother craves a word with you.

**ROMEO.** What is her mother?

**NURSE.**　　　　　　　　Marry, bachelor,
　　Her mother is the lady of the house,
　　And a good lady, and a wise and virtuous.
　　I nursed her daughter that you talked withal.
115　I tell you, he that can lay hold of her
　　Shall have the chinks.[26]

24. **O . . . urged!** Romeo is
saying, in substance, that
he is happy. Juliet calls his
kiss a sin, for now he can
take it back—by another
kiss.
25. **by th' book** as if you were
following a manual of
courtly love.
26. **chinks** cash.
27. **My life . . . debt** Since
Juliet is a Capulet,
Romeo's life is at the
mercy of the enemies of
his family.

**ROMEO.**　　　　　　　　Is she a Capulet?
　　O dear account! My life is my foe's debt.[27]

**BENVOLIO.** Away, be gone; the sport is at the best.

**ROMEO.** Ay, so I fear; the more is my unrest.

**CAPULET.** Nay, gentlemen, prepare not to be gone;

120   We have a trifling foolish banquet towards.[28]
   Is it e'en so?[29] Why then, I thank you all.
   I thank you, honest gentlemen. Good night.
   More torches here! Come on then; let's to bed.

125   Ah, sirrah, by my fay,[30] it waxes late;
   I'll to my rest.           [*Exit all but* JULIET *and* NURSE.]

**JULIET.** Come hither, nurse. What is yond gentleman?

**NURSE.** The son and heir of old Tiberio.

**JULIET.** What's he that now is going out of door?

130   **NURSE.** Marry, that, I think, be young Petruchio.

**JULIET.** What's he that follows here, that would not dance?

**NURSE.** I know not.

**JULIET.** Go ask his name—If he is married,

28. **towards** being prepared.
29. **Is . . . so?** Is it the case that you really must leave?
30. **fay** faith.

**Literary Analysis**

**Dialogue and Stage Directions** How can you tell that the dialogue that follows line 126 is a private conversation?

**Reading Check**

How does Romeo get Juliet to kiss him?

My grave is like to be my wedding bed.

135 **NURSE.** His name is Romeo, and a Montague,
The only son of your great enemy.

**JULIET.** My only love, sprung from my only hate!
Too early seen unknown, and known too late!
Prodigious[31] birth of love it is to me
140    That I must love a loathèd enemy.

**NURSE.** What's this? What's this?

**JULIET.**               A rhyme I learnt even now.
Of one I danced withal.      [*One calls within,* "JULIET."]

**NURSE.**             Anon, anon!
Come, let's away; the strangers all are gone.    [*Exit all.*]

**31. Prodigious** monstrous; foretelling misfortune.

---

## Critical Thinking

Cite textual evidence to support your responses.

@ 1. **Key Ideas and Details (a)** Based on Act I, what do you know about Romeo's life and Juliet's life? **(b) Compare and Contrast:** Use details from the text to show how their personalities are similar and different.

@ 2. **Key Ideas and Details (a)** What information about the two households is presented in the Prologue? **(b) Connect:** How does Juliet's comment in Act I, Scene v, lines 137–138, echo the Prologue? Explain your response.

@ 3. **Key Ideas and Details Analyze:** How do the comments of Mercutio and Benvolio add to your understanding of Romeo's character? Explain your answer.

@ 4. **Key Ideas and Details (a) Analyze:** What threats to Romeo and Juliet's love already exist in Act I? **(b) Speculate:** How do you think Romeo and Juliet will react to these threats? Explain your response.

@ 5. **Integration of Knowledge and Ideas Evaluate:** Based on Romeo's behavior in Act I, do you think Shakespeare accurately portrays a teenager in love? Explain.

@ 6. **Integration of Knowledge and Ideas** How do the differences between Romeo and Juliet define their relationship? Explain. *[Connect to the Big Question: Do our differences define us?]*

# After You Read | The Tragedy of Romeo and Juliet, Act I

## Literary Analysis: Dialogue and Stage Directions

© **1. Key Ideas and Details** Using a chart like the one shown, explain what the **dialogue** involving the Nurse, Juliet, and Lady Capulet in Act I, Scene iii, reveals about each character.

| Character | Dialogue | | Reveals |
|---|---|---|---|
| | | → | |

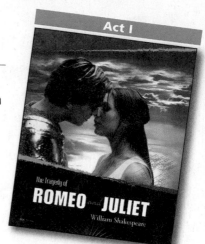

Act I

The Tragedy of
ROMEO and JULIET
William Shakespeare

© **2. Craft and Structure (a)** Identify three examples of **stage directions** that do more than simply dictate characters' movements on and off stage. **(b)** Explain what each direction tells about the characters and the action.

## Reading Skill: Summarize

**3.** Use **text aids** to restate Capulet's scolding of Tybalt in Act I, Scene v, lines 77–87, in your own words.

**4. (a)** Using text aids to clarify her meaning, explain the play on words in Juliet's speech in Act I, Scene v, lines 96–99.
**(b) Summarize** her speech in a few sentences.

## Vocabulary

© **Acquisition and Use** An **oxymoron** is a phrase combining contradictory or opposing ideas, often used as a figure of speech for poetic effect. Review the vocabulary list on page 804. Then, explain the meaning of each phrase and tell why each one is an oxymoron.

**1.** pernicious blessing

**2.** augmenting scarcity

**3.** flattering grievance

**4.** honorable transgression

**5.** cooperative adversary

**6.** cheerful oppression

**Word Study** Use the context of the sentences and what you know about the **Latin prefix *trans-*** to explain your answer to each question.

**1.** Can you *transfer* information from the Internet to a computer?
**2.** If the operation of a government office is *transparent,* will people know what is going on?

### Word Study

The **Latin prefix *trans-*** means "across," "over," or "through."

**Apply It** Explain how the prefix *trans-* contributes to the meanings of these words. You may consult a dictionary if necessary.

transport
translucent
transition

## Do our *differences* define us?

**While You Read** Continue to notice the differences between Romeo and Juliet. Decide whether these differences have a strong effect on the way their relationship develops.

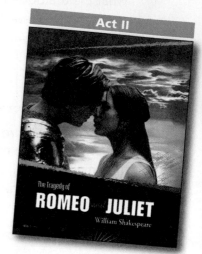

### © Common Core State Standards

Meet these standards with *The Tragedy of Romeo and Juliet*, **Act II** (p. 834).

**Reading Literature**

**2.** Determine a theme or central idea of a text; provide an objective summary of the text. *(Reading Skill: Summarize)*

**5.** Analyze how an author's choices concerning how to structure a text, order events within it, and manipulate time create such effects as mystery, tension, or surprise. *(Literary Analysis: Blank Verse)*

**Spiral Review: RL.9-10.3**

## Vocabulary

Read each word and its definition. Decide whether you know the word well, know it a little bit, or do not know it at all. After you read, see how your knowledge of each word has increased.

- **procure** (prō kyoor´) *v.* get; obtain (p. 843) *The hungry man tried to procure food. procurement n. procurable adj.*

- **predominant** (prē däm´ ə nənt) *adj.* of or having stronger influence (p. 845) *Despite some disagreement, the predominant tone of the meeting was one of unity. predominantly adv. dominant adv. dominate v.*

- **intercession** (in´ tər sesh´ ən) *n.* act of pleading on another's behalf (p. 846) *Thanks to the intercession by Andy and Paula, Jim was allowed into the concert without a ticket. intercede v.*

- **sallow** (sal´ ō) *adj.* of a sickly, pale-yellowish hue (p. 846) *When her sickness passed, her face no longer looked sallow. sallowness n.*

- **lamentable** (lam´ ən tə bəl) *adj.* distressing; sad (p. 848) *His lack of concern about his health is lamentable. lament v. lamentably adv.*

- **unwieldy** (un wēl´ dē) *adj.* awkward; clumsy (p. 854) *Joe's sprained ankle made him unwieldy on the dance floor. wield v.*

### Word Study

The **Latin prefix pro-** means "before," "forward."

In this play, Juliet promises to **procure** the opportunity to come to Romeo, if his intentions are to marry her. She means she will take steps beforehand so that she can see him.

# Literary Analysis: Blank Verse

**Blank verse** is unrhymed poetry written in a meter called iambic pentameter. A line of iambic pentameter has five stressed syllables, each preceded by an unstressed syllable, as in the following example:

- Bŭt sóft! Whăt líght thrŏugh yónděr wíndŏw bréaks?
- Ĭt ís thĕ eást, ănd Júlĭĕt ís thĕ sún!

Much of *The Tragedy of Romeo and Juliet* is written in blank verse. Shakespeare uses its formal meter to reinforce character rank. Important or aristocratic characters typically speak in blank verse. Minor or comic characters often do not speak in verse. This deliberate change in style has an impact on the tone and mood of the character's interactions.

# Reading Skill: Summarize

**Summarizing** is briefly stating the main ideas in a piece of writing. Stopping periodically to summarize what you have read helps you to check your comprehension before you read further.

Summarizing is especially useful when reading a play that has long passages of blank verse. When you encounter one of these passages, **read in sentences**—just as if you were reading a poem. Pause according to the punctuation instead of at the end of each line. As you become more accustomed to the form, you will be able to increase your speed.

Once you have grasped the meanings of individual sentences in blank verse, you can more easily and accurately summarize long passages.

## Using the Strategy: Summarizing Chart

Use a chart like this one to summarize passages in this act of the drama.

| Passage | Sentences | Summary |
|---|---|---|
| What's Montague? It is nor hand, nor foot, / Nor arm, nor face, nor any other part / Belonging to a man. O, be some other name! / What's in a name? That which we call a rose / By any other name would smell as sweet. | ① What's Montague? ② It is nor hand, nor foot, Nor arm, nor face, nor any other part Belonging to a man. ③ O, be some other name! ④ What's in a name? ⑤ That which we call a rose By any other name would smell as sweet. | Montague is just a name; it's not who Romeo physically is, but Juliet wishes he had another name because of what she knows it represents. |

# ACT II

## Review and Anticipate

Act I reveals a bitter, long-standing feud between the Montagues and the Capulets. It also introduces the play's title characters, who meet at a feast and immediately fall in love, only to discover that they come from opposing sides of the feud.

Based on what you have learned about the personalities of Romeo and Juliet, how do you expect them to respond to their love for each other and to the problems it poses? How do you think their families will react?

## Prologue

[*Enter* CHORUS.]

**CHORUS.** Now old desire[1] doth in his deathbed lie,
    And young affection gapes to be his heir;[2]
That fair[3] for which love groaned for and would die,
    With tender Juliet matched, is now not fair.
5  Now Romeo is beloved and loves again,
    Alike bewitchèd[4] by the charm of looks;
But to his foe supposed he must complain,[5]
    And she steal love's sweet bait from fearful hooks.

1. **old desire** Romeo's love for Rosaline.
2. **young . . . heir** Romeo's new love for Juliet is eager to replace his love for Rosaline.
3. **fair** beautiful woman (Rosaline).
4. **Alike bewitchèd** Both Romeo and Juliet are enchanted.
5. **complain** address his words of love.

Being held a foe, he may not have access
10 To breathe such vows as lovers use to swear,
And she as much in love, her means much less
To meet her new belovèd anywhere;
But passion lends them power, time means to meet,
Temp'ring extremities with extreme sweet.[6]

[*Exit.*]

*Scene i. Near Capulet's orchard.*

[*Enter* ROMEO *alone.*]

**ROMEO.** Can I go forward when my heart is here?
Turn back, dull earth,[1] and find thy center[2] out.

[*Enter* BENVOLIO *with* MERCUTIO. ROMEO *retires.*]

**BENVOLIO.** Romeo! My cousin Romeo! Romeo!

**MERCUTIO.**                                          He is wise.
And, on my life, hath stol'n him home to bed.

5 **BENVOLIO.** He ran this way and leapt this orchard wall.
Call, good Mercutio.

**MERCUTIO.**                          Nay, I'll conjure[3] too.
Romeo! Humors! Madman! Passion! Lover!
Appear thou in the likeness of a sigh;
Speak but one rhyme, and I am satisfied!
10 Cry but "Ay me!" Pronounce but "love" and "dove";
Speak to my gossip[4] Venus one fair word,
One nickname for her purblind son and heir,
Young Abraham Cupid, he that shot so true
When King Cophetua loved the beggar maid!
15 He heareth not, he stirreth not, he moveth not;
The ape is dead,[5] and I must conjure him.
I conjure thee by Rosaline's bright eyes,
By her high forehead and her scarlet lip,
By her fine foot, straight leg, and quivering thigh,
20 And the demesnes that there adjacent lie,
That in thy likeness thou appear to us!

**BENVOLIO.** And if he hear thee, thou wilt anger him.

**MERCUTIO.** This cannot anger him. 'Twould anger him
To raise a spirit in his mistress' circle
25 Of some strange nature, letting it there stand
Till she had laid it and conjured it down.

---

**6. Temp'ring . . . sweet** easing their difficulties with great delights.

**1. dull earth** lifeless body.
**2. center** heart, or possibly soul (Juliet).

**3. conjure** recite a spell to make Romeo appear.

**4. gossip** merry old lady.
**5. The ape is dead** Romeo, like a trained monkey, seems to be playing.

**Literary Analysis**
**Blank Verse** Based on the meter of this speech, how can you tell that Mercutio is an aristocratic character?

That were some spite; my invocation
Is fair and honest; in his mistress' name,
I conjure only but to raise up him.

30 **BENVOLIO.** Come, he hath hid himself among these trees
To be consorted[6] with the humorous[7] night.
Blind is his love and best befits the dark.

**MERCUTIO.** If love be blind, love cannot hit the mark.
Now will he sit under a medlar[8] tree
35 And wish his mistress were that kind of fruit
As maids call medlars when they laugh alone.
O, Romeo, that she were, O that she were
An open *et cetera*, thou a pop'rin pear!
Romeo, good night. I'll to my truckle bed;[9]
40 This field bed is too cold for me to sleep.
Come, shall we go?

**BENVOLIO.**                    Go then, for 'tis in vain
To seek him here that means not to be found.

[*Exit with others.*]

*Scene ii. Capulet's orchard.*

**ROMEO.** [*Coming forward*] He jests at scars that never felt a
          wound.

[*Enter* JULIET *at a window.*]

But soft! What light through yonder window breaks?
It is the East, and Juliet is the sun!
Arise, fair sun, and kill the envious moon,
5 Who is already sick and pale with grief
That thou her maid art far more fair than she.
Be not her maid, since she is envious.
Her vestal livery[1] is but sick and green,
And none but fools do wear it. Cast it off.
10 It is my lady! O, it is my love!
O, that she knew she were!
She speaks, yet she says nothing. What of that?
Her eye discourses; I will answer it.
I am too bold; 'tis not to me she speaks.
15 Two of the fairest stars in all the heaven,
Having some business, do entreat her eyes
To twinkle in their spheres[2] till they return.
What if her eyes were there, they in her head?

6. **consorted** associated.
7. **humorous** humid; moody, like a lover.

8. **medlar** applelike fruit.

9. **truckle bed** trundlebed, placed under a larger bed when not in use.

**Literary Analysis**
**Blank Verse** Which line in Romeo's speech breaks the pattern of five stressed syllables per line?

1. **livery** clothing or costume worn by a servant.

2. **spheres** orbits.

**Reading Check**
Whom does Romeo see at the window?

The brightness of her cheek would shame those stars
20 As daylight doth a lamp; her eyes in heaven
Would through the airy region stream so bright
That birds would sing and think it were not night.
See how she leans her cheek upon that hand,
O, that I were a glove upon that hand,
That I might touch that cheek!

**JULIET.**                                    Ay me!

25 **ROMEO.**                              She speaks.
O, speak again, bright angel, for thou art
As glorious to this night, being o'er my head,
As is a wingèd messenger of heaven
Unto the white-upturnèd wond'ring eyes
30 Of mortals that fall back to gaze on him
When he bestrides the lazy puffing clouds
And sails upon the bosom of the air.

**JULIET.** O Romeo, Romeo! Wherefore art thou Romeo?[3]
Deny thy father and refuse thy name;
35 Or, if thou wilt not, be but sworn my love,
And I'll no longer be a Capulet.

▼ **Critical Viewing**
Which line of dialogue in this scene might this photograph capture? **[Connect]**

3. **Wherefore . . . Romeo?**
Why are you Romeo—a Montague?

**ROMEO.** [*Aside*] Shall I hear more, or shall I speak at this?

**JULIET.** Tis but thy name that is my enemy.
Thou art thyself, though not[4] a Montague.
40     What's Montague? It is nor hand, nor foot,
Nor arm, nor face, nor any other part
Belonging to a man. O, be some other name!
What's in a name? That which we call a rose
By any other name would smell as sweet.
45     So Romeo would, were he not Romeo called,
Retain that dear perfection which he owes[5]
Without that title. Romeo, doff[6] thy name;
And for thy name, which is no part of thee,
Take all myself.

**ROMEO.**            I take thee at thy word.
50     Call me but love, and I'll be new baptized;
Henceforth I never will be Romeo.

**JULIET.** What man art thou, thus bescreened in night,
So stumblest on my counsel?[7]

**ROMEO.**                By a name
I know not how to tell thee who I am.
55     My name, dear saint, is hateful to myself
Because it is an enemy to thee.
Had I it written, I would tear the word.

**JULIET.** My ears have yet not drunk a hundred words
Of thy tongue's uttering, yet I know the sound.
60     Art thou not Romeo, and a Montague?

**ROMEO.** Neither, fair maid, if either thee dislike.

**JULIET.** How camest thou hither, tell me, and wherefore?
The orchard walls are high and hard to climb,
And the place death, considering who thou art,
65     If any of my kinsmen find thee here.

**ROMEO.** With love's light wings did I o'erperch[8] these walls;
For stony limits cannot hold love out,
And what love can do, that dares love attempt.
Therefore thy kinsmen are no stop to me.

70 **JULIET.** If they do see thee, they will murder thee.

**ROMEO.** Alack, there lies more peril in thine eye
Than twenty of their swords! Look thou but sweet,
And I am proof[9] against their enmity.

---

4. **though not** even if you were not.

**Reading Skill
Summarize** Briefly summarize Juliet's speech about Romeo's name.

5. **owes** owns; possesses.
6. **doff** remove.

7. **counsel** secret thoughts.

**Literary Analysis
Blank Verse** How do the stressed syllables in line 57 reinforce Romeo's meaning?

8. **o'erperch** fly over.

9. **proof** protected, as by armor.

**Reading Check**

Why does Romeo say his name is hateful to him?

**JULIET.** I would not for the world they saw thee here.

75 **ROMEO.** I have night's cloak to hide me from their eyes;
And but[10] thou love me, let them find me here.
My life were better ended by their hate
Than death proroguèd,[11] wanting of thy love.

**JULIET.** By whose direction found'st thou out this place?

80 **ROMEO.** By love, that first did prompt me to inquire.
He lent me counsel, and I lent him eyes.
I am no pilot; yet, wert thou as far
As that vast shore washed with the farthest sea,
I should adventure[12] for such merchandise.

85 **JULIET.** Thou knowest the mask of night is on my face;
Else would a maiden blush bepaint my cheek
For that which thou hast heard me speak tonight.
Fain would I dwell on form[13]—fain, fain deny
What I have spoke; but farewell compliment![14]
90 Dost thou love me? I know thou wilt say "Ay";
And I will take thy word. Yet, if thou swear'st,
Thou mayst prove false. At lovers' perjuries,
They say Jove laughs. O gentle Romeo,
If thou dost love, pronounce it faithfully.
95 Or if thou thinkest I am too quickly won,
I'll frown and be perverse[15] and say thee nay,
So thou wilt woo; but else, not for the world.
In truth, fair Montague, I am too fond,[16]
And therefore thou mayst think my havior light;[17]
100 But trust me, gentleman, I'll prove more true
Than those that have more cunning to be strange.[18]
I should have been more strange, I must confess,
But that thou overheard'st, ere I was ware,
My truelove passion. Therefore pardon me,
105 And not impute this yielding to light love,
Which the dark night hath so discoverèd.[19]

**ROMEO.** Lady, by yonder blessèd moon I vow,
That tips with silver all these fruit-tree tops—

**JULIET.** O, swear not by the moon, th' inconstant moon,
110 That monthly changes in her circle orb,
Lest that thy love prove likewise variable.

10. **And but** unless.

11. **proroguèd** postponed.

12. **adventure** risk a long journey, like a sea adventurer.
13. **Fain . . . form** eagerly would I follow convention (by acting reserved).
14. **compliment** conventional behavior.

15. **be perverse** act contrary to my true feelings.
16. **fond** affectionate.
17. **my havior light** my behavior immodest or unserious.
18. **strange** distant and cold.

19. **discoverèd** revealed.

**ROMEO.** What shall I swear by?

**JULIET.**                    Do not swear at all;
    Or if thou wilt, swear by thy gracious self,
    Which is the god of my idolatry,
    And I'll believe thee.

115 **ROMEO.** If my heart's dear love—

**JULIET.** Well, do not swear. Although I joy in thee,
    I have no joy of this contract[20] tonight.
    It is too rash, too unadvised, too sudden;
    Too like the lightning, which doth cease to be
120    Ere one can say it lightens. Sweet, good night!
    This bud of love, by summer's ripening breath,
    May prove a beauteous flow'r when next we meet.
    Good night, good night! As sweet repose and rest
    Come to thy heart as that within my breast!

125 **ROMEO.** O, wilt thou leave me so unsatisfied?

**JULIET.** What satisfaction canst thou have tonight?

**ROMEO.** Th'exchange of thy love's faithful vow for mine.

**Literary Analysis**
**Blank Verse** The five stressed syllables of lines 112 and 115 are split between the two speakers. What does this weaving together of dialogue suggest about the speakers' relationship?

**20. contract** betrothal.

 **Reading Check**
Why does Juliet tell Romeo not to swear his love by the moon?

The Tragedy of Romeo and Juliet, Act II **841**

**JULIET.** I gave thee mine before thou didst request it;
    And yet I would it were to give again.

130  **ROMEO.** Wouldst thou withdraw it? For what purpose, love?

**JULIET.** But to be frank[21] and give it thee again.
    And yet I wish but for the thing I have.

    My bounty[22] is as boundless as the sea,
    My love as deep; the more I give to thee,
135  The more I have, for both are infinite,
    I hear some noise within. Dear love, adieu!

[NURSE *calls within.*]

    Anon, good nurse! Sweet Montague, be true.
    Stay but a little, I will come again.         [*Exit.*]

---

## LITERATURE IN CONTEXT

### Culture Connection

**Falconry**

When Juliet longs for "a falc'ners voice," she is referring to someone who practices falconry, the sport of hunting with falcons. Falcons are swift, hawk-like birds of prey. The falconer trains the bird to respond to a combination of physical and vocal commands.

**During Shakespeare's time, one's rank in society determined the kind of bird one could own:**

| Rank | Type of Bird |
| --- | --- |
| King | Gyr falcon |
| Prince | Peregrine falcon (male) |
| Knight | Saker falcon |
| Squire | Lanner falcon |
| Lady | Merlin (female) |
| Yeoman (landowner) | Goshawk |
| Servants, children | Kestrel |

### Connect to the Literature

Why do you think Juliet wishes Romeo would respond to her voice as a falcon does to the falconer's commands?

◄ Falconry began as a way to obtain food but gradually evolved into the "sport of kings."

Thick leather gloves protected the falconer from the bird's talons. ▶

**ROMEO.** O blessèd, blessèd night! I am afeard,
140  Being in night, all this is but a dream,
Too flattering-sweet to be substantial.[23]

[*Enter* JULIET *again.*]

**JULIET.** Three words, dear Romeo, and good night indeed.
If that thy bent[24] of love be honorable,
Thy purpose marriage, send me word tomorrow,
145  By one that I'll procure to come to thee,
Where and what time thou wilt perform the rite;
And all my fortunes at thy foot I'll lay
And follow thee my lord throughout the world.

**NURSE.** [*Within*] Madam!

150  **JULIET.** I come anon.—But if thou meanest not well,
I do beseech thee—

**NURSE.**      [*Within*] Madam!

**JULIET.**                    By and by[25] I come.—
To cease thy strife[26] and leave me to my grief.
Tomorrow will I send.

**ROMEO.**                    So thrive my soul—

**JULIET.** A thousand times good night!                    [*Exit.*]

155  **ROMEO.** A thousand times the worse, to want thy light!
Love goes toward love as schoolboys from their books;
But love from love, toward school with heavy looks.

[*Enter* JULIET *again.*]

**JULIET.** Hist! Romeo, hist! O for a falc'ner's voice
To lure this tassel gentle[27] back again!
160  Bondage is hoarse[28] and may not speak aloud,
Else would I tear the cave where Echo[29] lies
And make her airy tongue more hoarse than mine
With repetition of "My Romeo!"

**ROMEO.** It is my soul that calls upon my name.
165  How silver-sweet sound lovers' tongues by night,
Like softest music to attending ears!

**JULIET.** Romeo!

**ROMEO.**      My sweet?

**JULIET.**                    What o'clock tomorrow
Shall I send to thee?

23. **substantial** real.
24. **bent** purpose; intention.

**Vocabulary**
**procure** (prō kyoor´)
*v.* get; obtain

25. **By and by** at once.
26. **strife** efforts.

**Literary Analysis**
**Blank Verse** Based on the fact that Romeo and Juliet speak in blank verse, what can you conclude about their character rank?

27. **tassel gentle** male falcon.
28. **Bondage is hoarse** Being bound in by my family restricts my speech.
29. **Echo** In classical mythology, the nymph Echo, unable to win the love of Narcissus, wasted away in a cave until nothing was left of her but her voice.

Reading Check

Why can't Juliet speak loudly to Romeo?

**ROMEO.** By the hour of nine.

**JULIET.** I will not fail. 'Tis twenty year till then.
170 I have forgot why I did call thee back.

**ROMEO.** Let me stand here till thou remember it.

**JULIET.** I shall forget, to have thee still stand there,
Rememb'ring how I love thy company.

**ROMEO.** And I'll stay, to have thee still forget,
175 Forgetting any other home but this.

**JULIET.** 'Tis almost morning. I would have thee gone—
And yet no farther than a wanton's[30] bird,
That lets it hop a little from his hand,
Like a poor prisoner in his twisted gyves,[31]
180 And with a silken thread plucks it back again,
So loving-jealous of his liberty.

**ROMEO.** I would I were thy bird.

**JULIET.** Sweet, so would I.
Yet I should kill thee with much cherishing.
Good night, good night! Parting is such sweet sorrow
185 That I shall say good night till it be morrow. [*Exit.*]

**ROMEO.** Sleep dwell upon thine eyes, peace in thy breast!
Would I were sleep and peace, so sweet to rest!
Hence will I to my ghostly friar's[32] close cell,[33]
His help to crave and my dear hap[34] to tell. [*Exit.*]

### Scene iii. Friar Lawrence's cell.

[*Enter* FRIAR LAWRENCE *alone, with a basket.*]

**FRIAR.** The gray-eyed morn smiles on the frowning night,
Check'ring the eastern clouds with streaks of light;
And fleckèd[1] darkness like a drunkard reels
From forth day's path and Titan's burning wheels.[2]
5 Now, ere the sun advance his burning eye
The day to cheer and night's dank dew to dry,
I must upfill this osier cage[3] of ours
With baleful[4] weeds and precious-juicèd flowers.
The earth that's nature's mother is her tomb.
10 What is her burying grave, that is her womb;
And from her womb children of divers kind[5]
We sucking on her natural bosom find,
Many for many virtues excellent,

---

30. **wanton's** spoiled, playful child's.
31. **gyves** (jīvz) chains.

**Reading Skill**
**Summarize** Briefly state the main points of the Friar's speech in lines 1–30.

32. **ghostly friar's** spiritual father's.
33. **close cell** small room.
34. **dear hap** good fortune.

1. **fleckèd** spotted.
2. **Titan's burning wheels** wheels of the sun god's chariot.
3. **osier cage** willow basket.
4. **baleful** poisonous.
5. **divers kind** different kinds.

None but for some, and yet all different.

15 O, mickle[6] is the powerful grace[7] that lies
In plants, herbs, stones, and their true qualities;
For naught so vile that on the earth doth live
But to the earth some special good doth give;
Nor aught so good but, strained[8] from that fair use,
20 Revolts from true birth,[9] stumbling on abuse.
Virtue itself turns vice, being misapplied,
And vice sometime by action dignified.

[*Enter* ROMEO.]

Within the infant rind[10] of this weak flower
Poison hath residence and medicine power;[11]
25 For this, being smelt, with that part cheers each part;[12]
Being tasted, stays all senses with the heart.[13]
Two such opposèd kings encamp them still[14]
In man as well as herbs—grace and rude will;
And where the worser is predominant,
30 Full soon the canker[15] death eats up that plant.

**ROMEO.** Good morrow, father.

**FRIAR.**                          *Benedicite!*[16]
What early tongue so sweet saluteth me?
Young son, it argues a distemperèd head[17]
So soon to bid good morrow to thy bed.
35 Care keeps his watch in every old man's eye,
And where care lodges, sleep will never lie;
But where unbruisèd youth with unstuffed[18] brain
Doth couch his limbs, there golden sleep doth reign,
Therefore thy earliness doth me assure
40 Thou art uproused with some distemp'rature;[19]
Or if not so, then here I hit it right—
Our Romeo hath not been in bed tonight.

**ROMEO.** That last is true. The sweeter rest was mine.

**FRIAR.** God pardon sin! Wast thou with Rosaline?

45 **ROMEO.** With Rosaline, my ghostly father? No.
I have forgot that name and that name's woe.

**FRIAR.** That's my good son! But where hast thou been then?

**ROMEO.** I'll tell thee ere thou ask it me again.
I have been feasting with mine enemy,
50 Where on a sudden one hath wounded me
That's by me wounded. Both our remedies

6. **mickle** great.
7. **grace** divine power.
8. **strained** turned away.
9. **Revolts . . . birth** conflicts with its real purpose.
10. **infant rind** tender skin.
11. **and medicine power** and medicinal quality has power.
12. **with . . . part** with that quality—odor—revives each part of the body.
13. **stays . . . heart** kills (stops the working of the five senses along with the heart).
14. **still** always.
15. **canker** destructive caterpillar.

**Vocabulary**
**predominant** (prē däm´ ə nənt) *adj.* of or having stronger influence

16. *Benedicite!* God bless you!
17. **distemperèd head** troubled mind.

18. **unstuffed** not filled with cares.
19. **distemp'rature** illness.

**Literary Analysis**
**Blank Verse** What sets the Friar's lines apart from normal blank verse?

**Reading Check**
What plan do Romeo and Juliet make for the following day?

20. **physic** (fiz´ ik) medicine.
21. **My . . . foe** my plea also helps my enemy (Juliet, a Capulet).
22. **and . . . drift** and simple in your speech.
23. **Riddling . . . shrift** A confusing confession will get you uncertain forgiveness. The Friar means that unless Romeo speaks clearly, he will not get clear and direct advice.
24. **And . . . save** and we are united in every way, except for (save).
25. **brine** salt water (tears).

26. **fall** be weak or inconstant.
27. **strength** constancy; stability.
28. **doting** being infatuated.
29. **badst** urged.

30. **grace** favor.
31. **allow** give.
32. **Thy . . . spell** your love recited words from memory with no understanding of them.

Within thy help and holy physic[20] lies.
I bear no hatred, blessèd man, for, lo,
My intercession likewise steads my foe.[21]

55   **FRIAR.** Be plain, good son, and homely in thy drift.[22]
      Riddling confession finds but riddling shrift.[23]

  **ROMEO.** Then plainly know my heart's dear love is set
      On the fair daughter of rich Capulet;
      As mine on hers, so hers is set on mine,
60       And all combined, save[24] what thou must combine
      By holy marriage. When and where and how
      We met, we wooed, and made exchange of vow,
      I'll tell thee as we pass; but this I pray,
      That thou consent to marry us today.

65   **FRIAR.** Holy Saint Francis! What a change is here!
      Is Rosaline, that thou didst love so dear,
      So soon forsaken? Young men's love then lies
      Not truly in their hearts, but in their eyes.
      Jesu Maria! What a deal of brine[25]
70       Hath washed thy sallow cheeks for Rosaline!
      How much salt water thrown away in waste
      To season love, that of it doth not taste!
      The sun not yet thy sighs from heaven clears,
      Thy old groans ring yet in mine ancient ears.
75       Lo, here upon thy cheek the stain doth sit
      Of an old tear that is not washed off yet.
      If e'er thou wast thyself, and these woes thine,
      Thou and these woes were all for Rosaline.
      And art thou changed? Pronounce this sentence then:
80       Women may fall[26] when there's no strength[27] in men.

  **ROMEO.** Thou chidst me oft for loving Rosaline.

  **FRIAR.** For doting,[28] not for loving, pupil mine.

  **ROMEO.** And badst[29] me bury love.

  **FRIAR.**                     Not in a grave
      To lay one in, another out to have.

85   **ROMEO.** I pray thee chide me not. Her I love now
      Doth grace[30] for grace and love for love allow.[31]
      The other did not so.

  **FRIAR.**                 O, she knew well
      Thy love did read by rote, that could not spell.[32]

But come, young waverer, come go with me.
90 In one respect I'll thy assistant be;
   For this alliance may so happy prove
   To turn your households' rancor³³ to pure love.

   **ROMEO.** O, let us hence! I stand on³⁴ sudden haste.

   **FRIAR.** Wisely and slow. They stumble that run fast.     [*Exit all.*]

### Scene iv. A street.

[*Enter* BENVOLIO *and* MERCUTIO.]

   **MERCUTIO.** Where the devil should this Romeo be? Came he not
      home tonight?

   **BENVOLIO.** Not to his father's. I spoke with his man.

   **MERCUTIO.** Why, that same pale hardhearted wench, that
5      Rosaline,
      torments him so that he will sure run mad.

   **BENVOLIO.** Tybalt, the kinsman to old Capulet,
      Hath sent a letter to his father's house.

   **MERCUTIO.** A challenge, on my life.

10 **BENVOLIO.** Romeo will answer it.

   **MERCUTIO.** Any man that can write may answer a letter.

   **BENVOLIO.** Nay, he will answer the letter's master, how he dares,
      being dared.

   **MERCUTIO.** Alas, poor Romeo, he is already dead: stabbed
15      with a white wench's black eye; run through the ear
      with a love song; the very pin of his heart cleft with the
      blind bow-boy's butt-shaft;¹ and is he a man to encounter
      Tybalt?

   **BENVOLIO.** Why, what is Tybalt?

20 **MERCUTIO.** More than Prince of Cats.² O, he's the courageous
      captain of compliments.³ He fights as you sing
      pricksong⁴—keeps time, distance, and proportion; he
      rests his minim rests,⁵ one, two, and the third in your
      bosom! The very butcher of a silk button,⁶ a duelist, a
25      duelist! A gentleman of the very first house,⁷ of the first
      and second cause.⁸ Ah, the immortal *passado*! The
      *punto reverso*! The hay!⁹

   **BENVOLIO.** The what?

   **MERCUTIO.** The pox of such antic, lisping, affecting

---

33. **rancor** hatred.
34. **stand on** insist on.

**Literary Analysis
Blank Verse** In what way is Mercutio's and Benvolio's speech in this scene different from what it was earlier in Act II?

1. **blind bow-boy's butt-shaft** Cupid's blunt arrow.
2. **Prince of Cats** Tybalt, or a variation of it, is the name of the cat in medieval stories of Reynard the Fox.
3. **captain of compliments** master of formal behavior.
4. **as you sing pricksong** with attention to precision.
5. **rests . . . rests** observes all formalities.
6. **button** exact spot on his opponent's shirt.
7. **first house** finest school of fencing.
8. **the first and second cause** reasons that would cause a gentleman to challenge another to a duel.
9. *passado*! . . . *punto reverso*! . . . hay! lunge . . . backhanded stroke . . . home thrust.

**Reading Check**

What does the Friar think Romeo and Juliet's love will do for the Capulets and Montagues?

---

**10. The pox . . . accent** May the plague strike these absurd characters with their phony manners.

**Vocabulary**
**lamentable** (lam´ ən tə bəl) *adj.* distressing; sad

**11. these pardon-me's** these men who are always saying "Pardon me."
**12. Without . . . herring** worn out.
**13. numbers** verses of love poems.

**14. slip** escape. *Slip* is also a term for a counterfeit coin.

30 fantasticoes—these new tuners of accent![10] "By Jesu, a very good blade! A very tall man! A very good whore!" Why, is not this a lamentable thing, grandsir, that we should be thus afflicted with these strange flies, these fashionmongers, these pardon-me's,[11] who stand so 35 much on the new form that they cannot sit at ease on the old bench? O, their bones, their bones!

[*Enter* ROMEO.]

**BENVOLIO.** Here comes Romeo! Here comes Romeo!

**MERCUTIO.** Without his roe, like a dried herring.[12] O flesh, flesh, how art thou fishified! Now is he for the numbers[13] 40 that Petrarch flowed in. Laura, to his lady, was a kitchen wench (marry, she had a better love to berhyme her), Dido a dowdy, Cleopatra a gypsy, Helen and Hero hildings and harlots, Thisbe a gray eye or so, but not to the purpose. Signior Romeo, *bonjour!* 45 There's a French salutation to your French slop. You gave us the counterfeit fairly last night.

**ROMEO.** Good morrow to you both. What counterfeit did I give you?

**MERCUTIO.** The slip,[14] sir, the slip. Can you not conceive?

## LITERATURE IN CONTEXT

### History Connection

#### Mercutio's Allusions
The women Mercutio names as he taunts Romeo are famous figures in European literature and history. Laura was the name of a woman to whom the Italian poet Petrarch addressed much of his love poetry. Dido, according to Roman mythology, was the queen of Carthage and love interest of Aeneas, the founder of Rome. Cleopatra was the famed Egyptian queen with whom Julius Caesar and later Mark Antony fell in love. Helen, Hero, and Thisbe are all legendary beauties in Greek mythology. Mercutio mocks Romeo by saying that Romeo thinks none of them compare with Rosaline.

### Connect to the Literature

Why is Mercutio's use of grand references and exaggerated language a fitting way to tease Romeo?

**ROMEO.** Pardon, good Mercutio. My business was great,
    and in such a case as mine a man may strain courtesy.

**MERCUTIO.** That's as much as to say, such a case as yours
    constrains a man to bow in the hams.[15]

**ROMEO.** Meaning, to curtsy.

55 **MERCUTIO.** Thou hast most kindly hit it.

**ROMEO.** A most courteous exposition.

**MERCUTIO.** Nay, I am the very pink of courtesy.

**ROMEO.** Pink for flower.

**MERCUTIO.** Right.

60 **ROMEO.** Why, then is my pump[16] well-flowered.

**MERCUTIO.** Sure wit, follow me this jest now till thou hast
    worn out thy pump, that, when the single sole of it is
    worn, the jest may remain, after the wearing, solely
    singular.[17]

65 **ROMEO.** O single-soled jest, solely singular for the singleness![18]

**MERCUTIO.** Come between us, good Benvolio! My wits faints.

**ROMEO.** Swits and spurs, swits and spurs; or I'll cry a
    match.[19]

**MERCUTIO.** Nay, if our wits run the wild-goose chase, I
    am done; for thou hast more of the wild goose in one of
70     thy wits than, I am sure, I have in my whole five. Was I
    with you there for the goose?

**ROMEO.** Thou wast never with me for anything when thou
    wast not there for the goose.

**MERCUTIO.** I will bite thee by the ear for that jest.

75 **ROMEO.** Nay, good goose, bite not!

**MERCUTIO.** Thy wit is a very bitter sweeting;[20] it is a most sharp
    sauce.

**ROMEO.** And is it not, then, well served in to a sweet goose?

**MERCUTIO.** O, here's a wit of cheveril,[21] that stretches from an
80     inch narrow to an ell broad!

**ROMEO.** I stretch it out for that word "broad," which added
    to the goose, proves thee far and wide a broad goose.

15. **hams** hips.

16. **pump** shoe.
17. **when . . . singular** the jest will outwear the shoe and will then be all alone.
18. **O . . . singleness!** O thin joke, unique for only one thing—weakness!
19. **Swits . . . match** Drive your wit harder to beat me or else I will claim victory in this match of word play.

**Literary Analysis**
**Blank Verse** Why do you think Romeo does not speak in blank verse in this conversation with his friends?

20. **sweeting** kind of apple.
21. **cheveril** easily stretched kid leather.

Reading Check
How does Romeo respond when Mercutio says that Romeo gave his friends "the slip" the night before?

**MERCUTIO.** Why, is not this better now than groaning for
love? Now art thou sociable, now art thou Romeo; now

85      art thou what thou art, by art as well as by nature. For
this driveling love is like a great natural[22] that runs
lolling[23] up and down to hide his bauble[24] in a hole.

**BENVOLIO.** Stop there, stop there!

**MERCUTIO.** Thou desirest me to stop in my tale against the
hair.[25]

90   **BENVOLIO.** Thou wouldst else have made thy tale large.

**MERCUTIO.** O, thou art deceived! I would have made it
short; for I was come to the whole depth of my tale,
and meant indeed to occupy the argument[26] no longer.

**ROMEO.** Here's goodly gear![27]

[*Enter* NURSE *and her Man,* PETER.]

95       A sail, a sail!

**MERCUTIO.** Two, two! A shirt and a smock.[28]

**NURSE.** Peter!

**PETER.** Anon.

**NURSE.** My fan, Peter.

100  **MERCUTIO.** Good Peter, to hide her face; for her fan's the
fairer face.

**NURSE.** God ye good morrow, gentlemen.

**MERCUTIO.** God ye good-den, fair gentlewoman.

**NURSE.** Is it good-den?

105  **MERCUTIO.** 'Tis no less, I tell ye; for the bawdy hand of the
dial is now upon the prick of noon.

**NURSE.** Out upon you! What a man are you!

**ROMEO.** One, gentlewoman, that God hath made, himself to mar.

**NURSE.** By my troth, it is well said. "For himself to mar,"

110      quoth 'a? Gentlemen, can any of you tell me where I
may find the young Romeo?

**ROMEO.** I can tell you; but young Romeo will be older
when you have found him than he was when you sought
him. I am the youngest of that name, for fault[29] of a

115      worse.

---

**22. natural** idiot.
**23. lolling** with tongue hanging out.
**24. bauble** toy.
**25. the hair** natural inclination.

**26. occupy the argument** talk about the matter.
**27. goodly gear** good stuff for joking (Romeo sees Nurse approaching).
**28. A shirt and a smock** a man and a woman.

**Literary Analysis**
**Blank Verse** How does Shakespeare reveal Romeo and Mercutio's intelligence even when they are not speaking in blank verse?

**29. fault** lack.

**NURSE.** You say well.

**MERCUTIO.** Yea, is the worst well? Very well took,[30] i' faith!
Wisely, wisely.

**NURSE.** If you be he, sir, I desire some confidence[31] with you.

120 **BENVOLIO.** She will endite him to some supper.

**MERCUTIO.** A bawd, a bawd, a bawd! So ho!

**ROMEO.** What hast thou found?

**MERCUTIO.** No hare, sir; unless a hare, sir, in a lenten pie,
that is something stale and hoar ere it be spent.

[*He walks by them and sings.*]

125            An old hare hoar,
           And an old hare hoar,
               Is very good meat in Lent;
           But a hare that is hoar
           Is too much for a score
130                When it hoars ere it be spent.

30. **took** understood.

31. **confidence** Nurse means
"conference."

**Reading Check**

Who interrupts Romeo
and his friends to ask
about Romeo?

Romeo, will you come to your father's? We'll to dinner thither.

**ROMEO.** I will follow you.

**MERCUTIO.** Farewell, ancient lady. Farewell, [*singing*] "Lady, lady, lady."[32]

[*Exit* MERCUTIO, BENVOLIO.]

135   **NURSE.** I pray you, sir, what saucy merchant was this that was so full of his ropery?[33]

**ROMEO.** A gentleman, nurse, that loves to hear himself talk and will speak more in a minute than he will stand to in a month.

140   **NURSE.** And 'a[34] speak anything against me, I'll take him down, and 'a were lustier than he is, and twenty such Jacks; and if I cannot, I'll find those that shall. Scurvy knave! I am none of his flirt-gills;[35] I am none of his skainsmates.[36] And thou must stand by too, and suffer
145   every knave to use me at his pleasure!

**PETER.** I saw no man use you at his pleasure. If I had, my weapon should quickly have been out, I warrant you. I dare draw as soon as another man, if I see occasion in a good quarrel, and the law on my side.

150   **NURSE.** Now, afore God, I am so vexed that every part about me quivers. Scurvy knave! Pray you, sir, a word; and, as I told you, my young lady bid me inquire you out. What she bid me say, I will keep to myself; but first let me tell ye, if ye should lead her in a fool's paradise, as
155   they say, it were a very gross kind of behavior, as they say; for the gentlewoman is young; and therefore, if you should deal double with her, truly it were an ill thing to be off'red to any gentlewoman, and very weak[37] dealing.

160   **ROMEO.** Nurse, commend[38] me to thy lady and mistress. I protest unto thee—

**NURSE.** Good heart, and i' faith I will tell her as much. Lord, Lord, she will be a joyful woman.

**ROMEO.** What wilt thou tell her, nurse? Thou dost not
165   mark me.

**NURSE.** I will tell her, sir, that you do protest, which, as I take it, is a gentlemanlike offer.

---

32. **"Lady . . . lady"** line from an old ballad, "Chaste Susanna."
33. **ropery** Nurse means "roguery," the talk and conduct of a rascal.

34. **'a** he.

35. **flirt-gills** common girls.
36. **skainsmates** criminals; cutthroats.

**Spiral Review**
**Character** What do Nurse's comments to Romeo reveal about her feelings for Juliet?

37. **weak** unmanly.

38. **commend** convey my respect and best wishes.

**ROMEO.** Bid her devise
Some means to come to shrift[39] this afternoon;

170 And there she shall at Friar Lawrence' cell
Be shrived and married. Here is for thy pains.

**NURSE.** No, truly, sir; not a penny.

**ROMEO.** Go to! I say you shall.

**NURSE.** This afternoon, sir? Well, she shall be there.

175 **ROMEO.** And stay, good nurse, behind the abbey wall.
Within this hour my man shall be with thee
And bring thee cords made like a tackled stair.[40]
Which to the high topgallant[41] of my joy
Must be my convoy[42] in the secret night.

180 Farewell. Be trusty, and I'll quit[43] thy pains.
Farewell. Commend me to thy mistress.

**NURSE.** Now God in heaven bless thee! Hark you, sir.

**ROMEO.** What say'st thou, my dear nurse?

**NURSE.** Is your man secret? Did you ne'er hear say,

185 Two may keep counsel, putting one away?[44]

**ROMEO.** Warrant thee my man's as true as steel.

**NURSE.** Well, sir, my mistress is the sweetest lady. Lord,
Lord! When 'twas a little prating[45] thing—O, there is a
nobleman in town, one Paris, that would fain lay knife

190 aboard;[46] but she, good soul, had as lieve[47] see a toad,
a very toad, as see him. I anger her sometimes, and tell
her that Paris is the properer man; but I'll warrant
you, when I say so, she looks as pale as any clout[48]
in the versal world.[49] Doth not rosemary and Romeo

195 begin both with a letter?

**ROMEO.** Ay, nurse; what of that? Both with an R.

**NURSE.** Ah, mocker! That's the dog's name.[50] R is for the—
No; I know it begins with some other letter; and she
hath the prettiest sententious[51] of it, of you and rosemary,

200 that it would do you good to hear it.

**ROMEO.** Commend me to thy lady.

**NURSE.** Ay, a thousand times. [*Exit* ROMEO.] Peter!

**PETER.** Anon.

205 **NURSE.** Before, and apace.[52]                    [*Exit, after* PETER.]

---

**39. shrift** confession.

**Reading Skill
Summarize** Read in
sentences to summarize
Romeo's instructions
to the Nurse in lines
175–181.

**40. tackled stair** rope ladder.
**41. topgallant** summit.
**42. convoy** conveyance.
**43. quit** reward; pay you back
for.

**44. Two . . . away** Two can
keep a secret if one is
ignorant, or out of the way.
**45. prating** babbling.
**46. fain . . . aboard** eagerly
seize Juliet for himself.
**47. had as lieve** would as
willingly.
**48. clout** cloth.
**49. versal world** universe.
**50. dog's name** *R* sounds like
a growl.
**51. sententious** Nurse means
"sentences"—clever, wise
sayings.
**52. Before, and apace** Go
ahead of me, and quickly.

**Literary Analysis
Blank Verse** What is
the effect of hearing
Romeo's blank verse
after long passages of
prose?

**Reading
Check**
What does Romeo ask
the Nurse to tell Juliet?

*Scene v. Capulet's orchard.*

[*Enter* JULIET.]

> **JULIET.** The clock struck nine when I did send the nurse;
>> In half an hour she promised to return.
>> Perchance she cannot meet him. That's not so.
>> O, she is lame! Love's heralds should be thoughts,
> 5   Which ten times faster glides than the sun's beams
>> Driving back shadows over low'ring¹ hills.
>> Therefore do nimble-pinioned doves draw Love,²
>> And therefore hath the wind-swift Cupid wings.
>> Now is the sun upon the highmost hill
> 10   Of this day's journey, and from nine till twelve
>> Is three long hours; yet she is not come.
>> Had she affections and warm youthful blood,
>> She would be as swift in motion as a ball;
>> My words would bandy her³ to my sweet love,
> 15   And his to me.
>> But old folks, many feign⁴ as they were dead—
>> Unwieldy, slow, heavy and pale as lead.

[*Enter* NURSE *and* PETER.]

>> O God, she comes! O honey nurse, what news?
>> Hast thou met with him? Send thy man away.

> 20  **NURSE.** Peter, stay at the gate.          [*Exit* PETER.]

> **JULIET.** Now, good sweet nurse—O Lord, why lookest thou sad?
>> Though news be sad, yet tell them merrily;
>> If good, thou shamest the music of sweet news
>> By playing it to me with so sour a face.

> 25  **NURSE.** I am aweary, give me leave⁵ awhile.
>> Fie, how my bones ache! What a jaunce⁶ have I!

> **JULIET.** I would thou hadst my bones, and I thy news.
>> Nay, come, I pray thee speak. Good, good nurse, speak.

> **NURSE.** Jesu, what haste? Can you not stay a while?
> 30   Do you not see that I am out of breath?

> **JULIET.** How art thou out of breath when thou hast breath
>> To say to me that thou art out of breath?
>> The excuse that thou dost make in this delay
>> Is longer than the tale thou dost excuse.
> 35   Is thy news good or bad? Answer to that.

---

**1. low'ring** darkening.
**2. Therefore . . . Love** therefore, doves with quick wings pull the chariot of Venus, goddess of love.

**3. bandy her** send her rapidly.

**Vocabulary**
**unwieldy** (un wēl′ dē) *adj.* awkward; clumsy

**4. feign** act.

**5. give me leave** excuse me; give me a moment's rest.
**6. jaunce** rough trip.

Say either, and I'll stay the circumstance.[7]
Let me be satisfied, is't good or bad?

**NURSE.** Well, you have made a simple[8] choice; you know
not how to choose a man. Romeo? No, not he. Though
40   his face be better than any man's, yet his leg excels all
men's; and for a hand and a foot, and a body, though
they be not to be talked on, yet they are past compare.
He is not the flower of courtesy, but, I'll warrant him,
as gentle as a lamb. Go thy ways, wench; serve God.
45   What, have you dined at home?

**JULIET.** No, no. But all this I did know before.
What says he of our marriage? What of that?

**NURSE.** Lord, how my head aches! What a head have I!
It beats as it would fall in twenty pieces.
50   My back a[9] t'other side—ah, my back, my back!
Beshrew[10] your heart for sending me about
To catch my death with jauncing up and down!

**JULIET.** I' faith, I am sorry that thou art not well.
Sweet, sweet, sweet nurse, tell me, what says my love?

55   **NURSE.** Your love says, like an honest gentleman, and a
courteous, and a kind, and a handsome, and, I warrant,
a virtuous—Where is your mother?

**JULIET.** Where is my mother? Why, she is within.
Where should she be? How oddly thou repliest!
60   "Your love says, like an honest gentleman,
'Where is your mother?'"

**NURSE.**                    O God's Lady dear!
Are you so hot?[11] Marry come up, I trow.[12]
Is this the poultice[13] for my aching bones?
Henceforward do your messages yourself.

65   **JULIET.** Here's such a coil![14] Come, what says Romeo?

**NURSE.** Have you got leave to go to shrift today?

**JULIET.** I have.

**NURSE.** Then hie you hence to Friar Lawrence' cell;
There stays a husband to make you a wife.
70   Now comes the wanton[15] blood up in your cheeks:
They'll be in scarlet straight at any news.
Hie you to church: I must another way,

7. **stay the circumstance** wait for the details.
8. **simple** foolish; simpleminded.

9. **a** on.
10. **Beshrew** shame on.

**Literary Analysis**
**Blank Verse** What might Shakespeare be indicating about the Nurse's character by having her switch between prose and blank verse?

11. **hot** impatient; hot-tempered.
12. **Marry . . . trow** Indeed, cool down, I say.
13. **poultice** remedy.
14. **coil** disturbance.
15. **wanton** excited.

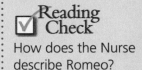

**Reading Check**
How does the Nurse describe Romeo?

**Literary Analysis**
**Blank Verse** What effect is created by making Juliet's last line rhyme with the Nurse's last line?

To fetch a ladder, by the which your love
Must climb a bird's nest soon when it is dark.
75   I am the drudge, and toil in your delight:
But you shall bear the burden soon at night.
Go; I'll to dinner; hie you to the cell.

**JULIET.** Hie to high fortune! Honest nurse, farewell.

[*Exit all.*]

### Scene vi. Friar Lawrence's cell.

[*Enter* FRIAR LAWRENCE *and* ROMEO.]

**FRIAR.** So smile the heavens upon this holy act
That afterhours with sorrow chide us not![1]

**ROMEO.** Amen, amen! But come what sorrow can,
It cannot countervail[2] the exchange of joy
5   That one short minute gives me in her sight.
Do thou but close our hands with holy words,
Then love-devouring death do what he dare—
It is enough I may but call her mine.

**FRIAR.** These violent delights have violent ends
10   And in their triumph die, like fire and powder,[3]
Which, as they kiss, consume. The sweetest honey

1. **That . . . not!** that the future does not punish us with sorrow.
2. **countervail** equal.
3. **powder** gunpowder.

▶ **Critical Viewing**
Which details in this picture reflect the feelings Romeo and Juliet have for each other? **[Interpret]**

Is loathsome in his own deliciousness
And in the taste confounds[4] the appetite.
Therefore love moderately: long love doth so;
15   Too swift arrives as tardy as too slow.

[*Enter* JULIET.]

Here comes the lady. O, so light a foot
Will ne'er wear out the everlasting flint.[5]
A lover may bestride the gossamers[6]
That idles in the wanton summer air,
20   And yet not fall; so light is vanity.[7]

**JULIET.** Good even to my ghostly confessor.

**FRIAR.** Romeo shall thank thee, daughter, for us both.

4. **confounds** destroys.

5. **flint** stone.
6. **gossamers** spider webs.
7. **vanity** foolish things that cannot last.

The Tragedy of Romeo and Juliet, Act II  **857**

**JULIET.** As much to him,[8] else is his thanks too much.

25 **ROMEO.** Ah, Juliet, if the measure of thy joy
Be heaped like mine, and that thy skill be more
To blazon it,[9] then sweeten with thy breath
This neighbor air, and let rich music's tongue
Unfold the imagined happiness that both
Receive in either by this dear encounter.

30 **JULIET.** Conceit, more rich in matter than in words,
Brags of his substance, not of ornament.[10]
They are but beggars that can count their worth;
But my true love is grown to such excess
I cannot sum up sum of half my wealth.

35 **FRIAR.** Come, come with me, and we will make short work;
For, by your leaves, you shall not stay alone
Till Holy Church incorporate two in one.              [*Exit all.*]

8. **As . . . him** the same greeting to him.
9. **and . . . it** and if you are better able to proclaim it.

10. **Conceit . . . ornament** Understanding does not need to be dressed up in words.

---

## Critical Thinking

Cite textual evidence to support your responses.

© 1. **Key Ideas and Details (a)** Where do Romeo and Juliet first mutually declare their love? **(b) Interpret:** What role does darkness play in the scene?

© 2. **Key Ideas and Details (a)** What weakness in Romeo does the Friar point out before agreeing to help? **(b) Compare and Contrast:** How do the Friar's motives differ from the couple's motives? Explain your response.

© 3. **Key Ideas and Details (a)** For whom does Juliet wait in Act II, Scene v? **(b) Analyze:** What are her feelings as she waits? Explain your answer.

© 4. **Integration of Knowledge and Ideas  Evaluate:** Why do you think the love scene in Capulet's garden is one of the most famous dramatic scenes in all literature? Explain.

© 5. **Integration of Knowledge and Ideas** Have the differences between Romeo and Juliet affected their relationship? Use details from the text to support your response. *[Connect to the Big Question: Do our differences define us?]*

## After You Read

### The Tragedy of Romeo and Juliet, Act II

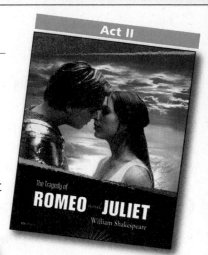

Act II

The Tragedy of
ROMEO and JULIET
William Shakespeare

## Literary Analysis: Blank Verse

ⓒ **1. Craft and Structure** Copy the following passages of **blank verse.** Then, indicate the pattern of accented (ˊ) and unaccented (˘) syllables in each line. **(a)** Act II, Scene ii, lines 43–51 **(b)** Act II, Scene vi, lines 3–8

ⓒ **2. Craft and Structure** Using a chart like the one shown, rewrite the following two lines, marking stressed and unstressed syllables. Then, identify the key words stressed in each line, and explain what meaning is conveyed. **(a) ROMEO.** Can I go forward when my heart is here? **(b) JULIET.** But my true love is grown to such excess.

| Blank Verse Pattern | Key Words | Significance |
|---|---|---|
|  |  |  |

ⓒ **3. Craft and Structure (a)** Identify the aristocratic and common people in Acts I and II based on whether or not they speak in blank verse. **(b)** Why might Shakespeare have chosen blank verse for aristocrats?

## Reading Skill: Summarize

**4. (a)** How many sentences are in lines 1–8 of Act II, Scene v?
**(b)** Write a **summary** of these lines.

## Vocabulary

ⓒ **Acquisition and Use** Answer each question. Then, explain your answer.

**1.** Where would you go to *procure* groceries?

**2.** What is the *predominant* feeling at a celebration?

**3.** How many people are needed for an *intercession* to occur?

**4.** Is a *sallow* complexion a sign of good health?

**5.** If a situation is *lamentable*, are people likely to be happy about it?

**6.** Is an *unwieldy* package something you would want to carry far?

**Word Study** Use the context of the sentences and what you know about the **Latin prefix pro-** to explain your answer to each question.

**1.** If you make a *proposal,* have you suggested a course of action?

**2.** If you are *proactive,* are you waiting for something to occur?

### Word Study

The **Latin prefix pro-** means "before," "forward."

**Apply It** Explain how the prefix *pro-* contributes to the meanings of these words. Consult a dictionary if necessary.

**program**
**project**
**prorate**

## Before You Read | The Tragedy of Romeo and Juliet, Act III

 **THE BIG Q** **Do our *differences* define us?**

**While You Read** Look for the steps that Romeo and Juliet try to take to overcome their differences—and think about the new separations they are developing among friends and family.

Act III

The Tragedy of
ROMEO and JULIET
William Shakespeare

## © Common Core State Standards

Meet these standards with *The Tragedy of Romeo and Juliet,* **Act III** (p. 862).

**Reading Literature**
**2.** Determine a theme or central idea of a text; provide an objective summary of the text. *(Reading Skill: Summarize)*
**Spiral Review: RL.9–10.3**
**5.** Analyze how an author's choices concerning how to structure a text, order events within it, and manipulate time create such effects as mystery, tension, or surprise. *(Literary Analysis: Dramatic Speeches)*

## Vocabulary

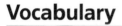

Read each word and its definition. Decide whether you know the word well, know it a little bit, or do not know it at all. After you read, see how your knowledge of each word has increased.

- **gallant** (gal´ ənt) *adj.* brave and noble (p. 868) *We called the fire-fighters* gallant, *but they said they were just doing their job.* gallantly *adv.* gallantry *n.*

- **fray** (frā) *n.* noisy fight (p. 869) *The crew argued, but the captain stayed above the* fray. fray *v.* frayed *adj.*

- **martial** (mär´ shəl) *adj.* military; warlike (p. 869) *The band played* martial *music to honor the soldiers.* martialist *n.*

- **exile** (eks´ īl´) *v.* banish (p. 870) *Years ago, rulers would* exile *criminals to faraway places.* exiler *n.*

- **eloquence** (el´ ə kwəns) *n.* speech that is graceful and persuasive (p. 871) *The* eloquence *of her speech moved the audience.* eloquent *adj.* eloquently *adv.*

- **fickle** (fik´ əl) *adj.* changeable (p. 884) *His* fickle *sense of style made buying clothes for him difficult.* fickleness *n.*

### Word Study

The **Latin root -*loque-*** means "talk," "speak," or "say."

In Act III, Juliet says that everyone who speaks Romeo's name speaks **eloquence.** She means that the name itself is a graceful, vivid expression.

# Literary Analysis: Dramatic Speeches

In most plays, the dramatic action takes place through **dialogue**—the conversations between characters. Some playwrights, however, make use of specialized dialogue in the form of **dramatic speeches.**

- **Soliloquy:** a lengthy speech in which a character—usually alone on stage—expresses his or her true thoughts or feelings. Soliloquies are unheard by other characters.
- **Aside:** a character revealing his or her true thoughts or feelings in a remark that is unheard by other characters.
- **Monologue:** a lengthy speech by one character. Unlike a soliloquy or an aside, a monologue is addressed to other characters.

Characters' speeches reflect their individual character traits, and Shakespeare often uses dialogue and action to emphasize differences between characters. As you read, look for **foils,** or characters whose words and actions show you clear personality contrasts.

# Reading Skill: Summarize

**Summarizing** is briefly stating the main points in a piece of writing. Before you summarize a passage of a play by Shakespeare, **paraphrase** it, or restate the lines in your own words. Compare these two versions of a speech by Romeo:

**Shakespeare's version:** "This gentleman, the Prince's near ally, / My very friend, hath got his mortal hurt / In my behalf. . . ."

**Paraphrase:** My good friend, a close relative of the prince, has been fatally wounded in defending me.

Once you have paraphrased small portions of text, you can more easily and accurately summarize an entire passage.

### Using the Strategy: Summarizing Chart

Use a chart like this one to paraphrase and summarize the text.

| Text | Paraphrase | Summary |
| --- | --- | --- |
| "I pray thee, good Mercutio, let's retire. The day is hot, the Capulets abroad, And, if we meet, we shall not 'scape a brawl, For now, these hot days, is the mad blood stirring." | Please, Mercutio, let's leave. It's hot out, and the Capulets are around. And if we meet up with them, we will most likely fight, because on these hot days we have fight in us. | Benvolio is trying to convince Mercutio to leave the public place they are meeting in, because he is afraid a brawl with the Capulets is inevitable. |

# Act III

## Review and Anticipate

In Act II, Romeo and Juliet express their mutual love and enlist the aid of Juliet's nurse and Friar Lawrence to arrange a secret marriage ceremony. As the act closes, the young couple is about to be married. Before performing the ceremony, the Friar warns, "These violent delights have violent ends. . . ." How might this statement hint at events that will occur in Act III or later in the play?

**Scene i. A public place.**

[*Enter* MERCUTIO, BENVOLIO, *and* MEN.]

    **BENVOLIO.** I pray thee, good Mercutio, let's retire.
       The day is hot, the Capulets abroad,
       And, if we meet, we shall not 'scape a brawl,
       For now, these hot days, is the mad blood stirring.

5  **MERCUTIO.** Thou art like one of these fellows that, when he
       enters the confines of a tavern, claps me his sword upon the
       table and says, "God send me no need of thee!" and by the
       operation of the second cup draws him on the drawer,[1] when
       indeed there is no need.

10 **BENVOLIO.** Am I like such a fellow?

    **MERCUTIO.** Come, come, thou art as hot a Jack in thy mood as
       any in Italy; and as soon moved to be moody, and as soon
       moody to be moved.[2]

1. **and . . . drawer** and by the effect of the second drink, draws his sword against the waiter.
2. **and . . . moved** and as quickly stirred to anger as you are eager to be so stirred.

Reading
Check

Why does Benvolio want to get off the street?

**Literary Analysis
Dramatic Speeches**
Which details of
Mercutio's speech
indicate that it is a
monologue and not a
soliloquy?

15 **MERCUTIO.** Nay, and there were two such, we should have none
shortly, for one would kill the other. Thou! Why, thou wilt
quarrel with a man that hath a hair more or a hair less in
his beard than thou hast. Thou wilt quarrel with a man for
cracking nuts, having no other reason but because thou
20 hast hazel eyes. What eye but such an eye would spy out
such a quarrel? Thy head is as full of quarrels as an egg is
full of meat; and yet thy head hath been beaten as addle³ as
an egg for quarreling. Thou hast quarreled with a man for
coughing in the street, because he hath wakened thy dog
25 that hath lain asleep in the sun. Didst thou not fall out with
a tailor for wearing his new doublet⁴ before Easter? With
another for tying his new shoes with old riband?⁵ And yet
thou wilt tutor me from quarreling!⁶

3. **addle** scrambled; crazy.

4. **doublet** jacket.
5. **riband** ribbon.
6. **tutor . . . quarreling**
instruct me not to quarrel.
7. **fee simple** complete
possession.
8. **an hour and a quarter**
length of time that a man
with Mercutio's fondness
for quarreling may be
expected to live.
9. **O simple!** O stupid!

**BENVOLIO.** And I were so apt to quarrel as thou art, any man
30 should buy the fee simple⁷ of my life for an hour and a
quarter.⁸

**MERCUTIO.** The fee simple? O simple!⁹

[*Enter* TYBALT, PETRUCHIO, *and* OTHERS.]

**BENVOLIO.** By my head, here comes the Capulets.

**MERCUTIO.** By my heel, I care not.

35 **TYBALT.** Follow me close, for I will speak to them.
Gentlemen, good-den. A word with one of you.

**MERCUTIO.** And but one word with one of us? Couple it with
something; make it a word and a blow.

**TYBALT.** You shall find me apt enough to that, sir, and you will
40 give me occasion.¹⁰

**Reading Skill
Summarize** How would
you paraphrase the
exchange between Tybalt
and Mercutio?

10. **occasion** cause; reason.
11. **consortest** associate
with.
12. **Consort** associate with;
"consort" also meant a
group of musicians.
13. **discords** harsh sounds.
14. **Zounds** exclamation of
surprise or anger ("By
God's wounds").

**MERCUTIO.** Could you not take some occasion without giving?

**TYBALT.** Mercutio, thou consortest¹¹ with Romeo.

**MERCUTIO.** Consort?¹² What, dost thou make us minstrels?
And thou make minstrels of us, look to hear nothing but
45 discords.¹³ Here's my fiddlestick; here's that shall make you
dance. Zounds,¹⁴ consort!

**Literary Analysis
Dramatic Speeches**
How does the dialogue
here set Mercutio and
Benvolio as foils?

**BENVOLIO.** We talk here in the public haunt of men.
Either withdraw unto some private place,
Or reason coldly of your grievances,
50 Or else depart. Here all eyes gaze on us.

**MERCUTIO.** Men's eyes were made to look, and let them gaze.
　　I will not budge for no man's pleasure, I.

[*Enter* ROMEO.]

　　**TYBALT.** Well, peace be with you, sir. Here comes my man.[15]

　　**MERCUTIO.** But I'll be hanged, sir, if he wear your livery.[16]
55　　Marry, go before to field,[17] he'll be your follower!
　　Your worship in that sense may call him man.

　　**TYBALT.** Romeo, the love I bear thee can afford
　　No better term than this: thou art a villain.[18]

　　**ROMEO.** Tybalt, the reason that I have to love thee
60　　Doth much excuse the appertaining[19] rage
　　To such a greeting. Villain am I none.
　　Therefore farewell. I see thou knowest me not.

15. **man** man I am looking for; "man" also meant "manservant."
16. **livery** servant's uniform.
17. **field** dueling place.
18. **villain** low, vulgar person.
19. **appertaining** appropriate.

**Reading Check**

What are Mercutio and Benvolio arguing about?

**TYBALT.** Boy, this shall not excuse the injuries
That thou hast done me; therefore turn and draw.

65 **ROMEO.** I do protest I never injured thee,
But love thee better than thou canst devise[20]
Till thou shalt know the reason of my love;
And so, good Capulet, which name I tender[21]
As dearly as mine own, be satisfied.

70 **MERCUTIO.** O calm, dishonorable, vile submission!
*Alla stoccata*[22] carries it away.                          [*Draws.*]
Tybalt, you ratcatcher, will you walk?

**TYBALT.** What wouldst thou have with me?

**MERCUTIO.** Good King of Cats, nothing but one of your
75     nine lives. That I mean to make bold withal,[23] and, as
you shall use me here-after, dry-beat[24] the rest of the
eight. Will you pluck your sword out of his pilcher[25]
by the ears? Make haste, lest mine be about your
ears ere it be out.

80 **TYBALT.** I am for you.                                    [*Draws.*]

**ROMEO.** Gentle Mercutio, put thy rapier up.

**MERCUTIO.** Come, sir, your *passado*!                       [*They fight.*]

**ROMEO.** Draw, Benvolio; beat down their weapons.
Gentlemen, for shame! Forbear this outrage!
85     Tybalt, Mercutio, the Prince expressly hath

20. **devise** understand; imagine.
21. **tender** value.

22. *Alla stoccata* at the thrust—an Italian fencing term that Mercutio uses as a nickname for Tybalt.

23. **make bold withal** make bold with; take.
24. **dry-beat** thrash.
25. **pilcher** scabbard.

▼▶ **Critical Viewing**
Which details in these photographs suggest that a duel is about to take place? **[Analyze]**

Forbid this bandying in Verona streets.
Hold, Tybalt! Good Mercutio!

[TYBALT *under* ROMEO'S *arm thrusts* MERCUTIO *in, and flies.*]

**MERCUTIO.**                              I am hurt.
A plague a[26] both houses! I am sped.[27]
Is he gone and hath nothing?

**BENVOLIO.**                              What, art thou hurt?

90 **MERCUTIO.** Ay, ay, a scratch, a scratch. Marry, 'tis enough.
Where is my page? Go, villain, fetch a surgeon.     [*Exit* PAGE.]

**ROMEO.** Courage, man. The hurt cannot be much.

**MERCUTIO.** No, 'tis not so deep as a well, nor so wide as
a church door; but 'tis enough, 'twill serve. Ask for
95 me tomorrow, and you shall find me a grave man. I
am peppered,[28] I warrant, for this world. A plague a
both your houses! Zounds, a dog, a rat, a mouse, a

**Reading Check**
What is the outcome of the duel between Tybalt and Mercutio?

cat, to scratch a man to death! A braggart, a rogue,
a villain, that fights by the book of arithmetic![29] Why

100 the devil came you between us? I was hurt under
your arm.

**ROMEO.** I thought all for the best.

**MERCUTIO.** Help me into some house, Benvolio,
Or I shall faint. A plague a both your houses!

105 They have made worms' meat of me. I have it,[30]
And soundly too. Your houses! [*Exit* MERCUTIO *and* BENVOLIO.]

**ROMEO.** This gentleman, the Prince's near ally,[31]
My very friend, hath got his mortal hurt
In my behalf—my reputation stained

110 With Tybalt's slander—Tybalt, that an hour
Hath been my cousin. O sweet Juliet,
Thy beauty hath made me effeminate
And in my temper soft'ned valor's steel!

[*Enter* BENVOLIO.]

**BENVOLIO.** O Romeo, Romeo, brave Mercutio is dead!

115 That gallant spirit hath aspired[32] the clouds,
Which too untimely here did scorn the earth.

**ROMEO.** This day's black fate on moe[33] days doth depend;[34]
This but begins the woe others must end.

[*Enter* TYBALT.]

**BENVOLIO.** Here comes the furious Tybalt back again.

120 **ROMEO.** Alive in triumph, and Mercutio slain?
Away to heaven respective lenity,[35]
And fire-eyed fury be my conduct[36] now!
Now, Tybalt, take the "villain" back again
That late thou gavest me; for Mercutio's soul

125 Is but a little way above our heads,
Staying for thine to keep him company.
Either thou or I, or both, must go with him.

**TYBALT.** Thou, wretched boy, that didst consort him here,
Shalt with him hence.

**ROMEO.** This shall determine that.
[*They fight.* TYBALT *falls.*]

130 **BENVOLIO.** Romeo, away, be gone!

The citizens are up, and Tybalt slain.
Stand not amazed. The Prince will doom thee death
If thou art taken. Hence, be gone, away!

**ROMEO.** O, I am fortune's fool![37]

**BENVOLIO.**                                        Why dost thou stay?

[*Exit* ROMEO.]

[*Enter* CITIZENS.]

135   **CITIZEN.** Which way ran he that killed Mercutio?
Tybalt, that murderer, which way ran he?

**BENVOLIO.** There lies that Tybalt.

**CITIZEN.**                                        Up, sir, go with me.
I charge thee in the Prince's name obey.

[*Enter* PRINCE, OLD MONTAGUE, CAPULET, *their* WIVES, *and all.*]

**PRINCE.** Where are the vile beginners of this fray?

140   **BENVOLIO.** O noble Prince, I can discover[38] all
The unlucky manage[39] of this fatal brawl.
There lies the man, slain by young Romeo,
That slew thy kinsman, brave Mercutio.

**LADY CAPULET.** Tybalt, my cousin! O my brother's child!
145   O Prince! O cousin! Husband! O, the blood is spilled
Of my dear kinsman! Prince, as thou art true,
For blood of ours shed blood of Montague.
O cousin, cousin!

**PRINCE.** Benvolio, who began this bloody fray?

150   **BENVOLIO.** Tybalt, here slain, whom Romeo's hand did slay.
Romeo, that spoke him fair, bid him bethink
How nice[40] the quarrel was, and urged withal
Your high displeasure. All this—utterèd
With gentle breath, calm look, knees humbly bowed—
155   Could not take truce with the unruly spleen[41]
Of Tybalt deaf to peace, but that he tilts[42]
With piercing steel at bold Mercutio's breast;
Who, all as hot, turns deadly point to point,
And, with a martial scorn, with one hand beats
160   Cold death aside and with the other sends
It back to Tybalt, whose dexterity
Retorts it. Romeo he cries aloud,
"Hold, friends! Friends, part!" and swifter than his tongue,
His agile arm beats down their fatal points,

**37. fool** plaything.

**Vocabulary**
**fray** (frā) *n.* noisy fight

**38. discover** reveal.
**39. manage** course.

**40. nice** trivial.

**41. spleen** angry nature.
**42. tilts** thrusts.

**Vocabulary**
**martial** (mär´ shəl)
*adj.* military

**Reading Check**
Who does Benvolio say
started the brawl?

Literary Analysis
**Dramatic Speeches**
Which details of
Benvolio's speech
suggest that he is trying
to portray Romeo
favorably?

43. **envious** full of hatred.
44. **entertained** considered.

165   And 'twixt them rushes; underneath whose arm
      An envious[43] thrust from Tybalt hit the life
      Of stout Mercutio, and then Tybalt fled;
      But by and by comes back to Romeo,
      Who had but newly entertained[44] revenge,
170   And to't they go like lightning; for, ere I
      Could draw to part them, was stout Tybalt slain;
      And, as he fell, did Romeo turn and fly.
      This is the truth, or let Benvolio die.

   **LADY CAPULET.** He is a kinsman to the Montague;
175   Affection makes him false, he speaks not true.
      Some twenty of them fought in this black strife,
      And all those twenty could but kill one life.
      I beg for justice, which thou, Prince, must give.
      Romeo slew Tybalt; Romeo must not live.

180 **PRINCE.** Romeo slew him; he slew Mercutio.
      Who now the price of his dear blood doth owe?

45. **His fault . . . Tybalt** by
killing Tybalt, he did what
the law would have done.

   **MONTAGUE.** Not Romeo, Prince; he was Mercutio's friend;
      His fault concludes but what the law should end,
      The life of Tybalt.[45]

**Vocabulary**
**exile** (eks´ īl´) v. banish

185 **PRINCE.**                    And for that offense
      Immediately we do exile him hence.
      I have an interest in your hate's proceeding.

46. **My blood** Mercutio was
related to the Prince.
47. **amerce** punish.

      My blood[46] for your rude brawls doth lie a-bleeding;
      But I'll amerce[47] you with so strong a fine
190   That you shall all repent the loss of mine.
      I will be deaf to pleading and excuses;
      Nor tears nor prayers shall purchase out abuses.
      Therefore use none. Let Romeo hence in haste,
      Else, when he is found, that hour is his last.

48. **attend our will** await my
decision.

195   Bear hence this body and attend our will.[48]
      Mercy but murders, pardoning those that kill.
                              [*Exit with others.*]

### Scene ii. Capulet's orchard.
[*Enter* JULIET *alone.*]

1. **fiery-footed steeds**
horses of the sun god,
Phoebus.
2. **Phoebus' lodging** below
the horizon.
3. **Phaëton** Phoebus' son,
who tried to drive his
father's horses but was
unable to control them.

   **JULIET.** Gallop apace, you fiery-footed steeds,[1]
      Towards Phoebus' lodging![2] Such a wagoner
      As Phaëton[3] would whip you to the west
      And bring in cloudy night immediately.

5　　Spread thy close curtain, love-performing night,
　　That runaways' eyes may wink,[4] and Romeo
　　Leap to these arms untalked of and unseen.
　　Lovers can see to do their amorous rites,
　　And by their own beauties; or, if love be blind,
10　It best agrees with night. Come, civil night,
　　Thou sober-suited matron all in black,
　　And learn me how to lose a winning match,
　　Played for a pair of stainless maidenhoods.
　　Hood my unmanned blood, bating in my cheeks,[5]
15　With thy black mantle till strange[6] love grow bold,
　　Think true love acted simple modesty,
　　Come, night; come, Romeo; come, thou day in night;
　　For thou wilt lie upon the wings of night
　　Whiter than new snow upon a raven's back.
20　Come, gentle night; come, loving, black-browed night;
　　Give me my Romeo; and when I shall die,
　　Take him and cut him out in little stars,
　　And he will make the face of heaven so fine
　　That all the world will be in love with night
25　And pay no worship to the garish sun.
　　O, I have bought the mansion of a love,
　　But not possessed it; and though I am sold,
　　Not yet enjoyed. So tedious is this day
　　As is the night before some festival
30　To an impatient child that hath new robes
　　And may not wear them. O, here comes my nurse,

[*Enter* NURSE, *with cords.*]

　　And she brings news; and every tongue that speaks
　　But Romeo's name speaks heavenly eloquence.
　　Now, nurse, what news? What hast thou there, the cords
　　That Romeo bid thee fetch?

35　**NURSE.**　　　　　　　　　　　Ay, ay, the cords.

　　**JULIET.** Ay me! What news? Why dost thou wring thy hands?

　　**NURSE.** Ah, weraday![7] He's dead, he's dead, he's dead!
　　We are undone, lady, we are undone!
　　Alack the day! He's gone, he's killed, he's dead!

　　**JULIET.** Can heaven be so envious?

40　**NURSE.**　　　　　　　　　　Romeo can,
　　Though heaven cannot. O Romeo, Romeo!
　　Who ever would have thought it? Romeo!

**Literary Analysis**
**Dramatic Speeches**
How can you tell that
Juliet's speech is a
soliloquy?

4. **That runaways' eyes may
wink** so that the eyes of
busybodies may not see.
5. **Hood . . . cheeks** hide the
untamed blood that makes
me blush.
6. **strange** unfamiliar.

**Spiral Review**
**Character** What
does Juliet reveal
about herself in this
soliloquy?

**Vocabulary**
**eloquence** (el´ ə kwəns)
*n.* speech that is graceful
and persuasive

7. **Ah, weraday!** alas!

**Reading**
**Check**
What punishment does
the Prince order for
Romeo?

**JULIET.** What devil art thou that dost torment me thus?
    This torture should be roared in dismal hell.
45    Hath Romeo slain himself? Say thou but "Ay,"
    And that bare vowel "I" shall poison more
    Than the death-darting eye of cockatrice.
    I am not I, if there be such an "Ay,"[8]
    Or those eyes' shot[9] that makes thee answer "Ay."
50    If he be slain, say "Ay"; or if not, "No."
    Brief sounds determine of my weal or woe.

**NURSE.** I saw the wound, I saw it with mine eyes,
    (God save the mark![10]) here on his manly breast.
    A piteous corse,[11] a bloody piteous corse;
55    Pale, pale as ashes, all bedaubed in blood,
    All in gore-blood. I sounded[12] at the sight.

**JULIET.** O, break, my heart! Poor bankrout,[13] break at once!
    To prison, eyes; ne'er look on liberty!
    Vile earth, to earth resign;[14] end motion here,
60    And thou and Romeo press one heavy bier![15]

**NURSE.** O Tybalt, Tybalt, the best friend I had!
    O courteous Tybalt! Honest gentleman!
    That ever I should live to see thee dead!

**JULIET.** What storm is this that blows so contrary?[16]
65    Is Romeo slaught'red, and is Tybalt dead?
    My dearest cousin, and my dearer lord?
    Then, dreadful trumpet, sound the general doom![17]

8. **"Ay"** yes.
9. **eyes' shot** the Nurse's glance.
10. **God save the mark!** May God save us from evil!
11. **corse** corpse.
12. **sounded** swooned; fainted.
13. **bankrout** bankrupt.
14. **Vile . . . resign** let my body return to the earth.
15. **bier** platform on which a corpse is displayed before burial.
16. **contrary** in opposite directions.
17. **dreadful . . . doom** let the trumpet that announces doomsday be sounded.

For who is living, if those two are gone?

**NURSE.** Tybalt is gone, and Romeo banishèd;
70     Romeo that killed him, he is banishèd.

**JULIET.** O God! Did Romeo's hand shed Tybalt's blood?

**NURSE.** It did, it did! Alas the day, it did!

**JULIET.** O serpent heart, hid with a flow'ring face!
Did ever dragon keep so fair a cave?
75     Beautiful tyrant! Fiend angelical!
Dove-feathered raven! Wolvish-ravening lamb!
Despisèd substance of divinest show!
Just opposite to what thou justly seem'st—
A damnèd saint, an honorable villain!
80     O nature, what hadst thou to do in hell
When thou didst bower the spirit of a fiend
In mortal paradise of such sweet flesh?
Was ever book containing such vile matter
So fairly bound? O, that deceit should dwell
In such a gorgeous palace!

**Reading Skill Summarize** Briefly summarize Juliet's remarks about Romeo in lines 73–84.

85   **NURSE.**                          There's no trust,
No faith, no honesty in men; all perjured,
All forsworn,[18] all naught, all dissemblers.[19]
Ah, where's my man? Give me some aqua vitae.[20]
These griefs, these woes, these sorrows make me old.
Shame come to Romeo!

18. **forsworn** are liars.
19. **dissemblers** hypocrites.
20. **aqua vitae** brandy.

90   **JULIET.**                         Blistered be thy tongue
For such a wish! He was not born to shame.
Upon his brow shame is ashamed to sit;
For 'tis a throne where honor may be crowned
Sole monarch of the universal earth.
95     O, what a beast was I to chide at him!

**NURSE.** Will you speak well of him that killed your cousin?

**JULIET.** Shall I speak ill of him that is my husband?
Ah, poor my lord, what tongue shall smooth thy name
When I, thy three-hours wife, have mangled it?
100    But wherefore, villain, didst thou kill my cousin?
That villain cousin would have killed my husband.
Back, foolish tears, back to your native spring!
Your tributary[21] drops belong to woe,
Which you, mistaking, offer up to joy.
105    My husband lives, that Tybalt would have slain;

21. **tributary** in tribute.

**Reading Check**
What is Juliet's initial reaction to Romeo's involvement in Tybalt's death?

**Literary Analysis
Dramatic Speeches**
What makes this speech
a monologue but not a
soliloquy?

And Tybalt's dead, that would have slain my husband.
All this is comfort; wherefore weep I then?
Some word there was, worser than Tybalt's death,
That murd'red me. I would forget it fain;
110  But O, it presses to my memory
Like damnèd guilty deeds to sinners' minds!
"Tybalt is dead, and Romeo—banishèd."
That "banishèd," that one word "banishèd,"
Hath slain ten thousand Tybalts. Tybalt's death
115  Was woe enough, if it had ended there;
Or, if sour woe delights in fellowship
And needly will be ranked with[22] other griefs,
Why followed not, when she said "Tybalt's dead,"
Thy father, or thy mother, nay, or both,
120  Which modern[23] lamentation might have moved?
But with a rearward[24] following Tybalt's death,
"Romeo is banishèd"—to speak that word
Is father, mother, Tybalt, Romeo, Juliet,
All slain, all dead. "Romeo is banishèd"—
125  There is no end, no limit, measure, bound,
In that word's death; no words can that woe sound.
Where is my father and my mother, nurse?

**NURSE.** Weeping and wailing over Tybalt's corse.
Will you go to them? I will bring you thither.

130  **JULIET.** Wash they his wounds with tears? Mine shall be spent,
When theirs are dry, for Romeo's banishment.
Take up those cords. Poor ropes, you are beguiled,
Both you and I, for Romeo is exiled.
He made you for a highway to my bed;
135  But I, a maid, die maiden-widowèd.
Come, cords; come, nurse. I'll to my wedding bed;
And death, not Romeo, take my maidenhead!

**NURSE.** Hie to your chamber. I'll find Romeo
To comfort you. I wot[25] well where he is.
140  Hark ye, your Romeo will be here at night.
I'll to him; he is hid at Lawrence' cell.

**JULIET.** O, find him! Give this ring to my true knight
And bid him come to take his last farewell. [*Exit with* NURSE]

22. **needly . . . with** must be
accompanied by.

23. **modern** ordinary.
24. **rearward** follow up;
literally, a rear guard.

25. **wot** know.

*Scene iii. Friar Lawrence's cell.*
[*Enter* FRIAR LAWRENCE.]

 **FRIAR.** Romeo, come forth; come forth, thou fearful man.
   Affliction is enamored of thy parts,[1]
   And thou art wedded to calamity.

[*Enter* ROMEO.]

 **ROMEO.** Father, what news? What is the Prince's doom?[2]
5  What sorrow craves acquaintance at my hand
   That I yet know not?

 **FRIAR.**       Too familiar
   Is my dear son with such sour company.
   I bring thee tidings of the Prince's doom.

 **ROMEO.** What less than doomsday[3] is the Prince's doom?

10 **FRIAR.** A gentler judgment vanished[4] from his lips—
   Not body's death, but body's banishment.

 **ROMEO.** Ha, banishment? Be merciful, say "death";
   For exile hath more terror in his look,
   Much more than death. Do not say "banishment."

15 **FRIAR.** Here from Verona art thou banishèd.
   Be patient, for the world is broad and wide.

 **ROMEO.** There is no world without[5] Verona walls,
   But purgatory, torture, hell itself.
   Hence banishèd is banished from the world,
20  And world's exile is death. Then "banishèd"
   Is death mistermed. Calling death "banishèd,"
   Thou cut'st my head off with a golden ax
   And smilest upon the stroke that murders me.

 **FRIAR.** O deadly sin! O rude unthankfulness!
25  Thy fault our law calls death;[6] but the kind Prince,
   Taking thy part, hath rushed[7] aside the law,
   And turned that black word "death" to "banishment."
   This is dear mercy, and thou seest it not.

 **ROMEO.** 'Tis torture, and not mercy. Heaven is here,
30  Where Juliet lives; and every cat and dog
   And little mouse, every unworthy thing,
   Live here in heaven and may look on her;
   But Romeo may not. More validity,[8]
   More honorable state, more courtship lives
35  In carrion flies than Romeo. They may seize

**1. Affliction . . . parts**
misery is in love with your
attractive qualities.

**2. doom** final decision.

**3. doomsday** my death.
**4. vanished** escaped; came
forth.

**5. without** outside.
**6. Thy fault . . . death** for
what you did our law
demands the death
penalty.
**7. rushed** pushed.
**8. validity** value.

**Reading Skill
Summarize**
Paraphrase Romeo's
complaint in lines 29–33,
and then summarize
his reaction to his
banishment.

Reading
Check
What punishment does
the Friar say Romeo
could have received for
his crime?

On the white wonder of dear Juliet's hand
And steal immortal blessing from her lips,
Who, even in pure and vestal modesty,
Still blush, as thinking their own kisses sin;
40  But Romeo may not, he is banishèd.
Flies may do this but I from this must fly;
They are freemen, but I am banishèd.
And sayest thou yet that exile is not death?
Hadst thou no poison mixed, no sharp-ground knife,
45  No sudden mean$^9$ of death, though ne'er so mean,$^{10}$
But "banishèd" to kill me—"banishèd"?
O friar, the damnèd use that word in hell;
Howling attends it! How hast thou the heart,
Being a divine, a ghostly confessor,
50  A sin-absolver, and my friend professed,
To mangle me with that word "banishèd"?

**FRIAR.** Thou fond mad man, hear me a little speak.

**ROMEO.** O, thou wilt speak again of banishment.

**FRIAR.** I'll give thee armor to keep off that word;
55  Adversity's sweet milk, philosophy,
To comfort thee, though thou art banishèd.

9. **mean** method.
10. **mean** humiliating.

## Romeo and Juliet Through the Years

These illustrations and images from various productions of *Romeo and Juliet* mark the timelessness of Shakespeare's most dramatized piece. The core qualities of the play, including its theme and language, have moved forward into the present with updated costumes and props, diverse casts, and new technology.

Frontispiece for the 1599 edition

Movie – 1916
Romeo and Juliet

Book illustration – 1905

**ROMEO.** Yet "banishèd"? Hang up philosophy!
    Unless philosophy can make a Juliet,
    Displant a town, reverse a prince's doom,
60    It helps not, it prevails not. Talk no more.

**FRIAR.** O, then I see that madmen have no ears.

**ROMEO.** How should they, when that wise men have no eyes?

**FRIAR.** Let me dispute[11] with thee of thy estate.[12]

**ROMEO.** Thou canst not speak of that thou dost not feel.
65    Wert thou as young as I, Juliet thy love,
    An hour but married, Tybalt murderèd,
    Doting like me, and like me banishèd,
    Then mightst thou speak, then mightst thou tear thy hair,
    And fall upon the ground, as I do now,
70    Taking the measure of an unmade grave.

[*Knock.*]

**FRIAR.** Arise, one knocks. Good Romeo, hide thyself.

**ROMEO.** Not I; unless the breath of heartsick groans
    Mistlike infold me from the search of eyes. [*Knock.*]

**Reading Skill Summarize**

Summarize Romeo's ideas in lines 57–60. What do they suggest about his state of mind?

11. **dispute** discuss.
12. **estate** condition; situation.

Reading Check

How does Romeo view his banishment?

Movie – 1936
Poster and balcony scene.
(Director: George Cukor
Actors: Norma Shearer and Leslie Howard)

Movie – 1968
Balcony scene.
(Director: Franco Zeffirelli
Actors: Leonard Whiting and Olivia Hussey)

**13. By and by!** In a minute! (said to the person knocking).

**14. simpleness** silly behavior (Romeo does not move).

**FRIAR.** Hark, how they knock! Who's there? Romeo, arise;
75  Thou wilt be taken.—Stay awhile!—Stand up; [*Knock.*]
     Run to my study.—By and by![13]—God's will,
     What simpleness[14] is this.—I come, I come! [*Knock.*]
     Who knocks so hard? Whence come you? What's your will?

[*Enter* NURSE.]

**NURSE.** Let me come in, and you shall know my errand.
     I come from Lady Juliet.

80  **FRIAR.**                         Welcome then.

**NURSE.** O holy friar, O, tell me, holy friar,
     Where is my lady's lord, where's Romeo?

**FRIAR.** There on the ground, with his own tears made drunk.

**NURSE.** O, he is even in my mistress' case,
85   Just in her case! O woeful sympathy!
     Piteous predicament! Even so lies she,
     Blubb'ring and weeping, weeping and blubb'ring.
     Stand up, stand up! Stand, and you be a man.
     For Juliet's sake, for her sake, rise and stand!
90   Why should you fall into so deep an O?[15]

**Literary Analysis
Dramatic Speeches**
What does this brief speech by the Nurse reveal about her relationship with Romeo?

**15. O** cry of grief.

Stage production – 1990s
Royal Shakespeare Company

Stage production – 2004
Royal Shakespeare Company
Friar and Juliet.

Ballet – 2001
Kirov Ballet of St. Petersburg, Russia.

**ROMEO.** [*Rises.*] Nurse—

**NURSE.** Ah sir, ah sir! Death's the end of all.

**ROMEO.** Spakest thou of Juliet? How is it with her?
Doth not she think me an old murderer,
95 Now I have stained the childhood of our joy
With blood removed but little from her own?
Where is she? And how doth she? And what says
My concealed lady[16] to our canceled love?

**NURSE.** O, she says nothing, sir, but weeps and weeps;
100 And now falls on her bed, and then starts up,
And Tybalt calls; and then on Romeo cries,
And then down falls again.

**ROMEO.**                                          As if that name,
Shot from the deadly level[17] of a gun,
Did murder her; as that name's cursèd hand
105 Murdered her kinsman. O, tell me, friar, tell me,
In what vile part of this anatomy
Doth my name lodge? Tell me, that I may sack[18]
The hateful mansion.

[*He offers to stab himself, and* NURSE *snatches the dagger away.*]

**16. concealed lady** secret bride.

**17. level** aim.
**18. sack** plunder.

### Reading Check

What does Romeo nearly do before the Nurse stops him?

Stage production
– 2004
Royal Shakespeare
Company
Fight scene.

Verona, Italy
Balcony and Juliet

Illustration – 2006

**FRIAR.**                          Hold thy desperate hand.
Art thou a man? Thy form cries out thou art;

110  Thy tears are womanish, thy wild acts denote
The unreasonable fury of a beast.
Unseemly[19] woman in a seeming man!
And ill-beseeming beast in seeming both![20]
Thou hast amazed me. By my holy order,

115  I thought thy disposition better tempered.
Hast thou slain Tybalt? Wilt thou slay thyself?
And slay thy lady that in thy life lives,
By doing damnèd hate upon thyself?
Why railest thou on thy birth, the heaven, and earth?

120  Since birth and heaven and earth, all three do meet
In thee at once; which thou at once wouldst lose.
Fie, fie, thou shamest thy shape, thy love, thy wit,[21]
Which, like a usurer,[22] abound'st in all,
And usest none in that true use indeed

125  Which should bedeck[23] thy shape, thy love, thy wit.
Thy noble shape is but a form of wax,
Digressing from the valor of a man;
Thy dear love sworn but hollow perjury,
Killing that love which thou hast vowed to cherish;

130  Thy wit, that ornament to shape and love,
Misshapen in the conduct[24] of them both,
Like powder in a skilless soldier's flask,[25]
Is set afire by thine own ignorance,
And thou dismemb'red with thine own defense.[26]

135  What, rouse thee, man! Thy Juliet is alive,
For whose dear sake thou wast but lately dead.[27]
There art thou happy.[28] Tybalt would kill thee,
But thou slewest Tybalt. There art thou happy.
The law, that threat'ned death, becomes thy friend

140  And turns it to exile. There art thou happy.
A pack of blessings light upon thy back;
Happiness courts thee in her best array;
But, like a misbehaved and sullen wench,[29]
Thou puts up[30] thy fortune and thy love.

145  Take heed, take heed, for such die miserable.
Go get thee to thy love, as was decreed,
Ascend her chamber, hence and comfort her.
But look thou stay not till the watch be set,[31]
For then thou canst not pass to Mantua,

150  Where thou shalt live till we can find a time
To blaze[32] your marriage, reconcile your friends,

Beg pardon of the Prince, and call thee back
With twenty hundred thousand times more joy
Than thou went'st forth in lamentation.
155 Go before, nurse. Commend me to thy lady,
And bid her hasten all the house to bed,
Which heavy sorrow makes them apt unto.³³
Romeo is coming.

**NURSE.** O Lord, I could have stayed here all the night
160 To hear good counsel. O, what learning is!
My lord, I'll tell my lady you will come.

**ROMEO.** Do so, and bid my sweet prepare to chide.³⁴
[NURSE *offers to go in and turns again.*]

**NURSE.** Here, sir, a ring she bid me give you, sir.
Hie you, make haste, for it grows very late. [*Exit.*]

165 **ROMEO.** How well my comfort is revived by this!

**FRIAR.** Go hence; good night; and here stands all your state:³⁵
Either be gone before the watch be set,
Or by the break of day disguised from hence.
Sojourn³⁶ in Mantua. I'll find out your man,
170 And he shall signify³⁷ from time to time
Every good hap to you that chances here.
Give me thy hand. 'Tis late. Farewell; good night.

**ROMEO.** But that a joy past joy calls out on me,
It were a grief so brief to part with thee.
175 Farewell. [*Exit all.*]

*Scene iv. A room in Capulet's house.*
[*Enter old* CAPULET, *his* WIFE, *and* PARIS.]

**CAPULET.** Things have fall'n out, sir, so unluckily
That we have had no time to move¹ our daughter.
Look you, she loved her kinsman Tybalt dearly,
And so did I. Well, we were born to die.
5 'Tis very late; she'll not come down tonight.
I promise you, but for your company,
I would have been abed an hour ago.

**PARIS.** These times of woe afford no times to woo.
Madam, good night. Commend me to your daughter.

10 **LADY.** I will, and know her mind early tomorrow;
Tonight she's mewed up to her heaviness.²

**Reading Skill**
**Summarize** Briefly state the main points of the Friar's speech to Romeo.

33. **apt unto** likely to do.

34. **chide** rebuke me (for slaying Tybalt).

35. **here . . . state** this is your situation.

36. **Sojourn** remain.
37. **signify** let you know.

1. **move** discuss your proposal with.
2. **mewed . . . heaviness** locked up with her sorrow.

Reading
Check
What reason do the Capulets give Paris to explain why Juliet cannot see him?

**CAPULET.** Sir, Paris, I will make a desperate tender[3]

Of my child's love. I think she will be ruled

In all respects by me; nay more, I doubt it not.

15 Wife, go you to her ere you go to bed;

Acquaint her here of my son[4] Paris' love

And bid her (mark you me?) on Wednesday next—

But soft! What day is this?

**PARIS.** Monday, my lord.

**CAPULET.** Monday! Ha, ha! Well, Wednesday is too soon.

20 A[5] Thursday let it be—a Thursday, tell her,

She shall be married to this noble earl.

Will you be ready? Do you like this haste?

We'll keep no great ado[6]—a friend or two;

For hark you, Tybalt being slain so late,

25 It may be thought we held him carelessly,[7]

Being our kinsman, if we revel much.

Therefore we'll have some half a dozen friends,

And there an end. But what say you to Thursday?

**PARIS.** My lord, I would that Thursday were tomorrow.

30 **CAPULET.** Well, get you gone. A Thursday be it then.

Go you to Juliet ere you go to bed;

Prepare her, wife, against[8] this wedding day.

Farewell, my lord.—Light to my chamber, ho!

Afore me,[9] it is so very late

35 That we may call it early by and by.

Good night.                    [*Exit all.*]

3. **desperate tender** risky offer.
4. **son** son-in-law.

5. **A** on.

6. **We'll . . . ado** We will not make a great fuss.
7. **held him carelessly** did not respect him enough.

### Reading Skill
### Summarize

Summarize Lord Capulet's remarks about the timing of Juliet's marriage to Paris.

8. **against** for.
9. **Afore me** indeed (a mild oath).

*Scene v. Capulet's orchard.*
[*Enter* ROMEO *and* JULIET *aloft.*]

**JULIET.** Wilt thou be gone? It is not yet near day.

It was the nightingale, and not the lark,

That pierced the fearful hollow of thine ear.

Nightly she sings on yond pomegranate tree.

5 Believe me, love, it was the nightingale.

**ROMEO.** It was the lark, the herald of the morn;

No nightingale. Look, love, what envious streaks

Do lace the severing[1] clouds in yonder East.

Night's candles[2] are burnt out, and jocund day

10 Stands tiptoe on the misty mountaintops.

I must be gone and live, or stay and die.

1. **severing** parting.
2. **Night's candles** stars.

### Literature Connection

**The Nightingale and the Lark**

The nightingale and the lark are two birds that appear frequently in literature, particularly in poetry. Both birds are admired for their beautiful singing, and they also have symbolic associations. The nightingale and its song are traditionally associated with night; the lark and its song with dawn. Shakespeare draws on these associations in this exchange between Romeo and Juliet.

Lark

### Connect to the Literature

Why do Romeo and Juliet have negative associations with the lark at this point in the play?

**JULIET.** Yond light is not daylight; I know it, I.
It is some meteor that the sun exhales³
To be to thee this night a torchbearer
15 And light thee on thy way to Mantua.
Therefore stay yet; thou need'st not to be gone.

**ROMEO.** Let me be ta'en, let me be put to death.
I am content, so thou wilt have it so.
I'll say yon gray is not the morning's eye,
20 'Tis but the pale reflex of Cynthia's brow;⁴
Nor that is not the lark whose notes do beat
The vaulty heaven so high above our heads.
I have more care to stay than will to go.
Come, death, and welcome! Juliet wills it so.
25 How is't, my soul? Let's talk; it is not day.

**JULIET.** It is, it is! Hie hence, be gone, away!
It is the lark that sings so out of tune,
Straining harsh discords and unpleasing sharps.⁵
Some say the lark makes sweet division;⁶
30 This doth not so, for she divideth us.
Some say the lark and loathèd toad change eyes;⁷
O, now I would they had changed voices too,
Since arm from arm that voice doth us affray,⁸
Hunting thee hence with hunt's-up⁹ to the day.
35 O, now be gone! More light and light it grows.

**ROMEO.** More light and light—more dark and dark our woes.

3. **exhales** sends out.

4. **reflex . . . brow** reflection of the moon (Cynthia was a name for the moon goddess).

5. **sharps** shrill high notes.
6. **division** melody.
7. **change eyes** exchange eyes (because the lark has a beautiful body with ugly eyes and the toad has an ugly body with beautiful eyes).
8. **affray** frighten.
9. **hunt's-up** morning song for hunters.

### Reading Check

What do the Capulets plan for Juliet on Thursday?

[*Enter* NURSE.]

**NURSE.** Madam!

**JULIET.** Nurse?

**NURSE.** Your lady mother is coming to your chamber.
40 The day is broke; be wary, look about.      [*Exit.*]

**JULIET.** Then, window, let day in, and let life out.

**ROMEO.** Farewell, farewell! One kiss, and I'll descend.

[*He goeth down.*]

**JULIET.** Art thou gone so, love-lord, ay husband-friend?
I must hear from thee every day in the hour,
45 For in a minute there are many days.
O, by this count I shall be much in years[10]
Ere I again behold my Romeo!

**ROMEO.** Farewell!
I will omit no opportunity
50 That may convey my greetings, love, to thee.

**JULIET.** O, think'st thou we shall ever meet again?

**ROMEO.** I doubt it not; and all these woes shall serve
For sweet discourses[11] in our times to come.

**JULIET.** O God, I have an ill-divining[12] soul!
55 Methinks I see thee, now thou art so low,
As one dead in the bottom of a tomb.
Either my eyesight fails, or thou lookest pale.

**ROMEO.** And trust me, love, in my eye so do you.
Dry sorrow drinks our blood.[13] Adieu, adieu!      [*Exit.*]

60 **JULIET.** O Fortune, Fortune! All men call thee fickle.
If thou art fickle, what dost thou[14] with him
That is renowned for faith? Be fickle, Fortune,
For then I hope thou wilt not keep him long
But send him back.

[*Enter* MOTHER.]

65 **LADY CAPULET.** Ho, daughter! Are you up?

**JULIET.** Who is't that calls? It is my lady mother.
Is she not down so late,[15] or up so early?
What unaccustomed cause procures her hither?[16]

**LADY CAPULET.** Why, how now, Juliet?

---

**Reading Skill**
**Summarize** Identify the key points of the farewell conversation between Romeo and Juliet.

10. **much in years** much older.

11. **discourses** conversations.

12. **ill-divining** predicting evil.

13. **Dry sorrow . . . blood** It was once believed that sorrow drained away the blood.
14. **dost thou** do you have to do.

**Vocabulary**
**fickle** (fik´ əl) *adj.*
changeable

15. **Is she . . . late** Has she stayed up so late?
16. **What . . . hither?** What unusual reason brings her here?

**JULIET.**                                 Madam, I am not well.

70 **LADY CAPULET.** Evermore weeping for your cousin's death?
    What, wilt thou wash him from his grave with tears?
    And if thou couldst, thou couldst not make him live.
    Therefore have done. Some grief shows much of love;
    But much of grief shows still some want of wit.

75 **JULIET.** Yet let me weep for such a feeling[17] loss.

**LADY CAPULET.** So shall you feel the loss, but not the friend
    Which you weep for.

**JULIET.**                               Feeling so the loss,
    I cannot choose but ever weep the friend.

**LADY CAPULET.** Well, girl, thou weep'st not so much for his death
80     As that the villain lives which slaughtered him.

**JULIET.** What villain, madam?

**LADY CAPULET.**                         That same villain Romeo.

**JULIET.** [*Aside*] Villain and he be many miles asunder.[18]—
    God pardon him! I do, with all my heart;
    And yet no man like he doth grieve my heart.

85 **LADY CAPULET.** That is because the traitor murderer lives.

**JULIET.** Ay, madam, from the reach of these my hands.
    Would none but I might venge my cousin's death!

**LADY CAPULET.** We will have vengeance for it, fear thou not.
    Then weep no more. I'll send to one in Mantua,
90     Where that same banished runagate[19] doth live,
    Shall give him such an unaccustomed dram[20]
    That he shall soon keep Tybalt company;
    And then I hope thou wilt be satisfied.

**JULIET.** Indeed I never shall be satisfied
95     With Romeo till I behold him—dead[21]—
    Is my poor heart so for a kinsman vexed.
    Madam, if you could find out but a man
    To bear a poison, I would temper[22] it;
    That Romeo should, upon receipt thereof,
100     Soon sleep in quiet. O, how my heart abhors
    To hear him named and cannot come to him,
    To wreak[23] the love I bore my cousin
    Upon his body that hath slaughtered him!

**17. feeling** deeply felt.

**18. asunder** apart.

**Literary Analysis**
**Dramatic Speeches**
What qualities of an aside do you find in line 82?

**19. runagate** renegade; runaway.
**20. unaccustomed dram** unexpected dose of poison.

**21. dead** Juliet is deliberately ambiguous here. Her mother thinks *dead* refers to Romeo. But Juliet is using the word with the following line, in reference to her heart.
**22. temper** mix; weaken.

**23. wreak** (rēk) avenge; express.

**Reading Check**
What are Lady Capulet's plans for Romeo?

**LADY CAPULET.** Find thou the means, and I'll find such a man.
105    But now I'll tell thee joyful tidings, girl.

**JULIET.** And joy comes well in such a needy time.
What are they, I beseech your ladyship?

**LADY CAPULET.** Well, well, thou hast a careful[24] father, child;
One who, to put thee from thy heaviness,
110    Hath sorted out[25] a sudden day of joy
That thou expects not nor I looked not for.

**JULIET.** Madam, in happy time![26] What day is that?

**LADY CAPULET.** Marry, my child, early next Thursday morn
The gallant, young, and noble gentleman,
115    The County Paris, at Saint Peter's Church,
Shall happily make thee there a joyful bride.

**JULIET.** Now by Saint Peter's Church, and Peter too,
He shall not make me there a joyful bride!
I wonder at this haste, that I must wed
120    Ere he that should be husband comes to woo.
I pray you tell my lord and father, madam,
I will not marry yet; and when I do, I swear
It shall be Romeo, whom you know I hate,
Rather than Paris. These are news indeed!

125  **LADY CAPULET.** Here comes your father. Tell him so yourself,
And see how he will take it at your hands.

[*Enter* CAPULET *and* NURSE.]

**CAPULET.** When the sun sets the earth doth drizzle dew,
But for the sunset of my brother's son
It rains downright.
130    How now? A conduit,[27] girl? What, still in tears?
Evermore show'ring? In one little body
Thou counterfeits a bark,[28] a sea, a wind:
For still thy eyes, which I may call the sea,
Do ebb and flow with tears; the bark thy body is,
135    Sailing in this salt flood; the winds, thy sighs,
Who, raging with thy tears and they with them,
Without a sudden calm will overset
Thy tempest-tossèd body. How now, wife?
Have you delivered to her our decree?

140  **LADY CAPULET.** Ay, sir; but she will none, she gives you
thanks.[29]
I would the fool were married to her grave!

---

24. **careful** considerate.
25. **sorted out** selected.

26. **in happy time** just in time.

**Literary Analysis**
**Dramatic Speeches**
How does Lady Capulet's dialogue here show Paris as a foil to Romeo?

27. **conduit** water pipe.

28. **bark** boat.

**Reading Skill**
**Summarize**
Summarize the comparison Lord Capulet makes in lines 130–138.

29. **she will none . . . thanks** she will have nothing to do with it, thank you.

**CAPULET.** Soft! Take me with you,[30] take me with you, wife.
How? Will she none? Doth she not give us thanks?
Is she not proud?[31] Doth she not count her blest,
145    Unworthy as she is, that we have wrought[32]
So worthy a gentleman to be her bride?

**JULIET.** Not proud you have, but thankful that you have.
Proud can I never be of what I hate,
But thankful even for hate that is meant love.

150  **CAPULET.** How, how, how, how, chopped-logic?[33] What is this?
"Proud"—and "I thank you"—and "I thank you not"—
And yet "not proud"? Mistress minion[34] you,
Thank me no thankings, nor proud me no prouds,
But fettle[35] your fine joints 'gainst Thursday next
155    To go with Paris to Saint Peter's Church,
Or I will drag thee on a hurdle[36] thither.
Out, you greensickness carrion![37] Out, you baggage![38]
You tallow-face![39]

**LADY CAPULET.**          Fie, fie! What, are you mad?

**JULIET.** Good father, I beseech you on my knees,
160    Hear me with patience but to speak a word.

**CAPULET.** Hang thee, young baggage! Disobedient wretch!
I tell thee what—get thee to church a Thursday
Or never after look me in the face.
Speak not, reply not, do not answer me!
165    My fingers itch. Wife, we scarce thought us blest
That God had lent us but this only child;
But now I see this one is one too much,
And that we have a curse in having her.
Out on her, hilding![40]

**NURSE.**                    God in heaven bless her!
170    You are to blame, my lord, to rate[41] her so.

**CAPULET.** And why, my Lady Wisdom? Hold your tongue,
Good Prudence. Smatter with your gossips, go![42]

**NURSE.** I speak no treason.

**CAPULET.**                    O, God-i-god-en!

**NURSE.** May not one speak?

**CAPULET.**                    Peace, you mumbling fool!
175    Utter your gravity[43] o'er a gossip's bowl,
For here we need it not.

---

30. **Soft! Take . . . you** Wait a minute. Let me understand you.
31. **proud** pleased.
32. **wrought** arranged.

33. **chopped-logic** contradictory, unsound thought and speech.
34. **Mistress minion** Miss Uppity; overly proud.
35. **fettle** prepare.
36. **hurdle** sled on which prisoners were taken to their execution.
37. **greensickness carrion** anemic lump of flesh.
38. **baggage** naughty girl.
39. **tallow-face** wax-pale face.

**Literary Analysis Dramatic Speeches** What feelings and personality traits does Lord Capulet reveal in this brief speech?

40. **hilding** worthless person.

41. **rate** scold; berate.

42. **Smatter . . . go!** Go chatter with the other old women.
43. **gravity** wisdom.

**Reading Check**
Rather than Paris, whom does Juliet threaten to marry?

**LADY CAPULET.** You are too hot.

**CAPULET.** God's bread![44] It makes me mad.
    Day, night; hour, tide, time; work, play;
    Alone, in company; still my care hath been
180    To have her matched; and having now provided
    A gentleman of noble parentage,
    Of fair demesnes,[45] youthful, and nobly trained,
    Stuffed, as they say, with honorable parts,[46]
    Proportioned as one's thought would wish a man—
185    And then to have a wretched puling[47] fool,
    A whining mammet,[48] in her fortune's tender,[49]
    To answer "I'll not wed, I cannot love;
    I am too young, I pray you pardon me"!
    But, and you will not wed, I'll pardon you!
190    Graze where you will, you shall not house with me.
    Look to't, think on't; I do not use to jest.
    Thursday is near; lay hand on heart, advise:[50]
    And you be mine, I'll give you to my friend;
    And you be not, hang, beg, starve, die in the streets,
195    For, by my soul, I'll ne'er acknowledge thee,
    Nor what is mine shall never do thee good.
    Trust to't. Bethink you. I'll not be forsworn.[51]    [*Exit.*]

**JULIET.** Is there no pity sitting in the clouds
    That sees into the bottom of my grief?
200    O sweet my mother, cast me not away!
    Delay this marriage for a month, a week;
    Or if you do not, make the bridal bed
    In that dim monument where Tybalt lies.

**LADY CAPULET.** Talk not to me, for I'll not speak a word.
205    Do as thou wilt, for I have done with thee.    [*Exit.*]

**JULIET.** O God!—O nurse, how shall this be prevented?
    My husband is on earth, my faith in heaven.[52]
    How shall that faith return again to earth
    Unless that husband send it me from heaven
210    By leaving earth?[53] Comfort me, counsel me.

---

**44. God's bread!** By the holy Eucharist!

**45. demesnes** property.
**46. parts** qualities.
**47. puling** whining.

**48. mammet** doll.
**49. in . . . tender** when good fortune is offered her.

**50. advise** consider.

### Reading Skill
### Summarize
Summarize the threat that Lord Capulet makes to Juliet in this monologue.

**51. forsworn** made to violate my promise.

**52. my faith in heaven** my marriage vow is recorded in heaven.
**53. leaving earth** dying.

Alack, alack, that heaven should practice stratagems[54]
Upon so soft a subject as myself!
What say'st thou? Hast thou not a word of joy?
Some comfort, nurse.

215 **NURSE.**                     Faith, here it is.
Romeo is banished; and all the world to nothing[55]
That he dares ne'er come back to challenge[56] you;
Or if he do, it needs must be by stealth.
Then, since the case so stands as now it doth,
I think it best you married with the County.
220 O, he's a lovely gentleman!
Romeo's a dishclout to him.[57] An eagle, madam,
Hath not so green, so quick, so fair an eye
As Paris hath. Beshrew my very heart,
I think you are happy in this second match,
225 For it excels your first; or if it did not,
Your first is dead—or 'twere as good he were
As living here and you no use of him.

**JULIET.** Speak'st thou from thy heart?

**NURSE.** And from my soul too; else beshrew them both.

230 **JULIET.** Amen!

▶ **Critical Viewing** In what ways
does this picture suggest Juliet's
vulnerability? Explain. **[Interpret]**

54. **stratagems** tricks; plots.

55. **all . . . nothing** the odds
are overwhelming.
56. **challenge** claim.

57. **a dishclout to him** a
dishcloth compared with
him.

**Reading Check**

How do the Capulets re-
spond to the Nurse's at-
tempts to defend Juliet?

**58. be absolved** receive
forgiveness for my sins.

**59. Ancient damnation!** Old
devil!

**60. Thou . . . twain** You will
from now on be separated
from my trust.

**Literary Analysis**
**Dramatic Speeches**
What feelings toward her
Nurse does Juliet reveal
in this soliloquy?

**NURSE.** What?

**JULIET.** Well, thou hast comforted me marvelous much.
Go in; and tell my lady I am gone,
Having displeased my father, to Lawrence' cell,
235     To make confession and to be absolved.[58]

**NURSE.** Marry, I will; and this is wisely done.          [*Exit.*]

**JULIET.** Ancient damnation![59] O most wicked fiend!
Is it more sin to wish me thus forsworn,
Or to dispraise my lord with that same tongue
240     Which she hath praised him with above compare
So many thousand times? Go, counselor!
Thou and my bosom henceforth shall be twain.[60]
I'll to the friar to know his remedy.
If all else fail, myself have power to die.          [*Exit.*]

Cite textual
evidence to
support your
responses.

## Critical Thinking

ⓒ **1. Key Ideas and Details (a)** Make a three-column chart. In the
first column, write the remark regarding the Montagues and
Capulets that Mercutio makes three times as he is dying.
**(b) Infer:** In the second column, explain what Mercutio means by
this exclamation. **(c) Interpret:** In the third column, explain how
his remark reinforces ideas set forth in the play's Prologue.

ⓒ **2. Key Ideas and Details (a)** How and why does Romeo kill Tybalt?
**(b) Interpret:** What does Romeo mean when he says, after killing
Tybalt, "I am fortune's fool"?

ⓒ **3. Key Ideas and Details (a) Analyze:** Describe the clashing
emotions Juliet feels when the Nurse reports Tybalt's death and
Romeo's punishment. **(b) Compare and Contrast:** In what ways
are Romeo's and Juliet's reactions to Romeo's banishment similar
and different? Explain.

ⓒ **4. Integration of Knowledge and Ideas Draw Conclusions:**
How might Tybalt's death have been avoided?

ⓒ **5. Integration of Knowledge and Ideas** How have the differences
between Romeo and Juliet returned to threaten their future
together? Explain. *[Connect to the Big Question: Do our
differences define us?]*

## After You Read | The Tragedy of Romeo and Juliet, Act III

Act III

## Literary Analysis: Dramatic Speeches

ⓒ **1. Key Ideas and Details (a)** What thoughts and feelings does Juliet express in the **soliloquy** that opens Scene ii of Act III? **(b)** When Juliet makes an **allusion** to Phoebus and Phaëton, what is she hoping will happen?

ⓒ **2. Key Ideas and Details** What criticisms of Romeo does the Friar address in his Scene iii **monologue** beginning, "Hold thy desperate hand"?

ⓒ **3. Key Ideas and Details** In Act III, Scene v, when her mother refers to Romeo as a villain, Juliet utters the **aside,** "Villain and he be many miles asunder." What has happened? Why does Juliet speak only to the audience?

ⓒ **4. Key Ideas and Details (a)** How would you describe the personalities of each of the following characters: Romeo, Tybalt, Benvolio, Mercutio. **(b)** Which of these men are **foils** to each other? Explain.

## Reading Skill: Summarize

**5. (a) Paraphrase** lines 29–51 in Act III, Scene iii. **(b)** Write a few sentences that **summarize** what Romeo says to the Friar. Then summarize the events of Act III.

## Vocabulary

ⓒ **Acquisition and Use** Identify which two words in each group are **synonyms** and which one is an **antonym** of the other two. Explain your response.

**1.** gallant, courageous, cowardly

**2.** fray, truce, brawl

**3.** exile, banishment, welcome

**4.** martial, peaceful, warlike

**5.** eloquence, expressiveness, inarticulateness

**6.** fickle, unpredictable, constant

**Word Study** Use the context of the sentences and what you know about the **Latin root -loque-** to explain your answer to each question.

**1.** Would a *colloquialism* be out of place when used among friends?

**2.** What would you expect to happen at a *colloquium* on William Shakespeare?

### Word Study

The **Latin root -loque-** means "talk," "speak," or "say."

**Apply It** Explain how the root *-loque-* contributes to the meanings of these words. Consult a dictionary if necessary.

**ventriloquist**
**soliloquy**
**loquacious**

## Before You Read | The Tragedy of Romeo and Juliet, Act IV

# Do our *differences* define us?

**While You Read** Look for the ways that the feud between the Montagues and the Capulets continues to drive the young lovers apart. Then, decide whether the actions they take are wise or foolish.

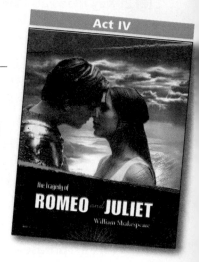

Act IV

The Tragedy of
ROMEO and JULIET
William Shakespeare

## © Common Core State Standards

Meet these standards with *The Tragedy of Romeo and Juliet,* **Act IV** (p. 894).

**Reading Literature**
**2.** Determine a theme or central idea of a text; provide an objective summary of the text. *(Reading Skill: Summarize)*

**5.** Analyze how an author's choices concerning how to structure a text, order events within it, and manipulate time create such effects as mystery, tension, or surprise. *(Literary Analysis: Dramatic Irony)*

**Language**
**5.a.** Interpret figures of speech in context and analyze their role in the text. *(Literary Analysis: Comic Relief and Puns)*
**Spiral Review: RL.9-10.3**

## Vocabulary

Read each word and its definition. Decide whether you know the word well, know it a little bit, or do not know it at all. After you read, see how your knowledge of each word has increased.

- **pensive** (pen´ siv) *adj.* deeply thoughtful (p. 896) *She listened intently, looking pensive.* pensively *adv.* pensiveness *n.*

- **vial** (vī´ əl) *n.* small bottle containing medicine or other liquids (p. 898) *The vial was filled with expensive perfume.*

- **enjoined** (en joind´) *v.* ordered (p. 900) *The jurors were enjoined not to discuss the case.* enjoin *v.* enjoinment *n.*

- **wayward** (wā´ wərd) *adj.* headstrong (p. 900) *The wayward boy did not listen to anyone and insisted on working alone.* waywardly *adv.* waywardness *n.*

- **dismal** (diz´ məl) *adj.* causing gloom or misery (p. 901) *The dismal sight of his abandoned house made the old man sad.* dismally *adv.*

- **loathsome** (lōth´ səm) *adj.* disgusting; detestable (p. 903) *The loathsome smell of rotten eggs filled the laboratory.* loathe *v.* loathing *n.*

### Word Study

The **Latin prefix en-** means "in," "into," or "within."

In Act IV, Juliet says she is **enjoined** by Friar Lawrence to be ruled by her father. She means that Friar Lawrence wants her to join with her father by obeying his wishes.

# Literary Analysis: Dramatic Irony

**Dramatic irony** is a contradiction between what a character thinks and what the audience knows to be true. Dramatic irony engages the audience emotionally; tension and suspense build as the audience waits for the truth to be revealed to the characters.

Shakespeare understood the importance of providing a balance of tragic and comic elements in his plays. Injecting humor into an otherwise tragic plot allows the audience to experience a range of reactions to the events unfolding onstage. These comic elements are used thoughout the play:

- **Comic relief:** the introduction of a humorous character or situation into an otherwise tragic scene.

- **Puns:** plays on words using a word with multiple meanings or two words that sound alike but have different meanings. For example, the dying Mercutio makes a pun using the word *grave:* "Ask for me tomorrow, and you shall find me a grave man."

As you read, notice how Shakespeare uses dramatic irony, comic relief, and puns to balance strong emotion with humor and wit.

**PHLit Online!**
www.PHLitOnline.com

**Hear It!**
- Selection summary audio
- Selection audio

**See It!**
- Get Connected video
- Background video
- More about the author
- Vocabulary flashcards

**Do It!**
- Interactive journals
- Interactive graphic organizers
- Self-test
- Internet activity
- Grammar tutorial
- Interactive vocabulary games

# Reading Skill: Summarize

To summarize long passages of Shakespearean dialogue, you should **break down long sentences** into shorter units of meaning.

- If a sentence contains multiple subjects or verbs, separate it into smaller sentences with one subject and one verb.

- If a sentence contains colons, semicolons, or dashes, treat these marks as periods in order to make shorter sentences.

## Using the Strategy: Summarizing Chart

Use a chart like this one to help you break down long sentences.

| Line of Dialogue | Line in Smaller Sentences | Summary |
|---|---|---|
| Immoderately she weeps for Tybalt's death, / And therefore have I little talked of love; / For Venus smiles not in a house of tears. | 1. Immoderately she weeps for Tybalt's death. <br> 2. Therefore have I little talked of love. <br> 3. Venus smiles not in a house of tears. | Paris has not talked of love with Juliet because she is crying over Tybalt's death. |

# Act IV

## Review and Anticipate

Romeo and Juliet are married for only a few hours when disaster strikes. In Act III, Juliet's cousin Tybalt kills Mercutio, and then Romeo kills Tybalt. This leads to Romeo's banishment from Verona. To make matters worse, Juliet's parents are determined to marry her to Paris. Will Romeo and Juliet ever be able to live together as husband and wife? What, if anything, can the lovers now do to preserve their relationship?

*Scene i. Friar Lawrence's cell.*

[*Enter* FRIAR LAWRENCE *and* COUNTY PARIS.]

**FRIAR.** On Thursday, sir? The time is very short.

**PARIS.** My father¹ Capulet will have it so,
And I am nothing slow to slack his haste.²

**FRIAR.** You say you do not know the lady's mind.
5     Uneven is the course;³ I like it not.

**PARIS.** Immoderately she weeps for Tybalt's death,
And therefore have I little talked of love;
For Venus smiles not in a house of tears.
Now, sir, her father counts it dangerous

1. **father** future father-in-law.
2. **I . . . haste** I will not slow him down by being slow myself.
3. **Uneven . . . course** irregular is the plan.

### Reading Check

What is the Friar's complaint to Paris about the impending wedding?

10      That she do give her sorrow so much sway,
        And in his wisdom hastes our marriage
        To stop the inundation[4] of her tears,
        Which, too much minded[5] by herself alone,
        May be put from her by society.
15      Now do you know the reason of this haste.

**FRIAR.** [*Aside*] I would I knew not why it should be slowed.—
        Look, sir, here comes the lady toward my cell.

[*Enter* JULIET.]

**PARIS.** Happily met, my lady and my wife!

**JULIET.** That may be, sir, when I may be a wife.

20 **PARIS.** That "may be" must be, love, on Thursday next.

**JULIET.** What must be shall be.

**FRIAR.**                          That's a certain text.[6]

**PARIS.** Come you to make confession to this father?

**JULIET.** To answer that, I should confess to you.

**PARIS.** Do not deny to him that you love me.

25 **JULIET.** I will confess to you that I love him.

**PARIS.** So will ye, I am sure, that you love me.

**JULIET.** If I do so, it will be of more price,[7]
        Being spoke behind your back, than to your face.

**PARIS.** Poor soul, thy face is much abused with tears.

30 **JULIET.** The tears have got small victory by that,
        For it was bad enough before their spite.[8]

**PARIS.** Thou wrong'st it more than tears with that report.

**JULIET.** That is no slander, sir, which is a truth;
        And what I spake, I spake it to my face.

35 **PARIS.** Thy face is mine, and thou hast sland'red it.

**JULIET.** It may be so, for it is not mine own.
        Are you at leisure, holy father, now,
        Or shall I come to you at evening mass?

**FRIAR.** My leisure serves me, pensive daughter, now.
40      My lord, we must entreat the time alone.[9]

**PARIS.** God shield[10] I should disturb devotion!
    Juliet, on Thursday early will I rouse ye.
    Till then, adieu, and keep this holy kiss.         [*Exit.*]

**JULIET.** O, shut the door, and when thou hast done so,
45    Come weep with me—past hope, past care, past help!

**FRIAR.** O Juliet, I already know thy grief;
    It strains me past the compass of my wits.[11]
    I hear thou must, and nothing may prorogue[12] it,
    On Thursday next be married to this County.

50 **JULIET.** Tell me not, friar, that thou hearest of this,
    Unless thou tell me how I may prevent it.
    If in thy wisdom thou canst give no help,
    Do thou but call my resolution wise
    And with this knife I'll help it presently.[13]
55    God joined my heart and Romeo's, thou our hands;
    And ere this hand, by thee to Romeo's sealed,
    Shall be the label to another deed,[14]
    Or my true heart with treacherous revolt
    Turn to another, this shall slay them both.
60    Therefore, out of thy long-experienced time,
    Give me some present counsel; or, behold,
    'Twixt my extremes and me[15] this bloody knife
    Shall play the umpire, arbitrating[16] that
    Which the commission of thy years and art
65    Could to no issue of true honor bring.[17]
    Be not so long to speak. I long to die
    If what thou speak'st speak not of remedy.

**FRIAR.** Hold, daughter. I do spy a kind of hope,
    Which craves[18] as desperate an execution
70    As that is desperate which we would prevent.
    If, rather than to marry County Paris,
    Thou hast the strength of will to slay thyself,
    Then is it likely thou wilt undertake
    A thing like death to chide away this shame,
75    That cop'st with death himself to scape from it;[19]
    And, if thou darest, I'll give thee remedy.

**JULIET.** O, bid me leap, rather than marry Paris,
    From off the battlements of any tower,
    Or walk in thievish ways,[20] or bid me lurk

---

**10. shield** forbid.

**11. past . . . wits** beyond the ability of my mind to find a remedy.
**12. prorogue** delay.

**13. presently** at once.
**14. Shall . . . deed** shall give the seal of approval to another marriage contract.
**15. 'Twixt . . me** between my misfortunes and me.
**16. arbitrating** deciding.
**17. Which . . . bring** which the authority that derives from your age and ability could not solve honorably.

**Literary Analysis**
**Dramatic Irony** Which two meanings of the word "long" does Juliet use to make a pun in line 66?

**18. craves** requires.
**19. That cop'st . . . it** that bargains with death itself to escape from it.
**20. thievish ways** roads where criminals lurk.

**Reading Check**

What does Juliet threaten to do to avoid marrying Paris?

21. **charnel house** vault for bones removed from graves to be reused.
22. **reeky** foul-smelling.
23. **chapless** jawless.

80 Where serpents are; chain me with roaring bears,
Or hide me nightly in a charnel house,[21]
O'ercovered quite with dead men's rattling bones,
With reeky[22] shanks and yellow chapless[23] skulls;
Or bid me go into a new-made grave
85 And hide me with a dead man in his shroud—
Things that, to hear them told, have made me tremble—
And I will do it without fear or doubt,
To live an unstained wife to my sweet love.

**FRIAR.** Hold, then. Go home, be merry, give consent
90 To marry Paris. Wednesday is tomorrow.
Tomorrow night look that thou lie alone;
Let not the nurse lie with thee in thy chamber.
Take thou this vial, being then in bed,
And this distilling liquor drink thou off;
95 When presently through all thy veins shall run
A cold and drowsy humor;[24] for no pulse
Shall keep his native[25] progress, but surcease;[26]
No warmth, no breath, shall testify thou livest;
The roses in thy lips and cheeks shall fade
100 To wanny ashes,[27] thy eyes' windows[28] fall
Like death when he shuts up the day of life;
Each part, deprived of supple government,[29]
Shall, stiff and stark and cold, appear like death;
And in this borrowed likeness of shrunk death
105 Thou shalt continue two-and-forty hours,
And then awake as from a pleasant sleep.
Now, when the bridegroom in the morning comes
To rouse thee from thy bed, there art thou dead.
Then, as the manner of our country is,
110 In thy best robes uncovered on the bier[30]
Thou shalt be borne to that same ancient vault
Where all the kindred of the Capulets lie.
In the meantime, against[31] thou shalt awake,
Shall Romeo by my letters know our drift;[32]
115 And hither shall he come; and he and I

**Vocabulary**
**vial** (vī′ əl) *n.* small bottle containing medicine or other liquids

24. **humor** fluid; liquid.
25. **native** natural.
26. **surcease** stop.
27. **wanny ashes** to the color of pale ashes.
28. **eyes' windows** eyelids.
29. **supple government** ability for maintaining motion.

30. **uncovered on the bier** displayed on the funeral platform.
31. **against** before.
32. **drift** purpose; plan.

Will watch thy waking, and that very night
Shall Romeo bear thee hence to Mantua.
And this shall free thee from this present shame,
If no inconstant toy$^{33}$ nor womanish fear
120     Abate thy valor$^{34}$ in the acting it.

    **JULIET.** Give me, give me! O, tell not me of fear!

    **FRIAR.** Hold! Get you gone, be strong and prosperous
In this resolve. I'll send a friar with speed
To Mantua, with my letters to thy lord.

125 **JULIET.** Love give me strength, and strength shall help afford.
Farewell, dear father.           [*Exit with* FRIAR.]

### Scene ii. Hall in Capulet's house.

[*Enter* FATHER CAPULET, MOTHER, NURSE, *and* SERVINGMEN, *two or three.*]

    **CAPULET.** So many guests invite as here are writ.

                [*Exit a* SERVINGMAN.]

Sirrah, go hire me twenty cunning$^{1}$ cooks.

    **SERVINGMAN.** You shall have none ill, sir; for I'll try$^{2}$ if they can lick their fingers.

5     **CAPULET.** How canst thou try them so?

    **SERVINGMAN.** Marry, sir, 'tis an ill cook that cannot lick his own fingers.$^{3}$ Therefore he that cannot lick his fingers goes not with me.

    **CAPULET.** Go, begone.

                [*Exit* SERVINGMAN.]

We shall be much unfurnished$^{4}$ for this time.
10     What, is my daughter gone to Friar Lawrence?

    **NURSE.** Ay, forsooth.$^{5}$

    **CAPULET.** Well, he may chance to do some good on her.
A peevish self-willed harlotry it is.$^{6}$

[*Enter* JULIET.]

    **NURSE.** See where she comes from shrift with merry look.

15     **CAPULET.** How now, my headstrong? Where have you been gadding?

---

**33. inconstant toy** passing whim.

**34. Abate thy valor** Lessen your courage.

**Literary Analysis**

**Dramatic Irony** What information does Juliet now have that Romeo does not?

**1. cunning** skillful.

**2. try** test.

**3. 'tis . . . fingers** It is a bad cook who will not taste his own cooking.

**4. unfurnished** unprepared.

**5. forsooth** in truth.

**6. A peevish . . . it is** It is the ill-tempered, selfish behavior of a woman without good breeding.

**Reading Check**

According to the Friar, how will Romeo learn of Juliet's plan to meet him?

**Vocabulary**
**enjoined** (en joind´)
*v.* ordered

7. **behests** requests.

8. **fall prostrate** lie face down in humble submission.

9. **becomèd** suitable; proper.

**Literary Analysis**
**Dramatic Irony** What is ironic about Lord Capulet's relief in this scene?

10. **bound** indebted.
11. **closet** private room.
12. **ornaments** clothes.

13. **short . . . provision** lacking time for preparation.

14. **deck up her** dress her; get her ready.
15. **What, ho!** Capulet is calling for his servants.

**Vocabulary**
**wayward** (wā´ wərd)
*adj.* headstrong

**JULIET.** Where I have learnt me to repent the sin
Of disobedient opposition
To you and your behests,[7] and am enjoined
By holy Lawrence to fall prostrate[8] here
20 To beg your pardon. Pardon, I beseech you!
Henceforward I am ever ruled by you.

**CAPULET.** Send for the County. Go tell him of this.
I'll have this knot knit up tomorrow morning.

**JULIET.** I met the youthful lord at Lawrence' cell
25 And gave him what becomèd[9] love I might,
Not stepping o'er the bounds of modesty.

**CAPULET.** Why, I am glad on't. This is well. Stand up.
This is as't should be. Let me see the County.
Ay, marry, go, I say, and fetch him hither.
30 Now, afore God, this reverend holy friar,
All our whole city is much bound[10] to him.

**JULIET.** Nurse, will you go with me into my closet[11]
To help me sort such needful ornaments[12]
As you think fit to furnish me tomorrow?

35 **LADY CAPULET.** No, not till Thursday. There is time enough.

**CAPULET.** Go, nurse, go with her. We'll to church tomorrow.

[*Exit* JULIET *and* NURSE.]

**LADY CAPULET.** We shall be short in our provision.[13]
'Tis now near night.

**CAPULET.**                    Tush, I will stir about,
And all things shall be well, I warrant thee, wife.
40 Go thou to Juliet, help to deck up her.[14]
I'll not to bed tonight; let me alone.
I'll play the housewife for this once. What, ho![15]
They are all forth; well, I will walk myself
To County Paris, to prepare up him
45 Against tomorrow. My heart is wondrous light,
Since this same wayward girl is so reclaimed.

[*Exit with* MOTHER.]

*Scene iii. Juliet's chamber.*

[*Enter* JULIET *and* NURSE.]

**JULIET.** Ay, those attires are best; but, gentle nurse,
   I pray thee leave me to myself tonight;
   For I have need of many orisons[1]
   To move the heavens to smile upon my state,[2]
5  Which, well thou knowest, is cross[3] and full of sin.

[*Enter* MOTHER.]

**LADY CAPULET.** What, are you busy, ho? Need you my help?

**JULIET.** No, madam; we have culled[4] such necessaries
   As are behoveful[5] for our state tomorrow.
   So please you, let me now be left alone,
10 And let the nurse this night sit up with you:
   For I am sure you have your hands full all
   In this so sudden business.

**LADY CAPULET.**                    Good night.
   Get thee to bed, and rest: for thou hast need.

                    [*Exit* MOTHER *and* NURSE.]

**JULIET.** Farewell! God knows when we shall meet again.
15 I have a faint cold fear thrills through my veins
   That almost freezes up the heat of life.
   I'll call them back again to comfort me.
   Nurse!—What should she do here?
   My dismal scene I needs must act alone.
20 Come, vial.
   What if this mixture do not work at all?
   Shall I be married then tomorrow morning?
   No, no! This shall forbid it. Lie thou there.

                    [*Lays down a dagger.*]

   What if it be a poison which the friar
25 Subtly hath minist'red[6] to have me dead,
   Lest in this marriage he should be dishonored
   Because he married me before to Romeo?
   I fear it is; and yet methinks it should not,
   For he hath still been tried[7] a holy man.
30 How if, when I am laid into the tomb,
   I wake before the time that Romeo
   Come to redeem me? There's a fearful point!

**Spiral Review**
**Character** What is Juliet's motivation for deceiving the Nurse?

1. **orisons** prayers.
2. **state** condition.
3. **cross** selfish; disobedient.

**Reading Skill**
**Summarize** Briefly state the reasons Juliet gives her Nurse and Lady Capulet for why she should be alone.

4. **culled** chosen.
5. **behoveful** desirable; appropriate.

**Vocabulary**
**dismal** (diz´ məl) *adj.* causing gloom or misery

6. **minist'red** given me.

7. **tried** proved.

**Reading Check**
How does Juliet regain her parents' favor?

Shall I not then be stifled in the vault,
To whose foul mouth no healthsome air breathes in,
35 And there die strangled ere my Romeo comes?
Or, if I live, is it not very like
The horrible conceit[8] of death and night,
Together with the terror of the place—
As in a vault, an ancient receptacle
40 Where for this many hundred years the bones
Of all my buried ancestors are packed;
Where bloody Tybalt, yet but green in earth,[9]
Lies fest'ring in his shroud; where, as they say,
At some hours in the night spirits resort—
45 Alack, alack, is it not like[10] that I,
So early waking—what with loathsome smells,
And shrieks like mandrakes[11] torn out of the earth,
That living mortals, hearing them, run mad—
O, if I wake, shall I not be distraught,[12]
50 Environèd[13] with all these hideous fears,
And madly play with my forefathers' joints,
And pluck the mangled Tybalt from his shroud,
And, in this rage, with some great kinsman's bone
As with a club dash out my desp'rate brains?
55 O, look! Methinks I see my cousin's ghost
Seeking out Romeo, that did spit his body
Upon a rapier's point. Stay, Tybalt, stay!
Romeo, Romeo, Romeo, I drink to thee.

[*She falls upon her bed within the curtains.*]

8. **conceit** idea; thought.

9. **green in earth** newly entombed.

10. **like** likely.

**Vocabulary**
**loathsome** (lō*th*′ səm)
*adj.* disgusting;
detestable

11. **mandrakes** plants with forked roots that resemble human legs. The mandrake was believed to shriek when uprooted and cause the hearer to go mad.

12. **distraught** insane.

13. **Environèd** surrounded.

**Reading Skill**
**Summarize** Summarize the fears that Juliet expresses in this soliloquy.

Reading
Check

What does Juliet do after her mother and the Nurse leave her chambers?

◀ **Critical Viewing** In what way do the colors in this photograph enhance the mood of the scene? **[Analyze]**

## Scene iv. Hall in Capulet's house.

[*Enter* LADY OF THE HOUSE *and* NURSE.]

    **LADY CAPULET.** Hold, take these keys and fetch more spices,
      nurse.

    **NURSE.** They call for dates and quinces[1] in the pastry.[2]

[*Enter old* CAPULET.]

    **CAPULET.** Come, stir, stir, stir! The second cock hath crowed,
      The curfew bell hath rung, 'tis three o'clock.
5     Look to the baked meats, good Angelica;[3]
      Spare not for cost.

    **NURSE.**                Go, you cotquean,[4] go,
      Get you to bed! Faith, you'll be sick tomorrow
      For this night's watching.[5]

    **CAPULET.** No, not a whit. What, I have watched ere now
10    All night for lesser cause, and ne'er been sick.

    **LADY CAPULET.** Ay, you have been a mouse hunt[6] in your time;
      But I will watch you from such watching now.
                        [*Exit* LADY *and* NURSE.]

    **CAPULET.** A jealous hood,[7] a jealous hood!

[*Enter three or four* FELLOWS *with spits and logs and baskets.*]
                            Now, fellow,
      What is there?

15    **FIRST FELLOW.** Things for the cook, sir; but I know not what.

    **CAPULET.** Make haste, make haste. [*Exit* FIRST FELLOW.] Sirrah,
      fetch drier logs.
      Call Peter; he will show thee where they are.

    **SECOND FELLOW.** I have a head, sir, that will find out logs
      And never trouble Peter for the matter.

20    **CAPULET.** Mass,[8] and well said; a merry whoreson, ha!
      Thou shalt be loggerhead.[9]
                     [*Exit* SECOND FELLOW, *with the others.*]
             Good faith, 'tis day.
      The County will be here with music straight,
      For so he said he would.           [*Play music.*]
               I hear him near.
      Nurse! Wife! What, ho! What, nurse, I say!

---

**1. quinces** golden, apple-shaped fruits.

**2. pastry** baking room.

**3. Angelica** This is probably the Nurse's name.

**4. cotquean** (kat´ kwēn´) man who does housework.

**5. watching** staying awake.

**6. mouse hunt** woman chaser.

**7. jealous hood** jealousy.

**8. Mass** by the Mass (an oath).

**9. loggerhead** blockhead.

**Literary Analysis**
**Dramatic Irony** Reread lines 16–21. In what way does Capulet's pun in line 21 contribute to the mood of Scene iv?

[*Enter* NURSE.]

25      Go waken Juliet; go and trim her up.
        I'll go and chat with Paris. Hie, make haste,
        Make haste! The bridegroom he is come already:
        Make haste, I say.                               [*Exit.*]

## Scene v. *Juliet's chamber.*

     **NURSE.** Mistress! What, mistress! Juliet! Fast,¹ I warrant her,
        she.
        Why, lamb! Why, lady! Fie, you slugabed.²
        Why, love, I say! Madam; Sweetheart! Why, bride!
        What, not a word? You take your pennyworths now;
5       Sleep for a week; for the next night, I warrant,
        The County Paris hath set up his rest
        That you shall rest but little. God forgive me!
        Marry, and amen. How sound is she asleep!
        I needs must wake her. Madam, madam, madam!
10      Ay, let the County take you in your bed;
        He'll fright you up, i' faith. Will it not be?
                                    [*Draws aside the curtains.*]
        What, dressed, and in your clothes, and down again?³
        I must needs wake you. Lady! Lady! Lady!
        Alas, alas! Help, help! My lady's dead!
15      O weraday that ever I was born!
        Some aqua vitae, ho! My lord! My lady!

[*Enter* MOTHER.]

     **LADY CAPULET.** What noise is here?

     **NURSE.**                          O lamentable day!

     **LADY CAPULET.** What is the matter?

     **NURSE.**                          Look, look! O heavy day!

     **LADY CAPULET.** O me, O me! My child, my only life!
20      Revive, look up, or I will die with thee!
        Help, help! Call help.

[*Enter* FATHER.]

     **CAPULET.** For shame, bring Juliet forth; her lord is come.

     **NURSE.** She's dead, deceased; she's dead, alack the day!

     **LADY CAPULET.** Alack the day, she's dead, she's dead, she's
        dead!

1. **Fast** fast asleep.
2. **slugabed** sleepyhead.

**Literary Analysis
Dramatic Irony** In what
way does the Nurse's
carefree chatter add to
the irony of the scene?

3. **down again** back in bed.

Reading
Check
What does the Nurse find
when she draws aside
the curtains in Juliet's
chamber?

**CAPULET.** Ha! Let me see her. Out alas! She's cold,
    Her blood is settled, and her joints are stiff;
    Life and these lips have long been separated.
    Death lies on her like an untimely frost
    Upon the sweetest flower of all the field.

**NURSE.** O lamentable day!

30  **LADY CAPULET.**          O woeful time!

**CAPULET.** Death, that hath ta'en her hence to make me wail,
    Ties up my tongue and will not let me speak.

[*Enter* FRIAR LAWRENCE *and the* COUNTY PARIS, *with* MUSICIANS.]

**FRIAR.** Come, is the bride ready to go to church?

**CAPULET.** Ready to go, but never to return.
35    O son, the night before thy wedding day
    Hath Death lain with thy wife. There she lies,
    Flower as she was, deflowerèd by him.
    Death is my son-in-law, Death is my heir;
    My daughter he hath wedded. I will die
40    And leave him all. Life, living, all is Death's.

**PARIS.** Have I thought, love, to see this morning's face,
    And doth it give me such a sight as this?

**LADY CAPULET.** Accursed, unhappy, wretched, hateful day!
    Most miserable hour that e'er time saw
45    In lasting labor of his pilgrimage!
    But one, poor one, one poor and loving child,
    But one thing to rejoice and solace[4] in,
    And cruel Death hath catched it from my sight.

**NURSE.** O woe! O woeful, woeful, woeful day!
50    Most lamentable day, most woeful day
    That ever ever I did yet behold!
    O day, O day, O day! O hateful day!
    Never was seen so black a day as this.
    O woeful day! O woeful day!

55  **PARIS.** Beguiled,[5] divorcèd, wrongèd, spited, slain!
    Most detestable Death, by thee beguiled,
    By cruel, cruel thee quite overthrown.
    O love! O life!—not life, but love in death!

**CAPULET.** Despised, distressèd, hated, martyred, killed!
60    Uncomfortable[6] time, why cam'st thou now
    To murder, murder our solemnity?[7]

**Literary Analysis**
**Dramatic Irony** In what way does the Friar's question add to the dramatic irony of the scene?

4. **solace** find comfort.
5. **Beguiled** cheated.

6. **Uncomfortable** painful, upsetting.
7. **solemnity** solemn rites.

### Culture Connection

**Rosemary**

When the Capulets discover Juliet apparently dead, the Friar advises, "Dry up your tears and stick your rosemary / On this fair corse." Rosemary is an evergreen herb that traditionally signifies remembrance, loyalty, and love. Shakespeare often included references to herbs in his plays for symbolic purposes, and rosemary is one herb that turned up often in his works. *Hamlet, King Lear, The Winter's Tale,* and *Pericles* all include references to rosemary as a symbol of remembrance.

**Connect to the Literature**

Why do you think the Friar tells the Capulets to lay a sprig of rosemary on Juliet's body?

O child, O child! My soul, and not my child!
Dead art thou—alack, my child is dead,
And with my child my joys are burièd!

65 **FRIAR.** Peace, ho, for shame! Confusion's cure lives not
In these confusions.[8] Heaven and yourself
Had part in this fair maid—now heaven hath all,
And all the better is it for the maid.
Your part in her you could not keep from death,
70 But heaven keeps his part in eternal life.
The most you sought was her promotion,
For 'twas your heaven she should be advanced;
And weep ye now, seeing she is advanced
Above the clouds, as high as heaven itself?
75 O, in this love, you love your child so ill
That you run mad, seeing that she is well.[9]
She's not well married that lives married long,
But she's best married that dies married young.
Dry up your tears and stick your rosemary[10]
80 On this fair corse, and, as the custom is,
And in her best array bear her to church:
For though fond nature[11] bids us all lament,
Yet nature's tears are reason's merriment.[12]

8. **Confusion's . . . confusions** The remedy for this calamity is not to be found in these outcries.

9. **well** blessed in heaven.

10. **rosemary** evergreen herb signifying love and remembrance.

11. **fond nature** mistake-prone human nature.

12. **Yet . . . merriment** While human nature causes us to weep for Juliet, reason should cause us to be happy (since she is in heaven).

## Reading Check

What does the Friar recommend that the Capulets do when they discover Juliet and believe she is dead?

**CAPULET.** All things that we ordainèd festival[13]
85      Turn from their office to black funeral—
     Our instruments to melancholy bells,
     Our wedding cheer to a sad burial feast;
     Our solemn hymns to sullen dirges[14] change;
     Our bridal flowers serve for a buried corse;
90      And all things change them to the contrary.

**FRIAR.** Sir, go you in; and, madam, go with him;
     And go, Sir Paris. Everyone prepare
     To follow this fair corse unto her grave.
     The heavens do low'r[15] upon you for some ill;
95      Move them no more by crossing their high will.

        [*Exit, casting rosemary on her and shutting the curtains.*
                   *The* NURSE *and* MUSICIANS *remain.*]

**FIRST MUSICIAN.** Faith, we may put up our pipes and be gone.

**NURSE.** Honest good fellows, ah, put up, put up!
     For well you know this is a pitiful case.[16]          [*Exit.*]

**FIRST MUSICIAN.** Ay, by my troth, the case may be amended.

[*Enter* PETER.]

100 **PETER.** Musicians, O, musicians, "Heart's ease," "Heart's ease"!
     O, and you will have me live, play "Heart's ease."

**FIRST MUSICIAN.** Why "Heart's ease"?

**PETER.** O, musicians, because my heart itself plays "My heart is
     full."
     O, play me some merry dump[17] to comfort me.

105 **FIRST MUSICIAN.** Not a dump we! 'Tis no time to play now.

**PETER.** You will not then?

**FIRST MUSICIAN.** No.

**PETER.** I will then give it you soundly.

**FIRST MUSICIAN.** What will you give us?

110 **PETER.** No money, on my faith, but the gleek.[18] I will give
     you[19] the minstrel.[20]

---

**13. ordainèd festival** planned to be part of a celebration.

**14. dirges** funeral hymns.

**Literary Analysis**
**Dramatic Irony** In what way does the dramatic irony of the Friar's words heighten the play's suspense?

**15. low'r** frown.

**16. case** situation; instrument case.

**17. dump** sad tune.

**18. gleek** scornful speech.
**19. give you** call you.
**20. minstrel** a contemptuous term (as opposed to "musician").

**FIRST MUSICIAN.** Then will I give you the serving-creature.

**PETER.** Then will I lay the serving-creature's dagger on
    your pate.
    I will carry no crotchets.[21] I'll *re* you, I'll *fa* you. Do you
    note me?

115 **FIRST MUSICIAN.** And you *re* us and *fa* us, you note us.

**SECOND MUSICIAN.** Pray you put up your dagger, and put out
    your wit.
    Then have at you with my wit!

**PETER.** I will dry-beat you with an iron wit, and put up my iron
    dagger. Answer me like men.
120     "When griping grief the heart doth wound,
       And doleful dumps the mind oppress,
    Then music with her silver sound"—
    Why "silver sound"? Why "music with her silver sound"?
    What say you, Simon Catling?

125 **FIRST MUSICIAN.** Marry, sir, because silver hath a sweet sound.

**PETER.** Pretty! What say you, Hugh Rebeck?

**21. crotchets** whims; quarter
notes.

**Literary Analysis**
**Dramatic Irony** What kind of mood does the pun in line 127 help to create in this scene?

**22. cry you mercy** beg your pardon.

**SECOND MUSICIAN.** I say "silver sound" because musicians sound for silver.

**PETER.** Pretty too! What say you, James Soundpost?

130 **THIRD MUSICIAN.** Faith, I know not what to say.

**PETER.** O, I cry you mercy,²² you are the singer. I will say for you. It is "music with her silver sound" because musicians have no gold for sounding.
"Then music with her silver sound
135 With speedy help doth lend redress." [*Exit.*]

**FIRST MUSICIAN.** What a pestilent knave is this same!

**SECOND MUSICIAN.** Hang him, Jack! Come, we'll in here, tarry for the mourners, and stay dinner. [*Exit with others.*]

## Critical Thinking

Cite textual evidence to support your responses.

1. **Key Ideas and Details (a)** What is Friar Lawrence's plan for Juliet? **(b) Analyze:** Why do you think Juliet trusts the Friar? Explain using details from the text.

2. **Key Ideas and Details (a)** What three fears does Juliet reveal in her Act IV, Scene iii, soliloquy? **(b) Interpret:** What does the soliloquy reveal about her personality? Explain your response.

3. **Integration of Knowledge and Ideas (a) Evaluate:** Do you think drinking the potion is a brave act or a foolish act? Explain. **(b) Draw Conclusions:** How has Juliet changed in the course of the play? Give details to explain.

4. **Integration of Knowledge and Ideas (a)** In what way do Juliet's ideas about love differ from her parents' ideas? **(b)** What do Juliet's rebellious actions reveal about her? *[Connect to the Big Question: Do our differences define us?]*

## After You Read | The Tragedy of Romeo and Juliet, Act IV

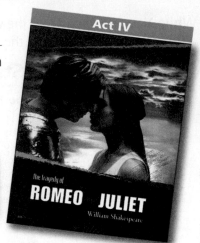

Act IV

The Tragedy of
ROMEO JULIET
William Shakespeare

## Literary Analysis: Dramatic Irony

**©** **1. Craft and Structure** In what way is Juliet's encounter with Paris in Friar Lawrence's cell an instance of **dramatic irony?**

**©** **2. Craft and Structure** Complete a chart like the one shown to demonstrate why Capulet's statement in Act IV, Scene iv, line 25, is dramatic irony.

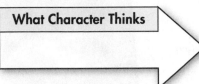

| What Character Thinks | What Audience Knows |

**©** **3. Craft and Structure** Explain how Capulet's encounter with the fellows in Act IV, Scene iv, represents an example of **comic relief.**

**©** **4. Craft and Structure** **(a)** Explain the **pun** in the Nurse's exchange with the First Musician in Act IV, Scene v, lines 97–98. **(b)** How is the conversation that follows among the musicians and Peter an example of comic relief?

## Reading Skill: Summarize

**5. (a) Summarize** lines 50–59 of Juliet's monologue to Friar Lawrence in Act IV, Scene i. **(b)** Then, summarize all of Act IV. Break long sentences into smaller ones to clarify speakers' thoughts.

## Vocabulary

**©** **Acquisition and Use** Indicate whether each of the following statements is *True* or *False*. Revise the sentences that are false to make them true.

**1.** Clowns make children laugh by appearing *pensive*.

**2.** If you have been *enjoined* to attend an event, you should not go.

**3.** A *wayward* person would probably dislike orders.

**4.** If you were in a *dismal* mood, you would be good company.

**5.** A *loathsome* meal is not likely to be eaten quickly.

**6.** A *vial* would be a good container for a cough syrup.

**Word Study** Use the context of the sentences and what you know about the **Latin prefix en-** to explain your answer to each question.

**1.** Would a terrible insult *enrage* you?

**2.** What happens when someone *enlists* in the armed forces?

---

### Word Study

The **Latin prefix en-** means "in," "into," "within."

**Apply It** Explain how the prefix *en-* contributes to the meanings of these words. Consult a dictionary if necessary.

encage

entrap

entreat

---

Extended Study: The Tragedy of Romeo and Juliet **911**

# Before You Read | The Tragedy of Romeo and Juliet, Act V

**While You Read** Consider the ways that differences in this drama lead to a tragic end. Then, decide if the events had to happen this way.

 ## Common Core State Standards

Meet these standards with *The Tragedy of Romeo and Juliet,* **Act V** (p. 914).

**Reading Literature**

**2.** Determine a theme or central idea of a text; provide an objective summary of the text. *(Reading Skill: Summarize)*

**7.** Analyze the representation of a subject or a key scene in two different artistic mediums, including what is emphasized or absent in each treatment. *(Research and Technology: Film Review)*

**Writing**

**1.** Write arguments to support claims in an analysis of substantive topics or texts, using valid reasoning and relevant and sufficient evidence. *(Writing: Persuasive Letter)*

**1.c.** Use words, phrases, and clauses to link the major sections of the text, create cohesion, and clarify the relationships between claim(s) and reasons, between reasons and evidence, and between claim(s) and counterclaims. *(Writing: Persuasive Letter)*

**4.** Produce clear and coherent writing in which the development, organization, and style are appropriate to task, purpose, and audience. *(Writing: Editorial)*

**Speaking and Listening**

**1.** Initiate and participate effectively in a range of collaborative discussions. *(Speaking and Listening: Mock Trial)*

**4.** Present information, findings, and supporting evidence clearly, concisely, and logically such that listeners can follow the line of reasoning. *(Research and Technology: Annotated Flowchart)*

**Language**

**1.b.** Use various types of phrases and clauses to convey specific meanings and add variety and interest to writing or presentations. *(Conventions: Participles and Participial Phrases; Gerunds and Gerund Phrases)*

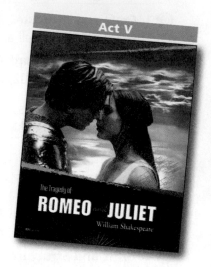

Act V

The Tragedy of
ROMEO and JULIET
William Shakespeare

# Vocabulary

Read each word and its definition. Decide whether you know the word well, know it a little bit, or do not know it at all. After you read, see how your knowledge of each word has increased.

- **remnants** (rem´ nənts) *n.* what is left over; remainders (p. 917) *The <u>remnants</u> of the house still stood after the fire.*

- **penury** (pen´ yo͞o rē) *n.* extreme poverty (p. 917) *His choice was either to find work or to live in <u>penury</u>. penurious adj.*

- **disperse** (di spʉrs´) *v.* to break up and scatter in all directions; spread about; distribute widely (p. 918) *Our group will <u>disperse</u> flyers about the fundraiser in the mall. dispersal n. dispersion n. dispersible adj.*

- **haughty** (hôt´ ē) *adj.* arrogant (p. 921) *He acts <u>haughty</u> onstage but humble offstage. haughtily adv. haughtiness n.*

- **ambiguities** (am´ bə gyo͞o´ ə tēz) *n.* statements or events whose meanings are unclear (p. 927) *Voters were confused by the <u>ambiguities</u> in the candidate's speech. ambiguous adj. ambiguously adv.*

- **scourge** (skʉrj) *n.* instrument for inflicting punishment (p. 929) *Longer practices were the <u>scourge</u> that the coach used to punish the players for their laziness.*

## Word Study

The **Latin prefix** *ambi-* means "both."

In this drama, the Prince says he wants to clear up the **ambiguities** and learn the truth. He means that the facts are uncertain and can be understood from two or more points of view.

## Literary Analysis: Tragedy and Motive

A **tragedy** is a drama in which the major character, who is of noble stature, meets with disaster or great misfortune. The tragic hero's downfall is usually the result of one of the following:

- *fate*, or the idea of a pre-planned destiny
- a serious character flaw
- some combination of both

**Motive** is an important element of a tragic hero's character. A character's motives guide his or her thoughts or actions. Often, the hero's motives are basically good but misguided. As a result, the hero suffers a tragic fate that may seem undeserved.

Although tragedies are sad, they can also be uplifting and instructive. They can teach us about ourselves. They can show the greatness and nobility of the human spirit when faced with grave challenges. As you read the final act of *Romeo and Juliet,* consider what positive message the tragic events ultimately convey.

## Reading Skill: Summarize

**Summarizing** is briefly stating the central ideas in a piece of writing. In summarizing the action, it is useful to first **identify causes and effects.**

- A *cause* is an event, action, or emotion that produces a result.
- An *effect* is the result produced by the cause.

Tragedies often involve a chain of causes and effects that advance the plot and lead to the tragic outcome. Recognizing the sequence will help you summarize plots like the one in this play.

### Using the Strategy: Cause-and-Effect Chart

As you read Act V, use a chart like this one to record causes and effects.

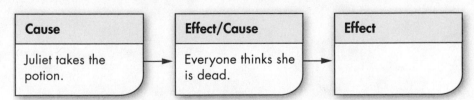

| Cause | Effect/Cause | Effect |
|-------|--------------|--------|
| Juliet takes the potion. | Everyone thinks she is dead. | |

# Act V

## Review and Anticipate

To prevent her marriage to Paris, Juliet has taken the Friar's potion and, as Act V begins, is in a temporary deathlike sleep. Her unsuspecting family plans her funeral. Meanwhile, the Friar has sent a messenger to Mantua to tell Romeo of the ruse, so that he may return and rescue Juliet from her family tomb. What do you think might go wrong with the Friar's plan?

*Scene i. MANTUA. A STREET.*

[*Enter* ROMEO.]

    **ROMEO.** If I may trust the flattering truth of sleep,[1]
      My dreams presage[2] some joyful news at hand.
      My bosom's lord[3] sits lightly in his throne,
      And all this day an unaccustomed spirit
5    Lifts me above the ground with cheerful thoughts.
      I dreamt my lady came and found me dead
      (Strange dream that gives a dead man leave to think!)
      And breathed such life with kisses in my lips
      That I revived and was an emperor.
10   Ah me! How sweet is love itself possessed,
      When but love's shadows[4] are so rich in joy!

[*Enter* ROMEO'S MAN, BALTHASAR, *booted.*]
      News from Verona! How now, Balthasar?

1. **flattering . . . sleep** pleasing illusions of dreams.
2. **presage** foretell.
3. **bosom's lord** heart.

4. **shadows** dreams; unreal images.

**Reading Check**
Why is Romeo in a good mood?

Dost thou not bring me letters from the friar?
How doth my lady? Is my father well?
15 How fares my Juliet? That I ask again,
For nothing can be ill if she be well.

**MAN.** Then she is well, and nothing can be ill.
Her body sleeps in Capels' monument,[5]
And her immortal part with angels lives.
20 I saw her laid low in her kindred's vault
And presently took post[6] to tell it you.
O, pardon me for bringing these ill news,
Since you did leave it for my office,[7] sir.

**ROMEO.** Is it e'en so? Then I defy you, stars!
25 Thou knowest my lodging. Get me ink and paper
And hire post horses. I will hence tonight.

5. **Capels' monument** the Capulets' burial vault.
6. **presently took post** immediately set out on horseback.
7. **office** duty.

**Literary Analysis**
**Tragedy and Motive** In what way does Romeo's remark in line 24 reinforce fate's role in the tragedy?

**MAN.** I do beseech you, sir, have patience.
Your looks are pale and wild and do import
Some misadventure.[8]

**ROMEO.**                                   Tush, thou art deceived.
30  Leave me and do the thing I bid thee do.
Hast thou no letters to me from the friar?

**MAN.** No, my good lord.

**ROMEO.**                         No matter. Get thee gone.
And hire those horses. I'll be with thee straight.

*[Exit* BALTHASAR.]

Well, Juliet, I will lie with thee tonight.
35  Let's see for means. O mischief, thou art swift
To enter in the thoughts of desperate men!
I do remember an apothecary,[9]
And hereabouts 'a dwells, which late I noted
In tatt'red weeds, with overwhelming brows,
40  Culling of simples.[10] Meager were his looks,
Sharp misery had worn him to the bones;
And in his needy shop a tortoise hung,
An alligator stuffed, and other skins
Of ill-shaped fishes; and about his shelves
45  A beggarly account[11] of empty boxes,
Green earthen pots, bladders, and musty seeds,
Remnants of packthread, and old cakes of roses[12]
Were thinly scatterèd, to make up a show.
Noting this penury to myself I said,

8. **import / Some misadventure** suggest some misfortune.

9. **apothecary** one who prepares and sells drugs and medicines.
10. **In tatt'red . . . simples** in torn clothing, with overhanging eyebrows, sorting out herbs.
11. **beggarly account** small number.
12. **cakes of roses** pressed rose petals (used for perfume).

**Vocabulary**
**remnants** (rem´ nənts) *n.* what is left over; remainders
**penury** (pen´ yōō rē) *n.* extreme poverty

Reading Check

What does Romeo learn from Balthasar?

**Vocabulary**
**disperse** (di spʉrs´) v.
to break up and scatter
in all directions; spread
about; distribute widely

13. **caitiff** miserable.

14. **ducats** (duk´ ets) gold
coins.
15. **soon-speeding gear** fast-
working stuff.

16. **trunk** body.
17. **utters** sells.

50 "And if a man did need a poison now
Whose sale is present death in Mantua,
Here lives a caitiff[13] wretch would sell it him."
O, this same thought did but forerun my need,
And this same needy man must sell it me.
55 As I remember, this should be the house.
Being holiday, the beggar's shop is shut.
What, ho! Apothecary!

[*Enter* APOTHECARY.]

**APOTHECARY.** Who calls so loud?

**ROMEO.** Come hither, man. I see that thou art poor.
Hold, there is forty ducats.[14] Let me have
60 A dram of poison, such soon-speeding gear[15]
As will disperse itself through all the veins
That the life-weary taker may fall dead,
And that the trunk[16] may be discharged of breath
As violently as hasty powder fired
65 Doth hurry from the fatal cannon's womb.

**APOTHECARY.** Such mortal drugs I have; but Mantua's law
Is death to any he that utters[17] them.

---

## LITERATURE IN CONTEXT

### History Connection

**Plague Searchers**
The Black Plague, or Black Death, was a disease
that swept through Europe, Asia, and the
Middle East during the 1300s, with outbreaks
continuing until 1400. It is thought that as
much as a third of Europe's population died of
the disease between 1347 and 1351. During an
outbreak of plague, officials would appoint
plague searchers to quarantine people infected
with the disease and dispose of victims'
remains. In *Romeo and Juliet*, Friar John is
quarantined by plague searchers who fear he
has been infected. As a result, he is unable to
deliver Friar Lawrence's letter to Romeo.

### Connect to the Literature

In what way does the Black Death contribute
to the tragedy in *Romeo and Juliet?*

**ROMEO.** Art thou so bare and full of wretchedness
　　　And fearest to die? Famine is in thy cheeks,
70　　Need and oppression starveth in thy eyes,
　　　Contempt and beggary hangs upon thy back:
　　　The world is not thy friend, nor the world's law;
　　　The world affords no law to make thee rich;
　　　Then be not poor, but break it and take this.

75　**APOTHECARY.** My poverty but not my will consents.

**ROMEO.** I pay thy poverty and not thy will.

**APOTHECARY.** Put this in any liquid thing you will
　　　And drink it off, and if you had the strength
　　　Of twenty men, it would dispatch you straight.

80　**ROMEO.** There is thy gold—worse poison to men's souls,
　　　Doing more murder in this loathsome world,
　　　Than these poor compounds[18] that thou mayst not sell.
　　　I sell thee poison; thou hast sold me none.
　　　Farewell. Buy food and get thyself in flesh.
85　　Come, cordial[19] and not poison, go with me
　　　To Juliet's grave; for there must I use thee.　　　　[*Exit all.*]

### Scene ii. *Friar Lawrence's cell.*

[*Enter* FRIAR JOHN, *calling* FRIAR LAWRENCE.]

**JOHN.** Holy Franciscan friar, brother, ho!

[*Enter* FRIAR LAWRENCE.]

**LAWRENCE.** This same should be the voice of Friar John.
　　　Welcome from Mantua. What says Romeo?
　　　Or, if his mind be writ, give me his letter.

5　**JOHN.** Going to find a barefoot brother out,
　　　One of our order, to associate[1] me
　　　Here in this city visiting the sick,
　　　And finding him, the searchers of the town,
　　　Suspecting that we both were in a house
10　　Where the infectious pestilence did reign,
　　　Sealed up the doors, and would not let us forth,
　　　So that my speed to Mantua there was stayed.

**LAWRENCE.** Who bare my letter, then, to Romeo?

**JOHN.** I could not send it—here it is again—
15　　Nor get a messenger to bring it thee,
　　　So fearful were they of infection.

**Spiral Review**
**Conflict** What conflicting motivations does the Apothecary face?

**Literary Analysis**
**Tragedy and Motive** What is the apothecary's motive for selling Romeo the poison?

18. **compounds** mixtures.
19. **cordial** health-giving drink.

**Reading Skill**
**Summarize** Briefly state the causes and effects of Friar John's failure to deliver Friar Lawrence's letter.

1. **associate** accompany.

**Reading Check**
What does Romeo plan to do with the apothecary's help?

2. **nice** trivial.
3. **full of charge, / Of dear import** urgent and important.

4. **beshrew** blame.
5. **accidents** happenings.

**LAWRENCE.** Unhappy fortune! By my brotherhood,
The letter was not nice,[2] but full of charge,
Of dear import;[3] and the neglecting it
20    May do much danger. Friar John, go hence,
Get me an iron crow and bring it straight
Unto my cell.

**JOHN.**          Brother, I'll go and bring it thee.    [*Exit.*]

**LAWRENCE.** Now must I to the monument alone.
Within this three hours will fair Juliet wake.
25    She will beshrew[4] me much that Romeo
Hath had no notice of these accidents;[5]
But I will write again to Mantua,
And keep her at my cell till Romeo come—
Poor living corse, closed in a dead man's tomb!    [*Exit.*]

*Scene iii. A churchyard; in it a monument belonging to the Capulets.*

[*Enter* PARIS *and his* PAGE *with flowers and sweet water.*]

1. **aloof** apart.

2. **lay . . . along** lie down flat.

**PARIS.** Give me thy torch, boy. Hence, and stand aloof.[1]
Yet put it out, for I would not be seen.
Under yond yew trees lay thee all along,[2]
Holding thy ear close to the hollow ground.
5    So shall no foot upon the churchyard tread
(Being loose, unfirm, with digging up of graves)
But thou shalt hear it. Whistle then to me,
As signal that thou hearest something approach.
Give me those flowers. Do as I bid thee, go.

3. **adventure** chance it.

10 **PAGE.** [*Aside*] I am almost afraid to stand alone
Here in the churchyard; yet I will adventure.[3]    [*Retires.*]

4. **sweet** perfumed.

5. **obsequies** memorial ceremonies.
6. **cross** interrupt.

**PARIS.** Sweet flower, with flowers thy bridal bed I strew
    (O woe! thy canopy is dust and stones)
Which with sweet[4] water nightly I will dew;
15      Or, wanting that, with tears distilled by moans.
The obsequies[5] that I for thee will keep
Nightly shall be to strew thy grave and weep.   [**BOY** *whistles.*]
The boy gives warning something doth approach.
What cursèd foot wanders this way tonight
20    To cross[6] my obsequies and true love's rite?
What, with a torch? Muffle me, night, awhile.    [*Retires.*]

[*Enter* ROMEO, *and* BALTHASAR *with a torch, a mattock, and a crow of iron.*]

**ROMEO.** Give me that mattock and the wrenching iron.
    Hold, take this letter. Early in the morning
    See thou deliver it to my lord and father.
25    Give me the light. Upon thy life I charge thee,
    Whate'er thou hearest or seest, stand all aloof
    And do not interrupt me in my course.
    Why I descend into this bed of death
    Is partly to behold my lady's face,
30    But chiefly to take thence from her dead finger
    A precious ring—a ring that I must use
    In dear employment.[7] Therefore hence, be gone.
    But if thou, jealous,[8] dost return to pry
    In what I farther shall intend to do,
35    By heaven, I will tear thee joint by joint
    And strew this hungry churchyard with thy limbs.
    The time and my intents are savage-wild,
    More fierce and more inexorable[9] far
    Than empty[10] tigers or the roaring sea.

40 **BALTHASAR.** I will be gone, sir, and not trouble ye.

**ROMEO.** So shalt thou show me friendship. Take thou that.
    Live, and be prosperous; and farewell, good fellow.

**BALTHASAR.** [*Aside*] For all this same, I'll hide me hereabout.
    His looks I fear, and his intents I doubt.    [*Retires.*]

45 **ROMEO.** Thou detestable maw,[11] thou womb of death,
    Gorged with the dearest morsel of the earth,
    Thus I enforce thy rotten jaws to open,
    And in despite[12] I'll cram thee with more food.

                   [ROMEO *opens the tomb.*]

**PARIS.** This is that banished haughty Montague
50    That murd'red my love's cousin—with which grief
    It is supposed the fair creature died—
    And here is come to do some villainous shame
    To the dead bodies. I will apprehend[13] him.
    Stop thy unhallowèd toil, vile Montague!
55    Can vengeance be pursued further than death?
    Condemnèd villain, I do apprehend thee.
    Obey, and go with me; for thou must die.

**ROMEO.** I must indeed; and therefore came I hither.
    Good gentle youth, tempt not a desp'rate man.

**Literary Analysis**

**Tragedy and Motive** What different motives do Paris and Romeo have for visiting Juliet's tomb?

7. **dear employment** important business.
8. **jealous** curious.

9. **inexorable** uncontrollable.
10. **empty** hungry.

11. **maw** stomach.

12. **despite** scorn.

**Vocabulary**
**haughty** (hôt´ ē)
*adj.* arrogant

13. **apprehend** seize; arrest.

Reading Check

How does Paris react to seeing Romeo at Juliet's tomb?

## Reading Skill
### Summarize

Summarize the causes that you think will produce a tragic effect in the confrontation between Romeo and Paris.

14. **conjurations** solemn appeals.
15. **felon** criminal.

16. **peruse** look over.
17. **betossèd** upset.
18. **attend** give attention to.

19. **lanthorn** windowed structure on top of a room to admit light; also, a lantern.
20. **feasting presence** chamber fit for celebration.
21. **keepers** jailers.
22. **ensign** banner.

## Literary Analysis
### Tragedy and Motive

What tragic mistake does Romeo make regarding Juliet's appearance?

60 Fly hence and leave me. Think upon these gone;
Let them affright thee. I beseech thee, youth,
Put not another sin upon my head
By urging me to fury. O, be gone!
65 By heaven, I love thee better than myself,
For I come hither armed against myself.
Stay not, be gone. Live, and hereafter say
A madman's mercy bid thee run away.

**PARIS.** I do defy thy conjurations.[14]
And apprehend thee for a felon[15] here.

70 **ROMEO.** Wilt thou provoke me? Then have at thee, boy!
[*They fight.*]

**PAGE.** O Lord, they fight! I will go call the watch.

[*Exit.* PARIS *falls.*]

**PARIS.** O, I am slain! If thou be merciful,
Open the tomb, lay me with Juliet.                    [*Dies.*]

**ROMEO.** In faith, I will. Let me peruse[16] this face.
75 Mercutio's kinsman, noble County Paris!
What said my man when my betossèd[17] soul
Did not attend[18] him as we rode? I think
He told me Paris should have married Juliet.
Said he not so, or did I dream it so?
80 Or am I mad, hearing him talk of Juliet,
To think it was so? O, give me thy hand,
One writ with me in sour misfortune's book!
I'll bury thee in a triumphant grave.
A grave? O, no, a lanthorn,[19] slaught'red youth,
85 For here lies Juliet, and her beauty makes
This vault a feasting presence[20] full of light.
Death, lie thou there, by a dead man interred.

[*Lays him in the tomb.*]

How oft when men are at the point of death
Have they been merry! Which their keepers[21] call
90 A lightning before death. O, how may I
Call this a lightning? O my love, my wife!
Death, that hath sucked the honey of thy breath,
Hath had no power yet upon thy beauty.
Thou art not conquered. Beauty's ensign[22] yet
95 Is crimson in thy lips and in thy cheeks,
And death's pale flag is not advancèd there.

Tybalt, liest thou there in thy bloody sheet?
O, what more favor can I do to thee
Than with that hand that cut thy youth in twain
100  To sunder[23] his that was thine enemy?
Forgive me, cousin! Ah, dear Juliet,
Why art thou yet so fair? Shall I believe
That unsubstantial Death is amorous,[24]
And that the lean abhorrèd monster keeps
105  Thee here in dark to be his paramour?
For fear of that I still will stay with thee
And never from this pallet[25] of dim night
Depart again. Here, here will I remain
With worms that are thy chambermaids. O, here
110  Will I set up my everlasting rest
And shake the yoke of inauspicious[26] stars
From this world-wearied flesh. Eyes, look your last!

23. **sunder** cut off.

24. **amorous** full of love.

25. **pallet** bed.
26. **inauspicious** promising misfortune.

What happens to Paris at Juliet's tomb?

27. **dateless** eternal.
28. **engrossing** all-encompassing.
29. **conduct** guide (poison).
30. **pilot** captain (Romeo himself)

115    Arms, take your last embrace! And, lips, O you
       The doors of breath, seal with a righteous kiss
       A dateless[27] bargain to engrossing[28] death!
       Come, bitter conduct;[29] come, unsavory guide!
       Thou desperate pilot,[30] now at once run on
       The dashing rocks thy seasick weary bark!
       Here's to my love! [*Drinks.*] O true apothecary!
120    Thy drugs are quick. Thus with a kiss I die.          [*Falls.*]

[*Enter* FRIAR LAWRENCE, *with lanthorn, crow, and spade.*]

31. **speed** help.
32. **stumbled** stumbling was thought to be a bad omen.
33. **grubs** worms.

    **FRIAR.** Saint Francis be my speed![31] How oft tonight
        Have my old feet stumbled[32] at graves! Who's there?

    **BALTHASAR.** Here's one, a friend, and one that knows you well.

    **FRIAR.** Bliss be upon you! Tell me, good my friend,
125     What torch is yond that vainly lends his light
        To grubs[33] and eyeless skulls? As I discern,
        It burneth in the Capels' monument.

    **BALTHASAR.** It doth so, holy sir; and there's my master,
        One that you love.

    **FRIAR.**                          Who is it?

▼ **Critical Viewing**
What feelings in the scene does this image convey? **[Analyze]**

**BALTHASAR.**               Romeo.

**FRIAR.** How long hath he been there?

130 **BALTHASAR.**                          Full half an hour.

**FRIAR.** Go with me to the vault.

**BALTHASAR.**                          I dare not, sir.
My master knows not but I am gone hence,
And fearfully did menace me with death
If I did stay to look on his intents.

135 **FRIAR.** Stay then; I'll go alone. Fear comes upon me.
O, much I fear some ill unthrifty³⁴ thing.

**BALTHASAR.** As I did sleep under this yew tree here,
I dreamt my master and another fought,
And that my master slew him.

**FRIAR.**                          Romeo!
140 Alack, alack, what blood is this which stains
The stony entrance of this sepulcher?
What mean these masterless³⁵ and gory swords
To lie discolored by this place of peace?     [*Enters the tomb.*]
Romeo! O, pale! Who else? What, Paris too?
145 And steeped in blood? Ah, what an unkind³⁶ hour
Is guilty of this lamentable chance!
The lady stirs.                          [JULIET *rises.*]

**JULIET.** O comfortable³⁷ friar! Where is my lord?
I do remember well where I should be,
150 And there I am. Where is my Romeo?

**FRIAR.** I hear some noise. Lady, come from that nest
Of death, contagion, and unnatural sleep.
A greater power than we can contradict
Hath thwarted our intents. Come, come away.
155 Thy husband in thy bosom there lies dead;
And Paris too. Come, I'll dispose of thee
Among a sisterhood of holy nuns.
Stay not to question, for the watch is coming.
Come, go, good Juliet. I dare no longer stay.

160 **JULIET.** Go, get thee hence, for I will not away.     [*Exit* FRIAR.]
What's here? A cup, closed in my truelove's hand?
Poison, I see, hath been his timeless³⁸ end.
O churl!³⁹ Drunk all, and left no friendly drop
To help me after? I will kiss thy lips.

**Literary Analysis**
**Tragedy and Motive** In what way is Friar Lawrence's late arrival another example of chance contributing to this tragedy?

**34. unthrifty** unlucky.

**35. masterless** discarded (without masters).

**36. unkind** unnatural.

**37. comfortable** comforting.

**38. timeless** untimely; too soon.
**39. churl** rude fellow.

**Literary Analysis**
**Tragedy and Motive** Why do you think Friar Lawrence wants to "dispose of Juliet" in a sisterhood of nuns?

**Reading Check**
How does Juliet react when she wakes up?

40. **restorative** medicine.

165　Haply some poison yet doth hang on them
　　To make me die with a restorative.⁴⁰　　　　[*Kisses him.*]
　　Thy lips are warm!

**CHIEF WATCHMAN.** [*Within*] Lead, boy. Which way?

41. **happy** convenient; opportune.

**JULIET.** Yea, noise? Then I'll be brief. O happy⁴¹ dagger!
　　　　　　　　　　　　　　　[*Snatches* ROMEO'S *dagger.*]
170　This is thy sheath; there rust, and let me die.
　　　　　　　　　　　　　[*She stabs herself and falls.*]

[*Enter* PARIS' BOY *and* WATCH.]

**BOY.** This is the place. There, where the torch doth burn.

**CHIEF WATCHMAN.** The ground is bloody. Search about the
　　churchyard.

42. **attach** arrest.

　　Go, some of you; whoe'er you find attach.⁴²
　　　　　　　　　　　　　[*Exit some of the* WATCH.]
　　Pitiful sight! Here lies the County slain;
175　And Juliet bleeding, warm, and newly dead,
　　Who here hath lain this two days burièd.
　　Go, tell the Prince; run to the Capulets;
　　Raise up the Montagues; some others search.
　　　　　　　　　　　　[*Exit others of the* WATCH.]
　　We see the ground whereon these woes do lie,

43. **ground** cause.
44. **without circumstance descry** see clearly without details.

180　But the true ground⁴³ of all these piteous woes
　　We cannot without circumstance descry.⁴⁴

[*Enter some of the* WATCH, *with* ROMEO'S MAN, BALTHASAR.]

**SECOND WATCHMAN.** Here's Romeo's man. We found him in the
　　churchyard.

**CHIEF WATCHMAN.** Hold him in safety till the Prince come
　　hither.

[*Enter* FRIAR LAWRENCE *and another* WATCHMAN.]

**Literary Analysis
Tragedy and
Motive** How might the tragic ending have been averted if Paris, Romeo, and the Friar had come to Juliet's tomb in a different order?

**THIRD WATCHMAN.** Here is a friar that trembles, sighs and
　　weeps.
185　We took this mattock and this spade from him
　　As he was coming from this churchyard's side.

**CHIEF WATCHMAN.** A great suspicion! Stay the friar too.

[*Enter the* PRINCE *and* ATTENDANTS.]

**PRINCE.** What misadventure is so early up,
  That calls our person from our morning rest?

[*Enter* CAPULET *and his* WIFE *with others.*]

190 **CAPULET.** What should it be, that is so shrieked abroad?

**LADY CAPULET.** O, the people in the street cry "Romeo,"
  Some "Juliet," and some "Paris"; and all run
  With open outcry toward our monument.

**PRINCE.** What fear is this which startles in your ears?

195 **CHIEF WATCHMAN.** Sovereign, here lies the County Paris slain;
  And Romeo dead; and Juliet, dead before,
  Warm and new killed.

**PRINCE.** Search, seek, and know how this foul murder comes.

**CHIEF WATCHMAN.** Here is a friar, and slaughtered Romeo's man,
200   With instruments upon them fit to open
  These dead men's tombs.

**CAPULET.** O heavens! O wife, look how our daughter bleeds!
  This dagger hath mista'en, for, lo, his house[45]
  Is empty on the back of Montague,
205   And it missheathèd in my daughter's bosom!

**LADY CAPULET.** O me, this sight of death is as a bell
  That warns my old age to a sepulcher.

[*Enter* MONTAGUE *and others.*]

**PRINCE.** Come, Montague; for thou art early up
  To see thy son and heir more early down.

210 **MONTAGUE.** Alas, my liege,[46] my wife is dead tonight!
  Grief of my son's exile hath stopped her breath.
  What further woe conspires against mine age?

**PRINCE.** Look, and thou shalt see.

**MONTAGUE.** O thou untaught! What manners is in this,
215   To press before thy father to a grave?

**PRINCE.** Seal up the mouth of outrage[47] for a while,
  Till we can clear these ambiguities
  And know their spring, their head, their true descent;
  And then will I be general of your woes[48]
220   And lead you even to death. Meantime forbear,
  And let mischance be slave to patience.[49]
  Bring forth the parties of suspicion.

**FRIAR.** I am the greatest, able to do least,
    Yet most suspected, as the time and place

225    Doth make against me, of this direful[50] murder;
    And here I stand, both to impeach and purge[51]
    Myself condemnèd and myself excused.

**PRINCE.** Then say at once what thou dost know in this.

**FRIAR.** I will be brief, for my short date of breath[52]

230    Is not so long as is a tedious tale.
    Romeo, there dead, was husband to that Juliet;
    And she, there dead, that's Romeo's faithful wife.
    I married them; and their stol'n marriage day
    Was Tybalt's doomsday, whose untimely death

235    Banished the new-made bridegroom from this city;
    For whom, and not for Tybalt, Juliet pined.
    You, to remove that siege of grief from her,
    Betrothed and would have married her perforce
    To County Paris. Then comes she to me

240    And with wild looks bid me devise some mean
    To rid her from this second marriage,
    Or in my cell there would she kill herself.
    Then gave I her (so tutored by my art)
    A sleeping potion; which so took effect

245    As I intended, for it wrought on her
    The form of death. Meantime I writ to Romeo
    That he should hither come as[53] this dire night
    To help to take her from her borrowed grave,
    Being the time the potion's force should cease,

250    But he which bore my letter, Friar John,
    Was stayed by accident, and yesternight
    Returned my letter back. Then all alone
    At the prefixèd hour of her waking
    Came I to take her from her kindred's vault;

255    Meaning to keep her closely[54] at my cell
    Till I conveniently could send to Romeo.
    But when I came, some minute ere the time
    Of her awakening, here untimely lay
    The noble Paris and true Romeo dead.

260    She wakes; and I entreated her come forth
    And bear this work of heaven with patience;
    But then a noise did scare me from the tomb,
    And she, too desperate, would not go with me,
    But, as it seems, did violence on herself.

265    All this I know, and to the marriage

Her nurse is privy;[55] and if aught in this
Miscarried by my fault, let my old life
Be sacrificed some hour before his time
Unto the rigor[56] of severest law.

270 **PRINCE.** We still have known thee for a holy man.
Where's Romeo's man? What can he say to this?

**BALTHASAR.** I brought my master news of Juliet's death;
And then in post he came from Mantua
To this same place, to this same monument.
275 This letter he early bid me give his father,
And threat'ned me with death, going in the vault,
If I departed not and left him there.

**PRINCE.** Give me the letter. I will look on it.
Where is the County's page that raised the watch?
280 Sirrah, what made your master[57] in this place?

**BOY.** He came with flowers to strew his lady's grave;
And bid me stand aloof, and so I did.
Anon comes one with light to ope the tomb;
And by and by my master drew on him;
285 And then I ran away to call the watch.

**PRINCE.** This letter doth make good the friar's words,
Their course of love, the tidings of her death;
And here he writes that he did buy a poison
Of a poor 'pothecary and therewithal
290 Came to this vault to die and lie with Juliet.
Where be these enemies? Capulet, Montague,
See what a scourge is laid upon your hate,
That heaven finds means to kill your joys with love.
And I, for winking at[58] your discords too,
295 Have lost a brace[59] of kinsmen. All are punished.

**CAPULET.** O brother Montague, give me thy hand.
This is my daughter's jointure,[60] for no more
Can I demand.

**MONTAGUE.**          But I can give thee more;
For I will raise her statue in pure gold,
300 That whiles Verona by that name is known,
There shall no figure at such rate[61] be set
As that of true and faithful Juliet.

**CAPULET.** As rich shall Romeo's by his lady's lie—
Poor sacrifices of our enmity![62]

---

**55. privy** secretly informed about.

**56. rigor** strictness.

**57. made your master** was your master doing.

**Vocabulary**
**scourge** (skʉrj) *n.* instrument for inflicting punishment

**58. winking at** closing my eyes to.
**59. brace** pair (Mercutio and Paris).
**60. jointure** wedding gift; marriage settlement.
**61. rate** value.
**62. enmity** hostility.

Reading Check

How does the Friar explain his role in the fate of Romeo and Juliet?

63. **glooming** cloudy; gloomy.

**Literary Analysis**

**Tragedy and**

**Motive** What might be Lord Montague's motive for the promise he makes to Lord Capulet?

305 **PRINCE.** A glooming[63] peace this morning with it brings.
The sun for sorrow will not show his head.
Go hence, to have more talk of these sad things;
Some shall be pardoned, and some punishèd;
For never was a story of more woe
310 Than this of Juliet and her Romeo.                    [*Exit all.*]

## Critical Thinking

**Cite textual evidence to support your responses.**

1. **Key Ideas and Details (a)** In Act V, Scene i, what causes Romeo to exclaim, "Then I defy you, stars"? **(b) Interpret:** In what way are Romeo's words consistent with what you know of his character?

2. **Key Ideas and Details (a)** Identify at least three events that cause the Friar's scheme to fail. **(b) Analyze:** Why is it not surprising that the scheme fails?

3. **Integration of Knowledge and Ideas (a)** How does the relationship between the feuding families change at the end of the play? **(b) Draw Conclusions:** Were the deaths of Romeo and Juliet necessary for this change to occur? Explain. **(c) Make a Judgment:** Is the end of long-term violence between their families a fair exchange for the deaths of Romeo and Juliet? Explain your response.

4. **Integration of Knowledge and Ideas** Did Romeo and Juliet have any control over the differences that separated them and led to their tragic end? Explain. *[Connect to the Big Question: Do our differences define us?]*

## After You Read | The Tragedy of Romeo and Juliet, Act V

## Literary Analysis: Tragedy and Motive

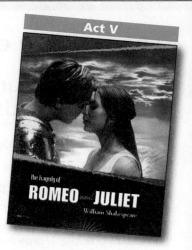

Act V

**ⓒ 1. Key Ideas and Details (a)** Use a chart like the one shown to identify details of the elements that contribute to the **tragedy** in the play. **(b)** Explain which element you think is most responsible for the tragic events.

| Romeo and Juliet's Personalities | Fate or Chance | Other Causes |
|---|---|---|
| | | |

**ⓒ 2. Key Ideas and Details (a)** What is the Friar's **motive** for helping Romeo and Juliet? **(b)** To what extent is he responsible for their tragedy? Explain.

**ⓒ 3. Integration of Knowledge and Skills** What theme or message does Shakespeare convey through the tragic events in the play?

**ⓒ 4. Integration of Knowledge and Ideas** What positive message about the human spirit, if any, does this tragic play offer? Explain.

## Reading Skill: Summarize

**5. (a)** What events cause Romeo and Paris to arrive at Juliet's tomb at the same time? **(b)** What is the effect of this? Explain your answer.

**6. (a)** Analyze the chain of causes and effects that leads to the tragic ending. **(b) Summarize** the events that occur at the tomb.

## Vocabulary

**ⓒ Acquisition and Use** Identify the word in each group that does not belong with the others. Explain your response.

**1.** remnants, future, past

**2.** penury, poor, wealthy

**3.** haughty, proud, insecure

**4.** ambiguities, absolute, uncertain

**5.** scourge, pleasure, happiness

**6.** disperse, scatter, collect

**Word Study** Use the context of the sentences and what you know about the **Latin prefix ambi-** to explain your answer to each question.

**1.** Would you know how to respond if someone asked an *ambiguous* question?

**2.** Is an *ambivalent* person unsure of what he or she wants in life?

### Word Study

The **Latin prefix ambi-** means "both."

**Apply It** Explain how the prefix *ambi-* contributes to the meanings of these words. Consult a dictionary if necessary.

ambivalent
ambient
ambidextrous
ambition

**PERFORMANCE TASKS**
# Integrated Language Skills

## The Tragedy of Romeo and Juliet

### Conventions: Participles and Participial Phrases, Gerunds and Gerund Phrases

A **participle** is a verb form that is used as an adjective.

A **present participle** ends in *-ing*. The past participle of a regular verb ends in *-ed*. A **participial phrase** is a group of words that functions as an adjective in the sentence and contains a participle.

| Present Participle | *growing* child |
|---|---|
| Past Participle | *troubled* child |
| Participial Phrase | *Focusing intently,* the driver stopped in time. |

A **gerund** is a verb form that acts as a noun.

It can function as a subject, an object, a predicate noun, or the object of a preposition. A **gerund phrase** is a gerund and its modifiers. A gerund phrase, also called a **noun phrase,** also acts as a noun.

| Subject | *Remodeling* the building's style was a good idea. |
|---|---|
| Direct Object | Michael enjoys *painting.* |
| Predicate Noun | His favorite sport is *fishing.* |
| Object of the Preposition | Lucille never gets tired of *singing.* |
| Gerund Phrase | The *loud, shrill howling* continued all morning. |

**Practice A** Identify the participle or gerund in each sentence.

1. Suffering greatly, Romeo emptied the vial.
2. The young men seemed to enjoy fighting.
3. The doomed lovers yearned for each other.
4. Loud weeping spread through Verona.

Ⓒ **Reading Application** In *The Tragedy of Romeo and Juliet,* find one sentence that uses a participle or participle phrase and one that uses a gerund or gerund phrase.

**Practice B** In each sentence, change one of the verbs to a participle or a gerund. Then, use that word or phrase to combine the two sentences.

1. Tybalt wanted to kill Romeo. It was his only thought.
2. Juliet felt great sorrow. She held the knife.
3. Capulet wanted his daughter married. He gave her to Paris.
4. He thought of Juliet. It was his greatest joy.

Ⓒ **Writing Application** Write two sentences following the models in the second chart above.

**PH** **WRITING COACH**  Further instruction and practice are available in *Prentice Hall Writing Coach.*

# Writing

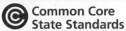 **Common Core State Standards**

L.9-10.1.b; W.9-10.1, W.9-10.4
[For the full wording of the standards, see page 912.]

**Argumentative Text** Imagine that you are the editor of a newspaper in Verona at the time of the play. Write an **editorial** addressing the Prince's response to the deaths of Tybalt and Mercutio.

- Reread the Prince's dialogue in Act III, Scene i.
- Decide whether Romeo's sentence was appropriate, and explain whether you agree or disagree with the Prince's order.
- Write the editorial, supporting your ideas with details from Act III, Scenes i–iii.

Share your editorial with classmates, and encourage them to write letters to the editor in support of or in opposition to your editorial.

**Argumentative Text** As Friar Lawrence, write a **persuasive letter** to both Lord Capulet and Lord Montague. Urge them to end their feud.

- Make a list of factual evidence and emotional pleas that support your argument. Consider appealing to the families' sense of logic and ethical beliefs.
- Begin your draft by explaining the benefits of marriage and the benefits of becoming allies rather than enemies.
- Use persuasive techniques, such as powerful word choice, repetition, and rhetorical questions, to strengthen your argument.

**Grammar Application** Make sure to use participles, participial phrases, gerunds, and gerund phrases correctly in your editorial and persuasive letter.

## Writing Workshop: *Work in Progress*

**Prewriting for How-to Essay** For a how-to essay you may write, record five tasks that you do well. Choose one and complete each of these steps:

Use this prewriting activity to prepare for the **Writing Workshop** on page 1002.

1. Make a list of steps necessary to complete your task.
2. Visualize performing the task step by step. After you have finished visualizing, go back and add any missed steps to your list.
3. Use stick figures to make a "cartoon frame" for each step on your list. Add dialogue bubbles to each frame and write a sentence in which you explain the step.

Save your work in your writing portfolio.

## Integrated Language Skills

## Speaking and Listening

**Comprehension and Collaboration** Select a scene from *The Tragedy of Romeo and Juliet* and plan a **staged performance** with classmates. Choose a scene with at least three characters. Then, plan and rehearse the scene. Follow these steps:

- Decide who will play each role.

- As you rehearse, use appropriate gestures, body movements, and eye contact that convey the qualities of your character. Adjust your tone of voice and speed of delivery to dramatize the performance.

- Pause periodically during your rehearsal to assess the group's work. Take turns critiquing the performance. Express your thoughts clearly and convey your criticism in a respectful way. As others present criticism, listen carefully and ask questions to clarify comments. Discuss ways to respond to comments and to improve the performance.

When you are ready, perform the scene for the class, and invite comments and feedback from the audience.

**Comprehension and Collaboration** As a class, conduct a **mock trial** to investigate the causes of the tragedy in *The Tragedy of Romeo and Juliet.* Follow these steps:

- Assign roles for the main characters of the play, the lawyers, and the judge. The rest of the class should serve as the jury.

- Take depositions, or statements in which each character tells the story from his or her perspective. Lawyers should follow up the statements of witnesses with questions to clarify and expand on the witnesses' stories.

- All participants should use appropriate gestures, eye contact, and a speaking voice that projects the correct tone and mood.

- Choose language—formal, informal, slang, or jargon—that fits the social, cultural, and professional status of each character.

Jury members should listen carefully to distinguish between valid claims and *propaganda*—arguments that twist or ignore facts to present a biased and distorted picture of events. Listeners should also evaluate the clarity, quality, effectiveness, and coherence of each speaker's arguments, evidence, and delivery.

When the trial is completed, the jury members should present their verdict, explaining which characters bear the most blame for the tragedy.

# Research and Technology

 **Common Core State Standards**

SL.9-10.1, SL.9-10.4;
RL9-10.7
[For the full wording of the standards, see page 912.]

**Presentation of Knowledge and Ideas** Conduct research to create an **annotated flowchart** that accurately displays and explains the structure of the nobility in sixteenth-century Verona. Your flowchart should show the relative positions of the Prince, Count Paris, the Montagues, and the Capulets.

- Use both primary and secondary sources as you learn more about the time period in which the story unfolds.
- Evaluate the validity and reliability of the information you research and the sources you use.
- Organize your text and images logically.
- Remember to document sources for both ideas and images, using standard citation style. (For more on citing sources, see page R36.)

Present your flowchart to the class, explaining where you located information.

**Presentation of Knowledge and Ideas** With a small group, view a filmed version of *Romeo and Juliet,* and then write a **film review**. It might be a movie version, a filmed stage production, or a filmed version of the ballet. Take notes as you view, using the following questions to guide your note taking:

- What specific effects contribute to the beauty or artistry of the film?
- How do the movements of the actors or dancers communicate the play's ideas?
- How does the film use music, stage sets, and camerawork to convey mood?
- How do key scenes in the film compare to those in the written version? If scenes are changed or omitted in the filmed version, how does the change affect meaning?

After viewing, use your notes to draft your review. Be sure to highlight the key differences between the filmed version and the written version, and explain which version you thought was more effective. Finally, present your review to the class.

**Presentation of Knowledge and Ideas** With a partner, create a **multimedia presentation** on Renaissance music. Use library or Internet resources to collect examples of music that would have been played by the musicians in Act IV, Scene v. Find pictures of instruments from the period as well. Record accurate bibliographic information about your sources, using correct citation style.

Present your findings in class using available props, visual aids, and electronic media. Then, lead a discussion about the music and its effects on listeners.

**PHLit Online!**
www.PHLitOnline.com

- Interactive graphic organizers
- Grammar tutorial
- Interactive journals

# Test Practice: Reading

## Summarize

### Drama Selection

**Directions:** *Read the selection. Then, answer the questions.*

*The stage is dark. A spotlight shines on two young women sitting on a bench. Both wear plain, long dresses in a 19th-century style. It is evident from their posture and position that the two women are strangers.*

**SARAH.** *(turning shyly to the other woman on the bench)* Did you attend the Women's Rights Convention today? Did you hear Sojourner Truth?

**ABIGAIL.** *(looking startled and then annoyed)* I would never get mixed up with that nonsense!

**SARAH.** *(gaining confidence)* I also felt that way before I went to the convention. The struggle for women's rights may seem impossible, but it is not. Some women have overcome so much already. Don't you believe that you deserve equal rights? (*Abigail nods and leans towards Sarah, appearing interested.*) Let me tell you about Sojourner Truth's speech. Her words may inspire you just as they inspired me.

**1.** Which sentence best summarizes the first set of stage directions?

  **A.** The stage is mostly dark, with one blindingly bright spotlight shining.

  **B.** A spotlight shines on two women in 19th-century dresses seated on a bench.

  **C.** There are two young women.

  **D.** One woman in a long, plain dress sits next to another woman in a long, plain dress.

**2.** Which statement best summarizes the action in the scene?

  **A.** Sarah meets Abigail and begins to tell her about Sojourner Truth's speech.

  **B.** Sarah witnesses Sojourner Truth's speech at a convention.

  **C.** Sojourner Truth attends a Women's Rights Convention and gives a speech that many women find inspirational.

  **D.** Abigail is originally not interested in women's rights, but becomes curious.

**3.** How does Sarah feel about the Women's Rights Convention?

  **A.** She is inspired by the convention.

  **B.** She wants to speak at a convention.

  **C.** The convention speakers annoy her.

  **D.** The convention was too short for her.

**4.** Which sentence should be left out of a summary of this scene?

  **A.** Sarah attended a convention.

  **B.** Sarah was excited about equal rights.

  **C.** Sojourner Truth's speech inspired Sarah.

  **D.** Sarah and Abigail wore plain dresses.

## Writing for Assessment

Write a three-sentence summary of the scene. Be sure to use your own words and include only the main ideas in your summary.

## Nonfiction Selection

**Directions:** *Read the selection. Then, answer the questions.*

Women's rights activist and abolitionist Sojourner Truth was born in 1797 in New York State. She was born into slavery and spent the early years of her life enslaved, Suffering brutalities too numerous to mention. When she escaped slavery in 1827, she retrieved her son who had been sold to a plantation owner in Alabama at age five. As a free woman, Sojourner Truth took it upon herself to fight for the rights of slaves and women and to help those freed after the Civil War. Sojourner Truth's best-known speech "Ain't I a Woman?" was given at the Women's Rights Convention in Akron, Ohio. Over the years, Sojourner Truth traveled the country preaching and speaking out for women's rights and the abolition of slavery. She was a powerful force in both movements.

**1.** Into how many basic units of thought can sentence 2 be broken?

   **A.** one
   **B.** two
   **C.** three
   **D.** four

**2.** Which sentence *best* summarizes the first three sentences of the selection?

   **A.** Sojourner Truth suffered greatly when she was enslaved from 1797 to 1827.
   **B.** Sojourner Truth, women's rights activist, abolitionist, and former slave, was born in 1797 in New York.
   **C.** Sojourner Truth was a women's rights activist who lived through and fought against slavery.
   **D.** Abolitionist and former slave Sojourner Truth was born in New York in 1797.

**3.** What did Sojourner Truth make her life's work after she escaped slavery?

   **A.** teaching other freed slaves
   **B.** fighting for the rights of the oppressed
   **C.** keeping public speaking engagements
   **D.** writing speeches to deliver at conventions

**4.** Which sentence *best* summarizes the selection?

   **A.** Born in 1797, Sojourner Truth was enslaved; she rescued her son from slavery after she herself escaped.
   **B.** Sojourner Truth was born in 1797 in New York and lived as a slave until 1827, when she escaped.
   **C.** Sojourner Truth gave a famous speech at a convention for women's rights.
   **D.** Sojourner Truth escaped slavery to become a powerful force in the women's rights and abolitionist movements.

## Writing for Assessment

**Connecting Across Texts**
How does reading the biography of Sojourner Truth help you understand Sarah's reaction to her speech? Give your response in a paragraph. Use details from both passages.

**www.PHLitOnline.com**
- Online practice
- Instant feedback

# Reading for Information

## Analyzing Functional and Expository Texts

### Atlas Entry

### Travel Brochure

 **Common Core State Standards**

**Reading Informational Text**
**3.** Analyze how the author unfolds an analysis or series of ideas or events, including the order in which the points are made, how they are introduced and developed, and the connections that are drawn between them.

**Writing**
**2.** Write informative/explanatory texts to examine and convey complex ideas, concepts, and information clearly and accurately through the effective selection, organization, and analysis of content. *(Timed Writing)*

**Language**
**4.c.** Consult general and specialized reference materials, both print and digital, to find the pronunciation of a word or determine or clarify its precise meaning, its part of speech, or its etymology.
**6.** Acquire and use accurately grade-appropriate general academic and domain-specific words and phrases; demonstrate independence in gathering vocabulary knowledge when considering a word or phrase important to comprehension or expression.

## Reading Skill: Analyze Text Information

Reading about the same subject across different types of informational documents provides a more complete understanding of that subject. Here the subject is Italy. **Examine the sequence** in which information is presented in each document and critique its logic. To do this, **analyze** which details are emphasized and whether that information is in a logical order. Text features, such as maps and headings, can give clues about the sequence of information and can also aid understanding of the text.

| Feature | How the Feature Aids Understanding |
|---|---|
| title or heading | states a broad topic |
| subheading | organizes details and support by subtopic |
| bold print | draws readers' attention to key words or details |
| map | provides broad overview of a particular place (geography, location, distance) |
| image | illustrates and clarifies details mentioned in the text |

### Content-Area Vocabulary

These words appear in the selections that follow. You may also encounter them in other content-area texts.

- **peninsula (pə nin´ sə lə)** *n.* land mass almost completely surrounded by water

- **temperate (tem´ pər it)** *adj.* not very hot and not very cold

- **Renaissance (ren´ə säns´)** *n.* term meaning "rebirth"; period in Europe (14th-17th centuries) when the arts and sciences flourished after a long period of inactivity

# ITALY

Adapted from *Dorling Kindersley World Reference Atlas*

## ITALY

Total Land Area : 294 060 sq. km
(301 270 sq. miles)

**POPULATION**

over 1 000 000
over 500 000
over 100 000
over 50 000
over 10 000

**LAND HEIGHT**

3000m/9843ft
2000m/6562ft
1000m/3281ft
500m/1640ft
200m/656ft
Sea Level

Note that location names are given in the official language of Italy, Italian.

# ITALY

**Official Name:** *Italian Republic*
**Capital:** *Rome*
**Population:** *57.2 million*
**Currency:** *the euro*
**Official Language:** *Italian*

Lying in southern Europe, Italy comprises the famous boot-shaped **peninsula** stretching 500 miles into the Mediterranean and a number of islands—Sicily and Sardinia being the largest. The Alps form a natural boundary to the north, while the Apennine Mountains run the length of the peninsula. The south is an area of seismic activity, epitomized by the volcanoes of Mounts Etna and Vesuvius. United under ancient Roman rule, Italy subsequently developed into a series of competing kingdoms and states, not fully reunited until 1870. Italian politics was dominated by the Christian Democrats (CD) from 1945 to 1992 under a system of political patronage and a succession of short-lived governments. Investigations into corruption from 1992 on led to the demise of this system in the elections of 1994.

## CLIMATE

Southern Italy has a Mediterranean climate; the north is more **temperate**. Summers are hot and dry, especially in the south. Temperatures range from 75°F to over 81°F in Sardinia and Sicily. Southern winters are mild; northern ones are cooler and wetter. The mountains usually experience heavy snow. The Adriatic coast suffers from cold winds such as the bora.

## TRANSPORTATION

 Leonardo da Vinci (Fiumicino), Rome 15.55m passengers

 791 ships (10.13m dwt)

Many of Italy's key routes are congested. The trans-Apennine *autostrada* (expressway) from Bologna to Florence is being doubled in size. A high-speed train program (*treno ad alta velocità*—TAV) is planned to link Turin, Milan, Venice, Bologna, Florence and Naples to Rome. Most of Italy's exports travel by road, via Switzerland and Austria. Only 16% goes by sea.

## TOURISM

 27.5m visitors

 Up 4% in 1994

Italy has been a tourist destination since the 16th century and probably invented the concept. Roman Popes consciously aimed to make their city the most beautiful in the world to attract travelers. In the 18th century, Italy was the focus of any Grand Tour. Today, its many unspoilt centers of Renaissance culture continue to make Italy one of the world's major tourism destinations. The industry accounts for 3% of Italy's GDP, and hotels and restaurants employ one million out of a working population of 21 million.

Most visitors travel to the northern half of the country, to cities such as Rome, Florence, Venice and Padova. Many are increasingly traveling to the northern lakes. Beach resorts such as Rimini attract a large, youthful crowd in summer. Italy is also growing in popularity as a skiing destination.

## PEOPLE

 Italian, German, French, Rhaeto-Romanic, Sardinian

 505 people per sq. mile

Italy is a remarkably homogeneous society. Most Italians are Roman Catholics, and Italy has far fewer ethnic minorities than its EU neighbors. Most are fairly recent immigrants from Ethiopia, the Philippines and Egypt. A sharp rise in illegal immigration in the 1980's and 1990's, from North and West Africa, Turkey and Albania, generated a right-wing backlash and tighter controls. It became a major election issue in 1993 and a factor in the rise of the federalist Northern League.

# Italy

## from *Liberty Travel: Europe*

Italy's illustrious history is evident everywhere you go and each city treasures its own collection of cultural masterpieces.

The picturesque qualities of its cityscape and its rich cultural history give Rome an air of romance. Begin your exploration at the Spanish Steps or the Piazza St. Maria Maggiore, popular meeting places where visitors mix easily with locals. In the Holy See, you can spend days perusing the vast collections of the Vatican Museum & Gallery. Michelangelo's frescoes in the Sistine Chapel continue to mesmerize tourists and pilgrims alike.

Florence is Europe's capital of beauty and the birthplace of the **Renaissance**. Must-sees here include the Academy and Uffizi galleries, which house some of the world's finest collections of paintings and sculptures. The Duomo boasts sculptures by Michelangelo, and the Palazzo Vecchio is a splendid palace dating back to 1299.

Venice lives up to its reputation. Every bit as beautiful as you imagine, it is built on 120 tiny islands networked by canals, an elegant feat of engineering. A ride in a romantic gondola and a walk through the quaint streets are quintessential ways to tour the city. In St. Mark's Square, watch the figures in the Clock Tower signal the end of the day as you sip a rich coffee blend at Florian's historic botega de caffè.

A visit to Milan is an encounter with the height of Italian fashion and sophistication. The spired cathedral in the central Piazza del Duomo is aptly inspiring. You can easily find a table at one of Milan's many fine restaurants, but you'll have to make reservations to view da Vinci's Last Supper in the church of Santa Maria delle Grazie.

Each of the old Mediterranean seaside towns of the Amalfi Coast has its own distinct character. Highlights include the church of Santa Maria Assunta in Positano, Villa Cimbrone and Villa Rufolo in Ravello, and the views from the "Amalfi Drive," a narrow cliff-top route to Sorrento.

String together the jewel cities of Italy and create one unforgettable vacation.

This first paragraph gives a general statement about visiting the country of Italy. Following paragraphs discuss specific Italian cities.

# Rome Sightseeing

### Monumental Rome

Marvel at the glory of Rome via guided bus tour •
View the Piazza della Repubblica Fontana di Trevi.
Castel Sant'Angelo, and St. Peter's Basilica, home of
Michelangelo's Pietà • Tour stops at the Pantheon,
Piazza Navona and St. Peter's • Half day, mornings

### Naples & Pompeii

Ride via deluxe motorcoach along the toll road A1,
nicknamed Autostrada del Sole (Sun Highway) to
Naples • In Naples, see the Mergellina, Lungomare
Caracciolo, the Royal Palace, and the San Carlo
Theatre • Continue to ancient Pompeii for lunch •
Visit the beautifully restored ruins of Pompeii where,
in AD 79, the eruption of Mt. Vesuvius buried portions
of the city and some of its inhabitants in volcanic
ash and pumice • Take in panoramic views of the
Tyrrhenian Sea • Return to Rome • Full day

### Florence

Ride via deluxe motorcoach along the Autostrada
del Sole superhighway to Florence for a day of art
and architecture • Visit the Cathedral of Santa Maria
del Fiore, Giotto's Bell Tower and Baptistry, and
the Academy Gallery, where Michelangelo's David
resides • Lunch in a Florentine restaurant • Proceed
to the Piazza Santa Croce for free time and shopping • End the day with a stop at the Piazzale
Michelangelo for a panoramic view of Florence and
the scenic Ponte Vecchio • Return to Rome • Full day

### Illuminated Rome

Tour begins on the elegant Via Veneto • See the
Aurelian Walls. Triton Fountain, and Quirinal Square
with the Presidential Palace • Stop at the famous
Trevi Fountain • Pass through Piazza Venezia and
see the Colosseum and Theatre of Marcellus • After
a visit to Piazza Navona, it's on to Castel Sant' Angelo
and St. Peter's Basilica in Vatican City • Departs 8pm •
Daily

Subheadings direct the reader to specific information about the different tours available.

Photos depict locations mentioned in the text and indicate to the reader what is being discussed in this section of the brochure.

## Comparing Functional and Expository Texts

 **1. Craft and Structure (a) Analyze text information** by comparing and contrasting the types and **sequences of information** in the atlas entry and the travel brochure. **(b)** How does the sequence of information in each text aid the reader's understanding? **(c)** What idea connects the first and second pages of the travel brochure?

### Content-Area Vocabulary

**2. (a)** Use a dictionary to explain how the meanings of *temperature* and *intemperately* are related to *temperate*. **(b)** Name another *temperate peninsula* in the world, besides Italy. **(c)** List two works of art that are associated with the *Renaissance*. **(d)** What era, in your opinion, represents a *renaissance* in popular music? Explain.

## Timed Writing

**Explanatory Text: Essay**

**Format**
The prompt directs you to write a brief explanatory essay. Therefore, your response should be three to five paragraphs in length and should provide facts and explanations.

Using information from the atlas entry, write a brief explanatory essay that gives an overview of Italy as a tourist destination. Use information from both the graphics and text to describe the country's size and location, its land and climate, and its people. Also note any key facts that would help tourists make the most of their visit. (35 minutes)

**Academic Vocabulary**
When you *describe* something, you use details, examples, and vivid language to form a picture in your reader's mind.

### 5-Minute Planner

Complete these steps before you begin to write:

1. Read the prompt carefully and completely.

2. Review both documents, including graphics and text. Take notes about key facts and details that you will include in your essay.

3. Decide in what order you will present your information. Choose an order that is logical. Then, create an outline for your essay. **TIP** Review the sequences of information in the atlas entry and travel brochure. Consider the best sequence to use in your essay.

4. Refer to your notes and use your outline as you draft your essay.

## Comparing Archetypal Themes

An **archetype** is a plot, character, image, or setting that appears in literature, mythology, and folklore from around the world and throughout history. Archetypes represent universal themes and truths about life and are said to mirror the working of the human mind. The following are some common archetypes:

- Characters: the hero; the outcast; the fool
- Plot types: the quest, or search; the task
- Symbols: water as a symbol of life; fire as a symbol of power

A **theme** is the central idea, message, or insight of a literary work. **Archetypal stories** can be thought of as original models on which other versions are based.

**Archetypal themes** develop or explore fundamental or universal ideas. Ill-fated love is one archetypal theme that appears in literature from all over the world. A complex character's fall from grace is another archetypal theme. Works of literature can differ for a variety of reasons in their presentations of the same archetypal theme. For example, the values of the work's era, the author's purpose, and the author's culture and language may affect how a writer presents a universal theme.

As you read Ovid's "Pyramus and Thisbe," a classic tale from ancient Rome, make comparisons to Shakespeare's treatment of a similar tale in two of his works: *The Tragedy of Romeo and Juliet* and the comedy *A Midsummer Night's Dream*. Consider how Shakespeare draws on the original source to develop his story and theme in both the full-length tragedy and the subplot of the comedy. Use a chart like the one shown to organize your observations.

|  | **Similarities** | **Differences** |
|---|---|---|
| **Characters** |  |  |
| **Events** |  |  |

### Common Core State Standards

**Reading Literature**

**3.** Analyze how complex characters develop over the course of a text, interact with other characters, and advance the plot or develop the theme.

**9.** Analyze how an author draws on and transforms source material in a specific work (e.g., how Shakespeare treats a theme or topic from Ovid or the Bible or how a later author draws on a play by Shakespeare).

**Writing**

**2.** Write informative/explanatory texts to examine and convey complex ideas, concepts, and information clearly and accurately through the effective selection, organization, and analysis of content.

**PHLit Online!**
www.PHLitOnline.com

- Vocabulary flashcards
- Interactive journals
- More about the authors
- Selection audio
- Interactive graphic organizers

# Do our *differences* define us?

## Writing About the Big Question

In these selections, the main characters fall in love despite the differences that separate them. Use this sentence starter to develop your ideas about the Big Question:

The **differences** between two people can be less important than _____.

# Meet the Authors

## Ovid (43 B.C.–A.D. 17)

### Author of "Pyramus and Thisbe"

Educated in Rome, Ovid began his career writing poems about love and pleasure. However, the emperor Augustus wanted citizens to focus on morality and work toward an ideal Roman state. In response, Ovid decided to write about myths and traditional stories, such as "Pyramus and Thisbe."

**Achievement and Exile** After completing his masterpiece, *Metamorphoses,* in A.D. 8, Ovid was banished to a remote village. The reasons for his banishment are not entirely clear, but the emperor might have felt that Ovid's work endangered public morals. Although he continued to write, he was never allowed to return to Rome.

## William Shakespeare (1564–1616)

### Author of *A Midsummer Night's Dream*

Perhaps the greatest of all playwrights, William Shakespeare was born in the town of Stratford-on-Avon and gained his successes in the flourishing theatrical world of London. He worked as an actor, a playwright, and part owner of a theater company, earning enough to retire to Stratford in 1610.

**Kings and Clowns, Lovers and Villains** Shakespeare's 37 plays are populated with a wide range of characters who embody the depth and variety of human experience. No writer has played a more significant role in shaping the English language and English literature.

# Pyramus and Thisbe

### ✌ Ovid ✌    *retold by* **Edith Hamilton**

# Background

**Background** The tale of Pyramus and Thisbe appears in Book IV of *Metamorphoses,* Ovid's greatest achievement. A poem of nearly 12,000 lines, it tells a series of stories beginning with the creation of the world and ending with the death of Julius Caesar. In each story, someone or something undergoes a change. Divided into fifteen books, the stories are linked by clever transitions, so that the entire work reads as one long, uninterrupted tale.

Once upon a time the deep red berries of the mulberry tree[1] were white as snow. The change in color came about strangely and sadly. The death of two young lovers was the cause.

Pyramus and Thisbe, he the most beautiful youth and she the loveliest maiden of all the East, lived in Babylon, the city of Queen Semiramis, in houses so close together that one wall was common to both. Growing up thus side by side they learned to love each other. They longed to marry, but their parents forbade. Love, however, cannot be forbidden. The more that flame is covered up, the hotter it burns. Also love can always find a way. It was impossible that these two whose hearts were on fire should be kept apart.

In the wall both houses shared there was a little chink.[2] No one before had noticed it, but there is nothing a lover does not notice. Our two young people discovered it and through it they were able to whisper sweetly back and forth. Thisbe on one side, Pyramus on the other. The hateful wall that separated them had become their means of reaching each other. "But for you we could touch, kiss," they would say. "But at least you let us speak together. You give a passage for loving words to reach loving ears. We are not ungrateful." So they would talk, and as night came on and they must part, each would press on the wall kisses that could not go through to the lips on the other side.

Every morning when the dawn had put out the stars, and the sun's rays had dried the hoarfrost on the grass, they would steal to the crack and, standing there, now utter words of burning love and now lament their hard fate, but always in softest whispers. Finally a day came when they could endure no longer. They decided that that very night they would try to slip away and steal out through the city into the open country where at last they could be together in freedom. They agreed to meet at a well-known place, the Tomb of Ninus, under a tree there, a tall mulberry full of snow-white berries, near which a cool spring bubbled up. The plan pleased them and it seemed to them the day would never end.

---

1. **mulberry** (mul′ ber′ rē) **tree** *n.* tree with an edible, purplish-red fruit.
2. **chink** (chiŋk) *n.* narrow opening; crack.

◀ **Critical Viewing**
What do you think the girl is feeling as she listens through the crack in the wall? **[Speculate]**

**Literary Analysis**
**Archetypal Theme**
What is the main obstacle the lovers face?

**Vocabulary**
**lament** (lə ment′) *v.* express deep sorrow; mourn

**Reading Check**
How do Pyramus and Thisbe communicate with each other?

**Literary Analysis**
**Archetypal Theme**
What does Thisbe's "bold" behavior suggest about the power of love?

**Vocabulary**
**inevitable** (in ev´ i tə bəl) *adj.* unavoidable; certain

At last the sun sank into the sea and night arose. In the darkness Thisbe crept out and made her way in all secrecy to the tomb. Pyramus had not come; still she waited for him, her love making her bold. But of a sudden she saw by the light of the moon a lioness. The fierce beast had made a kill; her jaws were bloody and she was coming to slake her thirst in the spring. She was still far enough away for Thisbe to escape, but as she fled she dropped her cloak. The lioness came upon it on her way back to her lair and she mouthed it and tore it before disappearing into the woods. That is what Pyramus saw when he appeared a few minutes later. Before him lay the bloodstained shreds of the cloak and clear in the dust were the tracks of the lioness. The conclusion was inevitable. He never doubted that he knew all. Thisbe was dead. He had let his love, a tender maiden, come alone to a place full of danger, and not been there first to protect her. "It is I who killed you," he said. He lifted up from the trampled dust what was left of the cloak and kissing it again and again carried it to the mulberry tree. "Now,"

he said, "you shall drink my blood too." He drew his sword and plunged it into his side. The blood spurted up over the berries and dyed them a dark red.

Thisbe, although terrified of the lioness, was still more afraid to fail her lover. She ventured to go back to the tree of the tryst, the mulberry with the shining white fruit. She could not find it. A tree was there, but not one gleam of white was on the branches. As she stared at it, something moved on the ground beneath. She started back shuddering. But in a moment, peering through the shadows, she

**◄ Critical Viewing**
Explain the similarities and differences between this lioness and the one Thisbe sees. **[Compare and Contrast]**

saw what was there. It was Pyramus, bathed in blood and dying. She flew to him and threw her arms around him. She kissed his cold lips and begged him to look at her, to speak to her. "It is I, your Thisbe, your dearest," she cried to him. At the sound of her name he opened his heavy eyes for one look. Then death closed them.

She saw his sword fallen from his hand and beside it her cloak stained and torn. She understood all. "Your own hand killed you," she said, "and your love for me. I too can be brave. I too can love. Only death would have had the power to separate us. It shall not have that power now." She plunged into her heart the sword that was still wet with his life's blood.

The gods were pitiful at the end, and the lovers' parents too. The deep red fruit of the mulberry is the everlasting memorial of these true lovers, and one urn holds the ashes of the two whom not even death could part.

**Literary Analysis**

**Archetypal Theme** In deciding to return to the tree, is Thisbe guided more by love or by reason? Explain.

## Critical Thinking

*Cite textual evidence to support your responses.*

1. **Key Ideas and Details (a)** How do the parents feel about the romance between Pyramus and Thisbe? **(b) Analyze Cause and Effect:** What actions do Pyramus and Thisbe take as a result of their parents' feelings? **(c) Make a Judgment:** Do you think Pyramus and Thisbe or their parents are more responsible for the tragic outcome?

2. **Key Ideas and Details (a)** What does the chink in the wall enable the couple to do? **(b) Speculate:** How might the story be different if the chink did not exist?

3. **Integration of Knowledge and Ideas (a) Draw Conclusions:** What does the mulberry tree symbolize in this story? **(b) Analyze:** In what way does this symbol reinforce the story's theme?

4. **Integration of Knowledge and Ideas Speculate:** Do you think this story will continue to appeal to readers in the future? Why or why not?

5. **Integration of Knowledge and Ideas (a)** How do Pyramus and Thisbe's wishes differ from that of their families? **(b)** In what way did those differences lead to tragedy? *[Connect to the Big Question: Do our differences define us?]*

*from*

# A Midsummer Night's Dream

## William Shakespeare

*Background* In *A Midsummer Night's Dream*, Shakespeare creates comedy out of misunderstandings, magic transformations, and the interactions of characters from three different worlds: the noble class, the working class, and the realm of the fairy spirits. In this scene, several local craftsmen (the "Clowns") prepare to put on a play for the duke's wedding. Robin, the fairy king's jester, discovers the actors and decides to play a trick on one of them. All of this happens as Titania, the queen of the fairies, sleeps nearby. The actors do not know that Titania is under a spell that will cause her to fall in love with the first person she sees upon waking.

### Act III, Scene i

*With* TITANIA *still asleep onstage, enter the* CLOWNS, BOTTOM, QUINCE, SNOUT, STARVELING, SNUG, *and* FLUTE.

**BOTTOM.** Are we all met?

**QUINCE.** Pat,[1] pat. And here's a marvels convenient place for our rehearsal. This green plot shall be our stage, this hawthorn brake[2] our tiring-house,[3] and we will do it in
5　action as we will do it before the Duke.

**BOTTOM.** Peter Quince?

**QUINCE.** What sayest thou, bully[4] Bottom?

**BOTTOM.** There are things in this comedy of Pyramus and Thisbe that will never please. First, Pyramus must draw a
10　sword to kill himself, which the ladies cannot abide. How answer you that?

**SNOUT.** By 'r lakin,[5] a parlous fear.

**STARVELING.** I believe we must leave the killing out, when all is done.[6]

◀ **Critical Viewing**
How would you describe Titania in the image shown here?

**1. pat** exactly; right on time.
**2. brake** thicket.
**3. tiring house** room used for dressing, or attiring.
**4. bully** jolly fellow.
**5. By 'r lakin** shortened version of "By your ladykin (little lady)."
**6. when all is done** after all.

Reading Check

Who is asleep onstage when the Clowns enter?

**BOTTOM.** Not a whit! I have a device to make all well. Write me a prologue, and let the prologue seem to say we will do no harm with our swords, and that Pyramus is not killed indeed. And, for the more better assurance, tell them that I, Pyramus, am not Pyramus, but Bottom the weaver. This will put them out of fear.

20

**QUINCE.** Well, we will have such a prologue, and it shall be written in eight and six.[7]

**BOTTOM.** No, make it two more. Let it be written in eight and eight.

25

**SNOUT.** Will not the ladies be afeard of the lion?

**STARVELING.** I fear it, I promise you.

**BOTTOM.** Masters, you ought to consider with yourself, to bring in God shield us! a lion among ladies is a most dreadful thing. For there is not a more fearful wildfowl than your lion living, and we ought to look to it.

30

**SNOUT.** Therefore another prologue must tell he is not a lion.

**BOTTOM.** Nay, you must name his name, and half his face must be seen through the lion's neck, and he himself must speak through, saying thus, or to the same defect: "Ladies," or "Fair ladies, I would wish you," or "I would request you," or "I would entreat you not to fear, not to tremble! My life for yours. If you think I come hither as a lion, it were pity of my life.[8] No, I am no such thing. I am a man as other men are." And there indeed let him name his name and tell them plainly he is Snug the joiner.

35

40

---

7. **eight and six** ballad meter containing alternating eight- and six-syllable lines.

**Literary Analysis**
**Archetypal Theme**
How do the Clowns plan to soften their presentation of the lion?

8. **it were . . . my life** risky for me.

---

## LITERATURE IN CONTEXT

### Science Connection

#### Almanacs

When Bottom calls for an almanac, he is referring to a type of book that was very popular in Elizabethan times. The almanac was essentially a calendar, but it also provided lists of upcoming natural events, such as tides, full moons, and eclipses. The book was especially useful to farmers because it included gardening tips and weather predictions. Almanacs of various kinds are still published and consulted today.

### Connect to the Literature

Do you think the "Clowns" are wise to rely on the accuracy of the almanac with regard to moonlight? Why or why not?

**QUINCE.** Well, it shall be so. But there is two hard things: that is, to bring the moonlight into a chamber, for you know Pyramus and Thisbe meet by moonlight.

**SNOUT.** Doth the moon shine that night we play our play?

45 **BOTTOM.** A calendar, a calendar! Look in the almanac. Find out moonshine, find out moonshine.

QUINCE *takes out a book.*

**QUINCE.** Yes, it doth shine that night.

**BOTTOM.** Why, then, may you leave a casement of the great chamber window, where we play, open, and the moon may
50 shine in at the casement.

**QUINCE.** Ay, or else one must come in with a bush of thorns[9] and a lantern and say he comes to disfigure[10] or to present the person of Moonshine. Then there is another thing: we must have a wall in the great chamber, for Pyramus and
55 Thisbe, says the story, did talk through the chink of a wall.

**SNOUT.** You can never bring in a wall. What say you, Bottom?

**BOTTOM.** Some man or other must present Wall. And let him have some plaster, or some loam, or some roughcast[11] about him to signify wall, or let him hold his fingers thus,
60 and through that cranny shall Pyramus and Thisbe whisper.

**QUINCE.** If that may be, then all is well. Come, sit down, every mother's son, and rehearse your parts. Pyramus, you begin. When you have spoken your speech, enter into
65 that brake, and so every one according to his cue.

*Enter* ROBIN *invisible to those onstage.*

**ROBIN.** *(aside)*
What hempen homespuns[12] have we swaggring
   here
So near the cradle[13] of the Fairy Queen?
What, a play toward?[14] I'll be an auditor—
An actor too perhaps, if I see cause.

70 **QUINCE.** Speak, Pyramus.—Thisbe, stand forth.

**BOTTOM.** *(as Pyramus)*
Thisbe, the flowers of odious savors sweet—

**QUINCE.** Odors, odors!

**BOTTOM.** *(as Pyramus)*
        . . . odors savors sweet.
So hath thy breath, my dearest Thisbe dear—

9. **a bush of thorns** according to legend, the man in the moon collected firewood on Sundays and was thus banished to the sky.
10. **disfigure** Quince means figure, as in "symbolize" or "stand for."
11. **plaster . . . roughcast** three different blended materials, each used for plastering walls.

12. **hempen homespuns** characters wearing clothing homemade from hemp, probably from the country.
13. **cradle** bower where Titania sleeps.
14. **toward** being rehearsed.

**Reading Check**

How do the Clowns plan to present the wall that separates Pyramus and Thisbe?

But hark, a voice! Stay thou
but here awhile.
75 And by and by I will to thee
appear. *(He exits.)*

**ROBIN.** *(aside)*
A stranger Pyramus than
e'er played here.

*(He exits.)*

**FLUTE.** Must I speak now?

**QUINCE.** Ay, marry, must you, for
you must understand he goes
80 but to see a noise that he
heard and is to come again.

**Flute.** *(as Thisbe)*
Most radiant Pyramus,
most lily-white of hue,
Of color like the red
rose on triumphant[15]
brier,
Most brisky juvenal[16] and
eke[17] most lovely Jew,[18]
85 As true as truest horse, that yet would never tire.
I'll meet thee, Pyramus, at Ninny's tomb.[19]

**QUINCE.** "Ninus tomb," man! Why, you must not speak that
yet. That you answer to Pyramus. You speak all your
part[20] at once, cues and all.— Pyramus, enter. Your cue is
90 past. It is "never tire."

**FLUTE.** O!

*(As Thisbe)* As true as truest horse, that yet would never
tire.

*Enter* ROBIN, *and* BOTTOM *as Pyramus with the ass-head.*[21]

**BOTTOM.** *(as Pyramus)*
If I were fair, fair Thisbe, I were[22] only thine.

**QUINCE.** O monstrous! O strange! We are haunted. Pray,
95 masters, fly, masters! Help!

QUINCE, FLUTE, SNOUT, SNUG, *and* STARVELING *exit.*

**ROBIN.** I'll follow you. I'll lead you about a round,[23]
Through bog, through bush, through brake, through
brier.
Sometime a horse I'll be, sometime a hound,
A hog, a headless bear, sometime a fire.[24]

▶ **Critical Viewing**
How would Bottom
feel if he knew how
he looked to others?
**[Speculate]**

15. **triumphant** splendid;
magnificent.
16. **juvenal** juvenile; a young
person.
17. **eke** also.
18. **Jew** shortening of "jewel"
to complete the rhyme.
19. **Ninny's tomb** refers to
Ninus, legendary founder
of biblical city of Nineveh.
20. **part** script containing
stage cues, which Flute
is accused of missing or
misreading.
21. **with the ass-head**
wearing an ass-head.
22. **were** would be.
23. **about a round** in a
roundabout, like a circle
dance.
24. **fire** will-o'-the-wisp.

100 And neigh, and bark, and grunt, and roar, and burn,
Like horse, hound, hog, bear, fire, at every turn.

*(He exits.)*

**BOTTOM.** Why do they run away? This is a knavery of them
to make me afeard.

*Enter* SNOUT.

**SNOUT.** O Bottom, thou art changed! What do I see on thee?

105 **BOTTOM.** What do you see? You see an ass-head of your
own, do you? *(SNOUT exits.)*

*Enter* QUINCE.

**QUINCE.** Bless thee, Bottom, bless thee! Thou art
translated![25] *(He exits.)*

**BOTTOM.** I see their knavery. This is to make an ass of me,
110 to fright me, if they could. But I will not stir from this
place, do what they can. I will walk up and down here,
and I will sing, that they shall hear I am not afraid.
*(He sings.) The ouzel cock,[26] so black of hue,*
*With orange-tawny bill,*
115 *The throstle[27] with his note so true,*
*The wren with little quill—[28]*

**TITANIA.** *(waking up)*
What angel wakes me from my flow'ry bed?

**BOTTOM.** *(sings)*
*The finch, the sparrow, and the lark,*
120 *The plainsong cuckoo[29] gray,*
*Whose note full many a man doth mark*
*And dares not answer "nay"—[30]*
for, indeed, who would set his wit to so foolish a bird? Who
would give a bird the lie[31] though he cry "cuckoo" never so?[32]

**TITANIA.**
125 I pray thee, gentle mortal, sing again.
Mine ear is much enamored of thy note,
So is mine eye enthralled to thy shape,
And thy fair virtue's force perforce doth move me[33]
On the first view to say, to swear, I love thee.

130 **BOTTOM.** Methinks, mistress, you should have little reason
for that. And yet, to say the truth, reason and love keep little
company together nowadays. The more the pity that some

▲ **Critical Viewing**
How do Titania and
Bottom seem to feel
about each other in this
image? **[Describe]**

34. **gleek** jest; joke.
35. **rate** value; rank.
36. **still doth tend** still
    serves.

honest neighbors will not make them friends. Nay, I can
gleek³⁴ upon occasion.

**TITANIA.**

135    Thou art as wise as thou art beautiful.

**BOTTOM.** Not so neither; but if I had wit enough to get out of
this wood, I have enough to serve mine own turn.

**TITANIA.**

Out of this wood do not desire to go.
Thou shalt remain here whether thou wilt or no.
140    I am a spirit of no common rate.³⁵
The summer still doth tend³⁶ upon my state,
And I do love thee. Therefore go with me.
I'll give thee fairies to attend on thee,
And they shall fetch thee jewels from the deep
145    And sing while thou on pressèd flowers dost sleep.

And I will purge thy mortal grossness[37] so
That thou shalt like an airy spirit go.—
Peaseblossom, Cobweb, Mote,[38] and Mustardseed!

*Enter four Fairies:* PEASEBLOSSOM, COBWEB,
MOTE, *and* MUSTARDSEED.

**PEASEBLOSSOM.** Ready.

150 **COBWEB.** And I.

**MOTE.** And I.

**MUSTARDSEED.** And I.

**ALL.** Where shall we go?

**TITANIA.**
Be kind and courteous to this gentleman.
155 Hop in his walks and gambol in his eyes;
Feed him with apricocks and dewberries.[39]
With purple grapes, green figs, and mulberries;
The honey-bags steal from the humble-bees,
And for night-tapers crop their waxen thighs
160 And light them at the fiery glowworms' eyes
To have my love to bed and to arise;
And pluck the wings from painted butterflies
To fan the moonbeams from his sleeping eyes.
Nod to him, elves, and do him courtesies.

165 **PEASEBLOSSOM.** Hail, mortal!

**COBWEB.** Hail!

**MOTE.** Hail!

**MUSTARDSEED.** Hail!

**BOTTOM.** I cry your Worships mercy,[40] heartily.—I beseech
170 your Worship's name.

**COBWEB.** Cobweb.

**BOTTOM.** I shall desire you of more acquaintance, good
Master Cobweb. If I cut my finger, I shall make bold with
you.[41]—Your name, honest gentleman?

175 **PEASEBLOSSOM.** Peaseblossom.

**BOTTOM.** I pray you, commend me to Mistress Squash,[42]
your mother, and to Master Peascod,[43] your father. Good
Master Peaseblossom, I shall desire you of more
acquaintance, too.—Your name, I beseech you, sir?

180 **MUSTARDSEED.** Mustardseed.

---

37. **mortal grossness** the physical, mortal state of human beings.

38. **Mote** a speck, but also moth, as this word was pronounced similarly.

39. **apricocks and dewberries** apricots and blackberries.

## Literary Analysis
### Archetypal Theme
How do Titania's commands emphasize the absurdity of her feelings toward Bottom?

40. **cry. . . mercy** beg your pardon.

41. **Master . . . you** cobwebs were used to stop bleeding.

42. **squash** an unripe pea pod.

43. **peascod** a ripe pea pod.

**Reading Check**
How does Titania want the fairies to treat Bottom?

**BOTTOM.** Good Master Mustardseed, I know your patience[44] well. That same cowardly, giantlike ox-beef hath devoured many a gentleman of your house. I promise you, your kindred hath made my eyes water ere now. I desire you of

185    more acquaintance, good Master Mustardseed.

**TITANIA.** Come, wait upon him. Lead him to my bower.
The moon, methinks, looks with a watery eye,
And when she weeps, weeps every little flower,
Lamenting some enforcèd chastity.[45]

190    Tie up my lover's tongue. Bring him silently.

*They exit.*

## Critical Thinking

*Cite textual evidence to support your responses.*

1. **Key Ideas and Details (a)** What are the Clowns trying to accomplish in this scene? **(b) Analyze Cause and Effect:** What events prevent their success? Explain.

2. **Key Ideas and Details (a)** How is Bottom transformed?
**(b) Infer:** Is Bottom aware of his transformation? Explain.
**(c) Analyze:** Does the transformation alter Bottom's personality as well as his appearance? Why or why not?

3. **Key Ideas and Details (a)** Who is Titania? **(b) Analyze:** In what ways does the match between Titania and Bottom mock typical portrayals of romantic love?

4. **Integration of Knowledge and Ideas Analyze:** Does Bottom's transformation actually reveal a truth about his character? Explain.

5. **Key Ideas and Details (a) Summarize:** What alterations to script and costumes do the Clowns plan in order to minimize the frightening aspects of their play? **(b) Speculate:** Do you think the Clowns' eventual audience will enjoy their production of "Pyramus and Thisbe"? Explain.

6. **Integration of Knowledge and Ideas (a)** What are the major differences between Titania and Bottom? **(b)** What similarities help them overcome their differences? **(c)** Do you think their differences or their similarities will matter more in the end? Explain. *[Connect to the Big Question: Do our differences define us?]*

| After You Read | **Pyramus and Thisbe • *from*** **A Midsummer Night's Dream** |  |
| --- | --- | --- |

## Comparing Archetypal Themes

**© 1. Key Ideas and Details** Use a chart like the one shown to identify the characters, obstacles, and main events depicted in the scene Bottom and his friends rehearse in *A Midsummer Night's Dream,* the full version of *The Tragedy of Romeo and Juliet,* and Ovid's "Pyramus and Thisbe."

| Selection | Characters | Obstacles | Main Events |
| --- | --- | --- | --- |
| A Midsummer Night's Dream | | | |
| The Tragedy of Romeo and Juliet | | | |
| Pyramus and Thisbe | | | |

**© 2. Craft and Structure (a)** Using your chart, explain how Shakespeare draws on and transforms Ovid's story in both *A Midsummer Night's Dream* and *Romeo and Juliet.* **(b)** What are the differences in the ways the three selections present this theme?

**© 3. Integration of Knowledge and Ideas (a)** Why is Titania and Bottom's love ill-fated? **(b)** How do these reasons compare to the obstacles faced by Romeo and Juliet or Pyramus and Thisbe?

## ⏱ Timed Writing

### Explanatory Text: Essay

In an essay, compare the way Shakespeare uses the characters and events from "Pyramus and Thisbe" in *The Tragedy of Romeo and Juliet* with the way he uses them in *A Midsummer Night's Dream.* Discuss why Shakespeare might explore the same story in both a tragedy and a comedy. **(40 minutes)**

### 5-Minute Planner

1. Read the prompt carefully and completely.
2. Gather your ideas by jotting down answers to these questions:
   - How do the different settings and characters in each of Shakespeare's plays affect the two presentations of the archetypal theme?
   - How do you think Shakespeare wanted audiences to feel about the ill-fated love in each play?
3. Reread the prompt, and then draft your essay.

# Writing Workshop

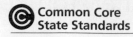 **Common Core State Standards**

**Writing**

**2.** Write informative/explanatory texts to examine and convey complex ideas, concepts and information clearly and accurately through the effective selection, organization, and analysis of content.

**2.a.** Introduce a topic; organize complex ideas, concepts, and information to make important connections and distinctions; include formatting when useful to aiding comprehension.

**2.b.** Develop the topic with well-chosen, relevant, and sufficient facts, extended definitions, concrete details, quotations, or other information and examples appropriate to the audience's knowledge of the topic.

**2.d.** Use precise language and domain-specific vocabulary to manage the complexity of the topic.

**2.f.** Provide a concluding statement or section that follows from and supports the information or explanation presented.

**4.** Produce clear and coherent writing in which the development, organization, and style are appropriate to task, purpose, and audience.

## Write an Explanatory Text

### Exposition: How-to Essay

**Defining the Form** A **how-to essay** provides step-by step instructions for completing a specific task. The best how-to essays are clearly written so readers can avoid mistakes and follow the best path to a desired outcome. You might use elements of the how-to essay in repair instructions, travel directions, recipes, training manuals, and problem solving.

**Assignment** Write a how-to essay about an activity or a process that you know well. Include these elements:

- ✓ *specific, well-chosen, and sufficient information* presented in logical sequence
- ✓ *step-by-step directions* for each stage in the process
- ✓ *examples* and *concrete definitions* that demonstrate key concepts
- ✓ *instructions* that anticipate readers' questions
- ✓ error-free grammar, including use of *modifying phrases*

To preview the criteria on which your how-to essay may be judged, see the rubric on page 965.

 **Writing Workshop:** *Work in Progress*

Review the work you did on page 933.

## Prewriting/Planning Strategy

Choose a topic by thinking about some of your daily activities. Select as a topic an activity that involves several steps you feel confident about explaining.

**List the materials.** Write down all the materials, tools, and information your readers will need to accomplish the activity you plan to describe. First, make a list of items needed. Then, note all of the steps involved, in the order in which they occur. Take time to identify basic rules of behavior—for example, about safety, care of equipment, or working with others. Be sure to list all technical terms and notations accurately.

| Items or Tools Needed | Steps in Process | Rules to Follow |
|---|---|---|
|  |  |  |

# Getting Organized

The **organization** of an essay is the order in which the information is put together. Organization is especially important in a how-to essay because readers have to understand completely in order to do the task. There are two kinds of organization to think about as you plan your essay:

- The order of steps in the task you are describing
- The order of information in your essay

**Organizing the Steps** How-to essays are usually organized in chronological order. Often, the easiest way to start is to list things that need to be done as you think of them. When you finish listing, number them in the order they need to be completed. Include preparation as one of the steps. Think about what materials you need to have on hand. For example, in preparing for a part in a play, your steps might include the following:

1. Get a copy of the play you can mark up.

2. Read the play thoroughly.

3. Read it a second time while underlining the lines you will read.

4. Reread your lines and think about your character.

**Organizing the Essay** An effective how-to essay has three main parts: introduction, body, and conclusion. In your introduction, identify your task and give readers a reason to read your essay. In the body, explain the process in step-by-step order. Finally, write a conclusion that emphasizes the importance of the process you have explained. Use the chart shown to help you organize your essay.

---

**Organizing Information**

1. State the purpose of your how-to-essay.

2. List the materials and conditions necessary to complete the activity.

3. Provide examples to demonstrate the activity.

4. List steps to complete in consecutive order.

5. Suggest solutions to common problems when performing the activity.

6. Present your final thoughts in a conclusion.

---

**PH WRITING COACH**

Further instruction and practice are available in *Prentice Hall Writing Coach*.

# Drafting Strategies

**Begin writing.** Once you have planned your how-to essay, begin your first draft. Refer to your notes, and present your directions simply and clearly.

**Use formatting.** To present information that must be followed in a specific order, use numbered lists. Use bulleted lists to present items that do not have to be followed step by step. For example, use a bulleted list to present materials that are needed or to list precautions.

**Use graphic devices.** Locate or create graphics to reinforce your instructions, and place them at appropriate points in your essay. If you have access to a computer, use graphics features to create helpful diagrams and drawings.

**Define unfamiliar terms.** How-to essays often require the inclusion of specialized language that may be unfamiliar to your readers. To avoid confusion, be sure to explain any terms that you think your readers might not know—especially when describing complex tasks.

# Revising Strategies

**Revise for clarity.** Look over your draft to identify instructions, steps, or information that may be unclear to your reader. Mark these sections, and then go back to them, rewriting or adding language that better explains your points. If the order in which you have explained the steps is confusing, rearrange paragraphs to create a better flow of information.

**Common Core State Standards**

**Writing**

**2.a.** Introduce a topic; organize complex ideas, concepts, and information to make important connections and distinctions; include formatting, graphics, and multimedia when useful to aiding comprehension.

**2.c.** Use appropriate and varied transitions to link the major sections of the text, create cohesion, and clarify the relationships among complex ideas and concepts.

**2.d.** Use precise language and domain-specific vocabulary to manage the complexity of the topic.

**5.** Develop and strengthen writing as needed by planning, revising, editing, rewriting, or trying a new approach, focusing on addressing what is most significant for a specific purpose and audience.

**Language**

**1.b.** Use various types of phrases and clauses to convey specific meanings and add variety and interest to writing or presentations.

---

**Model: Revising for Clarity**

    I was totally unprepared for the reading. We were all gathered

on the stage and I didn't recognize the ~~line~~ prompt when the director fed it to me.

    Memorizing all my lines was the first challenge.... The director asked us to do a read-through of the play just to get comfortable with saying the lines as a cast.

The writer clarifies the writing by using a more precise term. The writer changes the order of the paragraphs to follow chronological order.

---

**Revise for transitions.** Look for sections in your draft that need transitional language to connect the steps. In this example, the words *first* and *then* would make the instruction easier to understand.

*First* study the character and *then* think how you can express the character's personality.

# Revising to Combine Sentences With Phrases

To avoid a series of too many simple sentences, combine some sentences by converting the idea in one sentence into a modifying phrase in another.

**Identifying Modifying Phrases** An **appositive phrase** is a group of words that clarifies the meaning of a noun or pronoun. The following sentences can be combined using an appositive phrase.

**Original:** Sophia is a talented actress. She has appeared in more than twenty productions.

**Combined:** Sophia, *a talented actress,* has appeared in more than twenty productions. (appositive phrase)

**Verbal phrases,** which use verbs as nouns, adjectives, or adverbs, can also be used to combine sentences. Verbal phrases may be classified as participial, gerund, and infinitive, depending on their function.

| Participle | Gerund | Infinitive |
|---|---|---|
| *Finding himself alone onstage,* Aaron paced nervously. | *Meeting with new people* is difficult for some people. | The director's advice was *to focus first on learning the lines.* |
| Adjective modifies *Aaron* | Noun acts as subject of sentence | Noun acts as complement of verb *was* |

When adding a modifying phrase to a sentence, place the phrase close to the word it modifies. A misplaced modifier can confuse readers.

**Misplaced:** *Hanging from a silken thread,* Jeremy noticed a spider. (Participial phrase seems to modify *Jeremy.*)

**Correct:** Jeremy noticed a spider *hanging from a silken thread.*

**Combining With Phrases** Follow these steps to revise a series of short sentences by using phrases to combine them.

1. Express the information from one sentence as an appositive or a verbal phrase.
2. Insert the phrase in a new sentence, locating it near the word or words being modified.
3. Make sure that the revised sentence is punctuated correctly.

> **PH WRITING COACH**
> Further instruction and practice are available in *Prentice Hall Writing Coach.*

### Grammar in Your Writing
Review your draft, looking for short sentences that might be combined using appositive, participial, gerund, or infinitive phrases. Consider combining these sentences.

## Preparing for a Dramatic Role

One of the first challenges of a new dramatic role is the task of memorizing lines. Use the following guidelines to memorize lines more efficiently:

1. Read the entire play at least twice to familiarize yourself with the setting and situations. When performing, it is essential to know what is going on around you in order to provide the appropriate reactions.

    > The numbering system allows Carmen to present information logically.

2. Highlight or underline all your lines to identify when your character speaks.

3. Begin to concentrate solely on your parts. Look at the script scene by scene, memorizing one or two scenes a day, depending on how much time you have. Reading the lines out loud speeds up the process by making the lines more memorable.

    > By offering time suggestions, Carmen anticipates readers' questions and concerns.

4. Once you feel confident enough, begin to "run" your lines. Read them aloud, with another person reading the other characters' lines. This prepares you for being onstage with other actors.

5. When you begin rehearsing with fellow cast members, you will be able to try out different ways of saying things, and you'll start to develop your character. Here are the steps to use when developing a character:

    - If your role is based on a real person, research that person or observe someone in a similar situation. Try to find out as much information as you can so that you can play the part realistically.

        > Advice about conducting research elaborates on Carmen's earlier suggestions.

    - If you are playing a fictional character, study the script closely. The character's words can tell you about his or her feelings, likes, and dislikes.
    - Once you have learned some aspects of your character, begin to delve into the mind and soul of the person. Make up an entire life story for your character. The more you know about the person, the easier it is to put yourself in his or her place. Think of a past experience to relate to something your character is going through. Bring the emotions you felt in that situation to your character's situation.
    - Finally, conduct general conversations with other cast members, with each of you speaking from your own character's point of view. Ask things like "How do you feel about me?" and "How do you think I feel about you?" This lets you know how you are perceived by the other actors/characters in the play and allows you to react more realistically.

        > These ideas explain the value of each strategy.

6. After each rehearsal, consider what worked well and what felt wrong to you. Use your after-rehearsal notes as feedback to improve your next performance.

# Editing and Proofreading

Check your draft for errors in spelling, grammar, and punctuation.

**Focus on formatting.** If you include bullets or numbered lists in your essay, be sure that you use these elements consistently in your final draft. Check that numbers are consecutive and that bullets are the same size and shape. In addition, check that spacing is consistent and appropriate.

# Publishing and Presenting

Consider one of the following ways to share your writing:

**Deliver an oral presentation.** Share your essay with classmates and give an instructional presentation in which you accurately utilize technical terms and notations. If the process you describe can be done in a classroom, have a classmate demonstrate the steps as you describe them. Ask for feedback about the clarity of your presentation.

**Prepare a how-to manual.** With a group of classmates, compile several how-to essays into a booklet. Add step-by-step photographs or illustrations to your instructions. Make the collection available to the class.

# Reflecting on Your Writing

Jot down your answers to this question:

*How did writing a how-to essay help you understand the process you outlined?*

# Rubric for Self-Assessment

Find evidence in your writing to address each category. Then, use the rating scale to grade your work.

| Criteria | Rating Scale |
|---|---|
| | not very      very |
| **Focus:** How specific is your focus? | 1　2　3　4　5 |
| **Organization:** How logical is your organization of the process into steps? | 1　2　3　4　5 |
| **Support/Elaboration:** How effective are your examples in demonstrating key concepts? | 1　2　3　4　5 |
| **Style:** How well do your instructions anticipate readers' questions? | 1　2　3　4　5 |
| **Conventions:** How correct is your grammar, especially your use of modifying phrases? | 1　2　3　4　5 |
| **Sentence Fluency:** How well have you combined sentences to eliminate a series of too many simple sentences? | 1　2　3　4　5 |

**Spiral Review**

Earlier in this unit, you learned about **participles and participial phrases** and **gerunds and gerund phrases** (p. 932). Check your essay to be sure you have used these forms correctly.

Drama

Build your skills and improve your comprehension of drama with this selection.

Read **"The Inspector-General"** to learn how it might feel to travel about in disguise and hear what people have to say about you.

 Common Core State Standards

Meet these standards with **"The Inspector General"** (p. 968).

**Reading Literature**
**1.** Cite strong and thorough textual evidence to support analysis of what the text says explicitly as well as inferences drawn from the text. *(Reading Skill: Draw Conclusions)*

**5.** Analyze how an author's choices concerning how to structure a text, order events within it, and manipulate time create such effects as mystery, tension, or surprise. *(Literary Analysis: Comedy)*

**Spiral Review RL.9-10.3**

**Writing**
**3.** Write narratives to develop real or imagined experiences or events using effective technique, well-chosen details, and well-structured event sequences. **3.a.** Engage and orient the reader by setting out a problem, situation, or observation, establishing one or multiple point(s) of view, and introducing a narrator and/or characters; create a

smooth progression of experiences or events. **3.b.** Use narrative techniques, such as dialogue, pacing, description, reflection, and multiple plot lines, to develop experiences, events, and/or characters. **3.c.** Use a variety of techniques to sequence events so that they build on one another to create a coherent whole. *(Writing: Play)*

**7.** Conduct short as well as more sustained research projects to answer a question or solve a problem. *(Research and Technology: Informational Chart)*

**Language**
**1.** Demonstrate command of the conventions of standard English grammar and usage when writing or speaking. **1.b.** Use various types of phrases and clauses to convey specific meanings and add variety and interest to writing or presentations. *(Conventions: Main and Subordinate Clauses)*

# Literary Analysis: Comedy

**Comedy** is a form of drama that is lighter in mood than tragedy, ends happily, and aims primarily to amuse. The humor in comic plays may arise from one or more of the following elements:

- Funny character names and fast-paced, witty dialogue
- **Incongruous situations,** such as a woman in high heels stomping grapes or a clown conducting a meeting
- Character misunderstandings and mistaken identities

Humor is often created by **dramatic irony,** a form of irony that occurs when the audience knows or understands something that the character does not. As a result, the characters' statements and behavior are often misguided or inappropriate, provoking laughter from the knowing audience. As you read, look for ways in which the author creates dramatic irony by providing information to the audience while withholding it from the characters.

# Reading Skill: Draw Conclusions

A **conclusion** is an inference based on a number of details in a text. In drawing conclusions about a play, consider stated and implied information. The following strategies can help you draw conclusions about characters in a play:

- Consider what the **dialogue** reveals about characters' personalities and circumstances.
- Read **stage directions** closely for details about the scene and about characters' appearances and behavior.
- Note other details that could prove essential to the plot or ideas.

## Using the Strategy: Conclusion Chart

As you read, use a chart like the one shown to record conclusions you draw about characters.

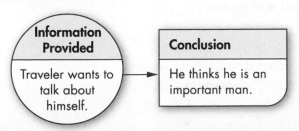

**Information Provided**

Traveler wants to talk about himself.

**Conclusion**

He thinks he is an important man.

**D**o our *differences* define us?

## Writing About the Big Question

In "The Inspector-General," the Inspector-General dresses in disguise so people won't know he's on official business. He is different from those around him, though, and the truth is hard to conceal. Use this sentence starter to develop your ideas about the Big Question.

A person's **background** may be difficult to conceal because _____.

**While You Read** Look for clues about the Inspector-General's identity.

## Vocabulary

Read each word and its definition. Decide whether you know the word well, know it a little bit, or do not know it at all. After you read, see how your knowledge of each word has increased.

- **incognito** (in´ käg nēt´ ō) *adj.* with true identity unrevealed or disguised; under an assumed name (p. 970) *The movie star was incognito because she hoped to have some privacy.*

- **anonymous** (ə nän´ ə məs) *adj.* without a known or acknowledged name (p. 970) *Wishing to remain anonymous, the writer sent an unsigned letter. anonymously adv.*

- **trundle** (trun´ dəl) *v.* roll along (p. 970) *While we were chatting, the shopping cart began to trundle down the aisle. trundling v.*

- **discreetly** (di skrēt´ lē) *adv.* without drawing attention (p. 972) *The candidate avoided embarrassment by discreetly straightening his crooked tie during the debate. discreet adj. discreetness n.*

- **cunning** (kun´ iŋ) *adj.* skilled in deception (p. 972) *The small but cunning animal is usually able to outwit and escape its predators. cunningly adv.*

- **telegraph** (tel´ ə graf´) *n.* an apparatus or system that converts a coded message into electric impulses and sends it to a distant receiver (p. 974) *The telegraph was invented to send messages quickly. telegraph v. telegraphic adj. telegraphically adv.*

### Word Study

The **Latin root -nym-** or **-nom-** means "name."

In this selection, the Inspector-General receives an **anonymous** letter, summoning him to a small town. The letter was *anonymous* because there was no name on it.

# Meet
# Anton Chekhov
## (1860–1904)

## Author of
## The Inspector-General

The grandson of a former serf who had purchased his freedom, Anton Chekhov grew up in a small Russian coastal town. He later attended medical school in Moscow, where he began writing humorous stories. Writing soon became his major focus.

**Passion and Compassion** Chekhov wrote many short stories as well as several acclaimed plays, including *The Seagull* (1896), *Uncle Vanya* (1897), and *The Three Sisters* (1901). His characters range from old peasants to young society women, from those whom life has treated kindly, to those who are disappointed. Chekhov treats them all with respect and sympathy. His humor and ability to portray characters of great depth and authenticity have helped make Chekhov a beloved author.

## BACKGROUND FOR THE PLAY

### Inspectors General

"The Inspector-General" is set in imperial Russia, when the country was ruled by an emperor, or czar. To oversee the many officials in Russia's vast expanse, the czars employed inspectors-general. They observed how local schools, courts, and hospitals were functioning. Many citizens resented the czar's authority, however, and inspectors-general were often unwelcome.

## Did You Know?
**Chekhov married a famous actress, Olga Knipper.**

# The Inspector-General

## Anton Chekhov
### adapted by Michael Frayn

*The curtain goes up to reveal falling snow and a cart facing away from us. Enter the* STORYTELLER, *who begins to read the story. Meanwhile, the* TRAVELER *enters. He is a middle-aged man of urban appearance, wearing dark glasses and a long overcoat with its collar turned up. He is carrying a small traveling bag. He climbs into the cart and sits facing us.*

**STORYTELLER.** The Inspector-General. In deepest incognito, first by express train, then along back roads, Pyotr Pavlovich Posudin[1] was hastening toward the little town of N, to which he had been summoned by an anonymous letter. "I'll take them by surprise," he thought to himself. "I'll come down on them like a thunderbolt out of the blue. I can just imagine their faces when they hear who I am . . ." [*Enter the* DRIVER, *a peasant, who climbs onto the cart, so that he is sitting with his back to us, and the cart begins to trundle slowly away from us.*] And when he'd thought to himself for long enough, he fell into conversation with the driver of the cart. What did he talk about? About himself, of course. [*Exit the* STORYTELLER.]

---

1. **Pyotr Pavlovich Posudin** (pyō' tər päv lō' vich pō syōō' dən)

**Vocabulary**
**incognito** (in' käg nēt' ō) *adj.* with true identity unrevealed or disguised; under an assumed name
**anonymous** (ə nän' ə məs) *adj.* without a known or acknowledged name
**trundle** (trun' dəl) *v.* roll along

**TRAVELER.** I gather you've got a new Inspector-General in these parts.

**DRIVER.** True enough.

**TRAVELER.** Know anything about him? [*The driver turns and looks at the* TRAVELER, *who turns his coat collar up a little higher.*]

**DRIVER.** Know anything about him? Of course we do! We know everything about all of them up there! Every last little clerk—we know the color of his hair and the size of his boots! [*He turns back to the front, and the* TRAVELER *permits himself a slight smile.*]

**TRAVELER.** So, what do you reckon? Any good, is he? [*The* DRIVER *turns around.*]

**DRIVER.** Oh, yes, he's a good one, this one.

**TRAVELER.** Really?

**DRIVER.** Did one good thing straight off.

**TRAVELER.** What was that?

**DRIVER.** He got rid of the last one. Holy terror he was! Hear him coming five miles off! Say he's going to this little town. Somewhere like we're going, say. He'd let all the world know about it a month before. So now he's on his way, say, and it's like thunder and lightning coming down the road. And when he gets where he's going he has a good sleep, he has a good eat and drink— and then he starts. Stamps his feet, shouts his head off. Then he has another good sleep, and off he goes.

**TRAVELER.** But the new one's not like that?

**DRIVER.** Oh, no, the new one goes everywhere on the quiet, like. Creeps around like a cat. Don't want no one to see him, don't want no one to know who he is. Say he's going to this town down the road here. Someone there sent him a letter on the sly, let's say. "Things going on here you should know about." Something of that kind. Well, now, he creeps out of his office, so none of them up there see him go. He hops on a train just like anyone else, just like you or me. Then when he gets off he don't go jumping into a cab or nothing fancy. Oh, no. He wraps himself up from head to toe so you can't see his face, and he wheezes away like an old dog so no one can recognize his voice.

**TRAVELER.** Wheezes? That's not wheezing! That's the way he talks! So I gather.

◀ **Crtical Viewing**
How might the people of a small town like this react to the arrival of an inspector? **[Speculate]**

**Reading Skill**
**Draw Conclusions**
What conclusion about the Inspector-General can you draw from the stage direction that he "permits himself a slight smile"?

**Reading Check**
Why is the Inspector-General traveling to the town?

**DRIVER.** Oh, is it? But the tales they tell about him. You'd laugh till you burst your tripes![2]

**TRAVELER.** [*sourly*]. I'm sure I would.

**DRIVER.** He drinks, mind!

**TRAVELER.** [*startled*]. Drinks?

**DRIVER.** Oh, like a hole in the ground. Famous for it.

**TRAVELER.** He's never touched a drop! I mean, from what I've heard.

**DRIVER.** Oh, not in public, no. Goes to some great ball—"No thank you, not for me." Oh, no, he puts it away at home! Wakes up in the morning, rubs his eyes, and the first thing he does, he shouts, "Vodka!" So in runs his valet with a glass. Fixed himself up a tube behind his desk, he has. Leans down, takes a pull on it, no one the wiser.

**TRAVELER.** [*offended*]. How do you know all this, may I ask?

**DRIVER.** Can't hide it from the servants, can you? The valet and the coachman have got tongues in their heads. Then again, he's on the road, say, going about his business, and he keeps the bottle in his little bag. [*The* TRAVELER *discreetly pushes the traveling bag out of the* DRIVER'S *sight*.] And his housekeeper . . .

**TRAVELER.** What about her?

**DRIVER.** Runs circles around him, she does, like a fox round his tail. She's the one who wears the trousers.[3] The people aren't half so frightened of him as they are of her.

**TRAVELER.** But at least he's good at his job, you say?

**DRIVER.** Oh, he's a blessing from heaven, I'll grant him that.

**TRAVELER.** Very cunning—you were saying.

**DRIVER.** Oh, he creeps around all right.

**TRAVELER.** And then he pounces, yes? I should think some people must get the surprise of their life, mustn't they?

**DRIVER.** No, no—let's be fair, now. Give him his due. He don't make no trouble.

**TRAVELER.** No, I mean, if no one knows he's coming . . .

**DRIVER.** Oh, that's what he thinks, but we all know.

---

2. **tripes** (trīps) *n.* parts of the stomach, usually of an ox or a sheep, when used as food.
3. **wears the trousers** has the greatest authority; is really in charge.

White Night, 1901, Edvard Munch, Photo: J. Lathion ©Nasjonalgalleriet 1997, ©2003 The Munch Museum/The Munch-Ellingsen Group/Artists Rights Society (ARS), NY

**TRAVELER.** You know?

**DRIVER.** Oh, some gentleman gets off the train at the station back there with his greatcoat up to his eyebrows and says, "No, I don't want a cab, thank you, just an ordinary horse and cart for me." Well, we'd put two and two together, wouldn't we! Say it was you, now, creeping along down the road here. The lads would be down there in a cab by now! By the time you got there the whole town would be as regular as clockwork! And you'd think to yourself, "Oh, look at that! As clean as a whistle! And they didn't know I was coming!" No, that's why he's such a blessing after the other one. This one believes it!

**TRAVELER.** Oh, I see.

▲ **Critical Viewing**
How does the countryside depicted in this painting compare to the setting of the play? **[Compare and Contrast]**

© **Spiral Review**
**Character** What does the dialogue reveal about the Inspector-General's character?

The Inspector-General **973**

**Vocabulary**
**telegraph** (tel´ ə graf´)
*n.* an apparatus or sys-
tem that converts a
coded message into elec-
tric impulses and sends
it to a distant receiver

**Reading Skill**
**Drawing Conclusions**
What conclusion can
you draw based on the
Traveler's sudden order
to turn around?

**DRIVER.** What, you thought we wouldn't know him? Why, we've got the electric telegraph these days! Take today, now. I'm going past the station back there this morning, and the fellow who runs the buffet comes out like a bolt of lightning. Arms full of baskets and bottles. "Where are you off to?" I say. "Doing drinks and refreshments for the Inspector-General!" he says, and he jumps into a carriage and goes flying off down the road here. So there's the old Inspector-General, all muffled up like a roll of carpet, going secretly along in a cart somewhere—and when he gets there, nothing to be seen but vodka and cold salmon!

**TRAVELER.** [*shouts*]. Right—turn around, then . . . !

**DRIVER.** [*to the horse*]. Whoa, boy! Whoa! [*To the* TRAVELER.] Oh, so what's this, then? Don't want to go running into the Inspector-General, is that it? [*The* TRAVELER *gestures impatiently for the* DRIVER *to turn the cart around.* DRIVER *to the horse.*] Back we go, then, boy. Home we go. [*He turns the cart around, and the* TRAVELER *takes a swig from his traveling bag.*] Though if I know the old devil, he's like as not turned around and gone home again himself. [*Blackout.*]

## Critical Thinking

Cite textual evidence to support your responses.

ⓒ **1. Key Ideas and Details (a)** What does the Traveler do when the Driver mentions that the Inspector-General keeps a flask of vodka? **(b) Infer:** What does this action tell you about the Traveler?

ⓒ **2. Key Ideas and Details (a)** According to the Driver, what preparations does the town make for the Inspector-General's arrival? **(b) Interpret:** Why does the Driver's account provoke the Traveler's demand to turn around?

ⓒ **3. Craft and Structure (a)** How does the dramatic irony in the story work to create humor? **(b) Analyze:** How might the story be considered an incongruous situation?

ⓒ **4. Integration of Knowledge and Ideas (a)** Why did the Inspector-General want to hide his background? **(b)** How was the driver able to determine the Inspector-General's identity? **[Connect to the Big Question: Do our differences define us?]**

## Literary Analysis: Comedy

© **1. Craft and Structure** Note specific ways in which "The Inspector-General" does or does not meet these criteria for **comedy:** It ends happily; it uses witty dialogue; it presents an incongruous or comic situation; it seeks to amuse.

© **2. Craft and Structure (a)** What information, conveyed by the Storyteller, sets up the **dramatic irony** in "The Inspector-General"? **(b)** Identify an exchange between the Driver and the Traveler that highlights the dramatic irony of the situation.

## Reading Skill: Draw Conclusions

**3.** What **conclusions** can you draw about the character of the Traveler based on the stage directions *sourly, startled,* and *offended* that precede three of his lines?

**4.** What conclusions can you draw about the character of the Driver based on his dialogue with the Traveler? Explain your answer.

**5.** Who do you think is the wiser and cleverer man, the Driver or the Traveler? Explain.

## Vocabulary

© **Acquisition and Use** Indicate whether each statement is *True* or *False.* Explain your answers. Then, revise false sentences to make them true.

**1.** Someone making an *anonymous* donation wants recognition.

**2.** A tricycle is something that might *trundle.*

**3.** The best way to send a message *discreetly* is to shout.

**4.** If a man is *cunning,* he may not always tell the truth.

**5.** Movie stars sometimes travel *incognito* so they can escape notice.

**6.** People once used the *telegraph* to send packages and letters.

**Word Study** Use the context of the sentences and what you know about the **Latin root -nym-** or **-nom-** to explain your answer to each question.

**1.** Is scientific *nomenclature* for different animals hard to remember?

**2.** Do you think someone who is only the *nominal* Inspector-General would fulfill the responsibilities of the job?

### Word Study

The **Latin root -nym-** or **-nom-** means "name."

**Apply It** Explain how the root -nym- or -nom- contributes to the meanings of these words. Consult a dictionary if necessary.

synonym
nominate
misnomer

# Integrated Language Skills

## The Inspector-General

### Conventions: Main and Subordinate Clauses

> A **clause** is a group of words that contains a subject and a verb. It can be a **main** (independent) **clause** or a **subordinate** (dependent) **clause.**

A main clause can stand by itself as a complete sentence. It may be used by itself, be connected to another independent clause, or be connected to a subordinate clause. In contrast, a subordinate clause cannot stand by itself. It needs additional information to make sense. Subordinate clauses can function as noun, adjective, or adverbial clauses. Subordinate clauses include subordinating conjunctions such as _however, although, when, if, after,_ or _because._

| Main Clause | Subordinate Clause |
|---|---|
| The Inspector-General hoped | that someone would speak up. |
| A man got off the train | which was stopped at the station. |
| The cart raced down the road | as fast as the horse could run. |

**Practice A** Identify each of the following as a main or subordinate clause. Then, add to each subordinate clause to make it a complete sentence.

1. when the train stopped
2. after the Inspector-General climbed into the cart
3. the driver turned the cart around
4. he shoved the satchel out of sight

**Reading Application** In "The Inspector-General," find one example of a main clause that stands alone and one example of a subordinate clause.

**Practice B** Combine each of the following pairs of sentences into one sentence by changing one main clause into a subordinate clause.

1. The Inspector-General was a clever man. He dressed in disguise.
2. He thought to himself. He would surprise the townspeople.
3. He came to town. Everyone knew.
4. The driver smiled to himself. The Inspector-General got back on the train.

**Writing Application** Write two sentences about "The Inspector-General" that are made up only of main clauses. Then, write two sentences that include at least one subordinate clause.

**PH WRITING COACH** Further instruction and practice are available in _Prentice Hall Writing Coach._

# Writing

 **Common Core State Standards**

L.9-10.1.b; W.9-10.3,
W.9-10.3.a, W.9-10.3.b,
W.9-10.3.c ,W.9-10.7
[For the wording of the standards, see page 966.]

**Narrative Text** Write a brief **play** in which students outwit a bully. Create *dramatic irony* by including scenes in which the audience knows something the bully does not know.

- Use a realistic school setting and dialogue that sounds true to life.

- Write to entertain and teach without being cruel.

- Make sure that your play includes narrative elements including a conflict and its resolution.

Rehearse your play with classmates and perform it for your class. Use any available props within the classroom to bring your setting to life. Also deliver your dialogue convincingly to convey a true-to-life feeling.

**Grammar Application** Make sure to use main and subordinate clauses correctly as you write your play.

## Writing Workshop: *Work in Progress*

**Prewriting for Research Report** For a research report you may be asked to write, discuss details in "The Inspector-General" drawn from historical research—for example, note details about language, dress, writing, or theatrical practices of the day. Keep these in your portfolio.

Use this prewriting activity to prepare for the **Writing Workshop** on page 1002.

# Research and Technology

**Build and Present Knowledge** Use library and Internet resources to research what life was like in Russia during the rule of the czars, including the role of inspectors-general at that time. Organize your findings in an **informational chart**. Follow these steps:

- Take careful notes and observe which key terms, research tools, and processes help you locate the best information.

- Identify topics to include in your report, such as typical jobs; freedoms; and role of government.

- As you gather details, identify the distinctions between the relative value and significance of the data, facts, and ideas you find. Decide what information is most important and which details may support these larger ideas. Eliminate irrelevant information.

- Make sure the formatting of your chart enhances your information.

- To finalize your work, write an introductory paragraph that explains the purpose of your chart. Then, list your sources. Use a style manual, such as an MLA handbook, for assistance.

# Test Practice: Reading

## Draw Conclusions

### Fiction Selection

**Directions:** *Read the selection. Then, answer the questions.*

It was the summer of 2006, and the Clark High School baseball team was playing in the state championship. Their rivals, the Morristown Tigers, had defeated the Clark Eagles earlier in the season. Jack was going to see the championship game, and he was ecstatic. Although he had played in the first four games of the season with the Eagles, an ankle injury had put him on the sideline for the rest of the season. Now, he couldn't wait to cheer his team on to victory.

Jack made it to his seats just before the game began. The Eagles were the first to score. Then, the Tigers took the lead. Jack was on the edge of his seat. He kept cheering with all his might. His classmate Tony, an out-fielder, tied the score in the sixth inning with a home run. With two runs in the ninth inning, the Eagles won the game and the championship. Jack was surrounded by fans cheering wildly. Jack jumped out of his seat and hurried to the field to congratulate his friends. He could not wait until next year when he would again join his team on the field.

1. What can you conclude based on the fact that the Tigers defeated the Eagles earlier in the season?

   A. The Eagles could lose to the Tigers.
   B. The Eagles are better than the Tigers.
   C. The Tigers are an undefeated team.
   D. The Tigers want to win more than the Eagles.

2. Based on the details in the selection, one can conclude that Jack—

   A. is a student at Clark High School.
   B. has decided to quit baseball.
   C. believes that the Tigers are an unbeatable team.
   D. prefers hockey to baseball.

3. What can you conclude about Jack's feelings about the game?

   A. He was angry he could not play.
   B. His injury prevented him from enjoying the game.
   C. He hoped the Eagles would win.
   D. He wanted to learn the rules of baseball.

4. The fans near Jack cheered wildly because—

   A. they were excited their team had won.
   B. Jack had caught a home run ball.
   C. Tony had just hit a home run.
   D. they were proud of the Tigers.

### Writing for Assessment

What can you conclude were the high and low points for Jack in the game? Write a paragraph in which you support your answer with details.

# Nonfiction Selection

**Directions:** *Read the selection. Then, answer the questions.*

The National Baseball Hall of Fame and Museum, located in Cooperstown, New York, draws many fans of baseball each year. First opened on June 12, 1939, the museum includes artifacts from baseball's past, exhibits on famous players and coaches, and plaques for every member of the hall of fame. Over the years, the museum has changed a great deal. Visits to the museum now begin with "The Baseball Experience," a digitally-enhanced, multimedia experience designed to appeal to baseball fans of all ages. The museum offers more than just entertainment, though; it also includes a research library, utilized by baseball scholars as they study what is often called "America's Favorite Pastime." Whether you want to study baseball or just experience the joy of the sport, a visit to Cooperstown will have a lot to offer you.

1. What can you conclude about the author's perspective on the National Baseball Hall of Fame and Museum?

   A. The author believes it is not worth visiting.
   B. The author is arguing that the museum should close its doors.
   C. The author wants the museum to raise its prices.
   D. The author thinks the museum may appeal to a variety of people.

2. Based on this passage, what conclusion can you draw about the museum?

   A. The museum is not very successful.
   B. Only older people visit the museum.
   C. The hall of fame plaques are the best part of the museum.
   D. The museum highlights different aspects of baseball.

3. Based on the details of the selection, "America's Favorite Pastime" is a nickname for—

   A. museums.
   B. baseball.
   C. research.
   D. multimedia presentations.

4. Based on this selection, what conclusion can you draw about Cooperstown?

   A. Many people visit Cooperstown in order to go to the National Baseball Museum.
   B. Cooperstown should open a new art museum.
   C. People who live in Cooperstown get annoyed with the large number of tourists.
   D. Cooperstown is the capital city of New York State.

## Writing for Assessment

**Connecting Across Texts**
Would Jack enjoy visiting the National Baseball Museum? Explain your answer in a paragraph. Use details from both passages.

**PHLit Online!**
www.PHLitOnline.com
• Online practice
• Instant feedback

# Reading for Information

## Analyzing Expository Texts

### Web Site

### Web Encyclopedia Entry

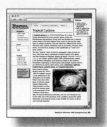

**Common Core State Standards**

**Reading Informational Text**
**3.** Analyze how the author unfolds an analysis or series of ideas or events, including the order in which the points are made, how they are introduced and developed, and the connections that are drawn between them.

**Language**
**6.** Acquire and use accurately grade-appropriate general academic and domain-specific words and phrases.

## Reading Skill: Evaluate Sources

When you **extend the ideas** presented in a text, you consider and build on those ideas. One way to do this is through **evaluating the source**—judging the validity and reliability of the information presented. Extending the ideas in a source will allow you to connect those ideas to other sources on similar issues and draw general conclusions about your topic. Use this checklist to help you evaluate sources.

---

**Evaluating Sources**

- Is the main idea fully supported by the evidence?
- Are the author's arguments logical and valid?
- Does support consist of specific facts?
- Can the evidence presented be verified?
- Is the material presented in an impartial way?
- Who is the author or sponsor of the site?
  - For Web sites, what is the URL ending? (e.g., ".edu" and ".gov" tend to be the most reliable sites)
  - Is the source current?

---

## Content-Area Vocabulary

These words appear in the selections that follow. You may also encounter them in other content-area texts.

- **meteorological** (mē´ tē ər ə loj´ ə kəl) *adj.* related to the science and study of atmosphere and weather

- **atmospheric** (at´ mə sfir´ ik) *adj.* referring to the air that surrounds Earth

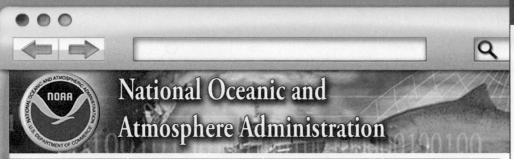

**Features:**

- home page with links to other pages
- informative text for research or leisure reading
- photos or other images

## National Oceanic and Atmosphere Administration

| Home | Contacts | Media | Search |

### Weather Page
Fujita Tornado Damage Scale

**Category F0:** Light Damage (<73 mph); Some damage to chimneys and sign boards, branches broken off trees, shallow-rooted trees pushed over.

**Category F1:** Moderate Damage (73–112 mph); Peels surface off roofs; mobile homes pushed off foundations or overturned; moving autos blown off road.

**Category F2:** Considerable Damage (113–157 mph); Roofs torn off frame houses; mobile homes demolished; boxcars over-turned; large trees snapped or uprooted; light-object missiles generated; cars lifted off ground.

**Category F3:** Severe Damage (158–206 mph); Roofs and some walls torn off well-constructed houses, trains overturned; most trees in forest uprooted; heavy cars lifted off ground and thrown.

**Category F4:** Devastating Damage (207–260 mph); Well-constructed houses leveled; structure with weak foundations blown off some distance; cars thrown and large missiles generated.

**Category F5:** Incredible Damage (261–318 mph); Strong frame houses lifted off foundations and swept away; automobile sized missiles fly through the air in excess of 100 meters (109 yards); trees debarked.

# Tornadoes

Tornadoes are one of nature's most violent storms. In an average year, about 1,000 tornadoes are reported across the United States, resulting in 80 deaths and over 1,500 injuries. A tornado is a violently rotating column of air extending from a thunderstorm to the ground. The most violent tornadoes are capable of tremendous destruction with wind speeds of 250 mph or more. Damage paths can be in excess of one mile wide and 50 miles long.

Tornadoes come in all shapes and sizes and can occur anywhere in the U.S. at any time of the year. In the southern states, peak tornado season is March through May, while peak months in the northern states are during the summer.

### Preparedness Guides

- Are you prepared for <u>Nature's Most Violent Storms</u>? A preparedness guide including safety information for schools prepared by the National Weather Service, FEMA and the American Red Cross.
- <u>Thunderstorms and Camping Safety</u>
- <u>Weather Safety for Kids</u> - Owlie Skywarn's Weather Book about Tornadoes

> You can extend ideas presented on this text by following links to other Web pages.

## More Info

- <u>Weather Glossary for Storm Spotters</u>
- <u>Storm Reports</u> - includes monthly tornado statistics, deadly tornadoes, current severe weather reports and more from the National Weather Service's Storm Prediction Center.
- <u>Tornadoes of the 20th Century</u> - a list of the more notable tornado out-breaks that occurred in the U.S. during the 20th century.

Owlie's
Front Page

View My Safety
Tips About . . .

Tornadoes
  Watches
  Warnings

Lightning

Flash Floods

Hurricanes

Winter Weather

Carbon Monoxide

## National Weather Service

Owlie Skywarn's Weather Book
Watch Out...Storms Ahead!

# TORNADO!

If you ever see a big black cloud with a funnel-like extension beneath it, watch out. It could be a tornado.

A tornado looks like a funnel with the fat part at the top. Inside it, winds may be swirling around at 3,000 miles per hour. If it goes through a town, the tornado could flatten houses and buildings, lift up cars and trucks, shatter mobile homes into splinters. Sometimes the path is narrow, but everything in the path gets wrecked. But you don't always see the funnel. It may be raining too hard. Or the tornado may come at night. Listen for the tornado's roar. Some people say it sounds like a thousand trains.

## What to do if...

**You are in your house**    **You are downtown or in a shopping mall**    **You are outside**

**You are in school**    **You are in a mobile home**    **In Conclusion...**

Last updated June 22, 20__

The Web site indicates how recently its information was updated.

Educators and students should send their questions to the NOAA outreach team.

# WIKIPEDIA
### The Free Encyclopedia

**Navigation**
- Main Page
- Contents
- Current Events
- Random Article

**Search**

[ ]

(GO)

**Toolbox**
- Upload File
- Add to File
- Special Pages
- Cite this Page

The entry presents specific facts about the behavior of tropical cyclones.

| Article | Discussion | Edit Article | History |

**Features:**
- online access
- photographs or illustrations
- links to related topics and Web sites
- text written for a general audience

# Tropical Cyclone

A **tropical cyclone** is a **meteorological** term for a storm system characterized by a low pressure system center and thunderstorms that produces strong wind and flooding rain. A tropical cyclone feeds on the heat released when moist air rises and the water vapor it contains condenses. They are fueled by a different heat mechanism than other cyclonic windstorms such as nor'easters, European windstorms, and polar lows, leading to their classification as "warm core" storm systems.

The term "tropical" refers to both the geographic origin of these systems, which form almost exclusively in tropical regions of the globe, and their formation in Maritime Tropical air masses. The term "cyclone" refers to such storms' cyclonic nature, with counterclockwise rotation in the Northern Hemisphere and clockwise rotation in the Southern Hemisphere. Depending on their location and strength, tropical cyclones are referred to by various other names, such as **hurricane, typhoon, tropical storm, cyclonic storm,** and **tropical depression.**

Many tropical cyclones develop when the **atmospheric** conditions around a weak disturbance in the atmosphere are favorable. Others form when other types of cyclones acquire tropical characteristics. Tropical systems are then moved by steering winds in the troposphere; if the conditions remain favorable, the tropical disturbance intensifies, and can even develop an eye. On the other end of the spectrum, if the conditions around the system deteriorate or the tropical cyclone makes landfall, the system weakens and eventually dissipates.

This section describes the criteria the sponsors use to judge what entry information is included in this Web encyclopedia.

You can extend the ideas presented here about the reputations of third-party sources and connect them to the Web site on pages 981–982.

# Wikipedia: Verifiability

The threshold for inclusion in Wikipedia is **verifiability, not truth.** "Verifiable" in this context means that readers should be able to check that material added to Wikipedia has already been published by a reliable source. Editors should provide a reliable source for quotations and for any material that is challenged or is likely to be challenged, or it may be removed.

## Burden of evidence

The burden of evidence lies with the editor who adds or restores material. All quotations and any material **challenged or likely to be challenged** should be attributed to a reliable, published source using an inline citation. The source should be cited clearly and precisely to enable readers to find the text that supports the article content in question.

## Sources

Articles should rely on reliable, third-party published sources with a reputation for fact-checking and accuracy. Reliable sources are necessary both to substantiate material within articles and to give credit to authors and publishers in order to avoid plagiarism and copyright violations. Sources should directly support the information as it is presented in an article and should be appropriate to the claims made: exceptional claims require exceptional sources.

All articles must adhere to Wikipedia's neutrality policy, fairly representing all majority and significant-minority viewpoints that have been published by reliable sources, in rough proportion to the prominence of each view. Tiny-minority views and fringe theories need not be included, except in articles devoted to them.

In general, the most reliable sources are peer-reviewed journals and books published in university presses; university-level textbooks; magazines, journals, and books published by respected publishing houses; and mainstream newspapers.

## Comparing Expository Texts

© **1. Integration of Knowledge and Ideas (a) Evaluate** the Web site and the Web encyclopedia entry by comparing and contrasting their reliability as sources on types of extreme weather. **(b)** Which source do you judge to be more reliable? Explain.

### Content-Area Vocabulary

**2. (a)** Explain the parts of speech and meanings of the following words: *meteorology, meteorologically, meteoric, meteoroid.* **(b)** Use each word in a sentence that shows its meaning.

## Timed Writing

**Argument: Evaluation**

> **Format**
> The prompt directs you to write an evaluation. Therefore, your response should include observations and judgments about the elements mentioned in the prompt.

Write an evaluation of the Web encyclopedia entry as a source for research about tropical cyclones. Assess the usefulness of the information presented, and draw conclusions about its validity and reliability. Use details and examples from the text to support your evaluations and conclusions. (30 minutes)

> **Academic Vocabulary**
> When you *assess,* you make a determination about something's value.

### 5-Minute Planner

Complete these steps before you begin to write:

**1.** Read the prompt carefully and completely. Look at the highlighted words to help you understand the assignment.

**2.** Review the Web encyclopedia entry on tropical cyclones. Note details that help you understand the subject. Decide how useful the information in the entry would be if you were researching tropical cyclones.

**3.** Review the Web encyclopedia's statement regarding the verifiability of information on the site. Based on that statement, decide whether you think the information in the entry is completely reliable. **TIP Extend ideas** presented in the statement on verifiability by considering whether information in the entry could be verified using another reliable source.

**4.** Make notes and create a rough outline for your evaluation. Then, refer to your outline as you draft your response.

## Comparing Satire

**Satire** is writing that exposes and makes fun of the foolishness and faults of an individual, an institution, a society, or a situation. Although a satire may make readers laugh, it may also aim to correct the flaws that it criticizes. Some satires address serious social problems, while others explore less important subjects. Satirical writings vary in style and tone, level of *subtlety,* and the writer's attitude toward the subject and the audience. A satire may have the following characteristics:

- It may be gentle and sympathetic or angry and bitter in tone.

- It might use *sarcasm* or *irony*—language that means the opposite of what it says.

- It may exaggerate faults to make them both funny and obvious.

In addition, the perspective of the satirist plays a key role. Some satirists write as outside onlookers, while others include themselves as objects of the satire. Skilled satirists reveal their targets with subtleties in the text rather than elements that are overly obvious.

As you read these selections, answer questions like those in the chart to better understand and evaluate the satire in each one.

> ### Questions About Satire
>
> **Subject**
> - What or whom is ridiculed?
> - Is the topic serious or trivial?
> - Does the writer include him- or herself as an object of the satire?
>
> **Tone**
> - Is the tone gentle or harsh?
> - Does the writer use sarcasm or irony?
>
> **Purpose**
> - Is the satire funny?
> - Does the satirist want to correct the flaws he/she exposes?

 **Common Core State Standards**

**Reading Literature**
**4.** Determine the meaning of words and phrases as they are used in the text, including figurative and connotative meanings; analyze the cumulative impact of specific word choices on meaning and tone.

**Writing**
**2.** Write informative/explanatory texts to examine and convey complex ideas, concepts, and information clearly and accurately through the effective selection, organization, and analysis of content.
**2.a.** Intoduce a topic; organize complex ideas, concepts, and information to make important connections and distinctions.
**2.b.** Develop the topic with well-chosen, relevant, and sufficient facts, extended definitions, concrete details, quotations, or other information and examples appropriate to the audience's knowledge of the topic.

**PHLit Online!**
www.PHLitOnline.com

- Vocabulary flashcards
- Interactive journals
- More about the authors

- Selection audio
- Interactive graphic organizers

# Do our *differences* define us?

## Writing About the Big Question

Both these selections use people's differences to satirize an element of life or society. Use this sentence starter to develop your ideas about the Big Question.

When writers expose what is foolish in society, we can learn that our **differences** _____.

# Meet the Authors

## Oscar Wilde (1854–1900)

### Author of *The Importance of Being Earnest*

Oscar Wilde was educated in Dublin and at Oxford University, where he became notorious for his wit. While he wrote poems and celebrated works of fiction, it was in his plays that Wilde's genius found its voice.

**The Importance of Being Funny** In a series of brilliant comedies, including *A Woman of No Importance* and *An Ideal Husband*, Wilde targeted the strait-laced manners and hypocrisy of English society in the 1890s. His masterpiece is *The Importance of Being Earnest*, a drama about Victorian values that still entertains audiences today.

## Henry Alford (b. 1962)

### Author of *Big Kiss*

Henry Alford calls himself an "investigative humorist," a comic journalist who unearths humor wherever it hides. Armed with dry wit and charm, he uncovers what makes popular culture funny, amazing, or outrageous.

**Comic Escapades** *Big Kiss: One Actor's Desperate Attempt to Claw His Way to the Middle* chronicles Alford's adventures as he tries to become an actor. He faces humiliation at the hands of acting teachers and directors, but he relishes his minor victory as an extra in *Godzilla*.

*from*

# The Importance of Being Earnest

## Oscar Wilde

The following excerpt is from Act I of *The Importance of Being Earnest*. The play takes place in England in the 1890s, during the reign of Queen Victoria, a time when elegance, manners, and social status were of great importance. In this scene, John Worthing, nicknamed Jack, visits the London apartment of his friend Algernon. Jack loves Algernon's cousin, Gwendolen. In order to maintain his spotless reputation at his home in the country, Jack takes on a different identity when he is in the city. When he is out in the country, he pretends to have a brother named Ernest, and when he visits London, Jack pretends to be Ernest. Gwendolen knows nothing about Jack's real name or his double identity.

## CHARACTERS

John Worthing, JP                    Algernon
Lady Bracknell
Hon. Gwendolen Fairfax

LADY BRACKNELL *and* ALGERNON *go into the music room,* GWENDOLEN *remains behind.*

**JACK.** Charming day it has been, Miss Fairfax.

**GWENDOLEN.** Pray don't talk to me about the weather, Mr Worthing. Whenever people talk to me about the weather, I always feel quite certain that they mean something else. And that makes me so nervous.

**JACK.** I do mean something else.

**GWENDOLEN.** I thought so. In fact, I am never wrong.

**JACK.** And I would like to be allowed to take advantage of Lady Bracknell's temporary absence. . . .

**GWENDOLEN.** I would certainly advise you to do so. Mamma has a way of coming back suddenly into a room that I have often had to speak to her about.

**JACK.** *(nervously)* Miss Fairfax, ever since I met you I have admired you more than any girl . . . I have ever met since . . . I met you.

**GWENDOLEN.** Yes, I am quite aware of the fact. And I often wish that in public, at any rate, you had been more demonstrative. For me you have always had an irresistible fascination. Even before I met you I was far from indifferent to you. *(Jack looks at her in amazement)* We live, as I hope you know, Mr Worthing, in an age of ideals. The fact is constantly mentioned in the more expensive monthly magazines, and has reached the provincial pulpits I am told; and my ideal has always been to love someone of the name of Ernest. There is something in that name that inspires absolute confidence. The moment Algernon first mentioned to me that he had a friend called Ernest, I knew I was destined to love you.

**JACK.** You really love me, Gwendolen?

**GWENDOLEN.** Passionately!

**JACK.** Darling! You don't know how happy you've made me.

> **Literary Analysis**
> **Satire** Which words here make fun of Gwendolen's haughtiness?

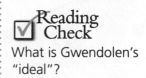

> **Reading Check**
> What is Gwendolen's "ideal"?

◀ **Critical Viewing** Judging from the actor playing Jack in this photograph, what do you think Jack will be like? **[Predict]**

**GWENDOLEN.** My own Ernest!

**JACK.** But you don't really mean to say that you couldn't love me if my name wasn't Ernest?

**GWENDOLEN.** But your name is Ernest.

**JACK.** Yes, I know it is. But supposing it was something else? Do you mean to say you couldn't love me then?

**GWENDOLEN.** (*glibly*) Ah! that is clearly a metaphysical speculation, and like most metaphysical speculations has very little reference at all to the actual facts of real life, as we know them.

**JACK.** Personally, darling, to speak quite candidly, I don't much care about the name Ernest. . . . I don't think the name suits me at all.

**GWENDOLEN.** It suits you perfectly. It is a divine name. It has music of its own. It produces vibrations.

**JACK.** Well, really, Gwendolen, I must say that I think there are lots of other much nicer names. I think Jack, for instance, a charming name.

**GWENDOLEN.** Jack? . . . No, there is very little music in the name Jack, if any at all, indeed. It does not thrill. It produces absolutely no vibrations. . . . I have known several Jacks, and they all, without exception, were more than usually plain. Besides, Jack is a notorious domesticity for John! And I pity any woman who is married to a man called John. She would probably never be allowed to know the entrancing pleasure of a single moment's solitude. The only really safe name is Ernest.

**JACK.** Gwendolen, I must get christened at once—I mean we must get married at once. There is no time to be lost.

**GWENDOLEN.** Married, Mr Worthing?

**JACK.** (*astounded*) Well . . . surely. You know that I love you, and you led me to believe, Miss Fairfax, that you were not absolutely indifferent to me.

---

**Literary Analysis**
**Satire** What is ironic about Gwendolen's fascination with the name Ernest and her feelings for Jack?

▶ **Critical Viewing**
How would you describe the expression on Jack's face in the image at right? **[Describe]**

**GWENDOLEN.** I adore you. But you haven't proposed to me yet. Nothing has been said at all about marriage. The subject has not even been touched on.

**JACK.** Well . . . may I propose to you now?

**GWENDOLEN.** I think it would be an admirable opportunity. And to spare you any possible disappointment, Mr Worthing, I think it only fair to tell you quite frankly beforehand that I am fully determined to accept you.

**JACK.** Gwendolen!

**GWENDOLEN.** Yes, Mr Worthing, what have you got to say to me?

**JACK.** You know what I have got to say to you.

**GWENDOLEN.** Yes, but you don't say it.

**JACK.** Gwendolen, will you marry me? *(Goes on his knees)*

**GWENDOLEN.** Of course I will, darling. How long you have been about it! I am afraid you have had very little experience in how to propose.

**JACK.** My own one, I have never loved anyone in the world but you.

**GWENDOLEN.** Yes, but men often propose for practice. I know my brother Gerald does. All my girlfriends tell me so. What wonderfully blue eyes you have, Ernest! They are quite, quite blue. I hope you will always look at me just like that, especially when there are other people present.

*(Enter LADY BRACKNELL)*

**LADY BRACKNELL.** Mr Worthing! Rise, sir, from this semi-recumbent posture. It is most indecorous.

**GWENDOLEN.** Mamma! *(He tries to rise; she restrains him)* I must beg you to retire. This is no place for you. Besides, Mr Worthing has not quite finished yet.

**LADY BRACKNELL.** Finished what, may I ask?

**GWENDOLEN.** I am engaged to Mr Worthing, mamma.

*(They rise together)*

**LADY BRACKNELL.** Pardon me, you are not engaged to anyone. When you do become engaged to someone, I, or your father, should his health permit him, will inform you of the fact. An engagement should come on a young girl as a surprise, pleasant or unpleasant, as the case may be. It is hardly a matter that she could be allowed to arrange for herself. . . . And now I have a few questions to put to you, Mr Worthing. While I am making these inquiries, you, Gwendolen, will wait for me below in the carriage.

**GWENDOLEN.** *(reproachfully)* Mamma!

**Literary Analysis**
**Satire** What does Lady Bracknell's use of elaborate expressions suggest about her character?

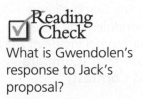

**Reading Check**

What is Gwendolen's response to Jack's proposal?

**LADY BRACKNELL.** In the carriage, Gwendolen!

*GWENDOLEN goes to the door. She and JACK blow kisses to each other behind LADY BRACKNELL'S back. LADY BRACKNELL looks vaguely about as if she could not understand what the noise was. Finally turns round*

Gwendolen, the carriage!

**GWENDOLEN.** Yes, mamma.

*Goes out, looking back at JACK*

**LADY BRACKNELL.** *(sitting down)* You can take a seat, Mr Worthing. *(Looks in her pocket for note-book and pencil)*

**JACK.** Thank you, Lady Bracknell, I prefer standing.

**LADY BRACKNELL.** *(pencil and note-book in hand)* I feel bound to tell you that you are not down on my list of eligible young men, although I have the same list as the dear Duchess of Bolton has. We work together, in fact. However, I am quite ready to enter your name, should your answers be what a really affectionate mother requires. How old are you?

**JACK.** Twenty-nine.

**LADY BRACKNELL.** A very good age to be married at. I have always been of opinion that a man who desires to get married should know either everything or nothing. Which do you know?

**JACK.** *(after some hesitation)* I know nothing, Lady Bracknell.

**LADY BRACKNELL.** I am pleased to hear it. I do not approve of anything that tampers with natural ignorance. Ignorance is like a delicate exotic fruit; touch it and the bloom is gone. The whole theory of modern education is radically unsound. Fortunately in England, at any rate, education produces no effect whatsoever. If it did, it would prove a serious danger to the upper classes, and probably lead to acts of violence in Grosvenor Square. What is your income?

**JACK.** Between seven and eight thousand a year.

**LADY BRACKNELL.** *(makes a note in her book)* In land, or in investments?

**JACK.** In investments, chiefly.

**LADY BRACKNELL.** That is satisfactory. What between the duties expected of one during one's lifetime, and the duties exacted from one after one's death, land has ceased to be either a profit or a pleasure. It gives one position, and prevents one from keeping it up. That's all that can be said about land.

**JACK.** I have a country house with some land, of course, attached to it, about fifteen hundred acres, I believe; but I don't depend

---

**Literary Analysis**
**Satire** Is Lady Bracknell truly "a really affectionate mother"? Explain.

**Vocabulary**
**ignorance** (ig′ nə rəns) *n.* lack of knowledge

▶ **Critical Viewing**
How do these actresses' portrayals of Lady Bracknell and Gwendolen compare to your mental image of the characters? **[Compare and Contrast]**

on that for my real income. In fact, as far as I can make out, the poachers are the only people who make anything out of it.

**LADY BRACKNELL.** A country house! How many bedrooms? Well, that point can be cleared up afterwards. You have a town house, I hope? A girl with a simple, unspoiled nature, like Gwendolen, could hardly be expected to reside in the country.

**JACK.** Well, I own a house in Belgrave Square, but it is let by the year to Lady Bloxham. Of course, I can get it back whenever I like, at six months' notice.

**LADY BRACKNELL.** Lady Bloxham? I don't know her.

**JACK.** Oh, she goes about very little. She is a lady considerably advanced in years.

**LADY BRACKNELL.** Ah, nowadays that is no guarantee of respectability of character. What number in Belgrave Square?

**JACK.** 149.

**LADY BRACKNELL.** *(shaking her head)* The unfashionable side. I thought there was something. However, that could easily be altered.

**JACK.** Do you mean the fashion, or the side?

**LADY BRACKNELL.** *(sternly)* Both, if necessary, I presume. What are your politics?

**JACK.** Well, I am afraid I really have none. I am a Liberal Unionist.

**LADY BRACKNELL.** Oh, they count as Tories. They dine with us. Or come in the evening, at any rate. Now to minor matters. Are your parents living?

**JACK.** I have lost both my parents.

**LADY BRACKNELL.** Both? . . . That seems like carelessness. Who was your father?

**Literary Analysis**
**Satire** Does Gwendolen really have a "simple, unspoiled, nature"? Explain.

**Spiral Review**
**Character** What do you learn about Lady Bracknell's character from her comments about the house in Belgrave Square?

**Reading Check**
What kind of list does Lady Bracknell keep?

He was evidently a man of some wealth. Was he born in what the Radical papers call the purple of commerce, or did he rise from the ranks of the aristocracy?

**JACK.** I am afraid I really don't know. The fact is, Lady Bracknell, I said I had lost my parents. It would be nearer the truth to say that my parents seem to have lost me. . . . I don't actually know who I am by birth. I was . . . well, I was found.

**LADY BRACKNELL.** Found!

**JACK.** The late Mr Thomas Cardew, an old gentleman of a very charitable and kindly disposition, found me, and gave me the name of Worthing, because he happened to have a first-class ticket for Worthing in his pocket at the time. Worthing is a place in Sussex. It is a seaside resort.

**LADY BRACKNELL.** Where did the charitable gentleman who had a first-class ticket for this seaside resort find you?

**JACK.** (*gravely*) In a hand-bag.

**LADY BRACKNELL.** A hand-bag?

**JACK.** (*very seriously*) Yes, Lady Bracknell. I was in a hand-bag— a somewhat large, black leather handbag, with handles to it— an ordinary hand-bag in fact.

**LADY BRACKNELL.** In what locality did this Mr James, or Thomas, Cardew come across this ordinary hand-bag?

**JACK.** In the cloak-room at Victoria Station. It was given to him in mistake for his own.

**LADY BRACKNELL.** The cloak-room at Victoria Station?

**JACK.** Yes. The Brighton line.

**LADY BRACKNELL.** The line is immaterial. Mr Worthing, I confess I feel somewhat bewildered by what you have just told me. To be born, or at any rate bred, in a hand-bag, whether it had handles or not, seems to me to display a contempt for the ordinary decencies of family life that reminds one of the worst excesses of the French Revolution. And I presume you know what that unfortunate movement led to? As for the particular locality in which the hand-bag was found, a cloak-room at a railway station might serve to conceal a social indiscretion—has probably, indeed, been used for that purpose before now—but it could hardly be regarded as an assured basis for a recognized position in good society.

**JACK.** May I ask you then what you would advise me to do? I need hardly say I would do anything in the world to ensure Gwendolen's happiness.

**Literary Analysis**
**Satire** How does Jack's explanation of being "found" make fun of the Victorian value of proper lineage and family ties?

**Literary Analysis**
**Satire** Explain how Lady Bracknell's use of exaggeration adds to the satire.

**LADY BRACKNELL.** I would strongly advise you, Mr Worthing, to try and acquire some relations as soon as possible, and to make a definite effort to produce at any rate one parent, of either sex, before the season is quite over.

**JACK.** Well, I don't see how I could possibly manage to do that. I can produce the hand-bag at any moment. It is in my dressing-room at home. I really think that should satisfy you, Lady Bracknell.

**LADY BRACKNELL.** Me, sir! What has it to do with me? You can hardly imagine that I and Lord Bracknell would dream of allowing our only daughter—a girl brought up with the utmost care—to marry into a cloak-room, and form an alliance with a parcel? Good morning, Mr Worthing!

*Lady Bracknell sweeps out in majestic indignation*

**JACK.** Good morning! (ALGERNON, *from the other room, strikes up the Wedding March.* JACK *looks perfectly furious, and goes to the door)* For goodness' sake don't play that ghastly tune, Algy! How idiotic you are!

**Literary Analysis**
**Satire** How does Lady Bracknell's final demand add to the satire?

## Critical Thinking

*Cite textual evidence to support your responses.*

1. **Key Ideas and Details (a)** How does Gwendolen respond to Jack's proposal? **(b) Infer:** How would you describe Gwendolen's feelings for Jack?

2. **Key Ideas and Details (a)** According to Lady Bracknell, how should a young girl learn she is engaged? **(b) Infer:** What do Lady Bracknell's remarks suggest about Victorian attitudes toward marriage and family?

3. **Key Ideas and Details (a) Summarize:** Write a summary of the personal information that Lady Bracknell needs from Jack. **(b) Interpret:** In what ways does Lady Bracknell find Jack both acceptable and unacceptable as a possible husband? **(c) Assess:** Based on her judgment of Jack, describe Lady Bracknell's character.

4. **Integration of Knowledge and Ideas (a) Interpret:** What values does Lady Bracknell hold dear? Explain. **(b) Compare and Contrast:** How do you think Lady Bracknell's values compare to the values of most people today?

5. **Integration of Knowledge and Ideas (a)** Which qualities in Jack are most important to Gwendolen and her mother? **(b)** What do you think the author suggests is more important than these differences? Support your answer. *[Connect to the Big Question: Do our differences define us?]*

# from BIG KISS

## ONE ACTOR'S ATTEMPT TO CLAW HIS WAY TO THE MIDDLE

### Henry Alford

In the acting profession, as in life, you must make the most of your tiny allotment. He who waits until he has been cast as Othello to pull out all the stops is setting himself up for disappointment—it will be Othello, not Desdemona,[1] who is strangled in this production. So when a classmate told me she was helping to cast extras for the remake of *Godzilla,* I quickly recommended myself for duty. I clearly had not slayed them at improv camp in Wisconsin; here was an opportunity to channel my feelings of disappointment into bravura acting. And perhaps, in so doing, to achieve every extra's dream: to be awarded a line of dialogue.

My classmate called me two days later and said that the filming, to be done that Sunday, would involve prodigious amounts of stage rain. I assured her that I was no stranger to adverse meteorological conditions, natural and man-made, and, as such, could "play wet." The pay for non-Screen Actors Guild[2] talent was seventy-five dollars; I needed to be available all day and night. I was to wear a raincoat and carry a black umbrella.

The harbinger[3] of location shooting in a metropolitan area is a table on the sidewalk, heaped high with haggard bagels. When

**Literary Analysis**
**Satire** Which details make Alford's role as an extra sound important?

---

1. **Othello . . . Desdemona** In Shakespeare's play, Othello kills his wife, Desdemona, because he believes she had an affair. He later discovers she had been faithful, and his grief causes him to kill himself.
2. **Screen Actors Guild** (SAG) labor union for performers.
3. **harbinger** (här´ bin jər) *n.* something that comes before to give an indication of what follows.

I arrived at the appointed location in the Financial District that Sunday morning at six-thirty, although the chaos I found there—Teamsters[4] bickering over sports scores, thick black cables veining the streets as if to depict the late stages of arteriosclerosis—had all the earmarks of filmmaking, I did not see the telltale breadstuffs and so was moved to ask the first walkie-talkie-wielding individual I saw, "Where are the bagels?"

"Are you SAG or non-SAG?" she asked.

"Non."

"You're in the tent."

She pointed to a huge, dun-colored tent around which loitered hundreds of men and women, many of whom were also wearing raincoats and carrying umbrellas. "My people," I exclaimed. I walked over to the tent and, seeing a line formed at one of the twenty or so tables thereunder, queued up. Four minutes later the casting people had checked my name off on a list and I had been given a voucher, the form by which I would be paid.

All was actor-clogged; I could barely find an empty seat at a table. I was glad I finally did—we proceeded to wait for two hours. During this time, small groups of us were presented to a young, unshaven man from Wardrobe who was, by turns, exhausted and sniffy. He looked at the camouflage cap that the fortysomething gentleman ahead of me in line was wearing and said, "I don't know anyone who would wear that cap." Then he scanned me—that is to say, my tan raincoat, my black umbrella, and my wingtips encased in black rubbers—and yawned, "You're fine."

Shortly thereafter we were herded down to the set in groups of thirty or forty. The set was Federal Hall, the majestic site of George Washington's inauguration, rich in Corinthian columns and impressive stairways, which dead-ends Broad Street in the manner of a lion's gaping jaws. Halfway up its main stairs was a podium, festooned with red, white, and blue bunting and a sign reading RE-ELECT MAYOR EBERT. I wondered aloud, "Where's the reptile?"

The self-appointed expert in my group explained, "They're gonna blue-screen[5] him in later."

We lined up on the sidewalk and then, one by one, walked through a small, cordoned-off area where a sweet, pale, bespectacled man was handing out props. It looked like about a third of the extras were being given still cameras and two thirds were being given placards reading RE-ELECT EBERT.

"I hope I get a camera," the woman standing behind me in line said.

---

4. **Teamsters** (tēm´ stərz) *n.* members of a large labor union for truck drivers and other occupations.
5. **blue-screen** *v.* film against a blue background, in order to apply special effects later.

**Spiral Review**
**Character** What do the details in this paragraph reveal about the narrator?

**Literary Analysis**
**Satire** What does the word "herded" convey about the experience of extras?

**Reading Check**
What instructions does Alford's friend give him?

Eager to be filmed shooting at Godzilla, I responded, "I hope I get a Taser."

Moments later I was handed three props—a fake 35-millimeter camera, a fanny pack, and a press badge. I looked at the badge. The first thing I noticed was that the photo on it was of the man who had just handed it to me. Hovering over the photo was the name Sean Haworth and the call letters WAQR. These call letters sounded more like radio than TV to me; but then why was I carrying a still camera?

Rather than let this seeming contradiction bother me, I decided to base my character interpretation on it. What if Sean Haworth labored under the impression that if he took a good enough photograph it would be aired on the radio? Wouldn't this, character-wise, raise the stakes, and imbue him with the driven quality that makes for an interesting dramatic character? Poor Sean, you can almost hear the editorial staff at WAQR whispering over the water cooler. If only he understood that ours is an aural medium.

But five minutes later an assistant director who had assembled about a hundred of us in front of Federal Hall took away my camera.

"I based my character interpretation on that!" I exclaimed, hoping that this would translate to him as "Serious actor. Could handle a line of dialogue."

"I need it for up front," he reported tersely, then walked to the front of the crowd.

One of my fellow colleagues—a vivacious English as a Second Language tutor and sometime actress in her early thirties with whom I had fallen into conversation back in the tent—witnessed my loss of camera and counseled, "You were probably overpropped anyway."

"Yes," I responded, "my work was getting proppy."

We proceeded to work for almost eleven hours, lunch break included, on variations of a single shot. In it, about four hundred of us New Yorkers are standing in the rain, listening to Mayor Ebert (Michael Lerner) give a speech. All of a sudden, we hear a thump. Some of the crowd—those born between January and April, to be precise—look behind them, down Broad Street, whence the sound originates. The mayor continues to netter on when thump! May through August now look down the street, too, expressing restlessness, a sense of discomfort, the vague possibility that this little piece of earth they call their own will soon be rent asunder.

## Media Connection

### Recipe for a Monster

He's big, he's green, he's mean, and his breath is radioactive. Godzilla—named "Gojira" in his native Japan—has been stomping on Tokyo since 1954, when he made his movie debut. A dinosaur transformed into a giant monster as the result of atomic testing, Godzilla's appearance was created by scientists and sculptors using the ingredients below.

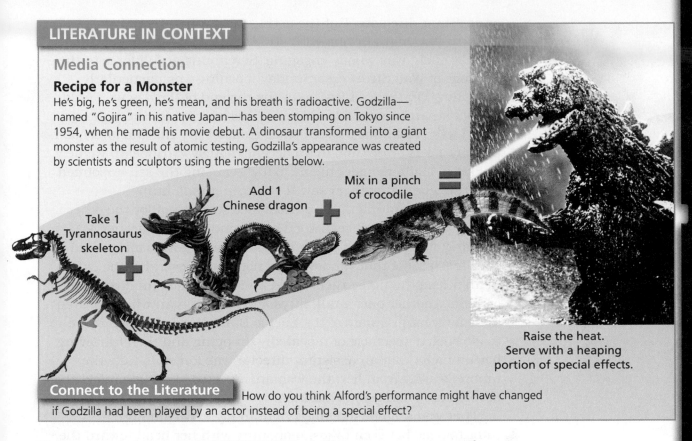

Take 1 Tyrannosaurus skeleton

Add 1 Chinese dragon

Mix in a pinch of crocodile

Raise the heat.
Serve with a heaping portion of special effects.

**Connect to the Literature** How do you think Alford's performance might have changed if Godzilla had been played by an actor instead of being a special effect?

Then seconds later a third THUMP!: Godzilla appears, causing the crowd, regardless of natal season, to shriek with abandon, perhaps to drop umbrellas or placards, and to run off in a prescribed direction.

Since I was born in February, my prescribed direction was straight ahead, up the thirty or so stairs of Federal Hall. So, hearing my thump, I would look behind me down Broad Street in highly nuanced, ever-burgeoning panic; erupt into a despair-tinged, Edvard Munch-calibre scream[6] on hearing the third thump; run northward, negotiating my way through what was, by now, a very festival of bad acting; ascend the stairs two at a time; look behind me again while closing my umbrella (note the elegant adherence to decorum, even in the face of apocalypse); and then hurl my body against Federal Hall's massive stone doors in an attempt to gain entry.

I loved this work. I would be hard-pressed to recount any event from my personal or professional life that more accurately typified the phrase crazy fun. Yes, my colleagues and I encountered much wetness; the rain machines were assiduous in their ministrations. Moreover, no lines of dialogue were being doled out by the director

**Vocabulary**
**assiduous** (ə sijˊ o͞o əs)
*adj.* done with constant and careful attention

Reading
Check

How do the film-makers divide the crowd of extras into groups?

---

6. **Edvard Munch-calibre scream** an outcry with the intensity of *The Scream*, a famous painting by Norwegian artist Edvard Munch [munk] (1863–1944), which shows a person screaming.

or assistant directors. But the acting task at hand wedded blitzkrieg-strength drama with stuntman-strength athleticism and, as such, was wholly engaging. Screaming at full force in the canyons of Wall Street on a Sunday morning was particularly liberating. On the first few takes (by the end of the day we would do more than twenty) I would yell, "There he is!" By the eighth take I was screaming, "Here comes trouble!" By the late afternoon, punchy, I was shrieking, in an accent vaguely Caribbean, vaguely Cockney, "'Zilla monster ate me baby!" causing the self-appointed expert to glare at me and say, "Let's keep it real, huh?"

This statement might have chastened were it not for the other extras. Seldom have I seen such a preponderance of scenery-chewing; my colleagues' every utterance and movement seemed to offer ready proof that vaudeville[7] is not dead. Several of the extras, in an attempt to make themselves noticed, would run directly at the camera. Another one, a tall, fiftysomething woman who appeared to be a recent graduate of the Lucille Ball School of Clown Makeup, made such a spectacle of repeatedly dropping and then retrieving her umbrella that an assistant director was forced to take the umbrella away from her; the woman, divested of her gimmick, then devoted her energies to shrieking.

"That woman just screamed right in my eardrum," the ESL tutor told me between takes, motioning with her head toward the offender.

"Yes," I acknowledged, "her work is particularly broad."

---

**7. vaudeville** (vôd′ vil) old-fashioned stage shows of mixed specialty acts, including songs, dances, and comic skits.

## Critical Thinking

**Cite textual evidence to support your responses.**

1. **Key Ideas and Details** **(a)** According to Alford's opening paragraph, what is every extra's dream? **(b) Analyze:** Even though his dream does not come true, does he still feel his experience was worthwhile? Explain.

2. **Key Ideas and Details** **(a)** What are Alford and the other extras required to do during the scene? **(b) Generalize:** What do they actually do? **(c) Analyze:** Why do they do so much more than required?

3. **Integration of Knowledge and Ideas** **(a)** What tricks do the extras try to make themselves "different" for the camera? **(b)** How do these tricks backfire? **(c)** What or whom do you think the author is mocking, or making fun of? Explain. *[Connect to the Big Question: Do our differences define us?]*

## Comparing Satire

**©** **1. Craft and Structure (a)** Use a chart like the one shown to identify elements of satire in both *The Importance of Being Earnest* and *Big Kiss*. **(b)** Explain specific ways in which both selections use humor to expose people's foolishness or flaws.

| Selection | Subject of the Satire | Foolishness or Faults Exposed | Author's Tone or Attitude |
|---|---|---|---|
| The Importance of Being Earnest | | | |
| Big Kiss | | | |

**©** **2. Integration of Knowledge and Ideas (a)** Which selection satirizes serious social issues, and which one satirizes trivial or light-hearted issues? **(b)** Which selection is harsher toward the people it satirizes? Explain.

## ⏱ Timed Writing

### Explanatory Text: Essay

The perspective, or vantage point, of the writer helps shape the satire. In *The Importance of Being Earnest,* Wilde is not part of the events he satirizes. In the excerpt from *The Big Kiss,* Alford is a participant in the action. In an essay, discuss how these different perspectives affect the satire. **(35 minutes)**

### 5-Minute Planner

1. Read the prompt carefully and completely.
2. Note your answers to the following questions:
   - What purpose do you think Wilde had in writing this play about Victorian society?
   - What subtle hints in the text reveal Wilde's view of his characters?
   - Does Alford's point of view make him more or less sympathetic to the other actors he satirizes?
   - How do Alford's inner thoughts add to the humor of the satire?
   - Which text clues suggest Alford's level of seriousness about his topic?
   - Which satire do you think is more successful? Why?
3. Reread the prompt. Then, refer to your notes and draft your essay.

# Writing Workshop

 **Common Core
State Standards**

**Writing**

**5.** Develop and strengthen
writing as needed by planning,
revising, editing, rewriting, or
trying a new approach, focusing
on addressing what is most
significant for a specific purpose
and audience.

**7.** Conduct short as well as more
sustained research projects to
answer a question (including a
self-generated question) or solve
a problem; narrow or broaden
the inquiry when appropriate.

**8.** Gather relevant information
from multiple authoritative print
and digital sources, using
advanced searches effectively;
assess the usefulness of each
source in answering the research
question.

## Write an Informative Text

### Research Writing: Research Report

**Defining the Form** A **research report** presents and interprets information gathered through the extensive study of a subject. You might use elements of a research report in writing lab reports, documentaries, annotated bibliographies, histories, and persuasive essays.

**Assignment** Write a research report on a subject that is both interesting and worth exploring in depth. Include these elements:

✓ a *thesis statement* that is clearly expressed

✓ *factual support* from a variety of reliable, credited sources

✓ a *clear organization* that includes an *introduction,* a *body,* and a *conclusion*

✓ a *bibliography* or *works-cited list* that provides a complete listing of research sources formatted in an approved style.

✓ error-free grammar, including use of *adverb clauses*

To preview the criteria on which your report may be judged, see the rubric on page 1013.

 **Writing Workshop:** *Work in Progress*

Review the work you did on page 977.

## WRITE GUY
*Jeff Anderson, M.Ed.*

### What Do You Notice?

**Examples that Build an Argument**

This excerpt is from Alan Axelrod's historical research study *Nothing To Fear: Lessons in Leadership from FDR.* Read it several times.

*He could then and there have given in to the fog of fear, but he chose not to. He chose instead to understand polio, to see clearly the extent of his disability, and then to assess—also clearly—his options for overcoming that disability.*

What do you notice about these sentences? Discuss your observations with a partner. Consider how you can use examples to build an argument in your research report.

**Reading-Writing Connection**

To get a feel for research writing, read the selection from *Nothing To Fear* by Alan Axelrod on page 567.

# Prewriting/Planning Strategies

**Brainstorm for categories.** Identify an area of general interest and list specific related categories. For example, from the area of art, you might list sculpture, painting, and ceramics. Repeat the process: from painting, you might list Impressionism, Cubism, and Pop Art. Continue listing categories until you find a topic to research.

**Review notebooks.** Flip through the notebooks you keep for each class in school to find subjects or ideas that spark your interest. Choose one of these as the topic of your research paper.

**Identify an open-ended research question.** Before you begin, compose a question about your topic. This question may become your thesis statement, or it may lead up to it. The question will also help focus your research into a comprehensive but flexible search plan, as well as prevent you from gathering details that are too broad for your purpose. As you continue to learn more about your topic as you research, you may find it necessary to change, refocus, or adapt your original question.

   **Question:** *How did the Impressionist school of painting begin?*

**PHLit**
**Online!**
www.PHLitOnline.com
• Author video: Writing Process
• Author video: Rewards of Writing

# Gathering Details Through Research

**Use a variety of primary and secondary sources.** To get a full view of your topic, use *primary sources* (firsthand or original accounts, such as interview transcripts and newspaper articles) and *secondary sources* (accounts that are not original, such as encyclopedia entries).

**Find appropriate sources.** Analyze and apply evaluative criteria to assess that your sources are appropriate to the purpose of your report and your audience. You may find the information you need to answer your research question in specialized and authoritative resources, such as almanacs (for social, cultural, and natural statistics), government publications (for law, government programs, and subjects such as agriculture), and information services. Also, consider consumer, workplace, and public documents. Consult your librarian on the best sources to use. You can find sources of specific information through an online search, a card catalog, or by using more advanced tools:

* **Databases:** Access databases of information to find appropriate sources. For example, the Modern Language Association (MLA) database indexes articles on topics within the humanities.

* **Indexes:** Locate magazine or newspaper articles by consulting the *Readers' Guide to Periodical Literature.*

# Gathering Details Through Research *(continued)*

**Question your sources.** As you locate information, choose sources representing a variety of viewpoints. If you find information you do not trust, consult a second source to verify its validity.

**Record and organize information.** Take notes as you locate and connect pertinent information from multiple sources, and keep a reference list of every source you use. This will help you to make distinctions between the relative value and significance of specific data, facts, and ideas.

- **Source Cards:** Create a card that identifies the author, title, publisher, city, date of publication, and page number of each source you consult. For Internet sources, record the name and Web address of the site, and the date you accessed the information.

- **Note cards:** For each item of information, create a separate note card that includes both the fact or idea and its source.

**Quote accurately.** Responsible research begins with the first note you take. Be sure to quote and paraphrase your sources accurately so you can iden-tify these sources later. In your notes, circle all quotations and paraphrases to distinguish them from your own comments. When photocopying from a source, include the copyright infor-mation. Also, remember to include the Web addresses of printouts from online sources.

**Sample *Readers' Guide* Entry**

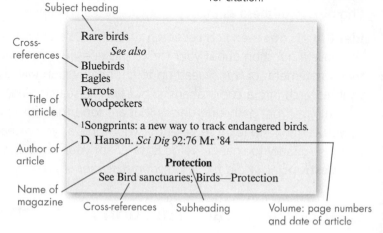

**Source Card** [A]

Marsh, Peter, M.D. *Eye to Eye: How People Interact.* Topsfield, MA: Salem House Publishers, 1988.

(p. 54)

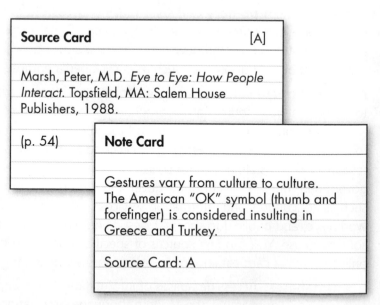

**Note Card**

Gestures vary from culture to culture. The American "OK" symbol (thumb and forefinger) is considered insulting in Greece and Turkey.

Source Card: A

# Drafting Strategies

**Propose a thesis statement.** Write a sentence that takes a position and can be supported by most of your research. A thesis statement is a controlling idea that gives your essay coherence.

- **Sample Thesis Statement:** *Claude Monet's use of light in his water lily paintings typifies Impressionist techniques.*

**Choose a text structure.** Use your thesis statement and knowledge of your audience to choose an organizational structure. Consider these options:

- **Chronological order:** Present events in the order in which they occur. This is ideal for reporting a subject's history.

- **Order of importance:** Present details in order of increasing or decreasing significance. This is ideal for building an argument.

- **Comparison and contrast:** Present similarities and differences. This is ideal for addressing two or more subjects.

**Write an outline.** Review your note cards and build a road map that shows your plan for integrating and presenting key information. In an outline, use headings to identify the main idea in each section, and order these ideas so they flow logically. Use this outline to develop your draft.

**Make direct references to sources.** Use these methods to incorporate the facts, examples, and quotations you have found:

- **Direct Quotation:** Enclose a writer's exact words in quotation marks. Omissions should not alter the intent of the passage. Indicate omitted words with **ellipses,** or dots.

- **Paraphrase:** Restate a writer's specific ideas in your own words, accurately reflecting the writer's meaning.

- **Summary:** Condense an extended idea into a brief statement in your own words to introduce background information or review key ideas.

**Credit your sources.** To avoid **plagiarism**—presenting another's work as your own—include documentation every time you use another writer's ideas. Note the author's last name and the page numbers of material used. Later, use these notes to create formal citations in a bibliography or works-cited list at the end of your paper.

**Plan for visuals.** You may include visual aids, such as charts, maps, and graphs, to organize and display information in your report. Whenever you include additional information—whether it is visuals or quotations—be sure to make a clear link from your thesis to the data you include and reference.

# Revising Strategies

**Evaluate your sources.** Underline any fact in your draft that may not have a trustworthy source. For example, you may have found information from a newspaper or a Web site known for sensationalizing or exaggerating events. Confirm this information through a more reliable source, such as an established encyclopedia, a scholarly Web site, or a reputable newspaper.

 **Common Core State Standards**

**Writing**

**5.** Develop and strengthen writing as needed by planning, revising, editing, rewriting, or trying a new approach, focusing on addressing what is most significant for a specific purpose and audience.

**6.** Use technology, including the Internet, to produce, publish, and update individual or shared writing products, taking advantage of technology's capacity to link to other information and to display information flexibly and dynamically.

**Language**

**3.a.** Write and edit work so that it conforms to the guidelines in a style manual appropriate for the discipline and writing type.

> **Model: Evaluating Sources**
> A good way for people to convey a positive message is to avoid certain movements. ~~When people cross their arms it is always a sign of panic.~~
>
> The writer found that this claim was supported by only one source. Since it was not important to her basic argument, she chose to delete it.

**Revise to vary word choice.** Except for specific terminology required by your topic, avoid overuse of particular words and expressions. Review your draft to identify words that you may have overused. For each, use a dictionary and thesaurus to generate a list of possible synonyms, and substitute them as appropriate.

**Example Synonym Banks**

**invention:**  innovation, development, contrivance, device

**theory:**  belief, policy, system, position, idea, supposition

**Peer Review**

Exchange drafts with a partner. As you read each other's reports, circle or highlight words that recur repeatedly. Working together, identify replacements to improve word variety in the writing.

**Revise to follow a consistent research format.** As you finalize your report, be sure that it meets your teacher's criteria for length, format, and documentation of sources. The Modern Language Association (MLA) requires standardized parenthetical citations of sources and a works-cited list that includes only the sources used in the report.

To credit sources within a research paper, include direct documentation in the form of footnotes, endnotes, or parenthetical citations. At the end of your paper, provide a reference list giving complete bibliographic information. If possible, use the footnoting function in a word processing program to aid your efforts.

# Writers on Writing

## Gary L. Blackwood On Showing, Not Telling

> Gary L. Blackwood is the author of the excerpt from *The Shakespeare Stealer* (p. 787).

To me, research is as much fun as beachcombing: You never know what fascinating items you're going to find. Since books are generally more reliable than the Internet, I do most of my beachcombing in libraries. I know that some people consider nonfiction dull, but I find good nonfiction more compelling than a novel, because I know the events really happened. Who could invent a story as singular and mysterious as that of Kaspar Hauser, which I came upon while researching my four-volume work *Unsolved History*?

*"It helps to read sentences aloud."*
—Gary L. Blackwood

### Professional Model:

### from *Perplexing People,*
a volume in the *Unsolved History* series published by Benchmark Books (Marshall Cavendish), Sept. 2005

~~Sometime in the afternoon of~~ *On* May 26, 1828, a peculiar boy of about sixteen appeared, seemingly from nowhere, on a street in the German city of Nuremberg. His clothing was shabby and ill-fitting and he walked with a ~~peculiar~~ *strange* waddling gait, as though intoxicated. His face wore a vacant expression; he spoke and understood only a few words. Within a year he would become one of the ~~best known and most discussed~~ *most celebrated and controversial* people in Europe. . . .

The police questioned the boy, but his replies consisted of two phrases in ungrammatical German: "Don't know" and "I want to be a horseman as my father is." When they gave him paper and a pen ~~and asked to write his name and address,~~ he produced a series of scribbles, of which only two were intelligible: "cavalryman" and "Kaspar Hauser."

Writing can be factual without also being sleep-inducing. I try to liven things up by using vivid adjectives.

To add interest and a feeling of authenticity, I use a lot of quotes from primary sources—people who actually witnessed or participated in the events or chroniclers of the time.

Good prose—whether it's fiction or nonfiction—is clear and concise. I do a lot of cutting of superfluous words and phrases, and I may reword a sentence half a dozen times before I'm satisfied with it.

# Documenting Sources

You must give proper credit to the people whose ideas and words you have borrowed. Failing to do this raises legal and ethical issues. Libel, slander, copyright infringement, and plagiarism are serious accusations. Good writers are thorough and accurate in citing all of their sources.

When citing sources, follow a specific format. Modern Language Association (MLA) style calls for citations in parentheses directly following the material being cited.

- For print works, provide the author's or editor's name followed by a page number. If the work does not have an author, use a keyword or phrase from the title.

  **Citing a Print Work:** . . . body language makes up approximately 65 percent of human communication (Aylesworth 3).

- For Web sources, give the author's name and the title of the article, if any, or title of the site.

  **Citing a Web Source:** <u>Unsolvedmysteries.com</u> describes a lottery winner whose dreams reveal a winning ticket ("Winning the Lottery").

At the end of your report, give information for each source you cite. MLA style calls for an alphabetical *Works Cited* list.

- For books, give the author's name (last name first), the title of the work, the city of publication, the name of the publisher, and the year of publication.

  **Entry for a Book:** Aylesworth, Thomas G. *Understanding Body Talk.* New York: F. Watts, 1979.

- For articles in periodicals, give the author's last name, first name, title of the article, the name of the magazine, the date of the issue, the volume and issue number, and the pages of the article. For any month with more than four letters, abbreviate the month by using the first three letters followed by a period.

  **Entry for a Periodical Article:** Kreisler, Kristin V. "Why We Dream What We Dream." *Reader's Digest.* Feb. 1995: 28.

- For Web sites, give any of the following information that is available, in this order: author's name, title of the page, title of the site, date of last update, and name of the sponsoring organization. Give the date you consulted the site and its full URL, or Web address.

  **Entry for a Web Site:** "Winning the Lottery in Your Dreams." *Unsolved Mysteries.* 11 March 2000. <u>http://unsolvedmysteries.com/usm397.html</u>

For more information on citing sources using MLA style, see page R36.

**Common Core State Standards**

**Writing**
**8.** Gather relevant information from multiple authoritative print and digital sources, avoiding plagiarism and following a standard format for citation.

**Language**
**1.b.** Use various types of phrases and clauses to convey specific meanings and add variety and interest to writing or presentations.
**3.a.** Write and edit work so that it conforms to the guidelines in a style manual appropriate for the discipline and writing type.

# Revising to Combine Sentences Using Adverb Clauses

**Adverb clauses** can be used to combine information from two sentences into one sentence. Often, the revised sentence will make the intended meaning more obvious.

**Two sentences:**  I joined the panel. Jay is the leader.

**Combined:**  I joined the panel because Jay is the leader.

**Identifying Adverb Clauses** A clause is any group of words with a subject and a verb. An *independent clause* can stand by itself as a complete sentence; a *subordinate clause* is not complete because it does not express a full idea. An *adverb clause* is a subordinate clause that modifies a verb, an adjective, or another adverb in a sentence. It begins with a subordinating conjunction that tells *where, when, in what way, to what extent, under what condition,* or *why.*

**When:**  *After I read the report,* I agreed with the mayor.

**Condition:**  Dan will ask for a refund *if you will go with him.*

**In what way:**  The bulldog yawned *as if he were utterly bored.*

**Why:**  I drew a map *so that they would not get lost.*

> **PH | WRITING COACH**
>
> Further instruction and practice are available in *Prentice Hall Writing Coach.*

**Combining Sentences** When combining two short sentences using adverb clauses, follow these steps:

1. Look for a relationship between the ideas of the two clauses.

2. Select the appropriate subordinate conjunction to show that relationship. Place the adverb clause at the beginning or end of the combined sentence—wherever it conveys your intent more clearly.

3. Use a comma to separate a subordinate clause only when it begins a sentence.

### Grammar in Your Writing

Review several paragraphs of your report and highlight any consecutive short sentences that you find. Look for a possible adverbial relationship (*where, when, in what way,* and so on) in two of the sentences. Following the steps outlined here, combine the sentences using an appropriate subordinating conjunction.

| Common Subordinate Conjunctions | | | |
| --- | --- | --- | --- |
| after | because | since | when |
| although | before | so that | whenever |
| as | even though | unless | whether |
| as soon as | if | until | while |

## Student Model: Lyndsey Regan, Canyon Country, CA

### Body Language

When we speak to other people, they are not only listening to our actual words, but sensing our facial expression, tone of voice, gestures, level of eye contact, posture, and movements as well. Nonverbal communication, or body language, makes up approximately 65 percent of human communication (Aylesworth 3). Body language has a major impact on how others perceive what we say. It can also be a tool for miscommunication when the speaker and listener are from different cultures or are communicating through technology that deprives them of visual cues. In fact, we often realize the importance of body language only when we cannot interpret someone else's body language correctly.

In *Eye to Eye: How People Interact*, Dr. Peter Marsh explains that before we speak, our gestures, posture, and facial expressions are already broadcasting messages to those around us. While we are speaking, these gestures continue to communicate messages—usually clarifying what we are saying, but sometimes contradicting us in telltale ways (Marsh 116–119).

Often, body language is an unconscious act that triggers the most developed senses in other people—hearing and sight (Aylesworth 18). That is why body language is such a great way to emphasize words and ideas. Many people take advantage of this. Advertisers, for example, cast actors in their commercials who use body language that appeals to viewers.

Studies have shown that people's body language changes when they are not telling the truth (Vrij, Edward, Roberts, and Bull 239–263). If someone's body language is inconsistent with what he or she is saying, people tend to believe what the body is telling them. A good way for people to convey a positive message is to avoid certain movements, like fidgeting or letting your eyes wander. Instead, good communicators maintain steady eye contact, nod in agreement, and smile. You may notice that people on television, like hosts of infomercials and talk-shows, generally display this positive body language when speaking.

The opening line captures the reader's attention by presenting a surprising perspective.

Lyndsey expresses her thesis statement clearly and concisely.

Lyndsey smoothly introduces a research source and explains the ideas it provided.

Body language is usually learned, but it can also be inherited. It is affected by age, gender, background, and situation. The meaning of body language can change depending on cultural context. According to Dr. Marsh, each culture has developed its own repertoire of symbolic gestures, many with original associations that have now long been forgotten (Marsh 53–54). This sometimes causes people to be alarmed by foreign visitors or nervous around people when they visit new countries.

In the United States, people have a wide variety of regional influences because the country is a melting pot of diverse cultures. A gesture that means the same thing throughout the Unite States is the "OK" sign made with the thumb and forefinger. This gesture is interpreted similarly in some European countries, but if you were to perform this sign in Greece or Turkey, it would be considered very insulting (Marsh 54).

There are other cultural differences in body language within Europe. In Germany, body language often reflects social status, and Germans often use body language for emphasis. Italian gestures are often passionate, emotional expressions communicated with the face, arms, and shoulders. Italians often use body language to clarify themselves or to express urgency. In France, people tend to use more formal gestures. They are generally not as expressive or insistent as Italians. The body language of the French is not nearly as casual as we are used to in America (Ruesch and Kees 23–25). As you can see by exploring a few examples from different cultures, there are many differences in body language. Therefore, when you communicate with people from other countries, take special care in your use of body language.

Technological advancements in our society affect the way we communicate. For example, when we speak on the telephone, we are unable to see the person on the other end of the line. The message that a person may be trying to convey may be misinterpreted without the additional visual information provided by his or her body language. With electronic mail, there is no visual or verbal communication whatsoever. As a result, people cannot completely understand the meaning of what is being communicated. Therefore, people using e-mail should be careful about what they write. To avoid miscommunication, communicating the old-fashioned way—in person—may be the best approach.

Whenever Lyndsey presents a specific piece of evidence that is not her own idea or common knowledge, she cites it using the appropriate format.

Lyndsey's organizational structure is logical and clear. First, she discusses how body language is used in a variety of cultures. Next, she gives examples of what happens when we do not have body language to guide us.

In conclusion, body language is a significant component of communication, even though we are often not aware of it. Body language, like facial expression and gestures, frequently enables people to clearly understand one another, but we must remember that people cannot always be read like a book. With cultural differences, body language can take on different meanings, and this allows for potential miscommunication. Changes in technology present a different kind of problem, but with a similar result. When body language cannot be seen, people may misinterpret the meaning of the communicator, making them angry or confused. As you can see, the additional information we provide with our body language plays a major role in how we communicate our thoughts and ideas.

## Works-Cited List

Aylesworth, Thomas G. *Understanding Body Talk.* New York: F. Watts, 1979.

Marsh, Peter, M.D. *Eye to Eye: How People Interact.* Topsfield, MA: Salem House Publishers, 1988.

Ruesch, Jurgen, and Weldon Kees. *Nonverbal Communication: Notes on the Visual Perception of Human Relations.* Berkeley, CA: University of California Press, 1969.

Vrij, Aldert, Katherine Edward, Kim P. Roberts, and Ray Bull. "Detecting Deceit via Analysis of Verbal and Nonverbal Behavior." *Journal of Nonverbal Behavior,* Winter 2000: 239–263.

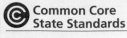

**Common Core
State Standards**

**Language**
**3.a.** Write and edit work so that it conforms to the guidelines in a style manual appropriate for the discipline and writing type.

After her conclusion, Lyndsey presents the complete information for the works cited in her report using MLA format, a common style for citation.

# Editing and Proofreading

Review your draft to correct errors in format, grammar, and spelling.

**Focus on format.** Follow the manuscript requirements by including an appropriate title page, pagination, spacing and margins, and citations. Make sure you have used the preferred system for crediting sources in your paper and for bibliographical sources at the end. Double-check all punctuation and capitalization.

**Notice unusual consonant groupings.** Some words are difficult to spell because they contain unusual letter combinations. Certain consonant groupings, such as the *rh* in *rhythm*, don't occur in many words. Other consonant groups are hard to hear (ex<u>h</u>ilarating) or contain a silent letter (sil<u>h</u>ouette). Be sure to double-check these problematic words.

# Publishing and Presenting

Consider one of the following ways to share your writing:

**Deliver an oral presentation.** Read your research report aloud to your classmates, or consider recreating the report as a multimedia presentation using presentation software. Add appropriate visual aids as needed, such as charts, maps, and graphs.

**Organize a panel discussion.** If several of your classmates have written on a similar topic, plan a discussion to compare and contrast your findings. Speakers can summarize their research before opening the panel to questions from the class.

# Reflecting on Your Writing

Jot down your answers to this question:

*How did writing a research report affect your understanding of your topic?*

# Rubric for Self-Assessment

Find evidence in your writing to address each category. Then, use the rating scale to grade your work.

**Spiral Review**

Earlier in the unit, you learned about **main and subordinate clauses** (p. 976). Review your research report to be sure that no subordinate clause stands by itself.

**PH  WRITING COACH**

Further instruction and practice are available in *Prentice Hall Writing Coach*.

| Criteria | Rating Scale |
|---|---|
| | not very                     very |
| **Focus:** How clear is your thesis statement? | 1   2   3   4   5 |
| **Organization:** How logical and consistent is your organization? | 1   2   3   4   5 |
| **Support/Elaboration:** How effective and varied is your support? | 1   2   3   4   5 |
| **Style:** How well do you summarize background information? | 1   2   3   4   5 |
| **Conventions:** According to an accepted format, how complete and accurate are your citations? | 1   2   3   4   5 |

# Vocabulary Workshop

## Borrowed and Foreign Words

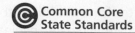
**Common Core**
**State Standards**

**Language**
**3.** Apply knowledge of language to understand how language functions in different contexts, to make effective choices for meaning or style, and to comprehend more fully when reading or listening.

**4.c.** Consult general and specialized reference materials, both print and digital, to find the pronunciation of a word or determine or clarify its precise meaning, its part of speech, or its etymology.

**4.d.** Verify the preliminary determination of the meaning of a word or phrase.

English has more words than any other language. Many of these words are taken directly from other languages. At first, these new words are treated as **foreign words.**

Over time, as the words become common in everyday speech, most of them are accepted into the language and are considered to be English. Words that enter the languages in this way are called **borrowed words.** You use them every day. The first chart shows some common borrowed words that are now part of the English language.

| Borrowed Words | Original Language |
|---|---|
| ballet, cavalry, infantry, bigot | French |
| cargo, canyon, ranch, tornado | Spanish |
| chipmunk (Algonquian), pecan (Illinois), raccoon (Virginia Algonquian), moccasin (Algonquian) | Native American |
| bandanna, pajamas, thug, shampoo | Hindi |
| kindergarten, hamburger, dollar, vandal | German |

Some words are not fully adopted into the language and are always treated as foreign words. Some of these words are written in italics. Dictionaries often indicate those that should be italicized. See how many of these words you know.

| | | |
|---|---|---|
| *au courant* | up-to-date, informed on current affairs | French |
| *mot juste* | the exact, appropriate word | French |
| *carpe diem* | seize the day, or live for the day | Latin |
| *nom de plume* | a pen name | French |
| *caveat emptor* | let the buyer beware | Latin |

**Practice A** Look up each of these foreign words in a dictionary. Identify the original language and write the definition.

1. ad infinitum
2. *cause célèbre*
3. pro bono

4. ex post facto
5. *bon mot*
6. *mea culpa*

**Practice B** Complete each sentence with the correct borrowed or foreign word from the box. Identify the original language. Then, use a print or online dictionary to verify the accuracy of each choice.

| embargo | status quo | desperado | mesa | *mano a mano* |
| algebra | RSVP | onslaught | sushi | *fait accompli* |

1. After turning in his report, Alexis declared it a _____ .

2. Joshua really enjoyed eating the _____ until someone told him it was raw fish.

3. It was a steep climb to the top of the _____ , but then the ground became level.

4. I usually do well in _____ , but that one equation puzzled me.

5. "Tyler," said the smaller boy, "I challenge you to a game of basketball _____ ."

6. The card said _____ , so I immediately called Megan and accepted the invitation.

7. He was not a common thief, but a dangerous _____ wanted in ten states.

8. The United States declared an _____ on all goods from the country until hostilities ended.

9. The fort quickly fell before the _____ of the invaders.

10. Helena hated the _____ so she began working to make changes.

**Comprehension and Collaboration**

Use these words in a paragraph: *persona non grata, voilà, coup de grace, per se.* Then, meet with a partner and critique each other's word usage. Read the paragraphs aloud, being careful to pronounce the words correctly. Verify your definitions and pronunciations in a dictionary.

**Activity** Prepare four notecards like the one shown. Then, write one of these foreign words on each card: *hoi polloi, savoir faire, vis-à-vis, ad hoc.* Look up each word in a print or online dictionary. Write the definition, the pronunciation, and a sentence that clearly shows each meaning.

Word:

Definition:

Sentence:

# Communications Workshop

## Multimedia Presentation of a Research Report

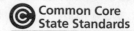

**Common Core
State Standards**

**Speaking and Listening**
**1.d.** Respond thoughtfully to diverse perspectives, summarize points of agreement and disagreement, and, when warranted, qualify or justify their own views and understanding and make new connections in light of the evidence and reasoning presented.
**5.** Make strategic use of digital media in presentations to enhance understanding of findings, reasoning, and evidence and to add interest.

Modern classrooms offer students several ways to add sound and visuals to a verbal report. Students may choose from an array of equipment to make multimedia presentations. The following strategies will help you develop and deliver a multimedia presentation of a research report.

### Learn the Skills

**Organizing Content** Your choice of media depends on the equipment and software available to you, your topic, and your target audience. Use the following tips:

- Use a two-column format for your outline. Arrange the content of your report in the left column; plan media elements in the right column. Use this same pattern in your final script: Run your speaking text in the left column and your media cues in the right.

- Use media strategically. Incorporate audio, video, and graphic elements where they will be the most effective. Media should enhance your audience's understanding of material in a presentation.

- Choose media appropriate to your content. Dry recitation of statistics can be replaced with colorful graphs and charts to enhance the appeal and accuracy of your presentation. If your report is historical, incorporate music from the time period. Photographs or video images may clarify complex procedures.

- Distribute media use evenly throughout your report to make it easier for you to manage the equipment and to maintain audience interest.

**Preparing the Presentation** An effective multimedia presentation is the result of planning and practice. These tips may help you prepare:

- If possible, rehearse your presentation in the room where it will take place. Check sight lines to make sure that your visual materials will be seen by all of your audience. Do a sound check as well.

- Make sure that words on your slides are readable; do not put too much content on any one slide.

- Practice shifting from spoken content to media elements. Plan what you will do and say if any piece of equipment fails.

# Practice the Skills

**Ⓒ Presentation of Knowledge and Ideas** Use what you've learned in this workshop to perform the following task.

> ## ACTIVITY: Give a Multimedia Presentation
>
> Use a research report from your portfolio as the basis of a multimedia presentation. Plan and practice your presentation using the guidelines from page 1016. Remember the following important points:
> - Create a script based on your research report that includes media elements.
> - Choose media relating to your content.
> - Use media evenly throughout the report.
> - Media should enhance your key points.

As your classmates make their presentations, use the Presentation Checklist below to offer them some feedback. Your classmates will also use the checklist to analyze your presentation.

> ### Presentation Checklist
>
> **Presentation Content**
> Does the presentation meet the requirements of the activity?
> Check all that apply.
> ☐ The media related to the content.
> ☐ Media was used evenly throughout the report.
> ☐ Media helped listeners to understand key points.
>
> **Presentation Delivery**
> Did the speaker use the media successfully?
> ☐ Equipment functioned properly.
> ☐ Media was visible and audible.
> ☐ Transitions between media uses were smooth.

**Ⓒ Comprehension and Collaboration** With a small group, discuss the presentations you have viewed. Consider the ways in which media added to your understanding of information in each presentation. Ask what group members learned from multimedia presentations that they could not have learned from reading research reports. Determine which presentations used media most effectively, and why. If there are multiple perspectives, summarize points of agreement and disagreement.

# Cumulative Review

## I. Reading Literature

**Directions:** *Read the passage. Then, answer each question that follows.*

**Common Core
State Standards**

RL.9-10.3, RL.9-10.4; W.9-10.3.b;
L.9-10.4.a
[For the full wording of the standards,
see the standards chart in the front of
your textbook.]

*The stage is dark. Bill, a somewhat scrawny, brainy-looking teenager, stands center stage. A spotlight shines on him as he begins his speech.*

**BILL.** *(dramatically)* To be or not to be: that is the question. At least that's what Hamlet said. Of course, this is not life and death, but it could be social suicide. I don't want to be a tattletale. But I also don't want to be an <u>accomplice</u> to cheating—I don't want to help break the rules. What to do? *(with a sigh)* Jack—the football team captain—knows that I know he cheated. He caught me looking his way as he glanced at the cheat sheet he had on his arm. After Mrs. Lundy's class, he confronted me. "I have to pass this test to stay on the team. I can count on you not to rat me out, right?" he said menacingly. I said I wouldn't. But why should he get away with cheating? It's not right. If I tell, he will know it's me. I'll lose my social life—the little I have. I will be an outcast. What do I do? I need help.

*The curtain falls. It opens to show a guidance counselor's office stage right. The older guidance counselor sits behind a desk. Bill walks in to see the guidance counselor, Mr. Peters. Bill has a look of concern on his face.*

**MR. PETERS.** *(in a friendly tone as Bill enters)* So you wanted to talk to me about something, Bill? You making plans for college already? *(pauses and looks at Bill)* Don't look so worried. *(smiles and offers Bill a seat)*

**BILL.** *(nervously)* Actually, I need a different kind of help, Mr. Peters. I don't know what to do. If I just tell you the basics, will you help me decide?

**MR. PETERS.** Let's give it a shot. I will certainly try to help.

**BILL.** *(looks around to make sure no one is listening)* I caught someone cheating. He knows I saw it and told me not to rat him out. I don't want people to think I am a rat, but I also don't want to be an accomplice to cheating. We both have a lot to lose if I tell. I don't know what to do.

**MR. PETERS.** *(smiling knowingly)* I think you know what you need to do.

**BILL.** *(resigned)* I guess you are right. I will talk to Mrs. Lundy at lunch. *The curtain falls.*

1. What do you learn from the first set of **stage directions?**

   A. how Bill acts
   B. how Bill feels
   C. how the stage looks
   D. how Mr. Peters' office is set up

2. What **allusion** does Bill make in his first speech?

   A. to a speech he gave
   B. to a news report
   C. to the play *Hamlet*
   D. to a TV show

3. Which of Bill's speaking parts is a **soliloquy?**

   A. first
   B. second
   C. third
   D. fourth

4. What makes Bill's speech a **soliloquy** instead of a **monologue?**

   A. He addresses another character.
   B. He makes a brief remark to the audience.
   C. He is thinking aloud alone on the stage.
   D. He is talking about another character.

5. Based on the **dialogue** and **stage directions,** how would you best describe Mr. Peters?

   A. harsh
   B. smug
   C. funny
   D. caring

6. Which element of **drama** is missing from this selection?

   A. aside
   B. dialogue
   C. stage directions
   D. conflict

7. **Vocabulary** Which word is closest in meaning to the underlined word *accomplice?*

   A. friend
   B. accessory
   C. tattletale
   D. teacher

8. The set of **stage directions** beginning "The curtain falls. It opens…" describes everything *except*—

   A. Bill's expression.
   B. where Mr. Peters is in his office.
   C. Mr. Peters' physical appearance.
   D. why Bill enters the office.

9. Bill's **dialogue** with Mr. Peters reveals—

   A. Bill and Mr. Peters will remain friendly for years.
   B. Mr. Peters believes that Bill cheated on his test and will not confess.
   C. Mr. Peters has advised Bill previously.
   D. Bill trusts Mr. Peters' opinion very much.

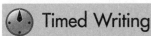 Timed Writing

10. **Write** a ten-sentence **monologue** that Bill might deliver to Mrs. Lundy. Be sure he directly addresses the teacher. **Explain** the situation and **describe** his fears in the monologue.

# II. Reading Informational Text

**Directions:** *Read the passage. Then, answer each question that follows.*

**Common Core
State Standards**

**RI.9-10.1; W.9-10.5; L.9-10.3, L.9-10.4.a.**
[For the full wording of the standards, see the standards chart in the front of your textbook.]

## Planet Protection: The EPA

Taking care of the environment is an issue that seems to be constantly reported by the media. Although it may seem that protecting the climate has just become an issue recently, helping the environment is nothing new. One organization devoted to this purpose is the Environmental Protection Agency.

The Environmental Protection Agency (EPA) was founded in 1970 to limit pollution, monitor pesticide use, and ensure clean air and water for all. Since that time, the EPA has been involved in everything from cleaning up oil spills to enforcing laws that make sure drinking water in the United States is safe.

The EPA has recently established the U.S. Climate Change Site in order to provide information to the public about the state of global warming, what is known, and what is still questionable. According to the EPA, we know that the earth's temperature has increased over 1 degree in the last century. Their sources suggest that the temperature will continue to increase. However, scientists are unsure of how quickly and drastically the increase will occur. Scientists are working on proving theories about climate change, thus allowing them to make more accurate predictions about events to come.

The EPA Web site states, "Climate change may be a big problem, but there are many little things we can do to make a difference." The site suggests a variety of ways that people, old and young, can make small changes to take better care of the environment. Although improving the environment may seem to be a <u>daunting</u> task that is too much for one person, these tips can help guide people to small daily changes that do make a difference.

**1. Vocabulary** What is the best definition for *daunting?*

**A.** incredibly difficult

**B.** oddly intelligent

**C.** kindly attentive

**D.** extremely responsible

**2.** How do you know the quotation in the last paragraph is from a reliable source?

**A.** It comes from a Web site.

**B.** It is from the coverage of a current event.

**C.** It comes from a media outlet.

**D.** It is from a respected organization.

**3.** You might scan this article to learn—

**A.** its general focus.

**B.** everything about the EPA.

**C.** what the letters "EPA" represent.

**D.** all the causes of climate change.

**4.** According to the article, how sure are scientists about the effects to come from global warming?

**A.** They are not sure at all.

**B.** They are somewhat sure.

**C.** They are extremely sure.

**D.** They have no doubt.

# III. Writing and Language Conventions

## Exposition: How-to Essay

**Directions:** *Read the passage. Then, answer each question that follows.*

(1) One of the easiest and most basic commands to teach your dog is *Sit.* (2) With a little practice, the right technique, and a few treats, you will have a dog that knows how to sit on command. (3) The dog will pick it up within a few brief training sessions. (4) Use the following procedure:

(5) • Gather small training treats.
(6) • Next, stand in front of your dog.
(7) • Then, hold the treat in your hand. (8) Place your hand in front of the dog's nose. (9) Then, move the treat over its head toward the tail as you say your dog's name and "Sit." (10) The dog's head and nose should follow the treat and the rear end should hit the ground. (11) Be sure not to hold the treat too high or the dog will jump up to get it.
(12) • When the dog's hindquarters hit the ground, say "Good sit" and immediately give the dog the treat. (13) Do not give the dog the treat if it doesn't sit. (14) Start over again.
(15) • Repeat.

**1.** How is the how-to essay **organized?**

   **A.** in step-by-step order
   **B.** in spatial order
   **C.** in chronological order
   **D.** in order of importance

**2.** How should sentences 7 and 8 be **combined?**

   **A.** Before you hold your hand in front of the dog's nose, hold the treat there.
   **B.** When holding the treat with your hand.
   **C.** Then, holding the treat in your hand, place it in front of the dog's nose.
   **D.** Then, hold the treat in your hand.

**3.** What **word choice** in sentence 1 establishes the level of difficulty of the task?

   **A.** easiest, most basic
   **B.** One, easiest
   **C.** commands, teach
   **D.** teach, *Sit*

**4.** Which best describes the **structure** of the instruction?

   **A.** paragraphs
   **B.** list
   **C.** anecdotes
   **D.** charts

**5.** What would clarify the step in sentence 15?

   **A.** Replace "Repeat" with "Do again."
   **B.** Move sentence 15 earlier in the passage.
   **C.** Explain how many times you should repeat.
   **D.** Describe why this technique works.

**6.** Which **transition word** belongs in sentence 5?

   **A.** Then
   **B.** Later
   **C.** First
   **D.** Next

# Performance Tasks

**Common Core
State Standards**

RL.9-10.3, RL.9-10.4, RL.9-10.5;
W.9-10.2, W.9-10.9.a; SL.9-10.1;
SL.9-10.4
[For the complete wording of the
standards, see the standards chart in
the front of your textbook.]

**Directions:** *Follow the instructions to complete the tasks below
as required by your teacher.*

*As you work on each task, incorporate both general academic
vocabulary and literary terms you learned in this unit.*

## Writing

### Task 1: Literature [RL.9-10.9; W.9-10.2, W.9-10.9.a]
#### Analyze Theme in Related Works

*Write an essay in which you analyze how Shakespeare
draws on the work of Ovid to convey a theme.*

- Explain that you will discuss similarities and
differences between Ovid's "Pyramus and Thisbe"
and Shakespeare's *Romeo and Juliet.*

- Identify specific ways in which the story and the
play are similar and different. Consider main
characters, minor characters, settings, and events.
For each work, describe the reasons that
characters act as they do. Finally, explain the
themes each work expresses.

- Choose an organizational style that allows you to
express ideas clearly and logically. Use a variety of
transitional words and phrases to clarify the
relationships among ideas.

- Include a clear thesis statement, explaining what
you believe to be the theme of both works. Use
well-chosen details and quotations to support
your interpretation.

- Provide a clear and concise conclusion that
summarizes your analysis.

### Task 2: Literature [RL.9-10.3; W.9-10.9.a]
#### Analyze a Complex Character

*Write an essay in which you analyze a complex
character in a literary work from this unit.*

- Explain which work and character you will discuss.
Summarize the plot and describe the character's
role in the story.

- Present a well-reasoned analysis of the character's
actions and motivations. Explain whether the
character has multiple or conflicting motivations.

- Explain how the character interacts with other
characters. Discuss whether the character changes
over the course of the work, and describe the
nature of any changes.

- Explain specific ways in which the character's
behavior, thoughts, statements, and actions
advance the plot and help to express the theme.

- Cite specific details and use quotations from the
work to support your ideas.

### Task 3: Literature [RL.9-10.5; W.9-10.2]
#### Analyze Structural Choices

*Write an essay in which you analyze the role of a
dramatic speech or section of dialogue in a work
from this unit.*

- State which play and which soliloquy, monologue,
or section of dialogue you will discuss.

- Explain why the example you chose is important
to the plot and theme of the work as a whole.

- Summarize the circumstances in which the
speech or dialogue is delivered. Explain why
you think the playwright chose to include this
speech or dialogue at this point in the play.

- Interpret the message conveyed in the speech or
dialogue. Consider both explicit and implicit
meanings.

- Cite specific details to support your ideas.

# Speaking and Listening

## Task 4: Literature [RL.9-10.3; SL.9-10.4]
**Present a Tragic Character**

*Deliver a speech in which you discuss how a complex character from a play in this unit qualifies as a tragic figure.*

- Begin your speech by presenting background for the play—its setting and plot. Then, introduce the character and describe him or her in detail, including his or her role in the plot.

- Consider your audience, purpose, and task as you compose and deliver your presentation. Include information your audience needs in order to understand the general concept of a tragic figure as well as details about your character's choices, motivations, thoughts, and feelings.

- Present your information and supporting evidence clearly, concisely, and logically so that your audience can understand your ideas. Use relevant examples and quotations from the drama to support your analysis.

- End with a memorable conclusion that restates the key elements of your analysis.

## Task 5: Literature [RL.9-10.2; SL.9-10.1]
**Analyze the Development of a Theme**

*Lead a small-group discussion about the theme expressed in a literary work from this unit.*

- Conduct your own analysis of the text and prepare handouts in which you state your interpretation of the theme. Cite specific details from the beginning, middle, and end of the work that support your point of view.

- Write down three questions you have about the theme and its development throughout the play.

- Share your handouts with the group. Then, ask the first of your questions to start the discussion. Pose your remaining questions as the discussion continues.

- As you lead the discussion, respond thoughtfully to group members' ideas. Work with your group to arrive at a shared understanding of the theme.

## Task 6: Literature [RL.9-10.4; SL.9-10.4]
**Analyze Word Choice and Tone**

*Deliver a visual presentation in which you analyze the cumulative impact of word choice on tone in a literary work from this unit.*

- State which work you chose and summarize its key elements—setting, character, events, and insight, or theme.

- Define the tone of the work. Cite at least three specific word choices that contribute to this tone.

- Discuss the denotative and connotative meanings of each word you chose. Explain how the connotations of the words contribute to the overall tone of the work.

- Incorporate visuals, such as drawings or photographs, that illustrate specific word choices and the overall tone of the work you chose.

- Present your information clearly, concisely, and logically so that listeners can follow your line of reasoning.

> **THE BIG ?**
>
> **Do our differences define us?**
> At the beginning of Unit 5, you participated in a discussion about the Big Question. Now that you have completed the unit, write a response to the question. Discuss how your initial ideas have either changed or been reinforced. Cite specific examples from the literature in this unit, from other subject areas, and from your own life to support your ideas. Use Big Question vocabulary words (see p. 779) in your response.

# Featured Titles

In this unit, you have read a variety of dramatic works. Continue to read on your own. Select works that you enjoy, but challenge yourself to explore new playwrights and works of increasing depth and complexity. The titles suggested below will help you get started.

## Literature

### Our Town
by Thornton Wilder
Harper Collins, 2003                    EXEMPLAR TEXT

This Pulitzer Prize–winning **drama** explores the daily lives of the citizens of Grover's Corners, a typical American small town. Through everyday events and conversations, the play's characters reveal the impermanence of life and the desperate need to value every moment, no matter how ordinary.

### The Glass Menagerie
by Tennessee Williams          EXEMPLAR TEXT

In his first major **drama,** Williams shows what happens when the lid is lifted off lives of quiet desperation. The situation appears simple. Tom Wingfield, a man frustrated with his dead-end life, invites a friend to meet his sister Laura. However, when Tom's fragile sister and overprotective mother meet his friend, the consequences prove complicated—and devastating.

### A Pocket Full of Rye
by Agatha Christie
Signet, 2004

Agatha Christie is a famous name in the world of **mystery fiction.** Her brilliant amateur detective Miss Marple solves crimes that appear unsolvable to everyone else. In this case, the crimes are murders that leave behind clues referring to childhood nursery rhymes that baffle the police.

### The Giant's House
by Elizabeth McCracken
The Dial Press, 1996

An unlikely romance blossoms in this **novel** when a lonely librarian falls for a gigantic young man researching his height problems. As the two fall in love, they start to see the world through one another's eyes.

### The Shakespeare Stealer
by Gary Blackwood
Dutton, 1998

In this **novel,** the young orphan Widge is ordered by his greedy master to steal Shakespeare's new play, *Hamlet.* Welcomed in the theater by Shakespeare's actors, Widge must betray his new friends or risk everything.

### Twentieth-Century American Drama          EXEMPLAR TEXT

The **plays** in this volume speak powerfully about the American mind and spirit during the twentieth century, capturing the experiences that define us as Americans and as people. Through these pages, get acquainted with some giants of the American theater—Lorraine Hansberry, Arthur Miller, Thornton Wilder, and Tennessee Williams.

## Informational Texts

### American Speeches          EXEMPLAR TEXT

This collection of famous American **speeches** features works from some of the country's most memorable speakers, including Martin Luther King, Jr., and Patrick Henry.

### Reaching Out
by Francisco Jiménez

In this award-winning **autobiography,** the son of Mexican immigrants shares his experiences as the first member of his family to attend university. As Jiménez adjusts to university life, his family's traditions of hard work and determination help him overcome the challenges of poverty and prejudice.

# Preparing to Read Complex Texts

**Attentive Reading** As you read literature on your own, bring your imagination and questions to the text. The questions shown below and others that you ask as you read will help you learn and enjoy literature even more.

 **Common Core State Standards**

**Reading Literature/Informational Text**
**10.** By the end of grade 9, read and comprehend literature, including stories, dramas, poems, and literary nonfiction in the grades 9–10 text complexity band proficiently, with scaffolding as needed at the high end of the range.

## When reading drama, ask yourself...

- Who is the main character? What struggles does this character face?
- What other characters are important? How do these characters relate to the main character?
- Is there more than one conflict? If so, how do they connect?
- What is the setting of the play? Does the setting cause conflicts or affect the characters' actions? Why or why not?
- Is there more than one setting? If so, do the settings create different moods or conflicts?
- Are the characters, setting, and events believable? Why or why not?
- Does the play end happily, sadly, or somewhere in between? How does the ending make me feel?
- What theme or insight do I think the play conveys? Is that theme or insight important and true?

**Key Ideas and Details**

- How is the play structured? How many acts does it have? What events unfold in each act?
- Are there multiple plots—a main plot and a subplot? If so, how do the different plots relate to each other?
- Does the dialogue sound authentic and believable? Why or why not?
- What do the stage directions tell me about the characters and situations? In what other ways do I learn about the characters?
- At what point in the play do I feel the most concern for the characters? Why?
- What point of view does the main character express? Do other characters express similar points of view? If not, is this difference a point of conflict?
- If characters express different points of view, which one do I think the playwright shares? Why? Which point of view do I share? Why?

**Craft and Structure**

- What do I find most interesting, unusual, or powerful about this play?
- In what ways is the play similar to or different from others I have read or seen?
- What insights have I gained from reading this play?
- What actors would I choose to play the roles in this play?
- If I were to be cast in this play, which role would I want? Why?
- If I were directing this play, how might I stage it?
- After reading this play, do I want to read others by this playwright? Why or why not?

**Integration of Ideas**

THE BIG
?

# Do *heroes* have responsibilities?

# Themes in Literature: Heroism

**PHLit**
**Online!**
www.PHLitOnline.com

**Hear It!**
• Selection summary audio
• Selection audio
• BQ Tunes

**See It!**
• Author videos
• Big Question video
• Get Connected videos
• Background videos
• More about the authors
• Illustrated vocabulary words
• Vocabulary flashcards

**Do It!**
• Interactive journals
• Interactive graphic organizers
• Grammar tutorials
• Interactive vocabulary games
• Test practice

# Do *heroes* have responsibilities?

Heroes are all around us. We find them in literature and in the real world. Heroes sometimes show strength of character and an unusual depth of wisdom. They make important choices and selflessly get involved when others might stand back. Heroes may serve others and fight for justice. Often, they exhibit outstanding courage, honesty, and leadership, but sometimes they do not have any of these qualities. They can be ordinary, unassuming people who somehow stand up in a crisis and act in heroic ways. Think about who heroes are and what makes them take action. Is it character? Is it a sense of responsibility?

## Exploring the Big Question

**Collaboration: One-on-One Discussion** Start thinking about the Big Question by listing heroes whom you know about. They might be people you know personally or have read about in works of nonfiction, such as biographies, history books, or newspapers. They might be characters you have watched on TV shows or in movies or read about in works of fiction. To help identify heroes you already know about, describe a hero from each of these categories:

- A person whose courageous act saves or protects those who are in danger

- Someone who chooses honesty or integrity over self-interest

- A leader who guides others to success

- A person who sacrifices himself or herself to help others

- Someone who acts to help others without a desire for reward or recognition

    After you have completed your list, share it with a partner. As you describe each person on your list, provide details that show why he or she is a hero. As your partner reads from his or her list, listen carefully and ask questions if the description or the qualities of a hero that your partner has chosen are not clear to you. Then, use the Big Question vocabulary as you discuss whether a sense of responsibility motivated the heroes on your lists. Work actively to clarify, challenge, and enrich each other's ideas. Finally, come to an agreement on the qualities that make up a hero, select one or two examples of a hero who has such qualities, and present your findings to the class.

**Connecting to the Literature** Each reading in this unit will give you additional insight into the Big Question.

**PHLit Online!**
www.PHLitOnline.com
- Big Question video
- Illustrated vocabulary words
- Interactive vocabulary games
- BQ Tunes

# Learning Big Question Vocabulary

**Acquire and Use Academic Vocabulary** Academic vocabulary is the language you encounter in textbooks and on standardized tests. Review the definitions of these academic vocabulary words.

> **choices** (choí sez) *n.* a variety of possibilities that a person can select from
>
> **hero** (hir´ o) *n.* a person who is admired for brave or noble actions
>
> **identify** (i den´ tə fí) *v.* define who someone is or what something is
>
> **intentions** (in ten´ shənz) *n.* aims or purposes that a person has in mind
>
> **serve** (surv) *v.* perform duties for another person or be useful to him or her

Use these words as you complete Big Question activities in this unit that involve reading, writing, speaking, and listening.

**Gather Vocabulary Knowledge** Additional Big Question words are listed below. Categorize the words by deciding whether you know each one well, know it a little bit, or do not know it at all.

> | | | |
> |---|---|---|
> | character | justice | standard |
> | honesty | morality | wisdom |
> | imitate | obligation | |
> | involvement | responsibility | |

Then, do the following:

1. Work with a partner to write each word on one side of an index card and its definition on the other side.
2. Verify each definition by looking the word up in a print or online dictionary. Revise your definitions as needed.
3. Place the cards with the words facing up in a pile.
4. Take turns drawing a word card, pronouncing the word, and making a true or false statement that uses the word and is related to ideas of heroism and responsibility. Here is an example: *Thoughtlessness is typical of a heroic character.* Invite your partner to determine whether the statement is true or false.

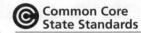

# Theme and the Oral Tradition

Stories from the oral tradition teach a culture's central values and beliefs. They also convey universal themes.

**Oral Tradition** Storytellers and poets of long ago did not write down the tales they told. Instead, they learned the stories and poems of their culture from others and recited them from memory. The term **oral tradition** refers to the literature they passed down through the ages by word of mouth. Eventually, these spoken stories and poems were retold in writing.

The tales of love, ambition, and friendship in the oral tradition do more than entertain. They record the history, customs, beliefs, and values of the cultures from which they sprang. The **points of view,** or perspectives on life, expressed in this literature reflect the **cultural experiences** of the tellers—the basic experiences that shaped life in their society. For example, the stories of a warrior culture tell of battle and adventure, heroism and sacrifice. Experiences of war along with the emphasis placed on bravery and loyalty form the **social and cultural context** for such tales—the values, beliefs, and experiences the tales reflect and affirm.

**Themes** Like much literature, works in the oral tradition convey **themes**—deeper meanings or insights. A **universal theme** is an insight into life and human nature that appears in the literature of many different times and cultures.

Universal themes concern fundamental ideas such as the importance of heroism, the strength of loyalty, the power of love, the responsibilities of leadership, the struggle between good and evil, and the dangers of greed.

Storytellers in the oral tradition often explore universal themes, and they frequently do so using archetypes. An **archetype** is an element that recurs throughout the literature of different cultures. Character types, plot patterns, images, and symbols all may be archetypes, as in the examples shown below.

---

**Example: Archetypes**
- The **trickster** is a clever person or animal who can fool others but often gets into trouble through curiosity.
- In the **hero's quest,** a clever or brave person undergoes a series of tests or trials while on a search for something of great importance.
- The character of the hero is often called the **protagonist,** and his **antagonist** is the character or force that opposes him. Often, the opposing force is a **monster,** a nonhuman or semi-human figure that menaces society and must be destroyed by the hero.

---

The **hero's quest** follows an archetypal plot pattern similar to the one shown here.

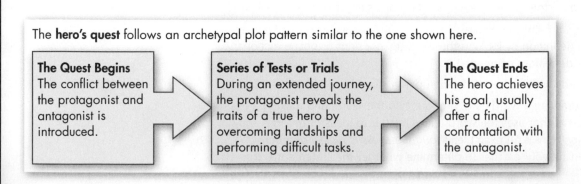

| **The Quest Begins** | **Series of Tests or Trials** | **The Quest Ends** |
|---|---|---|
| The conflict between the protagonist and antagonist is introduced. | During an extended journey, the protagonist reveals the traits of a true hero by overcoming hardships and performing difficult tasks. | The hero achieves his goal, usually after a final confrontation with the antagonist. |

## Forms from the Oral Tradition

Across cultures, storytellers in the oral tradition developed specific narrative forms. Among these forms are myths, folk tales, legends, and epics.

Narratives in each of these forms express the values, ideals, and behaviors held important by the culture from which they came. They also reflect the oral nature of the tradition. For example, epics may feature *epithets,* or descriptive phrases that are repeated when a character is named. These epithets may have helped storytellers memorize the story. They might also have helped listeners recognize and remember the characters.

### Literary Forms in the Oral Tradition

| Form | Characteristics | Example |
|------|-----------------|---------|
| **Myth** | • describes the actions of gods or heroes or explains the origins of elements of nature<br>• is present in the literature of every ancient culture. Ancient Greek and Roman myths are known as **classical mythology.** | Prometheus, son of the Greek god Zeus, defies his father and the other gods by giving fire to humans. |
| **Folk Tale** | • follows a simple formula<br>• deals with heroics, adventure, magic, or romance<br>• frequently contains animal characters with human traits, such as the trickster coyote<br>• includes fables and fairy tales | A poor fisherman catches a golden fish. The fish and the man strike a deal: in exchange for its freedom, the fish will grant the man a wish. The man agrees, but he and his wife become greedy and demand more wishes. The fish vanishes, leaving the fisherman in poverty once more. |
| **Legend** | • recounts the adventures of a hero from the past<br>• relates events that may or may not be based on a historical truth<br>• includes tall tales, which feature exaggeration | Stories of Davy Crockett portray this real-life hero as a superhero who frees the sun, uses lightning to fly, and defeats the entire British navy. |
| **Epic** | • is a long narrative poem<br>• describes the deeds of a larger-than-life hero<br>• combines features of myths and legends<br>• depicts a hero who usually goes on a dangerous journey or quest; the hero is helped or hindered by supernatural creatures or gods<br>• gives a detailed portrait of a culture | The ancient Mesopotamian king Gilgamesh, who is part human and part god, displays wisdom and strength as he struggles against the gods, nature, and his own human weaknesses. |

## In This Section

**Theme and the Oral Tradition**

**Determining Themes**

**Analyzing Point of View and Cultural Experience**

**Close Read: Theme and Point of View**
• Model Text
• Practice Text

**After You Read**

 Common Core State Standards

RL.9-10.2, RL.9-10.6
[For the full wording of the standards, see the standards chart in the front of your textbook.]

# Determining Themes

## At the center of a literary work is its theme—the insight or message that its details combine to convey.

 **Common Core State Standards**

**Reading Literature**

**2.** Determine a theme or central idea of a text and analyze in detail its development over the course of the text, including how it emerges and is shaped and refined by specific details; provide an objective summary of the text.

**6.** Analyze a particular point of view or cultural experience reflected in a work of literature from outside the United States, drawing on a wide reading of world literature.

The **theme,** or central insight or message of a literary work, may be stated directly. For example, a fable ends with a statement of the moral of the story, such as "He who hesitates is lost." Frequently, however, the theme of a work is **implied,** or suggested, by story details. Readers can determine an implied theme by analyzing the way storytellers pattern details.

**Development of Themes** To introduce and develop a theme, writers create patterns of events and actions or of contrasts between characters and their fates. As the story unfolds, new events may reinforce these patterns or alter them, suggesting new ideas to readers.

By identifying such patterns as you read, you will gain clues to the implied theme. Restating the patterns in general terms will help you reach a conclusion about an implied theme, as shown in the following example:

| Title | "Midas and the Golden Touch" |
|---|---|
| **Pattern** | Everything King Midas touches turns to gold, including his beloved daughter. |
| **Generalized Restatement** | Driven by greed, a person destroys what he loves. |
| **Theme** | Greed can destroy all that is good in a person's life. |

**Determining Universal Themes** In the oral tradition, universal themes—themes found in the literature of many cultures—are often

conveyed through the use of **archetypes,** or recurring elements common to many stories. Your ability to recognize these archetypes as the story develops and to interpret their meanings can help you determine a story's universal themes, as in the following example:

| Story | **The Tortoise and the Hare** A tortoise and a hare compete in a race. The hare assumes he will win and stops for a nap. The tortoise keeps going and wins. |
|---|---|
| **Archetypes** | • Overconfident, boastful character (hare)<br>• Quiet, confident character (tortoise)<br>• Plot pattern: Competition in which a weaker character succeeds because of the pride of a stronger character |
| **Universal Themes** | • Slow and steady wins the race.<br>• Too much pride can have bad results. |

**Culturally Specific Themes** Not all themes in the oral tradition are universal. Some are specific to the time and the culture in which the story originated. These themes reflect the specific social and cultural backgrounds of their authors. Generally, they do not apply to people in modern cultures. Still, they provide an interesting window into the values, beliefs, and customs of bygone eras.

# Analyzing Point of View and Cultural Experience

## Authors' cultural backgrounds influence their points of view.

**Point of View** An author's **point of view,** or perspective, consists of his or her attitudes toward, and beliefs about, a subject. Point of view determines how the writer approaches a subject. An author's point of view is influenced in part by his or her cultural experiences—the basic experiences, beliefs, and values that shape life in his or her society.

Literature in the oral tradition usually expresses a cultural—rather than an individual—point of view. By contrast, works of modern literature usually express an author's unique and individual point of view. This point of view may even be critical of the author's own culture. In both cases, it is important for readers to recognize the point of view and cultural experiences that shape a literary text.

### Examples

| Author's Cultural Experiences |
|---|
| The history, beliefs, values, and behavior of a specific group |

↓

| Author's Point of View, or Perspective |
|---|
| The author's attitude—feelings, opinions, and ideas—about a subject; the author's view of the world |

**Cultural Experience and Purpose** The author's **purpose** is his or her main reason for writing. Writers usually write **to entertain, to inform or explain,** or **to persuade.** Although entertainment was a means for getting the attention of listeners, storytellers in the oral tradition also felt responsible for preserving the identity of their culture. Through stories and poems, they reminded people of their history; they communicated values to younger members of their group; and they shared religious beliefs.

Storytellers were more than just entertainers; they served as historians, teachers, and advisors.

Modern writers may also create literature with more than one purpose in mind. For example, an author might write a story that includes information about a serious problem in the world, and at the same time provide readers with a satisfying narrative that entertains.

**Changing Points of View** As stories were passed among generations and cultures, details changed to reflect different values and attitudes. Consider this example of a story that has been retold in numerous cultures.

---

**Example: Cinderella**

After Cinderella's mother dies, her father remarries and leaves Cinderella with his new wife and her two daughters. Cinderella is enslaved by the unreasonable demands of her cruel stepmother and stepsisters. She attends the King's ball and she meets the Prince. Eventually, Cinderella and the Prince marry and live happily ever after.

| Culture/ Version | Cultural Viewpoint | Specific Details |
|---|---|---|
| German tale retold by the Brothers Grimm in 1812 | Medieval view: Cruelty and violence are part of the world. | At the end, birds peck out the eyes of the stepsisters. |
| American version, based on a retelling by the French writer Charles Perrault in 1697 | Modern view: Violence and cruelty should be hidden from children's view. | At the end, Cinderella forgives her stepsisters and invites them to live in the castle. |

# Close Read: Theme and Point of View

Recognizing theme and point of view in literature will enrich your reading experience and broaden your appreciation of the written word.

From the oral tradition to works of modern literature, stories and poems teach us about life, other cultures, and ourselves. They also express distinctive points of view of the world. To convey themes and express point of view, storytellers use a variety of literary elements as well as details that reflect their cultural experiences. Note that nonfiction writers, too, may incorporate literary elements into their works. For example, a work of literary nonfiction may express its writer's point of view as it conveys a central idea, or theme. Analyze literary elements as you read to draw conclusions about theme and point of view. Use the tips in the chart to guide you.

## Clues to Theme and Point of View

### Archetype
As you read, look for

- essential opposites, such as good and evil, or dark and light;
- character types, such as the hero, the trickster, the warrior, or the mysterious guide;
- patterns of events, such as a sequence of obstacles, or a series of riddles.

### Characters
As you read, notice

- what you learn about characters from their appearances, thoughts, actions, and words;
- ways in which characters' values, beliefs, and struggles reflect the cultural context of the work;
- what insight into life characters' actions and ultimate fates suggest.

### Social and Cultural Context
As you read, think about

- cultural practices described in the text;
- values and beliefs suggested by characters' actions, thoughts, and statements;
- the writer's background, including his or her culture, geographic location, and beliefs.

### Direct Statements or Observations
As you read, notice

- any direct statements or observations characters make about themselves or their situations;
- any direct statements the author makes about his or her values, background, or beliefs.

### Setting
The time and place in which a work takes place may shed light on the theme and cultural point of view. As you read, consider

- the **setting**—when and where the story occurs;
- what insights about the world the setting suggests—for example, whether the setting is hostile or friendly, fertile or arid, unforgiving or welcoming.

### Word Choice and Sentence Patterns
As you read, look for

- descriptive details that help express the writer's point of view;
- words with strong positive or negative connotations, or associations, suggesting a point of view;
- repeated sentence patterns that emphasize particular ideas.

# Model

**About the Text** The *Ramayana* is one of the famous epic poems of India. The poet Valmiki wrote the earliest surviving version in the ancient Indian language of Sanskrit some time after 300 B.C. Grounded in Hindu culture, the poem tells the life story of Rama, who embodies the spirit of the Hindu god Vishnu.

## from the *Ramayana* retold by R. K. Narayan

***Background:*** *As an adult, Rama is about to inherit the throne from his father when evil plots result in his banishment from the kingdom. For fourteen years, he wanders in exile with his wife, Sita, and his brother, Lakshmana. During this time, Sita is kidnapped by the evil giant Ravana, chief of a group of rakshasas, or demons. His name means "He who makes the universe scream." Rama sets out to rescue Sita with the help of Hanuman, the monkey god, and a huge battle ensues. This selection opens as the battle is reaching its climax.*

### Rama and Ravana in Battle

Every moment, news came to Ravana of fresh disasters in his camp. One by one, most of his commanders were lost. No one who went forth with battle cries was heard of again. Cries and shouts and the wailings of the widows of warriors came over the chants and songs of triumph that his courtiers arranged to keep up at a loud pitch in his assembly hall. Ravana became restless and abruptly left the hall and went up on a tower, from which he could obtain a full view of the city. He surveyed the scene below but could not stand it. One who had spent a lifetime in destruction, now found the gory spectacle intolerable. Groans and wailings reached his ears with deadly clarity. . . . This was too much for him. He felt a terrific rage rising within him, mixed with some admiration for Rama's valor. He told himself, "The time has come for me to act by myself again."

He hurried down the steps of the tower, returned to his chamber, and prepared himself for the battle. He had a ritual bath and performed special prayers to gain the benediction of Shiva; donned his battle dress, matchless armor, armlets, and crowns. He had on a protective armor for every inch of his body. . . .

When he emerged from his chamber, his heroic appearance was breathtaking. He summoned his chariot, which could be drawn by horses or move on its own if the horses were hurt or killed. People stood aside when he came out of the palace and entered his chariot. "This is my resolve," he said to himself: "Either that woman Sita, or my wife Mandodari, will soon have cause to cry and roll in the dust in grief. Surely, before this day is done, one of them will be a widow."

The gods in heaven noticed Ravana's determined move and felt that Rama would need all the support they could muster. They requested Indra to send down his special chariot for Rama's use. When the chariot appeared at his camp, Rama was deeply impressed with the magnitude and brilliance of the vehicle. . . .

Rama fastened his sword, slung two quivers full of rare arrows over his shoulders, and climbed into the chariot.

---

**Archetype** Sita's kidnapping sets up the conflict between Rama and Ravana. This struggle is an archetype that expresses an important universal theme—the question of whether good or evil ultimately triumphs.

**Characters** The narrator reveals Ravana's disturbed state of mind as Ravana prepares to face Rama. These details develop one important theme— evil is associated with a lack of self-control.

**Social and Cultural Context** Shiva is the Hindu god of destruction. This reference would have special meaning for members of the Hindu religion.

**Social and Cultural Context** The gods' support for Rama reflects Hindu belief in a moral universe and is key to the story's cultural point of view.

## Model continued

**Word Choice** The use of descriptive phrases creates a vivid picture of the scene. The mood of excitement and chaos reflects the author's perspective—the battle will be exciting.

**Characters** In the heat of battle, Rama is calm, wise, and rational. The contrast between Rama's and Ravana's states of mind helps refine an important theme—good is associated with rational thought and action, evil with disorder.

**Social and Cultural Context** Omens, or events regarded as signs of the future, were often taken quite seriously in ancient cultures.

**Word Choice** The phrase "his own doom" reveals that Rama will triumph over Ravana. This outcome develops the universal theme that good triumphs over evil.

The beat of war drums, the challenging cries of soldiers, the trumpets, and the rolling chariots speeding along to confront each other, created a deafening mixture of noise. While Ravana had instructed his charioteer to speed ahead, Rama very gently ordered his chariot driver, "Ravana is in a rage; let him perform all the antics he desires and exhaust himself. Until then be calm; we don't have to hurry forward. Move slowly and calmly, and you must strictly follow my instructions; I will tell you when to drive faster."

Ravana's assistant and one of his staunchest supporters, Mahodara—the giant among giants in his physical appearance—begged Ravana, "Let me not be a mere spectator when you confront Rama. Let me have the honor of grappling with him. Permit me to attack Rama."

"Rama is my sole concern," Ravana replied. "If you wish to engage yourself in a fight, you may fight his brother Lakshmana."

Noticing Mahodara's purpose, Rama steered his chariot across his path in order to prevent Mahodara from reaching Lakshmana. Whereupon Mahodara ordered his chariot driver, "Now dash straight ahead, directly into Rama's chariot."

The charioteer, more practical-minded, advised him, "I would not go near Rama. Let us keep away." But Mahodara, obstinate and intoxicated with war fever, made straight for Rama. He wanted to have the honor of a direct encounter with Rama himself in spite of Ravana's advice; and for this honor he paid a heavy price, as it was a moment's work for Rama to destroy him, and leave him lifeless and shapeless on the field. Noticing this, Ravana's anger mounted further. He commanded his driver, "You will not slacken now. Go." Many ominous signs were seen now—his bowstrings suddenly snapped; the mountains shook; thunders rumbled in the skies; tears flowed from the horses' eyes; elephants with decorated foreheads moved along dejectedly. Ravana, noticing them, hesitated only for a second, saying, "I don't care. This mere mortal Rama is of no account, and these omens do not concern me at all." Meanwhile, Rama paused for a moment to consider his next step; and suddenly turned towards the armies supporting Ravana, which stretched away to the horizon, and destroyed them. He felt that this might be one way of saving Ravana. With his armies gone, it was possible that Ravana might have a change of heart. But it had only the effect of spurring Ravana on; he plunged forward and kept coming nearer Rama and his own doom.

# Independent Practice

**About the Text** In this excerpt from *The Carolina Way*, Coach Dean Smith, who describes himself as an "open-minded dictator," offers his perspectives on how to build and maintain a winning team, whether in sports, business, or any other area of life.

## "Play Hard; Play Together; Play Smart" from *The Carolina Way* by Dean Smith with John Kilgo

I never went into a season as North Carolina's head coach thinking we'd just plug things into the previous year's plan and duplicate ourselves. As I said, we never had the same team return, and there were any number of other variables from one year to the next. We couldn't have had the long run of success that we enjoyed if we'd been too stubborn to change and come up with new ideas and different ways to play the game.

I will repeat this several times in this book: Don't fear change. Sometimes change can refresh a stale team; sometimes it's mandated by changing personnel; sometimes the rules of the game change. We adapted each year to hide our weaknesses and accentuate our strengths.

Although we didn't have a system at North Carolina, we certainly had a philosophy. We believed in it strongly and didn't stray very far from it. It pretty much stayed the same from my first year as head coach. It was our mission statement; our strategic plan, our entire approach in a nutshell: Play hard; play smart; play together.

*Hard* meant with effort, determination, and courage; *together* meant unselfishly, trusting your teammates, and doing everything possible not to let them down; *smart* meant with good execution and poise, treating each possession as if it were the only one in the game.

That was our philosophy; we believed that if we kept our focus on those tenets, success would follow. Our North Carolina players seldom heard me or my assistants talk about winning. Winning would be the by-product of the process. There could be no shortcuts.

Making winning the ultimate goal usually isn't good teaching. Tom Osborne, the great former football coach of the University of Nebraska, said that making winning the goal can actually get in the way of winning. I agree. So many things happened in games that were beyond our control: the talent and experience of the teams; bad calls by officials; injuries; bad luck.

By sticking to our philosophy, we asked realistic things from our players. A player could play hard. He could play unselfishly and do things to help his teammates succeed. He could play intelligently if we did the job in practice as coaches. We measured our success by how we did in those areas.

**Setting** Dean Smith coached basketball at the University of North Carolina from 1961 through 1997. In what way, if any, might this setting be important to the development of his theme?

**Direct Statements and Observations** Smith explains each of the beliefs that make up his philosophy. What do these direct statements tell you about his point of view on basketball?

## Practice continued

**Social and Cultural Context** American culture is not the only one that values fierce competition. The oral tradition shows that many ancient cultures engaged in competitions as a means of proving superiority. What does Smith's reaction to the player at the Air Force Academy show about the difference between his values and those commonly held in his culture?

**Sentence Patterns** In what way does the repetition of sentences help emphasize and develop Smith's theme?

**Social and Cultural Context** What words and phrases in this sentence are specific to the culture of basketball? Why does Smith include them here?

When we put these elements together, the players had fun, one of my goals as their coach. I wanted our players to enjoy the experience of playing basketball for North Carolina. Each player on our team knew he was important. Each did a terrific job of sharing the ball, which also made the game enjoyable for more players. All won and lost as a team.

Of course it is easier to talk about playing hard, playing smart, and playing together than it is to do all three. It begins by the recruiting of unselfish players, who subscribe to the philosophy of team over individual. In a summer physical education class I once taught at the Air Force Academy there was one young man who shot every time he touched the ball. Exasperated from watching him, I pulled his four teammates off the court. He asked who would throw the ball inbounds to him. "You understand that it takes at least one more player," I said to him.

### Playing Hard

Maybe a player wasn't the fastest, the tallest, or the most athletic person on the court. In the course of any given game that was out of his control. But each of them could control the effort with which he played. "Never let anyone play harder than you," I told them. "That is part of the game you can control." If another team played harder than we did, we had no excuse for it. None. We worked on it in every practice. If a player didn't give maximum effort, we dealt with it right then. We stopped practice and had the entire team run sprints for the offending player. We played a style of basketball that was physically exhausting and made it impossible for a player to go full throttle for forty minutes. When he got tired, he flashed the tired signal, a raised fist, and we substituted for him. He could put himself back in the game once he had rested. We didn't want tired players on the court because they usually tried to rest on defense. That wouldn't work in our plan. Therefore we watched closely in practice and in games to make sure players played hard. If they slacked off, it was important to catch them and get them out of the game, or if it occurred in practice, to have the entire team run.

### Playing Together

One of the first things I did at the beginning of preseason practice was to spell out for our players the importance of team play. Basketball is a game that counts on togetherness. I pointed out that seldom, if ever, did the nation's leading scorer play on a ranked team. He certainly didn't play on a championship team. I made them understand that our plan would fall apart if they didn't take care of one another: set screens; play team defense; box out; pass to the open man. One man who failed to do his job unselfishly could undermine the efforts of the four other players on the court.

### Playing Smart

We taught and drilled until we made the things we wanted to see become habits. The only way to have a smart team is to have one that is fundamentally sound. We didn't skimp on fundamentals. We worked on them hard in practice and repeated them until they were down cold. We didn't introduce something and then move away from it before we had nailed it. Our entire program was built around practice, which we will talk more about in a later chapter. Practice, competitive games, late-game situations, and my relationship with our players are what I've missed most since I retired from coaching. We expected our team to execute well and with precision. If we practiced well and learned, we could play smart. It was another thing we could control. . . .

I stay in touch with many members of my extended family, former Carolina basketball players. These men have brought great happiness to my life. Ninety-six percent of them earned their college degrees, and one-third of those continued their studies at graduate and professional schools. It's the way a teacher's career should be judged. Our former players are doing great things for people in all walks of life.

The Carolina Way isn't the only way, that's for certain. But playing hard, playing smart, playing together certainly worked well for us.

Our trophy case is full, but far more important, our Museum of Good Memories runneth over.

**Point of View** How does Smith measure his success? How does his attitude reinforce the theme of the selection?

## After You Read

### Play Hard; Play Together; Play Smart *from* The Carolina Way

**1. Key Ideas and Details** Write an **objective summary** of "Play Hard; Play Together; Play Smart." Remember that an objective summary should not include your personal reaction to the selection and should include just the most important ideas and details.

**2. Key Ideas and Details Infer:** What is Dean Smith's main purpose for writing "Play Hard; Play Together; Play Smart"? Explain.

**3. Key Ideas and Details (a) Cite:** Name two factors in sports that, according to Smith, are beyond a team's control.
**(b) Drawing Conclusions:** In what way might Smith's point of view on coaching help a team deal with the unexpected?

**4. Key Ideas and Details Cite:** According to Smith, how should a teacher's career be judged?

**5. Craft and Structure Analyze:** How does Smith's point of view influence the organization of main ideas in the text?

**6. Integration of Knowledge and Ideas (a) Analyze:** Using a chart like the one shown, analyze the values that Smith emphasized as a basketball coach. In the first column, list the three values that Smith taught. In the second column, give an example of how Smith promoted each value among his players. In the third column, suggest ways that Smith's values could apply to other areas of life.

| Value | Specific Examples | Application to Life |
|---|---|---|
|  |  |  |

**(b) Collaborate:** In a small group, discuss your findings, and add new insights to your chart.

# Preparing to Read the *Odyssey*

*Homer's epic poems celebrate the legendary heroes and heritage of a great culture.*

## Historical Background: Ancient Greece

The world of ancient Greece included the Greek mainland, dipping down from continental Europe, and western Asia Minor, the Asian part of present-day Turkey. It also included hundreds of islands in the Aegean (ē jē´ ən) Sea, the arm of the Mediterranean Sea between mainland Greece and Asia Minor, and in the Ionian (ī ō´ nē ən) Sea, the arm of the Mediterranean to the west of mainland Greece. Odysseus, the legendary hero of Homer's *Odyssey*, was said to be the ruler of Ithaca, one of the western islands.

**The Minoans and Mycenaeans**   Nearly a thousand years before Odysseus would have lived, Greek civilization rose to greatness on Crete, another island south of the mainland. By about 2000 B.C., a sophisticated society called the Minoan (mi nō´ ən) civilization had developed on Crete. Judging by the archaeological evidence, the Minoans produced elegant stone palaces and fine carvings and metalwork. They also developed a writing system, preserved on a few hundred of the clay tablets on which they wrote. Scholars call that writing system Linear A and have yet to decipher it.

For several centuries, Minoan civilization dominated the Greek world. Then, in about 1450 B.C., it collapsed rather suddenly, perhaps due to earthquakes and invasion. With the weakening of Minoan culture, the Mycenaeans (mī´sə nē´ ənz) became the dominant force in the Greek world. Originating on mainland Greece, the Mycenaeans had swept south and into Crete. Strongly influenced by Minoan civilization, the Mycenaeans too had a palace culture, an economy based on trade, and a writing system that mostly used clay tablets. Evidence of their writing is found in Knossos and Chania on Crete as well as in Mycenae, Pylos, and Thebes, three of their mainland strongholds. Because the Mycenaeans spoke an archaic, or older, form of Greek, scholars have been able to decipher their writing, known as Linear B. It was used primarily to keep palace records.

Sir Arthur Evans, the British archaeologist who worked extensively on Crete, named Minoan civilization for King Minos (mī´ näs), a ruler of Crete in Greek mythology.

◀ ▲ The photograph above shows a reconstruction of one wall of The Palace of Minos at Knossos, Crete. The photo at left shows a fresco, or wall painting, from the palace's interior.

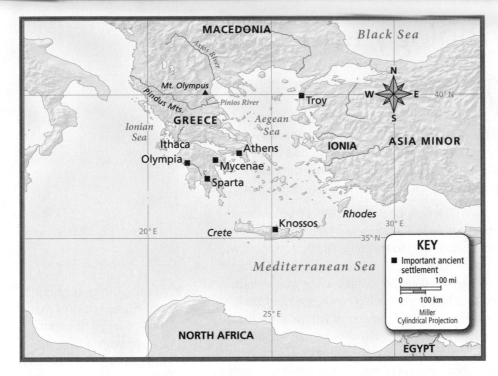

◄ Ancient Greece included mainland territories and hundreds of islands clustered in the the Aegean and Ionian Seas. Odysseus' kingdom of Ithaca is a small island in the Ionian Sea.

**Legendary Conflicts**  The writing and archaeological remains suggest early cities with large central palaces and thick protective walls, each ruled by a wanax, or king. Others in society included priests, slaves, workers in trades or crafts, administrative officials, and a warrior class. The Mycenaens wore armor in battle, in which they engaged with apparent frequency. Their warfare with Troy, on the northwest coast of Asia Minor, has become one of the most famous military ventures of all time—the Trojan War. If there really was a King Odysseus, he would have been a key player in that conflict.

Scholars date the Trojan War to somewhere around 1200 B.C. Shortly thereafter, Mycenaean civilization collapsed as the Greek world fell into chaos and confusion. For some three hundred years, writing seems to have disappeared in what is often called the Greek Dark Ages. Then, in about 850 B.C., Greece began emerging from this darkness, spurred by flourishing trade throughout the Mediterranean region. Along with the economic boom came a resurgence of the arts and learning that peaked with the epic poems of Homer. These poems—the *Iliad* and the *Odyssey*—chronicle the Trojan War and the subsequent adventures of the hero Odysseus.

**The Rise of City-States**  After Homer's time, Greek civilization grew more organized and sophisticated. Smaller communities organized as city-states—cities that functioned independently, as countries do. Among them were Sparta, known for its military prowess, and Athens, the birthplace of democracy. Though rivalries sometimes led to warfare among city-states, the Greeks still recognized their common heritage as Hellenes, as they by then usually called themselves. They coordinated efforts to fight common enemies, such as the Persians. They participated in the Olympic games, which records indicate began in 776 B.C. Together, too, they saw the works of Homer as pillars of their heritage, two great epics that celebrated their common past and its heroes.

> The Greek word for "city-state" is *polis*, the origin of our words *metropolis* and *politics*.

# Greek Mythology and Customs

*All aspects of Greek culture reflected belief in the Olympian gods.*

Ancient Greek religion was based on a belief in many gods. Zeus was king of the gods; Hera, his beautiful and powerful wife. Other gods and goddesses were associated with different aspects of nature or human behavior. The most important ones were said to dwell on Mount Olympus, the tallest mountain in Greece, where Zeus sat on a throne of gold. These Olympians, however, were not the first gods.

**The Titans are Overthrown** The early poet Hesiod (hē´ sē əd) wrote a mythic account of the origin of the gods in *Theogony*, a work the Greeks revered almost as much as Homer's epics. According to that origin myth, first there was Chaos, a dark, empty void. Out of Chaos came the Earth, personified as the goddess Gaea. The Earth generated the skies, personified as the god Uranus, who with Gaea produced the giant gods known as Titans. Cronus, the chief Titan, ruled the universe until he was displaced by his three sons, who split the universe among them. Zeus, the most powerful of these sons, became ruler of the heavens. His brother Poseidon became ruler of the seas. The third brother, Hades, became ruler of the underworld, a dark region also called Hades, which was inhabited by shades of the dead.

The Greek gods were powerful, but they were not all-powerful: even Zeus had to bow to fate. The gods displayed many human qualities and were often vengeful and quarrelsome. They were also quick to slap down human beings guilty of hubris (hyo͞o´ or ho͞o´ bris), or excessive pride. To appease the gods, human beings performed sacrifices, which often involved the killing of animals. In the *Odyssey*, Odysseus makes several sacrifices to plead for divine aid on his journey home.

**Celebrating the Gods** The Greeks worshipped the gods in temples dedicated to many gods or just one. The Parthenon in Athens, for instance, was a temple dedicated to the goddess Athena. The Greeks also celebrated their gods at great festivals such as the Olympic games, which were dedicated to Zeus.

The Greeks believed in prophecy, which they associated with the god Apollo. In the *Odyssey*, Odysseus journeys all the way to the underworld to consult the blind prophet Tiresias (tī rē´ sē əs), who continues to have the gift of prophecy even though he has died. The Greeks also believed in myths, stories about gods and heroes that they used to explain the world around them. The *Iliad* and the *Odyssey* drew on these myths; however, for future generations of ancient Greeks, Homer's two epics—like Hesiod's *Theogony*—took on the aura of myths themselves.

▼ Apollo, the god of light and music (among many other things), is often shown with a lyre, the stringed instrument from which the English word *lyric* derives.

# Gods in Greek Mythology

You may be more familiar with the Roman names for the Greek gods. The ancient Romans accepted Greek mythology, but they had their own names for its gods and heroes. For example, they called Odysseus *Ulysses*. For each Greek god listed below, the Roman equivalent is also given.

**Zeus** (zōōs) king of the gods and ruler of the heavens; Roman *Jupiter*, sometimes called *Jove*

**Hera** (her´ ə) wife of Zeus and goddess of married women; Roman *Juno*

**Poseidon** (pō sī´ dən) god of the seas; Roman *Neptune*

**Hades** (hā´ dēz) god of the underworld; Roman *Pluto*

**Aphrodite** (af´ rə dītē) goddess of love and beauty; Roman *Venus*

**Ares** (er' ēz) god of war; Roman *Mars*

**Apollo** (əp ol´ ō) god of prophecy and music; also called Phoebus (fè' bəs); Roman *Apollo*

**Artemis** (är´ tə mis) goddess of the hunt and the moon; Roman *Diana*

**Athena** (ə thē´ nə) goddess of wisdom, skills, and war; Roman *Minerva*

**Hephaestus** (hē fes´ təs) god of fire and metalwork; Roman *Vulcan*

**Hermes** (hʉr´ mēz) god of commerce and cunning; messenger of the gods; Roman *Mercury*

**Demeter** (di mē' tər) goddess of the harvest; Roman *Ceres* (sīr´ ez)

**Dionysus** (dī´ ən ī´səs) god of wine and revelry, also called Bacchus (bak´ əs); Roman *Dionysus* or *Bacchus*

**Hestia** (hes´ tē ə) goddess of home and hearth; Roman *Vesta*

**Helios** (hē´ lē os´) sun god; Roman *Sol*

**Uranus** (yōō rə´ nəs) sky god supplanted by his son Cronus; Roman *Uranus*

**Gaea** (jē´ ə) earth goddess and mother of the Titans and Cyclopes; Roman *Tellus* or *Terra*

**Cronus** (krō´ nəs) Titan who ruled the universe before his son Zeus dethroned him; Roman *Saturn*

**Rhea** (rē´ ə) wife of Cronus and mother of Zeus; Roman *Cybele* (sib´ ə lē)

**Cyclops** (sī´ klops) any one of three Titans who forged thunderbolts for Zeus; plural, Cyclopes (sī´ klō pēs)

**The Fates** three goddesses who wove the threads of each person's life: Clotho (klō´ thō) spun the thread; Lachesis (lak´ i sis) measured out the amount of thread; Atropos (a´ trə pis) snipped the thread

**The Muses** (myōō´ ziz) nine goddesses who presided over the arts and sciences, including Calliope (kə lī´ ə pē´), the Muse of epic poetry

▼ Poseidon, god of the sea, was also the god of earthquakes and horses. His symbols include the trident, a three-pronged spear.

# HOMER *epic poet*

## THE POEMS ATTRIBUTED TO HOMER STILL INFLUENCE LITERATURE AND CULTURE TODAY.

*Homer is the legendary poet credited with writing the* Iliad *and the* Odyssey. *These epics, known for their sweeping scope, gripping stories, and vivid style, have captured readers' imaginations for almost 3,000 years.*

**Was there really a Homer?** No one can prove his existence with any certainty, for no authentic record of Homer's life exists. Tradition has it that he was born in Ionia in western Asia Minor, perhaps on the island of Chios, and that he was blind. The location is not unreasonable, for Ionia was a center of poetry and learning, where eastern and western cultures met and new intellectual currents were born. Descriptions of Asia Minor in the *Iliad* show in-depth knowledge of the landscape; moreover, both the *Iliad* and the *Odyssey* contain plot elements found in the world's first known epic, *Gilgamesh*, which by Homer's era had traveled from Mesopotamia (present-day Iraq) to become familiar in Asia Minor. For example, the hero Gilgamesh visits the underworld, just like the hero of the *Odyssey*; he also has a very good friend who is killed, just like Achilles has in the *Iliad*.

Most efforts to date Homer's life place him somewhere between 850 and 750 B.C. As a Greek oral poet, it is unlikely he lived much later, for by then writing had been reintroduced to Greek culture. The details in Homer's epics make clear that the poems were orally composed and that the *Iliad* was written first and probably some years before the *Odyssey*. The two epics differ in style: the *Iliad* is a single long, highly dramatic narrative, while the *Odyssey* is episodic and reads more like an adventure novel than a drama. For these reasons, some scholars even speculate that the epics were composed by two different poets

**Inspiring Poems** Whatever the truth about Homer may be, no one disputes the quality of the two epics with which he is credited. The ancient Greeks revered the *Iliad* and the *Odyssey*. They recited the poems at religious festivals and had children memorize them in school. All the Greek writers and philosophers who came after Homer drew on the two epics. Their influence spread to Rome and beyond, and they became foundational works of western literature. Even in modern times, great works from James Joyce's *Ulysses* to Derek Walcott's *Omeros* have been directly inspired by Homer's verse.

# The Epic Form

An **epic** is a long narrative poem that relates important events in the history or folklore of the culture that produced it. Its central character, or **epic hero,** is a larger-than-life figure who embodies traits that the culture values. Typical among those characteristics are physical strength, bravery, high birth, fame, and effective skills as a leader and in battle.

The *Iliad* and the *Odyssey* influenced virtually all the great western epics that followed them. From the *Aeneid*, the great epic of ancient Rome, to *Beowulf*, the foundational epic of Old English; from *The Divine Comedy*, the masterful epic by the Italian poet Dante, to *Paradise Lost*, the brilliant epic by Britain's John Milton—all had Homer's epics as models. Literary devices in Homer's epics are often imitated in these later works, even though many of the later epics were not orally composed. Influential literary devices found in Homer's epics include the following:

- **Opening invocation to the Muse:** The speaker of the poem asks the Muse for inspiration.

- **Starting the story in medias res,** or "in the middle of things": Beginning (after the invocation) with action instead of background information helps capture audience attention.

- **Lofty style:** Elegant language stresses the nobility of the subject.

- **Objective tone:** By keeping an emotional distance, the poet focuses attention on the story.

- **Meter,** or a fixed rhythmic pattern: A strong meter helps the oral poet remember the lines. In the original Greek, the *Odyssey* uses hexameter, or six beats to a line, which helps create a fast pace.

- **Epithet,** a characterizing phrase for a person, place, or thing: Recurring epithets are easy to remember and can help fill out the meter. Some examples of Homer's epithets include "rosy-fingered dawn" and "son of Laertes" for Odysseus.

- **Epic simile,** a long comparison over many lines: Such similes were another way to fill out the meter and aid the poet's memory.

Ionia, from where Homer may have come, was on the west coast of Asia Minor. The Ionian Sea, where Odysseus's island of Ithaca lies, is off the west coast of Greece. The duplicated names are likely no coincidence; Greek speakers from Ionia probably migrated to the west of Greece and brought the name with them (just as British settlers often brought British place names to America).

▼ The island of Ionia, Homer's possible birthplace, as it appears today

# Before You Read

## *from the* **Odyssey, Part 1**

 **Epic**

Build your skills and improve your comprehension of epic literature with this selection.

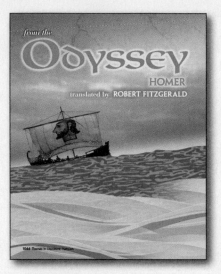

Read the **Odyssey** to learn about a hero of the ancient world, his long journey home, and the choices he makes.

## Common Core State Standards

Meet these standards with Part 1 of the **Odyssey** (p. 1044).

**Reading Literature**
**3.** Analyze how complex characters develop over the course of a text, interact with other characters, and advance the plot or develop the theme. *(Literary Analysis: Epic Hero)*

**Spiral Review: RL.9-10.2**
**5.** Analyze how an author's choices concerning how to structure a text, order events within it, and manipulate time create such effects as mystery, tension, or surprise. *(Literary Analysis: Epic Hero)*

**6.** Analyze a particular point of view or cultural experience reflected in a work of literature from outside the United States, drawing on a wide reading of world literature. *(Reading Skill: Historical and Cultural Context)*

**Writing**
**3.** Write narratives to develop real or imagined experiences or events using effective technique, well-chosen details, and well-structured event sequences. **3.a.** Engage and orient the reader by setting out a problem, situation, or observation, establishing one or multiple point(s) of view,

and introducing a narrator and/or characters. **3.b.** Use narrative techniques, such as dialogue, pacing, description, reflection, and multiple plot lines. **3.c.** Use a variety of techniques to sequence events so that they build on one another to create a coherent whole. **3.d.** Use precise words and phrases, telling details, and sensory language to convey a vivid picture of the experiences, events, setting, and/or characters. *(Writing: Everyday Epic)*

**Speaking and Listening**
**1.** Initiate and participate effectively in a range of collaborative discussions. **1.a.** Come to discussions prepared, having read and researched material under study. **1.b.** Work with peers to set individual roles as needed. *(Speaking and Listening: Conversation)*

**Language**
**1.** Demonstrate command of the conventions of standard English grammar and usage when writing or speaking. *(Conventions: Simple and Compound Sentences)*

# Literary Analysis: Epic Hero

An **epic hero** is the larger-than-life character in an **epic**—a long narrative poem about important events in the history or folklore of a culture. The epic hero demonstrates traits that are valued by the society. The character's traits can be communicated in narration as well as through dialogue. Here, Odysseus speaks about his own courage and leadership:

> Now, by the gods, I drove my big hand spike
> deep in the embers, charring it again,
> and cheered my men along with battle talk
> to keep their courage up; no quitting now.

Traditional epics like the *Odyssey* use specific plot devices, or structures, that both provide background information and allow the story to unfold in an exciting way. For example, many epics begin *in medias res* ("in the middle of things"), meaning that major events occurred before events in the poem begin. The audience is, thus, thrust into the middle of the action. In addition, the hero's adventures are often recounted in a **flashback,** a scene that interrupts a narrative to relate earlier events. Consider how these structural elements added excitement and tension to the story for Homer's original audiences and continue to affect readers today.

# Reading Skill: Historical and Cultural Context

The **historical and cultural context** of a work is the backdrop of details of the time and place in which the work is set or in which it was written. These details include specific events, beliefs, and customs. When you read a work from another time and culture, **use background and prior knowledge** to analyze the influence of the historical and cultural context—the themes and issues important at that time and place.

- Read the author biography, footnotes, and other text aids.
- Note how characters' behavior and attitudes reflect the historical and cultural context.

## Using the Strategy: Context Chart

As you read, use a chart like the one shown to note the influences of ancient Greek culture in Homer's *Odyssey*.

| Historical/Cultural Detail | Background | Analysis |
|---|---|---|
| "Now Zeus the lord of cloud roused in the north a storm against the ships...." | Zeus is king of the gods in Greek mythology. | The *Odyssey* reflects a belief that the gods participate actively in the lives of mortals. |

## Making Connections *from the* Odyssey, Part 1

**Do _heroes_ have responsibilities?**

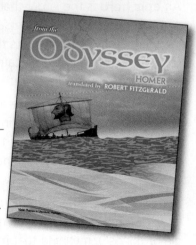

### Writing About the Big Question

In Part 1 of the *Odyssey,* Homer describes the hero Odysseus' long and dangerous journey home. Use these sentence starters to develop your ideas about the Big Question.

A **hero** has an **obligation** to _____ because _____.

The **choices** he or she makes are looked at closely and even scrutinized because _____.

**While You Read** Look for characteristics that define the epic hero and take note of the ways in which Odysseus looks after his men.

### Vocabulary

Read each word and its definition. Decide whether you know the word well, know it a little bit, or do not know it at all. After you read, see how your knowledge of each word has increased.

- **plundered** (plun´ dərd) *v.* took goods by force; looted (p. 1045) *The fierce pirates captured the merchant ship and plundered it.* plunderous *adj.* plunderer *n.*

- **dispatched** (di spacht´) *v.* finished quickly (p. 1053) *Remarkably, she dispatched the assignment an hour before anyone else did.*

- **assuage** (ə swāj´) *v.* calm; pacify (p. 1065) *Gentle words may assuage their anger.* assuaged *v.* assuagement *n.*

- **bereft** (bē reft´) *adj.* deprived (p. 1068) *Bereft of sleep, she struggled to stay awake during the movie.* bereavement *n.*

- **ardor** (är´ dər) *n.* passion; enthusiasm (p. 1073) *The audience cheered their favorite characters with ardor.* ardent *adj.*

- **insidious** (in sid´ ē əs) *adj.* characterized by craftiness and betrayal (p. 1077) *The traitor's insidious actions led to the city's downfall.* insidiously *adv.* insidiousness *n.*

---

### Word Study

The **Old English prefix be-** means "around," "make," or "covered with."

In this selection, Tiresias warns Odysseus that he will be **bereft** of his companions. Tiresias means that Odysseus will lose his companions. **Bereft** is a form of **bereave,** which means "made to suffer a loss."

## Background for the Story

# THE TROJAN WAR

*In the* Iliad, *Homer focuses on the final year of the Trojan War; in the* Odyssey, *he tells what happened to one of the key warriors afterward.*

**It Begins with Strife** According to legend, the Trojan War began when Eris, goddess of strife, brought among the gods a golden apple inscribed "To the fairest." Hera, Athena, and Aphrodite all wanted that apple. They asked Paris, son of the king of Troy, to decide which of them deserved it. Each tried to bribe him: Hera offered power; Athena, wisdom; and Aphrodite, the world's most beautiful woman. The famous Judgment of Paris was that Aphrodite was the fairest. Soon, on a diplomatic mission to Sparta, Paris met Helen, the world's most beautiful woman and Sparta's queen. With Aphrodite's help, the two fell in love and eloped. When Menelaus (**men´ ə lā´ əs**), king of Sparta, could not persuade the Trojans to send his wife, Helen, back, he went to his brother Agamemnon (**ag´ ə mem´ nän**), king of Mycenae and the most powerful Greek leader. Agamemnon called on all the Greek rulers to honor a pact and go to Troy to fight to bring Helen home. The Greeks agreed and sailed to Troy. They laid siege to the city but for ten long years could not breach its impregnable walls.

**War Crimes and Punishment** Agamemnon might have been a more powerful king and Achilles (**ə kil´ ēz**) a superior warrior, but Odysseus, king of Ithaca, was cleverest of them all. He devised a scheme in which the Greeks left a great wooden horse outside the walls of Troy and tricked the Trojans into taking it inside. That night, the Greeks hiding inside the horse—Odysseus among them—slipped out, unlocked the gates of the city, and allowed their fellow warriors to come swarming in to defeat the Trojans and sack the city. The fighting was brutal and destructive. King Priam (**prī´ əm**), Paris's father, for example, was killed while he was praying. The Greeks' behavior angered many of the gods, who made their voyages home very difficult.

Odysseus was no exception. Following the Greek victory, he set sail for Ithaca but encountered a series of perilous misadventures that made his journey last ten years. It is this difficult, adventure-filled journey that Homer's *Odyssey* recounts.

> "Trojan" is the adjective form of the ancient city of Troy. It is also the name for a person from Troy.

> Named for Odysseus, the *Odyssey* gave rise to our English word *odyssey*, meaning "an extended journey."

▼ The Trojan horse, as depicted in the film *Troy* (Warner Brothers, 2004)

*from the*

# Odyssey

## HOMER

### translated by ROBERT FITZGERALD

# PART 1

# The Adventures of Odysseus

*In the opening verses, Homer addresses the muse of epic poetry. He asks her help in telling the tale of Odysseus.*

> Sing in me, Muse,[1] and through me tell the story
> of that man skilled in all ways of contending,
> the wanderer, harried for years on end,
> after he plundered the stronghold
> 5  on the proud height of Troy.[2]
>
> He saw the townlands
> and learned the minds of many distant men,
> and weathered many bitter nights and days
> in his deep heart at sea, while he fought only
> to save his life, to bring his shipmates home.
> 10  But not by will nor valor could he save them,
> for their own recklessness destroyed them all—
> children and fools, they killed and feasted on
> the cattle of Lord Helios,[3] the Sun,
> and he who moves all day through heaven
> 15  took from their eyes the dawn of their return.
> Of these adventures, Muse, daughter of Zeus,[4]
> tell us in our time, lift the great song again.

Note: In translating the *Odyssey,* Fitzgerald spelled Greek names to suggest the sound of the original Greek. In these excerpts, more familiar spellings have been used. For example, Fitzgerald's "Kirkê," "Kyklops," and "Seirênês" are spelled here as "Circe," "Cyclops," and "Sirens."

1. **Muse** (myo͞oz) any one of the nine goddesses of the arts, literature, and sciences; the spirit that is thought to inspire a poet or other artist.
2. **Troy** (trɔi) city in northwest Asia Minor; site of the Trojan War.

**Vocabulary**
**plundered** (plun´ dərd) *v.* took goods by force; looted

3. **Helios** (hē´ lē äs´) sun god.
4. **Zeus** (zo͞os) king of the gods.

# CHARACTERS

**Alcinous** (al sin´ ō əs)—king of the Phaeacians, to whom Odysseus tells his story

**Odysseus** (ō dis´ ē əs)—king of Ithaca

**Calypso** (kə lip´ sō)—sea goddess who loved Odysseus

**Circe** (sʉr´ sē)—enchantress who helped Odysseus

**Zeus** (zo͞os)—king of the gods

**Apollo** (ə päl´ ō)—god of music, poetry, prophecy, and medicine

**Agamemnon** (ag´ ə mem´ nän´)—king and leader of Greek forces

**Poseidon** (pō sī´ dən)—god of sea, earthquakes, horses, and storms at sea

**Athena** (ə thē´ nə)—goddess of wisdom, skills, and warfare

**Polyphemus** (päl´ i fē´ məs)—the Cyclops who imprisoned Odysseus

**Laertes** (lā ʉr´ tēz´)—Odysseus' father

**Cronus** (krō´ nəs)—Titan ruler of the universe; father of Zeus

**Perimedes** (per´ ə mē´ dēz)—member of Odysseus' crew

**Eurylochus** (yo͞o ril´ ə kəs)—another member of the crew

**Tiresias** (tī rē´ sē əs)—blind prophet who advised Odysseus

**Persephone** (pər sef´ ə nē)—wife of Hades

**Telemachus** (tə lem´ ə kəs)—Odysseus and Penelope's son

**Sirens** (sī´ rənz)—creatures whose songs lure sailors to their deaths

**Scylla** (sil´ ə)—sea monster of gray rock

**Charybdis** (kə rib´ dis)—enormous and dangerous whirlpool

**Lampetia** (lam pē´ shə)—nymph

**Hermes** (hʉr´ mēz´)—herald and messenger of the gods

**Eumaeus** (yo͞o mē´ əs)—old swineherd and friend of Odysseus

**Antinous** (an tin´ ō əs)—leader among the suitors

**Eurynome** (yo͞o rin´ ə mē)—housekeeper for Penelope

**Penelope** (pə nel´ ə pē)—Odysseus' wife

**Eurymachus** (yo͞o ri´ mə kəs)—suitor

**Amphinomus** (am fin´ ə məs)—suitor

## Sailing from Troy

*Ten years after the Trojan War, Odysseus departs from the goddess Calypso's island. He arrives in Phaeacia, ruled by Alcinous. Alcinous offers a ship to Odysseus and asks him to tell of his adventures.*

"I am Laertes'[5] son, Odysseus.

                        Men hold me

formidable for guile[6] in peace and war:

20     this fame has gone abroad to the sky's rim.

My home is on the peaked sea-mark of Ithaca[7]
under Mount Neion's wind-blown robe of leaves,
in sight of other islands—Dulichium,
Same, wooded Zacynthus—Ithaca

25     being most lofty in that coastal sea,
and northwest, while the rest lie east and south.
A rocky isle, but good for a boy's training;
I shall not see on earth a place more dear,
though I have been detained long by Calypso,[8]

30     loveliest among goddesses, who held me
in her smooth caves, to be her heart's delight,
as Circe of Aeaea,[9] the enchantress,
desired me, and detained me in her hall.
But in my heart I never gave consent.

35     Where shall a man find sweetness to surpass
his own home and his parents? In far lands
he shall not, though he find a house of gold.

What of my sailing, then, from Troy?

                        What of those years

of rough adventure, weathered under Zeus?

40     The wind that carried west from Ilium[10]
brought me to Ismarus, on the far shore,
a strongpoint on the coast of Cicones.[11]
I stormed that place and killed the men who fought.
Plunder we took, and we enslaved the women,

45     to make division, equal shares to all—
but on the spot I told them: 'Back, and quickly!
Out to sea again!' My men were mutinous,[12]
fools, on stores of wine. Sheep after sheep

5. **Laertes** (lā ʉr´ tēz´)
6. **guile** (gīl) *n.* craftiness; cunning.
7. **Ithaca** (it*h*´ ə kə) island off the west coast of Greece.

**Literary Analysis**
**Epic Hero** For what quality does Odysseus say he is famous?

8. **Calypso** (kə lip´ sō) sea goddess who loved Odysseus.
9. **Circe** (sʉr´ sē) **of Aeaea** (ē´ ē ə)
10. **Ilium** (il´ ē əm) Troy.

11. **Cicones** (si kō´ nēz)
12. **mutinous** (myoot´´n əs) *adj.* rebellious.

**Reading Check**

Who has asked Odysseus to tell his tale?

they butchered by the surf, and shambling cattle,
50  feasting,—while fugitives went inland, running
to call to arms the main force of Cicones.
This was an army, trained to fight on horseback
or, where the ground required, on foot. They came
with dawn over that terrain like the leaves
55  and blades of spring. So doom appeared to us,
dark word of Zeus for us, our evil days.
My men stood up and made a fight of it—
backed on the ships, with lances kept in play,
from bright morning through the blaze of noon
60  holding our beach, although so far outnumbered;
but when the sun passed toward unyoking time,
then the Achaeans,[13] one by one, gave way.
Six benches were left empty in every ship
that evening when we pulled away from death.
65  And this new grief we bore with us to sea:
our precious lives we had, but not our friends.
No ship made sail next day until some shipmate
had raised a cry, three times, for each poor ghost
unfleshed by the Cicones on that field.

# The Lotus-Eaters

70      Now Zeus the lord of cloud roused in the north
a storm against the ships, and driving veils
of squall moved down like night on land and sea.
The bows went plunging at the gust; sails
cracked and lashed out strips in the big wind.
75  We saw death in that fury, dropped the yards,
unshipped the oars, and pulled for the nearest lee:[14]
then two long days and nights we lay offshore
worn out and sick at heart, tasting our grief,
until a third Dawn came with ringlets shining.
80  Then we put up our masts, hauled sail, and rested,
letting the steersmen and the breeze take over.

I might have made it safely home, that time,
but as I came round Malea the current
took me out to sea, and from the north
85  a fresh gale drove me on, past Cythera.
Nine days I drifted on the teeming sea
before dangerous high winds. Upon the tenth

**13. Achaeans** (ə kē′ ənz) *n.* Greeks; here, Odysseus' men.

**Reading Skill
Historical and Cultural
Context** What beliefs and values are reflected in lines 65–69?

**14. lee** (lē) *n.* area sheltered from the wind.

**Literary Analysis
Epic Hero** What words in line 82 remind you that this part is a flashback?

we came to the coastline of the Lotus-Eaters,
who live upon that flower. We landed there
90  to take on water. All ships' companies
mustered alongside for the mid-day meal.
Then I sent out two picked men and a runner
to learn what race of men that land sustained.
They fell in, soon enough, with Lotus-Eaters,
95  who showed no will to do us harm, only
offering the sweet Lotus to our friends—
but those who ate this honeyed plant, the Lotus,
never cared to report, nor to return:
they longed to stay forever, browsing on
100  that native bloom, forgetful of their homeland.
I drove them, all three wailing, to the ships,
tied them down under their rowing benches,
and called the rest: 'All hands aboard;
come, clear the beach and no one taste
105  the Lotus, or you lose your hope of home.'
Filing in to their places by the rowlocks
my oarsmen dipped their long oars in the surf,
and we moved out again on our sea faring.

**Literary Analysis**
**Epic Hero** Which characteristics of an epic hero does Odysseus show in this episode?

## Critical Thinking

1. **Key Ideas and Details (a)** While on Ismarus, in what ways do Odysseus' men disobey orders? **(b) Analyze Cause and Effect:** What is the result of this disobedience? **(c) Speculate:** What lesson might Odysseus take away from this experience?

2. **Key Ideas and Details (a)** What happens to the men who eat the Lotus? **(b) Infer:** What does this episode suggest about the main problem that Odysseus has with his men? **(c) Evaluate:** Do you think Odysseus responds appropriately to the three men who long to stay with the Lotus-Eaters? Why or why not?

3. **Key Ideas and Details (a)** Note two points at which Odysseus mentions a desire to return home. **(b) Infer:** What significant role might his longing for home play in Odysseus' epic journey?

4. **Integration of Knowledge and Ideas (a)** In this episode, does Odysseus prove himself to be a hero? **(b)** What responsibilities does he demonstrate, if any? *[Connect to the Big Question: Do heroes have responsibilities?]*

*Cite textual evidence to support your responses.*

# The Cyclops

**15.** **Cyclopes** (sī klō′ pēz′) *n.* plural form of Cyclops (sī′ klăps′), race of giants with one eye in the middle of the forehead.

In the next land we found were Cyclopes,[15]
110    giants, louts, without a law to bless them.
In ignorance leaving the fruitage of the earth in mystery
to the immortal gods, they neither plow
nor sow by hand, nor till the ground, though grain—
wild wheat and barley—grows untended, and
115    wine-grapes, in clusters, ripen in heaven's rains.
Cyclopes have no muster and no meeting,
no consultation or old tribal ways,
but each one dwells in his own mountain cave
dealing out rough justice to wife and child,
120    indifferent to what the others do. . . .

As we rowed on, and nearer to the mainland,
at one end of the bay, we saw a cavern
yawning above the water, screened with laurel,
and many rams and goats about the place
125    inside a sheepfold—made from slabs of stone
earthfast between tall trunks of pine and rugged
towering oak trees.
                     A prodigious[16] man
slept in this cave alone, and took his flocks
to graze afield—remote from all companions,
130    knowing none but savage ways, a brute
so huge, he seemed no man at all of those
who eat good wheaten bread; but he seemed rather
a shaggy mountain reared in solitude.
We beached there, and I told the crew
135    to stand by and keep watch over the ship:
as for myself I took my twelve best fighters
and went ahead. I had a goatskin full
of that sweet liquor that Euanthes' son,
Maron, had given me. He kept Apollo's[17]
140    holy grove at Ismarus; for kindness
we showed him there, and showed his wife and child,
he gave me seven shining golden talents[18]
perfectly formed, a solid silver winebowl,
and then this liquor—twelve two-handled jars
145    of brandy, pure and fiery. Not a slave
in Maron's household knew this drink; only
he, his wife and the storeroom mistress knew;

**Reading Skill**
**Historical and**
**Cultural Context** Based on Odysseus' criticism of the Cyclopes, what kind of society do you think the Greeks valued?

**16. prodigious** (prō dij′ əs) *adj.* enormous.

**Reading Skill**
**Historical and Cultural Context** What does this passage reveal about ancient Greek attitudes toward the importance of community?

**17. Apollo** (ə päl′ ō) god of music, poetry, prophecy, and medicine.

**18. talents** units of money in ancient Greece.

and they would put one cupful—ruby-colored,
honey-smooth—in twenty more of water,
150   but still the sweet scent hovered like a fume
over the winebowl. No man turned away
when cups of this came round.

                              A wineskin full
I brought along, and victuals[19] in a bag,
for in my bones I knew some towering brute
155   would be upon us soon—all outward power,
a wild man, ignorant of civility.

We climbed, then, briskly to the cave. But Cyclops
had gone afield, to pasture his fat sheep,
so we looked round at everything inside:
160   a drying rack that sagged with cheeses, pens
crowded with lambs and kids,[20] each in its class:
firstlings apart from middlings, and the 'dewdrops,'
or newborn lambkins, penned apart from both.
And vessels full of whey[21] were brimming there—
165   bowls of earthenware and pails for milking.
My men came pressing round me, pleading:

                                    'Why not
take these cheeses, get them stowed, come back,
throw open all the pens, and make a run for it?
We'll drive the kids and lambs aboard. We say
170   put out again on good salt water!'

                              Ah,
how sound that was! Yet I refused. I wished
to see the cave man, what he had to offer—
no pretty sight, it turned out, for my friends.
We lit a fire, burnt an offering,
175   and took some cheese to eat; then sat in silence
around the embers, waiting. When he came
he had a load of dry boughs[22] on his shoulder
to stoke his fire at suppertime. He dumped it
with a great crash into that hollow cave,
180   and we all scattered fast to the far wall.
Then over the broad cavern floor he ushered
the ewes he meant to milk. He left his rams
and he-goats in the yard outside, and swung
high overhead a slab of solid rock

**19. victuals** (vit′ əlz) *n.* food or other provisions.

**20. kids** young goats.

**21. whey** (hwā) *n.* thin, watery part of milk separated from the thicker curds.

**Literary Analysis**
**Epic Hero** What character flaw does the hero Odysseus reveal by refusing to leave the cave?

**22. boughs** (bouz) *n.* tree branches.

**Reading Check**

Where is Cyclops when Odysseus and his men enter the cave?

**23. withy** (with´ ē) *adj.* made from tough, flexible twigs.

185 to close the cave. Two dozen four-wheeled wagons,
with heaving wagon teams, could not have stirred
the tonnage of that rock from where he wedged it
over the doorsill. Next he took his seat
and milked his bleating ewes. A practiced job

190 he made of it, giving each ewe her suckling;
thickened his milk, then, into curds and whey,
sieved out the curds to drip in withy[23] baskets,
and poured the whey to stand in bowls
cooling until he drank it for his supper.

195 When all these chores were done, he poked the fire,
heaping on brushwood. In the glare he saw us.

'Strangers,' he said, 'who are you? And where from?
What brings you here by seaways—a fair traffic?
Or are you wandering rogues, who cast your lives

200 like dice, and ravage other folk by sea?'

We felt a pressure on our hearts, in dread
of that deep rumble and that mighty man.
But all the same I spoke up in reply:
'We are from Troy, Achaeans, blown off course

205 by shifting gales on the Great South Sea;
homeward bound, but taking routes and ways
uncommon; so the will of Zeus would have it.
We served under Agamemnon,[24] son of Atreus—
the whole world knows what city

**24. Agamemnon** (ag´ ə mem´ nän´) king who led the Greek army during the Trojan War.

210 he laid waste, what armies he destroyed.
It was our luck to come here; here we stand,
beholden for your help, or any gifts
you give—as custom is to honor strangers.
We would entreat you, great Sir, have a care

215 for the gods' courtesy; Zeus will avenge
the unoffending guest.'

He answered this
from his brute chest, unmoved:

'You are a ninny,
or else you come from the other end of nowhere,
telling me, mind the gods! We Cyclopes

220 care not a whistle for your thundering Zeus
or all the gods in bliss; we have more force by far.

**Reading Skill
Historical and Cultural
Context** What ancient Greek beliefs regarding the gods, military might, and respect for strangers does Odysseus express in his words to the Cyclops?

I would not let you go for fear of Zeus—
you or your friends—unless I had a whim[25] to.
Tell me, where was it, now, you left your ship—
225  around the point, or down the shore, I wonder?'

He thought he'd find out, but I saw through this,
and answered with a ready lie:

                                   'My ship?
Poseidon[26] Lord, who sets the earth a-tremble,
broke it up on the rocks at your land's end.
230  A wind from seaward served him, drove us there.
We are survivors, these good men and I.'

Neither reply nor pity came from him,
but in one stride he clutched at my companions
and caught two in his hands like squirming puppies
235  to beat their brains out, spattering the floor.
Then he dismembered them and made his meal,
gaping and crunching like a mountain lion—
everything: innards, flesh, and marrow bones.
We cried aloud, lifting our hands to Zeus,
240  powerless, looking on at this, appalled;
but Cyclops went on filling up his belly
with manflesh and great gulps of whey,
then lay down like a mast among his sheep.
My heart beat high now at the chance of action,
245  and drawing the sharp sword from my hip I went
along his flank to stab him where the midriff
holds the liver. I had touched the spot
when sudden fear stayed me: if I killed him
we perished there as well, for we could never
250  move his ponderous doorway slab aside.
So we were left to groan and wait for morning.

When the young Dawn with fingertips of rose
lit up the world, the Cyclops built a fire
and milked his handsome ewes, all in due order,
255  putting the sucklings to the mothers. Then,
his chores being all dispatched, he caught
another brace[27] of men to make his breakfast,
and whisked away his great door slab

---

**25. whim** (hwim) *n.* sudden thought or wish to do something.

**26. Poseidon** (pō sī′ dən) god of the sea, earthquakes, horses, and storms at sea.

**Literary Analysis**
**Epic Hero** In what way does Odysseus' response show that he is "formidable for guile"?

**Literary Analysis**
**Epic Hero** How do lines 244–250 show Odysseus' ability to think ahead?

**Vocabulary**
**dispatched** (di spacht′) *v.* finished quickly

**27. brace** (brās) *n.* pair.

Reading Check

What does Odysseus tell the Cyclops happened to his ship?

28. **cap a quiver** (kwiv´ ər) close a case holding arrows.
29. **din** (din) *n.* loud, continuous noise; uproar.
30. **Athena** (ə thē´ nə) goddess of wisdom, skills, and warfare.
31. **felled green and left to season** chopped down and exposed to the weather to age the wood.
32. **lugger** (lug´ ər) *n.* small sailing vessel.

**Literary Analysis**
**Epic Hero** What heroic qualities does Odysseus reveal as he plots against the Cyclops?

**Literary Analysis**
**Epic Hero** What plan do you think Odysseus has in mind by offering the Cyclops the wine?

to let his sheep go through—but he, behind,
260   reset the stone as one would cap a quiver.[28]
There was a din[29] of whistling as the Cyclops
rounded his flock to higher ground, then stillness.
And now I pondered how to hurt him worst,
if but Athena[30] granted what I prayed for.
265   Here are the means I thought would serve my turn:

a club, or staff, lay there along the fold—
an olive tree, felled green and left to season[31]
for Cyclops' hand. And it was like a mast
a lugger[32] of twenty oars, broad in the beam—
270   a deep-sea-going craft—might carry:
so long, so big around, it seemed. Now I
chopped out a six foot section of this pole
and set it down before my men, who scraped it;
and when they had it smooth, I hewed again
275   to make a stake with pointed end. I held this
in the fire's heart and turned it, toughening it,
then hid it, well back in the cavern, under
one of the dung piles in profusion there.
Now came the time to toss for it: who ventured
280   along with me? whose hand could bear to thrust
and grind that spike in Cyclops' eye, when mild
sleep had mastered him? As luck would have it,
the men I would have chosen won the toss—
four strong men, and I made five as captain.

285   At evening came the shepherd with his flock,
his woolly flock. The rams as well, this time,
entered the cave: by some sheepherding whim—
or a god's bidding—none were left outside.
He hefted his great boulder into place
290   and sat him down to milk the bleating ewes
in proper order, put the lambs to suck,
and swiftly ran through all his evening chores.
Then he caught two more men and feasted on them.
My moment was at hand, and I went forward
295   holding an ivy bowl of my dark drink,
looking up, saying:

                      'Cyclops, try some wine.
Here's liquor to wash down your scraps of men.
Taste it, and see the kind of drink we carried

under our planks. I meant it for an offering
300  if you would help us home. But you are mad,
unbearable, a bloody monster! After this,
will any other traveler come to see you?'

He seized and drained the bowl, and it went down
so fiery and smooth he called for more:

305  'Give me another, thank you kindly. Tell me,
how are you called? I'll make a gift will please you.
Even Cyclopes know the wine grapes grow
out of grassland and loam in heaven's rain,
but here's a bit of nectar and ambrosia!'[33]

310  Three bowls I brought him, and he poured them down.
I saw the fuddle and flush come over him,
then I sang out in cordial tones:

▲ **Critical Viewing**
What traits does this
image of the Cyclops
illustrate? **[Interpret]**

33. **nectar** (nek´ tər) **and
ambrosia** (am brō´ zhə)
drink and food of the
gods.

Reading
Check

What does Odysseus
plan to do with the
stake that he and his
men make?

            'Cyclops,
you ask my honorable name? Remember
the gift you promised me, and I shall tell you.
315 My name is Nohbdy: mother, father, and friends,
everyone calls me Nohbdy.'

               And he said:
'Nohbdy's my meat, then, after I eat his friends.
Others come first. There's a noble gift, now.'


Even as he spoke, he reeled and tumbled backward,
320 his great head lolling to one side; and sleep
took him like any creature. Drunk, hiccuping,
he dribbled streams of liquor and bits of men.


Now, by the gods, I drove my big hand spike
deep in the embers, charring it again,
325 and cheered my men along with battle talk
to keep their courage up: no quitting now.
The pike of olive, green though it had been,
reddened and glowed as if about to catch.
I drew it from the coals and my four fellows
330 gave me a hand, lugging it near the Cyclops
as more than natural force nerved them; straight
forward they sprinted, lifted it, and rammed it
deep in his crater eye, and leaned on it
turning it as a shipwright turns a drill
335 in planking, having men below to swing
the two-handled strap that spins it in the groove.
So with our brand we bored[34] that great eye socket
while blood ran out around the red-hot bar.
Eyelid and lash were seared; the pierced ball
340 hissed broiling, and the roots popped.

                  In a smithy
one sees a white-hot axehead or an adze
plunged and wrung in a cold tub, screeching steam—
the way they make soft iron hale and hard—:
just so that eyeball hissed around the spike.
345 The Cyclops bellowed and the rock roared round him,
and we fell back in fear. Clawing his face
he tugged the bloody spike out of his eye,
threw it away, and his wild hands went groping;

**Reading Skill Historical and Cultural Context** What cultural values are represented in Odysseus' reference to "the gods" in line 323?

**34. bored** (bôrd) *v.* made a hole in.

then he set up a howl for Cyclopes
350   who lived in caves on windy peaks nearby.
Some heard him; and they came by divers[35] ways
to clump around outside and call:

                                    'What ails you,
Polyphemus?[36] Why do you cry so sore
in the starry night? You will not let us sleep.
355   Sure no man's driving off your flock? No man
has tricked you, ruined you?'

                                    Out of the cave
the mammoth Polyphemus roared in answer:

'Nohbdy, Nohbdy's tricked me, Nohbdy's ruined me!'

To this rough shout they made a sage[37] reply:

360   'Ah well, if nobody has played you foul
there in your lonely bed, we are no use in pain
given by great Zeus. Let it be your father,
Poseidon Lord, to whom you pray.'

                                    So saying
they trailed away. And I was filled with laughter
365   to see how like a charm the name deceived them.
Now Cyclops, wheezing as the pain came on him,
fumbled to wrench away the great doorstone
and squatted in the breach with arms thrown wide
for any silly beast or man who bolted—
370   hoping somehow I might be such a fool.
But I kept thinking how to win the game:
death sat there huge; how could we slip away?
I drew on all my wits, and ran through tactics,
reasoning as a man will for dear life,
375   until a trick came—and it pleased me well.
The Cyclops' rams were handsome, fat, with heavy
fleeces, a dark violet.

                                    Three abreast

I tied them silently together, twining
cords of willow from the ogre's bed;
380   then slung a man under each middle one
to ride there safely, shielded left and right.

35. **divers** (dī´ vərz) *adj.*
    several; various.

36. **Polyphemus** (päl´ i fē´
    məs)

37. **sage** (sāj) *adj.* wise.

**Literary Analysis
Epic Hero** What does
Odysseus' gleeful
response to his success-
ful trick reveal about his
character?

Reading
Check

What do the other
Cyclopes think Polyphe-
mus is saying when he
says, "Nohbdy's tricked
me"?

So three sheep could convey each man. I took
the woolliest ram, the choicest of the flock,
and hung myself under his kinky belly,
385   pulled up tight, with fingers twisted deep
in sheepskin ringlets for an iron grip.
So, breathing hard, we waited until morning.

When Dawn spread out her fingertips of rose
the rams began to stir, moving for pasture,
390   and peals of bleating echoed round the pens
where dams with udders full called for a milking.
Blinded, and sick with pain from his head wound,
the master stroked each ram, then let it pass,
but my men riding on the pectoral[38] fleece
395   the giant's blind hands blundering never found.
Last of them all my ram, the leader, came,
weighted by wool and me with my meditations.
The Cyclops patted him, and then he said:

'Sweet cousin ram, why lag behind the rest
400   in the night cave? You never linger so,
but graze before them all, and go afar
to crop sweet grass, and take your stately way
leading along the streams, until at evening
you run to be the first one in the fold.
405   Why, now, so far behind? Can you be grieving
over your Master's eye? That carrion rogue[39]
and his accurst companions burnt it out
when he had conquered all my wits with wine.
Nohbdy will not get out alive, I swear.
410   Oh, had you brain and voice to tell
where he may be now, dodging all my fury!
Bashed by this hand and bashed on this rock wall
his brains would strew the floor, and I should have
rest from the outrage Nohbdy worked upon me.'

415   He sent us into the open, then. Close by,
I dropped and rolled clear of the ram's belly,
going this way and that to untie the men.
With many glances back, we rounded up
his fat, stiff-legged sheep to take aboard,
420   and drove them down to where the good ship lay.

**38. pectoral** (pek´ tə rəl) *adj.*
located in or on the chest.

**39. carrion** (kar´ ē ən) **rogue**
(rōg) repulsive scoundrel.

**Literary Analysis**
**Epic Hero** What details
of this speech show that
Polyphemus is far less
clever than Odysseus?

◄ **Critical Viewing**
How does this image
compare with your
mental picture of the
Cyclops? **[Analyze]**

Reading
Check
How do the men escape
from the Cyclops' cave?

► **Critical Viewing**
Odysseus and his sur-
viving men escape in
their ship as the blinded
Cyclops hurls boulders
and curses. How does
this illustration compare
to your mental image of
the scene? **[Analyze]**

**Spiral Review**
**Universal Theme**
What universal theme
does the fight between
Odysseus and the
Cyclops suggest?

**Literary Analysis**
**Epic Hero** Despite his
heroism, what human
weaknesses does Odys-
seus reveal as he sails
away?

We saw, as we came near, our fellows' faces
shining; then we saw them turn to grief
tallying those who had not fled from death.
I hushed them, jerking head and eyebrows up,
425    and in a low voice told them: 'Load this herd;
move fast, and put the ship's head toward the breakers.'
They all pitched in at loading, then embarked
and struck their oars into the sea. Far out,
as far off shore as shouted words would carry,
430    I sent a few back to the adversary:
'O Cyclops! Would you feast on my companions?
Puny, am I, in a cave man's hands?
How do you like the beating that we gave you,
you damned cannibal? Eater of guests
435    under your roof! Zeus and the gods have paid you!'

The blind thing in his doubled fury broke
a hilltop in his hands and heaved it after us.
Ahead of our black prow it struck and sank
whelmed in a spuming geyser, a giant wave
440    that washed the ship stern foremost back to shore.
I got the longest boathook out and stood
fending us off, with furious nods to all
to put their backs into a racing stroke—
row, row, or perish. So the long oars bent
445    kicking the foam sternward, making head
until we drew away, and twice as far.
Now when I cupped my hands I heard the crew
in low voices protesting:

                                        'Godsake, Captain!
Why bait the beast again? Let him alone!'

450    'That tidal wave he made on the first throw
all but beached us.'

                                        'All but stove us in!'
'Give him our bearing with your trumpeting,
he'll get the range and lob a boulder.'

                                                'Aye
He'll smash our timbers and our heads together!'
455    I would not heed them in my glorying spirit,

but let my anger flare and yelled:

                               'Cyclops,
if ever mortal man inquire
how you were put to shame and blinded, tell him
Odysseus, raider of cities, took your eye:

460    Laertes' son, whose home's on Ithaca!'

At this he gave a mighty sob and rumbled:
'Now comes the weird[40] upon me, spoken of old.
A wizard, grand and wondrous, lived here—Telemus,[41]
a son of Eurymus;[42] great length of days

465    he had in wizardry among the Cyclopes,
and these things he foretold for time to come:
my great eye lost, and at Odysseus' hands.
Always I had in mind some giant, armed
in giant force, would come against me here.

470    But this, but you—small, pitiful and twiggy—
you put me down with wine, you blinded me.
Come back, Odysseus, and I'll treat you well,
praying the god of earthquake[43] to befriend you—
his son I am, for he by his avowal

475    fathered me, and, if he will, he may
heal me of this black wound—he and no other
of all the happy gods or mortal men.'

Few words I shouted in reply to him:

'If I could take your life I would and take

480    your time away, and hurl you down to hell!
The god of earthquake could not heal you there!'

At this he stretched his hands out in his darkness
toward the sky of stars, and prayed Poseidon:

'O hear me, lord, blue girdler of the islands,

485    if I am thine indeed, and thou art father:
grant that Odysseus, raider of cities, never
see his home: Laertes' son, I mean,
who kept his hall on Ithaca. Should destiny
intend that he shall see his roof again

490    among his family in his father land,
far be that day, and dark the years between.

---

**40. weird** (wird) *n.* fate or destiny.
**41. Telemus** (tel e´ məs)
**42. Eurymus** (yo͞o rim´ əs)

**43. god of earthquake** Poseidon.

**Reading Skill**
**Historical and Cultural Context** What do lines 472–493 suggest about ancient Greek beliefs about the gods' involvement in the mortal world?

Let him lose all companions, and return
under strange sail to bitter days at home.'
In these words he prayed, and the god heard him.
495 Now he laid hands upon a bigger stone
and wheeled around, titanic for the cast,
to let it fly in the black-prowed vessel's track.
But it fell short, just aft the steering oar,
and whelming seas rose giant above the stone
500 to bear us onward toward the island.

                                                                  There
as we ran in we saw the squadron waiting,
the trim ships drawn up side by side, and all
our troubled friends who waited, looking seaward.
We beached her, grinding keel in the soft sand,
505 and waded in, ourselves, on the sandy beach.
Then we unloaded all the Cyclops' flock
to make division, share and share alike,
only my fighters voted that my ram,
the prize of all, should go to me. I slew him
510 by the seaside and burnt his long thighbones
to Zeus beyond the stormcloud, Cronus'[44] son,
who rules the world. But Zeus disdained my offering:
destruction for my ships he had in store
and death for those who sailed them, my companions.
515 Now all day long until the sun went down
we made our feast on mutton and sweet wine,
till after sunset in the gathering dark
we went to sleep above the wash of ripples.

When the young Dawn with fingertips of rose
520 touched the world, I roused the men, gave orders
to man the ships, cast off the mooring lines;
and filing in to sit beside the rowlocks
oarsmen in line dipped oars in the gray sea.
So we moved out, sad in the vast offing,[45]
525 having our precious lives, but not our friends.

**Literary Analysis**
**Epic Hero** What admirable quality does Odysseus show by dividing the sheep among his men?

44. **Cronus** (krō´ nəs)
Titan who was ruler
of the universe until
he was overthrown
by his son Zeus.

45. **offing** (ôf´ iŋ) *n.* distant
part of the sea visible from
the shore.

Reading
Check

What does the Cyclops
ask for in his prayer to
Poseidon?

# The Land of the Dead

46. **Aeolia** (ē ō´ lē ə) . . .
    **Aeolus** (ē´ ə ləs)

*Odysseus and his men sail to Aeolia, where Aeolus,[46] king of the winds, sends Odysseus on his way with a gift: a sack containing all the winds except the favorable west wind. When they are near home, Odysseus' men open the sack, letting loose a storm that drives them back to Aeolia. Aeolus casts them out, having decided that they are detested by the gods. They sail for seven days and arrive in the land of the Laestrygonians,[47] a race of cannibals. These creatures destroy all of Odysseus' ships except the one he is sailing in. Odysseus and his reduced crew escape and reach Aeaea, the island ruled by the sorceress-goddess Circe. She transforms half of the men into swine. Protected by a magic herb, Odysseus demands that Circe change his men back into human form. Before Odysseus departs from the island a year later, Circe informs him that in order to reach home he must journey to the land of the dead, Hades, and consult the blind prophet Tiresias.*

47. **Laestrygonians**
    (les tri gō´ nē ənz)

48. **singing nymph . . . hair**
    Circe.

**Reading Skill**
**Historical and Cultural Context** What details here suggest that the source of wind was mysterious to ancient Greeks?

> We bore down on the ship at the sea's edge
> and launched her on the salt immortal sea,
> stepping our mast and spar in the black ship;
> embarked the ram and ewe and went aboard
> 530 in tears, with bitter and sore dread upon us.
> But now a breeze came up for us astern—
> a canvas-bellying landbreeze, hale shipmate
> sent by the singing nymph with sunbright hair;[48]
> so we made fast the braces, took our thwarts,
> 535 and let the wind and steersman work the ship
> with full sail spread all day above our coursing,
> till the sun dipped, and all the ways grew dark
> upon the fathomless unresting sea.
>
>                By night
> our ship ran onward toward the Ocean's bourne,
> 540 the realm and region of the Men of Winter,
> hidden in mist and cloud. Never the flaming
> eye of Helios lights on those men
> at morning, when he climbs the sky of stars,
> nor in descending earthward out of heaven;
> 545 ruinous night being rove over those wretches.
> We made the land, put ram and ewe ashore,

and took our way along the Ocean stream
to find the place foretold for us by Circe.
There Perimedes and Eulylochus[49]
550   pinioned[50] the sacred beasts. With my drawn blade
I spaded up the votive[51] pit, and poured
libations[52] round it to the unnumbered dead:
sweet milk and honey, then sweet wine, and last
clear water; and I scattered barley down.
555   Then I addressed the blurred and breathless dead,
vowing to slaughter my best heifer for them
before she calved, at home in Ithaca,
and burn the choice bits on the altar fire;
as for Tiresias, I swore to sacrifice
560   a black lamb, handsomest of all our flock.
Thus to assuage the nations of the dead
I pledged these rites, then slashed the lamb and ewe,
letting their black blood stream into the wellpit.
Now the souls gathered, stirring out of Erebus,[53]
565   brides and young men, and men grown old in pain,
and tender girls whose hearts were new to grief;
many were there, too, torn by brazen lanceheads,
battle-slain, bearing still their bloody gear.
From every side they came and sought the pit
570   with rustling cries; and I grew sick with fear.
But presently I gave command to my officers
to flay those sheep the bronze cut down, and make
burnt offerings of flesh to the gods below—
to sovereign Death, to pale Persephone.[54]
575   Meanwhile I crouched with my drawn sword to keep
the surging phantoms from the bloody pit
till I should know the presence of Tiresias.[55]

One shade came first—Elpenor, of our company,
who lay unburied still on the wide earth
580   as we had left him—dead in Circe's hall,
untouched, unmourned, when other cares compelled us.
Now when I saw him there I wept for pity
and called out to him:
                   'How is this, Elpenor,
how could you journey to the western gloom
585   swifter afoot than I in the black lugger?'
He sighed, and answered:

**49.** **Perimedes** (per´ ə mē´
dēz) and Eurylochus (yoō
ril´ ə kəs)

**50.** **pinioned** (pin´ yənd) v.
confined or shackled.

**51.** **votive** (vōt´ iv) adj. done
to fulfill a vow or express
thanks.

**52.** **libations** (lī bā´ shənz)
n. wine or other liquids
poured upon the ground
as a sacrifice or offering.

## Vocabulary
**assuage** (ə swāj´)
v. calm; pacify

**53.** **Erebus** (er´ ə bəs) dark
region under the earth
through which the dead
pass before entering the
realm of Hades.

**54.** **Persephone** (pər sef´ ə
nē) wife of Hades.

**55.** **Tiresias** (tī rē´ sē əs)

### Reading Check
What does Circe say that
Odysseus must do in
order to reach home?

*Odysseus in the Land of the Dead from Homer's The Odyssey*, N.C. Wyeth, Brandywine River Museum

                'Son of great Laertes,
Odysseus, master mariner and soldier,
bad luck shadowed me, and no kindly power;
ignoble death I drank with so much wine.
590   I slept on Circe's roof, then could not see
the long steep backward ladder, coming down,
and fell that height. My neckbone, buckled under,
snapped, and my spirit found this well of dark.
Now hear the grace I pray for, in the name
595   of those back in the world, not here—your wife
and father, he who gave you bread in childhood,
and your own child, your only son, Telemachus,[56]
long ago left at home.

                     When you make sail
and put these lodgings of dim Death behind,
600   you will moor ship, I know, upon Aeaea Island;
there, O my lord, remember me, I pray,
do not abandon me unwept, unburied,
to tempt the gods' wrath, while you sail for home;
but fire my corpse, and all the gear I had,
605   and build a cairn[57] for me above the breakers—
an unknown sailor's mark for men to come.
Heap up the mound there, and implant upon it
the oar I pulled in life with my companions.'

He ceased, and I replied:

                  'Unhappy spirit,
610   I promise you the barrow and the burial.'

So we conversed, and grimly, at a distance,
with my long sword between, guarding the blood,
while the faint image of the lad spoke on.
Now came the soul of Anticlea, dead,
615   my mother, daughter of Autolycus,[58]
dead now, though living still when I took ship
for holy Troy. Seeing this ghost I grieved,
but held her off, through pang on pang of tears,
till I should know the presence of Tiresias.
620   Soon from the dark that prince of Thebes[59] came forward
bearing a golden staff; and he addressed me:

---

◀ **Critical Viewing**
What can you infer about ancient Greek beliefs concerning death and the afterlife from lines 555–577 on page 1065 and from this illustration? **[Infer]**

**56. Telemachus** (tə lem´ ə kəs)
**57. cairn** (kern) *n.* conical heap of stones built as a monument.

**58. Autolycus** (ô täl´ i kəs)

**59. Thebes** (thēbz)

**Reading Skill
Historical and Cultural
Context** What ancient Greek values and beliefs are suggested by Elpenor's requests?

**Reading
Check**
What does Elpenor's spirit ask of Odysseus?

'Son of Laertes and the gods of old,
Odysseus, master of landways and seaways,
why leave the blazing sun, O man of woe,
625   to see the cold dead and the joyless region?
Stand clear, put up your sword;
let me but taste of blood, I shall speak true.'

At this I stepped aside, and in the scabbard
let my long sword ring home to the pommel silver,
630   as he bent down to the somber blood. Then spoke
the prince of those with gift of speech:

                                'Great captain,
a fair wind and the honey lights of home
are all you seek. But anguish lies ahead;
the god who thunders on the land prepares it,
635   not to be shaken from your track, implacable,
in rancor for the son whose eye you blinded.
One narrow strait may take you through his blows:
denial of yourself, restraint of shipmates.
When you make landfall on Thrinacia first
640   and quit the violet sea, dark on the land
you'll find the grazing herds of Helios
by whom all things are seen, all specch is known.
Avoid those kine,[60] hold fast to your intent,
and hard seafaring brings you all to Ithaca.
645   But if you raid the beeves, I see destruction
for ship and crew. Though you survive alone,
bereft of all companions, lost for years,
under strange sail shall you come home, to find
your own house filled with trouble: insolent men
650   eating your livestock as they court your lady.
Aye, you shall make those men atone in blood!
But after you have dealt out death—in open
combat or by stealth—to all the suitors,
go overland on foot, and take an oar,
655   until one day you come where men have lived
with meat unsalted, never known the sea,
nor seen seagoing ships, with crimson bows
and oars that fledge light hulls for dipping flight.
The spot will soon be plain to you, and I
660   can tell you how: some passerby will say,
"What winnowing fan is that upon your shoulder?"

---

**Reading Skill
Historical and Cultural
Context** What ancient
Greek value is reflected
in the "narrow strait"
that Tiresias describes
(lines 637–638)?

**60. kine** (kīn) *n.* cattle.

**Vocabulary
bereft** (bē reft´)
*adj.* deprived

Halt, and implant your smooth oar in the turf
and make fair sacrifice to Lord Poseidon:
a ram, a bull, a great buck boar; turn back,
665  and carry out pure hecatombs[61] at home
to all wide heaven's lords, the undying gods,
to each in order. Then a seaborne death
soft as this hand of mist will come upon you
when you are wearied out with rich old age,
670  your country folk in blessed peace around you.
And all this shall be just as I foretell.'

**61. hecatombs** (hek´ ə
tōmz´) *n.* large-scale
sacrifices to the gods in
ancient Greece; often, the
slaughter of 100 cattle at
one time.

# Critical Thinking

**1. Key Ideas and Details (a)** Before the meeting with the Cyclops, what had Odysseus received from Maron at Ismarus? **(b) Generalize:** What does the encounter with Maron reveal about ancient Greek attitudes regarding hospitality?

**2. Key Ideas and Details (a)** How do Odysseus and his companions expect to be treated by the Cyclops? **(b) Infer:** What "laws" of behavior and attitude does Polyphemus violate?

**3. Key Ideas and Details (a) Summarize:** How do Odysseus and his crew escape from the Cyclops? **(b) Evaluate:** What positive and negative character traits does Odysseus demonstrate in his adventure with the Cyclops?

**4. Integration of Knowledge and Ideas (a) Compare and Contrast:** Compare and contrast Odysseus' reactions to the three ghosts he meets in the Land of the Dead—Elpenor, Anticlea, and Tiresias. **(b) Analyze:** What character trait does Odysseus display in the Land of the Dead that he did not reveal earlier?

**5. Key Ideas and Details (a) Summarize:** What difficulty does Tiresias predict for the journey to come? **(b) Speculate:** Why would Odysseus continue, despite the grim prophecies?

**6. Integration of Knowledge and Ideas Assess:** Judging from Tiresias' prediction, which heroic qualities will Odysseus need to rely upon as he continues his journey? Explain.

**7. Integration of Knowledge and Ideas (a)** What are Odysseus' responsibilities as he reaches the land of the Cyclopes? **(b)** How well does he fulfill these responsibilities? *[Connect to the Big Question: Do heroes have responsibilities?]*

Cite textual
evidence to
support your
responses.

*Circe Meanwhile Had Gone Her Ways...*, 1924, William Russell Flint Collection of the New York Public Library, Special Collections/ Art Resources

# The Sirens

*Odysseus returns to Circe's island. The goddess reveals his course to him and gives advice on how to avoid the dangers he will face: the Sirens, who lure sailors to their destruction; the Wandering Rocks, sea rocks that destroy even birds in flight; the perils of the sea monster Scylla and, nearby, the whirlpool Charybdis;[62] and the cattle of the sun god, which Tiresias has warned Odysseus not to harm.*

As Circe spoke, Dawn mounted her golden throne,
and on the first rays Circe left me, taking
her way like a great goddess up the island.
675   I made straight for the ship, roused up the men
to get aboard and cast off at the stern.
They scrambled to their places by the rowlocks
and all in line dipped oars in the gray sea.
But soon an offshore breeze blew to our liking—
680   a canvas-bellying breeze, a lusty shipmate
sent by the singing nymph with sunbright hair.
So we made fast the braces, and we rested,
letting the wind and steersman work the ship.
The crew being now silent before me, I
685   addressed them, sore at heart:

                             'Dear friends,
more than one man, or two, should know those things
Circe foresaw for us and shared with me,
so let me tell her forecast: then we die
with our eyes open, if we are going to die,
690   or know what death we baffle if we can. Sirens
weaving a haunting song over the sea
we are to shun, she said, and their green shore
all sweet with clover; yet she urged that I
alone should listen to their song. Therefore
695   you are to tie me up, tight as a splint,
erect along the mast, lashed to the mast,
and if I shout and beg to be untied,
take more turns of the rope to muffle me.'

I rather dwelt on this part of the forecast,
700   while our good ship made time, bound outward down
the wind for the strange island of Sirens.

◀ **Critical Viewing**
The sorceress Circe both helps and hinders Odysseus on his journey home. What can you tell about Circe from this illustration? **[Deduce]**

**Literary Analysis**
**Epic Hero** What does Odysseus reveal about his character by sharing information with his men?

Reading
Check
What instructions does Odysseus give his ship-mates as they prepare to deal with the Sirens?

Then all at once the wind fell, and a calm
came over all the sea, as though some power
lulled the swell.

                                    The crew were on their feet
705    briskly, to furl the sail, and stow it; then,
each in place, they poised the smooth oar blades
and sent the white foam scudding by. I carved
a massive cake of beeswax into bits
and rolled them in my hands until they softened—
710    no long task, for a burning heat came down
from Helios, lord of high noon. Going forward
I carried wax along the line, and laid it
thick on their ears. They tied me up, then, plumb
amidships, back to the mast, lashed to the mast,
715    and took themselves again to rowing. Soon,
as we came smartly within hailing distance,
the two Sirens, noting our fast ship
off their point, made ready, and they sang:

**Reading Skill**
**Historical and Cultural Context** What does Odysseus' mention of Helios reveal about ancient Greek beliefs regarding astronomical events?

> *This way, oh turn your bows,*
720    > *Achaea's glory,*
> *As all the world allows—*
> *Moor and be merry.*

> *Sweet coupled airs we sing.*
> *No lonely seafarer*
725    > *Holds clear of entering*
> *Our green mirror.*

> *Pleased by each purling note*
> *Like honey twining*
> *From her throat and my throat,*
730    > *Who lies a-pining?*

> *Sea rovers here take joy*
> *Voyaging onward,*
> *As from our song of Troy*
> *Graybeard and rower-boy*
735    > *Goeth more learnèd.*

> *All feats on that great field*
> *In the long warfare,*
> *Dark days the bright gods willed,*
> *Wounds you bore there,*

**Literary Analysis**
**Epic Hero** Which details in the Sirens' song are designed to flatter the epic hero?

740 *Argos' old soldiery*[63]
    *On Troy beach teeming,*
    *Charmed out of time we see.*
    *No life on earth can be*
    *Hid from our dreaming.*

745 The lovely voices in ardor appealing over the water
made me crave to listen, and I tried to say
'Untie me!' to the crew, jerking my brows;
but they bent steady to the oars. Then Perimedes
got to his feet, he and Eurylochus,
750 and passed more line about, to hold me still.
So all rowed on, until the Sirens
dropped under the sea rim, and their singing
dwindled away.

                My faithful company
rested on their oars now, peeling off
755 the wax that I had laid thick on their ears;
then set me free.

## Scylla and Charybdis

But scarcely had that island
faded in blue air than I saw smoke
and white water, with sound of waves in tumult—
a sound the men heard, and it terrified them.
760 Oars flew from their hands; the blades went knocking
wild alongside till the ship lost way,
with no oar blades to drive her through the water.
Well, I walked up and down from bow to stern,
trying to put heart into them, standing over
765 every oarsman, saying gently,

                        'Friends,
have we never been in danger before this?
More fearsome, is it now, than when the Cyclops
penned us in his cave? What power he had!
Did I not keep my nerve, and use my wits
770 to find a way out for us?

**63. Argos' old soldiery** soldiers from Argos, a city in ancient Greece.

**Vocabulary**
**ardor** (är´ dər) *n.* passion; enthusiasm

**Spiral Review**
**Universal Theme**
What details in this scene suggest the importance of having loyal friends and companions?

**Reading Check**
How does Odysseus keep his shipmates from hearing the Sirens sing?

Literary Analysis
**Epic Hero** What parts
of Odysseus' speech
demonstrate his strength
as a leader?

Now I say
by hook or crook this peril too shall be
something that we remember.

Heads up, lads!
We must obey the orders as I give them.
Get the oar shafts in your hands, and lay back
775   hard on your benches; hit these breaking seas.
Zeus help us pull away before we founder.
You at the tiller, listen, and take in
all that I say—the rudders are your duty;
keep her out of the combers and the smoke;[64]
780   steer for that headland; watch the drift, or we
fetch up in the smother, and you drown us.'

That was all, and it brought them round to action.
But as I sent them on toward Scylla,[65] I
told them nothing, as they could do nothing.
785   They would have dropped their oars again, in panic,
to roll for cover under the decking. Circe's
bidding against arms had slipped my mind,
so I tied on my cuirass[66] and took up
two heavy spears, then made my way along
790   to the foredeck—thinking to see her first from there,
the monster of the gray rock, harboring
torment for my friends. I strained my eyes
upon the cliffside veiled in cloud, but nowhere
could I catch sight of her.

And all this time,
795   in travail,[67] sobbing, gaining on the current,
we rowed into the strait—Scylla to port
and on our starboard beam Charybdis, dire
gorge[68] of the salt seatide. By heaven! when she
vomited, all the sea was like a cauldron
800   seething over intense fire, when the mixture
suddenly heaves and rises.

The shot spume
soared to the landside heights, and fell like rain.
But when she swallowed the sea water down
we saw the funnel of the maelstrom,[69] heard
805   the rock bellowing all around, and dark
sand raged on the bottom far below.
My men all blanched against the gloom, our eyes

64. **the combers** (kōm´ ərs)
**and the smoke** the large
waves that break on the
beach and the ocean
spray.

65. **Scylla** (sil´ ə)

66. **cuirass** (kwi ras´) *n.* armor
for the upper body.

67. **travail** (trə vāl´) *n.* very
hard work.

68. **gorge** (gôrj) *n.* throat or
gullet.

69. **maelstrom** (māl´ strəm) *n.*
large, violent whirlpool.

◄ **Critical Viewing**
How does this image
compare with the
description of Scylla in
the scene? **[Compare
and Contrast]**

were fixed upon that yawning mouth in fear
of being devoured.

                            Then Scylla made her strike,
810   whisking six of my best men from the ship.
      I happened to glance aft at ship and oarsmen
      and caught sight of their arms and legs, dangling
      high overhead. Voices came down to me
      in anguish, calling my name for the last time.

815   A man surfcasting on a point of rock
      for bass or mackerel, whipping his long rod
      to drop the sinker and the bait far out,

Reading
Check

What demand does
Odysseus make of his
men as they approach
the rough waters?

will hook a fish and rip it from the surface
to dangle wriggling through the air:

so these
820    were borne aloft in spasms toward the cliff.

She ate them as they shrieked there, in her den,
in the dire grapple, reaching still for me—
and deathly pity ran me through
at that sight—far the worst I ever suffered,
825    questing the passes of the strange sea.

We rowed on.
The Rocks were now behind; Charybdis, too,
and Scylla dropped astern.

## The Cattle of the Sun God

In the small hours of the third watch, when stars
that shone out in the first dusk of evening
830    had gone down to their setting, a giant wind
blew from heaven, and clouds driven by Zeus
shrouded land and sea in a night of storm;
so, just as Dawn with fingertips of rose
touched the windy world, we dragged our ship
835    to cover in a grotto, a sea cave
where nymphs had chairs of rock and sanded floors.
I mustered all the crew and said:

'Old shipmates,
our stores are in the ship's hold, food and drink;
the cattle here are not for our provision,
840    or we pay dearly for it.

Fierce the god is
who cherishes these heifers and these sheep:
Helios; and no man avoids his eye.'

To this my fighters nodded. Yes. But now
we had a month of onshore gales, blowing
845    day in, day out—south winds, or south by east.
As long as bread and good red wine remained
to keep the men up, and appease their craving,
they would not touch the cattle. But in the end,
when all the barley in the ship was gone,

**Literary Analysis**
**Epic Hero** What quality of heroic leadership does Odysseus show in lines 823–825?

**Reading Skill**
**Historical and Cultural Context** Which details here suggest that ancient Greeks believed the gods controlled the weather?

**Reading Skill**
**Historical and Cultural Context** How does this passage show that ancient Greeks believed their gods had human-like emotions?

850 hunger drove them to scour the wild shore
with angling hooks, for fishes and seafowl,
whatever fell into their hands; and lean days
wore their bellies thin.

                                    The storms continued.
So one day I withdrew to the interior
855 to pray the gods in solitude, for hope
that one might show me some way of salvation.
Slipping away, I struck across the island
to a sheltered spot, out of the driving gale.
I washed my hands there, and made supplication
860 to the gods who own Olympus,[70] all the gods—
but they, for answer, only closed my eyes
under slow drops of sleep.

                                    Now on the shore Eurylochus
made his insidious plea:

                                    'Comrades,' he said,
'You've gone through everything; listen to what I say.
865 All deaths are hateful to us, mortal wretches,
but famine is the most pitiful, the worst
end that a man can come to.

                                    Will you fight it?
Come, we'll cut out the noblest of these cattle
for sacrifice to the gods who own the sky;
870 and once at home, in the old country of Ithaca,
if ever that day comes—
we'll build a costly temple and adorn it
with every beauty for the Lord of Noon.[71]
But if he flares up over his heifers lost,
875 wishing our ship destroyed, and if the gods
make cause with him, why, then I say: Better
open your lungs to a big sea once for all
than waste to skin and bones on a lonely island!'

Thus Eurylochus; and they murmured 'Aye!'
880 trooping away at once to round up heifers.
Now, that day tranquil cattle with broad brows
were gazing near, and soon the men drew up
around their chosen beasts in ceremony.
They plucked the leaves that shone on a tall oak—
885 having no barley meal—to strew the victims,
performed the prayers and ritual, knifed the kine

**70. Olympus** (ō lim´ pəs) Mount Olympus, home of the gods.

**Vocabulary**
**insidious** (in sid´ ē əs) *adj.* characterized by craftiness and betrayal

**71. Lord of Noon** Helios.

**Literary Analysis**
**Epic Hero** How are the values of Eurylochus different from those of Odysseus?

Reading
Check
Who owns the heifers and sheep on the island?

### Geography Connection

**Real Places and Imaginary Events in the *Odyssey***

Odysseus' journey carries him to real places, including Troy, Sparta, and the Strait of Gibraltar. However, in the story, many of these real places are populated by imaginary creatures, such as the Cyclops and the Sirens. The combination of real places and fantastic events is part of the story's appeal.

**Connect to the Literature**  How does the inclusion of real places make the story's imaginary events more believable?

and flayed each carcass, cutting thighbones free
to wrap in double folds of fat. These offerings,
with strips of meat, were laid upon the fire.
890 Then, as they had no wine, they made libation
with clear spring water, broiling the entrails first;
and when the bones were burnt and tripes shared,
they spitted the carved meat.

                              Just then my slumber
left me in a rush, my eyes opened,
895 and I went down the seaward path. No sooner
had I caught sight of our black hull, than savory
odors of burnt fat eddied around me;
grief took hold of me, and I cried aloud:

'O Father Zeus and gods in bliss forever,
900 you made me sleep away this day of mischief !
O cruel drowsing, in the evil hour!
Here they sat, and a great work they contrived.'[72]

**72. contrived** (kən trīvd´) v.
thought up; devised.

Lampetia[73] in her long gown meanwhile
had borne swift word to the Overlord of Noon:
905 'They have killed your kine.'

And the Lord Helios

burst into angry speech amid the immortals:

'O Father Zeus and gods in bliss forever,
punish Odysseus' men! So overweening,
now they have killed my peaceful kine, my joy
910 at morning when I climbed the sky of stars,
and evening, when I bore westward from heaven.
Restitution or penalty they shall pay—
and pay in full—or I go down forever
to light the dead men in the underworld.'

915 Then Zeus who drives the stormcloud made reply:
'Peace, Helios: shine on among the gods,
shine over mortals in the fields of grain.
Let me throw down one white-hot bolt, and make
splinters of their ship in the winedark sea.'

920 —Calypso later told me of this exchange,
as she declared that Hermes[74] had told her.
Well, when I reached the sea cave and the ship,
I faced each man, and had it out; but where
could any remedy be found? There was none.
925 The silken beeves[75] of Helios were dead.
The gods, moreover, made queer signs appear:
cowhides began to crawl, and beef, both raw
and roasted, lowed like kine upon the spits.

Now six full days my gallant crew could feast
930 upon the prime beef they had marked for slaughter
from Helios' herd; and Zeus, the son of Cronus,
added one fine morning.

All the gales

had ceased, blown out, and with an offshore breeze
we launched again, stepping the mast and sail,
935 to make for the open sea. Astern of us
the island coastline faded, and no land
showed anywhere, but only sea and heaven,
when Zeus Cronion piled a thunderhead
above the ship, while gloom spread on the ocean.

**73. Lampetia** (lam pē′ shə)
a nymph.

**74. Hermes** (hʉr′ mēz′) n. god
who serves as herald and
messenger of the other
gods.

**75. beeves** (bēvz) n. alternate
plural form of "beef."

**Literary Analysis**
**Epic Hero** What details
in lines 920–921 clarify
the flashback presented
here?

**Reading**
**Check**

What do Odysseus'
shipmates do while he
is sleeping?

La Nef de Telemachus (The Ship of Telemachus), New York Public Library Picture Collection

940　We held our course, but briefly. Then the squall
　　struck whining from the west, with gale force, breaking
　　both forestays, and the mast came toppling aft
　　along the ship's length, so the running rigging
　　showered into the bilge.

　　　　　　　　　　　　　　　　On the afterdeck

945　the mast had hit the steersman a slant blow
　　bashing the skull in, knocking him overside,
　　as the brave soul fled the body, like a diver.
　　With crack on crack of thunder, Zeus let fly
　　a bolt against the ship, a direct hit,

950　so that she bucked, in reeking fumes of sulphur,
　　and all the men were flung into the sea.
　　They came up 'round the wreck, bobbing awhile
　　like petrels[76] on the waves.

　　　　　　　　　　　　　　　No more seafaring

　　homeward for these, no sweet day of return;

955　the god had turned his face from them.

　　　　　　　　　　　　　　　　　　I clambered

　　fore and aft my hulk until a comber
　　split her, keel from ribs, and the big timber
　　floated free; the mast, too, broke away.
　　A backstay floated dangling from it, stout

960　rawhide rope, and I used this for lashing
　　mast and keel together. These I straddled,
　　riding the frightful storm.

　　　　　　　　　　　　　　　　　Nor had I yet

　　seen the worst of it: for now the west wind
　　dropped, and a southeast gale came on—one more

965　twist of the knife—taking me north again,
　　straight for Charybdis. All that night I drifted,
　　and in the sunrise, sure enough, I lay
　　off Scylla mountain and Charybdis deep.
　　There, as the whirlpool drank the tide, a billow

970　tossed me, and I sprang for the great fig tree,
　　catching on like a bat under a bough.
　　Nowhere had I to stand, no way of climbing,
　　the root and bole[77] being far below, and far
　　above my head the branches and their leaves,

975　massed, overshadowing Charybdis pool.
　　But I clung grimly, thinking my mast and keel
　　would come back to the surface when she spouted.

◀ **Critical Viewing**
In the *Odyssey*, Odysseus'
son Telemachus searches
for his father in a ship
like this one. From what
you observe in the
painting, how does this
ship compare with
modern ships? **[Compare
and Contrast]**

**76. petrels** (pe′ trəlz) *n.* small,
　　dark sea birds.

**Literary Analysis**
**Epic Hero** Which of
Odysseus' heroic qualities
does he demonstrate in
this passage?

**77. bole** (bōl) *n.* tree trunk.

Reading
Check

How is Odysseus' ship
destroyed?

And ah! how long, with what desire, I waited!
till, at the twilight hour, when one who hears
980 and judges pleas in the marketplace all day
between contentious men, goes home to supper,
the long poles at last reared from the sea.

Now I let go with hands and feet, plunging
straight into the foam beside the timbers,
985 pulled astride, and rowed hard with my hands
to pass by Scylla. Never could I have passed her
had not the Father of gods and men,[78] this time,
kept me from her eyes. Once through the strait,
nine days I drifted in the open sea
990 before I made shore, buoyed up by the gods,
upon Ogygia[79] Isle. The dangerous nymph
Calypso lives and sings there, in her beauty,
and she received me, loved me.

                                        But why tell
the same tale that I told last night in hall
995 to you and to your lady? Those adventures
made a long evening, and I do not hold
with tiresome repetition of a story."

**78. Father . . . men** Zeus.

**79. Ogygia** (ō jij´ ē ə)

**Literary Analysis**
**Epic Hero** In what way do lines 994–997 remind you that Odysseus is telling his story to an audience?

## Critical Thinking

*Cite textual evidence to support your responses.*

© 1. **Key Ideas and Details (a)** In the episode of the Lotus-Eaters, how does Odysseus handle the men who ate the lotus? **(b) Interpret:** What does Odysseus understand that his men do not?

© 2. **Key Ideas and Details (a)** In the episode of the Cattle of the Sun God, why does the crew kill the cattle? **(b) Interpret:** How does Odysseus react to this action? **(c) Analyze:** What does Odysseus' reaction show about the importance of the gods to him?

© 3. **Integration of Knowledge and Ideas (a) Evaluate:** The *Odyssey* has entertained people for thousands of years. Why do you think it has remained such an enduring work of literature? **(b) Discuss:** In a small group, share your ideas. As a group, choose one response to share with the class.

© 4. **Integration of Knowledge and Ideas** Could Odysseus have prevented his men from eating the cattle of Helios and so saved their lives? Explain. *[Connect to the Big Question: Do heroes have responsibilities?]*

# After You Read | *from the* **Odyssey, Part 1**

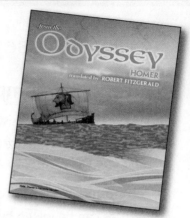

## Literary Analysis: Epic Hero

© **1. Key Ideas and Details (a)** Using a chart like the one shown, identify three other actions that the **epic hero** Odysseus performs.
**(b)** For each action, identify the character trait that it reveals. **(c)** Then,
explain which character traits the ancient Greeks admired most.

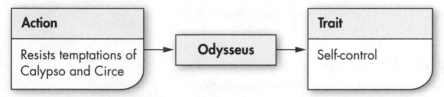

| Action | | Trait |
|---|---|---|
| Resists temptations of Calypso and Circe | → **Odysseus** → | Self-control |

© **2. Craft and Structure** Odysseus recounts most of the action in
Part 1 in the form of a **flashback.** List the events of Part 1 in
chronological sequence, beginning with the end of the Trojan War.

© **3. Key Ideas and Details** The epic hero recounts his own adventures. In what way does this affect your reaction to the events he
describes? Explain.

## Reading Skill: Historical and Cultural Context

**4.** Consider the **historical and cultural context** of Homer's *Odyssey.*
What role do ancient Greek religious beliefs play in the epic?

**5.** What abilities or features of modern technology could have helped
Odysseus on his journey had they been available in ancient times?

## Vocabulary

© **Acquisition and Use** Identify the word in each group that does not
belong.

**1.** plundered, robbed, donated

**2.** dispatched, hesitated, completed

**3.** assuage, soothe, increase

**4.** bereft, after, without

**5.** ardor, spirit, fear

**6.** insidious, traitorous, friendly

**Word Study** Use the context of the sentences and what you know about
the **Old English prefix be-** to explain your answer to each question.

**1.** If people *begrudge* your success, are they happy for you?

**2.** What might happen if a sailing ship were *becalmed*?

### Word Study

The **Old English prefix
be-** means "around,"
"make," or "covered
with."

**Apply It** Explain how
the prefix *be-* contrib-
utes to the meanings of
these words. Consult a
dictionary if necessary.

bemuse
belittle
befriend

*from the* Odyssey, Part 1 **1083**

# Integrated Language Skills

## *from the* Odyssey, Part 1

### Conventions: Simple and Compound Sentences

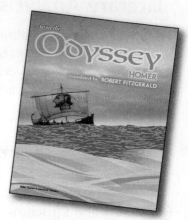

A **simple sentence** consists of a single independent clause.

Although a simple sentence is just one independent clause with one subject and one verb, the subject, verb, or both may be compound.

A **compound sentence** consists of two or more independent clauses.

The clauses can be joined by a comma and a coordinating conjunction or by a semicolon. The coordinating conjunctions are *and, but, or, nor, for, yet,* and *so.*

| Simple sentence | He remembered an old story. |
|---|---|
| Simple sentence with compound subject | He and she remembered an old story. |
| Compound sentence | They laughed together, and they remembered an old story. |

**Practice A** Identify each of the following sentences as simple or compound. For compound sentences, identify the coordinating conjunction.

1. Odysseus led his ship through the perils of Scylla and Charybdis.
2. The Cyclops captured the Greeks, and he ate some of them.
3. The men were starving, but Odysseus commanded them not to eat Helios' cattle.
4. Calypso and Circe both helped and hindered Odysseus.

© **Reading Application** In the *Odyssey,* find one simple sentence and one compound sentence.

**Practice B** Combine each pair of simple sentences to form a compound sentence. Use a comma and coordinating conjunction or a semicolon to separate the clauses.

1. Odysseus yelled insults at Polyphemus. The Cyclopes hurled a rock at the ship.
2. The Sirens sang. The ship sailed on.
3. Scylla swooped down on the ship. She grabbed six men.
4. The men screamed for help. Odysseus stood by helplessly.

© **Writing Application** Write four sentences about your response to the *Odyssey.* Use two simple sentences and two compound sentences.

**PH WRITING COACH** Further instruction and practice are available in *Prentice Hall Writing Coach.*

# Writing

 **Common Core State Standards**

L.9-10.1; W.9-10.3,
W.9-10.3.a, W.9-10.3.b,
W.9-10.3.c; SL.9-10.1,
SL.9-10.1.a, SL.9-10.1.b
[For the full wording of the standards, see page 1040.]

**Narrative Text** Write an **everyday epic.** Choose an ordinary daily event, and write an account that makes it seem larger than life. Recite your work for the class.

- Outline the plot of your story, adding points in the action where you can demonstrate your hero's traits, such as generosity and bravery. Include extreme challenges and plan appearances by gods and monsters.

- Use multiple points of view. Begin with the voice of a speaker outside the story, and then have one of the characters tell the tale.

- Use the models you find in the *Odyssey* to help you incorporate figurative language to accurately describe scenes for your reader.

- Reveal the emotions of your characters through dialogue.

**Grammar Application** As you write your epic, use a variety of sentence types, including both simple and compound.

### Writing Workshop: *Work in Progress*

**Prewriting for Technical Document** To choose a topic for a Technical Document you may write, list tasks that you do well. For example, you might be good at using a computer program, or you might know how to use an outdated tool that not many people can work anymore. You might be a skilled party planner. Save this Task List in your writing portfolio.

Use this prewriting activity to prepare for the **Writing Workshop** on page 1138.

# Speaking and Listening

**Presentation of Ideas** With two classmates, improvise a **conversation** among ordinary Greeks discussing Odysseus' exploits. Each character's statements should reflect the ancient Greek values shown in the *Odyssey*.

- Plan your conversation for an audience of contemporaries—imagine that they, like your characters, also live in Greece during the time the *Odyssey* takes place.

- Work together to assign specific roles for each participant.

- As a group, sketch out the general direction the conversation will take. Leave room for improvisation, but agree about a broad plan.

- As you speak, use verbal techniques such as tone, volume, and change of pace to add realism and interest to your conversation.

- In addition, use nonverbal techniques, such as gestures, facial expressions, and eye contact to help convey your message.

Practice your conversation, including the verbal and nonverbal presentation techniques. Then, present the conversation to your class, using the techniques you rehearsed with your group.

**PHLit**
**Online!**
www.PHLitOnline.com
- Interactive graphic organizers
- Grammar tutorial
- Interactive journals

# Before You Read | *from the* Odyssey, Part 2

## Ⓒ Epic

Build your skills and improve your comprehension of epic literature with this selection.

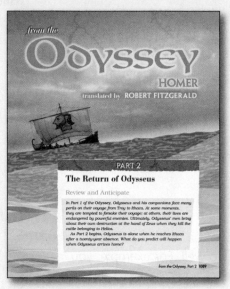

Read the **Odyssey** to learn about Odysseus' return to Ithaca and the battle he must wage to regain his home.

## Ⓒ Common Core State Standards

Meet these standards with Part 2 of the **Odyssey** (p. 1089).

### Reading Literature
**4.** Determine the meaning of words and phrases as they are used in the text, including figurative and connotative meanings; analyze the cumulative impact of specific word choices on meaning and tone. *(Literary Analysis: Epic Simile)*

**6.** Analyze a particular point of view or cultural experience reflected in a work of literature from outside the United States, drawing on a wide reading of world literature. *(Reading Skill: Historical and Cultural Context)*

### Writing
**4.** Produce clear and coherent writing in which the development, organization, and style are appropriate to task, purpose, and audience. *(Writing: Biography)*

### Speaking and Listening
**1.** Initiate and participate effectively in a range of collaborative discussions with diverse partners, building on others' ideas and expressing their own clearly and persuasively. **3.** Evaluate a speaker's point of view, reasoning, and use of evidence and rhetoric, identifying any fallacious reasoning or exaggerated or distorted evidence. *(Speaking and Listening: Debate)*

### Language
**1.** Demonstrate command of the conventions of standard English grammar and usage when writing or speaking. *(Conventions: Complex and Compound-Complex Sentences)*

**6.** Acquire and use accurately general academic and domain-specific words and phrases. *(Vocabulary: Word Study)*

# Literary Analysis: Epic Simile

An **epic simile** is an elaborate comparison that may extend for several lines and that may use the words *like, as, just as,* or *so.* Unlike a normal simile, which draws a comparison to a single image, an epic simile might recall an entire place or story. In Part 1, lines 268–271, Odysseus uses an epic simile to describe the size of the tree from which he creates a weapon.

> And it was like a mast / a lugger of twenty oars, broad in the beam— / a deep-sea-going craft—might carry: / so long so big around, it seemed.

As you read, notice how Homer uses epic similes—sometimes called Homeric similes—to bring descriptions to life.

# Reading Skill: Historical and Cultural Context

The **historical and cultural context** of a work is the time and place in which it is set or was written. Details in a work reflect the beliefs and customs of that time and place. When you **identify influences on your own reading and responses,** you become aware of your own cultural context and how it affects your understanding of literature. Follow these steps:

- Keep your own beliefs and customs in mind.
- Notice the ways in which your reactions to ideas and situations in the work differ from the reactions of the characters.
- Consider whether your reactions reflect your cultural values.

## Using the Strategy: Cultural Influences Chart

As you read, use a chart like this one to note the differences between your own beliefs and values and those reflected in the *Odyssey.*

| Detail in Text |
|---|
| Odysseus says he and his crew plundered Ismarus. |

| Meaning for Characters | Meaning in My Culture |
|---|---|
| Winners can take valuables from the defeated. | Looting is shameful. |

## Making Connections · *from the* **Odyssey, Part 2**

# Do *heroes* have responsibilities?

## Writing About the Big Question

In Part 2 of the *Odyssey*, Homer describes Odysseus' arrival home and the confrontation with suitors who are there to marry his wife and steal his lands. Use this sentence starter to develop your ideas about the Big Question.

The true **character** of a **hero** can be seen when _____.

**While You Read** Look for Odysseus' reactions to the challenges he faces. Also, note examples of the responsibilities Odysseus may have and what he does to fulfill them.

## Vocabulary

Read each word and its definition. Decide whether you know the word well, know it a little bit, or do not know it at all. After you read, see how your knowledge of each word has increased.

- **dissemble** (di sem′ bəl) *v.* conceal under a false appearance; disguise (p. 1090) *The spy was able to <u>dissemble</u> and seem like a patriot.*
  *dissemblance n. resemble v.*

- **incredulity** (in′ krə dōō′ lə tē) *n.* unwillingness or inability to believe (p. 1092) *During the eclipse, they were silent with <u>incredulity</u>.*
  *incredulous adj. incredible adj.*

- **bemusing** (bē myōōz′ iŋ) *v.* stupefying or muddling (p. 1095) *After <u>bemusing</u> the audience, the speaker received little applause.*
  *bemusement n. amuse v.*

- **equity** (ek′ wit ē) *n.* fairness; justice (p. 1100) *Laws are meant to treat everyone with <u>equity</u>.* *equitable adj. inequity n.*

- **maudlin** (môd′ lin) *adj.* tearfully and foolishly sentimental (p. 1101) *The scene in which the lost dog finally returned home evoked <u>maudlin</u> responses from the audience.* *maudlinly adv. maudlinness n.*

- **contempt** (kən tempt′) *n.* disdain or scorn (p. 1108) *A good athlete shows respect, not <u>contempt</u>, for an opponent.* *contemptible adj.*

### Word Study

The **Latin prefix** *dis-* means "away," "apart," or "not."

In this selection, the goddess Athene tells Odysseus not to **dissemble**, or not disguise himself, from his son Telemachus.

*from the*

# Odyssey

## HOMER

### translated by ROBERT FITZGERALD

## PART 2

# The Return of Odysseus

## Review and Anticipate

*In Part 1 of the* Odyssey, *Odysseus and his companions face many perils on their voyage from Troy to Ithaca. At some moments, they are tempted to forsake their voyage; at others, their lives are endangered by powerful enemies. Ultimately, Odysseus' men bring about their own destruction at the hand of Zeus when they kill the cattle belonging to Helios.*

*As Part 2 begins, Odysseus is alone when he reaches Ithaca after a twenty-year absence. What do you predict will happen when Odysseus arrives home?*

# "Twenty years gone, and I am back again . . ."

*Odysseus has finished telling his story to the Phaeacians. The next day, young Phaeacian noblemen conduct him home by ship. He arrives in Ithaca after an absence of twenty years. The goddess Athena appears and informs him of the situation at home. Numerous suitors, believing Odysseus to be dead, have been continually seeking the hand of his wife, Penelope, in marriage, while overrunning Odysseus' palace and enjoying themselves at Penelope's expense. Moreover, they are plotting to murder Odysseus' son, Telemachus, before he can inherit his father's lands. Telemachus, who, like Penelope, still hopes for his father's return, has journeyed to Pylos and Sparta to learn what he can about his father's fate. Athena disguises Odysseus as a beggar and directs him to the hut of Eumaeus,[1] his old and faithful swineherd. While Odysseus and Eumaeus are eating breakfast, Telemachus arrives. Athena then appears to Odysseus.*

1. **Eumaeus** (yōō mē´ əs)

▶ **Critical Viewing**
What can you tell about Eumaeus from this illustration? **[Infer]**

**Vocabulary**
**dissemble** (di sem´ bəl)
*v.* conceal under a false appearance; disguise

. . . From the air
she walked, taking the form of a tall woman,
handsome and clever at her craft, and stood
1000  beyond the gate in plain sight of Odysseus,
unseen, though, by Telemachus, unguessed,
for not to everyone will gods appear.
Odysseus noticed her; so did the dogs,
who cowered whimpering away from her. She only
1005  nodded, signing to him with her brows,
a sign he recognized. Crossing the yard,
he passed out through the gate in the stockade
to face the goddess. There she said to him:
"Son of Laertes and the gods of old,
1010  Odysseus, master of landways and seaways,
dissemble to your son no longer now.
The time has come: tell him how you together
will bring doom on the suitors in the town.
I shall not be far distant then, for I
1015  myself desire battle."

Saying no more,
she tipped her golden wand upon the man,
making his cloak pure white, and the knit tunic
fresh around him. Lithe and young she made him,
ruddy with sun, his jawline clean, the beard

**Reading Skill
Historical and Cultural
Context** What do lines
1021–1029 suggest
about the way ancient
Greeks responded to the
presence of a god?

2. **oblation** (äb lā´ shən) *n.*
offing to a god.

ⓒ
**Spiral Review
Archetypes** Is the
encounter described
in lines 1034–1035
an example of an
archetype? Why or
why not?

**Vocabulary
incredulity** (in´ krə d o͞o´
lə tē) *n.* unwillingness
or inability to believe

1020 no longer gray upon his chin. And she
withdrew when she had done.
                              Then Lord Odysseus
reappeared—and his son was thunderstruck.
Fear in his eyes, he looked down and away
as though it were a god, and whispered:

                                    "Stranger,
1025 you are no longer what you were just now!
Your cloak is new; even your skin! You are
one of the gods who rule the sweep of heaven!
Be kind to us, we'll make you fair oblation[2]
and gifts of hammered gold. Have mercy on us!"

1030 The noble and enduring man replied:

"No god. Why take me for a god? No, no.
I am that father whom your boyhood lacked
and suffered pain for lack of. I am he."

Held back too long, the tears ran down his cheeks
1035 as he embraced his son.
                              Only Telemachus,
uncomprehending, wild
with incredulity, cried out:
                              "You cannot
be my father Odysseus! Meddling spirits
conceived this trick to twist the knife in me!
1040 No man of woman born could work these wonders
by his own craft, unless a god came into it
with ease to turn him young or old at will.
I swear you were in rags and old,
and here you stand like one of the immortals!"

1045 Odysseus brought his ranging mind to bear
and said:
                              "This is not princely, to be swept
away by wonder at your father's presence.
No other Odysseus will ever come,
for he and I are one, the same; his bitter
1050 fortune and his wanderings are mine.
Twenty years gone, and I am back again
on my own island.

                    As for my change of skin,
      that is a charm Athena, Hope of Soldiers,
      uses as she will; she has the knack
1055  to make me seem a beggar man sometimes
      and sometimes young, with finer clothes about me.
      It is no hard thing for the gods of heaven
      to glorify a man or bring him low."

      When he had spoken, down he sat.
                              Then, throwing
1060  his arms around this marvel of a father
      Telemachus began to weep. Salt tears
      rose from the wells of longing in both men,
      and cries burst from both as keen and fluttering
      as those of the great taloned hawk,
1065  whose nestlings farmers take before they fly.
      So helplessly they cried, pouring out tears,
      and might have gone on weeping so till sundown,
      had not Telemachus said:

                              "Dear father! Tell me
      what kind of vessel put you here ashore
1070  on Ithaca? Your sailors, who were they?
      I doubt you made it, walking on the sea!"

      Then said Odysseus, who had borne the barren sea:

      "Only plain truth shall I tell you, child.
      Great seafarers, the Phaeacians, gave me passage
1075  as they give other wanderers. By night
      over the open ocean, while I slept,
      they brought me in their cutter,[3] set me down
      on Ithaca, with gifts of bronze and gold
      and stores of woven things. By the gods' will
1080  these lie all hidden in a cave. I came
      to this wild place, directed by Athena,
      so that we might lay plans to kill our enemies.
      Count up the suitors for me, let me know
      what men at arms are there, how many men.
1085  I must put all my mind to it, to see
      if we two by ourselves can take them on
      or if we should look round for help."

**Literary Analysis
Epic Simile** To what are Odysseus' and Telemachus' cries compared in the epic simile in lines 1063–1065?

3. **cutter** (kut´ər) n. small, swift ship or boat carried aboard a large ship to transport personnel or supplies.

Reading Check

Why is Telemachus initially doubtful that the man before him is Odysseus, his father?

Telemachus replied:

> "O Father, all my life your fame
> as a fighting man has echoed in my ears—
1090 > your skill with weapons and the tricks of war—
> but what you speak of is a staggering thing,
> beyond imagining, for me. How can two men
> do battle with a houseful in their prime?[4]
> For I must tell you this is no affair
1095 > of ten or even twice ten men, but scores,
> throngs of them. You shall see, here and now.
> The number from Dulichium alone
> is fifty-two picked men, with armorers,
> a half dozen; twenty-four came from Same,
1100 > twenty from Zacynthus; our own island
> accounts for twelve, high-ranked, and their retainers,
> Medon the crier, and the Master Harper,
> besides a pair of handymen at feasts.
> If we go in against all these
1105 > I fear we pay in salt blood for your vengeance.
> You must think hard if you would conjure up
> the fighting strength to take us through."

Odysseus
who had endured the long war and the sea answered:

> "I'll tell you now.
1110 > Suppose Athena's arm is over us, and Zeus
> her father's, must I rack my brains for more?"

Clearheaded Telemachus looked hard and said:

> "Those two are great defenders, no one doubts it,
> but throned in the serene clouds overhead;
1115 > other affairs of men and gods they have
> to rule over."

And the hero answered:
> "Before long they will stand to right and left of us
> in combat, in the shouting, when the test comes—
> our nerve against the suitors' in my hall.
1120 > Here is your part: at break of day tomorrow
> home with you, go mingle with our princes.
> The swineherd later on will take me down

**Reading Skill**
**Historical and Cultural Context** What does Odysseus' statement in lines 1109–1111 suggest about ancient Greek beliefs about the gods' interest in human affairs?

the port-side trail—a beggar, by my looks,
hangdog and old. If they make fun of me
1125 in my own courtyard, let your ribs cage up
your springing heart, no matter what I suffer,
no matter if they pull me by the heels
or practice shots at me, to drive me out.
Look on, hold down your anger. You may even
1130 plead with them, by heaven! in gentle terms
to quit their horseplay—not that they will heed you,
rash as they are, facing their day of wrath.
Now fix the next step in your mind.

                                Athena,
counseling me, will give me word, and I
1135 shall signal to you, nodding: at that point
round up all armor, lances, gear of war
left in our hall, and stow the lot away
back in the vaulted storeroom. When the suitors
miss those arms and question you, be soft
1140 in what you say: answer:

                         'I thought I'd move them
out of the smoke. They seemed no longer those
bright arms Odysseus left us years ago
when he went off to Troy. Here where the fire's
hot breath came, they had grown black and drear.
1145 One better reason, too, I had from Zeus:
suppose a brawl starts up when you are drunk,
you might be crazed and bloody one another,
and that would stain your feast, your courtship.
    Tempered
iron can magnetize a man.'
                                Say that.
1150 But put aside two broadswords and two spears
for our own use, two oxhide shields nearby
when we go into action. Pallas Athena
and Zeus All-Provident will see you through,
bemusing our young friends.
                         Now one thing more.
1155 If son of mine you are and blood of mine,
let no one hear Odysseus is about.
Neither Laertes, nor the swineherd here,
nor any slave, nor even Penelope.

## LITERATURE IN CONTEXT

### Cultural Connection

**Athena**
Athena was the goddess of wisdom, skills, and warfare. When she helps Odysseus in this epic, it is not the first time that she offers assistance to a Greek hero. In Homer's *Iliad*, Athena helps the Greek hero Achilles defeat the Trojan warrior Hector. Athena favored Achilles for his unmatched skill in battle, but Odysseus was her favorite among the Greeks. He displayed not only skill in warfare, but also ingenuity and cunning.

### Connect to the Literature

Which of Odysseus' deeds in the *Odyssey* might have helped him to earn Athena's favor? Explain.

**Vocabulary**
**bemusing** (bē myo͞oz´ iŋ) *v.* stupefying or muddling

Reading
Check

How does Odysseus tell his son to respond if the suitors "practice shots" on Odysseus?

But you and I alone must learn how far
1160    the women are corrupted; we should know
how to locate good men among our hands,
the loyal and respectful, and the shirkers[5]
who take you lightly, as alone and young."

## Argus

*Odysseus heads for town with Eumaeus. Outside the palace,*
*Odysseus' old dog, Argus, is lying at rest as his long-absent*
*master approaches.*

                              While he spoke
an old hound, lying near, pricked up his ears
1165    and lifted up his muzzle. This was Argus,
trained as a puppy by Odysseus,
but never taken on a hunt before
his master sailed for Troy. The young men, afterward,
hunted wild goats with him, and hare, and deer,
1170    but he had grown old in his master's absence.
Treated as rubbish now, he lay at last
upon a mass of dung before the gates—
manure of mules and cows, piled there until
fieldhands could spread it on the king's estate.
1175    Abandoned there, and half destroyed with flies,
old Argus lay.

                      But when he knew he heard
Odysseus' voice nearby, he did his best
to wag his tail, nose down, with flattened ears,
having no strength to move nearer his master.
1180    And the man looked away,
wiping a salt tear from his cheek; but he
hid this from Eumaeus. Then he said:

"I marvel that they leave this hound to lie
here on the dung pile;
1185    he would have been a fine dog, from the look of him,
though I can't say as to his power and speed
when he was young. You find the same good build
in house dogs, table dogs landowners keep
all for style."

**5. shirkers** (shʉrk´ ərz) *n.*
people who get out of
doing what needs to be
done.

▼ **Critical Viewing**
What can you infer
about the ancient Greeks
based on the fact that
they depicted their gods
on everyday objects
like this urn? **[Infer]**

And you replied, Eumaeus:

1190 "A hunter owned him—but the man is dead
in some far place. If this old hound could show
the form he had when Lord Odysseus left him,
going to Troy, you'd see him swift and strong.
He never shrank from any savage thing
1195 he'd brought to bay in the deep woods; on the scent
no other dog kept up with him. Now misery
has him in leash. His owner died abroad,
and here the women slaves will take no care of him.
You know how servants are: without a master
1200 they have no will to labor, or excel.
For Zeus who views the wide world takes away
half the manhood of a man, that day
he goes into captivity and slavery."

Eumaeus crossed the court and went straight forward
1205 into the megaron[6] among the suitors:
but death and darkness in that instant closed
the eyes of Argus, who had seen his master,
Odysseus, after twenty years.

## The Suitors

*Still disguised as a beggar, Odysseus enters his home.*
*He is confronted by the haughty[7] suitor Antinous.[8]*

But here Antinous broke in, shouting:

"God!

1210 What evil wind blew in this pest?

Get over,

stand in the passage! Nudge my table, will you?
Egyptian whips are sweet
to what you'll come to here, you nosing rat,
making your pitch to everyone!
1215 These men have bread to throw away on you
because it is not theirs. Who cares? Who spares
another's food, when he has more than plenty?"

---

**Reading Skill**
**Historical and**
**Cultural Context** How
do Eumaeus' beliefs
about servitude and slav-
ery compare with those
of your own culture?

6. **megaron** (meg´ ə rön) *n.*
great, central hall of the
house, usually containing
a center hearth.

7. **haughty** (hôt´ ē) *adj.*
arrogant.

8. **Antinous** (an tin´ ō əs)

**Reading Check**

How does Antinous react
to Odysseus, who is
disguised as a beggar?

With guile Odysseus drew away, then said:

"A pity that you have more looks than heart.
1220 You'd grudge a pinch of salt from your own larder
to your own handyman. You sit here, fat
on others' meat, and cannot bring yourself
to rummage out a crust of bread for me!"

Then anger made Antinous' heart beat hard,
1225 and, glowering under his brows, he answered:

                                                    "Now!
You think you'll shuffle off and get away
after that impudence?[9] Oh, no you don't!"

The stool he let fly hit the man's right shoulder
on the packed muscle under the shoulder blade—
1230 like solid rock, for all the effect one saw.
Odysseus only shook his head, containing
thoughts of bloody work, as he walked on,
then sat, and dropped his loaded bag again
upon the door sill. Facing the whole crowd
1235 he said, and eyed them all:

                                            "One word only,
my lords, and suitors of the famous queen.
One thing I have to say.
There is no pain, no burden for the heart
when blows come to a man, and he defending
1240 his own cattle—his own cows and lambs.
Here it was otherwise. Antinous
hit me for being driven on by hunger—
how many bitter seas men cross for hunger!
If beggars interest the gods, if there are Furies[10]
1245 pent in the dark to avenge a poor man's wrong, then may
Antinous meet his death before his wedding day!"

Then said Eupeithes' son, Antinous:

                                                "Enough.
Eat and be quiet where you are, or shamble elsewhere,
unless you want these lads to stop your mouth
1250 pulling you by the heels, or hands and feet,
over the whole floor, till your back is peeled!"

---

**Reading Skill
Historical and
Cultural Context** What
conflicting values does
this exchange between
Antinous and Odysseus
reveal?

**9. impudence** (im´ pyo͞o
dəns) *n.* quality of being
shamelessly bold;
disrespectful.

**Reading Skill
Historical and Cultural
Context** What values
regarding the use of
physical force are evident
in this speech?

**10. Furies** (fyo͝or´ ēz) *n.* three
terrible female spirits
who punish the doers of
unavenged crimes.

But now the rest were mortified, and someone
spoke from the crowd of young bucks to rebuke him:

"A poor show, that—hitting this famished tramp—
1255  bad business, if he happened to be a god.
You know they go in foreign guise, the gods do,
looking like strangers, turning up
in towns and settlements to keep an eye
on manners, good or bad."

But at this notion

1260  Antinous only shrugged.

Telemachus,

after the blow his father bore, sat still
without a tear, though his heart felt the blow.
Slowly he shook his head from side to side,
containing murderous thoughts.

Penelope

1265  on the higher level of her room had heard
the blow, and knew who gave it. Now she murmured:

"Would god you could be hit yourself, Antinous—
hit by Apollo's bowshot!"

**Reading Skill
Historical and Cultural
Context** What ancient
Greek belief is conveyed
in this suitor's speech?

Reading
Check

How does Penelope
regard Antinous?

                                          And Eurynome[11]
            her housekeeper, put in:

                "He and no other?
    1270    If all we pray for came to pass, not one
            would live till dawn!"

                                          Her gentle mistress said:

            "Oh, Nan, they are a bad lot; they intend
            ruin for all of us; but Antinous
            appears a blacker-hearted hound than any.
    1275    Here is a poor man come, a wanderer,
            driven by want to beg his bread, and everyone
            in hall gave bits, to cram his bag—only
            Antinous threw a stool, and banged his shoulder!"

            So she described it, sitting in her chamber
    1280    among her maids—while her true lord was eating.
            Then she called in the forester and said:

            "Go to that man on my behalf, Eumaeus,
            and send him here, so I can greet and question him.
            Abroad in the great world, he may have heard
    1285    rumors about Odysseus—may have known him!"

## Penelope

*In the evening, Penelope interrogates the old beggar.*

            "Friend, let me ask you first of all:
            who are you, where do you come from, of what nation
            and parents were you born?"

                                          And he replied:
            "My lady, never a man in the wide world
    1290    should have a fault to find with you. Your name
            has gone out under heaven like the sweet
            honor of some god-fearing king, who rules
            in equity over the strong: his black lands bear
            both wheat and barley, fruit trees laden bright,
    1295    new lambs at lambing time—and the deep sea
            gives great hauls of fish by his good strategy,
            so that his folk fare well.

**Spiral Review**
**Archetype**
Odysseus hides his
true identity from
Penelope. How
does this behavior
suggest the trickster
archetype?

**Vocabulary**
**equity** (ek´ wit ē)
*n.* fairness; justice

O my dear lady,

this being so, let it suffice to ask me
of other matters—not my blood, my homeland.
1300　Do not enforce me to recall my pain.
My heart is sore; but I must not be found
sitting in tears here, in another's house:
it is not well forever to be grieving.
One of the maids might say—or you might think—
1305　I had got maudlin over cups of wine."

And Penelope replied:

"Stranger, my looks,

my face, my carriage,[12] were soon lost or faded
when the Achaeans crossed the sea to Troy,
Odysseus my lord among the rest.
1310　If he returned, if he were here to care for me,
I might be happily renowned!
But grief instead heaven sent me—years of pain.
Sons of the noblest families on the islands,
Dulichium, Same, wooded Zacynthus,[13]
1315　with native Ithacans, are here to court me,
against my wish; and they consume this house.
Can I give proper heed to guest or suppliant
or herald on the realm's affairs?

How could I?

wasted with longing for Odysseus, while here
1320　they press for marriage.

Ruses[14] served my turn

to draw the time out—first a close-grained web
I had the happy thought to set up weaving
on my big loom in hall. I said, that day:
'Young men—my suitors, now my lord is dead,
1325　let me finish my weaving before I marry,
or else my thread will have been spun in vain.
It is a shroud I weave for Lord Laertes
when cold Death comes to lay him on his bier.
The country wives would hold me in dishonor
1330　if he, with all his fortune, lay unshrouded.'
I reached their hearts that way, and they agreed.
So every day I wove on the great loom,
but every night by torchlight I unwove it;
and so for three years I deceived the Achaeans.

**Vocabulary**
**maudlin** (môd´ lin)
*adj.* tearfully and fool-ishly sentimental

**12. carriage** (kar´ ij) *n.* posture.

**13. Zacynthus** (za sin´ *th*us)

**14. ruses** (ro͞oz´ iz) *n.* tricks.

**Reading Skill**
**Historical and Cultural Context** How do the ancient Greek ideas in Penelope's speech about honoring the dead compare to modern ideas?

**Reading Check**

How was Penelope able to delay marriage for three years?

The Trial of the Bow from Homer's *The Odyssey*, N.C. Wyeth, Brandywine River Museum

But when the seasons brought a fourth year on,
as long months waned, and the long days were spent,
through impudent folly in the slinking maids
they caught me—clamored up to me at night;
I had no choice then but to finish it.
And now, as matters stand at last,
I have no strength left to evade a marriage,
cannot find any further way; my parents
urge it upon me, and my son
will not stand by while they eat up his property.
He comprehends it, being a man full-grown,
able to oversee the kind of house
Zeus would endow with honor.
But you too
confide in me, tell me your ancestry.
You were not born of mythic oak or stone."

*Penelope again asks the beggar to tell about himself. He makes up a tale in which Odysseus is mentioned and declares that Penelope's husband will soon be home.*

"You see, then, he is alive and well, and headed
homeward now, no more to be abroad
far from his island, his dear wife and son.
Here is my sworn word for it. Witness this,
god of the zenith, noblest of the gods,[15]
and Lord Odysseus' hearthfire, now before me:
I swear these things shall turn out as I say.
Between this present dark and one day's ebb,
after the wane, before the crescent moon,
Odysseus will come."

## The Challenge

*Pressed by the suitors to choose a husband from among them, Penelope says she will marry the man who can string Odysseus' bow and shoot an arrow through twelve axhandle sockets. The suitors try and fail. Still in disguise, Odysseus asks for a turn and gets it.*

And Odysseus took his time,
turning the bow, tapping it, every inch,
for borings that termites might have made

◀ **Critical Viewing** The winner of the archery contest will win Penelope's hand in marriage. What details or artistic techniques capture the tension in this scene? **[Interpret]**

15. **god of the zenith, noblest of the gods** Zeus.

**Reading Check**
What means does Penelope decide she will use to choose a husband?

while the master of the weapon was abroad.
The suitors were now watching him, and some
jested among themselves:

                                    "A bow lover!"

1365   "Dealer in old bows!"

                                "Maybe he has one like it
at home!"

                          "Or has an itch to make one for himself."

"See how he handles it, the sly old buzzard!"

And one disdainful suitor added this:
"May his fortune grow an inch for every inch he bends it!"

1370 But the man skilled in all ways of contending,
satisfied by the great bow's look and heft,
like a musician, like a harper, when
with quiet hand upon his instrument
he draws between his thumb and forefinger
1375 a sweet new string upon a peg: so effortlessly
Odysseus in one motion strung the bow.
Then slid his right hand down the cord and plucked it,
so the taut gut vibrating hummed and sang
a swallow's note.

                        In the hushed hall it smote the suitors
1380 and all their faces changed. Then Zeus thundered
overhead, one loud crack for a sign.
And Odysseus laughed within him that the son
of crooked-minded Cronus had flung that omen down.
He picked one ready arrow from his table
1385 where it lay bare: the rest were waiting still
in the quiver for the young men's turn to come.
He nocked[16] it, let it rest across the handgrip,
and drew the string and grooved butt of the arrow,
aiming from where he sat upon the stool.

**▲ Critical Viewing**
Does the hunter pictured
here show the same
grace as does Odysseus
in lines 1370–1392?
Explain. **[Compare
and Contrast]**

16. **nocked** (näkt) set an
    arrow into the bowstring.

                                        Now flashed

1390    arrow from twanging bow clean as a whistle
        through every socket ring, and grazed not one,
        to thud with heavy brazen head beyond.

                                        Then quietly
        Odysseus said:

                                        "Telemachus, the stranger
        you welcomed in your hall has not disgraced you.
1395    I did not miss, neither did I take all day
        stringing the bow. My hand and eye are sound,
        not so contemptible as the young men say.
        The hour has come to cook their lordships' mutton—
        supper by daylight. Other amusements later,
1400    with song and harping that adorn a feast."

        He dropped his eyes and nodded, and the prince
        Telemachus, true son of King Odysseus,
        belted his sword on, clapped hand to his spear,
        and with a clink and glitter of keen bronze
1405    stood by his chair, in the forefront near his father.

# Critical Thinking

**1. Key Ideas and Details (a)** Who does Telemachus think Odysseus is when they first reunite? **(b) Compare and Contrast:** Compare Odysseus' emotions with those of Telemachus at their reunion.

**2. Key Ideas and Details (a)** Describe Antinous' treatment of Odysseus. **(b) Analyze Cause and Effect:** Why do you think Antinous treats Odysseus as he does?

**3. Integration of Knowledge and Ideas (a)** What does Odysseus tell Penelope about himself? **(b) Infer:** Why do you think Odysseus chooses not to reveal his identity to his wife? **(c) Take a Position:** Is it wrong for Odysseus to deceive Penelope? Explain your response.

**4. Integration of Knowledge and Ideas (a)** Which of Odysseus' responsibilities are revealed in this section? **(b)** Do you think he manages them heroically? Explain your response. *[Connect to the Big Question: Do heroes have responsibilities?]*

Cite textual evidence to support your responses.

**The Slaughter of the Suitors** from Homer's **The Odyssey**, N.C. Wyeth. Licensed by ASAP Worldwide.
Photo courtesy of the Archives of the American Illustrators Gallery, NYC.
©Copyright 2000 National Museum of American Illustration, Newport, RI. www.americanillustration.org

# Odysseus' Revenge

Now shrugging off his rags the wiliest[17] fighter of the islands
leapt and stood on the broad doorsill, his own bow in his
   hand.
He poured out at his feet a rain of arrows from the quiver
and spoke to the crowd:

         "So much for that. Your clean-cut game is over.
1410  Now watch me hit a target that no man has hit before,
if I can make this shot. Help me, Apollo."

He drew to his fist the cruel head of an arrow for Antinous
just as the young man leaned to lift his beautiful drinking
   cup,
embossed, two-handled, golden: the cup was in his fingers:
1415  the wine was even at his lips: and did he dream of death?
How could he? In that revelry[18] amid his throng of friends
who would imagine a single foe—though a strong foe
   indeed—
could dare to bring death's pain on him and darkness on his
   eyes?
Odysseus' arrow hit him under the chin
1420  and punched up to the feathers through his throat.

Backward and down he went, letting the winecup fall
from his shocked hand. Like pipes his nostrils jetted
crimson runnels, a river of mortal red,
and one last kick upset his table
1425  knocking the bread and meat to soak in dusty blood.
Now as they craned to see their champion where he lay
the suitors jostled in uproar down the hall,
everyone on his feet. Wildly they turned and scanned
the walls in the long room for arms; but not a shield,
1430  not a good ashen spear was there for a man to take and
   throw.
All they could do was yell in outrage at Odysseus:

"Foul! to shoot at a man! That was your last shot!"
"Your own throat will be slit for this!"
            "Our finest lad is down!
You killed the best on Ithaca."
        "Buzzards will tear your eyes out!"

**17. wiliest** (wīl´ ē əst) *adj.*
craftiest; slyest.

◀ **Critical Viewing** Do
you think this illustration
presents the slaughter
of the suitors accurately?
Explain. **[Evaluate]**

**18. revelry** (rev´ əl rē) *n.* noisy
festivity.

**Reading Skill
Historical and
Cultural Context**
Does the manner in
which Odysseus kills
Antinous agree with your
idea of a "fair fight"?
Explain.

Reading
Check
Whom does Odysseus
kill first?

For they imagined as they wished—that it was a wild shot,
an unintended killing—fools, not to comprehend
they were already in the grip of death.
But glaring under his brows Odysseus answered:

"You yellow dogs, you thought I'd never make it
1440 home from the land of Troy. You took my house to
      plunder. . .
You dared bid for my wife while I was still alive.
Contempt was all you had for the gods who rule wide
      heaven,
contempt for what men say of you hereafter.
Your last hour has come. You die in blood."

1445 As they all took this in, sickly green fear
pulled at their entrails, and their eyes flickered
looking for some hatch or hideaway from death.
Eurymachus[19] alone could speak. He said:

"If you are Odysseus of Ithaca come back,
1450 all that you say these men have done is true.
Rash actions, many here, more in the countryside.
But here he lies, the man who caused them all.
Antinous was the ringleader, he whipped us on
to do these things. He cared less for a marriage
1455 than for the power Cronion has denied him
as king of Ithaca. For that
he tried to trap your son and would have killed him.
He is dead now and has his portion. Spare
your own people. As for ourselves, we'll make
1460 restitution of wine and meat consumed,
and add, each one, a tithe of twenty oxen
with gifts of bronze and gold to warm your heart.
Meanwhile we cannot blame you for your anger."

Odysseus glowered under his black brows
1465 and said:
              "Not for the whole treasure of your fathers,
all you enjoy, lands, flocks, or any gold
put up by others, would I hold my hand.
There will be killing till the score is paid.
You forced yourselves upon this house. Fight your way out,
1470 or run for it, if you think you'll escape death.

I doubt one man of you skins by."

They felt their knees fail, and their hearts—but heard
Eurymachus for the last time rallying them.
"Friends," he said, "the man is implacable.
1475 Now that he's got his hands on bow and quiver
he'll shoot from the big doorstone there
until he kills us to the last man.
                                        Fight, I say,
let's remember the joy of it. Swords out!
Hold up your tables to deflect his arrows.
1480 After me, everyone: rush him where he stands.
If we can budge him from the door, if we can pass
into the town, we'll call out men to chase him.
This fellow with his bow will shoot no more."

He drew his own sword as he spoke, a broadsword of fine
    bronze,
1485 honed like a razor on either edge. Then crying hoarse and
    loud
he hurled himself at Odysseus. But the kingly man let fly
an arrow at that instant, and the quivering feathered butt
sprang to the nipple of his breast as the barb stuck in his
    liver.
The bright broadsword clanged down. He lurched and fell
    aside,
1490 pitching across his table. His cup, his bread and meat,
were spilt and scattered far and wide, and his head slammed
    on the ground.
Revulsion, anguish in his heart, with both feet kicking out,
he downed his chair, while the shrouding wave of mist closed
    on his eyes.

Amphinomus now came running at Odysseus,
1495 broadsword naked in his hand. He thought to make
the great soldier give way at the door.
But with a spear throw from behind Telemachus hit him
between the shoulders, and the lancehead drove
clear through his chest. He left his feet and fell
1500 forward, thudding, forehead against the ground.
Telemachus swerved around him, leaving the long dark
    spear
planted in Amphinomus. If he paused to yank it out

**Literary Analysis**
**Epic Simile** Why is the
comparison of Euryma-
chus' sharp sword to a
razor only a simile and
not an epic simile?

Reading
Check

What does Eurymachus
offer Odysseus to try to
calm his anger?

someone might jump him from behind or cut him down with
    a sword
at the moment he bent over. So he ran—ran from the tables
1505    to his father's side and halted, panting, saying:

"Father let me bring you a shield and spear,
a pair of spears, a helmet.
I can arm on the run myself; I'll give
outfits to Eumaeus and this cowherd.
1510    Better to have equipment."

                           Said Odysseus:
"Run then, while I hold them off with arrows
as long as the arrows last. When all are gone
if I'm alone they can dislodge me."

                           Quick
upon his father's word Telemachus
1515    ran to the room where spears and armor lay.
He caught up four light shields, four pairs of spears,
four helms of war high-plumed with flowing manes,
and ran back, loaded down, to his father's side.
He was the first to pull a helmet on
1520    and slide his bare arm in a buckler strap.
The servants armed themselves, and all three took their
    stand
beside the master of battle.

                        While he had arrows
he aimed and shot, and every shot brought down
one of his huddling enemies.
1525    But when all barbs had flown from the bowman's fist,
he leaned his bow in the bright entryway
beside the door, and armed: a four-ply shield
hard on his shoulder, and a crested helm,
horsetailed, nodding stormy upon his head,
1530    then took his tough and bronze-shod spears. . . .

> *Aided by Athena, Odysseus, Telemachus, Eumaeus, and other faithful herdsmen kill all the suitors.*

And Odysseus looked around him, narrow-eyed,
for any others who had lain hidden
while death's black fury passed.

**Reading Skill
Historical and Cultural
Context** What cultural
values are reflected in
Telemachus' behavior
toward his father?

In blood and dust

he saw that crowd all fallen, many and many slain.

1535 Think of a catch that fishermen haul in to a half-moon bay
in a fine-meshed net from the whitecaps of the sea:
how all are poured out on the sand, in throes for the salt sea,
twitching their cold lives away in Helios' fiery air:
so lay the suitors heaped on one another.

## Penelope's Test

*Penelope tests Odysseus to prove he really is her husband.*

1540 Greathearted Odysseus, home at last,
was being bathed now by Eurynome
and rubbed with golden oil, and clothed again
in a fresh tunic and a cloak. Athena
lent him beauty, head to foot. She made him
1545 taller, and massive, too, with crisping hair
in curls like petals of wild hyacinth
but all red-golden. Think of gold infused
on silver by a craftsman, whose fine art
Hephaestus[20] taught him, or Athena: one
1550 whose work moves to delight: just so she lavished
beauty over Odysseus' head and shoulders.
He sat then in the same chair by the pillar,
facing his silent wife, and said:

"Strange woman,

the immortals of Olympus made you hard,
1555 harder than any. Who else in the world
would keep aloof as you do from her husband
if he returned to her from years of trouble,
cast on his own land in the twentieth year?

Nurse, make up a bed for me to sleep on.
1560 Her heart is iron in her breast."

Penelope

spoke to Odysseus now. She said:

"Strange man,

if man you are . . . This is no pride on my part

**Literary Analysis**
**Epic Simile** Which aspects of the slain suitors' appearance does the epic simile in lines 1535–1539 emphasize?

**Literary Analysis**
**Epic Simile** Which details in the epic simile in lines 1547–1551 compare Odysseus' hair to a work of art?

20. **Hephaestus** (hē fes′ təs) god of fire and metalworking.

**Reading Check**
Who helps Odysseus defeat the suitors?

nor scorn for you—not even wonder, merely.
I know so well how you—how he—appeared

1565 boarding the ship for Troy. But all the same . . .

Make up his bed for him, Eurycleia.
Place it outside the bedchamber my lord
built with his own hands. Pile the big bed
with fleeces, rugs, and sheets of purest linen."

1570 With this she tried him to the breaking point,
and he turned on her in a flash raging:

"Woman, by heaven you've stung me now!
Who dared to move my bed?
No builder had the skill for that—unless

1575 a god came down to turn the trick. No mortal
in his best days could budge it with a crowbar.
There is our pact and pledge, our secret sign,
built into that bed—my handiwork
and no one else's!

An old trunk of olive

1580 grew like a pillar on the building plot,
and I laid out our bedroom round that tree,
lined up the stone walls, built the walls and roof,
gave it a doorway and smooth-fitting doors.
Then I lopped off the silvery leaves and branches,

1585 hewed and shaped that stump from the roots up
into a bedpost, drilled it, let it serve
as model for the rest. I planed them all,
inlaid them all with silver, gold and ivory,
and stretched a bed between—a pliant web

1590 of oxhide thongs dyed crimson.

There's our sign!
I know no more. Could someone else's hand
have sawn that trunk and dragged the frame away?"

Their secret! as she heard it told, her knees
grew tremulous and weak, her heart failed her.

1595 With eyes brimming tears she ran to him,
throwing her arms around his neck, and kissed him,
murmuring:

"Do not rage at me, Odysseus!

**Literary Analysis**
**Epic Simile** Explain why the simile comparing the olive trunk to a pillar is not an epic simile.

◀ **Critical Viewing**
How does this image
convey the events in
text? **[Connect]**

No one ever matched your caution! Think
what difficulty the gods gave: they denied us
1600 life together in our prime and flowering years,
kept us from crossing into age together.
Forgive me, don't be angry. I could not
welcome you with love on sight! I armed myself
long ago against the frauds of men,
1605 impostors who might come—and all those many
whose underhanded ways bring evil on! . . .
But here and now, what sign could be so clear
as this of our own bed?
No other man has ever laid eyes on it—
1610 only my own slave, Actoris, that my father
sent with me as a gift—she kept our door.
You make my stiff heart know that I am yours."

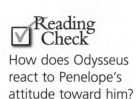

**Reading Check**

How does Odysseus
react to Penelope's
attitude toward him?

21. **abyss** (ə bis´) *n.* ocean depths.

Now from his breast into his eyes the ache
of longing mounted, and he wept at last,
1615  his dear wife, clear and faithful, in his arms,
longed for as the sunwarmed earth is longed for by a
     swimmer
spent in rough water where his ship went down
under Poseidon's blows, gale winds and tons of sea.
Few men can keep alive through a big surf
1620  to crawl, clotted with brine, on kindly beaches
in joy, in joy, knowing the abyss[21] behind:
and so she too rejoiced, her gaze upon her husband,
her white arms round him pressed as though forever.

## The Ending

*Odysseus is reunited with his father. Athena commands that peace prevail between Odysseus and the relatives of the slain suitors. Odysseus has regained his family and his kingdom.*

## Critical Thinking

Cite textual evidence to support your responses.

1. **Key Ideas and Details (a)** When Odysseus returns to his home, who helps him? **(b) Interpret:** What does the varying social status of Odysseus' helpers suggest about his character?

2. **Key Ideas and Details (a)** What planning does Odysseus do before he battles the suitors? **(b) Analyze:** How does his planning help him defeat his opponents?

3. **Key Ideas and Details (a)** What is Penelope's test, and how does Odysseus pass it? **(b) Infer:** Why does Penelope feel the need to test Odysseus even though he has abandoned his disguise? **(c) Interpret:** Is the mood after the test altogether happy? Explain.

4. **Integration of Knowledge and Ideas** Are Odysseus' actions in dealing with the suitors consistent with his actions in earlier episodes of the epic? Support your response.

5. **Integration of Knowledge and Ideas (a)** Do you think Odysseus kills the suitors to fulfill his responsibilities? Explain. **(b)** Is Odysseus' revenge justified? Why or why not? *[Connect to the Big Question: Do heroes have responsibilities?]*

# After You Read | *from the* Odyssey, Part 2

## Literary Analysis: Epic Simile

**©** **1. Craft and Structure (a)** Using a chart like the one shown, analyze the **epic simile** in lines 1613–1624.

| Items Being Compared | Details of Epic Simile | Purpose |
|---|---|---|
|  |  |  |

**(b)** Why is this simile a powerful and fitting image for the conclusion of the *Odyssey*?

## Reading Skill: Historical and Cultural Context

**2. (a)** What attitudes and values are reflected in Odysseus' actions toward the suitors? **(b)** What do his actions suggest about the **cultural and historical context** of Homer's *Odyssey* and the attitudes and values of ancient Greeks? Explain your answer.

**3. (a)** Name one of Odysseus' cultural beliefs, attitudes, or practices that is similar to an idea or a tradition in your own culture. **(b)** Name one that is significantly different. **(c)** Are Odysseus' values unique to his culture, or are they universal? Explain.

## Vocabulary

**©** **Acquisition and Use** Indicate whether each statement is *True* or *False*. Explain your answers. Then, revise false sentences to make them true.

**1.** People sometimes *dissemble* in order to hide their true feelings.

**2.** An event that is common and predictable evokes *incredulity*.

**3.** If road signs are *bemusing* drivers, the signs are working well.

**4.** A good judge is one with a strong sense of *equity*.

**5.** A pep band should play *maudlin* songs if it wants to excite fans.

**6.** Successful salespeople always show *contempt* for customers.

**Word Study** Use the context of the sentences and what you know about the **Latin prefix dis-** to explain your answer to each question.

**1.** If a reporter *discloses* the source of information, does she tell where she got the information?

**2.** If you are *disheartened* by some news, do you feel better?

### Word Study

The **Latin prefix dis-** means "away," "apart," or "not."

**Apply It** Explain how the prefix *dis-* contributes to the meanings of these words. Consult a dictionary if necessary.

**dispute**
**dishevel**
**disembark**

**PERFORMANCE TASKS**
# Integrated Language Skills

## *from the* Odyssey, Part 2

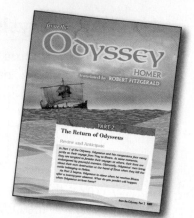

### Conventions: Complex and Compound-Complex Sentences

Sentences can be classified by the number of dependent and independent clauses they contain. An *independent clause* contains a subject and a verb and can stand alone as a sentence. A *dependent* or *subordinate clause* contains a subject and a verb but cannot stand as a sentence. It begins with a subordinate conjunction such as *when, although, because, before, since,* or *while.*

A **complex sentence** consists of one independent clause and one or more subordinate clauses.

A **compound-complex sentence** consists of two or more independent clauses and one or more subordinate clauses.

As with compound sentences, the independent clauses in compound-complex sentences are connected by a comma and a coordinating conjunction.

| Complex sentence | Compound-complex sentence |
| --- | --- |
| When the lights came on, he saw the audience. | When the lights came on, he saw the audience, and he waved to his parents. |

**Practice A** Identify each sentence as complex or compound-complex. Identify the independent clauses and the subordinate clauses.

1. Because Odysseus was disguised, Penelope did not recognize her husband.
2. When Odysseus strung the bow, the suitors were amazed, and they stopped laughing.
3. Telemachus grabbed a sword, and he stood by his father while they fought.
4. Although there were many suitors, Odysseus killed every one of them.

**Ⓒ Reading Application** In the *Odyssey,* find one complex sentence and one compound-complex sentence.

**Practice B** Combine the simple sentences to form one new sentence, as directed by the sentence type indicated in parentheses.

1. Argus recognized Odysseus. He died. (complex)
2. Odysseus strung the bow. Telemachus looked on. (complex)
3. Odysseus tested the bow. The suitors mocked him. They called him names. (compound-complex)
4. He shot the arrow. It passed through each ring. The suitors were awed. (compound-complex)

**Ⓒ Writing Application** Write six simple sentences about the *Odyssey.* Choose from among these sentences to build two complex sentences and two compound-complex sentences.

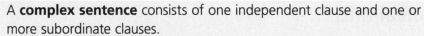

**PH WRITING COACH** | Further instruction and practice are available in *Prentice Hall Writing Coach.*

# Writing

**Informative Text** Write a short **biography** of Odysseus based on details in the *Odyssey*. Present the basic facts of his life and adventures, and hold your reader's attention by describing the dramatic situations in detail.

- List events in the *Odyssey* that are suitable for your biography. Focus on events that reveal the character of Odysseus.

- Include quotations from the epic to add detail and depth.

- Share your biography with classmates, and compare the events you each chose to include. In your discussion, consider what makes some events more significant than others.

**Grammar Application** As you write your biography, use a variety of sentence types, including complex and compound-complex sentences.

## Writing Workshop: *Work in Progress*

**Prewriting for Technical Document** From your Task List, choose a topic for your Technical Document. Think about the steps in the task and the order in which the instructions should be presented. Make an outline to plan your document. Save this Organizational Outline in your portfolio.

# Speaking and Listening

**Comprehension and Collaboration** Conduct a **debate** to decide whether Odysseus should be prosecuted for the murders of Penelope's suitors. Follow these steps to effectively practice the art of persuasion and debate:

- Divide into two opposing teams.

- With teammates, prepare a rational argument expressing your position. Be sure to support this logical assertion with details from the *Odyssey*.

- Plan an introduction to your remarks, a body that includes your arguments, and a conclusion that summarizes your position.

- Consider techniques to enhance your arguments. For example, you might use changes in tone and rhythm, gestures, and eye contact.

- During the debate, listen carefully and evaluate the opposing team's facts and reasoning so you can respond effectively.

Present your argument before the class, and ask your audience to decide which team was more persuasive.

**Common Core State Standards**

L.9-10.1; W.9-10.4; SL.9-10.1, SL.9-10.3
[For the full wording of the standards, see page 1086.]

Use this prewriting activity to prepare for the **Writing Workshop** on page 1138.

**www.PHLitOnline.com**
- Interactive graphic organizers
- Grammar tutorial
- Interactive journals

# Test Practice: Reading

## Cultural and Historical Context

### Fiction Selection

**Directions:** *Read the selection. Then, answer the questions.*

Sue rolled out of bed and crept over to the family laptop. Since she had been diagnosed with mononucleosis—the "kissing disease" as her best friend Lisa kept teasing her—everything required extra effort. Updating her weblog was the only thing she could find energy to do.

"Mono, Day 9," she typed. "I cannot believe that I've missed so much school. I'm so glad it is almost summer vacation. The doctor tells me to rest and drink fluids; these days, when people can get laser eye surgery, you would think they would be able to do more for this. The Web says the same thing, though, so I guess the doctor's right. My doctor is usually correct, but doing extra research cannot hurt. At least I have the computer to keep me busy. E-mail me if you want. I want to know what is going on with everyone at school." With that, Sue slid back into bed for a nap.

**1.** Based on the cultural and historical context of this passage, a reader can infer that Sue probably lives—

  **A.** in the future.
  **B.** at a boarding school.
  **C.** in the 1950s.
  **D.** in the present day.

**2.** Which details suggest that Sue values technology?

  **A.** She keeps a weblog and she researches her illness online.
  **B.** She knows what a laptop is and she is glad it is almost summer vacation.
  **C.** She enjoys e-mail and she follows her doctor's advice.
  **D.** She questions the lack of available treatments and she knows she should rest.

**3.** Based on the details in this passage, one can infer that Sue believes her illness is—

  **A.** punishment for a poor decision.
  **B.** an inconvenience.
  **C.** a terrifying ordeal.
  **D.** an exciting adventure.

**4.** Based on the details in this passage, one can conclude Sue believes that a doctor's advice—

  **A.** never leads to a quick recovery.
  **B.** can and should be questioned.
  **C.** is usually confusing.
  **D.** should be trusted in all cases.

### Writing for Assessment

Imagine that Sue lived in ancient times. Write a paragraph describing how the experience of having mononucleosis might be different. Use details from this passage as a guide.

## Nonfiction Selection

**Directions:** *Read the selection. Then, answer the questions.*

Between 1347 and 1353, the Black Death, or bubonic plague, killed one out of every three people in Europe. The disease was first spread by fleas on rats. Rats were common in Europe at the time and few people paid attention to them. People threw garbage into the streets, and the rats thrived in these unsanitary conditions. The plague could also be spread from person to person through the air. Therefore, most doctors would not treat people who were infected. The few who did treat people wore a leather mask with a beak filled with herbs. They believed the herbs would keep them from being infected. Doctors often treated patients by "bleeding" them. They thought that draining excess blood would balance bodily fluids and make the patient better. This practice made the problem worse. In all, over 25 million people died from the Black Death in Europe alone—more than in any war in history.

1. Which of the following details help you infer that people at the time did not know the source of the plague?

   **A.** People allowed conditions in which rats could thrive.

   **B.** The plague could be spread from person to person through the air.

   **C.** Doctors would not treat infected people.

   **D.** The plague was called the Black Death.

2. Which detail suggests that people at the time did not understand the connection between filth and disease?

   **A.** The plague was first spread by fleas.

   **B.** People threw garbage into the streets.

   **C.** Doctors thought spices prevented infection.

   **D.** Doctors wore masks to treat patients.

3. Which of the following is *not* a logical assumption about Europe in the 1300s, based on details in the passage?

   **A.** People were not prepared for a plague like the Black Death.

   **B.** Antibiotic medicines were not available.

   **C.** People did not fully understand how diseases spread.

   **D.** People did not trust doctors.

4. Based on the passage, what can you conclude about medical science during the plague?

   **A.** It was less advanced than medical science today.

   **B.** It was the same as medical science today.

   **C.** Doctors only used herbs to treat illness.

   **D.** Doctors did not believe that herbs had any use in medicine.

## Writing for Assessment

**Connecting Across Texts**
The Black Death was especially terrible because people misunderstood its causes and treatments. How is people's understanding of illness related to the time and place in which they live? Support your answer using details from both passages and your own knowledge.

**PHLit Online!**
www.PHLitOnline.com
- Online practice
- Instant feedback

# Reading for Information

## Analyzing Argumentative Texts

### Commentary

### Movie Review

**Common Core State Standards**

**Reading Informational Text**
**6.** Determine an author's point of view or purpose in a text and analyze how an author uses rhetoric to advance that point of view or purpose.

**Writing**
**1.a.** Introduce precise claim(s), distinguish the claim(s) from alternate or opposing claims, and create an organization that establishes clear relationships among claim(s), counterclaims, and evidence.

**Language**
**4.b.** Identify and correctly use patterns of word changes that indicate different meanings or parts of speech.
**6.** Acquire and use accurately general academic and domain-specific words and phrases, sufficient for reading, writing, speaking, and listening at the college and career readiness level.

## Reading Skill: Identify Characteristics of Various Types of Texts

To analyze an informational text, begin by **identifying characteristics of the text.** For example, if you read a text about a historical event, first determine the author's purpose for writing and his or her central, or main, idea. Then, examine the sources used as support for the main idea, including whether they are primary sources—firsthand accounts— or secondary sources—accounts by those who did not see the event. Next, evaluate the sources to decide if they are trustworthy and effective as support. Finally, extend the ideas presented in a text by identifying questions you have that are left unanswered and by researching to find out more about the topic. As you read, consider these questions:

| Extending Ideas | Questions to Ask |
|---|---|
| Analysis | • What is the text about? What details are presented? <br> • What are the characteristics or features of the text? |
| Evaluation | • How well are the main ideas presented and supported? <br> • Does the text achieve its purpose? |
| Elaboration | • What connections can I make with the text? <br> • What additional ideas and questions do I have? |

### Content-Area Vocabulary

These words appear in the selections that follow. You may also encounter them in other content-area texts.

- **conventional** (kən ven′ shə nəl) *adj.* following custom and traditional models

- **footage** (foot′ ij) *n.* any length of film that has been shot

# A Hero in Our Midst

### by Justice Paul E. Pfeifer

**Sept. 13, 2006**

This week marks the fifth anniversary of the Sept. 11 terrorist attacks on the United States. The news that day was nothing but grim; horror unleashed on a large scale. But recently, those of us who work at the Supreme Court of Ohio discovered an unexpected ray of light that emerged from the darkness of that day, and in the process learned a lesson about bravery and humility, and that greatness can be right before your eyes without you even knowing it.

> Analyzing this paragraph reveals that the author discusses events he was not personally involved in, indicating that this commentary is a secondary source.

Last month Paramount Pictures released a movie about the attack in New York City. The film, entitled *World Trade Center*, was directed by Oliver Stone—the man who makes movies that sometimes raise almost as much controversy as they do cash. This time, Stone has made a pretty **conventional** film that tells the true story of two New York City Port Authority police officers who were trapped under the crumbled towers.

While the movie focuses primarily on the police officers—John McLoughlin and Will Jimeno—there are two other characters vital to the story: the two Marines who found the trapped men and led others to their rescue.

One of the Marines, Staff Sergeant David Karnes, was actually two years out of the Corps and working as an accountant in Connecticut at the time. When he heard about the attacks that morning, Karnes put on his old uniform and headed into the city to help with rescue efforts.

In the days following Sept. 11, Karnes spoke with the press and his story is well chronicled in the movie.

The other man, known only as Sergeant Thomas, remained something of a mystery. Karnes encountered Thomas in the chaos surrounding the collapsed towers, teamed up with him to search the wreckage, and then, after the rescue, never saw him again. Like a mythic figure of old, Thomas had seemingly just appeared where people were in peril, performed his heroics, then vanished into the mist and confusion.

> Extending the ideas in this paragraph might lead you to research how filmmakers were able to depict a character they knew so little about.

For five years no one knew who he was, though the police and other authorities searched for him. The filmmakers sought him as well. When they came up empty, the movie was made without knowing any more about Sergeant Thomas.

But when commercials for the film began appearing on television, the movie, you might say, found Sergeant Thomas. When he saw the previews he recognized his character on the screen. After nearly five years of silence, Sergeant Thomas finally decided to come forward.

Sergeant Thomas is actually Jason Thomas. And, as it turns out, Jason is now a security officer here at the Supreme Court of Ohio, in Columbus. For more than two years Jason has kept a watchful eye over all of us, and no one at the court—not his close friends or his casual acquaintances—had ever heard about his role on Sept. 11.

And it's not as if Jason is easy to miss. He is a mountain of a man, a broad-shouldered former football player who exudes—and inspires—confidence. If you didn't know Jason had been a Marine, you would think he ought to become one. They should use him for the recruitment posters.

But until the movie came out, this quiet man never felt the need to speak of what he'd done. . . .

That morning, Jason was dropping off his newborn daughter at his mother's house on Long Island before heading off to class. His mother met him on the porch and told him that a plane had hit one of the twin towers. Sensing this wasn't a freak accident, Jason's first words to her were: "They got us."

Although Jason had been out of the Marine Corps for a year, his uniform was in the trunk of his car. Why was it there? Because he was in the middle of moving, and he didn't want his most valued possession—his Marine uniform —getting lost among the boxes.

Donning his uniform, he told his mother to contact his wife, Kirsti, who worked in midtown Manhattan, to tell her that he was headed to the crash site. "I had all this military training," he said. "That's my city. I felt compelled to help out." His mother didn't try to stop him. "She knew it would be a waste of words. . . ."

As he got out of his car, the smoke and ash engulfed him. Sticking his head into his shirt for air, he crouched down as the world went dark around him. Then, while dozens ran for safety away from the buildings, Jason Thomas bowed his back and ran toward the fallen towers.

What makes a man run into danger rather than from it? Part of it, Jason said, is his upbringing. His parents taught him—and his ten brothers and six sisters—to never leave someone behind. "You go together, you come back together," their mother always told them.

And then there's the Marine training. Robert Kaplan, a journalist who was embedded with the Marines in Fallujah, has written that running into gunfire "rather than seeking cover from it goes counter to every human survival instinct—trust me." But in Fallujah, Kaplan saw Marines—without being ordered— running straight into the direction of fire time and again.

Although they didn't know it, John McLoughlin and Will Jimeno—trapped and dying beneath a mountain of concrete and steel—were about to reap the benefits of Jason Thomas's Marine training, and the sense of duty, instilled by his parents, to help those in need.

**Sergeant Jason Thomas**

> One characteristic of a commentary is that the author offers his own opinions and feelings about his subject.

> It is characteristic of a commentary to pose questions and then answer them. You can extend these ideas by analyzing the text and forming your own questions for research.

Sign In/Register

Search by Movie ▼     Search by Actor ▼

MENU    |    **EDITORIAL REVIEW**    |    NEWS    |    TRAILERS    |

**Features:**
- a reviewer's opinion of the movie
- a summary of the plot
- names of the actors and the roles they play
- general information about the film and its makers

# WORLD TRADE CENTER

## Movie Review *by Rebecca Murray*

After the Twin Towers fell on September 11, 2001, only 20 people were pulled from the rubble alive. *20 people.* Port Authority Police Sergeant John McLoughlin and Officer Will Jimeno were numbers 18 and 19. *World Trade Center* is their story, told through the eyes of Jimeno, McLoughlin and their families. There's no political agenda or finger-pointing. *World Trade Center* is very simply a tale of hope, courage and survival on one of America's darkest days.

The film begins with the central characters going through the mundane motions of preparing for work, lining up for duty, and then heading out on patrol. From there the events of 9/11 unfold with the officers racing to the Twin Towers. Focus shifts from outside the Towers to inside, swiftly narrowing the story to spotlight a small group of Port Authority officers led by Sergeant McLoughlin (played by Nicolas Cage).

Of course the officers don't have a grasp on the full picture and, without knowing just how bad things will ultimately become, set out gathering equipment for a rescue operation that never has time to materialize. They get no further than the concourse level when the Tower falls. McLoughlin and Jimeno (Michael Pena) become pinned 20 feet below the surface under piles of twisted metal and burning rubble. Critically injured, the men spend hours keeping each other awake as their families cling to the hope they'll somehow make it out alive.

If you didn't know this was an Oliver Stone movie going in, chances are you won't know it as you leave the theater unless you stay for the credits. Stone refrained from inserting his own view of the events into this story and tonally, visually, and substance-wise, *World Trade Center* is nothing like any of his previous films. Stone not only didn't include his own politics in the movie, but also chose not to include **footage** of the planes hitting the buildings, the Towers actually collapsing, or other all-too-familiar scenes from that horrific day. None of that sort of footage would have benefited the story and Stone, to his credit, manages to show the scope of the devastation just by focusing on the specific area surrounding Jimeno and McLoughlin.

**Movie Photos**

> One characteristic of a movie review is that the reviewer summarizes the plot of the film.

> It is typical of a movie review to include comparisons to the filmmaker's other works. You can extend these ideas by connecting the information given here to what you may know about other films.

Sign In/Register

Search by Movie ▼    Search by Actor ▼

MENU | **EDITORIAL REVIEW** | NEWS | TRAILERS

**More Photos**

   *World Trade Center* is only the second major feature film to focus on the horrible events of 9/11 so comparisons to Paul Greengrass' *United 93* are inevitable. Unfortunately for Stone's film, *United 93* not only made it to theaters first but also did a better job of capturing the extreme anxiety of the day - and even did a far better job of involving the audience emotionally. Because Stone's *World Trade Center* is not just the story of the two men trapped in the ruins of the Towers but also the story of their wives and families, Stone's film is forced to devote time away from the rescue operation of Jimeno and McLoughlin. Not to take anything away from the suffering the real Donna McLoughlin and Allison Jimeno went through waiting for word on their husbands, screenwriter Andrea Berloff's script and Stone's direction fail to adequately capture what must have been the most difficult day in the lives of both women. Instead of furthering the film's heart wrenching story, when the focus shifts to the homes of Jimeno and McLoughlin, the movie bogs down and loses intensity.

   As for the performances in *World Trade Center,* Stone has to be commended for casting against type and getting the best out of his eclectic group of actors. Cage in particular gives a powerful performance as Sergeant McLoughlin. At least half of Cage's time onscreen is spent trapped in rubble, leaving only his voice and facial expressions to hold our attention. Cage pulls it off, giving one of the most tightly controlled performances of his career. . . .

   Shot in New York with the cooperation of the Port Authority Police Department and the brave men and women involved in Jimeno and McLoughlin's rescue, *World Trade Center* tries hard to get the story right. The filmmakers should be applauded for doing their research and keeping the politics out of this particular story.

   *World Trade Center* moves a little too slow—the pacing's not quite right—but otherwise it's a decent film and one that's a fitting tribute to the best in people during the worst of times.

Characteristically, the movie review ends with a summary of the reviewer's opinions about the film.

## Comparing Argumentative Texts

**1. Craft and Structure (a)** In what ways are the **characteristics** and features of the commentary and the movie review similar and different? **(b)** Analyze the characteristics of each text to determine how the authors use them to advance their purposes for writing and to introduce and develop their central ideas.

### Content-Area Vocabulary

**2. (a)** Remove the suffix -*al* from the word *conventional*. Using a print or an online dictionary, explain how removing the suffix alters the meaning of the word and its part of speech. **(b)** Then, use the words *conventional* and *convention* in a sentence that shows their meanings.

## Timed Writing

### Argumentative Text: Critique

> **Format**
> The prompt directs you to write a critique. Therefore, your response should offer judgments and opinions about the review, supported by evidence and examples.

Write a critique of the movie review. Analyze the types of details presented and evaluate the strength of those details as support for the reviewer's claims. Consider whether the review leaves important questions unanswered and whether the text reveals too much of the plot. Use details from the text to support your critique. (40 minutes)

> **Academic Vocabulary**
> When you *analyze* a text, you examine it in detail. When you *evaluate* a text, you judge its value or worth.

### 5-Minute Planner

Complete these steps before you begin to write:

**1.** Read the prompt carefully, noting highlighted key words.

**2.** Skim the movie review. Make notes about whether the reviewer's claims are sufficiently supported by the details provided. **TIP** Make a two-column chart, noting claims in one column and supporting details or evidence in the other. Then, consult your chart to make your evaluation.

**3.** Consider whether the reviewer reveals too much or too little about the plot of the film. Support your judgment with specific details. Note any additional questions you have about the movie.

**4.** Sketch a rough outline for your critique. Then, refer to your notes and outline as you write.

# Comparing Literary Works

## Comparing Contemporary Interpretations

A **contemporary interpretation** of a literary work is a new piece of writing that a modern-day author bases on an older work. Even when they are based on the same work, contemporary interpretations can differ widely in purpose and theme. Each writer's cultural and historical backgrounds, attitudes, and beliefs profoundly affect his or her perceptions of the older work and influence the creation of the new work.

Writers draw from classic, traditional, or simply well-known source material for a variety of reasons, such as the following:

- Timeless or universal themes that are relevant to modern-day life
- Recognizable characters, settings, and conflicts
- Established meaning and importance
- Quick introduction of complex ideas
- Basis for additional interpretation and new layers of meaning

The characters and events of Homer's *Odyssey* are timeless and universal in their appeal. They have inspired many contemporary interpretations, including the poems you are about to read. By reinventing and transforming Homer's tales, modern-day writers shed new light on Homer's ancient words.

Contemporary interpretations of literature from ages past can be viewed as extended allusions to the ancient or traditional texts. An **allusion** is a reference to a well-known person, place, event, or work of literature or art. As you read, use a chart like the one shown to note the extended allusion each poet makes to Homer's *Odyssey*. Then, think about the ways in which the allusion helps each poet express a new, modern meaning.

| Poem | Allusion to the *Odyssey* | Meaning |
|------|---------------------------|---------|
|      |                           |         |

### Common Core State Standards

**Reading Literature**

**7.** Analyze the representation of a subject or a key scene in two different artistic mediums.

**9.** Analyze how an author draws on and transforms source material in a specific work.

**Writing**

**2.** Write informative/explanatory texts to examine and convey complex ideas, concepts, and information clearly and accurately through the effective selection, organization, and analysis of content.

**2.a.** Introduce a topic; organize complex ideas, concepts, and information to make important connections and distinctions.

**9.** Draw evidence from literary or informational texts to support analysis, reflection, and research.

**www.PHLitOnline.com**

- Vocabulary flashcards
- Interactive journals
- More about the authors

- Selection audio
- Interactive graphic organizers

# Do *heroes* have responsibilities?

## Writing About the Big Question

In these selections, characters have different ways of living up to their responsibilities. Use these sentence starters to develop your ideas about the Big Question.

In my own life, I know I am **responsible** for _____.

If I do not live up to this **obligation,** one consequence might be _____.

When I make **responsible choices,** one positive result is _____.

# Meet the Authors

## Edna St. Vincent Millay (1892–1950)
### Author of "An Ancient Gesture" (p. 1128)

Edna St. Vincent Millay is remembered for her artistic experimentation and her rebelliousness. Her poetry collection *The Harp Weaver and Other Poems* (1923) earned her a Pulitzer Prize.

## Margaret Atwood (b. 1939)
### Author of "Siren Song" (p. 1130)

Much of Margaret Atwood's writing is about what it means to be a woman in a period of social change. In "Siren Song," Atwood presents another of her themes—the role of mythology in people's lives.

## Derek Walcott (b. 1930)
### Author of *The Odyssey* (p. 1132)

Born in St. Lucia, an island in the Caribbean Sea, Walcott writes poems that reflect his background. In 1992, he won the Nobel Prize in Literature. "Prologue" and "Epilogue" are from his stage version of *The Odyssey*.

## Constantine Cavafy (1863–1933)
### Author of "Ithaca" (p. 1135)

Constantine Cavafy was born to Greek parents in Alexandria, Egypt. "Ithaca" showcases his creative method: using Greek mythology to speak to the modern reader.

# An Ancient Gesture

## Edna St. Vincent Millay

I thought, as I wiped my eyes on the corner of my apron:
Penelope did this too.
And more than once: you can't keep weaving all day
And undoing it all through the night;
5  Your arms get tired, and the back of your neck gets tight;
And along towards morning, when you think it will never
  be light,
And your husband has been gone, and you don't know
  where, for years,
Suddenly you burst into tears;
There is simply nothing else to do.

10  And I thought, as I wiped my eyes on the corner of my apron:
This is an ancient gesture, authentic, antique,
In the very best tradition, classic, Greek;
Ulysses[1] did this too.
But only as a gesture,—a gesture which implied
15  To the assembled throng that he was much too moved
  to speak.
He learned it from Penelope . . .
Penelope, who really cried.

---

1. **Ulysses** Latin name for Odysseus.

**Literary Analysis Contemporary Interpretations** What connection does the speaker make between herself and Penelope?

**Vocabulary**
**authentic** (ô then´ tik) *adj.* genuine

◄ **Analyze Representations** How does the representation of Penelope in this painting compare to her portrayal in the poem? **[Interpret]**

## Critical Thinking

Cite textual evidence to support your responses.

1. **Key Ideas and Details (a)** What is the "ancient gesture"? **(b) Summarize:** According to the speaker, what caused Penelope to employ this gesture? **(c) Infer:** Why might the speaker have made a similar gesture?

2. **Key Ideas and Details (a)** According to the speaker, who else made this ancient gesture? **(b) Compare and Contrast:** How did this gesture differ from Penelope's? **(c) Analyze:** What do the different qualities of their gestures show about these characters?

3. **Integration of Knowledge and Ideas (a) Assess:** What questions about the speaker are left unanswered? **(b) Analyze Cause and Effect:** What effect do these unanswered questions create?

4. **Integration of Knowledge and Ideas (a)** According to this interpretation, does Odysseus live up to his responsibility as a husband? Explain. **(b)** Who do you think the author felt was the hero in the *Odyssey*—Penelope or Odysseus? *[Connect to the Big Question: Do heroes have responsibilities?]*

# SIREN SONG

## Margaret Atwood

This is the one song everyone
would like to learn: the song
that is irresistible:

the song that forces men
5   to leap overboard in squadrons
even though they see the beached skulls

the song nobody knows
because anyone who has heard it
is dead, and the others can't remember.

10  Shall I tell you the secret
and if I do, will you get me
out of this bird suit?[1]

**Literary Analysis**
**Contemporary Interpretations** What allusion do lines 4–9 make to the *Odyssey?*

---

**1. bird suit** Sirens are usually represented as half bird and half woman.

I don't enjoy it here
squatting on this island
15  looking *picturesque* and mythical

with these two feathery maniacs,
I don't enjoy singing
this trio, fatal and valuable.

I will tell the secret to you,
20  to you, only to you.
Come closer. This song

is a cry for help: Help me!
Only you, only you can,
you are unique

25  at last. Alas
it is a boring song
but it works every time.

## Critical Thinking

1. **Key Ideas and Details (a)** In the first stanza, what song does the speaker say everyone wants to learn? **(b) Analyze Cause and Effect:** What does this song have the power to do?

2. **Key Ideas and Details (a)** What does the speaker want in exchange for revealing the song's secret? **(b) Interpret:** Why does the speaker want to make this deal?

Cite textual evidence to support your responses.

3. **Integration of Knowledge and Ideas (a) Analyze:** Why do you think the speaker's compliment in lines 23 and 24 is so effective? **(b) Make Generalizations:** What might the speaker be saying about the relationships between men and women?

4. **Key Ideas and Details (a) Summarize:** How does the speaker feel about her song and its secret? **(b) Support:** Which details in the poem support your answer?

5. **Integration of Knowledge and Ideas (a)** How does the Siren affect heroes? Explain. **(b)** Do you think the Siren should be held responsible for her effect on heroes? Why or why not? *[Connect to the Big Question: Do heroes have responsibilities?]*

# Prologue and Epilogue from the

# Odyssey

## Derek Walcott

**PROLOGUE**

> *Sound of surf.*

**BILLY BLUE** *(Sings)*

> Gone sing 'bout that man because his stories please us,
> Who saw trials and tempests for ten years after Troy.

> I'm Blind Billy Blue, my main man's sea-smart Odysseus,
> Who the God of the Sea drove crazy and tried to destroy.

5    Andra moi ennepe mousa polutropon hos mala polla . . .[1]
> The shuttle of the sea moves back and forth on this line,

> All night, like the surf, she shuttles and doesn't fall
> Asleep, then her rosy fingers at dawn unstitch the design.

> When you hear this chord
> *(Chord)*

>                            Look for a swallow's wings

10   A swallow arrowing seaward like a messenger

> Passing smoke-blue islands, happy that the kings
> Of Troy are going home and its ten years' siege is over.

> So my blues drifts like smoke from the fire of that war,
> Cause once Achilles was ashes, things sure fell apart.

15   Slow-striding Achilles, who put the hex on Hector
> A swallow twitters in Troy. That's where we start.
> *(Exit.)*

---

**1. Andra moi. . .** the first line of Homer's *Odyssey* in Greek.

**Literary Analysis**
**Contemporary**
**Interpretations** What actions in lines 6–8 reflect the *Odyssey*? Explain.

**Vocabulary**
**siege** (sēj) *n.* encirclement of a fortified place by an opposing armed force intending to take it

## EPILOGUE

**BILLY BLUE** *(Sings)*

> I sang of that man against whom the sea still rages,
> Who escaped its terrors, that despair could not destroy,
>
> Since that first blind singer, others will sing down the ages
> 20   Of the heart in its harbour, then long years after Troy,
> after Troy.
>
> And a house, happy for good, from a swallow's omen,
> Let the trees clap their hands, and the surf whisper amen.
>
> For a rock, a rock, a rock, a rock-steady woman
> Let the waves clap their hands and the surf whisper amen.
>
> 25   For that peace which, in their mercy, the gods allow men.
> *(Fade. Sound of surf.)*

**Literary Analysis**
**Contemporary Interpretations** Which words suggest that the story of the *Odyssey* will always be meaningful?

**Spiral Review**
**Cultural Context**
What aspect of Derek Walcott's Caribbean background might these lines suggest?

## Critical Thinking

Cite textual evidence to support your responses.

1. **Key Ideas and Details (a)** Who is the speaker's "main man"? **(b) Interpret:** What is the speaker's attitude toward this "main man"?

2. **Key Ideas and Details (a) Infer:** What type of music does the speaker sing? **(b) Analyze:** Considering the loneliness, death, and defeat that occur in Homer's *Odyssey*, why is the speaker's musical style appropriate?

3. **Key Ideas and Details (a)** How is Penelope described in the Epilogue? **(b) Infer:** What seems to be the speaker's attitude toward Penelope?

4. **Integration of Knowledge and Ideas Generalize:** Overall, which elements from Homer's *Odyssey* seem most interesting to Walcott?

5. **Integration of Knowledge and Ideas (a)** Which details suggest that the poet felt a responsibility to show respect for Homer's *Odyssey?* **(b)** Do you think Billy Blue feels responsible for sharing Odysseus' story? Why or why not? *[Connect to the Big Question: Do heroes have responsibilities?]*

# Ithaca

## Constantine Cavafy

When you start on your journey to Ithaca,
then pray that the road is long,
full of adventure, full of knowledge.
Do not fear the Lestrygonians[1]
5  and the Cyclopes and the angry Poseidon.
You will never meet such as these on your path,
if your thoughts remain lofty, if a fine
emotion touches your body and your spirit.
You will never meet the Lestrygonians,
10 the Cyclopes and the fierce Poseidon,
if you do not carry them within your soul,
if your soul does not raise them up before you.

Then pray that the road is long.
That the summer mornings are many,
15 that you will enter ports seen for the first time
with such pleasure, with such joy!
Stop at Phoenician markets,
and purchase fine merchandise,
mother-of-pearl and corals, amber and ebony,
20 and pleasurable perfumes of all kinds,
buy as many pleasurable perfumes as you can;
visit hosts of Egyptian cities,
to learn and learn from those who have knowledge.

---

1. **Lestrygonians** (les tri gō′ nē ənz) *n.* cannibals who destroy all of Odysseus'
ships except his own and kill the crews.

◄ **Critical Viewing**
Which aspects of
this image relate to
Odysseus' journey?
**[Connect]**

**Vocabulary**
**lofty** (lôf ′ tē) *adj.* very
high; noble

Reading
Check

What advice does the
speaker give about meet-
ing the Lestrygonians?

Always keep Ithaca fixed in your mind.
25 To arrive there is your ultimate goal.
But do not hurry the voyage at all.
It is better to let it last for long years;
and even to anchor at the isle when you are old,
rich with all that you have gained on the way,
30 not expecting that Ithaca will offer you riches.

Ithaca has given you the beautiful voyage.
Without her you would never have taken the road.
But she has nothing more to give you.

And if you find her poor, Ithaca has not defrauded you.
35 With the great wisdom you have gained, with so much
    experience,
You must surely have understood by then what Ithaca
    means.

**Literary Analysis**
**Contemporary
Interpretations**
How does Odysseus'
desire for an end to his
journey differ from the
contemporary poet's atti-
tude toward the journey?

**Vocabulary**
**defrauded** (dē frôd´ əd)
*v.* cheated

# Critical Thinking

 **Cite textual evidence to support your responses.**

1. **Key Ideas and Details (a)** According to the speaker, how can you avoid meeting the Lestrygonians, the Cyclopes, and Poseidon? **(b) Infer:** Why might a person carry such terrors as these in his or her own soul?

2. **Key Ideas and Details (a)** What three things does the speaker say you should pray for on the journey to Ithaca? **(b) Connect:** What activities and pleasures are linked to these prayers?

3. **Key Ideas and Details (a)** According to the speaker, why is Ithaca important? **(b) Interpret:** What might Ithaca symbolize for the poet?

4. **Integration of Knowledge and Ideas (a) Interpret:** What message is conveyed in the last three lines of the poem? **(b) Assess:** Do you agree with this message? Explain.

5. **Integration of Knowledge and Ideas (a) Speculate:** What advice might the speaker have given to Odysseus during his long journey? **(b) Take a Position:** Do you agree with this advice? Explain.

6. **Integration of Knowledge and Ideas (a)** What does the "journey to Ithaca" symbolize? **(b)** Do you think people have a responsibility to take a "journey to Ithaca" in their own lives? Why or why not? *[Connect to the Big Question: Do heroes have responsibilities?]*

## Comparing Contemporary Interpretations

**1. Craft and Structure** The author of each contemporary interpretation in this section uses Homer's work as inspiration for new ideas. Use a chart like the one shown to explain how each poem is like and unlike Homer's *Odyssey*.

**2. Key Ideas and Details** Select one poem in this section, and identify the comment the poet is making about modern life. Support your explanation with details from your completed chart.

**3. Craft and Structure (a)** Identify an allusion in at least two of the poems. **(b)** Explain what the reference adds to the meaning of the poem. **(c)** Tell which allusion you think is more (or most) effective, and why.

## ⏱ Timed Writing

### Explanatory Text: Essay

Each writer in this section draws on Homer's epic to communicate a message suited to today's world. In an essay, compare how each poet uses classical allusions in combination with his or her own perspective. Support your ideas with evidence from the text. **(40 minutes)**

### 5-Minute Planner

1. Read the prompt carefully and completely.
2. Think about these questions and jot down ideas for your essay:
   - What is each poet's main message?
   - What makes each poet's allusion appropriate for his or her message?
   - In what ways does each poem shed new light on the events or characters of the *Odyssey*?
3. Choose and plan an organizational strategy for your essay.
4. Reread the prompt. Then, refer to your notes as you draft your essay.

# Writing Workshop

 **Common Core State Standards**

**Writing**

**2.** Write informative/explanatory texts to examine and convey complex ideas, concepts, and information clearly and accurately through the effective selection, organization, and analysis of content.

**2.a.** Introduce a topic; organize complex ideas, concepts, and information to make important connections and distinctions; include formatting, graphics, and multimedia when useful to aiding comprehension.

**2.b.** Develop the topic with well-chosen, relevant, and sufficient facts, extended definitions, concrete details, quotations, or other information and examples appropriate to the audience's knowledge of the topic.

**2.d.** Use precise language and domain-specific vocabulary to manage the complexity of the topic.

**5.** Develop and strengthen writing as needed by planning, revising, editing, rewriting, or trying a new approach, focusing on addressing what is most significant for a specific purpose and audience.

## Write Explanatory Text

### Technical Document

**Defining the Form** Technical writing conveys information and ideas logically while providing details and specifications. A technical manual can identify the steps to take to complete a task. You might use elements of this type of writing in instruction manuals, rule books, and assembly directions.

**Assignment** Write a manual for others to use when completing a task, such as how to wrap a gift, how to establish an exercise routine, how to take meeting minutes, or how to work together to resolve conflicts. Include these elements:

✓ *ideas* logically and correctly conveyed

✓ *detailed and accurate specifications*

✓ *scenarios*, *definitions*, and *examples* to aid comprehension

✓ *understandable abbreviations* and *legible writing*

✓ error-free grammar, especially correct use of *sentence fragments and run-ons*

To preview the criteria on which your manual may be judged, see the rubric on page 1143.

 **Writing Workshop:** *Work in Progress*

Review the work you did on pages 1085 and 1117.

## Prewriting/Planning Strategy

**Identify the information you will need to share.** Before you write, think about how someone would successfully complete the task you will explain. Consider your audience and what they need to learn the task you have chosen. List the necessary materials, and any specific skills you may need to detail. Complete a chart like the one shown to help you prepare to write your manual. If necessary, conduct research to learn more about your topic.

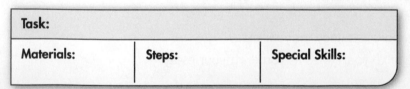

| Task: | | |
|---|---|---|
| **Materials:** | **Steps:** | **Special Skills:** |

# Expressing Your Ideas

**Ideas** are the basis for any form of writing, even technical writing. To provide instruction on how to accomplish a task, you must express your ideas clearly and organize them logically. Think about the obvious steps you take to complete the process, record them logically, and then review them to make sure you didn't miss anything.

**Teach your audience.** The main purpose of constructing a manual is to teach your audience how to accomplish a task. Begin by laying the groundwork for the task you will explain. You may need to define any new vocabulary. Provide a sufficient number of examples, scenarios, and clarifications related to your purpose to help your audience learn a new skill and complete the task in a variety of situations.

**Use visual aids.** Remember that visual aids can be helpful tools to convey basic information. It may be helpful to provide diagrams, charts, or maps. Alternatively, you might prepare a demonstration using presentation software. A labeled illustration like the one shown would be very helpful in a manual on bicycle repair.

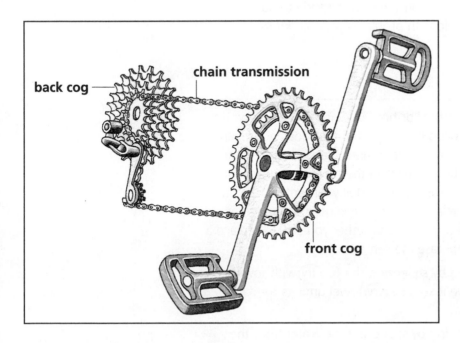

# Drafting Strategies

**Organize details in step-by-step order.** Because most manuals describe a process that takes place over time, chronological order is often the most effective organization.

**Choose the best format.** Paragraphs are not always the best way to present information meant to instruct or explain. Your readers will have different needs at different times:

- A reader who is considering doing the activity outlined in your manual will want a quick overview of materials and steps.

- A reader who is in the middle of following your instructions will need to locate a step quickly.

- A reader who is looking for special tips or background information will want additional information.

To meet the needs of each of these readers, consider these formatting possibilities as you draft:

- Present essential steps as a series of numbered points or in a bulleted list for ease of reading.

- Organize information below specific headings.

- Provide additional information in separate sections, such as boxes inset alongside your main instructions. You may decide to build a troubleshooting chart to help with problems your reader may encounter.

# Revising Strategies

**Evaluate repeated words.** A manual or how-to guide should be written in a formal style with straightforward language, but that does not mean it has to be boring. As you revise, incorporate more precise language or technical vocabulary that would help to explain the topic of your manual to the reader. Avoid overuse of words that may dull your writing. Go back through your draft to find and circle words you have used several times. Review the words you have circled to decide whether you should replace a word with a synonym or even rephrase the sentence.

**Draft:** Dry each part of your dog by squeezing the fur dry with towels. When the dog is mostly dry, have it sit on a dry towel until its fur completely dries.

**Revision:** Dry each part of your dog by squeezing the water from the fur with towels. When the dog is barely damp, have it sit on a fresh towel until its fur completely dries.

**Common Core State Standards**

**Writing**
**2.a.** Organize complex ideas, concepts, and information to make important connections and distinctions; include formatting, graphics, and multimedia when useful to aiding comprehension.
**2.d.** Use precise language and domain-specific vocabulary to manage the complexity of the topic.
**2.e.** Establish and maintain a formal style and objective tone while attending to the norms and conventions of the discipline in which they are writing.

**Language**
**1.** Demonstrate command of the conventions of standard English grammar and usage when writing or speaking.
**2.** Demonstrate command of the conventions of standard English punctuation when writing.

# Revising to Correct Fragments and Run-ons

A **fragment** is a group of words that does not express a complete thought but is punctuated as if it were a sentence. A **run-on** is two or more complete sentences that are not properly joined or separated.

**Identifying and Correcting Fragments** Fragments express incomplete thoughts. Often, they offer information that belongs to a nearby sentence. Correct fragments by attaching them to sentences.

> **Fragment:** They waited at the bus stop. *Huddled under an umbrella.*
>
> **Revised:** They waited at the bus stop, huddled under an umbrella.

Other fragments can be corrected through expansion—adding the words needed to make a complete sentence.

> **Fragment:** *As long as you agree to help.*
>
> **Expanded:** I will wash the car as long as you agree to help.

**Identifying and Correcting Run-ons** Run-ons include sentences that are fused with no punctuation at all or that are linked by only a comma.

> **Fused:** She speaks Spanish fluently she does not speak Italian at all.
>
> **Comma splice:** She speaks Spanish fluently, she does not speak Italian at all.

**PH WRITING COACH**

Further instruction and practice are available in *Prentice Hall Writing Coach*.

### Three Ways to Correct a Run-on Sentence

| | |
|---|---|
| Use an appropriate end mark to separate a run-on into two sentences. Begin the second sentence with a capital letter. | She speaks Spanish fluently. She does not speak Italian at all. |
| Use a comma and a coordinating conjunction, such as *and, but, or, for,* and *nor,* to combine two related independent clauses. | She speaks Spanish fluently, but she does not speak Italian at all. |
| Use a semicolon to connect two closely related ideas. | She speaks Spanish fluently; she does not speak Italian at all. |

### Grammar in Your Writing

Scan your technical document for fragments and run-ons by looking for sentences that seem too short or too long. Neatly correct any sentence problems you find using the strategies that have been presented.

# Student Model: C.J. Geeza, San Juan Capistrano, CA

 **Common Core State Standards**

**Language**
**2.c.** Spell correctly.

## Taking Meeting Minutes

One day, you just might get asked to take meeting notes for a meeting you are attending. Whether it is a business, sports, or student council meeting, taking meeting notes is important because notes capture discussion and decisions. It's easy to understand meeting notes if you break it down into five simple steps.

1. **Get Yourself Ready**—This first step in writing meaningful meeting minutes takes place before the meeting has started. Make sure you go to the meeting ready to listen objectively. Meeting minutes are usually the official record of what happened, so it is important to be accurate. Decide how you are going to record information. This could be a computer or pen and paper. If you're using your computer, you might want to consider sitting next to an outlet. A great hint is to use the meeting agenda, or an organized layout of the topics that are going to be discussed, to create an outline for your note taking. This will make it easier to move between topics as the meeting progresses. Make a map of the seating arrangement and write down names so you can make sure you know who said what.

2. **Just the Facts**—This next part is the most important part of taking meeting minutes. Start by writing down the date, time the meeting starts and ends, and who is and is not in attendance for the meeting. Listen to who is speaking and what is said. It's better to summarize what is said rather than to go into great detail. Do not make the mistake of recording every single comment. Be objective—your opinion is not needed.

3. **Make a Draft**—You should not wait too long before you write a draft of the meeting minutes using your notes. Use complete sentences and provide detail on the items discussed, major points raised, and decisions made. Be sure not to take sides in any arguments in your writing, as your job is only to record the meeting, not to cause more conflict. After you are finished with your draft, go back and revise it. You can organize your minutes by adding bullet points or numbers. Cut out any unimportant information not related to the meeting. Also, make sure the reader can point out important topics and comments by underlining, boldfacing, color coding, etc.

4. **Get it Right**—Compare your notes and final copy in order to make sure that you have covered all the content you wanted to include. Make sure that you only use one system of bullets and numbering. Check the spelling of names and words, grammar, and punctuation.

5. **Get it Out**—Making copies of your meeting minutes is a great idea. This way, you can give a copy to the people who were not at the meeting so they know what happened and a copy to those in attendance as a friendly reminder about any follow-up needed.

Meeting notes are an effective way to document the details and action items of a meeting. Learning to listen objectively and record notes accurately is a skill that will be used in the workplace. Like any other skill, the more you do it the better you become at it.

In the opening paragraph, C.J. explains what meeting minutes are before instructing how to take them.

Providing organizational tips teaches the reader how to effectively note what is said in the meeting.

The numbering system and headings allow C.J. to present information logically for the reader.

C.J. uses a conclusion to tie the steps together as an essay.

# Editing and Proofreading

Check your draft for errors in spelling, grammar, and punctuation.

**Review basic spelling skills.** When you edit and proofread your writing, make sure you spell everything correctly. Review common errors in usage and check words you often confuse. Confirm word formation rules, such as adding prefixes, suffixes, and changing spellings.

**Focus on legibility.** Make sure revisions are clear and readable. Draw a single line through a word to delete it. Use a caret (^) to show where words or letters need to be added. Underline letters three times to show that they need to be capitalized.

# Publishing and Presenting

Consider one of the following ways to share your writing:

**Print a manual.** Make a clean copy of your final draft. Enter your instructions into a word-processing program and print out a manual for others to consult.

**Create a podcast.** Use your manual as the basis for a podcast script. Record your podcast, making sure you express your organization clearly.

# Reflecting on Your Writing

**Writer's Journal** Jot down your answers to this question:

*How did writing directions for the process you chose help you understand it better?*

# Rubric for Self-Assessment

Find evidence in your writing to address each category. Then, use the rating scale to grade your work.

**Spiral Review**

Earlier in the unit, you learned about **simple and compound sentences** (p. 1084) and **complex and compound-complex sentences** (p. 1116). Make sure you have properly constructed these sentence types in your instructions.

| Criteria | Rating Scale |
|---|---|
| | not very          very |
| **Focus:** How clearly does your manual focus on the task at hand? | 1  2  3  4  5 |
| **Organization:** How logical is your organization? | 1  2  3  4  5 |
| **Support/Elaboration:** How effectively do you include specific details, examples, and descriptions to support your instruction? | 1  2  3  4  5 |
| **Style:** How well does your style match your audience's needs? | 1  2  3  4  5 |
| **Conventions:** How correct is your grammar, especially avoiding fragments and run-ons? | 1  2  3  4  5 |
| **Ideas:** How clearly do you express your ideas through instruction? | 1  2  3  4  5 |

## © Leveled Texts

Build your skills and improve your comprehension of short stories with texts of increasing complexity.

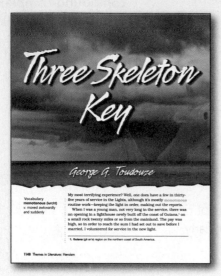

Read **"Three Skeleton Key"** to experience the unexpected dangers of life at an isolated lighthouse.

Read **"The Red-headed League"** to learn how a brilliant detective's mind works as he tracks a thief.

## © Common Core State Standards

Meet these standards with either **"Three Skeleton Key"** (p. 1148) or **"The Red-headed League"** (p. 1166).

**Reading Literature**
**3.** Analyze how complex characters develop over the course of a text, interact with other characters, and advance the plot or develop the theme. *(Literary Analysis: Protagonist and Antagonist; Reading Skill: Comparing and Contrasting Characters)*

**Writing**
**3.d.** Use precise words and phrases, telling details, and sensory language to convey a vivid picture of the experiences, events, setting, and/or characters. *(Writing: Journal Entries)*

**7.** Conduct short as well as more sustained research projects to answer a question or solve a problem; synthesize multiple sources on the subject, demonstrating understanding of the subject under investigation. *(Research and Technology: Report)*

**Speaking and Listening**
**2.** Integrate multiple sources of information presented in diverse media or formats evaluating the credibility and accuracy of each source. *(Research and Technology: Report)*

**5.** Make strategic use of digital media in presentations to enhance understanding of findings, reasoning, and evidence and to add interest. *(Research and Technology: Report)*

**Language**
**2.** Demonstrate command of the conventions of standard English capitalization, punctuation, and spelling when writing. *(Conventions: Commas and Dashes)*

**5.** Demonstrate understanding of figurative language, word relationships, and nuances in word meanings. *(Vocabulary: Analogies)*

# Literary Analysis: Protagonist and Antagonist

The **protagonist** is the chief character in a literary work. Some literary works also have an **antagonist**—a character or force that opposes the protagonist. The antagonist is often another character, but may also be an external force, such as nature. The conflict between the protagonist and antagonist is essential to the story. It usually drives the plot and may also be a key to the story's deeper meaning, or theme.

- The protagonist's motives may be universally understood feelings and goals, such as curiosity or the search for love.
- The protagonist's conflict with the antagonist may represent a universal struggle, such as the conflict between good and evil.

## Using the Strategy: Protagonist and Antagonist Chart

As you read, fill in a chart like the one shown.

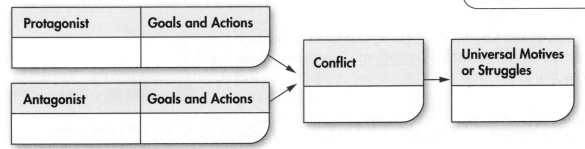

# Reading Skill: Compare and Contrast Characters

**Comparing and contrasting characters** is recognizing and thinking about their similarities and differences. You can compare different characters in a work, characters from different works, or a single character at different points. As you read, **generate questions** about each character. Your answers will show you important differences and similarities.

- What are the character's actions?
- What are the character's reasons for his or her actions?
- What qualities does the character demonstrate?

PHLit • Online!
www.PHLitOnline.com

**Hear It!**
- Selection summary audio
- Selection audio

**See It!**
- Get Connected video
- Background video
- More about the author
- Vocabulary flashcards

**Do It!**
- Interactive journals
- Interactive graphic organizers
- Self-test
- Internet activity
- Grammar tutorial
- Interactive vocabulary games

# Do *heroes* have responsibilities?

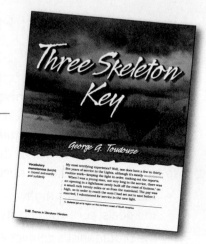

## Writing About the Big Question

In "Three Skeleton Key," three men who are staying on a tiny island confront an unexpected and dangerous enemy. Use this sentence starter to develop your ideas about the Big Question.

> Some people often **choose** to take on the **responsibility** that can come with the role of **hero** because _____.

**While You Read** Look for choices the protagonist makes for his group and think about his responsibility for their situation.

## Vocabulary

Read each word and its definition. Decide whether you know the word well, know it a little bit, or do not know it at all. After you read, see how your knowledge of each word has increased.

- **monotonous** (mə nät´ 'n əs) *adj.* having little or no variation (p. 1148) *The speaker lectured with a <u>monotonous</u> voice that made it difficult to pay attention.* monotonously *adv.* monotony *n.* monotone *n.*

- **provisions** (prə vizh´ ənz) *n.* something provided, prepared, or supplied for the future (p. 1150) *The scouts carried enough <u>provisions</u> to last them the entire hike.* provisioned *v.* provide *v.*

- **lurched** (lʉrcht) *v.* moved awkwardly and suddenly (p. 1152) *The newborn calf <u>lurched</u> forward as it tried to stand.*

- **diminution** (dim´ ə nōō´ shən) *n.* lessening (p. 1156) *The players' <u>diminution</u> of enthusiasm caused them to play poorly.* diminutive *adj.*

- **incessantly** (in ses´ ənt lē) *adv.* continuing in a way that seems endless; continually; unceasingly (p. 1156) *The wind blew so <u>incessantly</u> during the storm that the streets were covered with toppled garbage cans when it was over.* incessant *adj.* cease *v.*

- **derisive** (di rī´ siv) *adj.* mocking (p. 1159) *The critic's <u>derisive</u> laugh offended the artist.* derisively *adv.* derisiveness *n.*

### Word Study

The **Latin root -min-** means "small," "little," or "less."

In this selection, the narrator says there were so many rats, they could not see any **diminution,** or lessening, of their numbers when some were eaten by sharks.

# Meet
# George G. Toudouze
## (1877–1971)

## Author of
## *Three Skeleton Key*

The award-winning writer, editor, and scholar George Gustave Toudouze was born in Paris, France.

**Writer of the Sea** A maritime expert, Toudouze wrote nineteen books about the ocean and served as chief editor of *The French Maritime and Colonial League.* He also earned a doctorate of letters at the Sorbonne, one of the oldest and most distinguished universities in the world. He went on to become a professor of history and dramatic literature at the Paris Conservatory. His claim to fame, however, rests entirely upon one story, "Three Skeleton Key," which was published in 1937 in *Esquire* magazine.

### DID YOU KNOW?
"Three Skeleton Key" is the only one of Toudouze's stories to appear in English.

## BACKGROUND FOR THE STORY

### Lighthouses
A lighthouse, or "light," is a tower built on an island or other prominent point to warn ships away from treacherous areas near a coast. The tower is usually several stories high, with a large, bright, movable light at the top. Most lighthouses are now automated, but they used to be occupied by people who maintained and operated the light, moving the beam across the water when a ship approached. A lighthouse is often located on a key, which is a small island or a reef near a larger land mass.

# Three Skeleton Key

## George G. Toudouze

**Vocabulary**
**monotonous** (mə nät´ 'n əs) *adj.* having little or no variation

My most terrifying experience? Well, one does have a few in thirty-five years of service in the Lights, although it's mostly monotonous routine work—keeping the light in order, making out the reports.

When I was a young man, not very long in the service, there was an opening in a lighthouse newly built off the coast of Guiana,[1] on a small rock twenty miles or so from the mainland. The pay was high, so in order to reach the sum I had set out to save before I married, I volunteered for service in the new light.

---

1. **Guiana** (gē an´ ə) region on the northern coast of South America.

Three Skeleton Key, the small rock on which the light stood, bore a bad reputation. It earned its name from the story of the three convicts who, escaping from Cayenne[2] in a stolen dugout canoe, were wrecked on the rock during the night, managed to escape the sea but eventually died of hunger and thirst. When they were discovered, nothing remained but three heaps of bones, picked clean by the birds. The story was that the three skeletons, gleaming with phosphorescent light,[3] danced over the small rock, screaming. . . .

---

2. **Cayenne** (kī en´) capital city of French Guiana.
3. **phosphorescent** (fäs´ fə res´ ənt) light a glowing light produced by certain natural chemical reactions.

☑ Reading Check

How did Three Skeleton Key get its name?

**Literary Analysis
Protagonist and
Antagonist** Which
details in the story's first
four paragraphs suggest
that the narrator is the
central character in this
story?

But there are many such stories, and I did not give the warnings of the old-timers at the Isle de Sein[4] a second thought. I signed up, boarded ship, and in a month I was installed at the light.

Picture a gray, tapering cylinder, welded to the solid black rock by iron rods and concrete, rising from a small island twenty odd miles from land. It lay in the midst of the sea, this island, a small, bare piece of stone, about one hundred fifty feet long, perhaps forty wide. Small, barely large enough for a man to walk about and stretch his legs at low tide.

This is an advantage one doesn't find in all lights, however, for some of them rise sheer from the waves, with no room for one to move save within the light itself. Still, on our island, one must be careful, for the rocks were treacherously smooth. One misstep and down you would fall into the sea—not that the risk of drowning was so great, but the waters about our island swarmed with huge sharks who kept an eternal patrol around the base of the light.

**Vocabulary
provisions** (prə vizh´
ənz) *n.* something pro-
vided, prepared, or sup-
plied for the future

Still, it was a nice life there. We had enough provisions to last for months, in the event that the sea should become too rough for the supply ship to reach us on schedule. During the day we would work about the light, cleaning the rooms, polishing the metalwork and the lens and reflector of the light itself, and at night we would sit on the gallery and watch our light, a twenty thousand candle-power lantern, swinging its strong, white bar of light over the sea from the top of its hundred-twenty-foot tower. Some days, when the air would be very clear, we could see the land, a thread-like line to the west. To the east, north and south stretched the ocean. Landsmen, perhaps, would soon have tired of that kind of life, perched on a small island off the coast of South America for eighteen weeks, until one's turn for leave ashore came around. But we liked it there, my two fellow-tenders and myself—so much so that, for twenty-two months on end with the exception of shore leaves, I was greatly satisfied with the life on Three Skeleton Key.

**Reading Skill
Contrasting Characters**
What difference in the
characters' ages does the
narrator point out?

I had just returned from my leave at the end of June, that is to say mid-winter in that latitude, and had settled down to the routine with my two fellow-keepers, a Breton[5] by the name of Le Gleo and the head-keeper, Itchoua, a Basque[6] some dozen years or so older than either of us.

Eight days went by as usual, then on the ninth night after my return, Itchoua, who was on night duty, called Le

---

4. **Isle de Sein** (ēl´ də sen´) island off the northwestern coast of France.
5. **Breton** (bret´ 'n) person born or living in Brittany, a region on the northwestern coast of France.
6. **Basque** (bask) member of a people who inhabit a region between Spain and France on the Bay of Biscay.

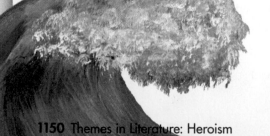

Gleo and me, sleeping in our rooms in the middle of the tower, at two in the morning. We rose immediately and, climbing the thirty or so steps that led to the gallery, stood beside our chief.

Itchoua pointed, and following his finger, we saw a big three-master, with all sail set, heading straight for the light. A queer course, for the vessel must have seen us, our light lit her with the glare of day each time it passed over her.

Now, ships were a rare sight in our waters, for our light was a warning of treacherous reefs, barely hidden under the surface and running far out to sea. Consequently we were always given a wide berth, especially by sailing vessels, which cannot maneuver as readily as steamers.

No wonder that we were surprised at seeing this three-master heading dead for us in the gloom of early morning. I had immediately recognized her lines, for she stood out plainly, even at the distance of a mile, when our light shone on her.

She was a beautiful ship of some four thousand tons, a fast sailor that had carried cargoes to every part of the world, plowing the seas unceasingly. By her lines she was identified as Dutch-built, which was understandable as Paramaribo and Dutch Guiana are very close to Cayenne.

Watching her sailing dead for us, a white wave boiling under her bows, Le Gleo cried out:

"What's wrong with her crew ? Are they all drunk or insane? Can't they see us?"

Itchoua nodded soberly, looked at us sharply as he remarked: "See us? No doubt—if there is a crew aboard!"

"What do you mean, chief?" Le Gleo had started, turned to the Basque, "Are you saying that she's the Flying Dutchman?"[7]

His sudden fright had been so evident that the older man laughed:

"No, old man, that's not what I meant. If I say that no one's aboard, I mean she's a derelict."

Then we understood his queer behavior. Itchoua was right. For some reason, believing her doomed, her crew had abandoned her.

▲ **Critical Viewing**
How does this photograph of a Dutch sailing ship help establish the time period of the story?
**[Connect]**

*One misstep and down you would fall into the sea...*

**Reading Check**

In the middle of the night, what surprising sight does Itchoua show his companions?

---

7. **Flying Dutchmwan** fabled ghost ship doomed to sail forever

**Vocabulary**
**lurched** (lᵊrcht) *v.* moved
awkwardly and suddenly

Then she had righted herself and sailed on, wandering with the wind.

The three of us grew tense as the ship seemed about to crash on one of our numerous reefs, but she suddenly lurched with some change of the wind, the yards swung around, and the derelict came clumsily about and sailed dead away from us.

In the light of our lantern she seemed so sound, so strong, that Itchoua exclaimed impatiently:

"But why the devil was she abandoned? Nothing is smashed, no sign of fire—and she doesn't sail as if she were taking water."

Le Gleo waved to the departing ship:

"Bon voyage!"[8] he smiled at Itchoua and went on. "She's leaving us, chief, and now we'll never know what—"

"No she's not!" cried the Basque. "Look! She's turning!"

As if obeying his words, the derelict three-master stopped, came about and headed for us once more. And for the next four hours the vessel played around us—zigzagging, coming about,[9] stopping, then suddenly lurching forward. No doubt some freak of current and wind, of which our island was the center, kept her near us.

Then suddenly, the tropic dawn broke, the sun rose and it was day, and the ship was plainly visible as she sailed past us. Our light extinguished, we returned to the gallery with our glasses and inspected her.

The three of us focused our glasses on her poop,[10] saw standing out sharply, black letters on the white background of a life-ring, the stenciled name:

"*Cornelius-de-Witt,* Rotterdam."

We had read her lines correctly, she was Dutch. Just then the wind rose and the *Cornelius-de-Witt* changed course, leaned to port and headed straight for us once more. But this time she was so close that we knew she would not turn in time.

"Thunder!" cried Le Gleo, his Breton soul aching to see a fine ship doomed to smash upon a reef, "She's going to pile up! She's gone!"

I shook my head:

"Yes, and a shame to see that beautiful ship wreck herself. And we're helpless."

There was nothing we could do but watch. A ship sailing with all sail spread, creaming the sea with her forefoot as she runs before the wind, is one of the most beautiful sights in the world—but this time I could feel the tears stinging my eyes as I saw this fine ship headed for her doom.

**Reading Skill**
**Contrasting**
**Characters** In what
ways are Le Gleo's and
the narrator's reactions
to the doomed ship
similar and different?

---

8. **Bon voyage** (bän′ voi äzh′) French for "pleasant journey;" a farewell to a traveler.
9. **coming about** changing direction according to the direction of the wind.
10. **poop** (po͞op) *n.* raised deck at the rear of a sailing ship.

All this time our glasses were riveted on her, and we suddenly cried out together:

"The rats!"

Now we knew why this ship, in perfect condition, was sailing without her crew aboard. They had been driven out by the rats. Not those poor specimens of rats you see ashore, barely reaching the length of one foot from their trembling noses to the tip of their skinny tails, wretched creatures that dodge and hide at the mere sound of a footfall.

No, these were ships' rats, huge, wise creatures, born on the sea, sailing all over the world on ships, transferring to other, larger ships as they multiply. There is as much difference between the rats of the land and these maritime rats as between a fishing smack and an armored cruiser.

The rats of the sea are fierce, bold animals. Large, strong and intelligent, clannish and seawise, able to put the best of mariners to shame with their knowledge of the sea, their uncanny ability to foretell the weather.

And they are brave, these rats, and vengeful. If you so much as harm one, his sharp cry will bring hordes of his fellows to swarm over you, tear you and not cease until your flesh has been stripped from the bones.

The ones on this ship, the rats of Holland, are the worst, superior to other rats of the sea as their brethren are to the land rats. There is a well-known tale about these animals.

A Dutch captain, thinking to protect his cargo, brought aboard his ship—not cats—but two terriers, dogs trained in the hunting,

**Reading Skill Contrasting Characters** In what way are the rats on the *Cornelius-de-Witt* different from other rats in the world?

**Reading Check**
What detail do the men notice that shows that the crew of the *Cornelius-de-Witt* did not abandon ship?

*The rats of the sea are fierce, bold animals.*

fighting and killing of vicious rats. By the time the ship, sailing from Rotterdam, had passed the Ostend light, the dogs were gone and never seen again. In twenty-four hours they had been overwhelmed, killed and eaten by the rats.

At times, when the cargo does not suffice, the rats attack the crew, either driving them from the ship or eating them alive. And studying the *Cornelius-de-Witt*, I turned sick, for her small boats were all in place. She had not been abandoned.

Over her bridge, on her deck, in the rigging, on every visible spot, the ship was a writhing mass—a starving army coming towards us aboard a vessel gone mad!

Our island was a small spot in that immense stretch of sea. The ship could have grazed us, passed to port or starboard with its ravening cargo—but no, she came for us at full speed, as if she were leading the regatta at a race, and impaled herself on a sharp point of rock.

There was a dull shock as her bottom stove in, then a horrible crackling as the three masts went overboard at once, as if cut down with one blow of some gigantic sickle. A sighing groan came as the water rushed into the ship, then she split in two and sank like a stone.

But the rats did not drown. Not these fellows! As much at home in the sea as any fish, they formed ranks in the water, heads lifted, tails stretched out, paws paddling. And half of them, those from the forepart of the ship, sprang along the masts and onto the rocks in the instant before she sank. Before we had time even to move, nothing remained of the three-master save some pieces of wreckage floating on the surface and an army of rats covering the rocks left bare by the receding tide.

Thousands of heads rose, felt the wind and we were scented, seen! To them we were fresh meat, after possible weeks of starving. There came a scream, composed of innumerable screams, sharper than the howl of a saw attacking a bar of iron, and in the one motion, every rat leaped to attack the tower!

We barely had time to leap back, close the door leading onto the gallery, descend the stairs and shut every window tightly. Luckily the door at the base of the light, which we never could have reached in time, was of bronze set in granite and was tightly closed.

**Literary Analysis**
**Protagonist and Antagonist** What details here might make readers sympathetic toward the narrator? Why?

▼ **Critical Viewing** Which details in the photograph make these rats appear fearsome, like the ones in "Three Skeleton Key"? **[Analyze]**

The horrible band, in no measurable time, had swarmed up and over the tower as if it had been a tree, piled on the embrasures of the windows, scraped at the glass with thousands of claws, covered the lighthouse with a furry mantle and reached the top of the tower, filling the gallery and piling atop the lantern.

Their teeth grated as they pressed against the glass of the lantern-room, where they could plainly see us, though they could not reach us. A few millimeters of glass, luckily very strong, separated our faces from their gleaming, beady eyes, their sharp claws and teeth. Their odor filled the tower, poisoned our lungs and rasped our nostrils with a pestilential, nauseating smell. And there we were, sealed alive in our own light, prisoners of a horde of starving rats.

That first night, the tension was so great that we could not sleep. Every moment, we felt that some opening had been made, some window given away, and that our horrible besiegers were pouring through the breach. The rising tide, chasing those of the rats which had stayed on the bare rocks, increased the numbers clinging to the walls, piled on the balcony—so much so that clusters of rats clinging to one another hung from the lantern and the gallery.

With the coming of darkness we lit the light, and the turning beam completely maddened the beasts. As the light turned, it successively blinded thousands of rats crowded against the glass, while the dark side of the lantern-room gleamed with thousands of points of light, burning like the eyes of jungle beasts in the night.

All the while we could hear the enraged scraping of claws against the stone and glass, while the chorus of cries was so loud that we had to shout to hear one another. From time to time, some of the rats fought among themselves and a dark cluster would detach itself, falling into the sea like a ripe fruit from a tree. Then we would see phosphorescent streaks as triangular fins slashed the water— sharks, permanent guardians of our rock, feasting on our jailors.

The next day we were calmer, and amused ourselves by teasing the rats, placing our faces against the glass which separated us. They could not fathom the invisible barrier which separated them from us, and we laughed as we watched them leaping against the heavy glass.

But the day after that, we realized how serious our position was. The air was foul; even the heavy smell of oil within our stronghold could not dominate the fetid odor of the beasts massed around us, and there was no way of admitting fresh air without also admitting the rats.

The morning of the fourth day, at early dawn, I saw the wooden framework of my window, eaten away from the outside, sagging

**Literary Analysis**
**Protagonist and Antagonist** With what external force are the narrator, Le Gleo, and Itchoua now in conflict?

**Reading Skill Comparing Characters** In what way do the sharks and the rats behave similarly?

Reading Check
What do the rats do almost immediately after landing on the island?

inwards. I called my comrades and the three of us fastened a sheet of tin in the opening, sealing it tightly. When we had completed the task, Itchoua turned to us and said dully:

"Well—the supply boat came thirteen days ago, and she won't be back for twenty-nine." He pointed at the white metal plate sealing the opening through the granite—"If that gives way—" he shrugged—"they can change the name of this place to Six Skeletons Key."

The next six days and seven nights, our only distraction was watching the rats whose holds were insecure fall a hundred and twenty feet into the maws of the sharks—but they were so many that we could not see any diminution in their numbers.

Thinking to calm ourselves and pass the time, we attempted to count them, but we soon gave up. They moved incessantly, never still. Then we tried identifying them, naming them.

One of them, larger than the others, who seemed to lead them in their rushes against the glass separating us, we named "Nero";[11] and there were several others whom we had learned to distinguish through various peculiarities.

But the thought of our bones joining those of the convicts was always in the back of our minds. And the gloom of our prison fed these thoughts, for the interior of the light was almost completely

11. **Nero** (nir′ ō) (a.d. 37–68) Roman emperor who was notoriously cruel.

*—"they can change the name of this place to Six Skeletons Key."*

dark, as we had to seal every window in the same fashion as mine, and the only space that still admitted daylight was the glassed-in lantern-room at the very top of the tower.

Then Le Gleo became morose and had nightmares in which he would see the three skeletons dancing around him, gleaming coldly, seeking to grasp him. His maniacal, raving descriptions were so vivid that Itchoua and I began seeing them also.

It was a living nightmare, the raging cries of the rats as they swarmed over the light, mad with hunger; the sickening, strangling odor of their bodies—

True, there is a way of signaling from light-houses. But to reach the mast on which to hang the signal we would have to go out on the gallery where the rats were.

There was only one thing left to do. After debating all of the ninth day, we decided not to light the lantern that night. This is the greatest breach of our service, never committed as long as the tenders of the light are alive; for the light is something sacred, warning ships of danger in the night. Either the light gleams, a quarter hour after sundown, or no one is left alive to light it.

Well, that night, Three Skeleton Light was dark, and all the men were alive. At the risk of causing ships to crash on our reefs, we left it unlit, for we were worn out—going mad!

**Literary Analysis**
**Protagonist and Antagonist** In addition to the rats, what other problems do the men face?

Reading Check

What happens in Le Gleo's nightmares?

Three Skeleton Key  **1157**

**Literary Analysis**
**Protagonist and**
**Antagonist** What do
you think motivates the
narrator and Le Gleo to
risk their own lives to
help Itchoua?

At two in the morning, while Itchoua was dozing in his room, the sheet of metal sealing his window gave way. The chief had just time enough to leap to his feet and cry for help, the rats swarming over him.

But Le Gleo and I, who had been watching from the lantern-room, got to him immediately, and the three of us battled with the horde of maddened rats which flowed through the gaping window. They bit, we struck them down with our knives—and retreated.

We locked the door of the room on them, but before we had time to bind our wounds, the door was eaten through and gave way, and we retreated up the stairs, fighting off the rats that leaped on us from the knee-deep swarm.

I do not remember, to this day, how we ever managed to escape. All I can remember is wading through them up the stairs, striking them off as they swarmed over us; and then we found ourselves, bleeding from innumerable bites, our clothes shredded, sprawled across the trapdoor in the floor of the lantern-room—without food or drink. Luckily, the trapdoor was metal set into the granite with iron bolts.

The rats occupied the entire light beneath us, and on the floor of our retreat lay some twenty of their fellows, who had gotten in with us before the trapdoor closed, and whom we had killed with our knives. Below us, in the tower, we could hear the screams of the rats as they devoured everything edible that they found. Those on the outside squealed in reply, and writhed in a horrible curtain as they stared at us through the glass of the lantern-room.

Itchoua sat up, stared silently at his blood trickling from the wounds on his limbs and body, and running in thin streams on the floor around him. Le Gleo, who was in as bad a state (and so was I, for that matter) stared at the chief and me vacantly, started as his gaze swung to the multitude of rats against the glass, then suddenly began laughing horribly:

"Hee! Hee! The Three Skeletons! Hee! Hee! The Three Skeletons are now six skeletons! Six skeletons!"

He threw his head back and howled, his eyes glazed, a trickle of saliva running from the corners of his mouth and thinning the blood flowing over his chest. I shouted to him to shut up, but he did not hear me, so I did the only thing I could to quiet him—I swung the back of my hand across his face.

The howling stopped suddenly, his eyes swung around the room, then he bowed his head and began weeping softly, like a child.

Our darkened light had been noticed from the mainland, and as dawn was breaking, the patrol was there to investigate the failure of our light. Looking through my binoculars, I could see the horrified

**Reading Skill**
**Contrasting**
**Characters** What
differences between the
narrator and Le Gleo
do their reactions make
clear?

expression on the faces of the officers and crew when, the daylight strengthening, they saw the light completely covered by a seething mass of rats. They thought, as I afterwards found out, that we had been eaten alive.

But the rats had also seen the ship, or had scented the crew. As the ship drew nearer, a solid phalanx[12] left the light, plunged into the water and, swimming out, attempted to board her. They would have succeeded, as the ship was hove to, but the engineer connected his steam to a hose on the deck and scalded the head of the attacking column, which slowed them up long enough for the ship to get under way and leave the rats behind.

Then the sharks took part. Belly up, mouths gaping, they arrived in swarms and scooped up the rats, sweeping through them like a sickle through wheat. That was one day that sharks really served a useful purpose.

The remaining rats turned tail, swam to the shore, and emerged dripping. As they neared the light, their comrades greeted them with shrill cries, with what sounded like a derisive note predominating. They answered angrily and mingled with their fellows. From the several tussles that broke out, they resented being ridiculed for their failure to capture the ship.

But all this did nothing to get us out of our jail. The small ship could not approach, but steamed around the light at a safe distance, and the tower must have seemed fantastic, some weird, many-mouthed beast hurling defiance at them.

Finally, seeing the rats running in and out of the tower through the door and the windows, those on the ship decided that we had perished and were about to leave when Itchoua, regaining his senses, thought of using the light as a signal. He lit it and, using a plank placed and withdrawn before the beam to form the dots and dashes, quickly sent out our story to those on the vessel.

Our reply came quickly. When they understood our position—how we could not get rid of the rats, Le Gleo's mind going fast, Itchoua and myself covered with bites, cornered in the lantern-room without food or water—they had a signalman send us their reply.

---

**12. phalanx** (fā´ laŋks´) *n.* group of individuals advancing in a close, compact formation.

**Vocabulary**
**derisive** (di rī´ siv) *adj.* mocking

**Reading Check**
What do the men do that results in the arrival of a patrol ship?

His arms swinging like those of a windmill, he quickly spelled out: "Don't give up. Hang on a little longer! We'll get you out of this!"

Then she turned and steamed at top speed for the coast, leaving us little reassured.

She was back at noon, accompanied by the supply ship, two small coast guard boats, and the fire boat—a small squadron. At twelve-thirty the battle was on.

After a short reconnaissance,[13] the fire boat picked her way slowly through the reefs until she was close to us, then turned her powerful jet of water on the rats. The heavy stream tore the rats from their places, hurled them screaming into the water where the sharks gulped them down. But for every ten that were dislodged, seven swam ashore, and the stream could do nothing to the rats within the tower. Furthermore, some of them, instead of returning to the rocks, boarded the fire boat, and the men were forced to battle them hand to hand. They were true rats of Holland, fearing no man, fighting for the right to live!

---

13. **reconnaissance** (ri kän´ ə səns) *n.* exploratory survey or examination.

**Reading Skill Comparing Characters** What similarity between the rats and the men does the narrator's remark about the rats reveal?

▼ **Critical Viewing** Based on this photograph, how easily do you think the sharks could attack the rats? Explain. **[Evaluate]**

Nightfall came, and it was as if nothing had been done, the rats were still in possession. One of the patrol boats stayed by the island; the rest of the flotilla[14] departed for the coast. We had to spend another night in our prison. Le Gleo was sitting on the floor, babbling about skeletons, and as I turned to Itchoua, he fell unconscious from his wounds. I was in no better shape and could feel my blood flaming with fever.

Somehow the night dragged by, and the next afternoon I saw a tug, accompanied by the fire boat, coming from the mainland with a huge barge in tow. Through my glasses, I saw that the barge was filled with meat.

Risking the treacherous reefs, the tug dragged the barge as close to the island as possible. To the last rat, our besiegers deserted the rock, swam out and boarded the barge reeking with the scent of freshly cut meat. The tug dragged the barge about a mile from shore, where the fire boat drenched the barge with gasoline. A well placed incendiary shell from the patrol boat set her on fire.

The barge was covered with flames immediately, and the rats took to the water in swarms, but the patrol boat bombarded them with shrapnel from a safe distance, and the sharks finished off the survivors.

A whaleboat from the patrol boat took us off the island and left three men to replace us. By nightfall we were in the hospital in Cayenne.

---

**14. flotilla** (flō til´ ə) *n.* small fleet.

**Spiral Review**
**Archetypes** How is the narrator different from the typical hero?

**Literary Analysis**
**Protagonist and Antagonist** In what way does human intelligence ultimately overcome the rats' brutality?

**Reading Check**
What does the fire boat do to attack the rats? What is the result?

*They were true rats of Holland, fearing no man, fighting for the right to live!*

What became of my friends? Well, Le Gleo's mind had cracked and he was raving mad. They sent him back to France and locked him up in an asylum,[15] the poor devil; Itchoua died within a week; a rat's bite is dangerous in that hot, humid climate, and infection sets in rapidly.

As for me—when they fumigated[16] the light and repaired the damage done by the rats, I resumed my service there. Why not? No reason why such an incident should keep me from finishing out my service there, is there?

Besides—I told you I liked the place—to be truthful, I've never had a post as pleasant as that one, and when my time came to leave it forever, I tell you that I almost wept as Three Skeleton Key disappeared below the horizon.

---

**15. asylum** (ə sī ′ ləm) *n.* institution for the care of the mentally ill.
**16. fumigated** (fyoo ′ mə gāt′ id) *v.* disinfected with fumes.

## Critical Thinking

Cite textual evidence to support your responses.

**1. Key Ideas and Details (a)** How do the rats come to the lighthouse? **(b) Infer:** What impression of the rats does this method of arrival create? **(c) Summarize:** Explain how the rescuers defeat the rats.

**2. Integration of Knowledge and Ideas (a)** What does Itchoua say about the name of the island and what will happen if the window seal gives way? **(b) Infer:** What does he mean by this remark? **(c) Interpret:** How does this remark create suspense and add meaning to the story's title?

**3. Key Ideas and Details (a) Categorize:** Which details portray the rats as intelligent and organized and which portray them as mindlessly vicious? **(b) Evaluate:** Does Toudouze make you believe that actual rats would be capable of the actions he describes? Explain.

**4. Integration of Knowledge and Ideas (a)** Is the narrator a hero? Explain. **(b)** Do the narrator's actions reflect a sense of responsibility toward the other characters? Why or why not? *[Connect to the Big Question: Do heroes have responsibilities?]*

## Literary Analysis: Protagonist and Antagonist

**1. Craft and Structure (a)** Identify the **protagonist** in the narrative. **(b)** What is the protagonist's goal? **(c)** Why are readers interested in whether the protagonist achieves his goal?

**2. Craft and Structure (a)** Identify the **antagonist. (b)** What is the antagonist's goal?

**3. Integration of Knowledge and Ideas (a)** Why is the story's conflict interesting? **(b)** What universal struggle does this conflict represent?

## Reading Skill: Comparing and Contrasting Characters

**4. (a)** Complete a Venn diagram to **compare and contrast** the narrator's outlook at the beginning of the story with his outlook at the end of the story. **(b)** Explain whether the narrator has or has not changed as a result of his experience.

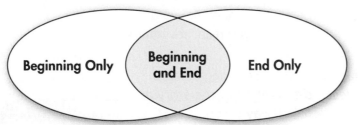

Beginning Only    Beginning and End    End Only

## Vocabulary

**Acquisition and Use Analogies** show the relationships between pairs of words. Use a word from the list on page 1146 to complete each analogy.

**1.** enlargement : increase :: _____ : decrease

**2.** glided : graceful :: _____ : clumsy

**3.** complimentary : praise :: _____ : ridicule

**4.** infrequently : rarely :: _____ : constantly

**5.** gasoline : automobile :: _____ : people

**6.** exciting : exhilarating :: _____ : boring

**Word Study** Use the context of the sentences and what you know about the **Latin root -min-** to explain your answer to each question.

**1.** Would a very hungry man want a *diminutive* sandwich?

**2.** Does exercise *minimize* the risk of heart attacks?

### Word Study

The **Latin root -min-** means "small," "little," or "less."

**Apply It** Explain how the root -*min*- contributes to the meanings of these words. Consult a dictionary if necessary.

minimum
minority
diminish

# Do *heroes* have responsibilities?

## Writing About the Big Question

In "The Red-headed League," Sherlock Holmes sets out to solve a peculiar mystery involving men with brilliant red hair. Use these sentence starters to develop your ideas about the Big Question.

When a crime is being committed, a **hero** will _____.

The hero's **involvement** may show his or her **character** because

_____.

**While You Read** Look for Sherlock Holmes's motivations for solving the mystery and decide whether his actions make him a hero.

## Vocabulary

Read each word and its definition. Decide whether you know the word well, know it a little bit, or do not know it at all. After you read, see how your knowledge of each word has increased.

- **embellish** (em bel´ ish) *v.* decorate or improve by adding details; ornament; adorn (p. 1167) *Max decided to embellish the story as he noticed his listeners losing interest halfway through.* *embellishment n.*

- **endeavored** (en dev´ ərd) *v.* made an earnest attempt to achieve or succeed; tried (p. 1168) *Jennifer endeavored to rank among the top ten students in her class.* *endeavor n/v.*

- **introspective** (in´ trə spek´ tiv) *adj.* having to do with looking into one's own thoughts and feelings (p. 1178) *The touching movie put me in an introspective mood.* *introspection n. introspectively adv.*

- **vex** (veks) *v.* annoy (p. 1180) *My allergies continued to vex me throughout the spring.* *vexing adj. vexation n. vexatiously adv.*

- **formidable** (fôr´ mə də bəl) *adj.* awe-inspiring (p. 1180) *Mt. Everest is a formidable sight.* *formidably adv. formidability n.*

- **tenacious** (tə nā´ shəs) *adj.* holding firmly to your point or beliefs; persistent; stubborn (p. 1183) *The tenacious man could not admit that he was wrong.* *tenacity n. tenaciousness n. tenaciously adv.*

### Word Study

The **Latin root -spect-** means "see," "look," or "examine."

In this selection, Sherlock Holmes describes a German music program as **introspective** because it helps him look into his own thoughts.

# Meet
# Sir Arthur Conan Doyle
### (1859–1930)

## Author of
## The Red-headed League

Sir Arthur Conan Doyle began his career as a doctor. He also pursued a career in writing. In a few years, he sold his first novel, *A Study in Scarlet*, which introduced Sherlock Holmes to the world.

**The World's Favorite Detective** It is likely that Conan Doyle modeled Sherlock Holmes on Dr. Joseph Bell, a professor of his who could diagnose illnesses from clues that other physicians had missed. Conan Doyle made the narrator of the Holmes mysteries Dr. John Watson. In the stories, Watson greatly admires Holmes but can never match his friend's powers of observation and reasoning.

Readers grew to love Sherlock Holmes. When Conan Doyle killed him off in a story in 1893, readers protested so strongly that the author was forced to bring back the beloved detective.

### DID YOU KNOW?

Although Holmes is often depicted in a plaid cape and a deerstalker hat, the stories never mention such clothing.

## BACKGROUND FOR THE STORY

**Sherlock Holmes**

This story is one of many tales about the exploits of one of the world's most famous fictional detectives, Sherlock Holmes. Often depicted wearing a plaid cape and a deerstalker cap, Sherlock Holmes is widely recognized by people around the world.

# The Red-Headed League

## Sir Arthur Conan Doyle

I had called upon my friend, Mr. Sherlock Holmes, one day in the autumn of last year and found him in deep conversation with a very stout, florid-faced, elderly gentleman with fiery red hair. With an apology for my intrusion, I was about to withdraw when Holmes pulled me abruptly into the room and closed the door behind me.

"You could not possibly have come at a better time, my dear Watson," he said cordially.

"I was afraid that you were engaged."

"So I am. Very much so."

"Then I can wait in the next room."

"Not at all. This gentleman, Mr. Wilson, has been my partner and helper in many of my most successful cases, and I have no doubt that he will be of the utmost use to me in yours also."

The stout gentleman half rose from his chair and gave a bob of greeting, with a quick little questioning glance from his small, fat-encircled eyes.

"Try the settee,"[1] said Holmes, relapsing into his armchair and putting his finger tips together, as was his custom when in judicial moods. "I know, my dear Watson, that you share my love of all that is bizarre and outside the conventions and humdrum routine of everyday life. You have shown your relish for it by the enthusiasm which has prompted you to chronicle, and, if you will excuse my saying so, somewhat to embellish so many of my own little adventures."

"Your cases have indeed been of the greatest interest to me," I observed.

"You will remember that I remarked the other day, just before we went into the very simple problem presented by Miss Mary Sutherland, that for strange effects and extraordinary combinations we must go to life itself, which is always far more daring than any effort of the imagination."

"A proposition which I took the liberty of doubting."

"You did, Doctor, but none the less you must come round to my view, for otherwise I shall keep on piling fact upon fact on you until your reason breaks down under them and acknowledges me to be right. Now, Mr. Jabez Wilson here has been good enough to call upon me this morning, and to begin a narrative which promises to be one of the most singular which I have listened to for some time. You have heard me remark that the strangest and most unique things are very often connected not with the larger but with the smaller crimes, and occasionally, indeed, where there is room for doubt whether any positive crime has been committed. As far as I have heard it is impossible for me to say whether the present case is an instance of crime or not, but the course of events is certainly among the most singular that I have ever listened to. Perhaps, Mr. Wilson, you would have the great kindness to recommence your

---

**1. settee** (se tē´) *n.* small sofa.

**Reading Skill
Comparing
Characters** According to Holmes, what do he and Watson have in common?

**Vocabulary
embellish** (em bel´ ish) *v.* decorate or improve by adding details; ornament; adorn

**Literary Analysis
Protagonist and
Antagonist** What details in Holmes's speech here help present him as a protagonist?

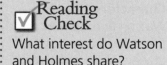

Reading
Check
What interest do Watson and Holmes share?

narrative. I ask you not merely because my friend Dr. Watson has not heard the opening part but also because the peculiar nature of the story makes me anxious to have every possible detail from your lips. As a rule, when I have heard some slight indication of the course of events, I am able to guide myself by the thousands of other similar cases which occur to my memory. In the present instance I am forced to admit that the facts are, to the best of my belief, unique."

The portly client puffed out his chest with an appearance of some little pride and pulled a dirty and wrinkled newspaper from the inside pocket of his great coat. As he glanced down the advertisement column, with his head thrust forward and the paper flattened out upon his knee, I took a good look at the man and endeavored, after the fashion of my companion, to read the indications which might be presented by his dress or appearance.

I did not gain very much, however, by my inspection. Our visitor bore every mark of being an average commonplace British tradesman, obese, pompous, and slow. He wore rather baggy gray shepherd's check trousers, a not over-clean black frock coat, unbuttoned in the front, and a drab waistcoat with a heavy brassy Albert chain, and a square pierced bit of metal dangling down as an ornament. A frayed top hat and a faded brown overcoat with a wrinkled velvet collar lay upon a chair beside him. Altogether, look as I would, there was nothing remarkable about the man save his blazing red head, and the expression of extreme chagrin and discontent upon his features.

Sherlock Holmes's quick eye took in my occupation, and he shook his head with a smile as he noticed my questioning glances. "Beyond the obvious facts that he has at some time done manual labor, that he takes snuff,[2] that he is a Freemason,[3] that he has been in China, and that he has done a considerable amount of writing lately, I can deduce nothing else."

---

**Vocabulary**
**endeavored** (en dev´ ərd) v. made an earnest attempt to achieve or succeed; tried

**Reading Skill**
**Contrasting Characters** How are Watson and Holmes different in terms of their powers of observation?

---

2. **snuff** (snuf) n. powdered tobacco.
3. **Freemason** member of a secret society.

Mr. Jabez Wilson started up in his chair, with his forefinger upon the paper, but his eyes upon my companion.

"How, in the name of good fortune, did you know all that, Mr. Holmes?" he asked. "How did you know, for example, that I did manual labor? It's as true as gospel, for I began as a ship's carpenter."

"Your hands, my dear sir. Your right hand is quite a size larger than your left. You have worked with it, and the muscles are more developed."

"Well, the snuff, then, and the Freemasonry?"

"I won't insult your intelligence by telling you how I read that, especially as, rather against the strict rules of your order, you use an arc-and-compass breastpin."

"Ah, of course, I forgot that. But the writing?"

"What else can be indicated by that right cuff so very shiny for five inches, and the left one with the smooth patch near the elbow where you rest it upon the desk?"

"Well, but China?"

"The fish that you have tattooed immediately above your right wrist could only have been done in China. I have made a small study of tattoo marks and have even contributed to the literature of the subject. That trick of staining the fishes' scales of a delicate pink is quite peculiar to China. When, in addition, I see a Chinese coin hanging from your watch-chain, the matter becomes even more simple."

Mr. Jabez Wilson laughed heavily. "Well, I never!" said he. "I thought at first that you had done something clever, but I see that there was nothing in it, after all."

"I begin to think, Watson," said Holmes, "that I make a mistake in explaining. '*Omne ignotum pro magnifico*,'[4] you know, and my poor little reputation, such as it is, will suffer shipwreck if I am so candid. Can you not find the advertisement, Mr. Wilson?"

"Yes, I have got it now," he answered with his thick red finger planted halfway down the column. "Here it is. This is what began it all. You just read it for yourself, sir."

I took the paper from him and read as follows:

To THE RED-HEADED LEAGUE:

On account of the bequest of the late Ezekiah Hopkins, of Lebanon, Pennsylvania, U. S. A., there is now another vacancy open

Reading Check

What facts about Mr. Wilson does Holmes deduce based on Wilson's appearance?

---

4. ***Omne ignotum pro magnifico*** (äm′ nā ig nō′ təm prō mag nē′ fē kō) Latin for "Whatever is unknown is magnified."

### Pound Conversions

The advertisement that concerns Mr. Wilson announces a salary of four pounds a week. The pound is the monetary unit of Great Britain. Its equivalency in American dollars fluctuates depending on current economic conditions. At the time Doyle wrote the story, one British pound equaled about $4.85, so four pounds would have equaled about $19.40. This was considered a large amount at the time in which the story is set, particularly for easy work.

Why might an offer of a large sum of money "for purely nominal services" be cause for suspicion?

**Literary Analysis
Protagonist and
Antagonist** Which details in the description of Vincent Spaulding attract Holmes's notice?

which entitles a member of the League to a salary of £4 a week for purely nominal services. All red-headed men who are sound in body and mind, and above the age of twenty-one years, are eligible. Apply in person on Monday, at eleven o'clock, to Duncan Ross, at the offices of the League, 7 Pope's Court, Fleet Street.

"What on earth does this mean?" I ejaculated after I had twice read over the extraordinary announcement.

Holmes chuckled and wriggled in his chair, as was his habit when in high spirits. "It is a little off the beaten track, isn't it?" said he. "And now, Mr. Wilson, off you go at scratch and tell us all about yourself, your household, and the effect which this advertisement had upon your fortunes. You will first make a note, Doctor, of the paper and the date."

"It is *The Morning Chronicle* of April 27, 1890. Just two months ago."

"Very good. Now, Mr. Wilson?"

"Well, it is just as I have been telling you, Mr. Sherlock Holmes," said Jabez Wilson, mopping his forehead; "I have a small pawnbroker's business at Coburg Square, near the City. It's not a very large affair, and of late years it has not done more than just give me a living. I used to be able to keep two assistants, but now I only keep one; and I would have a job to pay him but that he is willing to come for half wages so as to learn the business."

"What is the name of this obliging youth?" asked Sherlock Holmes.

"His name is Vincent Spaulding, and he's not such a youth, either. It's hard to say his age. I should not wish a smarter assistant, Mr. Holmes; and I know very well that he could better himself and earn twice what I am able to give him. But, after all, if he is satisfied, why should I put ideas in his head?"

"Why, indeed? You seem most fortunate in having an employee who comes under the full market price. It is not a common experience among employers in this age. I don't know that your assistant is not as remarkable as your advertisement."

"Oh, he has his faults, too," said Mr. Wilson. "Never was such a fellow for photography. Snapping away with a camera when he ought to be improving his mind, and then diving down into the cellar like a rabbit into its hole to develop his pictures. That is his main fault, but on the whole he's a good worker. There's no vice in him."

"He is still with you, I presume?"

"Yes, sir. He and a girl of fourteen, who does a bit of simple cooking and keeps the place clean—that's all I have in the house, for I am a widower and never had any family. We live very quietly, sir, the three of us; and we keep a roof over our heads and pay our debts, if we do nothing more.

"The first thing that put us out was that advertisement. Spaulding, he came down into the office just this day eight weeks, with this very paper in his hand, and he says:

"'I wish to the Lord, Mr. Wilson, that I was a red-headed man.'

"'Why that?' I asks.

"'Why,' says he, 'here's another vacancy on the League of the Red-headed Men. It's worth quite a little fortune to any man who gets it, and I understand that there are more vacancies than there are men, so that the trustees are at their wits' end what to do with the money. If my hair would only change color, here's a nice little crib all ready for me to step into.'

"'Why, what is it, then?' I asked. You see, Mr. Holmes, I am a very stay-at-home man, and as my business came to me instead of my having to go to it, I was often weeks on end without putting my foot over the doormat. In that way I didn't know much of what was going on outside, and I was always glad of a bit of news.

"'Have you never heard of the League of the Red-headed Men?' he asked with his eyes open.

"'Never.'

"'Why, I wonder at that, for you are eligible yourself for one of the vacancies.'

"'And what are they worth?' I asked.

"'Oh, merely a couple of hundred a year, but the work is slight, and it need not interfere very much with one's other occupations.'

"Well, you can easily think that that made me prick up my ears, for the business has not been over-good for some years, and an extra couple of hundred would have been very handy.

"'Tell me all about it,' said I.

"'Well,' said he, showing me the advertisement, 'you can see for

**Reading Skill Contrasting Characters** In what ways does Wilson's lack of awareness of the outside world present a contrast to Holmes and Watson?

**Reading Check** Who is eligible for the position in the advertisement?

The Red-headed League **1171**

yourself that the League has a vacancy, and there is the address where you should apply for particulars. As far as I can make out, the League was founded by an American millionaire, Ezekiah Hopkins, who was very peculiar in his ways. He was himself red-headed, and he had a great sympathy for all red-headed men; so when he died it was found that he had left his enormous fortune in the hands of trustees, with instructions to apply the interest to the providing of easy berths to men whose hair is of that color. From all I hear it is splendid pay and very little to do.

"'But,' said I, 'there would be millions of red-headed men who would apply.'

"'Not so many as you might think,' he answered. 'You see it is really confined to Londoners, and to grown men. This American had started from London when he was young, and he wanted to do the old town a good turn. Then, again, I have heard it is no use your applying if your hair is light red, or dark red, or anything but real bright, blazing, fiery red. Now, if you cared to apply, Mr. Wilson, you would just walk in; but perhaps it would hardly be worth your while to put yourself out of the way for the sake of a few hundred pounds.'

"Now, it is a fact, gentlemen, as you may see for yourselves, that my hair is of a very full and rich tint, so that it seemed to me that if there was to be any competition in the matter I stood as good a chance as any man that I had ever met. Vincent Spaulding seemed to know so much about it that I thought he might prove useful so I just ordered him to put up the shutters for the day and to come right away with me. He was very willing to have a holiday,[5] so we shut the business up and started off for the address that was given us in the advertisement.

"I never hope to see such a sight as that again, Mr. Holmes. From north, south, east, and west every man who had a shade of red in his hair had tramped into the city to answer the advertisement. Fleet Street was choked with red-headed folk, and Pope's Court looked like a coster's orange barrow.[6] I should not have thought there were so many in the whole country as were brought together by that single advertisement. Every shade of color they were—straw, lemon, orange, brick, Irish-setter, liver, clay; but, as Spaulding said, there were not many who had the real vivid flame-colored tint. When I saw how many were waiting, I would have given it up in despair; but Spaulding would not hear of it. How he did it I could not imagine, but he pushed and pulled and butted until he got me through the crowd, and right up to the steps which led to the office. There was a double stream upon the stair, some going up in hope, and some coming back dejected; but we wedged in as well as we could and soon found ourselves in the office."

**Reading Skill Contrasting Characters** Who seems more invested in Wilson's joining the Red-headed League—Wilson or Spaulding? Explain.

---

5. **holiday** day off from work; vacation.
6. **coster's orange barrow** pushcart of a seller of oranges.

"Your experience has been a most entertaining one," remarked Holmes as his client paused and refreshed his memory with a huge pinch of snuff. "Pray continue your very interesting statement."

"There was nothing in the office but a couple of wooden chairs and a deal table, behind which sat a small man with a head that was even redder than mine. He said a few words to each candidate as he came up, and then he always managed to find some fault in them which would disqualify them. Getting a vacancy did not seem to be such a very easy matter, after all. However, when our turn came the little man was much more favorable to me than to any of the others, and he closed the door as we entered, so that he might have a private word with us.

"'This is Mr. Jabez Wilson,' said my assistant, 'and he is willing to fill a vacancy in the League.'

"'And he is admirably suited for it,' the other answered. 'He has every requirement. I cannot recall when I have seen anything so fine.' He took a step backward, cocked his head on one side, and gazed at my hair until I felt quite bashful. Then suddenly he plunged forward, wrung my hand, and congratulated me warmly on my success.

"'It would be injustice to hesitate,' said he. 'You will, however, I am sure, excuse me for taking an obvious precaution.' With that he seized my hair in both his hands, and tugged until I yelled with the pain. 'There is water in your eyes,' said he as he released me. 'I perceive that all is as it should be. But we have to be careful, for we have twice been deceived by wigs and once by paint. I could tell you tales of cobbler's wax which would disgust you with human nature.' He stepped over to the window and shouted through it at the top of his voice that the vacancy was filled. A groan of disappointment came up from below, and the folk all trooped away in different directions until there was not a red head to be seen except my own and that of the manager.

"'My name,' said he, 'is Mr. Duncan Ross, and I am myself one of the pensioners upon the fund left by our noble benefactor. Are you a married man, Mr. Wilson? Have you a family?'

"I answered that I had not.

"His face fell immediately.

"'Dear me!' he said gravely, 'that is very serious indeed! I am sorry to hear you say that. The fund was, of course, for the propagation and spread of the red-heads as well as for their maintenance. It is exceedingly unfortunate that you should be a bachelor.'

"My face lengthened at this, Mr. Holmes, for I thought that I was not to have the vacancy after all; but after thinking it over for a few minutes he said that it would be all right.

**Reading Skill Contrasting Characters** In what way is the man's behavior toward Mr. Wilson different from his behavior toward the other candidates?

**Reading Check** Who helps Wilson push through the crowd of men applying for the Red-headed League?

"'In the case of another,' said he, 'the objection might be fatal, but we must stretch a point in favor of a man with such a head of hair as yours. When shall you be able to enter upon your new duties?'

"'Well, it is a little awkward, for I have a business already,' said I.

"'Oh, never mind about that, Mr. Wilson!' said Vincent Spaulding. 'I should be able to look after that for you.'

"'What would be the hours?' I asked.

"'Ten to two.'

"Now a pawnbroker's business is mostly done of an evening, Mr. Holmes, especially Thursday and Friday evening, which is just before pay-day; so it would suit me very well to earn a little in the mornings. Besides, I knew that my assistant was a good man, and that he would see to anything that turned up.

"'That would suit me very well,' said I. 'And the pay?'

"'Is £4 a week.'

"'And the work?'

"'Is purely nominal.'

"'What do you call purely nominal?'

"'Well, you have to be in the office, or at least in the building, the whole time. If you leave, you forfeit your whole position forever. The will is very clear upon that point. You don't comply with the conditions if you budge from the office during that time.'

"'It's only four hours a day, and I should not think of leaving,' said I.

"'No excuse will avail,' said Mr. Duncan Ross; 'neither sickness nor business nor anything else. There you must stay, or you lose your billet.'[7]

"'And the work?'

"'Is to copy out the Encyclopedia Britannica. There is the first volume of it in that press. You must find your own ink, pens, and blotting-paper, but we provide this table and chair. Will you be ready tomorrow?'

"'Certainly,' I answered.

"'Then, good-bye, Mr. Jabez Wilson, and let me congratulate you

**Literary Analysis**
**Protagonist and Antagonist** Which details in the description of Wilson's responsibilities make Ross seem like a suspicious character?

---

7. **billet** (bil´ it) *n.* position; job.

once more on the important position which you have been fortunate enough to gain.' He bowed me out of the room, and I went home with my assistant, hardly knowing what to say or do, I was so pleased at my own good fortune.

"Well, I thought over the matter all day, and by evening I was in low spirits again; for I had quite persuaded myself that the whole affair must be some great hoax or fraud, though what its object might be I could not imagine. It seemed altogether past belief that anyone could make such a will, or that they would pay such a sum for doing anything so simple as copying out the Encyclopedia Britannica. Vincent Spaulding did what he could to cheer me up, but by bedtime I had reasoned myself out of the whole thing. However, in the morning I determined to have a look at it anyhow, so I bought a penny bottle of ink, and with a quill-pen, and seven sheets of foolscap paper, I started off for Pope's Court.

"Well, to my surprise and delight, everything was as right as possible. The table was set out ready for me, and Mr. Duncan Ross was there to see that I got fairly to work. He started me off upon the letter A, and then he left me; but he would drop in from time to time to see that all was right with me. At two o'clock he bade me good-day, complimented me upon the amount that I had written, and locked the door of the office after me.

"This went on day after day, Mr. Holmes, and on Saturday the manager came in and planked down four golden sovereigns for my week's work. It was the same next week, and the same the week after. Every morning I was there at ten, and every afternoon I left at two. By degrees Mr. Duncan Ross took to coming in only once of a morning, and then, after a time, he did not come in at all. Still, of course, I never dared to leave the room for an instant, for I was not sure when he might come, and the billet was such a good one, and suited me so well, that I would not risk the loss of it.

"Eight weeks passed away like this, and I had written about Abbots and Archery and Armor and Architecture and Attica, and hoped with diligence that I might get on to the B's before very long. It cost me something in foolscap, and I had pretty nearly filled a shelf with my writings. And then suddenly the whole business came to an end."

"To an end?"

"Yes, sir. And no later than this morning. I went to my work as

**Reading Check**
Who offers to look after Wilson's pawnbroker business while he is at his other job?

usual at ten o'clock, but the door was shut and locked, with a little square of cardboard hammered on to the middle of the panel with a tack. Here it is, and you can read for yourself."

He held up a piece of white cardboard about the size of a sheet of notepaper. It read in this fashion:

THE RED-HEADED LEAGUE IS DISSOLVED.
October 9, 1890.

**Reading Skill**
**Contrasting**
**Characters** How do the reactions of Watson and Holmes to the announcement compare with Mr. Wilson's? Explain.

Sherlock Holmes and I surveyed this curt announcement and the rueful face behind it, until the comical side of the affair so completely overtopped every other consideration that we both burst out into a roar of laughter.

"I cannot see that there is anything very funny," cried our client, flushing up to the roots of his flaming head. "If you can do nothing better than laugh at me, I can go elsewhere."

"No, no," cried Holmes, shoving him back into the chair from which he had half risen. "I really wouldn't miss your case for the world. It is most refreshingly unusual. But there is, if you will excuse my saying so, something just a little funny about it. Pray what steps did you take when you found the card upon the door?"

"I was staggered, sir. I did not know what to do. Then I called at the offices round, but none of them seemed to know anything about it. Finally, I went to the landlord, who is an accountant living on the ground floor, and I asked him if he could tell me what had become of the Red-headed League. He said that he had never heard of any such body. Then I asked him who Mr. Duncan Ross was. He answered that the name was new to him.

"'Well,' said I, 'the gentleman at No. 4.'

"'What, the red-headed man?'

"'Yes.'

**Literary Analysis**
**Protagonist and**
**Antagonist** What does William Morris's dishonesty about his identity suggest about his character?

"'Oh,' said he, 'his name was William Morris. He was a solicitor[8] and was using my room as a temporary convenience until his new premises were ready. He moved out yesterday.'

"'Where could I find him?'

"'Oh, at his new offices. He did tell me the address. Yes, 17 King Edward Street, near St. Paul's.'

"I started off, Mr. Holmes, but when I got to that address it was a manufactory of artificial kneecaps, and no one in it had ever heard of either Mr. William Morris or Mr. Duncan Ross."

"And what did you do then?" asked Holmes.

"I went home to Saxe-Coburg Square, and I took the advice of my assistant. But he could not help me in any way. He could only say

---

8. **solicitor** (sə lis´ it ər) *n.* member of the legal profession.

that if I waited I should hear by post. But that was not quite good enough, Mr. Holmes. I did not wish to lose such a place without a struggle, so, as I had heard that you were good enough to give advice to poor folk who were in need of it, I came right away to you."

"And you did very wisely," said Holmes. "Your case is an exceedingly remarkable one, and I shall be happy to look into it. From what you have told me I think that it is possible that graver issues hang from it than might at first sight appear."

"Grave enough!" said Mr. Jabez Wilson. "Why, I have lost four pound a week."

"As far as you are personally concerned," remarked Holmes, "I do not see that you have any grievance against this extraordinary league. On the contrary, you are, as I understand, richer by some £30, to say nothing of the minute knowledge which you have gained on every subject which comes under the letter A. You have lost nothing by them."

"No, sir. But I want to find out about them, and who they are, and what their object was in playing this prank—if it was a prank—upon me. It was a pretty expensive joke for them, for it cost them two and thirty pounds."

"We shall endeavor to clear up these points for you. And, first, one or two questions, Mr. Wilson. This assistant of yours who first called your attention to the advertisement—how long had he been with you?"

"About a month then."

"How did he come?"

"In answer to an advertisement."

"Was he the only applicant?"

"No, I had a dozen."

"Why did you pick him?"

"Because he was handy and would come cheap."

"At half-wages, in fact."

"Yes."

"What is he like, this Vincent Spaulding?"

**Literary Analysis**
**Protagonist and Antagonist** What reason might Holmes have for being suspicious of Vincent Spaulding?

 Reading Check

What reasons does Mr. Wilson give for hiring Vincent Spaulding?

"Small, stout-built, very quick in his ways. No hair on his face, though he's not short of thirty. Has a white splash of acid upon his forehead."

Holmes sat up in his chair in considerable excitement. "I thought as much," said he. "Have you ever observed that his ears are pierced for earrings?"

"Yes, sir. He told me that a gypsy had done it for him when he was a lad."

"Hum!" said Holmes, sinking back in deep thought. "He is still with you?"

"Oh, yes, sir; I have only just left him."

"And has your business been attended to in your absence?"

"Nothing to complain of, sir. There's never very much to do of a morning."

"That will do, Mr. Wilson. I shall be happy to give you an opinion upon the subject in the course of a day or two. Today is Saturday, and I hope that by Monday we may come to a conclusion."

"Well, Watson," said Holmes when our visitor had left us, "what do you make of it all?"

"I make nothing of it," I answered frankly. "It is a most mysterious business."

"As a rule," said Holmes, "the more bizarre a thing is the less mysterious it proves to be. It is your commonplace, featureless crimes which are really puzzling, just as a commonplace face is the most difficult to identify. But I must be prompt over this matter."

"What are you going to do, then?" I asked.

"To smoke," he answered. "It is quite a three pipe problem, and I beg that you won't speak to me for fifty minutes." He curled himself up in his chair, with his thin knees drawn up to his hawk-like nose, and there he sat with his eyes closed and his black clay pipe thrusting out like the bill of some strange bird. I had come to the conclusion that he had dropped asleep, and indeed was nodding myself, when he suddenly sprang out of his chair with the gesture of a man who has made up his mind and put his pipe down upon the mantelpiece.

"Sarasate[9] plays at the St. James's Hall this afternoon," he remarked. "What do you think, Watson? Could your patients spare you for a few hours?"

"I have nothing to do today. My practice is never very absorbing."

"Then put on your hat and come. I am going through the City first, and we can have some lunch on the way. I observe that there is a good deal of German music on the program, which is rather more to my taste than Italian or French. It is introspective, and I want to introspect. Come along!"

---

9. **Sarasate** (sä rä sä´ tä) Spanish violinist and composer.

**Literary Analysis**
**Protagonist and Antagonist** What does Holmes's expectation of reaching a conclusion in two days reveal about his character?

**Vocabulary**
**introspective** (in´ trə spek´ tiv) *adj.* having to do with looking into one's own thoughts and feelings

We traveled by the Underground as far as Aldersgate; and a short walk took us to Saxe-Coburg Square, the scene of the singular story which we had listened to in the morning. It was a poky, little, shabby-genteel place, where four lines of dingy two-storied brick houses looked out into a small railed-in enclosure, where a lawn of weedy grass and a few clumps of faded laurel bushes made a hard fight against a smoke-laden and uncongenial atmosphere. Three gilt balls and a brown board with "JABEZ WILSON" in white letters, upon a corner house, announced the place where our red-headed client carried on his business. Sherlock Holmes stopped in front of it with his head on one side and looked it all over, with his eyes shining brightly between puckered lids. Then he walked slowly up the street, and then down again to the corner, still looking keenly at the houses. Finally he returned to the pawnbroker's, and, having thumped vigorously upon the pavement with his stick two or three times, he went up to the door and knocked. It was instantly opened by a bright-looking, clean-shaven young fellow, who asked him to step in.

"Thank you," said Holmes, "I only wished to ask you how you would go from here to the Strand."

"Third right, fourth left," answered the assistant promptly, closing the door.

"Smart fellow, that," observed Holmes as we walked away. "He is, in my judgment, the fourth smartest man in London, and for daring I am not sure that he has not a claim to be third. I have known something of him before."

"Evidently," said I, "Mr. Wilson's assistant counts for a good deal in this mystery of the Red-headed League. I am sure that you inquired your way merely in order that you might see him."

"Not him."

"What then?"

"The knees of his trousers."

"And what did you see?"

"What I expected to see."

"Why did you beat the pavement?"

"My dear doctor, this is a time for observation, not for talk. We are spies in an enemy's country. We know something of Saxe-Coburg Square. Let us now explore the parts which lie behind it."

The road in which we found ourselves as we turned round the corner from the retired Saxe-Coburg Square presented as great a contrast to it as the front of a picture does to the back. It was one

**Reading Skill**
**Comparing**
**Characters** Based on Holmes's remark about Spaulding, what trait do the two men share? Explain.

Reading Check
Which aspect of Spaulding's appearance does Holmes want to observe?

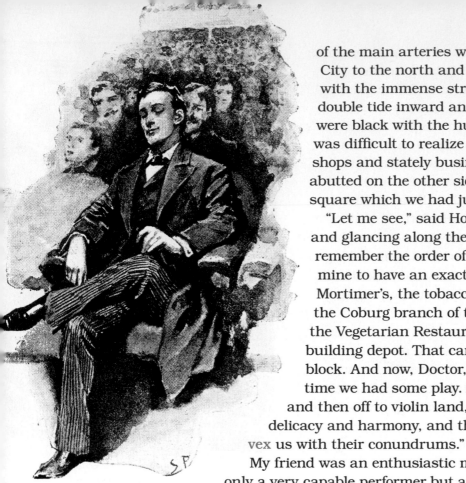

of the main arteries which conveyed the traffic of the City to the north and west. The roadway was blocked with the immense stream of commerce flowing in a double tide inward and outward, while the footpaths were black with the hurrying swarm of pedestrians. It was difficult to realize as we looked at the line of fine shops and stately business premises that they really abutted on the other side upon the faded and stagnant square which we had just quitted.

"Let me see," said Holmes, standing at the corner and glancing along the line, "I should like just to remember the order of the houses here. It is a hobby of mine to have an exact knowledge of London. There is Mortimer's, the tobacconist, the little newspaper shop, the Coburg branch of the City and Suburban Bank, the Vegetarian Restaurant, and McFarlane's carriage-building depot. That carries us right on to the other block. And now, Doctor, we've done our work, so it's time we had some play. A sandwich and a cup of coffee, and then off to violin land, where all is sweetness and delicacy and harmony, and there are no red-headed clients to vex us with their conundrums."

My friend was an enthusiastic musician, being himself not only a very capable performer but a composer of no ordinary merit. All the afternoon he sat in the stalls wrapped in the most perfect happiness, gently waving his long, thin fingers in time to the music, while his gently smiling face and his languid, dreamy eyes were as unlike those of Holmes, the sleuthhound, Holmes the relentless, keen-witted, ready-handed criminal agent, as it was possible to conceive. In his singular character the dual nature alternately asserted itself, and his extreme exactness and astuteness represented, as I have often thought, the reaction against the poetic and contemplative mood which occasionally predominated in him. The swing of his nature took him from extreme languor to devouring energy; and, as I knew well, he was never so truly formidable as when, for days on end, he had been lounging in his armchair amid his improvisations and his black-letter editions. Then it was that the lust of the chase would suddenly come upon him, and that his brilliant reasoning power would rise to the level of intuition, until those who were unacquainted with his methods would look askance at him as on a man whose knowledge was not that of other mortals. When I saw him that afternoon so enwrapped in the music at St. James's Hall I felt that an evil time might be coming upon those whom he had set himself to hunt down.

"You want to go home, no doubt, Doctor," he remarked as we emerged.

**Vocabulary**

**vex** (veks) *v.* annoy

**formidable** (fôr´ mə də bəl) *adj.* awe-inspiring

"Yes, it would be as well."

"And I have some business to do which will take some hours. This business at Coburg Square is serious."

"Why serious?"

"A considerable crime is in contemplation. I have every reason to believe that we shall be in time to stop it. But today being Saturday rather complicates matters. I shall want your help tonight."

"At what time?"

"Ten will be early enough."

"I shall be at Baker Street at ten."

"Very well. And, I say, Doctor, there may be some little danger, so kindly put your army revolver in your pocket." He waved his hand, turned on his heel, and disappeared in an instant among the crowd.

I trust that I am not more dense than my neighbors, but I was always oppressed with a sense of my own stupidity in my dealings with Sherlock Holmes. Here I had heard what he had heard, I had seen what he had seen, and yet from his words it was evident that he saw clearly not only what had happened but what was about to happen, while to me the whole business was still confused and grotesque. As I drove home to my house in Kensington I thought over it all, from the extraordinary story of the red-headed copier of the Encyclopedia down to the visit to Saxe-Coburg Square, and the ominous words with which he had parted from me. What was this nocturnal expedition, and why should I go armed? Where were we going, and what were we to do? I had the hint from Holmes that this smooth-faced pawnbroker's assistant was a formidable man—a man who might play a deep game. I tried to puzzle it out, but gave it up in despair and set the matter aside until night should bring an explanation.

It was a quarter past nine when I started from home and made my way across the Park, and so through Oxford Street to Baker Street. Two hansoms were standing at the door, and as I entered the passage I heard the sound of voices from above. On entering his room I found Holmes in animated conversation with two men, one of whom I recognized as Peter Jones, the official police agent, while the other was a long, thin, sadfaced man, with a very shiny hat and oppressively respectable frock coat.

"Ha! our party is complete," said Holmes, buttoning up his

peajacket and taking his heavy hunting crop from the rack. "Watson, I think you know Mr. Jones, of Scotland Yard? Let me introduce you to Mr. Merryweather, who is to be our companion in tonight's adventure."

"We're hunting in couples again, Doctor, you see," said Jones in his consequential way. "Our friend here is a wonderful man for starting a chase. All he wants is an old dog to help him to do the running down."

"I hope a wild goose may not prove to be the end of our chase," observed Mr. Merryweather gloomily.

"You may place considerable confidence in Mr. Holmes, sir," said the police agent loftily. "He has his own little methods, which are, if he won't mind my saying so, just a little too theoretical and fantastic, but he has the makings of a detective in him. It is not too much to say that once or twice, as in that business of the Sholto murder and the Agra treasure, he has been more nearly correct than the official force."

"Oh, if you say so, Mr. Jones, it is all right," said the stranger with deference. "Still, I confess that I miss my rubber.[10] It is the first Saturday night for seven-and-twenty years that I have not had my rubber."

"I think you will find," said Sherlock Holmes, "that you will play for a higher stake tonight than you have ever done yet, and that the play will be more exciting. For you, Mr. Merryweather, the stake will be some £30,000; and for you, Jones, it will be the man upon whom you wish to lay your hands."

**Reading Skill Comparing Characters** Despite their differences, in what ways are Sherlock Holmes and John Clay similar?

"John Clay, the murderer, thief, smasher, and forger. He's a young man, Mr. Merryweather, but he is at the head of his profession, and I would rather have my bracelets on him than on any criminal in London. He's a remarkable man, is young John Clay. His grandfather was a royal duke, and he himself has been to Eton[11] and Oxford.[12] His brain is as cunning as his fingers, and though we meet signs of him at every turn, we never know where to find the man himself. He'll crack a crib[13] in Scotland one week, and be raising money to build an orphanage in Cornwall the next. I've been on his track for years and have never set eyes on him yet."

"I hope that I may have the pleasure of introducing you tonight. I've had one or two little turns also with Mr. John Clay, and I agree with you that he is at the head of his profession. It is past ten, however, and quite time that we started. If you two will take the first hansom, Watson and I will follow in the second."

Sherlock Holmes was not very communicative during the long

---

**10. rubber** a term for a type of card game.
**11. Eton** famous British secondary school for boys.
**12. Oxford** oldest university in Great Britain.
**13. crack a crib** commit burglary.

drive and lay back in the cab humming the tunes which he had heard in the afternoon. We rattled through an endless labyrinth of gas-lit streets until we emerged into Farrington Street.

"We are close there now," my friend remarked. "This fellow Merryweather is a bank director, and personally interested in the matter. I thought it as well to have Jones with us also. He is not a bad fellow, though an absolute imbecile in his profession. He has one positive virtue. He is as brave as a bulldog and as tenacious as a lobster if he gets his claws upon anyone. Here we are, and they are waiting for us."

We had reached the same crowded thoroughfare in which we had found ourselves in the morning. Our cabs were dismissed, and, following the guidance of Mr. Merryweather, we passed down a narrow passage and through a side door, which he opened for us. Within there was a small corridor, which ended in a very massive iron gate. This also was opened, and led down a flight of winding stone steps, which terminated at another formidable gate. Mr. Merryweather stopped to light a lantern, and then conducted us down a dark, earth-smelling passage, and so, after opening a third door, into a huge vault or cellar, which was piled all round with crates and massive boxes.

"You are not very vulnerable from above," Holmes remarked as he held up the lantern and gazed about him.

"Nor from below," said Mr. Merryweather, striking his stick upon the flags which lined the floor. "Why, dear me, it sounds quite hollow!" he remarked, looking up in surprise.

"I must really ask you to be a little more quiet!" said Holmes severely. "You have already imperiled the whole success of our expedition. Might I beg that you would have the goodness to sit down upon one of those boxes, and not to interfere?"

The solemn Mr. Merryweather perched himself upon a crate, with a very injured expression upon his face, while Holmes fell upon his knees upon the floor and, with the lantern and a magnifying lens, began to examine minutely the cracks between the stones. A few seconds sufficed to satisfy him, for he sprang to his feet again and put his glass in his pocket.

"We have at least an hour before us," he remarked, "for they can hardly take any steps until the good pawnbroker is safely in bed. Then they will not lose a minute, for the sooner they do their work

**Vocabulary**
**tenacious** (tə nā´ shəs) *adj.* holding firmly to your point or beliefs; persistent; stubborn

Reading Check

Where does Mr. Merryweather lead Holmes and his companions?

**Literary Analysis**
**Protagonist and**
**Antagonist** What kind
of enemy does Holmes
anticipate he and his
companions will face?

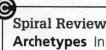

**Spiral Review**
**Archetypes** In what
ways is Holmes's case a
type of hero's quest?

the longer time they will have for their escape. We are at present, Doctor—as no doubt you have divined—in the cellar of the City branch of one of the principal London banks. Mr. Merryweather is the chairman of directors, and he will explain to you that there are reasons why the more daring criminals of London should take a considerable interest in this cellar at present."

"It is our French gold," whispered the director. "We have had several warnings that an attempt might be made upon it."

"Your French gold?"

"Yes. We had occasion some months ago to strengthen our resources and borrowed for that purpose 30,000 napoleons from the Bank of France. It has become known that we have never had occasion to unpack the money, and that it is still lying in our cellar. The crate upon which I sit contains 2,000 napoleons packed between layers of lead foil. Our reserve of bullion is much larger at present than is usually kept in a single branch office, and the directors have had misgivings upon the subject."

"Which were very well justified," observed Holmes.

"And now it is time that we arranged our little plans. I expect that within an hour matters will come to a head. In the meantime, Mr. Merryweather, we must put the screen over that dark lantern."

"And sit in the dark?"

"I am afraid so. I had brought a pack of cards in my pocket, and I thought that, as we were a *partie carrée*,[14] you might have your rubber after all. But I see that the enemy's preparations have gone so far that we cannot risk the presence of a light. And, first of all, we must choose our positions. These are daring men, and though we shall take them at a disadvantage, they may do us some harm unless we are careful. I shall stand behind this crate, and do you conceal yourselves behind those. Then, when I flash a light upon them, close in swiftly. If they fire, Watson, have no compunction about shooting them down."

I placed my revolver, cocked, upon the top of the wooden case behind which I crouched. Holmes shot the slide across the front of his lantern and left us in pitch darkness—such an absolute darkness as I have never before experienced. The smell of hot metal remained to assure us that the light was still there, ready to flash out at a moment's notice. To me, with my nerves worked up to a pitch of expectancy, there was something depressing and subduing in the sudden gloom, and in the cold dank air of the vault.

"They have but one retreat," whispered Holmes. "That is back through the house into Saxe-Coburg Square. I hope that you have done what I asked you, Jones?"

"I have an inspector and two officers waiting at the front door."

---

14. **partie carrée** (pär tē´ cä rā´) French for "group of four."

"Then we have stopped all the holes. And now we must be silent and wait."

What a time it seemed! From comparing notes afterwards it was but an hour and a quarter, yet it appeared to me that the night must have almost gone, and the dawn be breaking above us. My limbs were weary and stiff, for I feared to change my position; yet my nerves were worked up to the highest pitch of tension, and my hearing was so acute that I could not only hear the gentle breathing of my companions, but I could distinguish the deeper, heavier in-breath of the bulky Jones from the thin, sighing note of the bank director. From my position I could look over the case in the direction of the floor. Suddenly my eyes caught the glint of a light.

At first it was but a lurid spark upon the stone pavement. Then it lengthened out until it became a yellow line, and then, without any warning or sound, a gash seemed to open and a hand appeared; a white, almost womanly hand, which felt about in the center of the little area of light. For a minute or more the hand, with its writhing fingers, protruded out of the floor. Then it was withdrawn as suddenly as it appeared, and all was dark again save the single lurid spark which marked a chink between the stones.

Its disappearance, however, was but momentary. With a rending, tearing sound, one of the broad, white stones turned over upon its side and left a square, gaping hole, through which streamed the light of a lantern. Over the edge there peeped a clean-cut, boyish face, which looked keenly about it, and then, with a hand on either side of the aperture, drew itself shoulder-high and waist-high, until one knee rested upon the edge. In another instant he stood at the side of the hole and was hauling after him a companion, lithe and small like himself, with a pale face and a shock of very red hair.

"It's all clear," he whispered. "Have you the chisel and the bags? Great Scott! Jump, Archie, jump, and I'll swing for it."

Sherlock Holmes had sprung out and seized the intruder by the collar. The other dived down the hole, and I heard the sound of rending cloth as Jones clutched at his skirts. The light flashed upon the barrel of a revolver, but Holmes's hunting crop came down on the man's wrist, and the pistol clinked upon the stone floor.

"It's no use, John Clay," said Holmes blandly. "You have no chance at all."

"So I see," the other answered with the utmost coolness. "I fancy that my pal is all right, though I see you have got his coattails."

"There are three men waiting for him at the door," said Holmes.

"Oh, indeed! You seem to have done the thing very completely. I must compliment you."

"And I you," Holmes answered. "Your red-headed idea was very

**Literary Analysis Protagonist and Antagonist** What details of Watson's account help build the suspense of the conflict?

**Reading Skill Comparing Characters** In what ways is the first burglar's appearance similar to that of Vincent Spaulding?

Reading Check
What color is Clay's accomplice's hair?

new and effective."

"You'll see your pal again presently," said Jones. "He's quicker at climbing down holes than I am. Just hold out while I fix the derbies."[15]

"I beg that you will not touch me with your filthy hands," remarked our prisoner as the handcuffs clattered upon his wrists. "You may not be aware that I have royal blood in my veins. Have the goodness, also, when you address me always to say 'sir' and 'please.'"

"All right," said Jones with a stare and a snigger. "Well, would you please, sir, march upstairs, where we can get a cab to carry your Highness to the police station?"

"That is better," said John Clay serenely. He made a sweeping bow to the three of us and walked quietly off in the custody of the detective.

"Really, Mr. Holmes," said Mr. Merryweather as we followed them from the cellar, "I do not know how the bank can thank you or repay you. There is no doubt that you have detected and defeated in the most complete manner one of the most determined attempts at bank robbery that have ever come within my experience."

"I have had one or two little scores of my own to settle with Mr. John Clay," said Holmes. "I have been at some small expense over this matter, which I shall expect the bank to refund, but beyond that I am amply repaid by having had an experience which is in many ways unique, and by hearing the very remarkable narrative of the Red-headed League."

"You see, Watson," he explained in the early hours of the morning as we sat over a glass of whisky and soda in Baker Street, "it was perfectly obvious from the first that the only possible object of this rather fantastic business of the advertisement of the League, and the copying of the Encyclopedia, must be to get this not over-bright pawnbroker out of the way for a number of hours every day. It was a curious way of managing it, but, really, it would be difficult to

**Reading Skill Contrasting Characters** What difference between Holmes and Clay is revealed by Holmes's refusal to accept a reward?

---

15. **derbies** handcuffs.

suggest a better. The method was no doubt suggested to Clay's ingenious mind by the color of his accomplice's hair. The £4 a week was a lure which must draw him, and what was it to them, who were playing for thousands? They put in the advertisement, one rogue has the temporary office, the other rogue incites the man to apply for it, and together they manage to secure his absence every morning in the week. From the time that I heard of the assistant having come for half wages, it was obvious to me that he had some strong motive for securing the situation."

"But how could you guess what the motive was?"

"Had there been women in the house, I should have suspected a mere vulgar intrigue. That, however, was out of the question. The man's business was a small one, and there was nothing in his house which could account for such elaborate preparations, and such an expenditure as they were at. It must, then, be something out of the house. What could it be? I thought of the assistant's fondness for photography, and his trick of vanishing into the cellar. The cellar! There was the end of this tangled clue. Then I made inquiries as to this mysterious assistant and found that I had to deal with one of the coolest and most daring criminals in London. He was doing something in the cellar—something which took many hours a day for months on end. What could it be, once more? I could think of nothing save that he was running a tunnel to some other building.

"So far I had got when we went to visit the scene of action. I surprised you by beating upon the pavement with my stick. I was ascertaining whether the cellar stretched out in front or behind. It was not in front. Then I rang the bell, and, as I hoped, the assistant answered it. We have had some skirmishes, but we had never set eyes upon each other before. I hardly looked at his face. His knees were what I wished to see. You must yourself have remarked how worn, wrinkled, and stained they were. They spoke of those hours of burrowing. The only remaining point was what they were burrowing for. I walked round the corner, saw that the City and Suburban Bank abutted on our friend's premises, and felt that I had solved my problem. When you drove home after the concert I called upon Scotland Yard and upon the chairman of the bank directors, with the result that you have seen."

"And how could you tell that they would make their attempt tonight?" I asked.

"Well, when they closed their League offices that was a sign that they cared no longer about Mr. Jabez Wilson's presence—in other words, that they had completed their tunnel. But it was essential

**Literary Analysis**
**Protagonist and Antagonist** What was Clay's (Spaulding's) motivation in arranging for Wilson to be out of the house?

Reading Check
What was the motive behind the Red-headed League?

that they should use it soon, as it might be discovered, or the bullion might be removed. Saturday would suit them better than any other day, as it would give them two days for their escape. For all these reasons I expected them to come tonight."

"You reasoned it out beautifully," I exclaimed in unfeigned admiration. "It is so long a chain, and yet every link rings true."

"It saved me from ennui,"[16] he answered, yawning. "Alas! I already feel it closing in upon me. My life is spent in one long effort to escape from the commonplaces of existence. These little problems help me to do so."

"And you are a benefactor of the race," said I.

He shrugged his shoulders. "Well, perhaps, after all, it is of some little use," he remarked. "'*L'homme c'est rien—l'oeuvre c'est tout*,'[17] as Gustave Flaubert wrote to George Sand."[18]

---

16. **ennui** (än' wē') *n.* boredom.
17. **L'homme c'est rien—l'oeuvre c'est tout** (lum sä rē en' luvr sä tōō) French for "Man is nothing—the work is everything."
18. **Gustave Flaubert** (gōōs täv' flō ber') **. . . George Sand** notable French novelists of the nineteenth century.

---

## Critical Thinking

Cite textual evidence to support your responses.

1. **Key Ideas and Details (a)** Why does Jabez Wilson visit Sherlock Holmes? **(b) Infer:** Why does Holmes find Wilson's story interesting?

2. **Key Ideas and Details (a)** What happens the night of the attempted burglary? **(b) Analyze Cause and Effect:** Which clues found at Saxe-Coburg Square lead to Holmes's solution of the mystery? **(c) Speculate:** What details could have been misinterpreted, leading to an incorrect conclusion? Explain your response.

3. **Integration of Knowledge and Ideas (a)** What remark does Holmes make about commonplace crimes? **(b) Infer:** What does Holmes mean? **(c) Interpret:** What does his remark suggest about the qualities that make a great detective?

4. **Integration of Knowledge and Ideas** Would you call Holmes a hero? Why or why not? *[Connect to the Big Question: Do heroes have responsibilities?]*

## Literary Analysis: Protagonist and Antagonist

**1. Craft and Structure (a)** Identify the **protagonist** in the narrative. **(b)** What is the protagonist's goal? **(c)** Why are readers interested in whether the protagonist achieves his goal?

**2. Craft and Structure (a)** Identify the **antagonist. (b)** What is the antagonist's goal?

**3. Integration of Knowledge and Ideas (a)** Why is the story's conflict interesting? **(b)** What universal struggle does this conflict represent?

## Reading Skill: Comparing and Contrasting Characters

4. Use a Venn diagram to compare and contrast Holmes's character at the beginning and end of the story. Does he change? Explain.

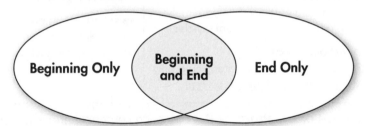

## Vocabulary

**Acquisition and Use  Analogies** show the relationship between pairs of words. Use a word from the list on page 1164 to complete each analogy.

**1.** kind : gentle :: _____ : fearsome

**2.** burn : candle :: _____ : problem

**3.** descending : downward :: _____ : inward

**4.** lose : misplace :: _____ : exaggerate

**5.** brutal : kind :: _____ : indecisive

**6.** inquire : ask :: _____ : attempt

**Word Study** Use the context of the sentences and what you know about the **Latin root -spec-** to explain your answer to each question.

**1.** Might a *prospector* hope to find gold or silver?

**2.** If you take a new *perspective*, might you have new ideas?

### Word Study

The **Latin root -*spec*-** means "see," "look," or "examine."

**Apply It** Explain how the root -*spec*- contributes to the meanings of these words. Consult a dictionary if necessary.

spectacle
inspector
spectator

# Integrated Language Skills

## Three Skeleton Key •
## The Red-headed League

## Conventions: Using Commas and Dashes

Use **commas** when you need to indicate a short pause in your writing. Two basic principles guide all comma usage.

Use a **dash** to indicate an abrupt change of thought, a dramatic interruption, or a summary statement.

| Use Commas to Separate... | Use Commas to Set Off... | Use Dashes to Indicate... |
|---|---|---|
| **Two independent clauses in a compound sentence**<br>I turned the ignition key<u>, but</u> the car did not start. | **An introductory word, phrase, or clause**<br><u>Coincidentally,</u> we all ended up at the same beach. | **An abrupt change of thought**<br>That man stole all that money—I don't even want to think about it. |
| **Three or more words, phrases, or clauses in a series**<br>He spoke <u>with passion, with gravity, and with sorrow</u>. | **Parenthetical or nonessential expressions**<br>The magazine<u>, which I unfortunately misplaced,</u> had some great articles. | **To set off an interrupting idea**<br>John—his mom calls him Sweetie Pie—has a great sense of humor. |
| **Parts of dates, places, or certain titles**<br>We went to <u>Sonoma, California,</u> for the weekend. | **Direct quotations**<br>President Roosevelt declared<u>, "The only thing we have to fear is fear itself."</u> | **To set off a summary statement**<br>Lemon, lime, or orange—deciding which flavor to pick was difficult. |

**Practice A** Identify the rule that the commas or dashes in each of these sentences follow.

1. The men called out, "Rats!"

2. Incredibly, the ship was covered with rats.

3. The rats, which were on the ship, leaped to the island.

4. The rats climbed, squealed, and chewed.

5. The lighthouse —if you could believe it—was under seige.

Ⓒ **Reading Application** In "Three Skeleton Key," find three sentences with commas that follow three different rules.

**Practice B** Copy each sentence, and add commas or dashes where they are necessary. Indicate which rule(s) you are following.

1. The man was stout elderly and red-headed.

2. Mr. Watson opened the door but he saw that Holmes was not alone.

3. Blonde or red-headed which is preferable?

4. After he had thought for some minutes Holmes leaped to his feet.

5. "Stop" the constable called out.

Ⓒ **Writing Application** Write four sentences about stories of suspense. Use commas in each sentence. Demonstrate correct usage of at least three rules.

**PH** **WRITING COACH** Further instruction and practice are available in *Prentice Hall Writing Coach*.

# Writing

**Common Core
State Standards**

**L.9-10.2; W.9-10.3.d,
W.9-10.7; SL.9-10.2,
SL.9-10.5.**
[For the full wording of the
standards, see page 1144.]

**Narrative Text** Imagine that you are one of the characters in the story you read. Choose a character other than the narrator in "Three Skeleton Key," or write as Dr. Watson in "The Red-headed League." Write three **journal entries** describing the events in the story as they unfold.

- Review the story and create a timeline for the major events.
- Decide which days you will record in your journal.
- As the character, write your thoughts about what happens each day.
- Use descriptive words and phrases to capture the events, setting, and characters memorably.

As you write, stay in character, making sure that your journal reflects any changes that the character experiences in the story.

**Grammar Application** Use commas and dashes correctly as you write your entries, especially in nonrestrictive phrases, contrasting expressions, and parenthetical information.

**Writing Workshop:** *Work in Progress*

**Prewriting for Comparison and Contrast** For a comparison-and-contrast essay you may write, choose two places that you know well. For each, note the purpose, sound, and look of the place. Save your list.

Use this prewriting activity to prepare for
the **Writing Workshop** on page 1234.

# Research and Technology

**Build and Present Knowledge** Prepare an **oral report** about a topic from the story you read.

- If you read "Three Skeleton Key," conduct research about ship's rats and how these rats differ from other rats.
- If you read "The Red-headed League," research criminology. Find information on fingerprinting, lie detectors, and police sketches.

Follow these steps to complete the assignment.

- Before you begin, generate research questions about your topic. Use the questions to direct and focus your research.
- Consult multiple sources, such as the Internet, encyclopedias, and other reference books. Make sure to verify information from one source with another.
- Then, compare what you learn to details presented in the story.
- To help you organize and present the information you find, develop visual aids using computer software or other technology.

Present your report to your class and invite questions. As others give reports, evaluate their information and techniques and ask questions.

**PHLit
Online!**
www.PHLitOnline.com
- Interactive graphic organizers
- Grammar tutorial
- Interactive journals

## Leveled Texts

Build your skills and improve your comprehension of types of nonfiction
with texts of increasing complexity.

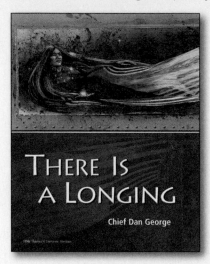

Read **"There Is a Longing"** to
learn about the dreams and goals
of a Native American leader.

Read **"Glory and Hope"** to see how
the leader of a reborn African nation
celebrates liberty.

## Common Core State Standards

Meet these standards with either **"There is a Longing"** (p. 1196) or **"Glory and Hope"** (p. 1202).

### Reading Informational Text
**3.** Analyze how the author unfolds an analysis or series of
ideas or events, including the order in which the points are
made, how they are introduced and developed, and the
connections that are drawn between them. *(Reading Skill:
Compare and Contrast)*

**6.** Determine an author's point of view or purpose in a
text and analyze how an author uses rhetoric to advance
that point of view or purpose. *(Literary Analysis:
Philosophical Assumptions)*

### Writing
**2.** Write informative/explanatory texts. **2.b.** Develop the
topic with well-chosen, relevant, and sufficient facts,
extended definitions, concrete details, quotations, or other
information and examples appropriate to the audience's
knowledge of the topic. **2.e.** Establish and maintain a
formal style and objective tone while attending to the
norms and conventions of the discipline in which they are
writing. *(Writing: Letter)*

### Speaking and Listening
**1.a.** Come to discussions prepared, having read and
researched material under study; explicitly draw on that
preparation to stimulate a thoughtful well-reasoned
exchange of ideas. **1.c.** Propel conversations by posing and
responding to questions; actively incorporate others into
the discussion; clarify conclusions. *(Speaking and Listening:
Panel Discussion)*

### Language
**2.** Demonstrate command of the conventions of standard
English capitalization, punctuation, and spelling when
writing. *(Conventions: Colons, Semicolons, and
Ellipsis Points)*

**6.** Acquire and use accurately grade-appropriate general
academic and domain-specific words and phrases; gather
vocabulary knowledge when considering a word or phrase
important to comprehension or expression. *(Vocabulary:
Word Study)*

# Literary Analysis: Philosophical Assumptions

An **author's purpose,** or goal, is shaped by his or her **philosophical assumptions,** or basic beliefs. Philosophical assumptions can be based on many factors, such as political beliefs, moral or ethical values, and cultural influences. In some cases, the author may use these basic beliefs to support his or her argument. The response of the **audience,** or readers, may depend on whether they share the author's basic beliefs.

To read critically, identify the author's basic beliefs and assumptions in the work. The author may state such beliefs directly or may suggest them in details and varied types of language, such as words that carry positive or negative associations. As you read, decide whether you accept these beliefs and whether the audience would be likely to accept them. Then, evaluate whether these assumptions help the author achieve his or her purpose.

## Using the Strategy: Assumptions Chart

As you read, use a chart like the one shown to record your ideas.

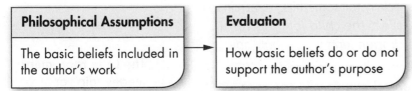

| Philosophical Assumptions | Evaluation |
|---|---|
| The basic beliefs included in the author's work | How basic beliefs do or do not support the author's purpose |

# Reading Skill: Compare and Contrast

When you **compare and contrast,** you recognize similarities and differences. In persuasive writing, authors often use a compare-and-contrast organization to help readers see the similarities and differences between one point of view and another. As you read, **use self-monitoring techniques** like these to make sure you understand the comparisons and contrasts:

- Identify the things or ideas being compared.
- Restate the similarities and differences in your own words.
- Explain the significance of the similarities and differences.

If you cannot identify, restate, or explain the author's points, reread to clarify and to find words or phrases that were unclear.

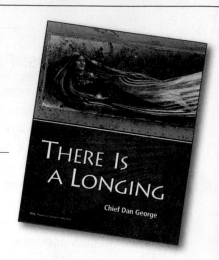

# Do *heroes* have responsibilities?

## Writing About the Big Question

In his speech, Chief Dan George says his power to make war is gone, but he longs to serve his people. Use these sentence starters to develop your ideas about the Big Question.

Not all **heroes** know they are heroes because _____.

A leader can be a true **hero** when he or she _____.

**While You Read**  Look for ways in which Chief Dan George accepts the responsibilities of leadership. Consider whether he is a hero.

## Vocabulary

Read each word and its definition. Decide whether you know the word well, know it a little bit, or do not know it at all. After you read, see how your knowledge of each word has increased.

- **longing** (lôŋ´ iŋ) *n.* a yearning, especially for something unattainable (p. 1197) *The passing dessert cart left the child longing for a piece of cake during the whole dinner.* long *v.* longingly *adv.*

- **determination** (dē tʉr´ mi nā´ shən) *n.* firm intention (p. 1197) *The runner's determination enabled him to win the race.* determined *adj.*

- **endurance** (en dʊr´ əns) *n.* ability to withstand hardship over time (p. 1197) *Surviving the hurricane required courage and endurance.* endure *v.* enduring *adj.*

- **emerge** (ē mʉrj´) *v.* come into existence; become visible or known (p. 1197) *Joe's parents hoped that after college he would emerge as a strong candidate for the business world.* emerging *adj.* emergent *adj.*

- **humbly** (hum´ blē) *adv.* in a manner that is not proud or arrogant; modestly (p. 1198) *Shannon accepted her award humbly, thanking everyone who helped her achieve it.* humble *adj.* humbled *v.*

- **segment** (seg´ mənt) *n.* a division or section (p. 1198) *Claire approached each segment of the test cautiously because the directions seemed to change with every one.* segmented *adj.*

### Word Study

The **Latin root -*merg*-** means "dip" or "plunge."

In this selection, Chief Dan George says the young of his nation will **emerge** from years of study, as if rising up from the waters. They will take their place in society.

## Author of
# THERE IS A LONGING

Chief Dan George had many careers, including actor and writer. Chief of a Salish Band of Native Americans in British Columbia, Canada, he was deeply concerned about improving the relationships between Native Americans and other North Americans.

**Celebrity Activist** Chief Dan George used the prominence he gained from his film and television roles to raise public awareness about the plight of Canada's native peoples. By the 1960s, he had become an unofficial spokesman for Native Americans and the environment. Throughout all of his endeavors against injustice, he always advocated peace over violence.

## BACKGROUND FOR THE SPEECH

### The Struggle of Native Americans

When Europeans settled in the Americas, they encountered tribal peoples who had lived on the land for thousands of years. Their initial fear and prejudice led to violence, and many native tribes were destroyed. Nevertheless, Native American culture survived. Today, Native Americans continue to discover ways to succeed in the twenty-first century while maintaining their own cultural identity.

## DID YOU KNOW?

Chief Dan George was nominated for an Academy Award as Best Supporting Actor for his role in the movie *Little Big Man*.

# THERE IS
# A LONGING

## Chief Dan George

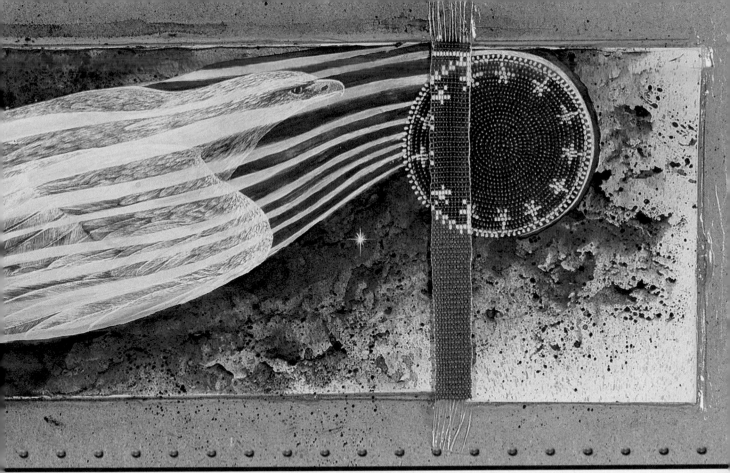

*We the People,* Kathy Morrow, Original scratchboard painting with hand-loomed beadwork. Courtesy of the artist.

There is a longing in the heart of my people
to reach out and grasp that which is needed
for our survival. There is a longing among
the young of my nation to secure for themselves
5  and their people the skills that will
provide them with a sense of worth and
purpose. They will be our new warriors.
Their training will be much longer and
more demanding than it was in olden days.
10 The long years of study will demand more
determination; separation from home and
family will demand endurance. But they
will emerge with their hand held forward,
not to receive welfare, but to grasp the
15 place in society that is rightly ours.
I am a chief, but my power to make war
is gone, and the only weapon left to me
is speech. It is only with tongue and speech
that I can fight my people's war.

▲ **Critical Viewing**
Which images in
this painting reflect
ideas found in the
speech? **[Analyze]**

**Vocabulary**
**longing** (lôŋˊ iŋ) *n.* a
yearning, especially for
something unattainable

**determination**
(dē tʉrˊ mi nāˊ shən)
*n.* firm intention

**endurance** (en dʊʊrˊ əns)
*n.* ability to withstand
hardship over time

**emerge** (ē mʉrjˊ) *v.*
come into existence;
become visible or known

There Is a Longing **1197**

20 Oh, Great Spirit![1] Give me back the courage
of the olden Chiefs. Let me wrestle with
my surroundings. Let me once again,
live in harmony with my environment.
Let me humbly accept this new culture
25 and through it rise up and go on. Like
the thunderbird[2] of old, I shall rise again
out of the sea; I shall grab the instruments
of the white man's success—his
education, his skills. With these new tools
30 I shall build my race into the proudest
segment of your society. I shall see our
young braves and our chiefs sitting in
the houses of law and government, ruling
and being ruled by the knowledge and
35 freedoms of our great land.

---

1. **Great Spirit** for many Native Americans, the greatest power or god.
2. **thunderbird** powerful supernatural creature that was thought to produce thunder by flapping its wings and to produce lightning by opening and closing its eyes. In the folklore of some Native American nations, the thunderbird is in constant warfare with the powers beneath the waters.

## Critical Thinking

Cite textual evidence to support your responses.

1. **Key Ideas and Details (a)** What does Chief Dan George say is his community's longing? **(b) Infer:** What is his greatest fear?

2. **Key Ideas and Details (a)** What training will the new warriors have to endure? **(b) Analyze:** Why does Chief Dan George believe that this training is necessary?

3. **Key Ideas and Details (a) Infer:** In what way is Chief Dan George different from the "olden" chiefs? **(b) Interpret:** What does the chief mean when he refers to fighting a war "with tongue and speech"?

4. **Integration of Knowledge and Ideas Assess:** Do you think the chief's goal of achieving success through education and skills is the best means for improving his people's lives? Explain your response.

5. **Integration of Knowledge and Ideas** Chief Dan George talks about fighting his people's war with "tongue and speech." Can someone who fights only with such weapons be a hero? *[Connect to the Big Question: Do heroes have responsibilities?]*

## Literary Analysis: Philosophical Assumptions

**1. Key Ideas and Details (a)** What is Chief Dan George's **purpose** in writing? **(b)** What are the **philosophical assumptions,** or beliefs, that shape his purpose?

**2. Key Ideas and Details (a)** For what **audience** did Chief Dan George originally write? **(b)** What details in the text indicate his intended audience? **(c)** Do you think his intended audience shared his basic beliefs? Support your answer with details from the text.

**3. Integration of Knowledge and Ideas** Using Chief Dan George's speech as an example, explain how the audience for a speech can change over time.

## Reading Skill: Compare and Contrast

**4. (a)** Use a chart like the one shown to record the ideas Chief Dan George presents about the past, present, and future.

| Past | Present | Future |
|------|---------|--------|
|      |         |        |

**(b)** Explain the point Chief Dan George makes by **comparing and contrasting** his ideas about the past, present, and future.

## Vocabulary

**Acquisition and Use** Indicate whether each statement is *True* or *False*. Explain your answers. Then, revise any sentences that are false to make them true.

**1.** Difficult tasks require *determination* to be completed.

**2.** Rock climbing requires less *endurance* than television watching.

**3.** When a winner responds *humbly* to a victory, he or she claims to be the world's greatest champion.

**4.** No one really wants to *emerge* from a time of pain or unpleasantness.

**5.** Only fortunate people have a *longing* to improve their lives.

**6.** Students are one *segment* of our society.

**Word Study** Use the context of the sentences and what you know about the **Latin root -merg-** to explain your answer to each question.

**1.** In an *emergency,* is someone in serious, unexpected trouble?

**2.** Is a *submersible* a ship built to float on the surface of the water?

### Word Study

The **Latin root -merg-** means "dip" or "plunge."

**Apply It** Explain how the root -merg- contributes to the meanings of these words. Consult a dictionary if necessary.
immerge
submerge
merger

# Do *heroes* have responsibilities?

Glory and Hope

Nelson Mandela

## Writing About the Big Question

In his speech, Nelson Mandela celebrates the liberty newly gained by his country and pleads for national reconciliation and liberty. Use these sentence starters to develop your ideas about the Big Question.

When a leader promises to **serve** his or her nation, he or she has an **obligation** to follow through because _____. The leader may become a **heroic** figure to many because _____.

**While You Read** Look for the values that Mandela celebrates and the goals that he has set. Consider whether you believe he is a hero.

## Vocabulary

Read each word and its definition. Decide whether you know the word well, know it a little bit, or do not know it at all. After you read, see how your knowledge of each word has increased.

- **distinguished** (di stiŋ´ gwisht) *adj.* having an air of distinction; celebrated for excellence; renowned (p. 1202) *The distinguished gentleman stood and bowed to the crowd that acknowledged him. distinguish v. distinct adj.*

- **confer** (kən fʉr´) *v.* give (p. 1202) *The school will confer an honorary degree on the singer. conferable adj.*

- **intimately** (in´ tə mət lē) *adv.* in a close manner; familiarly (p. 1202). *Because they had worked together for years, Sandy and her colleagues knew each other intimately. intimate adj. intimacy n.*

- **pernicious** (pər nish´ əs) *adj.* destructive (p. 1203) *A pernicious insect destroyed the tree. perniciously adv. perniciousness n.*

- **covenant** (kuv´ ə nənt) *n.* agreement or contract, especially a sacred one (p. 1203) *They made a covenant to be friends forever.*

- **reconciliation** (rek´ ən sil´ ē ā´ shən) *n.* the settling of a conflict or argument; agreement; compromise (p. 1204) *Maryanne hoped she would come to some sort of reconciliation with her daughter after their terrible fight. reconcile v. reconcilable adj.*

### Word Study

The **Latin root -fer-** means "carry" or "produce."

In this selection, Mandela says that by celebrating the change in South Africa, they will **confer,** or carry, glory and hope on their new liberty.

# Nelson Mandela
## (b. 1918)

## Author of
# Glory and Hope

Nelson Rolihlahla Mandela was born in South Africa, a nation whose white government maintained a strict policy of apartheid, or legal discrimination against blacks. In 1944, Mandela began protesting apartheid. Twenty years later, after several arrests, he was sentenced to life in prison for acts of protest.

**Freedom for a Man and a Nation** In 1990, after long years of imprisonment, Mandela was released. He continued to fight for equal rights for all South Africans. In 1991, apartheid was finally abolished and, in 1993, Mandela and South African president F. W. de Klerk shared the Nobel Prize for Peace. The next year, Mandela became the first black man to be elected president of South Africa. He retired from public life in 1999, and he currently lives in his birthplace, Qunu, Transkei.

### Did You Know?
Robben Island, Mandela's prison for so many years, has now been turned into a learning center.

## BACKGROUND FOR THE SPEECH
### Apartheid

In Afrikaans, one of the languages of South Africa, *apartheid* means "apartness." Apartheid is the policy of segregation and discrimination that was once practiced against nonwhites by the South African government. When apartheid became law in 1948, it affected housing, education, and transportation. In order to help end apartheid, many nations reduced trade with South Africa. Apartheid was finally abolished in 1991.

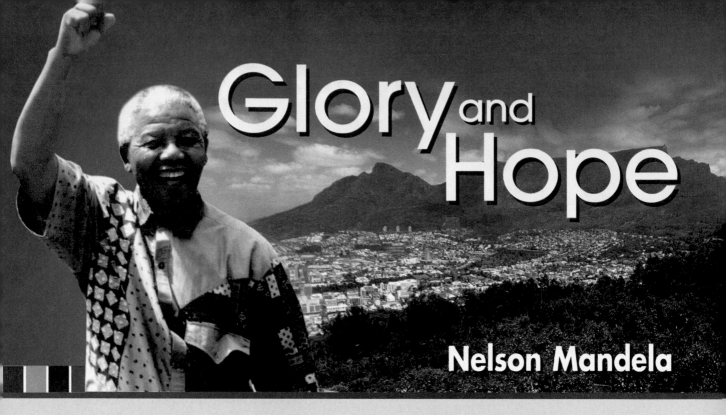

# Glory and Hope

## Nelson Mandela

**Vocabulary**

**distinguished**
(di stiŋ´ gwisht´) *adj.*
having an air of
distinction; celebrated
for excellence; renowned

**confer** (kən fʉr´) *v.* give

**intimately**
(in´ tə mət lē´) *adj.* In a
close manner; familiarly

**Reading Skill
Comparing and
Contrasting** What
important difference does
Mandela point out about
South Africa's future as
compared to its past?

Your majesties, your royal highnesses, distinguished guests,
comrades and friends: Today, all of us do, by our presence here,
and by our celebrations in other parts of our country and the world,
confer glory and hope to newborn liberty.

Out of the experience of an extraordinary human disaster that
lasted too long must be born a society of which all humanity will be
proud.

Our daily deeds as ordinary South Africans must produce an
actual South African reality that will reinforce humanity's belief in
justice, strengthen its confidence in the nobility of the human soul
and sustain all our hopes for a glorious life for all.

All this we owe both to ourselves and to the peoples of the world
who are so well represented here today.

To my compatriots, I have no hesitation in saying that each one of
us is as intimately attached to the soil of this beautiful country as
are the famous jacaranda trees of Pretoria and the mimosa trees of
the bushveld.[1]

Each time one of us touches the soil of this land, we feel a sense of
personal renewal. The national mood changes as the seasons change.

We are moved by a sense of joy and exhilaration when the grass
turns green and the flowers bloom.

That spiritual and physical oneness we all share with this
common homeland explains the depth of the pain we all carried in

---

1. **bushveld** (bōōsh´ velt) *n.* South African grassland with abundant shrubs and thorny
   vegetation.

our hearts as we saw our country tear itself apart in terrible conflict, and as we saw it spurned, outlawed and isolated by the peoples of the world, precisely because it has become the universal base of the pernicious ideology and practice of racism and racial oppression.

We, the people of South Africa, feel fulfilled that humanity has taken us back into its bosom, that we, who were outlaws not so long ago, have today been given the rare privilege to be host to the nations of the world on our own soil.

We thank all our distinguished international guests for having come to take possession with the people of our country of what is, after all, a common victory for justice, for peace, for human dignity.

We trust that you will continue to stand by us as we tackle the challenges of building peace, prosperity, nonsexism, nonracialism and democracy.

We deeply appreciate the role that the masses of our people and their democratic, religious, women, youth, business, traditional and other leaders have played to bring about this conclusion. Not least among them is my Second Deputy President, the Honorable F. W. de Klerk.

We would also like to pay tribute to our security forces, in all their ranks, for the distinguished role they have played in securing our first democratic elections and the transition to democracy, from bloodthirsty forces which still refuse to see the light.

The time for the healing of the wounds has come.

The moment to bridge the chasms that divide us has come.

The time to build is upon us.

We have, at last, achieved our political emancipation. We pledge ourselves to liberate all our people from the continuing bondage of poverty, deprivation, suffering, gender and other discrimination.

We succeeded to take our last steps to freedom in conditions of relative peace. We commit ourselves to the construction of a complete, just and lasting peace.

We have triumphed in the effort to implant hope in the breasts of the millions of our people. We enter into a covenant that we shall build the society in which all South Africans, both black and white, will be able to walk tall, without any fear in their hearts, assured of their inalienable right to human dignity—a rainbow nation at peace with itself and the world.

As a token of its commitment to the renewal of our country, the new Interim Government of National Unity will, as a matter of urgency, address the issue of amnesty for various categories of our people who are currently serving terms of imprisonment.

We dedicate this day to all the heroes and heroines in this country and the rest of the world who sacrificed in many ways and surrendered their lives so that we could be free.

**Vocabulary**
**pernicious** (pər nish´ əs)
*adj.* destructive

**Spiral Review**
**Universal Theme**
How do Mandela's words in the three short paragraphs that begin with "The time for the healing of the wounds has come" evoke a possible theme of hope and rebirth?

**Vocabulary**
**covenant** (kuv´ ə nənt)
*n.* agreement or contract, especially a sacred one

Reading
Check
What does Mandela say must be born "out of the experience of an extraordinary human disaster"?

Their dreams have become reality. Freedom is their reward.

We are both humbled and elevated by the honor and privilege that you, the people of South Africa, have bestowed on us, as the first President of a united, democratic, nonracial and nonsexist South Africa, to lead our country out of the valley of darkness.

We understand it still that there is no easy road to freedom.

We know it well that none of us acting alone can achieve success.

We must therefore act together as a united people, for national reconciliation, for nation building, for the birth of a new world.

Let there be justice for all.

Let there be peace for all.

Let there be work, bread, water and salt for all.

Let each know that for each the body, the mind and the soul have been freed to fulfill themselves.

Never, never and never again shall it be that this beautiful land will again experience the oppression of one by another and suffer the indignity of being the skunk of the world.

The sun shall never set on so glorious a human achievement!

Let freedom reign. God bless Africa!

**Vocabulary**
**reconciliation**
(rek´ ən sil´ ē ā´ shən) *n.*
the settling of a conflict
or argument; agreement;
compromise

## Critical Thinking

Cite textual evidence to support your responses.

1. **Key Ideas and Details (a)** What does Nelson Mandela say is "newborn" in his country? **(b) Interpret:** What emotion does the word "newborn" add to his remarks?

2. **Key Ideas and Details (a)** Into what "covenant" does Mandela say the South African people are now entering? **(b) Generalize:** Which ideas in the speech are especially important for safeguarding the human rights of all people throughout today's world?

3. **Key Ideas and Details (a) Interpret:** What do the words "glory" and "hope" mean? **(b) Connect:** How does the title of the speech connect with the ideas that Mandela conveys? Explain your response.

4. **Integration of Knowledge and Ideas Take a Position:** Basing your answer on Mandela's speech, what do you think was the new leader's greatest challenge? Explain.

5. **Integration of Knowledge and Ideas** Based on what you know about Nelson Mandela from his speech, would you call him a hero? Explain. *[Connect to the Big Question: Do heroes have responsibilities?]*

## Literary Analysis: Philosophical Assumptions

**1. Key Ideas and Details (a)** What is Nelson Mandela's **purpose** in his speech? **(b)** What are the **philosophical assumptions,** or beliefs, that shape his purpose?

**2. Key Ideas and Details (a)** For what **audience** did Nelson Mandela originally speak? **(b)** What details in the text indicate his intended audience? **(c)** Do you think his intended audience shared his basic beliefs? Support your answer with details from the text.

**3. Integration of Knowledge and Ideas** Using Nelson Mandela's speech as an example, explain how the audience for a speech can change over time.

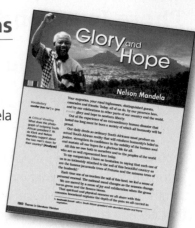

## Reading Skill: Compare and Contrast

**4. (a)** Use a chart like the one shown to record the ideas Nelson Mandela presents about the past, present, and future.

| Past | Present | Future |
|------|---------|--------|
|      |         |        |

**(b)** Explain the point that Nelson Mandela makes by **comparing and contrasting** his ideas about the past, present, and future.

## Vocabulary

**Acquisition and Use** Indicate whether each statement is *True* or *False*. Explain your answers. Then, revise any sentences that are false to make them true.

**1.** A signature serves to *confer* authenticity to a document.

**2.** A *pernicious* idea is always welcome at a team meeting.

**3.** Each party in a *covenant* hopes that the other party will break it.

**4.** A *distinguished* guest is well-known to many people.

**5.** If you're *intimately* involved in an event, you know little about it.

**6.** If you make a *reconciliation* with a friend with whom you've quarreled, you might sit down together and talk things through.

**Word Study** Use the context of the sentences and what you know about the **Latin root -fer-** to explain your answer to each question.

**1.** Does an unhappy and *vociferous* shopper complain quietly?

**2.** Why might an employer ask for a *referral* from a teacher?

### Word Study

The **Latin root -fer-** means "carry" or "produce."

**Apply It** Explain how the root -fer- contributes to the meanings of these words. Consult a dictionary if necessary.

ferry
fertile
transfer

# Integrated Language Skills

## There Is a Longing • Glory and Hope

### Conventions: Colons, Semicolons, and Ellipsis Points

Punctuation helps a writer clarify the meaning of a sentence.

A **colon** is used mainly to list items following an independent clause. A **semicolon** is used to join independent clauses that are closely related. A semicolon is also used to separate independent clauses or items in a series that already contain several commas.

**Ellipsis points** (. . .) are punctuation marks that show that something has not been expressed. Ellipsis points usually indicate one of the following:

- words that have been left out of a quotation
- a series that continues beyond the items mentioned
- time passing or action occurring in a narrative

| Colon | Semicolon | Ellipsis Points |
|---|---|---|
| The flowers seemed human: nodding, bending, dancing. | The teacher lifted the desk herself; the sight greatly impressed the students. | He struck out... but the end of the game would surprise them all. |

**Practice A** Explain the use of the colon, semicolon, or ellipsis points in each sentence.

1. Chief Dan George was a chief; he wanted to lead his people to a better future.

2. "I am a chief," he said, "but . . . the only weapon left to me is speech."

3. Chief Dan George expected great things for his people: education, participation in government, and freedom.

4. He spoke softly . . . and quietly sat down.

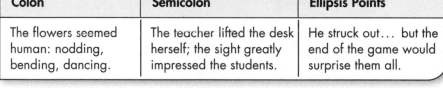 **Writing Application** Write three sentences about the opening image of "There Is a Longing." Use a colon, semicolon, and ellipsis points in your sentences.

**Practice B** Copy these sentences, adding colons, semicolons, or ellipsis points wherever necessary.

1. Nelson Mandela talked of the past, talked of the celebration in the present, and talked of.

2. Mandela had spent years working for liberty the years had brought him to this moment.

3. He wanted many things for his country justice, peace, work, and food for all.

4. The work was long the goal was liberty they celebrated the achievement.

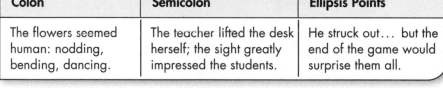 **Writing Application** Write three sentences about Nelson Mandela's facial and bodily expressions in the opening image of "Glory and Hope." Use a colon, semicolon, and ellipsis points in your writing.

**PH WRITING COACH** Further instruction and practice are available in *Prentice Hall Writing Coach*.

# Writing

**Common Core State Standards**

L.9-10.2; W.9-10.2,
W.9-10.2.b, W.9-10.2.e;
SL.9-10.1.a, SL.9-10.1.c
[For the full wording of the standards, see page 1192.]

**Informative Text** Write a **letter** to the author of the speech you read expressing what you found most inspiring.

- List words that describe how the speech makes you feel. Next to each word, write the line or lines that evoke that emotion.

- Tell the author why you are writing and why you think the speech has a message for *all* readers.

- As you draft, use a friendly yet respectful tone, and maintain focus throughout your letter.

- Use formal business letter format. *(For an example, see page R34.)*

**Grammar Application** Make sure you have used colons, semicolons, and ellipsis points properly in your letter.

**Writing Workshop:** *Work in Progress*

**Prewriting for Comparison and Contrast** Review the Comparison List in your writing portfolio. Think about the two places you have listed. Next, jot down emotions you connect with each one. Then, use a Venn diagram to compare and contrast the two places. Save your Comparison work.

Use this prewriting activity to prepare for the **Writing Workshop** on page 1234.

# Speaking and Listening

**Comprehension and Collaboration** In a group, hold a **panel discussion** to talk about the kind of world you hope future generations will enjoy. Keep in mind the issues that the speech you read addresses. Consider these tips:

- In order to discuss the issues in greater depth with other panel members, review the speech you read and note the key points the author makes.

- Using note cards, jot down the key ideas and important details from the speech you read.

- Use your note cards to help you respond to questions and convey details that you wish to share, such as key points from the speech or memorable lines.

- During the discussion, show respect for everyone's opinions and speak in turn.

When the discussion ends, analyze the process to decide how to improve future discussions.

**www.PHLitOnline.com**
- Interactive graphic organizers
- Grammar tutorial
- Interactive journals

# Test Practice: Reading

## Compare and Contrast

### Fiction Selection

**Directions:** *Read the selection. Then, answer the questions.*

Ron and Chris both smiled as they entered the student council meeting. Each one was sure he had the best idea for the school's charity fundraiser. Chris, guitarist for the school's most popular band, spoke first. "We should have a Hawaiian-style luau! We can have food and hula dancing, and I can play Hawaiian music on my guitar. It will be great!"

Ron, the captain of the basketball team, spoke next. "That sounds like fun, but everyone knows that people in this town love basketball more than anything else. We should challenge the other school in town to a basketball game for charity."

"Maybe we can do both," Chris replied. "We can have the basketball game, and then invite people to stay afterward for the luau. We can even give a preview of the music and dancing at halftime during the game."

"Great idea! I have a perfect name for the event," said Ron, grinning. Then they both said together, "Hula Hoops for Charity!"

**1.** What common goal do Chris and Ron have at the beginning of the passage?

   **A.** They both want to raise money for charity.
   **B.** They both want to organize a luau.
   **C.** They both want to organize a basketball game.
   **D.** They both want the same name for the charity event.

**2.** In which of the following ways are Chris and Ron *different*?

   **A.** Chris is a musician and Ron is a basketball player.
   **B.** Chris wants to hold a charity fundraiser and Ron does not.
   **C.** Chris is a member of the student council and Ron is not.
   **D.** Chris cares more than Ron about the charity fundraiser.

**3.** Based on the details in this passage, one way that Chris and Ron are *similar* is that their—

   **A.** schoolwork is not difficult for them.
   **B.** plans will not require any organization.
   **C.** interests influence their fundraising ideas.
   **D.** popularity is very important to them.

**4.** Which of the following statements about Chris and Ron's original ideas is *not* true?

   **A.** Chris wants to organize a luau.
   **B.** Ron wants to organize a basketball game.
   **C.** Both boys think that a luau would be fun.
   **D.** Both boys dislike each other's ideas.

## Writing for Assessment

In a paragraph, explain why you think Chris and Ron started out with different ideas but were able to agree in the end. Support your answer with details from the passage.

## Nonfiction Selection

**Directions:** *Read the selection. Then, answer the questions.*

In 1796, the United States faced a challenge. George Washington had been the clear choice to be the first president of the young nation. Now, after two terms in office, the popular president was retiring. America had to elect a new president. The two leading candidates were Thomas Jefferson and John Adams. Jefferson was tall, thin, and soft-spoken. Adams was short and stocky, and loved to argue. The two men had worked closely together in the cause for American independence. They had formed a strong friendship, but it had been strained in recent years by political differences. Adams was from the North and favored industry and a strong central government. Jefferson was from the South and favored farming and strong state governments. The vote between the two candidates was close, but Adams was elected president. According to the Constitution at that time, Jefferson—who received the second highest number of votes—was to be made vice president. Although Adams and Jefferson had different visions for the country, they knew they would have to put aside their differences and work together for the good of the nation they had helped to found.

**1.** Which of the following statements about Adams and Jefferson is *true*?

A. They had the same views on government.
B. They wanted America to be successful.
C. They were both tall.
D. They were both from the North.

**2.** Which detail conveys Adams's and Jefferson's different visions for the United States?

A. Adams craved power and Jefferson did not.
B. Jefferson wanted to carry out Washington's vision; Adams did not.
C. Adams favored strong central government; Jefferson favored state government.
D. Adams believed in a strong military; Jefferson supported farming.

**3.** Why was it especially important for the two men to look beyond their differences?

A. Both men ran for president.
B. The nation had just been created.
C. Both men were friends with Washington.
D. Jefferson had to be Adams's vice president.

**4.** Which statement *contrasts* the two men?

A. Adams favored industry, while Jefferson favored farming.
B. Both were for strong central government.
C. Jefferson and Adams worked together for American independence.
D. Adams and Jefferson served as president and vice president, respectively.

## Writing for Assessment

**Connecting Across Texts**
How is the relationship between Adams and Jefferson similar to the relationship between Chris and Ron? Which one is more complex? Write an essay in which you explain your answer using details from both passages.

www.PHLitOnline.com
• Online practice
• Instant feedback

# Reading for Information

## Analyzing Expository Texts

### News Article

### Online Posting

**Common Core State Standards**

**Reading Informational Text**
**6.** Determine an author's point of view or purpose in a text and analyze how an author uses rhetoric to advance that point of view or purpose.

**Writing**
**2.b.** Develop the topic with well-chosen, relevant, and sufficient facts, extended definitions, concrete details, quotations, or other information and examples appropriate to the audience's knowledge of the topic. *(Timed Writing)*

**Language**
**4.b.** Identify and correctly use patterns of word changes that indicate different meanings or parts of speech.
**4.c.** Consult general and specialized reference materials, both print and digital, to find the pronunciation of a word or determine or clarify its precise meaning, its part of speech, or its etymology.

## Reading Skill: Analyze Primary Sources

A **primary source** is a firsthand account of events or experiences. Unlike a secondary source, in which a person describes events from an outside perspective, a primary source presents information from the perspective of someone with immediate knowledge of the events. The writer's beliefs and attitudes—his or her point of view—will usually inform the ideas, emotions, and reactions he or she describes.

Use these questions to help you **analyze** each author's point of view or perspective and extend the ideas they present:

---

**Questions for Analyzing Primary Sources**

- How was the writer or speaker involved in the events he or she describes?
- Is the account biased or neutral?
- What is the writer or speaker's tone, or attitude, toward the topic?
- What details are included, and what details may have been left out?
- What additional information about this topic might be available from other sources?

---

### Content-Area Vocabulary

These words appear in the selections that follow. You may also encounter them in other content-area texts.

- **debut** (dā byōō) *n.* first appearance before the public as a performer or player
- **pedagogical** (ped´ ə goj´ ə kəl, ped´ ə gō´ jə kəl) *adj.* relating to teaching or educational methods
- **contemporary** (kən tem´ pə rer´ ē) *adj.* belonging to or living in the same period of time

# Dodgers Celebrate Jackie Robinson Day

by John Nadel
*Associated Press*
Sports Writer

News Article

**Features:**

- information about a current event or issue
- photos and captions
- quotes from participants in the events
- text written for a general audience

AP Photo/Jeff Lewis

The Los Angeles Dodgers, all wearing No. 42 in honor of Jackie Robinson, line up before the baseball game against the San Diego Padres on Jackie Robinson Day, Sunday, April 15, 2007, in Los Angeles. Robinson broke major league baseball's color barrier on April 15, 1947, with the Brooklyn Dodgers, and the sport celebrated the 60th anniversary of his debut.

LOS ANGELES

Apr. 16, 2007—No. 42 was everywhere for the Los Angeles Dodgers. Scampering around the bases, knocking hits to all fields, and coming away with an easy victory. The Dodgers did all they could to honor Jackie Robinson on the 60th anniversary of his major league debut before and during the game.

Robinson broke major league baseball's color barrier on April 15, 1947, with the Brooklyn Dodgers, and the sport celebrated the anniversary throughout the country Sunday, when more than 200 players, managers and coaches wore No. 42 in his honor.

Included in that total was every member of the Dodgers.

"I think it was special for everybody to put No. 42 on," said Russell Martin, who had three hits, three runs scored, two RBIs and a stolen base. "We had a blast out there today. There was a little added pressure wearing that number."

The Dodgers stole five bases, their most in a game since Aug. 23, 1999, when they stole seven in a game at Milwaukee in a 9–3 victory over San Diego on Sunday night.

"It seems like there were a lot of Jackies out there," Martin said, referring to Robinson's base-stealing ability.

The national celebration of Jackie Robinson Day was centered at Dodger Stadium, not far from where Robinson grew up in Pasadena. He would become the first athlete to earn letters in four sports at UCLA, and he served in the U.S. Army during World War II before making his debut with the Dodgers at age 27.

"The whole team wearing No. 42, it kind of goes sour if we don't win," winning pitcher Randy Wolf said. "It was great. There were a lot of special people here. It's a special day and I think they did it right."

Martin grew up in Montreal hearing about Robinson from his father, a 62-year-old African Canadian.

"Jackie Robinson is one of my dad's favorite baseball players, and I probably learned a lot about him just by hearing stories my dad told me about him. My dad's a good storyteller, so I just used to sit there while he told me stories about Jackie and how he played, how good a baseball player he was, and how fast he was...."

The many quotations in this primary source support the author's topic. You might extend the ideas in this quotation by finding out the specifics of Jackie Robinson's career.

Before the game, commissioner Bud Selig called Robinson an American hero.

"I've often said that baseball's most powerful moment in its really terrific history was Jackie Robinson's coming into baseball," Selig said. "It's an incredible story not just for baseball, but for society."

> This primary source includes facts, statistics, and detailed information.

Hank Aaron and Frank Robinson threw out ceremonial first pitches, and fellow Hall of Famers Joe Morgan and Dave Winfield were on hand, joined by actors Courtney B. Vance and Marlon Wayans. Academy Award winner Jennifer Hudson sang "The Star-Spangled Banner."

Adding a personal touch were Robinson's widow, Rachel, and two Dodgers who knew him. Broadcaster Vin Scully paid tribute to Rachel Robinson, and Don Newcombe, Robinson's former teammate and a longtime Dodgers executive, looked on.

San Diego's Mike Cameron, who also wore No. 42, said this was a day he'd never forget.

"It was a pretty special moment to have all of the household names here, all of the Hall of Famers, and to get a chance to go out and play in probably one of the biggest games that I'll play in this year besides going to the playoffs," he said.

Padres pitcher Chris Young (1-1), making his first start since signing a four-year, $14.5 million contract, allowed five runs in two-plus innings, and it would have been worse had Kevin Cameron not worked out of a bases-loaded, no-out jam in the third.

"I was terrible," Young said. "I just never found my rhythm and never found my groove. I put the guys in a hole early in the game and it was just too much to overcome."

Young wrote about Robinson for his 2002 Princeton thesis, and said that in doing the work, he learned a tremendous respect and appreciation for the former Dodgers' star.

"I can't imagine, having to go through that, the courage it took, the discipline, and just how successful he was," said Young, a 27-year-old right-hander from Dallas. "I mean, he wasn't just successful integrating the game. He was a great baseball player. He's a Hall of Fame baseball player. He wouldn't allow himself to fail, and that's tremendous."

Selig presented Mrs. Robinson with the Commissioner's Historic Achievement Award for her work with the Jackie Robinson Foundation, formed in 1973 to raise scholarship money for qualified minorities. Robinson died in October 1972 at age 53.

> Rachel Robinson, Jackie's widow, works with the Jackie Robinson Foundation. You might extend the ideas presented here by visiting the Jackie Robinson Foundation Web site.

"She's made an enormous impact on our sport," Selig said. "We are an institution with enormous social responsibilities. She keeps us focused on that."

Robinson retired following the 1956 season after the Dodgers traded him to the rival Giants and was elected to the Hall of Fame in 1962.

His impact has been lasting. Mrs. Robinson said 1,100 scholarship students have graduated from college and 266 are presently in school.

"We needed to find a way to hold onto him," Mrs. Robinson said of her late husband. "Jack's legacy is all over the place."

Online Posting

**Features:**

- the personal experiences of the author
- information about events presented from the perspective of the author
- informal text written for an audience with a specific interest

# The Academy of American Poets

## *Emily Dickinson Poetfans:*
### *Sharyn Moore and her students*

The author gives a first-hand account of her experiences as a teacher, indicating that this text is a primary source.

Finding poetry and a poet for college-bound international students is a **pedagogical** puzzle. Do I want someone funny, someone simple? Do I want symbolism, metaphor, rhythm, or clarity? Do I need someone **contemporary**; someone who will relate to these young adults from Japan, Brazil, Italy, or Saudi Arabia?

Emily Dickinson. Her verses are short; use symbolism; present idioms and vocabulary that can be guessed in context; set an obtainable challenge to meaning and contemporary application; and, surprisingly enough, are accessible to our multi-national student body.

For an elective course entitled "Here's Hollywood," ("Fame is a fickle food / Upon a shifting plate...") idiom, metaphor and new vocabulary lead to discussion, contemporary analogies and the realization, "I can understand poetry, in English!"

An advanced level reading of a news magazine article on war and its victims ("Hope is the thing with feathers / That perches in the soul…") leads to a commitment on the part of the students to practice peace and hold hope….

Miss Dickinson's poetry has been used for dictation, vocabulary, grammar analysis, discussion, debate, journal entries, essays, film tie-ins, and, most of all, has made amazing contributions to cross-cultural understanding and global connections. Take an American woman of letters, apply her verse to issues in current culture, and global youth begin to talk about fame, hope, and death. What educator could help but be an ardent fan?

*Sharyn Moore*
*Santa Monica, California*

## Comparing Expository Texts

 **1. Key Ideas and Details** **(a) Analyze primary sources** by describing how the authors of the article and the posting were involved in the events they describe. **(b)** What underlying attitudes and values, or points of view, does each author bring to the writing? **(c)** Which specific words and phrases best reflect the authors' points of view toward their subjects? Explain your choices.

### Content-Area Vocabulary

**2. (a)** Consider the words *pedagogic* and *pedagogical*. Explain how a change in suffix alters the meaning and part of speech of the base word *pedagogy*. If necessary, consult a dictionary for help. **(b)** Use each word in a sentence that shows its meaning.

## Timed Writing

### Explanatory Text: Expository Essay

> **Format**
> The prompt directs you to write an expository essay. Therefore, your writing should present information or discuss ideas.

Using information from the news article, write an expository essay in which you discuss the significance of Jackie Robinson's contributions to baseball and to the lives of his fans. Support your ideas with details and examples from the text. (40 minutes)

> **Academic Vocabulary**
> When you *discuss* a subject in an essay, you write about various aspects of that subject in detail.

### 5-Minute Planner

Complete these steps before you begin to write:

1. Read the prompt carefully and completely.

2. Develop the topic by reviewing the news article to find details and make notes about Jackie Robinson's accomplishments and their impact on baseball and on people's lives. Organize your supporting details cohesively, using transitions to link the facts and examples you choose to include.
   **TIP** Look for firsthand testimonies in which people describe how Jackie Robinson's achievements affected them personally.

3. Extend ideas presented in the news article by considering how Jackie Robinson's accomplishments might have affected the lives of people beyond those mentioned in the news article. Provide a concluding statement that supports the ideas in your essay. Make a quick list of your ideas.

4. Use your notes and your list to create a rough outline. Then, use your outline to help you organize and write your essay.

# Comparing Literary Works

## Comparing Tall Tale and Myth

A **tall tale** is a type of folk tale that is characterized by *hyperbole*, or overstatement. Tall tales usually contain larger-than-life heroes, far-fetched situations, amazing feats, and a great deal of humor. Tall tales are a kind of legend, a traditional story about the past that is often based on historical fact. Many tall tales come from the American frontier and reflect the ideas of that period. The purpose of a tall tale is to entertain readers and audiences.

A **myth** is an ancient story that is intended to explain the actions of gods or human heroes, the reasons for certain traditions, or the causes of natural features and events. Every culture has its own collection of myths, or mythology. Originally religious in nature, myths often express the central values of the people who created them.

In general, tall tales describe how humans make things happen on their own, while myths tell how gods shape human life. These qualities are reflected in the types of **heroes** featured in the two forms. Mythic heroes have the following attributes:

- Divine parents and supernatural aid
- Special knowledge or weapons
- Ability to achieve impossible tasks

By contrast, the heroes in tall tales are outsized, but nevertheless human. They are able to perform amazing feats because of their great size, strength, cleverness, or sheer force of will.

**Cultural Values** Both forms are deeply rooted in the oral tradition and express the values of the cultures in which they developed. Modern authors Harold W. Felton and Edith Hamilton honor these origins as they draw upon source material and make it their own. "Pecos Bill and the Cyclone" is told in the energetic American tall-tale tradition, full of bold, unexplained impossibility. "Perseus" is told in the classic tradition of the Greek myths. As you read, use a chart like the one shown to compare and contrast the heroes in these selections.

### Common Core State Standards

**Reading Literature**

**7.** Analyze the representation of a subject or a key scene in two different artistic mediums.

**9.** Analyze how an author draws on and transforms source material in a specific work.

**Writing**

**2.** Write informative/explanatory texts to examine and convey complex ideas, concepts, and information clearly and accurately.

**2.a.** Introduce a topic; organize complex ideas, concepts, and information to make important connections and distinctions.

|  | Human or partly divine? | Performs amazing feats? | Receives divine aid? | Story has humor and exaggeration? |
|---|---|---|---|---|
| **Pecos Bill** |  |  |  |  |
| **Perseus** |  |  |  |  |

www.PHLitOnline.com

- Vocabulary flashcards
- Interactive journals
- More about the authors
- Selection audio
- Interactive graphic organizers

# Do *heroes* have responsibilities?

## Writing About the Big Question

Both these selections present larger-than-life heroes who must face certain danger. Use this sentence starter to develop your ideas about the Big Question.

The level of danger in a situation is/is not important when assessing heroism because _____

For someone to be heroic, his or her intentions must be _____.

# Meet the Authors

## Harold W. Felton (1902–1991)

### Author of "Pecos Bill: The Cyclone"

Harold William Felton practiced law and worked for the Internal Revenue Service, but over the years, he became increasingly interested in the legends and folklore of the United States.

**Collector and Reteller** Felton published collections of stories about folk heroes and the cowboys of the West. His book *Legends of Paul Bunyan* contains more than one hundred folk tales about the great logger.

## Edith Hamilton (1867–1963)

### Author of "Perseus"

Edith Hamilton was a groundbreaking educator who helped found the Bryn Mawr School in Baltimore, the first college preparatory school for women. She taught a generation of young women not to limit their goals simply because they were not men.

**Modern Woman, Ancient Tales** After leaving Bryn Mawr, Hamilton began writing articles about ancient Greece, which she later turned into a book entitled *The Greek Way* (1930). Her other books include *The Roman Way* (1932) and *Mythology* (1942), which are both beautifully crafted retellings of the Greek myths.

# PECOS BILL

## THE CYCLONE

### HAROLD W. FELTON

**Literary Analysis**

**Tall Tale and Myth**
Which description in the first paragraph contains hyperbole?

One of Bill's greatest feats, if not the greatest feat of all time, occurred unexpectedly one Fourth of July. He had invented the Fourth of July some years before. It was a great day for the cowpunchers.[1] They had taken to it right off like the real Americans they were. But the celebration had always ended on a dismal note. Somehow it seemed to be spoiled by a cyclone.

---

1. **cowpunchers** (koʊ´ pun´ chərz) *n.* cowboys.

Bill had never minded the cyclone much. The truth is he rather liked it. But the other celebrants ran into caves for safety. He invented cyclone cellars for them. He even named the cellars. He called them "'fraid holes." Pecos wouldn't even say the word "afraid." The cyclone was something like he was. It was big and strong too. He always stood by musing pleasantly as he watched it.

The cyclone caused Bill some trouble, though. Usually it would destroy a few hundred miles of fence by blowing the postholes away. But it wasn't much trouble for him to fix it. All he had to do was to go and get the postholes and then take them back and put the fence posts in them. The holes were rarely ever blown more than twenty or thirty miles.

In one respect Bill even welcomed the cyclone, for it blew so hard it blew the earth away from his wells. The first time this happened, he thought the wells would be a total loss. There they were, sticking up several hundred feet out of the ground. As wells they were useless. But he found he could cut them up into lengths and sell them for postholes to farmers in Iowa and Nebraska. It was very profitable, especially after he invented a special posthole saw to cut them with. He didn't use that type of posthole himself. He got the prairie dogs to dig his for him. He simply caught a few gross[2] of prairie dogs and set them down at proper intervals. The prairie dog would dig a hole. Then Bill would put a post in it. The prairie dog would get disgusted and go down the row ahead of the others and dig another hole. Bill fenced all of Texas and parts of New Mexico and Arizona in this manner. He took a few contracts and fenced most of the Southern Pacific right of way too. That's the reason it is so crooked. He had trouble getting the prairie dogs to run a straight fence.

As for his wells, the badgers dug them. The system was the same as with the prairie dogs. The labor was cheap so it didn't make much difference if the cyclone did spoil some of the wells. The badgers were digging all of the time anyway. They didn't seem to care whether they dug wells or just badger holes.

One year he tried shipping the prairie dog holes up north, too, for postholes. It was not successful. They didn't keep in storage and they couldn't stand the handling in shipping. After they were installed they seemed to wear out quickly. Bill always thought the difference in climate had something to do with it.

---

2. **gross** (grōs) *n.* twelve dozen.

◀ **Critical Viewing**
Which details in this image suggest that this selection is a tall tale? Explain. **[Analyze]**

**Literary Analysis**
**Tall Tale and Myth**
Which realistic details here add humor?

Reading Check

Where does Pecos Bill get the postholes he sells to farmers in Iowa and Nebraska?

**Literary Analysis**
**Tall Tale and Myth**
Which details give this
tall tale a particularly
American flavor?

It should be said that in those days there was only one cyclone. It was the first and original cyclone, bigger and more terrible by far than the small cyclones of today. It usually stayed by itself up north around Kansas and Oklahoma and didn't bother anyone much. But it was attracted by the noise of the Fourth of July celebration and without fail managed to put in an appearance before the close of the day.

On this particular Fourth of July, the celebration had gone off fine. The speeches were loud and long. The contests and games were hard fought. The high point of the day was Bill's exhibition with Widow Maker, which came right after he showed off Scat and Rat.[3] People seemed never to tire of seeing them in action. The mountain lion was almost useless as a work animal after his accident, and the snake had grown old and somewhat infirm, and was troubled with rheumatism in his rattles. But they too enjoyed the Fourth of July and liked to make a public appearance. They relived the old days.

Widow Maker had put on a good show, bucking as no ordinary horse could ever buck. Then Bill undertook to show the gaits[4] he had taught the palomino.[5] Other mustangs at that time had only two gaits. Walking and running. Only Widow Maker could pace. But now Bill had developed and taught him other gaits. Twenty-seven in all. Twenty-three forward and three reverse. He was very proud of the achievement. He showed off the slow gaits and the crowd was eager for more.

He showed the walk, trot, canter, lope, jog, slow rack, fast rack, single foot, pace, stepping pace, fox trot, running walk and the others now known. Both men and horses confuse the various gaits nowadays. Some of the gaits are now thought to be the same, such as the rack and the single foot. But with Widow Maker and Pecos Bill, each one was different. Each was precise and to be distinguished from the others. No one had ever imagined such a thing.

Then the cyclone came! All of the people except Bill ran into the 'fraid holes. Bill was annoyed. He stopped the performance. The remaining gaits were not shown. From that day to this horses have used no more than the gaits Widow Maker exhibited that day. It is unfortunate that the really fast gaits were not shown. If they were, horses might be much faster today than they are.

Bill glanced up at the cyclone and the quiet smile on his face faded into a frown. He saw the cyclone was angry. Very, very angry indeed.

---

3. **Widow Maker . . . Scat and Rat.** Widow Maker is a mustang, a type of wild horse. Scat is Bill's mountain lion, and Rat is Bill's pet rattlesnake.
4. **gaits** (gāts) *n.* foot movements of a horse.
5. **palomino** (pal′ ə mē′ nō) *n.* golden-tan or cream-colored horse that has a white, silver, or ivory tail and, often, white spots on the face and legs.

The cyclone had always been the center of attention. Everywhere it went people would look up in wonder, fear and amazement. It had been the undisputed master of the country. It had observed Bill's rapid climb to fame and had seen the Fourth of July celebration grow. It had been keeping an eye on things all right.

In the beginning, the Fourth of July crowd had aroused its curiosity. It liked nothing more than to show its superiority and power by breaking the crowd up sometime during the day. But every year the crowd was larger. This preyed on the cyclone's mind. This year it did not come to watch. It deliberately came to spoil the celebration. Jealous of Bill and of his success, it resolved to do away with the whole institution of the Fourth of July once and for all. So much havoc and destruction would be wrought that there would never be another Independence Day Celebration. On that day, in future years, it would circle around the horizon leering and gloating. At least, so it thought.

The cyclone was resolved, also, to do away with this bold fellow who did not hold it in awe and run for the 'fraid hole at its approach. For untold years it had been the most powerful thing in the land. And now, here was a mere man who threatened its position. More! Who had usurped its position!

When Bill looked at the horizon and saw the cyclone coming, he recognized the anger and rage. While a cyclone does not often smile, Bill had felt from the beginning that it was just a grouchy fellow who never had a pleasant word for anyone. But now, instead of merely an unpleasant character, Bill saw all the viciousness of which an angry cyclone is capable. He had no way of knowing that the cyclone saw its kingship tottering and was determined to stop this man who threatened its supremacy.

But Bill understood the violence of the onslaught even as the monster came into view. He knew he must meet it. The center of the cyclone was larger than ever before. The fact is, the cyclone had been training for this fight all winter and spring. It was in best form and at top weight. It headed straight for Bill intent on his destruction. In an instant it was upon him. Bill had sat quietly and silently on the great pacing mustang. But his mind was working rapidly. In the split second between his first sight of the monster and the time for action he had made his plans. Pecos Bill was ready! Ready and waiting!

Green clouds were dripping from the cyclone's jaws. Lightning flashed from its eyes as it swept down upon him. Its plan was to envelop Bill in one mighty grasp. Just as it was upon him, Bill turned Widow Maker to its left. This was a clever move for the cyclone was right-handed, and while it had been training hard to

**Spiral Review**
**Universal Theme**
Why do you think that the cyclone is given human characteristics in this tale?

Reading Check
Why is the cyclone angry with Bill?

## Science Connection

### Cyclones

A cyclone is an area of rapidly spinning winds that is associated with severe thunderstorms. The rotating winds can reach speeds of 250 miles per hour and are capable of lifting even very heavy objects into the column of circulating air. Cyclones develop when warm and cold masses of air collide, causing abrupt changes in wind speed and direction. Cyclones that were over a mile wide and that have spread damage along a fifty-mile path have been recorded. Unlike Pecos Bill, most people are smart enough to take shelter underground when they see a cyclone coming.

### Connect to the Literature

Why might a literary character like Bill be especially beloved by people who live in areas affected by cyclones?

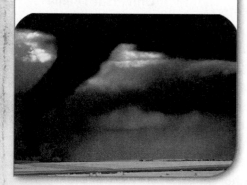

get its left in shape, that was not its best side. Bill gave rein to his mount. Widow Maker wheeled and turned on a dime which Pecos had, with great foresight and accuracy, thrown to the ground to mark the exact spot for this maneuver. It was the first time that anyone had thought of turning on a dime. Then he urged the great horse forward. The cyclone, filled with surprise, lost its balance and rushed forward at an increased speed. It went so fast that it met itself coming back. This confused the cyclone, but it did not confuse Pecos Bill. He had expected that to happen. Widow Maker went into his twenty-first gait and edged up close to the whirlwind. Soon they were running neck and neck.

At the proper instant Bill grabbed the cyclone's ears, kicked himself free of the stirrups and pulled himself lightly on its back. Bill never used spurs on Widow Maker. Sometimes he wore them for show and because he liked the jingling sound they made. They made a nice accompaniment for his cowboy songs. But he had not been singing, so he had no spurs. He did not have his rattlesnake for a quirt.[6] Of course there was no bridle. It was man against monster! There he was! Pecos Bill astride a raging cyclone, slick heeled and without a saddle!

The cyclone was taken by surprise at this sudden turn of events. But it was undaunted. It was sure of itself. Months of training had given it a conviction that it was invincible. With a mighty heave, it twisted to its full height. Then it fell back suddenly, twisting and turning violently, so that before it came back to earth, it had turned around a thousand times. Surely no rider could ever withstand such an attack. No rider ever had. Little wonder. No one had ever ridden a cyclone before. But Pecos Bill did! He fanned the tornado's ears with his hat and dug his heels into the demon's flanks and yelled, "Yipee-ee!"

The people who had run for shelter began to come out. The audience further enraged the cyclone. It was bad enough to be disgraced by having a man astride it. It was unbearable not to have thrown him. To have all the people see the failure was too much! It got down flat on the ground and rolled over and over. Bill retained his seat throughout this ruse. Evidence of this desperate but futile stratagem[7] remains today. The great Staked Plains, or as the Mexicans call it, Llano Estacado is

---

**6. quirt** (kwʉrt) *n.* riding whip with a braided lash and a short handle.

**7. futile** (fyo͞ot´'l) **stratagem** (strat´ ə jəm) useless or hopeless plan.

the result. Its small, rugged mountains were covered with trees at the time. The rolling of the cyclone destroyed the mountains, the trees, and almost everything else in the area. The destruction was so complete, that part of the country is flat and treeless to this day. When the settlers came, there were no landmarks to guide them across the vast unmarked space, so they drove stakes in the ground to mark the trails. That is the reason it is called "Staked Plains." Here is an example of the proof of the events of history by careful and painstaking research. It is also an example of how seemingly inexplicable geographical facts can be explained.

It was far more dangerous for the rider when the cyclone shot straight up to the sky. Once there, the twister tried the same thing it had tried on the ground. It rolled on the sky. It was no use. Bill could not be unseated. He kept his place, and he didn't have a sky hook with him either.

As for Bill, he was having the time of his life, shouting at the top of his voice, kicking his opponent in the ribs and jabbing his thumb in its flanks. It responded and went on a wild bucking rampage over the entire West. It used all the bucking tricks known to the wildest broncos as well as those known only to cyclones. The wind howled furiously and beat against the fearless rider. The rain poured. The lightning flashed around his ears. The fight went on and on. Bill enjoyed himself immensely. In spite of the elements he easily kept his place. . . .

The raging cyclone saw this out of the corner of its eye. It knew then who the victor was. It was twisting far above the Rocky Mountains when the awful truth came to it. In a horrible heave it disintegrated! Small pieces of cyclone flew in all directions. Bill still kept his seat on the main central portion until that rained out from under him. Then he jumped to a nearby streak of lightning and slid down it toward earth. But it was raining so hard that the rain put out the lightning. When it fizzled out from under him, Bill dropped the rest of the way. He lit in what is now called Death Valley. He hit quite hard, as is apparent from the fact that he so compressed the place that it is still two hundred and seventy-six feet below sea level. The Grand Canyon was washed out by the rain, though it must be understood that this happened after Paul Bunyan had given it a good start by carelessly dragging his ax behind him when he went west a short time before.

The cyclones and the hurricanes and the tornadoes nowadays are the small pieces that broke off of the big cyclone Pecos Bill rode. In fact, the rainstorms of the present day came into being in the same way. There are always skeptics, but even they will recognize

**Literary Analysis**
**Tall Tale and Myth** In his encounter with the cyclone, which details show Bill's physical strength and lack of fear?

**Vocabulary**
**skeptics** (skep´ tiks) *n.* people who doubt accepted ideas

**Literary Analysis**
**Tall Tale and Myth** According to the tale, how does Bill create a natural phenomenon?

**Reading Check**
What unusual feat does Bill complete with the cyclone?

the logic of the proof of this event. They will recall that even now it almost always rains on the Fourth of July. That is because the rainstorms of today still retain some of the characteristics of the giant cyclone that met its comeuppance at the hands of Pecos Bill.

Bill lay where he landed and looked up at the sky, but he could see no sign of the cyclone. Then he laughed softly as he felt the warm sand of Death Valley on his back. . . .

It was a rough ride though, and Bill had resisted unusual tensions and pressures. When he got on the cyclone he had a twenty-dollar gold piece and a bowie knife in his pocket. The tremendous force of the cyclone was such that when he finished the ride he found that his pocket contained a plugged nickel[8] and a little pearl-handled penknife. His two giant six-shooters were compressed and transformed into a small water pistol and a popgun.

It is a strange circumstance that lesser men have monuments raised in their honor. Death Valley is Bill's monument. Sort of a monument in reverse. Sunk in his honor, you might say. Perhaps that is as it should be. After all, Bill was different. He made his own monument. He made it with his hips, as is evident from the great depth of the valley. That is the hard way.

**Literary Analysis**
**Tall Tale and Myth**
Which details in this paragraph are examples of humorous exaggeration?

---

8. **plugged nickel** fake nickel.

## Critical Thinking

Cite textual evidence to support your responses.

1. **Key Ideas and Details (a)** What term does Bill use to refer to the cyclone cellars? **(b) Interpret:** What do you learn about the character of Pecos Bill from his reaction to the cellars?

2. **Key Ideas and Details (a)** What word is Bill unwilling to say aloud? **(b) Draw Conclusions:** How does his resolve never to say this word explain, in part, why he is a folk hero?

3. **Key Ideas and Details (a) Interpret:** What are three human characteristics of the cyclone? **(b) Compare:** How does the cyclone resemble Pecos Bill himself?

4. **Integration of Knowledge and Ideas (a)** How does Pecos Bill ultimately show responsibility to his community? Explain.
   **(b)** Do you think Bill has a responsibility to use his special abilities to help his community, or can he choose not to? Explain. *[Connect to the Big Question: Do heroes have responsibilities?]*

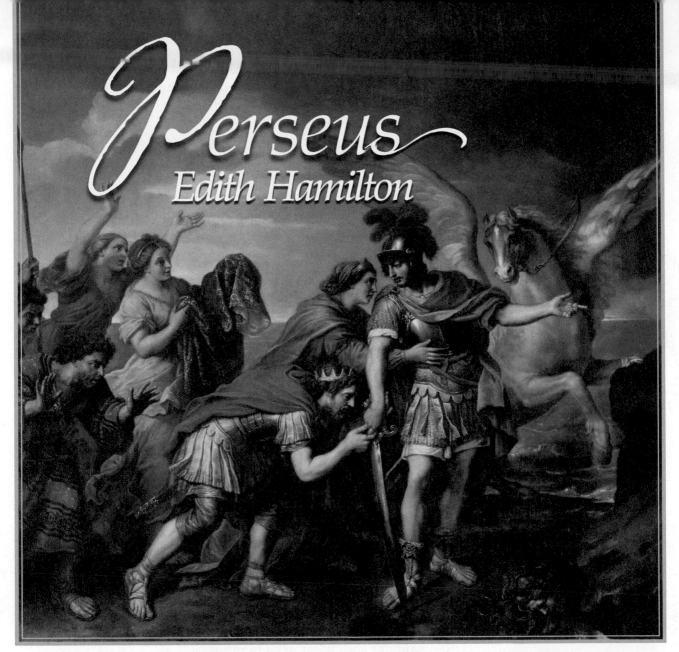

# Perseus
## Edith Hamilton

▲ **Critical Viewing**
The man with the sword is Perseus as an adult. Judging from this painting, how do you think others perceive him?
**[Interpret]**

King Acrisius [a kris´ ē əs] of Argos had only one child, a daughter, Danaë [dan´ ā ē]. She was beautiful above all the other women of the land, but this was small comfort to the King for not having a son. He journeyed to Delphi to ask the god if there was any hope that some day he would be the father of a boy. The priestess told him no, and added what was far worse: that his daughter would have a son who would kill him.

The only sure way to escape that fate was for the King to have Danaë instantly put to death—taking no chances, but seeing to it himself. This Acrisius would not do. His fatherly affection was not strong, as events proved, but his fear of the gods was. They visited with terrible punishment those who shed the blood of kindred.

Acrisius did not dare slay his daughter. Instead, he had a house built all of bronze and sunk underground, but with part of the roof open to the sky so that light and air could come through. Here he shut her up and guarded her.

> So Danaë endured, the beautiful,
> To change the glad daylight for brass-bound walls,
> And in that chamber secret as the grave
> She lived a prisoner. Yet to her came
> Zeus in the golden rain.

As she sat there through the long days and hours with nothing to do, nothing to see except the clouds moving by overhead, a mysterious thing happened, a shower of gold fell from the sky and filled her chamber. How it was revealed to her that it was Zeus who had visited her in this shape we are not told, but she knew that the child she bore was his son.

For a time she kept his birth secret from her father, but it became increasingly difficult to do so in the narrow limits of that bronze house and finally one day the little boy—his name was Perseus—was discovered by his grandfather. "Your child!" Acrisius cried in great anger. "Who is his father?" But when Danaë answered proudly, "Zeus," he would not believe her. One thing only he was sure of, that the boy's life was a terrible danger to his own. He was afraid to kill him for the same reason that had kept him from killing her, fear of Zeus and the Furies who pursue such murderers. But if he could not kill them outright, he could put them in the way of tolerably certain death. He had a great chest made, and the two placed in it. Then it was taken out to sea and cast into the water.

In that strange boat Danaë sat with her little son. The daylight faded and she was alone on the sea.

> When in the carven chest the winds and waves
> Struck fear into her heart she put her arms,
> Not without tears, round Perseus tenderly
> She said, "O son, what grief is mine.
> But you sleep softly, little child,
> Sunk deep in rest within your cheerless home,
> Only a box, brass-bound. The night, this darkness visible,
> The scudding waves so near to your soft curls,
> The shrill voice of the wind, you do not heed,
> Nestled in your red cloak, fair little face."

Through the night in the tossing chest she listened to the waters that seemed always about to wash over them. The dawn came, but with no comfort to her for she could not see it. Neither could she see that around them there were islands rising high above the sea, many islands. All she knew was that presently a wave seemed to lift

**Literary Analysis**
**Tall Tale and Myth**
Which elements of Perseus' story so far suggest that he will be a mythic hero?

them and carry them swiftly on and then, retreating, leave them on something solid and motionless. They had made land; they were safe from the sea, but they were still in the chest with no way to get out.

Fate willed it—or perhaps Zeus, who up to now had done little for his love and his child—that they should be discovered by a good man, a fisherman named Dictys. He came upon the great box and broke it open and took the pitiful cargo home to his wife who was as kind as he. They had no children and they cared for Danaë and Perseus as if they were their own. The two lived there many years, Danaë content to let her son follow the fisherman's humble trade, out of harm's way. But in the end more trouble came. Polydectes [pol i dek´ tēz], the ruler of the little island, was the brother of Dictys, but he was a cruel and ruthless man. He seems to have taken no notice of the mother and son for a long time, but at last Danaë attracted his attention. She was still radiantly beautiful even though Perseus by now was full grown, and Polydectes fell in love with her. He wanted her, but he did not want her son, and he set himself to think out a way of getting rid of him.

There were some fearsome monsters called Gorgons who lived on an island and were known far and wide because of their deadly power. Polydectes evidently talked to Perseus about them; he probably told him that he would rather have the head of one of them than anything else in the world. This seems practically certain from the plan he devised for killing Perseus. He announced that he was about to be married and he called his friends together for a celebration, including Perseus in the invitation. Each guest, as was customary, brought a gift for the bride-to-be, except Perseus alone. He had nothing he could give. He was young and proud and keenly mortified. He stood up before them all and did exactly what the King had hoped he would do, declared that he would give him a present better than any there. He would go off and kill Medusa and bring back her head as his gift. Nothing could have suited the King better. No one in his senses would have made such a proposal. Medusa was one of the Gorgons,

> And they are three, the Gorgons, each with wings
> And snaky hair, most horrible to mortals.
> Whom no man shall behold and draw again
> The breath of life,

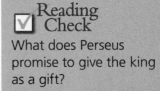

▲ **Critical Viewing**
Which scene in the story does this art illustrate?
**[Connect]**

**Vocabulary**
**mortified** (môrt´ ə f īd´) *adj.* extremely embarrassed

✓ Reading Check
What does Perseus promise to give the king as a gift?

for the reason that whoever looked at them were turned instantly into stone. It seemed that Perseus had been led by his angry pride into making an empty boast. No man unaided could kill Medusa.

But Perseus was saved from his folly. Two great gods were watching over him. He took ship as soon as he left the King's hall, not daring to see his mother first and tell her what he intended, and he sailed to Greece to learn where the three monsters were to be found. He went to Delphi, but all the priestess would say was to bid him seek the land where men eat not Demeter's golden grain, but only acorns. So he went to Dodona, in the land of oak trees, where the talking oaks were which declared Zeus's will and where the Selli lived who made their bread from acorns. They could tell him, however, no more than this, that he was under the protection of the gods. They did not know where the Gorgons lived.

When and how Hermes and Athena came to his help is not told in any story, but he must have known despair before they did so. At last, however, as he wandered on, he met a strange and beautiful person. We know what he looked like from many a poem, a young man with the first down upon his cheek when youth is loveliest, carrying, as no other young man ever did, a wand of gold with wings at one end, wearing a winged hat, too, and winged sandals. At sight of him hope must have entered Perseus' heart, for he would know that this could be none other than Hermes, the guide and the giver of good.

This radiant personage told him that before he attacked Medusa he must first be properly equipped, and that what he needed was in the possession of the nymphs of the North. To find the nymphs' abode, they must go to the Gray Women who alone could tell them the way. These women dwelt in a land where all was dim and shrouded in twilight. No ray of sun looked ever on that country, nor the moon by night. In that gray place the three women lived, all gray themselves and withered as in extreme old age. They were strange creatures, indeed, most of all because they had but one eye for the three, which it was their custom to take turns with, each removing it from her forehead when she had had it for a time and handing it to another.

All this Hermes told Perseus and then he unfolded his plan. He would himself guide Perseus to them. Once there Perseus must keep hidden until he saw one of them take the eye out of her forehead to pass it on. At that moment, when none of the three could see, he must rush forward and seize the eye and refuse to give it back until they told him how to reach the nymphs of the North.

He himself, Hermes said, would give him a sword to attack Medusa with—which could not be bent or broken by the Gorgon's scales, no matter how hard they were. This was a wonderful gift, no doubt, and yet of what use was a sword when the creature to be struck by it could turn the swordsman into stone before he was within striking distance? But another great deity was at hand to help. Pallas Athena stood beside Perseus. She took off the shield of polished bronze which covered her breast and held it out to him. "Look into this when you attack the Gorgon," she said. "You will be able to see her in it as in a mirror, and so avoid her deadly power."

Now, indeed, Perseus had good reason to hope. The journey to the twilight land was long, over the stream of Ocean and on to the very border of the black country where the Cimmerians dwell, but Hermes was his guide and he could not go astray. They found the Gray Women at last, looking in the wavering light like gray birds, for they had the shape of swans. But their heads were human and beneath their wings they had arms and hands. Perseus did just as Hermes had said, he held back until he saw one of them take the eye out of her forehead. Then before she could give it to her sister, he snatched it out of her hand. It was a moment or two before the three realized they had lost it. Each thought one of the others had it. But Perseus spoke out and told them he had taken it and that it would be theirs again only when they showed him how to find the nymphs of the North. They gave him full directions at once; they would have done anything to get their eye back. He returned it to them and went on the way they had pointed out to him. He was bound, although he did not know it, to the blessed country of the Hyperboreans [hī per bō´ rē anz], at the back of the North Wind, of which it is said: "Neither by ship nor yet by land shall one find the wondrous road to the gathering place of the Hyperboreans." But Perseus had Hermes with him, so that the road lay open to him, and he reached that host of happy people who are always banqueting and holding joyful revelry. They showed him great kindness: they welcomed him to their feast, and the maidens dancing to the sound of flute and lyre paused to get for him the

**Literary Analysis**
**Tall Tale and Myth**
Which details in this paragraph show Perseus' special status as a mythic hero?

**Literary Analysis**
**Tall Tale and Myth**
What heroic qualities does Perseus reveal in his encounter with the Gray Women?

**Vocabulary**
**revelry** (rev´ əl rē) *n.* noisy merrymaking

**Reading Check**
Who comes to Perseus' aid?

**Spiral Review**
**Universal Theme**
What is significant about the gifts Perseus receives?

**Literary Analysis**
**Tall Tale and Myth**
What special knowledge helps Perseus kill Medusa?

gifts he sought. These were three: winged sandals, a magic wallet which would always become the right size for whatever was to be carried in it, and, most important of all, a cap which made the wearer invisible. With these and Athena's shield and Hermes' sword Perseus was ready for the Gorgons. Hermes knew where they lived, and leaving the happy land the two flew back across Ocean and over the sea to the Terrible Sisters' island.

By great good fortune they were all asleep when Perseus found them. In the mirror of the bright shield he could see them clearly, creatures with great wings and bodies covered with golden scales and hair a mass of twisting snakes. Athena was beside him now as well as Hermes. They told him which one was Medusa and that was important, for she alone of the three could be killed; the other two were immortal. Perseus on his winged sandals hovered above them, looking, however, only at the shield. Then he aimed a stroke down at Medusa's throat and Athena guided his hand. With a single sweep of his sword he cut through her neck and, his eyes still fixed on the shield with never a glance at her, he swooped low enough to seize the head. He dropped it into the wallet which closed around it. He had nothing to fear from it now. But the two other Gorgons had awakened and, horrified at the sight of their sister slain, tried to pursue the slayer. Perseus was safe; he had on the cap of darkness and they could not find him.

> So over the sea rich-haired Danaë's son,
> Perseus, on his winged sandals sped,
> Flying swift as thought.
> In a wallet of silver,
> A wonder to behold,
> He bore the head of the monster,
> While Hermes, the son of Maia,
> The messenger of Zeus,
> Kept ever at his side.

On his way back he came to Ethiopia and alighted there. By this time Hermes had left him. Perseus found, as Hercules was later to find, that a lovely maiden had been given up to be devoured by a horrible sea serpent. Her name was Andromeda and she was the daughter of a silly vain woman,

> That starred Ethiop queen who strove
> To set her beauty's praise above
> The sea-nymphs, and their power offended.

She had boasted that she was more beautiful than the daughters of Nereus, the Sea-god. An absolutely certain way in those days to draw down on one a wretched fate was to claim superiority in anything over any deity[1]; nevertheless people were perpetually doing so. In this case the punishment for the arrogance the gods detested fell not on Queen Cassiopeia [kas´ ē ō pē´ ə], Andromeda's mother, but on her daughter. The Ethiopians were being devoured in numbers by the serpent; and, learning from the oracle that they could be freed from the pest only if Andromeda were offered up to it, they forced Cepheus [sē fəs], her father, to consent. When Perseus arrived the maiden was on a rocky ledge by the sea, chained there to wait for the coming of the monster. Perseus saw her and on the instant loved her. He waited beside her until the great snake came for its prey; then he cut its head off just as he had the Gorgon's. The headless body dropped back into the water; Perseus took Andromeda to her parents and asked for her hand, which they gladly gave him.

With her he sailed back to the island and his mother, but in the house where he had lived so long he found no one. The fisherman Dictys' wife was long since dead, and the two others, Danaë and the man who had been like a father to Perseus, had had to fly and hide themselves from Polydectes, who was furious at Danaë's refusal to marry him. They had taken refuge in a temple, Perseus was told. He learned also that the King was holding a banquet in the palace and all the men who favored him were gathered there. Perseus instantly saw his opportunity. He went straight to the palace and entered the hall. As he stood at the entrance, Athena's shining buckler on his breast, the silver wallet at his side, he drew the eyes of every man there. Then before any could look away he held up the Gorgon's head; and at the sight one and all, the cruel King and his servile courtiers, were turned into stone. There they sat, a row of statues, each, as it were, frozen stiff in the attitude he had struck when he first saw Perseus.

When the islanders knew themselves freed from the tyrant it was easy for Perseus to find Danaë and Dictys. He made Dictys king of the island, but he and his mother decided that they would go back with Andromeda to Greece and try to be reconciled to Acrisius, to

---

1. **deity** (dē´ ə tē) *n.* a god.

▲ **Analyze Representations** In what ways does this painting emphasize Perseus' physical strength and bravery? What other details in the myth are suggested in the painting? **[Interpret]**

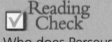

**Reading Check**
Who does Perseus rescue from the sea serpent?

see if the many years that had passed since he had put them in the chest had not softened him so that he would be glad to receive his daughter and grandson. When they reached Argos, however, they found that Acrisius had been driven away from the city, and where he was no one could say. It happened that soon after their arrival Perseus heard that the King of Larissa, in the North, was holding a great athletic contest, and he journeyed there to take part. In the discus-throwing when his turn came and he hurled the heavy missile, it swerved and fell among the spectators. Acrisius was there on a visit to the King, and the discus struck him. The blow was fatal and he died at once.

So Apollo's oracle was again proved true. If Perseus felt any grief, at least he knew that his grandfather had done his best to kill him and his mother. With his death their troubles came to an end. Perseus and Andromeda lived happily ever after. Their son, Electryon, was the grandfather of Hercules.

Medusa's head was given to Athena, who bore it always upon the aegis, Zeus's shield, which she carried for him.

**Literary Analysis**
**Tall Tale and Myth**
How do the events at the end of the story relate to situations described at the beginning?

## Critical Thinking

Cite textual evidence to support your responses.

ⓒ 1. **Key Ideas and Details** **(a)** Why does Perseus set out to kill Medusa? **(b) Infer:** What detail of Perseus' background might have led Athena and Hermes to help Perseus in his quest?

ⓒ 2. **Key Ideas and Details** **(a) Summarize:** Explain the weapons Perseus uses and the actions he takes to kill Medusa.
**(b) Hypothesize:** What might have happened to Perseus if he had not received help from the gods?

ⓒ 3. **Integration of Knowledge and Ideas** **(a) Interpret:** What lesson do you think this ancient myth taught its first audiences?
**(b) Extend:** In what ways is this myth still relevant today? Explain.

ⓒ 4. **Integration of Knowledge and Ideas** **(a)** How does Perseus' connection with the gods contribute to his stature as a hero?
**(b)** How do his plans and deeds reflect his heroic responsibilities?
*[Connect to the Big Question: Do heroes have responsibilities?]*

## Comparing Tall Tale and Myth

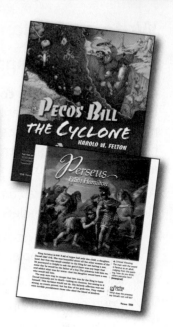

© **1. Craft and Structure** Use a chart like the one shown to identify the **tall tale** elements in "Pecos Bill: The Cyclone."

| Larger-than-life hero | Far-fetched situations | Amazing feats | Humor | Hyperbole |
|---|---|---|---|---|
| | | | | |

© **2. Craft and Structure (a)** What divine actions does the **myth** of Perseus describe? **(b)** In what ways is Perseus a typical **mythic hero**?

© **3. Key Ideas and Details (a)** What weapons, skills, and knowledge does Pecos Bill use to defeat the cyclone? **(b)** What weapons, skills, and knowledge does Perseus use to defeat Medusa? **(c)** In what ways are Pecos Bill's and Perseus' achievements similar and different?

© **4. Integration of Knowledge and Ideas (a)** What makes Pecos Bill a hero? **(b)** What makes Perseus a hero?

## ⏱ Timed Writing

### Explanatory Text: Essay

The heroes of tall tales and myths usually represent aspects of the cultures that create them. At the same time, every hero embodies some universal qualities—traits that are valued in all cultures. In an essay, compare and contrast the values that Pecos Bill and Perseus represent. **(40 minutes)**

### 5-Minute Planner

**1.** Read the prompt carefully and completely.

**2.** Think about these questions and jot down ideas for your essay.

   • Whom does each hero respect? What does each one fear?

   • What does each hero desire? What does each one accomplish?

   • Does the hero act primarily on his own behalf or on behalf of others?

   • How does each hero reflect the culture that created him?

**3.** List the main ideas you want to include in your essay. Then, number the ideas in the order you will discuss them.

**4.** Reread the prompt. Then, refer to your notes as you draft your essay.

# Writing Workshop

 **Common Core
State Standards**

**Writing**
**2.** Write informative/explanatory texts to examine and convey complex ideas, concepts, and information clearly and accurately through the effective selection, organization, and analysis of content.

**5.** Develop and strengthen writing as needed by planning, revising, editing, rewriting, or trying a new approach, focusing on addressing what is most significant for a specific purpose and audience.

## Write an Explanatory Text

### Exposition: Comparison-and-Contrast Essay

**Defining the Form** A **comparison-and-contrast essay** is a written exploration of the similarities and differences between or among two or more things. You may use elements of this type of writing in essays on historical figures and events, consumer reports, or essays on works of art, literature, or music.

**Assignment** Write a comparison-and-contrast essay about two events, ideas, or historical leaders. Include these elements:

✓ an *analysis* and *discussion* of the similarities and differences between two things, people, places, or ideas

✓ *accurate, factual details* about each subject

✓ a *purpose* for comparing and contrasting

✓ a *balanced presentation* of each subject using either *subject-by-subject* or *point-by-point organization*

✓ error-free grammar, including *varied sentence structure and length*

To preview the criteria on which your comparison-and-contrast essay may be judged, see the rubric on page 1241.

 **Writing Workshop:** *Work in Progress*

Review the work you did on pages 1191 and 1207.

**WRITE GUY**
*Jeff Anderson, M.Ed.*

### What Do You Notice?

**Methods of Comparing and Contrasting**

The following passage is from the 1911 Texas Almanac's "Automobiles in Texas." Read the passage several times.

*Ten years ago an automobile was a curiosity in the leading cities of Texas. Five years ago the people in many counties had never seen what was then known as the horseless carriage. Today it is estimated that the number of automobiles in actual service in Texas will reach nearly 30,000 and that over $40,000,000 is invested in the machines.*

Jot down what you notice about this passage and share your thoughts with a partner. Consider how you can use methods of comparing and contrasting in your essay.

**Reading-Writing Connection**

To get a feel for comparison-and-contrast writing, read "The News" by Neil Postman on page 478.

# Prewriting/Planning Strategies

**PHLit Online!**
www.PHLitOnline.com
- Author video: Writing Process
- Author video: Rewards of Writing

**Explore categories.** Working with a group, make a list of categories that your intended audience would find interesting, such as famous athletes, famous artists, vacation spots, or favorite foods. Then, choose one category and discuss it in greater depth. Identify specific topics within the category that present clear similarities and differences.

**Find related pairs.** Explore topics in terms of clear opposites, clear similarities, or close relationships. Start with names of people, places, objects, or ideas. Note related subjects that come to mind, as well as relationships that interest you. Choose one of these idea pairs to develop.

**Specify your purpose.** To identify a purpose for your essay, consider the following possibilities:

- To persuade—You may want readers to accept your opinion that one subject is preferable to another.

- To explain—You may want readers to understand something special about the subjects.

- To describe—You may want readers to understand the basic similarities and differences between your subjects.

**Use specific criteria.** When you compare and contrast, you should examine specific criteria as a basis for your writing. Use a three-column chart like the one shown to identify criteria and the similarities and differences between subjects.

| Criteria | Reading Literature | Listening to Music |
|---|---|---|
| **Entertainment value** | Very entertaining, requires you to use your imagination | Entertaining, helping change your mood or making you feel like dancing |
| **Attention needed** | Requires your full attention and concentration | Allows listener to do other things |
| **Portability/ Necessary materials** | Extremely portable, books and e-readers can fit in most bags, light is always needed, batteries needed if flashlight is used | Portable if using a CD or MP3 player, batteries or electricity may be needed |

# Drafting Strategies

**Prepare to compare.** Look at your Criteria chart. Use the details from your chart to fill in a Venn diagram, separating it into similarities and differences, helping you prepare to organize your essay. Record similarities in the space where the circles overlap, and note differences in the outer sections of the circles.

**Common Core State Standards**

**Writing**

**2.a.** Organize complex ideas, concepts, and information to make important connections and distinctions.

**2.b.** Develop the topic with well-chose, relevant, and sufficient facts.

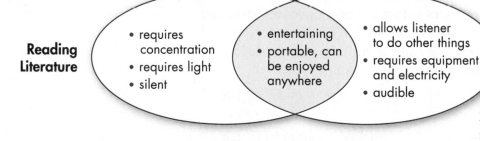

**Reading Literature**
- requires concentration
- requires light
- silent

- entertaining
- portable, can be enjoyed anywhere

- allows listener to do other things
- requires equipment and electricity
- audible

**Listening to Music**

**2.c.** Use appropriate and varied transitions to link the major sections of the text, create cohesion, and clarify the relationships among complex ideas and concepts.

**Choose an organization.** Select an organization that suits your topic. Point-by-point and subject-by-subject plans are the most common types of organization used in comparison-and-contrast writing.

- **Point-by-point organization:** Move between your subjects as you discuss points of comparison. First, compare one element (or criterion) of both subjects, and then address another element of both subjects. Continue this process until you have covered all the features. This method allows you to sharpen your points of similarity and difference.

- **Subject-by-subject organization:** Compare your subjects as complete units. First, discuss all the features of one subject; then, discuss all the features of the other. This format allows you to focus on one subject at a time, but be sure to address the same features and devote equal time to each subject.

**Add transitions.** For either type of organization, use transitional words or phrases to connect your ideas. To make comparisons, use words such as *similarly, in comparison,* or *likewise.* If you are contrasting ideas, use transitions such as *on the other hand, in contrast,* or *however.*

**Support generalizations with specifics.** Whether your purpose in comparing and contrasting two subjects is to describe, to persuade, or to explain, provide enough detail to fully develop your points. Support your statements about similarities and differences with a sufficient number of facts, examples, and other forms of evidence that clearly relate to your ideas and are well suited to your audience.

---

**Point-by-Point Plan**

Point 1
- Subject A
- Subject B

Point 2
- Subject A
- Subject B

---

**Subject-by-Subject Plan**

Subject A
- Point 1
- Point 2

Subject B
- Point 1
- Point 2

---

## Writers on Writing

# Coach Dean Smith with John Kilgo
## On Word Choice

> Dean Smith and John Kilgo are the co-authors of the excerpt from *The Carolina Way* (p. 1037).

John Kilgo, my co-author, took notes of our conversations related to this book and put my ideas into written form. I have strong feelings about what I want my words to convey, which means we did extensive rewriting and revising. When we finally signed off on a chapter, it was always shorter, sharper in focus, and less repetitive than the original.

### Professional Model:

### from *"The Carolina Way"*

A steady focus on taking care of the little things, attending diligently to the many details involved with building a team, helped us produce a mind-set that ⟵ enhanced our ability to handle the big things. . . . Here are some of the so-called little things that we integrated into our program:

Punctuality: Players knew I arrived early for meetings and practices, and I expected everyone to be there and ready to go. . . . Tardiness is the ~~definition~~ ˄height of ⟵ arrogance. In effect, you're saying, "My time is more important than yours." Being on time is being consider-ate of others. . . .

Swearing: We discouraged it in our program. When a player cursed in practice, the entire team ran for him. . . . This is not an easy subject to talk about because it can sound ~~sanctimonious~~ ˄pious. . . . However, I believe ⟵ that anger can be expressed without using profanity.

Top priority: We checked on the class attendance of our players, as well as their grades and academic progress.

We used the phrase "produce a mind-set," because it's important for readers to know that our program had a strong philosophy concerning team-building techniques that we instilled in our players beginning with the first day they stepped on campus.

We first wrote that tardiness is the "definition" of arrogance, but changed it to "height of arrogance" on the rewrite. Using "height of arrogance" seemed to more strongly emphasize how unacceptable tardiness was in our program.

We first used "sanctimonious" in describing the difficulty in even discussing the subject of swearing, but changed it to "pious," which sounds less "preachy," or at least we thought so at the time. Also, words have a rhythm, and "pious" just seemed to fit better here.

# Revising Strategies

**Revise to make comparisons and contrasts clear.** Using two different colors, mark your draft to distinguish between the two subjects you discuss. Whether you have used point-by-point or subject-by-subject organization, this color coding will clearly reveal if you have organized a balanced presentation of both subjects. If necessary, you can expand or reduce coverage of one of your subjects to achieve balance. Next, evaluate the places where the two colors—and subjects—meet. Add transitional words to make the shifts clear.

**Common Core State Standards**

**Writing**
**2.c.** Use appropriate and varied transitions to link the major sections of the text, create cohesion, and clarify the relationships among complex ideas and concepts.
**2.d.** Use precise language and domain-specific vocabulary to manage the complexity of the topic.

**Language**
**1.b.** Use various types of phrases and clauses to convey specific meanings and add variety and interest to writing or presentations.

### Model: Revising for Clarity

Reading literature and listening to music are two of my favorite pastimes.

^Reading literature is an excellent source of entertainment, taking me to worlds away from today. Listening to music is also fun. I can dance around the house while I do my chores.

Both
^Reading and listening to music can be enjoyed most anywhere.

However,
^It is better to have quiet when I try to read.

> The author uses the transitions "both" and "however" to move more fluidly from one idea to the next.

**Revise to add specifics.** To achieve your purpose and to help your readers understand the comparisons you make, add enough detail to explain the differences and similarities you see. Look for places where you can add related information that strengthens your description or analysis, such as well-chosen facts, quotations, definitions, or examples.

### Peer Review

Exchange drafts with a partner. As you read each other's essays, circle any vague language that you find. Consider choices that will convey the meaning more precisely. Then, discuss with your reader specific details that would make your comparisons more vivid. Incorporate these details into your draft.

**Vague:** In contrast to literature, popular music forms a soundtrack for our lives.

**Specific:** In contrast to literature that we must read to enjoy, popular music, like the Top 40 tunes we hear on the radio, forms a soundtrack for our lives. We can enjoy it as we drive, shop, or even fall asleep at night.

# Varying Sentence Structure and Length

A sequence of sentences of the same length and structural pattern can have a tedious effect on readers. You can make your paragraphs more interesting and readable by varying sentence length, introducing new sentence beginnings, and inverting subject-verb order.

**Vary Sentence Length** If you find an unbroken series of long sentences, look for an opportunity to include a short sentence. Since the short sentence will draw the reader's attention, use it to emphasize an important detail or idea. Be sure that it is a complete thought and not a fragment.

> **Original:**   Memories of long hours of practice, the brutal weather, the aches and bruises of an endless season were erased by the single fact that we had won the championship.
>
> **Revised:**   Memories of long hours of practice, the brutal weather, the aches and bruises of an endless season were erased by a single fact. We had won the championship.

**Vary Sentence Beginnings** If you have written a series of sentences beginning with a noun or pronoun, look for opportunities to start sentences with different parts of speech. Look at these techniques:

> **Adverb clause:** *Anywhere you go,* you will still find most people care about others.
>
> **Prepositional phrase:** *After a long Saturday of work,* Sarah did not feel like going out.
>
> **Complement:** *Most interesting to me* was an electronic display of the battlefield. (complement of the verb *was*)
>
> **Direct object:** *Our report* I gave to the editor; my opinion I kept to myself. (object of the verb *gave*)

**PH   WRITING COACH**

Further instruction and practice are available in *Prentice Hall Writing Coach.*

**Vary Subject-Verb Order** You can vary sentence beginnings by reversing the usual subject-verb order.

> **Original:**   The mystery guest is here at last.
>
> **Inverted:**   Here at last is the mystery guest.

### Grammar in Your Writing

As you review the three longest paragraphs in your draft, examine the length and pattern of each sentence to look for ways to improve variety. Change sentence lengths, alter sentence beginnings, and invert subject-verb order to add interest to your writing.

# Student Model: Lauren De Loach, Bernice, LA

## Ambivalence

When I consider my conflicting feelings about my hometown, I see that there are things that I love and hate about living in Bernice, Louisiana, a nineties version of Mayberry. I love the security of a small town, and I hate it. I love the way that my town is not clouded by the smog of a city, and I hate it too. I love it and I hate that I love it.

I love and hate the security in my town for a number of reasons. I love it because I know that it is my dog scratching at my door at 5:30 in the morning and not some dangerous stranger. In my town, a fifteen-car traffic jam is front-page news. On the other hand, I hate that it gets a little boring sometimes. I don't want criminals at my door, but a little excitement would be nice.

I am fond of the size of Bernice and I detest it, too. I'm glad that only fifteen cars is a major traffic jam. But I hate that I have to drive sixteen miles to the nearest major store. I love and hate that my town is so small that I know everybody's first, middle, and last names. I like it because I have a "tab" at the grocery store and the drug store, so that eliminates the necessity of carrying money. I hate that everybody knows me because that means that everybody finds out about whom I'm dating, whom I once dated, my height, weight, and age. I also hate that we all know each other so well that the most entertaining news we can come up with to put in the *Bernice Banner* is that Peggy Jane and her brother JC visited their Aunt Goosey Lou in the nursing home. But by knowing everyone so well, I've made friends who are trustworthy because we know all of one another's deepest secrets.

Even though I say that I detest some things, home wouldn't be home without these silly quirks. I love that my parents and their friends are known as the "elite group" because they have traveled beyond Texas, Arkansas, and Mississippi. I love saying that I have read the *Iliad* to people who think I would not read such a book. I know that it sounds like I love the provincialism that small towns can impose, but the smells of fresh-cut grass and the gardenia bush outside my door are what make my home my home.

This is what I love and what I hate, but I don't really. The overall feeling I get from living in Bernice is ambivalence. I love it and I hate that I love such goofy things. But the parts of home that seem so trivial are the ones that make you who you are. That makes a place your home.

**Lauren's essay will compare two feelings: what she loves and what she hates about her hometown.**

**Using a point-by-point organization, Lauren addresses the first contrast in her attitudes about her town: She feels ambivalence about its security.**

**These facts support Lauren's ideas and opinions.**

**Lauren's comparison allows her to be funny, but it also helps her reflect on her ideas.**

# Editing and Proofreading

Check your draft to correct errors in spelling, grammar, and punctuation.

**Focus on compound sentences.** Comparison-and-contrast essays often contain compound sentences—those with two independent clauses joined by a semicolon or a coordinating conjunction, such as *or*, *and*, or *but*. Check that you have correctly punctuated these sentences.

| | |
|---|---|
| **Conjunction:** | I liked the chili, but it was spicy. |
| **Semicolon:** | I rushed out; I was late for the bus. |

## Publishing and Presenting

Consider one of the following ways to share your writing:

**Deliver an oral presentation.** Read your comparison-and-contrast essay aloud to an audience of your classmates. If possible, include props or visuals to enhance the reading.

**Make a poster.** Present your comparison-and-contrast findings visually in a poster. Use a graphic organizer, such as a Venn diagram, to show the similarities and differences of your subjects. If possible, add photographs and illustrations to show the distinctive elements of your subjects.

## Reflecting on Your Writing

**Writer's Journal** Jot down your answers to this question:
*How did writing about your topic help you understand it?*

## Rubric for Self-Assessment

Find evidence in your writing to address each category. Then, use the rating scale to grade your work.

**Spiral Review**
Earlier in the unit, you learned about **commas and dashes** (p. 1190) and **colons, semicolons, and ellipsis points** (p. 1206). Make sure you have used these punctuation marks properly in your essay.

| Criteria | Rating Scale<br>*not very*       *very* |
|---|---|
| **Focus:** How clear is your purpose for comparing and contrasting? | 1   2   3   4   5 |
| **Organization:** How balanced is your organization? | 1   2   3   4   5 |
| **Support/Elaboration:** How accurate and factual are the details you use to support your ideas? | 1   2   3   4   5 |
| **Style:** How effectively do you use transitions to clarify ideas? | 1   2   3   4   5 |
| **Conventions:** How correct is your grammar, especially related to your use of varied sentence structure and length? | 1   2   3   4   5 |

# Vocabulary Workshop

## Idioms, Jargon, and Technical Terms

 **Common Core State Standards**

**Language**
**4.c.** Consult general and specialized reference materials, both print and digital, to find the pronunciation of a word or determine or clarify its precise meaning, its part of speech, or its etymology.
**5.a.** Interpret figures of speech in context and analyze their role in the text.

An **idiom** is an expression that is characteristic of a language, region, community, or class of people. It cannot be understood literally. For example, *I'm all ears* does not mean "I am made of ears" but rather "I'm listening intently." "Throw in the towel" has nothing to do with fabric; instead, it refers to a boxer's act of forfeiting a match. Now, the phrase has reached past sports to become an idiom that is understood to mean "give up." Many dictionaries list idioms at the end of the entry for the main word in the idiom.

Many fields of study, work, and play have **technical terms.** These are words that may be familiar, but they have specialized meanings in the particular field. Examples from the field of computers include *software, hard drive, Internet,* and *USB port.* Technical terms help people who share knowledge of the field communicate more effectively.

Like technical terms, **jargon** is the specialized words and phrases used in a specific field. While it is frequently useful, jargon can sometimes appear to be scientific or technical but instead is vague and meaningless.

| Jargon | Meaning |
|--------|---------|
| The vehicle's internal combustion engine became depleted of its distilled mixture of hydrocarbons. | The car ran out of gas. |
| This moisturizing cleansing bar is hot off the shelf. | This soap is brand new. |
| Stakeholders in our school environment need new text resources. | Students in our school need new textbooks. |

**Practice A** Match the definition in the box with the underlined jargon in each sentence. Use context clues to figure out the meanings.

| screen | clarinet | new sidewalks |
|--------|----------|---------------|
| car-washer | black eye | |

**1.** When the baseball hit me in the face, I ended up with a <u>periorbital hematoma.</u>

**2.** On the large <u>monitor</u>, I can see more of the document at once.

**3.** The jazz musician put his <u>licorice stick</u> to his lips and played.

4. The <u>vehicle appearance operative</u> washed and dried the car.

5. <u>Public infrastructure upgrades</u> are needed so people can walk around more safely.

**Practice B** Identify the idiom in each sentence and write a definition for each. If you are unsure of the meaning of the word or phrase, check your definition in a print or online dictionary.

1. She let us down by not showing up for the game.

2. I am up to my ears in homework.

3. Marvin, please cool it and sit down over there.

4. It's been a long day, so I'm going to turn in.

5. Jurors must try to keep an open mind during the trial.

6. Let's just nip this problem in the bud.

7. What are you driving at?

8. Your question has put the salesperson on the spot.

9. If you cheat in that game, I will blow the whistle on you.

10. I'm going to whip this team into shape.

**Activity** Prepare five note cards like the one shown. Write each of the following words and its definition on a card. Look the word up in a dictionary and find both a common and a technical meaning. Write the technical meaning on the card and identify the professional field in which that meaning is commonly used.

mouse    spare    snake    key    single

| |
| --- |
| **Word:** |
| |
| **Common Definition:** |
| |
| **Field:** |
| |
| **Technical Definition:** |
| |

**Comprehension and Collaboration**

Education is a specialized field. Work with several classmates and create a glossary of technical terms that apply to education. You might begin with words like *computer lab, activity bus,* and *hall pass.* Discuss how these terms may not be familiar to people outside of education.

# Communications Workshop

## Comparing Media Coverage

Both visual images and non-visual texts present events and communicate information. Comparing and contrasting how the media uses images and text to communicate will help you to develop your media literacy skills.

**Common Core State Standards**

**Reading Informational Text**
**7.** Analyze various accounts of a subject told in different mediums, determining which details are emphasized in each account.

## Learn the Skills

Analyze and then compare and contrast the ways in which events and information are conveyed in various types of media.

**Comparing and Contrasting Presentation** News events can be described with words or with images, or both. As you look at media coverage, compare and contrast the way in which text and/or images such as graphics, illustrations, and photographs bring events to life for readers.

- *When examining non-visual texts, ask:* In what order are the events described? What event, if any, is identified as most important or critical? What words or phrases indicate the importance of the event?

- *When viewing visual images, ask:* What event does the image capture? Why was this particular image chosen? What point of view does the image reveal?

**Comparing and Contrasting Communication** Once you have analyzed the presentation of events, compare and contrast the ways in which the information is communicated. Ask these questions:

- In what ways is the information in the text and the visual similar and different?
- Which treatment, the text or visual, gives more detailed information?
- Which treatment, the text or visual, has more impact? Why?

### Twin Pandas Reach Critical Milestone

Veterinarians at the Beijing Zoo have announced that twin pandas born in September are now expected to survive. Their mother, Yong Yong, was unable to nurse them from birth. The zoo staff quickly intervened, but the future of the young pandas was uncertain. Now that the pandas have survived their first seven weeks, veterinarians are optimistic that the pandas will survive.

When asked how long the pandas will require care

▲ **1.** This article describes an event. Compare and contrast how this article and the photograph present the event.

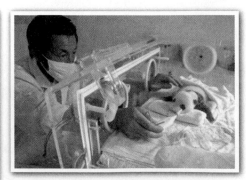

▲ **2.** This photograph shows a scene that is part of the event the text describes. Compare and contrast how the photograph and the text communicate information.

## Practice the Skills

Apply what you have learned and use the discussion guide below to complete the activity.

---

### ACTIVITY: Compare and Contrast Text and Visuals

With a partner, analyze two pairings of image and text that report on the same subject. Use the encyclopedia entry shown below as your first pairing. Then, research print and online sources to locate another example of text and images addressing the same subject. Take notes on both pairings as you analyze ways in which the visual and the text present events and communicate information. Discuss similarities and differences between the texts and the visuals using the discussion guide below. Then, write and present a summary of your findings to your class.

---

**San Francisco Earthquake**

## Damage from the San Francisco Earthquake

The San Francisco earthquake of 1906 had its epicenter near San Francisco, but the effects of the quake reached from southern Oregon to Los Angeles. Those who experienced the quake described it as about a minute of forceful shaking and powerful shocks.

The conditions of the earthquake challenged the views of contemporary scientists and resulted in extensive studies by scientists of the time. The insights that resulted from their research are the basis for

---

Use a **discussion guide** like this to compare and contrast how events are presented and information is communicated in visual images and non-visual texts.

1. **Compare:** What event is depicted both in the visual and in the text?

2. **Contrast:** What aspect of the event does the text describe that the visual does not? What aspect of the event does the visual bring to life that the text does not?

3. **Compare and contrast:** What overall information, or main idea, is communicated by the visual alone? What overall information is communicated by the text alone?

4. **Evaluate:** Would the encyclopedia entry be as effective if it contained text only? Would your second example be as effective as text only? Why or why not?

5. **Generalize:** What generalizations might you make about the kinds of information that are best conveyed with visuals and the kinds of information that seem better suited to text?

# Cumulative Review

**Common Core
State Standards**

RL.9-10.2, RL.9-10.6; L.9-10.4.a,
L.9-10.5.a
[For the full wording of the standards,
see the standards chart in the front of
your textbook.]

## I. Reading Literature

**Directions:** *Read the passage. Then, answer each question
that follows.*

Dimitri's hands held tight to the rocks around him as Aeolus, the god
of winds, pummeled him from all angles. As he clung to the side of the
volcano with a lion's courage, he remembered his visit to the oracle.

His journey to the oracle had taken eight long days of traveling through
the Greek countryside. When he arrived, he felt his journey must have been
a mistake. Deaf in one ear, he thought he could never be a hero. He should
leave before the priestesses serving the oracle laughed at his question.

Dimitri was about to turn around and return home when a priestess
with hair as black as night spotted him. "Come with me," she said. "You
have a question that must be asked." She led him into a large room.

"I want to silence the volcano next to my village. People are dying. I
must help. How can I do it?" he said abruptly to the priestess.

"I will ask the oracle for you," she said. Moments later, she returned.
"I have your answer. You must scale the volcano and listen for the magma
to sing its song. When it sings, and not before, you must drop this stone
into it. Then will the volcano rest." As the priestess spoke, she rested a
flaming red crystal in Dimitri's palm.

"I. . . " he stuttered, "I cannot hear in one ear. How can I hear the
volcano's song?"

"You will," she said. "The oracle is never wrong. Go and be brave."

Now, has he struggled to hold on to the side of the volcano, he felt
himself strengthened by her words. With a lion's courage, he lifted one
foot, then the other, against the raving of the mad wind until he stood
at the top of the volcano. Opening before him, the gaping mouth of the
volcano seemed ready to swallow anyone who came near. The sides of
the volcano poked out like huge lips, and the magma inside lashed from
side to side as a tongue would in an angry mouth. The wind blew louder
around him, and Dimitri felt a moment's hesitation. Then, with a lion's
courage, he rested his head against the rock and leaned forward into the
volcano. It seemed all he could hear was the howling of the wind. Then,
dimly, he could make out what sounded like the notes of a long-forgotten
song. It seemed to be calling his name, begging him to stop holding on to
the rocks and to lean just a little further over the side.

Before the hypnotic song could <u>befuddle</u> his reason and make him fall
into the volcano, Dimitri stood against the wind and took out the red crystal. He dropped it into the volcano, and suddenly the noise stopped.

1. Which of the following could be considered the **theme** of this selection?

   A. Only take a risk if you know what will happen.
   B. Slow and steady wins the race.
   C. If you believe in yourself, you will succeed.
   D. Nature is too powerful to overcome.

2. Which traditional quality of an **epic hero** does Dimitri demonstrate?

   A. bravery
   B. superhuman intelligence
   C. disrespect for the gods
   D. self-doubt

3. In what way is Aeolus, the god of winds, an **antagonist** in this selection?

   A. Aeolus is a powerful god.
   B. Aeolus obviously hates the oracle and will do anything to destroy it.
   C. Readers do not learn a great deal about Aeolus.
   D. Aeolus tries to stop the hero Dimitri from completing his mission.

4. What purpose is <u>not</u> fulfilled the **flashback**?

   A. to give information about Dimitri's mission
   B. to introduce another character
   C. to make readers doubt Dimitri's chance for success
   D. to teach readers more about Greek religion

5. Which of the following is <u>not</u> a characteristic of myths and is <u>not</u> present in the selection?

   A. a basis in historical truth
   B. a role played by gods
   C. a protagonist who teaches values
   D. a significant role for natural phenomena

6. **Epics** usually include all of the following except—

   A. a heroic central character.
   B. humor.
   C. adventures.
   D. adversity, or challenges to be overcome.

7. **Vocabulary** Which word is closest in meaning to the underlined word *befuddle*?

   A. strengthen
   B. identify
   C. imitate
   D. confuse

8. What is the significance of the **epic simile** in this selection?

   A. It emphasizes the size and power of the volcano.
   B. It shows the beauty of the priestess's hair.
   C. It demonstrates how far Dimitri journeyed to get to the oracle.
   D. It helps the reader get a mental picture of the red crystal.

9. **Repetition** of the phrase "with a lion's courage" emphasizes—

   A. Dimitri's bravery.
   B. the strength of the gods.
   C. the frightening challenges Dimitri faces.
   D. the ferociousness of the volcano.

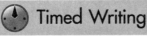 Timed Writing

10. **Write** a five-line **epic simile** comparing an occurrence in your life to a natural event. Use "like" or "as" to state the comparison. Develop your **simile** fully.

 **GO ON**

# II. Reading Informational Text

**Directions:** *Read the passage. Then, answer each question that follows.*

**Common Core
State Standards**

RI.9-10.2; L.9-10.1, L.9-10.2,
L.9-10.3
[For the full wording of the standards, see the standards chart in the front of your textbook.]

*Encyclopedia Entry*

**Bill of Rights** The Bill of Rights is the list of the first ten amendments added to the Constitution of the United States of America. Some delegates at the Constitutional Convention believed that our Constitution was missing the limitation put on government to guarantee certain individual rights. The Bill of Rights was adopted in 1791. James Madison played a crucial role in the process of creation and <u>ratification</u>, or confirmation, of the document.

*Biography*

James Madison (1751–1836) was born in Port Conway, Virginia. He attended the College of New Jersey, which is now Princeton. After he graduated in 1771, he began his political career. Madison eventually went on to become the fourth president of the United States. However, his major contribution to the country came before his presidency. He served as a delegate to the Constitutional Convention of 1787, drafting much of the document of the Constitution. In addition, he was a proponent and author of the Bill of Rights, which eventually tipped the scale for ratification of the Constitution.

*Public Document*

**Bill of Rights**

**Amendment I:** Congress shall make no law respecting an establishment of religion, or prohibiting the free exercise thereof; or abridging the freedom of speech, or of the press; or the right of the people peaceably to assemble, and to petition the government for a redress of grievances.

**1. Vocabulary** What is the best definition for *ratification?*

  **A.** investment in
  **B.** proponent of
  **C.** approval of
  **D.** designation of

**2.** Which text should you consult to learn more about the author of the Bill of Rights?

  **A.** biography
  **B.** the Constitution
  **C.** encyclopedia
  **D.** history text

**3.** What rights are protected by Amendment I of the Bill of Rights?

  **A.** freedom to bear arms
  **B.** freedom of dress
  **C.** freedom of speech and press
  **D.** protection from unnecessary search

**4.** Which two texts are secondary sources?

  **A.** encyclopedia entry and biography
  **B.** encyclopedia entry and public document
  **C.** biography and public document
  **D.** none of the above

# III. Writing and Language Conventions

**Directions:** *Read the passage. Then, answer each question that follows.*

## Recording Meeting Minutes

(1) How could anyone copy down every single word said at a meeting?
(2) Although some people may say you need to do it. (3) It is impossible!
(4) To take meeting minutes, you only need to worry about getting the
basic ideas. (5) Follow these guidelines to take appropriate meeting minutes.

(6) Make sure that the notes you write are brief and direct. (7) When
taking notes be sure to use clear abbreviations. (8) Use a highlighter or
underlining to indicate important topics or decisions that have been made.
(9) Recording meeting minutes may sound as tough as climbing Mount
Everest, but it is not. (10) If everyone can understand your minutes, you
have done an excellent job.

1. What is the *best* correction of the sentence **fragment** in sentence 2?

   **A.** Although some people may say you need to do it, it is impossible!
   **B.** Though some people may say you need to do it.
   **C.** Although it is impossible, although some people say you need to do it.
   **D.** Though you may need to, impossible!

2. Where in sentence 7 should a **comma** be added?

   **A.** after "taking"
   **B.** after "notes"
   **C.** after "sure"
   **D.** no comma needed

3. Which **transitional word** could be added to the beginning of sentence 6 for clarity?

   **A.** First,
   **B.** Finally,
   **C.** Afterward,
   **D.** Often,

4. To improve the organization of these instructions, the author may want to—

   **A.** delete sentence 4.
   **B.** include an illustration.
   **C.** create a new paragraph beginning at sentence 9.
   **D.** switch the order of sentences 9 and 10.

5. In what way should sentence 9 be revised to create a more formal **tone**?

   **A.** Replace "as tough as climbing Mount Everest" with "challenging."
   **B.** Remove "recording."
   **C.** Replace "but it is not" with "but it never is."
   **D.** Replace "it is not" with "but it is more like hiking up a hill."

# Performance Tasks

**Directions:** *Follow the instructions to complete the tasks below as required by your teacher.*

*As you work on each task, incorporate both general academic vocabulary and literary terms you learned in this unit.*

<table>
<tr><td>© Common Core<br>State Standards</td></tr>
</table>

**RL.9-10.2, RL.9-10.3, RL.9-10.6, RL.9-10.9; RI.9-10.3, RI.9-10.6; W.9-10.9.a–b; SL.9-10.3, SL.9-10.4; L.9-10.2.a**

[For the full wording of the standards, see the standards chart in the front of your textbook.]

## Writing

### © Task 1: Informational Text [RI.9-10.6; W.9-10.9.b]
**Analyze the Author's Purpose and Rhetoric**

*Write an essay in which you determine the author's purpose and analyze his or her use of rhetoric in a nonfiction work from this unit.*

- State which work you chose. Briefly explain who the author is and the circumstances under which he or she wrote the work.

- Identify the author's main purpose by explaining the goals he or she wanted to achieve in writing the work. Explain whether the author states his or her purpose explicitly or merely suggests it. Cite details from the work to support your ideas.

- Identify at least two words, phrases, sentences, or other uses of language that you think help advance the author's purpose for writing. Explain your position.

- Provide a concluding statement that supports the ideas you expressed earlier in your essay.

### © Task 2: Literature [RL.9-10.9; L.9-10.2.a]
**Analyze an Author's Interpretation of Source Material**

*Write an essay in which you analyze how an author from this unit draws on and transforms a theme or topic from an older work.*

- Select a work from this unit that interprets, draws upon, or makes an allusion to an older work of literature.

- Organize your ideas in an outline that compares the two works.

- Begin your essay by introducing the selection you chose and briefly summarizing its content. Then,

explain the source work, summarizing its content and explaining how it is used in the later work.

- Explain how the source material enriches the modern selection. In particular, analyze how the material influences the plot, character, meaning, or tone of the work you chose.

- Cite strong and thorough textual evidence from both works to support your ideas.

- Provide a strong conclusion that summarizes how references to the older work make your chosen selection more understandable and enjoyable.

- Use punctuation such as colons and semicolons correctly.

### © Task 3: Literature [RL.9-10.6; W.9-10.9.a]
**Analyze Cultural Perspective**

*Write an essay in which you analyze the cultural perspective conveyed in a literary work from this unit. The work must have been written outside the United States.*

- State which work you chose and briefly summarize it. Explain the cultural perspective the work expresses.

- Analyze how the cultural experience or perspective influences the selection's content and contributes to the overall meaning and tone of the work.

- Explain the theme or message of the work and show with specific examples how that message is influenced by the author's cultural perspective.

- Establish and maintain a formal style and objective tone.

- Provide a concluding statement that follows from and supports the explanation you have presented.

# Speaking and Listening

## ⓔ Task 4: Literature [RL.9-10.3; SL.9-10.4]
### Analyze a Complex Hero

*Deliver an oral report in which you analyze a heroic character in a work of literature from this unit.*

- Introduce the character and explain how the character's actions, dialogue, and interactions with other characters convey heroic qualities.

- Show how the character develops over the course of the work, analyzing how events and relationships with other characters reinforce the character's heroism.

- Cite specific examples from the work to show whether the character's actions suggest a hero's quest or a universal theme.

- Present your information and supporting evidence clearly, concisely, and logically so that your audience can understand your ideas.

- Employ correct grammar and an appropriate speaking style.

## ⓔ Task 5: Literature [RL.9-10.2; SL.9-10.3, SL.9-10.4]
### Analyze Theme

*Deliver a presentation in which you analyze the theme in a literary work from this unit and consider whether it is universal.*

- Explain which work you chose and provide at least two interesting facts about its author or the culture it represents.

- Briefly summarize the work, and state the theme it expresses. Cite specific details from the work that support your interpretation.

- Discuss whether the theme the work expresses is universal—one shared by people across time and from different cultures. Cite specific details.

- Add interest to your presentation by including visuals, such as photographs or drawings.

- Explain or define terms with which your audience may not be familiar. Present information clearly, concisely, and logically so that listeners can follow your reasoning.

- Conclude with a summarizing statement.

## ⓔ Task 6: Informational Text [RI.9-10.3; SL.9-10.3, SL.9-10.4]
### Analyze the Structure of a Work

*Deliver an oral presentation in which you demonstrate how an author organizes ideas in a nonfiction work from this unit.*

- Explain which work you chose and briefly summarize the author's main purpose and central idea.

- Identify the order in which the author unfolds his or her ideas. Cite specific methods the author uses to introduce and develop ideas.

- Demonstrate how the author makes connections among ideas. Identify transitional words and phrases, examples, or repetition.

- Use a visual aid to make your ideas clear to your audience. Options include a handout with an annotated outline, a series of note cards or posters, or the use of display technology.

- Present your information clearly, concisely, and logically so your listeners can follow your reasoning.

---

**THE BIG Q**

**Do heroes have responsibilities?**
At the beginning of Unit 6, you participated in a discussion of the Big Question. Now that you have completed the unit, write a response to the question. Discuss how your initial ideas have either changed or been reinforced. Cite specific examples from the literature in this unit, other subject areas, and your own life to support your ideas. Use Big Question vocabulary words (see p. 1029) in your response.

# Featured Titles

In this unit, you have read a wide variety of thematically related literary works. Continue to explore thematic connections in literature. Select works that you enjoy, but challenge yourself to explore new writers and works of increasing depth and complexity. The titles suggested below will help you get started.

## Literature

### Fathers and Sons
by Ivan Turgenev                    EXEMPLAR TEXT

 This 1862 **novel** set in Russia delves into the gap that has grown between a generation of parents and children who differ greatly in their philosophies. As the young demand social change, the old cling desperately to tradition.

### Revolutionary Petunias and Other Poems
by Alice Walker                    EXEMPLAR TEXT

 Known for her bold honesty and poetic language, Walker crafts a collection of **poetry** that explores the similarities between revolution and love.

### The War of the Worlds
by H. G. Wells
Signet, 1986

 This classic **science-fiction novel** is the book that launched a thousand Hollywood alien invasion movies. It imagines that Martians, intent on obliterating the human race, land on Earth. As the Martians mow down everything in their path, readers are left to wonder who, if anyone, can defend the planet against these seemingly invincible foes.

### The Odyssey
by Homer
Translated by Robert Fagles                    EXEMPLAR TEXT

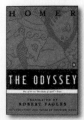 When the hero Odysseus begins his voyage home after the Trojan War, he has no idea his travels will lead him to seductive goddesses, man-eating monsters, and vengeful gods. Read this **epic tale** to decide for yourself if Odysseus is the ultimate hero.

## Informational Texts

### Joan of Arc
by Mary Gordon

 This **biography** tells the remarkable story of the short life of a peasant named Joan. After hearing a voice she believed was God's, she left her family and home behind to lead the French army to victory over the British.

### The Carolina Way
by Dean Smith and Gerald Bell with John Kilgo

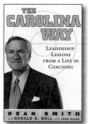 Dean Smith, the coach of the University of North Carolina men's basketball team for almost 40 years, shares his strategies for leadership, teamwork, and winning with integrity in this **nonfiction** book.

### The Story of Science: Newton at the Center
by Joy Hakim                    EXEMPLAR TEXT

An examination of the accomplishments and lives of several scientists, this work of **nonfiction** includes interesting stories and facts that present some engaging aspects of science.

### Nelson Mandela
by Laaren Brown and Lenny Hort

 This **biography** of Nelson Mandela describes his struggles against an unjust government and how he survived 27 years as a political prisoner as South Africa emerged out of the dark ages of apartheid.

# Preparing to Read Complex Texts

**Attentive Reading** As you read literature on your own, bring your imagination and questions to the text. The questions shown below and others that you ask as you read will help you learn and enjoy literature even more.

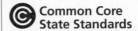

## Common Core State Standards

**Reading Literature/Informational Text**
**10.** By the end of grade 9, read and comprehend literature, including stories, dramas, poems, and literary nonfiction in the grades 9–10 text complexity band proficiently, with scaffolding as needed at the high end of the range.

---

## When reading texts from the oral tradition, ask yourself...

- What type of text is this? Is it an epic, a myth, a tale, or a legend? What types of characters, events, and ideas do I expect to find in this text?
- From what culture does this text come? What do I know about that culture?
- Does my knowledge of the culture lead me to expect certain qualities in this text? If so, what are my expectations?
- Does the text meet my expectations? Why or why not?
- What elements of the culture do I see in the text? For example, do I notice beliefs, foods, or settings that have meaning for the people of this culture?
- Does the text express a moral or theme that has meaning for modern readers? Why or why not?

**Key Ideas and Details**

- Is this text a retelling by a modern author? If so, does the author change the text for modern readers?
- How do I think the text on the page is different from the text when it was originally related, sung, or performed? Which parts of the text might a performer have exaggerated or altered?
- Does the text include characters and tell a story? If so, are the characters and plot interesting?
- What do I notice about the language, including descriptions and dialogue? How does the language compare to that of modern texts?
- Does the text include symbols? If so, do they have special meanings in the original culture of the text? Do they also have meanings in modern life?
- Does the text include patterns of events or repetitions of statements or images? If so, which ones? What is the effect?

**Craft and Structure**

- How does this text round out the picture of the culture I might get from a nonfiction source, such as an encyclopedia entry?
- Does this text express universal ideas or values—those that are common to people in many different cultures and time periods?
- Does this text seem like others I have read or heard? Why or why not?
- Do I know of any modern versions of this text? How are they similar to or different from this one?
- If I were researching this culture for a report, would I include passages from this text? If so, what would those passages show?
- Do I enjoy reading this text and others like it? Why or why not?

**Integration of Ideas**

# Resources

# Glossary

Big Question vocabulary appears in **blue type**. High-utility Academic vocabulary is <u>underlined.</u>

## A

**abash** (uh BASH) *v.* embarrass

**abdicated** (AB duh kayt uhd) *v.* gave up formally

**absurdity** (ab SUR duh tee) *n.* something ridiculous or nonsensical

**accentuated** (ak SEHN chu ayt uhd) *v.* emphasized; heightened the effect of

**accept** (ak SEHPT) *v.* take something that is given

**accumulated** (uh KYOO myuh layt uhd) *v.* piled up, collected, or gathered together, especially over a period of time

**acquiesced** (ak wee EHST) *v.* agreed or consented quietly without protest, but without enthusiasm

**adversary** (AD vuhr sehr ee) *n.* person who opposes or fights against another

**afflicted** (uh FLIHKT ihd) *v.* suffering or sickened

**allotment** (uh LOT muhnt) *n.* share; portion

**aloofness** (uh LOOF nehs) *n.* emotional distance

**ambiguities** (am buh GYOO uh teez) *n.* statements or events whose meanings are unclear

<u>**ambiguous**</u> (am BIHG yoo uhs) *adj.* having more than one meaning

**amicably** (AM uh kuh blee) *adv.* in a friendly manner

**amid** (uh MIHD) *prep.* among; in the middle of

**analysis** (uh NAL uh sis) *n.* careful examination by studying something's elements or parts

**anguish** (ANG gwihsh) *n.* great pain or suffering

**anonymous** (uh NON uh muhs) *adj.* without a known or acknowledged name

**antagonize** (an TAG uh nyz) *v.* make an enemy of

**apex** (AY pehks) *n.* highest point; peak

<u>**appreciate**</u> (uh PREE shee ayt) *v.* be aware of the value of

**archaic** (ahr KAY ihk) *adj.* from an earlier time; ancient

**ardor** (AHR duhr) *n.* passion; enthusiasm

**arduous** (AHR joo uhs) *adj.* difficult; laborious

<u>**argument**</u> (AHR gyuh muhnt) *n.* discussion in which there is disagreement

<u>**articulate**</u> (ahr TIHK yuh layt) *v.* express an idea clearly

<u>**articulate**</u> (ahr TIHK yuh liht) *adj.* able to express oneself clearly

**assiduous** (uh SIHJ oo uhs) *adj.* done with constant and careful attention; diligent

**assimilated** (uh SIHM uh layt uhd) *v.* took in or absorbed

**assimilated** (uh SIHM uh layt uhd) *adj.* having been taken in fully

**assuage** (uh SWAYJ) *v.* calm; pacify

<u>**assumption**</u> (uh SUHMP shuhn) *n.* something taken for granted

**atonement** (uh TOHN muhnt) *n.* act of making up for a wrongdoing or an injury

**attributes** (AT rihb yoots) *n.* characteristics or qualities of a person or thing

**augmenting** (awg MEHNT ihng) *v.* increasing; enlarging

**authentic** (aw THEHN tihk) *adj.* genuine; true

**aware** (uh WAIR) *adj.* knowing something because you have experienced it or have been informed of it

**awestruck** (AW struhk) *adj.* filled with wonder

**awry** (uh RY) *adj.* not straight or in the right direction

**azure** (AZH uhr) *adj.* blue

## B

**background** (BAK grownd) *n.* facts that cause or explain something

**bafflement** (BAF uhl muhnt) *n.* puzzlement; bewilderment

**balmy** (BAHL mee) *adj.* having the qualities of balm; soothing, mild, pleasant

**barren** (BAR uhn) *adj.* empty; having little or no vegetation

**battle** (BAT uhl) *n.* a fight between two opposing forces

**battle** (BAT uhl) *v.* fight or struggle

**beguiling** (bih GY lihng) *v.* tricking; charming

**belief** (bih LEEF) *n.* something accepted to be true

**bemusing** (bih MYOOZ ihng) *v.* stupefying; muddling

**benevolently** (buh NEHV uh luhnt lee) *adv.* in a well-meaning way

**bereft** (bih REHFT) *adj.* deprived

**bias** (BY uhs) *n.* mental leaning or inclination; partiality

**bilingual** (by LIHNG gwuhl) *adj.* using two languages

**blight** (blyt) *n.* something that destroys or prevents growth

**bulging** (BUHLJ ihng) *adj.* swelling

## C

**candor** (KAN duhr) *n.* sharp honesty or frankness in expressing oneself

**cascade** (kas KAYD) *n.* small steep waterfall; anything suggesting such a waterfall

**censure** (SEHN shuhr) *n.* strong disapproval

<u>**character**</u> (KAR ihk tuhr) *n.* qualities that make a person unique

**choices** (choys uhz) *n.* variety of things someone can choose from

**circumstance** (SUR kuhm stans) *n.* situation; event

**clarify** (KLAR uh fy) *v.* make something more clear or understandable

**clasps** (klasps) *v.* grips

**collective** (kuh LEHK tihv) *adj.* put together as a group; gathered into a whole

**communication** (kuh myoo nuh KAY shuhn) *n.* sharing information

**compensation** (kom puhn SAY shuhn) *n.* anything that makes up for a loss, damage, or debt

**compete** (kuhm PEET) *v.* try to win against an opponent

**competition** (kom puh TIHSH uhn) *n.* rivalry; act of competing

**comprehend** (kom prih HEHND) *v.* understand

**comprehension** (kom prih HEHN shuhn) *n.* act of understanding something

**conceded** (kuhn SEED uhd) *v.* admitted as true or valid; acknowledged

**concept** (KON sehpt) *n.* idea; notion

**concessions** (kuhn SEHSH uhnz) *n.* things given or granted as privileges

**condolences** (kuhn DOH luhns uhz) *n.* expressions of sympathy with another in grief

**confer** (kuhn FUR) *v.* give; bestow upon

**confines** (KON fynz) *n.* boundaries or bounded region; border; limit

**conformity** (kuhn FAWR muh tee) *n.* being in agreement with customs or rules

**connection** (kuh NEHK shuhn) *n.* joining of two or more things or ideas

**conspicuous** (kuhn SPIHK yoo uhs) *adj.* attracting attention by being unexpected, unusual, outstanding, or egregious; striking

**contempt** (kuhn TEHMPT) *n.* disdain or scorn

**context** (KON tehkst) *n.* parts of a sentence immediately next to or surrounding a word that determine its exact meaning

**controversy** (KON truh vur see) *n.* discussion of a question in which opposing opinions clash; debate; argument

**convince** (kuhn VIHNS) *v.* persuade by argument or evidence

**cooperate** (koh OP uh rayt) *v.* work together to achieve something

**countenance** (KOWN tuh nuhns) *n.* face

**covenant** (KUHV uh nuhnt) *n.* agreement or contract, especially a sacred one

**credible** (KREHD uh buhl) *adj.* believable

**creed** (kreed) *n.* statement of belief

**culture** (KUHL chuhr) *n.* ideas, customs, skills and arts of a group of people in a specific time in history

**cunning** (KUHN ihng) *adj.* skilled in deception

**curtailed** (kur TAYLD) *v.* cut short; reduced

# D

**daunting** (DAWNT ihng) *adj.* intimidating

**defaulted** (dih FAWLT uhd) *v.* failed to do something or be somewhere when required or expected; failed to make payment when due

**defend** (dih FEHND) *v.* support a position with evidence or justifications

**deferred** (dih FURD) *adj.* put off until a future time

**defiance** (dih FY uhns) *n.* open, bold resistance to authority

**defrauded** (dih FRAWD uhd) *v.* cheated

**degenerate** (dih JEHN uh rayt) *v.* grow worse

**dejection** (dih JEHK shuhn) *n.* lowness of spirits; depression

**deleterious** (dehl uh TIHR ee uhs) *adj.* harmful to health or well-being

**demonstrative** (dih MON struh tihv) *adj.* showing feelings openly

**demure** (dih MYUR) *adj.* modest

**depravity** (dih PRAV uh tee) *n.* crookedness; corruption

**depreciate** (dih PREE shee ayt) *v.* reduce in value

**derisive** (dih RY sihv) *adj.* showing contempt or ridicule; mocking

**desolate** (DEHS uh liht) *adj.* forlorn; wretched

**despotic** (dehs POT ihk) *adj.* like an absolute ruler or tyrant

**desultory** (DEHS uhl tawr ee) *adj.* aimless; random

**determination** (dih tur muh NAY shuhn) *n.* firm intention

**determine** (dih TUR muhn) *v.* cause something to happen in a certain way; control

**differences** (DIHF uhr uhns uhz) *n.* qualities that make things not the same; ways in which things are not the same

**differentiate** (dihf uh REHN shee ayt) *v.* see or express what makes two or more things different from each other

**diffused** (dih FYOOZD) *v.* spread out

**dilapidated** (duh LAP uh day tihd) *adj.* broken down

**diminution** (dihm uh NOO shuhn) *n.* lessening

**discerning** (duh ZUR nihng) *adj.* having good judgment or understanding

**discipline** (DIHS uh plihn) *n.* training that develops self-control, character, or orderliness and efficiency

**disclosed** (dihs KLOHZD) *v.* revealed; made known

**disconsolately** (dihs KON suh liht lee) *adv.* very unhappily

**discreet** (dihs KREET) *adj.* careful about what one says or does; prudent; keeping silent or preserving confidences when necessary

**discreetly** (dihs KREET lee) *adv.* without drawing attention

**discriminate** (dihs KRIHM uh nayt) *v.* see the differences between things; to act against someone because of prejudice

**discuss** (dihs KUHS) *v.* consider a topic in writing or speaking

**disgrace** (dihs GRAYS) *n.* loss of respect, honor, or esteem; shame

**disheveled** (dih SHEHV uhld) *adj.* untidy

**dishevelment** (dih SHEHV uhl muhnt) *n.* disorder; messiness

**dismal** (DIHZ muhl) *adj.* causing gloom or misery

**dispatched** (dihs PACHT) *v.* finished quickly

**disperse** (dihs PURS) *v.* break up and scatter in all directions; spread about; distribute widely

**disputed** (dihs PYOOT uhd) *adj.* contested; argued about

**dissemble** (dih SEHM buhl) *v.* conceal under a false appearance; disguise

**distinguished** (dihs TIHNG gwihsht) *adj.* having an air of distinction; celebrated for excellence; eminent; famous

**distort** (dihs TAWRT) *v.* twist out of shape

**distraught** (dihs TRAWT) *adj.* very troubled or confused

**diverged** (duh VURJD) *v.* branched out in different directions

**droll** (drohl) *adj.* funny in an odd or understated way

**duration** (du RAY shuhn) *n.* the time that a thing continues or lasts

## E

**elation** (ih LAY shuhn) *n.* feeling of exultant joy; pride; high spirits

**eloquence** (EHL uh kwuhns) *n.* speech or writing that is graceful and persuasive

**embellish** (ehm BEHL ihsh) *v.* decorate or improve by adding details; ornament; adorn

**emerge** (ih MURJ) *v.* come into existence; become visible or known

**emitting** (ih MIHT ihng) *v.* sending out

**empathy** (EHM puh thee) *n.* ability to understand and share someone else's feelings

**emulate** (EHM yuh layt) *v.* imitate (a person or thing admired)

**enamored** (ehn AM uhrd) *v.* filled with love and desire; charmed

**encroaching** (ehn KROHCH ihng) *adj.* intruding in a sneaky way

**endeavor** (ehn DEHV uhr) *n.* an earnest attempt or effort

**endeavored** (ehn DEHV uhrd) *v.* made an earnest attempt to achieve or succeed; tried

**endurance** (ehn DUR uhns) *n.* ability to withstand hardship over time

**enigma** (ih NIHG muh) *n.* mystery

**enjoined** (ehn JOYND) *v.* ordered

**entailed** (ehn TAYLD) *v.* caused or required as a necessary consequence; involved; necessitated

**enthralled** (ehn THRAWLD) *v.* held as in a spell; captivated

**enumerated** (ih NOO muh rayt ihd) *v.* named one by one; specified, as in a list

**equity** (EHK wuh tee) *n.* quality of being fair; fairness; justice

**esteem** (ehs TEEM) *n.* favorable opinion; high regard; respect

**evanescent** (ehv uh NEHS uhnt) *adj.* temporary; tending to disappear

**evidence** (EHV uh duhns) *n.* proof

**exchange** (ehks CHAYNJ) *n.* act of trading something

**exchange** (ehks CHAYNJ) *v.* trade

**exile** (EHG zyl) *v.* banish

**explicit** (ehk SPLIHS iht) *adj.* clearly stated

**extrapolating** (ehk STRAP uh layt ihng) *v.* arriving at a conclusion by inferring from known facts

## F

**fact** (fakt) *n.* a thing that has actually happened or that is true

**faltered** (FAWL tuhrd) *v.* acted hesitantly; showed uncertainty; wavered; flinched

**feasible** (FEE zuh buhl) *adj.* capable of being done or carried out; practicable; possible

**feeling** (FEE lihng) *n.* emotion that a person is aware of

**feisty** (FYS tee) *adj.* full of spirit; energetic

**fertile** (FUR tuhl) *adj.* rich in nutrients that promote growth

**fester** (FEHS tuhr) *v.* become infected; form pus

**feud** (fyood) *n.* bitter, protracted, and violent quarrel, especially between clans or families

**fickle** (FIHK uhl) *adj.* changeable

**forebears** (FAWR bairz) *n.* ancestors

**forgo** (fawr GOH) *v.* do without; abstain from; give up

**formality** (fawr MAL uh tee) *n.* attention to established rules or customs

**formidable** (FAWR muh duh buhl) *adj.* awe-inspiring

**fortitude** (FAWR tuh tood) *n.* the strength to bear misfortune and pain calmly and patiently

**fray** (fray) *n.* noisy fight

**furtive** (FUR tihv) *adj.* sneaky; hidden

**futile** (FYOO tuhl) *adj.* useless; hopeless

## G

**gallant** (GAL uhnt) *adj.* brave and noble

**grievance** (GREE vuhns) *n.* something that is thought to be unjust and a reason to feel resentment; complaint

**grotesque** (groh TEHSK) *adj.* having a strange, bizarre design; shocking or offensive

## H

**hallowed** (HAL ohd) *adj.* sacred

**haughty** (HAW tee) *adj.* arrogant

**hero** (HIHR oh) *n.* someone who is admired for brave or noble actions

**honesty** (ON uh stee) *n.* quality of being truthful

**humble** (HUHM buhl) *adj.* modest; having humility

**humbly** (HUHM buh lee) *adv.* in a manner that is not proud or arrogant; modestly

# I

**identify** (y DEHN tuh fy) *v.* say who someone or something is

**ignorance** (IHG nuhr uhns) *n.* lack of knowledge or education

**illuminate** (ih LOO muh nayt) *v.* light up; make something clearer

**imitate** (IHM uh tayt) *v.* copy the actions of another

**immaculate** (ih MAK yuh liht) *adj.* perfectly correct; without a flaw, fault or error

**imminent** (IHM uh nuhnt) *adj.* likely to happen soon

**impassive** (ihm PAS ihv) *adj.* showing no emotion

**impenetrable** (ihm PEHN uh truh buhl) *adj.* that cannot be passed through; that cannot be solved or understood; unfathomable

**implications** (ihm pluh KAY shuhnz) *n.* indirect results

**imposition** (ihm puh ZIHSH uhn) *n.* introduction of something such as a rule, tax, or punishment

**incessantly** (ihn SEHS uhnt lee) *adv.* continuing in a way that seems endless; continually; unceasingly

**incognito** (ihn kog NEE toh) *adj.* with true identity unrevealed or disguised; under an assumed name

**incredulity** (ihn kruh DOO luh tee) *n.* unwillingness or inability to believe

**individuality** (ihn duh vihj oo AL uh tee) *n.* state of being one of a kind

**indolently** (IHN duh luhnt lee) *adv.* lazily; idly

**induction** (ihn DUHK shuhn) *n.* installation; initiation

**inevitability** (ihn ehv uh tuh BIHL uh tee) *n.* quality of being certain to happen

**inevitable** (ihn EHV uh tuh buhl) *adj.* unavoidable; certain

**infallibility** (ihn fal uh BIHL uh tee) *n.* condition of not being likely to fail

**information** (ihn fuhr MAY shuhn) *n.* facts or knowledge about something

**informed** (ihn FAWRMD) *v.* gave someone information

**informed** (ihn FAWRMD) *adj.* having much knowledge, information, or education

**inscrutable** (ihn SKROO tuh buhl) *adj.* baffling; mysterious

**insidious** (ihn SIHD ee uhs) *adj.* characterized by craftiness and betrayal

**insight** (ihn syt) *n.* ability to have a deep understanding of something

**insinuatingly** (ihn SIHN yu ayt ihng lee) *adv.* suggesting indirectly; implying

**insolent** (IHN suh luhnt) *adj.* boldly disrespectful

**instigates** (IHN stuh gayts) *v.* urges on; stirs up

**instinct** (IHN stihngkt) *n.* behavior or response that one is born with

**intentions** (ihn TEHN shuhnz) *n.* aims or purposes of an action

**intercession** (ihn tuhr SEHSH uhn) *n.* act of pleading on another's behalf

**interlopers** (ihn tuhr LOHP erz) *n.* people who meddle in others' affairs; trespassers

**interminably** (ihn TUR muh nuh blee) *adv.* endlessly

**intermission** (ihn tuhr MIHSH uhn) *n.* any kind of break; more specifically, a break during a performance

**interpret** (ihn TUR priht) *v.* understand or explain the meaning of something

**interpretation** (ihn tur pruh TAY shuhn) *n.* explanation of the meaning of something

**intimately** (IHN tuh miht lee) *adv.* in a close manner; with a special or close knowledge; closely; jointly; familiarly

**introspective** (ihn truh SPEHK tihv) *adj.* having to do with looking into one's own thoughts and feelings

**involvement** (ihn VOLV muhnt) *n.* state of being included in something

**iridescent** (ihr uh DEHS uhnt) *adj.* showing colors that seem to change in different lights

**issue** (IHSH oo) *n.* subject for debate or discussion

# J

**jibed** (jybd) *v.* changed direction

**judicious** (joo DIHSH uhs) *adj.* showing good judgment

**justice** (JUHS tihs) *n.* quality of fairness and impartiality

# L

**ladle** (LAY duhl) *n.* long-handled, cuplike spoon for dipping out liquids

**lament** (luh MEHNT) *v.* express deep sorrow; mourn

**lamentable** (LAM uhn tuh buhl) *adj.* distressing; sad

**languid** (LANG gwihd) *adj.* drooping; weak

**legacy** (LEHG uh see) *n.* something handed down from an ancestor

**lithe** (lyth) *adj.* flexible

**loathsome** (LOHTH suhm) *adj.* disgusting; detestable

**lofty** (LAWF tee) *adj.* very high; noble

**longing** (lawng ihng) *n.* strong, persistent desire or craving, especially for something unattainable or distant; yearning

**lurched** (lurcht) *v.* moved awkwardly and suddenly

# M

**maladies** (MAL uh deez) *n.* diseases

**malodorous** (mal OH duhr uhs) *adj.* having a bad smell

**mammoth** (MAM uhth) *adj.* enormous

**manipulate** (muh NIHP yuh layt) *v.* handle or control

**martial** (MAHR shuhl) *adj.* military; warlike

**maudlin** (MAWD luhn) *adj.* tearfully and foolishly sentimental

**meaning** (MEE nihng) *n.* what is referred to or understood

**mediate** (MEE dee ayt) *v.* bring about agreement between people who disagree

**medium** (MEE dee uhm) *n.* particular way of communicating information and news to people, such as a newspaper or a television broadcast

**melancholy** (MEHL uhn kol ee) *adj.* sad; gloomy

**menacing** (MEHN his ihng) *v.* threatening

**metaphysical** (meht uh FIHZ uh kuhl) *adj.* spiritual; beyond the physical

**meticulously** (muh TIHK yuh luhs lee) *adv.* very carefully and precisely

**miraculously** (muh RAK yuh luhs lee) *adv.* in an amazing way; as though by a miracle

**momentous** (moh MEHN tuhs) *adj.* very important

**monotone** (MON uh tohn) *n.* uninterrupted repetition of the same tone; utterance of successive syllables or words without change of pitch or key

**monotonous** (muh NOT uh nuhs) *adj.* going on in the same tone without variation

**morality** (muh RAL uh tee) *v.* principles that someone uses to decide if behavior is right or wrong

**moribund** (MAWR uh buhnd) *adj.* slowly dying

**mortified** (MAWR tuh fyd) *adj.* extremely embarrassed

**multitude** (MUHL tuh tood) *n.* large number of persons or things, especially when gathered together or considered as a unit

**muted** (myoot ihd) *adj.* weaker; less intense

## N

**naive** (nah EEV) *adj.* unsophisticated; innocent

**novice** (NOV ihs) *adj.* new to an activity; inexperienced

**nurturing** (NUR chuhr ihng) *n.* the raising or promoting the development of; training, educating, fostering

## O

**obligation** (ob luh GAY shuhn) *n.* something that must be done

**oblivion** (uh BLIHV ee uhn) *n.* forgetfulness; the state of being unconscious or of not noticing what is happening

**obstinacy** (OB stuh nuh see) *n.* stubbornness

**ominous** (OM uh nuhs) *adj.* threatening

**oppression** (uh PREHSH uhn) *n.* act of being weighed down or held back by worries or problems; keeping others down by the unjust use of power.

## P

**pallid** (PAL ihd) *adj.* pale

**pallor** (PAL uhr) *n.* unnatural paleness

**palpable** (PAL puh buhl) *adj.* able to be felt; easily perceived

**palpitating** (PAL puh tayt ihng) *adj.* beating rapidly; throbbing

**pandemonium** (pan duh MOH nee uhm) *n.* any place or scene of wild disorder, noise, or confusion; chaos

**paradoxical** (PAR uh DOK suh kuhl) *adj.* seemingly full of contradictions

**penetrated** (PEHN uh trayt uhd) *v.* broke through

**pensive** (PEHN sihv) *adj.* thinking deeply or seriously; thoughtful

**penury** (PEHN yuhr ee) *n.* extreme poverty

**perceive** (puhr SEEV) *v.* become aware of

**perennial** (puh REHN ee uhl) *adj.* happening over and over; perpetual

**permeate** (PUR mee ayt) *v.* spread or flow throughout

**pernicious** (puhr NIHSH uhs) *adj.* causing great injury or ruin; destructive

**perplexes** (pehr PLEHKS uhz) *v.* confuses or puzzles

**perspective** (puhr SPEHK tihv) *n.* point of view

**pertinent** (PUR tuh nuhnt) *adj.* having some connection with the matter at hand; relevant; to the point

**perverse** (puhr VURS) *adj.* different from what is considered right or reasonable

**picturesque** (pihk chuh REHSK) *adj.* like or suggesting a picture; lovely to look at; attractive and interesting

**pious** (PY uhs) *adj.* having or showing religious devotion

**placidly** (PLAS ihd lee) *adv.* calmly; quietly

**plundered** (PLUHN duhrd) *v.* took goods by force; looted

**poignant** (POY nuhnt) *adj.* emotionally touching

**pondered** (PON duhrd) *v.* thought deeply about

**ponderously** (PON duhr uhs lee) *adv.* in a labored and dull way; in a boring and serious way

**potential** (puh TEHN shuhl) *n.* possibility

**precariously** (prih KAIR ee uhs lee) *adv.* insecurely

**preceded** (pree SEED uhd) *v.* came before in time, place, order, rank, or importance

**precipitous** (prih SIHP uh tuhs) *adj.* steep; sheer

**precluded** (prih KLOOD ihd) *v.* prevented

**predominant** (prih DOM uh nuhnt) *adj.* having dominating influence over others

**preliminaries** (prih LIHM uh nehr eez) *n.* steps or events before the main one

**preposterous** (prih POS tuhr uhs) *adj.* so contrary to nature, reason, or common sense as to be laughable; absurd; ridiculous

**presumed** (prih ZOOMD) *adj.* taken for granted; accepted as true, lacking proof to the contrary; supposed

**pretentious** (prih TEHN shuhs) *adj.* grand in a showy way

**prevail** (prih VAYL) *v.* gain the advantage or mastery; be victorious; triumph

**procure** (pruh KYUR) *v.* get; obtain

**prodigious** (pruh DIHJ uhs) *adj.* enormous

**prodigy** (PROD uh jee) *n.* person who is amazingly talented or intelligent, especially a child of highly unusual talent or genius

**profound** (pruh FOWND) *adj.* deep; intense

**profoundly** (pruh FOWND lee) *adv.* deeply

**provisions** (pruh VIHZH uhnz) *n.* something provided, prepared, or supplied for the future

**prudence** (PROO duhns) *n.* a sensible and careful attitude; economy

**pungent** (PUHN juhnt) *adj.* producing a sharp smell

**purged** (purjd) *v.* cleansed

# R

**raggedy** (RAG uh dee) *adj.* somewhat ragged and torn; tattered

**rancor** (RANG kuhr) *n.* bitter hate

**ravenous** (RAV uh nuhs) *adj.* wildly hungry

**react** (ree AKT) *v.* do something in response to something else

**reciprocate** (rih SIHP ruh kayt) *v.* return

**reckless** (REHK lihs) *adj.* careless; rash

**recoiling** (rih KOYL ihng) *v.* staggering back

**reconciliation** (rehk uhn sihl ee AY shuhn) *n.* the settling of a conflict or argument; agreement; compromise

**reels** (reelz) *n.* frames or spools on which thread, wire, tape, film, or a net is wound

**refrain** (rih FRAYN) *v.* hold back

**relationship** (rih LAY shuhn shihp) *n.* connection between two or more people or things

**remnants** (REHM nuhnts) *n.* what is left over; remainders

**renegade** (REHN uh gayd) *adj.* disloyal; traitorous

**research** (rih SURCH) *n.* careful study in some field of knowledge

**research** (rih SURCH) *v.* perform careful study

**resolution** (rehz uh LOO shuhn) *n.* part of a narrative in which the plot is unraveled

**respite** (REHS piht) *n.* rest; relief

**resplendent** (rih SPLEHN duhnt) *adj.* shinning brightly

**respond** (rih SPOND) *v.* reply or react

**responsibility** (rih spon suh BIHL uh tee) *n.* having to answer to someone or something else; being accountable for success or failure

**retort** (rih TAWRT) *n.* sharp or clever reply

**retribution** (reht ruh BYOO shuhn) *n.* payback; punishment for a misdeed

**revelry** (REHV uhl ree) *n.* noisy merrymaking

**revered** (rih VIHRD) *adj.* regarded with great respect and awe

**reverie** (REHV uhr ee) *n.* dreamy thinking and imagining

**revival** (rih VY vuhl) *n.* a bringing or coming back into use, attention, or being after a decline

**riddled** (RIHD uhld) *adj.* affected throughout by something unpleasant

**rifled** (RY fuhld) *v.* ransacked and robbed; searched quickly through a cupboard or drawer

**rueful** (ROO fuhl) *adj.* feeling sorrow or regret

# S

**sallow** (SAL oh) *adj.* of a sickly, pale-yellowish color

**scarred** (skahrd) *adj.* marked or dented

**scourge** (skurj) *n.* instrument for inflicting punishment

**scruples** (SKROO puhlz) *n.* misgivings about something one feels is wrong

**segment** (SEHG muhnt) *n.* division or section

**seizure** (SEE zhuhr) *n.* sudden and brief loss of consciousness and body control

**senses** (SEHNS uhz) *n.* physical ways in which a person or animal learns about the world: sight, hearing, touch, taste, and smell

**sensory** (SEHN suhr ee) *adj.* relating to the senses of sight, sound, taste, touch, or smell

**serve** (surv) *v.* work for; to be useful for

**shriveled** (SHRIHV uhld) *adj.* shrunken and wrinkled

**siege** (seej) *n.* encirclement of a fortified place by an opposing armed force intending to take it

**similarity** (sihm uh LAR uh tee) *n.* state of being alike

**skeptics** (SKEHP tihks) *n.* doubters; disbelievers

**solitude** (SOL uh tood) *n.* the state of being solitary, or alone; seclusion, isolation, or remoteness

**sources** (SAWRS uhz) *n.* places where things begin or are found

**speculate** (SPEHK yuh layt) *v.* think about or make up theories about a subject; guess at

**spurn** (spurn) *v.* reject with contempt or disdain

**stalks** (stawks) *v.* walks in a stiff, haughty, or grim manner

**standard** (STAN duhrd) *n.* idea to which other things are compared

**standard** (STAN duhrd) *adj.* normal; average

**statistics** (stuh TIHS tihks) *n.* science of collecting, analyzing, and using mathematical data

**stout** (stowt) *adj.* sturdy

**stranded** (STRAN dihd) *adj.* in a place or situation from which one needs help to leave

**submerged** (suhb MURJD) *adj.* covered with water or the like

**subsided** (suhb SYD ihd) *v.* settled down; became less active or intense

**subverting** (suhb VURT ihng) *v.* overthrowing or destroying something established

**succumbed** (suh KUHMD) *v.* gave way; yielded

**suffice** (suh FYS) *v.* be enough

**surreal** (suh REE uhl) *adj.* strange, like something from a dream

**survival** (suhr VY vuhl) *n.* the state of continuing to exist

## T

**tantalizingly** (tan tuh LY zihng lee) *adv.* in a teasing way

**telegraph** (TEHL uh graf) *n.* an apparatus or system that converts a coded message into electric impulses and sends it to a distance receiver

**temporal** (TEHM puhr uhl) *adj.* having to do with time

**tenacious** (tih NAY shuhs) *adj.* holding firmly to beliefs; persistent; stubborn; adamant

**tenement** (TEHN uh muhnt) *n.* apartment house, often run-down

**transgression** (trans GREHSH uhn) *n.* wrongdoing; sin

**treble** (TREHB uhl) *n.* high-pitched voice or sound

**trundle** (TRUHN duhl) *v.* roll along

**truth** (trooth) *n.* corresponding with reality or fact

**tumultuous** (too MUHL chu uhs) *adj.* greatly disturbed; in an uproar

## U

**understanding** (uhn duhr STAN dihng) *n.* ability to get the meaning of something; ability to think or learn

**unique** (yoo NEEK) *adj.* one of a kind

**unpalatable** (uhn PAL uh tuh buhl) *adj.* distasteful; unpleasant

**unrequited** (uhn rih KWY tuhd) *adj.* not returned or repaid

**unwieldy** (uhn WEEL dee) *adj.* awkward; clumsy

**usurped** (yoo SURPT) *v.* took power or position without right

## V

**values** (VAL yooz) *n.* beliefs accepted by an individual

**venture** (VEHN chuhr) *n.* risky action

**verify** (VEHR uh fy) *v.* make sure something is true; confirm

**vex** (vehks) *v.* annoy

**vial** (vyl) *n.* small bottle containing medicine or other liquids

**vigilant** (VIHJ uh luhnt) *adj.* watchful

**vile** (vyl) *adj.* evil; wicked

**volumes** (VOL yuhmz) *n.* sets of the issues of a periodical over a fixed period of time, usually a year; books

**voluminously** (vuh LOO muh nuhs lee) *adv.* fully; in great volume

## W

**wail** (wayl) *n.* lament; cry of deep sorrow

**war** (wawr) *n.* armed conflict between people

**warp** (wawrp) *v.* twist; distort

**wayward** (WAY wuhrd) *adj.* headstrong

**wheezed** (hweez) *v.* breathed hard with a breathy sound

**wisdom** (WIHZ duhm) *n.* ability to make good judgments based on knowledge and experience

**woeful** (WOH fuhl) *adj.* full of sorrow

**woes** (wohz) *n.* great sorrows

**writhing** (RYTH ihng) *v.* twisting; turning

# Spanish Glossary

El vocabulario de Gran Pregunta aparece en **azul**. El vocabulario academico de alta utilidad esta **subraydo**.

## A

**abash / avergonzar** *v.* apenar

**abdicated / abdicó** *v.* renunció formalmente

**absurdity / absurdo** *s.* algo ridículo o un disparate

**accentuated / acentuó** *v.* enfatizó; realzó el efecto de

**accept / aceptar** *v.* recibir algo que se da

**accumulated / acumuló** *v.* amontonado, recopilado o reunido, especialmente durante algún lapso de tiempo

**acquiesced / accedió** *v.* consintió o se doblegó calladamente sin protestar, pero sin entusiasmo

**adversary / adversario** *s.* persona que se opone o lucha contra otra

**afflicted / afligió** *v.* que sufrió o padeció de

**allotment / asignación** *s.* parte; porción

**aloofness / retraimiento** *s.* calidad de estar distante o apartado

**ambiguities / ambigüedades** *s.* declaraciones o eventos cuyos significados no son claros

**ambiguous / ambiguo** *adj.* que tiene más de un significado

**amicably / amigablemente** *adv.* de manera amistosa

**amicably / amistosamente** *adv.* de manera amigable

**amid / entre** *prep.* en medio de; rodeado por

**anguish / angustia** *s.* gran dolor o sufrimiento

**anonymous / anónimo** *adj.* sin nombre conocido o reconocido

**antagonize / contrariar** *v.* enemistar

**apex / cima** *s.* punto más alto; cumbre

**appreciate / apreciar** *v.* reconocer el valor de algo

**archaic / arcaico** *adj.* de épocas pasadas; antiguo

**ardor / ardor** *s.* pasión; entusiasmo

**arduous / arduo** *adj.* difícil; laborioso

**argument / discusión** *s.* intercambio de ideas cuando hay un desacuerdo

**articulate / articulado** *adj.* capaz de expresarse con claridad

**articulate / elocuente** *adj.* que se expresa con claridad y facilidad

**assiduous / asiduo** *adj.* hecho con atención constante y cuidadosa; diligente

**assimilated / asimiló** *v.* ingirió o absorbió

**assimilated / asimilado** *adj.* algo o alguien que ha sido completamente absorbido

**assuage / apaciguar** *v.* calmar; sosegar

**assumption / suposición** *s.* algo que se da por sentado

**atonement / desagravio** *s.* acción de enmendar algún agravio o perjuicio

**attributes / atributos** *s.* características o cualidades de una persona o cosa

**augmenting / aumentando** *v.* incrementando; haciendo más grande

**authentic / auténtico** *adj.* genuino; verdadero

**aware / consciente** *adj.* saber algo por haberlo experimentado o por haber sido informado de ello

**awestruck / pasmado** *adj.* maravillado

**awry / ladeado** *adj.* estar mal puesto o torcido

**azure / azur** *adv.* azul celeste

## B

**background / antecedentes** *s.* hechos que causan o explican algo

**bafflement / desconcierto** *s.* perplejidad; dificultad de comprensión

**balmy / balsámico** *adj.* que tiene las cualidades del bálsamo; apacible, suave, agradable

**battle / batalla** *s.* pelea entre fuerzas armadas

**battle / combatir** *v.* pelear o luchar

**barren / árido** *adj.* desértico; que tiene poca o ninguna vegetación

**beguiling / cautivar** *v.* engañar; encantar

**belief / creencia** *s.* algo que se acepta como cierto

**bemusing / aturdiendo** *v.* confundir; desconcertar

**benevolently / benévolamente** *adv.* de manera bien intencionada

**bereft / desprovisto** *adj.* despojado, privado de

**bias / predisposición** *s.* inclinación o tendencia mental; parcialidad

**bilingual / bilingüe** *adj.* que usa dos idiomas

**blight / plaga** *s.* algo que destruye o impide el crecimiento

**bulging / protuberante** *adj.* abultado

## C

**candor / franqueza** *s.* marcada honestidad o sinceridad al expresarse

**cascade / cascada** *s.* pequeño salto de agua empinado; cualquier cosa que se asemeje a un salto de agua

**censure / censura** *s.* firme desaprobación

**character / carácter** *s.* cualidades que hacen única a una persona

**choices / elecciones** s. variedad de cosas de donde uno puede seleccionar

**circumstance / circunstancia** s. situación; evento

**clarify / aclarar** v. hacer que algo sea más claro y comprensible

**clasps / agarra** v. sujeta con firmeza

**collective / colectivo** adj. conformado como grupo; reunido en uno solo

**communication / comunicación** s. intercambio de información

**compensation / compensación** s. cualquier cosa que sirve para subsanar una pérdida, daño o deuda

**compete / competir** v. tratar de ganar contra un adversario

**competition / competencia** s. rivalidad; acción de competir

**comprehend / comprender** v. entender

**comprehension / comprensión** s. acción de entender algo

**comprehension / comprensión** s. entendimiento

**conceded / concedió** v. admitió como cierto o válido; reconoció

**concept / concepto** s. idea; noción

**concessions / concesiones** s. cosas otorgadas o cedidas como privilegios

**condolences / condolencias** s. manifestaciones de compasión hacia otra persona que sufre

**confer / conferir** v. conceder; otorgar

**confines / confines** s. fronteras o zona fronteriza; borde; límite

**conformity / conformidad** s. estar de acuerdo con costumbres o normas

**connection / conexión** s. unión de dos o más cosas o ideas

**conspicuous / conspicuo** adj. que atrae la atención por ser inesperado, inusual, sobresaliente o notorio; impresionante

**contempt / desprecio** s. desdén o menosprecio

**context / contexto** s. partes de una oración cercanas a una palabra que determinan su significado exacto

**controversy / controversia** s. discusión de un asunto en el que chocan las opiniones divergentes

**countenance / semblante** s. rostro

**covenant / pacto** s. convenio o acuerdo, especialmente uno sagrado

**convince / convencer** v. persuadir mediante argumentos o evidencia

**cooperate / cooperar** v. trabajar conjuntamente para lograr algo

**credible / creíble** adj. verosímil

**creed / credo** s. declaración de creencias

**culture / cultura** s. ideas, costumbres, destrezas y arte de un grupo de personas de una época específica en la historia

**cunning / astuto** adj. hábil en el engaño

**curtailed / restringió** v. acortó; redujo

# D

**daunting / amedrentador** adj. intimidante

**defaulted / incumplió** v. dejó de hacer algo o no compareció en alguna parte cuando era requerido o esperado; faltó a un pago a su vencimiento

**defend / defender** v. proteger contra ataques

**deferred / difirió** v. postergó a una fecha futura

**defiance / desafío** s. franca y descarada resistencia a la autoridad

**defrauded / estafó** v. engañó

**degenerate / degenerar** v. empeorar

**dejection / desaliento** s. desánimo; depresión

**deleterious / nocivo** adj. perjudicial para la salud o el bienestar

**demonstrative / expresivo** adj. que demuestra abiertamente los sentimientos

**demure / reservado** adj. modesto

**depravity / depravación** s. deshonestidad; corrupción

**depreciate / depreciar** v. disminuir su valor

**derisive / burlón** adj. que muestra desprecio o ridiculiza; mofador

**desolate / desolado** adj. afligido; desconsolado

**despotic / despótico** adj. como un gobernante absoluto o tirano

**desultory / vago** adj. sin rumbo; aleatorio

**determination / determinación** s. firme intención

**determine / determinar** v. ocasionar que algo ocurra de cierta forma

**differences / diferencias** s. características que hacen que las cosas sean disímiles; maneras en que las cosas no son iguales

**differentiate / diferenciar** v. ver o expresar lo que hace que dos o más cosas sean diferentes entre sí

**diffused / difundió** v. diseminó

**dilapidated / desmoronado** adj. ruinoso

**diminution / disminución** s. reducción

**discerning / perspicaz** adj. tener buen juicio o comprensión

**discipline / disciplina** s. entrenamiento que desarrolla el dominio de sí mismo, carácter, o el orden y eficiencia

**disclosed / divulgó** v. reveló; hizo público

**disconsolately / desconsoladamente** adv. muy desdichadamente

**discreet / discreto** adj. cuidadoso con lo que dice o hace; prudente; que calla o mantiene confidencias cuando es necesario

**discreetly / discretamente** adv. sin llamar la atención

**discriminate / discriminar** v. distinguir las diferencias entre las cosas; actuar en contra de alguien por prejuicio

**discuss / discutir** v. hablar sobre algo

**disgrace / deshonra** s. pérdida del respeto, honor, o estima; vergüenza

**disheveled / desordenado** adj. desarreglado

**dishevelment / desorden** s. desarreglo; desaseo

**dismal / melancólico** *adj.* que ocasiona tristeza o desolación

**dispatched / despachó** *v.* terminó con prontitud

**disperse / dispersar** *v.* romper y desparramar en todas direcciones; esparcir; distribuir ampliamente

**disputed / disputado** *adj.* en litigio; contencioso

**dissemble / disimular** *v.* ocultar bajo una falsa apariencia; disfrazar

**distinguished / distinguido** *adj.* que tiene un aire de distinción; reconocido por su excelencia; eminente; famoso

**distort / distorsionar** *v.* enredar hasta perder la forma original

**distraught / afligido** *adj.* muy alterado o confundido

**diverged / bifurcó** *v.* ramificó en diferentes direcciones

**droll / gracioso** *adj.* divertido de manera comedida

**duration / duración** *s.* el tiempo en que algo continúa o permanece

# E

**elation / entusiasmo** *s.* sentimiento de júbilo; orgullo; alborozo

**eloquence / elocuencia** *s.* elegancia y persuasión en el discurso o la escritura

**embellish / embellecer** *v.* decorar o mejorar agregando detalles; ornamentar; adornar

**emerge / surgir** *v.* nacer como algo nuevo o mejorado; tornarse visible o conocido

**emitting / emitir** *v.* despedir

**empathy / empatía** *s.* capacidad de comprender y compartir los sentimientos de otra persona

**emulate / emular** *v.* imitar (a una persona o cosa que se admira)

**enamored / enamoró** *v.* lleno de amor y deseo; encantado

**encroaching / de manera usurpadora** *adj.* invadir de manera furtiva

**endeavor / intento** *s.* tentativa o esfuerzo formal

**endeavored / intentó** *v.* hizo un esfuerzo formal para conseguir o lograr algo; trató

**endurance / resistencia** *s.* capacidad para soportar adversidades

**enigma / enigma** *s.* misterio

**enjoined / impuso** *v.* exigió

**entailed / implicó** *v.* causó o requirió como consecuencia necesaria; involucró; obligó

**enthralled / embelesó** *v.* mantuvo como hechizado; cautivó

**enumerated / enumeró** *v.* nombró uno a uno; especificó, como en una lista

**esteem / estima** *s.* opinión favorable; aprecio; respeto

**evanescent / evanescente** *adj.* temporal; tendiente a desaparecer

**evidence / evidencia** *s.* prueba

**exchange / intercambio** *s.* acción de comerciar algo

**exchange / intercambiar** *v.* comerciar

**exile / exiliar** *v.* desterrar

**explicit / explícito** *adj.* expresado con claridad

**extrapolating / extrapolando** *v.* llegando a una conclusión por deducción de hechos conocidos

# F

**fact / hecho** *s.* algo que realmente ocurrió o que es cierto

**faltered / titubeó** *v.* actuó de forma vacilante; mostró incertidumbre; flaqueó; se acobardó

**feasible / factible** *adj.* capaz de hacerse o realizarse; viable; posible

**feeling / sentimiento** *s.* emoción de la que están conscientes las personas

**feisty / determinado** *adj.* lleno de coraje; vigoroso

**fertile / fértil** *adj.* rico en nutrientes que promueven el crecimiento

**fester / enconar** *v.* infectar; formar pus

**feud / lucha** encarnizada *s.* amargas, prolongadas y violentas disputas, especialmente entre clanes o familias

**fickle / voluble** *adj.* cambiante

**forebears / antepasados** *s.* ascendientes

**forgo / privar** *v.* contenerse de; abstenerse de; renunciar a

**formality / formalidad** *s.* atención a normas o costumbres establecidas

**formidable / formidable** *adj.* impresionante

**fortitude / fortaleza** *s.* fuerza para soportar el infortunio y el dolor con calma y paciencia

**fray / refriega** *s.* pelea escandalosa

**furtive / furtivo** *adj.* a hurtadillas; oculto

**futile / fútil** *adj.* inútil; sin remedio

# G

**gallant / gallardo** *adj.* valiente y noble

**grotesque / grotesco** *adj.* que tiene un diseño extraño, raro; extraño o inusual de manera tal que resulta repugnante u ofensivo

# H

**hallowed / santificado** *adj.* sagrado

**haughty / altanero** *adj.* arrogante

**hero / héroe** *s.* alguien a quien se admira por sus acciones valientes o nobles

**honesty / sinceridad** *s.* calidad de ser veraz

**humble / humilde** *adj.* modesto; que tiene humildad

**humbly / humildemente** *adv.* de tal manera que no es soberbio ni arrogante; modestamente

# I

**identify / identificar** v. describir lo que es una persona o cosa

**ignorance / ignorancia** s. falta de conocimiento o educación

**illuminate / iluminar** v. alumbrar; aclarar

**imitate / imitar** v. copiar las acciones de otro

**immaculate / impecable** adj. en perfectas condiciones; sin defectos, faltas o errores

**imminent / inminente** adj. que probablemente ocurrirá pronto

**impassive / impasible** adj. que no muestra emoción alguna

**impenetrable / impenetrable** adj. que no se puede atravesar; que no puede ser resuelto o entendido; insondable

**implications / implicaciones** s. consecuencias indirectas

**imposition / imposición** s. introducción de algo como una norma, impuesto o castigo

**incessantly / incesantemente** adv. que sigue de forma que pareciera interminable; continuamente; constantemente

**incognito / incógnito** adj. sin revelar la verdadera identidad; bajo un nombre ficticio

**incredulity / incredulidad** s. renuencia o incapacidad para creer

**individuality / individualidad** s. condición de ser único

**indolently / indolentemente** adv. con pereza; ociosamente

**induction / instalación** s. inclusión; iniciación

**inevitability / inevitabilidad** s. calidad de que ciertamente ocurrirá

**inevitable / inevitable** adj. ineludible; con seguridad

**infallibility / infalibilidad** s. condición de que no puede fallar

**information / información** s. hechos o conocimientos sobre algo

**informed / informado** adj. que tiene mucho conocimiento, información o educación

**informed / informó** v. le dio información a alguien

**insight / perspicacia** s. capacidad de tener una profunda comprensión sobre algo

**inscrutable / inescrutable** adj. desconcertante; misterioso

**insidious / insidioso** adj. que se caracteriza por su astucia y traición

**insinuatingly / de manera** insinuante adv. que sugiere indirectamente; que implica

**insolent / insolente** adj. descaradamente irrespetuoso

**instigates / instiga** v. fomenta; promueve

**instinct / instinto** s. conducta o respuesta con la que se nace

**intentions / intenciones** s. objetivos o propósitos de una acción

**intercession / intercesión** s. acción de abogar por otra persona

**interlopers / intrusos** s. personas que interfieren en los asuntos de otros; invasores

**interminably / interminablemente** adv. que no tiene fin

**intermission / intermedio** s. cualquier tipo de interrupción; más específicamente, el entreacto durante una función de teatro

**interpret / interpretar** v. entender o explicar el significado de algo

**interpretation / interpretación** s. explicación del significado de algo

**intimately / íntimamente** adv. de forma cercana; con conocimiento especial o estrecho; celosamente; conjuntamente; familiarmente

**introspective / introspectivo** adj. que tiene que ver con el análisis de sus propios pensamientos y sentimientos

**involvement / participación** s. condición de estar incluido en algo

**iridescent / iridiscente** adj. que muestra colores que parecen cambiar de acuerdo a los diferentes tipos de luz

**issue / asunto** s. tema para debate o discusión

# J

**jibed / viró** v. cambió de dirección

**judicious / juicioso** adj. que muestra buen juicio

**justice / justicia** s. calidad de equidad e imparcialidad

# L

**ladle / cazo** s. cucharón hondo de mango largo usado para servir líquidos

**lament / lamentar** v. expresar profunda tristeza; penar

**lamentable / lamentable** adj. angustioso; penoso

**languid / lánguido** adj. flojo; débil

**legacy / legado** s. algo heredado de un antepasado

**lithe / ágil** adj. flexible

**loathsome / odioso** adj. repugnante; detestable

**lofty / elevado** adj. muy alto; noble

**longing / añoranza** s. fuerte y persistente deseo o antojo, particularmente por algo inalcanzable o distante; nostalgia

**lurched / sacudió** v. se movió torpe y repentinamente

# M

**maladies / dolencias** s. enfermedades

**malodorous / maloliente** adj. que tiene mal olor

**mammoth / gigante** adj. enorme

**manipulate / manipular** v. manejar o controlar

**martial / marcial** adj. de corte militar

**maudlin / llorón** adj. lloroso y tontamente sentimental

**meaning / significado** s. de qué trata o qué se entiende por algo

**mediate / mediar** v. interceder para que las partes que están en desacuerdo lleguen a un acuerdo

**medium / medio** *s.* manera particular de comunicar información y noticias a la gente, como un periódico o un programa de televisión

**melancholy / melancolía** *s.* tristeza; pesimismo

**menacing / amenazar** *v.* intimidar

**metaphysical / metafísico** *adj.* espiritual; que traspasa lo físico

**meticulously / meticulosamente** *adv.* de manera muy cuidadosa y precisa

**miraculously / milagrosamente** *adv.* de manera sorprendente; como por milagro

**momentous / trascendental** *adj.* muy importante

**monotone / monotonía** *s.* repetición ininterrumpida de un mismo tono; pronunciación de sílabas o palabras sucesivas sin cambiar el tono o tonalidad

**monotonous / monótono** *adj.* seguir en el mismo tono sin variación

**morality / moralidad** *v.* principios que sirven para decidir si el comportamiento es correcto o incorrecto

**moribund / moribundo** *adj.* que muere lentamente

**mortified / avergonzado** *adj.* extremadamente humillado

**multitude / multitud** *s.* gran cantidad de personas o cosas, especialmente cuando se juntan o se consideran una unidad

**muted / silencioso** *adj.* más débil; menos intenso

# N

**naive / ingenuo** *adj.* poco sofisticado; inocente

**novice / novato** *adj.* nuevo en cualquier actividad; sin experiencia

**nurturing / formación** *s.* crianza o fomento del desarrollo; capacitación, educación, crianza

# O

**obligation / obligación** *s.* algo que se debe hacer

**oblivion / olvido** *s.* falta de memoria; condición de estar inconsciente o inadvertido de lo que ocurre

**obstinacy / obstinación** *s.* terquedad

**ominous / siniestro** *adj.* amenazante

**oppression / opresión** *s.* sensación de estar agobiado o reprimido por preocupaciones, problemas o el uso injusto del poder

# P

**pallid / pálido** *adj.* lívido

**pallor / palidez** *s.* lividez poco natural

**palpable / palpable** *adj.* capaz de sentirse; percibido con facilidad

**palpitating / palpitante** *adj.* que late rápidamente; que pulsa

**pandemonium / pandemonio** *s.* cualquier lugar o escena de desorden, ruido o confusión desenfrenada; caos

**paradoxical / paradójico** *adj.* aparentemente lleno de contradicciones

**penetrated / penetró** *v.* traspasó

**pensive / pensativo** *adj.* que reflexiona profunda o seriamente

**penury / penuria** *s.* extrema pobreza

**perceive / percibir** *v.* darse cuenta de

**perennial / perenne** *adj.* que ocurre una y otra vez; perpetuo

**permeate / penetrar** *v.* extenderse o fluir a través

**pernicious / pernicioso** *adj.* que causa gran perjuicio o ruina; destructivo

**perplexes / desconcierta** *v.* confunde o deja perplejo

**perspective / perspectiva** *s.* punto de vista

**pertinent / pertinente** *adj.* que tiene alguna conexión con el asunto entre manos; relevante; al grano

**perverse / perverso** *adj.* distinto de lo que se considera correcto o razonable

**picturesque / pintoresco** *adj.* que sugiere o que se parece a una pintura; hermoso a la vista

**pious / piadoso** *adj.* que tiene o muestra fervor religioso

**placidly / plácidamente** *adv.* tranquilamente; sosegadamente

**plundered / saqueó** *v.* que tomó mercancías por la fuerza; robó

**poignant / conmovedor** *adj.* que suscita emociones

**pondered / sopesó** *v.* consideró profundamente

**ponderously / pesadamente** *adv.* de manera forzada y monótona; de forma aburrida y seria

**potential / potencial** *s.* posibilidad; habilidades que se necesitan para triunfar

**precariously / precariamente** *adv.* de manera insegura

**preceded / precedió** *v.* que estaba antes en tiempo, lugar, orden, rango o importancia

**precipitous / escarpado** *adj.* abrupto; vertical

**precluded / impidió** *v.* imposibilitó

**predominant / predominante** *adj.* que tiene influencia dominante sobre otros

**preliminaries / preparativos** *s.* pasos o eventos antes del principal

**preposterous / absurdo** *adj.* tan contrario a la naturaleza, la razón o el sentido común que es irrisorio; ilógico; ridículo

**presumed / supuesto** *adj.* dado por sentado; aceptado como cierto, a falta de prueba de lo contrario; asumido

**pretentious / pretencioso** *adj.* magnífico de manera ostentosa

**prevail / prevalecer** *v.* obtener la ventaja o el dominio; salir victorioso; triunfar

**procure / procurar** *v.* lograr; obtener

**prodigious / prodigioso** *adj.* enorme

**prodigy / prodigio** *s.* persona que es increíblemente talentosa o inteligente, particularmente un niño de talento extraordinario; genio

**profound / profundo** *adj.* hondo; intenso

**profoundly / profundamente** *adv.* intensamente

**provisions / suministros** *s.* algo que se provee, prepara o suple para el futuro

**prudence / prudencia** *s.* actitud racional y cuidadosa; economía

**pungent / acre** *adj.* que produce un olor penetrante

**purged / depuró** *v.* purificó

# R

**raggedy / andrajoso** *adj.* bastante harapiento y roto; hecho jirones

**rancor / rencor** *s.* odio implacable

**ravenous / voraz** *adj.* con hambre desmesurada

**react / reaccionar** *v.* hacer algo en respuesta a otra cosa

**reciprocate / corresponder** *v.* devolver

**reckless / temerario** *adj.* descuidado; descabellado

**recoiling / retrocediendo** *v.* dando marcha atrás

**reconciliation / reconciliación** *s.* resolución de un conflicto o disputa; acuerdo; compromiso

**reels / carretes** *s.* marcos o rollos en los que se arrolla hilo, alambre, cinta o red

**refrain / abstener** *v.* contenerse

**relationship / relación** *s.* conexión entre dos o más personas o cosas

**remnants / remanentes** *s.* sobrantes; restos

**renegade / renegado** *adj.* desleal; traicionero

**research / investigación** *s.* estudio profundo en algún campo del conocimiento

**research / investigar** *v.* realizar estudio profundo

**resolution / resolución** *s.* parte de una narrativa en la que se desenmaraña la trama

**respite / respiro** *s.* descanso; alivio

**resplendent / resplandeciente** *adj.* radiantemente iluminado

**respond / responder** *v.* contestar o reaccionar

**responsibility / responsabilidad** *s.* tener que responder ante alguien o algo; tener que rendir cuentas por el éxito o el fracaso

**retort / réplica** *s.* respuesta cortante o astuta

**retribution / castigo** *s.* restitución; escarmiento por una falta cometida

**revelry / parranda** *s.* fiesta ruidosa

**revered / venerado** *adj.* tratado con gran respeto y admiración

**reverie / ensueño** *s.* pensamiento e imaginación soñadora

**revival / restablecimiento** *s.* traer o devolver al uso, atención o naturaleza después de un descenso

**riddled / plagado** *adj.* afectado completamente

**rifled / desvalijó** *v.* saqueó y robó; buscó rápidamente en un armario o gaveta

**rueful / arrepentido** *adj.* que siente tristeza o remordimiento

# S

**sallow / amarillento** *adj.* de color enfermizo, pálido maciliento

**scarred / cicatrizado** *adj.* marcado o abollado

**scourge / azote** *s.* instrumento para imponer un castigo

**scruples / escrúpulos** *s.* dudas sobre algo que uno siente que es incorrecto

**segment / segmento** *s.* división o sección

**seizure / ataque** *s.* breve y repentina pérdida del conocimiento y del control corporal

**senses / sentidos** *s.* formas físicas con las que una persona o animal aprende sobre el mundo: vista, oído, tacto, gusto y olfato

**sensory / sensorial** *adj.* relativo a los sentidos de la vista, oído, gusto, tacto y olfato

**serve / servir** *v.* trabajar para; ser útil para

**shriveled / marchito** *adj.* seco y arrugado

**siege / sitio** *s.* cercamiento de un lugar fortificado por fuerzas armadas opositoras con el fin de tomarlo

**similarity / similitud** *s.* condición de ser parecidos

**skeptics / escépticos** *s.* aquéllos que dudan; aquéllos que no creen

**skeptics / escépticos** *s.* personas que dudan y cuestionan las ideas generalmente aceptadas

**solitude / soledad** *s.* condición de estar solitario o solo; reclusión, aislamiento o alejamiento

**sources / fuentes** *s.* lugares en donde comienzan o se encuentran las cosas

**speculate / especular** *v.* pensar o inventar teorías sobre un tema; adivinar

**spurn / desdeñar** *v.* rechazar con desprecio o desdén

**stalks / taconea** *v.* que camina de manera arrogante, ceremoniosa y severa

**standard / norma** *s.* concepto contra el que se comparan otras cosas

**standard / estándar** *adj.* normal; promedio

**statistics / estadísticas** *s.* ciencia de recoger, analizar y usar datos matemáticos

**stout / sólido** *adj.* robusto

**stranded / varado** *adj.* desamparado en un lugar o situación donde se necesita ayuda para salir

**submerged / sumergido** *adj.* cubierto con agua o algo similar

**subsided / disminuyó** *v.* se calmó; se volvió menos activo o intenso

**subverting / trastornando** *v.* derribando o destruyendo algo establecido

**succumbed / sucumbió** *v.* se rindió; cedió

**suffice / bastar** *v.* ser suficiente

**surreal / surrealista** *adj.* extraño, como algo salido de un sueño

**survival / supervivencia** *s.* condición de continuar existiendo

## T

**tantalizingly / tentadoramente** *adv.* de manera provocativa

**telegraph / telégrafo** *s.* aparato o sistema que convierte un mensaje codificado en impulsos eléctricos y lo envía a un receptor distante

**temporal / temporal** *adj.* que tiene que ver con el tiempo

**tenacious / tenaz** *adj.* que se mantiene firme en sus creencias; persistente; terco; decidido

**tenement / casa de vecindad** *s.* vivienda, a menudo en malas condiciones

**transgression / transgresión** *s.* infracción; pecado

**treble / tiple** *s.* voz o sonido muy agudo

**trundle / rodar** *v.* ir rodando

**truth / verdad** *s.* que corresponde a realidades o hechos

**tumultuous / tumultuoso** *adj.* muy agitado; en un alboroto

## U

**understanding / entendimiento** *s.* capacidad de comprender el significado de algo; capacidad para pensar o aprender

**unique / único** *adj.* exclusivo

**unpalatable / desagradable** *adj.* repugnante; molesto

**unrequited / no correspondido** *adj.* no reciprocado ni devuelto

**unwieldy / abultado** *adj.* incómodo; torpe

**usurped / usurpó** *v.* tomó el poder o posición sin derecho

## V

**values / valores** *s.* convicciones aceptadas por una persona

**venture / ventura** *s.* acción riesgosa

**verify / verificar** *v.* asegurarse de que algo es cierto; corroborar

**vex / fastidiar** *v.* irritar

**vial / frasco** *s.* envase pequeño que contiene medicamento u otros líquidos

**vigilant / vigilante** *adj.* alerta

**vile / vil** *adj.* malévolo; malvado

**volumes / volúmenes** *s.* conjuntos de ejemplares de periódicos que abarcan un lapso de tiempo fijo, generalmente un año; libros

**voluminously / voluminosamente** *adv.* completamente; de gran volumen

## W

**wail / gemido** *s.* lamento; grito de profundo dolor

**war / guerra** *s.* conflicto armado entre pueblos

**warp / torcer** *v.* retorcer; distorsionar

**wayward / avieso** *adj.* caprichoso

**wheezed / resolló** *v.* respiró con silbido

**wisdom / sabiduría** *s.* capacidad de emitir buenos juicios con base en el conocimiento y la experiencia

**woeful / afligido** *adj.* lleno de dolor

**woes / aflicciones** *s.* grandes tristezas

**writhing / retorcer** *v.* contorsionar; serpentear

# Literary Terms

**ACT** See *Drama.*

**ALLEGORY** An *allegory* is a story or tale with two or more levels of meaning—a literal level and one or more symbolic levels. The events, setting, and characters in an allegory are symbols for ideas and qualities.

**ALLITERATION** *Alliteration* is the repetition of initial consonant sounds. Writers use alliteration to give emphasis to words, to imitate sounds, and to create musical effects. In the following line from Edgar Allan Poe's "The Raven" (p. 710), there is alliteration of the *w* sound: Once upon a midnight dreary, while I pondered weak and weary, . . .

**ALLUSION** An *allusion* is a reference to a well-known person, place, event, literary work, or work of art. In O. Henry's "The Gift of the Magi" (p. 260), the title and details of the story refer to the biblical account of the Magi, wise men who brought gifts to the baby Jesus.

**ANALOGY** An *analogy* makes a comparison between two or more things that are similar in some ways but otherwise unalike.

**ANECDOTE** An *anecdote* is a brief story about an interesting, amusing, or strange event told to entertain or to make a point. In the excerpt from "A Lincoln Preface" (p. 500), Carl Sandburg tells anecdotes about Abraham Lincoln. See also *Narrative.*

**ANTAGONIST** An *antagonist* is a character or force in conflict with a main character, or protagonist.

**ANTICLIMAX** Like a climax, an *anticlimax* is a turning point in a story. However, an anticlimax is always a letdown. It's the point at which you learn that the story will not turn out the way you had expected. In Thayer's "Casey at the Bat" (p. 696), the anticlimax occurs when Casey strikes out instead of hitting a game-winning run.

**ARCHETYPE** An *archetype* is a type of character, detail, image, or situation that appears in literature throughout history. Some critics believe that archetypes reveal deep truths about human experience.

**ARGUMENT** See *Persuasion.*

**ASIDE** An *aside* is a short speech delivered by a character in a play in order to express his or her true thoughts and feelings. Traditionally, the aside is directed to the audience and is presumed to be inaudible to the other actors.

**ASSONANCE** *Assonance* is the repetition of vowel sounds followed by different consonants in two or more stressed syllables. Assonance is found in the phrase "weak and weary" in Edgar Allan Poe's "The Raven" (p. 710).

**ATMOSPHERE** See *Mood.*

**AUTOBIOGRAPHY** An *autobiography* is a form of nonfiction in which a writer tells his or her own life story. An autobiography may tell about the person's whole life or only a part of it. An example of an autobiography is the excerpt from *A White House Diary* (p. 104).

See also *Biography* and *Nonfiction.*

See also *Oral Tradition.*

**BIOGRAPHY** A *biography* is a form of nonfiction in which a writer tells the life story of another person. Biographies have been written about many famous people, historical and contemporary, but they can also be written about "ordinary" people. An example of a biography is the excerpt from *Arthur Ashe Remembered* (p. 508).

See also *Autobiography* and *Nonfiction.*

**BLANK VERSE** *Blank verse* is poetry written in unrhymed iambic pentameter lines. This verse form was widely used by William Shakespeare.

See also *Meter.*

**CHARACTER** A *character* is a person or an animal that takes part in the action of a literary work. The main character, or protagonist, is the most important character in a story. This character often changes in some important way as a result of the story's events. In Richard Connell's "The Most Dangerous Game" (p. 214), Rainsford is the main character and General Zaroff is the antagonist, or character who opposes the main character.

Characters are sometimes classified as round or flat, dynamic or static. A *round character* shows many different traits—faults as well as virtues. A *flat character* shows only one trait. A *dynamic character* develops and grows during the course of the story; a static character does not change.

See also *Characterization* and *Motivation.*

**CHARACTERIZATION** *Characterization* is the act of creating and developing a character. In *direct characterization,* the author directly states a character's traits.

For example, at the beginning of "The Necklace" (p. 332), Maupassant directly characterizes Madame Loisel: "She was one of those pretty, charming young women. . . ."

In *indirect characterization,* an author provides clues about a character by describing what a character looks like, does, and says, as well as how other characters react to him or her. It is up to the reader to draw conclusions about the character based on this indirect information.

The most effective indirect characterizations usually result from showing characters acting or speaking.

See also *Character.*

**CLIMAX** The *climax* of a story, novel, or play is the high point of interest or suspense. The events that make up the rising action lead up to the climax. The events that make up the falling action follow the climax.

See also *Conflict, Plot,* and *Anticlimax.*

**COMEDY** A *comedy* is a literary work, especially a play, that has a happy ending. Comedies often show ordinary characters in conflict with society. These conflicts are resolved through misunderstandings, deceptions, and concealed identities, which result in the correction of moral faults or social wrongs. Types of comedy include *romantic comedy,* which involves problems among lovers, and the *comedy of manners,* which satirically challenges the social customs of a sophisticated society. Comedy is often contrasted with tragedy, in which the protagonist meets an unfortunate end.

**COMIC RELIEF** *Comic relief* is a technique that is used to interrupt a serious part of a literary work by introducing a humorous character or situation.

**CONFLICT** A *conflict* is a struggle between opposing forces. Characters in conflict form the basis of stories, novels, and plays.

There are two kinds of conflict: external and internal. In an *external conflict,* the main character struggles against an outside force. This force may be another character, as in Richard Connell's "The Most Dangerous Game" (p. 214), in which Rainsford struggles with General Zaroff. The outside force could also be the standards or expectations of a group, such as the family prejudices that Romeo and Juliet struggle against. Their story (p. 806) shows them in conflict with society. The outside force may be nature itself, a person-against-nature conflict. The two men who are trapped by a fallen tree in Saki's "The Interlopers" (p. 270) face such a conflict.

An *internal conflict* involves a character in conflict with himself or herself. In "Checkouts" (p. 82), two young people who meet by chance in a supermarket agonize over whether they should speak to each other.

See also *Plot.*

**CONNOTATION** The *connotation* of a word is the set of ideas associated with it in addition to its explicit meaning.

See also *Denotation.*

**CONSONANCE** *Consonance* is the repetition of final consonant sounds in stressed syllables with different vowel sounds, as in *hat* and *sit.*

**CONTEMPORARY INTERPRETATION** A *contemporary interpretation* is a literary work of today that responds to and sheds new light on a well-known, earlier work of literature. Such an interpretation may refer to any aspect of the older work, including plot, characters, settings, imagery, language, and theme. Edna St. Vincent Millay's poem "An Ancient Gesture" (p. 1128), for example, provides a modern perspective on the characters Penelope and Odysseus in the *Odyssey.*

**COUPLET** A *couplet* is a pair of rhyming lines, usually of the same length and meter. In the following couplet from a poem by William Shakespeare, the speaker comforts himself with the thought of his love:

> For thy sweet love remember'd such wealth brings
>
> That then I scorn to change my state with kings.

See also *Stanza.*

**DENOTATION** The *denotation* of a word is its dictionary meaning, independent of other associations that the word may have. The denotation of the word *lake,* for example, is an inland body of water. "Vacation spot" and "place where the fishing is good" are connotations of the word *lake.*

See also *Connotation.*

**DESCRIPTION** A *description* is a portrait in words of a person, a place, or an object. Descriptive writing uses sensory details, those that appeal to the senses: sight, hearing, taste, smell, and touch. Description can be found in all types of writing. Rudolfo Anaya's essay "A Celebration of Grandfathers" (p. 444) contains descriptive passages.

**DIALECT** *Dialect,* the form of language spoken by people in a particular region or group, may involve changes to the pronunciation, vocabulary, and sentence structure of standard English. An example from Mark Twain's "The Invalid's Story" (p. 362) is a character's use of the term *yourn* for *yours*.

**DIALOGUE** A *dialogue* is a conversation between characters that may reveal their traits and advance the action of a narrative. In fiction or nonfiction, quotation marks indicate a speaker's exact words, and a new paragraph usually indicates a change of speaker. Following is an exchange between the narrator and his frail younger brother, Doodle, in "The Scarlet Ibis" (p. 384):

> "Aw, come on Doodle," I urged. "You can do it. Do you want to be different from everybody else when you start school?"
>
> "Does it make any difference?"

Quotation marks are not used in a *script*, the printed copy of a play. Instead, the dialogue follows the name of the speaker, as in this example from Chekhov's *The Inspector General* (p. 970):

> **DRIVER.** Oh, yes, he's a good one, this one.

**DICTION** *Diction* refers to an author's choice of words, especially with regard to range of vocabulary, use of slang and colloquial language, and level of formality. These lines from Ernest Lawrence Thayer's poem "Casey at the Bat" (p. 696) are an example of colloquial, informal diction: "It looked extremely rocky for the Mudville nine that day; / The score stood two to four; with but an inning left to play."

See also *Connotation* and *Denotation*.

**DIRECT CHARACTERIZATION**
See *Characterization*.

**DRAMA** A *drama* is a story written to be performed by actors. The script of a drama is made up of *dialogue*—the words the actors say—and *stage directions*, which are comments on how and where action happens.

The drama's *setting* is the time and place in which the action occurs. It is indicated by one or more sets, including furniture and backdrops, that suggest interior or exterior scenes. *Props* are objects, such as a sword or a cup of tea, that are used onstage.

At the beginning of most plays, a brief *exposition* gives the audience some background information about the characters and the situation. Just as in a story or novel, the plot of a drama is built around characters in conflict.

Dramas are divided into large units called *acts*, which are divided into smaller units called scenes. A long play may include many sets that change with the *scenes*, or it may indicate a change of scene with lighting.

See also *Dialogue, Genre, Stage Directions,* and *Tragedy. Romeo and Juliet* (p. 806) is a long play in five acts.

**DRAMATIC IRONY** See *Irony.*

**DRAMATIC MONOLOGUE** A *dramatic monologue* is a poem in which a character reveals himself or herself by speaking to a silent listener.

**DRAMATIC POETRY** *Dramatic poetry* is poetry that utilizes the techniques of drama. The dialogue used in Edgar Allan Poe's "The Raven" (p. 710) makes it dramatic dialogue. A *dramatic monologue* is a poem spoken by one person, addressing a silent listener.

**END RHYME** See *Rhyme.*

**EPIC** An *epic* is a long narrative poem about the deeds of gods or heroes. Homer's *Odyssey* (p. 1044) is an example of epic poetry. It tells the story of the Greek hero Odysseus, the king of Ithaca.

An epic is elevated in style and usually follows certain patterns. The poet begins by announcing the subject and asking a Muse—one of the nine goddesses of the arts, literature, and sciences—to help. An *epic hero* is the larger-than-life central character in an epic. Through behavior and deeds, the epic hero displays qualities that are valued by the society in which the epic originated.

See also *Epic Simile* and *Narrative Poem.*

**EPIC SIMILE** An *epic simile,* also called *Homeric simile,* is an elaborate comparison of unlike subjects. In this example from the *Odyssey* (p. 1044), Homer compares the bodies of men killed by Odysseus to a fisherman's catch heaped up on the shore:

> Think of a catch that fishermen haul in to a
>     half-moon bay
> in a fine-meshed net from the whitecaps of the sea:
> how all are poured out on the sand, in throes
>     for the salt sea,
> twitching their cold lives away in Helios' fiery air:
>     so lay the suitors heaped on one another.

See also *Figurative Language* and *Simile.*

**EPIPHANY** An *epiphany* is a character's sudden flash of insight into a conflict or situation. At the end of Judith

Ortiz Cofer's story "American History" (p. 240), for example, the central character experiences an epiphany.

**ESSAY** An *essay* is a short nonfiction work about a particular subject. While classification is difficult, four types of essays are sometimes identified.

A *descriptive essay* seeks to convey an impression about a person, place, or object. In "A Celebration of Grandfathers" (p. 444), Rudolfo Anaya describes the cultural values that his grandfather and other "old ones" from his childhood passed down.

A *narrative essay* tells a true story. In "The Washwoman" (p. 26), Isaac Bashevis Singer tells of his childhood in Poland.

An *expository essay* gives information, discusses ideas, or explains a process. In "Single Room, Earth View" (p. 468), Sally Ride explains what it is like to be in outer space.

A *persuasive essay* tries to convince readers to do something or to accept the writer's point of view. Pete Hamill's "Libraries Face Sad Chapter" (p. 530) is a persuasive essay.

See also *Description, Exposition, Genre, Narration, Nonfiction,* and *Persuasion.*

**EXPOSITION** *Exposition* is writing or speech that explains a process or presents information. In the plot of a story or drama, the exposition is the part of the work that introduces the characters, the setting, and the basic situation.

**EXTENDED METAPHOR** In an *extended metaphor,* as in regular metaphor, a writer speaks or writes of a subject as though it were something else. An extended metaphor sustains the comparison for several lines or for an entire poem.

See also *Figurative Language* and *Metaphor.*

**EXTERNAL CONFLICT** See *Conflict.*

**FALLING ACTION** See *Plot.*

**FANTASY** A *fantasy* is highly imaginative writing that contains elements not found in real life. Examples of fantasy include stories that involve supernatural elements, stories that resemble fairy tales, and stories that deal with imaginary places and creatures.

See also *Science Fiction.*

**FICTION** *Fiction* is prose writing that tells about imaginary characters and events. The term is usually used for novels and short stories, but it also applies to dramas and narrative poetry. Some writers rely on their imaginations alone to create their works of fiction. Others base their fiction on actual events and people, to which they add invented characters, dialogue, and plot situations.

See also *Genre, Narrative,* and *Nonfiction.*

**FIGURATIVE LANGUAGE** *Figurative language* is writing or speech not meant to be interpreted literally. It is often used to create vivid impressions by setting up comparisons between dissimilar things.

Some frequently used figures of speech are *metaphors, similes,* and *personifications.*

See also *Literal Language.*

**FLASHBACK** A *flashback* is a means by which authors present material that occurred earlier than the present tense of the narrative. Authors may include this material in a character's memories, dreams, or accounts of past events.

**FOIL** A *foil* is a character who provides a contrast to another character. In *Romeo and Juliet* (p. 806), the fiery temper of Tybalt serves as a foil to the good nature of Benvolio.

**FOOT** See *Meter.*

**FORESHADOWING** *Foreshadowing* is the use in a literary work of clues that suggest events that have yet to occur. This technique helps create suspense, keeping readers wondering about what will happen next.

See also *Suspense.*

**FREE VERSE** *Free verse* is poetry not written in a regular pattern of meter or rhyme. Like Whitman's "I Hear America Singing" (p. 750), however, it may use parallelism and various sound devices.

**GENRE** A *genre* is a category or type of literature. Literature is commonly divided into three major genres: poetry, prose, and drama. Each major genre is in turn divided into smaller genres, as follows:

1. Poetry: Lyric Poetry, Concrete Poetry, Dramatic Poetry, Narrative Poetry, and Epic Poetry

2. Prose: Fiction (Novels and Short Stories) and Nonfiction (Biography, Autobiography, Letters, Essays, and Reports)

3. Drama: Serious Drama and Tragedy, Comic Drama, Melodrama, and Farce

See also *Drama, Poetry,* and *Prose.*

**HAIKU** The *haiku* is a three-line verse form. The first and third lines of a haiku each have five syllables. The second line has seven syllables. A haiku seeks to convey a single vivid emotion by means of images from nature.

**HOMERIC SIMILE** See *Epic Simile.*

**HYPERBOLE** A *hyperbole* is a deliberate exaggeration or overstatement. In Mark Twain's "The Notorious Jumping Frog of Calaveras County," the claim that Jim Smiley would follow a bug as far as Mexico to win a bet is a hyperbole. As this example shows, hyperboles are often used for comic effect.

**IAMB** See *Meter.*

**IDIOM** An *idiom* is an expression that is characteristic of a language, region, community, or class of people. *Idiomatic expressions* often arise from figures of speech and therefore cannot be understood literally. In "The Invalid's Story" (p. 362), for example, a character uses the idiom *throw up the sponge,* meaning "surrender."

See also *Dialect.*

**IMAGE** An *image* is a word or phrase that appeals to one or more of the five senses—sight, hearing, touch, taste, or smell. Writers use images to re-create sensory experiences in words.

See also *Description.*

**IMAGERY** *Imagery* is the descriptive or figurative language used in literature to create word pictures for the reader. These pictures, or images, are created by details of sight, sound, taste, touch, smell, or movement.

**INDIRECT CHARACTERIZATION**
See *Characterization.*

**INTERNAL** See *Conflict.*

**INTERNAL RHYME** See *Rhyme.*

**IRONY** *Irony* is the general term for literary techniques that portray differences between appearance and reality, or expectation and result. In *verbal irony,* words are used to suggest the opposite of what is meant. In *dramatic irony,* there is a contradiction between what a character thinks and what the reader or audience knows to be true. In *irony of situation,* an event occurs that directly contradicts the expectations of the characters, the reader, or the audience.

**LEGEND** See *Oral Tradition.*

**LITERAL LANGUAGE** *Literal language* uses words in their ordinary senses. It is the opposite of *figurative*

*language.* If you tell someone standing on a diving board to jump in, you speak literally. If you tell someone on the street to jump in a lake, you are speaking figuratively.

See also *Figurative Language.*

**LYRIC POEM** A *lyric poem* is a highly musical verse that expresses the thoughts, observations, and feelings of a single speaker.

**MAIN CHARACTER** See *Character.*

**METAPHOR** A *metaphor* is a figure of speech in which one thing is spoken of as though it were something else. Unlike a simile, which compares two things using *like* or *as,* a metaphor implies a comparison between them. In "Dreams" (p. 621), Langston Hughes uses a metaphor to show what happens to a life without dreams:

> . . . if dreams die
>
> Life is a broken-winged bird
>
> That cannot fly.

See also *Extended Metaphor* and *Figurative Language.*

**METER** The *meter* of a poem is its rhythmical pattern. This pattern is determined by the number and types of stresses, or beats, in each line. To describe the meter of a poem, you must scan its lines. Scanning involves marking the stressed and unstressed syllables, as shown with the following two lines from "I Wandered Lonely as a Cloud" by William Wordsworth (p. 622):

> Ĭ wán|dĕřed lońe|lў ás| ă clóud
>
> Thăt floáts | ŏn hígh| o'ĕr váles| ănd hílls.

As you can see, each strong stress is marked with a slanted line (´) and each unstressed syllable with a horseshoe symbol (˘). The stressed and unstressed syllables are then divided by vertical lines (|) into groups called *feet.* The following types of feet are common in English poetry:

1. *Iamb:* a foot with one unstressed syllable followed by a stressed syllable, as in the word "again"

2. *Trochee:* a foot with one stressed syllable followed by an unstressed syllable, as in the word "wonder"

3. *Anapest:* a foot with two unstressed syllables followed by one strong stress, as in the phrase "on the beach"

4. *Dactyl:* a foot with one strong stress followed by two unstressed syllables, as in the word "wonderful"

5. *Spondee:* a foot with two strong stresses, as in the word "spacewalk"

Depending on the type of foot that is most common in them, lines of poetry are described as *iambic, trochaic, anapestic,* and so forth.

Lines are also described in terms of the number of feet that occur in them, as follows:

1. *Monometer:* verse written in one-foot lines
   All things
   Must pass
   Away.

2. *Dimeter:* verse written in two-foot lines
   Thomas | Jefferson
   What do | you say
   Under the | gravestone
   Hidden | away?

   —Rosemary and Stephen Vincent Benét,
   "Thomas Jefferson, 1743–1826"

3. *Trimeter:* verse written in three-foot lines
   I know | not whom | I meet
   I know | not where | I go.

4. *Tetrameter:* verse written in four-foot lines

5. *Pentameter:* verse written in five-foot lines

6. *Hexameter:* verse written in six-foot lines

7. *Heptameter:* verse written in seven-foot lines

**Blank verse,** used by Shakespeare in *Romeo and Juliet* (p. 806), is poetry written in unrhymed iambic pentameter.

**Free verse,** used by Walt Whitman in "I Hear America Singing" (p. 750), is poetry that does not follow a regular pattern of meter and rhyme.

**MONOLOGUE** A *monologue* in a play is a speech by one character that, unlike a *soliloquy,* is addressed to another character or characters. An example from Shakespeare's *Romeo and Juliet* (p. 806) is the speech by the Prince of Verona in Act 1, Scene i, lines 72–94.

See also **Soliloquy.**

**MONOMETER** See **Meter.**

**MOOD** *Mood,* or *atmosphere,* is the feeling created in the reader by a literary work or passage. The mood is often suggested by descriptive details. Often the mood can be described in a single word, such as lighthearted, frightening, or despairing. Notice how this passage from Edgar Allan Poe's "The Cask of Amontillado" (p. 60) contributes to an eerie, fearful mood:

"The niter!" I said; "see, it increases. It hangs like moss upon the vaults. We are below the river's bed. The

drops of moisture trickle among the bones. Come, we will go back ere it is too late."

See also **Tone.**

**MORAL** A *moral* is a lesson taught by a literary work, especially a fable—many fables, for example, have a stated moral at the end. It is customary, however, to discuss contemporary works in terms of the themes they explore, rather than a moral that they teach.

**MOTIVATION** *Motivation* is a reason that explains or partially explains why a character thinks, feels, acts, or behaves in a certain way. Motivation results from a combination of the character's personality and the situation he or she must deal with. In "Checkouts" (p. 82), the main character is motivated by conflicting feelings.

See also **Character** and **Characterization.**

**MYTH** A *myth* is a fictional tale that describes the actions of gods and heroes or explains the causes of natural phenomena. Unlike legends, myths emphasize supernatural rather than historical elements. Many cultures have collections of myths, and the most familiar in the Western world are those of the ancient Greeks and Romans. "Perseus" (p. 1225) is a retelling of a famous ancient Greek myth.

See also **Oral Tradition.**

**NARRATION** *Narration* is writing that tells a story. The act of telling a story in speech is also called narration. Novels and short stories are fictional narratives. Nonfiction works—such as news stories, biographies, and autobiographies—are also narratives. A narrative poem tells a story in verse.

See also **Anecdote, Essay, Narrative Poem, Nonfiction, Novel,** and **Short Story.**

**NARRATIVE** A *narrative* is a story told in fiction, nonfiction, poetry, or drama.

See also **Narration.**

**NARRATIVE POEM** A *narrative poem* is one that tells a story. "Casey at the Bat" (p. 696) is a humorous narrative poem about the last inning of a baseball game. Edgar Allan Poe's "The Raven" (p. 710) is a serious narrative poem about a man's grief over the loss of a loved one.

See also **Dramatic Poetry, Epic,** and **Narration.**

**NARRATOR** A *narrator* is a speaker or character who tells a story. The writer's choice of narrator determines the story's **point of view,** which directs the type and amount of information the writer reveals.

When a character in the story tells the story, that character is a *first-person narrator.* This narrator may be a major character, a minor character, or just a witness. Readers see only what this character sees, hear only what he or she hears, and so on. The first-person narrator may or may not be reliable. We have reason, for example, to be suspicious of the first-person narrator of Edgar Allan Poe's "The Cask of Amontillado" (p. 60).

When a voice outside the story narrates, the story has a *third-person narrator.* An omniscient, or all-knowing, third-person narrator can tell readers what any character thinks and feels. For example, in Guy de Maupassant's "The Necklace" (p. 332), we know the feelings of both Monsieur and Madame Loisel. A limited third-person narrator sees the world through one character's eyes and reveals only that character's thoughts. In James Thurber's "The Secret Life of Walter Mitty" (p. 128), the narrator reveals only Mitty's experiences and feelings.

See also **Speaker.**

**NONFICTION** *Nonfiction* is prose writing that presents and explains ideas or that tells about real people, places, ideas, or events. To be classified as nonfiction, a work must be true. "Single Room, Earth View" (p. 468) is a nonfictional account of the view of Earth from space.

See also **Autobiography, Biography,** and **Essay.**

**NOVEL** A *novel* is a long work of fiction. It has a plot that explores characters in conflict. A novel may also have one or more subplots, or minor stories, and several themes.

**NOVELLA** A *novella* is a work of fiction that is longer than a short story but shorter than a novel.

**OCTAVE** See **Stanza.**

**ONOMATOPOEIA** *Onomatopoeia* is the use of words that imitate sounds. *Whirr, thud,* and *hiss* are examples.

**ORAL TRADITION** The *oral tradition* is the passing of songs, stories, and poems from generation to generation by word of mouth. Many folk songs, ballads, fairy tales, legends, and myths originated in the oral tradition.

See also **Myth.**

**OXYMORON** An *oxymoron* is a combination of words, or parts of words, that contradict each other. Examples are "deafening silence," "honest thief," "wise fool," and "bittersweet." This device is effective when the apparent contradiction reveals a deeper truth, as in Act 2, Scene ii, line 184, of *Romeo and Juliet* (p. 806) when Juliet bids goodbye to Romeo: "Parting is such *sweet sorrow.*"

**PARADOX** A *paradox* is a statement that seems contradictory but actually may be true. Because a paradox is surprising, it catches the reader's attention.

**PARALLELISM** See **Rhetorical Devices.**

**PENTAMETER** See **Meter.**

**PERSONIFICATION** *Personification* is a type of figurative language in which a nonhuman subject is given human characteristics. William Wordsworth personifies daffodils when he describes them as "Tossing their heads in sprightly dance" (p. 626).

See also **Figurative Language.**

**PERSUASION** *Persuasion* is writing or speech that attempts to convince the reader to adopt a particular opinion or course of action. An *argument* is a logical way of presenting a belief, conclusion, or stance. A good argument is supported with reasoning and evidence.

**PLOT** *Plot* is the sequence of events in a literary work. In most novels, dramas, short stories, and narrative poems, the plot involves both characters and a central conflict. The plot usually begins with an *exposition* that introduces the setting, the characters, and the basic situation. This is followed by the *inciting incident,* which introduces the central conflict. The conflict then increases during the *development* until it reaches a high point of interest or suspense, the *climax.* All the events leading up to the climax make up the *rising action.* The climax is followed by the *falling action,* which leads to the *denouement,* or *resolution,* in which a general insight or change is conveyed.

**POETRY** *Poetry* is one of the three major types of literature, the others being prose and drama. Most poems make use of highly concise, musical, and emotionally charged language. Many also make use of imagery, figurative language, and special devices of sound such as rhyme. Poems are often divided into lines and stanzas and often employ regular rhythmical patterns, or meters. However, some poems are written out just like prose, while others are written in free verse.

See also **Genre.**

**POINT OF VIEW** See **Narrator.**

**PROSE** *Prose* is the ordinary form of written language. Most writing that is not poetry, drama, or song is considered prose. Prose is one of the major genres of literature and occurs in two forms: fiction and nonfiction.

See also **Fiction, Genre,** and **Nonfiction.**

**PROTAGONIST** The protagonist is the main character in a literary work.

See also *Antagonist* and *Character.*

**PUN** A *pun* is a play on words involving a word with two or more different meanings or two words that sound alike but have different meanings. In *Romeo and Juliet* (p. 806), the dying Mercutio makes a pun involving two meanings of the word *grave,* "serious" and "burial site": "Ask for me tomorrow, and you shall find me a grave man" (Act 3, Scene i, lines 92–93).

**QUATRAIN** A *quatrain* is a stanza or poem made up of four lines, usually with a definite rhythm and rhyme scheme.

**REPETITION** *Repetition* is the use of any element of language—a sound, a word, a phrase, a clause, or a sentence—more than once.

Poets use many kinds of repetition. Alliteration, assonance, rhyme, and rhythm are repetitions of certain sounds and sound patterns. A refrain is a repeated line or group of lines. In both prose and poetry, repetition is used for musical effects and for emphasis.

See also *Alliteration, Assonance, Rhyme,* and *Rhythm.*

**RESOLUTION** See *Plot.*

**RHETORICAL DEVICES** *Rhetorical devices* are special patterns of words and ideas that create emphasis and stir emotion, especially in speeches or other oral presentations. *Parallelism,* for example, is the repetition of a grammatical structure in order to create a rhythm and make words more memorable. In his "I Have a Dream" speech (p. 542), Martin Luther King, Jr., uses parallel statements beginning, "I have a dream that . . ."

Other common rhetorical devices include *restatement,* expressing the same idea in different words, and *rhetorical questions,* questions with obvious answers.

**RHYME** *Rhyme* is the repetition of sounds at the ends of words. *End rhyme* occurs when the rhyming words come at the ends of lines, as in "The Desired Swan Song" by Samuel Taylor Coleridge:

> Swans sing before they die—'twere no bad thing
> Should certain persons die before they sing.

*Internal rhyme* occurs when the rhyming words appear in the same line, as in the first line of Edgar Allan Poe's "The Raven" (p. 710):

> Once upon a midnight *dreary,* while I pondered, weak and *weary,*

*Exact rhyme* involves the repetition of words with the same vowel and consonant sounds, like *ball* and *hall. Slant rhyme* involves the repetition of words that sound alike but do not rhyme exactly, like *grove* and *love.*

See also *Repetition* and *Rhyme Scheme.*

**RHYME SCHEME** A *rhyme scheme* is a regular pattern of rhyming words in a poem. The rhyme scheme of a poem is indicated by using different letters of the alphabet for each new rhyme. In an *aabb* stanza, for example, line 1 rhymes with line 2 and line 3 rhymes with line 4. William Wordsworth's poem "I Wandered Lonely as a Cloud" (p. 622) uses an *ababcc* rhyme pattern:

> I wandered lonely as a cloud       a
> That floats on high o'er vales and hills,       b
> When all at once I saw a crowd,       a
> A host, of golden daffodils;       b
> Beside the lake, beneath the trees,       c
> Fluttering and dancing in the breeze.       c

Many poems use the same pattern of rhymes, though not the same rhymes, in each stanza.

See also *Rhyme.*

**RHYTHM** *Rhythm* is the pattern of *beats,* or *stresses,* in spoken or written language. Some poems have a very specific pattern, or meter, whereas prose and free verse use the natural rhythms of everyday speech.

See also *Meter.*

**RISING ACTION** See *Plot.*

**ROUND CHARACTER** See *Character.*

**SATIRE** A *satire* is a literary work that ridicules the foolishness and faults of individuals, an institution, society, or even humanity in general.

**SCENE** See *Drama.*

**SCIENCE FICTION** *Science fiction* is writing that tells about imaginary events involving science or technology. Many science-fiction stories are set in the future. Arthur C. Clarke's "If I Forget Thee, Oh Earth . . ." (p. 162) is set on the moon after a nuclear disaster on Earth.

See also *Fantasy.*

**SENSORY LANGUAGE** *Sensory language* is writing or speech that appeals to one or more of the senses.

See also *Image.*

**SESTET** See *Stanza.*

**SETTING** The *setting* of a literary work is the time and place of the action. Time can include not only the historical period—past, present, or future—but also a specific year, season, or time of day. Place may involve not only the geographical place—a region, country, state, or town—but also the social, economic, or cultural environment.

In some stories, setting serves merely as a backdrop for action, a context in which the characters move and speak. In others, however, setting is a crucial element.

See also *Mood.*

**SHORT STORY** A *short story* is a brief work of fiction. In most short stories, one main character faces a conflict that is resolved in the plot of the story. Great craftsmanship must go into the writing of a good story, for it has to accomplish its purpose in relatively few words.

See also *Fiction* and *Genre.*

**SIMILE** A *simile* is a figure of speech in which the words *like* or *as* are used to compare two apparently dissimilar items. The comparison, however, surprises the reader into a fresh perception by finding an unexpected likeness. In "Dream Deferred" (p. 620), Langston Hughes uses the simile "Does it dry up/like a raisin in the sun?" to discuss a dream deferred.

**SOLILOQUY** A *soliloquy* is a long speech expressing the thoughts of a character alone on stage. In William Shakespeare's *Romeo and Juliet* (p. 806), Romeo gives a soliloquy after the servant has fled and Paris has died (Act V, Scene iii, lines 74–120).

See also *Monologue.*

**SONNET** A *sonnet* is a fourteen-line lyric poem, usually written in rhymed iambic pentameter. The *English,* or *Shakespearean,* sonnet consists of three quatrains (four-line stanzas) and a couplet (two lines), usually rhyming *abab cdcd efef gg.* The couplet usually comments on the ideas contained in the preceding twelve lines. The sonnet is usually not printed with the stanzas divided, but a reader can see distinct ideas in each. See the Sonnet 30 by William Shakespeare on page 754.

The *Italian,* or *Petrarchan,* sonnet consists of an octave (eight-line stanza) and a sestet (six-line stanza). Often, the octave rhymes *abbaabba* and the sestet rhymes *cdecde.* The octave states a theme or asks a question. The sestet comments on or answers the question.

See also *Lyric Poem, Meter,* and *Stanza.*

**SOUND DEVICES** A *sound device* is a technique used by a poet to emphasize the sound relationships among words in order to create musical and emotional effects and emphasize a poem's meaning. These devices include *alliteration, consonance, assonance, onomatopoeia,* and *rhyme.*

**SPEAKER** The *speaker* is the imaginary voice assumed by the writer of a poem. In many poems, the speaker is not identified by name. When reading a poem, remember that the speaker within the poem may be a person, an animal, a thing, or an abstraction. The speaker in the following stanza by Emily Dickinson is a person who has died:

> Because I could not stop for Death—
>
> He kindly stopped for me—
>
> The Carriage held but just Ourselves—
>
> And Immortality.

**STAGE DIRECTIONS** *Stage directions* are notes included in a drama to describe how the work is to be performed or staged. These instructions are printed in italics and are not spoken aloud. They are used to describe sets, lighting, sound effects, and the appearance, personalities, and movements of characters.

See also *Drama.*

**STANZA** A *stanza* is a repeated grouping of two or more lines in a poem that often share a pattern of rhythm and rhyme. Stanzas are sometimes named according to the number of lines they have—for example, a *couplet,* two lines; a *quatrain,* four lines; a *sestet,* six lines; and an *octave,* eight lines.

**STATIC CHARACTER** See *Character.*

**STYLE** *Style* refers to an author's unique way of writing. Elements determining style include diction; tone; characteristic use of figurative language, dialect, or rhythmic devices; and syntax, or typical grammatical structures and patterns.

See also *Diction* and *Tone.*

**SURPRISE ENDING** A *surprise ending* is a conclusion that violates the expectations of the reader but in a way that is both logical and believable.

O. Henry's "The Gift of the Magi" (p. 260) and Guy de Maupassant's "The Necklace" (p. 332) have surprise endings. Both authors were masters of this form.

**SUSPENSE** *Suspense* is a feeling of uncertainty about the outcome of events in a literary work. Writers create suspense by raising questions in the minds of their readers.

**SYMBOL** A *symbol* is anything that stands for something else. In addition to having its own meaning and reality, a symbol also represents abstract ideas. For example, a flag is a piece of cloth, but it also represents the idea of a country. Writers sometimes use conventional symbols like flags. Frequently, however, they create symbols of their own through emphasis or repetition. In James Hurst's "The Scarlet Ibis" (p. 384), for example, the ibis symbolizes the character named Doodle. Both are beautiful and otherworldly.

**TALL TALE** A *tall tale* is a type of folk tale that contains some or all of these features: humor, hyperbole, far-fetched situations, highly imaginative language, and a hero who performs outrageous feats. Tall tales originated during the development of the American frontier and are a particularly American form of folk tale. "Pecos Bill: The Cyclone" (p. 1218) is an example of a tall tale.

**THEME** A *theme* is a central message or insight into life revealed through a literary work.

The theme of a literary work may be stated directly or implied. When the theme of a work is implied, readers think about what the work suggests about people or life.

*Archetypal themes* are those that occur in folklore and literature across the world and throughout history. Ill-fated love, the theme of *Romeo and Juliet* (p. 806), is an example of such a theme.

**TONE** The *tone* of a literary work is the writer's attitude toward his or her audience and subject. The tone can often be described by a single adjective, such as *formal* or *informal, serious* or *playful, bitter* or *ironic.* When O. Henry discusses the young couple in "The Gift of the Magi" (p. 260), he uses a sympathetic tone.

See also *Mood.*

**TRAGEDY** A *tragedy* is a work of literature, especially a play, that results in a catastrophe, a disaster or great misfortune, for the main character, or *tragic hero.* In ancient Greek drama, the main character was always a significant person—a king or a hero—and the cause of the tragedy was a *tragic flaw,* or weakness, in his or her character. In modern drama, the main character can be an ordinary person, and the cause of the tragedy can be some evil in society itself. Tragedy not only arouses fear and pity in the audience but also, in some cases, conveys a sense of the grandeur and nobility of the human spirit.

Shakespeare's *Romeo and Juliet* (p. 806) is a tragedy. Romeo and Juliet both suffer from the tragic flaw of impulsiveness. This flaw ultimately leads to their deaths.

See also *Drama.*

**UNDERSTATEMENT** An *understatement* is a figure of speech in which the stated meaning is purposely less than (or "under") what is really meant. It is the opposite of *hyperbole,* which is a deliberate exaggeration.

**UNIVERSAL THEME** A *universal theme* is a message about life that can be understood by most cultures. Many folk tales and examples of classic literature address universal themes such as the importance of courage, the effects of honesty, or the danger of greed.

**VERBAL IRONY** See *Irony.*

**VILLANELLE** A *villanelle* is a nineteen-line lyric poem written in five three-line stanzas and ending in a four-line stanza. It uses two rhymes and repeats two refrain lines that appear initially in the first and third lines of the first stanza. These lines then appear alternately as the third line of subsequent three-line stanzas and, finally, as the last two lines of the poem.

**VISUAL ESSAY** A *visual essay* is an exploration of a topic that conveys its ideas through visual elements as well as language. Like a standard essay, a visual essay presents an author's views of a single topic. Unlike other essays, however, much of the meaning in a visual essay is conveyed through illustrations or photographs.

**VOICE** *Voice* is a writer's distinctive "sound" or way of "speaking" on the page. It is related to such elements as word choice, sentence structure, and tone. It is similar to an individual's speech style and can be described in the same way—fast, slow, blunt, meandering, breathless, and so on.

Voice resembles *style,* an author's typical way of writing, but style usually refers to a quality that can be found throughout an author's body of work, while an author's voice may sometimes vary from work to work.

See also *Style.*

# Tips for Discussing Literature

As you read and study literature, discussion with other readers can help you understand, enjoy, and develop interpretations of what you read. Use the following tips to practice good speaking and listening skills while participating in group discussions of literature.

- ## Understand the purpose of your discussion

  When you discuss literature, your purpose is to broaden your understanding and appreciation of a work by testing your own ideas and hearing the ideas of others. Stay focused on the literature you are discussing, and keep your comments relevant to that literature. Starting with one focus question will help keep your discussion on track.

- ## Communicate effectively

  Effective communication requires thinking before speaking. Plan the points that you want to make, and decide how you will express them. Organize these points in logical order, and cite details from the work to support your ideas. Jot down informal notes to help keep your ideas focused.

  Remember to speak clearly, pronouncing words slowly and carefully so that others can understand your points. Also, keep in mind that some literature touches readers deeply—be aware of the possibility of counterproductive emotional responses, and work to control them. Negative emotional responses can also be conveyed through body language, so work to demonstrate respect in your demeanor as well as in your words.

- ## Encourage everyone to participate

  While some people are comfortable participating in discussions, others are less eager to speak up in groups. However, everyone should work to contribute thoughts and ideas. To encourage the entire group's participation, try the following strategies:

  - If you enjoy speaking, avoid monopolizing the conversation. After sharing your ideas, encourage others to share theirs.

  - Try different roles. For example, have everyone take turns being the facilitator or host of the discussion.

  - Use a prop, such as a book or gavel. Pass the prop around the group, allowing whomever is holding the prop to have the floor.

- ## Make relevant contributions

  Especially when responding to a short story, a poem, or a novel, avoid simply summarizing the plot. Instead, consider *what* you think might happen next, *why* events take place as they do, or *how* a writer provokes a response in you. Let your ideas inspire deeper thought or discussion about the literature.

- ## Consider other ideas and interpretations

  A work of literature can generate a wide variety of responses in different readers—and that can make your discussions exciting. Be open to the idea that many interpretations can be valid. To support your own ideas, point to the events, descriptions, characters, or other literary elements in the work that produced your interpretation. To consider someone else's ideas, decide whether details in the work support the interpretation he or she presents. Be sure to convey your criticism of the ideas of others in a respectful and supportive manner.

## • Ask questions and extend the contributions of others

Get in the habit of asking questions to help you clarify your understanding of another reader's ideas. You can also use questions to call attention to possible areas of confusion, to points that are open to debate, or to errors.

In addition, offer elaboration of the points that others make by providing examples and illustrations. To move a discussion forward, pause occasionally to summarize and evaluate tentative conclusions reached by the group members. Then, continue the discussion with a fresh understanding of the material and ideas you have already covered.

## • Manage differing opinions and views

Each participant brings his or her own personality, experiences, ideas, cultural background, likes and dislikes to the experience of reading, making disagreement almost inevitable. As differences arise, be sensitive to each individual's point of view. Do not personalize disagreements, but keep them focused on the literature or ideas under discussion.

When you meet with a group to discuss literature, use a chart like the one shown to analyze the discussion.

| Work Being Discussed: | |
|---|---|
| Focus Question: | |
| Your Response: | Another Student's Response: |
| Supporting Evidence: | Supporting Evidence: |

# Literary Criticism

*Criticism* is writing that explores the meaning and techniques of literary works, usually in order to evaluate them. Writing criticism can help you think through your experience of a work of literature and can also help others deepen their own understanding. All literary criticism shares similar goals:

- *Making Connections* within or between works, or between a work of literature and its context
- *Making Distinctions* or showing differences between elements of a single work or aspects of two or more works
- *Achieving Insights* that were not apparent from a superficial reading
- *Making a Judgment* about the quality or value of a literary work

Critics use various *theories of literary criticism* to understand, appreciate, and evaluate literature. Some theories focus on the context of the work while others focus on the work itself. Sometimes critics combine one or more theories. These charts show a few examples of the many theories of criticism:

| Focus on Contexts | |
|---|---|
| **Human Experience** | **Mythic Criticism** Explores universal situations, characters, and symbols called archetypes as they appear in a literary work. |
| **Culture and History** | **Historical Criticism** Analyzes how circumstances or ideas of an era influence a work |
| **Author's Life** | **Biographical Criticism** Explains how the author's life sheds light on the work |

| Focus on the Work Itself |
|---|
| **Formal Criticism** Shows how the work reflects characteristics of the genre, or literary type, to which it belongs |

## Examples of Literary Theories in Action

- *Mythic Criticism:* discussing how Robert Frost's "The Road Not Taken," p. 724, explores the archetypal situation of choice at a fork in the road
- *Historical Criticism:* showing how American frontier life led to the use of exaggeration in "Pecos Bill: The Cyclone," p. 1218
- *Biographical Criticism:* showing that Edgar Allan Poe's loss of his parents at an early age influenced the theme of "The Raven," p. 710
- *Formal Criticism:* showing how "The Scarlet Ibis," p. 384, displays short-story elements like plot, setting, character, symbol, and theme

# Literary Movements

Our literary heritage has been shaped by a number of literary movements, directions in literature characterized by shared assumptions, beliefs, and practices. This chart shows, in chronological order, some important literary movements. While these movements developed at particular historical moments, all of them may still influence individual writers working today.

| Movement | Beliefs and Practices | Examples |
|---|---|---|
| **Classicism**<br>Europe during the Renaissance (c. 1300–1650) | • Looks to classical literature of ancient Greece and Rome as models<br>• Values logic, clarity, balance, and restraint<br>• Prefers "ordered" nature of parks and gardens | the clarity and restraint of Robert Frost's verse ("The Road Not Taken," p. 724) |
| **Romanticism**<br>Europe during the late 1700s and the early 1800s | • Rebels against Classicism<br>• Values imagination and emotion<br>• Focuses on everyday life | the celebration of the natural world in Rachel Carson's writings ("Silent Spring," p. 167) |
| **Realism**<br>Europe and America from the mid–1800s to the 1890s | • Rebels against Romanticism's search for the ideal<br>• Focuses on everyday life | the faithful rendering of Pueblo life in Leslie Marmon Silko's fiction ("The Man to Send Rain Clouds," p. 292) |
| **Naturalism**<br>Europe and America during the late 1800s and early 1900s | • Assumes people cannot choose their fate but are shaped by psychological and social forces<br>• Views society as a competitive jungle | the portrayal of characters as victims of social pressures and psychology in Guy de Maupassant's fiction ("The Necklace," p. 332) |
| **Modernism**<br>Worldwide between 1890 and 1945 | • In response to WWI, questions human reason<br>• Focuses on studies of the unconscious and the art of primitive peoples<br>• Experiments with language and form | the experiments with language in E. E. Cummings's poetry ("maggie and milly and molly and may," p. 732) |
| **Post-Modernism**<br>Worldwide after 1945; still prevalent today | • Includes an eclectic mix of styles, such as parody, magical realism, and dark humor.<br>• Often rebels against reason. | the magical realism in Isabel Allende's fiction ("Uncle Marcos," p. 138) |

# Tips for Improving Reading Fluency

When you were younger, you learned to read. Then, you read to expand your experiences or for pure enjoyment. Now, you are expected to read to learn. As you progress in school, you are given more and more material to read. The tips on these pages will help you improve your reading fluency, or your ability to read easily, smoothly, and expressively.

## Keeping Your Concentration

One common problem that readers face is the loss of concentration. When you are reading an assignment, you might find yourself rereading the same sentence several times without really understanding it. The first step in changing this behavior is to notice that you do it. Becoming an active, aware reader will help you get the most from your assignments. Practice using these strategies:

- Cover what you have already read with a note card as you go along. Then, you will not be able to reread without noticing that you are doing it.

- Set a purpose for reading beyond just completing the assignment. Then, read actively by pausing to ask yourself questions about the material as you read.

- Use the Reading Strategy instruction and notes that appear with each selection in this textbook.

- Stop reading after a specified period of time (for example, 5 minutes) and summarize what you have read. To help you with this strategy, use the Reading Check questions that appear with each selection in this textbook. Reread to find any answers you do not know.

## Reading Phrases

Fluent readers read phrases rather than individual words. Reading this way will speed up your reading and improve your comprehension. Here are some useful ideas:

- Experts recommend rereading as a strategy to increase fluency. Choose a passage of text that is neither too hard nor too easy. Read the same passage aloud several times until you can read it smoothly. When you can read the passage fluently, pick another passage and keep practicing.

- Read aloud into a tape recorder. Then, listen to the recording, noting your accuracy, pacing, and expression. You can also read aloud and share feedback with a partner.

- Use the *Prentice Hall Listening to Literature* audiotapes or CDs to hear the selections read aloud. Read along silently in your textbook, noticing how the reader uses his or her voice and emphasizes certain words and phrases.

## Understanding Key Vocabulary

If you do not understand some of the words in an assignment, you may miss out on important concepts. Therefore, it is helpful to keep a dictionary nearby when you are reading. Follow these steps:

- Before you begin reading, scan the text for unfamiliar words or terms. Find out what those words mean before you begin reading.
- Use context—the surrounding words, phrases, and sentences—to help you determine the meanings of unfamiliar words.
- If you are unable to understand the meaning through context, refer to the dictionary.

## Paying Attention to Punctuation

When you read, pay attention to punctuation. Commas, periods, exclamation points, semicolons, and colons tell you when to pause or stop. They also indicate relationships between groups of words. When you recognize these relationships you will read with greater understanding and expression. Look at the chart below.

| Punctuation Mark | Meaning |
|---|---|
| comma | brief pause |
| period | pause at the end of a thought |
| exclamation point | pause that indicates emphasis |
| semicolon | pause between related but distinct thoughts |
| colon | pause before giving explanation or examples |

## Using the Reading Fluency Checklist

Use the checklist below each time you read a selection in this textbook. In your Language Arts journal or notebook, note which skills you need to work on, and chart your progress each week.

| Reading Fluency Checklist |
|---|
| ❑ Preview the text to check for difficult or unfamiliar words. |
| ❑ Practice reading aloud. |
| ❑ Read according to punctuation. |
| ❑ Break down long sentences into the subject and its meaning. |
| ❑ Read groups of words for meaning rather than reading single words. |
| ❑ Read with expression (change your tone of voice to add meaning to the word). |

Reading is a skill that can be improved with practice. The key to improving your fluency is to read. The more you read, the better your reading will become.

# Types of Writing

Good writing can be a powerful tool used for many purposes. Writing can allow you to defend something you believe in or show how much you know about a subject. Writing can also help you share what you have experienced, imagined, thought, and felt. The three main types of writing are argument, informative/explanatory, and narrative.

## Argument

When you think of the word *argument*, you might think of a disagreement between two people, but an argument is more than that. An argument is a logical way of presenting a belief, conclusion, or stance. A good argument is supported with reasoning and evidence.

Argument writing can be used for many purposes, such as to change a reader's point of view or opinion or to bring about an action or a response from a reader.

There are three main purposes for writing a formal argument:

- to change the reader's mind
- to convince the reader to accept what is written
- to motivate the reader to take action, based on what is written

The following are some types of argument writing:

**Advertisements** An advertisement is a planned message meant to be seen, heard, or read. It attempts to persuade an audience to buy a product or service, accept an idea, or support a cause. Advertisements may appear in print, online, or in broadcast form.

Several common types of advertisements are public-service announcements, billboards, merchandise ads, service ads, and political campaign literature.

**Persuasive Essay** A persuasive essay presents a position on an issue, urges readers to accept that position, and may encourage a specific action. An effective persuasive essay

- Explores an issue of importance to the writer
- Addresses an issue that is arguable
- Uses facts, examples, statistics, or personal experiences to support a position
- Tries to influence the audience through appeals to the readers' knowledge, experiences, or emotions
- Uses clear organization to present a logical argument

Forms of persuasion include editorials, position papers, persuasive speeches, grant proposals, advertisements, and debates.

## Informative/Explanatory

Informative/explanatory writing should rely on facts to inform or explain. Informative/explanatory writing serves some closely related purposes: to increase readers' knowledge of a subject, to help readers better understand a procedure or process, or to provide readers with an enhanced comprehension of a concept. It should also feature a clear introduction, body, and conclusion. The following are some examples of informative/explanatory writing:

**Cause-and-Effect Essay** A cause-and-effect essay examines the relationship between events, explaining how one event or situation causes another. A successful cause-and-effect essay includes

- A discussion of a cause, event, or condition that produces a specific result
- An explanation of an effect, outcome, or result
- Evidence and examples to support the relationship between cause and effect
- A logical organization that makes the explanation clear

**Comparison-and-Contrast Essay** A comparison-and-contrast essay analyzes the similarities and differences between or among two or more things. An effective comparison-and-contrast essay

- Identifies a purpose for comparison and contrast
- Identifies similarities and differences between or among two or more things, people, places, or ideas
- Gives factual details about the subjects
- Uses an organizational plan suited to the topic and purpose

**Descriptive Writing** Descriptive writing creates a vivid picture of a person, place, thing, or event. Most descriptive writing includes

- Sensory details—sights, sounds, smells, tastes, and physical sensations
- Vivid, precise language
- Figurative language or comparisons
- Adjectives and adverbs that paint a word picture
- An organization suited to the subject

Types of descriptive writing include descriptions of ideas, observations, travel brochures, physical descriptions, functional descriptions, remembrances, and character sketches.

**Problem-and-Solution Essay** A problem-and-solution essay describes a problem and offers one or more solutions to it. It describes a clear set of steps to achieve a result. An effective problem-and-solution essay includes

- A clear statement of the problem, with its causes and effects summarized for the reader
- The most important aspects of the problem
- A proposal of at least one realistic solution
- Facts, statistics, data, or expert testimony to support the solution
- A clear organization that makes the relationship between problem and solution obvious

**Research Writing** Research writing is based on information gathered from outside sources. A research paper—a focused study of a topic—helps writers explore and connect ideas, make discoveries, and share their findings with an audience. An effective research paper

- Focuses on a specific, narrow topic, which is usually summarized in a thesis statement
- Presents relevant information from a wide variety of sources
- Uses a clear organization that includes an introduction, body, and conclusion
- Includes a bibliography or works-cited list that identifies the sources from which the information was drawn

Other types of writing that depend on accurate and insightful research include multimedia presentations, statistical reports, annotated bibliographies, and experiment journals.

**Workplace Writing** Workplace writing is probably the format you will use most after you finish school. In general, workplace writing is fact-based and meant to communicate specific information in a structured format. Effective workplace writing

- Communicates information concisely
- Includes details that provide necessary information and anticipate potential questions
- Is error-free and neatly presented

Common types of workplace writing include business letters, memorandums, résumés, forms, and applications.

# Narrative

Narrative writing conveys experience, either real or imaginary, and uses time to provide structure. It can be used to inform, instruct, persuade, or entertain. Whenever writers tell a story, they are using narrative writing. Most types of narrative writing share certain elements, such as characters, a setting, a sequence of events, and, often, a theme. The following are some types of narration:

**Autobiographical Writing** Autobiographical writing tells a true story about an important period, experience, or relationship in the writer's life. Effective autobiographical writing includes

- A series of events that involve the writer as the main character
- Details, thoughts, feelings, and insights from the writer's perspective
- A conflict or an event that affects the writer
- A logical organization that tells the story clearly
- Insights that the writer gained from the experience

Types of autobiographical writing include autobiographical sketches, personal narratives, reflective essays, eyewitness accounts, and memoirs.

**Short Story** A short story is a brief, creative narrative. Most short stories include

- Details that establish the setting in time and place
- A main character who undergoes a change or learns something during the course of the story
- A conflict or a problem to be introduced, developed, and resolved
- A plot, the series of events that make up the action of the story
- A theme or message about life

Types of short stories include realistic stories, fantasies, historical narratives, mysteries, thrillers, science-fiction stories, and adventure stories.

# Writing Friendly Letters

## Writing Friendly Letters

A friendly letter is much less formal than a business letter. It is a letter to a friend, a family member, or anyone with whom the writer wants to communicate in a personal, friendly way. Most friendly letters are made up of five parts:

- ✔ the heading
- ✔ the salutation, or greeting
- ✔ the body
- ✔ the closing
- ✔ the signature

The purpose of a friendly letter is often one of the following:

- ✔ to share personal news and feelings
- ✔ to send or to answer an invitation
- ✔ to express thanks

## Model Friendly Letter

In this friendly letter, Betsy thanks her grandparents for a birthday present and gives them some news about her life.

11 Old Farm Road
Topsham, Maine 04011

April 14, 20—

Dear Grandma and Grandpa,

Thank you for the sweater you sent me for my birthday. It fits perfectly, and I love the color. I wore my new sweater to the carnival at school last weekend and got lots of compliments.

The weather here has been cool but sunny. Mom thinks that "real" spring will never come. I can't wait until it's warm enough to go swimming.

School is going fairly well. I really like my Social Studies class. We are learning about the U.S. Constitution, and I think it's very interesting. Maybe I will be a lawyer when I grow up.

When are you coming out to visit us? We haven't seen you since Thanksgiving. You can stay in my room when you come. I'll be happy to sleep on the couch. (The TV is in that room!!)

Well, thanks again and hope all is well with you.

Love,

Betsy

> The **heading** includes the writer's address and the date on which he or she wrote the letter.

> The **body** is the main part of the letter and contains the basic message.

> Some common **closings** for personal letters include "Best Wishes," "Love," "Sincerely," and "Yours Truly."

# Writing Business Letters

## Formatting Business Letters

Business letters follow one of several acceptable formats. In **block format,** each part of the letter begins at the left margin. A double space is used between paragraphs. In **modified block format,** some parts of the letter are indented to the center of the page. No matter which format is used, all letters in business format have a heading, an inside address, a salutation or greeting, a body, a closing, and a signature. These parts are shown and annotated on the model business letter below, formatted in modified block style.

## Model Business Letter

In this letter, Yolanda Dodson uses modified block format to request information.

The **heading** shows the writer's address and organization (if any) and the date.

Students for a Cleaner Planet
c/o Memorial High School
333 Veteran's Drive
Denver, CO 80211

January 25, 20—

The **inside address** indicates where the letter will be sent.

Steven Wilson, Director
Resource Recovery Really Works
300 Oak Street
Denver, CO 80216

Dear Mr. Wilson:

A **salutation** is punctuated by a colon. When the specific addressee is not known, use a general greeting such as "To whom it may concern:"

Memorial High School would like to start a branch of your successful recycling program. We share your commitment to reclaiming as much reusable material as we can. Because your program has been successful in other neighborhoods, we're sure that it can work in our community. Our school includes grades 9–12 and has about 800 students.

Would you send us some information about your community recycling program? For example, we need to know what materials can be recycled and how we can implement the program.

The **body** of the letter states the writer's purpose. In this case, the writer requests information.

At least fifty students have already expressed an interest in getting involved, so I know we'll have the people power to make the program work. Please help us get started.

Thank you in advance for your time and consideration.

Sincerely,

*Yolanda Dodson*

Yolanda Dodson

The **closing** "Sincerely" is common, but "Yours truly" or "Respectfully yours" are also acceptable. To end the letter, the writer types her name and provides a **signature.**

# Writing a Résumé

## Writing a Résumé

A résumé summarizes your educational background, work experiences, relevant skills, and other employment qualifications. It also tells potential employers how to contact you. An effective résumé presents the applicant's name, address, and phone number. It follows an accepted résumé organization, using labels and headings to guide readers.

A résumé should outline the applicant's educational background, life experiences, and related qualifications using precise and active language.

## Model Résumé

With this résumé, James, a college student, hopes to find a full-time job.

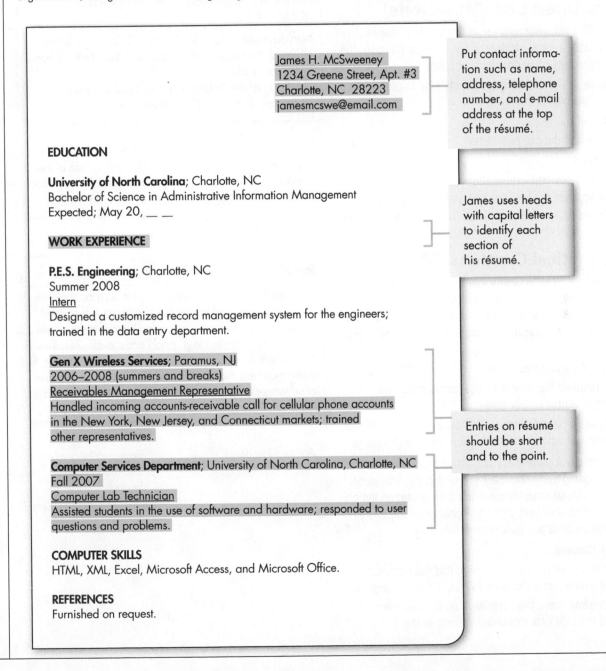

James H. McSweeney
1234 Greene Street, Apt. #3
Charlotte, NC  28223
jamesmcswe@email.com

Put contact information such as name, address, telephone number, and e-mail address at the top of the résumé.

**EDUCATION**

**University of North Carolina**; Charlotte, NC
Bachelor of Science in Administrative Information Management
Expected; May 20, __ __

James uses heads with capital letters to identify each section of his résumé.

**WORK EXPERIENCE**

**P.E.S. Engineering**; Charlotte, NC
Summer 2008
Intern
Designed a customized record management system for the engineers; trained in the data entry department.

**Gen X Wireless Services**; Paramus, NJ
2006–2008 (summers and breaks)
Receivables Management Representative
Handled incoming accounts-receivable call for cellular phone accounts in the New York, New Jersey, and Connecticut markets; trained other representatives.

**Computer Services Department**; University of North Carolina, Charlotte, NC
Fall 2007
Computer Lab Technician
Assisted students in the use of software and hardware; responded to user questions and problems.

Entries on résumé should be short and to the point.

**COMPUTER SKILLS**
HTML, XML, Excel, Microsoft Access, and Microsoft Office.

**REFERENCES**
Furnished on request.

# Citing Sources and Preparing Manuscript

In research writing, cite your sources. In the body of your paper, provide a footnote, an endnote, or a parenthetical citation, identifying the sources of facts, opinions, or quotations. At the end of your paper, provide a bibliography or a works-cited list, a list of all the sources you cite. Follow an established format, such as Modern Language Association (MLA) Style.

## Works-Cited List (MLA Style)

A works-cited list must contain accurate information sufficient to enable a reader to locate each source you cite. The basic components of an entry are as follows:

- Name of the author, editor, translator, or group responsible for the work
- Title of the work
- Place and date of publication
- Publisher

For print materials, the information required for a citation generally appears on the copyright and title pages of a work. For the format of works-cited list entries, consult the examples at right and in the chart on page R37.

## Parenthetical Citations (MLA Style)

A parenthetical citation briefly identifies the source from which you have taken a specific quotation, factual claim, or opinion. It refers the reader to one of the entries on your works-cited list. A parenthetical citation has the following features:

- It appears in parentheses.
- It identifies the source by the last name of the author, editor, or translator.
- It gives a page reference, identifying the page of the source on which the information cited can be found.

**Punctuation** A parenthetical citation generally falls outside a closing quotation mark but within the final punctuation of a clause or sentence. For a long quotation set off from the rest of your text, place the citation at the end of the excerpt without any punctuation following.

### Special Cases

- If the author is an organization, use the organization's name, in a shortened version if necessary.
- If you cite more than one work by the same author, add the title or a shortened version of the title.

---

### Sample Works-Cited Lists (MLA 7th Edition)

Carwardine, Mark, Erich Hoyt, R. Ewan Fordyce, and Peter Gill. *The Nature Company Guides: Whales, Dolphins, and Porpoises.* New York: Time-Life, 1998. Print.

"Discovering Whales." *Whales on the Net.* 1998. Whales in Danger Information Service. Web. 18 Oct. 1999.

Neruda, Pablo. "Ode to Spring." *Odes to Opposites.* Trans. Ken Krabbenhoft. Ed. and illus. Ferris Cook. Boston: Little, 1995. Print.

*The Saga of the Volsungs.* Trans. Jesse L. Byock. London: Penguin, 1990. Print.

> List an anonymous work by title.

> List both the title of the work and the collection in which it is found.

---

### Sample Parenthetical Citations

It makes sense that baleen whales such as the blue whale, the bowhead whale, the humpback whale, and the sei whale (to name just a few) grow to immense sizes (Carwardine, Hoyt, and Fordyce 19–21). The blue whale has grooves running from under its chin to partway along the length of its underbelly. As in some other whales, these grooves expand and allow even more food and water to be taken in (Ellis 18–21).

> Author's last name

> Page numbers where information can be found

# MLA Style for Listing Sources

| | |
|---|---|
| **Book with one author** | Pyles, Thomas. *The Origins and Development of the English Language.* 2nd ed. New York: Harcourt, 1971. Print. |
| **Book with two or three authors** | McCrum, Robert, William Cran, and Robert MacNeil. *The Story of English.* New York: Penguin, 1987. Print. |
| **Book with an editor** | Truth, Sojourner. *Narrative of Sojourner Truth.* Ed. Margaret Washington. New York: Vintage, 1993. Print. |
| **Book with more than three authors or editors** | Donald, Robert B., et al. *Writing Clear Essays.* Upper Saddle River: Prentice, 1996. Print. |
| **Single work in an anthology** | Hawthorne, Nathaniel. "Young Goodman Brown." *Literature: An Introduction to Reading and Writing.* Ed. Edgar V. Roberts and H. E. Jacobs. Upper Saddle River: Prentice, 1998. 376–385. Print. <br>[Indicate pages for the entire selection.] |
| **Introduction to a work in a published edition** | Washington, Margaret. Introduction. *Narrative of Sojourner Truth.* By Sojourner Truth. Ed. Washington. New York: Vintage, 1993. v–xi. Print. |
| **Signed article from an encyclopedia** | Askeland, Donald R. "Welding." *World Book Encyclopedia.* 1991 ed. Print. |
| **Signed article in a weekly magazine** | Wallace, Charles. "A Vodacious Deal." *Time* 14 Feb. 2000: 63. Print. |
| **Signed article in a monthly magazine** | Gustaitis, Joseph. "The Sticky History of Chewing Gum." *American History* Oct. 1998: 30–38. Print. |
| **Newspaper** | Thurow, Roger. "South Africans Who Fought for Sanctions Now Scrap for Investors." *Wall Street Journal* 11 Feb. 2000: A1+. Print. <br>[For a multipage article that does not appear on consecutive pages, write only the first page number on which it appears, followed by the plus sign.] |
| **Unsigned editorial or story** | "Selective Silence." Editorial. *Wall Street Journal* 11 Feb. 2000: A14. Print. <br>[If the editorial or story is signed, begin with the author's name.] |
| **Signed pamphlet or brochure** | [Treat the pamphlet as though it were a book.] |
| **Work from a library subscription service** | Ertman, Earl L. "Nefertiti's Eyes." *Archaeology* Mar.–Apr. 2008: 28–32. *Kids Search.* EBSCO. New York Public Library. Web. 18 June 2008 <br>[Indicate the date you accessed the information.] |
| **Filmstrips, slide programs, videocassettes, DVDs, and other audiovisual media** | *The Diary of Anne Frank.* Dir. George Stevens. Perf. Millie Perkins, Shelley Winters, Joseph Schildkraut, Lou Jacobi, and Richard Beymer. 1959. Twentieth Century Fox, 2004. DVD. |
| **CD-ROM (with multiple publishers)** | Simms, James, ed. *Romeo and Juliet.* By William Shakespeare. Oxford: Attica Cybernetics; London: BBC Education; London: Harper, 1995. CD-ROM. |
| **Radio or television program transcript** | "Washington's Crossing of the Delaware." *Weekend Edition Sunday.* Natl. Public Radio. WNYC, New York. 23 Dec. 2003. Television transcript. |
| **Internet Web page** | "Fun Facts About Gum." NACGM site. 1999. National Association of Chewing Gum Manufacturers. Web. 19 Dec. 1999 <br>[Indicate the date you accessed the information.] |
| **Personal interview** | Smith, Jane. Personal interview. 10 Feb. 2000. |

All examples follow the style given in the *MLA Handbook for Writers of Research Papers,* seventh edition, by Joseph Gibaldi.

# Guide to Rubrics

## What is a rubric?

A rubric is a tool, often in the form of a chart or a grid, that helps you assess your work. Rubrics are particularly helpful for writing and speaking assignments.

To help you or others assess, or evaluate, your work, a rubric offers several specific criteria to be applied to your work. Then, the rubric helps you or an evaluator indicate your range of success or failure according to those specific criteria. Rubrics are often used to evaluate writing for standardized tests.

Using a rubric will save you time, focus your learning, and improve the work you do. When you know what the rubric will be before you begin writing a persuasive essay, for example, you will be aware as you write of specific criteria that are important in that kind of essay. As you evaluate the essay before giving it to your teacher, you will focus on the specific areas that your teacher wants you to master—or on areas that you know present challenges for you. Instead of searching through your work randomly for any way to improve it or correct its errors, you will have a clear and helpful focus on specific criteria.

## How are rubrics constructed?

Rubrics can be constructed in several different ways.

- Your teacher may assign a rubric for a specific assignment.
- Your teacher may direct you to a rubric in your textbook.
- Your teacher and your class may construct a rubric for a particular assignment together.
- You and your classmates may construct a rubric together.
- You may create your own rubric with criteria you want to evaluate in your work.

## How will a rubric help me?

A rubric will help you assess your work on a scale. Scales vary from rubric to rubric but usually range from 6 to 1, 5 to 1, or 4 to 1, with 6, 5, or 4 being the highest score and 1 being the lowest. If someone else is using the rubric to assess your work, the rubric will give your evaluator a clear range within which to place your work. If you are using the rubric yourself, it will help you make improvements to your work.

What are the types of rubrics?

- A **holistic rubric** has general criteria that can apply to a variety of assignments. See p. R-40 for an example of a holistic rubric.
- An **analytic rubric** is specific to a particular assignment. The criteria for evaluation address the specific issues important in that assignment. See p. R-39 for examples of analytic rubrics.

# Sample Analytic Rubrics

## Rubric With a 4-point Scale

*The following analytic rubric is an example of a rubric to assess a persuasive essay. It will help you evaluate focus, organization, support/elaboration, and style/convention.*

| | Focus | Organization | Support/Elaboration | Style/Convention |
|---|---|---|---|---|
| 4 | Demonstrates highly effective word choice; clearly focused on task. | Uses clear, consistent organizational strategy. | Provides convincing, well-elaborated reasons to support the position. | Incorporates transitions; includes very few mechanical errors. |
| 3 | Demonstrates good word choice; stays focused on persuasive task. | Uses clear organizational strategy with occasional inconsistencies. | Provides two or more moderately elaborated reasons to support the position. | Incorporates some transitions; includes few mechanical errors. |
| 2 | Shows some good word choices; minimally stays focused on persuasive task. | Uses inconsistent organizational strategy; presentation is not logical. | Provides several reasons, but few are elaborated; only one elaborated reason. | Incorporates few transitions; includes many mechanical errors. |
| 1 | Shows lack of attention to persuasive task. | Demonstrates lack of organizational strategy. | Provides no specific reasons or does not elaborate. | Does not connect ideas; includes many mechanical errors. |

## Rubric With a 6-point Scale

*The following analytic rubric is an example of a rubric to assess a persuasive essay. It will help you evaluate presentation, position, evidence, and arguments.*

| | Presentation | Position | Evidence | Arguments |
|---|---|---|---|---|
| 6 | Essay clearly and effectively addresses an issue with more than one side. | Essay clearly states a supportable position on the issue. | All evidence is logically organized, well presented, and supports the position. | All reader concerns and counterarguments are effectively addressed. |
| 5 | Most of essay addresses an issue that has more than one side. | Essay clearly states a position on the issue. | Most evidence is logically organized, well presented, and supports the position. | Most reader concerns and counterarguments are effectively addressed. |
| 4 | Essay adequately addresses issue that has more than one side. | Essay adequately states a position on the issue. | Many parts of evidence support the position; some evidence is out of order. | Many reader concerns and counterarguments are adequately addressed. |
| 3 | Essay addresses issue with two sides but does not present second side clearly. | Essay states a position on the issue, but the position is difficult to support. | Some evidence supports the position, but some evidence is out of order. | Some reader concerns and counterarguments are addressed. |
| 2 | Essay addresses issue with two sides but does not present second side. | Essay states a position on the issue, but the position is not supportable. | Not much evidence supports the position, and what is included is out of order. | A few reader concerns and counterarguments are addressed. |
| 1 | Essay does not address issue with more than one side. | Essay does not state a position on the issue. | No evidence supports the position. | No reader concerns or counterarguments are addressed. |

# Sample Holistic Rubric

Holistic rubrics such as this one are sometimes used to assess writing assignments on standardized tests. Notice that the criteria for evaluation are focus, organization, support, and use of conventions.

| Points | Criteria |
|---|---|
| **6 Points** | • The writing is strongly focused and shows fresh insight into the writing task.<br>• The writing is marked by a sense of completeness and coherence and is organized with a logical progression of ideas.<br>• A main idea is fully developed, and support is specific and substantial.<br>• A mature command of the language is evident, and the writing may employ characteristic creative writing strategies.<br>• Sentence structure is varied, and writing is free of all but purposefully used fragments.<br>• Virtually no errors in writing conventions appear. |
| **5 Points** | • The writing is clearly focused on the task.<br>• The writing is well organized and has a logical progression of ideas, though there may be occasional lapses.<br>• A main idea is well developed and supported with relevant detail.<br>• Sentence structure is varied, and the writing is free of fragments, except when used purposefully.<br>• Writing conventions are followed correctly. |
| **4 Points** | • The writing is clearly focused on the task, but extraneous material may intrude at times.<br>• Clear organizational pattern is present, though lapses may occur.<br>• A main idea is adequately supported, but development may be uneven.<br>• Sentence structure is generally fragment free but shows little variation.<br>• Writing conventions are generally followed correctly. |
| **3 Points** | • Writing is generally focused on the task, but extraneous material may intrude at times.<br>• An organizational pattern is evident, but writing may lack a logical progression of ideas.<br>• Support for the main idea is generally present but is sometimes illogical.<br>• Sentence structure is generally free of fragments, but there is almost no variation.<br>• The work generally demonstrates a knowledge of writing conventions, with occasional misspellings. |
| **2 Points** | • The writing is related to the task but generally lacks focus.<br>• There is little evidence of organizational pattern, and there is little sense of cohesion.<br>• Support for the main idea is generally inadequate, illogical, or absent.<br>• Sentence structure is unvaried, and serious errors may occur.<br>• Errors in writing conventions and spellings are frequent. |
| **1 Point** | • The writing may have little connection to the task and is generally unfocused.<br>• There has been little attempt at organization or development.<br>• The paper seems fragmented, with no clear main idea.<br>• Sentence structure is unvaried, and serious errors appear.<br>• Poor word choice and poor command of the language obscure meaning.<br>• Errors in writing conventions and spelling are frequent. |
| **Unscorable** | The paper is considered unscorable if:<br>• The response is unrelated to the task or is simply a rewording of the prompt.<br>• The response has been copied from a published work.<br>• The student did not write a response.<br>• The response is illegible.<br>• The words in the response are arranged with no meaning.<br>• There is an insufficient amount of writing to score. |

# Student Model

## Persuasive Writing

This persuasive letter, which would receive a top score according to a persuasive rubric, is a response to the following writing prompt, or assignment:

**With the increased use of technology in the workplace, the skills that high-school graduates must possess have changed. Write a letter to your principal advocating new technology courses that could give high-school graduates a competitive edge.**

Dear Principal:

I am writing to alert you to an urgent need in our school's curriculum. We need computer graphics courses!

> The letter begins with an engaging introduction that clearly states the persuasive focus.

Although you would have to find funds to buy the equipment, I've concluded that setting up this course would well be worth it. By adding this course, you would be adding many high paying career options for students. Computer graphics is a type of art, and businesses all around us involve art in some form. You see computer graphics in commercials, movies, news broadcasts, weather broadcasts, architectural design, and business presentations. Workers with computer graphics skills are well paid because they are in such high demand.

You may argue that the school already has computer science classes. Good point! I'm in a computer science class and it is mainly programming. Once we did have an assignment to design a graphic of a pumpkin. You wouldn't believe how much coding it takes to get a simple, animated drawing. In order to get a really creative image with definite lines, shading, lifelike colors, and texture, you need to use computer graphics software designed especially for that purpose. With software, you can make images that move and talk smoothly and environments with realistic colors and lighting. This is the same graphics software that businesses use for commercials, movies, and brochures. Students should be learning how to use this software.

> The author effectively counters an opposing argument to increase the persuasive power of her own argument.

Most important, computer graphics is a subject area that allows students to express their creativity. Adding a computer graphics course would have a positive effect on students. Course participants would enjoy doing their assignments, so they would earn good grades and turn in creative work. The energy and enthusiasm they would bring to their projects would catch the attention of the community at large. As a result, they would make the school and the principal look good.

> A positive argument that is well supported enhances the letter's persuasive appeal.

As you can see, adding a computer graphics course could be a very profitable idea for you, the students, and the community. You would be ensuring the success of the students who desire an art or computer career. You would be opening hundreds of different career pathways. Wouldn't it be great to know you were the reason for these students' success? Thanks for your time and consideration.

Sincerely,
Dawn Witherspoon

# 21st-Century Skills

New technology has created many new ways to communicate. Today, it is easy to contribute information to the Internet and send a variety of messages to friends far and near. You can also share your ideas through photos, illustrations, video, and sound recordings. *21st-Century Skills* gives you an overview of some ways you can use today's technology to create, share, and find information. Here are the topics you will find in this section.

- ✔ Blogs
- ✔ Multimedia Elements
- ✔ Social Networking
- ✔ Podcasts
- ✔ Widgets & Feeds
- ✔ Wikis

## BLOGS

A **blog** is a common form of online writing. The word *blog* is a contraction of *Web log*. Most blogs include a series of entries known as *posts*. The posts appear in a single column and are displayed in reverse chronological order. That means that the most recent post is at the top of the page. As you scroll down, you will find earlier posts.

Blogs have become increasingly popular. Researchers estimate that 75,000 new blogs are launched every day. Blog authors are often called *bloggers*. They can use their personal sites to share ideas, songs, videos, photos, and other media. People who read blogs can often post their responses with a comments feature found in each new post.

Because blogs are designed so that they are easy to update, bloggers can post new messages as often as they like, often daily. For some people blogs become a public journal or diary, in which they share their thoughts about daily events.

### Types of Blogs

Not all blogs are the same. Many blogs have a single author, but others are group projects. These are some common types of blog:

- ✔ Personal blogs often have a general focus. Bloggers post their thoughts on any topic they find interesting in their daily lives.

- ✔ Topical blogs focus on a specific theme, such as movie reviews, political news, class assignments, or health-care opportunities.

---

### Web Safety

Always be aware that information you post on the Internet can be read by everyone with access to that page. Once you post a picture or text, it can be saved on someone else's computer, even if you later remove it.

Using the Internet safely means keeping personal information personal. Never include your address (e-mail or real), last name, or telephone numbers. Avoid mentioning places you can be frequently found. Never give out passwords you use to access other Web sites and do not respond to e-mails from people you do not know.

---

## Anatomy of a Blog

Here are some of the features you can include in a blog.

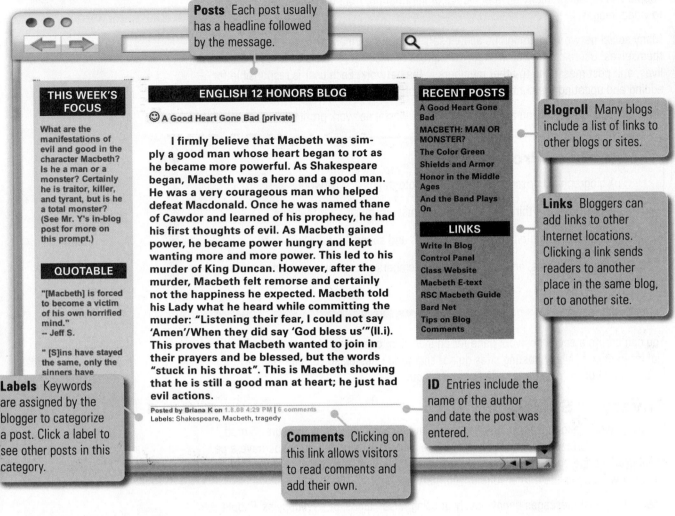

**Posts** Each post usually has a headline followed by the message.

**THIS WEEK'S FOCUS**

What are the manifestations of evil and good in the character Macbeth? Is he a man or a monster? Certainly he is traitor, killer, and tyrant, but is he a total monster? (See Mr. Y's in-blog post for more on this prompt.)

**QUOTABLE**

"[Macbeth] is forced to become a victim of his own horrified mind."
-- Jeff S.

" [S]ins have stayed the same, only the sinners have

**ENGLISH 12 HONORS BLOG**

☺ A Good Heart Gone Bad [private]

    I firmly believe that Macbeth was simply a good man whose heart began to rot as he became more powerful. As Shakespeare began, Macbeth was a hero and a good man. He was a very courageous man who helped defeat Macdonald. Once he was named thane of Cawdor and learned of his prophecy, he had his first thoughts of evil. As Macbeth gained power, he became power hungry and kept wanting more and more power. This led to his murder of King Duncan. However, after the murder, Macbeth felt remorse and certainly not the happiness he expected. Macbeth told his Lady what he heard while committing the murder: "Listening their fear, I could not say 'Amen'/When they did say 'God bless us'"(II.i). This proves that Macbeth wanted to join in their prayers and be blessed, but the words "stuck in his throat". This is Macbeth showing that he is still a good man at heart; he just had evil actions.

Posted by **Briana K** on 1.8.08 4:29 PM | 6 comments
Labels: Shakespeare, Macbeth, tragedy

**RECENT POSTS**

A Good Heart Gone Bad
**MACBETH: MAN OR MONSTER?**
The Color Green
Shields and Armor
Honor in the Middle Ages
And the Band Plays On

**LINKS**

Write In Blog
Control Panel
Class Website
Macbeth E-text
RSC Macbeth Guide
Bard Net
Tips on Blog Comments

**Blogroll** Many blogs include a list of links to other blogs or sites.

**Links** Bloggers can add links to other Internet locations. Clicking a link sends readers to another place in the same blog, or to another site.

**Labels** Keywords are assigned by the blogger to categorize a post. Click a label to see other posts in this category.

**Comments** Clicking on this link allows visitors to read comments and add their own.

**ID** Entries include the name of the author and date the post was entered.

## Creating a Blog

Keep these hints and strategies in mind to help you create an interesting and fair blog:

- ✔ Focus each blog entry on a single topic.

- ✔ Vary the length of your posts. Sometimes, all you need is a line or two to share a quick thought. Other posts will be much longer.

- ✔ Choose font colors and styles that can be read easily.

- ✔ Many people scan blogs rather than read them closely. You can make your main ideas pop out by using clear or clever headlines and boldfacing key terms.

- ✔ Give credit to other people's work and ideas. State the names of people whose ideas you are quoting or add a link to take readers to that person's blog or site.

- ✔ If you post comments, try to make them brief and polite.

# SOCIAL NETWORKING

Social networking means any interaction between members of an online community. People can exchange many different kinds of information, from text and voice messages to video images.

Many social network communities allow users to create permanent pages that describe themselves. Users create home pages to express themselves, share ideas about their lives, and post messages to other members in the network. Each user is responsible for adding and updating the content on his or her profile page.

Here are some features you are likely to find on a social network profile:

## Features of Profile Pages

- A biographical description, including photographs and artwork.

- Lists of favorite things, such as books, movies, music, and fashions.

- Playable media elements such as videos and sound recordings.

- Message boards, or "walls" in which members of the community can exchange messages.

You can create a social network page for an individual or a group, such as a school or special interest club. Many hosting sites do not charge to register, so you can also have fun by creating a page for a pet or a fictional character.

## Privacy in Social Networks

Social networks allow users to decide how open their profiles will be. Be sure to read introductory information carefully before you register at a new site. Once you have a personal profile page, monitor your privacy settings regularly. Remember that any information you post will be available to anyone in your network.

Users often post messages anonymously or using false names, or *pseudonyms.* People can also post using someone else's name. Judge all information on the net critically. Do not assume that you know who posted some information simply because you recognize the name of the post author. The rapid speed of communication on the Internet can make it easy to jump to conclusions—be careful to avoid this trap.

## Tips for Sending Effective Messages

Technology makes it easy to share ideas quickly, but writing for the Internet poses some special challenges, as well. The writing style for blogs and social networks is often very conversational. In blog posts and comments, instant messages, and e-mails, writers often express themselves very quickly, using relaxed language, short sentences, and abbreviations. However, in a conversation, we get a lot of information from a speaker's tone of voice and body language. On the Internet, those clues are missing. As a result, Internet writers often use italics or bracketed labels to indicate emotions. Another alternative is using emoticons—strings of characters that give visual clues to indicate emotion:

| | | |
|---|---|---|
| **:-)** smile (happy) | **:-(** frown (unhappy) | **;-)** wink (light sarcasm) |

Use these strategies to communicate effectively when using technology:

- ✔ Reread your messages. Before you click *Send,* read your message through and make sure that your tone will be clear to the reader.

- ✔ Do not jump to conclusions—ask for clarification first. Make sure you really understand what someone is saying before you respond.

- ✔ Use abbreviations your reader will understand.

## WIDGETS & FEEDS

A **widget** is a small application that performs a specific task. You might find widgets that give weather predictions, offer dictionary definitions or translations, provide entertainment such as games, or present a daily word, photograph, or quotation.

A **feed** is a special kind of widget. It displays headlines taken from the latest content on a specific media source. Clicking on the headline will take you to the full article.

Many social network communities and other Web sites allow you to personalize your home page by adding widgets and feeds.

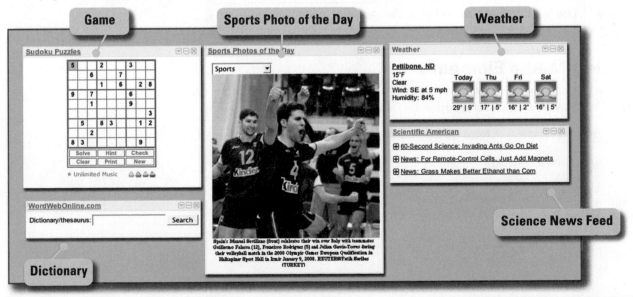

# MULTIMEDIA ELEMENTS

One of the great advantages of communicating on the Internet is that you are not limited to using text only. When you create a Web profile or blog, you can share your ideas using a wide variety of media. In addition to widgets and feeds (see page R45), these media elements can make your Internet communication more entertaining and useful.

| Graphics | |
|---|---|
| **Photographs** | You can post photos taken by digital cameras. |
| **Illustrations** | Artwork can be created using computer software. You can also use a scanner to post a digital image of a drawing or sketch. |
| **Charts, Graphs, and Maps** | Charts and graphs can make statistical information clear. Use spreadsheet software to create these elements. Use Internet sites to find maps of specific places. |

| Video | |
|---|---|
| **Live Action** | Digital video can be recorded by a camera or recorded from another media source. |
| **Animation** | Animated videos can also be created using software. |

| Sound | |
|---|---|
| **Music** | Many social network communities make it easy to share your favorite music with people who visit your page. |
| **Voice** | Use a microphone to add your own voice to your Web page. |

## Editing Media Elements

You can use software to customize media elements. Open source software is free and available to anyone on the Internet. Here are some things you can do with software:

✔ Crop a photograph to focus on the subject or brighten an image that is too dark.

✔ Transform a drawing's appearance from flat to three-dimensional.

✔ Insert a "You Are Here" arrow on a map.

✔ Edit a video or sound file to shorten its running time.

✔ Add background music or sound effects to a video.

# PODCASTS

A **podcast** is a digital audio or video recording of a program that is made available on the Internet. Users can replay the podcast on a computer, or download it and replay it on a personal audio player. You might think of podcasts as radio or television programs that you create yourself. They can be embedded on a Web site or fed to a Web page through a podcast widget.

## Creating an Effective Podcast

To make a podcast, you will need a recording device, such as a microphone or digital video camera, as well as editing software. Open source editing software is widely available and free of charge. Most audio podcasts are converted into the MP3 format. Here are some tips for creating a podcast that is clear and entertaining:

- ✔ Listen to several podcasts by different authors to get a feeling for the medium. Make a list of features and styles you like and also those you want to avoid.

- ✔ Test your microphone to find the best recording distance. Stand close enough to the microphone so that your voice sounds full, but not so close that you create an echo.

- ✔ Create an outline that shows your estimated timing for each element.

- ✔ Be prepared before you record. Rehearse, but do not create a script. Podcasts are best when they have a natural, easy flow.

- ✔ Talk directly to your listeners. Slow down enough so they can understand you.

- ✔ Use software to edit your podcast before publishing it. You can edit out mistakes or add additional elements.

# WIKIS

A **wiki** is a collaborative Web site that lets visitors create, add, remove, and edit content. The term comes from the Hawaiian phrase *wiki wiki,* which means "quick." Web users at a wiki are both the readers and the writers of the site. Some wikis are open to contributions from anyone. Others require visitors to register before they can edit the content.

All of the text in these collaborative Web sites was written by people who use the site. Articles are constantly changing, as visitors find and correct errors and improve texts.

Wikis have both advantages and disadvantages as sources of information. They are valuable open forums for the exchange of ideas. The unique collaborative writing process allows entries to change over time. However, entries can also be modified incorrectly. Careless or malicious users can delete good content and add inappropriate or inaccurate information.

You can change the information on a wiki, but be sure your information is correct and clear before you add it. Wikis keep track of all changes, so your work will be recorded and can be evaluated by other users.

# Rules of Debate

A **debate** is a structured contest based on a formal discussion of opinion. In essence, it is a battle of intellect and verbal skill. The goal is mastering the art of persuasion. Who can best express, argue, and support opinions on a given topic? Who can best refute an argument, showing that the opponent's points are invalid? Which team, in the end, can convince the judges that their argument is the most sound?

## Teams

A **formal debate** is conducted with two teams—an Affirmation team and a Negative team. As the names suggest, the Affirmation team is responsible for presenting the "pro" side of an issue, while the Negative team presents the "con" side of the issue. Each team has a main purpose and will offer both constructive and rebuttal speeches, practicing the art of persuasion and debate.

**Affirmation team** The Affirmation team as a whole carries the burden of proof for the debate. They must prove there is a problem. To do so, they need to cite credible sources, include relevant details, and present and support valid points. Each team member has a specific job. The first speaker has the most responsibility. He or she must

- define the issue or problem

- introduce the team line—a one-line summary of the team's position on the issue

- identify the point of the argument each speaker will discuss

The remaining team members have the job of presenting and supporting the main points of the argument.

**Negative team** Though the Negative team does not carry the burden of proof, the team must show that there is no problem or that the Affirmation team's solutions are invalid. Though their purpose is to rebut an argument, the rebuttal technique calls for a formation of their own argument. They must argue against the Affirmation team. To construct their argument, they must use—like the Affirmation team—credible sources, relevant details, and valid points. They should incorporate any available statistics, pertinent facts, or applicable testimonies to bolster their argument. Even though the first speaker of the Affirmation team lays out each point of the argument, the Negative team speakers cannot address points that have not been thoroughly discussed by an Affirmation team member.

## Structure

Just like most other contests, debates have a set structure. Debates are divided into halves. The first half begins with the constructive speeches from both teams, which last ten minutes each.

After the first half, there is a short intermission. Then, the second half begins with the Negative team. This half is reserved for the rebuttal speeches, which last five minutes each and include rebuttals and refutations. This is each team's chance to rebuild their arguments that the other team broke down (rebuttal), and put forth evidence to show the other team is wrong (refutation). Although the Negative team begins the argument in the second half, every debate begins and ends with the Affirmation team.

## Structure of Debate

| 1st Half: Constructive Speeches (10 minutes each) | 2nd Half: Rebuttal Speeches (5 minutes each) |
|---|---|
| 1st Affirmative Team Speaker | 1st Negative Team Speaker |
| 1st Negative Team Speaker | 1st Affirmative Team Speaker |
| 2nd Affirmative Team Speaker | 2nd Negative Team Speaker |
| 2nd Negative Team Speaker | 2nd Affirmative Team Speaker |
| 3rd Affirmative Team Speaker | 3rd Negative Team Speaker |
| 3rd Negative Team Speaker | 3rd Affirmative Team Speaker |

# Speeches—Content, Organization, and Delivery

**Debate speeches** are the result of practicing the art of persuasion. To be effective, speakers must include pertinent content, use clear and logical organization, and have a powerful delivery. These combined elements make a strong speech.

**Content** Debates often focus on concrete issues that can be proved or disproved. The basis for a debate speech is its content. The Affirmation team should first determine their position. They should be sure to include any facts and/or statistics that concretely support the argument. Speech writers should cite specific instances and occurrences that solidify their position. Writers might also include testimonies or ideas from professionals. Finally, the Affirmation team needs to propose possible solutions to the problem or issue and examine the costs and effects of those solutions.

Though the Negative team does not have to state a position—their position is automatically the opposing position—they still need to include facts, statistics, testimony, and descriptions of specific instances or occurrences to make their counterpoints. They need to analyze the Affirmation team's proposed solutions and explain why they will not work. In essence, the Negative team must construct an argument around the Affirmation team's argument.

**Organization** Debate speeches are organized like other speeches and essays. They should have an introduction, transitions, body, and conclusion. The speeches should have clear main points and supporting details for those points. Because a debate is a structured discussion, there will be a specific order of points and the speakers who present them must be identified. Speakers can use note cards to help them stick to the planned organization, but they should only use brief notes, never reading directly from the cards.

**Delivery** The manner in which a speech is delivered can make or break the argument. The impression the speaker makes on the audience, including the judges, is key. To make a good impression, the speaker must present the material with confidence. He or she can portray confidence by forming a connection with the audience through eye contact, glancing away only briefly to consult notes. A speaker should focus on his or her voice, varying the tone, volume, and pace appropriately. Body movements should not include fidgeting or nervous movement. They should only be used if they are deliberate and help express or underscore a point. Finally, speakers should be concise, focusing on vivid and clear word choice and using words that emphasize the point.

# Scoring

Debates are scored much like other contests. Each side is judged on the content and delivery of their speeches. Judges contemplate different elements of content and delivery in order to determine the number of points to give each team. They might ask themselves the questions in the chart below in order to determine the score.

Finally, judges look at the observation of debate etiquette. Speakers are expected to be mature and respectful of their opponents. Speakers should never attack an opponent, but instead should attack the argument. Judges will deduct points for personal attacks.

## Scoring Criteria

| Content | Delivery |
| --- | --- |
| Were arguments convincing? | Were speakers able to speak extemporaneously? |
| Were arguments supported with credible, valid and relevant reasons? | Were body movements deliberate and effective? |
| Were refutations and rebuttals effective? | Did speakers make a connection with the audience? |
| Were speakers confident and knowledgeable? | Did speakers stay within their time limits? |

## Parts of Speech

**Nouns**  A noun names a person, place, or thing. Common nouns name any one of a class of people, places, or things. Proper nouns name specific people, places, or things.

| Common Noun | Proper Noun |
|---|---|
| city | Washington, D.C. |

Use *apostrophes* with nouns to show ownership. Add an apostrophe and *s* to show the **possessive case** of most singular nouns. Add just an apostrophe to show the possessive case of plural nouns ending in *s* or *es*. Add an apostrophe and s to show the possessive case of plural nouns that do not end in *s* or *es*.

**Pronouns**  A **pronoun** is a word that stands for a noun or for a word that takes the place of a noun.

A **personal pronoun** refers to (1) the person speaking, (2) the person spoken to, or (3) the person, place, or thing spoken about.

| | Singular | Plural |
|---|---|---|
| First Person | I, me, my, mine | we, us, our, ours |
| Second Person | you, your, yours | you, your, yours |
| Third Person | he, him, his, she, her, hers, it, its | they, them, their, theirs |

A **reflexive pronoun** ends in -*self* or -*selves* and adds information to a sentence by pointing back to a noun or pronoun earlier in the sentence.

> As I said these words I busied *myself* among the pile of bones of which I have before spoken.
> —"The Cask of Amontillado," p. 60

An **intensive pronoun** ends in -*self* or -*selves* and simply adds emphasis to a noun or a pronoun in the same sentence.

> The best playground, however, was the dark alley *itself*.
> —"Rules of the Game," p. 316

**Demonstrative pronouns** (*this, these, that,* and *those*) direct attention to a specific person, place, or thing.

> *These* are the juiciest pears I have ever tasted.

A **relative pronoun** begins a subordinate (relative) clause and connects it to another idea in the sentence.

> The poet *who* wrote "Fire and Ice" is Robert Frost.
> The poet *whom* I admire is Frost.

An **interrogative pronoun** is used to begin a question. The five interrogative pronouns are *what, which, who, whom, whose.*

An **indefinite pronoun** refers to a person, place, or thing, often without specifying which one.

> *Some* of the flowers were in bloom.
> *Everybody* chose something.

**Verbs**  A **verb** is a word that expresses time while showing an action, a condition, or the fact that something exists.

An **action verb** indicates the action of someone or something. An action verb is **transitive** if it directs action toward someone or something named in the same sentence.

> Marcos accepted their bouquets . . .
> —"Uncle Marcos," p. 138

An action verb is **intransitive** if it does not direct action toward something or someone named in the same sentence.

> "He nodded and smiled a lot."
> —"American History," p. 240

A **linking verb** is a verb that connects the subject of a sentence with a noun or pronoun that renames or describes the subject. All linking verbs are intransitive.

> Life *is* a broken-winged bird . . .
> —"Dreams," p. 621

A **helping verb** is a verb that can be added to another verb to make a verb phrase.

> Nor *did* I suspect that these experiences could be part of a novel's meaning.

**Adjectives**  An **adjective** describes a noun or a pronoun or gives a noun or a pronoun a more specific meaning. Adjectives answer these questions:

| | |
|---|---|
| What kind? | *blue* lamp, *large* tree |
| Which one? | *this* table, *those* books |
| How many? | *five* stars, *several* buses |
| How much? | *less* money, *enough* votes |

The articles *the, a,* and *an* are adjectives. *An* is used before a word beginning with a vowel sound.

A noun may sometimes be used as an adjective.

> *diamond* necklace          *summer* vacation

**Adverbs**  An **adverb** modifies a verb, an adjective, or another adverb. Adverbs answer the questions *Where? When? In what way?* or *To what extent?*

> He could stand *there*. (modifies verb *stand*)
> He was *blissfully* happy. (modifies adjective *happy*)
> It ended *too* soon. (modifies adverb *soon*)

**Prepositions**  A **preposition** relates a noun or a pronoun that appears with it to another word in the sentence.

> the scene *before* the end          stood *near* me

**Conjunctions** A **conjunction** connects other words or groups of words. A **coordinating conjunction** connects similar kinds or groups of words.

mother *and* father        simple *yet* stylish

**Correlative conjunctions** are used in pairs to connect similar words or groups of words.

*both* Sue *and* Meg        *neither* he *nor* I

A **subordinating conjunction** connects two complete ideas by placing one idea below the other in rank or importance.

You would know him *if* you saw him.

**Interjections** An **interjection** expresses feeling or emotion and functions independently of a sentence.

"*Oh*, my poor, poor, Mathilde!"
    —"The Necklace," p. 332

# Sentences, Phrases, and Clauses

**Sentences** A **sentence** is a group of words with a subject and a predicate. Together, these parts express a complete thought.

I closed my eyes and pondered my next move.
    — "Rules of the Game," p. 316

A **fragment** is a group of words that does not express a complete thought.

The Swan Theater in London

A **run-on** is two or more complete sentences run together without punctuation.

A **direct object** is a noun or pronoun that receives the action of a transitive verb.

An **indirect object** is a noun or pronoun that appears with a direct object and names the person or thing that something is given to or done for.

**The Four Structures of Sentences** There are two kinds of clauses: independent and subordinate. These can be used to form four basic sentence structures: *simple, compound, complex,* and *compound-complex.*

A **simple sentence** consists of a single independent clause.

A **compound sentence** consists of two or more independent clauses.

The clauses in a compound sentence can be joined by a comma and a coordinating conjunction (*and, but, for, not, or, so, yet*) or by a semicolon (;).

A **complex sentence** consists of one independent clause and one or more subordinate clauses.

The independent clause in a complex sentence is often called the *main clause* to distinguish it from the subordinate clause or clauses.

A **compound-complex sentence** consists of two or more independent clauses and one or more subordinate causes.

**Phrases** A **phrase** is a group of words, without a subject and a verb, that functions in a sentence as one part of speech.

A **prepositional phrase** is a group of words that includes a preposition and a noun or a pronoun that is the object of the preposition.

outside my window        below the counter

An **adjective phrase** is a prepositional phrase that modifies a noun or a pronoun by telling *what kind* or *which one.*

The wooden gates *of that lane* stood open.

An **adverb phrase** is a prepositional phrase that modifies a verb, an adjective, or an adverb by pointing out *where, when, in what way,* or *to what extent.*

". . . I could sleep without closing my eyes . . ."
    —"The Most Dangerous Game," p. 215

An **appositive phrase** is a noun or pronoun with modifiers, placed next to a noun or a pronoun to add information and details.

"It is a very great pleasure and honor to welcome Mr. Sanger Rainsford, *the celebrated hunter,* to my home."
    —"The Most Dangerous Game," p. 215

A **participial phrase** is a participle with its modifiers or complements. The entire phrase acts as an adjective.

"Try the settee," said Holmes, *relapsing into his armchair . . .*
    —"The Red-headed League," p. 1166

A **gerund phrase** is a gerund with modifiers or a complement, all acting together as a noun.

*The baying of the hounds* drew nearer, . . .
    —"The Most Dangerous Game," p. 215

An **infinitive phrase** is an infinitive (*to* and a verb) with modifiers, complements, or a subject, all acting together as a single part of speech.

I continued, as was my wont, *to smile in his face,* . . .
    —"The Cask of Amontillado," p. 60

**Clauses** A **clause** is a group of words with a subject and a verb.

An **independent clause** has a subject and a verb and can stand by itself as a complete sentence.

A **subordinate clause** has a subject and a verb but cannot stand by itself as a complete sentence; it can only be part of a sentence.

An **adjective clause** is a subordinate clause that modifies a noun or a pronoun by telling *what kind* or *which one.*

Walter Mitty stopped the car in front of the building *where his wife went to have her hair done.*
    —"The Secret Life of Walter Mitty," p. 128

An **adverb clause** modifies a verb, an adjective, an adverb, or a verbal by telling *where, when, in what way, to what extent, under what condition,* or *why.*

> The hunter shook his head several times, *as if he was puzzled.*
> —"The Most Dangerous Game," p. 215

A **noun clause** is a subordinate clause that acts as a noun.

> . . . I discovered *that the intoxication had worn off* . . .
> —"The Cask of Amontillado," p. 60

**Parallelism** involves using similar grammatical structures to express similar ideas. Sentences with parallel structure contain repeated grammatical patterns or repeated types of phrases or clauses within a sentence.

> Marguerite has a great love *for art, for children,* and *for teaching.*

## The Four Principal Parts of Verbs

Tenses are formed from principal parts and helping verbs.

A verb has four **principal parts:** the present, the present participle, the past, and the past participle.

**Pronoun Case** The **case** of a pronoun is the form it takes to show its use in a sentence. There are three pronoun cases: nominative, objective, and possessive.

The **nominative case** is used to rename the subject of the sentence. The nominative case pronouns are *I, you, he, she, it, we, you, they.*

> As the subject: *She* is brave.
> Renaming the subject: The leader is *she.*

The **objective case** is used as the direct object, indirect object, or object of the preposition. The objective case pronouns are *me, you, him, her, us, you, them.*

> **As a direct object:** Our manager praised her.
> **As an indirect object:** Give him the new product.
> **As an object of the preposition:** The coach gave pointers to me.

The **possessive case** is used to show ownership. The possessive pronouns are *my, you, his, her, its, our, their, mine, yours, his, hers, its, ours, theirs.*

**Subject and Verb Agreement** A singular verb must be used with a singular subject; a plural verb must be used with a plural subject.

> *Reegan is* going home now.
> Many *storms are* the cause of beach erosion.

In a sentence with combined singular and plural subjects, the verb should agree with the subject closest to it.

> Either the *cats* or the *dog is* hungry.
> Neither *Angie* nor her *sisters were* present.

**Antecedents** are the nouns (or the words that take the place of nouns) to which pronouns refer.

A personal pronoun must agree with its antecedent in number and gender. *Number* indicates whether a pronoun is singular or plural.

Some pronouns and nouns also indicate one of three *genders:* masculine, feminine, or neuter.

Use a singular personal pronoun to refer to two or more singular antecedents joined by *or* or *nor.*

Use a plural personal pronoun to refer to two or more antecedents joined by *and.*

**Degrees of Comparison** Most adjectives and adverbs have different forms to show degrees of comparison.

The three degrees of comparison are the *positive,* the *comparative,* and the *superlative.*

Use the comparative degree to compare two people, places, or things. Use the superlative degree to compare three or more people, places, or things.

Use *more* or *most* to form the comparative and superlative degrees of all modifiers with three or more syllables.

Memorize the irregular comparative and superlative forms of certain adjectives and adverbs.

The most commonly used irregular modifiers are listed in the following chart. Notice that some modifiers differ only in the positive degree. For instance, the modifiers *bad, badly,* and *ill* all have the same comparative and superlative forms (*worse, worst*).

## Capitalization and Punctuation

**Capitalization** Capitalize the first word of a sentence and also the first word in a quotation if the quotation is a complete sentence.

> I said to him, "My dear Fortunato, you are luckily met."
> —"The Cask of Amontillado," p. 60

Capitalize all proper nouns and adjectives.

> O. Henry     Ganges River     Great Wall of China

Capitalize a person's title when it is followed by the person's name or when it is used in direct address.

> Madame     Dr. Mitty     General Zaroff

Capitalize titles showing family relationships when they refer to a specific person, unless they are preceded by a possessive noun or pronoun.

> Uncle Marcos     Granddaddy Cain

Capitalize the first word and all other key words in the titles of books, periodicals, poems, stories, plays, paintings, and other works of art.

> *Odyssey*     "I Wandered Lonely as a Cloud"

# Punctuation

**End Marks** Use a **period** to end a declarative sentence, an imperative sentence, an indirect question, and most abbreviations.

Mr. Jabez Wilson laughed heavily.
—"The Red-headed League," p. 1166

Use a **question mark** to end a direct question, an incomplete question, or a statement that is intended as a question.

"What do you expect me to do with that?"
—"The Necklace," p. 332

Use an **exclamation mark** after a statement showing strong emotion, an urgent imperative sentence, or an interjection expressing strong emotion.

Free at last! Free at last!
Thank God almighty, we are Free at last!
—"I Have a Dream," p. 542

**Commas** Use a **comma** before the coordinating conjunction to separate two independent clauses in a compound sentence.

All at once . . . she came upon a superb diamond necklace, and her heart started beating with overwhelming desire.
—"The Necklace," p. 332

Use commas to separate three or more words, phrases, or clauses in a series.

My brothers and I would peer into the medicinal herb shop, watching old Li dole out onto a stiff sheet of white paper the right amount of insect shells, saffron-colored seeds, and pungent leaves for his ailing customers.
—"Rules of the Game," p. 316

Use commas to separate adjectives of equal rank. Do not use commas to separate adjectives that must stay in a specific order.

The big cottonwood tree stood apart from a small group of winterbare cottonwoods which grew in the wide, sandy arroyo.
—"The Man to Send Rain Clouds," p. 292

His present turned out to be a box of intricate plastic parts.
—"Rules of the Game," p. 316

Use a comma after an introductory word, phrase, or clause.

When Marvin was ten years old, his father took him through the long, echoing corridors . . .
—"If I Forget Thee, Oh Earth . . . ," p. 162

Use commas to set off parenthetical and nonessential expressions.

An evil place can, so to speak, broadcast vibrations of evil.
—"The Most Dangerous Game," p. 215

Use commas with places, dates, and titles.

Poe was raised in Richmond, Virginia.
On September 1, 1939, World War II began.
Dr. Martin Luther King, Jr., was born in 1929.

Use a comma to set off a direct quotation, to prevent a sentence from being misunderstood, and to indicate the omission of a common verb in a sentence with two or more clauses.

Michele said, "I'm going to the game tonight."

*Faulty:* She stifled the sob that rose to her lips and lay motionless.

*Revised:* She stifled the sob that rose to her lips, and lay motionless.

In the *Odyssey*, the Cyclops may symbolize brutishness; the Sirens, knowledge.

**Semicolons** Use a **semicolon** to join independent clauses that are not already joined by a conjunction.

The lights of cities sparkle; on nights when there was no moon, it was difficult for me to tell the Earth from the sky. . . .
—"Single Room, Earth View," p. 468

Use a semicolon to join independent clauses separated by either a conjunctive adverb or a transitional expression.

Edward Way Teale wrote nearly thirty books; moreover, he was also an artist and a naturalist.

Use semicolons to avoid confusion when independent clauses or items in a series already contain commas.

Unable to afford jewelry, she dressed simply; but she was as wretched as a *déclassée*, for women have neither caste nor breeding—in them beauty, grace, and charm replace pride of birth.
—"The Necklace," p. 332

**Colons** Use a **colon** in order to introduce a list of items following an independent clause.

The authors we are reading include a number of poets: Robert Frost, Lewis Carroll, and Emily Dickinson.

Use a colon to introduce a formal quotation.

I have a dream that one day this nation will rise up and live out the true meaning of its creed: "We hold these truths to be self-evident; . . ."
—"I Have a Dream," p. 542

**Quotation Marks** A **direct quotation** represents a person's exact speech or thoughts and is enclosed in quotation marks.

"This great nation will endure as it has endured, will revive and will prosper," said President Franklin D. Roosevelt.
—"First Inaugural Address," p. 552

An **indirect quotation** reports only the general meaning of what a person said or thought and does not require quotation marks.

> I went up to her, put my arms around her, and said something to her.
> —from *A White House Diary*, p. 104

Always place a comma or a period inside the final quotation mark.

> "There," he said, "there's something for you."
> —"The Necklace," p. 332

Place a question mark or an exclamation mark inside the final quotation mark if the end mark is part of the quotation; if it is not part of the quotation, place it outside the final quotation mark.

> "That pig will devour us, greedily!"
> —"The Golden Kite, the Silver Wind," p. 396
> Have you ever read the poem "Dreams"?

Use single quotation marks for a quotation within a quotation.

> " 'But,' said I, 'there would be millions of red-headed men who would apply.' "
> —"The Red-headed League," p. 1067

Use quotation marks around the titles of short written works, episodes in a series, songs, and titles of works mentioned as parts of a collection.

> "I Hear America Singing"        "Pride"

**Dashes** Use **dashes** to indicate an abrupt change of thought, a dramatic interrupting idea, or a summary statement.

> The streets were lined with people—lots and lots of people—the children all smiling, placards, confetti, people waving from windows.
> —from *A White House Diary*, p. 104

**Parentheses** Use **parentheses** to set off asides and explanations only when the material is not essential or when it consists of one or more sentences.

> One last happy moment I had was looking up and seeing Mary Griffith . . . (Mary for many years had been in charge of altering the clothes which I purchased) . . .
> —from *A White House Diary*, p. 104

**Hyphens** Use a **hyphen** with certain numbers, after certain prefixes, with two or more words used as one word, and with a compound modifier coming before a noun.

> seventy-six        Post-Modernist

**Apostrophes** Add an **apostrophe** and -*s* to show the possessive case of most singular nouns.

> Thurmond's wife        the playwright's craft

Add an apostrophe to show the possessive case of plural nouns ending in -*s* and -*es*.

> the sailors' ships        the Wattses' daughter

Add an apostrophe and -*s* to show the possessive case of plural nouns that do not end in -*s* or -*es*.

> the children's games        the people's friend

Use an apostrophe in a contraction to indicate the position of the missing letter or letters.

> You'll be lonely at first, they admitted, but you're so nice you'll make friends fast.
> —"Checkouts," p. 82

# Glossary of Common Usage

**among, between:** *Among* is usually used with three or more items. *Between* is generally used with only two items.

> *Among* the poems we read this year, Margaret Walker's "Memory" was my favorite.
> Mark Twain's "The Invalid's Story" includes a humorous encounter *between* the narrator and a character named Thompson.

**around:** In formal writing, *around* should not be used to mean *approximately* or *about*. These usages are allowable, however, in informal writing or in colloquial dialogue.

> Shakespeare's *Romeo and Juliet* had its first performance in *approximately* 1595.
> Shakespeare was *about* thirty when he wrote this play.

**as, because, like, as to:** The word *as* has several meanings and can function as several parts of speech. To avoid confusion, use *because* rather than *as* when you want to indicate cause and effect.

> *Because* Cyril was interested in the history of African American poetry, he decided to write his report on Paul Laurence Dunbar.

Do not use the preposition *like* to introduce a clause that requires the conjunction *as*.

> Dorothy Parker conversed *as* she wrote—wittily.

The use of *as to* for *about* is awkward and should be avoided.

> Rosa has an interesting theory *about* E. E. Cummings's unusual typography in his poems.

# Index of Skills

Boldface numbers indicate pages where terms are defined.

## Reading

## Reading Skills

## Word Origins (Etymology)

## Writing

### Writing Applications

## Writing Strategies

**Prewriting:**

Persuasive techniques, include, 582
Position, state, 582
Problem profile, create, 173
Purpose
    clarify, 757
    specify, 1235
Questions
    answer, 489
    identify open-ended, 1003
    jot down, 463
Quote accurately, 1004
Repetition, 933
Rhetorical questions, 933
Scene, bring to life, 687
Sensory words list, 641, 667
Sentence Starters, use, 173
Sight list, make, 641
Sources
    find appropriate, 1003
    question, 1004
    use variety of, 1003
Text structure, choose, 345
Thesis statement, write, 583
Timeline, use, 94
Tone, setting, **513**
Top-ten list, make, 757
Topic, decide on, 739
Vague language, avoid, 95
Venn diagram, use, 1207
Visual aids, use, 1139
Vivid words, choose, 687
Voice, create, 513
Word choice, 95, 687, 933

**Drafting:**

Anecdote, consider, 174
Arguments, anticipate/evaluate, 174, 584
Audience, consider, 688, 758
Chronological order, use, 404
Comparable situations, describe, 174
Conflict, emphasize, 96
Description, use, 308
Details
    organize, 1140
    provide supporting, 758
    select, 174
Dialogue, create, 308
Evidence
    provide, 584
    use logical, 404
Examples, use, 174, 758
Expert opinion, provide, 174, 584
Fact and opinion, distinguish between, 584
Flow chart, 96
Format, select, 514
Formatting, use, 962
Graphic devices, use, 962
Ideas, organize, 758
Instructions, organize, 1140
Main point, identify, 96

McCracken, Elizabeth on, 175
Observations, provide personal, 584
Order of importance, use, 404
Organization, choose, 688, 1236
Outline, use, 584, 1005
Pace action, 96
Paragraph development, use TRI method, 404
Paraphrases, use, 758
Point of view, develop, 308
Problem, outline, 174
Quotations, use, 758
Scenario, consider, 174
Sources
    credit, 1005
    make direct references to, 1005
Specifics, support generalizations with, 1236
Statistics, provide, 174, 584
Suspense, create, 96
Testimonials, provide, 584
Text structure, choose, 1005
Thesis, identify, 758
Thesis statement, propose, 1005

**Revising:**

Audience, consider, 688
    cause and effect, clarify, 406
Clarity, provide, 962
Combining sentences, 406, 1009
Comparisons and contrasts, clarify, 1238
Criticism, check words of, 760
Details
    eliminate irrelevant, 688
    revise, 760
Format, follow consistent, 1006
Fragments, identifying and correcting, 1141
Generalizations, support, 176
Impression, strengthen main, 688
Inconsistent verb tenses, identify, 309
Indefinite pronoun use, 407
Information, eliminate unnecessary, 760
Language, use active, 308
Parallelism, create, 587
Peer review, use, 176, 406, 586, 760, 1006, 1238
Praise, check words of, 760
Prepositional phrases, identify, 689
Possessive nouns, form correct, 97
Pronoun-antecedent agreement, identify correct, 177
Quotations, use, 761
Readers' concerns, address, 586
Run-ons, identifying and correcting, 1141
Sentences
    beginnings, vary, 96, 1239
    combine, 406, 515, 963
    fix choppy, 515
    highlight nonsupporting, 760

length, vary, 1239
    patterns, vary, 689
Sequence of events, maintain effective, 308
Sources, evaluate, 1006
Specifics, add, 1238
    Subject-verb agreement, identify correct, 407
Subject-verb order, vary, 1239
Synonym banks, use, 1006
Thesis, underline, 760
Transitions, provide, 962
Vocabulary, evaluate, 176
Voice, highlight active, 514
Word choice, revise to vary, 1006
Words, choose powerful, 586

**Student Models:**

Autobiographical narrative, 98
Business letter, 516
Cause-and-effect essay, 408
Comparison-and contrast essay, 1240
Descriptive essay, 690
Editorial, 588
How-to essay, 964
Problem-and-solution essay, 178
Research report, 1010
Response/Review, 762
Short story, 310
Technical document, 1142

**Professional Models:**

Cause-and-effect essay (Choy), 405
Comparison and contrast essay (Smith), 1237
Fiction (McCracken), 175
Persuasive editorial (Walker), 585
Research report (Blackwood), 1007
Response to literature (Mora), 759

**Writer's Toolbox:**

Conventions, 97, 309, 407, 587, 761, 1141
Ideas, 1139
Organization, 307, 961
Pronoun-antecedent agreement, 177
Sentence fluency, 515, 689, 963, 1009, 1239
Voice, 513
Word choice, 687

**Editing/Proofreading:**

Accuracy, focus on, 517
Common usage problems, correct, 763
Compound sentences, focus on, 1241
Dates, focus on, 99
Errors, check for, 409
Facts, focus on, 99
Format, focus on, 965, 1013
Legibility, focus on, 1143
Lists, focus on, 965
Problematic words, double-check, 1013

# Research and Technology

## Media Literacy

# Index of Features

Boldface numbers indicate pages where terms are defined.

# Index of Authors and Titles

**Notes:** Page numbers in *italics* refer to biographical information; nonfiction and informational text appear in red.

# Acknowledgments

Grateful acknowledgment is made to the following for copyrighted material:

**The Academy of American Poets** "Pablo Neruda Poetfans" by Alberto Meza from *http://poets.org/viewmedia.php/prmMID/19607*. "Emily Dickinson Poetfans" by Sharyn Moore from *http://poets.org/viewmedia.php/prmMID/19605*. Copyright © 1997-2007 by The Academy of American Poets. Used by permission of the Academy of American Poets.

**American Broadcasting Companies, Inc.** "No. 42 Jackie Robinson" by John Nadel from *http://abcnews.go.com/Sports/wireStory?id=3044174*. Copyright © 2007 ABCNews Internet Ventures. Used courtesy of ABC News.

**Arte Publico Press, Inc.** "A Voice" by Pat Mora from *Communion* by Pat Mora. Copyright © 1991 Arte Publico Press—University of Houston. Used by permission of the publisher.

**Ballantine Books** "New Road Chicken Pies" from *The Book Lover's Cookbook* by Shaunda Kennedy Wenger and Janet Kay Jensen. Copyright © 2003 by Shaunda Kennedy Wenger and Janet Kay Jensen. Used by permission of Ballantine Books, a division of Random House, Inc.

**Bantam Doubleday Dell Publishing** "Tell Me a Riddle" by Tillie Olsen from *Delta Book, Doubleday*. "Things Fall Apart" by Chinua Achebe from *Anchor Books, Doubleday*. All rights reserved.

**Susan Bergholz Literary Services** "Twister Hits Houston" from *My Wicked Wicked Ways* by Sandra Cisneros. Copyright © 1987 by Sandra Cisneros. Published by Third Woman Press and in hardcover by Alfred A. Knopf. From *A Celebration of Grandfathers* by Rudolfo Anaya. Copyright © 1983 by Rudolfo Anaya. First published in New Mexico Magazine, March 1983. "My English" by Julia Alvarez from *Something to Declare* by Julia Alvarez. Published by Plume, an imprint of Penguin Group (USA), in 1999 and originally in hardcover by Algonquin Books of Chapel Hill. Copyright © 1998 by Julia Alvarez. Used by permission of Third Woman Press and Susan Bergholz Literary Services, New York, NY and Lamy, NM. All rights reserved.

**Gary I. Blackwood** From *The Shakespeare Stealer* by Gary I. Blackwood. Copyright © 2003 by Gary I. Blackwood. Used by permission of the author.

**Tyroneca Booker** "The Day of the Storm" by Ty Booker from *Katrina, In Their Own Words* edited by Richard Louth. All works copyrighted © 2006 by the individual authors. Southeastern Louisiana Writing Project, Publisher. Southeastern Louisiana University, Hammond, Louisiana, 70402. Used by permission of Tyroneca Booker.

**Georges Borchardt, Inc.** "The Glass Menagerie" by Tennessee Williams. Copyright © 1945, renewed 1973 by The University of the South. Reprinted by permission.

**Brandt & Hochman Literary Agents, Inc.** "The Most Dangerous Game" from *The Most Dangerous Game* by Richard Connell. Copyright © 1924 by Richard Connell. Copyright renewed © 1952 by Louise Fox Connell. "Sonata For Harp and Bicycle" from *The Green Flash and Other Tales of Horror* by Joan Aiken. Copyright © 1957, 1958, 1959, 1960, 1965, 1968, 1969, 1971 by Joan Aiken. Used by permission of Brandt & Hochman Literary Agents, Inc. Any copying or redistribution of the text is expressly forbidden.

**Curtis Brown, Ltd.** "Uncoiling" by Pat Mora. First appeared in *Daughters of the Fifth Sun*, published by Riverhead Press. Copyright © 1995. Used by permission of Curtis Brown, Ltd.

**The Bukowski Agency** "The Jade Peony" by Wayson Choy. First published in the *UBC Alumni Chronicle*, Vol. 34, No. 4, Winter 1979. Copyright by Wayson Choy 1977. The novel The Jade Peony, based on this story, is published in the United States by The Other Press. Used by permission of The Bukowski Agency.

**California State Parks** Railtown 1897 State Historic Park, Filming on Location: The Movie Railroad from *www.csrmf.org/railtown/doc.asp?id=13*. Copyright © 2001 California State Railroad Museum Foundation. All rights reserved. Used by permission of California State Parks.

**Jonathan Clowes Ltd.** "The Red-headed League" from *The Adventures of Sherlock Holmes* by Sir Arthur Conan Doyle. Copyright © 1996 Sir Arthur Conan Doyle Copyright Holders. Used by kind permission of Jonathan Clowes Ltd., London, on behalf of Andrea Plunket, the Administrator of the Sir Arthur Conan Doyle Copyrights.

**Don Congdon Associates, Inc.** "The Golden Kite, the Silver Wind" by Ray Bradbury from *Epoch*, February 1953. Copyright © 1953 by Epoch Associates; renewed 1981 by Ray Bradbury. Used by permission of Don Congdon Associates, Inc.

**Catherine Costello** "There is No Word For Goodbye" by Mary Tall Mountain from *There Is No Word for Goodbye: Poems by Mary Tall Mountain*. Copyright © 1994 by Tall Mountain Estate. Used by permission of Catherine Costello. All rights reserved.

**Dell Publishing, a div of Random House, Inc.** From *The Giant's House* by Elizabeth McCracken, copyright © 1996 by Elizabeth McCracken. Used by permission of The Dial Press/Dell Publishing, a division of Random House, Inc.

**Dunow Carlson Lerner Agency** "Desiderata" by Elizabeth McCracken from *http://www.randomhouse.com/boldtype/0397/mccracken/*. Copyright © 1996 by Elizabeth McCracken. Used by permission of Dunow Carlson Lerner Agency.

**Stephen Edwards** "Rock Climbing Equipment and Techniques" by Stephen Edwards from *http://alumnus.caltech.edu/~sedwards/climbing/techniques.html*. Used by permission of Stephen Edwards.

**eSchool News** "Georgia School Displays iPod Ingenuity" by eSchool News Staff and wire service reports from *http://www.eschoolnews.com/news/showStory.cfm?ArticleID=6211*. Copyright © 2007 eSchool News. All rights reserved. Used by permission of eSchool News.

**Faber and Faber Limited** "The Horses" by Edwin Muir from *Collected Poems by Edwin Muir*, copyright © 1960 by Willa Muir. "Macavity: The Mystery Cat" by T. S. Eliot from *Old Possum's Book of Practical Cats* by T. S. Eliot. Copyright © 1939 by T. S. Eliot and renewed 1967 by Esme Valerie Eliot. Used by permission of Faber and Faber Limited.

**Farrar, Straus & Giroux, LLC** "Prologue and Epilogue" by Derek Walcott from *The Odyssey: A Stage Version* by Derek Walcott. Copyright © 1993 by Derek Walcott. "The Washwoman" by Isaac Bashevis Singer from *A Day of Pleasure* by Isaac Bachevis Singer. Copyright © 1969 by Isaac Bashevis Singer. "Part 1: The Adventures of Odysseus" and "Part 2: The Return of Odysseus" from *The Odyssey* by Homer, translated by Robert Fitzgerald. Copyright © 1961, 1963 by Robert Fitzgerald. Copyright renewed 1989 by Benedict r. C. Fitzgerald, on behalf of the Fitzgerald children. Used with permission of Farrar, Straus and Giroux, LLC.

**Florida Railroad Museum, Inc.** Florida Gulf Coast Railroad Museum from *www.frrm.org/information.html*. Copyright © 2006 Florida Railroad Museum, Inc. Used by permission of Florida Railroad Museum, Inc.

**Fresno State University Communications** "iPods Join Educational Toolkit at Fresno State" by Megan Jacobsen from FresnoStateNews January 17, 2007, *www.fresnostatenews.com/2007/01/podcasts.htm*. Used courtesy of FresnoStateNews.com.

**Professor Anthony I. Gooch** From *Cassell's Spanish-English English-Spanish Dictionary* by Anthony Gooch and Angel Garcia de Paredes. Copyright © 1978 by Macmillan Publishing Company, a division of Macmillan, Inc. Used by permission of Professor Anthony I. Gooch.

**Graywolf Press** "Fifteen" from *The Way It Is: New and Selected Poems* by William Stafford. Copyright © 1966, 1998 by the Estate of William Stafford. Used by permission of Graywolf Press, Saint Paul, MN.

**Harcourt Education Limited** "The Girl Who Can" by Ama Ata Aidoo from *Opening Spaces: An Anthology of Contemporary African Women's Writing*, edited by Yvonne Vera. Used by permission of Harcourt Education.

**Harcourt, Inc.** "The Writer" from *The Mind-Reader* by Richard Wilbur. Copyright © 1971 by Richard Wilbur. "Women" by Alice Walker from *Revolutionary Petunias & Other Poems*, copyright © 1970 and renewed 1998 by Alice Walker. From *A Lincoln Preface*, copyright 1953 by Carl Sandburg and renewed 1981 by Margaret Sandburg, Janet Sandburg, and Helga Sandburg Crile. "Macavity: The Mystery Cat" from *Old Possum's Book of Practical Cats* by T. S. Eliot. Copyright 1939 by T. S. Eliot and renewed 1967 by Esme Valorie Eliot. "Ithaca" by Constantine Cavafy from *The Complete Poems of Cavafy*. English translation copyright © 1961 and renewed 1989 by Rae Dalven. Used by permission of Harcourt, Inc. This material may not be reproduced in any form or by any means without the prior written permission of the publisher.

**HarperCollins Publishers, Inc.** "Summer" from *Brown Angels: An Album of Pictures and Verse* by Walter Dean Myers. Copyright © 1993 by Walter Dean Myers. Used by permission of HarperCollins Publishers.

**Harvard University Press** "Much madness is divinest sense" from *The Poems of Emily Dickinson*, Thomas H. Johnson, ed., Cambridge, Mass.: The Belknap Press of Harvard University Press, Copyright © 1951, 1955, 1979, 1983 by the President and Fellows of Harvard College. Used by permission of the publishers and the Trustees of Amherst College. Reprinted by permission of the publishers and the Trustees of Amherst College from *The Poems of Emily Dickinson*, Thomas H. Johnson, ed., Cambridge, Mass.: The Belknap Press of Harvard University Press, Copyright (c) 1951, 1955, 1979, 1983 by the President and Fellows of Harvard College.

**Hawaiian Lifeguard Association** "Beach and Ocean Safety Signs" by Staff from *www.aloha.com*. Copyright © 1986, 2001 Hawaiian Lifeguard Association. All rights (and lefts) reserved. Used with permission.

**David Hilbun** "Hope" by David Hilbun from *Katrina, In Their Own Words* edited by Richard Louth. All works copyrighted © 2006 by the individual authors. Southeastern Louisiana Writing Project, Publisher. Southeastern Louisiana University, Hammond, Louisiana, 70402. Used by permission of David Hilbun.

**Helmut Hirnschall** "There is a Longing . . ." by Chief Dan George & Helmut Hirnschall from *My Heart Soars*. Copyright © 1974 by Chief Dan George and Helmut Hirnschall. Used by permission of Helmut Hirnschall.

**The Barbara Hogenson Agency, Inc.** "The Secret Life of Walter Mitty" by James Thurber from *My World-And Welcome To It*. Copyright © 1942 by James Thurber. Copyright © renewed 1970 by Rosemary A. Thurber. Used by permission from The Barbara Hogenson Agency, Inc.

**Henry Holt and Company, Inc.** "Talk" by Harold Courlander and George Herzog from *The Cow-Tail Switch and Other West African Stories* by Harold Courlander and George Herzog, © 1947, 1974 by Harold Courlander. "Fire and Ice" by Robert Frost from *The Poetry of Robert Frost*, edited by Edward Connery Lathem. Copyright © 1951 by Robert Frost. Used by permission of Henry Holt and Company, LLC.

**Houghton Mifflin Company, Inc.** "Siren Song" from *Selected Poems, 1965-1975* by Margaret Atwood. Copyright © 1976 by Margaret Atwood. Excerpt from "A Fable for Tomorrow" from *Silent Spring* by Rachel Carson. Copyright © 1962 by Rachel I. Carson, renewed 1990 by Roger Christie. "All Watched Over by Machines of Loving Grace" from *The Pill Versus the Springhill Mine Disaster* by Richard Brautigan. Copyright © 1968 by Richard Brautigan. Used by permission of Houghton Mifflin Company. All rights reserved.

**HowStuffWorks, Inc.** "How Podcasting Works" by Stephanie Watson from *http://computer.howstuffworks.com/podcasting.htm*. Copyright © 1998-2007 HowStuffWorks, Inc. Courtesy of How Stuff Works.com.

**James r. Hurst** "The Scarlet Ibis" by James Hurst, published in *The Atlantic Monthly*, July 1960. Copyright © 1988 by James Hurst. Used by permission of the author.

**International Creative Management, Inc.** "Libraries Face Sad Chapter" by Pete Hamill from *www.petehamill.com*. Copyright © 2002 by Pete Hamill. Used by permission of International Creative Management, Inc.

**Japan Publications, Inc.** "Temple bells die out" by Basho; and "Dragonfly catcher" and "Bearing no flowers" by Chiyojo, translated by Daniel C. Buchanan, from *One Hundred Famous Haiku* by Daniel C. Buchanan. Copyright © 1973 by Japan Publications. Used by permission of Japan Publications, Inc.

**Lyndon b. Johnson Library** From *A White House Diary* by Lady Bird Johnson. Used with permission of the Lyndon b. Johnson Library.

**The Estate of Dr. Martin Luther King, Jr. c/o Writer's House LLC** "I Have a Dream" by Dr. Martin Luther King, Jr. from *The Words Of Martin Luther King, Jr.* Copyright © 1963 Martin Luther King Jr., copyright renewed © 1991 Coretta Scott King. Used by arrangement with The Heirs to the Estate of Martin Luther King Jr., c/o Writers House as agent for the proprietor New York, NY.

**Alfred A. Knopf, a division of Random House, Inc.** "Pecos Bill: The Cyclone" from *Pecos Bill: Texas Cowpuncher* by Harold W. Felton, illustrated by Aldren A. Watson, copyright © 1949 by Alfred A. Knopf, a division of Random House, Inc. Copyright © renewed 1976 by Harold W. Felton. "Dreams" from *The Collected Poems of Langston Hughes* by Langston Hughes. Copyright © 1994 by The Estate of Langston Hughes. "The News" from *Conscientious Objections* by Neil Postman, copyright © 1988 by Neil Postman. "Dream Deferred" from *The Collected Poems of Langston Hughes* by Langston Hughes. Copyright © 1994 by The Estate of Langston Hughes. "Uncle Marcos" by Isabel Allende, translated by Magda Bogin, from *The House of the Spirits* by Isabel Allende, copyright © 1985 by Alfred A. Knopf, a division of Random House, Inc. Used by permisson of Alfred A. Knopf, a division of Random House, Inc.

**Learned Hand** "I Am An American Day" address by Learned Hand. New York City, May 21, 1944.

**Liberty Travel, Inc.** "Italy Travel Guide" from *Liberty Travel Brochure.* Copyright © 2006 Liberty Travel, Inc. Used by permission of Liberty Travel, Inc.

**Little, Brown and Company, Inc.** "Pyramus and Thisbe" and "Perseus" from *Mythology* by Edith Hamilton. Copyright © 1942 by Edith Hamilton; Copyright © renewed 1969 by Dorian Fielding Reid and Doris Fielding Reid. Used by permission of Little Brown & Company.

**Liveright Publishing Corporation** "maggie and milly and molly and may" by E. E. Cummings from *Complete Poems, 1904-1962* by E.E. Cummings, edited by George J. Frimage. Copyright © 1956, 1984, 1991 by the Trustees for the E. E. Cummings Trust. Used by permission of Liveright Publishing Corporation.

**Andrew MacAndrew** "The Necklace" by Guy de Maupassant, translated by Andrew MacAndrew, from *Boule de Suif and Selected Stories* by Guy de Maupassant, New York, NAL, 1964, pp. 143-151. Translation copyright © 1964 by Andrew MacAndrew. Used by permission of Marie-Christine MacAndrew.

**Massachusetts Institute of Technology** "Team Builds 'Sociable' Robot" by Elizabeth A. Thomson from *Massachusetts Institute of Technology News Office February 14, 2001, http://web.mit.edu/news-office/2001/kismet-0214.html.* Copyright © 2001. Used by permission of MIT News Office.

**John McPhee** "Arthur Ashe Remembered" by John McPhee, first published in *The New Yorker*, March 1, 1993. Used by permission of the author.

**Methuen Publishing, Ltd.** "The Inspector-General" from *The Sneeze: Plays and Stories* by Anton Chekhov, translated and adapted by Michael Frayn, published by Methuen Drama. Originally from An Awl in a Sack by Anton Chekhov, 1885. Used by permission of Methuen Publishing, Ltd.

**Edna St. Vincent Millay Society** "An Ancient Gesture" by Edna St. Vincent Millay from *Collected Poems*, HarperCollins. Copyright © 1954, 1982 by Norma Millay Ellis. All rights reserved. Used by permission of Elizabeth Barnett, literary executor.

**NASA Johnson Space Center** "Space Shuttle Basics" by Staff from *www.nasa.gov.* "Launch Schedule 101/ NASA's Shuttle and Rocket Missions" from *www.nasa.gov/missions/highlights/schedule101.html.* "Robotics Education Project" by Staff from *http://robotics.arc.nasa.gov/.* Copyright © National Aeronautics and Space Administration.

**Charles Neider** "The Invalid's Story" by Mark Twain from *The Complete Sketches and Tales of Mark Twain*, edited by Charles Neider: Copyright © 1977 by Charles Neider. Used by permission of Charles Neider.

**The New York Times Syndication Sales Corp. Headquarters** "World Trade Center Movie Review" by Rebecca Murray from *http://movies.about.com/od/worldtradecenter/fr/wtcreview080806. htm.* Copyright © 2007 by Rebecca Murray. Used with permission of About, Inc., a part of The New York Times Company. All rights reserved.

**NJ TRANSIT** Port Jervis & Pascack Valley Lines from *MTA Train Schedule: Metro-North Railroad.* Copyright © 2006 NJ Transit. Used by permission of NJ TRANSIt.

**Northwestern University Press** "Sonnets on Love XIII" from *Sonnets on Love and Death* by Jean de Sponde translated by David r. Slavitt. English translation copyright © 2001 by David r. Slavitt. Published 2001. Evanston: Northwestern University Press, 2001. Used by permission of Northwestern University Press. All rights reserved. http://www.nupress.northwester.edu.

**W. W. Norton & Company, Inc.** "The War Against the Trees" from *The Collected Poems* by Stanley Kunitz. Copyright © 2000 by Stanley Kunitz. Used by permission of W.W. Norton & Company, Inc.

**Naomi Shihab Nye** "Daily" by Naomi Shihab Nye from *Hugging The Jukebox* by Naomi Shihab Nye. Copyright © 1982 All rights reserved. Used by permission of the author.

**Orchard Books, an imprint of Scholastic Inc.** "Checkouts" adapted from *A Couple of Kooks and Other Stories About Love* by Cynthia Rylant. Published by Scholastic Inc./Orchard Books. Copyright © 1990 by Cynthia Rylant. Used by permission of Scholastic, Inc.

**Oxford University Press, Canada** "Siren Song" by Margaret Atwood from *Selected Poems 1966-1984.* Copyright © Margaret Atwood 1990. Used by permission of Oxford University Press Canada.

**Oxford University Press, Inc.** "The Horses" by Edwin Muir from *Collected Poems* by Edwin Muir. Copyright © 1960 by Willa Muir. Used by permission of Oxford University Press, Inc.

**Penguin Group (USA) Inc. & Wallace Literary Agency, Inc.** "Rama and Ravana in Battle," from *The Ramayana* by R.K. Narayan, copyright © 1972 by R.K. Narayan. Used by permission.

**The Penguin Press** "Play Hard; Play Together; Play Smart" by Dean Smith and Gerald D. Bell with John Kilgo from *The Carolina Way: Leadership Lessons From A Life In Coaching.* Copyright © 2004 by Dean E. Smith. Used by permission of The Penguin Press, a division of Penguin Group (USA) Inc.

# Credits

## Photo Credits

xii–xiii: Sean Davey/CORBIS; xiv–xv: Sean Davey/CORBIS; xvi–xvii: Images.com/CORBIS; xviii–xix: Images.com/CORBIS; xx–xxi: Images.com/CORBIS; xxii–xxiii: Images.com/CORBIS; xxvi–xxvii: © Diana Ong/SuperStock; xxviii–xxix: Nice One Productions/CORBIS; xxx–xxxi: Nice One Productions/CORBIS; xlviii Thomas Owen Jenkins/Shutterstock; **Gr09 U1** 1: © Catherine Cabrol/Kipa/CORBIS; 2: © Dave Cutler/Images.com; 3: © Johner/ Johner Images/ Getty Images; 5: Images.com/CORBIS; 6: CALVIN AND HOBBES © 1994 Watterson. Reprinted with permission of UNIVERSAL PRESS SYNDICATE. All rights reserved.; 9: Alberto Giacometti, *Man Pointing*, 1947. Bronze, 70 1/2 x 40 3/4 x 16 3/8". The Museum of Modern Art/Licensed by Scala-Art Resource, NY. Gift of Mrs. John D. Rockefeller 3rd. © 2004 Artists Rights Society (ARS), New York/ADAGP, Paris.; 10: © Lisa Haney /Images.com; 12: Christooph Wilhelm/Getty Images; 13: © Bob Winsett/CORBIS; 15: *Library*, 2003 (acrylic on wood), Crook, P.J. (b. 1945) /Private Collection, /The Bridgeman Art Library International; 17: Michael S. Lewis/CORBIS; 17: bkgrnd. Nick Belton/ istockphoto.com; 18: Maria Ferrari/SuperStock; 18–19: bkgrnd. Nick Belton/ istockphoto.com; 20: akg-images; 20: bkgrnd. Nick Belton/ istockphoto.com; 25: t. Robert Maass/CORBIS; 25: b. Lee Snider/CORBIS; 26: *The Oldest Inhabitant*, 1876, Julian Alden Weir, oil on canvas, 65 1/2 x 32" Signed, upper left. Butler Institute of American Art, Youngstown, Ohio; 26: bkgrnd. Lee Snider/CORBIS; 29: Erich Lessing/Art Resource, NY; 30: The Washerwomen, from the 'Tableau de Paris' series, engraved by C. Motte, c.1830–40 (colour litho), Delarue, Fortune (b. 1794) (after)/Musee de la Ville de Paris, Musee Carnavalet, Paris, France, Archives Charmet/The Bridgeman Art Library International; 31: Lee Snider/CORBIS; 32: *The Oldest Inhabitant* (detail), 1876, Julian Alden Weir, oil on canvas, 65 1/2 x 32" Signed, upper left. Butler Institute of American Art, Youngstown, Ohio; 35: t. Getty Images; 35: b. © Ashok Rodrigues/istockphoto.com; 36: t. istockphoto.com; 36: b. © Ashok Rodrigues/istockphoto.com; 37: CORBIS; 48: Royalty Free © Vladimir Piskunov/Dreamtime.com; 49: John Heseltine/© Dorling Kindersley; 49: bkgrnd. istockphoto.com; 50: Canberra Bicycle Museum and Resource Centre, Australia; 52: © Dorling Kindersley; 54: Royalty Free/ PhotoDisc/ Getty Images; 55: tl. © Dorling Kindersley; 55: tr. istockphoto.com; 55: b. Canberra Bicycle Museum and Resource Centre, Australia; 56: rt. istockphoto.com; 56: tl. Royalty Free/ C Squared Studios/PhotoDisc/ Getty Images; 56: rb. istockphoto.com; 59: t. Bettmann/CORBIS; 60–61: © Held Collection/The Bridgeman Art Library International; 62: istockphoto.com; 62–63: border. istockphoto.com; 64: RF Digital Vision/ Getty Images; 64–65: border. istockphoto.com; 66: t. istockphoto.com; 66: b. istockphoto.com; 67: l. © Holton Collection/SuperStock; 67: r. istockphoto.com; 68: l. istockphoto.com; 68: r. istockphoto.com; 75: Barnabas Kindersley/© Dorling Kindersley; 76: © Foodfolio/ Image State/ Jupiter Images; 77: t. © GK Hart/Vikki Hart/ Getty Images; 77: b. © Peter Kubal/Photographers Direct; 78: t. © GK Hart/Vikki Hart/ Getty Images; 78: b. © C.Fleurent/ photocuisine/ CORBIS; 81: b. Ama Ata Aidoo; 82–83: istockphoto.com; 84: istockphoto.com; 85: RF © Tim Jones/ Digital Vision/ Getty Images; 86: © Ron Giling/Peter Arnold, Inc.; 88: © Ron Giling/Peter Arnold, Inc.; 90: Barnabas Kindersley/© Dorling Kindersley; 91: l. Corel Professional Photos CD-ROM™; 91: r. Corel Professional Photos CD-ROM™; 92: © Ron Giling/Peter Arnold, Inc.; 103: © Archive Photos; 104: Bettmann/CORBIS; 104: bkgrnd. istockphoto.com; 105: l. Art Rickerby/Time & Life Pictures/Getty Images; 105: m. © CORBIS; 105: r. © Bettmann/ CORBIS; 106: tl. Audio Visual Archives at the John F. Kennedy Library; 106: tr. istockphoto.com; 106: tm. CORBIS Sygma; 106: m. Courtesy of The Peace Corps; 106: b. Bettmann/CORBIS; 107: l. © Randy Faris/ CORBIS; 107: m. © Bettmann/CORBIS; 107: r. © Bettmann/ CORBIS; 108: t. Loretta Hostettler/istockphoto.com; 108: bl.

Art Rickerby/ Time & Life Pictures/Getty Images; 108: bm. Bettmann/CORBIS; 108: br. © Wally McNamee/CORBIS; 109: l. Bettmann/CORBIS; 109: m. Keystone/ Hulton Archive/ Getty images; 109: r. Lisa Svara/ istockphoto.com; 110: istockphoto.com; 113: Copyright© by Julia Alvarez/Bill Eichner. Reprinted by permission of Susan Bergholz Literary Services, NY. All Rights reserved.; 114: t. istockphoto.com; 114: b. RF Terry Vine/Blend Images/Getty Images; 114–115: istockphoto.com; 116: RF Medioimages/Photodisc/Getty Images; 119: l. istockphoto.com; 119: r. RF George Marks/Retrofile/Getty Images; 120: RF Terry Vine/ Blend Images/Getty Images; 127: CORBIS; 128–129: istockphoto.com; 129: istockphoto.com; 130: © Ufuk Zivana/ istockphoto.com; 131: l. RF Tetra Images/Getty Images; 131: r. RF Joshua Ets-Hokin/ PhotoDisc/ Getty Images; 132: l. Hulton-Deutsch/CORBIS; 132: r. Comstock Select/ CORBIS; 132: inset. RF Rubberball/ Getty Images; 133: RF Joshua Ets-Hokin/ PhotoDisc/Getty Images; 134: istockphoto.com; 137: t. AFP/Getty Images; 137: m. RF © Brownie Harris/CORBIS; 137: b. RF PhotoDisc/ Jules Frazier/ Getty Images; 138: Images.com/CORBIS; 139: RF© Tom Grill/ CORBIS; 140: istockphoto.com; 141: istockphoto.com; 142: Bettmann/CORBIS; 142–143: istockphoto.com; 145: Bettmann/CORBIS; 147: l. RF © Brownie Harris/ CORBIS; 147: r. RF PhotoDisc/ Jules Frazier/ Getty Images; 148: Images.com/CORBIS; 156: Courtesy of NJ Transit; 157: l. istockphoto.com; 157: r. istockphoto.com; 157: br. © Ted Streshinsky/ CORBIS; 157: istockphoto.com; 157: t. courtesy of the Florida Railroad Museum; 157: t. Randy Mayes/ istockphoto.com; 158: mr. © NRM/SSPL/The Image Works; 158: br. © Wolfgang Kaehler/ CORBIS; 158: istockphoto.com; 158: mr. courtesy of SouthEastern Railway Museum; 158: b. courtesy of SouthEastern Railway Museum; 161: t. AP/Wide World Photos; 161: b. Photofest; 162: NASA; 164: t. NASA; 164: b. NASA; 165: © RF - ER Productions; 166: © RF - Natphotos/ DigitalVisions/ Getty Images; 167: © Momatiuk - Eastcott/ CORBIS; 168–169: © Ed Freeman/Stone/Getty Images; 175: Prentice Hall; 182: © Michael Newman/Photo Edit; 190 (CL) ©Sophie Bassouls/Sygma/Corbis, (BR) ©The Granger Collection, NY, (TR) Getty Images **Gr09 U2** 192–193: Sean Davey/ CORBIS; 194: Associated Press; 197: © Images.com/CORBIS; 198: www.CartoonStock.com; 199: 20th Century Fox/Photofest; 201: © David Forbert/SuperStock; 201: border. istockphoto.com; 202: © Andrew Gunners/ Digital Vision/ Getty Images; 206: Pearson Education/ PH School Division; 208: Alan Carey/Photo Researchers, Inc.; 213: t. The New York Times/Redux Pictures; 221: Sovfoto/Eastfoto; 233: bkgrnd. Hulton Archive/Getty Images Inc.; 233: t. Getty Images; 233: m. The Imperial War Museum London; 233: b. Jane Burton/© Dorling Kindersley; 239: Miriam Berkely/Authorpix; 240: Ralph Fasanella, "Sunday Afternoon - Stickball Game" (1953). 40 X 36, oil on canvas. Courtesy A.C.A. Galleries, N.Y.; 249: CORBIS; 252: Robert Harding World Imagery; 259: t. Bettmann/CORBIS; 259: b. Corel Professional Photos CD-ROM™; 260: © Christie's Images; 262: *Hairdresser's Window*, 1907, John Sloan, oil on canvas, 1947.240, Wadsworth Atheneum, Hartford, Ct. The Ella Gallup Sumner and Mary Catlin Sumner Collection Fund; 263: Corel Professional Photos CD-ROM™; 269: t. E.O. Hoppe/ Stringer/Time Life Pictures/Getty Images; 269: b. © Ingram Publishing/ SuperStock; 270–271: © Ghislain & Marie David de Lossy/ Getty Images; 272: © Mel Curtis/ Stockbyte/ Getty Images; 273: © PhotoAlto/Ale Ventura/ Getty Images; 274–275: © Ken Redding/CORBIS; 276: © Ingram Publishing/SuperStock; 285: istockphoto.com; 287: © Adam Woolfitt/ CORBIS; 290: istockphoto.com; 291: t. © Nancy Crampton; 291: b. © Marilyn Silverstone /Magnum Photos; 295: *Feast Day*, San Juan Pueblo, 1921, William Penhallow Henderson, National Museum of American Art, Smithsonian Institution; Given in Memory of Joshua C. Taylor/Art Resource, New York; 298–299: © Steve Allen/ TIB/ Getty images; 299: border. istockphoto.com; 300–301: border. istockphoto.com; 301: Sheldon Collins/CORBIS; 302: Historical Picture Archive/CORBIS; 302–303: border. istockphoto.com; 304: border. istockphoto.com;

## Staff Credits

The people who made up the Pearson Prentice Hall Literature team—representing design, editorial, editorial services, education technology, manufacturing and inventory planning, market research, marketing services, planning and budgeting, product planning, production services, project office, publishing processes, and rights and permissions—are listed below. Boldface type denotes the core team members.

**Tobey Antao, Margaret Antonini,** Rosalyn Arcilla, Penny Baker, James Ryan Bannon, Stephan Barth, **Tricia Battipede,** Krista Baudo, Rachel Beckman, Julie Berger, Lawrence Berkowitz, Melissa Biezin, **Suzanne Biron,** Rick Blount, **Marcela Boos, Betsy Bostwick,** Kay Bosworth, Jeff Bradley, Andrea Brescia, Susan Brorein, Lois Brown, **Pam Carey,** Lisa Carrillo, **Geoffrey Cassar,** Patty Cavuoto, Doria Ceraso, Jennifer Ciccone, Jaime Cohen, Rebecca Cottingham, Joe Cucchiara, Jason Cuoco, **Alan Dalgleish, Karen Edmonds, Irene Ehrmann,** Stephen Eldridge, **Amy Fleming,** Dorothea Fox, Steve Frankel, Cindy Frederick, Philip Fried, Diane Fristachi, Phillip Gagler, **Pamela Gallo,** Husain Gatlin, **Elaine Goldman,** Elizabeth Good, John Guild, Phil Hadad, Patricia Hade, Monduane Harris, Brian Hawkes, Jennifer B. Heart, Martha Heller, John Hill, Beth Hyslip, Mary Jean Jones, Grace Kang, Nathan Kinney, Roxanne Knoll, **Kate Krimsky,** Monisha Kumar, Jill Kushner, Sue Langan, Melisa Leong, Susan Levine, Dave Liston, **Mary Luthi, George Lychock, Gregory Lynch, Joan Mazzeo, Sandra McGloster,** Eve Melnechuk, Kathleen Mercandetti, Salita Metha, Artur Mkrtchyan, Karyn Mueller, Alison Muff, Christine Mulcahy, Kenneth Myett, Elizabeth Nemeth, Stefano Nese, Carrie O'Connor, April Okano, Kim Ortell, Sonia Pap, Raymond Parenteau, Dominique Pickens, Linda Punskovsky, **Sheila Ramsay,** Maureen Raymond, Mairead Reddin, **Erin Rehill-Seker, Renée Roberts, Laura Ross,** Bryan Salacki, Sharon Schultz, Jennifer Serra, **Melissa Shustyk,** Rose Sievers, Christy Singer, Yvonne Stecky, **Cynthia Summers,** Steve Thomas, Merle Uuesoo, Roberta Warshaw, Patricia Williams, Daniela Velez

## Additional Credits

Lydie Bemba, Victoria Blades, Denise Data, Rachel Drice, Eleanor Kostyk, Jill Little, Loraine Machlin, Evan Marx, Marilyn McCarthy, Patrick O'Keefe, Shelia M. Smith, Lucia Tirondola, Laura Vivenzio, Linda Waldman, Angel Weyant